COLLINS
Modern Encyclopedia
IN COLOUR

COLLINS
Modern Encyclopedia
IN COLOUR

 COLLINS LONDON AND GLASGOW

ISBN 0 00 434304 2

Text copyright © 1969 William Collins Sons & Co., Ltd., Glasgow and London

Illustrations copyright © 1969 N.V. Uitgeversmaatschappij Elsevier, Amsterdam-Brussels

Printed in the Netherlands

Foreword

This completely new encyclopedia combines a thoroughly up-to-date and authorita-tive text, international in outlook, with a profusion of colour illustrations, maps and diagrams.

The range of subjects covered is very wide and breaks much new ground, providing a wealth of really useful information in a concise and easily digested form. Subjects often neglected in other works of reference will be found here, but not at the expense of traditional areas. Technical subjects are presented in simple language and related to daily life.

The full-colour illustrations on every page are a special feature of this encyclopedia. They have been especially chosen to aid readability and supplement the text on a wide variety of subjects including natural science, art, technology and history.

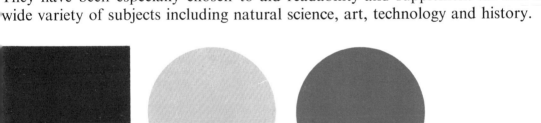

Abbreviations used in this Encyclopedia

D	Anno Domini	diam.	diameter	m.	married, metre(s)	rly.	railway(s)
gric.	agricultural	E	East, eastern, easterly, eastwards	max.	maximum	Russ.	Russian
mer.	American			Med.	Mediterranean	S	South, southern, southerly, southwards
pprox.	approximately	eccles.	ecclesiastical	mi.	mile(s)		
.S.	Anglo-Saxon	educ.	educational	Min.	Minister, Ministry	Scot.	Scottish
t. wt.	atomic weight	Eng.	English			sec.	second(s)
tmos.	atmospheric	esp.	especially	min.	minute(s), minimum	Sec.	Secretary
ress,	pressure	est.	estimate(d)			Soc.	Society
ustral.	Australian	estab.	established, establishment	mm.	millimetre(s)	Sp.	Spanish
utobiog.	autobiography, autobiographical			M.P.	Member of Parliament (UK)	sp. gr.	specific gravity
		fl.	floruit (Latin: lived)			St(e)	Saint(e)
v.	average			Mt(s).	Mountain(s)	t.	ton(s)
	born	Fr.	French	myth.	mythology	temp.	temperate
C	Before Christ	FRS	Fellow of the Royal Society	N	North, northern northerly, northwards	trib.	tributary
rit.	British					trop.	tropical
	circa	ft.	foot, feet			UN	United Nations
	central	Ger.	German	NT	New Testament	v.	versus
ap.	capital	Gk.	Greek	O.E.	Old English	vol.	volume
ent.	century, centuries	gm.	gramme(s)	orig.	originally	W	West, western, westerly, westwards
		Gov.	Governor	OT	Old Testament		
nem.	chemical	govt.	government	oz.	ounce(s)		
n.	centimetre(s)	hr.	hour(s)	parl.	parliament(ary)	wt.	weight
o.	Company, County	ht.	height	polit.	political	yd.	yard(s)
		in.	inch(es)	pop.	population	yr.	year(s)
. of E.	Church of England	Inc.	Incorporated	P.M.	Prime Minister		
		incl.	including	pres.	president(ial)		
. of S.	Church of Scotland	indust.	industrial	prob.	probably		
		Is.	Island(s)	prov.	province, provincial		
olloq.	colloquial(ly)	Ital.	Italian				
omm.	Communist	Jap.	Japanese	Pty.	Party (Australia)		
ons.	Conservative (UK)	k.	knot(s)				
		L.	Lake	pub.	published		
ıb.	cubic	Lab.	Labour (UK)	R.	River		
vt.	hundredweight	Lat.	Latin	R.C.	Roman Catholic		
	died	lb.	pound(s)				
ept.	department	Lib.	Liberal (UK)	repub.	republic(an)		

Managing Editor: J. B. Foreman, M.A. (St. Andrews)

Executive Editor: Patricia Bascom, B.A. Hons. (London) L.G.S.M.

Editors: Janet France, B.Sc. Hons. (Liverpool)
Jennifer Fulton, M.A. Hons. (Aberdeen)
David Grant, M.A. (Glasgow)
Linda Lane, B.A. (Radcliffe College)
Alison Langlands, M.A. (Aberdeen)
James Mallory, B.A. (McGill)
Jean S. A. Robertson, M.A. Hons. (Glasgow)
K. Jane Rust

Administration: Charles Wacher
Margaret McCormack
Marianne Leonardt, B.A. Hons. (Bristol)

Production: Ronald Mongredien

Computer-typeset by C. Tinling & Co., Ltd., Prescot, England.
Printed by Smeets Lithographers, Weert, Holland.
Bound by Proost en Brandt n.v., Amsterdam, Holland.

A

Aachen [Fr: **Aix-la-Chapelle**], city, West Germany, in coal mining area of North Rhine-Westphalia near Dutch and Belgian borders. Machinery, rubber, textile manufacturing. Founded in Roman times; Charlemagne built palace and founded cathedral (rebuilt 10th cent.). Annexed by France (1801); awarded to Prussia 1814. Pop. (1965) 177,000.

Aalborg, city and port of NE Jutland, Denmark, on S shore of Limfjord. One of oldest towns of Denmark, trade centre since 11th cent. Pop. (1965) 100,000.

Aalsmeer, town of North Holland prov., Netherlands. Fertile sandy soil suitable for horticulture; exports plants and bulbs. Pop. c. 1,400.

Aalto, [**Hugo**] **Alvar Henrik** (1898–), Finnish architect and furniture designer. Adapted traditional Finnish architecture to suit environment and modern functional requirements. Pioneered construction of functional furniture using plywood.

Aaltonen, Waino (1894– 1966), Finnish sculptor. Began as painter but later worked esp. in granite, producing massive human figures, and also portrait busts. *See* illus. p. 10.

aardvark, antbear, earth pig, *Orycteropus afer,* large nocturnal burrowing mammal of Africa. Long snout, extensile tongue and strong claws. Feeds on ants and termites.

aardwolf, *Proteles cristatus,* mammal of hyena family. Found in scrubland of S and E Africa. Striped coat, 5-toed forefeet and erectile mane; feeds on carrion and insects.

Aargau, canton of N Switzerland. Area: 542 sq. mi.; cap. Aarau. Fertile region crossed by Aare R. Germany forms N border on the Rhine. Agriculture important. People mainly German-speaking Protestants. Pop. (1966) 361,000.

Aarhus, city of E Jutland, Denmark, port on Aarhus Bay. Commercial and indust. centre, 2nd largest Danish city. Contains 13th cent. cathedral. Pop. (1965) 118,000.

Aaron, in OT, founder and head of Jewish priesthood. With Moses, led the Jews out of Egypt. Made the golden calf and participated in its worship.

Aasen, Ivar Andreas (1813– 96), Norwegian philologist and linguist. Estab. accepted literary and spoken language (*Landsmaal*), based on spoken Norwegian dialects. Published *Grammar* (1848) and *Dictionary of Norse* (1850).

abacá *see* MANILA HEMP.

abacus, calculating device usually consisting of frame with beads which move along either in parallel grooves or on parallel rods.

Abadan, inland port, E Iran, on Shatel-Arab River. Large oil refineries. Pop. (1966) 272,962.

Abakan, town and cap. of Khakass autonomous region, Krasnoyarsk territory, Siberia, USSR. At confluence of Yenisei and Abakan rivers. Pop. (1965 est.) 71,000.

abalone, ear shell, sea-ear, large snail of genus *Haliotis* found on Pacific coast from California to Mexico. Perforated flattened shell. Flesh used as food and shell as source of mother-of-pearl.

Abbasid or **Abbaside,** Arabic dynasty, descended from Abbas, uncle of Mohammed. Held caliphate (749– 1258); overthrown by Hulago Khan.

Abbe, Cleveland (1838– 1916), Amer. meteorologist. Instrumental in formation of US govt. weather service.

Abbe, Ernst (1840– 1905), Ger. physicist. Invented Abbe refractometer and Jena glass. Bought (1888) and reorganized Zeiss optical works.

Abbevillian or **Acheulian culture,** culture identified with lower Paleolithic Age and related to similar C African culture. Evidence discovered by archaeologists at Abbeville and Acheul in N France.

Abbey, Edwin Austin (1852– 1911), Amer. artist, famed for book illustrations. Official painter of coronation of Edward VII.

abbey, in Christian religion, building

Potplants growing in a nursery at Aalsmeer

in which a community of at least 12 monks or nuns live, ruled by an abbot or abbess. First abbey founded (c. AD 529) by St Benedict at Monte Cassino, Italy.

Abbey Theatre, theatrical company founded during Irish literary revival of early 1900's by W. B. Yeats, A. E. Housman and Lady Gregory. In its theatre in Dublin works by Synge, O'Casey and Vincent Carroll received their 1st presentation.

Abbot, Charles Greeley (1872–), Amer. astrophysicist. Completed mapping of infra-red solar spectrum; perfected instruments for measuring solar heat.

Abbot, Maude E. (1896– 1940), Canadian pathologist and bacteriologist. Best known for work on pathological anatomy and histories of medicine and nursing.

Abbotsford, home of Sir Walter Scott in Roxburghshire, Scotland. On S bank of R. Tweed near Melrose. Built to his own design (1811– 24). Contains collection of relics.

Abbott, George (1889–), Amer. theatrical producer, director and dramatist. Adapted themes from Shakespeare's *Comedy of Errors*; co-author with J. C. Holm, and director of *Three Men on a Horse*;

Aardvark: Diagram shows hollow cheek teeth, which are steadily worn away by friction, and solid lower teeth, which grow steadily in compensation.

co-author with P. Dunning, of *Broadway* (1926).

Abbott, Sir John Joseph Caldwell (1821–93), Canadian politician. Solicitor-general (1862). Lost seat over PACIFIC SCANDAL (1873). Re-elected (1880), appointed to Senate (1887); succeeded Sir John A. Macdonald as P.M. (1891). Resigned following year.

ABC powers, term for loose entente between Argentina, Brazil and Chile in early 20th cent. Several agreements (1899–1905) aimed to counter US domination in South America.

Abd-el-Krim (*c.* 1882–1962), Moroccan tribal leader in the Rif. Defeated (1925) by Sp. and Fr. forces; deported to Reunion Is. Escaped (1947) to lead N African independence movements.

abdomen, in animals interior cavity of trunk, below diaphragm. Enclosed by muscular wall of several layers and lined by membrane (peritoneum). Contains stomach, intestines, liver, spleen, pancreas and kidneys.

Abdul Hamid I (1725–89), Turkish sultan (1774–89); signed (1774) peace treaty of KUCHUK KAINARJI with Russia; renewed war (1787).

Abdul Hamid II (1842–1918), Turkish sultan (1876–1909). Noted for despotic and brutal policies, esp. Armenian massacres (1894–6). Instituted pro-German foreign policy. Deposed by Young Turks (1909) under Enver Pasha.

Abdul Mejid I (1823–61), Ottoman Sultan (1839–61). Despite reactionary opposition, achieved military, legal, educ. reforms. Opposed Russia in Crimea (1853–6).

Abdullah (1882–1951), 1st king of Jordan (1946–51), led Arab revolt against Turks (1916–18). Lost Hejaz to Ibn Saud (1924). Led Arab legion against Israel (1948). Assassinated.

Abdur Rahman (1844–1901), emir of Afghanistan. Began modernization of kingdom with introduction of some western institutions.

Abdur Rahman III (891–961), Moorish ruler of Córdoba, Spain. As emir (from 912), centralized govt. of Moslem Spain. Took title of caliph (929).

Abel, in OT, 2nd son of Adam and Eve. Killed by his jealous brother Cain (*Gen.* iv. 1–8).

Abel, Sir Frederick Augustus (1826–1902), Eng. chemist. Improved manufacture of guncotton; with Dewar, invented cordite. Devised Abel test for finding flash point of petroleum.

Abel, John Jacob (1857–1938), Amer. pharmacologist. Isolated adrenalin (1898); achieved crystallization of insulin (1926).

Aaltonen's statue of Paavo Nurmi, standing in front of the Olympic Stadium in Helsinki

Abel, Niels Henrik (1802–29), Norwegian mathematician. Best known for work on theory of elliptic functions.

Abélard, Pierre (1079–1142), Fr. scholastic philosopher and theologian. Regarded as founder of University of Paris. His conceptualism, holding that both particular objects and universal concepts are real, antagonized clergy; accused of heresy. Applied logic to test truths of faith in *Sic et Non*. Popularly remembered for tragic love affair with Héloïse and their exchange of letters, incl. his advice on the conduct of her convent.

abelia, genus of mainly E Asian shrubs of family Caprifoliaceae with white, pink or reddish flowers.

Abenaki Confederacy, former polit. alliance of several NE North Amer. Indian tribes of E Algonkian linguistic stock. In 17th cent., joined French against New England colonists. Later moved N to Canada.

Abeokuta, industrial town of Nigeria, W Africa. On Ogun R. Name also of prov. of SW Nigeria. Pop. (1963) 187,000.

Abercrombie, Lascelles (1881–1938), Eng. poet and critic. Published *Interludes and Poems* (1908), *Deborah* (play, 1913) and *Principles of English Prosody* (1923).

Abercrombie, Sir [Leslie] Patrick (1879–1957), Eng. architect and town planner. His *County of London Plan* (1943) and *Greater London Plan* (1944) formed basis of post-war development of London. Also prepared plans for Edinburgh, Plymouth, Sheffield.

Aberdare Mountains, mountain range of Kenya. Formerly major European settlement area.

Aberdeen, 4th Earl of *see* GORDON, GEORGE HAMILTON.

Aberdeen and Temair, 1st Marquis of *see* GORDON, JOHN CAMPBELL.

Aberdeen, city of NE Scotland, port of North Sea at mouths of Don and Dee rivers. County town of Aberdeenshire. Granite working, light engineering, tourism important. Major fish market. Pop. (1967) 182,000.

Aberdeen University, Aberdeen, Scotland, union (1860) of King's College (orig. College of St Mary in Nativity), founded 1494 and Marischal College, founded 1593.

Aberdeenshire, maritime county of NE Scotland. Area: 1,957 sq. mi.; county town, Aberdeen. Land rises to Cairngorm Mts. in SW. Drained by Dee and Don rivers. Agriculture, fishing, cattle raising (esp. Aberdeen Angus stock) important. Pop. (1967) 318,000.

Aberfan, town of Glamorgan, S Wales, scene of disaster (21 Oct. 1966) when coal tip engulfed school inflicting heavy loss of life.

Aberhart, William (1879–1943), Canadian politician. P.M. of Alberta (1935–43). A founder and leader of SOCIAL CREDIT party.

Abernathy, Ralph (1926–), Amer. religious leader and civil rights worker. Succeeded Martin Luther King, Jr. as head of Southern Christian Leadership Council (1968).

aberration, in astronomy, angular difference between true and apparent position of observed star, planet or other heavenly body. Caused by movement of observer in relation to other body while light is in transit to him. Used in calculations of actual motion of heavenly bodies, and of their distance from Earth.

aberration, in optics, failure of reflected or refracted light to form perfect image. Caused by imperfections of mirror or lens.

Aberystwyth, town in W Wales. Holiday resort, seat of college of University of Wales and of National Library. Pop. (1965 est.) 10,000.

Abidjan, cap. city of Repub. of Ivory Coast, W Africa. Sheltered deep water port since completion (1950) of Vridi Canal. Industries, food processing, sawmilling. Pop. (1963) 250,000.

Abilene, city of central Kansas, US. In 19th cent., major cattle market. Commercial centre of agric. area. Pop. (1960) 6,746.

Abimelech, in OT, son of Gideon who killed his 70 brothers, except for Jothan, in order to become king.

Abitibi, Fort, fur-trading post at mouth of Abitibi R., NE Ontario, estab. by Fr. traders 1686. Operated by Hudson's Bay Co. (1774–1914).

abjuration [Lat: denial on oath], renunciation under oath, of heresy and allegiance to, *e.g.* royal pretenders. In England, govt. employees were required (1701–1858) to abjure and renounce Stuart claims to throne.

Abkhazia, Abkhaz Autonomous SSR, region in NW Georgian SSR on Black Sea. Area: 3,360 sq. mi.; cap. Sukhumi; main city, Gagry. Agriculture and forestry important. Region colonized by Greeks (AD 6th cent.), later conquered by Turks. Became autonomous repub. of USSR in 1922.

Abney, Sir William de Wiveleslie (1843–1920), Brit. scientist. First to photograph infra-red region of solar spectrum.

abolitionists, in US history, advocates of abolition of Negro slavery. Campaign influenced by success (1833) of Brit. anti-slavery campaign. Leading figures were W. L. GARRISON and Wendell Phillips. Passage (1850) of Fugitive State Law strengthened movement in North and South and culminated in JOHN BROWN's abortive raid (1859) on Harpers Ferry. Unyielding attitude of abolitionists, major factor in bringing about Civil War.

abominable snowman *see* YETI.

aborigine [Lat: *ab origine,* from the beginning], inhabitants of a country who are believed to be orig. natives of the region. Term used esp. to refer to AUSTRALIAN ABORIGINES

abortion, in medicine, spontaneous or induced expulsion of foetus from the womb before 28th week of pregnancy. After 28th week known as miscarriage.

Aboukir, Abukir, village in Egypt at mouth of Nile. Aboukir Bay was scene of Nelson's victory in BATTLE OF THE NILE.

Diagram of abdomen showing layout of main organs

Abraham, Abram, in OT, Hebrew patriarch, *c.* 19th cent. BC. Forefather of the Jews through his son Isaac, and through Ishmael, of the Arabs. Founder of Israelite faith; by tradition instituted rite of circumcision on receiving God's promise of Canaan as promised land for his descendants. Complete trust in God exemplified by willingness to sacrifice his son Isaac.

Abraham, Plains of *see* PLAINS OF ABRAHAM.

Abramovitz, Max (1908–), Amer. architect. Designs include Philharmonic Hall at Lincoln Centre.

Abrams, Mark Alexander (1906–), Brit. sociologist. Chairman of Executive Committee Political and Economic Planning. Author of *Social Surveys and Social Action* (1951).

abrasive, material used for scouring, grinding or polishing. High-grade abrasives are emery, form of corundum (natural mineral) or artificial silicon-carbide or aluminium products. Quartz and pumice are low-grade varieties.

Abruzzi, Luigi Amedeo Giuseppe Maria Ferdinando Francesco, Duca degli (1873–1933), Ital. mountaineer and explorer, b. Madrid. Leader of Arctic expedition (1899). Made 1st

ascent (1909) of Bride Peak in Himalayas.

Abruzzi e Molise, region of C Italy, made up of provs. of Aquila, Campobasso, Chieti, Pescara and Teramo. Mainly mountainous, part of Apennine range. Produce includes olives, grapes, almonds.

Absalom, in OT, favourite son of David, king of Judah. Killed while leading rebellion against his father.

absenteeism, in industrial psychology, term for persistent absence from work, usually without good reason.

absinthe, highly toxic green-coloured liqueur flavoured with wormwood, anise and other aromatics; high alcoholic content. Now banned in most countries because of deleterious effect of wormwood.

absolute zero, temperature zero point on Kelvin Scale ($0°K$), where freezing point of water is $-273.16°K$. Theoretically, the point at which linear motions of all the molecules of a substance would cease, because of absence of heat energy.

absolutism, exercise of complete and unrestricted power of govt. by 1 individual or group. In Europe, absolute monarchy flourished

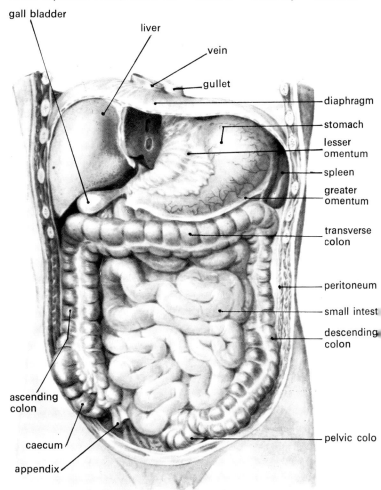

gall bladder — liver — vein — gullet — diaphragm — stomach — lesser omentum — spleen — greater omentum — transverse colon — peritoneum — small intest — descending colon — ascending colon — caecum — appendix — pelvic colo

ABSTRACT ART

16th–18th cent.; gradually declined (18th–19th cent.) with growth of liberal ideas. Theory of absolutism defended by THOMAS HOBBES. Absolutism appears in totalitarian forms of govt., *e.g.* fascism, Nazism.

abstract art, non-representational painting and sculpture. Originated in Europe *c.* 1910, dispensing with treatment of natural objects; achieves aesthetic and emotional impact by concentrating on relationships between line, tone, colour, texture and form. In painting, purest abstract style developed by Russ.-born Kandinsky (1910) and Dutch painter Mondrian. Romanian Constantin Brancusi probably leading abstract sculptor. Term covers various 20th cent. movements *e.g.* Fauvism, Cubism, expressionism.

abstract expressionism, school of Amer. abstract painting developed in New York City after World War 2; soon became prominent both in America and Europe. First Amer. school of painting to exert important influence on European art. Leading artists include Jackson Pollok, William de Kooning and Franck Kline.

absurd, 20th cent. philosophical term describing meaninglessness and loneliness of man's existence in an irrational world. Basis of much existentialist philosophy and literature. Leading philosophical exponents CAMUS and SARTRE, and of the absurd in drama, Beckett, Ionesco and Albee.

Abu Bakr, Abu Bekr (573–634), father-in-law of Mohammed, after whose death (632) became 1st Caliph.

Temple at Abu-Simbel

Lighters landing goods from ships moored offshore in Accra's shallow waters.

Added Mesopotamia to Moslem world and extended Islam as world religion.

Abu Dhabi, largest of TRUCIAL STATES on shore of Persian Gulf. Town of Abu Dhabi being developed.

Abu-Simbel or **Ipsambel,** site of 2 ancient (*c.* 1250 BC) temples carved from sandstone cliffs on Nile R., Egypt. Moved (1964–8) to higher ground to avoid submersion by lake created by Aswan High Dam.

abutilon, trop. Amer. shrub of genus *Abutilon.* One of flowering maples, cultivated for yellow, pink or white bell flowers. Also grown as house plant in temp. regions.

Abydos, ancient town in Asia Minor, on Hellespont; site of Xerxes' crossing to Greece (480 BC). Starting point of Leander's nightly swim to Sestos to meet Hero.

Abyssinia, another name for ETHIOPIA.

Abyssinian cat, breed of domesticated cat originating in Africa. Grey or brown fur with reddish undercoat.

acacia, leguminous trop. or sub-trop. tree of genus *Acacia* of family Leguminosae. Pinnate leaves with clusters of yellow or white flowers. Yields gum arabic, dyes, tanning aids, wood for furniture manufacturing. Species include cooba, *A. salicina,* an Austral. wattle. Mimosa is any plant of same genus or related genus *Mimosa.*

Académie Française, oldest of institutes comprising Institut de France. Founded (1635) as arbiter of Fr. language and culture. Prepared 1st standard dictionary of Fr. language (1639–94). Awards literary prizes annually.

academy, orig. name given to olive grove near Athens where Plato taught. Today name generally denotes learned societies whose function is to promote arts or sciences, normally financed by public money.

Academy Awards or **Oscars,** statuettes awarded annually in US by Academy of Motion Picture Arts and Sciences for outstanding achievements in cinema. Includes awards for year's best film, best leading and supporting performances, *etc.*

Acadia, former Fr. colony and region of E Canada. Region included Nova Scotia, New Brunswick, and Prince Edward Island. Chief town, Port Royal (founded 1605). Occupied by British 1710. Many Fr. settlers deported. Area ceded to UK by Treaty of Utrecht (1713).

Acadia, US National Park in Maine, estab. 1919. Area: 44 sq. mi. On Mount Desert Is. and promontory of mainland across Frenchman Bay.

acanthus, perennial herb of genus *Acanthus* of Med. region. Deeply cut, hairy shiny leaves. Stylized form of the leaf used as architectural ornament, esp. in Corinthian capitals, from *c.* 5th cent. BC.

Acapulco, city and port, Guerrero, SW Mexico. Settled 1530. Natural harbour; popular winter resort. Pop. (1963) 35,000.

Accault, Michel *see* ACO.

accelerator, in physics, device used to impart high speeds to charged particles. Linear and circular types are used esp. in nuclear research. Some examples are betatron, cyclotron and synchrotron.

accentor, name for certain Eurasian birds of Prunellidae family.

accessory, legal term covering someone suspected or accused of complicity in a crime. Accessory before the fact is someone who aids or incites commission of a crime. Accessory after the fact is someone who, knowing a crime to have been committed, assists perpetrator to evade arrest.

accipiter, name for member of genus of Old World hawks. Lives in woodlands. Has short wings and narrow tail. Preys on smaller birds.

accordion, portable keyboard wind instrument. Wind is supplied by bellows as in ORGAN. Invention variously attributed to Buschmann of Berlin (1822), Damien of Vienna (1829) and Bouton of Paris (1852).

accountancy, profession of recording and interpreting financial data concerning persons and organizations.

Accra, city and cap. of Repub. of Ghana, W Africa, on Gulf of Guinea. Industrial and manufacturing port, rly. terminal. Pop. (1966) 600,000.

acculturation, in sociology and anthropology, name for process by which values and modes of life are transmitted between individuals and groups.

accumulator, storage battery, device for storage of electric current.

Aceldama, in NT, field near Jerusalem purchased with 30 pieces of silver thrown down by Judas Iscariot after his betrayal of Jesus. Also site of his suicide by hanging. Called 'field of blood'.

acer, widely distributed genus of trees and shrubs of family Aceraceae. Simple or compound leaves, small clustered flowers followed by winged fruits. Species include the maples, *e.g.* box elder, *A. regundo.*

acetic acid, weak organic acid, a constituent of vinegar. Colourless liquid with pungent odour; miscible with water. Pure acid called glacial

Acacia longifolia, a type of mimosa

acetic acid; its compounds used in plastics, lacquers, medicines.

acetone, colourless water-soluble inflammable liquid, the simplest ketone. Usually derived by oxidation of isopropyl alcohol or by bacterial fermentation of carbohydrates. Used in paints and varnishes, as solvent for organic substances.

acetylcholine, compound of carbon, hydrogen, oxygen and nitrogen.

Widely distributed; dilates blood vessels. Isolated by O. Loewi (1921).

acetylene, colourless gas with ether-like odour. Produced by action of water on calcium carbide or partial oxidation of natural gas. Used in metal cutting, welding, as an illuminant and in organic synthesis.

acetylsalicylic acid *see* ASPIRIN.

Achaea, region of ancient Greece on Gulf of Corinth, N Peloponnese. Powerful by 1250 BC. First Achaean League formed before 5th cent. BC, dissolved by Philip of Macedon (338 BC). Second League formed 3rd cent. BC in opposition to Macedonian rule, opposed by Sparta; helped by Rome (198 BC), later dissolved by Romans (146 BC).

Achard, Franz Karl (1753–1821), Ger. chemist. Pioneer in development of sugar-beet industry for large scale production of sugar.

Achelous, river, longest in Greece (135 mi.). Rises in Pindus Mts., flows into Ionian Sea opposite Cephalonia. Formerly called Aspropotamos, 'white river'.

Acheron, in Gk. myth., one of the rivers of the underworld.

Acheson, Dean Gooderham (1893–1971), Amer. statesman. Instrumental in signing of North Atlantic Treaty (1949). Sec. of State (1949–53), opposed in Senate despite 'containment' policy against spread of Soviet influence.

Acheulian, term applied to phase of Paleolithic period. Named after Saint-Acheul, France, site of discovery of typical tools and implements. *See* also ABBEVILLIAN.

Achilles, in Gk. myth., son of Peleus and Thetis, Gk. hero in Trojan War, subject of ILIAD. Made invulnerable (except heel) when dipped in Styx R. by Thetis. Hidden on Scyros, but found by Odysseus and joined expedition to Troy. Quarrelled with Agamemnon who had taken his captive Briseis, when his own, Chryseis, was returned to her father. Achilles withdrew to his tent; only returned to battle after death of PATROCLUS. Slew Hector, son of Priam, and Penthesileia, queen of the Amazons. Shot in the heel by Paris or

Accipiter gentilis (Goshawk)

Apollo; later said to have lived immortal on island in Euxine Sea.

Achitophel *see* AHITHOPHEL.

acid, compound which gives hydrogen ions in water solution. Characterized by distinctive sour taste, ability to corrode metals, affect certain dyes; forms salts when reacting with bases.

acidosis, condition of human blood in which proportion of bicarbonate is considerably less than normal. May be caused by starvation, malnutrition, diabetes or liver affections.

acne, disease of sebaceous glands, common during adolescence. Characterized by pustular eruptions of the skin, esp. on face, back and chest.

Aco or **Accault, Michel** (*fl.* 1680–1702), Fr. explorer in N America. Made several expeditions with La Salle, esp. in Mississippi region.

Acoma, Ácoma, pueblo, W central New Mexico, US. Visited by expedition of Francisco Vasquez de Coronado (1540). Revolted 1599; joined 1680 uprising of Pueblo Indians. Main occupations, farming and pottery making. Language, Western Keresan. Pop. *c.* 1,500.

Aconcagua, extinct volcano (22,835 ft), W Argentina, in the Andes. First ascended 1897.

aconite, plant of genus *Aconitum,* esp. *A. napellus,* the common monkshood of Europe. Includes species with poisonous and medicinal properties.

acorn, ovoid fruit or nut of OAK. Consists of nut itself in cup-shaped base. Formerly used as food for pigs.

acorn squash, acorn-shaped N Amer. winter squash of genus *Cucurbita.* Has greenish or orange skin.

acorn worm, burrowing worm-like

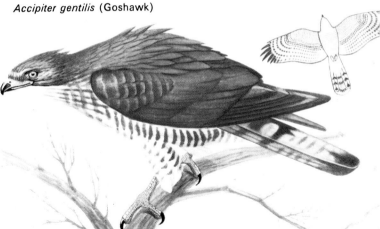

The Acropolis, Athens

hermichordate of class Enteropneusta with acorn-shaped mouth parts.

acoustics, branch of physics dealing with propagation and detection of sound. Scientific basis of music as it explains nature of musical sound and physical properties of sound-producing media.

Acre [Arabic: **Acca**; Hebrew: **Acco**], ancient city of N Israel. Taken by Arabs AD 683, captured and held by Crusaders (1104–1291). Assigned to Arabs at Partition of Palestine (1948) but occupied by Israeli forces. Pop. (1960) *c*. 18,000.

Acre, river of South America, rising near borders of Bolivia, Brazil and Peru, and flowing NE; a main trib. of Purús R. Brazil annexed most of surrounding area (1903), on payment of indemnity to Bolivia.

acropolis, in ancient Gk. towns, citadel built on piece of high ground. Buildings of Acropolis of Athens included PROPYLAEA, PARTHENON and Erectheum, mostly constructed under Cimon and Pericles. Other notable examples include Corinth and Lindos, Rhodes.

act, general term for law passed by legislative body, *e.g.* parliament.

act of God, in law, unforeseeable, unavoidable accident. Victim cannot normally claim damages.

Act of Settlement *see* SETTLEMENT, ACT OF.

Act of Supremacy, legislation passed by Eng. Parl. (1559) estab. sovereign as supreme head of Church of England.

Act of Union *see* UNION, ACTS OF.

Actaeon, in Gk. myth., son of Aristaeus and Autonoe, daughter of Cadmus. For offending Artemis transformed into a stag and devoured by his dogs.

actinium (Ac), radioactive metallic element. Formed from protoactinium, a radio-element of comparatively short life, by alpha radiation. Found esp. in pitchblende.

actinolite, mineral, a variety of amphibole. Occurs in green crystals or in masses.

actinomycetes, filamentous aerobic or anaerobic bacteria of family Actinomycetaceae. Certain species produce disease in man and animals.

Actium, ancient name of promontory in W Greece. Site of defeat of Antony and Cleopatra by Octavian (31 BC).

Acton, Lord *see* DALBERG-ACTON, JOHN EMERICH EDWARD.

Acts of the Apostles, 5th book of NT. Traditionally ascribed to St Luke. Written in Greek *c*. AD 60. Describes growth and spread of early Church.

actuary, statistician employed by govt. department, insurance company or other business. Calculates probabilities and risks involved in insurance, lotteries, *etc*.

acupuncture, form of medical treatment of Chinese origin. Consists of insertion of needles into certain specific portions of body.

adagio [Ital: at ease], in music, slow movement. In dancing, pas de deux of graceful, often complicated steps.

Adam [Hebrew: mankind], in OT, 1st man, created by God from dust. With Eve his wife, expelled by God from Garden of Eden for tasting forbidden fruit (*Gen.* i 26–v 5).

Adam, Adolphe Charles (1803–56), Fr. musician. Best known compositions *Cantique de Noël* and ballet *Giselle*.

Adam, Robert (1728–92), Brit. architect and designer. Architect to George III. With his brother **James Adam** (1730–94), designed Adelphi Terrace, London, and many houses incorporating classical principles and details learned on travels in Italy.

Adam de la Halle (*c*. 1237–85), Fr. dramatist and musician. His *Li Gieus de Robin et Marion* performed at Fr. court. Probably first drama with music.

Adamic, Louis (1899–1951), Amer. writer, b. Yugoslavia. Described his life as an immigrant in *Laughing in the Jungle* (1932). Criticized slow integration of immigrants to US in *My America* (1938).

Adams, Charles Francis (1807–86), Amer. diplomat and lawyer, son of J. Q. Adams. Minister to Great Britain (1861–8), aided Union cause during Civil War, esp. in incidents over *Trent* and *Alabama* ships.

Adams, Frank Dawson, FRS (1859–1942), Canadian geologist. Wrote *Birth and Development of the Geological Sciences* (1938).

Adams, Henry (1838–1918), Amer. historian. Works include *The Edu-*

The island of Patmos in the Aegean Sea

cation of Henry Adams and a study of Middle Ages. Brother, **Brooks Adams** (1848–1927) also historian. Propounded theory that Amer. democracy was doomed by its nature to decay.

Adams, John (1735–1826), 2nd US Pres. (1797–1801), Federalist. Patriot leader and Massachusetts representative to Continental Congress, defended Declaration of Independence (July 1776). Vice-Pres. (1789–97) under Washington. As Pres., retained polit. integrity despite Federalist-dominated Congress' attempts (*see* ALIEN AND SEDITION ACTS) to discredit Jeffersonian Democrats.

Adams, John Couch (1819–92), Eng. astronomer. Independently, but at same time as Leverrier, discovered planet Neptune (1845–6). Did extensive research on motion of Moon and investigated Leonid meteor shower.

Adams, John Quincy (1767–1848), 6th US Pres. (1825–9), Federalist. Son of Pres. John Adams, promulgated MONROE DOCTRINE as Sec. of State (1817–25). Elected Pres. by House of Representatives over Andrew Jackson after neither candidate had obtained majority of Electoral College votes. Congressman from Massachusetts (1831–48), opposed extension of slavery.

Adams, Leonie Fuller (1899–   ), Amer. poet. Works include *Those Not Elect* (1925) and *This Measure* (1933).

Adams, Roger (1889–   ), Amer. organic chemist. Published, with J. R. Johnson, standard work, *Laboratory Experiments in Organic Chemistry*. 1st to synthesize anaesthetics butyn and procaine.

Adams, Samuel (1722–1803), one of leaders in Amer. Revolution. Advocated total separation from Britain; instigated BOSTON TEA PARTY; signed Declaration of Independence.

Adams, Sherman (1899–), Amer. politician. Gov. (1948–52) of New Hampshire, special assistant with cabinet rank (1948–58) to Pres. Eisenhower. Resigned after involvement in tax fraud.

Adam's Peak, mountain (7,352 ft.) of S central Ceylon. Held sacred by Buddhists, Hindus, Moslems.

Adam's-needle, *Yucca filamentosa,* a yucca of US, grown as an ornamental.

Adamson, Joy-Friederike Victoria (1910–), Brit. naturalist and author. Books *Born Free* (1960) and *Living Free* (1961) describe unique relationship between humans and lioness Elsa.

Adana, city in S Turkey. Centre of cotton trade and tobacco industry. Pop.(1965) 291,000.

Addams, Charles (1912–), Amer. cartoonist. Work exemplifies macabre humour.

Addams, Jane (1860–1935), Amer. social worker. Co-founder (1899) of noted social settlement at Hull House, Chicago. Shared Nobel Peace Prize (1931).

addax, *Addax nasomacula,* large pale-coloured antelope of N Africa with spiral horns.

Addensell, Richard Stewart (1904–), Eng. composer. Wrote incidental music for stage and screen, best known work, *Warsaw Concerto.*

adder, *Vipera berus,* small poisonous snake of viper family. Common in Europe; also found in Asia, Africa, Australia. In US name is given to various harmless snakes, *e.g.* hognose snake.

adder's-tongue, name of several ferny plants. Some have flower or fruit spikes.

addiction, compulsive uncontrolled use of habit-forming substances, *e.g.* alcohol (*see* ALCOHOLISM), or drugs, beyond period of medical need, or under conditions harmful to society. Cessation may cause withdrawal symptoms, characterized by acute physical and mental distress.

Addington, Henry, 1st Viscount Sidmouth (1757–1844), Eng. Tory statesman, P.M. (1801–04). Repressive measures while Home Sec. helped provoke PETERLOO MASSACRE.

Addis Ababa, cap. of Ethiopia. Important commercial, educational and rail and road centre. Headquarters of UN Economic Commission for Africa. Industries, cotton-spinning,

Adder

tanning, tobacco processing. Pop. (1965) 560,000.

Addison, Joseph (1672–1719), Eng. writer and statesman. Co-founder with Richard Steele of the *Spectator.* Noted esp. for essays on manners and morals, characterized by wit and polished style. Excelled as delineator of character, *e.g.* the imaginary Sir Roger de Coverley.

Addison, Thomas (1793–1860), Eng. physician. Known for descriptions of Addison's disease and pernicious anaemia. First to correlate disease symptoms with changes in endocrine glands.

Addison's disease, pathological state caused by disease of the adrenal glands. Characterized by weakness, low blood pressure, loss of weight, irritability of alimentary canal and bronze colouring of the skin.

additive, inclusive term for wide range of chemicals added to provide substances with specific property. Examples are mould inhibitors, emulsifiers, food preservatives.

Adelaide, cap. of state of South Australia on Torrens R. Founded 1836. Industrial and educ. centre with university. Pop. (1966) 727,000.

Adelboden, town in Bern, C Switzerland. Health spa and winter sports resort in Engstligental in Bernese Oberland. Pop. *c.* 3,000.

Adélie Coast, region of Antarctica, in Australian quadrant between George V Land and Wilkes Land. Known for very high winds and deep glaciation. Sighted (1840) by Captain d'Urville.

Aden, former Brit. Crown Colony and protectorate comprising port of ADEN and state of Aden (17 sultanates and emirates). Violent reaction to Brit. rule, commenced (1963), resulted in setting up of People's Repub. of SOUTHERN YEMEN (1967).

Aden, port and cap. of Southern Yemen on Gulf of Aden. Flourishing oil and transshipment port, also market for surrounding territories. Pop. (1965 est.) 285,000.

Aden, Gulf of, arm of Arabian Sea, between Southern Yemen and Somali Republic. Port of Suez route.

Adenauer, Konrad (1876–1967), Ger. statesman. Founded Christian Democratic Union and became Chancellor of West Germany (1949). Pursued policies of co-operation with other W European nations, esp. through formation of European Economic Community (1957). Championed German reunification.

adenoids, masses of lymphoid tissue situated between nose and throat in humans. Nasal infection in children,

Adelboden, in the Bernese Oberland

Adjutant Bird

often results from overgrowth sometimes necessitating surgical removal.

adenosine triphosphate (ATP), complex organic compound consisting of adenine, ribose, and phosphate groups. Necessary in plant photo-synthesis, muscular and nervous systems, formation of nucleic acid.

Adige, river of N Italy. Rises in Rhaetian Alps, crosses Plain of Lombardy and enters Adriatic S of Venice. Main towns Merano, Trento and Verona.

Adirondack Forest Preserve, area in Adirondack Mts. containing many lakes. Popular tourist area.

Adirondack Mountains, group of mountains in NE New York state, US. Highest peak Mt. Marcy (5,344 ft.). Contains source of Hudson R.

adjutant stork, adjutant bird, adjutant crane, large stork of genus *Leptoptilos*. Dark plumage without feathers on head and neck; feeds on carrion, small aquatic animals and snakes. Species include *L. dubius* of India, up to 6 ft. tall.

Adler, Alfred (1870–1937), Austrian-Amer. psychiatrist. After studying with Freud, founded own school of individual psychiatry. Considered drive for power as influential as search

for sexual gratification. Works include *Organic Inferiority and Psychic Compensation* (1907).

Adler, Larry (1914–   ), Amer. harmonica player. 1st serious harmonica works composed for him by Vaughan Williams and Milhaud.

Admetus, in Gk. myth., king of Pherae, husband of Alcestis. Served by Apollo for 1 year. Ordained by Fates to early death, only avoidable if another died in his place. Alcestis then died, but Heracles, visiting Admetus, wrestled with Death and returned her to Admetus.

admiral, brightly-coloured butterfly of family Nymphalidae. Species include red admiral, *Vanessa atalanta,* with orange-red band on front wings, common in Europe and US; white admiral of genus *Limenitis,* esp. *L. arthemis* of NE N America with white bands on wings.

Admiralty Islands, volcanic group in Bismarck Archipelago, New Guinea, in SW Pacific Ocean. Area: *c.* 800 sq. mi. Administered by Australia as UN trust territory. Exports coconuts. Pop. *c.* 17,000.

Admiralty Range, coastal mountains of Antarctica at N end of the range W of Ross Sea, Victoria Land. Peaks reach 10,000 ft. Sighted (1841) by Sir James Clark Ross.

adobe, sun-dried brick made of sandy and silty clay mixed with straw. Introduced by Sp. explorers to Indians of Mexico and SW US. Only used in hot dry climate.

adolescence, stage of human development between PUBERTY and maturity. In law, ends with attainment of age of majority.

Adonis, in Gk. myth., beautiful son of Myrrha (or Smyrna) and her father, Cinyras of Cyprus. Loved by Aphrodite. Killed while hunting and claimed by Aphrodite and Persephone (queen of Underworld); Zeus finally decided that he should spend part of the year with each. Life and death of Adonis symbolic of course of vegetation.

Adour, river of SW France, *c.* 200 mi. long. Rising in Pyrenees, it flows NW and W, reaching Bay of Biscay near Biarritz.

Adrastus, in Gk. myth., king of Argos. Led unsuccessful expedition supporting Polyneices' claim to throne of Thebes (Seven against Thebes). Later headed expedition of Epigoni (sons of Seven against Thebes). Estab. Thersander, son of Polyneices, on throne, but died on return to Argos.

adrenal gland, suprarenal gland, either of 2 endocrine glands on upper

end of each kidney. Consists of inner part (medulla) which secretes adrenaline and outer layer (cortex) which produces hormones which influence sexual development, carbohydrate and protein metabolism.

adrenaline, hormone produced by medullary portion of ADRENAL GLAND. Causes rise in blood pressure.

Adrian, Edgar Douglas, 1st Baron Adrian (1889–   ), Eng. physiologist. Conducted important investigations of nervous system. Shared Nobel Prize for Physiology and Medicine (1932) with Sir Charles Sherrington for work on function of neuron.

Adrian IV, orig. Nicholas Breakspear (d. 1159), Eng. churchman and pope (1154–9). Gave Ireland as fief to Henry II of England. Involved in quarrels with Frederick Barbarossa and William I of Sicily.

Adrianople *see* EDIRNE.

Adriatic Sea, N part of Med. Sea lying between Italy and Balkan peninsula. Contains numerous islands. Main ports Trieste, Venice, Bari, Dubrovnik.

Advent [Lat: coming], in Christian calendar, 4-week period before Christmas. Commences on Sunday closest to 30 Nov.; 1st season of Christian year.

Adventists, evangelical sects who believe that second coming of Christ to earth is imminent. View prevalent in early Church, now held mainly by Seventh Day Adventists and Jehovah's Witnesses.

advertising, in commerce, use of mass communications media (press, television, *etc.*) to sell goods and services. Now conducted mainly by specialist agencies.

advocaat, Dutch beverage made from brandy and egg yolks.

advocate, in law, person appointed to plead cause of another, esp. in court or court-martial. In Scotland, term designates member of Bar of Scotland. Lord Advocate is senior law officer of the Crown in Scotland, responsible for criminal prosecutions.

Red Admiral Butterfly

Ady, Andre (1877–1919), Hungarian symbolist poet, known in English as Andrew Ady. Best known for *Uj Versek* (*New Poems*, 1906).

Adyge or **Adighe Autonomous Oblast,** admin. territory (since 1922) of SE European RSFSR. Area: *c.* 1,700 sq. mi.; cap. Maikop. Principal occupations agriculture, livestock raising, food-processing. Pop. *c.* 354,000.

Adzhar Autonomous Soviet Socialist Republic, Adzharistan, autonomous repub. of SW Georgian SSR. Area: 1,120 sq. mi.; cap. Batum. Chief products fruit, maize, tobacco, cotton and timber. Pop. (1965 est.) 288,000.

AE *see* RUSSELL, GEORGE WILLIAM.

aedile, in ancient Rome, office orig. held by 2 plebeians, involving admin. of temples, public buildings, games, *etc.* Supplemented by 2 *aediles curules* from patrician class (367 BC). Organized corn supply until replaced by special officers.

Aedui, Haedui, Hedui, Celtic people of ancient Gaul. Occupied area between Saône and Loire rivers. Their capital was Bibracte (present Autun). Rose up against Romans 52 BC.

Aegean Civilization, general term referring to early Gk. cultures, *e.g.* MINOAN CIVILIZATION of Crete and MYCENAEAN CIVILIZATION of Gk. mainland.

Aegean Sea, part of Med. Sea lying between Greece and Turkey. Connected to Sea of Marmara and Black Sea by Dardanelles. Contains numerous islands incl. Crete, Sporades, Cyclades, Dodecanese.

Aegeus, in Gk. myth., father of Theseus and king of Athens. Believing his son killed by Minotaur, threw himself into the sea (now called Aegean Sea).

Aegina, Aigina, island off SE Greece, in Gulf of Aegina, Aegean Sea. Area: 32 sq. mi.; chief town Aegina. Has sulphur springs.

Aegir or **Gymir** [Old Norse: Hlér], in Old Norse myth., giant and god of the ocean, husband of Ran. Principal water demon but personification of more peaceful aspects of the ocean.

aegis, in Gk. myth., attribute of Zeus and Athena. Represented as goatskin cloak worn over shoulders or over left arm like a shield; bordered with snakes, often with head of Medusa.

Aegisthus, in Gk. myth., son of Thyestes, the brother of Atreus. Adopted by Atreus and sent to kill Thyestes, but recognized by him; contrived death of Atreus. Lover of Clytemnestra, he slew her husband, Agamemnon, on his return from Troy.

Aeneas, in Gk. and Roman myth., son of Anchises and Aphrodite, and member of Trojan royal house. Left Troy with Anchises and son Ascanius after Trojan War; reached Africa, related adventures to Dido, queen of Carthage, finally arrived in Italy. After war against Latins led by Turnus, he founded Lavinium. Regarded as ancestor of Roman nation.

Aeneid, epic poem in 12 books, written (30–19 BC) by Vergil, after estab. of Augustus' principate. Based on legend of Aeneas, celebrates origin and growth of Roman empire.

Aeolian harp, Gk. stringed instrument designed to be played by the wind when hung in a favourable position. Named after Aeolus, Gk. king of the winds.

Aeolus, in Gk. myth., king of the winds. Gave Odysseus the adverse winds tied in leather bag. According to Vergil, kept winds in a cave.

aerodynamics, branch of fluid mechanics dealing with reaction of air or other gases to forces exerted upon them. Primarily concerned with principles governing flight of aircraft, space vehicles in Earth's atmosphere, *etc.*

aeroembolism, bends, disorder caused by too rapid decrease in atmospheric pressure. Causes gas bubbles of body nitrogen to block veins and arteries and gather in tissues. Characterized by nausea, paralysis, pains in abdomen and joints. Most commonly suffered by deep-sea divers. Also known as caisson disease or altitude sickness.

aeronautical engineering, branch of engineering concerned with design, propulsion, *etc.* of aircraft, rocket craft.

aeronautics, science of the design, construction and operation of all heavier-than-air craft. Also operation of airports and control of air traffic.

aeroplane [UK], **airplane** [US], powered heavier-than-air craft which derives lift from action of air against normally fixed wings. Included early

The Ponte Scaligero, spanning the Adige River at Verona

biplane (double-winged) types, monoplanes (incl. delta-wing shapes) and swing-wing types capable of sub- and supersonic flight.

Aeschylus (525–456 BC), Gk. tragic poet, b. near Athens. Author of *c.* 90 plays (some satirical) of which 7 survive, incl. *Agamemnon, Choëphoroe* and *Eumenides* ('Oresteia' trilogy). Regarded as founder of Gk. tragedy, introduced second actor, giving rise to true dialogue and dramatic action. Themes usually myth.; plays marked by idea of destiny working through divine will and human passion, also heredity of crime.

Aesculapius, Roman form of Gk. ASCLEPIUS, god of medicine and healing. Temple erected to him 293 BC on island in Tiber, also a sanatorium.

aesculus, genus of trees and shrubs of family Hippocastanaceae found in N temp. regions. Divided leaves, showy flowers and glossy seeds. Species include horse chestnut, *A. hippocastanum*, Asiatic tree introduced into Europe, and Ohio buckeye, *A. glabra* of central US.

Aesir, in Scandinavian myth., collective name for the 12 gods and 26 goddesses dwelling in ASGARD.

Lindos on Rhodes, an island in the south of the Aegean Sea

Aesop (*fl.* 6th cent. BC), traditional author of Gk. fables about animals; tales adapted to moral or satirical ending. Said to have been slave to Thracian Iadmon.

aesthetics, branch of philosophy concerned with nature of beauty. Plato contended that beauty lay in object itself; Epicurus that the nature of beauty is subjective.

Aetius, Flavius (*c.* 396–454), Roman general under Valentinian III. Strengthened N borders of empire, decisively defeated Attila and the Huns at Châlons-sur-Marne (451). Murdered on return to Rome.

Aetolians, people of ancient Greece, occupying region N of Gulf of Corinth. Fishing and farming principal occupations. Cities formed into

Aetolian League (4th cent. BC) to combat Macedonians.

Afar, nomadic pastoral tribe of NE Africa. Known to Arabs as Danakil.

Afars and the Issas, French Territory of the, formerly **French Somaliland,** Fr. territory on NE coast of Africa, on Gulf of Aden. Area: *c.* 9,000 sq. mi.; cap. Djibouti. Renamed (1967) to emphasize existence of 2 main ethnic

AFRICA

Height in Feet

10000'	3048m
6000'	1829m
3000'	914m
1500'	457m
600'	183m
Sea Level	
Land below Sea Level	

B. BURUNDI
F. FR. TERR. OF AFARS AND ISSAS
G. GAMBIA
N.T. NEUTRAL TERRITORY
P.G. PORTUGUESE GUINEA
R. RWANDA

| 0 | 200 | 400 | 600 | 800 | 1000 miles |
| 0 | 400 | 800 | 1200 | 1600 kms |

groups in population. Pop. (1961 est.) 81,000.

affidavit, in law, written declaration made on oath to legally authorized person, *e.g.* notary or justice of the peace.

Affleck, Raymond Tait (1922–   ), Canadian architect. Designed buildings for Expo '67 in Montreal.

afforestation, systematic planting of large areas of land with trees to create forests or replace those previously exploited or destroyed. Shelters cultivated land and provides timber.

Afghan hound, breed of hunting dog with long narrow head and long silky coat. Stands *c.* 27 in. high at the shoulder.

Afghanistan, kingdom of C Asia, bounded by Iran, Pakistan and USSR. Area: *c.* 250,000 sq. mi.; cap.

Kabul; main centres, Kandahar, Herat. Mountainous country dominated by Hindu Kush. Principal industries, agriculture, sheep raising. Crops include wheat, barley, rice, maize. Silks and carpets manufactured. Mineral resources include silver, copper, iron, lead, gold. Conquered by Alexander the Great (326 BC), later by Genghis Khan and Tamberlane. Russia and UK struggled for control at beginning of 20th cent. Independence estab. 1907. Became kingdom under Amanullah (1926). Main languages, Persian, Pashtu. Unit of currency, afghanis. Pop. (1964 est.) 15,227,000.

Africa, 2nd largest continent occupying approx. 20% of world's land area. Area: *c.* 11,684,000 sq. mi. Bounded on N by Med. Sea, on E by Red Sea, on S and SE by Indian Ocean, on W by Atlantic Ocean. Comprises plateau of ancient hard rock. Principal mountain systems are Atlas in NW, Drakensberg in SE and E central highlands, containing Mt. Kiliman-

jaro (19,565 ft.), continent's highest peak. Coastal regions in extreme N and S have Mediterranean climate and vegetation. Inland are vast arid deserts (Sahara, Libyan, Nubian in N; Kalahari in S). Equatorial savannah lands contain large game reserves. Along equator are jungles and rain forests. High lakes of E central Africa feed large rivers incl. Nile, Congo, Zambesi. Vast resources of iron ore, coal, copper, oil. High percentage of world's gold and diamonds mined in S. Africa may have had the earliest civilizations. Ancient Egypt had high cultural development before 3000 BC. N coast colonized by Romans after fall of Carthage (149 BC). Islam brought by Arab invaders (7th–11th cent.). European exploration begun 15th–16th cent. Continent extensively colonized (19th cent.) by France, Germany, Holland, Spain, Portugal, Italy and Britain. Independence achieved by most colonies in 20th cent. (esp. during 1950s and 1960s), with, however, persistence of European rule in, *e.g.* South Africa and Rhodesia. Pop. *c.* 270 million.

Afghan Hound

African art, carvings, sculptures, portraits, decorated ceremonial and domestic utensils produced esp. in W coast and Congo regions of Africa. Subject to gradual change, forms, esp. in sculptures and masks, highly stylized; associated with tribal religions or customs. Works of Benin kingdom (*fl.* 13th–17th cent.) include ivory gongs, musical instruments and relief representations (often in bronze) of court life. Later works include wood carvings of Bushango kingdom, detailed gold work of Ashanti tribe, secret society masks of Poro tribe,

Johannesburg, largest city in South Africa

Kano, an important Nigerian city

African Art: religious bronze relief from Benin Nigeria

The Taj Mahal, Agra

figures for ancestor worship of Fang tribes. In 20th cent. influenced Western art, esp. Cubism. Contact with other cultures has disrupted traditional art forms.

African lily, agapanthus, genus of S African herbs of Liliaceae family. Showy blue flowers.

Afrikaans, Germanic Indo-European language, derived from that of 17th cent. Dutch settlers in South Africa.

Afro-Asiatic languages, group comprising languages of Near East and N Africa. Formerly known as Hamito-Semitic languages.

Aga Khan, hereditary title bestowed by Queen Victoria on Hasan Ali Shah as reward for his services to Brit. govt. in India. He and his successors held to be direct descendants of Fatima, daughter of Mohammed and spiritual leaders of Ismaeli sect of Islam.

Agadir, city and port of SW Morocco. Scene (1911) of 'gunboat' incident when Fr. and Ger. interests clashed. Almost destroyed (1960) by earthquake. Pop. *c.* 16,000.

Agamemnon, in Gk. myth., son of Atreus and brother of Menelaus; husband of Clytemnestra and father of Electra, Iphigeneia, Chrysothemis and Orestes. Led Gk. expedition to TROJAN WAR, quarrelled with ACHILLES. Murdered by Clytemnestra and lover Aegisthus on return from Troy. Avenged by Orestes.

agamid, Old World lizard of family Agamidae related to New World iguana. Arboreal, terrestrial and semi-aquatic varieties; most are insectivorous.

Agana, city and cap. of Guam, island in W Pacific. Founded by Spanish (1668). Anderson US Air Force Base nearby. Pop. (1960) 1,642.

Aganippe, in Gk. myth., fountain near Mt. Helicon, Boeotia, Greece, sacred to the Muses. Believed to inspire those who drank its water.

Agardh, Karl Adolf (1785–1859), Swedish naturalist and polit. economist. Works include *Systema Algarum* (1824). His son **Jakob Georg Agardh** (1813–1901) distinguished as botanist. Author of *Theoria Systematis Naturalis Plantarum* (1858).

agaric, fungus of Agaricaceae family esp. of genus *Agaricus,* incl. mushrooms. Blade-shaped gills on underside of the cap.

Agassiz, Jean Louis Rodolphe (1807–73), Swiss naturalist, teacher and writer. Major work, *Contributions to the Natural History of the United States of America* (4 vols., 1857–62). Opposed Darwinian theory of evolution.

Agassiz, Lake, lake of Pleistocene era, *c.* 700 mi. long and 250 mi. wide. Named (1879) after Louis Agassiz. Formed by melting of continental ice sheet; as ice melted, water drained E into L. Superior and N into Hudson Bay, leaving many smaller lakes. Lake

bed now important N Amer. wheat-growing valley of Red R.

agate, variety of quartz with curved bands of 2 or more colours. Found in US, Brazil, Uruguay and India.

agave, genus of plants of family Amaryllidaceae, native to trop. America and SW US. Mescal, spirituous liquor, distilled from agave sap. Some cultivated for their fibre, *e.g.* sisal, or other economic purposes; others as ornamentals.

Agee, James (1909–55), Amer. novelist and film critic. Works include *Let Us Now Praise Famous Men* (1941), *A Death in the Family* (pub. 1957). Works on the cinema include *Agee on Film* (2 vols. pub. 1958–60).

Agen, cap. of Lot-et-Garonne department, SW France, on Garonne R. Centre of fruit growing region. Contains 11th cent. Gothic cathedral. Pop. *c.* 35,000.

Agence France-Presse, Fr. news agency with world-wide coverage. Developed after govt. took over *Agence Havas* (formed 1832).

agglomerate, in geology, rock composed of rounded or angular volcanic fragments.

aggression, in psychology, fundamental animal characteristic, linked with survival instinct. Freud postulated that in humans outwardly directed aggression, modified by social influences, was beneficial, but if inwardly directed led to personality disorders.

Agincourt, village of Pas-de-Calais department, N France. Site of victory of Henry V of England over French (1415).

Agnes, Saint (*fl.* 3rd cent. AD), child martyr, believed beheaded at age of 12 or 13. Patron saint of young maidens. According to superstition, girl may see face of future husband on St Agnes' Eve (20 Jan.).

Agnesi, Maria Gaetana (1718–99), Ital. mathematician, linguist and philosopher. Author of *Instituzioni Analitiche* (1748). Sister of composer Maria Teresa Agnesi.

Agnew, Spiro Theodore (1918–), Amer. politician. Governor of Maryland (1966–9). Republican Vice-Pres. (1969–) under Richard Nixon.

Agnon, [Shmuel] Yosef Halevi, orig. Shmuel Yosef Czaczkes (1888–1970), Hebrew writer. Author of *Agunot* (1909), *Temol Shilshom* (1945). With Nelly Sachs, awarded Nobel Prize for Literature (1966).

agnosticism [Gk: *agnostos,* unknowing], maintenance of continuing doubt about existence of a god or any ultimate being. Term 1st suggested by T. H. Huxley.

Agamid Lizard

Agnus Dei [Lat: lamb of God], sacramental chant of R.C. Church. Small wafer of wax blessed by pope during yr. of coronation and every 7 yr. thereafter.

Agoult, Marie Catherine Sophie de Flavigny, Comtesse d' (1805–76), Fr. authoress, mistress of Franz Liszt. Novels, written under pseudonym of Daniel Stern, include *Nélida*. Hist. works include *Histoire de la Révolution de 1848* (1851).

agouti, rabbit-like rodents of genera *Dasyprocta* and *Myoprocta* of S and central America and W Indies. Short hair and short ears; destructive to sugar cane.

Agra, city, W Uttar Pradesh, India, on Jumna R. Founded by Akbar (1566) as cap. of Mogul Empire. Rly. junction; cotton spinning and carpet manufacturing. Famous buildings include Taj Mahal, Pearl Mosque, Great Mosque. Pop. (1961) 509,108.

Agricola, Georgius see BAUER, GEORG.

Agricola, Gnaeus Julius (AD 40–93), Roman soldier and provincial governor, father-in-law of Tacitus. Served in Britain (AD 61), Asia (AD 64); gov. of Britain after election as consul (AD 77). Extended Roman power in Britain beyond Firth of Forth, defeating Caledonians at Mons Graupius (AD 83 or 84) and setting up chain of forts. Circumnavigated Britain.

agriculture, art or science of producing crops and livestock, using earth's natural resources. Aim is high production without soil exhaustion. Branches of agriculture include agronomy, agric. engineering, agric. economics, soil chemistry, animal husbandry, entomology, fish farming, horticulture, forestry.

Agrigento, city and tourist centre, S Sicily, Italy. Agric. market; exports sulphur, salt. Founded (*c.* 580 BC) as Acragas by Gk. colonists from Gela. Remains of Doric temples (6th–5th cent. BC). Pop. (1961) 47,094.

agrimony, plant of genus *Agrimonia* of rose family. Grows wild in N temp. regions and cultivated in herb gardens. Aromatic pinnate leaves with small yellow flowers. Species include *A. eupatoria*.

Agrippa, Marcus Vipsanius (*c.* 62–12 BC), Roman general and one of Augustus' military advisers, largely responsible for defeat of Antony at Actium (31 BC). Father of Agrippina, wife of Tiberius, later married Julia, daughter of Augustus.

Agulhas, Cape, most S point of continent of Africa.

Ahab, in OT, king of Israel (*c*

875–854 BC). Married Jezebel, princess of Sidon and introduced worship of Phoenician god Baal. Rebuked by Elijah. Killed in battle by Syrians.

Ahaggar or **Hoggar Mountains,** range with extensive plateau in C Sahara region. Peaks rise to 8,000–10,000 ft.

Ahasuerus see XERXES I.

Ahidjo, Ahmadou (1924–), Cameroon politician. P.M. (1958–9), Pres. (1960–1), Pres. of Federation of Cameroon (1961–).

Ahithophel, Achitophel, in OT, counsellor of King David and later of Absalom. Committed suicide.

Ahlin, Lars (1915–), Swedish writer. Novels include *If* (1946), *The Cinnamon Stick* (1953).

Ahmedabad, city of W India, cap. of Gujarat state. Centre of cotton-growing and textile manufacturing region. Has important Jain temple. Pop. (1966) 1,316,000.

Aidan or **Aedhan, Saint** (d. 651), Irish monk, founded church in Northumbria, 1st bishop of Lindisfarne. Started numerous churches and schools in N England.

Aiken, Conrad Potter (1889–), Amer. poet, anthologist and critic. Poetry includes collections *The Charnel Rose* (1918) and *Time in the Rock* (1936).

ailanthus, several trees of genus *Ailanthus,* esp. *A. altissima,* tree of heaven or stinkweed.

Ailleboust de Coulonge et d'Argentenay, Louis d' (1612–60), Fr. administrator in Canada. A founder and Gov. (1645–7) of colony of Ville-Marie (later Montreal) Gov. (1645–7). Gov. of New France (1648–51, 1657–8). Organized militia groups to combat Iroquois raids on fur trade routes.

Ain, department of E central France, formerly part of Burgundy. Area: 2,249 sq. mi.; cap. Bourg-en-Bresse. Predominantly agricultural, produces corn, wine, hemp. Plastics and textile industries. Winter sports resort. Pop. (1962) 327,146.

Aintree, Eng. racecourse near Liverpool, estab. 1839. Site of annual GRAND NATIONAL steeplechase.

Ainu, hairy, European-like people native to Japan whose language is unrelated to any other known language. Driven to N islands, fewer than 17,000 remain, supporting themselves by hunting and fishing.

air plant, epiphyte, general name for plants without roots in the soil. Grow on other plants, drawing water from the atmosphere. Category includes orchid, Spanish moss.

aircraft, heavier-than-air machine capable of sustained self-propelled

The Temple of Juno, Agrigento

flight. Term does not include the helicopter or jet-propelled ballistic rocket craft. Aircraft are supported by aerodynamic effect of air on wings (lifting surfaces), are normally provided with horizontal and vertical tailpieces to provide stability. Propul-

Agate: polished and cut stones (above) and brooch setting

Airedale terrier

sion is by motor-driven propeller, jet or rocket engine.

Airedale, large terrier with docked tail. Wiry black and tan coat; stands *c.* 22 in. high.

airship, lighter-than-air craft comprising form of balloon with attached means of propulsion and suspended compartment for passenger or freight carrying. Ger. Zeppelin type with rigid gas-carrying hull developed for bombing in World War 1. After war Brit. and Amer. types used for passenger-carrying, until destruction by fire of several incl. Brit. R101 (1930), after which production virtually ceased.

Aisne, department of NE France. Area: 2,868 sq. mi.; cap. Laon. Agriculture and stock raising important. Metal and textile industries. Aisne R. was site of several important battles in World War 1.

Aitken, William Maxwell, 1st Baron Beaverbrook (1879– 1964), Brit. newspaper owner and govt. adviser, b. Canada. Accumulated huge fortune before going (1910) to England. Leading advocate of imperialism through his newspapers, *Daily Express, Sunday Express* and *Evening Standard.* Member of Churchill's war cabinet (1940– 5).

Aix-en-Provence, city of Bouches-du-Rhône department, SE France. Founded by Romans (*c.* 122 BC) as Aquae Sextiae. Cap. of Provence (1501– 1789). Contains university (founded 1409). Pop. (1962) 67,943.

Aix-la-Chapelle *see* AACHEN.

Aix-la-Chapelle, Treaty of, settlement (1668) ending French invasion of Sp. Netherlands. France retained most of conquests in Flanders. Also name of treaty (1748) concluding War of Austrian Succession (1740– 8). Major results were ceding of Silesia to Prussia and upholding of Pragmatic Sanction, confirming Maria Theresa's right to inherit Habsburg possessions.

Ajaccio, cap. of Corsica, France.

Birthplace of Napoleon I. Winter health resort. Pop. (1962 est.) 33,000.

Ajax, in Gk. myth., Gk. warrior in Trojan War, son of Telamon. Failed in contest with Odysseus for armour of Achilles; slew flock of sheep mistaking them for his enemies, and in shame killed himself.

Ajax, in Gk. myth., son of Oileus, leader of Locrians at Trojan War. Attempted to ravish Cassandra near sacred image of Athena. Shipwrecked and killed on return from Troy.

Akbar the Great, orig. Jelal-ed-Din-Mohammed (1542– 1605), Mogul emperor of India (1556– 1605). Conquered Afghanistan and all of N India. Made sweeping reforms and insisted upon religious tolerance.

Akhenaton or **Ikhnaton,** orig. Amenhotep IV (d. *c.* 1354 BC), king of Egypt, son of Amenhotep III, husband of Nefertiti. Changed name to Akhenaton, built new cap. Akhetaton (modern Tel-el-Amarna). Efforts to uphold worship of Aton, the sun god, resulted in much internal unrest. Great era of Egyptian art.

Akhmatova, Anna, orig. Anna Andreyevna Gorenko (1888– 1966), Russ. poet. Early collections include *Evening* (1912), *Anno Domini* (1922). Officially criticized (1946) for avoiding polit. themes; found favour, however, in 1950s.

Akron, city of NE Ohio, US, on Little Cuyahoga R. Settled 1807. Industrial centre; manufactures automobile and aircraft parts, metal products, chemicals, machinery. Main rubber centre of US; rubber factory estab. 1870. Pop. (1960) 290,351.

Aksakov, Sergei Timofeyevich (1791– 1859), Russ. author. Wrote essays on the theatre. Best known for 3 autobiog. works, *The Family Chronicle* (1856), *Reminiscences* (1856), *Years of Childhood of Bagrov's Grandson* (1858).

Aksum or **Axum,** ancient town of Ethiopia, cap. of former Axumite kingdom. A centre of coptic religion.

Alabama, state of SE US. Area: 57,609 sq. mi.; cap. Montgomery; principal cities Birmingham, Mobile. Undulating plains with Cumberland Plateau in NE. Main crops, cotton and corn. Industry in Tennessee Valley. Mineral resources include petroleum, coal. Desegregation decision (1954) led to an increase in

racial conflict which continued into 1960s. Pop. (1960) 3,266,740.

Alabama dispute, case referred to international arbitration (1871– 2) after US Civil War. US awarded damages from Britain for losses to Union shipping caused by British-financed Confederate warships. Of Confederate ships involved, steam sloop *Alabama* had done most damage.

alabaster, fine-grained, translucent form of gypsum, white or lightly coloured, often streaked. Softer than marble, used for statues and ornaments.

Alacoque, Saint Marguerite Marie (1647– 90). Fr. nun. Founded R. C. devotion of Sacred Heart of Jesus. Canonized 1920.

Alain-Fournier *see* FOURNIER, HENRI ALBAN.

Alamannia *see* ALEMANNIA.

Alamein, coastal town of Egypt. Scene of decisive Allied victory in World War 2 (1942). Halted Ger. advance under Rommel into Egypt and opened way for Brit. march under Montgomery on Tripoli. See NORTH AFRICAN CAMPAIGN.

Alamo, fortified mission in San Antonio, Texas, US. Fewer than 200 Texans withstood lengthy siege by *c.* 6,000 Mexican troops under Santa Anna. Fell after all defenders had been killed or wounded.

Alamogordo, city of S New Mexico US, near Sacramento Mts. Settled 1898. Trade centre of livestock, timber; resort area. First atomic bomb exploded in desert nearby (16 July 1945). Pop. (1960) 21,723.

Alamosa, city of S Colorado, US, on Rio Grande. Founded 1878, centre of irrigated farm region.

Aland Islands, Finnish archipelago in Baltic Sea at entrance to Gulf of Bothnia. Area: 572 sq. mi.; main town, Mariehamn. Farming, shipping.

Albatross

Population largely Swedish-speaking. Ceded by Sweden to Russia (1809); incorporated by independent Finland (1917). Pop. (1967) 29,000.

Alarcón, Hernando de (*fl.* 16th cent.), Sp. explorer in SW US. Discovered Colorado R.

Alarcón, Pedro Antonio de (1833–91), Sp. novelist and diplomat. Best known for short novel *Three cornered Hat* (1874).

Alarcón y Mendoza, Juan Ruiz de (1580–1639), Sp. poet and comic dramatist. Plays included *La Verdad Sospechosa* (basis of Corneille's *Le Menteur*) and *El Tejedor de Segovia*.

Alaric I (*c.* AD 370–410), king of Visigoths. Commanded auxiliaries under Emperor Theodosius but left Roman service and was elected king of Visigoths (395). Invaded Italy (408), captured and sacked Rome (410).

Alaric II (d. 507), king of Visigoths of Spain and W Gaul. Estab. legal code based on Roman law. Killed in battle by Clovis, king of the Franks.

Alaska, Pacific state of US. Admitted to Union (1959). Area: 586,400 sq. mi.; cap. Juneau; main towns Anchorage, Fairbanks. Contains volcanic mountains rising to over 20,000 ft. (Mt. McKinley, highest in US, 20,270 ft.). Main river, Yukon. Settled by Russ. fur traders (18th cent.). Bought by US (1867). Discovery of gold (*c.* 1896) resulted in Gold Rush. Mineral resources include copper, mercury, uranium and coal. Some agriculture and herding of reindeer. Pop. (1960) 246,000.

Alaska Highway, N Amer. highway (1,523 mi. long) from Dawson Creek, British Columbia, Canada to Fairbanks, Alaska. Built (1942) by US army to supply forces in Alaska.

Alaska Range, mountain range S central Alaska, US. Mt. McKinley (20,270 ft.) highest point in North America.

Alava y Navarete, Ignacio Maria de (*c.* 1750–1817), Sp. naval officer and explorer. On voyage round the world (begun 1794) explored East Indies and coast of South America.

Alba or **Alva, Fernando Alvarez de Toledo, Duke of** (1508–82), Sp. soldier and administrator. Became regent (1567) in Netherlands for Philip II. Set up 'Court of Blood' (*c.* 18,000 executed) to crush rebellion; resigned 1573. Conquered Portugal (1580).

Alba Longa, city of Italy, according to Roman tradition founded *c.* 1152 BC by Ascanius, son of Aeneas. Ruled by succession of kings, destroyed by Romans *c.* 600 BC. Situated at or near modern Castel Gandolphe, 12 mi. SE of Rome.

Albanel, Charles (1616–96), Fr. Jesuit missionary and explorer in Canada. Led party overland from Quebec to Hudson Bay (1671–2).

Albania [Shqipnija], repub. of E Europe on Adriatic coast. Area: 10,631 sq. mi.; cap. Tirana; chief towns, Scutari, Korce. Occupied by

Serbs 7th–14th cent.; then part of Ottoman empire until 1912. Became monarchy (1928) under Ahmed Bey Zogu (King Zog I), overrun by Italians in World War 2. Chose to become repub. 1946. Mainly agric. with some mineral resources. Pop. (1966 est.) 1,914,000.

Albanian, Indo-European language with est. 2 million speakers in Albania.

Albany, cap. of state of New York, US. Most N port of Hudson R. Important shipping centre for grain, oil, *etc.* Manufactures include chemicals, paper, textiles. Pop. (1960) 129,700.

Albany Congress, meeting (1754) of delegates from 7 Amer. colonies held at Albany, N.Y. Benjamin Franklin's plan for unifying colonies rejected by legislatures and Brit. crown.

albatross, bird of genus *Diomedea* related to the petrels, generally found in S hemisphere. Largest seabird, with wingspan of up to 12 ft.; capable of long continuous flight. Species include black-browed albatross, *D. melanophrys,* with dark mark above the eye, and wandering albatross, *D. exulans,* with black wings.

Albee, Edward (1928–), Amer. dramatist. Plays, noted for biting modern dialogue, include *The Zoo Story* (1960), *Who's Afraid of Virginia Woolf?* (1962) and *Tiny Alice* (1964).

Albéniz, Isaac (1860–1909), Sp. pianist and composer. Wrote operas and songs; best known works, based on Sp. folk tunes and piano suites, include *Iberia* (1906–9).

Alberich, in Germanic legend, dwarf who guards magic ring of Nibelungs.

Alberoni, Giulio (1664–1752), Ital. statesman and cardinal at Sp. court. Negotiated marriage of Philip V and Elizabeth Farnese. Chief min. of Spain (1715–19). Exiled over disastrous effects of foreign policy.

Albert I (1875–1934), king of Bel

gium (1909–34). Headed resistance to Ger. invasion during World War I. Initiated social reforms in Belgium and Belgian Congo.

Albert Francis Charles Augustus Emmanuel of Saxe-Coburg-Gotha, Prince (1819–61), Prince Consort, husband of Queen Victoria. Interested in arts and scientific developments. Promoted Great Exhibition (1851).

Albert of Brandenburg (1490–1545), Ger. churchman. Became archbishop and Elector of Mainz. Appointed JOHANN TETZEL as his agent to sell indulgences in Germany.

Albert Nyanza, lake of E central Africa. Area: 2,004 sq. mi. Discovered by Samuel Baker (1864). Lies in Great Rift Valley, fed by Victoria Nile R. and drains into Albert Nile R.

Alberta, prov. of W Canada. Area: 255,285 sq. mi.; cap. Edmonton; main towns, Calgary, Lethbridge, Medicine Hat. Main range of Canadian Rockies on SW border. Rivers include Peace and Athabasca. Part of Hudson's Bay Co. territory until 1870. Received prov. status 1905. Mineral resources include petroleum and natural gas. Agriculture is main industry esp. cattle rearing and cereal growing. Pop. (1966) 1,463,203.

Albertus Magnus (*c.* 1200–1280), Dominican scholastic philosopher. Among many works was *Summa Theologiae,* in which he attempted to reconcile Aristotelian philosophy and Christian doctrine. Pupils included St Thomas Aquinas.

Albi, formerly Albigi, city and cap. of Tarn department, S France. Former centre of Albigensian heresy. Notable

Albert Nile River

medieval architecture, esp. Gothic cathedral. Pop. (1962) 40,309.

Albigensians or **Catharists,** religious group in S France, *fl.* 12th-13th cent. Regarded as heretics, adopted Manichean doctrine of duality of good and evil, held that Jesus lived only in semblance. Supported by Raymond VI of Toulouse; exterminated by Albigensian Crusade proclaimed by Pope Innocent III, and by Inquisition.

albinism, condition in humans, animals and plants, characterized by deficiency of pigmentation. In humans manifested by pale skin, white hair and pink eyes, resulting from congenital deficiency.

Albinus see ALCUIN.

Albion, ancient name for Britain, prob. of Celtic origin. Thought by Romans to refer to white (*albus*) cliffs of Dover.

albumin, albumen, in biochemistry, any of class of water-soluble proteins composed of nitrogen, carbon, hydrogen, oxygen and sulphur. Occurs in animal and vegetable juices and tissues. White of egg called albumen.

Albuquerque, Alfonso de (1453–1515), Portuguese navigator and colonist. Founded Portuguese empire in E. Conquered Goa, Malacca, Ceylon (1510–15).

Albuquerque, city, N central New Mexico, US, on Rio Grande. Founded 1706, new town planned 1880. Important indust., commercial and transportation centre; altitude makes it health resort. Pop. (1965) 241,000.

Alcaeus (*fl.* 7th-6th cent. BC), Gk. lyric poet, contemporary of Sappho. Fragments of poetry survive with polit. as well as personal themes. Credited with invention of Alcaic stanza.

Alcalá Zamora, Niceto (1877–1949),

The White Cliffs of Dover gave Britain its ancient name of Albion

Sp. statesman. Leader in revolution (1931), 1st pres. of Sp. repub. (1931–6). Pursued moderate and liberal policy.

Alcatraz, rocky island in San Francisco Bay, W California, US. Fortified by Spanish; used as military prison by US after 1859, as federal maximum security prison after 1933; closed 1963.

alcazar, Sp. fortress or citadel. Most famous is at Toledo, C Spain.

Alcestis see ADMETUS.

alchemy, art, prob. originating in Egypt, which sought to change one substance into another, esp. base metal into gold. Belief in philosopher's stone possibly originated in Alexandria. Influenced by Gk. philosophy and later by Moslems. Came to Europe (12th cent.) through Arabs, gradually developing into chemistry.

Alcibiades (*c.* 450–404 BC), Athenian noble and politician, educated by Pericles, and friend of Socrates. Leader in Peloponnesian War, defeated at Mantinea 418 BC; urged Sicilian Expedition 415 BC. Accused of sacrilege and recalled; fled to Sparta then to Persia. Recalled to Athens (411 BC), but defeated 406 BC in naval battle of Notium. Murdered in Phrygia.

Alcmaeon, in Gk. myth., son of Amphiaraus. Joined Epigoni against Thebes (*see* ADRASTUS). Slew mother Eriphyle; pursued by Furies. Married Arsinoë, gave her necklace of Harmonia which brought ill fortune to all who possessed it. Later married Callirhoe and gave her the necklace. Murdered by his sons.

Alcmene, in Gk. myth., wife of Amphitryon of Tiryus. Mother of twins, Heracles, son of Zeus, and Iphicles, son of Amphitryon.

alcohol, colourless, volatile inflammable intoxicating liquid. Ethylalcohol, intoxicating element of beer, wines and spirits, formed by fermenting action of yeast on starch and sugars present in grapes, grain, *etc.* Dangerous in pure form, alcohol is diluted with water in beverages. Various forms of pure alcohol used in chemical industry and as fuel.

Alcoholics Anonymous, organization formed (1934) to combat ALCOHOLISM. Provides clinics for inebriates, psychiatric and medical treatment and contacts with controlled alcoholics.

alcoholism, pathological condition caused by excessive consumption of alcoholic beverages. Biological consequences include cirrhosis of liver,

polyneuritis, affection of brain function leading to hallucinations, dietary and behavioural disorders.

Alcott, Louisa May (1832–88), Amer. children's novelist. Books include *Little Women* (1868), *Little Men* (1871), *Jo's Boys* (1886).

Alcuin or **Albinus** (*c.* 735–804), Eng. churchman and scholar at court of Charlemagne. Estab. study of the 7 liberal arts, later the curriculum of medieval W Europe.

Aldanov, Mark, orig. Mark Aleksandrovich Landau (1886–1957), Russ. author who became US citizen. Works include *The Fifth Seal* (1939), *The Escape* (1950).

aldehyde, in chemistry, any of class of organic compounds containing group (–CHO), yielding acids on oxidation, alcohol on reduction.

Alder, Kurt (1902–58), Ger. organic chemist. Shared Nobel Prize for Chemistry (1950) with Otto Diels for discovery and development of method of synthesizing of benzene ring hydrocarbons.

alder, deciduous shrub or tree of genus *Alnus* of cool temp. regions. Simple leaves bear catkins. Wood is water resistant; used for pumps, millwheels, bridges, *etc.*; bark yields brownish dye. Species include black alder, *A. ghitinosa.*

alderfly, dark-coloured insect of family Sialidae. Larvae are aquatic and predacious on other aquatic insects.

Alderney, one of CHANNEL ISLANDS. Area: $3\frac{1}{2}$ sq. mi.; cap. St Anne. Fertile soil, cattle grazing. Occupied by Germans (1940–5).

Aldrich, Nelson Wilmarth (1841–1915), Amer. politician and financier, concerned esp. with tariff protection. Instrumental in adoption of Payne-Aldrich Tariff Act (1909).

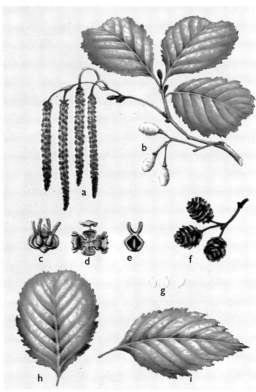

Common Alder: 1. winter silhouette, 2. in summer, 3. (a) male catkin, (b) female catkin, (c) female flower (d) male flower, (e) section of fruit, (f) cones, (g) seeds, (h) leaf of black alder, (i) leaf of grey alder.

Aldrich, Thomas Bailey (1836–1907), Amer. novelist, editor, dramatist. Edited *The Atlantic Monthly* and wrote *Marjorie Daw* (1873).

Aldrin, Edwin ('Buzz') *see* APOLLO PROJECT.

Aldus Manutius (1450–1515), Venetian humanist and printer. Estab. Aldine Press, with imprint of dolphin and anchor; issued series of editions of classical authors. Commissioned 1st italic type (1501).

ale, in UK, any light-coloured BEER. In US, beverage darker, heavier and more bitter than beer, containing *c.* 6% alcohol.

Aleichem, Sholem, orig. Solomon Rabinowitz (1859–1916), Yiddish writer. Best known for tragicomic tales of life among Russ. Jews in late 19th cent., esp. *Tevye der Milchiger* adapted for stage as *Fiddler on the Roof*.

Alekhine or **Aljechin, Aleksandr Aleksandrovich** (1892–1946), Russ. chess player. World champion 1927–35, 1937–46.

Alemán, Miguel (1902–   ), Mexican statesman. Pres. of Mexico (1946–52); consolidated prosperity of Mexico by industrialization, introduction of modern agric. methods, expansion of educ. system, and encouragement of foreign investment.

Alemanni, Germanic tribe occupying Rhenish lands in 5th cent. Dialects of SW Germany and Switzerland called Alemannic.

Alemannia or **Alamannia,** division of ancient Germany approx. from end of 3rd cent. Covered SW part of Germany, parts of Switzerland and Tyrol.

Alembert, Jean le Rond d' (1717–83), Fr. mathematician and philosopher. Co-editor of Diderot's *Encyclopédie*. Expressed principle (1742) in mechanics showing that Newton's 3rd law of motion applies to movable as well as stationary bodies.

Alençon, cap. of Orne department, NW France, at junction of Briante and Sarthe rivers. Manufactures lace, linen, pottery. Contains 15th cent. Church of Notre Dame. Pop. *c.* 22,000.

Aleppo, Alep, city in NW Syria. Centre of Hittite kingdom before 1000 BC, on caravan route to Baghdad. Flourished in Byzantine empire, taken by Arabs, later by Turks; site of much subsequent fighting. Products include silk and cotton, trading in wool, hides and fruit. Pop. (1965) 563,000.

Aletsch glacier, largest glacier in Europe (area: 66 sq. mi.); situated between Jungfrau and Aletschhorn, Bernese Oberland.

Aleutian Islands, chain of *c.* 150 volcanic islands extending 1,200 mi.

Toledo, showing the Alcazar (top right)

Marine algae: (left to right) Bladder Wrack, Tangle, Sargassum Weed, Giant Kelp

from SW Alaska across N Pacific. Discovered by Vitus Bering (1741), now US territory. Composed of 4 groups, with moderate damp climate, no trees, but dense vegetation. Fishing and fur trapping main occupations.

alewife, sawbelly, *Alosa pseudo-*

harengus, N Amer. fish of herring family. Used as food and in manufacture of oil and fertilizer.

Alexander VI, orig. Rodrigo de Borja (1431–1503), pope (1492–1503). Member of Sp. branch of Borgias among whom he distributed patronage. Proclaimed demarcation line separating Spanish and Portuguese colonies (1494).

Alexander [III] the Great (356–323 BC), king of Macedon (336–323 BC), son of Philip II. After subduing uprising of Gk. states, began (334 BC) conquest of W Asia by conquering Persian Empire through Asia Minor, then pushing into Bactria and India. Army refused to go further and Alexander forced to return to Susa (324 BC) after 8 yr. of marching. Attempted to estab. unity of culture in extensive empire; married Bactrian princess, Roxana. Died of fever, having achieved renown as general and leader.

Alexander I (1777–1825), emperor of Russia (1801–25). Succeeded his father Paul I, at whose murder he prob. connived. Failed in attempts at domestic reform. Joined alliance against Napoleon I (1805); military defeats led to peace at TREATY OF TILSIT (1807). Successfully countered Napoleon's attack on Russia (1812). After attending CONGRESS OF VIENNA (1814–15), promoted Holy Alliance in order to retain polit. status quo in Europe.

Alexander II (1818–81), emperor of Russia (1855–81), son of Nicholas I. After defeat in Crimean War and peasant disorders, initiated reforms in Russia, most important being Edict of Emancipation (1861) freeing serfs. Failure resulted in increasing terrorism. Assassinated by anarchist.

Alexander III (1845–94), emperor of Russia (1881–94). Increased police powers and took other

Totem pole of Red Indians indigenous to the Alexander Archipelago

measures to counter liberalism; persecuted Jews. Advocated peaceful foreign policy.

Alexander III (1241–86), king of Scotland (1249–86). Defeated Norwegians at Largs (1263), ending dispute over Western Isles.

Alexander (1888–1934), king of Yugoslavia (1921–34). Became regent of Kingdom of Serbs, Croats and Slovenes (1918). In 1929 made himself absolute ruler, dismissed parl. and abolished constitution, named country Yugoslavia. Assassinated in France.

Alexander, Harold Rupert Leofric George, Earl Alexander of Tunis (1891–1969), Brit. army officer. In World War 2, directed retreat from Dunkirk (1940) and Burma (1942). Led invasion of Italy through Sicily, becoming Allied commander-in-chief of Med. forces. Gov.-general of Canada (1946–52); UK Min. of Defence under Churchill (1952–4).

Alexander, Samuel (1859–1938), Brit. philosopher. Postulated system based on unity of space and time in works, notably *Space, Time and Deity* (1920).

Alexander, William, Earl of Stirling (c. 1567–1640), Scot. poet. Works include *Aurora* (1604) and love sonnets. Also wrote *An Encouragement to Colonies* (1624).

Alexander Archipelago, group of c. 1,100 islands off SE Alaska, US, incl. Chichagof Is., Admiralty Is., Prince of Wales Is. Area: 13,000 sq. mi. A submerged mountain system, islands rise steeply from the sea. Fishing, fur farming and logging are chief occupations.

Alexander Nevski, Saint (1220–63), grand duke of Vladimir-Suzdal. Russian hero after victory (1240) over Swedes on the Neva, from which he took his surname.

Alexander Obrenovich (1876–1903), king of Serbia (1899–1903). Took over govt. (1893), abolished liberal constitution. Scandalous marriage and subsequent repressive polit. measures ended in assassination of royal couple.

Alexander Severus, Marcus Aurelius, orig. Alexianus Bassianus (*c.* AD 208–235), Roman emperor (222–235). Succeeded Heliogabalus.

alexander, plant of family Umbelliferae, *e.g. Smyrnium olusatrum,* native to Europe and resembling celery. Formerly cultivated as pot herb.

Alexandra Feodorovna (1872–1918), empress of Russia, consort of Tsar Nicholas II. Dominated by RASPUTIN who encouraged her opposition to liberal reform. Shot with husband and family by Bolsheviks (1918).

Alexandria, city and Med. seaport, United Arab Repub., NW of Nile delta. Built 332 BC by Alexander the Great. Handles most of Egypt's foreign trade. Cap. (304–30 BC); centre of Hellenistic and Jewish culture. Became part of Roman Empire after 30 BC; in 642 fell to Arabs who moved cap. to Cairo. Main Brit. Med. naval base in both World Wars. Pop. (1960) 1,516,234.

Alexandrian codex, Gk. manuscript of the Scriptures (believed written 5th cent.), presented by Patriarch of Constantinople to Charles I of England (1628). Contains Septuagint version of complete OT. Now in British Museum.

Alexandrian Library, library founded at Alexandria, Egypt by Ptolemy I (*c.* 290 BC) and enlarged by Ptolemy II. Contained 400,000 volumes by *c.* 300 BC, 700,000 by 1st cent. BC. Said to have been destroyed by Caliph Omar AD 646.

alexandrine, in poetry, line of 12 or 13 syllables. Used in rhyming couplets of Classical Fr. drama (works of Corneille and Racine). In English used esp. by Spenser in *Faerie Queene.*

alexandrite, variety of chrysoberyl, green by daylight, red in artificial light. Used as gem stone.

Alexius [I] Comnenus (1048–1118), emperor of Byzantium (1081–1118). Supplanted Nicephorus III. Restored prestige of empire defending it against Norman invaders. Negotiated with leaders of 1st Crusade and persuaded them to recognize his claim to be suzerain of Antioch.

alfalfa, lucerne, *Medicago sativa,* European leguminous forage plant naturalized in most temp. regions. Trifoliate leaves and bluish purple flowers; grown mainly for hay;

Greek coin with head of Alexander the Great

adaptable to varying soils and climates.

Alfieri, Vittorio (1749–1803), Ital. poet and dramatist. Tragedies include *Cleopatra, Antigone, Oreste.* Collection of sonnets and odes, *L'America Libera* (1781–3) celebrate independence of US.

alfilaria, pin grass, *Erodium cicutarium,* European weed grown for forage in dry regions of SW US.

Alfonso [X] the Wise (1221–84), king of León and Castile (1252–82). Waged war with Moors (1261–6). Systematized legal code; made astronomical observations. Dethroned by his son Sancho.

Alfonso XIII (1886–1941), king of Spain (1886–1931). His mother, Maria Christina of Austria, served as regent until 1902. Unsatisfactory foreign policy and problems created by neutral position of Spain in World War 1, led to estab. of dictatorship (1923) under Primo de Rivera. Forced to go into exile with fall of dictatorship.

Alfonso III (1210–79), king of Portugal (1248–79). Completed reconquest of Portugal from Moors; stimulated trade.

Alfred the Great (849–99), king of Wessex (871–99). Danish threat to conquer England forced him to retreat (878) to Somerset, but subsequent victory at Ethandum routed Danes. Initiated programme of reform, codifying legal system through strong, centralized monarchy. Rebuilt navy, encouraged revival of clerical learning and took leading role in estab. Old

English literary prose. Sponsored writing of Anglo-Saxon Chronicle. Subject of many semi-legendary episodes.

algae, motile or non-motile chlorophyll-containing plants of phylum Thallophyta. Found in fresh and salt water. Range from unicellular forms, usually microscopic, to multicellular forms up to 100 ft. in length.

Algarve, prov. of S Portugal. Area:

Alfalfa

1,958 sq. mi.; cap. Faro. Settled by Phoenicians, prospered under Moors. Fruit grown; tuna fish and sardine industries. Pop. *c.* 315,000.

algebra, branch of mathematics dealing with general relative statements using letters and other symbols to represent numbers, values, *etc.* in description of such relationships.

Algeciras, city of Cádiz prov., S Spain, port on Med. Sea. Site of Brit. victory over Fr. and Sp. forces (1801). Pop. (1965) 66,317. **Algeciras Conference** (1906) estab. temporary settlement of rivalry between European powers for control of Morocco. Protection of Ger. interests assured, France and Spain authorized to police Morocco.

Alger, Horatio (1834–99), Amer. writer of books for boys. Wrote over 100 books depicting success achieved despite great odds.

Algeria, repub. of NW Africa. Area: *c.* 855,900 sq. mi.; cap. Algiers; principal cities Oran, Constantine.

Atlas Mts. separate Med. coastline and fertile Tell region. High semi-arid plateaus and Sahara Desert inland. Agriculture (cereals, fruits, vines), stock raising, fishing important. Mineral resources include phosphate, lead, silver, iron ore, zinc. Oil and natural gas discovered 1956. Annexed

Old and new architecture in Algiers

by France 1842. After World War 2, nationalist opposition to Fr. rule, led by Moslem Front de Libération Nationale (FLN), resulted in war (1954–62) with right-wing Secret Army Organization (OAS); independence achieved 1962. Official language, Arabic. Pop. (1966 est.) 12,102,000.

Algiers [Fr: **Alger**], cap. of Algeria, major port of N Africa on Med. Sea. Old Town dominated by 16th cent. Casbah (fortress); modern city built by French (19th cent.). Exports fruit, wine, iron ore. Seat of provisional Fr. govt. during World War 2. Pop. (1966) 897,352.

Algonkian, Amer. Indian linguistic group. Included Blackfoot, Cheyenne, Cree, Chippawa, Algonkin, Shawnee, Fox, Micmac and Mohegan tribes. Occupied large area of N America from Newfoundland to Rocky Mts.

Algonkin, Algonquin, N Amer. Indian tribe of Algonkian linguistic stock. Made alliance with Fr. settlers in Canada (early 17th cent.).

algorism, term denoting Arabic system of arithmetical notation. Uses figures 1, 2, 3, *etc.*

Algren, Nelson (1909–   ), Amer. novelist and short-story writer. His works, often describing slum conditions in Chicago, include *The Man with the Golden Arm* (1949), *A Walk on the Wild Side* (1956).

Alhambra [Arabic: the red], remains of Moorish buildings on hills above Granada, Spain. Built (1238–1354), extensively restored after 1828. Exceptional examples of Islamic architecture.

Ali (*c.* 600–661), 4th caliph and husband of Fatima; cousin and faithful follower of Mohammed. Rule witnessed beginning of Shiite-Sunnite divisions in Islam. Ali and son Husein regarded as important Shiite saints.

Ali Pasha (*c.* 1744–1822), Turkish governor of Yannina, orig. Albanian brigand leader. Rebelled against order of deposition (1820); assassinated by Turkish agent.

Alicante, prov. of Valencia, SE Spain. Area: 2,185 sq. mi.; cap. Alicante. Industries include tobacco, food processing, oil refining. Exports fruit and wine.

Alice Springs, town in Northern Territory, Australia. Forms terminus of Central Australian Rly. Pastoral and opal mining area. Pop. (1966) 4,000.

Alien and Sedition Acts, legislation passed (1798) by US Congress empowering pres. to expel aliens. Also provided for legal action against govt. critics. Sponsored by Federalists to counter Jeffersonian strength among immigrant voters.

alienation, in psychiatry, term used referring to feelings of depersonalization and withdrawal from reality.

alimentary canal, in mammals, tubular passage from mouth to anus concerned with intake of food, digestion, and disposal of residual waste products. Includes pharynx, oesophagus, stomach, small intestine, large intestine, rectum.

alkali, base, substance soluble in water and forming caustic solution which neutralizes acids and changes colour of indicator dyes. Used in manufacture of soap, glass, textiles drugs and paper. Important alkalis are compounds of calcium, sodium and potassium.

alkaloid, in chemistry, any of group of organic bases containing nitrogen and oxygen. Often of plant origin, used in medicine. Examples are caffeine, curare, heroin, quinine.

Al-Khowarizmi (*fl.* 820), Arabian mathematician, author of treatises on Hindu algebra and arithmetic. Supposedly gave name to algebra. Works, translated into Latin, much used as source books in medieval Europe.

All Saints' Day, in Christian calendar, 1 Nov. Feast day instituted by Pope Gregory IV in honour of all saints.

All Souls' Day, in Christian calendar, 2 Nov. Feast day commemorates all Christians who have died in the faith.

Allah, name for Supreme Being used by Moslems.

Allahabad, city of S Uttar Pradesh, India, at junction of Ganges and

Jumna rivers. Commercial and communications centre. Regarded by Hindus as holy city. Pop. (1965) 465,000.

Allan, Sir Hugh (1810–82), Canadian industrialist and ship-owner, b. Scotland. Involved in PACIFIC SCANDAL.

Allegheny Mountains, part of W Appalachian Mts. of US, extending from Pennsylvania S to Virginia. Generally over 2,800 ft., in places over 4,800 ft.

allegory, in literature, work expressing commentary or account of social, polit. or artistic ideas, using complex symbolism. Characters represent types or personifications. Examples include *The Faerie Queene* by Spenser, Bunyan's *Pilgrim's Progress.*

Allegro, John Marco (1923–   ), Eng. philologist, archaeologist and broadcaster. Has made extensive studies of DEAD SEA SCROLLS. Author of *Dead Sea Scrolls* (1956), *Discoveries in the Judaean Desert* (1968).

allele, allelomorph, in genetics, term for type of gene responsible for hereditary variation.

Allen, Ethan (1738–89), commander during Amer. Revolution. Organized Vermont militia known as Green Mountain Boys; captured Fort Ticonderoga (1775). Seized by British during attempt to invade Canada. Unsuccessfully advocated independence for Vermont.

Allen, Ned see ALLEYN, EDWARD.

Allen, Ralph (1913–66), Canadian journalist and novelist. His *Home Made Banners* (1946) and *The High White Forest* (1964) are about World War 2.

Allen, [William] Hervey (1889–1949), Amer. writer. Hist. novels include *Anthony Adverse* (1933).

Allen, Zachariah (1795–1882), Amer. inventor. Replaced cogwheels with belt lines in transmitting power. Said to have developed 1st central heating system to use hot air.

Allenby, Edmund Henry Hynman, 1st Viscount Allenby of Megiddo (1861–1936), Brit. army officer. Commander of Egyptian expeditionary force (1917–19), invaded Palestine and decisively defeated (1918) Turks at Samaria. Brit. high commissioner for Egypt (1919–25).

Allentown, indust. city of E Pennsylvania, US; situated N of Philadelphia. Orig. settled by Ger. religious groups. Trade centre for Pennsylvania Dutch farming region. Manufactures machinery, textiles, rolling stock, cement. Arms supply centre for colonists' army in Amer. Revolution. Pop. (1960) 108,347.

allergy, body disorder caused by hypersensitivity to emotional excitement, physical conditions or certain substances, *e.g.* pollen, hair, various foods. Allergic disorders include skin rashes, asthma, hay fever, digestive disturbances.

Alleyn, Edward (1566–1626), Eng. actor known as Ned Allen. Played leads in *Tamburlaine* and *Doctor Faustus.* Owner-manager with Philip Henslowe of several London theatres, incl. Globe and Fortune.

Alliance for Progress, programme of economic assistance instituted (1961) by US Pres. John Kennedy to help resolve economic and social problems of Latin Amer. countries. Capital investment, tax and land reforms pledged by members. Initial expenditure to last 10 yr.

Allies, term used to describe opponents of Central Powers (in World War 1) and AXIS (in World War 2). In both wars, most important members were Britain, France, US and Russia.

alligator, large reptile of genus *Alligator* of crocodile family. Swims with assistance of lashing movements of tail; feeds on fish and mammals; valued for its hide. *A. mississippiensis,* attaining length of 12 ft., inhabits S US. Smaller *A. sinensis* is found in Yangtze valley, China.

Allingham, Margery Louise (1904–66), Eng. writer of detective fiction. Works include *Tiger in the Smoke* and *The China Governess.*

allium, genus of bulbous plants of family Liliaceae found in Europe, N Africa, Asia and N America. Basal leaves, umbellate white, yellow or red flowers. Species include onion, garlic, chives, leek, shallot, all with characteristic odour.

allosaur, large extinct carnivorous dinosaur of genus *Allosaurus* from late Jurassic period of N America. Over 30 ft. in length with small forelegs and massive hind legs.

allotrophy, property of certain chem. elements (*e.g.* carbon, sulphur, phosphorus), existing in 2 or more distinct forms. Differ in physical properties and atomic arrangement, similar chem. properties.

alloy, metallic substance composed of mixture of 2 or more metals, or of a compound of metallic and non-metallic elements. Common alloys are brass (copper and zinc) steel (iron, carbon, manganese, nickel chromium).

Allport, Gordon Willard (1897–1967), Amer. psychologist. Works

The Alhambra, Granada

include *Personality; a psychological interpretation* (1937) and *Pattern and Growth in Personality* (1961).

allspice, berry of allspice tree, *Pimenta dioica.* Yields pungent aromatic spice.

Allston, Washington (1779–1843), Amer. romantic painter. Works include *Diana in the Chase* and *Elijah in the Desert.*

Allumettes, tribes of Algonkian Indians inhabiting Allumette Is. (now Morrison Is.) in Ottawa R.

alluvium, sedimentary material; usually clay, sand, gravel, *etc.,* deposited by running water. Term usually refers to geologically recent deposits laid down in stream channels and on flood plains of river valleys.

Allward, Walter Seymour (1876–1955), Canadian sculptor. Designed Canadian War Memorial at Vimy Ridge, France.

Alma, river of Crimean oblast of Russ. SFSR, flowing into Black Sea *c.* 20 mi. N of Sevastopol. First battle of Crimean War (1854) took place near its mouth.

Alma Ata, orig. Verny, city of USSR, cap. of Kazakh SSR. Market centre and fruit growing area. Industries, textiles, food processing, electrical goods. Pop. (1966) 634,000.

almanac, publication orig. containing astronomical, meteorological and eccles. data, based on calendar and often including astrological and prophetic material. Now usually refers to book of useful facts and statistics, published annually, *e.g. Whitaker's*

Alligator

Alsatian Dog

Aloe

Almanack [UK], *World Almanac* [US] and *Canadian Almanac.*

Almanach de Gotha, reference book of European royalty and nobility, giving details of administration and statistics of most countries. Published annually (1763–1944) at Gotha, Germany.

Almar, Christian (1826–98), Swiss Alpine guide. Made many notable 1st ascents with famous mountaineers, incl. Edward Whymper.

Alma-Tadema, Sir Lawrence (1836–1912), Brit. painter, b. Holland. Best known for representation of Egyptian, Gk. and Roman life.

Almeria, city and port of S Spain. Exports grapes and minerals. Important Moorish city (13th–15th cent.). Pop. *c.* 90,000.

Almohades or **Almohads,** Berber dynasty of Morocco and Spain (12th–13th cent.). Founded by Mohammed ibn Tumart (*c.* 1120) in opposition to ALMORAVIDES, displacing them by 1174. Defeated by Spain and Portugal (1212), by Merenide dynasty 1269.

Alps near St Moritz in the upper Engadine, Switzerland

almond, *Amygdalus prunus,* tree of warm temp. regions, native to W Asia. Fruit has nut-like stone or kernel which yields oil. Sweet almonds used in cooking and confectionery; oil used as lubricant for delicate mechanisms. Bitter almonds used in manufacture of flavouring extracts; the oil, cosmetics, medicine.

Almoravides or **Almoravids,** Berber dynasty of Morocco and Spain (11th–12th cent.). Founded by Abdullah ibn Yasin whose successors founded Marrakesh (1062), aided Spanish and Moors against Christians; displaced by ALMOHADES.

alnus, genus of alders, trees and shrubs of family Betulaceae found in N temp. regions and the Andes. Toothed leaves and small woody cone-like fruit.

aloe, genus of succulent plants of genus *Aloe* of family Liliaceae. Found chiefly in S Africa. Red or yellow flowers; yields drugs and hemp-like fibre.

Alonso, Alicia (1909–   ), Amer. ballerina and choreographer, b. Cuba. Founded (1948) Ballet Alicia Alonso, later called Ballet de Cuba.

Aloysius, Saint, orig. Luigi Gonzaga (1568–91), Ital. Jesuit. Renowned for purity. Patron saint of youth.

alpaca, domesticated mammal of S America, resembling LLAMA. Long, woolly fleece used commercially. Also name of lightweight cloth, made orig. of alpaca wool.

alpha particle, product of spontaneous disintegration of radioactive substances. Particle consists of 2 protons and 2 neutrons ejected with great velocity from nucleus.

alphabet, any system of recording language, esp. system in which almost every spoken sound is represented by a symbol (letter). Developed by Phoenicians (*c.* 1400 BC), transmitted from NW Semites to Greece (1st recorded *c.* 8th cent. BC), used in ancient Rome and forms basis of alphabets in W European and several recently written African and Asian languages. Cyrillic alphabet, developed separately from Greek, used in Russian. Hebrew and Arabic alphabets are also still in use.

Alpheus, in Gk. myth., god of R. Alpheus, rising in Arcadia and flowing through Elis. Fell in love with nymph ARETHUSA. Waters diverted by Heracles to clean stables of Augeas.

alpine aster, *Aster meritus,* Rocky Mountain herb with violet-purple flowers.

alpine rose, any of various European and Asiatic alpine rhododendrons.

Alps, major mountain system of Europe. Extends N from Gulf of Genoa through France, Switzerland, Germany, Austria and Yugoslavia. Many famous peaks over 14,000 ft., incl. Mont Blanc (highest in Europe, 15,781 ft.), Matterhorn (14,782 ft.), Eiger (13,000 ft.). Valleys contain beautiful lakes, incl. Geneva, Constance, Como, Maggiore. Resorts concentrated in Switzerland, France and Austria. Passes contain road and rail links.

Als, island off Denmark, separated from S Jutland by Als Sound. Area: 121 sq. mi.; chief city, Sonderberg. Agriculture and fruit-growing. Pop. *c.* 50,000.

Alsace and **Lorraine,** ancient provs. of NW France, part of Ger. empire until 17th cent. Alsace and NE Lorraine annexed by Germany after Franco-Prussian War (1871). France regained possession by Treaty of Versailles (1919). Now comprises Fr. departments of Moselle, Bas-Rhin and Haut-Rhin. Alsace has important industry; Lorraine mainly agric.

alsatian, German shepherd, sheep dog originating in N Europe. Long body, long bushy tail; smooth coat ranging in colour from grey-white to brindled, black-and-tan or black. Used esp. in police work and as guide dog for the blind.

Altai, mountain system of SW Siberia, Russ. SFSR, and of W Mongolia. Belukha (14,780 ft.) in Katum range is highest peak. Rich mineral deposits, incl. lead, zinc, silver.

Altaic, family of languages of Eurasia. Divided into W and E, of which Turkic and Mongolian are largest sub-groups.

Altamira, group of caves near Santander, N Spain. Prehistoric paintings of animals of Magdalenian period discovered 1880.

alternation of generations, in biology, alternation of asexual and sexual cycles in reproductive processes of an organism. Often known as metagenesis in plants.

Altgeld, John Peter (1847–1902),

Amer. polit. leader, b. Germany. Democrat governor of Illinois (1892–6). Opposed use of Federal troops against strikers at Pullman, Ill. (1894).

Althing, Icelandic parliament, first convened 930. Oldest European parl. body. Voted independence of Iceland from Denmark (1944).

altimeter, device for measuring altitude. Types in use include form of aneroid barometer and of radio wave transmitter and receiver.

alto, in singing, term used for highest male voice. Also lowest female voice.

alto clarinet *see* CLARINET.

alto flute *see* FLUTE.

altruism [Lat: of or to others], selfless service, acting for benefit of others without reward. Term first used by positivist philosopher Auguste Comte.

alum, double sulphate of potassium and aluminium. Name also applied to large number of double sulphates having similar formulae and crystal structure.

alumina, aluminium oxide, natural or synthetic oxide of aluminium, occurring naturally in pure crystal form as corundum.

aluminium [UK], **aluminum** [US] (Al), silvery-white metallic element. Resists corrosion, ductile and malleable; good conductor of heat and electricity. Produced commercially from bauxite by electrolysis of alumina. Used, pure or alloyed, where lightness is needed, *e.g.* aircraft, cooking utensils, electrical apparatus. Chief producers, US, USSR, Canada.

alumroot, herb of genus *Heuchera*, esp. N Amer. *H. americana.* Heart-shaped leaves and clusters of purplish flowers; roots have astringent properties.

Alva, Duke of *see* ALBA, FERNANDO ALVAREZ DE TOLEDO, DUKE OF.

Alvarado, Pedro de (1486–1541), Sp. conquistador, served under Hernán Cortés in conquest of Mexico.

Alpaca

Conquered Guatemala and Salvador; governor of Guatemala until killed fighting Mexican Indians.

Alvarez, Luis W[alter] (1911–   ), Amer. physicist. Awarded Nobel Prize for Physics (1968) for developing hydrogen bubble chamber, used to record tracks of charged nuclear particles.

alyssum, plant of genus *Alyssum* of family Cruciferae, native to Eurasia. Has small yellow or white flowers.

Amadis of Gaul, legendary medieval hero, subject of chivalric romances 1st composed in Spain or Portugal (13th or 14th cent.).

Amagar, island of Denmark, in the Oresund. N end occupied by part of Copenhagen. Pop. (1965) 178,184.

Amagasaki, city of S Honshu, Japan, on Osaka Bay. Indust. centre and port. Pop. (1965) 501,000.

Amalekites, Semitic tribe of Palestine. In OT, enemies of Israelites; defeated by Saul and David.

Amalfi, town of Campania, S Italy, on Gulf of Salerno. Popular tourist resort. Cathedral in Sicilian-Arabic style begun 10th cent. Pop. (1965) 7,163.

amalgam, metallic compound containing mercury. Silver and gold amalgams occur in natural deposits, most others man-made. Used in dental fillings, mirror manufacture.

Amalric or **Amaury,** Latin kings of Jerusalem. **Amalric II** (*c.* 1155–1205) succeeded to title by marrying daughter of Amalric I. Became king of Cyprus (1194).

Amalthaea, in Gk. myth., goat which suckled infant Zeus in Crete, or nymph who fed Zeus with goat's milk. Horn of goat, given power to provide whatever owner wished, known as Cornucopia (Horn of Plenty).

amanita, widely distributed agaric genus of white-spored fungus. Most species are poisonous.

amaranth, cosmopolitan plant of genus *Amaranthus*. Garden species cultivated for colourful foliage and showy flowers, *e.g.* Joseph's coat, love-lies-bleeding. Some species are weeds, *e.g.* pigweed, tumbleweed.

amaryllis, genus of bulbous S African plants of lily family. Species include belladonna lily, *Amaryllis (Atropa) belladonna*.

Amateur Athletic Association (AAA), governing body for men's athletics in England and Wales. Founded 1886. Organizes annual UK championships.

Amati, Andrea (*c.* 1520–1611), Ital. violin maker. Produced 1st instrument of modern shape. Founded family of string instrument makers which in-

Alpine Rose

Alpine Aster

cluded **Niccolo Amati** (1596–1684) who taught Antonio Stradivari.

Amaya, Carmen (1909–1963), Sp. dancer and choreographer. Leading exponent of flamenco dancing, found greatest success in S America.

Amaziah (d. *c.* 775 BC), king of Judah (*c.* 802– *c.* 775 BC), successor of Joash of Judah. Conquered Edom and attacked Joash of Israel who captured Amaziah and sacked Temple in Jerusalem.

Hippeastrum, one of the Amaryllis genus

Amazonite in raw (left) and polished state

Amazon River

Amazon, principal river (c. 3,500 mi.) of S America. Rises in Peruvian Andes in 2 major headstreams, Marañón and Ucayali, and flows across Brazil to Atlantic. Tributaries include Negro, Napo, Putumayo, Juruá, Madeira, Tapajós; main river ports, Manaus, Iquitos. Divides around Marajó Is.; S stream called Pará. Main resources include wild rubber, cacao, jute. Sparsely populated, mainly by Indians. Vicente Yáñez Pinzón explored lower river (1500); 1st crossing of continent via Amazon by Francisco de Orellana (1540–1).

amazonite, amazon stone, green feldspar mineral named after Amazon R., site of its 1st discovery.

Amazons, in Gk. myth., nation of female warriors, living around Eux-

Amethyst: raw and cut stones (top), amethyst and diamond ring settings (below)

ine Sea (Black Sea). Allied with Trojans in Trojan War, Queen Penthesileia slain by Achilles. As 9th labour Heracles required to obtain girdle of Amazon queen, Hippolyte. Theseus repelled Amazons' invasion of Attica, capturing Queen Hippolyte (or Antiope) who bore him Hippolytus.

amber, fossil resin of vegetable origin. Pale yellow, reddish or brownish in colour. Used as a gemstone.

ambergris, waxy secretion of sperm whale intestine. Found floating in trop. seas as yellow, grey, black or variegated mass. Used in manufacture of perfume.

Ambler, Eric (1909–   ), Eng. author. His suspense novels include *Journey Into Fear* (1940), *Passage of Arms* (1959).

Ambleside, village in Westmorland, England. Tourist centre of Lake District; associated with poet Wordsworth.

amblypod, primitive mammal of extinct order Pantodonta from Paleocene and Eocene eras. Massive body with short legs.

Amboina, Ambon, island of Moluccas, E Indonesia. Area: 314 sq. mi.; chief city and port Amboina. Exports copra, spices, sugar.

Ambrose, Saint (c. 340–397), Ger. churchman. One of fathers of Roman church. Created Bishop of Milan (374). Protagonist of orthodoxy against Arianism. Works include commentaries, hymns and treatises. Type of plainsong called Ambrosian Chant attributed to him.

ambrosia and **nectar,** in Gk. myth., the food and drink of the gods, giving qualities of immortality and beauty.

ambrosia beetle, small beetle of Ipidae or Scolytidae families. Bores into dead wood and cultivates ambrosia fungus on which it feeds.

Amen *see* AMMON.

Amenhotep or **Amenophis,** name of ancient Egyptian kings of 18th dynasty. During reign of **Amenhotep III** (1411–1375 BC) empire consolidated, many temples and monuments erected. Amenhotep IV became AKHENATON.

America, western hemisphere lands including NORTH AMERICA, SOUTH AMERICA, CENTRAL AMERICA, WEST INDIES. Term sometimes used as synonym for US.

American bison *see* BUFFALO.

American Civil Liberties Union, organization estab. 1920 to maintain and protect civil rights. Provides legal counsel, prepares briefs for many controversial cases. Financed by private contributions.

American Expeditionary Forces (AEF), official name of US troops sent to European front during World War 1. Commanded by John J. Pershing (1917–19).

American Federation of Labor-Congress of Industrial Organizations (AFL-CIO), Amer. labour organization founded 1881, reorganized (1886) as AFL representing craft unions. Led by Samuel Gompers in formative years. In 1935, dissenters formed Committee for Industrial Organization (later CIO), under J. L. Lewis, protested AFL's conservatism and exclusion of workers in growing mass-production industries. Two bodies merged (1955), electing George Meany as pres.

American Friends Service Committee, organization estab. (1917) by QUAKERS in US. Provides for overseas relief and reconstruction; shared Nobel Peace Prize (1947) with Service Council of Brit. Society of Friends.

American League, US professional baseball league estab. 1901. Comprises 8 charter members, 4 teams added in 1960s. New York Yankees team has won 29 league championships.

American lion, cougar, *Felix concolor,* large powerful cat formerly widespread over most of the Americas, now extinct in much of US and E Canada. Tawny brown in colour; longer limbed and less bulky than jaguar.

American Party *see* KNOW-NOTHING MOVEMENT.

American Robin

American Revolution or **American War of Independence,** uprising (1775–83) resulting in independence from Britain for the Thirteen Colonies of N America. By mid-18th cent., had begun demands for limited self-govt.; STAMP ACT (1765) opposed on slogan 'No taxation without representation'. Further resentment after Townshend Acts (1767), levying duty on Brit. manufactured goods, resulted in BOSTON MASSACRE (1770) and BOSTON TEA PARTY (1773). Parl. subsequently passed INTOLERABLE ACTS (1774); representatives of colonies listed grievances at Continental Congress of 1774. Conflict began (Apr. 1775) at Lexington. George Washington appointed to lead Continental Army; DECLARATION OF INDEPENDENCE adopted July, 1776. Badly-prepared volunteer army of colonialists defeated in Quebec campaign (1775–6); fighting inconclusive until Brit. defeat (Oct. 1777) at Saratoga. French gave rebels crucial aid and British were pushed N from Carolinas (1780–1) leading to Cornwallis' surrender (Oct. 1781) ending YORKTOWN CAMPAIGN and concluding hostilities. Treaty of Paris (1783) formally recognized national independence of US.

American robin, *Turdus migratorius,* large N Amer. thrush. Upper parts grey, breast dull red.

American States, Organization of *see* ORGANIZATION OF AMERICAN STATES.

America's Cup, international yachting trophy. Cup first awarded by Royal Yacht Squadron to schooner *America* after race around Isle of Wight. Presented (1857) to New York Yacht Club, subject to challenge by any foreign club, victory in 4 of 7 races needed to win.

Ames, Fisher (1758–1808), Amer. politician; Congressman from Massachusetts (1789–97). Supported policies of Alexander Hamilton, defended Jay's Treaty.

amethyst, coarsely crystallized quartz, violet or purple in colour. Used as a gem.

Amharic, Afro-Asian Semitic language; official language of Ethiopia, with *c.* 6 million speakers.

Amherst, Jeffrey Amherst, Baron (1717–97), Brit. army officer. Commanded Brit. forces at end of French and Indian Wars. Led successful siege of Louisburg (1758) and captured Montreal (1760).

Amherst College, liberal arts college for men, Amherst, Massachusetts, US. Orig. development of Amherst Academy; chartered 1825.

American Lion

Amherstburg, town on Detroit R., S Ontario, Canada. Fort Malden built 1796. In War of 1812, Brit. garrison and naval station, held by Amer. troops at end of war.

Amiel, Henri Frédéric (1821–81), Swiss poet and philosopher. Author of *Fragments d'un Journal Intime* (2 vols., pub. 1883).

Amiens, city of NE France. Industries, textiles, food processing, metalwork. Cathedral (13th cent.) is fine example of High Gothic architecture. Pop. (1962) 113,000.

amines, class of compounds derived from ammonia by replacement of 1 or more hydrogen atoms with organic groups. Used as solvents, rust-inhibiters and in anti-freeze mixtures.

amino acids, class of organic compounds containing carbon, hydrogen, oxygen and often sulphur. Certain amino acids necessary in metabolism; cannot be synthesized by human body and must be included in protein diet.

Amis, Kingsley (1922–), Eng. poet and novelist, one of 'angry young men' of 1950s. Works include *Lucky Jim* (1954), *The Anti-Death League* (1966).

Amman, cap. of Jordan, on Jabbok R. Centre of industry and commerce, royal residence. In Bible, appears as Rabbah. Contains Roman ruins. Pop. (1966) 300,000.

Ammanati, Bartolomeo (1511–92), Ital. sculptor and architect. Worked in Florence and Venice. Appointed architect to Cosimo de' Medici;

designed façade of Pitti Palace, Florence.

ammeter *see* GALVANOMETER.

Ammon, Amon, Amen, in ancient Egyptian religion, orig. god of Thebes, later imperial deity. Represented as ram or man with ram's head and horns. Had famous oracle at Siwa in Libyan Desert. Identified with Gk. Zeus and Roman Jupiter.

ammonia (NH_3), pungent-smelling gaseous compound, lighter than air and very soluble in water. Formed from atmospheric nitrogen or from coal-gas. Used as cleaner and water softener.

ammoniac, gum ammoniac, gum resin prepared from milky exudation from stem of *Dorema ammoniacum*, native to Iran, India, Siberia. Used in manufacture of porcelain cements and in medicine as an expectorant.

ammonite, flat spiral fossil shell of cephalopod mollusc of extinct order Ammonoidea. Common in Mesozoic era, extinct by end of Cretaceous.

Ammonites, ancient Semitic people, lived NW of Dead Sea on edge of Syrian Desert. Frequent conflict with Israel. Worshipped Moloch, offering human sacrifice.

amnesia, temporary or prolonged loss of memory. Caused by shock, fatigue, brain injury, alcohol or illness.

amoeba, microscopic one-celled animal of class Rhizopoda. Consists of naked mass of protoplasm; moves by pseudopodia, or false feet, which engulf food (minute animals, plants) in water.

Remains of a Roman city near Amman

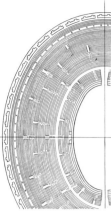

Amphitheatre: Left, plan of the Colosseum, Rome. Right, Roman amphitheatre at Pula, Yugoslavia

Amon see AMMON.

Amor, in Roman religion, god of love, son of Venus and brother of CUPID.

Amos, prophetic book of OT, written by Amos c. 750 BC. Made up of 3 parts, God's judgement on Gentiles and Israel; sermons on fate of Israel; visions of destruction, ending with redemption.

Amoy, city of Fukien prov., SE China, port on Amoy Is. Manufacturing centre; Yingtan-Amoy rly. (completed 1956) increased hinterland and trade range. Treaty port opened 1842. Pop. (1957) 224,300.

ampelopsis, woody vine of genus *Ampelopsis,* incl. pepper vine of S US. Blue, purple, yellow or orange berries.

Ampère, André Marie, FRS (1775–1836), Fr. physicist and mathematician. Known for work in electrodynamics; formulated Ampère's Law; studied relationship of electricity and magnetism.

ampere, unit of measurement in electricity. Named after André Marie Ampère.

amphibian, cold-blooded vertebrate of class Amphibia, comprising frogs, salamanders, caecilians. Adult is terrestrial, breathing by lungs and through moist glandular skin; larva is aquatic, breathing through gills.

amphibole, any of complex group of hydrous silicate minerals containing mainly calcium, magnesium, sodium, iron and aluminium. Includes hornblende, tremolite, asbestos, *etc.*

Amphilochus, in Gk. myth., brother of Alcmaeon one of Epigoni (*see* ADRASTUS). According to Homer, took part in Trojan War, celebrated as seer.

amphioxus, fishlike animal of LAN-CELET type, having certain vertebrate characteristics.

amphitheatre, circular or elliptical theatre with spectators' seats surrounding arena, used in ancient Rome for gladiatorial contests and exhibitions of wild beasts; arena sometimes flooded for mock sea battles. Colosseum, started under Vespasian, only survives in ruins.

Amphitrite, in Gk. myth., one of the Nereids. Wife of Poseidon and mother of Triton.

Amphitryon, in Gk. myth., grandson of Perseus, and husband of ALCMENE. Accidentally killed Electryon of Mycenae, Alcmene's father, fled to Thebes. Father of Iphicles.

Amritsar, city of NW Punjab, India, centre of Sikh religion. Manufactures silks, carpets. Site of conflict (1919) between Indian nationalists and Brit. forces. Pop. (1966) 403,000.

Amsterdam, constitutional cap. of Holland, on Ij inlet of Ijsselmeer. Major port connected by canals with North Sea and Rhine delta. Cultural, commercial centre of Netherlands. Diamond-cutting important. Contains University of Amsterdam (founded 1632). Pop. (1966) 863,000.

Amu Darya, Oxus, river of C Asia (1,350 mi.). Rises in Pamir Mts., flows down Hindu Kush; forms boundary between USSR and Afghanistan, enters Aral Sea through delta.

amulet, object worn as charm to ward off evil spirits, sometimes hung on doors or walls. Belief common to many cultures, now mostly found in primitive peoples. May be made of animal teeth, precious stone, *etc.,* sometimes with engraved symbols.

Amundsen, Roald (1872–1928), Norwegian polar explorer. Navigated

Typical 17th century house, Amsterdam

Bridge over the Amstel River, Amsterdam

Anaconda

North West Passage (1903–6), locating N magnetic pole. Reached S pole 34 days ahead of Robert Scott (Dec. 1911). Explored North East Passage (1918–20). Successfully flew over North Pole (1926) and was lost in search for crashed airship of Umberto Nobile.

Amur, river of E Asia, *c.* 1,770 mi. long. Rises in Mongolia, flows into Tatar Strait. Frozen for 6 months of year. Forms part of Sino-Soviet border, scene of border disputes.

amygdaloid, igneous and usually volcanic rock. Contains small cavities, produced by expansion of steam inside the rock before solidification. Cavities are later filled by deposits of various minerals, *e.g.* quartz, calcite, zeolites.

amygdaloidal lava, igneous and usually volcanic rock in which small cavities produced by expansion of steam have later been filled by deposits of minerals.

Amyot, Jacques (1513–93), Fr. churchman and humanist; Bishop of Auxerre (1570). Known for translation (1559) of Plutarch's *Lives,* basis for Thomas North's Eng. translation.

Amyot or **Amiot, Joseph** (1718–*c.* 1794), Fr. Jesuit missionary in China. Authority on Manchu language; one of the first to introduce Chinese literature, antiquities and customs to Europe.

Anabaptists, name for various Protestant sects (incl. MENNONITES) which deny validity of infant baptism. Applied historically to Ger. followers of Thomas Münzer (d. 1525), who preached separation of church and state, and were persecuted as heretics.

anabolism, in physiology, term for synthesis in living organisms of complex substances from simpler ones. *See* also METABOLISM.

anaconda, *Eunectes murinus,* large arboreal snake of family Boidae of trop. S America. Double row of large black spots along the back; nocturnal feeding, semi-aquatic.

Anacreon (*fl.* 6th cent. BC), Gk. lyric poet, b. Ionia. Poems mostly songs of wine and love, without depth of passion; only short fragments survive.

anaemia, disease resulting from deficiency of haemoglobin content of red blood corpuscles. Caused by loss of blood, characterized by pallor, weakness and breathlessness.

anaesthesia, loss of sensation deliberately caused by drugs known as ANAESTHETICS.

anaesthetics, drugs which act on higher nerve centres and cause unconsciousness; diethyl ether, nitrous oxide and cyclopropane most widely used. Local anaesthetics act on peripheral nerve endings in region of application; drugs used include novocaine and procaine. Refrigeration may be used to produce anaesthesia to reduce blood circulation. Chloroform 1st used as an anaesthetic by Sir James Simpson (1847).

Anaheim, city of S California, US. Founded by Germans (1857). Industrial centre of citrus fruit area. Site of Disneyland, built 1955; extensive tourist facilities. Pop. (1960) 104,184.

analcite, white or slightly coloured zeolite mineral. Occurs in various igneous rocks in crystal or massive form.

analogue computer, calculating device, esp. electronic, which determines magnitudes by measurements along scale rather than by digital counting. *See* COMPUTER.

analysis, qualitative, in chemistry, examination to discover nature of constituents of substance. Known as quantitative analysis when concerned with relative amount of constituents.

analytical chemistry *see* ANALYSIS, QUALITATIVE.

analytical geometry, branch of geometry using procedures of ALGEBRA. Position is stated analytically by co-ordinates.

Ananias, name of 3 biblical characters mentioned in the *Acts of the Apostles*: 1) a convert to Christianity who fell dead when rebuked by Paul for telling a lie. 2) disciple of Paul who cured latter of blindness in Damascus. 3) high priest who ordered mob to smite Paul.

anapaest, in poetry, metrical foot composed of 2 short syllables and 1 long.

anarchism, polit. theory based on principle of absolute freedom of individual. Proposes abolition of govt., legal systems, ownership of property and replacement by freely associating communities. Philosophical principle outlined by Zeno of Citium, advocated by Levellers (17th cent.), developed by Proudhon (19th cent.) and esp. by MIKHAIL BAKUNIN.

Anastasia (b. 1901), youngest daughter of Tsar Nicholas II of Russia. Generally assumed assassinated with rest of family (1918). Several women have claimed to be Anastasia without proving claim conclusively.

anathema [Gk: accursed], in Bible, object of consecration or execration. In R.C. Church, came to denote severest form of excommunication.

Anatolia, name for portion of Turkey which is ASIA MINOR.

Anatolian-Turkish, language of Turkic groups of Altaic family. Spoken by *c.* 25 million speakers over wide area from N Siberia to Turkey and Cyprus.

anatomy, science concerned with structure of plants and animals and with their dissection. Divided into embryology (pre-natal development), histology (structure and tissues) and cytology (structure and function of cells).

Anaxagoras (*c.* 500–430 BC), Gk. philosopher. Developed theory of universe as being composed of

The Anatomy Lesson of Professor Tulp by Rembrandt

Andalusian street scene

particles arranged by an omnipresent intelligence.

Anaximander (*c*. 611–547 BC), Gk. philosopher, astronomer and mathematician. Conceived world as sphere created from disordered mass of substance. Also drew map of Earth.

Anaximenes (*fl*. 6th cent. BC), Gk. philosopher. Postulated theory that air is origin of everything.

ancestor worship, religious practices based on belief that souls of the dead continue to be involved with living, esp. their descendants, and must be propitiated. Feature of most religions except Judaism, Christianity and Islam.

Anchises, in Gk. myth., member of royal house of Troy, father of Aeneas, borne him by Aphrodite. Saved at fall of Troy by Aeneas, accompanied him on his voyages, died in Sicily.

Anchorage, city of S central Alaska, on Cook Inlet. Market centre for fish.

Angelfish

In region with petroleum and iron ore deposits. Has international airport. Severe earthquake (1964). Pop. (1960) 44,237.

anchovy, small marine fish of family Engraulidae. *Engraulis encrasicholus*, found in Med. Sea, is used as food.

ancien régime, term used in history for monarchical system of govt. in France prior to, and abolished by, Fr. Revolution.

Andalusia, ancient prov., most S region of Spain. Comprises provs. of Almeria, Cádiz, Córdoba, Granada, Huelva, Jaen, Málaga, and Seville. Main cities, Seville, Málaga, Granada, Córdoba. Major river, Guadalquivir. Produces cereals, citrus fruit, grapes, olives. Mineral resources include copper, zinc, iron and lead.

Andaman and Nicobar Islands, Indian territory in Bay of Bengal. SW of Burma. Area: 3,215 sq. mi.; cap. Port Blair. Export timber and copra. Pop. *c*. 63,500.

Andean condor, *Vultur gryphus*, large New World vulture of family Cathartidae. One of largest flying birds of W hemisphere. Bare head and neck, dull black plumage, white neck ruff.

Andersen, Hans Christian (1805–75), Danish poet, novelist and author of fairy tales. Achieved prominence with novel *Improvisatoren* (1835). Subsequently published numerous collections of fairy tales, best known of which are 'The Ugly Duckling', 'The Brave Tin Soldier' and 'The Red Shoes'.

Andersen Nexø, Martin (1869–1954), Danish novelist. Most notable work *Pelle the Conquerer* (4 vols., 1906–10).

Anderson, Carl David (1905–), Amer. physicist. With Victor Hess, awarded Nobel Prize for Physics (1936) for discovery of positrons in cosmic radiation.

Anderson, Elizabeth Garrett (1836–1917), Brit. pioneer woman physician. Licensed to practice medicine (1865) by Scot. Society of Apothecaries. Became (1908) 1st woman mayor in England. Opened hospital in London named after her.

Anderson, Sir John, 1st Viscount Waverley (1882–1958), Brit. administrator. Gov. of Bengal (1932–7); Home Sec. (1939–40). Supervised installation of bomb shelters in World War 2 (type of shelter named after him). Chanc. of Exchequer (1943–5).

Anderson, Dame Judith, orig. Frances Margaret Anderson (1898–), Austral. actress. Noted for tragic roles, esp. Lady Macbeth and Medea.

Anderson, Marian (1902–), Amer. contralto. International reputation based esp. on rendering of Sibelius' songs and Negro spirituals.

Anderson, Maxwell (1888–1959), Amer. dramatist. Author of *What Price Glory?* (with Laurence Stallings, 1924). Hist. plays include *Elizabeth the Queen* (1930), *High Tor* (1937) and *The Bad Seed* (1954).

Anderson, Patrick (1915–), Canadian poet, b. England. Founded magazine *Preview* (1942). Works include *The White Centre* (1946), *The Colour as Naked* (1953).

Anderson, Sherwood (1876–1941), Amer. novelist and short-story writer. His *Winesburg, Ohio* (1919) is collection of short stories giving realistic picture of life and people in Midwest. Novels include *Poor White* (1920), *Dark Laughter* (1925).

Andersonville, village of SW Georgia, US. Nearby prison, now a state park, notorious for conditions during Civil War, when over 12,000 Union inmates died.

Andes, major mountain range of S America extending over 4,000 mi. from Cape Horn, most S extremity of continent, through Argentina, Chile, Bolivia, Peru, Ecuador, Colombia, Venezuela. Some mountains still active volcanoes. Highest peak is prob. Aconcagua (23,000 ft.). Rich mineral resources are little exploited because of inaccessibility.

Andhra Pradesh, state of SE India. Area: 106,052 sq. mi.; chief city, Hyderabad. Comprises former state of Andhra (inaugurated 1953), enlarged and renamed with addition of part of Hyderabad state (1956). Pop. (1967 est.) 35,980,000.

Andorra, state in Pyrenees Mts. between France and Spain. Area: 191 sq. mi.; cap. Andorra la Vella. Virtually independent, ruled by council and elected Syndic General, pays nominal tribute to Spain and France. Pop. (1965 est.) 14,408.

Andorra la Vella, cap. of Andorra. Tourist centre. Pop. (1961 est.) 2,200.

Andrade, Edward Neville da Costa (1887–), Brit. physicist. Publications include *Structure of the Atom* (1923) and *Simple Science* (1934, with Julian Huxley).

Andrassy, Julius, Count (1823–90), Hungarian statesman. Supported Kossuth during 1848–9 revolution. Returned from exile (1858), negotiated formation (1867) of Austro-Hungarian monarchy. Premier (1867–71), estab. defence force in Hungary. Foreign min. (1871–9) of Austro-Hungary, signed alliance with Germany.

European Wood Anemone

Andrea del Sarto (1486– 1531), Florentine Renaissance painter. Experimented with effect of light and dark colour masses. Best known works frescoes *Birth of the Virgin* (1514) and *Madonna del Sacco* (1525).

Andreanov Islands, one of groups making up ALEUTIAN ISLANDS archipelago.

Andres, Stefan (1906–   ), Ger. writer. Novels explore conflict between morals and society, incl. *Die Hochzeit der Feinde* (1947) and *Der Graue Regenbogen* (1959).

Andrew, Saint (d. *c.* AD 79), one of 12 disciples of Jesus. In NT worked with brother Peter, James and John as fisherman at Capernaum. Preached in Asia Minor and Greece. According to tradition, crucified on X-shaped cross. Patron saint of Scotland.

Andrew Albert Christian Edward, Prince (1960–   ), 2nd son of Elizabeth II of Great Britain.

Andrewes, Lancelot (1555– 1626), Eng. churchman and scholar. Successively Bishop of Chichester, Winchester and Ely. Helped in preparation of Authorized Version of Bible.

Andrews, Roy Chapman (1884– 1960), Amer. naturalist and explorer. Led expeditions to China, Tibet, Mongolia and Burma. Discovered important fossil fields and dinosaur eggs.

Andreyev, Leonid Nikolayevich (1871– 1919), Russ. writer. Left Russia during Revolution (1917). Works include novels *The Red Laugh* (1904), *The Seven Who Were Hanged* (1909) and *S.O.S.* (pub. 1920).

Andric, Ivo (1892–   ), Yugoslav writer, b. Bosnia. Wrote historical trilogy on Bosnia:*The Bridge on the Drina* (1945), *Bosnian Story* (Eng.

tr. 1963), *The Woman from Sarajevo* (1945). Awarded Nobel Prize for Literature (1961).

Androclus, Androcles (*fl.* AD 1st cent.), Roman slave. According to legend, spared in arena by lion from whose paw he had previously extracted a thorn.

androgen, sex hormone produced in male testes and in adrenal cortex. Stimulates male secondary characteristics.

Andromache, in Gk. myth., wife of Hector of Troy and mother of Astyanax. Allotted as captive to Neoptolemus at fall of Troy, later married Helenus, son of Priam.

Andromeda, in Gk. myth., daughter of Cepheus and Cassiopeia. Rescued from sea-monster by Perseus, later married to him. Andromeda, Cassiopeia, Cepheus and the monster (Cetrus) became constellations.

andromeda, Japanese andromeda, *Pieris japonica,* Asian evergreen shrub. Broad glossy leaves and clusters of whitish blossoms.

Andros, Sir Edmund (1637– 1714), Eng. colonial administrator. Gov. of Dominion of New England (1686– 89). Disliked for severity, opposed by Puritans under Cotton Mather, was deposed and returned to England.

Andros, Gk. island in Aegean Sea. Most N of Cyclades. Area: 145 sq. mi.; cap. Andros. Pop. (1961) 13,000.

androsterone, sex hormone usually present in male urine. Also obtained synthetically from cholesterol.

Androuet, Jacques (*c.* 1520– 84), Fr. architect. Helped introduce Ital. Renaissance architecture into France.

Aneirin or **Aneurin** (*fl.* 6th cent.), Welsh poet. Writings contained in *Book of Aneirin* (13th cent.) attributed to him.

anemometer, instrument for measuring and indicating wind velocity.

anemone, plant of genus *Anemone* of family Ranunculaceae, widely distributed in temp. and subarctic regions. Species include *A. quinquefolia,* spring wild flower with slender stem and delicate whitish blossoms; cultivated garden varieties with showy variously coloured flowers, *e.g.* European pasqueflower, *A. pulsatilla.*

aneroid, type of BAROMETER consisting of metal container containing partial vacuum. Surface reaction to atmos. pressure changes recorded on dial.

aneurism, aneurysm, abnormal dilation of wall of blood vessel, esp. artery, forming tumour. Caused by disease of blood vessel.

Part of the *Last Judgment* fresco by Fra Angelico

Angara, river of S central USSR (1,134 mi. long). Rises in L. Baikal. Has several hydro-electric power stations.

angel, in theology, celestial being. According to traditions of Judaism, Christianity and Islam, intermediate between God and man. Good angels are bearers of communications from God to man. Angels of hell are followers of Satan and tempt mankind.

Angel Falls, waterfall in Guiana highlands, S America. One of highest uninterrupted falls in world (3,212 ft.).

angelfish, butterfly fish, trop. fish of genera *Holocanthus* and *Pomacanthus* of trop. shore waters. Brightly coloured, spiny head and compressed body.

angelica, archangel, plant of genus *Angelica,* esp. *A. archangelica.* Cultivated in Europe for aromatic odour and root stalks which are candied and eaten; and for roots and seeds yielding oil used in perfume and liqueurs.

Angelico, Fra, orig. Guido di Pietro (1387– 1455), Ital. Dominican friar and fresco painter. Work characterized by simple style and fresh colours includes frescoes in convent of San Marco, Florence; chapel of Nicolas V in the Vatican.

Angell, Sir Norman, orig. Ralph Norman Angell Lane (1872– 1967), Brit. writer and pacifist. In *The Great Illusion* (1910) argued war econ-

Cathedral, Angers

omically unsound for victor as well as defeated. Awarded Nobel Peace Prize (1933).

angel's wing, bivalve mollusc of family Pholadidae. Bores holes in wood, clay, peat and rocks.

Angers, Félicité (1845–1924), Fr. Canadian novelist, wrote under name Laure Conan. Works include psychological novel *Angéline de Montbrun* (1881–2).

Angers, cap. of Maine-et-Loire department, W France and of former duchy, Anjou. On Maine R. Castle (built 13th cent.), cathedral remain. Pop. (1962) 134,000.

Angevin, dynastic name for members of several houses of Anjou. Includes Plantagenet line of English kings begun by Henry II who was also Count of Anjou. Second Angevin line estab. 1246 as branch of Capetian dynasty.

angina pectoris, heart disease characterized by sudden attacks of restricting chest pain (sometimes spreading down left arm) often as result of exercise. Caused by obstruction of coronary arteries, resulting in lack of oxygen to heart muscles.

angiosperm, plant of class Angiospermae, comprising seed plants (*e.g.* rose, orchid) which produce seeds enclosed in an ovary.

Angkor Thom, historic cap. of Khmer empire (6th–15th cent.) in W Cambodia. Now in ruins, remains indicate ornate architecture.

Angkor Wat, large sandstone Buddhist temple near Angkor Thom, Cambodia. Built *c.* 12th cent. during Khmer dynastic rule.

angle, in plane geometry, configuration made by 2 line segments extending from one point (vertex). Measured in degrees, with right angle made by 2 rotating lines through 90°. Angles smaller than 90° are acute, larger obtuse.

anglerfish, angler, *Lophius piscatorius,* European and Amer. marine fish of order Pediculati. Large broad depressed head, with wormlike filament for luring prey, and large mouth; reaches length of 3–5 ft.

Angles, Teutonic tribe of Denmark and N Germany (modern Schleswig-Holstein). East Anglia named after settlers in England. Said to have founded kingdoms of Mercia, Bernicia and Deira. *See* ANGLO-SAXONS.

Anglesey, island and county off N coast of Wales. Area: 261 sq. mi. Joined to mainland by road and rail bridges over Menai Straits. Principal town, Holyhead. Pop. (1961) 51,700.

Anglican Communion, churches in communion with Church of England. Includes Church of Ireland, Scot. Episcopal Church, Episcopal Church of US. Representatives meet every 10 yrs. at Lambeth Conference with the Archbishop of Canterbury presiding. *See* ENGLAND, CHURCH OF.

Anglo-Catholics *see* OXFORD MOVEMENT.

Anglo-Egyptian Sudan, name of NE African country, now Sudan. Administered jointly (1899–1955) by Britain and Egypt.

Anglo-Norman, French dialect introduced into England with Norman conquest (1066). Language of court and educated class until 14th cent.

Anglo-Saxon [Old English], Germanic language of Indo-European family. Developed in England *c.* 5th cent. by Germanic invaders. Dialects included Kentish, Mercian, Northumbrian and esp. West Saxon which

Modern architecture Luanda, Angola

became standard literary language at time of King Alfred. Evolved into Middle English c. 1050.

Anglo-Saxon Chronicle, account of English history written in Old English. Includes 4 distinct chronicles with additions, continuations, editings. Prob. begun (AD 891) under King Alfred.

Anglo-Saxon literature, written works of Old English. Poetry alliterative, written in 4-stress line influenced by Germanic, pagan heritage. Includes heroic epic *Beowulf,* Christian *Hymn of Caedmon,* lives of saints, Biblical translations, homilies. Prose mainly translations from Latin and the ANGLO-SAXON CHRONICLE.

Anglo-Saxons, general name for Germanic settlers in post-Roman Britain, incl. Angles, Saxons and Jutes, latter from Rhine mouth. Term used in contemporary parlance to refer to Anglo-American society, its values and attitudes.

Angola, Portuguese West Africa, overseas prov. of Portugal, SW Africa. Area: 488,000 sq. mi.; cap. Luanda; major towns Benguela, Lobito. Orig. part of Congo kingdom, coast settled by Portuguese (16th cent.), used as slave trade source. Industries include diamond mining and oil drilling. Lack of polit. autonomy led to civil war (1960). Pop. (1967 est.) 5,293,000.

Angora see ANKARA.

angostura bark, angostura, bitter aromatic bark of 2 S Amer. trees, *Galipea officinalis* and *G. cusparia.* Used in medicine and in preparation of liqueurs and bitters.

Angoulême, historic city of W France, cap. of Charente department. Has Byzantine cathedral (11th–12th cent.). Now centre of paper and wine-making industries. Pop. (1962) 50,187.

Angoumois, region and former prov. of W France surrounding ANGOULÊME.

Angra do Heroísmo, seaport, former cap. of Azores, on Terceira Is. Founded 1534. Exports wine and fruit. Pop. (1950) 13,860.

'angry young men', name applied to several Eng. writers of 1950s, esp. John Osborne (*Look Back in Anger*), Kingsley Amis (*Lucky Jim*), John Braine (*Room at the Top*). Works tended to attack estab. social order and traditional values.

Angström, Anders Jöns, FRS (1814–74), Swedish physicist. Pioneer of spectroscopy. Investigated spectrum of Sun and of aurora borealis. Unit for measuring wavelength of light named after him.

Anguilla, island of Lesser Antilles, W Indies. With St Kitts and Nevis, forms state in association with Britain. Area: 35 sq. mi.; cap. (on St Kitts) Basseterre. Declared independence, but occupied by Brit. troops (1969). Pop. (1960) 5,810.

Angus, county of E Scotland, N of Firth of Tay. Area: 873 sq. mi.; county town, Forfar; largest town, Dundee. County known as Forfarshire from 16th cent. until 1928. Agriculture and horticulture important; also manufacture of jute and linen. Pop. (1966) 279,000.

angwantibo, *Arctocebus calabarensis,* small lemur of W Africa. Long snout and rudimentary tail.

Anhalt, part of East Germany, former Ger. state. Became part of Ger. empire (1871); duchy until 1918.

Anhwei, Anhui, prov. of E China. Area: 56,000 sq. mi.; cap. Hofei. Main river, Yangtze-Kiang. Mainly agric. with some mining (iron and coal). Pop. (1957) 33,560,000.

anhydride, any chem. compound that reacts with water to form an acid. May be organic or inorganic.

anhydrite, calcium sulphate, mineral used in manufacture of sulphuric acid and plaster.

Aniachak, volcano in Aleutian range, W Alaska. Its crater is more than 6 mi. in diameter.

aniline, aromatic organic compound of carbon, hydrogen and nitrogen. May be obtained from coal tar or by reduction of nitrobenzene. Used in dye-stuffs, dyes, plastics, *etc.*

animal, name for group of living things ranging from protozoans to mammals. Distinguished from plants by consumption of organic substances. Also typically characterized by capacity for voluntary movement, by sexual reproduction and by more or less centralized nervous system.

animism, primitive religious belief that natural phenomena and inanimate objects can have souls. Also that these and human souls can exist apart from their bodies.

anise, *Pimpinella anisum,* herbaceous plant of Med. regions. Yields aniseed used in medicine, cookery, *etc.* for its liquorice-like flavour.

Anjou, former prov. of N France. County and duchy 10th–15th cent. Region includes part of Paris basin and valley of Loire. Products include wine, fruit, vegetables.

Ankara, Angora, cap. of Turkey, central Anatolia. Cap. of Roman prov. of Galatia. Replaced former cap. of Turkey, Istanbul, in 1923. Now trade, transport and educ. centre. Pop. (1965) 650,000.

Ann Arbor, city in Michigan, US. Centre of fruit growing region. Seat of University of Michigan (since 1837). Pop. (1960) 67,000.

Anna Comnena (1083–c. 1150), Byzantine princess. Took part in plot to seize throne from her brother, John II; retreated to convent, where she wrote *Alexiad,* history of reign of her father and of 1st Crusade.

Annam, former state of central Vietnam. Area: c. 58,000 sq. mi.; historic cap. Hué. Subjected to Chinese rule from 3rd cent. BC to 1428, when independent kingdom estab. French occupation during 19th cent. led to status as protectorate (1884–1954).

Annapolis, cap. of Maryland, US, on Severn R. near mouth of Chesapeake Bay. Commercial and shipping centre. Founded (1649) by Puritan exiles from Virginia. Contains US Naval Academy. Pop. (1960) 23,385.

Annapolis Royal, town of W Nova Scotia, Canada, on Annapolis R. Founded (1605) as Port Royal, estab. Fr. settlement in Acadia.

Annapurna, mountain in Nepalese Himalayas. Comprises 2 peaks, Annapurna I (26,502 ft.) first climbed 1950, and Annapurna II (26,041 ft.).

Anne or **Anna, Saint,** traditionally mother of the Virgin Mary. Several apocryphal gospels relate her life. Patron saint of Quebec.

Anne (1665–1714), queen of England, Scotland and Ireland (1702–14), daughter of James II. By Act of Union (1707) she became 1st queen of Great Britain and Ireland. Supported William of Orange during revolution of 1688. Greatly influenced during her reign by the Duke and Duchess of Marlborough. Foreign affairs dominated by WARS OF THE SPANISH SUCCESSION.

Anne Boleyn (c. 1507–36), second wife and queen of Henry VIII of England, and mother of Elizabeth I. Accused by Henry of adultery and beheaded.

Ankara, showing its ancient fortified walls

Anne Elizabeth Alice Louise, Princess (1950–), daughter of Queen Elizabeth II of Britain and Prince Philip.

Anne of Bohemia (1366–94), wife and queen of Richard II of England, daughter of Emperor Charles IV.

Anne of Britanny (1476–1514), queen of France, wife of Charles VIII and, after his death, of Louis XII.

Anne of Cleves (1515–57), fourth wife and queen of Henry VIII of England, chosen for the king by Thomas Cromwell. Marriage lasted for 6 months.

Anne of Denmark (1574–1619), wife and queen of James VI of Scotland and 1 of England. Mother of Charles I.

annealing, process by which materials are made less brittle and more ductile. Involves application of heat, then slow cooling.

annelid, segmented worm of phylum Annelida, incl. earthworms, leeches and various marine varieties.

Annigoni, Pietro (1910–), Ital. painter. Best known for portraits of Queen Elizabeth II, Prince Philip, Dame Margot Fonteyn.

annual, plant which germinates, flowers, seeds and dies within 1 yr., *e.g.* zinnia. Biennial completes life cycle in 2 yr., flowering 2nd yr.; perennial has life cycle of more than 2 yr.

Annunciation, Feast of the or **Lady Day,** R.C. holy day (25 Mar.) commemorating announcement to the

African antelopes

Virgin Mary, by angel Gabriel, that she was to be the mother of Christ.

anoa, *Anoa depressicornis,* small wild ox of Celebes. Related to the buffalo but has almost straight horns.

anode *see* ELECTRODE.

anodyne, drug used to ease pain, *e.g.* opium.

anole, iguaniid lizard of genus *Anolis* of N, Central and S America. Chiefly insectivorous; has ability to change colour of its skin.

Anouilh, Jean (1910–), Fr. dramatist. Recurrent theme is freshness and innocence of youth in conflict with staleness and sordidness of age. Plays include *Antigone* (1942), *The Waltz of the Toreadors* (1952), *Becket* (1959).

Ansbach, city in W Bavaria, West Germany. Grew around abbey (built 8th cent.). Residence of Hohenzollerns of Franconia (1331–1791). Pop. (1965) 33,000.

Anschluss [Ger: union], term given to Ger. annexation of Austria (1938).

Anselm, Saint (1033–1109), Brit. prelate, b. Italy. Became archbishop of Canterbury (1093). Allegiance to papacy resulted in conflict with William II and Henry I. Works include *Monologion, Proslogion* and *Cur Deus Homo?*

Ansermet, Ernest Alexandre (1883–1969), Swiss musician. Founded Orchestre de la Suisse-Romande (1918) in Geneva. Guest conductor on many tours of Europe and US.

Anson, George, Baron (1697–1762), Eng. naval officer. Circumnavigated the globe (1740–4) inflicting heavy damage on Sp. ships. Defeated (1747) Fr. convoy off Cape Finisterre. First Lord of the Admiralty (1751–6, 1757–62). Made important reforms in Brit. navy.

ant, insect of family Formicidae comprising thousands of widely distributed species. Lives in colonies with various castes performing special duties. Adult males are winged and short-lived, fertile females usually temporarily winged; remainder of colony made up of wingless sterile females called workers.

Antakya *see* ANTIOCH.

Antananarivo or **Tananarive,** cap. of Malagasy Repub., in C highlands of Madagascar. Industries include handicrafts, cotton cloth manufacture. Connected by rail to Tamatave port. Pop. (1965) 322,000.

Antar (*fl.* 6th cent.), Arabian tribal chief. Of slave origin, became popular hero and subject of Arabic romance *Antar.*

Antarctica, uninhabited, ice-covered continent of S Polar region. Area: *c.* 6

Antimony

million sq. mi. Partly mountainous, *e.g.* Mt. Markham 15,100 ft. High, ice-covered C plateau. Surrounding seas beneath pack-ice for part of the year. Almost no plant or animal life except algae and penguins.

antbear, great anteater, *Myrmecophaga jubata,* S Amer. mammal of order Edenta. Long tapering snout and extensile tongue; shaggy grey coat with black band. Feeds on ants and termites.

antbird, ant thrush, bird of family Formicariidae of trop. America. Feeds on ants and other insects.

anteater, any of several mammals feeding chiefly on ants and termites, *e.g.* antbear, spiny anteater, tamandua. Long narrow snout and tongue.

antelope, hoofed ruminant of family Bovidae found chiefly in Africa and Asia. Hollow unbranched horns; valued for its hide.

antelope brush, *Purshia tridentata,* deciduous shrub, native to W US. Grows in deserts and arid mountain regions.

antennae, in wireless transmission, aerials used to intercept radio waves. Built variously to accommodate specific transmission wavelength requirements.

antennae, in zoology, flexible, jointed appendages on head of insects and myriapods (1 pair) and crustaceans (2 pairs). Function mainly sensory (touch, smell) but in some crustaceans may be used for swimming or attachment.

anthem, short, religious choral work not based on the liturgy. Developed in Anglican Church in place of Latin motet, and now in general use.

Anthemius of Tralles (*fl.* 6th cent. AD), Gk. mathematician and architect. One of architects employed by Justinian to build church of Saint Sophia (Hagia Sophia) at Constantinople.

Anthony, Saint, also Anthony the Great (*c.* 251–*c.* 350), Egyptian hermit and founder of monasticism. Led solitary life near Nile R.

Community of ascetics gathered near him.

Anthony of Padua, Saint (1195–1231), Franciscan friar and theologian, b. Portugal. Taught in France and Italy. Canonized 1232.

Anthony, Susan Brownell (1820–1906), Amer. abolitionist and social reformer. Associated with Women's State Temperance Society of New York. Pres. of National American Woman Suffrage Association (1892–1900).

anthozoan, marine coelenterate of class *Anthozoa,* comprising corals, sea anemones, sea pens, *etc.*

anthracene, colourless, crystalline solid with high boiling and melting points. Found in coal tar, its derivatives used in producing dyes. It is 1st constituent of anthracene series of aromatic hydrocarbons.

anthracite, hard form of COAL, containing more carbon and fewer hydrocarbons than other forms. Burns with smokeless flame and has high heat-producing capacity.

anthrax, malignant infectious disease of cattle, sheep and other mammals incl. man. Caused by *Bacillus anthracis.*

anthropoid ape, tailless ape of family Pongidae. Anatomically resembling man, comprises gorillas, chimpanzees, orangutans and gibbons.

anthropology, scientific study of man. Developed as science in 19th cent. and deals with evolution, historical and geographical distribution, social and polit. organization, cultural relationships, *etc.*

anthropometry, science concerned with measurement of human body. Forms statistical and numerical aid to anthropology.

anthroposophy, philosophical system based on teaching of RUDOLPH STEINER. Maintains that mystical communion with the supernatural can be achieved by prescribed method of spiritual discipline.

antibiotic, chem. substance which can destroy or inhibit growth of microorganisms. Produced from certain bacteria and fungi. Sir Alexander Fleming observed and named 1st, penicillin (1928). Together with others, now widely used in medicine.

antibody, serum protein produced by body. Reacts to resist bacterial or viral infections.

Antichrist, in NT, term for personage who personifies opposition to Christ. Specifically denies incarnation and messianic role of Jesus. Attempts have been made to identify Antichrist with various hist. persons.

anticline, arched fold in sedimentary rocks caused by pressure on earth's crust. Beds or layers bend downwards in opposite directions from crest or fold axis.

Anti-Comintern Pact, agreement between Germany and Japan (1936). Stated policy of opposition to international communism.

Anti-Corn Law League *see* CORN LAWS.

Anticosti, island, E Quebec, Canada, at head of Gulf of St Lawrence. Length, 130 mi.; max. width, 30 mi. Lumbering main occupation. Discovered by Fr. explorer Jacques Cartier (1534); given to Jolliet but returned to Canada (1774); privately owned since 1895.

anticyclone, in meteorology, area of high atmospheric pressure from which air moves spirally outwards to areas of low pressure (cyclones). Air is deflected by rotation of Earth and tends to move clockwise in N hemisphere and anti-clockwise in S hemisphere.

anti-depressant, drug used to improve mental function and alleviate depression. Also called psychic energizer.

antidote, medicine prepared to counteract effects of poison or disease.

Antietam campaign, in US Civil War, unsuccessful attempt by Confederates under R. E. Lee to penetrate Maryland and Pennsylvania (Sept. 1862). Stonewall Jackson took Harpers Ferry, but Lee pushed back Northern army to Sharpsburg, Md. Battle (Sept. 17) near Antietam Creek, with much loss of life, resulted in repulse of Southern forces.

antifreeze, non-corrosive, stable, non-viscous substance which lowers freezing point of liquid in which it is dissolved. Ethylene glycol is used in cooling systems of water-cooled motors.

Antigone, in Gk. myth., daughter of Oedipus, king of Thebes, and Jocasta; sister of POLYNEICES and Eteocles. Accompanied father in exile to Colonus, returned to Thebes after his death. Despite prohibition of Creon,

Anoa

her uncle, performed funerary rites over Polyneices; as punishment immured in burial vault; hanged herself.

Antigonus I (*c.* 382–301 BC), Macedonian soldier and ruler. General under Alexander the Great, subsequently attempted to rebuild empire, but defeated by rival generals in wars of DIADOCHI.

Antigua, island of West Indies in Caribbean. Area: 171 sq. mi.; cap. St John's. Discovered by Columbus (1493), colonized by English (1632). One of 10 islands in short-lived West Indies Federation. Now state (with Barbuda) in association with Britain. Pop. (Antigua and Barbuda, 1960) 53,534.

Antigua, town in S central Guatemala. Former cap. of Sp. Guatemala. Centre of coffee growing region. Pop. (1964) 22,000.

antihistamine, name given to group of medicinal compounds which neutralize effects of HISTAMINE in human body. Used in treatment of allergies.

Antilles, name given to all islands of West Indies archipelago except BAHAMAS. Greater Antilles comprise Cuba, Hispaniola, Puerto Rico and neighbouring small islands; Lesser Antilles comprise Leeward and Windward Islands, Netherlands Antilles, Barbados, Trinidad and Tobago and Venezuelan islands.

anti-matter, in physics, matter composed of particles analogous to each other (*e.g.* electron and positron). Analogous particles, called antiparticles, are short-lived; destroy each other in reaction with ordinary particles. Decay caused by cosmic rays produces anti-matter.

antimony (Sb), brittle lustrous white metallic element. Occurs free or in

Hagia Sophia, Constantinople, designed by Anthemius of Tralles

Shipyards at Antwerp

combination. Chiefly used in alloys and in compounds in medicine.

antinomianism [Gk: against law], Christian doctrine advocating redemption through faith and repudiating moral teachings, esp. those of OT. Considered heretical until 17th cent.; belief upheld by Anabaptists.

Antioch, Antakya, ancient city of Turkey on Orontes R. Built on trade route from Euphrates R. to Med. Sea, made cap. of Roman prov. of Syria. Early Christian centre. Declined after Arab conquest (AD 638). Pop. (1965) 45,000.

Antiochus [III] the Great (d. 187 BC), king of Syria (223–187 BC). Extended empire before defeat by Romans at Magnesia (190 BC).

antioxidants, substances used as additives to prevent oxidation. Added to food, rubber, plastics, soap, *etc.* to slow down deterioration.

anti-particle *see* ANTI-MATTER.

Antiphon (*c.* 480–411 BC), Athenian orator and teacher of rhetoric. Executed as leader of unsuccessful oligarchic conspiracy (411). Important innovator of Attic prose. Extant

Triumphal Arch of Augustus at Aosta

ant innovator of Attic prose. Extant works include rhetorical exercises.

antipodes, places diametrically opposite on globe, separated by half circumference of Earth. Examples are London, England and Antipodes Islands, SE of New Zealand.

antirrhinum, plant of genus *Antirrhinum* of N hemisphere comprising the snapdragons.

anti-Semitism, antipathy towards Jews. Manifested before 19th cent. through persecution and restriction, as in GHETTO, for religious reasons. Subsequently practised for polit., social, or ethnic gains, culminating in policies of Nazi party in Germany. Hitler instigated extermination of *c.* 6 million Jews (1939–45).

antiseptic, substance which curbs growth of micro-organisms without killing them. Joseph Lister introduced use in surgery, esp. carbolic acid and iodine. Latest development is technique of asepsis, *i.e.* production of germ-free conditions for surgery.

anti-slavery movement *see* SLAVERY.

Antisthenes (*fl.* 400 BC), Gk. philosopher. Founded school of Cynics.

antitoxin, antibody formed by immunological response of a body to a toxin. Neutralizes the toxin. Can be given by injection for short-term effect, *e.g.* tetanus antitoxin.

anti-trust legislation *see* MONOPOLY.

antlion, insect of family Myrmeleontidae. Larva burrows in sand to lie in wait for ants or other insects.

Antofagasta, seaport of NW Chile on

Pacific, cap. of Antofagasta prov. Exports minerals, esp. nitrates. Pop. (1965) 112,000.

Antoine, André (1858–1943), Fr. theatre manager. Sponsored works of naturalist playwrights; his theatres became models for experimental drama.

Antonescu, Ion (1882–1946), Romanian military and polit. leader. Became premier (1940); estab. dictatorship and joined Axis powers in World War 2. Overthrown (1944), executed.

Antonine Wall, Roman turf and clay wall across C Scotland from R. Forth to R. Clyde. Begun under Antoninus Pius (*c.* AD 140), not repaired after 200.

Antoninus Pius [Titus Aurelius Fulvus Boionius Arrius Antoninus] (AD 86–161), Roman emperor, adopted heir of Hadrian. Reign marked by peace and sound admin.; also construction of Antonine Wall across C Scotland.

Antonio, orig. Antonio Ruiz Soler (1921–   ), Sp. dancer. Noted interpreter of Sp. national dance.

Antonioni, Michelangelo (1912–   ), Ital. film director. Films include *L'Avventura* (1960), *La Notte* (1961), *Blow Up* (1966).

Antonius, Marcus [Mark Antony] (*c.* 82–30 BC), Roman soldier, supporter of Julius Caesar, and co-consul (44 BC). Member of 2nd Triumvirate with Octavian and Lepidus (43 BC); defeated Brutus and Cassius at Philippi (42 BC). Received command of E provinces, but routed by Parthians (36 BC). Remained in Egypt with Cleopatra, defeated at Actium (31 BC), committed suicide.

antpipit, gnateater, small long-legged bird of family Tonopophagidae of S America.

Antrim, county of Northern Ireland. Area: 1,098 sq. mi.; county town, Antrim; main city, Belfast, cap. of Northern Ireland. Mainly agric. lowland with Giant's Causeway on N coast. Industry, esp. shipbuilding and textiles centred in Belfast. Pop. (1967) 716,000.

Antwerp, city of N Belgium on Scheldt R. Important commercial and banking centre (15th–16th cent.). Made military port by Napoleon I. Now major European port and a centre of world diamond-cutting industry. Pop. (1964) 657,000.

Anubis, in Egyptian religion, god of the dead. Usually shown as a black jackal or man with head of jackal. Sometimes identified with Gk. Hermes.

Anuradhapura, Anarajapura, ancient

cap. of Ceylon. Has Buddhist relics and is place of pilgrimage. Pop. *c.* 22,800.

anuran, amphibian of order Anura comprising frogs and toads. Characterized by long strong hind limbs suited to leaping and swimming, and absence of tail in adult stage.

anus, in mammals, posterior opening of alimentary canal, through which waste is excreted.

anxiety, in psychology, complex emotional state associated with fatigue and fear or dread of what is likely, or thought likely, to happen. Characteristic of certain mental disorders. Phobias and compulsions are extreme manifestations.

Anzengruber, Ludwig (1839–89), Austrian dramatist. Author of *Das vierte Gebot,* considered one of 1st naturalistic plays.

Anzio, seaport on W coast of C Italy.. Site of Roman town, Antium. Scene of landing (1944) of Allied troops in World War 2. Pop. (1965 est.) 15,000.

aorta, main blood vessel of arterial system. Conveys blood from left ventricle of heart.

Aosta, city, cap. of Valle d'Aosta, region of NW Italy. Pop. (1965) 30,000.

Aosta, Valle d', autonomous Alpine region of NW Italy. Area: 1,260 sq. mi.; cap. Aosta. Became duchy (1238), later part of Savoy, then Sardinia and finally Piedmont. Made free zone 1945. Pop. *c.* 100,000.

aoudad, Barbary sheep, *Ammotragus lervia,* wild sheep of N Africa. Long fringe of hair on throat, chest and forelegs.

Apache, N Amer. Indian tribes noted for warlike disposition, esp. against 19th cent. W expansion. Some 80,000 still live on reservations in US.

apartheid, legally enforced system of racial separation on grounds of colour. Enforced in Repub. of South Africa.

apatite, common mineral calcium fluophosphate. Varies in colour; occurs as hexagonal crystals or in masses. Used in manufacture of phosphate fertilizers.

ape *see* ANTHROPOID APE.

Apeldoorn, municipality of Gelderland prov., E central Netherlands. Rly. junction with manufacturing industries. Het Loo, summer palace of Dutch monarchs nearby. Pop. (1966) 115,000.

Apelles (*fl.* 4th cent. BC), Gk. painter. Celebrated in antiquity, none of his works survive. Court painter to Macedonian rulers.

Apennines, mountain system of Italy running from Maritime Alps S to tip of peninsula, *c.* 840 mi. Vesuvius and Etna are active volcanoes.

aphasia [Gk: speechlessness], disability characterized by inability to understand written or spoken words, or to express oneself by means of them. Usually caused by brain lesion.

aphid, plant louse, small soft-bodied insect of family Aphididae. Sucks sap from stems and leaves of plants. Carries certain virus diseases of plants. Also called green fly or blight.

aphorism, short, pithy statement of principles; a truism. Term 1st used for maxims of Hippocrates, *e.g.* 'Life is short, art is long'.

Aphrodite, in Gk. myth., goddess of love. Daughter of Zeus and Dione, or sprung from foam lathering round severed member of Uranus. Said to have emerged from the sea at Paphos or Cythera. Wife of Hephaestus, mother of Eros. Goddess of pure love (Aphrodite Urania) and of sexual lust (Aphrodite Pandemos). Identified by Romans with Venus.

apidae, family of social bees, incl. common honeybee and all stingless bees. Term formerly referred to all bees.

Apis, Hapi, Hap, in ancient Egyptian religion, sacred bull worshipped at Memphis. Orig. identified with Ptah, later name Apis was assimilated with Osiris to form Serapis.

apocalypse [Gk: uncovering], prophetic literature common in ancient Hebrew and Christian writings. Inspired by visions and full of veiled symbolism. NT book of REVELATION often known as the *Apocalypse.*

Apocrypha [Gk: *apokrupto,* hidden], books of OT, of doubtful authority, included in Gk. (Septuagint) and Latin (Vulgate) versions. Regarded as non-canonical by many Christians and Jews. Term has come to denote false or heretical literature.

Apollinaire, Guillaume, orig. Wilhelm Apollinaris de Kostrowitski (1880–1918), Fr. poet and critic. His *Cubist Painters* (1913) estab. CUBISM as school of painting. Collections of poetry include *Alcools* (1913) and *Calligrammes* (1918) in which he drew lines with the words. Regarded as forerunner of SURREALISM.

Apollo, in Gk. myth., son of Zeus and Leto, and brother of Artemis, born on Delos. God of prophecy, healing, purification and music, protector of flocks and herds, sometimes identified with the Sun. Cult centred at Delphi, temple guarded by dragon (Python), oracular utterances given by priestess (Pythia). In Roman religion, orig. god of healing, later of oracles.

Delphi, home of the oracle of Apollo

Apollo project, Amer. space programme culminating (July 1969) in moon landing by *Apollo XI* spacecraft. Astronauts aboard were Neil Armstrong (1st man on the moon), Buzz Aldrin and Michael Collins (who stayed in orbit).

Apollodorus (*fl.* 5th cent. BC), Gk. painter, b. Athens. Thought to be first to depict light and shade.

Apollodorus of Athens (b. *c.* 180 BC), Gk. scholar, latterly resident in Athens. Extant works are fragments of *On the Gods* and *Chronicle,* covering period after fall of Troy.

Apollodorus of Damascus (*fl.* 2nd cent. AD), Gk. town planner and architect, worked in Rome. Planned Forum of Trajan, designed Basilica and Trajan's Column. Banished by Hadrian (AD 129), later put to death.

Apollonius of Perga (*c.* 262–190 BC), Gk. mathematician of Alexandrian school, b. Perga, Pamphylia. First to use terms parabola, hyperbola, ellipse.

Apollonius of Tyrana (b. *c.* 4 BC), Pythagorean philosopher and mystic. Attained fame by pretended miraculous powers, travelled widely.

Apollonius Rhodius (*c.* 295–215 BC), Gk. poet and scholar, b. Alexandria. Author of *Argonautica,* epic in 4 books on legend of Jason and the Argonauts.

Apollyon, Gk. name for destroying angel mentioned in NT (*Revelation*).

apologetics, explanation and argument regarding religious belief. Major Christian apologists have been Augustine, Aquinas, Anselm, Abelard. Work has been fundamental in formulation of basic Christian theology.

apoplexy, stroke, loss of consciousness followed by coma, paralysis, loss of speech and other after-effects of varying severity. Caused by haemorrhage, thrombosis

Enquiring Children
by Karel Appel

or other damage to blood vessels of brain.

apostle, name given to TWELVE DISCIPLES of Jesus appointed by him to preach, baptise, exorcise and heal. Other major apostles include St Paul.

Apostles' creed, one of 3 basic statements of Christian faith. Used as prayer in R.C. and various Protestant churches. Prob. dates in present form from 6th cent.

apostolic succession, in Christian theology, belief that contemporary churchmen have inherited power of apostles. Basic tenet of Roman Catholic doctrine. Subject of continuing theological dispute between R.C. and Protestant churches.

Appalachian Trail, footway beginning in Georgia and stretching over 2,000 mi. to Maine along ridges of Appalachian Mts., US. Passes through 14 states.

Appalachians, general name for several mountain ranges extending SW from St Lawrence valley, Quebec prov., Canada, to Gulf Coast plain, Alabama, US. Include Catskill Mts.,

Allegheny Mts., Black Mts., Great Smoky Mts.

appeal, in law, application for hearing in higher court or tribunal.

Appel, Karel (1921–   ), Dutch abstract painter. Work, esp. murals, characterized by thick layers of paint.

appendix, vermiform appendix, in man, outgrowth of large intestine in lower right abdomen (caecum). Infection may result in appendicitis which usually makes removal of appendix necessary.

Appenzell, canton of NE Switzerland. Area: 163 sq. mi.; cap. Appenzell. Divided (1597) into Protestant Ausser-Rhoden and Catholic Inner-Rhoden. Agriculture, textiles, tourism main occupations. Pop. *c.* 62,000.

Appian Way [Lat: **Via Appia**], important Roman road running from Brindisi, S Italy to Rome (*c.* 350 mi.). Begun *c.* 312 BC under supervision of Appius Claudius Caecus.

apple, *Pyrus malus,* tree of rose family of temp. regions. Round red, yellow or green edible fruit. Economically important esp. in N America, Europe and Australasia. Several thousand varieties of cultivated apples divided into eating, cooking (*e.g.* crabapple) and cider types.

Apple of Discord, in Gk. myth., golden apple inscribed 'for the fairest' thrown among guests at wedding of Peleus and Thetis by Eris, only deity not invited. *See* PARIS.

applejack *see* CIDER.

Apples of the Hesperides, in Gk. myth., golden apples, fruit of tree given by Gaia to Hera on her marriage to Zeus and guarded by the Hesperides (daughters of the Evening Star) with help of dragon Ladon. Sought by Heracles as 11th labour.

Appleseed, Johnny *see* CHAPMAN, JOHN.

Appleton, Sir Edward Victor (1892–1965), Eng. physicist. Awarded Nobel Prize for Physics (1947) for studies of ionosphere, important in development of radar.

Appomattox Courthouse, building

near Appomattox, S Virginia, US, scene of Confederate General Lee's surrender to Ulysses S. Grant (9 April 1865), marking end of American Civil War.

apprenticeship, period of instruction in which pupil learns trade by working for skilled tradesman. Upon completing term, apprentice becomes journeyman (works for wages), then master. System was integral part of medieval guilds.

apricot, *Prunus armeniaca,* tree with downy, orange-coloured edible fruit. Native to the Far East, introduced into Europe and US.

April Fool's Day, 1 April, day in W hemisphere when ancient custom of playing practical jokes is carried on.

a priori, logical term opposite to *a posteriori*; hence deduction proceeding from cause to effect. If concept is independent of experience (*e.g.* God) it is said to be *a priori*. Modern logic regards *a priori* knowledge as formal and not informative, since it does not derive from matters of fact.

Apuleius, Lucius (*fl.* AD 2nd cent.), Roman rhetorician. His *Metamorphoses* or *The Golden Ass* is one of few remaining Latin romances. Also known to have written on scientific subjects.

Apulia, region in S Italy occupying southern third of Ital. Adriatic coast. Area: 7,442 sq mi.; cap. Bari. Fertile coastal plain and dry chalk plateau. Products, olives, almonds, wine. Pop. (1965) 3,409,000.

Aqaba, port on Gulf of Aqaba. Formerly Jordan's only access to sea, occupied by Israelis since June war of 1967.

Aqaba, Gulf of, NE arm of Red Sea between Sinai and Saudi Arabia. Passage of Israeli ships through Strait of Tiran, its mouth, one of issues in Arab-Israeli conflict (1967).

aqua vitae, early name for BRANDY.

aquamarine, transparent light blue or greenish blue variety of the mineral beryl (beryllium aluminium silicate). Used as gemstone.

aquarium, an artificially-constructed habitat for aquatic animals or plants. May be a tank, bowl, pond or museum. Precautions necessarily taken in construction to avoid water pollution.

Aquarius *see* ZODIAC.

aqueduct, artificial channel constructed for conducting water, usually by means of gravity; orig. built on arches over valley. Oldest example of Roman aqueducts Aqua Appia (*c.* 310 BC); longest modern aqueduct Coolgardie, Australia, 350 mi.

aquilegia, genus of herbs of family

Aquamarine: ring setting (left), raw and cut stone (right)

Arab from Saudi Arabia

Ranunculaceae. Species include the columbine of temp. regions; grows wild and cultivated as garden plant.

Aquinas, Saint Thomas (1225–74), Ital. theologian and scholastic philosopher. Joined Dominican order and became renowned as a teacher. Achieved triumph for scholasticism in controversy over interpretation of Aristotle. Founded school of philosophy known as Thomism. Synthesized official R.C. theology. Writings include *Summa Theologica* (1267–73), attempt to summarize all learning and demonstrate compatibility of intellect and faith.

Aquitaine, former independent duchy in SW France. Comprised area between Garonne R. and Pyrenees, at times stretching as far N as Loire R. After Roman occupation, conquered 1st by Visigoths (5th cent.) then by Franks (507); became kingdom (781) under Charlemagne's son, and duchy in 9th cent.; passed to Eng. crown on marriage (1152) of Eleanor of Aquitaine to Henry II. Regained (1453) by France at end of Hundred Years War.

Arab League, organization of Arab states formed (1945) to promote co-operation esp. in defence and economic affairs; instrumental in ensuring joint Arab action against existence of State of Israel. Collective security agreement came into force 1952, but after estab. (1958) of United Arab Repub., League's importance as unifying force in Arab world declined. Members are Algeria, Iraq, Jordan, Kuwait, Lebanon, Libya, Morocco, Saudi Arabia, Sudan, Syria, Tunisia, United Arab Repub., Yemen.

Arabia, desert peninsula in SW Asia. Area: *c.* 1,000,000 sq. mi. Mainly desert and steppe land with no perennial rivers and negligible rainfall; few fertile areas in SW. Inhabited mainly by nomadic Bedouin tribes. Prior to discovery (1932) of rich oil deposits, mainly in E, economy based on agriculture and horse breeding in the oases areas, pearl fishing, and revenue from pilgrims to holy cities

of Mecca and Medina. Rise of MOHAMMED in 7th cent. led to unification of small feuding tribes into force whose conquests spread in W to Spain and in E to India and borders of China. After 1517 ruled mainly by Turks until World War 1. Arabia then split up into various states and sheikhdoms, among which are Saudi Arabia and the Yemen.

Arabian art and architecture *see* ISLAMIC ART.

Arabian Sea, NW part of Indian Ocean between Arabia and India. Principal arms are Gulf of Aden leading to Red Sea and Gulf of Oman leading to Persian Gulf.

Arabic, Semitic language of Afro-Asiatic group, with over 50 million speakers in most of N Africa, Sudan, Arabian peninsula, Lebanon, Syria and Iraq.

Arabic numerals, number signs, 0123456789, of Indian origin, introduced by Arabs into European arithmetic during Middle Ages. Replaced Roman numerals incl. I, V, X, L, C, D, M, *etc.*

arabis, genus of herbs of family Cruciferae with white or purple flowers. Species include N Amer. rock cress, *A. canadensis,* with long curved pods, and tower mustard, *A. glabra,* a widely distributed cress.

Arab-Israeli Wars, series of conflicts, culminating on 3 occasions in outright war between Israel and Arab countries over existence in Palestine of independent Jewish state of Israel. Its proclamation (1948) led to immediate invasion by neighbouring Arab states; ended (1949) by UN armistice. Egyptian seizure (1956) of Suez Canal precipitated Sinai Campaign in which Israel succeeded in occupying Gaza strip and most of Sinai peninsula but gave up these gains on agreeing (Nov. 1956) to UN cease fire. Border clashes continued and 3rd war broke out in June, 1967, after

In the Ardennes

Arad, city in W Romania. Important indust. centre; leather, machinery, textiles, food processing. Pop. (1966) 136,912.

Arafat, hill near Mecca, Saudi Arabia. Site of prayer-giving during annual pilgrimage to Mecca.

Aragats, Mount, extinct volcano. (13,435 ft.) in N Armenian SSR. Site of astrophysical research centre.

Aragon, Louis (1897–   ), Fr. novelist, poet and journalist. Early member of dadaist and surrealist movements, later joined Communist party. Novels include *Les Cloches de Basle* (1934), *Les Beaux Quartiers* (1936). Later poetry relates experiences in Fr. resistance during World War 2.

Aragon, ancient kingdom of NE Spain in E Pyrenees. Captured by Visigoths after Roman occupation; Moorish possession (8th cent.); became kingdom 1035, united (1137) to Catalonia and (1479) with Castile, laying foundations of unified Spain.

Aragon, House of, Sp. and Ital. royal dynasty of Middle Ages. Founded by Ramiro I who became 1st king of Aragon (1035). Catalonia was united (1137) with Aragon; other territories ruled by separate branches of family. Marriage of Ferdinand II (Aragon) and Isabella (Castile) laid basis for kingdom of Spain; 2 houses merged with Habsburgs through Emperor Charles V.

Araguaia, river (*c.* 1,300 mi. long) rising in central Brazil. Flows northward into Tocantins R.

Arakan, region of W Burma, on Bay of Bengal. Scene of heavy fighting between Japanese and Brit. forces during World War 2.

Aral Sea, inland sea of USSR, in Kazakh SSR and Kara-Kalpak ASSR. Area: 25,659 sq. mi. Fed by Syr Darya and Amu Darya rivers. Has no outlet.

Aram, Eugene (1704–59), Eng. scholar. A skilled linguist, he pointed out affinity of Celtic to Indo-European. Executed for murder.

Aramaic, dead Semitic language of Afro-Asiatic family. Superseded by Arabic. Previously served as lingua franca in SW Asia.

Aran Islands, group of barren islands in Galway Bay, Co. Galway, Repub. of Ireland. Comprise Inishmore, Inisheer, Inishmaan.

Arapaho Indians, N Amer. Indians of Algonkian-Mosan linguistic stock, related to Blackfoot and Cheyenne. Approx. 2,000 live on reservations in Wyoming and Oklahoma.

Ararat, mountain (16,916 ft.) in E Turkey near border with Iran. In OT, landing place of Noah's Ark after the flood.

Araucanian Indians, S Amer. peoples who occupied much of present-day Chile. Fled to Argentina after Sp. conquest. Subjugated 1883.

araucaria, any pinaceous tree of genus *Araucaria* of S America and Australasia. Species include Chile pine.

Arawak, several S Amer. Indian tribes of Arawakan linguistic stock. Inhabited trop. forests of S America, often in conflict with Carib.

arbitration, means of resolving disputes. **Industrial arbitration** involves settlement between employer and employees through 3rd party's decision. **International arbitration** involves pacific settlement between states through mutually acceptable 3rd nation or through body such as International Court of Justice.

arborvitae, evergreen tree or shrub of genus *Thuja*. Has scale-like leaves, small cones. Species include Amer. northern white cedar, *T. occidentalis.* Western red cedar, *T. plicata,* is source for interior woodwork.

Arbuthnot, John (1667–1735), Scot. physician and writer. Physician to Queen Anne. A founder of the Scriblerus Club (*c.* 1713). Satirical pamphlets include *The History of John Bull* (1712).

arc, in electricity, luminous discharge produced when a current is passed between 2 electrodes. May constitute very bright source of light.

Arcadia, mountainous region of ancient Greece in C Peloponnese. Resisted Dorian invasion and later Spartan attacks. Many associations with Gk. myth., and with origins of Rome. Symbolizes idyllic pastoral existence.

Arcaro, George Edward ('Eddie') (1916–   ), Amer. jockey. Won 4,779 races in 31 yr. Won Kentucky Derby 5 times.

arch, curved structure erected over an opening; load supported by transmitting thrust on to supporting piers. Keystone (inserted in centre of arch) pushes stress outwards.

archaeology, the tracing of man's development by systematic examination and tabulation of excavated relics. Little interest shown in ancient remains until Renaissance, when Gk. and Roman pottery, coins, *etc.* became highly prized. Modern scientific archaeology pioneered by Darwin and Huxley.

archaeopteryx, primitive reptile-like bird of genus *Archaeopteryx.* Only a few specimens found from late Jurassic period of Europe having teeth and long feathered vertebrate tail.

Archaeozoic, Archean *see* GEOLOGICAL TABLE.

Archangel, cap. of Archangel oblast, USSR, port on White Sea. Has shipyards, pulp and paper mills. Major exporting centre for lumber. Pop. (1965 est.) 303,000.

archangels, in Christianity, Judaism and Islamic beliefs, chief ANGELS. They include Michael, Gabriel, Raphael.

archbishop, high dignitary in R.C. and episcopal Christian churches. The archbishops of Canterbury and York are principal dignitaries of Church of England.

Archer, William (1856–1924), Brit. dramatist and critic. Aided G.B. Shaw; introduced Ibsen to Eng. stage with translation (1888) of *Pillars of Society.*

archerfish, *Toxotes jaculatrix,* small fish of East Indies. Ejects drops of water from its mouth at insects causing them to fall into the water and be captured.

archery, art of shooting with bow and arrow, formerly practised in hunting and warfare, today solely a sport. Probably dates from before 35,000 BC. Decisive in battles in Middle Ages (Hastings, Crecy, Agincourt) until introduction of gunpowder.

Archimedes (*c.* 287–212 BC), Gk. mathematician, inventor, physicist. Fixed value of *pi,* devised methods for calculating areas bounded by curves, laid down principles of mechanics. Devised Archimedes' screw, instrument consisting of a screw within a cylinder and still used to raise water in Nile delta. Formulated **Archimedes' Principle,** stating buoyancy of solid body immersed in water is determined by force equalling weight of fluid displaced by solid.

archipelago, group of islands. Ancient name for Aegean Sea, then for its islands; now applied to any cluster of islands.

Archipenko, Alexander (1887–1964), Russ.-Amer. abstract sculptor. Works of female nude show cubist influence.

architecture, art of designing and constructing buildings, ideally aiming for maximum beauty and utility. Styles influenced by climate, materials and techniques available, social and cultural settings. Materials have included stone, brick, wood, metal, glass and, most recently, reinforced concrete.

Arcot, town of SE India. Capture (1751) by Robert Clive marked 1st important victory for British in struggle with France for control of India.

arctic fox, *Alopex lagopus,* small fox of N regions. Valued for bluish-grey fur which turns white in winter.

Arctic Ocean, sea situated over and around N Pole. Area: *c.* 5,440 sq. mi. Sections known as Barents Sea, Beaufort Sea, E Siberian Sea, Norwegian Sea, Greenland Sea, *etc.* Two-thirds covered by drifting pack ice. Site of US research by atomic-powered submarines.

Arctic regions, area of N hemisphere lying to N of tree-line, including Arctic Ocean and N Pole. Arctic conditions also found in Greenland, N areas of Siberia, Canada, Alaska and Iceland, inhabited in summer only by variety of animals incl. bears, seals.

Arcturus, star of 1st magnitude, most prominent in constellation Boötes. Mentioned by Hesiod and used by ancient navigators.

Arden, Elizabeth, orig. Florence Nightingale Graham (1874–1966), Amer. businesswoman. Estab. (1914) cosmetics business with branches in over 70 countries and prototype beauty farm in Arizona.

Arden, John (1930–), Eng. playwright. Plays of social protest include *Live Like Pigs* (1958), *Serjeant Musgrave's Dance* (1959).

Arden, site of ancient forest of S Warwickshire, England. Probable

Archery: medieval crossbowman

setting for Shakespeare's *As You Like It.*

Ardennes, wooded plateau in Belgium, France, Germany, Luxembourg; altitude 1,000–2,000 ft. Contains much peat; rugged landscape. Scene of heavy fighting in both World Wars.

Ardizzone, Edward Jeffrey Irving (1900–), Brit. artist. Official war artist (1940–5). Best known as book illustrator.

areca, palm of genus *Areca* of trop. Asia and Malay Archipelago. Species

Arctic Fox

include the betel palm, *A. catechu,* bearing a nut.

Arendt, Hannah (1906–), Ger.-Amer. polit. philosopher. Works include contributions to journals as well as *The Origins of Totalitarianism* (1951) and *On Revolution* (1963).

Areopagus, Athenian council of elders, principal council until early 5th cent. BC. Named after hill near Acropolis where Ares was tried for murder of Halirrhothius, son of Poseidon.

Arequipa, city of S Peru. Commercial centre. Founded (1540) by Pisarro, devastated by earthquake (1868). Pop. (1964) 147,000.

Ares, in Gk. myth., son of Zeus and Hera, and god of war, loved by Aphrodite. Appears as instigator of violence or as tempestuous lover. Identified by Romans with Mars.

Arethusa, in Gk. myth., nymph loved by river-god Alpheus; fled to Ortygia, island in harbour of Syracuse, Sicily, and transformed into fountain by

Argali

Artemis. Alpheus, flowing under the sea, finally united with fountain.

Aretino, Pietro (1492–1556), Ital. Renaissance writer. Satirized powerful people and social customs of the day. Best known for comedy *La Cortigiana* (1525).

Arezzo, city and cap. of Arezzo prov., Tuscany, central Italy. Etruscan and later Roman town; became cultural centre in Middle Ages. Medieval and Renaissance architecture. Pop. (1965) 74,245.

argali, argal, *Ovis ammon,* wild sheep of Asia. Long, thick, spirally curved horns.

Argall, Sir Samuel (d. 1626), Eng. colonist and adventurer. Went to Virginia (1609). Destroyed Fr. settlements incl. Port Royal, Acadia (now Annapolis Royal, Nova Scotia).

Argentina [República Argentina], repub. of S America. Area: 10,799,650 sq. mi.; cap. Buenos Aires. In W are Cordilleras, part of Andes Mts., rest of country mainly plains. Exploration and colonization begun 16th cent. by Spaniards. Argentina achieved independence mid-19th cent. Became dictatorship

under Juan Peron, overthrown by military revolt (1955). Industry based on agric. products, esp. meat, wool and grain. Main language, Spanish; religion, Roman Catholicism. Unit of currency, peso. Pop. (1966) 22,700,000.

argentite, dark lead-grey mineral, silver sulphide. An important ore of silver. Occurs in crystals and masses.

argol, crust of impure tartar deposited in wine casks during fermentation. Used as mordant in dyeing, in manufacture of tartaric acid and in fertilizers.

Argolis, area of Peloponnese, Greece, hinterland of Corinth. Mycenae was the chief city of all Greece.

argon (Ar), colourless, odourless chemically inactive gaseous element Occurs in air and some volcanic gases. Due to its inertness used for filling fluorescent and incandescent lamps and radio vacuum tubes.

Argonauts, in Gk. myth., heroes led by Jason when sent to bring Golden Fleece from Aeëtes of Colchis to Greece. Sailed in ship *Argo,* passing through the Symplegades and between Scylla and Charybdis Helped by Medea, Aeëtes daughter, Jason completed tasks set by Aeëtes, secured Fleece and returned to Greece.

Argos, town in ancient Greece, NE Peloponnese, centre of Argolis. Struggled against Sparta, rivalled Athens and Corinth, taken by Sparta (c. 494 BC). Revived under Roman rule after 146 BC.

Argus, in Gk. myth., herdsman charged by Hera to watch over Io. Had eyes all over his body. Slain by Hermes, eyes transferred to peacock's tail.

Argyll, Dukes of *see* CAMPBELL. Scot. noble family.

Argyllshire, maritime county of W Scotland. Area: 3,110 sq. mi.; county town, Inverary. Includes several islands off coast. Forestry, quarrying tourism main occupations. Pop. (1967 est.) 58,500.

aria, in music, composition for voice, esp. solo with orchestral accompaniment. A feature of operas, cantatas, oratorios since 1600.

Ariadne, in Gk. myth., daughter of Minos of Crete. Enabled Theseus to escape from labyrinth after slaying Minotaur by providing skein of thread which led him out of the maze. Married Theseus but deserted by him on Naxos, later found by Dionysus and married to him.

Arianism, in Christianity, heresy

Gaucho, the Argentinian cowboy

Argentinian cattle market

derived from doctrines of Arius of Alexandria (*fl.* 3rd-4th cent.) renouncing Trinity. Resulting conflict led to convening of Council of Nicaea (325) leading to its condemnation and eventual victory for Athanasius and orthodoxy. Arianism persisted in N Africa and Spain until 6th cent.

Aries *see* ZODIAC.

Arikara Indians, N Amer. tribe of Caddoan linguistic family of Hokan-Siouan stock. Inhabited Missouri R. area; hunted buffalo and grew maize.

Arion, semi-legendary Gk. poet, b. Lesbos; lived mostly at Corinth. Attributed with literary composition of dithyramb, and with invention of musical mode later used in tragedy.

Ariosto, Ludovico (1474–1533), Ital. poet. Works include Latin poems and plays; best known is epic poem *Orlando Furioso* (1516).

Aristarchus of Samos (*c.* 310–230 BC), Gk. philosopher and astronomer. Said to have been 1st to hold theory that Earth revolves round Sun; also set out method of estimating relative distances of Sun and Moon.

aristocracy [Gk: power of the best], in polit. theory, government by those owning wealth and property, esp. when inherited.

Aristophanes (*c.* 448-*c.* 380 BC), Gk. comic poet, b. Athens. Plays, concerned with political, literary and social satire, constitute form of Gk. Old Comedy. Eleven plays survive, incl. *The Clouds, The Wasps, The Birds, Lysistrata, The Frogs.*

Aristotle (384–322 BC), Gk. philosopher, pupil of Plato and tutor of Alexander the Great. Founded Peripatetic school at Athens (335 BC). Works cover logic, natural philosophy ethics, politics, rhetoric and poetry. In *Metaphysics,* universe

Typical countryside in Argolis

made up of hierarchy of existences, headed by God; nature of matter inherent in it, not separate entity. *Nicomachean Ethics* mainly study of ultimate end of conduct, *i.e.* the Good, accepted as happiness, esp. as caused by life of contemplation; virtue of character rather than intellect. In *Politics,* classification of types of rule, virtuous and enlightened monarchy most conducive to ideal state, limited democracy prob. best suited to practical contemporary state. Extant part of *Poetics* defines and analyses tragedy and epic poetry.

arithmetic [Gk: *arithmos,* number], term used for computation with positive real numbers (incl. fractions and decimals). Concerned with fundamental operations of addition, subtraction, multiplication and division.

Arizona, Rocky Mt. state of SW US. Area: 113,909 sq. mi.; cap. Phoenix; principal cities, Tucson, Yuma. Consists of high plateau drained by Colorado R.; contains Grand Can-

yon. High mountains and forests in centre. Mineral resources include copper, gold, silver, uranium. Agriculture facilitated by vast irrigation projects. Tourism important. Pop. (1960) 1,302,161.

Arizona cypress, *Cupressus arizonica,* evergreen tree of Arizona. Thick leaves and bluish-green cones; used as windbreak.

Ark, in OT, ship built by Noah to protect his family and animals from the flood (*Gen.* vi-ix).

ark shell, marine bivalve of family Arcidaes, esp. of genus *Arca.* Heavy external shell covering with toothed hinge.

Arkansas, state of SW US. Area: 53,104 sq. mi.; cap. Little Rock; principal cities, Fort Smith, Pine Bluff. Mountainous in N and W with Mississippi plains in S and E. Drained by Mississippi and Arkansas rivers. Main occupation agriculture, esp. cotton, rice, maize growing. Mineral resources include petroleum, bauxite; natural gas. Production of

Hoover Dam, Arizona

Remains of the ancient city of Argos

German half-armour
(1555)

timber important. Pop. (1960) 1,786,272.

Arkansas, river (c. 1,460 mi. long) of SW US. Rises in Rocky Mts. of Colorado, flows SE through Colorado, Kansas, Oklahoma, Arkansas to Mississippi R. Major irrigation and power projects.

Arkwright, Sir Richard (1732–92), Eng. inventor and manufacturer. Developed mechanical spinning processes which provided basis for mass-production in cotton industry. Introduced steam engine to Nottingham factory (1790).

Arlen, Michael, orig. Dikran Kouyoumdjian (1895–1956), Brit. novelist, b. Bulgaria. Author of *The Green Hat* (1924), subsequently dramatized and filmed. Other works include *The Flying Dutchman* (1939).

Arles, city of Provence, SE France, on Rhône delta. Silk and wine trades important. Centre of Roman Gaul, cap. of kingdom of Arles (933–1033), medieval cultural focus of Provence. Remains include Roman arena (built c. 200). Pop. (1962) 42,353.

Arlington, Henry Bennet, 1st Earl of (1618–85), Eng. courtier. Fought for Royalists during Civil War, created (1662) Sec. of State by Charles II after Restoration. Member of CABAL ministry.

Arlington National Cemetery, burial ground of Amer. war dead, opposite Washington, DC, in N Virginia, on Potomac R. Includes tomb of Unknown Soldier.

Arliss, George (1868–1946), Eng. actor. Stage and film role in *Disraeli*. Other films include *The Man Who Played God*.

arm, in man, upper limb of body, esp. from shoulder to wrist. Also refers to forelimb of any vertebrate.

Armada, Spanish, fleet sent by PHILIP II of Spain against England (1588). War galleons (130) launched to convey invading force, which was to seize throne for Philip. Suffered severe losses in Eng. Channel engagements with Eng. fleet under Charles Howard and Sir Francis Drake and returned home, incurring further losses by storm and shipwreck off Ireland. Less than half of fleet returned to Spain.

armadillo, any of various burrowing edentate mammals of family Dasypodidae. Found from Patagonia to parts of SW US. Body encased in flexible armour of strong bony plates, tail has bony rings. Feeds chiefly on insects. US species is *Dasypus,* nine-banded armadillo.

Armageddon, in OT and NT, battlefield where final conflict will be fought between powers of good and evil.

Armagh, county of N Ireland. Area: 488 sq. mi.; county town, Armagh. Agriculture main occupation. Town is seat of R.C. and Anglican archbishoprics. Pop. (1966) 125,000.

Armagnac, hist. region of SW France, now part of Gascony. Ancient cap. Auch. Noted for wine and brandy production.

Armavir, city of Krasnodar Territory, SW European RSFSR, on Kuban R. Rly. junction; machine and tool plants. Pop. (1965 est.) 131,000.

Armenia, former kingdom of Asia Minor, now part of NE Turkey and Armenian SSR. Conquered by Alexander the Great, later by Rome, Persia and Byzantines. Independence ended (1921) by Russo-Turkish treaty.

Giant Armadillo

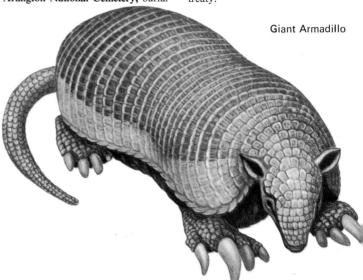

Armenian, branch of Indo-European family of languages. Over 3 million speakers in Asia Minor.

Armenian Soviet Socialist Republic, constituent repub., in Caucasus, S USSR. Area: 11,500 sq. mi.; cap. Erivan. Mountainous region rising to Mt. Aragats (13,432 ft.); irrigation facilitates production of wine, cotton. Pastures make wool important export. Territory incorporated (1828) by Russia from Persia. Pop. (1965 est.) 2,164,000.

Arminius (d. c. AD 21), Ger. chieftain. Organized rebellion against Romans and destroyed (AD 9) legions under Varus, arresting Roman conquest of Germany.

Arminius, Jacobus, orig. Jacob Harmensen (1560–1609), Dutch theologian. Teachings, formulated (1622) as **Arminianism** by Simon Episcopius, revised rigorous Calvinist doctrine of predestination. Influenced the Wesleys.

Armorica, ancient region of N France. Included present-day BRITTANY.

Armory Show, international modern art exhibition held at 69th Infantry Regiment Armory, New York City in 1913. Introduced modern art into N America. Impressionist and post impressionist paintings shown. Included works by Picasso, Braque, Matisse.

Armour, Thomas Donaldson ('Tommy') (1896–1968), Amer. golfer, b. Scotland. Victories include PGA Open (1930) and Brit. Open (1931).

armour, protective covering for persons, vehicles, naval vehicles and aircraft in warfare. Used since prehistoric times, metal armour becoming highly elaborate during Middle Ages. Declined in importance with introduction of firearms (16th cent.) and later of mobile warfare. In 20th cent., became important as protective device for ships, aircraft and tanks.

Armstrong, Edwin Howard (1890–1954), Amer. electrical engineer. Invented regenerative circuit for high-frequency oscillations (1912) and feed-back circuit (1914). Work on correction of static radio resulted in frequency modulation (FM).

Armstrong, Louis ('Satchmo') (1900–71), Amer. jazz trumpeter, band leader and singer. Influenced development of jazz.

Armstrong, Neil see APOLLO PROJECT.

Armstrong-Jones, Anthony Charles Robert, 1st Earl of Snowdon (1930–   ), husband of Brit. Princess Margaret Rose. Created peer (1961).

army, body of men, trained and armed for military combat on land. Large standing army developed with growth of Roman Empire, fulfilling need for occupation and pacification of foreign peoples. In feudal Europe, military service was obligatory among knights and yeomanry, but was eventually replaced with advent of mercenaries. CONSCRIPTION introduced during Napoleonic wars. During peacetime, most modern armies are made up of volunteers.

army ant, driver ant, legionary ant, chiefly trop. ant of suborder Dorylinae. Travels in vast swarms; preys mainly on arthropods.

army worm, larva of noctuid moth, *Pseudaletia unipuncta*. Usually moves in hordes, destructive to grain and other crops. Great pest in S and central US.

Arndt, Ernst Moritz (1769–1860), Ger. poet and historian. Much of his poetry was nationalistic, attacking Napoleon and calling for Ger. unification. Instrumental in abolition of serfdom in Pomerania (1806).

Arne, Thomas Augustine (1710–78), Eng. composer of songs, oratorios, operas and incidental music. Best known for music of song 'Rule Britannia' (1740).

Arnhem, municipality and city, cap. of Gelderland prov., E Netherlands. Industrial port on Rhine R. Dates from 10th cent. Site of defeat of Brit. air-borne troops in World War 2 (Sept. 1944). Pop. (1966) 130,399.

Arnhem Land, peninsula in Northern Territory, Australia, W of Gulf of Carpentaria. Contains aboriginal reservation (31,200 sq. mi.).

Arnim, [Ludwig] Achim von (1781–1831), Ger. Romantic writer. With Clemens Brentano, published folk song collection *Des Knaben Wunderhorn* (1806–8). Also wrote novel *Isabella von Ägypten* (1812).

Arno, Peter (1904–68), Amer. cartoonist. Works, published in *New Yorker* magazine, characterize well-known types.

Arno, river (150 mi. long) in central Italy. Rises in Apennine Mts., flows through Florence and Pisa into Ligurian Sea. Severe flood (1966) destroyed numerous Florentine art treasures.

Arnold, Benedict (1741–1801), Amer. army officer. Held commands during Amer. Revolution, but plotted to betray West Point garrison to British. Discovered, he escaped and later fought for British.

Arnold, Henry Harley ('Happy')

Arm

1. Axillary artery, behind collarbone
2. Collarbone (clavicle)
3. Greater pectoral muscle
4. Trapezius muscle
5. Deltoid muscle
6. Biceps muscle
7. Brachial artery
8. Radial artery
9. Radial nerve
10. Arterial arch
11. Palmar fascia

(1886–1950), Amer. army officer. Chief of Army Air Forces (1941–6). Wrote autobiog. *Global Mission* (1949).

Arnold, Matthew (1822–88), Eng. poet and literary critic. Deplored middle-class 19th cent. Eng. values in essays, *e.g. Literature and Dogma.* Poetry, as in 'Dover Beach' and 'The Scholar Gypsy', marked by Romantic pessimism.

Arnold, Thomas (1795–1842), Eng. scholar and educator, father of Matthew Arnold. As Headmaster of

Rugby (1827–42), broadened standards and curriculum.

Arnold of Brescia (c. 1090–1155), Ital. reformer and priest. Rebelled against papal govt. and criticized Church for owning property. Supported Abelard against heresy charges at Sens (1141). Excommunicated (1148); arrested and hanged in Rome.

Arnoldson, Klas Pontus (1844–1916), Swedish journalist. Advocated permanent neutrality of Scandinavian countries. Awarded Nobel Peace Prize (1908) with Fredrik Bajer.

Arnulf (c. 850–899), last Carolingian emperor (896–899). After leading rebellion which deposed his uncle Charles III, declared king of East Franks (887). Defeated Normans 891; invaded Italy 894 and 895. Crowned emperor at Rome (896) by Pope Formosus.

aromatic compound, in chemistry, any of class of organic compounds containing unsaturated ring of carbon atoms. Usually has agreeable odour (e.g. benzene, naphthalene).

Aroostook War, dispute (1839) over boundary of New Brunswick, Canada, and Maine, US. Truce averted fighting; border estab. 1842.

Arova, Sonia (1927–), Amer. ballet dancer, b. Bulgaria. Leading classical soloist, joined International Ballet (1941), Metropolitan Ballet (1947).

Arp, Jean or Hans (1887–1966), Fr. sculptor and painter. Associated with Ger. expressionist group, Blaue Reiter. Co-founder of Dada movement, best known for surrealistic sculptures.

arquebus or **harquebus,** small-calibre gun operated by matchlock, precursor of musket. Prominent in 16th cent. Ital. wars.

Arrabal, Fernando (1932–), Sp. dramatist. Leading exponent of 'theatre of the absurd'. Works include *The Automobile Graveyard* and *The Two Executioners.*

arrak, arak, alcoholic liquor, made mainly in Asian countries from fermented rice, molasses or coconut palm juice.

Artichoke

Arran, small island off W coast of Scotland, in county of Bute. Popular tourist centre. Fishing and agriculture main occupations.

Arras, city and cap. of Pas-de-Calais department, N France. Historic cap. of Artois, noted for tapestry-weaving in late Middle Ages. Pop. (1962) 36,242.

Arras, Treaty of, agreement (1482) between Louis XI of France and representatives of The Netherlands, following Mary of Burgundy's death. Mary's widower (later Emperor Maximilian I) retained Burgundian territory in Habsburg control; France acquired Duchy of Burgundy and Artois.

Arrau, Claudio (1903–), Chilean pianist. Noted for romantic style.

Arrhenius, Svante August, FRS (1859–1927), Swedish scientist. Awarded Nobel Prize for Chemistry (1903) for theory of electrolytic dissociation (ionization). Also worked on osmosis and toxins.

Arrighi, Ludovico degli (d. 1527), Ital. printer. Produced 1st handwriting manual.

arrow grass, family of perennial grasses. Species include *Triglochin maritima,* sometimes poisonous to cattle.

arrow wood, any of several shrubs, esp. of honeysuckle family. Several Amer. species formerly used by Indians to make arrows.

arrowhead, any aquatic perennial of genus *Sagittaria* of water plantain family. Has long stalked leaves shaped like arrowheads.

arrowroot, edible starch extracted from certain plants of trop. America. Garden species include *Maranta arundinacea,* grown for its decorative foliage.

arrow-worm, plankton worm of class Chaetognatha. Has narrow transparent body with row of grasping hooks on jaws.

arsenic (As), brittle white to steel-grey element of metallic lustre. Occurs in many ores, chiefly arsenopyrite. Used in glass manufacture, animal and insect poisons. Some compounds used medicinally.

art nouveau [Fr: new art], European and N Amer. movement in architecture, furniture design, interior decoration and the graphic arts at its height c. 1890–1910. Characterized by rejection of previous styles and romantic, highly decorative approach to creation of utilitarian objects. Leading exponents include Aubrey Beardsley, Antonio Gaudi, William Morris, Charles Rennie Mackintosh.

Artaud, Antonin (1895–1948), Fr. theatrical producer. Influenced theatre through theories in *The Theatre of Cruelty* (1935) and *Theatre and Its Double* (1938).

Artaxerxes II (c. 436–358 BC), king of Persia, son of Darius II. Crushed rebellion of Cyrus, but failed to recover Egypt. Reign witnessed decline and disintegration of empire.

Artemis, in Gk. myth., daughter of Zeus and Leto, and sister of Apollo, born on Delos. Virgin goddess of hunting, wild life, childbirth, also identified with the moon. Famous centre of cult at Ephesus, maternal aspects prominent. Identified by Romans with Diana.

artemisia, genus of herbaceous perennial herb of Compositae family. Native to temp. and arctic regions, has scented foliage and small rayless flowers. Species include wormwood, mugwort and sagebrush.

Artemovsk, city of E central Ukraine. Called Bakhmut until 1924. Industrial city of Donets basin; salt mines, mining equipment, metal working. Pop. (1965 est.) 74,000.

arterio-sclerosis, hardening and thickening of arterial walls. Frequently occurs in old age. May result in damage to any organ, esp. brain, heart, kidneys.

artery, vessel carrying blood from heart to body tissues (see BLOOD VESSEL). Largest arterial branch is aorta.

artesian well, fountain of water created by drilling into porous, water-bearing layer between 2 impervious strata. Hydrostatic pressure, dependent on slope and rainfall, causes water to rise.

Artevelde, Jacob van (c. 1290–1345),

Aruba

Flemish statesman. Obtained Flemish neutrality (1338) as head of Ghent city govt. during Anglo-French war; negotiated commercial treaty with England. His son, **Philip van Artevelde** (1340–82), led weavers' revolt (1381) against Count of Flanders, but was defeated after French intervention.

arthritis, term applied to group of diseases affecting joints, muscles and ligaments. Rheumatoid arthritis, most severely crippling form, causes inflammation of joint lining; joints of fingers, hands, knees become swollen and wasting of muscles follows. Osteo-arthritis results from degeneration of cartilage found at joint surfaces and overgrowth of bone at joint margin.

arthrodira, group of fishes of Devonian period; became extinct during Mississippian period. Sometimes as large as 30 ft., characterized by bony outer 'armour'.

arthropod, member of invertebrate animal phylum, Arthropoda, with more species (c. 700,000) than all other animal groups. Includes crustaceans, centipedes, insects, extinct

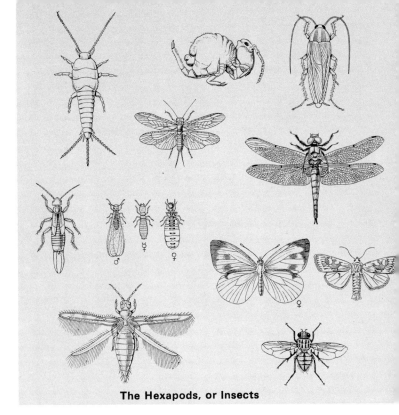

The Hexapods, or Insects

The largest phylum of the animal kingdom, the Arthropods: (1) Silverfish, 8-10 mm. (2) Springtail, 0.5-1 mm. (3) Cockroach, 11-12 mm. (4) Stonefly, 40-52 mm. (5) Four-spotted Dragonfly, 45-55 mm. (6) Earwig, 15 mm. (7) Termites (male, worker and female). (8) Cabbage Butterfly, 22 mm. (9) Stippled Moth, 19 mm (10) Pear Thrips, 1.5 mm. (11) Housefly. (12) Brown Centipede, 4 cm. (13) Giant Centipede, 25 cm. (14) Pillbug, 1.5 cm. (15) Millipede, 4 cm. (16) Sea-crab, 30 cm. (17) Shrimp, 6 cm. (18) Crayfish, 15 cm.

The Myriapods, or Centipedes

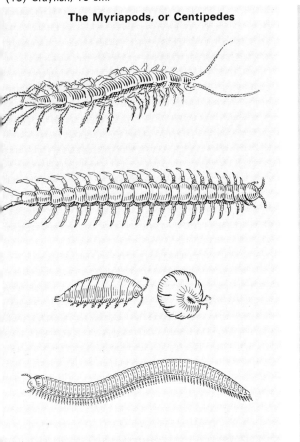

The Crustaceans

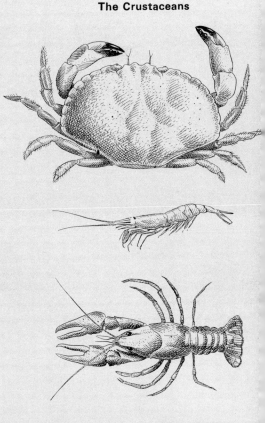

Symbol of Asclepius

trilobites. Has segmented body, jointed appendage, horny outer skeleton. Gills or trachea function as respiratory organ.

Arthur (*fl. c.* 6th cent.), warrior king of Britain, focal point of ARTHURIAN LEGEND.

Arthur, Chester Alan (1830–86), 21st US Pres. (1881–5), Republican. Nominated and elected Vice-Pres. (1880), became Pres. upon assassination of James Garfield. Supported

Ash (a) Twig with leaves (b) fruit (c) flowering twig (d) female florescence (e) male florescence (f) winged seed

civil service reform, prosecuted corruption in postal service and vetoed bill violating treaty with China.

Arthurian legend, body of literature dating from 6th cent. and centring on semi-legendary King Arthur. Earliest extant works are in Celtic literature. In Geoffrey of Monmouth's *Historiae* (12th cent.), Arthur became great Eng. national figure. Norman poet Wace (12th cent.) introduced Round Table, centre of court at Camelot. Legend grew with anonymously-written *Sir Gawain and the Green Knight* and Sir Thomas Malory's *Morte d'Arthur* and evolved with Arthur demonstrating his royal blood by removing sword Excalibur embedded in stone. Fatally wounded by treacherous Sir Mordred, Arthur taken to Avalon, whence he would return. Other figures include Lancelot of the Lake, heroic but faithless knight; Sir Galahad and Parsifal, who sought Holy Grail; Sir Gawain, Arthur's nephew; Guinevere, Arthur's queen, mistress of Lancelot; Merlin, the court magician.

artichoke, name for 2 different garden vegetables of Compositae family. *Cynara scolymus,* native to Africa, is French or globe artichoke, used in salads. Jerusalem artichoke, *Helianthus tuberosus,* is perennial sunflower; tuberous roots used as vegetable or livestock feed.

Articles of Confederation *see* CONFEDERATION, ARTICLES OF.

artificial insemination, artificial method of introducing semen from male into female to facilitate FERTILIZATION. Widely used in propagation of animals, esp. livestock. Sometimes used in humans when normal fertilization impossible.

artificial kidney, mechanical device which substitutes for the kidney. Operates outside the body removing waste products from the blood.

artificial respiration, restoration of breathing by manual or mechanical means. Air is forced into and out of lungs to estab. rhythm of inspiration and expiration. Methods include iron lung and mouth-to-mouth resuscitation.

artillery, term. orig. covering all military projectiles, now refers to heavy guns and troops operating them. Its use against fortifications ended impregnability of medieval castle.

artillery plant, *Pilea microphylla,* annual herb of trop. America. Small leaves and green flowers; pollen is discharged explosively when dry.

Artois, region of N France, in Pas-de-Calais department. Former

province; cap. Arras. Largely agric., extensive coal-mining. Under rule of Habsburgs from 1493 until 1640, when conquered by France. Scene of intensive fighting during World War 1.

Arts Council of Great Britain, organization estab. 1946 under Royal Charter to promote practice and appreciation of arts. Scot. and Welsh Arts Councils function independently.

Artzybashev, Mikhail Petrovich (1878–1927), Russ. writer. Author of novel *Sanine* (1907). Emigrated after Russ. Revolution (1917). His son, **Boris Artzybasheff** (1899–1965) illustrated books and periodicals.

Aruba, island of Netherlands Antilles, part of Curaçao, in Caribbean Sea. Area: *c.* 70 sq. mi. Site of large petroleum refinery.

arum, any plant of Araceae family, native mainly to trop. swamps and temp. Eurasia. Has heart-shaped leaves and spathe at base.

Arundel, Thomas Howard, 2nd Earl of (1585–1646), Eng. nobleman, art collector. Collection of ancient sculptures 'Arundel Marbles' donated (1667) to Oxford University.

arundinaria, genus of large bamboo grasses of Asia and Americas. Commonly known as cane.

Arunta, aboriginal people of C Australia.

Arup, Ove Nyquist (1895–), Eng. civil engineer. Known for artistic use of reinforced concrete. Awarded Royal Gold Medal for Architecture (1966).

Aryan, Hindu name for peoples speaking Indo-Iranian languages. Term used, without scientific basis, in Nazi ideology to designate Indo-European race.

asafetida, soft brown gum resin obtained from roots of plants of genus *Ferula.* Bitter acrid taste and unpleasant odour. Formerly used in medicine as a carminative and anti-spasmodic.

Asafiev, Boris (1884–1949), Russ. composer. Works include ballets (*e.g. The Fountain of Bakhchisarai*), operas and symphonies.

asbestos, any magnesium silicate mineral with fibrous structure; resistant to acid or fire. Often found in veins of rock. Used as pipe insulation, *etc.* Canada is leading producer.

Ascanius or **Iulus,** in Gk. and Roman myth., son of Aeneas, accompanied him to Italy after fall of Troy. Founded ALBA LONGA.

ascaris, genus of worm resembling earthworm. Longest, *Ascaris lumbricoides,* is parasite of human intestines.

Ascension, Christian festival cele-

Picturesque square in Ascona

brating departure from earth of Jesus. 40 days after the Resurrection.

Ascension, island of S Atlantic, part of Brit. colony of St Helena. Primarily used as naval station; main settlement, Georgetown.

asceticism [Gk: *asketes,* hermit], doctrine that renunciation of pleasures through rigorous self-discipline will lead to high spiritual or intellectual state.

Asch, Sholem (1880–1957), Amer. writer, b. Poland. Novels, reflecting conviction that Christianity is outgrowth of Judaism, include *The Nazarene* (1939) and *The Prophet* (1955).

Ascham, Roger (1515–68), Eng. writer and classical scholar. Tutor to Princess Elizabeth and Latin sec. (1553–8) to Queen Mary. Treatises

Asbestos as a raw mineral

include *Toxophilus* (1545), on archery, and *The Scholemaster* (1570).

Aschheim-Zonder test, A-Z test, test to determine human pregnancy in its early stages. Based on effects of subcutaneous injection of patient's urine on ovaries of an immature female mouse.

Asclepiades of Bithynia (d. 40 BC), Gk. physician. Rejected Hippocratic theories; founded Roman medical school.

Asclepius, in Gk. myth., god of medicine, son of Apollo and Coronis. Learned art of medicine from Cheiron the Centaur. Worshipped as god of healing, esp. at Epidaurus. Slain by Zeus for reviving Hippolytus. Serpent and cock sacred to him. Known as Aesculapius by Romans.

Ascona, town and tourist centre on L. Maggiore, Switzerland. Southern elevation has encouraged growth of sub-trop. vegetation.

ascorbic acid, crystalline vitamin occurring mainly in fruits (esp. citrus), vegetables and fresh tea leaves. Soluble in water; also called Vitamin C.

Ascot, town in Berkshire, SE England. Annual horse races held at nearby Ascot Heath since 1711.

asepsis *see* ANTISEPTIC.

Asgard or **Asaheim** [Old Norse: Asaheimr or Asgardhr], in Old Norse myth., heavenly realm of the gods and goddesses. Contained several regions, *e.g.* Valhalla, assembling-place of gods and heroes.

ash, any tree of genus *Fraxinus,* source of valuable timber. Includes common European ash, *F. excelsior* as well as white ash *F. americana* and black ash *F. nigra* of US.

Ash Wednesday, 1st day of Christian LENT, 40th weekday prior to Easter. Name derived from custom of sprinkling ashes on heads of clergy and laity.

Ashanti, region of central Ghana, mainly inhabited by Ashanti tribe. Series of 19th cent. wars with British resulted in defeat (1896) of Ashanti and annexation (1901) by colonists. Incorporated (1946) into Gold Coast colony.

Ashcan School, term applied to group of Amer. artists in New York, called 'The Eight'. Organized 1908, introduced modern European art to US. Group include Arthur Davies, Maurice Prendergast, William Glackens and Robert Henri.

Ashcroft, Dame Edith Margaret Emily ('Peggy') (1907–), Brit. actress. Known for both classical and modern theatrical roles.

Ashes, The, series of test matches in cricket between England and Australia. Dates from 1883, when defeated Austral. side presented England with urn containing ashes of burnt cricket stump.

Ashkelon, Ascalon, ancient city of Philistines, between Jaffa and Gaza on Med. coast. Centre of worship of goddess Astarte.

Ashkenazim, term applied to N European Jews. Distinguished from Sephardim, name for Jews of Iberian peninsula.

Ashkenazy, Vladimir (1937–), Russ. pianist. Winner of Tchaikovsky Piano Competition (1962) in Moscow.

Ashmole, Elias (1617–92), Eng. antiquarian. Founded Ashmolean Museum, Oxford, opened 1683.

Ashton, Sir Frederick William Mallandaine (1906–), Brit. ballet dancer and choreographer, b. Ecuador. Creations include *Façade* and *Enigma Variations.* Director of Royal Ballet.

Asia, largest and most populous continent of world. Stretches from Ural Mts., USSR, and Asia Minor in W to Bering Strait, Japan and Indonesia

Asia: Tokyo, Japan

Asia: Russian tundra

in E. Area: *c.* 16,700,000 sq. mi. Contains highest mountain ranges, incl. Himalayas. Major rivers are Ob and Yenisei in Siberia; Amur, Yangtze and Mekong in E and SE Asia; Ganges, Indus, Tigris and Euphrates, centres of earliest known civilizations, in S and SW Asia. S of cold Siberian tundra region is coniferous forestland, rich in fur-bearing animals. Wooded steppes merge into desert regions of W China. In SE are fertile, monsoon coastlands and river valleys of China, Japan, India and Indonesia, all densely populated, supported by rice crops. Development of industry and communications has increased area's potential. SW desert regions now exploited for vast oil reserves. Pop. *c.* 1,600,000,000.

Asia Minor or **Anatolia,** peninsula of W Asia. Mountainous region, now consists of Asiatic Turkey. Area provided contact between ancient Greece and Mesopotamia. Unified by Romans, subsequently under constant attack by Arabs while part of Byzantine Empire. Consolidated (13th–15th cent.) by Turks.

Asimov, Isaac (1920–), Amer.

scientist and writer, b. Russia. Best known for science fiction, *e.g. I, Robot* (1950). Also writes scientific books for general public, as in *The Genetic Code* (1963) and *The New Intelligent Man's Guide to Science* (1967).

Asmara, city and cap. of Eritrea, N Ethiopia. Rly. and cablecar link 7,300 ft. high city with port of Massawa. Pop. (1965) 132,000.

Asoka (d. 232 BC), Indian emperor of Maurya dynasty. Conquered most of India and Afghanistan, but abandoned wars after conversion to Buddhism.

asp, *Vipera aspis,* venomous snake related to viper, native to Balkans and Asia Minor. Egyptian queen, Cleopatra, said to have killed herself with an asp.

asparagus, *Asparagus officinalis,* perennial garden vegetable native to Eurasia, cultivated in Americas. Tender shoots considered delicacy by many. Decorative species include *A. plumosus.*

asparagus lettuce, *Lactuca sativa angustana,* common lettuce variety. Thick stem is edible.

asparagus pea, pod of edible seed of Goa bean, *Psophocarpus tetragonolobus.*

aspen, any of several species of poplars with flattened leaves. Includes *Populus tremula* of Europe as well as *P. tremuloides* and *P. grandidentata* of N America. Soft wood of some species is source of pulp.

asphalt, brownish-black bitumen found in natural deposits in trop. America. Artificially produced as by-product of petroleum, valuable in road construction.

asphodel, hardy stemless plant of genera *Asphodelus* and *Asphodeline,* native to Eurasia. Has showy flower spikes.

aspidistra, genus of Asiatic herbs of family Liliaceae. Has long basal leaves, bears flowers near ground.

aspirin, acetylsalicylic acid, non-toxic drug used to relieve minor pain and to reduce fever. Dangerous, esp. to children, in excessive doses.

Aspland, Gunnar (1885–1940), Swed. architect. Works include Town Hall of Göteborg (1934–7).

Asquith, Anthony (1902–68), Brit. film director. Films include *The Winslow Boy* (1949) and *The Importance of Being Earnest* (1952).

Asquith, Herbert Henry, 1st Earl of Oxford and Asquith (1852–1928), Brit. statesman, P.M. (1908–16). Championed free trade, instrumental in Liberal electoral victory of 1905; Chanc. of Exchequer (1905–8). As P.M., successfully challenged veto power of House of Lords; initiated social insurance programme; attempt to estab. Home Rule in Ireland failed. Resigned after heading coalition cabinet (1915–16) during World War 1.

ass any of several mammals of genus *Equus,* smaller than horse; domesticated variety known as donkey. Hardy and sure-footed, has small

Asia: Trees felled to clear ground for planting; a primitive method still much used

hooves, large head and long ears. Prob. domesticated in Near East (*c.* 4000 BC). Mule is hybrid between horse and ass; hinny between stallion and ass.

Assam, state of NE India. Area: 84,899 sq. mi.; cap. Shillong. Heavy rainfall facilitates growth of rice, tea and jute in fertile valleys. Subject to Burmese invasions from 13th cent. to 1826 when became part of Brit. India. Part of SW incorporated (1947) into East Pakistan. Pop. (1966) 13,450,000.

Assamese, member of Indic branch of Indo-European family of languages. Spoken almost exclusively in Assam state, India.

assassin bug, conenose, predaceous bug of family Reduviidae. Lives mostly on other insects; some attack mammals.

assegai, throwing weapon formerly used among certain African tribes. Made of hardwood, tipped with iron.

Asser, Tobias Michael Carel (1838–1913), Dutch statesman and jurist, promoter of international arbitration. Awarded Nobel Peace Prize (1911) with Alfred Fried.

assignats, promissory notes issued by Fr. govt. during First Republic. Demands on state issues were so high that they could not be repaid. By 1796 they were worth 0·03% of nominal value.

Assiniboin or **Assiniboine,** Siouan tribe of central N America. Formerly nomadic plainsdwellers. Now live on

Procession of St Francis's Day, Assisi

reserves in Alberta and Saskatchewan.

Assisi, town of Umbria, C Italy; birth-place of St Francis. Outside town is Santa Maria degli Angeli church. Pop. (1965) 24,800.

Associated Press (AP), Amer. news-gathering agency, H.Q. New York. Orig. organized (1848).

association, in psychology, conscious or unconscious tendency to link words and ideas. Basic method in treating patient by psychoanalysis, to reveal areas of repression and conflict, is to exploit this tendency.

Association football or **soccer,** in UK, game of FOOTBALL played in accordance with regulations of Football Association (FA).

Assur-bani-pal (d. *c.* 626 BC), king of Assyria (669–626 BC). Conquered Egypt, later lost it; suppressed revolt in Babylon and sacked city. Ruled while Assyria was at its cultural height; had renowned library at Nineveh.

Assyria, ancient empire of W Asia (*fl.* 9th-7th cent. BC). Originated in region of Ashur, on upper Tigris R., as small Semitic city-state. Imperial admin. set up (9th cent. BC) under Ashurnasirpal II. Gained ascendancy in Middle East, esp. under SARGON II, later Sen-

nacherib and Assur-bani-pal. Declined rapidly after secession of Egypt. Absorbed by Persian Empire.

Astaire, Fred (1899–   ), Amer. dancer and actor. Best known for films with Ginger Rogers, incl. *Flying Down to Rio* (1933) and *Top Hat* (1935).

Astarte, Semitic goddess of fertility, beauty and love. Sometimes considered as goddess of the moon. Identified with Ishtar and Gk. Aphrodite.

astatine, radio-active chem. element of halogen group. First prepared at University of California by E. Segrè and others (1940).

Astell, Mary (1666–1731), Eng. writer and feminist. Proposed scheme for woman's college in *Serious Proposal to the Ladies* (1694–7).

aster, perennial plant of genus *Aster* with small daisy-like flowers, often called wild aster. Most garden varieties derived from N Amer. fall-blooming species; grown as Michaelmas daises in Europe.

asteroid or **planetoid,** minor planet of Solar System. Over 1,600 recognized, most of which lie between Mars and Jupiter. Largest is Ceres.

asteroidea, class of echinoderms, comprising starfishes. Group has star-shaped body and loosely-knit skeleton.

asthma, condition characterized by difficulty in breathing. Frequently caused by allergy; sometimes result of psychosomatic disturbance.

astigmatism, defect of vision resulting from surface irregularities of lens or cornea of eye.

astilbe, genus of chiefly Asiatic perennials of family Saxifragaceae. Has ferny foliage and spikes of pastel flowers.

Aston, Francis William (1877–1945), Brit. scientist. Awarded Nobel Prize for Chemistry (1922) for discovery of isotopes in non-radioactive elements.

Astor, John Jacob (1763–1848), Amer. merchant, b. Germany. Amassed enormous fortune. His great-grandson, **William Waldorf Astor, 1st Viscount Astor** (1848–1919), founded Eng. branch of family. His daughter-in-law, **Nancy Witcher Astor, Viscountess Astor,** née Langhorne (1879–1964), became Brit. politician. As Conservative, 1st woman to sit in Parl. Promoted 'Cliveden set' (*see* CLIVEDEN) in 1930s.

Astrakhan, city of SE European Russ. SFSR, port on Volga delta. Transport and distribution centre; caviar processing. Pop. (1966) 361,000.

astringent, binding drug used in

medicine to alleviate haemorrhages and to stop gland secretions, *e.g.* tannic acid, copper sulphate or vegetable compounds.

astrolabe, ancient and medieval scientific instrument used to measure altitudes and position of the sun, moon and stars. Replaced by quadrant in 18th cent.

astrology, form of prediction based on theory that all events are determined by movement of heavenly bodies. Basis of ancient astronomy, from which it diverged after Copernicus. Forecasts of prospects for individuals commonly called horoscopes.

astronaut, one who travels outside gravitational pull of Earth's atmosphere, esp. pilot of spacecraft.

astronautics, science of locomotion outside Earth's atmosphere. Includes study of Earth's satellites and potential interplanetary travel.

astronomy, science dealing with the nature of heavenly bodies. Early associated with astrology. Early theories, collected by CLAUDIUS PTOLEMY displaced (16th cent.) by COPERNICUS' system. Studies of radiation, light and composition of stars and planets have contributed to astronomical knowledge.

astrophysics, branch of astronomy primarily concerned with physical and chemical composition of heavenly bodies. Also deals with their origin and evolution.

Asturias, region and former kingdom of NW Spain, on Bay of Biscay; historic cap. Oviedo. Coal, iron, zinc mined; cattle-raising and fishing chief occupations. Kingdom united (10th cent.) with Leon.

Asturias, Miguel Angel (1899–   ), Guatemalan writer. Best known works, drawing on Latin Amer. folk

Autumn Aster

legends, include *Hombres de Maiz* (1949) and *Mulata de Tal* (1963). Awarded Nobel Prize for Literature (1967).

Astyanax, in Gk. myth., son of Hector and Andromache of Troy. Born during Trojan War; thrown from walls by Greeks at fall of Troy.

Asunción, cap. of Paraguay, port and commercial centre on Paraguay R. Major town of Rio de la Plata region until rise of Buenos Aires. Pop. (1962) 305,000.

Aswan, city of Upper Egypt, below 1st cataract of Nile R. Ancient remains include tombs of VIth to XIIth dynasties. Pop. *c.* 30,000.

Aswan Dam, on Nile R., Upper Egypt. Completed 1902, provides storage facilities for water to irrigate Nile valley. Flood control, river navigation and hydro-electric power production to be developed upon completion of **Aswan High Dam** (begun 1960), *c.* 5 mi. to S of old dam.

asylum, sanctuary or place of refuge. In Middle Ages the Church provided asylum for civil criminals and offenders. Today, political asylum involves the right of one country to harbour refugees from another, under certain agreed conditions.

Atacama Desert, arid area of N Chile with narrow strip of coastal vegetation. Rich in nitrate and copper.

Atahualpa (d. 1533), last Inca ruler of Peru. Captured (1532) by Sp. conquistador Pizarro, who had him killed.

Atalanta, in Gk. myth., huntress, took part in Calydonian Boar Hunt, given its head by Meleager. Ran foot race with each suitor, those who lost the race put to death. Finally Hippomenes won his race by dropping 3 golden apples which Atalanta picked up.

Ataturk, Kemal *see* KEMAL PASHA, MUSTAFA.

atavism, term in physiology for re-appearance of genetic characteristic after lapse of one or more generations.

ataxia, lack of co-ordination of muscles resulting in erratic body movements. Caused by alcoholic or drug intoxication, or damage to central nervous system.

Ate, in Gk. myth., personification of folly or moral blindness, causing right and wrong, advantage and disadvantage to be indistinguishable. According to Homer, daughter of Zeus; in Hesiod, daughter of Eris.

Athabaska, Lake, in N Alberta and Saskatchewan, Canada, on edge of Laurentian plateau. Area: 3,058 sq. mi.; *c.* 200 mi. long.

Athaliah (d. *c.* 841 BC), in OT, queen

Mural showing papyrus boats of a type used to transport granite blocks for the pyramids down the Nile from Aswan

of Judah and daughter of Ahab and Jezebel. Succeeded murdered son Ahaziah. Killed in favour of Joash.

Athanasian Creed, statement of Catholic belief written *c.* 6th cent. Gives definition of Trinity and the Incarnation.

Athanasius, Saint (*c.* 295–373), Gk. cleric, patriarch of Alexandria. Instrumental in outlawing ARIANISM at Council of Nicaea (325), helped shape Catholic orthodoxy, esp. in *Discourses against the Arians* (*c.* 357).

Athapaskan or **Athabascan,** linguistic family of N Amer. Indians. Formerly distributed among tribes throughout W Canada and W US.

atheism, denial of existence of God or gods. Dates from ancient times, notable exponents include Socrates. To be distinguished from belief that knowledge of whether God can exist cannot be achieved by man, represented by AGNOSTICISM.

Athelstan (*c.* 895–939), king of Mercians and West Saxons, grandson of Alfred the Great. Subdued parts of Cornwall and Wales; defeated (937) Welsh, Scots and Danes at Brunanburh.

Athena or **Pallas Athene,** in Gk. myth., daughter of Zeus and Metis

Aswan high dam

and patron goddess of Athens. Protector of cities and patroness of arts and crafts, esp. weaving and spinning. Represented wearing armour, often with AEGIS. PARTHENON erected to her on Acropolis. Identified by Romans with Minerva.

Athens, cap. of Greece, on plain of Attica; cultural, religious and indust. centre. Earliest focus of Western civilization, maintained Greek hegemony during 5th cent. BC through naval power. Literature, art and architecture reached high level in Golden Age of Pericles; philosophy and science in 4th cent. BC. Polit. decline followed war with Sparta in

Ruins of the Propylaea on the Acropolis, Athens

The harbour at Piraeus, the port of Athens

The Acropolis, Athens

supply centre during Civil War, burned by General Sherman (1864). Pop. (1960) 487,000.

Atlantic Cable, submarine telegraph cable linking Britain and US. Successfully laid (1866) through efforts of Amer. financier Cyrus Field after 3 earlier attempts. Telephone cable laid 1956; cable link between UK and Canada completed 1961.

Atlantic Charter, programme drawn up (Aug. 1941) by P.M. Churchill of Britain and Pres. F. D. Roosevelt of US and stating general aims for post-war peace. Goals included in UN declaration of 1942.

Atlantic City, seaside resort, SE New Jersey, US. Also used as centre for conventions. Pop. (1965) 125,000.

Atlantic Ocean, 2nd largest ocean, extending from Arctic to Antarctic between Americas and Europe and Africa. Area: 31,830,000 sq. mi. Chief currents are Equatorials and their subsidiaries: Gulf Stream and Labrador in N, Brazil and Guinea in S. Greatest width is *c.* 5,000 mi., narrowest *c.* 1,700 mi.

Atlantis, legendary island in Atlantic Ocean, NW of Africa, mentioned by Plato and regarded as Utopian state. Reputedly attained high level of civilization; disappeared in earthquake.

Atlas, in Gk. myth., son of Titans Iapetus and Clymene. For part in Titans' revolt against Olympians required to carry the sky. Temporarily relieved of task by Heracles when on quest for Apples of Hesperides. Father of Pleiades and Hyades.

Atlas Mountains, mountain system of NW Africa. Rich in phosphates, extends from Morocco to Tunisia and S to Sahara.

PELOPONNESIAN WAR. Age of Athens passed with subjection by Macedon and later Rome (1st cent. BC); Athenian culture influenced both Roman and Byzantine rule, which ended 13th cent. Declined during Ottoman domination, became cap. of independent Greece. Landmarks of ancient Athens include Parthenon (on the Acropolis). Pop. (1961) 627,000.

athlete's foot *see* RINGWORM.

athletics, physical games and contests, divided into field (throwing, jumping, vaulting, *etc.*) and track

(running) events. Orig. organized by Greeks. Modern athletics dates from 19th cent. and received considerable impetus from estab. of international competitions, *e.g.* Olympic Games (1896).

Athos or **Akte,** most E peninsula of NE Greece, extends into Aegean Sea. Area belongs to Gk. Orthodox monks.

Atlanta, city and cap. of Georgia, US, on Chattahochee R. Textiles and steel produced. Town founded 1837. Vital Confederate communications and

Monastery of St Dionysius on Mount Athos

The Atom : (a) hydrogen atom showing nucleus, consisting of one proton, and one electron, atomic number 1; (b) helium atom with two electrons and nucleus consisting of two protons and two neutrons, atomic number 2; (c) lithium atom with three electrons and nucleus of three protons and three or four neutrons, atomic number 3; (d) neon atom with ten electrons and nucleus of ten protons and ten or twelve neutrons, atomic number 10.

a

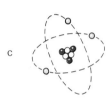

b

c

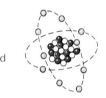

d

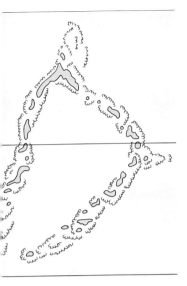

Plan and section of a coral atoll

atmosphere, air, gases, vapour enveloping Earth. Consists mainly of nitrogen (78%) and oxygen (21%). Troposphere, lowest layer, merges with stratosphere 5-10 mi. above Earth, beyond which lies ionosphere, properties of which enable it to reflect radio signals. Atmosphere forms shield to combat radiation and cosmic rays by absorbing and dispersing materials.

atoll, coral reef in shape of ring or horseshoe. Encloses a lagoon.

atom, in chemistry, smallest particle of matter which preserves characteristics of an element. Modern atomic theory dates from early 20th cent. discovery that atom is divisible. Internal structure comprises nucleus (proton and neutron) and electrons, moving in separate orbits around nucleus; proton has unit positive charge, neutron is neutral, electron has unit negative charge. Atomic number reflects number of protons in nucleus characterizing element. Atomic mass or weight determined by relation in scale based on carbon isotope.

atomic bomb, weapon deriving explosive force from conversion by fission of matter into atomic energy. Achieved by splitting (fission) nucleus of atom of element, usually uranium 235 or plutonium, explosion results from rapid rate of fissions. Intense heat and shock yield produces destruction and lingering radioactivity. Mass destruction wrought by US atomic bombs dropped (1945) on Japan led to attempts to achieve international nuclear disarmament.

Attic kylix (6th cent. BC) showing Dionysus and satyr

Aubergine, showing (left) *aubergines hollandaises*

atomic energy *see* ATOMIC BOMB.

Atomic Energy, International Conference on the Peaceful Uses of, series of meetings (begun 1955 in Geneva) set up under UN auspices to encourage exchange of data on non-military nuclear research. Subsequent conferences 1958, 1964.

Atomic Energy Authority [UK], govt. body (estab. 1954) responsible for research and development of uses of atomic energy.

Atomic Energy Commission [US], 5-man body (estab. 1946) set up to supervise peaceful uses of atomic energy. Members appointed by Pres., subject to Senate's approval.

Aton, Egyptian deity, became supreme god during religious revolution (14th cent. BC) of Akhenaton (Ikhnaton). Worshipped as creator and preserver of all life.

atonality, in music, absence of a key or tonal centre. Much of modern music has moved away from past definitions in treatment of concord and discord. Developed by Schoenberg, Webern and Berg.

Atonement, Day of [Hebrew: Yom Kippur], Jewish holy day, usually late Sept. or Oct. (Tishri). Solemn ritual observed, liturgy begins with Kol Nidre prayer.

Atreus, in Gk. myth., son of Pelops and brother of THYESTES; father of Agamemnon and Menelaus. Killed by AEGISTHUS and Thyestes.

atrium, either of 2 upper chambers on each side of the heart. Receives blood from veins and forces it into the ventricles.

atropine, poisonous alkaloid derived from DEADLY NIGHTSHADE. Used in moderate doses to dilute pupil of eye. Pain reliever and poison antidote.

Atropos, in Gk. myth., one of the Fates who cut the thread of human life.

Attenborough, Richard Samuel (1923–   ), Brit. actor and film producer. Best known for roles in *Brighton Rock* (1943) and *The Angry Silence* (1959). His brother, **David Frederick Attenborough** (1926–   ), leading television producer and naturalist.

Attica, region of E central Greece, mostly consisting of small interconnected plains. In early times contained several independent settlements, by 5th cent. BC dominated by Athens. Produces olives and vines, natural resources incl. silver, marble and clay. Attic pottery prominent in early 6th cent. BC. *See* illus. p. 61.

Attila (d. 453), king of the Huns. Captured most of Danubian frontier and E cities of Roman Empire; forced Rome to pay tribute. Invaded Gaul (451) when tributes ceased. Defeated at Châlons by Aetius. Renowned savagery prob. exaggerated.

Attis, Phrygian deity, associated with myth of Cybele as her consort and 1st eunuch priest. After death, caused by self-castration, spirit passed into pine tree; violets grew from his blood symbolizing death and revival of vegetation.

Attlee, Clement Richard, 1st Earl (1883–1967), Brit. statesman, P.M. (1945–51). Rose to Lab. Party leadership (1935), served as deputy leader in Churchill's wartime coalition cabinet (1942–5). As P.M. sponsored nationalization of major industries, instituted National Health Service and granted Indian independence. Succeeded (1955) as Party leader by Hugh Gaitskell.

Atum, in ancient Egyptian religion, original god of the Ennead (group of 9 related Egyptian deities). Father of Shu and Tefnut.

Atwood, George (1746–1807), Eng. mathematician and physicist. Invented Atwood's machine, device for studying motion of falling bodies.

Auber, Daniel François Esprit (1782–1871), Fr. composer. Operas, both comic and grand, include *La Muette de Portici* (1828) and *Fra Diavolo* (1830).

aubergine, deep purple fruit of egg-plant, *Solanum melongena*, native to India. Cultivated widely, esp. in Med. region.

Aubrey, John (1626–97), Eng. antiquary. Discovered (1648) prehistoric remains at Avebury. Author of *Brief Lives* (pub. 1813), containing portraits of famous men, incl. Bacon, Milton.

aubrietia, plant of genus *Aubrietia* of family Cruciferae, native to Med. region. Showy purplish flowers, often cultivated in rock gardens.

Aubusson, town in central France. Noted for tapestry and carpet-making dating from 15th cent.

Auchincloss, Louis Stanton (1917–   ), Amer. writer. Best known works are *The Injustice Collectors* (1950) and *The Romantic Egoist* (1954), both collections of short stories.

Auchinleck, Sir Claude John Eyre (1884–   ), Brit. army officer. In North African campaign, launched unsuccessful offensive (1942) into Libya. Became (1943) commander-in-chief in India.

Auckland, city and chief port of New Zealand, situated on N of North Island. Exports dairy products; chief industries, shipbuilding, sugar refining. Founded 1841, cap. until 1865. Pop. (1966) 149,989.

Auckland Islands, small uninhabited island group of extreme S Pacific. Area: 234 sq. mi. Discovered 1805; belong to New Zealand.

Auden, W[ystan] H[ugh] (1907–   ), Amer. poet, b. England. Leader of left-wing literary Oxford group, collaborated with Christopher Isherwood in verse plays *The Dog beneath the Skin* (1935), *The Ascent of F 6* (1936). Best known lyrics published in *Collected Poetry* (1945).

audio-visual aids, materials used in training or teaching through senses of hearing and sight. Instruction based on use of films, recordings, *etc.*

Audubon, John James (c.

1780–1851), Amer. naturalist. Pioneered ornithology with bird-banding experiments. Author of *The Birds of America* and *Ornithological Biography* (with William MacGillivray), both published in England.

Auenbrugger von Auenbrugg, Leopold (1722–1809), Austrian physician. First to introduce percussion as means of detecting chest diseases.

Augeas, in Gk. myth., king of Elis. Owned large herds of cattle whose stables Heracles was commanded to clean in one day (6th labour). Task accomplished by diverting R. Alpheus to flow through stables.

Augier, [Guillaume Victor] Emile (1820–89), Fr. dramatist. Works include *Le Gendre de Monsieur Poirier* (with Jules Sandeau, 1854), *Les Effrontés* (1861).

Augsburg, city of S Germany, cap. of Swabia, W Bavaria. Major commercial and banking centre (15th-16th cent.), home of Fugger family. Pop. (1965) 211,000.

Augsburg, League of, European alliance (1686) against Louis XIV of France by Habsburgs, Sweden and various German states. Joined by England and Holland (1689) to form Grand Alliance which ended in war (1688–97). *See* RYSWICK, TREATY OF.

Augsburg, Peace of, settlement (1555) of problems created within Holy Roman Empire by Reformation. Estab. principle that choice between Lutheranism and Catholicism was to be made by individual princes.

Augsburg Confession, official statement (written 1530) of Lutheran beliefs. Mainly the work of Melanchthon and endorsed by Luther.

Augurs, in ancient Rome, priestly college whose members interpreted auspices (entrails of animals, dreams, *etc.*) to ascertain the gods' favour or disfavour concerning an enterprise.

Augusta, city of E Georgia, US, on Savannah R. Market for cotton, indust. centre. City planned (1735), state cap. (1785–95). Munitions supply base during Civil War. Pop. (1960) 70,600.

Augustine, Saint (354–430), Roman Catholic theologian. Converted to Christianity (387), bishop of Hippo (396–430) in N Africa. Defended Christian faith against heretical beliefs. Most famous works are *City of God,* statement of reality and idealism in Christian life and doctrine, and autobiog. *Confessions.*

Augustine of Canterbury, Saint (d. *c.* 604), 1st archbishop of Canterbury, known as the 'Apostle of England'. Member of Benedictine order, sent (596) by Pope Gregory I on mission to England. Converted King Ethelbert of Kent (597) and introduced Roman doctrines to England.

Augustinians, religious orders in R.C. Church who live according to Rule of St Augustine of Hippo. First organized in 11th cent. Most famous house is hospice on Great St Bernard Pass, Swiss-Ital. border.

Augustus [Gaius Julius Caesar Octavianus], orig. Gaius Octavius (63 BC-AD 14), 1st Roman emperor, great-nephew and adopted son of Julius Caesar. Formed 2nd Triumvirate with Antony and Lepidus (43 BC), with Antony defeated Brutus and Cassius at Philippi (42 BC). Conflict with Antony culminated in defeat of Antony at Actium (31 BC), leaving Octavian sole master of Rome. Received title Augustus (27 BC) with further powers, marking end of republic (23 BC). Pacified and organized provinces, carried out moral and religious reforms. Rule marked by general peace and prosperity and known as Golden Age of literature, writers include Vergil, Horace, Ovid, Livy.

auk, diving bird of family Alcidae of N hemisphere. Webbed feet and short wings; usually black and white. Species include great auk, *Pinguinus impennis,* large flightless auk, extinct since mid-19th cent., formerly found in N seas of North Atlantic; razor-billed auk, *Alca torda,* of Amer. and European shores of N North Atlantic.

Aulis, small port of ancient Greece where Iphigenia, daughter of Agamemnon, was sacrificed to Artemis to enable Gk. fleet to sail to Troy.

Aurangzeb (1618–1707), Mogul emperor of India. Took throne after imprisoning father, Shah Jehan, and extended empire through military conquests. Destroyed Hindu temples.

Aurelian [Lucius Domitius Aurelianus] (*c.* AD 212–75), Roman military commander, proclaimed emperor by soldiers (AD 270). Repelled barbarian invasions esp. around Danube, captured Palmyra. Reincorporated Gaul into empire. Competent but severe ruler.

Aurelius, Marcus *see* MARCUS AURELIUS ANTONINUS.

Aureomycin, trademark for antibiotic, chlortetracycline.

auricula, *Primula auricula,* yellow primrose, native to Alpine Europe. Also called bear's-ear.

Aurignacian culture, prehistoric culture of Paleolithic man. Artifacts dating from period 1st discovered in caves near village of Aurignac, S France.

Auricula

Auriol, Vincent (1884–1966), Fr. statesman. Moderate Socialist, Pres. of republic (1947–54).

aurochs, *Bos primigenius,* species of Eurasian wild cattle. Extinct since 17th cent.

Aurora, in Roman religion, goddess of the dawn, identified with Gk. Eos.

aurora borealis, light phenomenon seen in the sky at night in N hemisphere, esp. in extreme N latitudes. Also known as 'northern lights'. In S hemisphere, similar luminous display is called aurora australis.

Auschwitz [Polish: **Oswiecim**], town of S Poland. Scene of extermination of 4 million (mainly Jewish) prisoners in Ger. concentration camp during World War 2.

Augsburg

Austen, Jane (1775–1817), Eng. novelist. Author of widely-read incisive and witty social satires. Major works are *Sense and Sensibility* (1811), *Pride and Prejudice* (1813), *Mansfield Park* (1814), *Emma* (1816), and *Northanger Abbey* and *Persuasion* (pub. together, 1818).

Austerlitz, village of W Czechoslovakia. Scene of Napoleon I's victory (Dec. 1805) over Russ. and Austrian forces. Austria forced out of war.

Austin, Alfred (1835–1913), Eng. poet. Popularity began with satirical *The Season* (1861). Later works included *Savonarola* (1881) and *Sacred and Profane Love* (1908). Created Poet Laureate (1896).

Austin, John (1911–60), Brit. philosopher. Emphasized investigation of ordinary linguistic usage. Works, published posthumously, *Sense and Sensibilia* and *How to Do Things with Words*.

Austin, Moses (1761–1821), Amer. pioneer. Gained Spanish permission to settle Texas. Scheme carried out by his son, **Stephen Fuller Austin** (1793–1836). Estab. settlements

between Colorado and Brazos rivers. Opposed Mexican rule, thus aiding separation of Texas.

Austin, state cap. and city of S central Texas, US. Voted (1839) cap. of Texas repub.; became (1870) permanent cap. of state. Irrigation projects of 1920s brought indust. prosperity. Pop. (1960) 186,500.

Australasia, islands of S Pacific, largest of which are Australia, New Zealand and New Guinea.

Australia, smallest of continents, lies between Indian and Pacific oceans. With island state of Tasmania, it

forms Australia, member of Brit. Commonwealth. Area: 2,971,081 sq. mi.; cap. Canberra; main cities, Sydney, Melbourne, Brisbane, Adelaide and Perth. W half of country is largely arid plateau, economic importance derived from extensive iron and gold deposits. Trop. forests predominate in NE, further S are Great Dividing Range and coal-mining regions of New South Wales. Staple products of interior are wool and grain. Distinctive animal life (kangaroo and platypus) and vegetation (eucalyptus). European settlement began after Brit. claim to E regions estab. (1770) by James Cook. Whole continent brought under Brit. rule

Coastline in Van Diemen's Gulf, Northern Territory, Australia

(1829). Independence (achieved 1901) brought states of New South Wales, Victoria, Queensland, South Australia, Western Australia and Tasmania together to form Commonwealth of Australia. Northern Territory and Australian Capital Territory (contains Canberra) administered by central govt. Official language, English; main religion, Protestantism.

Savannah in Arnhem Land, Northern Territory, Australia

Sydney Harbour Bridge, Australia

Unit of currency, Australian dollar. Pop. (1966) 11,751,000.

Australian aborigines, ethnic group of Austral. mainland (mainly N and NE). Nomadic hunters, they have primitive culture with complex religious rituals. Weapons include boomerang. Est. population is 70,000; most live on reservations, largest being Arnhem Land, Northern Territory.

Australian Alps, mountain ranges of SE Australia, part of Great Dividing Range. Contains Mt. Kosciusko (7,328 ft.) highest peak in Australia.

Australian Capital Territory, federal enclave of SE Australia, containing cap. Canberra. Area: 939 sq. mi. Region ceded (1911) by New South Wales. Pop. (1966) 86,000.

Austrasia, Frankish kingdom of early Middle Ages (6th-8th cent.), comprising E France and the Rhineland.

Austria [Österreich], federal repub. of central Europe. Area: 32,388 sq. mi.; cap. Vienna. Most of country crossed

by the Alps; main river, Danube. Predominantly agric.; chief industries (machinery, textiles) concentrated in Vienna basin. Nucleus of Austrian empire estab. by Charlemagne (791).

Land ceded (1276) to Habsburgs, after which ruled by Holy Roman emperors until 1806 when Empire was dissolved. Francis-Joseph incorporated Hungary under dual monarchy of Austro-Hungary after war with Prussia (1866). Monarchy collapsed after World War 1, Austria united with Germany (1938). Restored as repub. after World War 2, occupied by Allied troops until 1955. Main language, German; main religion, Roman Catholicism. Unit of currency, schilling. Pop. (1965) 7,323,000.

Austrian Succession, War of the, European conflict (1740–8) precipitated by Maria Theresa's succession to Habsburg lands challenged by Bavarian elector (later Emperor Charles VII). Frederick II, by claiming and invading Silesia, started war; withdrew (1745) after obtaining most of Silesia through Treaty of Dresden. Bavaria forced out after death (1745) of Charles VII when Austrian troops overran it. Subsequent hostilities inconclusive, war concluded by TREATY OF AIX-LA-CHAPELLE.

Austro-Hungary, Habsburg empire (1867–1918) formed out of compromise by Emperor Francis-Joseph after Austrian defeat (1866) by Prussia. Austria and Hungary both ruled by Habsburg emperor; known also as Dual Monarchy.

Austro-Prussian War, conflict (June-Aug. 1866), between Prussia, sup-

Palace of Schönbrunn, Vienna, Austria

ported by Italy, and Austria, allied with several German states. Prussia won quick victory, defeating Austrians at Sadowa. Peace of Prague resulted in Austria ceding Venetia to Italy; Prussia annexed Frankfurt, Hanover and Hesse-Kassel.

Authorized Version, English translation of the Bible, also called the King James Bible, 1st appeared 1611. It was prepared by group of Protestant theologians under general direction of Lancelot Andrewes.

autism, psychosis, esp. of children, characterized by withdrawal from contact with other humans. Mani-

Belvedere Palace, Vienna, Austria

The Europa Bridge near Innsbruck, Austria

fested by lapses into daydreams or fantasies.

autoclave, strong enclosed, lined metal vessel. Used as container for liquid when heated, enabling chem. reactions to occur under high pressure.

auto da fé [Portuguese: act of faith], ceremonial burning of heretics. In widest use during Inquisition in Spain and Portugal; last known use in Mexico, 1815.

autogiro or **gyroplane,** aircraft with unpowered, horizontal revolving wings and propeller and engine. First flown 1923, it departed from models of Wright brothers. Superseded by helicopter.

Autolycus, in Gk. myth., son of Hermes. Accomplished thief, with power of making himself and stolen goods invisible, finally outwitted by Sisyphus. Father of Anticlea, the mother of Odysseus.

automation, in industry, automatic regulation of performance by mechanical system. Process eliminates need for human control. Also *see* CYBERNETICS.

automobile, motor car, self-propelling vehicle, chiefly used to convey passengers, driven by INTERNAL COMBUSTION ENGINE. Developed late 19th cent. in Germany by Gottlieb Daimler (*c.* 1885) and in US, esp. by Henry Ford. By World War 1 steam-driven models had been largely replaced by gasoline models.

Automobile Association (AA), organization estab. (1905) to protect and uphold rights of motorists in UK. Largest body of its kind in the world.

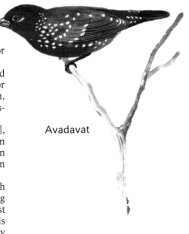

Avadavat

autonomy, freedom of self-determination and independence from external constraint. Polit. term refers to limited self-govt., often as a prelude to complete independence.

Auvergne, region of central France. Former prov., historic cap. Clermont. Volcanic Auvergne Mts. dominate fertile region.

Auxerre, cap. of Yonne department; NE France. Noted for medieval architecture, esp. 13th cent. Gothic cathedral and Church of St Germain. Centre of Chablis wine trade. Pop. (1962) 26,583.

auxin, plant hormone regulating amount, type and direction of plant growth. Derivatives used to force fruit production from unfertilized flowers.

avadavat, *Estrilda amandava,* waxbill native to SE Asia, domesticated in Europe and N America. Male has scarlet plumage with white dots on sides of breast.

Scenery in the Auvergne region of France

avalanche, vast mass of snow and ice at high altitude, accumulated until its own weight causes it to slide rapidly down mountain slope often carrying with it many tons of rock and inflicting extensive damage. In popular tourist areas, may be deliberately precipitated at announced times to ensure safety of skiers, *etc. See* LANDSLIDE.

Automobile drive showing (left to right) crankshaft and pistons, clutch, gears, universal joint and drive shaft

Aye-Aye

Avalon, in Arthurian legend, island to which the dying Arthur was taken. In Celtic mythology, paradise island of blessed souls.

Ave Maria or **Hail, Mary,** prayer to Virgin Mary fixed in present form by Pope Pius V (16th cent.). In R.C. practice, main prayer of the ROSARY.

Avebury, site of megalithic temple in Wiltshire, England, near Stonehenge. Large stones in a 450 yd. circle remain. Dates from Stone Age.

avens, perennial herb of genus *Geum* with yellow, white or red flowers. Species include girivale of N temp. regions.

Avernus, lake in S Italy near Naples. Because of sulphuric fumes regarded by Romans as entrance to hell.

Averroës or **Ibn-Rushd** (1126–98), Sp. Islamic philosopher, scholar. Works, esp. commentaries on Aristotle, written in Arabic, widely translated.

Avesta, collection of writings sacred to Zoroastrians and Parsees. Includes liturgies, hymns, devotion laws. Present form compiled (AD 3rd-4th cent.) from ancient writings.

aviation, operation of any heavier-than-air craft. History of aviation highlighted esp. by Wright brothers' first flight in heavier-than-air craft (US, 1903); Louis Bleriot's flight across English Channel (1909);

Alcock and Brown's trans-Atlantic flight (1919); Charles Lindbergh's solo Atlantic crossing (1927); Amelia Earhart's solo Atlantic crossing (1932); Wiley Post's solo flight round world (1933); 1st trans-Atlantic passenger service begun by Pan American Airways (1939); development of jet propulsion and supersonic flight for military and civilian purposes.

Avicenna or **Ibn Sina** (980–1037), Arabian philosopher and physician. His *Canon of Medicine* was standard medical text until 17th cent. Also known for interpretations of Aristotle.

Avignon, city and cap. of Vaucluse department, SE France. Noted for wine trade, silks. Residence of 7 popes (1309–78); papal possession (1348–1791). Pop. (1962) 75,181.

Ávila, cap. of Ávila prov., central Spain, on Adaja R. Centre of sheep raising and wheat district. Pop. (1965) 26,800.

Aviz, Portuguese ruling dynasty (1383–1580), taking name from village of Aviz, central Portugal. Granted to Knights of Calatrava which later became Order of Aviz. Its master became (1383) King John I.

avocado, avocado pear, trop. Amer. tree of genus *Persea,* esp. cultivated varieties originating in West Indies, Guatemala, Mexico. Yields pulpy green or purple pear-shaped edible fruit; also called alligator pear.

avocet, large long-legged shore bird of genus *Recurvirostra* related to snipe and stilt. Europe, N and S America, and Australia all have 1 species. Webbed feet and long slender upward-curving bill.

Avogadro, Amadeo, Conte di Quarenga (1776–1856), Ital. physicist and chemist. Formulated (1811) **Avogadro's law** stating that equal volumes of all gases under same temperature and pressure contain identical number of molecules.

avoirdupois, system of weight used in

UK and US: 16 drams=1 ounce, 16 ounces=1 pound, 28 pounds=1 quarter, 4 quarters (112 pounds)=1 hundred-weight, 20 hundred-weights =1 ton. Word of Fr. origin (Old French *aver de peis,* goods of weight); orig. applied to weighing of bulky goods. Estab. in England by 1340, became separate standard. Soon to be superseded in UK by METRIC SYSTEM.

Avon, 1st Earl of see EDEN, ROBERT ANTHONY.

Avon [Celtic: river], name of several rivers in England; most famous rises in Warwickshire and flows 96 mi. SW to Severn, through Rugby, Warwick, Stratford-on-Avon.

Awe, deep, narrow loch and river flowing from it, Argyllshire, Scotland. Length of loch 25 mi. Hydro-electric developments opened 1963.

Awolowo, Obafemi (1909–), Nigerian statesman, chief of Yoruba. Founded Action Group, P.M. of Western Region (1954–9). Sentenced to 10 yr. imprisonment (1963), released 1966.

Axis, coalition of states, active in World War 2. Headed by Germany, Italy, Japan; included Hungary, Rumania, Bulgaria, Slovakia, Croatia. Grew out of 1936 Ger.-Ital. alliance; Japan joined 1940.

Axminster, town of Devonshire, S England famous since mid-18th cent. for manufacture of carpets.

axolotl, larval salamander of genus *Ambystoma* found in lakes and ponds of SW US and Mexico. Capable of breeding in larval stage. Species include *A. mexicanus.*

Ayacucho, town of S Peru. Scene of victory (1824) against Spaniards guaranteeing Peruvian independence.

aye-aye, *Daubentonia madagascariensis,* nocturnal lemur found in Madagascar. Incisor teeth and long fingers with sharp nails.

Ayer, A[lfred] J[ules] (1910–), Brit. philosopher associated with logical positivism. Works include

Aztec art: Two headed snake in mosaic on wood base

Language, Truth, and Logic (1936),
Philosophy and Language (1960).

Ayesha, called by Mohammedans
Ummu al-Muminin (*c.* 611–678),
child-wife and favourite of Mohammed.

Aylesbury, county town of Buckinghamshire, England. Centre of fruit
growing and agric. region. Ducks
reared for export. Pop. (1967)
28,000.

Aymara, S Amer. Indians of Titcara
Basin in Peru and Bolivia. Survived
15th cent. domination by Incas.

Aymé, Marcel (1902–   ), Fr. writer
of satirical novels, short stories,
children's books. Works include *The
Green Mare* (1933).

Aymer of Valence (d. *c.* 1260), bishop
of Winchester, half brother of Henry
III of England. Dissolute behaviour
incurred hostility of barons and
contributed to outbreak (1263) of
Baron's war.

Ayr, county town of Ayrshire, SW
Scotland, on Firth of Clyde. Featured
in poetry of Robert Burns. Pop.
(1966) 45,000.

Ayrshire, maritime county of SW
Scotland. Area: 1,132 sq. mi.; county
town, Ayr; largest town, Kilmarnock;
international airport, Prestwick. Agriculture, esp. dairying, important.
Industries include mining. Pop. (1966)
348,000.

Ayub Khan, Mohammed (1907–   ),
Pakistani army officer and statesman.

Azalea Indica

Avignon, the famous St Benezet bridge (12th cent.) with the Palace of
the Popes in the background

Defence min. (1954–6); became pres.
after military coup (1958). Resigned
(1969).

Ayuthia, ancient cap. of Siam, in
S Thailand. Shipping centre; has
ruins of Buddhist temples. Pop. (1965)
33,000.

azalea, widely distributed genus of
shrubs or trees, now usually considered a subgenus of genus *Rhododendron*. Deciduous leaves and funnel-
shaped flowers of various colours.
Many varieties cultivated as house
plants. Species include Amer. flame
azalea, *Rhododendron (Azalea)
calendulaceum.*

Azana, Manuel (1881–1940), Sp.
statesman. Premier of repub.
(1931–3, 1936), attempted social
reform. Pres. (1936–9); fled to France
upon Franco's victory.

Azarde, federation of African tribes of
Sudan, C Africa.

Azerbaijan, constituent repub. of S
central USSR. Area: 33,430 sq.
mi.; cap. Baku; chief city Tabriz.
Agriculture includes sheep-rearing,
cotton, grape and tea-growing. Important oil resources near Baku.
Pop. (1965) 4,590,000.

Azerbaijan, region of NW Iran. Chief
towns, Tabriz and Rezayeh.

Azikiwe, Benjamin Nnamdi (1904–
   ), Nigerian statesman. Gov.-
general of Federation of Nigeria
(1960–3), Pres. of Nigeria (1963–6).

azimuth, in astronomy, term for
distance of star in angular measurement from the N or S point of
meridian.

Azores, group of 9 Portuguese islands
in N Atlantic Ocean. Area: 922 sq.
mi.; chief town (on San Miguel) Ponta
Delgada. Islands known to Carthaginians, rediscovered and annexed by
Portuguese (*c.* 1430). Pop. (1965)
327,500.

Azov, Sea of, shallow N bay of Black
Sea. Area: 14,000 sq. mi.; chief ports

Rostov-on-Don,   Taganrog   and
Kerch.

Aztec, name of Amer. Indian people
of C Mexico. Ruling race at time of
Sp. conquest (16th cent.). Spoke
Uto-Aztecan language.

Aztec civilization, culture of Aztec
people developed (12th cent.) on
Mayan and Toltec foundations.
Characterized by use of irrigation for
agriculture, fine weaving, intricate
metal-work, esp. gold, massive buildings erected by slave labour. Religion
was pantheistic, latterly involving
human sacrifice.

azurite, copper ore, blue in colour.
Occurs in association with malachite.

Aviation: Experimental vertical
take-off jet fighter

B

Baalbek or **Heliopolis** (city of the sun), ancient town in Lebanon devoted to worship of Baal, the sun-god. Prominent in Roman times.

Babbage, Charles (1792–1871), Eng. mathematician and inventor. Developed antecedent of modern computing machines. Helped found Royal Astronomical Soc. and wrote *Tables of Logarithms* (1827).

Babcock, Orville E. (1835–84), Amer. Union general in Civil War. Associated with notorious 'Whisky Ring' under Pres. Ulysses S. Grant; indicted (1875) for complicity in revenue frauds. Acquitted following Grant's intervention.

Babel, Isaac (1894–1941), Russ. writer regarded as master of miniature short story. Works include *Red Cavalry* (1926) and *Odessa Tales* (1924). Principal works in Yiddish.

Babel, Tower of, structure erected after the Flood by Noah's descendants in Babylonia. The plan to build a tower that would reach heaven was thwarted by Jehovah who 'confounded their language'. Tower of Babel now signifies a visionary scheme.

Bab-el-Mandeb, Strait of, strait separating Arabia and Africa; joins Red Sea and Gulf of Aden.

baboon, family of omnivorous African and Asiatic monkeys with long muzzles and large canine teeth. Lives in open country in family groups with hierarchical organization for protection and care of helpless members.

Babylon, ancient city of Mesopotamia, on Euphrates; became important (*c.* 1750 BC) when Hammurabi made it cap. of Babylonia. Destroyed by Assyrians (*c.* 689 BC), rebuilt and acquired reputation for luxury and sensual living in days of Nebuchadnezzar. The Hanging Gardens were one of Seven Wonders of the World. •

Babylonia, S part of Mesopotamian Empire in Asia Minor, centred in Babylon and Nineveh. Home of earliest cosmopolitan civilization, reached peak (*c.* 2100 BC) under HAMMURABI. After Hittite attacks (18th cent. BC) declined until 6th cent. BC when Nebuchadnezzar restored empire and rebuilt Babylon; taken by Persians (538 BC) who ruled until its capture by Alexander the Great (323 BC). Conquered (312 BC) in wars of DIADOCHI by Seleucus Nicutor, who replaced Babylon with Seleucia. Babylonians were skilled in handicraft and developed calendar based on astronomical observations. Present division of hour and degree into 60 comes from Babylonian system.

Babylonian captivity, in history of Israel, period from fall of Jerusalem (586 BC) to reconstruction of new Jewish state (*c.* 516 BC) in Palestine. Also refers to period (1309–78) of papal rule in Avignon, France.

Bacchanalia, celebrations held in ancient Rome in honour of Bacchus, god of wine.

Bacchus, Roman name for Gk. god Dionysus.

Bach, Carl Philipp Emanuel (1714–88), Ger. composer and harpsichordist. Son of J. S. Bach, he was a noted keyboard player and improviser. His *Essay on the Proper Method of Playing Keyboard Instruments* is a valuable guide. Compositions characteristic of mid-18th cent., in reaction against his father's polyphonic style.

Bach, Johann Christian (1735–82), Ger. composer and musician later known as 'the English Bach'; son of J. S. Bach. Eng. court favourite, he was first to play piano solos in England. Works include operas, an oratorio, church music, symphonies, piano and chamber music.

Bach, Johann Sebastian (1685–1750), Ger. musician. Held many court music directorships, the last at Leipzig (1723–50). Distinguished on violin, harpsichord, and organ. First composer to give keyboard instrument a concert role, he estab. piano concerto. Combined old polyphonic and new harmonic styles. Vast output included, except for opera, every current form of music. Of sacred and secular choral works, compositions for organ and harpsichord, and chamber music, best known are the *Magnificat, Mass in B Minor, The Well-Tempered Clavier,* and the *Brandenburg Concertos.* Standing as major composer achieved during 19th cent. revival.

Bach, Wilhelm Friedemann (1710–84), Ger. organist and composer, son of J. S. Bach. Compositions include works for harpsichord and organ, cantatas, and 9 symphonies.

Tower of Babel: 9th century ruins of a mosque and minaret at Samarra, Iraq. The tower is constructed in the manner of the Babylonian step-towers which are thought to have been similar to the tower of Babel

Yellow Baboon

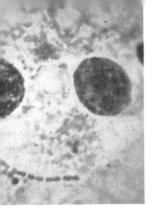

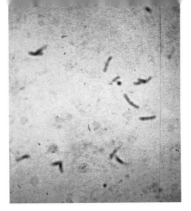

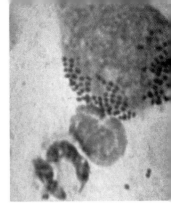

Bacteria: (1) spherical   (2) rod-shaped   (3) bacillus of anthrax

Backhaus, Wilhelm (1884–1969), Ger. pianist, formerly at Royal Manchester College of Music. Achieved world fame through tours.

backswimmer, *Notonectidae,* insect family distributed throughout world. Convex-keeled back suited to un-explained habit of swimming upside down; lighter than water, fastens itself below surface. Preys on crustaceans, insects and young fish and is eaten by waterfowl, toads and fish. N Amer. *N. undulata* particularly voracious.

Bacon, Francis, 1st Viscount St Albans, Lord Verulam (1561–1626), Eng. statesman and philosopher famous for *The Advancement of Learning* (1605) and *Novum Organum* (1620) and *Essays* (1597–1625). Argument that he was author of plays attributed to Shakespeare has persisted since 18th cent.

Bacon, Francis (1909–), Brit. artist, b. Dublin. Paintings, usually of solitary figures tormented with pain and fear, are in many collections.

Bacon, Nathaniel *see* BACON'S RE-BELLION.

Bacon, Roger (*c.* 1214–92), Eng. monk, philosopher and scientist, known as 'Doctor Mirabilis'. Advo-cated experimental over scholastic method of argument. *Opus Majus, Opus Minor* and *Opus Tertium,* written at request of Pope Clement IV, were attempts to systematize learning. Invented spectacles; writings contain prophecies of telescope, miscroscope, steam engines and aeroplane. Twice confined on suspicion of heresy.

Bacon's Rebellion (1676), uprising of Eng. colonists in Virginia, led by Nathaniel Bacon (1647–76) over exploitation of small farmers by England and local aristocracy. Bacon's unexpected death from fever resulted in collapse of rebellion.

bacteria, large class, Schizomycetes, of one-celled micro-organisms found in every living organism, throughout earth and stratosphere. Outnumber-ing all other species. Of 3 typical shapes: rod-shaped (*bacillus*); spheri-cal (*cocci*); and spiral or thread-like (*spirillum*). Some form ribbon colon-ies. *Flagellae,* thread-like extensions of cells, *i.e.* means of mobility, are universal in *spirilla,* common in *bacilli,* and rare in *cocci.* Aerobic bacteria need free oxygen, anaerobic do not; forms able to respire with or without free oxygen are called facultative anaerobes. Many are active in fermentation, conversion of dead organic material, and fixing of atmospheric nitrogen. Pathogenic (parasitic) bacteria, 'germs', produce wide range of plant and animal diseases. Reproduction by meiosis is rapid. Bacterial spore exhibits no life but may germinate to produce new cell. First observed by Antony van Leeuwenhoek (17th cent.), studies made by Louis Pasteur and Robert Koch (19th cent.) laid foundation for science of bacteriology.

Bactria, ancient name for Gk. king-dom, in modern N Afghanistan. Cap. Bactra (now Balkh). As satrapy of Persian Empire taken (328 BC) by Alexander the Great. Declared in-dependence (240 BC). Important as intermediary between Gk. and Oriental civilization. Fell (*c.* 130 BC) to nomadic Sakas.

Bactrian camel *see* CAMEL.

Baden-Powell, Robert Stevenson Smyth, 1st Baron (1857–1941), Brit. soldier, hero of siege of Mafeking (S African War) and founder of Boy Scouts Association.

Baden-Württemberg, Ger. state W of Bavaria, cap. Stuttgart; includes Ulm, Mannheim, Karlsruhe and Heidel-berg. Formed (1952) from states of Württemberg-Baden, Württemberg-Hohenzollern and Baden, all of which came into being after 1945.

Badlands, The, orig. term for arid, spectacularly eroded area of SW S Dakota, US; now used for any similar area. Typical features: deep gullies, saw-tooth divides, isolated spires, flat-topped buttes; located between plateau and lowland; infrequent but heavy rainfall.

badminton, game played by volleying shuttlecock (bird), small cork hemi-sphere with feathers attached, over a net using light gut-strung rackets. Played by 2 or 4 persons. Popular in 19th cent. England; introduced into US in 1890s.

The Neue Schlossplatz in Stuttgart, Baden-Württemberg

Palma, Balearic Islands

Badura-Skoda, Paul (1924–),
Austrian pianist; also writes on music;
has performed in Europe, US and
Australia.
Baedeker, Karl (1801–59), Ger.
printer; published popular series of
guidebooks.
Baekeland, Leo Hendrik (1863–
1944), Amer. chemist and inventor, b.
Belgium. Invented and manufactured
Velox process photographic papers.
Best known for invention of BAKE-
LITE.
Baer, Karl Ernst von, FRS (1792–
1876), Ger. biologist, founder of
comparative embryology. Discovered
mammalian egg and identified noto-
chord.
**Baeyer, [Johann Friedrich Wilhelm]
Adolf von** (1835–1917), Ger. organic
chemist, known for his synthesis of
indigo. Awarded Nobel Prize for
Chemistry (1905) for research on
organic dyestuffs and hydro-aromatic
compounds.
Baez, Joan (1941–), Amer. folk
singer and composer. Renowned for
traditional and modern Amer. folk
songs of protest.
Baffin Bay, between Baffin Is. and
Greenland, reaching depths of 9,000
ft.
Baffin Island, between Greenland and
Canadian mainland, largest of Arctic
Archipelago; named after William
Baffin (1584–1622). Area: 183,810
sq. mi. Whaling and fur trading are
main occupations of predominantly
Eskimo population. Coal and iron ore
mined. Pop. (1960) 2,754.
Bagehot, Walter (1826–77), Eng.
economist, social and literary critic.
Writings include *The English Con-
stitution* (1867), *Physics and Politics*
(1872) and *Literary Studies* (1879).
Editor of the *Economist* for 20 yr.
Baghdad, cap. of Iraq (since 1920), on
the Tigris, 25 mi. N of the Euphrates.
Trade centre since Assyrian times,
present city (founded 762) rose to
dominant commercial position. As
'Abode of Peace' it became a centre of
Islamic culture. Its period of greatest
glory is reflected in *Thousand and
One Nights.* Destroyed (1258) by
Mongols, it rose twice only to be
destroyed by Tamerlane (1400) and

again by Shah Ismail of Persia (1524).
Incorporated in Ottoman Empire
(1638). Pop. (1965) 1,745,000.
bagpipe, musical wind instrument
consisting of leather bag inflated by
either bellows or tube. Melody pipe or
chanter has finger holes; drones
produce continuous bass tone. Once
used in Europe and Asia, now chiefly
confined to Scotland, Brittany, Ireland, Poland and Sicily. Used in Scot.
Highland dancing.
Bahaism, religion founded in 19th
cent. by Baha Ullah (1817–92),
Persian religious leader. Bahaists
believe in the unity of all religions,
universal education, equality of the
sexes and world peace.
Bahamas, archipelago of *c.* 700
islands in Caribbean Sea extending
from Florida, US, towards Haiti.
Area: 5,386 sq. mi., Brit. colony; cap.
Nassau; principal islands include
Abaco, Andros, Cat Is., Eleuthera,
Grand Bahama, Inagua, Long Is. and
New Providence. Mild sub-trop.
climate promotes tourism, basis of
economy; nearly 1,000,000 tourists
visit annually. Tax advantages make it
attractive to investors. Other industries include rum, salt extraction
and handicrafts. Many of the islands
are undeveloped. First discovered by
Columbus (1492), Brit. jurisdiction
authorized by Treaty of Versailles
(1783). Internal self-govt. introduced
(1964). Currency, dollar. Pop. *c.*
145,000.
Bahrein, independent sheikdom,
under Brit. protection. Total area 400
sq. mi., comprising small group of 6
islands lying some 20 mi. off Arabia,
in Persian Gulf. Principal islands are
Bahrein and Muharraq, connected to
Manama, the cap. of Bahrein, by a 1½
mi. causeway. Climate is arid (annual
rainfall 4–5 in.), but irrigation enables
production of dates, citrus fruits,
almonds and vegetables. Until
recently centre of gulf pearl fishing
industry. Main source of revenue is
oil, discovered 1932; submarine pipe-
line connects Aramco oil fields in
Arabia to Bahrein. In 1958 Bahrein
became a free transit area. Pop.
195,000.
Baikal, lake in E Siberia, 1,640 ft.
above sea level. Area: 13,300 sq. mi.

Largest freshwater lake in Eurasia,
and the deepest (max. depth 5,500 ft.)
in the world. Contains unusual fish
species.
Bailey, Alfred (1905–), Canadian
poet and anthropologist. Author of
*The Conflict of European and East-
ern Algonkian Cultures, 1504–1700*
and *A Study in Canadian Civilization* (1937). Poetry includes *Songs of
the Saguenay and Other Poems*
(1927).
Baillargeon, Pierre (1916–), Fr.
Canadian writer. Founder of the
review *Amérique française*; best
known novel is *Les Médisances de
Claude Perrin* (1945).
Baja California, Lower California,
semi-arid, underdeveloped Mexican
peninsula S of California, US. It is *c.*
760 mi. long and 30–150 mi. wide.
Copper, silver and gold are mined,
and there are pearl fisheries. Agua
Caliente and Tijuana are border
resorts.
bakelite, phenol-formaldehyde resin
synthesized (1909) by Baekeland.
Resistant to corrosion and high
temperatures, an electrical insulator;
and used in production of varnishes,
adhesives and laminates.
Baker, Howland and Jarvis, 3 Pacific
atolls *c.* 1,650 mi. from Hawaii, now
under US jurisdiction.
Bakst, Leon Nikolaevich, orig. Leon
Rosenberg (1868–1924), Russ.
painter. International reputation
based on his sets for Diaghilev's
ballets.
Baku, cap. and port of Azerbaijanian
SSR, on W coast of Caspian Sea.
Once chief petroleum centre of USSR,
it has shipyards, oil refineries and
cable factories. Oil and gas wells were
once worshipped as shrines. Ruled by
Arabs, Turks, Persians, then annexed
(1806) by Russia. Pop. 1,164,000.
Bakunin, Mikhail Aleksandrovich
(1814–76), Russ. revolutionary and
anarchist. Active in 1848 Revolution;
exiled in Siberia, but escaped (1861).
Expelled (1872) from First International for opposition to Marxists.
Advocated freedom through anarchist philosophy.
Bala Java, section of Sevastopol, S
Ukrainian SSR, in the Crimea. Scene
of charge of the Light Brigade

Carvings on a
Hindu temple in
Bali

Bald Eagle

(Crimean War, 1854), celebrated in Tennyson's poem.

balalaika, Russ. guitar, usually with 3 strings, fretted fingerboard and triangular body.

balance of payments, statement of account of a country comprising the difference between values of imports and exports. Takes into account all gifts and foreign aid, capital, loans and gold transactions, and such items as shipping services abroad and interest on overseas investments.

balance of power, policy of preventing one nation from gaining sufficient power to threaten the security of other nations. Formulated by Metternich at Congress of Vienna (1815), it was leading principle in most 19th cent. European foreign policy.

Balanchine, orig. George Melitonovich Balanchivadze (1904–), Amer. dancer, choreographer and teacher. Trained at St Petersburg Imperial School of Ballet. From 1924, dancer and choreographer with many companies including that of Diaghilev; later director of New York City Ballet and School of American Ballet.

Balaton, largest lake in C Europe. Situated in Hungary; 48 mi. long; max. depth 35 ft.

bald eagle, *Haliaeetus leucocephalus,* rare and protected N Amer. bird of hawk family; black with white feathers on head, neck and tail. It mates for life; one brood reared annually. Lifespan *c.* 100 yr. Carnivorous and a carrion feeder, it is US national bird and appears on coat-of-arms.

Balder, Baldur, in Teutonic myth., son of Odin and god of light, summer, innocence and purity.

baldpate, type of WIGEON.

Baldwin, Faith [Cuthrell] (1893–), prolific Amer. novelist. Sentimental novels include *Those Difficult Years* (1925), *Medical Centre* (1940) and *Testament of Trust* (1960).

Baldwin, James (1924–), Amer. novelist and essayist. Works include

Go Tell It on the Mountain (1953), *Another Country* (1961) and *Nobody Knows My Name: More Notes of a Native Son* (1961). Most of his work shows concern for Amer. Negro.

Baldwin, Robert (1804–58), Canadian statesman. Member of the Province of Canada's Executive Council and Legislature in 1840s, advocated responsible government (afterwards achieved by Baldwin-LaFontaine Ministry, 1848–51).

Baldwin, Stanley, 1st Earl (1867–1947), Eng. statesman. Elected as Cons. M.P. after 20 yr. in family iron and steel business. Pres. of Board of Trade (1921), Chanc. of Exchequer (1922–3). Three times P.M.: 1st term (1923–4) ended over failure to obtain support for protectionist tariff policy; in 2nd term (1924–9) helped to end the General Strike (1926); his 3rd term (1935–7) marked by growing Axis threat and abdication of Edward VIII.

Balearic Islands, archipelago in Med. off E coast of Spain, forming Baleares prov. of Spain. Area: 1,936 sq. mi.; cap. Palma. The islands, esp. Majorca, Minorca, and Ibiza, are popular resorts. Chief occupations agriculture and fishing. Pop. 443,000.

Balenciaga, Cristóbal (1895–), Sp. fashion designer of international repute.

Balfour, Arthur James, 1st Earl of, (1848–1930), Brit. philosopher and statesman. First elected (1874) to House of Commons; entered cabinet (1886). Chief Sec. for Ireland, earned the title 'Bloody Balfour' for repression of Irish terrorism. Twice Cons. leader in Commons (1891–1902), succeeded his uncle (*see* CECIL, ROBERT A. T. GASCOYNE) as P.M. (1902). Leader of Opposition (1906–11); resigned over question of parl. reform. Member of wartime coalition cabinet and Foreign Sec. under Lloyd George (1916). Originated Balfour Declaration. Leader of Conservatives in House of Lords (1922).

Balfour Declaration (1917), assur-

ance, drawn up by Foreign Sec. Arthur Balfour, of Brit. protection for Jewish settlement of Palestine after its capture by Brit. forces.

Bali, island of Indonesia, E of Java. Area: 2,243 sq. mi.; cap. Singaradja. Mountainous with volcanoes; fertile plain in S. Culturally and economically important, chief products are copra, rice, coffee and teak. Hinduism dominant since 7th cent. Dutch first landed (1597). Pop. (1961) 1,782,529.

Balkan Wars (1912–13), 2 short wars for possession of Ottoman Empire's European territories. Serbo-Bulgarian alliance (1912) led to 1st war (Oct.) and Turkish expulsion from Europe saved the Constantinople area. Austria, Hungary and Italy, at a meeting of Great Powers in London, created (1913) an independent Albania, thwarting Serbia, which then demanded greater share of Macedonia from Bulgaria. Latter attacked Serbia (June 1913), only to be attacked by Romania, Greece and Turkey. Second Balkan War ended with Treaty of Bucharest (Aug. 1913), in which Bulgaria lost territory to all its enemies. Serbian territorial ambitions contributed to outbreak of World War 1.

Balkans, mountain range of Bulgaria extending for 350 mi., forming major divide between Danube and Meritza rivers. Botev Peak 7,793 ft., highest point.

Ball, John (d. 1381), Eng. priest, exponent of Wycliffe's doctrines; one of instigators of Peasant Rebellion (1381) under Watt Tyler. Executed after rebels dispersed.

Ball, John (1818–89), Eng. mountaineer and botanist. First pres. of Alpine Club (London). Crossed European Alpine chain 48 times; published *Alpine Guide* (1863).

ballad, orig. courtly dance song composed by minstrels; term now applied to narrative songs of popular origin. Classified according to subject: *i.e.* domestic, tragedy, historical, outlaw (Robin Hood or Jesse James), and Scot. coronach or lament ballad. Orally transmitted folk ballads became object of serious study in 19th cent. Literary ballads, usually characterized by four-line stanza with rhyming 2nd and 4th lines, and 3 or 4 accented line, date from the 14th cent.

ballade, poetic form set to music, *fl.* 13th and 14th cent. in Provence and Italy. Leading exponent, FRANÇOIS VILLON. Composers, esp. Chopin and Brahms, used term for dramatic piano pieces.

ballet, art form combining music,

'The Dancing School', 19th century impression of ballet by Edgar Degas

dance and mime, descended from court festivals of Ital. Renaissance. Developed as serious art form under patronage of Louis XIV who founded Académie Royale de Danse (1661) and Académie Royale de Musique (1669) to which he added a school for professional dancers (1713). These organizations became Paris Opera, still a centre of ballet production. Earliest notable ballet was *Ballet comique de la reine* (1581). After 1850, ballet declined until revived by Marius Petipa's attempts at stylistic unity by rigorous training of corps de ballet. Increasing popularity in 20th cent. due largely to the influence of the Ballets Russes of Diaghilev whose company included Michel Fokine, Léonide Massine, Vaslav Nijinsky, Anna Pavlova and George Balanchine. State-subsidized companies include Bolshoi (Moscow) and Royal Ballet (London). Contemporary ballet ranges from dance without plot or incident, to danced drama, lacking only speech, and its influence is apparent in opera, films, musical comedy and drama.

balloon, non-powered airship obtaining lift from bag filled with gas lighter than air, generally non-inflammable helium. Jacques and Joseph Montgolfier credited with invention (1783). Used for military observation since Napoleonic Wars; in World War 2, balloons held by cables were used in air defence. Balloons used for meteorological research; satellites of the Echo class are balloons launched from rockets.

balm, bee balm, *Melissa officinalis,* many branched lemon-scented perennial of thyme family with white, lipped flowers. Favourite plant of bees. Amer. bee balm is oswego tea.

Balmoral Castle, private residence of Brit. sovereign near Braemar, Aberdeenshire, Scotland.

balsa, corkwood *Ochroma lagopus,* tree of C and S America and W Indies. Strong, light wood used in modelmaking; raft in Kon-Tiki expedition (1947) was made of balsa trunks.

balsam, several trees, shrubs and plants which yield aromatic balsam. Orange balsam, *Impatiens capensis,* of N America; Himalayan balsam, *I. grandulifera,* showiest of the genus, grows wild beside rivers.

Baltic, part of Balto-Slavic branch of Indo-European languages, represented by Latvian (Lettish), Lithuanian and the now obsolete Old Prussian.

Baltic Sea, arm of Atlantic Ocean,

penetrating Scandinavia; *c.* 1,000 mi. long and 100 mi. wide. Narrow and shallow outlet makes it virtually a lake. Higher than the level of North Sea, low salinity and small tidal range subject it to long winter freeze-ups.

Baltimore, largest city in Maryland, US on Patapsco R. near Washington, DC. Important seaport, industrial and commercial centre; seat of Johns Hopkins University. First settled in 1700s. Incorporated as city (1794); developed shipbuilding industry around famous Baltimore clippers in early 1800s. During Civil War, inhabitants of Baltimore, technically loyal to Union, were violently pro-South. City rebuilt after disastrous fire. (1904). Pop. (1960) 939,000.

Baltimore, 1st Baron *see* CALVERT, GEORGE.

Baltimore oriole, hangnest, *Icterus galbula,* N Amer. insectivorous bird. Male, black and orange; nest, a small hanging bag woven from plant materials. State bird of Maryland.

Baluchistan, arid region of SE Iran, now united with Sistan (Seistan) prov. Area: 69,487 sq. mi. Pop. (1956) 428,608.

Balzac, Honoré de (1799–1850), Fr. novelist. *La Comédie Humaine* is a 'scientific' attempt to recreate Fr. society and depict in precise detail individuals of every class and profession. Novels include *Eugénie Grandet* (1833), *Le Père Goriot* (1835), and *La Cousine Bette* (1846).

Bamako, cap. of Republic of Mali, on upper Niger R. Port and terminus of Dakar-Niger Railway; trading centre for oil, cotton and peanuts. Pop. (1966) 135,000.

bamboo, cane, woody grass of the genera *Bambusa, Arundianaria, Phyllostachys,* and other trop. and sub-trop. varieties. Rapidly growing clump plant propagated by spreading underground roots; some attain 120 ft. *Bambusa arundinacea,* hard, durable with hollow stems, is used in

Banana flowers and immature fruit

buildings, furniture and utensils; also in paper-making. Young bamboo shoots are edible.

banana, *Musa sapientum,* large perennial Asian plant, now widespread in trop. regions of W hemisphere. Simple leaves, clustered flowers with edible fruits growing in large pendent bunches; rich in carbohydrates.

Banda, Hastings Kamazu (1902–), Pres. of Malawi (1966–). Campaigned from the Gold Coast (1953) against the Federation of Rhodesia and Nyasaland. Imprisoned during state of emergency after return (1958), but steadily gained power after independence (1964).

Bandaranaike, Sirimavo (1916–), Ceylonese P.M. (1960–65). Converted from Christianity to Buddhism on her marriage to Solomon Bandaranaike, later P.M. (1956). After husband's assassination (1959), she led her party to victory (1960).

bandicoot, nocturnal marsupial mammal of Australasia. Short-nosed bandicoot, *Isodon obesulus,* and long-nosed bandicoot, *Perameles nasuta,* are most common species. Rat-like; mainly carnivorous.

Bandung, city in W Java, SE of Djakarta. Site of Bandung Conference on Afro-Asian co-operation (1955). Pop. (1961) 973,000.

Banerjee, Tarashankar (1898–), Bengali novelist. Predominant concern: decay of landlord class. Best known for *Rai Kamal* (1934).

Banff National Park, Alberta, Canada, 1st Canadian national park (founded 1885). Area: 2,564 sq. mi. W of Calgary in E Rocky Mts; spectacular scenery, popular ski resort.

Banffshire, county of NE Scotland, mountainous in S. Area: 629 sq. mi.; county town, Banff. Main crop in lowlands is barley for distilleries; whisky is main industry. Pop. (1966) 45,000.

Bangalore, cap. of Mysore state, S India. Founded (1537), administrative seat of Mysore (1831). Major industrial and transport centre of S India, with varied industries incl. electronics and aircraft. Pop. (1965) 960,000.

Bangkok, cap. and principal port of Thailand. Industrial and transport centre; exports rice, teak, rubber and tin. Industries include shipbuilding, oil refining and rice milling. Old city, criss-crossed with canals, was sometimes known as 'Venice of the East'. Extensive reconstruction and modernization in European style in late 19th cent; buildings include Grand Palace and Royal Temple;

Bangladesh *see* PAKISTAN Buddhist monasteries. Pop. (1965) 1,800,000.

Bangui, cap. of Central African Republic and port on Ubangi River, founded (1890). Industries include textiles and food processing; has international airport. Pop. (1964) 111,000.

banjo, stringed musical instrument, thought to be of African origin; widely used in US by 19th cent. Negro minstrels and, in 20th cent., for 'ragtime' JAZZ form.

Bank of Canada, central bank of Canada, incorporated under Bank of Canada Act (1934). Regulates credit and currency by determining cash reserves available to chartered banks, each of which is required to maintain

Piccard's balloon on a Belgian postage stamp

Buddhist temple complex in Bangkok (top left)

Detail from a Coptic gospel book (1178-1180) depicting Baptism in the Jordan

Bantu dancers

minimum holdings in Bank of Canada.

Bank of England, central bank of Britain, founded (1694) as commercial bank. Popularly known as 'Old Lady of Threadneedle Street'. Bank Charter Act (1844) estab. present system: responsible for issue of bank notes, funding of national debts, *etc.* Nationalized 1945.

bank rate [UK], **discount rate** [US], rate at which Bank of England or US Federal Reserve Bank makes loans to commercial banks and other prime borrowers. High rate restricts borrowing and lending; low rate encourages expansion of credit. As instrument of monetary policy, bank rate used (19th cent.) to control international movements of capital; now used to curb inflation.

Bankhead, Tallulah (1903–68), Amer. film and stage actress. Known for wit and beauty, she achieved fame for dramatic and comic roles in New York and London.

banking, financial transactions through institutions primarily devoted to accepting deposits and making loans. Practised in classical times, large-scale banking in late Middle Ages dominated by Ital. families. Modern banking developed 18th–19th cent. in W Europe and US, with expansion of industry and trade. *See* FEDERAL RESERVE SYSTEM.

Banks, Sir Joseph (1743–1820), Eng. naturalist. Sailed round world (1768) with James Cook, collecting numerous botanical specimens, many of which were previously unclassified. Influential in establishing importance of Kew Gardens; Pres. of Royal Society (1778–1820).

Banks, Nathaniel Prentiss (1816–94), Amer. soldier and politician. Orig. Democrat, later Republican Gov-

ernor of Massachusetts (1858–60). Served in the Civil War, rising to rank of general in Union army.

Banks Island, most W island of Arctic Archipelago. Separated from N Canada by Amundsen Gulf, it is 250 by 225 mi. and consists of hilly plateaux, with scant Eskimo population. Discovered by Sir Robert McClure (1851).

banksia, bottle brush, genus of evergreen trees and shrubs of Proteaceae family named after Sir Joseph Banks. Widely distributed in S hemisphere, esp. Australia.

Bannister, Roger Gilbert (1929–   ), Brit. athlete. Practising physician, 1st man to run the mile in less than 4 min. (3 min. 59.4 sec.) at Oxford's Iffley Road track (May 1954).

Bannockburn, Battle of (1314), fought between Scots under Robert the Bruce, and English under Edward II. English routed by smaller Scot. army. Victory instrumental in securing Scot. independence.

banteng, *Bos sondaicus,* rare species of wild cattle of SE Asia, sometimes domesticated, with small slender horns. Lives in herds; calf is born yearly.

Bantic, most important family of Niger-Congo group of languages; spoken throughout much of C Africa.

Banting, Sir Frederick Grant (1891–1941), Canadian physiologist. With C. H. Best, isolated (1921) hormone, later called insulin, from pancreas. Awarded Nobel Prize for Physiology and Medicine (1923) with J. J. R. Macleod.

Bantu, group of ethnic and linguistic tribes of Africa S of Congo, thought to be descended from Hamitic and Negro stock. Shomo, Swahili, Zulu, Xhosa, Sotho and Herero-Ovambo are among 100 classified languages. Semi-nomadic and cattle-raising, they expanded S as population grew; some, such as Baganda (modern Uganda) were highly developed. Confederations arose opposing 19th cent. European settlement. Pop. (1963) 50,000,000.

banyan, *Ficus bengalensis,* tree of E India. Branches send out aerial roots which reach ground to form new trunks, creating sheltered space.

baobab, boojum, tree of *Andansonia* genus of Australia, Africa, India and S America. Large trunk adaptable to storage of water. African form, *A. digita,* is timber tree yielding edible fruit, monkey bread; bark used medicinally and in paper, cloth and rope-making.

baptism, initiation rite into Christian Church, in which person is sprinkled with or immersed in water. Symbolized repentance for John the Baptist.

Barabbas, in NT, thief, chosen in accordance with the Passover

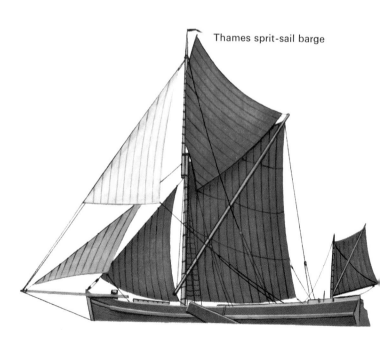

Thames sprit-sail barge

Barbary Ape

Barcelona, second largest city in Spain

custom (*Matt.* xxvii, 15–18), by the mob to be released instead of Christ by Pilate.

Barany, Robert (1876–1936), Austrian physician; specialist in otology, known for research in physiology and pathology of balancing apparatus in inner ear. Gave his name to special chair for testing air pilots. Awarded Nobel Prize for Physiology and Medicine (1914).

Barbados, island country of Brit. Commonwealth, in E Caribbean *c.* 200 mi. NE of Trinidad. Area: 166 sq. mi.; cap. Bridgetown. Sugar, molasses, and rum account for 90% of exports. Tourism is expanding rapidly. More than 80% of population is of African descent. English is main language. First settled by English (1627). Separate colony (1885) and independent (1966). Pop. (1965) 245,000.

Barbarossa *see* FREDERICK I.

barbary ape, magot, *Macaca sylvanus,* only monkey native to Europe; also found in N Africa. Welfare of the barbary apes of Gibraltar is entrusted to Brit. Army; said that if apes leave Gibraltar, so will British.

barbel, fish of genus *Barbus*. Lives in fresh, usually muddy water in Asia, Africa and Europe. *B. barbus,* common to Europe, is large, coarse fish, weighing 15–18 lb.

Barber, Samuel (1910–   ), Amer. composer. Won Pulitzer Prize for musical composition (1935, 1936). Works include operas, orchestral and chamber music, and songs.

barberry, any deciduous shrub of genus *Berberis*. Ornamental species includes Japanese barberry, *B. thumbergii*. The common European barberry, *B. vulgaris,* is also found in N America.

Barbirolli, Sir John (1889–1970), Eng. conductor. International career has included posts with Scottish Orchestra (1933–7), New York Philharmonic Orchestra (1937–43) and Hallé Orchestra (Manchester, England, 1943–58). From 1961 also conducted Houston (Texas) Symphony Orchestra.

barbiturates, phenobarbitone [UK], phenobarbitol [US], sedative-hypnotic drugs derived from barbituric acid; used anaesthetically and in treatment of insomnia, maniacal states, delirium tremens and epilepsy. They act on the central nervous system as sedatives and hypnotics.

Barbizon school, name given to a group of Fr. landscape painters who made their centre at Barbizon in the forest of Fontainebleau (1830–70). Members included Corot, Millet and Daubigny.

Barcelona, cap. of Barcelona prov. and chief city of Catalonia. Largest port in Spain; believed founded by Carthaginians, it flourished under Romans and Visigoths, fell to Moors (8th cent.), and was taken (801) by Charlemagne, who included it in his Spanish Marches. Barcelona's cloth trade grew rapidly and it became an important banking centre. Stronghold of Catalonia's separatist and radical politics, cap. of autonomous Catalan govt. (1932–39). Modern Barcelona's broad avenues and striking new buildings contrast with narrow streets and historic sites (Cathedral of Santa Eulalia) in the old quarter. Pop. 1,656,000.

Bardeen, John (1908–   ), Amer. physicist noted for research in magnetic and gravitational methods and theory of solid state. Awarded Nobel

'*The Gleaners*' by Millet, a member of the Barbizon School

Barites

Prize for Physics (1956) with W. H. Brattain and W. B. Shockley for work in developing transistor.

Bardot, Brigitte (1934–), Fr. film actress noted for her 'sex-kitten' roles. Career began in film *And God Created Woman*, directed by Roger Vadim.

Barents Sea, area of Arctic Ocean, bounded by Scandinavia, Spitsbergen and Novaya Zemlya. Floating ice in mid-summer makes it treacherous; Gulf Stream warms water in the S. Important fishing area, yielding cod, haddock and plaice.

barge, large boat, usually wooden, often flat-bottomed, used for transportation on sheltered waters. Common on the Nile in ancient Egypt. Modern barges propelled by sail or towed by horses or tugs. Self-propelled steel barges used on the Great Lakes of N America, for bulk transport. *See* illus. p 76.

Bari, seaport of S Italy. Agricultural market with various industries including oil refineries. Roman colony before passing to Goths, Lombards and Byzantines. Normans used it as base for crusades (1071). Became a Neapolitan duchy in Middle Ages. Port heavily damaged during World War 2. Romanesque basilica, with relics of St Nicholas of Bari, is a major place of pilgrimage. Pop. 335,000.

barites, barytes, heavy spar ($BaSO_4$), yellowish-white mineral occurring as flat orthorhombic crystals, or as massive, granular or stalactitic forms. Used in white paint, and as a filler in paper, linoleum and plastics.

baritone, male singing range with compass between bass and tenor.

barium, hard, silvery metallic element first isolated by Sir Humphry Davy (1808). Usually found in carbonate or sulphate state. Barium meals are used in X-rays of digestive tract.

bark beetles, beetles of family Scolytidae related to weevils, with brown compact body. Many species known as ENGRAVER BEETLE. Smaller European bark beetle, *Scolytus multistriatus,* introduced in US, where it is a serious pest. Like native Amer. elmbark beetle, *Hylurgopinus rufipes,* threatens existence of elm trees.

Barkla, Charles Glover (1877–1944), Eng. physicist. Awarded Nobel Prize for Physics (1917) for discovery of characteristic X-rays of elements.

barley, genus *Hordeum* of grass family, probably originating in Asia Minor and cultivated since prehistoric times. Most common cultivated form is *H. vulgare.* Unbranched stems rise in clumps and bearded seed heads extend from the grains. Now used to make malt.

barn owl, *Tyto alba,* long legged, very pale owl with white heart-shaped face. Most widely distributed land bird in the world, now scarce with demolition of old buildings which it frequented and through use of pesticides which can render it sterile. Its keen hearing enables it to catch prey in total darkness.

barnacle, marine crustacean of *Cirripedia* order, found on rocks, piers and the hulls of boats. Body enclosed in limy plates with space at top through which feathery appendages protrude and catch food. Species include the common European barnacle, *Balanus balanoides,* the Amer. *B. nubilis* and the goose barnacle, *Lepas anatifera.*

barnacle goose, *Branta leucopsis,* European goose appearing occasionally in N America. Has black and white plumage and white face. Breeds in the Arctic circle, migrating S in winter. In the Middle Ages this goose was thought to hatch from barnacles, and being considered fish, was eaten on days of abstinence.

Barnard, Christiaan (1922–), South African surgeon, first to

Barn Owl

Barnacle Goose

successfully perform heart transplant surgery on a human being.

Barnum, P[hineas] T[aylor] (1810–91), Amer. circus owner and impre-

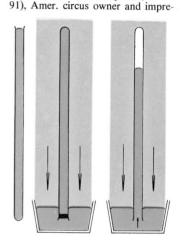

Diagram of Torricelli's Proof, the principle of the mercury barometer. A tube of mercury is upturned in a beaker of mercury. The tube empties to the point where the atmospheric pressure acting on the mercury in the beaker balances the weight of mercury in the tube. The amount of mercury supported depends on atmospheric pressure

sario. Made his name by extravagant advertising, and showing of freaks, incl. 'General Tom Thumb' and the original Siamese twins. His circus 'The Greatest Show on Earth' merged (1881) with most successful competitor to form Barnum and Bailey's Circus.

Baroja, Pio (1872–1956), Sp. writer and physician, whose novels reflect pessimistic view of life in which action is seen as the only way of combating the futility of the human situation. They include *Youth and Idolatry* (1917) and *The Tree of Knowledge* (1928).

barometer, instrument used to measure atmospheric pressure; comprises mercury-filled tube closed at upper end inverted in vessel containng mercury. Height of mercury in tube indicates atmos. press. Aneroid barometer uses metal box partially exhausted of air to measure atmos. press.

baroque, term applied, orig. to architecture, and later to art in general, of later 16th to early 18th cent. Europe. Its style is ornate and dramatic. 'Rococo', often wrongly used synonymously, applies to late baroque style, characterized by fantastic and grotesque ornamentation.

Barotseland, country in C Africa, protectorate of Zambia. Area: 63,000 sq. mi.; cap. Mongu. Limited autonomy retained when Brit. protection, later ceded to Zambia, accepted (1890–1900) by Barotse paramount chief on behalf of *c.* 25 tribes. Sources of Zambesi and its tribs. form heart of the region. Skilful use is made of the annual flood; population follows rise and fall of the waters. Livestock, grain, and teak are the main products. Pop. *c.* 300,000.

Barquisimeto, city in NW Venezuela, founded (1552) in highland area between Sierra Nevada de Mérida and Caribbean coastal range. Commercial centre on Pan American Highway. Good grazing country provides important cattle export trade. Rebuilt after earthquake (1812). Pop. 227,000.

barracuda, elongated fish of genus *Sphyraena,* with projecting lower jaw and sharp strong teeth. Only a few of the 20 species are dangerous, *e.g.,* the great barracuda, *S. barracuda.*

Barranquilla, city in N Colombia near mouth of Magdelena; founded (1629). Now an important Caribbean port and communications centre. Contains sugar refineries and textile mills. Pop. 493,000.

Barrault, Jean-Louis (1910–), Fr. actor, producer and outstanding mime. Films include *Les Enfants du Paradis* (1944) and *La Ronde* (1950).

barrel cactus, cactus of genus *Ferocactus* of Mexico and adjacent US, with strong, heavy spines. Compass cactus, *F. labispinus,* is best known.

barren strawberry, plant group, resembling strawberry. *Potentilla sterilis,* with white flowers, bears a dry fruit. US barren strawberry, *Wald-*

Examples of the Baroque style (1) Bernini's Trevi fountain in Rome. (2) The Theatine church of St Kajetan, Munich. (3) Detail from *Madonna Enthroned with Child* by Rubens. (4) Typical dress of the period

steinia fragarioides, with yellow flowers, resembles strawberry in leaf only.

Barrès, Maurice (1862–1923), Fr. novelist. His egoist trilogy *Le Culte du Moi* (1888–91) preceded socialist and nationalist awareness expressed in *Les Déracinés* (1897) and *Colette Baudoche* (1909).

Barrie, Sir J[ames] M[atthew], (1860–1937), Scot. novelist and dramatist. Author of fantasy *Peter Pan* (1904) and other whimsical plays, *e.g. The Admirable Crichton* (1902) and *Dear Brutus* (1917). Early novels set in Scotland.

barrister, member of upper branch of legal profession in England; has exclusive audience right in all superior courts, but appears only upon instructions of SOLICITOR. Potential barristers must join one of 4 Inns of Court. There are 2 grades, junior and Queen's Council. Scot. equivalent is advocate.

barrow, cairn or turf mound erected over burial place. Found in W Europe, dating from Neolithic period.

Barry, Jeanne Bécu, Comtesse du (1743–93), mistress of Louis XV of France. Installed at court (1769); notorious for her extravagance, she did not seek political influence. Retired on Louis XVI's accession (1774); guillotined in the Revolution.

Barry, Philip (1896–1949), Amer. playwright. Best known for his satirical comedies, esp. *The Philadelphia Story* (1939).

Barrymore, Ethel (1879–1959), Amer. actress, sister of John and Lionel. Versatile star on stage (*e.g. The Silver Box, The Corn is Green*) and also in films.

Barrymore, John (1882–1942), Amer. stage and film actor, brother of Ethel and Lionel. Distinguished on stage in *Peter Ibbetson, Richard III* and *Hamlet* (1922). Films include *Grand Hotel.*

Barrymore, Lionel (1878–1954), Amer. stage and film actor, brother of Ethel and John. Appeared on stage in

Basalt

Pantaloon and *Macbeth*; among first notable actors to star in films. Also famed for radio performances in Dickens' *Christmas Carol.*

Barth, John (1930–   ), Amer. novelist. Characterized by outrageous, often cruel, humour; novels include *The End of the Road* (1958) and *Giles Goat-Boy.*

Barth, Karl (1886–1968), Swiss Protestant theologian and educator. Early opponent of Nazi régime, deported to Switzerland (1935). Works concerned with return to doctrine of predestination; *Church Dogmatics* (include 4 vols., 1932–62).

Bartlett, John (1820–1905), Amer. compiler of *Familiar Quotations* (1855) and a Shakespeare concordance.

Bartok, Béla (1881–1945), Hungarian composer, pianist, collector of folk music (which influenced his own work). Among principal works: string quartets, orchestral suites, and set of piano pieces *Mikrokosmos.* Played and lectured in Europe and US.

Baruch, Bernard M[annes] (1870–1965), Amer. govt. adviser on economics, both official and voluntary. US representative to UN Atomic Energy Commission (1946).

barytes *see* BARITES.

basalt, widespread, basic, black, finely crystalline IGNEOUS ROCKS which make up the floor of the oceans. Occasionally outpours on continents as in the GIANTS CAUSEWAY, in Co. Antrim, N Ireland.

base, chem. compound yielding only a salt and water when mixed with an acid. Negatively charged, tastes bitter and feels soapy; in solution, it conducts electricity.

baseball, Amer. national game. Believed derived from Eng. game,

rounders. Abner Doubleday (1819–93) is credited with invention (1839) at Cooperstown, N.Y., where game's history is recorded in Hall of Fame and National Museum of Baseball. First organized game (1845); 1st professional team, Cincinnati Red Stockings (1869). Major League baseball is played by 24 teams divided between National and American Leagues. Leading teams from each League meet annually in World Series to determine champion.

Basic English, abbreviation for British American Scientific International Commercial English. One of the international languages, formulated by C. K. Ogden and I. A. Richards, it is claimed that its vocabulary of 850 English words is capable of expressing any concept and is intended to be an auxiliary language.

basil, several aromatic perennial herbs or shrubs of Labiatae family, native of Asia. Leaves of sweet basil, *Ocimum basilicum,* and bush basil, *O. suave,* are used in cookery.

Basil II (*c.* 954–1025), Byzantine emperor (976–1025), called Bulgaroktonos [Bulgar slayer]. Suppressed series of landowner revolts after 976. Annexed Bulgaria (1018) and extended E imperial frontier to the Caucasus.

Basil, Saint (*c.* 330–379), Gk. prelate, known as Basil the Great. Author of *The Longer Rule* and *The Shorter Rule,* basis for life of Basilian monks. As Bishop of Caesarea (370), established Nicene orthodoxy over Arianism in Byzantine East. Elegant defences of Catholic system are *On the Holy Ghost* and *Against Sinaurius.*

basilica, large Roman building in or near forum of a city. Earliest known built by Carlo the Elder (184 BC). With advent of Christianity, many

Basle, Switzerland

converted into churches. Orig. design, high central aisle and lower side aisles, adopted in many later churches.

basilisk, *Basiliscus basiliscus,* lizard of Iguana family of trop. America with an elevated crest along its back. Semi-aquatic, it can climb and run on its long hind legs. It feeds on plants and insects. Name was given to reptile of antiquity [Gk: *basileus,* a king], fabled king of serpents, also called cockatrice.

Baskerville, John (1707–75), Eng. type-designer and printer. Introduced influential type faces; his folio Bible (1763) was notable for its layout, excellent paper and ink.

theory which did not outlive the council itself.

Basov, Nikolai Gennadievich (1922–), Russ. physicist. Shared Nobel Prize (1964) for Physics with A. M. Procharov and C. H. Townes for work on lasers and masers and for contributions to field of quantum electronics.

Basque, one of few non Indo-European languages of Europe. A relic language, spoken in S France and N Spain by estimated 1,750,000.

Basque Provinces, region situated in W Pyrenees comprising Sp. Navarre and Basque Provinces and the Fr. districts of Labourd, Soule and Lower

ment of clarinet family. Invented *c.* 1770, now largely displaced by bass clarinet.

bassoon, orchestral woodwind instrument of oboe family. Wooden or metal tube is bent back on itself, reed being brought within reach of player's mouth by curved metal tube. Only contrabassoon is lower in pitch.

basswood, tree of genus *Tilia,* esp. *T. glabra.* Soft, strong wood is valued for furniture building.

Bastet, Egyptian goddess represented as a cat or cat-headed. City of Bubastis (House of Bastet) was named after her.

Bastille, former state prison in Paris.

1

2

1. Mouse-eared Bat
2. Common European Brown Bat

basketball, game played by 2 opposing teams of 5 players each on regulation court 94 ft. by 50 ft. Originated (1891) in US by James Naismith in Springfield, Mass. Professionally played since 1896; National Basketball Association (formed 1949) attracts wide following in US. Olympic event since 1936.

basking shark, *Cetorhinus maximus,* large shark, sometimes over 40 ft. long, common in the Atlantic. Name derived from habit of lying in sun; gill slits almost encircle this harmless fish.

Basle (Fr: **Bâle;** Ger: **Basel**), city in Basle canton, N Switzerland, major financial and industrial centre; Switzerland's chief railway junction and river port. Founded by Romans, it became an episcopal see (7th cent.), free imperial city (11th cent.), joined Swiss Confederation (1501), and accepted reformation (1523). An intellectual and artistic centre, notable buildings include 16th cent. town hall and 11th cent. cathedral Pop. (1965) 212,000.

Basle, Council of (1431–49), last of the great R.C. reform councils of the 15th cent. Beginning at Basle and continuing at Ferrara, Florence and Rome, it attempted to replace papal authority with that of the council, a

Navarre. Population differs in language and origin from its neighbours. Larger before Roman incursions, it resisted Visigoth, Moorish, and Frankish influence before creation (824) of Kingdom of Navarre. Sp. Basque conquered by Castile (1370), but retained some independence. General Franco conquered provinces (1937), after autonomy had been granted in 1936. N Basque provinces have been part of France since 1589 when Henry of Navarre ascended Fr. throne as Henry IV.

Basra, city in Iraq, 75 mi. from Persian Gulf. Exports petroleum products, wool, barley and dates. Founded (636) by Caliph Omar, Basra became cultural centre and declined with the Abbasid caliphates. Possession long contested by Persians and Turks. Importance revived by Baghdad railway link. Pop. 423,000.

bass, family of freshwater and marine fish. Popular game and food fish, feeds on crustaceans. Found primarily in N America.

Bass Strait, channel 80–150 mi. wide, between Tasmania and Victoria, Australia. Discovery by George Bass (1798) proved that Tasmania was not joined to Australia.

bass viol *see* VIOLA DA GAMBA.

basset horn, musical wind instru-

Built (1370) as fortress, used as prison (*c.* 1600). Stormed by Parisian mob (14 July 1789), marking outbreak of Fr. Revolution. Date is celebrated in France as national holiday.

Basuto, one of BANTU tribes.

Basutoland *see* LESOTHO.

bat, mammal of order *Chiroptera,* found in most trop. and temp. regions. Only true flying mammal, forelimbs modified to form membranous wings; suspends itself from claws when resting. Bats of colder regions hibernate in winter. Principal categories: large fruit-eating bats with good vision, *e.g.* flying fox; smaller insectivorous bats, more abundant, with poor eyesight compensated for by an echo-sounding system for flight and catching prey. Some bats are blood-sucking, *e.g.* VAMPIRE BAT.

Bataan, peninsula and province, W Luzon, Philippines Republic. Scene of intense fighting (World War 2 1942) in which US troops eventually surrendered to Japanese. Thousands of US prisoners of war died in subsequent Death March.

Batavia *see* DJAKARTA.

Bates, H[erbert] E[rnest] (1905–), Eng. writer. Author of novels, such as *Fair Stood the Wind for France* (1944), and short stories, many of which have been anthologized.

Bath, city of Somerset, England, *c.* 12 mi. SE of Bristol. Roman town, called Aquae Sulis, had extensive bath system using warm springs. Prospered during Middle Ages as wool and cloth town. Became famous spa in 18th cent., when planned streets and buildings were erected. Now residential and resort town with manufacturing and quarrying; 16th cent., abbey remains despite heavy damage of World War 2 air raids. Pop. (1960) 79,275.

batholith, mass of intruded igneous rock of unknown depth. Examples are Dartmoor and Bodmin Moor, England. Largest are those in Idaho, US, and Peru.

Bathsheba, in OT, wife of Uriah the Hittite. David brought about Uriah's death and married her. She bore him Solomon. (II *Sam.* xi 1–24).

Bathurst, port on W coast of Africa and cap. of The Gambia. Trading centre founded (1816) by British. Pop. (1963) 27,800.

Batista y Zaldivar, Fulgencio (1901–), Pres. of Cuba (1940–4, 1954–8). Military coup (1933) brought him to power; exiled (1945); another successful coup (1952) reinstated him. Discontent resulted in FIDEL CASTRO's revolutionary movement. Batista again fled Cuba (1959).

Baton Rouge, US city, state cap. of Louisiana. Built (1719) as fort by French. Major distributing and commercial centre, it has one of world's largest oil refineries; also heavy chemical plants. Pop. (1960) 194,000.

battery, group of cells used as source of electric current. Storage battery is principal current source and is a

Cross-section of accumulator battery showing plates and terminals

component of internal combustion engine.

battleship, large, armoured warship equipped with heavy guns. Evolved from ironclad warship of mid-18th cent., built of steel by 1870s. Britain's *Dreadnought,* completed in 1906, introduced 'all-big-gun' class of warship. Extensively used during World War 1, obsolete in World War 2 with development of aerial tactics, esp. dive bombing.

Baudelaire, Charles Pierre (1821–67), Fr. poet whose main theme is the inseparability of beauty and corruption. *Les Fleurs du Mal* (1857), condemned during his lifetime as obscene, now regarded as his masterpiece. Greatly influenced by Poe, whom he translated into French.

Baudouin (1930–), king of the Belgians (1951–). Son of Leopold III, joined father in exile (1944–50); became king on Leopold's abdication (1951).

Bauer, Georg, adopted name of Agricola (1494–1555), Ger. physician and scientist. Pioneer in scientific classifications of minerals; author of *De re metallica* (1566).

Baugh, Samuel Adrian (1914–), Amer. football player. All-Amer. backfield at Texas Christian University, later joined Washington Redskins of National Football League. Estab. many passing and kicking records during career (1937–52).

Bauhaus [literally 'building-house'], school of design, building, and craftsmanship, founded (1919) by Walter Gropius in Weimar, Germany; aimed at union of creative arts and technology of modern mass-production. Moved twice, to Dessau and later to Berlin; closed by the Nazis (1933). Its ideas and teaching have influenced both art and industrial design.

bauxite, aluminous hydrous residual deposit; white to red or brown mineral, chief source of aluminium and its compounds.

Bavaria [Ger: **Bayern**], former kingdom, now largest Ger. state; lies E of Baden-Württemberg along the Austrian border. Cap. Munich. Conquered (15 BC) by Romans, Bavaria came under Frankish rule (787). Wittelsbach family assumed duchy (1180). Napoleon made it a kingdom (1806). Bavaria joined Ger. Empire (1871) after supporting Austria during Austro-Prussian War (1866), but Wittelsbach king, Ludwig III, was not deposed until 1918.

Bax, Sir Arnold Edward Trevor (1883–1953), Eng. composer, influenced by Celtic literature and lore.

Quarrying for bauxite in Jamaica

His works include *Tintagel* and *A Garland for the Queen.* Master of the King's Music (1942–53).

bay lynx *see* BOBCAT.

bay tree, bay laurel, *Laurus nobilis,* evergreen shrub or tree of laurel family of Med. regions. Designation laureate comes from ancient custom of bestowing a wreath of bay leaves as mark of honour. Leaves now used as food flavouring.

Bayeux, town in Calvados department of Normandy, N France. Communications and agricultural centre with noted lace industry. The famous Bayeux tapestry, depicting scenes from Norman conquest of England, is in town's museum. Pop. (1960) 10,077.

Baylis, Lilian Mary (1874–1937), Eng. theatrical manager. Founded Old Vic Theatre Company, Sadler's Wells Opera, and Vic-Wells Ballet.

Bayly or **Barly** or **Baley, Charles** (*c.* 1630–80), Brit. adventurer. First overseas governor of Hudson's Bay Company (1669).

bayonet, blade clipped on to end of musket or rifle, introduced in late 17th cent. Invention made pike redundant.

Beaconsfield, Earl of *see* DISRAELI, BENJAMIN.

Beadle, George Wells (1903–), Amer. geneticist. Known for research on cytology and genetics; shared Nobel Prize for Physiology and Medicine (1958).

beaked whale, member of *Ziphiidae* family of medium-sized cetaceans with a distinct beak and 1 or 2 pairs of teeth. Best known genus is bottle-nosed whale, *Hyperoodon.*

bean, large kidney-shaped edible seed; an inexpensive source of protein. Species include runner bean, soya bean, haricot or navy bean.

Bean Goose

Bayeux Tapestry

bean goose, *Anser fabalis,* dark-coloured migratory goose with orange legs. Breeds in Arctic forests near water.

bearberry, *Arctostaphylos uva-ursi,* Amer. shrub with glossy red berries. Bears are said to be fond of the fruit, hence the name.

Beard, Charles Austin (1874–1948), Amer. historian. Helped promote cultural emphasis in the teaching of history. Wrote controversial *An Economic Interpretation of the Constitution* (1913), in which he studied conservative economic interests of delegates at US Constitutional Convention.

bearded lizard, *Amphibolurus barbatus,* lizard of the agamid family of the Austral. scrub. Has spines on its skin and a snout shield which, when swollen, looks like a beard. The whiplike tail is used for balance when animal is running on its hind legs.

Beardsley, Aubrey Vincent (1872–98), Eng. artist and book illustrator. His highly stylized drawings and posters, epitomizing ART NOUVEAU, became popular in mid-1960s.

Beatles, The, Eng. entertainers, 1st and most successful 'pop group', George Harrison (1943–), John Lennon (1940–), Paul McCartney (1942–), Ringo Starr [Richard Starkey] (1940–). The 'Liverpool Sound' changed 'pop' music and

caused it to be given serious critical consideration. Films include *A Hard Days Night* and *Help.*

Beaton, Sir Cecil (1904–). Eng. photographer, designer. Designs for theatre and cinema include *My Fair Lady.*

Beatty, David Beatty, 1st Earl (1871–1936), Brit. admiral. His fleet lured Ger. fleet at Battle of Jutland (1916), major naval encounter of World War 1. First Sea Lord (1919–27); created Earl (1919).

Beauchemin, Nérée (1850–1931), Fr. Canadian poet and physician. Exponent of regionalist school of poetry of Quebec called *Le Terroir. Patrie intime* (1828) expresses love for his native province.

Beaufort scale, measure of WIND velocity, varying from 0 for calm to 12 for hurricane force. Devised by Sir Francis Beaufort (1774–1857), Eng. admiral and hydrographer.

Beaumarchais, Pierre-Augustin Carron de (1732–99), Fr. dramatist. Edited and published first complete edition of works of Voltaire. Best remembered for plays *Barber of Seville* (1775) and *Marriage of Figaro* (1784), which inspired operas by Rossini and Mozart.

Beaumont, Francis (c. 1584–1616), Eng. dramatist. Name is always linked with that of his collaborator, John Fletcher. Their plays include

Philaster, and *The Maid's Tragedy.*

Beaumont, William (1785–1853), Amer. surgeon. Pioneer work on digestive processes contained in *Experiments and Observations on the Gastric Juice and the Physiology of Digestion* (1833), still a classic in medicine.

Beauregard, Pierre Gustave Toutant (1818–93), US Confederate army officer. In command at Charleston, where he ordered firing on FORT SUMTER. Promoted to full general after first battle of BULL RUN. Reinforced Lee in Virginia campaigns (1864). Settled in Louisiana as railroad pres. after the war.

Beauvoir, Simone de (1908–), Fr. novelist, essayist. A leading existentialist, her best-known book is essay on women, *The Second Sex* (1949). Novels include *The Mandarins* (1954) and *Les Belles Images* (1966).

beaver, *Castor fiber,* largest rodent of N hemisphere. Found in Europe, Asia and N America, particularly Canada; amphibious mammal with webbed hind feet and broad flattened tail. Feeds mainly on bark. Became rare due to demands for its fur and musk gland. Constructs 'lodges' in river banks and complex systems of dams and tunnels.

Beaverbrook, 1st Baron *see* AITKEN, WILLIAM MAXWELL.

Bechuanaland *see* BOTSWANA.

Beaver's dam showing lodges with insert showing specialised teeth and claws, used for building dams

Becket, Saint Thomas à, (1118–70). Eng. cleric and martyr. Befriended by Henry II, appointed chancellor (1155), archbishop of Canterbury (1162), but opposed King over taxation. Henry's attempt under Constitutions of Clarendon (1168) to secure jurisdiction over clergymen culminated in Becket's flight to Rome. Quarrel after his return (1170) ended with murder of Becket in Canterbury Cathedral; Henry's exact role never estab., but he did public penance (1174) at Thomas' tomb.

Beckett, Samuel (1906–), Irish dramatist and novelist. Work is mostly written in French. International reputation began with *Waiting for Godot* (1952). He was awarded the Nobel Prize for Literature (1969).

Becquerel, Antoine Henri (1852– 1908), Fr. physicist, famed for discovery of radioactivity (1896). Shared Nobel Prize for Physics (1903) for study of uranium and radioactive substances. Explored aspects of light, incl. polarization and absorption by crystals. Rays emitted by radioactive substance called 'Becquerel rays'.

bedbug, small cosmopolitan family, Cimicidae, of 30 species. Flat nocturnal ectoparasites of birds and mammals, require warm blood as food. Breed all year round, laying eggs in cracks; have a characteristic odour and survive without food for a year.

Beddoes, Thomas Lovell (1803–49), minor Eng. poet and playwright, author of *Death's Jest Book* (1850).

Bede or **Baeda** or **Beda, Saint** (673–735), Eng. scholar, historian and theologian. Known since 9th cent. as The Venerable Bede, and as author of *Ecclesiastical History of the English Nation.*

Bedford, John of Lancaster, Duke of *see* JOHN OF LANCASTER.

Bedfordshire, county of S Midlands, Eng. Area: 470 sq. mi.; county town, Bedford; main towns, Luton, Dunstable. Largely agric., wheat and garden products important. Industries include motor cars, textiles and engineering. Pop. (1966) 428,000.

Bedlington terrier, Eng. breed of dog with hardy woollen coat, narrow head and long tail. Tan, sandy or bluish coat.

Bedlington Terrier

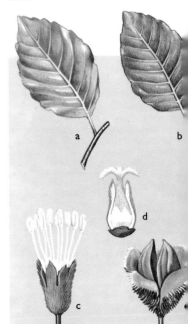

bee, *Apoidea,* group of insects of the order Hymenoptera of worldwide distribution. They have 2 pairs of membraneous wings, thick dense hair on body, large compound eyes, 3 occuli on head, antennae, and tube-like tongue for extracting nectar. Solitary bees nest in soil or hollow stems. The social bees include the BUMBLE BEE, CUCKOO BEE, HONEY BEES and small trop. stingless bees. Bees usually have a caste system involving queen, workers and drones.

beech, widespread family of trees typified by genus *Fagus,* with deep-green foliage, smooth grey bark and massive round trunk. Wood is used in furniture and building; popular hedging plant. Common species are European *Fagus sylvatica,* copper beech, *F. sylvatica capra,* and Amer. *F. grandifolia.*

beech drops, *Epiphegus virginiana,* low, wiry, dead-looking plant of the broomrape family, parasitic on beech and native of N America.

Beecham, Sir Thomas (1879–1961), Eng. conductor. Conducted the Beecham Symphony, Hallé, London Philharmonic, and Royal Philharmonic orchestras. Promoted opera; succeeded (1916) to his father's baronetcy.

Beecher, Henry Ward (1813–87), Amer. preacher, brother of HARRIET BEECHER STOWE. Renowned orator, championed anti-slavery, women's suffrage and evolutionary theory. Lawsuit against him by Theodore Tilton for adultery ended (1875) with jury's disagreement. Works include *Evolution and Religion* (1885).

bee-eater, family of birds, *Meropidae,* related to the kingfisher, found in Europe and Australia. Has brilliant plumage, long curved bill and pointed wings. These insectivorous migratory birds feed on bees and other stinging insects; nest underground.

beefwood, several Austral. trees of genus *Casuarina.* Hard, red wood is used in cabinet work. The beefwood, she-oak or ironwood, *C. equisetifolia,* bears cones.

beer, alcoholic beverage made by brewing and fermenting cereals, esp. malted barley, with hops. Britain, Germany, Czechoslovakia and the US, are the largest producers. The quantity of malt and water, as well as length of brewing, determine alcoholic content (usually 3 to 6 degrees).

Beerbohm, Sir Max (1872–1956), Eng. writer and caricaturist. Most famous work and only novel, *Zuleika Dobson* (1911). Brilliant caricatures contributed to legend of wit and satirical power.

Bee-eater

Beersheba, cap. of the Negev, Israel, 48 mi. SW of Jerusalem. Chiefly connected in Bible with Abraham, Hagar, Isaac and Elijah. Pop. (1960) 39,500.

beet, several varieties of biennial plants of genus *Beta,* grown for their roots or leaves. The sugar beet, *B. vulgaris,* native of Europe and grown in N America, provides two-fifths of the world's sugar. The garden beet [UK] beetroot, has red-veined leaves; edible root. Variety *cicla* is cultivated for leaves, known as beet spinach or Swiss chard.

Beethoven, Ludwig Van (1770– 1827), Ger. composer and pianist. Studied with his father and made his concert debut (1795). One of the most original and influential composers of all, among his best known works are orchestral, choral, chamber works, and piano sonatas; the *Third* (*Eroica*), *Fifth, Sixth* (*Pastoral*), and *Ninth* (*Choral*) symphonies; *Moon-*

Beech: (a) Leaf of Common Beech (b) Leaf of Copper Beech (c) Male flower (d) Female flower (e) Open fruit pod with 2 seeds *light Sonata, Mass in D,* and string quartets.

beetle, any insect of the order Coleoptera. Over 250,000 species exist, distributed in every habitat. Varying in size from $\frac{1}{16}$ in. to 5 in., all have biting jaws, 4 wings, the horny front pair covering the inner pair.

Beeton, Isabella Mary, née Mayson (1836–65), Eng. writer on cookery, domestic economy, and fashion. Famous for *Mrs Beeton's Book of Household Management* (1861).

begonia, genus of succulent herbs with ornamental leaves and red, pink, or white flowers, native of tropics. Cultivated varieties are divided into fibrous-rooted types which are mainly houseplants for winter blooming; and bulbous, tuberous and rhizomatous begonias.

Behan, Brendan (1923–64), Irish dramatist who gained fame with his first play *The Quare Fellow* (1956). Other works include *The Hostage* (1958) and *Borstal Boy* (1958).

Behar *see* BIHAR.

behaviourism, theory of human behaviour based on nervous activity in response to environmental stimuli. Introduced (1912) by JOHN B. WATSON, criterion was objective measurement of activity rather than subjective impression, substantiated by observations of animal behaviour, esp. Pavlov's conditioned reflex experiments. B. F. SKINNER focused on observable behaviour patterns, rejecting the unobservable.

behemoth [Heb. beasts], animal referred to in *Book of Job,* thought to be the hippopotamus.

Behn, Aphra (1640–89), Eng. playwright and authoress of romances. Employed by Charles II as spy in Antwerp at outbreak of Dutch War. Her works include *Oroonoko* (1688) and anticipate the 18th cent. novel.

Behring, Emil Adolph von (1854–1917), Ger. physician. Pioneer in serum therapy, demonstrated immunization against diphtheria (1890) and tetanus (1892) by injections of antitoxins; awarded Nobel Prize for Physiology and Medicine (1901).

Behrman, S[amuel] N[athaniel] (1893–), Amer. dramatist and scriptwriter, best known for his sophisticated comedies incl. *No Time for Comedy* (1939) and *But for Whom Charlie* (1964).

Beira, city in E central Mozambique, port on Indian Ocean, serving Rhodesia and Malawi. Founded (1891) as a terminus on a rly. to interior; now also a resort town. Pop. (1960 est.) 50,000.

Beirut, cap. (since 1941) and chief port of the Lebanon. In turn

Begonia

Phoenician, Roman, Frankish and Turkish city; disastrous earthquake (551). Pop. 500,000.

Bekesy, Georg von (1899–), Amer. biophysicist. Known particularly for his work on physical method of stimulation within the inner ear; awarded Nobel Prize for Physiology and Medicine (1961).

Belaney, George Stansfield (1888–1938), Canadian writer, known as 'Grey Owl'. Books include *The Men of the Last Frontier* (1931) and *The Adventures of Sajo and her Beaver People* (1935).

Belasco, David (1859–1931), Amer. actor, dramatist and theatrical producer. Of 400 plays, best known include *Zaya* (1898), *The Girl of the Golden West* (1905), and *Hearts of Oak* (with James A. Herne, 1879).

Belem, Pará, cap. of Pará State and chief port of N Brazil. At mouth of Amazon, it handles rubber, cocoa and timber. Prominent during late 19th cent. rubber boom. Contains state university. Pop. (1960) 402,000.

belemite, conical fossil several in.

long, consisting of internal calcareous rod of extinct animal; allied to cuttlefish. Existed from Jurassic to Upper Cretaceous periods.

Belfast, cap. and port of Northern Ireland. Supports shipbuilding, light and heavy industries and is centre of Irish linen manufacturing. Founded (1177) with building of ford over the Lagan. Contains Stormont (prov. parliament) and Queen's University. Pop. (1966) 399,000.

Belgae, Celtic people of N Gaul, joined by the Germanii *c.* 450 BC; given the name by Julius Caesar. By 55 BC a Belgic kingdom under Cassivelaunus had been formed in SE England and later spread westward. Improved standards of agriculture in Gaul and England.

Belgium, kingdom of W Europe. Area: 11,755 sq. mi., cap. Brussels. Constitutional monarchy with bicameral legislature and divided into 9 provinces. Industry concentrated in lowlands over Campine and Walloon

coal basins. Antwerp, Mons, Namur and Liège are centres of heavy and light industries, coal mining, chemicals, pharmaceuticals, textiles, and iron and steel production. One of world's chief zinc producers and a leader in shipping and transit trades. Cattle raising and market-gardening important. Ghent, Louvain, Brussels and Liège are university cities. Flemish and French spoken. Roman Catholicism is main religion. Ghent, Bruges and Ypres achieved prosperity and virtual independence through

Flat country behind the Belgian coast

Belgrade, Yugoslavia

their wool industry and trade. Dominated by the Netherlands, Austria and Spain (1477–1797). Prince Leopold of Saxe-Coburg-Gotha made king (1831). Dutch-Belgian Peace Treaty signed (1839) and the 'perpetual neutrality' of Belgium guaranteed by the major powers. Under Leopold II (1869–1909) industrialization and colonization, notably in the Congo, accompanied by labour unrest and rise of Socialist Party. Internal French-Flemish tension causes instability. Belgium was a founder member of Benelux customs union of Council of Europe, European coal and steel community and Common Market. Unit of currency, Belgian franc. Pop. (1966) 9,556,000.

Belgrade, cap. of Yugoslavia and Serbia. Industrial, polit., and cultural centre with varied industry. Occupied by Austria during World War 1; became cap. of kingdom of Serbians, Croats and Slovenes (1918) and of Yugoslavia upon creation (1929). Pop. (1964) 678,000.

Belize, cap. and seaport of Brit. Honduras. Exports trop. hardwoods. Pop. (1965 est.) 46,000.

Bell, Alexander Graham (1847–1922), Amer. scientist, b. Scotland. Invented telephone (1876), photophone which transmitted 1st wireless telephone message (1880), and produced 1st successful phonograph record.

Bell, Benjamin (1749–1806), Scot. surgeon. Experimented with methods of alleviating pain in surgical operations, and wrote a treatise on *Gonorrhea Virulenta* and *Lues Venerea* (1793), proving them to be 2 different diseases. His *System of Surgery* (6 vols., 1783–7), frequently reprinted and translated.

Bell, Sir Charles (1774–1842), Scot. surgeon. Most important contribution was discovery of distinct functions of the nerves, which he extended to the functional separation of sensory and motor nerves. Bell's Law and Bell's palsy are named after him.

Bell, Ellis, orig. EMILY BRONTË.

belladonna, deadly nightshade, *Atropa belladonna,* perennial plant of

nightshade family native of Europe and Asia and estab. in America. Known for centuries as a poison, the blackcurrant-like berries and leaves yield alkaloid drug atropine. Name comes from its cosmetic use by women to dilate pupils of the eyes.

Bellamy, Edward (1850–98), Amer. novelist and social reformer. Remembered mainly for his Utopian romance *Looking Backward* (1888), depicting triumphant socialist state of AD 2000.

Bellay, Joachim du (1522–60), Fr. poet, known as 'The French Ovid' and 'Prince of the Sonnet'. His *Défense et Illustration de la Langue Française* (1549) constituted the manifesto of group of poets known as the Pléiade.

Bellerophon, in Gk. myth., son of Glaucus of Corinth, or of Poseidon. Performed great deeds with help of winged horse, Pegasus; thrown from Pegasus' back and killed in attempt to reach Olympus.

Bellini, Giovanni (*c.* 1430–1516), Venetian painter. Known chiefly for his altarpieces. Among his pupils were Titian and Giorgione.

Bellini, Vincenzo (1801–35), Ital. opera composer. Work characterized by melodic style, elegance, and lyrical charm. His best-known operas are *La Sonnambula* (1831) and *Norma* (1831).

Belloc, [Joseph] Hilaire [Pierre] (1870–1953), Eng. poet, essayist and biographer, b. France. Best known for humorous verse, *The Bad Child's Book of Beasts* (1896) and *Cautionary Tales* (1907).

Bellona, Roman goddess of war sometimes identified with Gk. war-

goddess Enyo and with Nerio cult-partner of Mars.

Bellow, Saul (1915–   ), Amer. novelist, b. Canada. Works include picaresque *The Adventures of Augie March* (1953) and *Herzog* (1964).

bellwort, *Uvularia grandiflora,* Amer. plant with yellow, drooping, bell-shaped flowers. Its stem pierces leaf.

Belmonte, Juan (1892–1962), Sp. bullfighter. Considered by many as greatest matador of all, is credited with the introduction of modern daring style.

Belo Horizonte, cap. of Minas Gerais state, E Brazil. Built (1895–7) to replace Ouro Prêto as state cap. Opening of hydro-electric plant (1946) speeded industrial growth. Pop. (1960) 693,000.

Belorussian SSR *see* BYELORUSSIAN SSR.

Belshazzar (6th cent. BC), Babylonian general, son of Nabonidos. Until the decipherment of cuneiform inscriptions, he was known only from the book of *Daniel,* where he is represented as son of Nebuchadnezzar and last king of Babylon.

beluga, *Delphinapterus leucas,* genus of the toothed whale group related to the narwhal. Slow swimmer, inhabits Arctic seas and moves S in winter. Known as white whale, *c.* 14 ft. long, is prey of other whales.

Belukha, Byelukha, twin-peaked mountain, highest (15,157 ft.) in Altai system in C Asia on borders of USSR, China and Mongolia. It gives rise to 16 glaciers.

Belzoni, Giovanni Battista (1778–1823), Ital. archaeologist. Re-

Transfiguration by Giovanni Bellini

87

sponsible for transport of massive bust of Rameses II, known as the Colossus of Memnon, now in the Brit. Museum. One of the first men to stimulate interest in Egyptology.

Bemelmans, Ludwig (1898–1962), Amer. writer and painter, b. Austria. Works, illustrated with water colours and drawings, include *Madeleine* (1939), a book for children.

Ben Bella, Ahmed (1916–), Algerian statesman. After serving with Fr. army in World War 2, joined Algerian nationalist movement and became terrorist leader. Exiled (1949–56) before imprisonment by French. Released (1961), became premier with the help of army (1962). Elected pres. (1963), but deposed 2 years later by military coup.

Ben Gurion, David (1886–), Israeli statesman, 1st premier. Polish-born, active Zionist and Brit. supporter during World War 1. A leader of Mapai (Lab.) party, he was premier (1948–53) in newly-created Israeli state. Resigned, but returned for 2nd term (1955–63).

Ben Lawers, mountain in Perthshire, Scotland, 3,984 ft. Noted for wide variety of arctic and alpine plants.

Ben Nevis, highest peak in UK (4,406 ft.) in Inverness-shire, Scotland.

Benares, city in India on R. Ganges; railway and trade centre. Buddha preached at nearby Sarnath *c.* 500 BC. In 7th cent. AD Benares had many temples sacred to Siva; *c.* 1,000,000 pilgrims annually bathe in the Ganges. Educ. centre with a Hindu university. Pop. (1965) 527,000.

Benavente [y Martínez], Jacinto (1866–1954), Sp. dramatist. Noted for social satire and emphasis on rural life. Works include *Los Intereses Creados* (1907), Eng. tr., *Bonds of Interest* (1917). Awarded Nobel Prize for Literature (1922).

Benda, Julien (1867–1956), Fr. novelist and critic. Won recognition with *The Yoke of Pity* (1912). *La trahison des clercs* (1927) attacks sacrifice of artistry for practical gains.

Benedict, Ruth F[ulton] (1887–1948), Amer. anthropologist. Enlarged scope of anthropology through work on concept of culture motif and relation of personality to culture. Her most important work is *Patterns of Culture* (1934).

Benedictines, R.C. monastic order, estab. by St Benedict at Monte Cassino (529). Stressing communal living and work (motto: '*Laborare est orare*'), they did much to preserve learning in the Middle Ages. Among notable Benedictines were St Augustine, St Boniface, Gregory the Great.

Benares, on the Ganges, India

Benelux, economic union, of Belgium, the Netherlands, and Luxembourg, estab. (1958). Provides for abolition of trade restrictions. Economic union of Belgium and Luxembourg formed in 1922; in 1947 joined by the Netherlands in a customs union.

Beneš, Eduard (1884–1948), Czech statesman. Foreign Min. (1918–35), premier (1921–2), and pres. (1935–8, 1945–8). Joined T. G. MASARYK in exile (1915). Headed Czech provisional govt. in London during World War 2; re-elected pres. of post-war Czechoslovakia; resigned after Communist coup (1948).

Benét, Stephen Vincent (1898–1943), Amer. poet and novelist. Author of *John Brown's Body* (1928), poem on American Civil War.

Benevento, cap. 32 mi. NE of Naples, and prov. of C Italy. Roman colony and junction on Appian Way. Became seat of Duchy of Lombardy (571), part of papal possessions. Given by Napoleon to Charles de Talleyrand. United with Italy (1860).

Bengal, former state of NE India, divided (1947) between India and Pakistan. Consists largely of alluvial plain; main crops, rice, jute, tea. Iron smelting and steel rolling mills in W Bengal. E Bengal prov. of E Pakistan until 1971 war; W Bengal, state of India with area of 34,944 sq. mi., cap. Calcutta. Pop. (1961) 34,976,634.

Bengal, Bay of, N part of Indian Ocean between India and Andaman Is. From depth of 12,000 ft. in S it shelves rapidly to 50 mi. wide coastal shelf.

Bengali, Indo-European language, spoken in India and Pakistan by *c.* 70 million people.

Bengazi, Med. port and E cap. of Libya, on site of ancient city of Berenice. Made cap. by Turks and

Benedictine Abbey, Monte Cassino, Italy

Triumphal Arch of Trajan, Benevento

modernized by the Italians, who left in World War 2. Pop. 137,000.

Benjamin, in OT, youngest son of Jacob and Rachel; name means 'son of my right hand'. Benjamin's descendants, incl. Israel's 1st king, Saul, formed tribe of Benjamin.

Benjamin, Arthur (1893–1960), Austral. composer, pianist and teacher. Work includes symphonies, chamber music and film scores. *Jamaican Rumba* is well known.

Benjamin, Judah Philip (1811–84), Eng. lawyer and Confederate states-man, known in North as 'the brains of the Confederacy'. He was succes-sively Southern Attorney General, Sec. of War, and Sec. of State (1862–65). Wrote *A Treatise on the Law of Sale of Personal Property* (1868).

Benn, Gottfried (1886–1956), Ger. writer and physician. First volume of poems, *Morgue* (1912), uses his knowledge of medicine. Prose work *Der Ptolemaer* (1959) dispenses with rules of syntax and favours Expres-sionist style.

benne see SESAME SEED.

Bennett, [Enoch] Arnold (1867–1931), Eng. novelist whose books describe daily life in the Potteries region of Eng. Midlands. Works include *Anna of the Five Towns* (1902), *The Old Wives' Tale* (1908) and *Clayhanger* (1910).

Bennett, R[ichard] B[edford], 1st Viscount (1870–1947), Canadian statesman. Min. of Justice in several administrations; P.M. (1930–5).

Benny, Jack, orig. Jack Kubelsky (1894–), Amer. actor, radio and television comedian. Started as violin-ist, then switched to comedy revue, radio, films and television.

Benson, Ezra Taft (1899–), Amer. economist. Sec. of Agriculture (1953–61). Author of *Farmers at the Crossroads* (1956).

Bentham, Jeremy (1748–1832), Eng. philosopher and writer remembered for theory of 'utility' enunciated in *Introduction to Principles of Morals and Legislation* (1789). Worked out hedonist calculus, quantitative value of pain and pleasure as motives for action and evolved 'greatest happi-ness' principle that government

Berberis

should be activated to benefit the greatest number. With James Mill, founded *Westminster Review* (1824).

Bentinck, William Henry Cavendish, 3rd Duke of Portland (1738–1809), Brit. M.P. Lord Lieutenant of Ireland (1782); P.M. (1783) in coalition dominated by Charles James Fox and Lord Frederick North; Home Sec. under William Pitt (1794–1801). Sought union of Ireland with England. P.M. for 2nd term (1807–9).

Bentley, E[dmund] C[lerihew] (1875–1956), Eng. writer of detective fiction; originator of type of verse known as a clerihew. *Trent's Last Case* (1912) is a classic of detective fiction.

Bentley, Eric (1916–), Amer. dramatic critic, b. England. Brought work of Brecht to attention of Amer. public. Writings include *The Play-wright as Thinker* (1946) and *In Search of Theatre* (1953).

Benton, Thomas Hart (1782–1858), Amer. statesman. Senator (1821–51) and Congressman (1853–55) from Missouri. Drew up Pres. Jackson's Specie circular (1836), advocating hard money purchases. Supported Western development and financed JOHN FRÉMONT's early expeditions.

benzedrine, amphetamine, chemical substance used to stimulate central nervous system. Used in treatment of migraine and, with phenobarbitol, epilepsy. Also used to treat acute poisoning, *e.g.* by morphine and bar-biturates of central nervous system.

Beothuk, Indian tribe of E Canada, only about 500 of whom had survived when Cabot arrived in Newfoundland (1497); last died in 1829. Also called Red Indians by early European visitors, owing to their habit of smearing their bodies with red ochre.

Beowulf, O.E. epic of about 3,200 lines in alliterative verse. Earliest (prob. 7th–8th cent.) lengthy poem in any modern language. Based on Norse legends and historical events of 6th cent., it includes both pagan and Christian religious elements.

Berber, Hamitic peoples of N Africa, closely related to Europeans, Egypt-ians and Ethiopians. Desert pastor-alists, they became Muslims (10th cent.). Apart from Tuareg, who remain in Sahara, they are now settled agriculturalists.

Berber, family of Afro-Asian group of languages; includes 24 languages, with at least 11 million speakers in Morocco, Algeria and other parts of N Africa.

berberis, large important genus of

Front of the Cappella Colleoni, Bergamo

deciduous or evergreen shrubs with thorny stems. Many have red, purple, or black fruits. Garden varieties, *B. thunbergii,* Jap. barberry, and *B. stenophylla* of UK used as hedging for winter colour.

Berdyaev, Nicolai (1874–1948), Russ. theologian, philosopher and critic. His eclectic philosophy played part in the renaissance of religious and philosophical thought in early 20th cent. Russia. Expelled from Soviet Union (1922). Publications include *The Russian Revolution: Two Essays on its Implication in Religion and Psy-chology* (1931) and *Dostoevsky* (1938).

berg, warm dry wind of W coast of South Africa. Blows seawards from plateau, and is heated on descent. May last for 3 days, causing temperature to rise above 100°F, resulting in oppres-sive weather and crop damage.

Berg, Alban (1885–1935), Austrian composer. Student and exponent of ARNOLD SCHOENBERG, his principal works are the operas *Wozzeck* (1925) and *Lulu,* orchestral music incl. piano, violin chamber concertos; and string quartet, *Lyric Suite* (1926).

Bergamo, city of Lombardy, NE Italy. Has important textile industries, specializing in silk. Known for eccles. remains. Pop. (1961) 113,512.

bergamot, several plants incl. species of *Monarda,* native to N America, with oval leaves aromatic when crushed; sweet bergamot or oswego tea. *M. didyma,* is common in gardens. European bergamot is *Mentha aquitica.* Bergamot is also type of orange, *Citrus bergamia,* rind of which yields an oil used in perfumery.

Bergen, Norwegian seaport, com-mercial and cultural centre. German-occupied in World War 2. Of interest are Bergenhus Fort and nearby Haakon's Hall (1261), scientific insti-tutes, museums, a university (1948), and theatre of international repute. Pop. 117,000.

Bergius, Friedrich (1884–1949), Ger. chemist, devised practical process for manufacturing synthetic gasoline used by Germany in World War 2. Shared Nobel Prize for Chemistry (1931) for contribution to invention and development of chemical high-pressure techniques.

Bergman, Ingmar (1918–), Swedish stage and film producer. Internationally renowned as freelance producer of films incl. *The Seventh Seal* (1956–7), *Wild Strawberries* (1957), *The Silence* (1963) and *Persona* (1966).

Bergman, Ingrid (1915–), Swedish actress. Made Amer. film debut in *Intermezzo* (1939). Awarded 'Oscars' for roles in *Gaslight* (1944) and *Anastasia* (1956).

Bergman, Torbern Olof, FRS (1735–84), Swedish chemist and mineralogist. Furthered chemical analysis, classification of rocks and crystallography. Compiled tables of chemical reactions comparable in importance to modern atomic weight tables.

Bergson, Henri, (1859–1941), Fr. philosopher. Opposed prevailing positivist thought by espousing *élan vital* [life force] principle in evolution. Awarded Nobel Prize for Literature (1927) for his philosophical works.

Bering Sea, northward continuation of Pacific Ocean N of Aleutian Is. named after Vitus Bering

Brandenburg Gate, Berlin

Kurfürstendamm, a fashionable shopping street in West Berlin

(1680–1741). Pribiloff Is. are seal breeding grounds.

Beriosova, Svetlana (1932–), Eng. ballerina, b. Lithuania; danced with many companies, member of Royal Ballet since 1952. Created leading modern roles, *e.g. Pastorale,* and classical, *e.g. Swan Lake, Giselle.*

Berkeley, George (1685–1753), Eng. philosopher and bishop, b. Ireland. Known for his Principle *Esse est percipi* ('to be is to be perceived'), basis of *Treatise Concerning the Principles of Human Knowledge* (1710) which sets forth idea that reality consists of ideas in the mind of God. His concern with the relativity of space, time and motion anticipated Mach and Einstein.

Berkeley, Lennox Randal Francis (1903–), Eng. composer, pupil of Nadia Boulanger. Works include orchestral and chamber music, operas *Nelson* and *A Dinner Engagement,* and ballet, *The Judgement of Paris.*

Berkshire, inland Eng. county. Area: 724 sq. mi.; county town Reading; main towns, Abingdon, Newbury, Maidenhead. Windsor Castle is royal residence. Agriculture main industry, incl. fruit growing and animal husbandry. Pop. (1966) 586,000.

Berlin, city in N Germany on banks of the Spree, surrounded by Soviet-dominated E Germany. Grew rapidly

Bergen, Norway

from mid-18th cent. into cultural and commercial centre of Prussia. Cap. of Ger. Reich (1871–1945). Intensively bombed in World War 2 by Britain, Russia and US, and invaded by Soviet forces; subsequently divided into 4 sectors, Brit., Fr., Soviet and Amer., ruled by Allied Control Commission, from which USSR withdrew, creating separate govt. for its sector (1948). Proclaimed cap. of E Germany (1949). By 1957 4-power admin. had disappeared and Russians made several unsuccessful attempts to stop W influence. Pop. (1966) 3,400,000. *See* BERLIN WALL.

Berlin, Irving, orig. Israel Baline (1888–), Russian-born Amer. composer of popular songs and musicals. Works include *Alexander's Ragtime Band, I'm Dreaming of a White Christmas,* and musical *Annie Get Your Gun.*

Berlin Airlift, supply of foodstuffs and necessities to, and removal of exports from Berlin by W powers, after Russia imposed blockade (June 1948). Blockade ended (May 1949) but airlifts continued until Sept.

Berlin Philharmonic Orchestra, founded 1882. Conductors have included Hans von Bülow, Wilhelm Furtwängler, Herbert von Karajan Re-estab. in W Berlin (1945).

Berlin Wall, dividing E and W Berlin, erected by the E Germans (1961). Its 12 crossing points may be used only by those having special passes.

Berliner Ensemble, state theatre company of Ger. Democratic Repub. formed (1949) under direction of Helene Weigel (1900–), distinguished actress and widow of BRECHT.

Berlioz, [Louis] Hector, (1803–69) Fr. conductor and composer. Noted as pioneer of modern orchestration and creator of programme music. Works include *Symphonie Fantas-*

Bern

novelist. Intensity of his Catholic convictions lends bitter tone to his work dealing with struggle for soul of man between forces of good and evil. Novels include *Sous le Soleil de Satan* (1926) and *The Diary of a Country Priest* (1936).

Bernard, Claude (1813–78), Fr. physiologist. Pioneer in investigations of carbohydrate metabolism in chemistry of digestion and functions of pancreas, and in discovery of vasomotor system.

Bernard, Tristan or Paul Bernard (1866–1947), Fr. writer and dramatist. Plays include short farces, *e.g.* *L'Anglais tel qu'on le parle* (1899) and comedies, *e.g. Jules, Juliette et Julien* (1929). Novels include *Mémoires d'un jeune homme rangé* (1899) and *Amants et Voleurs* (1906).

Bernard of Clairvaux, Saint (*c.* 1090–1153), Fr. cleric. Led Innocent II's successful struggle for papacy and advised Pope Eugene III; his sermons launched 2nd Crusade. Protected Jews in Rhineland (1146). Treatises include *On the Steps of Humility and Pride* (*c.* 1125) and *On the Love of God* (*c.* 1127).

Berne, Eric (1910–70), Amer. psychiatrist. Popularly known for *Games People Play* (1966), pungent description of patterns of personal interaction. Other works include *Transactional Analysis* (1961).

Berne Convention *see* COPYRIGHT.

Bernese Oberland, area in Berne Canton, Switzerland, bounded by

tique, and choral works *Romeo et Juliet* and *La Damnation de Faust.*

Bermuda, Somers Is., Brit. crown colony of *c.* 100 small islands (only 20 inhabited) about 570 mi. off E US coast. Area: *c.* 20½ sq. mi., cap. Hamilton. Tourist centre and site of US naval and air bases. Named after Sp. discoverer Juan Bermudez (1515); first settled (1609) by Sir George Somers; administered by chartered company until taken over by Brit. Crown (1684). Currency, sterling. Pop. 51,000.

Bern, Berne, cap. of Swiss confederation. Founded (1191) as a military post; became free imperial city (1218); entered Swiss confederation (1353); cap. since 1848. Headquarters of international postal, telegraph, railway and copyright unions. Largely medieval in architecture, *e.g.* 15th cent. town hall and Gothic cathedral. Modern buildings include federal palace, museums and university. Pop. (1960 est.) 170,200.

Bernadette of Lourdes, Saint, orig. Bernadette Soubirous (1844–79), Fr. peasant girl to whom Virgin Mary appeared several times in vision revealing miraculous healing properties of the waters in a grotto at Lourdes. It has become one of the most famous R.C. shrines.

Bernadotte, Count Folke (1895–1948), Swed. internationalist, nephew of King Gustavus V, active in Red Cross. Appointed (1948) UN mediator in Palestine; assassinated in Jerusalem.

Bernadotte, Jean Baptiste Jules (1763–1844), King Charles XIV of

Sweden and Norway (1818–44). Fr. general under Bonaparte in Ital. Campaign (1796–7) and prominent in Austerlitz Campaign (1805). Created Marshal of the Empire (1804) and Prince of Ponte Corvo (1806). Chosen acting Crown Prince by Swed. govt. to succeed Charles XIII. With Brit. and Russ. aid, forced Danes and Napoleon to cede Norway to Sweden. Succeeding to throne (1818), he founded present dynasty.

Bernanos, Georges (1888–1948), Fr.

The Doldenhorn in the Bernese Oberland, Switzerland

St Peter's, Rome, with Bernini's colonnade

upper Rhône Valley in S and Lakes Brienz and Thun in N. Attracts tourists and mountaineers. Contains peaks Jungfrau, Eiger, Wetterhorn, Aletschhorn, Mönch and Finsteraarhorn, and largest glacier in Europe, the Aletsch. Grindelwald and Interlaken, are popular year-round resorts. Produces Emmenthal cheese known throughout the world.

Bernhardt, Sarah, orig. Henriette Rosine Bernard (1844–1923), Fr. actress. Triumphed at Comédie Française in productions of the classics, esp. Racine's *Phèdre*. Played *Hamlet* and created title role in Rostand's *L'Aiglon*.

Bernini, Giovanni Lorenzo, (1598–1680), Ital. architect and sculptor. Works include carvings of Apollo and Daphne and Colonnades at St Peter's, Rome.

Bernoulli, Daniel (1700–82), Swiss mathematician, son of Johann Bernoulli. Made important contributions in mathematics and advanced kinetic theory of gases and fluids.

Bernoulli, Jacob or James (1654–1705), Swiss mathematician, brother of Johann Bernoulli, famous for development of calculus. Also made valuable contributions to analytic geometry, theory of probability, and calculus of variations. 'Bernoulli's numbers' are named after him.

Bernoulli, Johann or John (1667–1748), Swiss mathematician, brother of Jacob and father of Daniel Bernoulli. Did much to develop integral calculus.

Bernstein, Leonard (1918–), Amer. musician, composer and con-

ductor. First US-born musical director of New York Philharmonic Orchestra, appointed 1958. Works include ballet *Fancy Free* (1944) and musical *West Side Story* (1957).

Berry, former prov. of France, now absorbed into departments of Cher and Indre. Successively possession of Rome, Visigoths, Aquitaine, Charlemagne and Viscounts of Bourges. Part of dowry of Eleanor of Aquitaine, it passed to England on her marriage to Henry II of England. After 1360, it was held as appanage for Fr. crown until absorbed (1601) into royal domain.

Berry, Charles Ferdinand, Duc de (1778–1820), younger son of Charles, comte d'Artois (later Charles X of France). Fought with Condé against Fr. Rev. His assassination was used by ultra-royalists to turn Louis XVIII against liberals.

Berthelot, Pierre Eugène Marcelin (1827–1907), Fr. chemist and statesman, pioneer of syntheses in organic chemistry. Notable for work on production of acetylene from hydrogen and carbon in electric arc; and for researches in explosives, dyestuffs and thermochemistry.

Berthollet, Claude Louis (1748–1822), Fr. chemist and physician. Discovered silver fulminate and chloric acid (1788), introduced chlorine bleaching, and collaborated on chemical nomenclature which is still basis of current system.

Berton, Pierre (1920–), Canad. writer known for provocative newspaper columns. Also wrote *Klondike: The Life and Death of the Last Great*

Goldrush (1958) and *The Comfortable Pew* (1965).

Berwickshire, county of SE Scotland. Area: 457 sq. mi.; county town, Duns. Main occupations fishing and manufacture of woollen textiles. Pop. (1966) 22,000.

beryl, very hard silicate of beryllium and aluminium. Crystals can be up to 18 ft. long. Ordinary beryl is opaque green, blue, yellow or white, but gem forms are EMERALD, AQUAMARINE.

Berzelius, Jöns Jakob, Baron (1779–1848), Swedish chemist. Discovered cerium (1803), selenium (1817), and thorium (1828). Improved blowpipe method of chemical analysis; determined atomic and molecular weights of substances, using oxygen as a standard; introduced present notation for writing chemical symbols and formulas.

Bes, in Egyptian myth., dwarf and buffoon of the gods, worshipped esp. in family. Presided over marriage, childbirth and toilet of women.

Besant, Annie (1847–1933), social reformer and theosophist, the first prominent English woman to advocate birth control. Prosecuted for obscenity on publication of Charles Knowlton's *The Fruits of Philosophy: or, The Private Companion of Young Married People*. Influenced by Bernard Shaw, she joined Fabian Society (1885). Organized the matchgirls union (1888).

Bessarabia, region of E Europe. Area: 13,012 sq. mi. Part of Moldavia since 15th cent., inhabited in turn by Slavs (6th cent.), Greeks (7th cent.) and Mongols (13th cent.). Administered

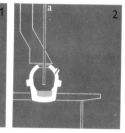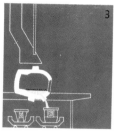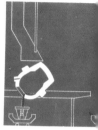

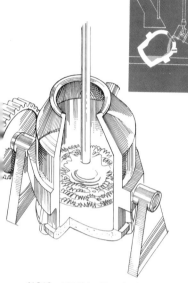

Bessemer Process: (1) The converter is loaded with 75% pig iron and 25% scrap iron. (2) Air is blown through the molten metal, oxidising the various elements, which leave the converter as a gas. (3) The layer of slag is poured off, leaving (4) the molten metal to be poured as steel.

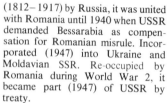

(1812–1917) by Russia, it was united with Romania until 1940 when USSR demanded Bessarabia as compensation for Romanian misrule. Incorporated (1947) into Ukraine and Moldavian SSR. Re-occupied by Romania during World War 2, it became part (1947) of USSR by treaty.

Bessborough, 9th Earl of *see* PONSONBY, VERE BRABAZON.

Bessemer, Sir Henry (1813–98), Eng. engineer and inventor. Famous for the Bessemer process for the manufacture of steel by decarbonization of melted pig iron by means of a blast of air.

Best, Charles Herbert (1899–), Canadian physiologist. Worked with F. C. Banting to discover use of insulin in treatment of diabetes (1921).

bestiary, allegorical work in prose or poetry with Christian or moral application describing appearance and habits of animals. Originated in Gk. work *Physiologus* (2nd cent. AD). Best-known works are those of Philippe de Thaon and Guillaume le Clare (12th cent.), and Richard de Fournival's *Bestiaire d'Amour*, which parodies bestiaries.

Betancourt, Romulo (1908–), Pres. of Venezuela (1945–8, 1959–64). Founded (1935) left-wing party, now *Accion Democratica*. Placed in power (1945) by a military coup, declared universal suffrage, instituted social reforms, and secured 50% oil profits for Venezuela.

betel palm, *Areca catechu,* Asiatic palm, source of betelnut, an astringent, orange, nutlike fruit, widely chewed in the E. Has stimulant effects and stains the teeth black.

Bethany, El Azariyeh, Biblical village on Mount of Olives, Jordan, where Lazarus and his sisters lived. A tower marks site of an abandoned Benedictine convent, beneath which is said to lie tomb of Lazarus. Pop. 1,118.

Bethe, Hans Albrecht, FRS (1906–), Amer. physicist, b. Germany. Nobel Prize for Physics (1967) for contributions to theory of nuclear reactions, esp. discoveries concerning energy production in stars.

Bethlehem, prosperous town of fertile district of Jordan, 5 mi. S of Jerusalem, reputed birthplace of Christ, and of David. Occupied by the Crusaders (1099), passed to the Muslims (1187), and restored to Christians (1229–44). A place of pilgrimage, contains Church of the Nativity and building marking site of Rachel's tomb.

Bethlehem, city of Pennsylvania, US, on the Lehigh River, 50 mi. NW of Philadelphia. Now centre of world's largest steel producing area. Home of annual Bach music festival. Pop. (1960) 75,408.

Bethune, Mary McLeod (1875–1955), Amer. educator. Founded (1904) Negro girls' school, now Bethune-Cookman College, Daytona, Florida. Consultant on inter-racial understanding at San Francisco Conference of UN (1945).

Betjeman, John (1906–), Eng. poet and architectural authority. Satirical light verse nostalgically evokes a passing way of Eng. life. Collections include *New Bats in Old Belfries* (1945), *A Few Late Chrysanthemums* (1955) and *Summoned by Bells* (1960).

betony, *Betonica officinalis,* European perennial of thyme family with spike of red-purple flowers, once used as remedy for many ills and thought to be good for soul as well as body. Wood betony is lousewort.

Bettelheim, Bruno (1903–), Amer. psychoanalyst, b. Vienna. Works include *Love is Not Enough* (1959), on the use of psychoanalysis and a controlled environment to treat psychosis in children; *The Informed*

Bethlehem, Jordan

Heart (1961) a study of concentration camps as an instrument of personality change, and *The Empty Fortress* (1967), only full-length work on AUTISM.

Betti, Ugo (1892–1953), Ital. poet, short-story writer and dramatist, noted for his dreamlike and fantastic style. His plays, predominantly pessimistic, include *La Padrona* (1927), and *Il Diluvio* (1943).

Bevan, Aneurin (1897–1960), Brit. politician. Coal miner and trade unionist, Labour M.P. (1929–60). As Min. of Health (1945–51), developed National Health Service; urged further socialization and opposed Ger. rearmament. Briefly expelled (1955) from Party for insubordination; unsuccessfully contested leadership with Clement Attlee. Married (1934) Jenny Lee.

Beveridge, William Henry, 1st Baron (1879–1963), Brit. economist. Famous for work for govt. (1908–19) on labour and food provisioning problems. Advocated state management to complement, not replace, individual initiative in report *Social Insurance and Allied Services (1942)* and *Full Employment in a Free Society* (1944).

Bevin, Ernest (1881–1951), Brit. statesman. Trade union official, merged unions to form powerful Transport and General Workers' Union, of which he became General Sec. (1921). Trade union representative (1930), favoured Commonwealth economic integration. Foreign Min. (1945–51), his anti-Soviet policy led to closer ties with US and laid the groundwork for NATO.

Bewick, Thomas (1753–1828), Eng. wood-engraver. Restored typographic harmony between printing and illustration. Best known for illustrations of animals and birds. His boxwood originals are collector's items.

bézique, card game usually for 2 players, forerunner of PINOCHLE. Primarily a melding game, though skill factor not so high as in piquet. Popular in England and France in 1860s.

Bhagavad Gita [Sanskrit: song of the blessed one], title of a cycle of the *Mahabharata* epic, containing much of basis of Hindu thought and philosophy.

Bhumibol, Adulyadej (1927–), king of Thailand (1946–). Educ. in Bangkok and Switzerland. Married Queen Sirikit (1950).

Bhutan, semi-indep. Himalayan kingdom. Area: 19,305 sq. mi., winter cap. Paro, summer cap. Thimphu. In return for annual allowance from

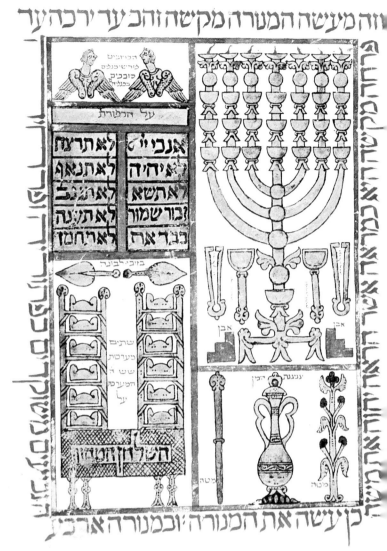

Part of a Hebrew Bible manuscript (dated 1299) from Perpignan

Britain the inhabitants agreed (1865) to refrain from raiding India. In 1949 Bhutan's foreign affairs were put under Indian control. Pop. (1965 est.) 770,000.

Biafra, region in SE Nigeria which seceded from Federation in 1967, plunging nation into war. Formerly known as E Region, its oil resources were vital to Nigerian development. Mass slaughter of the Ibo tribes in the N in late 1966 brought demands for autonomy. Repub. of Biafra proclaimed (1967); ensuing civil war ended (1970) with reoccupation.

Biarritz, town in Basses-Pyrénées department in SW France on the Bay of Biscay near Sp. border. A favourite residence of Napoleon III, now a resort. Pop. 22,922.

Bible, The [Gk. *ta biblia*, the books], body of sacred literature common to Jews and Christians. The canon, or standard list, of books making up OLD TESTAMENT is accepted by Jews and most Protestants; the APOCRYPHA, some books of which are accepted by the E Orthodox Church, is in part accorded recognition by the R.C. Church. The canon of the 27 books of NEW TESTAMENT is similar for all Christian churches.

Bibliographies, National, lists of current literature developed from compilations published from 1564 for Frankfurt Book Fair and later in Leipzig. National bibliographies of current literature usually in the care of national libraries. Oldest is *Bibliographie de la France* (1811–) while *US Cumulative Book Index* (1898–) is most comprehensive.

In Germany, the *Deutsche National-bibliographie* took over original Leipzig Book Fair catalogues (1931). *British National Bibliography* dates from 1950 and *Indian National Bibliography* from 1958.

bicycle, light, 2-wheeled vehicle based on 18th-cent. hobby-horse or dandy-horse, which consisted of 2 wooden wheels and crossbar on which the rider sat, propelling himself with his feet on the ground. First bicycle made (1840) in Scotland by Kirkpatrick MacMillan was dandy-horse with added pedals, seat, handlebars and driving rods. The boneshaker, 1st bicycle with rotary cranks was built (1865) in Paris. Later, light metal wheels with thin spokes and rubber tyres were introduced. The ordinary or pennyfarthing had larger front wheels giving higher gear ratio. The 'safety' bicycle invented (1876) by J. H. Lawson used geared transmission pedal and a crank-driven sprocket which transferred the motion to rear driving wheel by a chain and smaller rear sprocket.

Bidault, Georges (1899–), Fr. statesman. Premier (1949–50).

Biddle, Francis Beverley (1886–1968), Amer. lawyer and statesman, US Attorney-General (1941–5). Prosecuted 8 Ger. spies who landed on the E coast during World War 2. US member of International Military Tribunal which tried the principal Ger. war leaders at Nuremberg (1945–6). Works include *The World's Best Hope* (1949), *The Fear of Freedom* (1951) and autobiography, *A Casual Past* (1961).

Biddle, Nicholas (1786–1844), Amer. financier. Pres. of the Bank of the US (1823–36), he opposed Andrew Jackson's contention that bank charter was unconstitutional. His attempt to renew charter was defeated and bank

was renamed (1836) the Bank of the United States of Pennsylvania.

Biedermeier, Ger. style of decoration of the period 1815–50 resembling the Fr. Emp. style but simpler in design.

Bienville, Jean Baptiste Lemosne, Sieur de (1680–1768), Fr. explorer of lower Mississippi and Red Rivers (1699). Lieutenant of the Fr. king in Louisiana (1700), served as governor for varying periods (1701–43). Founded New Orleans (1718).

Bierce, Ambrose (1842–1914), Amer. newspaperman and satirist. Famous for *Devil's Dictionary* (1911), otherwise known as 'The Cynic's Word Book'.

Big Bend, US national park, W Texas, estab. 1944. Area: 708,221 acres. Amer. desert park, characterized by canyons cut by Rio Grande, and desert plains. Castle-like Chisos Mts. reach 4,000 ft.

big tree *see* SEQUOIA.

bighorn, Rocky Mountain sheep, *Ovis canadensis,* inhabiting Rockies from Alaska to Mexico. Massive horns of male form full circle; female has small upright horns. Lives in flocks and is remarkable for sure-footedness.

bignonia, small genus of Amer. and Jap. woody vines, named after Abbé Bignon, librarian of Louis XV. Best known species *B. radicans,* trumpet weeper, and *B. capreolata,* cross vine which is a partial evergreen of SE US.

Bihar, Behar, state of India, encompassing most fertile areas of lower and middle Ganges valley. Area: 67,196 sq. mi.; cap. Patna. Industries include iron and steel, fertilizers, coalmines, and tobacco. Pop. (1963) 46,500,000.

Bikini, atoll consisting of *c.* 20 islets, NW of Marshall Is., Micronesia. Used for Amer. atomic bomb tests (1946). Name given to woman's two-piece

Enamelled tin figures of the Biedermeier period (*c.* 1815-50)

swimsuit.

Bilbao, seaport, cap. of Viscaya prov., Spain, and chief Basque town. Original site on right bank of Nervión, founded (14th cent.), is example of medieval site laid out exactly to plan. New town on left bank built on modern, spacious lines from an 1876 plan. Exports iron ore, wine, lead and olive oil. Pop. (1960) 297,942.

bilberry, blaeberry, whortleberry, huckleberry [US], *Vaccinium myrtillus,* small, heath-like shrub with globular, edible, bluish-black fruit.

Bilbo, Theodore Gilmore (1877–1947), Amer. politician, twice governor of Mississippi (1916–20, 1928–32), known for advocacy of White Supremacy. Democratic senator (1935–47), died during Congressional investigation of charges of anti-Negro campaigning and bribery.

bilharziasis *see* SCHISTOSOMIASIS.

billiards, game played with tapered, leather-tipped stick (cue) and 3 ivory balls (cue ball and 2 object balls) on oblong cloth-covered slate table with cushioned edges. Eng. table has 6 pockets and scoring is by pocketing balls; Amer. or Fr. game is scored by specified hits of cue ball at object balls. World Professional Billiards Competition held annually.

Billingsgate, orig. gate of city of London near London Bridge. Fish-market nearby dates from 9th cent.

bindweed, widely distributed family of plants with long climbing stems. Species includes greater bindweed, *Calystegia sepium* and lesser or field bindweed, *Convolvulus arvensis* with white and pink flowers. Black bindweed, *Polygonum convolvulus,* of dock family is widespread.

Binet, Alfred (1857–1911), Fr. psychologist, developed intelligence tests and concept of mental age. Binet-Simon intelligence scale orig. used to measure retardedness through objective test based on simple problems. Revisions widely used in N

Big Bend National Park, Texas

America to test intelligence.

Bing, Rudolf (1902–), Vienneseborn opera impresario. First director of Edinburgh Festival (1947); became general manager of Metropolitan Opera House, New York (1950).

Bingham, Hiram (1875–1956), Amer. explorer, historian, educator and statesman, famous for discovery of MACCHU PICCHU, Peru. Senator from Connecticut (1925–33), later led 5 expeditions to S America, tracing routes of conquest and trade. Books include *The Monroe Doctrine* (1913) and *Lost City of the Incas* (1948).

Binyon, Laurence (1869–1943), Eng. poet and dramatist. Best known work is translation of Dante's *Divine Comedy*; poetry includes *The Burning of the Leaves* (1944). Author of *For the Fallen*, engraved on many Eng. war memorials.

biochemistry, science dealing with chemical transformation of inorganic compounds by living organisms. Two main branches: determination of

Roman 'bikini' clad figures in mosaic Piazza Armerena, Sicily

structures of organic compounds present in living organisms, *e.g.* plant pigments, vitamins, proteins, *etc*; elucidation of chemical means by which substances are utilized or made in living organism.

biology, science and study of living things comprising BOTANY and ZOOLOGY. Study of form and structure of an organism is morphology; of the functions, physiology; of reproduction and early growth, embryology; and of fossil remains palæontology.

birch, family of deciduous trees comprising alders, genus *Alnus,* and birches, *Betula*. Latter, hardy, with papery white bark, yields hard wood. Aromatic oil from sweet birch, *B. lenta,* used as wintergreen oil.

bird, feathered, warm-blooded vertebrate of class Aves, with forelimbs modified into wings. Nest built by most species for hatching of young from eggs.

bird of paradise, family of birds, *Paradiseidae,* of N Australia, New Guinea and adjacent islands. Males

are black with bizarre plumes or brightly coloured with elaborate ornamentation used in mating dances; females, dull-coloured and unadorned. One or 2 eggs laid yearly.

Birmingham, Eng. city 100 mi. NW of London, mentioned in Domesday Book (1085–6). Chartered (1889), diversified trades include engineering, car manufacture, chocolate production, gold and silver-smithing, and bicycles; two universities. Since World War 2, much of the city has been rebuilt, incl. the 'Bull Ring' shopping centre. Pop. (1961) 1,105,651.

Birmingham, largest city of Ala., US, leading industrial city of S. Founded (1871) on important iron and coalfields, near limestone, dolomite, graphite, marble, clay,

Silver Birch

Argonauts, abstract painting (1949) by Roger Bissière

sand, gravels, pyrites and quartz
deposits. Pig iron and steel leading
products, around which manufacturing industries have developed. Pop.
(1960) 340,887.

Birney, Earle (1904–   ), Canad. poet
and author. *David and Other Poems*
(1942) and *The Strait of Anian*
(1948) show skilful handling of forms
and language. In *Trial of a City and
other Verses* (1952) Vancouver is
used as prototype for urban life.

birth control *see* CONTRACEPTION.

Biscay, Bay of, arm of Atlantic
Ocean, bounded in NE and S by
France and Spain; named after
Basques of Viscaya. Varying cur-
rents and exposed position cause
storms.

**Bismarck, Prince Otto Eduard Leo-
pold** (1815–98), Ger. statesman.
Chief minister of Prussia (1862–90).
Formulated policies leading to defeat
of Austria (1866) and France (1871);
became chancellor with formation
(1871) of Ger. Empire. Autocratic
control (known as 'Iron Chancellor')
of domestic and foreign policies;
ineffective struggles against R.C.
Church (*see* KULTURKAMPF) and
socialism. Dismissed (1890) by
William II, who resented his
supremacy.

Bittern

Bismarck Archipelago, group of
islands, largest NEW BRITAIN, NEW
IRELAND and Lavongai, N of New
Guinea. Area: 19,200 sq. mi. With
other island groups and NE New
Guinea form Territory of New
Guinea. Discovered (1615); Ger.
territory (1884); UN trusteeship
(1947) under Austral. administration.
Mountainous, with several active
volcanoes. Copra main product. Pop.
is of Melanesian stock.

Bissau, cap. of Portuguese Guinea, W
Africa. Pop. (1965) 25,524.

Bissière, Roger (1888–1964), Fr.
painter; realist, then influenced by
Cubism before developing his own
abstract style.

bittern, several birds of heron family
with speckled plumage and long
pointed bills. Shy solitary bird, feeds
on water creatures and camouflages
itself among reeds by pointing its bill
upwards. Characteristic boom given
by male. Species include common
European bittern, *Botaurus stellaris*
and Amer. *B. lentiginosus.*

bitter-root, *Lewisia rediviva,* succulent Amer. plant with pink flowers.
State flower of Montana.

bittersweet, woody nightshade, *Solanum dulcamara,* sprawling Old
World plant of nightshade family now

naturalized in US. Poisonous plant, known as deadly nightshade, bittersweet, is also name of hardy ornamental woody vine, *Celastrus scadens*.

bituminous rock, rock containing high proportion of tar, ranging from bituminous coal and oil shales to the natural asphalt of Pitch Lake, Trinidad.

bivalve, *Bivalvia*, large class of aquatic mostly marine animals of phylum *Mollusca*, incl. oysters, clams and mussels with world-wide distribution. Body is enclosed between 2 calcareous valves forming hinged, sometimes toothed, shell; some species have retractable muscular foot. Food obtained by sifting minute particles out of water.

Bizet, Georges, orig. Alexandre César Léopold (1838– 75), Fr. opera composer best known for *Carmen*.

Björling, Jussi (1911– 60), Swedish opera singer who excelled in tenor roles in Ital. opera. Appeared at Metropolitan (New York), Covent Garden (London),La Scala (Milan).

Björnson, Björnstjerne (1832– 1910), Norwegian writer, journalist, polit. leader, major figure in Norweg. literature. As dramatist, attempted to destroy the Danish influence on the Norweg. theatre. Best-known works include *The Fisher Girl* (1868), *The Bankrupt* (1875) and *Beyond our Power* (1883– 95). Awarded Nobel Prize for Literature (1903).

Black, Joseph (1728– 99), Scot. chemist and physicist who investigated relationships between limestone and lime. Introduced terms calorie, specific heat and latent heat.

Black and Tan, irregular force enlisted in England for service in Ireland as auxiliaries to Royal Irish Constabulary during disturbances of 1919– 22. Name arose from the khaki colour of uniform worn with black accessories of the Royal Irish Constabulary.

black bear, *Ursus americanus*, N Amer. bear, smaller, rounder and less dangerous than the brown bear, well represented in the national parks. It breeds every other year, and spends much of the winter hibernating. Its glossy coat provides the bearskin hats of Brit. guardsmen.

Black Death *see* PLAGUE.

black-eyed susan, *Rudbeckia hirta*, species of cornflower native to N America. Biennial, *c.* 2 ft. high with dark-centred golden flowers. State flower of Maryland.

black fly, member of the family *Simuliidae*. Found near water, where

Black Swan

it lays its eggs. Persistent in search for blood.

Black Forest [Ger: Schwarzwald]. mt. range of SW Germany. Area: 2,320 sq. mi. Divided by a deep valley, the highest summits are in the S (Feldberg 4,905 ft.). Area in the N characterized by dense coniferous forests. Tourist centres Baden-Baden, Wildbad and Freudenstadt.

Black Hills, mountains of SW S Dakota and NE Wyoming covering *c.* 6,000 sq. mi. Highest point is Harney Peak (7,242 ft.). Minerals include gold, silver, coal, oil, beryllium and lithium.

Black Hole of Calcutta *see* CALCUTTA.

Black Hundred, name applied by their adversaries to the extreme right-wing groups in Russia in early 20th cent. Supported absolutism and nationalism, carried out pogroms against Jews and students, and estab. organizations with similar aims during the 1905 revolution.

'black power', belief dating from the 1960s, that Amer. Negro population can only assume its rightful role in society by having some autonomy. Its origins were threefold: frustrated hopes for equality based on legislative successes of the CIVIL RIGHTS movement; legitimation of violence following southern white terrorism against civil rights workers; feelings of powerlessness within a white 'power structure', often symbolized by the police. Tactics shifted from nonviolent (as advocated by MARTIN LUTHER KING and other civil rights leaders) to direct action.

Black Prince, epithet for Edward. Prince of Wales (1330– 76), eldest son of Edward III of England.

Black Sea, inland sea bounded by USSR, Turkey, Romania and Bul-

garia. Of low salinity, 720 mi. long, 380 mi. wide with maximum depth of 7,000 ft. Beaches and mild climate make it a favoured resort area. Literally black where the lower layer, containing hydrogen sulphide, can be seen through the exceptionally transparent upper layer.

black swan, *Cygnus atratus*, only native Austral. swan. Builds large nest on reeds and lays light green eggs.

black widow, *Latrodectus mactans*, black, venomous spider found in warm climates. Name derives from female's habit of devouring its mate after fertilization. Easily identified by the orange, hour-glass-shaped mark on the underside of the abdomen, is widely feared, but bite is seldom fatal.

blackberry *see* BRAMBLE.

blackbird, *Turdus merula*, of thrush family, common European garden songbird. The male has all black plumage and orange bill; albinos are quite common. Several Amer. blackbirds form family with orioles. The redwinged blackbird, *Agelaius phoeniceus*, most abundant land-bird in America, is migrant.

blackcap, several birds with black plumage on the head esp. *Sylvia atricapilla* of the Warbler family inhabiting woods of Europe.

Blackett, Patrick Maynard Stuart (1897–   ), Brit. physicist. Nobel Prize for Physics (1948) for work in improving and extending use of Wilson cloud chamber and for discoveries concerning cosmic rays.

Blackfoot, group of Algonkian Indians of upper Missouri and N Saskatchewan rivers and W to Rocky Mts.

black-headed gull, several gulls familiar on coasts and inland waters esp. *Larus ridibundus* [UK] and *L.*

Black Sea : the coast of Bulgaria

Black-headed Gull

atricilla [US]. A scavenger often found near towns, it has black head and breeds in colonies.

blackjack *see* VINGT-ET-UN.

Blackmore, Richard Doddridge (1825–1900), Eng. novelist whose best-known work is *Lorna Doone* (1869).

Blackpool, popular Eng. seaside resort in Lancashire. Main attractions are long sandy beach, 7 mi. of promenade, illuminations, a 520 ft. tower, winter gardens and piers. Pop. 150,000.

Blackstone, Sir William (1723–80), famous Eng. jurist and author of legal books. The first to hold the office of solicitor-general. His *Commentaries on the Laws of England* (1765–9), are the best-known history of the doctrines of Eng. law and have influenced jurisprudence in the US.

blackthorn, sloe, *Prunus spinosa,* European deciduous spiny tree or shrub of the Rose family. Short spikes of small, white flowers are followed by small, astringent fruits, sloes or sloe plums which are used to flavour sloegin.

Blackwell, Alice Stone (1857–1950), Amer. writer and advocate of women's suffrage. Wrote *American poems, Songs of Russia* and other books.

Blackwell, Elizabeth (1821–1910), Amer. physician b. England. First woman to be awarded MD in America (1849). Settled in England (1869).

Blackwood, Frederick Temple Hamilton-Temple, 1st Marquis of Dufferin and Ava (1826–1902). Governor-General of Canada (1872–8). Appointed after several Brit. political posts, his mistrust of P.M. Alexander Mackenzie led to appeasement of British Columbia, which was threatening secession (1876) pending construction of a connecting transcontinental railway, later built by Mackenzie's successor, Sir John A. Macdonald.

bladder *see* GALL BLADDER.

bladderwort, plant of genus *Utricularia,* of Eurasia and N America, esp. *U. vulgaris,* water plant with small bladders. It captures minute water animals and digests them.

bladderwrack, *Fucus vesiculosus,* alga *c.* 2 ft. high. Found on the coasts of arctic and temperate oceans. Tough leathery fronds have bladder-like gelatine-filled structures. Used as fertilizer and in cosmetics.

blaeberry *see* BILBERRY.

Blaine, James Gillespie (1830–93), Amer. statesman, often known as 'The Plumed Knight' from a speech by Robert G. Ingersoll nominating him for the presidency in the Republican convention (1876). He lost nomination because of charges of using political power for personal gain, but was nominated in 1884. His election defeat by Grover Cleveland was attributed to lack of R.C. support. As Sec. of State (1889), he conceived what was later first 'Pan-American Conference'.

Blair, David (1932–   ), Eng. principal dancer with Royal Ballet. Created roles in *Pineapple Poll* and *Harlequin in April.*

Blake, George, orig. George Behar (1922–   ), Brit. and Soviet spy. Appointed to Brit. Foreign Service (1947), he was indoctrinated by and worked for Communists (S Korea, 1950). Later imprisoned for espionage by Britain, he escaped (1966) to Russia.

Blake, Peter (1931–   ), Brit. painter of the 'Pop Art' school. Known for portraits of famous boxers and circus entertainers.

Blake, William (1757–1827), Eng. poet and artist. An engraver, he illustrated (with assistance of his wife, Catherine Boucher), his own and others' works. Poems show same metaphysical vision and simplicity as his engravings. *Songs of Innocence* (1789) and *Songs of Experience* (1794) have many haunting, short poems, *e.g.* 'The Tiger'. Much of his later work was devoted to developing mythological and religious theses.

Blanc, Louis (1811–82), Fr. politician and journalist. His *Organization du Travail* (1840) outlined social order based on principle, 'From each according to his abilities, to each according to his needs'. Leader in Revolution of 1848, fled to England after implication in unsuccessful workers' uprisings. Exile until 1871, he wrote *Histoire de la Revolution Française,* 12 vols. (1847–64). Returned to sit in Chamber of Deputies.

Blanca Peak, isolated mountain peak (14,363 ft.) in Colorado, US; it is in the Sierra Blanca, part of Rocky Mts.

Blanco Fombona, Rufino (1874–1944), Venezuelan poet, novelist and critic. Leader in campaign for Latin-Amer. union against N Amer. 'tyranny'. His novels, incl. *El Hombre de Hierro* (1907) and *El Hombre de Oro* (1916; Eng. *Man of Gold,* 1920), are characterized by social satire and political propaganda.

blank verse, unrhymed verse; in English, usually of iambic pentameters. Originated in Italy in 16th cent.; earliest work in unrhymed verse, Trissino's *Sofonisba* (1515). Introduced into Eng. by Henry Howard, Earl of Surrey; used in dramatic and epic verse from Shakespeare and Milton to present day.

Blankers-Koen, Fanny (1918–   ). Dutch athlete. Winner of 4 gold medals in 1948 Olympics track events. Established world records in 6 events (1938–51) in sprint and middle-distance running.

Blantyre, town in Malawi, Africa, named after David Livingstone's

Reproduction of William Bligh's ship HMS Bounty

Scot. birthplace. The oldest municipality in Malawi (founded 1876), and its main commercial centre. Industries include sawmilling, cement and tobacco manufacture. Amalgamated with Limbe (1956). Pop. (1958 est.) 46,150.

Blarney Stone, triangular stone in the wall of Blarney Castle, Co. Cork, Ireland. Persuasive powers supposed to be bestowed on those who kiss it.

Blatch, Harriet Eaton, née Stanton (1856–1940), Amer. suffrage leader and lecturer; daughter of ELIZABETH CADY STANTON. Founded Equality League of Self-Supporting Women (1907).

blazing star, several Amer. plants with purple or white flower clusters, e.g. the lily *Chamaillirum luteum* and the daisy *Liatrus scariosa*.

bleeding heart, *Dicentra spectabilis*, common garden plant of the fumitory family with deep-pink, drooping, heart-shaped flowers, native to Japan.

Blenheim, village, W Bavaria, Germany, 30 mi. NE of Ulm, on the Danube. Scene of the defeat of the French and Bavarians by the Austrians and English led by Marlborough (1704). Blenheim Palace, seat of the Dukes of Marlborough, was named after it.

blenny, numerous, usually small, fish of the family *Bleniidae*. It has elongated, often scaleless body, rounded tail and protective coloration; found near rocky shores in all regions. Some are freshwater species. Omnivorous, it crushes barnacles for food.

blesbok *see* BONTEBOK.

Bleuler, Paul E[ugen] (1857–1939), Swiss psychiatrist and neurologist. Revised concept of *dementia praecox*, introducing the term 'schizophrenia'.

Bligh, William (1754–1817), Eng. admiral. Chiefly remembered for mutiny on his ship HMS *Bounty*, 1789, during trading voyage in the Pacific. Set adrift with 18 of crew in small boat; sailed *c.* 4,000 mi. to Timor. Bligh was governor of New South Wales (1805–8).

blindness, partial or complete loss of sight, may be congenital; caused by injury or certain diseases, incl. cataract, glaucoma. Colour blindness is defective colour vision.

Bliss, Sir Arthur (1891–   ), Eng. composer. Master of the Queen's Music (1953). Principal works include ballets *Checkmate* and *Miracle in the Gorbals*.

blister beetle, member of widely-distributed family, *Meloidae*, generally with bright metallic colouring.

Spanish fly secretes a powerful blistering agent. Harmful to crops.

Blitzkrieg [Ger: lightning war], a form of large-scale surprise attack involving motorized forces with air support, developed by Germans in World War 2.

Blitzstein, Marc (1905–64), Amer. composer and pianist of militantly Democratic and pro-Labour ideas as in the opera *The Cradle Will Rock*. Also known for *Airborne Symphony*.

Blixen, Karen, Baroness, *see* DINESEN, ISAK.

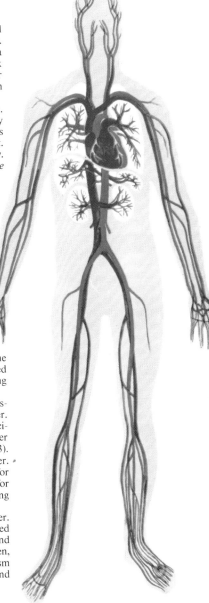

Blood Circulation

blizzard, furious wind driving fine particles of blinding snow. Orig. used to describe the N winds crossing the eastern US during the winter.

Bloch, Ernest (1880–1959), Swiss-born Amer. composer and teacher. Work has specific Jewish associations, e.g. *Schelomo* (1916). Other works include opera *Macbeth* (1903).

Bloch, Felix (1905–   ), Swiss-Amer. physicist. Awarded Nobel Prize for Physics (1952) with E. M. Purcell for developing a method of measuring magnetic fields in atomic nuclei.

Bloch, Konrad E. (1912–   ), Amer. biochemist, b. Germany. Awarded Nobel Prize for Physiology and Medicine (1964) with Feodor Lynen, for discoveries concerning mechanism and regulation of cholesterol, and fatty acid metabolism.

block flute *see* RECORDER.

Block Island, off Rhode Is., US. Area: 24 sq. mi., fishing and resort area.

Bloemfontein, cap. of Orange Free State, Republic of South Africa, 750 mi. from Cape Town. Founded (1846), captured (1900) in the Boer War by Lord Roberts.

Blok, Aleksandr Aleksandrovich (1880–1921), Russ. poet and playwright. Symbolic verse achieved prominence through cycle *Beautiful Lady* (1904). Later wrote nationalist epic *The Twelve* (1918).

blood, principal fluid of the circulatory system in higher vertebrates. Brings food and oxygen to body tissues and disposes of carbon dioxide and other wastes. Composed of PLASMA (55%) and cells (45%) comprising red corpuscles containing HAEMOGLOBIN, white corpuscles or LEUCOCYTES, and platelets or thrombocytes. BLOOD GROUPS are determined by reaction of red corpuscles of one type of blood with serum of another.

blood circulation, in birds and mammals, the movement of BLOOD through the HEART, the pulmonary circuit to exchange carbon dioxide for oxygen, and the systemic network of the body.

blood groups, classification into types

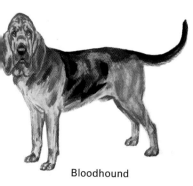

Bloodhound

of human blood according to the ability of blood serum from one group to cause agglutination of red cells of another. Classification, making blood transfusions possible, was first made (1900) by Karl Landsteiner.

blood pressure, exerted by blood on walls of blood vessels, esp. arteries.

blood sports, term used to refer to sport involving bloodshed. In Rom. times, men were often fatally gored in chariot racing and gladiatorial combat. Traces of Rom. lion-baiting and medieval bear-baiting have survived in BULLFIGHTING. Combat between animals, notably cockfighting in England, was once legal. Many spectacles ending in death have been declared illegal by most countries.

blood transfusion, transfer of blood from one mammal to another, first carried out successfully (1655). Discovery of BLOOD GROUPS (1900) and means of clot prevention, together with development of storage facilities, has made transfusion easier and widely practised.

blood types see BLOOD GROUPS.

blood vessels, in the higher vertebrates, vessels through which BLOOD CIRCULATION takes place. They comprise: arteries, carrying blood away from heart; veins, carrying blood towards heart; and capillaries, minute vessels which form subdivisions of arteries and then form first small veins. Aorta, largest artery in man, receives all of oxygenated blood pumped from heart, and distributes blood to branch arteries.

bloodhound, largish black and tan dog with long drooping ears, wrinkled forehead; highly developed power of smell. Ancestral stock of all Eng. tracking hounds.

bloodroot, Indian paint, *Sanguinaria canadensis,* plant of poppy family, with one leaf, red root and pretty, white, early-spring flower. Root possesses stimulant and emetic properties. Crimson sap was prized by Indians as decoration for the face and tomahawk.

bloodstone, quartz mineral, speckled red variety of CHALCEDONY, a semi-precious gemstone.

Bloody Assizes, name given to the trials conducted by Chief Justice Jeffreys in England (1685) after Monmouth Rebellion. More than 300 people were condemned to death, and hundreds were sold into slavery. Jeffreys became notorious because of ferocity with which trials were conducted.

Bloom, Claire (1931–), Brit. film actress. Member of the Old Vic Theatre Company (London), came to prominence in Charlie Chaplin's film, *Limelight.*

Bloomfield, Leonard (1887–1949), Amer. comparative philologist. Specialized in Germanic languages.

Bloomsbury group, name given to group of Eng. writers, artists, and philosophers who met *c.* 1906 in Bloomsbury, then an artistic, Bohemian district of London. Included Virginia and Leonard Woolf, E. M. Forster, Lytton Strachey, Roger Fry, John Maynard Keynes and Bertrand Russell.

Blue Tit

Blow, John (*c.* 1648–1708) Eng. composer, organist and teacher. Wrote church music and masques, incl. *Venus and Adonis.* Teacher of Henry Purcell.

blowfly, noisy insect of family Sarcophasidae or Calliphoridae, related to the flesh fly and the muscid fly. Familiar species are bluebottle fly and cluster fly. Maggots develop in and feed on living tissue, decomposing food, and carrion. The larva of sheep blowfly, *Lucilia sevicata* is well-known pest to sheep, esp. in Australia.

Blücher, Gebhard Leberecht von (1742–1819), Pruss. military officer. Helped recreate the Prussian opposition to Napoleon and lead the War of Liberation. Arrival of his troops at Waterloo (1815) contributed to Napoleon's defeat.

blue bull see NILGAI.

blue laceflower, *Trachymene coerulea,* delicate Austral. herb of carrot family with flat umbel of tiny blue flowers.

blue laws, regulating personal conduct in matters of conscience. Also used to describe legislation aimed at control of morals in Amer. colonies.

Blue Mountains, dissected plateau of New South Wales, Australia. Formed a barrier to settlement W of Sydney. Highest peak reaches 4,100 ft.; leading tourist area.

Blue Mountains, range of mountains in E Jamaica extending for 30 mi., rising to 7,520 ft., covered with dense forests and rich in bird life. Famous for coffee of same name.

Blue Ridge Mountains, forest range of the E Appalachians stretching from Georgia to Maryland, US.

Blue Team, The [Ital. *squada azzura*] Ital. bridge players who in 10 years (1957–67) won 9 world titles, 8 world championships and 1964 Olympiad. Captained by Carlo Alberto Perroux (non-playing).

blue tit, tom tit, *Parus caerulus,* European titmouse with yellow underparts and blue cap. This acrobatic bird is insectivorous.

blue wren, fairy wren, exquisitely coloured small wrens, genus *Malurus,* of the Austral. bush with long, jauntily-held tails.

bluebell, plant of many species, bearing blue, drooping, bell-shaped flowers, esp. *Campanula rotundifolia,* the HAREBELL, bluebell of Scotland, and the wild HYACINTH. *Endymion nonscriptus.* Found in Europe and N America. *See* SQUILL.

blueberry, several plants of genus *Vaccinium,* esp. the high bush blueberry, *V. corymbosum,* a profusely-branched N Amer. shrub. Sweet, edible berry, differs from huckleberry in containing numerous seeds.

bluebird, *Sialia sialia,* small N Amer. songbird of thrush family with reddish breast plumage. Insectivorous; state bird of NY and Missouri.

bluebonnet, *Lupinus subcarnosus,* annual plant of the lupin family, generally limited to Texas. The state flower, it is a protected plant.

bluebottle fly, blowfly of family Calliphoridae, related to the greenbottle fly, it develops in decaying matter and is notorious for carrying germs and dirt.

bluefish, *Pomatomus saltratrix,* species which travels in schools and preys on other fish. Young often called snappers.

Boa Constrictor

bluegrass, several grasses of the genus *Poa*, important in lawns and pastures; known as meadow grass in Brit. Kentucky bluegrass, *P. pratensis*, is particularly valuable as food for horses.

blue-green algae, *Cyanophyta*, simple plant phylum with blue pigment masking green. Widely distributed in unicellular or colonial bodies on moist soil, rocks and trees and in fresh and salt water; help mountain soil fertility and prevent erosion.

Blues, distinctive form of jazz songs with melancholy lyrics. Prob. derived from Negro work songs and spirituals. Typical Blues song is W. C. Handy's *St. Louis Blues* (1914).

bluestocking, term for a woman of intellectual interests. Orig. applied *c.* 1750 to ladies attending meetings in home of Elizabeth Montagu where discussion replaced cards and gossip.

bluets, innocence, *Houstonia coerulea,* delicate perennial plant of the bedstraw family native to N America, esp. common in New England. It has four-petalled bluish flowers with yellow eyes and small leaves at base of stem.

Blum, Léon (1872–1950), Fr. politician, entered politics through interest in social conditions. Head of coalition of Socialists, Radical Socialists and Communists—First Popular Front (1936–7), instigated far-reaching labour reform and proposed nationalization of industry. Arrested by Vichy government (1940), imprisoned by Germans (1942–5). Headed post-war Socialist cabinet (1946–7). Later became a moderate. Writings include *For All Mankind* (Eng. tr. 1946).

Blunden, Edmund (1896–   ), Eng. poet. Poetry collections include *A Hong KongHouse* (1967).

blusher, *Amanita rubescens,* edible fungus of agaric family found in

woodlands; flesh turns pink when touched.

Blyton, Enid Mary (*c.* 1885–1968) Eng. authoress. Prolific writer of books for children, best known for her fictional character 'Noddy' and for the adventures of 'The Famous Five' and 'The Secret Seven.'

boa, large snake of family Boidae; feeds on warm-blooded animals, killing by crushing. Young are hatched in body. Best known is the boa constrictor. *Constrictor constrictor,* of trop. America.

Boadicea, Boudicca (d. 62), Brit. queen of the Iceni in E Anglia. Led revolt (61) against Romans; defeated, she died, prob. of poison.

boar, *Sus scrofa,* wild pig found in the woodlands of Europe, N Africa, Asia, E Indies. Often subject of folklore.

Boas, Franz (1858–1942), Amer. anthropologist, b. Germany. Pioneer of linguistic analysis, his studies of Eskimoes and Indian tribes of British Columbia are classics.

bob white, *Colinus virginianus,* quail, often called a partridge, found throughout US. Favourite gamebird.

bobby, Eng. slang name for policeman, prob. derived from name of Sir Robert Peel.

bobcat, bay lynx, wildcat, *Felix rufa,* small lynx of N America. Powerful, usually nocturnal hunter. Name derived from short tail.

bobolink, *Dolichonyx oryzirorus,* N Amer. songbird related to the blackbird. Plumage is black and white. It migrates extensively within the range Canada to Paraguay.

bobsledding, winter sport in which two or four persons traverse course of icy, steeply-banked twisting inclines aboard a bobsled—an open, steel-bordered vehicle with sled-like runners. A development of tobogganning, it originated (19th cent.) in

Boccaccio : portrait by Andrea del Castagno

Switzerland. Olympic event since 1924.

Boccaccio, Giovanni (1313–75), Ital. prose-writer and poet. Most famous work, *Decameron,* is collection of charming, often licentious tales. Later rejected vernacular writing as sinful, and wrote scholarly works in Latin.

Boccherini, Luigi (1743–1805), Ital. composer and cellist. Prolific composer of chamber music.

Bodhisattva, in Buddhism, a future Buddha who postpones his apotheosis to assist others; often represented in art as youthful or feminine figures.

Bodleian Library, founded (1598) by Sir Thomas Bodley (1545–1613) at Oxford University. Famous for col-

Wild Boar

Bogotá Cathedral, Colombia

lection of rare books and manuscripts. Granted power to demand copies of all books published in UK under Copyright Act (1911).

Boehm, Theobald (1793–1881), Ger. musician and composer for flute. Inventor of key-mechanism facilitating finger control, and adapted to oboe, clarinet and bassoon.

Boer War (1899–1902), conflict between Britain and Transvaal Republic—Orange Free State alliance; result of protracted dispute between British and Boers (S Africans of Dutch descent). Immediate cause was Britain's refusal to withdraw troops from Transvaal. British forces. besieged at Ladysmith, Kimberley and Mafeking, were ascendant after Pretoria occupation (June, 1900). Peace signed May 1902. Defeated states granted self-government, and included (1909) in Union of South Africa. Also called South African War.

Boerhaave, Herman (1668–1738), Dutch scientist and physician, greatest science teacher of his age. One of first to envisage chemistry as independent science; recognized importance of temperature in chemical reactions; separated urea from urine.

Boethius, Anicius Manlius Severinus (c. 480–525), Roman philosopher. Imprisoned by Goths, wrote *The Consolations of Philosophy*, later translated by King Alfred, Chaucer and Queen Elizabeth I. Treatises were major source of medieval scholastic knowledge.

bog moss *see* SPHAGNUM.

bog myrtle, *Myrica gale,* deciduous bush or shrub of family Myricaceae of Europe and N America. Used to flavour beer before hops became popular.

Bogart, Humphrey (1899–1957), Amer. film actor, known for 'tough-guy' roles; began in Broadway theatre. Many successful films included *The Maltese Falcon, Casablanca* and *The African Queen.*

Bogotá, cap of Colombia, 8,500 ft. above sea level. Founded (1538) by Jiménez de Quesada: an archiepiscopal see, with a cathedral and several universities. Industries include iron and steel, textiles and tobacco. Pop. (1962) 1,329,230.

Bohemia, medieval European kingdom, cap. Prague. Became Habsburg crown land (16th cent.); joined (1918) Slovakia and Moravia to form CZECHOSLOVAKIA. Largely populated by Czechs.

Bohr, Niels [Henrik David] (1885–1962), Danish physicist; awarded Nobel Prize for Physics (1922) for concept of structure of the atom. Helped US research of atomic bomb.

Bois de Boulogne, park in the W of Paris covering 2,200 acres, given to city by Napoleon III. Contains race-courses, gardens and drives, notably Allée de Longchamp.

Bok, Edward William (1863–1930), Amer. editor, b. Holland. Edited (1889–1919) *Ladies' Home Journal* during its rise to popularity.

Bokhara *see* BUKHARA.

Boleslaus [I] the Brave (c. 966–1025), king of Poland (992–1025); 1st Polish ruler to call himself king. Emancipated Polish church from Ger. control. Campaigned successfully against Germany, Bohemia and Kiev, but failed to consolidate his acquisitions.

boletus, genus of fungi, some of which are poisonous. The cèpe, *B. edulis* is edible.

Bolger, Ray (1906–), Amer. actor and dancer. Films include *The Great Ziegfeld* (1936) and *The Wizard of Oz,* as well as New York stage title role in *Where's Charley?*

Bolívar, Simón (1783–1830), Amer. revolutionary, called the 'Liberator'; b. Venezuela, became a leader during 1810 revolution against Spain. After victory (1819) at Boyacá, elected pres. of Greater Colombia. Helped free Ecuador (1822), organized and created Peru and Bolivia. Meeting with Argentinian JOSÈ DE SAN MARTÍN, estab. him as leader of free S America (1824). Visions of united Sp. America never materialized and he resigned (1830) from presidency.

Bolivia [República de Bolivia], repub. of S America. Area: 412,772 sq. mi.; cap. La Paz (judiciary in Sucre). President, serving for only one term, is

Boletus edulis, edible fungus

vested with executive power. Two-thirds of population live in W Andean region (Altiplano). Region's tin deposits provide 25% of world supply and 66% of Bolivia's export earnings. Cocoa, coffee, and trop. fruits grown in fertile E region, once a major source of rubber and quinine. The jungle to the E is unexplored. There is little manufacture. Three-quarters of population of Quechua or Aymara stock, one-third does not speak the official language, Spanish. Incas ruled from 13th cent. until Sp. discovery of silver at Potosi (1530s). At independence (1825), Bolivia had sea coast, part of Amazon Basin, and most of Chaco, but had been reduced to its present boundaries by 1935. National govt. (1952–64) nationalized tin mines and instituted land reform. In 1964, a military coup led by General René Barrientos Ortũno succeeded and formed left-wing coalition govt. Unit of currency, Bolivian peso. Pop. (1965) 4,334,000.

Böll, Heinrich (1917–), Ger. writer. Works describing man's stupidity and hypocrisy include *The Train Was on Time* (1949), and *The Clown* (1963).

boll weevil, cotton boll weevil, *Autho-*

The Karlstein Palace, Bohemia

nomous grandis, grey weevil *c.* $\frac{1}{4}$ in. long. Eggs are laid in the cotton boll and larvae feed on the interior. Pest in Mexico, C America and US.

Bollingen Prize, award given by Paul Mellon, through the Bollingen Foundation, to US poets. Controversy arose (1949) over first award, given to Ezra Pound for his *Pisan Cantos,* Since 1950, Yale University Library has administered awards.

Bologna, city of N Italy, at foot of Apennines. Cultural and commercial centre, pre-Roman in origin. Papal rule (8th cent.) interrupted by 14th–15th cent. Guelph-Ghibelline strife, ended with Ital. unification (1860). University of Bologna (11th cent.) renowned for law school. Pop. (1965) 481,000.

Bolshevism, Russ. revolutionary movement that seized power (Oct. 1917). Term originated at Russ. Social Democratic Party Congress (1903) in London, when the radical wing led by Lenin prevailed in dispute. Russ. word *bolshe* means larger. Menshevism, contending faction, comes from *menshe,* smaller.

Bolshoi Theatre, principal opera and ballet theatre in Moscow; present building dates from 1856.

Bolt, Robert (1924–   ), Eng. dramatist. Plays include *Flowering Cherry* (1957) and *A Man for all Seasons* (1961), screenplay for which he won an 'Oscar' (1967).

Boltzmann, Ludwig (1844–1906), Austrian physicist known for his work on the kinetic theory of gases, and development of statistical mechanics, with J. C. Maxwell and J. W. Gibbs.

Bolyai, János (1802–60), Hungarian mathematician, co-discoverer (1823) of non-Euclidean geometry, generally credited to N. I. LOBACHEVSKY.

bombardier beetle, of genus *Brachimus,* small blue-grey and orange beetle which ejects volatile fluid when irritated.

Bombay, cap. and chief port of Maharashtra State, India. Built on several islands and reclaimed land, the only deep-water harbour of W India. Founded 13th cent., came under Mogul, Portuguese (1530) and Brit. (1662) rule. Headquarters of the Brit. East India Co. (1668–1858). It now handles much of India's trade, particularly textiles. Other major activities include tanning, engineering and banking. Pop. 4,654,000.

Bonaire Island, small island in Dutch W Indies.

Bonaparte, Jerome (1784–1860), king of Westphalia (1807–13), brother of NAPOLEON I. Marriage to an American annulled by Napoleon.

Bonaparte, Joseph (1768–1844), king of Naples (1800–8) and of Spain (1808–13), brother of Napoleon I. Inefficient in administering Naples, transferred to Spain, where unsuccessful defence of throne during Peninsular War forced abdication.

Bonaparte, Louis (1778–1846), king of Holland (1806–10), brother of NAPOLEON I. Married daughter of Josephine, Hortense de Beauharnais (1802). Napoleon forced him to abdicate for defying CONTINENTAL SYSTEM.

Bonaparte, Louis Napoleon *see* NAPOLEON III.

Bonaparte, Lucien (1775–1840). Fr. polit. leader, brother of NAPOLEON I. Pres. of Council of Five Hundred, aided Napoleon in coup d'état of 18 Brumaire (1799) by dispersing Council. Opposed establishment of empire and retired to Rome. Reconciled with brother (1814).

Bonaparte, Napoleon *see* NAPOLEON I.

Bonar Law. Andrew *see* LAW, ANDREW BONAR.

Bondfield, Margaret Grace (1873–1953), Brit. politician and trade unionist; 1st woman Cabinet member, Min. of Labour (1929–31) in Lab. govt.

Bondi, Hermann (1919–   ), Brit. mathematician of Austrian origin. Author of *Cosmology* (1952), formulated ideas of 'continuous creation' and a 'steady-state' universe.

bonds *see* SHARES.

bone, living tissue in vertebrates forming the SKELETON; manufactures constituents of blood, destroys old red cells, and stores minerals, esp. calcium and phosphorus, for the body.

boneset, *Eupatorium perfoliatium,* perennial herb of daisy family native to N America, with white-rayed flowers, and leaves pierced by the stem. The Indians first discovered its medicinal properties.

La Paz, Bolivia

bongo, *Brocerus eurycercus,* large forest antelope, with massive spiralling horns, of thick mountain forests of E Africa. Elusive ruminant, travels in small parties.

Bonhoeffer, Dietrich (1906–1945), Ger. Lutheran theologian. Joined Abwehr (1940) and involved in plot to assassinate Hitler. Arrested (1943) and later hanged. Fragmentary writ-

Bologna, Italy

Bombay:
monumental gate at the harbc

Bongo

The Parliament Building, Bonn

ings are collected in *Letters and Papers from Prison* and *Ethics*.

Boniface VIII, orig. Benedetto Caetani (1235–1303), pope (1249–1303). Interfered in Sicilian affairs and aggravated struggle between rival GUELPHS and GHIBELLINES; tried to stop Philip IV of France from collecting illegal taxes from clergy (*Clericis Laicos,* 1296). Philip retaliated by cutting off Fr. church contributions to Rome and later tried to depose Boniface. His *Unam sanctam* (1302) is the most extreme statement of papal jurisdiction over princes.

Bonin Islands, Pacific islands, 500 mi. SE of Japan, consisting of 4 major groups. Area: 40 sq. mi. Situated in unstable area, tiny islands appear and disappear periodically. Only 1 now inhabited. Not permanently settled until 1830. Annexed by Japan (1876); after World War 2 they were placed under US military administration. Only 11% of the land is cultivable. They are primarily of strategic importance. Pop. (1965) 203.

bonito, *Sarda sarda,* edible fish found in Atlantic coastal waters. Fast-moving, it has a series of finlets behind dorsal fin.

Bonn, cap. of Federal Repub. of Germany (since 1949) in NW Germany, on the Rhine. Dates from Roman times. Passed to Prussia in 1815. Noted for university and site of Beethoven's birthplace. Pop. (1960) 146,889.

Bonnet, Charles, FRS (1720–93), Swiss naturalist and philosopher. Credited with discovery of parthenogenesis. His philosophical works put forward utopian thesis.

bonsai, art of dwarfing trees in small containers by pruning roots and branches. Technique, 1st practised in China, pre-dates 13th cent. Specimens can be 300-400 years old, and are heirlooms in Japan.

bontebok, *Damaliscus pygargus,* antelope with white face and rump, and lyre-shaped horns. Once the rarest antelope in the world, conservation has ensured its survival. Comprises genus with blesbok, *D. albifrons.*

bony fish, order Teleostei of fish with skeleton composed mainly of bone, jaws and paired fins. Group contains most existing fish.

booby, goose-sized, heavily built, trop. seabird of gannet family. Name comes from Sp. *bobo,* (dunce) because of its apparent stupidity. A powerful, agile flier, it catches fish underwater. The Peruvian booby, *Sula variegata,* is a principal guano producer.

boogie woogie, type of piano jazz style popular in 1920s and 1930s in US.

boojum tree *see* BAOBAB.

book, group of pages bound together, at first handwritten, but now usually a collection of printed paper pages; used for recording information and literary work. Invention of printing in China (earliest known printed book *Diamond Sutra,* 868) and its introduction to Europe (14th cent.) made books universally accessible. Forerunners of the book include cuneiform tablets and rolled papyri. Book pages are fastened together either by machine process or manual art of bookbinding in which small numbers of pages are folded and sewn together, combined with others and glued to a cover.

Book of Changes *see* I-CHING.

Book of the Dead, collection of magic incantations, prayers and exorcisms, considered first of the Egyptian papyrus books. Used in ancient Egypt as guide for the dead on their journey through the underworld.

bookkeeping, systematic recording of money transactions; larger businesses require professional bookkeepers.

booklouse, dust louse of Psocoptera order. Small, wingless insect infesting old wood products. Feeds on paste and mould.

Boole, George (1815–64), Eng. mathematician and logician. Best known for *An Investigation of the Laws of Thought* (1854) in which he constructs his theory of a calculus, often called Boolean, on almost entirely original foundation.

boomslang [Eng: tree snake], *Dispholidus typus,* large, venomous, arboreal African snake. Has slim green and brown body and preys on birds.

Boone, Daniel (1734–1820), Amer. frontiersman. Known for his explor-

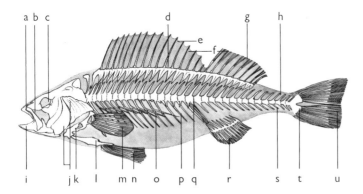

Bony Fish (a) premaxillary (b) upper jaw (c) parasphenoid (d) pterygiophore (e) fin rays (f) spiny-rayed dorsal fin (g) soft-rayed dorsal fin (h) upper vertebra (i) lower jaw (j) opercular (gill cover) (k) coracoid (l) basipterygium (m) pectoral fin (n) pelvic fin (o) epipleural rib (p) pleural rib (q) 1st caudal vertebra (r) anal fin (s) lower vertebra (t) hypural bones (u) caudal fin

ation and settlement of Kentucky in the 1770s. His adventures became part of Amer. folklore.

Boorstin, Daniel J. (1914–), Amer. educator and writer. Best known for *The Image* (1962) a study of Amer. self-deception; his works include series on US cultural history, beginning with *The Americans: The Colonial Experience* (1948).

Booth, Charles (1840–1916), Brit. social reformer. Pioneer in social survey method; headed group investigating poverty in London, *Life and Labour of the People in London*, (17 vols. 1891–1903).

Booth, John Wilkes (1838–65), Amer. actor. Confederate sympathizer, shot Pres. Abraham Lincoln (14 Apr. 1865) at Ford's Theatre, Washington. Killed two weeks later after frantic manhunt. His brother, **Edwin Booth** (1833–93), was first great Amer. actor of Shakespeare.

Booth, Shirley (1907–), Amer. actress, known for her starring roles in stage and screen versions of *Come Back, Little Sheba*, for which she won an 'Oscar'.

Boothe, Clare *see* LUCE, HENRY.

bootleggers, term referring to persons engaged in illegal distribution and sale of alcoholic spirits, particularly during US prohibition era.

bora, violent, cold, N or NE wind common on Adriatic coast. Similar to mistral.

boracic acid *see* BORIC ACID.

borage, Boraginaceae, family of hairy herbs, shrubs and trees of Asia and Europe, esp. Med. region. Also *Borago officinalis*, annual herb with deep blue flowers. Leaves are used in salads.

Borah, William E[dgar] (1865–1940), Amer. statesman. Senator from Idaho (1907–40); opposed US participation in world affairs through position as Chairman of Senate Foreign Relations Committee.

borax (sodium tetraborate), hydrated crystalline salt of sodium, boron, oxygen. Used as antiseptic, for cleaning textiles and metal surfaces, and in making glass and ceramics.

Bordeaux, city and cap. of Gironde department, SW France, on the Garonne; historic cap. of Aquitaine. A Roman site, it was under Eng. rule (1154–1453). Export centre for wines from Bordeaux region. Architecture (18th cent.) partly damaged in World War 2. Pop. (1962) 254,122.

Borden, Lizzie [Andrew] (1860–1927). Amer. spinster, accused of killing father and stepmother (1892),

but acquitted. Case has been widely treated in literature.

Borden, Sir Robert Laird (1854–1937), Canadian statesman. Elected to Parliament (1896), become leader (1901) of Cons. Party. P.M. during World War 1, resented for implementing conscription (1917). Head of coalition union govt. (1917–20), helped define new status of self-governing dominions in Brit. Empire.

Bordet, Jules, FRS (1870–1961), Belgian bacteriologist. Awarded Nobel Prize for Physiology and Medicine (1919) for his work on immunology.

Borge, Victor (1909–), Danish-born actor and pianist, known for his comic monologues.

Borges, Jorge Luis (1899–), Argentinian writer. Best known for *Labyrinths* (1962), collection of stories and essays.

Borgia, Sp.-Ital. noble family. Moved to Rome when **Alfonso de Borgia,** Archbishop of Valencia, became Pope Calixtus III (1455). His nephew, **Rodrigo Borgia** (*c.* 1431–1503), became Pope Alexander VI (1492). His son, **Cesare Borgia** (*c.* 1475–1507), became cardinal at 17, resigned after murder (1498) of brother at which he probably connived. Had his enemies strangled (1502) at castle of Sinigaglia. Julius II thwarted his ambitions by forcing him to restore misappropriated Papal possessions. Died fighting in service of king of Navarre. Vicious, ruthless, but imaginative, he was the model for Machiavelli's Prince. His sister, **Lucrezia Borgia** (1480–1519), won esteem for piety and beauty. **St Francis Borgia** (1510–1572), Sp. church reformer, was great-grandson of Alexander VI, Duke of Ganzia and courtier of Charles V.

Borglum, [John] Gutzon [de la Mothe] (1871–1941), Amer. sculptor who carved faces of the US presidents Washington, Jefferson, Lincoln, and Theodore Roosevelt on Mt. Rushmore, S Dakota.

boric acid, boracic acid, white crystalline, weakly acidic compound of boron, hydrogen and oxygen. Used as antiseptic (in solution) and eyewash;

toxic if taken internally.

Born, Max, FRS (1882–1970), Ger. physicist. Shared Nobel Prize for Physics (1954) with W. Bothe for work on quantum theory. Developed method of very accurate time measurement.

Borneo, largest island in Malay Archipelago and 3rd largest in world. Area: 286,969 sq. mi. Its 4 regions are Indonesian Borneo (about 70% of total area), Sabah, Sarawak and Brunei. Largely jungle and mountains; rivers are chief means of transport. Hot and humid climate, annual rainfall averaging over 100 in.; rice, rubber, maize, and sago are important crops. Oil is principal natural resource. Interior inhabited mainly by DYAKS; coastal areas by Chinese, Malays, and Javanese. Portuguese exploration preceded Dutch control (19th cent.). These territories, now called Kalimantan, became part of Indonesia (1949). Remaining areas are in Brit. Commonwealth. Pop. 2,750,000.

Bornholm, Danish island in Baltic Sea, SE of Sweden, chief town and port is Ronne. Low tableland, rocky and steep on N and W coasts; granite and kaolin extracted.

Borobudur, extensive 8th cent. temple remains in W Java, built (AD 750–850).

Borodin, Alexander [Porphyrevich] (1833–87), Russ. composer and chemist. Member of Russ. nationalist group of composers, 'The Five'. Works include opera *Prince Igor* ('Polovtsian Dances' are famous) and symphonies.

borough, burgh [Scot.], term for town in Brit. Is., unit of local govt. independent of county. Orig. sheltered or fortified place, after Norman times empowered by charter to administer its inhabitants. Widespread corruption in 18th and 19th cent. brought reform (1835) restricting local power to town council in specific terms. County borough exercises both city and county govt. power. 'Royal' precedes term when charter granted by Crown. In US, term refers to municipal corporation; also one of 5 divisions of New York City.

Borobudur, Java

Borodino, Battle of, fought (7 Sept. 1812) during Napoleonic Wars, at Borodino, near Moscow. Russ. forces under Mikhail Kutuzov engaged Napoleon's army in defence of Moscow. Victory disputed; *c.* 108,000 casualties.

boron, non-metallic element, yellowish-brown crystalline solid or brown amorphous powder. Not found in free state. Boron carbide is hardest man-made substance.

Borrow, George (1803–81), Eng. writer and philologist. Known for his partly autobiographical books on gypsies; they include *Lavengro* (1851), and *The Romany Rye* (1857).

borzoi, Russ. long-haired wolfhound. Has longish jaws, narrow chest and silky whitish coat.

Boscawen, Edward (1711–61), Brit. sailor present at capture of Porto Bello (1739). Played notable part in defeat of Fr. fleet off Cape Finisterre (1747). After distinguished naval career, became a Lord of the Admiralty (1751).

Bosch, Carl (1874–1940), Ger. chemist. Awarded Nobel Prize for Chemistry (1931) for adapting Haber process to achieve mass production.

Bosch, Hieronymus or **Jerom Bos** (*c.* 1460–1516), Flemish painter. Treated religious themes with fantastical and grotesque details. Favourite of Philip II.

Bose, Sir Jagadis Chandra (1858–1937), Indian physiologist. Known for study of plant life and invention of crescograph for measuring plant growth.

Bose, Satyendra Nath (1894–   ), Indian physicist whose work on Planck's law of radiation laid the foundation for the Bose-Einstein statistics.

Bosnia and Herzegovina, Balkan state, now Yugoslav constituent republic. Bosnia settled by Serbs (7th cent.), became kingdom (12th cent.) and annexed Herzegovina from Serbia (late 14th cent.); fell to Turkey (1463). Peasant rebellion (1875) led to Russ. intervention and Austro-Hungarian administration (1878). Archduke Francis Ferdinand's assassination at Sarajevo precipitated World War 1. Annexed by Serbia (1918); incorporated by Yugoslavia (1946).

Bosporus, Bosphorus, narrow strait joining Sea of Marmara with Black Sea; it separates Asia and Europe.

Bossuet, Jacques [Bénigne] (1627-1704), Fr. preacher and writer. Works include *Oraisons Funèbres*, and *Dis-*

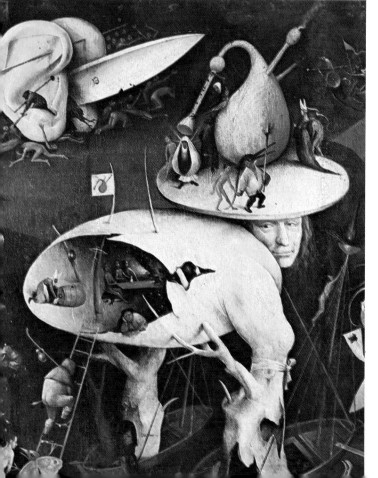

Detail from Hieronymus Bosch's *The Garden of Lusts*

Borzoi

cours sur l'histoire universelle (1681).

Boston, seaport and cap. of Mass., US. Estab. (1630) by John Winthrop. Inhabited by descendants of original Puritan settlers, and by large Irish and Ital. immigrant groups. Old 'Brahmin' families, *e.g.* Cabots, Lodges, Saltonstalls, made fortunes from shipping and textiles, building houses on Beacon Hill and Back Bay areas. Major financial and cultural centre (well known Boston Symphony Orchestra). Pop. 697,197.

Boston Massacre, pre-American Revolution incident (1770) in which 5 members of rioting crowd were killed by Brit. troops sent to Boston to protect customs commissioners.

Boston Tea Party, pre-American Revolution incident (1773) caused by retention of tea tax after repeal of Townshend Acts imposing duty on specified goods. Group of angry colonists, disguised as Indians, threw tea from 3 ships into Boston Harbour.

Boswell, James (1740–95), Author of celebrated biography *The Life of Samuel Johnson, LLD* (1791). Scot. lawyer, widely travelled in Europe, he spent much time in London where he frequented Johnson's coterie. His papers, recovered (20th cent.) by Col. Ralph H. Isham, have yielded *Private Papers* (18 vols., 1928–34), *Boswell's London Journal, 1762–63* (1950), and other volumes.

Bosworth Field, Leics., England. Scene of battle (1485) in which Henry Tudor defeated Richard III. Former then became Henry VII. Conflict ended the WARS OF THE ROSES.

botany, scientific study of plant life; comprising BIOLOGY together with ZOOLOGY. Plant classification begun by Aristotle and improved upon by Linnaeus. Studies of plant anatomy, embryology and reproduction made by 18th cent. Classification now made according to structure, environment and functions.

Botha, Louis (1862–1919), South African soldier and 1st P.M. of the Union of South Africa (1910–19). Commanded fellow Boer troops in the

Birth of Venus by Sandro Botticelli

South African War (1899–1902). Premier of Transvaal (1907–10); during World War 1, led force that conquered Ger. SW Africa.

Bothe, Walther (1891–1957), Ger. physicist. Awarded Nobel Prize for Physics (1954) with Max Born for research in cosmic radiation. Helped construct Germany's 1st cyclotron (1944).

Bothnia, Gulf of, shallow N arm of Baltic Sea between Sweden and Finland.

Bothwell, 4th Earl of *see* HEPBURN, JAMES.

Botswana, formerly Bechuanaland, repub. in S Africa and member of Brit. Commonwealth. Area: 222,000 sq. mi.; cap. Gaberones. Elective presidential system. Mainly arid plateau. Kalahari desert in S and W. Population lives primarily on self-administered reserves. Main occupation, cattle-raising; nearly half inhabitants seasonally employed in neighbouring Transvaal. Mineral deposits include manganese, asbestos, and copper from Shashi complex. Setswana is main language. Brit. protectorate from 1885 until independence (1965). Currency, South African rand. Pop. (1964) 593,000.

Botticelli, Sandro (*c.* 1444–1510), Florentine painter. Pupil of Fra Lippo Lippi; master of colour and rhythmic line. Famous for such paintings as *Spring, Venus, Allegory of Calumny* and for illustrations of *Divine Comedy.*

bottlebrush *see* BANKSIA.

bottlenosed dolphin, porpoise [US], *Tursiops truncatus,* cetacean of dolphin family; worldwide distribution esp. warmer waters. Its sociability and responsiveness to human contact has been subject of recent study.

bottlenosed whale, grey-black mammal with lighter underside of genus Hyperoodon, containing largest members of beaked whale family. Common in N Atlantic, moves in schools, feeding mainly on cuttlefish.

Botvinnik, Mikhail (1911–), Russ. chess player. World champion (1948–56, 1958, 1959, 1961).

Boucher [de Crèvecoeur] de Perthes, Jacques (1788–1868), Fr. archaeologist. Collected evidence of Stone Age culture in Somme Valley; failed to obtain recognition of findings for 20 years until acceptance (1859) by Royal Society.

Bougainville *see* SOLOMON ISLANDS.

Bougainville, Louis-Antoine, Comte de (1729–1811), Fr. scientist and navigator. Rediscovered Solomon Is. during voyage (1767–9) around the world; wrote accounts of N Amer. travels. Served in Fr. navy during Amer. Revolution.

bougainvillea, small genus of ornamental, trop. Amer. evergreen vines with brilliant red or purple flowers. Named after L.-A. de Bougainville.

Boulanger, Nadia Juliette (1887–), Fr. musician; influential 20th cent. teacher with many well-known composers among her pupils.

boulder clay, till, unstratified mixture of clay, sand, gravel and boulders left by retreating glacier. Found extensively in N Europe and N America.

Boumedienne, Houari (1927–), Algerian army officer, Pres. of Revolutionary Council. Commander-in-Chief of Algerian Forces and Min. of Defence (1962); helped Ahmed Ben Bella consolidate power after Algerian independence, succeeding him after military coup (1965).

Bourbaki, Nicolas, pseudonym used by group of Fr. mathematicians engaged since 1930s in preparing mathematical treatise, 25 volumes of which had appeared by 1960.

Bourbon, royal family, orig. French, branches of which ruled Spain, the Two Sicilies, and Parma. Robert of Clermont, son of Louis IX of France, m. (1272) Beatrice, Bourbon heiress, establishing the line. Antoine de Bourbon (1518–62) became king of Navarre through marriage. His son Henry IV was 1st Bourbon king of France (1589). They ruled France (except 1792–1814) until 1830 when Charles X was deposed. The Spanish Bourbons began (1700) with accession of Louis XIV's grandson, Philip V, to Spanish throne. Contested in 19th cent.; Alfonso XIII was deposed (1931). Present pretenders include Don Juan and his son Juan Carlos. Bourbon-Sicily, from the Sp. line, was founded (1759) by Ferdinand I of the Two Sicilies and ceased to rule when Francis II abdicated (1861). Bourbon-Parma founded (1748) by a younger son of Philip V of Spain and ended with deposition of Robert, 5th Duke of Parma (1860).

Bourke-White, Margaret (1904–71), Amer. journalist and photographer,

Bougainvillea

known for her photographic studies of social and economic conditions.

Bouts, Dierick (c. 1410–75), Dutch painter noted esp. for landscapes and altarpieces, 2 of which are in Brussels.

bouvier [des Flandres], breed of large varicoloured rough-coated dog used by shepherds and in police work. Originated in Belgium.

Bovet, Daniele, FRS (1907–), Ital. pharmacologist, b. Switzerland. Awarded Nobel Prize for Medicine and Physiology (1957) for work in developing anti-histamines, sulpha drugs, and muscle relaxants.

bovidae, ruminant wild CATTLE, distinguished by heavy, massive body, short broad neck, wet muzzle, and absence of tear ducts. Usually live in small herds of 5–20 females; young led by bull. Extant species belong to genus *Bibos* and include the gayal, gaur and banteng.

bow see ARCHERY.

Bowdler, Thomas (1754–1825), Eng. editor. Expurgations (esp. of Shakespeare) led to term 'bowdlerize'.

bowel see DIGESTION.

Bowell, Sir Mackenzie (1823–1917), Canadian P.M. (1894–7), b. England. Conservative cabinet minister and senator before becoming P.M. Resigned when leadership challenged after crisis over education in Manitoba.

Bowen, Elizabeth [Dorothea Cole] (1899–), Anglo-Irish novelist and short story writer. Works include *The Hotel* (1927), *The Death of the Heart* (1938).

bowerbird, any of Austral. bird group, related to the bird of paradise. Satin bowerbird, *Philonorhynchus violacens,* one of the best studied species, builds courtship bower decorated with shells, feathers, *etc.*

bowfin, mudfish, *Amia calva,* large freshwater fish of Amer. Midwest, only survivor of fish group abundant during the Jurassic and Cretaceous periods. Savage and voracious predator.

Bowlby, John (1907–), Brit. psychiatrist, prominent writer on maternal deprivation; author of *Maternal Care and Mental Health* (1950).

Bouvier

The Last Supper by Dierick Bouts

Bowles, Paul (1910–), Amer. composer and novelist. Wrote orchestral and ballet music, and an opera, *The Wind Remains* (1943). Novels include *The Hours After Noon* (1959).

bowling see TEN-PIN BOWLING.

bowls, lawn bowling [US], outdoor game dating from 13th cent., popular in UK. Played on green, divided into six rinks. Opponents alternately roll balls close to small white ball and attempt to dislodge those previously rolled. Rules governed by International Bowling Board.

box, evergreen shrub of genus *Buxus* of Europe and N Asia. Common variety, *B. sempervirens,* slow growing, used for clipped hedges.

box elder, *Acer negundo,* fast growing Amer. tree of maple family. Valued for shade, it has many garden varieties.

box tortoise or **turtle,** *Terrapene carolina,* shell-backed reptile of N Amer. brush country. Can withdraw entirely into its shell which is hinged and closes tightly.

boxer, sturdy short-coated dog of Ger. origin, descended from bulldog. Usually fawn coloured or brindle, characterized by protruding jaw.

Boxer Rebellion (1898–1900), uprising in China by the Boxers, secret society dedicated to removal of foreign influence. Revolt crushed by joint European, Jap. and Amer. forces. China forced to pay heavy indemnities.

boxfly, heavybodied fly of *Oestroidea* group of Europe, introduced into US, often parasitic. Horse boxfly, *Gasterophilus intestinalis,* and sheep boxfly (nostril fly), *Oestris oris,* are varieties.

boxing, sport of fighting with the fists, also called pugilism and prize fighting. Included in orig. Olympic games. Marquess of Queensberry's rules (introd. 1865) standard by 1889. Fought with padded gloves in ring c. 20 sq. ft. In modern Olympic Games since 1908.

Boyce, William (1710–79), Eng. composer and organist. Compiled *Cathedral Music* (3 vols., 1760–8).

Boyle, Robert (1627–91), Brit. chemist. First to distinguish between element and compound. Boyle's Law states that at constant temp., the volume of confined gas decreases in proportion to increase in pressure.

Boyne, Battle of the, confrontation (1690) near R. Boyne, E Ireland

Boxer

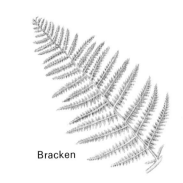

Bracken

Bracket Fungus

between Protestant William III (of Orange) and Catholic James II. William's victory thwarted James' attempt to regain British throne.

Brabant, former duchy of the Netherlands, comprising parts of present province of N Brabant and Belg. provinces of Antwerp and Brabant. Settled (5th cent.) by Franks; became independent duchy (12th cent.) and passed to house of Burgundy (1430). N part ceded to Netherlands (1609); S area remained Sp. until becoming part of Austrian Netherlands. United under Fr. rule (1794–1814). Now densely populated province of C Belgium.

brachiopod, lampshell, animal of exclusively marine phylum, *Brachiopoda,* represented since early Cambrian period by 3,000 fossils and 250 existing species. Soft body enclosed in bivalve symmetrical shell with articulating beak and teeth and anchoring stalk. Food introduced in current of water. Size varies from breadth of $\frac{1}{4}$ in. to 12 in. in fossil species, *Productus giganteus.*

bracken, brake, several species of fern esp. European and Amer. *Pteridium aquilinum,* with stout creeping stem which has sharp cutting ridge, and coarse branched spreading fronds. In some places a pernicious weed. Roots once used in beverages and tanning, and the fronds in thatching.

bracket fungus, shelf fungus, family

Flyweight	112 lb.
Bantamweight	113—119 lb.
Featherweight	120—125 lb.
Lightweight	126—132 lb.
Light Welterweight	133—139 lb.
Welterweight	140—147 lb.
Light Middleweight	148—156 lb.
Middleweight	157—165 lb.
Light Heavyweight	166—178 lb.
Heavyweight	179— lb.

Boxing weights as recognized by the Olympic Games.

of bracket-shaped fungi, *Polyporaceae,* with rough woody texture. Spores form in tubes opening to the air through pores. Most grow on dead timber.

Bradbury, Ray (1920–), successful Amer. writer of science fiction. Books include *The Illustrated Man* (1952), *The Golden Apples of the Sun* (1953) and *Fahrenheit 451* (1953).

Braddock, Edward (1695–1755), Brit. general. Commander-in-chief (1754) of Brit. forces in N America, he was killed following year near Fort Duquesne.

Bradford, William (1590–1657), Amer. colonist, a founder of Plymouth Colony. First elected governor (1621) and returned 30 times. Wrote *History of Plimoth Plantation.*

Bradley, A[ndrew] C[ecil] (1851–1934), Eng. literary critic whose best known works are *Shakespearean Tragedy* (1904) and *Oxford Lectures on Poetry* (1909).

Bradley, F[rancis] H[erbert] (1846–1924), Eng. philosopher, opponent of logical empiricism, maintaining that the absolute transcends contradictions between appearance and ideal. Works include *Ethical Studies* (1876), *Principles of Logic* (1883), and *Appearance and Reality* (1893).

Bradley, Omar [Nelson] (1893–), Amer. general who led US 1st Army in invasion of Normandy in World War 2, active in N African, Sicilian campaigns. First permanent Chairman of Joint Chiefs of Staff (1949–53).

Bradman, Sir Donald [George] (1908–), Austral. cricketer. Records include highest aggregate, highest score (334 at Leeds, 1930) and greatest number of centuries in England *v.* Australia test matches.

Brady, Mathew B. (1823–96), Amer. pioneer photographer. Known for his photographic record of the Civil War and his portraits of Lincoln.

Braemar, village and district of Deeside in Aberdeenshire, Scotland. Highland games are held annually. Balmoral Castle, holiday home of the Brit. sovereign, is in the district.

Braganza, ruling house of Portugal (1640–1910) descended from Alfonso, natural son of John I of Portugal, made Duke of Braganza (1442). His descendant, Duke John II, threw off Sp. rule and became King John IV of Portugal (1640). When Napoleon conquered Portugal, John VI fled to Brazil (1807–21). Dynasty ended when Portugal became republic (1910).

Bragg, Braxton (1817–76), US and Confederate army officer. Served in

US army during Seminole and Mexican campaigns. Succeeded Beauregard in command of Tennessee troops in Civil War. Victor at Chickamauga (1863).

Bragg, Sir William [Henry] (1862–1942), Brit. physicist. Awarded Nobel Prize for Physics (1915) with his son, Sir William [Lawrence] Bragg (1890–1971), for working out theory of X-ray diffraction and using it to determine structure of crystal.

Brahe, Tycho (1546–1601), Danish astronomer famous for design and construction of astronomical instruments and precise plotting of positions of stars and planets. Proposed a geostatic, heliocentric theory of the universe, the 'Tychonic system'.

Brahma, in Hinduism, the Absolute, or God conceived of as entirely personal, claimed by Brahmins as founder of Hinduism. First in divine triad, others being VISHNU and SIVA.

Brahmaputra, river 1,700 mi. long, rising in SW Tibet. Flowing E through

Braganza, Portugal

Tibet, it turns S into India to join the Ganges.

Brahmin, in Hinduism, member of caste representing priestly and meditative order.

Brahminism *see* HINDUISM.

Brahms, Johannes (1833–97), Ger. composer and pianist, b. Hamburg where, as a child, he played in taverns. Settled (1863) in Vienna, he devoted his life to composition and occasional tours. His best-known works include a requiem, piano and violin concertos, and chamber music. He also wrote 200 songs.

Braille, Louis (1809–52), Fr. teacher, blind from age of 3, who devised the system of raised-point writing named after him. Universally adopted for instruction of the blind; used for music as well as literature.

forehead, called pre-frontal or silent area, is apparently used in highest mental processes; (2) parietal lobe or sensory area receives sensations of warmth, cold, touch and general bodily movement; (3) temporal lobe or auditory area nearest to ears receives hearing impulses; (4) occipital lobe or visual area is at base of skull. Forming the stalk of the cerebrum are pathways of fibres, continuation of spinal cord containing much of the crossing-over of fibres linking left hemisphere to right-hand side of body and vice versa. Cerebellum, lying below rear regions of cerebral hemisphere assists muscular co-ordination. Electrical activity, measurable by electro-cardiogram, and known as brain wave patterns, is present from birth until death. Mem-

ularly used in 1960s to describe emigration from UK and Canada to US of people with specialized training, particularly scientists and technologists. Frequently cited as important factor in nation's economy.

Braine, John (1922–), Eng. novelist who established his reputation with *Room at the Top* (1957), an ironic account of an individual's struggle to free himself from his working-class background.

brainwashing (tr. of Chinese term), application of prolonged and intensive indoctrination in an attempt to induce a person to give up one set of beliefs and attitudes for another. Precedents can be found in the Sp. Inquisition and Puritan New England during 1730s. Used as means of correcting individual deviationist behaviour (Tsarist and Stalinist Russia) or as instrument of mass conversion (Communist China).

brake *see* BRACKEN.

Bramante, Donato (1444–1514), Ital. artist and architect. His Roman buildings considered most characteristic of high Renaissance style.

bramble [UK], **blackberry** [US]. *Rubus fructicosus*, low, rambling shrub with white flowers and black fruits. Amer. species include *R. alleghreniensis*. Edible berries made into jam or jelly. Once valued for orange dye yielded by roots, and as remedy for swellings and burns.

brambling, *Fringilla montifrigilla,* finch of N Europe and Asia, with conspicuous white rump. Male has orange shoulder patch.

Brand, Max orig. Frederick Faust (1892–1944), Amer. writer, best known for his westerns incl. *The Untamed* (1918) and *Destry Rides Again* (1930).

Brandeis, Louis Dembitz (1856–1941), Associate Justice of US Supreme Court (1916–39). Boston lawyer, opposed vested interests and monopolies. Brandeis University, founded (1948) in Waltham, Mass., is named after him.

Brandenburg, Prussian electorate, split since World War 2 between NE Poland and E Germany. First inhabited by ancient Germanic and Slavonic tribes, subjugated (12th cent.) by Albert the Bear and colonized with settlers from the Rhineland. His great-grandsons founded monasteries and towns, *e.g.* Berlin. Recognized (1356) as one of imperial electorates of Holy Roman Empire. Elector Frederick became King of Prussia as Frederick I (1701). With Prussia it became one of United Ger. provs. (1871).

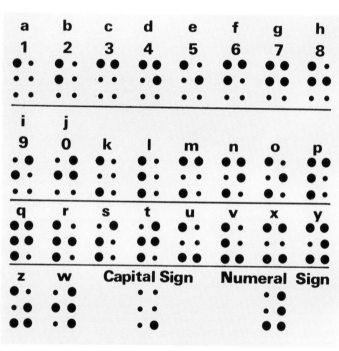

Braille alphabet, the larger dots within each six-dot 'braille cell' are raised in braille writing or printing; smaller dots are not represented. Other combinations of raised dots represent common words, phonetic and punctuation marks. The first 10 letters serve also as numbers. A special code has been worked out for musical notation

brain, in vertebrates, that part of central nervous system enclosed in skull. In man, composed of 14,000 million cells, weighs *c.* 2–3 lb. Cerebrum or cerebral cortex, is over $\frac{5}{6}$ of total and is divided into 2 cerebral hemispheres with 4 paired lobes; (1) frontal lobe or motor area controls muscular movement. Portion closer to

ory is thought to be changes in pattern of nerve cells in the cerebrum, in response to stimuli.

Brain, Dennis (1921–57) Eng. musician, noted for virtuosity on Fr. horn. Many works, incl. *Serenade* by Benjamin Britten, were written for him.

brain drain, journalistic term pop-

Brandes, Georg [Morris Cohen] 1842–1927), Danish literary critic. nvigorating influence on Danish hought. Works include biographies, *.g. Ibsen, Kierkegaard* (1877) and *Goethe* (1914–5).

Brando, Marlon (1924–), Amer. ctor, whose prominence on stage and creen was established by *A Streetcar Named Desire*. One of first to bring method acting to films; awarded Oscar for *On the Waterfront* (1954).

Brandon, Charles, 1st Duke of Suffolk (d. 1545), Eng. soldier and nobleman at court of Henry VIII. Led 2 invasions of France (1523, 1544) and PILGRIMAGE OF GRACE (1536).

Brandt, Willy, orig, Karl Herbert Frahm (1913–), Ger. political eader. Fled Nazi rule, becoming journalist. Mayor of West Berlin (1957–66), joined 1966 coalition govt. as Vice Chanc. and Foreign Min. Social Democrat Chancellor (1969–). Awarded Nobel Peace Prize (1971).

brandy, name for spirit distilled from any wine. Best known grape wine brandies are *Cognac*, from French town of that name, and *Armagnac* from Gascony in SW France. *Kirsch* is distilled from fermented cherry juice alone and *Slivovitz*, of E Europe, from plums. Characteristic light tawny colour acquired when left to mature in oak casks. Also applied to potable spirits, liqueurs and cordials, *e.g.* cherry and apricot brandies either distilled from cherries and apricots or merely flavoured with essence of the fruits.

Brant, Joseph, Indian name Thayendanegea (1742–1807), Mohawk Indian chief. During Amer. revolution aided British in ravaging Cherry Valley in New York (1778). Translated *Book of Common Prayer* into Mohawk language.

brant goose *see* BRENT GOOSE.

Braque, Georges (1882–1963), Fr. painter. Exponent of FAUVISM, and with Picasso one of creators of Cubism (1907).

Brasilia, new cap. of Brazil, situated in central highlands. Begun (1957), replaced Rio de Janeiro as cap. (1960). Planned by Lucio Costa; many buildings designed by OSCAR NIEMEYER. Pop. (1960) 141,172.

brass instruments *see* FRENCH HORN; TROMBONE; TRUMPET; TUBA.

Bratby, John (1928–), Brit. painter and writer. Known for his scenes of urban life and portraits of famous people. Novels include *Breakdown* (1960).

Brattain, Walter H[ouser] (1902–), Amer. physicist awarded Nobel Prize for Physics (1956) with William Shockley and John Bardeen for work in developing transistors and semiconductors.

Braun, Carl Ferdinand (1850–1918), Ger. physicist. Suggested use of binary compound crystals in radio and introduced coupled circuits into telegraphy. Awarded Nobel Prize for Physics (1909) with Guglielmo Marconi.

Still Life with Cards by Georges Braque

Bratislava, cap. of Slovakia, Czechoslovakia, large river port on Danube. Dates from Roman times; chartered (1291). Has 13th cent. castle and cathedral and 18th cent. Palace of Archbishops (now the city hall). Hungarian city (1541–1784). Transshipment centre, with engineering and chemical industries. Pop. (1961 est.) 255,000.

Brazil [República Federativa do Brasil], repub. of S America: federation of 22 states. Area: 3,280,000 sq. mi.; cap. Brasilia, principal cities. Rio de Janeiro, Sao Paulo and Belo Horizonte. Major geog. regions. 1) the N, dominated by Amazon basin: world's most extensive trop. rain forests. Yields rubber and manganese. 2) The central W includes lowlands of Paraguay basin; livestock, coffee, wheat. Largely underdeveloped. 3) the NE; fertile coast. Cattle and goat raising main occupations. 4) the E produces coffee, trop. fruits, cacao, sugar cane, tobacco, livestock and dairy products. Gold and diamonds mined; huge iron deposits. 5) the S produces coffee, cotton, cereals and

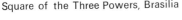

Square of the Three Powers, Brasilia

The Beggars by Pieter Breughel

livestock. First settled by Portuguese (1532), Independence from Portugal (1822); bloodless revolution made Brazil a repub. (1889). Official language, Portuguese. Unit of currency, the cruzeiro. Pop. (1967) 87,000,000.

brazilnut tree, *Bertholletia excelsa,* tree of nettle family, native of Brazil; leathery leaves. Large woody fruits contain about 20 3-sided edible oily seeds or nuts.

Brazza, Pierre Paul François Camille Savorgnan de (1852–1905), Fr. explorer. Estab. Fr. protectorate over the former kingdom of Makoko. Founded Brazzaville (1880).

Brazzaville, cap. of Congo Republic, founded (1880) by Fr. explorer BRAZZA. Situated on Stanley Pool of Congo R., opposite Kinshasa (Leopoldville), it has light metal and furniture industries. Centre of Free French Forces during World War 2. Pop. (1962 est,) 136,000.

breadfruit tree, *Artocarpus altilis,* native of Malaya, found throughout S Pacific; introduced into Americas by Capt. William Bligh. Large round fruit used as vegetable or as bread substitute.

bream, *Abramis brama,* freshwater food fish of CARP family of Europe and Asia. Small head, narrow deep body, and arched back with dull silver colouring on flanks.

Bream, Julian Alexander (1933–   ), Eng. guitarist and lutenist. Well known soloist, and leading exponent of classical guitar music.

breathing *see* RESPIRATION.

Brébeuf, Jean de (1593–1649), Fr. Jesuit missionary; founded Huron missions near Georgian Bay, Canada. In charge of these missions (1633–8, 1644–9); canonized (1930).

breccia, rock formed mainly of small angular fragments. Consists of cemented scree deposits, fault fractured rocks, or explosively fragmented volcanic rock.

Brecht [Eugen Friedrich] Bertolt (1898–1956), Ger. poet and dramatist; 1st success *The Threepenny Opera* (1928). Wrote most of his plays incl. *Mother Courage* (1939), *Galileo* (1939), *The Caucasian Chalk Circle* (1944–5) in Denmark and US. Best known for his theories of epic theatre, which form basis of work of BERLINER ENSEMBLE.

Breckinridge, John Cabell (1821–75), Amer. politician. Democratic Congressman from Kentucky (1851–5); Vice Pres. (1857–61). Division of Democrats (1860) led to nomination by southern faction. When Kentucky backed Union, joined Confederacy.

Brecknockshire, Breconshire, inland county of Wales, largely mountainous. Area: 860 sq. mi.; county town. Brecon (Brecknock). Pop. (1966) 55,000.

Bremen, city and seaport of W Germany, cap. of Bremen state, on the Weser, *c.* 60 mi. from its mouth. The river has been deepened and there are 3 harbours. Old city has buildings dating from Hanseatic League. Pop. 596,000. **State of Bremen,** formed (1946) comprises city and environs and **Bremerhaven,** a fishing centre and the outport for city of Bremen.

Brenner Pass, lower pass of Tyrolean Alps (4,495 ft.) on Austro-Italian border. Road built 1792; railway 1864–7.

brent, brant goose, *Branta bernicla,* small goose with black head and mainly dark plumage breeding in the Arctic; winters along the Atlantic coast of N America. Gregarious, more maritime than other geese, is edible and in some areas is protected.

Brentano, Clemens Maria (1778–1842), Ger. Romantic writer whose lyrics demonstrate the folk spirit also present in his *Märchen*. Creator of the 'folk legend' of the Lorelei.

Brest, city of Finistère department, NW France, on an inlet of Atlantic Ocean. Situated 313 mi. W of Paris, is chief naval base of France. Industry includes iron, steel and chemicals. Pop. (1962) 142,901.

Brest-Litovsk, Treaty of, peace treaty in World War 1, signed (1918) by Soviet Russia and the Central powers. Russia recognized independence of Ukraine and Georgia, confirmed independence of Finland, gave up Poland, the Baltic states, and part of Byelorussia to Germany and Austro-Hungary, and ceded Kars, Ardahan and Batum to Turkey. Terms renounced in the General Armistice (1918).

Brétigny, Treaty of (8 May 1360), concluded 2nd phase of Hundred Years War between England and France. Financial, dynastic and territorial in terms: King John II of France to be ransomed for 3,000,000 gold crowns; Edward III of England to abandon his claim to Fr. Crown; Aquitaine to be held in full sovereignty by Eng. king and territories of Poitou, Agenais, Périgord, Query, Limousin, Saintonge, Angoulême and Calais, to be ceded to Eng. king.

Breton *see* CELTIC.

Brent Goose

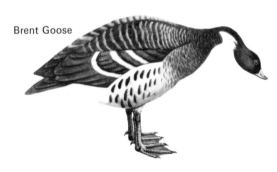

Breton, André (1896–1966), Fr. poet, novelist and critic; a founder and leader of the surrealist movement. Works include *Qu'est-ce-que le Surréalisme?* (1934; Eng. tr., *What is Surrealism?* 1936).

Bretton Woods Conference, name given to pre-UN Monetary and Financial Conference (July 1944), held at Bretton Woods, New Hampshire, US. Resulted in creation of the INTERNATIONAL MONETARY FUND and the INTERNATIONAL BANK FOR RECONSTRUCTION AND DEVELOPMENT.

Breuer, Josef (1842–1925), Austrian physician known for development of questioning under hypnosis to alleviate mental illness. In collaboration with Freud, wrote *Studien über Histerie.*

Breughel, Pieter (*c.* 1525–69), Flemish painter, foremost member of distinguished painting family. His naturalistic treatment of Flemish countryside and peasant life is shown esp. in *The Blind Leading the Blind* and *Peasant Wedding.*

Breuil, Abbé Henri (1877–1961), Fr. archaeologist, the acknowledged expert on the old Stone Age for almost 50 years. Travelled widely in Ethiopia, South Africa and China; correlated the classifications of prehistory to produce a systematized world-view.

Brewster, Sir David (1781–1868), Scot. physicist noted for discoveries connected with polarization of light. Invented kaleidoscope (1816) and perfected stereoscope (1849–50).

Brezhnev, Leonid Ilyich (1906–   ), first Sec. (since 1964) of Central Committee of Communist Party, USSR. Senior political officer during World War 2, became a secretary of Central Committee (1952) and Chairman of Presidium of Supreme Soviet (1960).

Briand, Aristide (1862–1932), Fr. statesman; premier (1909–21), foreign minister (1925–32). Chief architect of LOCARNO PACT and Kellogg-Briand Pact. Advocated co-operation with US and formation of United States of Europe. Awarded Nobel Peace Prize (1926) with Gustav Stresemann.

briar, sweetbriar, eglantine, thick-

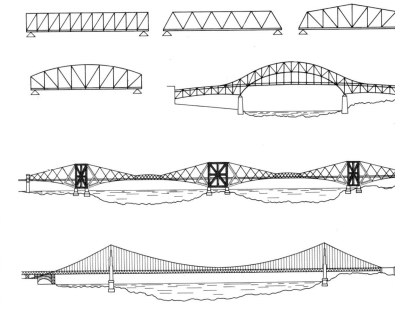

Methods of metal bridge construction

growing hedge-plant of Rose family, now naturalized in N America.

brickfielder, dry, hot, scorching wind blowing from desert interior of Australia.

bridge, structure to carry path, road, rly. or canal over gap or barrier. Most common types, cantilever, suspension, arch. Made of timber, masonry, concrete, iron or steel. Some of world's best known bridges include Forth Rly. Bridge, Scotland (cantilever), Brooklyn Bridge, New York (suspension), Sydney Harbour Bridge, Australia (steel arch), Golden Gate Bridge, San Francisco (suspension). Sectional Bailey Bridge invented in World War 2.

bridge, contract, card game developed from WHIST and auction bridge. First rules published (1914) but invention widely credited to Harold Vander-

bilt (1925). Rules governing tournament play determined by Portland Club, London, European Bridge League, and Amer. Contract Bridge League.

Bridge of Sighs, covered stone bridge in Venice, Italy, built (16th cent.) to connect ducal palace with prisons.

Bridges, Calvin Blackman (1889–1938), Amer. geneticist who identified chromosome as basis of heredity.

Bridges, Robert (1844–1930), Eng. poet and physician; Poet Laureate (1913–30). Works include *Poetical Works* (1912), *The Testament of Beauty* (1929).

Bridget, Saint, also known as **Brigid** and **Bride,** a patron saint of Ireland; founded Great Church and Monastery at Kildare.

Bridget of Sweden, Saint (*c.* 1304–73). Swedish saint, became nun

The City Hall, Bremen

Briar Rose

after death of husband, founded order of Bridgittines (1344). From *c.* 1350 lived in Rome and was involved in return of Urban V from Avignon.

Bridgetown, cap. of Barbados, W Indies. Commercial centre; exports sugar, rum, molasses. Pop. (1966) 94,000.

Bridgman, P[ercy] W[illiams] (1882–1961), Amer. physicist. Awarded Nobel prize for Physics

(1946) for high pressure experiments. Produced theory of 'operational analysis'.

Bridie, James, orig. Osborne Henry Mavor (1888–1951), Scot. playwright and physician. Works include *The Anatomist* (1931) *Dr Angelus* (1947) and *A Small Stir* (1949).

Brigantes, early people of N England (mainly Yorks.). Under their queen Cartimandua they formed a client-

state of Rome but were defeated (71 in Agricola's campaign; an unsuccessful revolt (155) led to the estab of many more Roman forts and settlements.

Briggs, Henry (*c.* 1556–1631), Eng mathematician. With JOHN NAPIER he constructed logarithmic system generally used today, known as Briggsian or common logarithms.

Brighton, Eng. seaside resort 51 mi. S

BRITISH ISLES

0   20   40   60   80   100 Miles
0 20 40 60 80 100 120 140 Kms.

© Collins-Longmans Atlases

of London. Fashionable health resort in 19th cent. Regency architecture includes Royal Pavilion built by Prince Regent (later George IV). Pop. 162,200.

brill, *Scophthalmus rhombus,* European marine flatfish of turbot family. Valued as food.

Brillat-Savarin, Anthelme (1755–1826), Fr. lawyer, politician and writer, author of witty *Physiology of Taste* (1825).

brimstone, *Gonepteryx rhanni,* spring butterfly of sulphur group common in Britain. One of the few butterflies to hibernate in the open.

Brisbane, cap. and chief port of Queensland, Australia, near mouth of Brisbane river in Moreton Bay; named after Sir Thomas Brisbane (1773–1840), Scot. soldier, astronomer and administrator. Settled (1824) as penal colony; opened (1842) to free settlers. Notable buildings are University of Queensland, national art gallery, museum, and Anglican and R.C. cathedrals. Exports wool, meat, gold, sugar and coal. Pop. (1966) 719,140.

Brissot de Warville, Jacques Pierre (1754–93), Fr. lawyer and pamphleteer instrumental in declaring war on Austria (1792). Wrote on French-US relations and founded abolitionist society; originated the phrase. 'Property is theft'. Executed after Jacobins overcame Girondists.

bristletail, small wingless insect of the orders *Thysanura* and *Entotrophi* with bristle-like caudal appendages and long slender legs. Widely distributed, most live in damp, sheltered places. Species include SILVERFISH, *Lepisma saccharina,* and firebrat, *Thermobia domestica.*

Bristol, Eng. city and seaport near Bristol Channel. Royal borough before 1066, later chartered as city

Brimstone Butterfly

(1155) and county (1375). By 18th cent. trade esp. in slaves and tobacco developed with Amer. colonies and W Indies. Exports grain and petroleum products; industries include engineering, aircraft, chocolate, tobacco, soap manufacture. Pop. (1966) 429,000.

British Broadcasting Corporation (BBC), public corporation responsible to parl. through BBC Director General. Chartered (1927) as a monopoly governing all phases of broadcasting: revision (1952) allowed the creation of the Independent Television Authority. There are 4 national and several local radio channels, operating on medium wave and frequency modulation, and 2 TV channels. Commonwealth and international services are provided. Operating costs paid for by income from licence fees and from the Treasury.

British Cameroons *see* CAMEROON.

British Columbia, Pacific prov. of Canada, comprising the width of the N Amer. Cordillera. Area: 366,255 sq. mi.; cap. Victoria. Main cities Vancouver, Victoria and Prince George. Discovered (1774) by Juan Perez of Spain and first explored by James Cook (1778); Alexander Mackenzie crossed the interior from the E (1793). Territory ceded to Britain (1790) and created a colony upon the discovery (1858) of gold. United with Vancouver Is. (1866), became a prov. (1871). Completion of Canadian Pacific Railway (1885) led to immigration and trade from the Orient. Forestry, mining, fishing (esp. salmon) and farming are major occupations and revenue sources. Provincial university, chartered (1908) is one of Canada's largest. Pop. (1967 est.) 1,947,000.

British Commonwealth of Nations *see* COMMONWEALTH OF NATIONS.

British Empire, estab. with colonization (1583) of Newfoundland, at its height (late 19th, early 20th cent.), largest empire in world history. Foundations laid with chartering of great trading enterprises, such as East India Co. and Hudson's Bay Co.; conquests in India, N America; colonizing in Africa, Australasia. Mercantilist stranglehold led to Amer. Revolution (1776). Dominion status (19th cent.) granted to various members. Canada being 1st (1867). STATUTE OF WESTMINSTER (1931) estab. COMMONWEALTH OF NATIONS and marked end of Brit. Empire.

British Guiana *see* GUYANA.

British Honduras, self-ruling Brit. crown colony, C America. Area: 8,867 sq. mi.; cap. Belize. flat and marshy, agriculture is main occupation. Once inhabited by aboriginal groups and site of Mayan civilization, population is of mixed Negro, Sp., Indian and Brit. stock. Sp. territory until 1798. 1st Brit. settlers (*c.* 1638)

The Royal Pavilion, Brighton

were prob. buccaneers. Status now in dispute with Guatemala. pop. (1968) 109,000.

British Indian Ocean Territory, Brit. colony estab. (1965) to provide strategic defence facilities for US and UK. Area: 72 sq. mi. Consists of Chagos Archipelago, Aldabra, Farquhar and Desroches Is. Administered from Victoria in Seychelles, it exports copra, fish and tortoiseshell. Pop. (1965) 1,400.

British Isles, a group of islands, area *c.* 121,600 sq. mi. off the NW coast of Europe, comprising ENGLAND, WALES, SCOTLAND, NORTHERN IRELAND, Republic of IRELAND (Eire) and islands round the coast. Population mainly descendants of European invaders. Politically divided into the United Kingdom, (UK) comprising Eng., Wales, Scot., N Ireland, and Republic of Ireland (Eire). England was unified under a Saxon king (9th cent.); Wales and Ireland were joined to it by end of 13th cent. In 1603 crowns of England and Scotland united under James I and VI; ACTS OF UNION (1707 and 1800) gave the UK Parl. at Westminster supreme authority. In 1922 the 26 counties of S Ireland became independent and formed the Republic of Ireland. Government of Ireland Act (1920) gave Northern Ireland power over domestic affairs.

British North America Act (1867), passed by the UK Parl. embodying the resolutions founding Confederation of the Dominion of Canada. Defined executive power; provided for division of federal and provincial legislative powers; safeguarded judicial independence;

Menhirs at Carnac, Brittany

provided for the admission of further provinces.

British Solomon Islands *see* SOLOMON ISLANDS.

British Somaliland *see* SOMALI REPUBLIC.

British Standards Institution (BSI), orig. Engineering Standards Committee, formed by various engineering bodies (1901), granted charter (1929); voluntarily prepared and published agreed manufacturing standards for their products. The BSI now covers over 60 major industries in the UK. Set up its Consumer Advisory Council (1955) to ensure consumer voice in matters previously preserve of traders and manufacturers. *Shopper's Guide* (1957–62) presented critical account and comparison of different consumer goods. Government-appointed Molony Committee (1959–62) led to formation of Government-sponsored Consumer Council. The official 'kite mark' guarantees objective standards of safety and quality.

Brittany [Bretagne], ancient prov. and duchy in NW peninsula of France. Area: 11,583 sq. mi. Famed for fishing, associated industries and naval installations of Brest and Lorient. An island plateau of relatively fertile land surrounded by a rocky coast; isolated until 19th cent. canal development. Original Celtic inhabitants conquered (56 BC) by Julius Caesar. Became Fr. (1532) after Anne of Brittany married Louis XII.

Britten, Edward Benjamin (1913–), Eng. composer. Works include operas *Peter Grimes* (1945), *Billy Budd* (1951) and *A War Requiem* (1962), as well as *Young person's guide to the orchestra*.

Brno, chief city of Moravia, S Czechoslovakia. Sited strategically, flourished in 13th and 14th cent. Besieged (1645) by Swedes, it was Napoleon's headquarters (1805) for Austerlitz. Industrial and communication centre, manufacturing textiles, machinery, tools, precision instruments. Pop. (1966) 330,000.

Broad, C[harlie] D[unbar] (1887–), Eng. philosopher and psychologist who devised theory of brain processes being both physical and mental. His books include *Perception, Physics and Reality* (1914).

broadbill, family of perching birds of trop. forests of Africa and Asia. Characterized by green or blue silky plumage and short wide bill.

broadcasting, transmission of sound or images by RADIO or TELEVISION. Its subject matter may be of entertainment, information, or educ. value. Sound broadcasting began *c.* 1920; TV broadcasting began 1936. Use of competing wavelengths caused severe interference necessitating international legislation. In US and Canada, broadcasting largely financed by advertising, in UK through licence fees and general taxation (except commercial TV under the Independent Television Authority).

Broadway, street in New York City which is also called the 'Great White Way'. Mid-Manhattan area famous as location of many theatres. Term 'off Broadway' refers to theatrical productions considered commercially unprofitable.

broccoli [UK], *Brassica oleracea,* varieties of winter and early spring cauliflower native to S Europe and cultivated widely in N temp. zones. Calabrese [US], is green, or sprouting broccoli.

Broch, Hermann (1886–1951), Austrian writer, best known for novel *Der Tod des Vergil* (1945), powerful blend of mythical and psychological elements.

brochs, massive drystone towers, *c.* 40 ft. high, mostly found in N and NW Scotland, usually dominating valleys or coastal farming country. Thought to have been refuges; inner spaces *c.* 30 ft. across. Among largest and most impressive pre-Roman remains in UK.

Brock, Sir Isaac (1769–1812), Brit. general and Canadian hero of War of 1812. Administrator of Upper Canada (1811), killed repelling Amer. attack at Queenston Heights.

Brock, Sir Russel (1903–), Brit. surgeon, authority on pulmonary stenosis and therapy for acquired cardiac defects.

Brockhaus, Friedrich Arnold (1772–1823) Ger. printer and publisher; founded (1805) firm famous mainly for its comprehensive reference books.

Broglie, Louis Victor, Prince de (1892–), Fr. physicist, awarded Nobel Prize for Physics (1929) for developing the theory of the wave character of atomic particles.

Broken Hill, mining town of New South Wales, Australia. Main centre of silver, lead and zinc mining since 1884. Pop. (1966) 30,000.

bromeliad, terrestrial or arboreal plant of the pineapple family, Bromeliaceae of trop. America, with glossy leaves and a spine-like flower; cultivated as house plants.

Bromfield, Louis (1896–1956), Amer. writer. Works include *Pleasant Valley* (1945), *Malabar Farm* (1948) and *The Rains Came* (1937).

bromine (Br), member of halogen group of elements, discovered (1825) in sea water by Antoine Jérôme Balard (1802–76). Occurs as bromides of sodium, potassium, magnesium and calcium in sea water and as silver bromide (Ag Br). Heavy volatile liquid, dark red in colour, its highly toxic vapour and liquid can produce severe burns. Used in manufacture of dyes, and in producing silver bromide used in photography.

Brontë, Charlotte (1816–55), Eng. novelist, sister of Emily, Anne and Bramwell. Gained immediate fame on publication of her most famous work *Jane Eyre* (1847).

Brontë, Emily (1818–48), Eng. novelist and poet famous for her single novel *Wuthering Heights* (1847).

brontosaurus [Gk. 'thunder lizard'], extinct semi aquatic quadruped of the dinosaur group, *c.* 70 ft. long, with long neck and tail. Weighed *c.* 30 tons, the brain weighing *c.* 1 lb. Bones of this herbivore have been found in

Broadway, New York

Jurassic and Cretaceous formations of US and elsewhere.

Bronx, The, borough of New York City, NE of Harlem river, co-extensive with Bronx County. Principal residential area, its recreational areas include Bronx Park, New York Zoological Park, Botanical Garden and Yankee Stadium.

Bronze Age, period *c.* 3500 BC characterized by use of bronze for tools and weapons. Preceded by use of stone, bone and wood and followed by adoption of iron as dominant metal.

Brooke, Rupert (1887–1915), Eng. Georgian poet and soldier; best known for his poems *The Great Lover* and *The Soldier*.

brooklime, *Veronica beccacunga,* sprawling perennial of the speedwell family with clusters of small blue flowers at the base of the leaves. Used as a salad plant in Europe and as a cure for scurvy. Species include *V. Americana.*

Brooklyn, borough of New York City, in SW Long Island, connected to Manhattan by 3 bridges and 3 tunnels, populous manufacturing centre, extensive residential areas. Settled by Dutch farmers and Walloons. Estab. (1645). Incorporated as village (1816) and chartered as city (1834), it now includes King's County.

Brooklyn Bridge, oldest (1883) of 3 bridges connecting Brooklyn to Manhattan, New York. Suspension-built with span of 1,595 ft.

Brooks, Cleanth (1906–   ), Amer. writer. *The Well Wrought Urn* (1947) influenced contemporary methods of teaching literature. Textbooks include *Understanding Poetry* (1938) and *Understanding Fiction* (1943) with R. P. Warren.

Brooks, Phillips (1835–93) Amer. cleric. Influential Episcopalian preacher at Trinity College, Boston (1869–91), Bishop of Massachusetts (1891). Works include published lectures and hymn, 'O Little Town of Bethlehem'.

Brooks, Van Wyck (1886–1963), Amer. literary historian interested in New England background; books include *The Flowering of New England* (1936) and *The Confident Years* (1952). Biographies include *The Ordeal of Mark Twain* (1920).

Brooks Range, most N part of Rocky Mountains in N Alaska, rising to 9,239 ft. and embracing several mountain chains.

broom, shrubs of 2 related genera, *Cytisus* and *Genista,* of pea family, with yellow, white or purple flowers. Common or Scotch broom. *C.*

Bromeliad

scoparius is naturalized in N America. Garden varieties include prostrate forms.

Broom, Robert (1866–1951), S African morphologist and palaeontologist, famous for the discovery (1936) of fossilized remains of the Australopithecines at Sterkfontein, South Africa.

broomcorn, *Sorghum vulgare technicum,* grass with a tough stem, native to trop. Asia and Africa, found in Europe, America and Russia. The long, slender, flexible, flower head used in broom-making. Grain is fed to cage birds.

broomrape, parasitic plant family, Orobanchaceae, native to Old World and western N America. They have fleshy scales and each species has its particular plant host.

Browder, Earl Russell (1891–   ), Amer. Communist leader, edited *Daily Worker* (1944–5), and was US pres. candidate (1936, 1940). Support of World War 2, opposed by USSR, resulted in removal from Comm. party (1946). Works include *Communism in the United States* (1935) and *War or Peace with Russia* (1947).

Brown, George (1818–80), Canadian newspaperman and statesman. Effectively advocated representation by

population in his paper *The Globe.* Entered politics (1851) as a Liberal, headed two-day govt. (1858), and supported coalition ministry pledged to achieve nationhood. Resigned 1865.

Brown, Joe (1930–   ), Eng. mountaineer, one of 1st 2 men to climb Kanchenjunga, and scale the W summit of Muztagh Tower (1956).

Brown, John (1800–59), Amer. abolitionist. Known as 'Old Brown of Osawatomie'. Fanatical in his conviction that slaves should be freed by force, he attacked Harper's Ferry with 21 men and seized US arsenal and armory (1859). Captured by soldiers led by Col. Robert E. Lee, tried for treason and hanged. His career has inspired many books and songs, incl. 'John Brown's Body'.

Brown, John Mason (1900–69), Amer. drama critic whose works include *The Modern Theatre in Revolt* (1928), *Broadway in Review* (1940) and *As They Appear* (1952).

Brown, Lancelot ('Capability') (1715–83), Eng. landscape gardener and Palladian architect. Laid out gardens at Kew and Blenheim, using isolated clumps of trees and undulating lawns surrounded by woodland.

Brown, Robert (1773–1858), Scot. botanist and botanical explorer, who collected plants in Australia. Observed Brownian movement (1827) and discovered cell nucleus (1831).

brown algae, brown to olive-green coloured algae, often with air bladders, *e.g.* bladder-wrack, *Fucus vesiculosus,* and a gelatinous surface, belong to phylum *Phaeophyta.* Mainly marine group abundant in colder latitudes. Some species are 70 yd. long.

brown bear, *Ursus arctos,* formerly European bear. Inhabits temp. forests in N hemisphere. One or 2 cubs born during hibernation, and raised with previous litter. Now largely eliminated from Europe.

brown rat, *Rattus norvegicus,* large

Brown Bear

Bruges, Belgium

rodent of Muridae family. Original home thought to be in C Asia, now estab. in most of the world.

Browne, Maurice (1881–1955), Brit. actor manager. With Ellen van Volkenberg, founded Chicago Little Theatre (1912). London productions included *Journey's End*.

Browne, Sir Thomas (1605–82), Eng. writer and physician, best known for *Religio Medici* (1642).

Brownell, Herbert, Jr. (1904–), Amer. politician. Served in New York state politics, managed Thomas E. Dewey's 1944 presidential campaign. Appointed Attorney General (1953–7) by Eisenhower.

Brownian motion, movement, unceasing random movement of small particles suspended in fluid. Caused by bombardment of particles by continuously moving molecules of fluid. Described by ROBERT BROWN who observed motion of microscopic pollen grains suspended in water.

Browning, Elizabeth Barrett (1806–61), Eng. poet, wife of Robert Browning. Their courtship, elopement and happy marriage is a celebrated literary romance. *Sonnets from the Portuguese* (1850), love sonnets to her husband, is her most famous work. *The Cry of the Children* (1843) protests against employment of children.

Browning, Robert (1812–89), Eng. poet who gained recognition, after 40 yr. of obscurity, with publication of *The Ring and The Book* (1868–9), series of dramatic monologues interpreting events from 12 different points of view. Earlier work included *Pippa Passes* (1841), *Dramatic Lyrics* (1847) and *Pauline* (1833). Poetry is notable for insight into character, use of dramatic monologue and forceful, colloquial English.

Brubeck, Dave (1920–), Amer. musician. Formed Modern Jazz Quartet (1951). Toured Europe and Middle East for US State Dept. (1960).

Bruce, James, 8th Earl of Elgin (1811–63), Gov.-General of Canada (1846–54), he successfully fostered responsible govt. (1848) by sanctioning measures of the Baldwin LaFontaine ministry.

Bruce, Thomas, 7th Earl of Elgin (1766–1841), Brit. diplomat and soldier famous for transportation to London of the Parthenon frieze known as the 'Elgin Marbles' (1806). Sculptures, attributed to Phidias, sold to nation for £35,000.

Bruch, Max (1838–1920), Ger. composer and conductor of many orchestras incl. Liverpool Philharmonic Society (1880–3). *Kol Nidrei* for cello and orchestra and G minor Violin Concerto are his best known works.

Bruchési, Jean (1901–), Fr. Canadian historian; pres. (1953) of the Royal Society of Canada. His *Histoire du Canada pour tous* (2 vols., 1934–6), honoured by the Fr. Academy, revised and reprinted as *Histoire du Canada* (1959). Essays include *Rappels* (1941), on Fr. literature, and *Evocations* (1947), on Canadian history.

Bruckner, Anton (1824–96), Austrian composer, organist and teacher. Disciple of Wagner, his work includes 9 symphonies, 4 masses and a string quintet.

Bruges, city of Belgium and cap. of W Flanders, connected to N Sea by Zeebrugge Canal. Founded in 9th cent., the wool industry of medieval Bruges made it a focal point of N Europe. Revived (19th cent.) with opening of canal. Important textile and lace-making centre; tourist attractions include medieval architecture and museums. Pop. (1964–5) 105,000.

Brulé, Etienne (*c.* 1592–1633), Fr. explorer who prob. arrived (1608) at Quebec with Champlain. Believed to be 1st white man to have visited L. Superior and L. Erie (1612–3). Killed in Huron country.

Brunei, Brit. protected sultanate, on NW coast of Borneo. Area: *c.* 2,200 sq. mi.; cap. Brunei town. Once a haven for pirates and slave trading centre, the British made it (1888) a protectorate. Association of Brunei, N Borneo, and Sarawak set up (1953). Brunei received first constitution (1959), the Brit. govt. remaining responsible for defence and external affairs, with the Sultan controlling internal affairs. Approx. 60% of population is Malay and 40% Chinese. Chief exports, oil and natural gas; rubber, coconut, sago and rice grown. Pop. 100,000.

Brunelleschi, Filippo (1377–1446), Florentine architect, credited with estab. of perspective. Famous for dome of Florence Cathedral (1420–36).

Brunhild, Brynhild, Brünnehilde, female warrior figure of Teutonic myth., prominent in the *Nibelungenlied* and other sagas.

Bruno, Giordano (1548–1600), Ital. philosopher and cosmologist who

Brussels, Belgium

believed that stars are other suns and that infinite universe contains finite worlds like the earth. Condemned by the Inquisition, he was burned at the stake.

Brunswick, Braunschweig, moated city of W Germany, on R. Oker, SE of Hanover. Member of Hanseatic League and one of N Germany's chief cities in Middle Ages, cap. of duchy of Brunswick from 1671. Active trade and industrial centre; manufactures food, iron, steel and pianos. Pop. (1960 est.) 242,489.

brush turkey, *Alectura lathami,* large bird of E Australia, its head and neck are bald, except for a few coarse hairs. Its eggs are laid in a mound of plant matter and incubated by heat of fermentation. The young are completely independent.

Brussels [Flemish: Brussel, Fr: Bruxelles], cap. of Belgium since 1830. Built as a Roman settlement on R. Senne, fortified (11th cent.) when it was a commercial centre on the trade route between Bruges and the Rhineland. Succeeded Bruges in the manufacture and marketing of woollens. Exploited and occupied during both World Wars. Now headquarters of NATO and the European Economic Community. There are celebrated art collections and old buildings. Pop. (1965) 1,066,000.

Brussels sprouts, *Brassica oleracea gemmifera,* vegetable of cabbage family. Small edible heads are borne on axis of stem.

brutalism, in architecture, use of rough exposed concrete masses giving impression of clashing movement as in work of Le Corbusier and Paul Rudolph.

Brutus, in ancient Rome a surname of the Junian family. **Lucius Junius Brutus** (*fl.* 510 BC), founder of Roman Republic, helped end the Tarquin dynasty after the rape of Lucrecia. Said to have killed his sons for plotting a Tarquin restoration. **Marcus Junius Brutus** (85–42 BC), partisan of Pompey, pardoned by Caesar after battle of Pharsalus, made gov. of Cisalpine Gaul (46 BC), but joined Cassius to murder Caesar (44 BC). Fighting for the republican cause in Macedonia was defeated by Antony

Dome of the Santa Maria del Fiore cathedral, Florence by Brunelleschi

and Octavian at Philippi (42 BC), and committed suicide. **Decimus Junius Brutus** (d. 43 BC), a kinsman, also a member of the conspiracy, despite being a favourite of Caesar's, refused to give up command in Gaul and was besieged and killed by Mark Antony.

Bryan, William Jennings (1860–1925), Amer. politician. As Democratic Congressman from Nebraska (1891–5) was associated with free silver movement. Famous 'Cross of Gold' speech led to first nomination (1896) for US presidency. Nominated again (1900, 1908). Gave support to Woodrow Wilson at 1912 Democratic convention. Sec. of State (1913–15), resigned over pro-World War 1 policy.

Bryant, William Cullen (1794–1878), Amer. poet and editor. Themes were the uncertainty of human life and permanence of nature. Works include *Thanatopsis* (1817) and translations of Homer.

Bryce, James, Viscount (1838–1922), Brit. historian and statesman. A Liberal, he held several diplomatic and cabinet posts. His *The American Commonwealth* (1888), is a classic interpretation of Amer. life.

Bryce Canyon, US National Park in SW Utah, estab. 1928. Area: 36,000 acres. Noted for beautiful colours of canyon walls.

bryophyta, small phylum of plant kingdom comprising mosses and liverworts. Widely distributed in water or moist habitats on banks, soil and rocks. Reproduction is normally by spores.

Buber, Martin (1878–1965), Jewish philosopher and theologian, best known for synthesizing Jewish mysticism and Christian existentialism as expounded, in *I and Thou* (1923).

Buchan, John *see* TWEEDSMUIR, 1ST BARON.

Buchanan, James (1791–1868), 15th US Pres. (1857–61), Democrat. US Senator (1834–45); Sec. of State (1845–9). Elected Pres. (1856), 1st bachelor ever to hold that office. Attempted to pursue moderate policy

Brown Rat

Budapest, capital of Hungary

Headquarters of official news agency, Bucharest

on slavery issue, but efforts to effect compromise met with suspicion by both North and South.

Bucharest, cap. of Romania since 1861, chief industrial and communication centre, manufacturing machinery, textiles, metals and chemicals. Seat of metropolitan of Eastern Orthodox Church, and R.C. archbishopric. Pop. (1964) 1,372,000.

Buchman, Frank *see* MORAL REARMAMENT.

Buchner, Eduard (1860–1917). Ger. biochemist. Awarded Nobel Prize for Chemistry (1907) for work on causes of fermentation.

Buck, Pearl S[ydenstricker] (1892–), Amer. novelist. Brought up in China, she spent much time doing missionary and welfare work. Most of her novels depict Chinese life, notably *The Good Earth* (1931). Awarded Nobel Prize for Literature (1938).

buckeye, Amer. shrubs and trees of genus *Aesculus* similar to horse chestnut but without sticky winter buds. Red buckeye, *A. pavia*, native of E US is small shrub with red flowers and smooth brown fruit; Ohio buckeye, *A. glabra,* popular ornamental tree, state tree of Ohio.

Buckingham Palace, official London residence of Brit. sovereign since

Queen Victoria's reign. Built (1703) for Duke of Buckingham; bought as private residence (1762) by George III. Reconstructed (1825–36) by John Nash. Contains finest private collection of paintings in Europe.

Buckinghamshire, inland county of England. Area: 746 sq. mi.; county town, Aylesbury; main towns, Marlow, Slough and Buckingham. Largely agric., industries include engineering, chemicals and confectionery. Pop. (1966) 542,000.

Buckley, William F[rank], Jr. (1925–), Amer. writer, known for arch-conservatism, wit and debating prowess. Works include *God and Man at Yale* (1951) and *Up From Liberalism* (1959).

buckthorn, family of deciduous and evergreen trees, *Rhamnaceae* and shrubs native to Europe and W and N Asia. Some species have thorny branches. Fruit has purgative properties and yields dye, Chinese green. Common buckthorn, *R. cathartica*, is hedge plant in America.

Budapest, cap. and largest city of Hungary, comprising Buda on one bank of Danube and Pest on other; united (1872). By 1917, leading commercial centre, its industrial population now accounts for half of Hungary's total; extensively damaged during World War 2 and 1956 uprising. Pop. (1966) 1,952,000.

Buddha [Sanskrit: 'enlightened one'], title of Siddhartha Gautama (*c.* 566–486 BC), Indian religious leader, founder of Buddhism. Renounced life of prince (*c.* 535 BC) for asceticism; founded an order which spread this religion.

Buddhism, religion of followers of Buddha, widespread in SE Asia, China and Japan; orig. related to Hinduism, it was in part reaction against it. Its 'four noble truths' are: life is pain; origin of

pain is desire; pain ceases when desire ceases; end desire by following 'noble eightfold path'. The path comprises right belief, right resolve, right speech, right conduct, right livelihood, right effort, rightmindedness, right ecstasy. Final goal is Nirvana, annihilation of self.

Budge, [John] Donald (1915–), Amer. tennis player, who scored the grand slam of tennis by winning US, Austral. Fr. and Brit. Singles championships (1938). Won Brit. (Wimbledon) title (1937).

budgerigar, *Melopsittacus undulatus*, commonest member of parrot family of Australia. In the wild, green with yellow head and long tapering blue tail; selective breeding has led to colour variations. Lives in nomadic flocks and eats seeds and grain. Two broods of about 9 eggs are laid yearly. Popular pet; first 'budgies' brought to England (1840s).

budget, govt. statement, issued annually, of revenue and expenditure of the previous year and estimated revenue and expenditure of forthcoming year. In UK, presented by Chanc. of the Exchequer to Commons, sitting as Committee of Ways and Means; elsewhere presented by finance minister. In US, executive budget recommendations (appropriations) supervised by Bureau of the Budget, after congressional approval.

Bueno, Maria (1939–), Brazilian tennis player. Women's champion at Wimbledon (1959, 1960, 1964) and at Forest Hills, NY (1959, 1963, 1964).

Buenos Aires, cap. (since 1862), chief port and railway terminus of Argentina. Has more than $\frac{1}{3}$ of country's population and is largest city of S hemisphere. Founded (1536) by Spanish. Captured by British, recaptured by Spanish (1806); citizens repulsed another Brit. attack (1807), but revolted against Spanish to establish a junta (1810). Financial and social

The Guard at Buckingham Palace London

Budgerigar

centre of Argentina. Pop. (1962) city 2,966,816; Greater Buenos Aires 6,762,629.

Buffalo, city and port in New York State, US, at end of L. Erie on Niagara R. Erie Canal (1825) and St Lawrence Seaway (1959) increased its role as one of leading commercial, industrial and transport centres of US. Largest grain-milling and distribution centre in the world. Pop. (1960) 1,054,000.

buffalo, wild cattle. Horns droop and sweep widely and hair is short and black, reddish or greyish. Wallows in mud; withstands humid climate as well as cold and survives on poor food. Some used as draught animals. Amer. bison, *Bison bison,* sometimes called buffalo. *See* CAPE BUFFALO; WATER BUFFALO.

buffalo bug *see* CARPET BEETLE.

buffalo fish, any of several large fish of genus *Letiobus,* of sucker family, found mostly in Mississippi valley. Has long, many-rayed fins. Many species are food fish.

Buffet, Bernard (1928–), Fr. cubist painter. Versatile range in graphics distinguished by linear rigidity; work widely reproduced.

Buffon, Comte Georges Louis Leclerc de, FRS (1707–88), Fr. naturalist and academician. Director (1739) of *Jardin du Roi,* Fr. zoological gardens, which he established as major centre of biological research. With others, incl. Daubenton, wrote *Histoire Naturelle* (1749–1804), 44 vols., 1st work to suggest animal evolution and minimise distinction between plants and animals.

Buganda, African kingdom, province of SE Uganda protectorate; cap. Kampala. Includes some islands in L. Victoria.

bugle, valveless form of trumpet which produces only natural harmonies.

Buisson, Ferdinand Edouard (1841–1932), Fr. educator and radical politician, chiefly responsible for estab. system of free compulsory secular education in France. Author of

Buffalo

Dictionnaire de Pédagogie. Shared Nobel Peace Prize (1927) with Ludwig Quidde.

Bujumbura, cap. and chief port of Burundi, L. Tanganyika, with hydroelectric plant and tea, clothing, brick and tile factories. Pop. (1963) 50,000.

Bukhara, Bokhara, Soviet town in Bukhara oblast of Uzbeck SSR; elevation of 1,200 ft. in centre of fertile oasis. Chief seat of Islamic culture after Mongol invasion (13th cent.), taken by Russians (1868). Has splendid mosques and palaces (9th–17th cent.). Pop. 60,000.

Bukharin, Nikolay Ivanovich (1888–1938), Russ. politician, and leading theorist of Bolshevik Party. Took part in October Revolution (1917) and became leader in Comintern, editor of *Pravda,* and *Izvestia* (1934). Supported Stalin in his rise to power in 1920s. Tried for treason (1938) during Great Purge and executed.

Bulawayo, 2nd largest city in Rhodesia. Founded (1893) on site chosen by last king of Matabeles; made city (1943). Manufactures metal goods, tires, bricks, textiles; processes food; and is headquarters of Rhodesian railway system. Pop. (1965) 237,000.

bulb, underground storage and reproductive structure of certain plants. Formed by swelling of leaf bases constructing sheath round embryo

flower, as distinct from corm, formed by swelling of stem, as in crocus; rhizome, also formed by stem swelling, as in iris; and tuber, formed by swollen underground branch, as in potato, or root as in dahlia.

bulbul, family of birds of genus *Pychonotus* native to Asia, Africa and Australia. Thrush-like with short wings and green, yellow, grey or brown plumage; some species have a crest. Gregarious songbirds, arboreal and mainly fruit-eating. Popular cage bird in Asia.

Bulgakov, Mikhail (1891–1940), Russ. writer and physician. First novel, *The White Guard,* dramatized and produced in London (1938). Best known for ironic and bizarre novels, *The Heart of a Dog* and *The Master and Margarita* (1938).

Bulganin, Nikolay Aleksandrovich (1895–), Russ. Communist leader. Marshal and deputy premier (1947), full member of Politburo (1948), Defence Min. under Stalin, and Premier (1955–8), with Khrushchev's support. Expelled from Central Committee of party (Sep. 1958).

Bulgaria, [Bulgariya], Balkan state of SE Europe. Area: 42,818 sq. mi. Cap. Sofia; other principal cities Plovdiv, Turnova and Varna. Danube, Maritsa and Struma principal rivers. Mineral resources include brown coal, iron ore, manganese, lead, zinc and

Bulb: from the base (a) grows flower bud (b); C_1 will replace original bulb when exhausted, C_2 is the reproductive shoot from which new bulb will develop; (d) are fleshy scales which contain food supplies; (e) are roots for absorbing nourishment

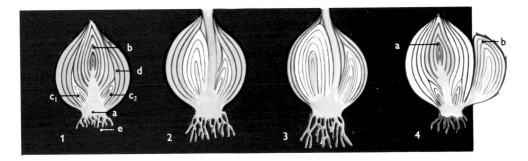

copper. Wheat, maize, barley, tobacco and fruit grown; livestock raised, meat and dairy produce exported. Traditionally agricultural country, now industrialized. Some oil extracted from Black Sea coast. Tourism expanding. Language Bulgarian. From mid-14th cent. subject to 500 yr. of Turkish rule. Turks defeated (1878) by Russian and Bulgarian freedom fighters. Declared independent (1905), joined Axis (1941), and invaded by Soviet troops (1944). Communist regime came to power, abolished monarchy and created People's Republic (Sep. 1946). Currency unit the Lev. Pop. 8,400,000.

Bulgarian, Slavic Indo European language, with 7 million speakers in Bulgaria. Uses Cyrillic alphabet.

Bulge, Battle of the, popular name for last Ger. offensive of World War 2 in the Ardennes on Western Front (Dec. 1944–July 1945).

bull, papal pronouncement, more solemn than brief or encyclical, traditionally sealed with lead. Also used to proclaim canonization of a saint.

Bull Moose Party *see* PROGRESSIVE PARTY.

Bull Run, Battles of (21 July 1861; 29–30 Aug. 1862); in Amer. Civil War, fought in NE Virginia, both Confederate victories.

bulldog, breed of dogs formerly used in bull-baiting. Squat, muscular, short haired and short legged animal, with highly developed jaw.

bullfighting, national spectacle of Spain, popular also in S France and S America, also Mexico. Matador, aided by banderilleros and picadors, makes passes with cape and man-

Bullfighting

oeuvres bull to tire it for kill. In Portugal the bull is not killed.

bullfinch, *Pyrrhulla pyrrhulla,* bird of finch family found in woodlands of Europe and Asia. Pink breast and throat; lays about 5 eggs yearly but only half the young survive predators, esp. jays.

Bullfinch, Thomas (1796–1867), Amer. teacher and writer, published *Age of Fable* (1855), an introduction to European mythology.

bullfrog, *Rana catesbeiana,* N Amer. frog up to 8 in. long. Greenish black, amphibian, hibernates in winter. Catches prey (insect, mouse, frog or bird) with tongue. Male has loud, bellowing mating call.

bullhead, any of several freshwater fishes, *e.g.* European bullhead or miller's thumb, *Cottus gobio,* aggressive and mainly nocturnal. Also some Amer. catfishes, *e.g. Ictalurus nebulosus,* which can live out of water for a time.

Bullinger, Heinrich (1504–75), Swiss Protestant reformer; succeeded Zwingli as Swiss leader. Helped compile 1st Helvetic Confession (1536). Joined John Calvin (1549) in drawing up *Consensus Tigurinus,* which helped to incline Swiss church to Calvinism.

Bullock, Alan [Louis Charles] (1918–), Brit. historian; works include *Hitler, a Study in Tyranny* (1952). Joint editor of *Oxford History of Modern Europe.*

Bülow, Hans Guido von (1830–94), Ger. pianist, music editor and conductor. Considered 1st virtuoso conductor; advocate of Liszt, Wagner and Brahms. Married Liszt's daughter who later left him for Wagner.

bulrush, several species of perennial sedge growing in wet land or water, esp. *Scirpus lacustris* [UK] and *S. validus* [US]. Soft green stems up to 8 ft. tall, terminal clusters of brownish flowers; reproduces by root spread.

bumble bee, humble bee, genus *Bombus,* social insects of worldwide distribution. Stout bodies covered with stiff orange, yellow or red hair; noisy flight and retractable sting.

Bunche, Ralph J. (1904–71), Amer. administrator; mediated for UN in truce in Palestine between Arabs and Jews (1968). US delegate (1944) at Dumbarton Oaks meeting which laid foundations of UN organization; head of trusteeship section of UN secretariat (1946). Awarded Nobel Peace Prize (1950). UN Under Sec.-General since 1968.

Bunin, Ivan [Alexeyevich] (1870–1953), Russ. poet and novelist;

published *The Dreams of Chang* and *Gentleman from San Francisco.* First Russ. writer to receive Nobel Prize for Literature (1933).

Bunker Hill, Battle of (17 June 1775), fought on neighbouring Breed's Hill. In Amer. Revolution, unsuccessful attempt by British to break colonists' siege of Boston.

Bunsen, Robert Wilhelm (1811–99), Ger. chemist, discoverer of caesium and rubidium. Investigated chemical action of light and formulated reciprocity law (1855) with Roscoe. Known for Bunsen burner, which enables high temperature gas flame to burn.

bunting, small, plump bird of finch family of genus *Emberiza;* insectivorous; many species are migratory. Species include yellowhammer, *E. citrinella,* ortolan bunting, *E. hortulana,* and reed bunting, *E. schoeniclus.* In US, buntings generally known as sparrows or finches.

Bunyan, John (1628–88), Eng. writer and preacher. Imprisoned (1660–72, 1675) for ignoring royal edicts banning nonconformist preaching. Devoted himself in jail to study and writing religious works, incl. part of his classic *Pilgrim's Progress* (1678).

Bunyan, Paul, Amer. legendary folk hero of NW forests. He and his ox, Babe, are frequently subject of 'tall tales'. His 1st mention in print was in advertising pamphlet published by Red River Lumber Co., *Paul Bunyan and his Big Blue Ox* (1914).

buoy, floating object used to moor ships, to mark courses and navigable limits of channels and to indicate sunken dangers such as isolated rocks, mined waters and telegraph cables.

buran, purga, cold, fierce N winter wind of Siberia and C Asia corresponding to blizzard. Carrying snow and ice particles, often up to gale force, below 20°F, it is dangerous to life. Also strong N summer wind in the area.

Burbage, James (d. 1597), Eng. actor and theatre-builder. Built 'The Theatre' (1556), 1st theatre in England intended specifically for stage performances. Acquired house at Blackfriars (1596) for plays during winter months. After his death his sons re-erected 'The Theatre', at Bankside, renaming it 'The Globe'.

Burbage, Richard (c. 1567–1619), Eng. actor, leading tragedian. Acted in orig. Shakespearean productions. He and his brother, Cuthbert, inherited shares in their father's theatres, ' The Theatre' and 'Black-

Burdock

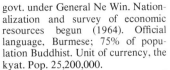

member of Samuel Johnson's circle. Influenced Whigs by stand on Amer. colonies through his speeches and writing, esp. *Thoughts on the Cause of the Present Discontents* (1770), advocating conciliation. He attempted to limit Crown patronage, exposed injustices in India and tried to make scapegoat of WARREN HASTINGS. Though he advocated practical reform, his *Reflections on the Revolution in France* (1790), made him the conservative spokesman of Europe and led to his break with Whigs (1791).

govt. under General Ne Win. Nationalization and survey of economic resources begun (1964). Official language, Burmese; 75% of population Buddhist. Unit of currency, the kyat. Pop. 25,200,000.

Burmese, Sino-Tibetan language; 15 million speakers in Burma.

Burmese cat, only natural breed of brown domestic cat. Silvery coated type, blue Burmese, has been bred. *See* illus. p. 125.

Burne-Jones, Sir Edward (1833–98), Eng. painter, one of the Pre-Raphaelite brotherhood.

Bumble bees : female, worker, male

friars', and transported 'The Theatre' to Bankside where it was reassembled as 'The Globe'.

Burbank, Luther (1849–1926), Amer. plant breeder. Created many new varieties of flowers, fruits and vegetables.

burbot, eelpout [US], **ling** [UK], freshwater fish of genus *Lota*, with large mouth and eel-like body, it has 2 small barbels on the nose and larger one on the chin. Species include European *Lota* and Amer. *L. maculosa* varieties.

Burckhardt, Jacob Christoph (1818–97), Swiss historian: published *The Civilization of the Renaissance in Italy* (1860), expressing view that culture patterns were peculiar to their age.

burdock, *Arctium lappa,* tall spreading large-leaved perennial plant native to Europe, found in N America.

Burger, Warren Earl (1907–), Amer. judge. Appointed (1969) Chief Justice of Supreme Court.

burgh, Scot. form of Eng. BOROUGH. Founded by charter from Scot. crown or by lords by royal licence; today may be royal, parliamentary, or police burgh. Has powers to elect own provost, bailies, council and magistrate. Scot. urban local government units also termed burghs.

Burgoyne, John (1722–92), Brit. general and statesman. Successful against Spanish in Seven Years War. Member of Parliament (1768); helped reform policy in India. Led poorly equipped, untrained Brit. force in Amer. Revolution and surrendered (1777) at Saratoga.

Burgundy, region of SE France. Kingdom created at fall of Roman Empire; became duchy (9th cent.) and remained powerful state until death of Charles the Bold (1477); annexed by Louis XI as prov. of France. Famous for wines, including Chablis and Burgundy.

Burke, Edmund (1729–97), Anglo-Irish political writer and statesman,

Burma, republic of SE Asia. Area: 261,789 sq. mi.; cap. Rangoon. Union of Burma comprises Burma, administrated directly by central govt., and federated states of Shan, Kachin, Karen, Kayah and Chin. Four main physical regions: 1) Alluvial Irrawaddy basin, one of main rice-growing areas of the world; rice constitutes 75% of Burma's exports. Oilfields exploited since 1871. Climate trop. 2) N and W mountain ranges rise to 19,000 ft. Mongolian tribes, incl. Kachins and Chins grow rice and

millet. The Arakan Yoma ranges are noted for teak and rubber. 3) The Karens of the Shan plateau and the mountainous Kayah state grow poor crops of maize, millet and upland rice. Tin, silver, lead, tungsten and teak are exploited. 4) Narrow coastal strip with over 200 in. annual rainfall. Rice, rubber and fruit grown. Burmese dynasties ruled until the annexation (19th cent.) by British who made it dependency of India. Separated from India (1937) and left Brit. Commonwealth (1957). Union of Burma estab. (1948) with surrounding areas joining as semi-autonomous states. Army took over govt. (1958), civil rule restored (1960), another army coup (1962) led to estab. of revolutionary

Burnet, Sir [Frank] Macfarlane, FRS (1899–), Austral. virologist and physician; awarded Nobel Prize for Medicine and Physiology (1960) with Sir Peter Brian Medawar, for their work in immunological tolerance.

Burnet rose, *Rosa pimpinellifolia, R. spinossissima,* dense shrub of rose family found near sea; unlike most wild roses has purple-black fruits.

Burney, Frances ('Fanny') (1752–1840), Eng. novelist. Her diary was published 1889. Novels include *Evelina* (1778), *Cecilia* (1782) and *Camilla* (1796).

burning bush, in OT, bush out of which voice of God spoke to Moses on Mt. Horab (*Exodus* iii 2), assuring Moses of deliverance of Israel from Egypt. Emblem of Presbyterian Church owing to its scriptural connotations and in remembrance of its early persecution.

Burns, Robert (1759–96), Scot. poet, considered Scotland's national poet. Most successful work, written in Scottish vernacular 'lallans', reveals mastery of verse-forms. Wrote lyrics on love, nature, and peasant life, merciless satires on spiritual and temporal pride. Best-known include *To a Mouse, To a Mountain Daisy, Holy Willie's Prayer* and longer poems, *The Cotter's Saturday Night* and *Tam o'Shanter.* His birthday, 25 January, is celebrated by Burns Suppers throughout the world.

Burnt Njal, hero of best-known early Icelandic Sagas. Plot concerns blood feud between Njal and Gunnar, resulting in murders, culminating in Njal's death by fire in his house.

Burr, Aaron (1756–1836), Amer. politician. Entered New York state politics (1784); US Senator (1791–7). Organized Republican victory in N.Y. election (1800). Tied with Thomas Jefferson for presidency; elected Vice Pres. by House of Representatives; killed Alexander Hamilton in duel (1804) after being defeated in N.Y. gubernatorial election. Involved in plan to colonize SW; tried for treason (1807); acquitted, left for England; later returned to US.

burrowing owl, *Speotyto cunicularia,* small owl, once common in America and the W Indies. Lives in burrows, feeds mainly on insects; more diurnal than other owls, migrates in winter.

Burton, Richard, orig. Richard Jenkins (1925–), Brit. actor. Shakespearean roles have included Henry V, Othello and Hamlet. Films include *Look Back in Anger, Becket, Who's Afraid of Virginia Woolf?*.

Burton, Sir Richard Francis (1821–90), Eng. diplomat, explorer, writer and linguist; translated *Arabian Nights* (16 vols., 1885–8). Journeyed (1853) to Mecca and Medina. Penetrated uncharted E central Africa; discovered L. Tanganyika; explored W Africa and Brazil.

Burundi, republic, formerly **Ruanda-Urundi**. Area: 10,747 sq. mi.; cap. Bujumbura. Borders on L. Tanganyika, Africa. High plateau region with

tropical climate and irregular rainfall. Country is mainly agricultural: chief crops are coffee and cotton; some minerals are mined. The official languages are French and Kirundi; Bantu and Kiswahili dialects are spoken. First European exploration (1894); soon after incorporated into German East Africa. After World War 1 territory was administered by Belgium under a League of Nations mandate and later (1946–62) as UN trust territory. Estab. as independent kingdom of Burundi. In 1965 king was deposed and P.M. proclaimed Burundi a republic, declaring himself president. Pop. 3,274,000.

burying beetle, nocturnal carrion beetle of genus *Necrophorus*. Amer. carrion beetle, *N. marginatus* has dull red markings on fore wings.

Busch, Adolf Georg Wilhelm (1891–1952), Ger. violinist and com-

poser. Soloist and leader of Busch String Quartet, partnered Rudolf Serkin. Composed choral symphonies, concertos, chamber works and songs.

Busch, Fritz (1890–1951), Ger. conductor. Best known as conductor (1934–9) of Glyndebourne Opera.

Busch, Wilhelm (1832–1908), Ger. humorist and illustrator, famous as writer of *Max and Montz* (1865), a satire of bourgeois complacency.

bush buck, harnessed antelope, *Tragelaphus scriptus,* small, trop. African antelope of savannah and forest, with dark red coat with white spots and stripes; male has spirally twisted lyre-shaped horns.

bush wolf, name for COYOTE.

bushbaby, galago, night ape, small African lemur of the loris family. Long-legged and agile nocturnal mammal with enormous eyes; soft thick silky fur, mainly insectivorous. Largest species is thick-tailed bushbaby, *Galago crassicandatus*.

bushido, ancient code of honour and conduct of Jap. nobility. Virtues are loyalty, austerity, self-sacrifice and indifference to pain. Basis for emperor worship.

bushmaster, *Lachesis mutus,* large venomous snake, of C and trop. S America. Most venomous is pit viper. Female lays eggs in burrows of other animals and protects them until they hatch. Colour and spotted markings make bushmaster almost invisible.

Bushmen, remnants of aboriginal race of S Africa, now confined to C and N Kalahari desert. Nomadic hunters living in groups of 50 to 100, famous for rock painting. Language distinguished by its 'clicks'.

business cycle, fluctuations in the economy of an industrialized nation reflected in periods of prosperity and economic recession, depressions and booms. Effects are more pronounced in the durable goods sector but are evident also in movements of national income, unemployment, prices, and profits.

Busoni, Ferruccio Benvenuto (1866–1924), Ital. pianist and composer. Better known as pianist, teacher, and arranger, esp. piano arrangements of J. S. Bach's organ pieces. Works include chamber music and many piano pieces.

bustard, family of large-bodied game birds of the Old World and Australia. Stout legs and short toes enable it to run swiftly. The great bustard *Otis tarda,* with 8 ft. wing-span, is largest European land bird. Found in England until 1838, still exists in parts of Europe and Asia. Other species

Buzzard

include the little bustard, *O. tetrax* and Austral. *Ardeotis australis* which kills snakes.

butcherbird, any of several species of shrike, esp. European *Lanius exubitor* and the N Amer. *L. borealis*, and some Austral. species of magpie. Name derives from the bird's habit of impaling or wedging its prey to facilitate eating. Prey includes large insects, small lizards and birds, mice and amphibians.

Bute, island in Firth of Clyde, W Scotland, forming, with Arran, Great and Little Cumbraes, Holy Isle, Inchmarnock and Pladda, county of Bute. Area: 218 sq. mi.; county town, Rothesay. Popular tourist resort. Pop. of county (1966) 13,000.

Bute, 3rd Earl of *see* STUART, JOHN.

Butenandt, Adolf (1903–), Ger. biochemist, awarded but forced to decline Nobel Prize for Chemistry (1939) with Leopold Ruzicka, for determining structure of progestin, and for isolating and naming androsterone.

Butler, Nicholas (1862–1947), Amer. educator. Promoted educational reform, helped establish Carnegie Endowment for International Peace. Shared Nobel Peace Prize (1931) with Jane Addams.

Butler, R[ichard] A[usten], Baron Butler of Saffron Walden (1902–), Brit. statesman. Entered Parliament (1929) as Conservative. As Minister of Education he piloted the Education Act (1944), providing free primary and secondary education for all. A leading Tory advocate of social reform, revised party policies while in opposition (1945–51) and led the country out of wartime austerity as Chanc. of the Exchequer (1951–5).

Butler, Samuel (1612–80), Eng. poet and satirist. Main work was poem

Byzantine Mosaic in San Vitale, Ravenna

Hudibras (1663–78), a satire on Puritan hypocrisy.

Butler, Samuel (1835–1902), Eng. novelist, translator and critic. Books include *Erewhon* (1872), an account of life in an imaginary half-utopian half-colonial country; *The Way of All Flesh* (1903) was an autobiog. novel. Opponent of 'mechanistic' Darwinism; critic of Christianity.

buttercup, herbs of Ranunculaceae family with alternate leaves and glossy yellow flowers, of cooler regions of N hemisphere, incl. anemone, crowfoot, celandine and buttercup. Pernicious weed, among species are tall perennial meadow buttercup [UK] bitter buttercup [US], *R. acris*; creeping buttercup, *R. repons* and bulbous buttercup, *R. bulbosus.*

butterfly bush, *Buddleia davidii,* shrub of *Buddleia* genus, downy white undersides to leaves and long spikes of scented mauve flowers, attracts butterflies. Native to China, popular garden plant.

butternut, *Juglans cinerea,* white walnut tree of walnut family of eastern N America; it is fast-growing and bears sweet edible nuts yielding oil. Kernel used in candy and ice-cream; also pickled.

buttcrwort, family, Lentibulariaceae, of insectivorous plants found in European bogs and wet moors, of genus *Pinguicula.* Common butterwort, *P. vulgaris,* hairy perennial with solitary flower, oblong sticky leaves have margins rolling inwards to trap insects.

buttonquail, genus *Turnix,* of quail family inhabiting dry bush of Africa, Australia and S Asia; *c.* 6 in. long, 3-toed, with booming call. Females more brightly coloured and belligerent than males and initiate courtship.

Buxtehude, Diderik (1637–1707), Danish organist and composer; compositions include organ and harpsichord pieces, and church cantatas.

buxus, genus of small evergreen trees and shrubs of box family native to S Europe and parts of Asia. Often cultivated in ornamental gardens.

buzzard, any of numerous heavily-built hawks with short broad wings and soaring flight. Diet includes rabbits, voles, mice, some birds, and carrion. Two young reared yearly. In US, buzzard refers to the vulture.

Byelorussian SSR, Belorussian SSR or **White Russia,** constituent republic of European Russia. Area: 80,150 sq. mi.; cap. Minsk. Occupies low-lying plain divided by Dnieper, Dvina and Nieman rivers; forested and sloping S to Pripet Marshes. During World War 1, occupied by Poland, but by end of World War 2, Russian once more. Chief occupations: agriculture, stock-raising, forestry. Pop. (1965) 8,533,000.

Byng, Julian Hedworth George, 1st Viscount Byng of Vimy (1862–1935), Gov.-General of Canada (1921–6). Brit. army officer commanding Canadian Corps during capture of Vimy Ridge (1917) in World War 1. At the end of his term as Gov.-General was faced with constitutional crisis precipitated by his refusal to grant P.M. Mackenzie King's request for dissolution of parl.

Byrd, Charlie (1925–), Amer. guitarist who introduced Sp. guitar into the jazz ensemble.

Byrd, Harry F[lood] (1887–1966), Amer. politician. Gov. of Virginia (1926–30). US Senator (1933–65); leader of conservative Democrats. His brother, **Richard Evelyn Byrd** (1888–1957) was aviator and explorer; 1st to fly over both N and S Poles. Led expeditions to Antarctica (1929, 1933). Later given charge of all US Antarctic activities.

Byrd, William (*c.* 1543–1623), Eng. musician, joint organist (1574) with Tallis of Chapel Royal.

Byrnes, James F[rancis] (1879–), Amer. politician. Entered politics as Democratic Congressman from S Carolina (1911–25); Senator (1931–41); Associate Justice of US Supreme Court (1941–2). As Sec. of State (1945–7) tried to mend post-war differences with the USSR. Opposed federal centralization tendencies during tenure as Gov. of S Carolina (1951–5).

Byron, Lord *see* GORDON, GEORGE.

Byzantine art, style of art blending Oriental and Hellenistic traditions, flourished in (Christian) Byzantine Empire from 5th cent. In architecture, substituted circular church building and pendentive cupola for straight lines of Roman basilica and introduced 3 aisles, apse, altar and bell tower. Much Christian symbolism originated in forms developed during this period. Main centres and remains are at Constantinople, Ravenna, and in E, Trebizond and Mistra.

Byzantine Empire, E part of Roman Empire, sometimes called the Eastern Empire. DIOCLETIAN divided administration among four emperors. This experiment led to 20 yrs. civil strife after his abdication (305). Reunited (324) by Constantine the Great, Byzantium dates from building of Constantinople (330) when its division from Rome acquired religious and national characteristics. It was Christian and Greek. From fall of Rome (476) until *c.* 1050, a major power and bulwark against Asian invasions. Ruled by absolute monarchy, it disappeared with fall of Constantinople (1453) to the Turks.

Byzantium, city on the shores of the Bosporus, on one of the 7 hills of modern Istanbul. First estab. (*c.* 657 BC), by Megarian colonists. Destroyed (196) by Romans. Constantine the Great chose (330) site for Constantinople, later capital of Byzantine Empire.

Burmese Cat

C

Cabal [Heb: *kabbalah*, hidden knowledge], secret group of advisers to Charles II of England. Name from initials of the members (Clifford, Arlington, Buckingham, Ashley and Lauderdale).

cabbage, *Brassica oleracea*, leafy vegetable of mustard family from which cauliflower, broccoli, kohl rabi, Brussels sprouts, kale and pe-tsai are derived. Native to E Europe, it has been cultivated for more than 4,000 years. Varieties are green, white and red, with varying leaf forms.

cabbage white butterfly, *Pieris brassicae*, larvae of which feed on cruciferous plants esp. cabbage.

cabinet, a group of executive advisers who themselves usually head administrative govt. departments. In UK, where the system originated, the cabinet has usually been a body of ministers selected from the majority party in House of Commons. The Brit. system has been widely imitated, particularly by Brit. Commonwealth countries. In continental European countries, where electoral procedure often leads to no overall parliamentary majority, cabinet members must be chosen from a coalition of competing parties. In US, cabinet members are not selected from either House of Congress and are responsible only to the Pres., who appoints them subject to Senate approval and may remove them at will.

Cabot, John (1450–98), Eng. navi-

Cactus *Astrophytum ornatum*

gator and explorer; prob. b. Italy. Went to England and obtained letters patent for voyage in search of route to Asia (1496). He reached the N Amer. shore somewhere between Labrador and Maine (1497). Discovery of the Grand Banks led to development of fishing industry.

Cabot, Sebastian (1483–1557), Eng. explorer, son of JOHN CABOT. Made maps for Henry VIII of England and Ferdinand of Spain. He explored Rio de la Plata and founded the Company of Merchant Adventurers of London to search for a NE passage to China which was not found until 19th cent.

cacao *see* COCOA.

cachalot, sperm whale, *Physeter catodon*, toothed whale of warmer ocean waters, up to 60 ft. long. The massive head has a cavity filled with spermaceti. It secretes AMBERGRIS.

Cacoyannis, Michael (1922–), Gk. film director, known for *Electra* (1960), *Zorba the Greek* (1964) and stage productions of *The Trojan Women* (1965) and *Mourning becomes Electra* (1967).

cactus, plant of family Cactaceae comprising several hundred species, native to wet and dry trop. regions of N and S America. Latter species adapt to drought. Genera include night blooming cactus *Cercus*, christmas cactus *Zygocactus*, and orchid cactus *Epiphylum*.

cactus moth, *Cactoblastis cactorum*, moth of family Pyralididae, destructive to cacti. Introduced to Australia to control prickly pear.

caddis fly, moth-like insect of order *Trichoptera*. Larva is used as bait.

Caddo, agricultural tribe of N Amer. plains Indians; occupied territory in Louisiana, Texas and Arkansas.

cadenza, orchestral pause near end of 1st or 3rd movement of concerto where soloist extemporizes. Since 19th cent. most are written down.

Cadiz, city and seaport of S Spain, cap. of Cadiz prov., on gulf of Cadiz. Founded by Phoenicians *c.* 1100 BC, flourished under Romans. Monopolized trade with Sp. America (18th cent.). Exports sherry, salt, olives, figs, cork and fish. Pop. (1966) 122,568.

cadmium, element, soft, white, divalent metal, stable at ordinary temperatures in dry air; compounds highly toxic.

Cadmus, in Gk. myth., son of Agenor. Sent with brothers to search for sister EUROPA (abducted by Zeus) and forbidden to return without her. Founded city of Thebes.

Caernarvonshire, county of NW

Saguaro or Giant Cactus

Wales. Area: 569 sq. mi.; county town, Caernarvon; main towns, Conway, Bangor. Main occupation agriculture; slate and light industry. Site of Snowdonia National Park. Pop. (1966) 120,000.

Caesar, Gaius Julius (*c.* 102–44 BC), Roman statesman, soldier and writer. Distinguished service in 2nd Mithridatic War (83–81 BC); praetor and *pontifex maximus* (62 BC). Formed 1st Triumvirate with Pompey and Crassus (60 BC), governor of Gaul (58–49 BC). Opposition from Pompey and Senate caused Civil War, ending in defeat of Pompey at Pharsalus (48 BC); pursued Pompey to Egypt, met Cleopatra. Murdered by conspirators under Brutus and Cassius (15 Mar. 44 BC). Re-estab. order and economy in Rome, noted for clemency. Books, *Gallic War* and *Civil War*, exceptionally lucid in style.

Caetano, Marcello (1906–), Portuguese lawyer and politician. Occupied political and university posts before succeeding ANTONIO SALAZAR as President (1969).

caffeine, alkaloid of xanthine group of stimulant drugs. Discovered acciden-

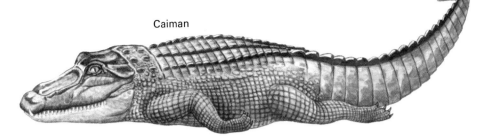

tally (1821) by Robiquet in coffee and by Oudry (1827) in tea.

Cagliostro, Count Alessandro di, orig. Giuseppe Balsamo (1743–95), Ital. adventurer. Travelled in Europe posing as physician and alchemist. Condemned (1789) as heretic and sorcerer by Inquisition; d. in prison.

Caillié, René (1799–1838), Fr. explorer. Entered Timbuktu in disguise after living among Arabs and learning their languages and customs.

caiman, reptile of ALLIGATOR family of C and S America. Species include black caiman, *Melanosuchus niger*; and broadnosed, *Caiman latirostius,* 6 ft. long, from E Brazil.

Cain, James M[allahan] (1892–), Amer. writer of crime fiction, best known for *The Postman Always Rings Twice* (1934).

cairn terrier, dog of Scot. origin, trained to rout animals out of burrows. Weight *c.* 15 lb. Colours are grey, brindle or sandy.

cairngorm, smoky-brown or smoky-yellow variety of crystalline QUARTZ, named after its Scot. locality.

Cairngorms, part of Grampian mountains, N Scotland, containing a nature reserve. Highest summit, Ben Macdhui (4,296 ft.). Popular skiing and climbing area.

Cairo, cap. of United Arab Republic, at head of Nile delta. Commercial and manufacturing centre of UAR. Founded (969) near ancient Egyptian cap., Memphis. Under Turkish rule (1517–1798); occupied by British (1882–1936). Contains citadel (built 12th cent.) and Moslem university in Mosque of El Azhar. Pop. (1966) 3,346,000.

Caithness, county of NE Scotland, most N point being John O'Groats; area: 686 sq. mi.; county town, Wick.

Cairo

Flat and treeless, sheep-rearing and fishing main occupations. Pop. (1966) 28,000.

calabrese *see* BROCCOLI.

Calais, important seaport of Pas-de-Calais department, N France. Eng. possession (1347–1558). Pop. (1964) 70,707.

Calchas, Gk. soothsayer who foretold length of Trojan War and declared that only sacrifice of Iphigenia in Aulis would enable Gk. fleet to sail and that restoration of Chryseis to her father would end plague in Gk. camp at Troy.

calcite ($CaCO_3$), common mineral form of calcium carbonate, usually white. Forms include chalk, marble, limestone.

calcium (Ca), greyish white metal prepared by electrolysis of calcium chloride. Found in many compound states. Essential constituent of living organisms, found in bones, teeth and sea shells. *See* CALCITE.

calculus, mathematical process of reasoning by use of symbols, orig. studied by ARCHIMEDES, and advanced by DESCARTES. *See* DIFFERENTIAL CALCULUS.

Calcutta, seaport in W Bengal, India. Founded by Britain (1690); captured by the Bengal nawab (1756) who imprisoned 146 people overnight in a small room (the 'Black Hole') leaving 23 survivors. Exports include jute and tea. Pop. (1965) 3,026,000.

Calder, Alexander (1898–), Amer. abstract sculptor best known for his 'mobiles' and 'stabiles', carefully balanced constructions of metal plates, rods and wires.

caldera, broad volcanic crater usually formed by subsidence, sometimes occupied by a lake. Best known in N America is Crater Lake, Oregon.

Calderón de la Barca, Pedro (1600–81), prolific Sp. dramatist. Soldier, court poet and priest (from 1651). Most famous works include *La vida es sueño, El magico prodigioso.*

Caldwell, Erskine Preston (1903–), Amer. author who observed with humour and sympathy predicament of Southern poor whites, *e.g.* in *Tobacco Road* (1932) and *God's Little Acre* (1933).

Caldwell, [Janet Miriam] Taylor (1900–), Amer. writer of historical and other novels, incl. *Dynasty of Death* (1938) and *Dear and Glorious Physician* (1959).

Caledonia, Roman name for N Britain used, mostly in literature, to denote all Scotland.

Calcite

Caledonian Canal, canal *c.* 62 mi. long, in N Scotland, constructed (1803–47) to link Lochs Ness, Oich, Lochy, Eil and Linnhe; connects the Moray Firth and Loch Linnhe.

calendar, systematic division of yr. into months and days. Ancient Chinese and Egyptian calendars based on phases of moon with adjustments to fit solar yr. Julius Caesar introduced Julian calendar (45 BC), dividing yr. into 365 days and inserting additional day every 4th yr., by 1582 inaccurate by 10 days. Pope Gregory XIII ordered readjustment, not adopted by Brit. dominions and N Amer. colonies until 1752. Christian calendar starts from accepted birth-date of Christ; Moslem from Hegira, flight of Mohammed to Medina (AD 622 in Julian calendar); used in United Arab Republic, Iran, Turkey, *etc.*

California

Calgary, city in Alberta, Canada. Communications, oil refining and meat packing centre. Pop. (1964) 323,000.

Calhoun, John Caldwell (1782– 1850), Amer. politician and philosopher; fighter for states' rights. Congressman and Senator from S Carolina, Sec. of War to James Monroe (1817–25), Vice Pres. to John Q. Adams (1825–9) and Andrew Jackson (1829–32). Split with Jackson during NULLIFICATION crisis (1832). Sec. of State (1844–5).

calico moth *See* TIGER MOTH.

Calicut *see* KOZHIKODE.

California, Pacific coast state of SW US. Area: 156,573 sq. mi.; cap. Sacramento; main towns, Los Angeles, San Francisco, Oakland and San Diego. Central Valley is walled by COAST RANGES and SIERRA NEVADA, farther S are vast wastes. Extensive irrigation necessary. Fruit and grains main agric. products. Exploration began 16th cent. and Spanish estab. 1st colony (1769). Control passed to Mexico (1822), but area ceded to US (1848); · state (1850). Gold strike (1848) and completion of 1st transcontinental railway (1869) brought settlers. Industrial development of S and real-estate boom (1920s) increased population. Petroleum, aircraft, textiles, film and tourist industries. Pop. (1964) 17,347,000.

California, University of, complex of 9 campuses organized under Californian state constitution, founded 1868. Campuses include Berkeley, Los Angeles and San Diego. Free Speech (1964) controversy at Berkeley sparked 1960s student unrest in US.

California grey whale, *Rhachianecres glaucus,* N Pacific whale up to 45 ft. long. Migrates from Arctic to warmer shallow waters.

California Institute of Technology, Pasadena, Calif., US, privately supported college (founded 1891), noted for scientific research.

Californian sea lion, *Zalophus,* variety of sea lion less than 9 ft. long, commonly trained for circuses.

Caligula (AD 12–41) [Lat: *caligae,* 'little boots'], nickname of Gaius Caesar Germanicus, 3rd Roman Emperor (37–41), succeeded Tiberius; later became insane. Said to have made his horse a consul. Assassinated by a tribune.

caliphate, temporal and spiritual headship of Islam, successors to Mohammed. First caliph, ABU BAKR. Title used by Selim I (1517), and Ottoman rulers until abolished (1924).

calla lily, plant native to trop. and S Africa. Best known species are *Zantedeschia rehmannii, Z. aethiopica* and *Z. elliottiana.*

Callaghan, Morley Edward (1903–), Canadian writer whose works include *That Summer in Paris* (1963)

describing his time in Paris with Hemingway, Scott Fitzgerald and James Joyce.

Callas, Maria Meneghini (1923–), Gk.-American opera singer. Soprano, specializes in Ital. operatic roles, esp. Rossini, Puccini, Verdi.

Callicrates (5th cent. BC), Gk. architect; builder, with Ictinus, of the Parthenon (447–432 BC).

calligraphy, art of elegant writing or penmanship; term is used esp. for works displaying Chinese characters or ornamental types of Arabic script.

Calliope, in Gk. and Roman myth., Muse of Epic Poetry.

calliope, steam organ, keyboard instrument, invented in America (1880s); comprises set of whistles blown by steam under pressure.

Calvert, George, 1st Baron Baltimore (*c.* 1580–1632), Brit. colonizer. Granted territory N of Potomac (1632), which became prov. of MARYLAND. His grandson, **Charles Calvert, 3rd Baron Baltimore** (1637– 1715), succeeded to proprietorship (1675), but was overthrown by revolt (1689).

Calvin, John (1509–64), Fr. Protestant theologian. Broke with Catholicism (1533) and became leader in REFORMATION. Calvinist doctrine stressed thrift, hard work, sobriety. Calvinist theology, set out in *Institute of the Christian Religion* (1536),

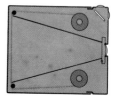

rejected papal authority, accepted justification by faith alone and systemized doctrine of PREDESTINATION.

Calvin, Melvin, FRS (1911–), Amer. chemist. Awarded Nobel Prize for Chemistry (1961) for studies of photosynthesis.

Calvinism, Protestant doctrine formulated by JOHN CALVIN. Adopted by

Camberwell
Beauty Butterfly

Covenanters in Scotland, Puritans in England and New England, Huguenots in France.

Calypso, in Gk. legend, daughter of Atlas; lived on island Ogygia where ODYSSEUS was stranded. Tried unsuccessfully to persuade him to remain with her.

calypso, humorous extemporized song, usually with topical or amatory theme, sung to traditional Caribbean melodies and accompaniment.

Camargue, La, marshy island 28 mi. long in Rhône delta, France. Cattle ranching in S; vines and rice in N. Provençal spoken and bulls bred for bullfighting.

camberwell beauty, mourning cloak, yellow edge, *Nymphalis antiopa,* butterfly of Europe and N America.

Cambodia, kingdom of SE Asia, prob. founded by Hindu migrants in 1st

cent. AD. Formerly a Fr. protectorate, declared independence during Indo-

Dromedary or single-humped riding Camel

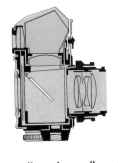

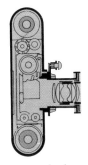

Eng. universities. Some Oxford scholars went to Cambridge (1209); first college, Peterhouse, founded (1284). Now composed of 26 colleges. Women granted full membership of the university (1948).

Cambridgeshire and **Isle of Ely,** flat inland county of England, incl. the Fens. Area 831 sq. mi.; county town, Cambridge. Produces grain, fruit and sugar beet. Isle of Ely is district within the Fens. Pop. (1966) 294,000.

Cambyses, king of Persia (529–521 BC), son of Cyrus the Great. Incorporated Phoenicia, Cyprus and Egypt into Persian Empire.

camel, mammal of Tylopod group allied to alpaca and vicuña. Bactrian camel, *Camelus bactrianus,* of cold rocky deserts of C Asia, has 2 dorsal humps of fatty tissue and a shaggy coat. Arabian camel, *C. dromedarius,* of N Africa and SW Asia, introduced into Australia, has 1 hump. The dromedary, a racing or riding form of Arabian camel, can survive for 2 weeks without water.

Cameroons and S section of Brit. Cameroons. Exports include cocoa. Rich mineral and metal resources. Came under German control (1885) as Kamerun, but divided among French and British after World War 1 as mandates. Independent (1960), joined by Brit. prov. (1961). Pop. (1966) 5,350,000.

Camilla, in Roman legend, daughter of Volscian king, joined Latins in war against AENEAS and killed.

Cameras: (from left to right) basic and modern box cameras; folding camera; 35mm miniature camera; reflex camera; half frame miniature camera.

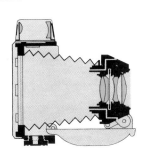

China war (1953). The Mekong river waters a fertile alluvial plain; rice and fish are chief products. Ancient ruins of Angkor Wat are great tourist attraction. Cap. is Phnôm-Penh. Pop. 6,320,000.

Cambodian *see* MON KHMER.
Cambrian *see* GEOLOGICAL TABLE.
Cambrian mountains *see* WALES.
Cambridge, Alexander Augustus Frederick William Alfred George, 1st Earl of Athlone (1874–1957), Brit. soldier and statesman. Distinguished service in South African War and World War 1 before appointments as Gov.-General of Union of South Africa (1923–31) and of Canada (1940–46).
Cambridge University, one of oldest

camellia, flowering evergreen shrub or small tree of Ternstroemiaceae family, native to Asia. Cultivated in warm climates and greenhouses. Most important economically is Tea Plant, *C. chinensis,* from India and China. Garden varieties belong to *C. japonica, C. sasanqua* and *C. reticulata,* and include both greenhouse and outdoor species.

camera, light-proof container with lens that focuses optical image to be recorded on black and white or colour film. *See* PHOTOGRAPHY.

Cameroon, Federal Republic of, [République Fédérale du Caméroun] equatorial W African country. Area: 183,581 sq. mi.; cap. Yaounde; main city, Douala. Comprises former Fr.

camomile, chamomile, *Anthemis,* genus of plants of aster family. Common European species, *A. nobilis,* is used for the astringent and bitter camomile tea.

camouflage, in warfare, disguise of military objectives with artificial vegetation or paint. In animals, adoption of protective colouring to match surroundings.

camouflage, in animals, phenomenon of adaptive coloration intended to conceal or disguise.

campanile, in architecture (esp. Ital.) a bell-tower, most commonly built beside or attached to a church. The most famous is probably the Leaning Tower of Pisa; St. Mark's, Venice, has another famous tower.

Canada: floating logs downriver to paper mills

University Avenue, Toronto

campanula, plant of Bellflower family with bell-shaped flowers. Found in temp. parts of N hemisphere and widely cultivated. Harebell *C. rotundifolia* and Canterbury bell *C. medium* are well-known species.

Campbell, Donald (1921–67), holder of world land speed record for wheel-driven car (429·311 mph) and world water speed record (328 mph) achieved on last and fatal attempt in *Bluebird K7.*

Campbell [Ignatius] Roy [Dunnachiel] (1902–57), South African poet and war correspondent. Best known work, *The Flaming Terrapin* (1924).

Campbell, Scot. noble family. **Archibald Campbell, 5th Earl of Argyll** (1530–73), inconsistent in his support of Mary, Queen of Scots; thought to have helped in Lord Darnley's murder. Later Lord Chanc. under James VI. **Archibald Campbell, 8th Earl and 1st Marquess of Argyll** (1607–61), statesman who, after surrender of Charles I (1646), tried to secure Presbyterian settlement in England; crowned Charles II in Scotland, but executed for treason at Restoration. His son, **Archibald Campbell, 9th Earl of Argyll** (1629–85), both Royalist and Protestant. Opposed extreme measures against Scots Presbyterians under Restoration. Beheaded for role in Monmouth rebellion against James II. **John Campbell, 2nd Duke of Argyll** and **Duke of Greenwich** (1678–1743), Scot. general; put down Jacobite rebellion (1715). His brother, **Archibald Campbell, 3rd Duke of Argyll** (1682–1761), Commissioner for the Union (1706); Scot. peer in United Parl. **John Douglas Sutherland Campbell, 9th Duke of Argyll** (1845–1914), Governor-General of Canada (1878–83). Elected to House of Commons as Liberal (1868) and Unionist (1895) before succeeding to title.

Campbell-Bannerman, Sir Henry (1836–1908), Brit. statesman. Entered Parliament (1868) as Liberal, was Sec. of the Admiralty (1882–4) and Sec. for Ireland (1884). Became party leader (1898) and P.M. (1905).

camphor, soft, white, translucent solid, essential oil from wood of CAMPHOR TREE. Volatile, antiseptic, with strong smell; mild anaesthetic and moth repellant.

camphor tree, *Laurus camphora,* tree of laurel family, native to China, Japan and Formosa. Camphor production historically important; most commercial camphor now synthetic.

campion, plant of pink family. Species include red campion, *Lychnis dioica,* pink flowered hairy perennial of Great Britain, moss campion, *Silene acaulis,* perennial alpine plentiful in Scotland and sea campion, *S. maritima.*

Campion, Edmond (c. 1540–81), Eng. b. Jesuit and martyr. Attempted to make converts and strengthen R.C. cause against Elizabeth I; was captured and executed.

Campion, Thomas (1567–1620), Eng. lutanist and poet, wrote songs to own music, collected in 3 *Books of Airs* (1601–17).

Campo Formio, Treaty of (Oct. 1797), Fr.-Austrian peace treaty at end of Napoleon's Ital. campaign. Austria ceded Austrian Netherlands to France and secretly promised France the left bank of the Rhine. The Venetian Republic was dissolved and most of it ceded to Austria; the Ionian Islands to France; the remainder to new Cisalpine Republic.

campos, trop. grasslands of C Brazil incl. Matto Grosso; cattle-grazing area.

Camus, Albert (1913–60), Fr. writer, b. Algeria. Considered existentialist, he stressed absurd in essay *The Myth of Sisyphus* (1942), but asserted humanist values in *The Plague* (1947). Other works include *The Rebel* (1952) and *The Outsider* (1942). Awarded Nobel Prize for Literature (1957).

Canaan, OT name for region W of Jordan occupied by Israelites after Exodus. Modern name Palestine.

Canada, constitutional monarchy and member of Brit. Commonwealth, occupying most of N half of N America. Area: 3,851,809 sq. mi.; cap. Ottawa; principal cities, Montreal, Toronto, Vancouver. Regions are 1) Appalachian, along Atlantic coast; small-scale farming and mining supplemented by fishing. 2) Fertile St Lawrence lowland, lying along L. Ontario and Erie and St Lawrence R. Lowland is main population and industrial centre. Motorcars and

heavy machinery manufactured. ST LAWRENCE SEAWAY created inland ports, increasing trade possibilities for petroleum, iron ore and produce from C plain region. 3) Laurentian Shield, separating W and E Canada. 4) Great wheat-producing central plain. 5) Cordillera, section of W coast mountain system of N America. Fishing, lumbering and mining are main occupations. Water resources of Rockies supply abundant hydroelectric power. Sparsely-populated N territories are rich in untapped mineral wealth. Diversified climate; conflicting ocean currents create much rainfall and fog at both coasts. Modern Canada has dual heritage:

Niagara Falls

Expo '67, Montreal: Habitat '67 scheme

Fr. exploration and colonization in NEW FRANCE and ACADIA during 16th and 17th cent. is preserved through Fr. Canadian language and culture surviving largely in Quebec Prov. Brit. trading interests, esp. HUDSON'S BAY COMPANY, flourished in 17th cent. Ensuing rivalry culminated in Fr. defeat on PLAINS OF ABRAHAM. Subsequent Brit. colonial rule laid foundations for Confederation. CONSTITUTIONAL ACT divided country into Upper and Lower Canada; W was opened through exploration and fur-trading. Independence with BRITISH NORTH AMERICA ACT (1867). Subsequent history influenced by: 1) westward expansion; 2) growth of economic and social ties with US; 3) preservation of institutional and ideological links with Great Britain, and of Fr.-Canadian culture. Predominantly English-speaking and Protestant, presence of large (30%) and vocal French-speaking and R.C. minority has led to pattern of checks and balances within federal system of govt. Currency unit, dollar. Pop. (1966) 20,014,880.

Canada goose, *Branta canadensis,* wild goose of N America. Introduced into Europe.

Canada thistle, creeping thistle, *Cirsium arvense,* perennial plant of daisy family with deep roots. Native of Europe but extensively naturalized throughout N America.

Canadian Broadcasting Corporation (CBC), estab. 1932, public body

Canada Goose

authorized to operate broadcasting stations and networks. Programmes in English and French. Radio and TV service financed through parliamentary grants and commercial revenues. Govt.-appointed Board of Broadcast Governors constituted under 1958 Broadcasting Act, regulates public and private stations.

Canadian National Railway (CNR), estab. 1922, publicly owned national railway system, operating greatest length of track (35,000 mi.) in N America. Incorporated after private rly. failure; incl. Canadian Northern and Intercolonial.

Canadian Pacific Railway (CPR), 1st Canadian transcontinental railway, completed 1885.

canal, artificial watercourse cut to join seas (Suez, Panama), river and lakes (St Lawrence Seaway), important river systems (Rhine, Marne) for transportation.

Canal Zone (non-self-governing US territories) *see* PANAMA CANAL ZONE.

Canaris, Wilhelm (1887–1945), Ger. admiral during and after World War 1. Chief of military intelligence (1935), later conspired against Hitler; executed after 1944 attempt to assassinate him.

canary, *Serinus canarius,* finch of the Canary Is. and the Azores. Popular songbird, domesticated (16th cent.) breeds in captivity. *See* ROLLER.

Canary Islands, Sp. archipelago in N Atlantic, 60 mi. off W coast of Africa. Area: 2,807 sq. mi. Islands form 2 provinces: Santa Cruz de Tenerife (Palma, Tenerife, Gomera and Hurro) and Las Palmas (Gran Canaria, Fuerteventura, Lanzarate). Mild climate and important tourist trade. Pop. 908,000.

canasta, card game, variation of RUMMY. Originated (1949) Montevideo. Rules set by Crockfords, London.

Canada Thistle

Cross-section of the St Lawrence Seaway Canal

Canaveral, Cape *see* KENNEDY, CAPE.

Canberra, cap. of Australia in Capital Territory, SE Australia. Built (1913) as cap. city; model of town planning. Pop. (1966) 92,199.

cancer, group of diseases characterized by abnormal uncontrolled growth of cells, in mammals, esp. humans. Cause unknown, but heredity, diet and environmental factors shown to be causative. Treatments include radiation, hormone treatment and surgery.

Cancer, Tropic of *see* TROPIC OF CANCER.

Candella, Felix (1910–), Mexican architect. Most significant works, Church of Our Lady of Miracles and Radiation Institute in Mexico City.

Canna Lily

candytuft, annual or perennial herb of CABBAGE family, native to S and W Europe. Globe candytuft, *Iberis umbellata,* is cultivated species.

cane *see* BAMBOO.

cankerworm, green caterpillar of several geometrid moths.

canna, Indian shot, genus of plants of Cannaceae family, native to trop. America and Asia. Large number of hortic. varieties; *C. indica* and *C. edulis* yield kind of arrowroot.

canna lily, species of arrowroot from W Indies and C America. Granules are very large. Also known as tous-les-mois or tulema.

cannabis, marijuana, hallucinatory, non-addictive drug prepared from dried flowers of Indian hemp, *Cannabis sativa,* which also produces HASHISH. Commonly smoked mixed with tobacco.

Cannae, ancient village of SE Italy where Hannibal (216 BC) defeated Romans under Paullus and Varro.

Cannes, Fr. resort in Alpes-Maritimes dept. on the Riviera 120 mi. E of Marseilles. Enclosed on E and W by Alps and Esterel Mts. Has annual film festival. Pop. 50,100.

Canning, George (1770–1827), Eng. Tory statesman. As Foreign Min. (1807–9) planned seizure of Danish fleet (1807) at Copenhagen. Opposed decisions of CONGRESS of VERONA; aided MONROE DOCTRINE; favoured Gk. independence. P.M. (1827).

cannon, smooth-bore piece of artillery, used until 19th cent., firing shot of 24–47 lb. Term now refers to large machine guns carried by fighter aircraft.

Cannon, Annie Jump (1863–1941), Amer. astronomer. Discovered over 300 variable stars, 5 new stars, and worked out classifications.

canoe, light, wooden or wood-framed boat covered with skin or bark. Common among primitive peoples, esp. in Pacific and N America. Propelled by single- or double-bladed paddles. Modern canvas canoe modelled on birch-bark form. Sport of canoeing dates from 19th cent. Introduced (1936) to Olympic Games.

canon, musical device in which a melody is closely followed by strict imitation at different pitch.

canon law, body of eccles. law which has grown up under the auspices of the R.C. Church. In England, it is observed by the C. of E. where it does not contravene the law of the land or the royal prerogative. Only the clergy are bound by it, unless the laws are authorized by Parliament or declared old custom. Rejected in Scotland after the Reformation, it has been retained in the laws of marriage, legitimacy and succession.

Cantabrians, mountain range forming a wall between the sea and plateau of C Spain. Average ht. 4,000-5,000 ft., highest peak Torre de Cerredo (8,678 ft.). Rich in iron and coal; rivers flowing from them provide hydro-electric power.

cantaloupe *see* MELON.

cantata, sacred or secular music of several movements. Popular in 18th cent. for soloists, orchestra and usually chorus; similar to oratorio but shorter.

Canterbury, city and county borough of Kent on R. Stour, 56 mi. SE of London. Since 597 eccles. cap. of England, Archbishop being Primate of England. Cathedral, scene of THOMAS À BECKET's murder, is

The Grand Canyon, Arizona

Canterbury Cathedral

12th–14th cent. Gothic Univ. of Kent founded at Canterbury (1965). Pop. (1961) 30,376.

Canterbury bell *see* CAMPANULA.

canterelle *see* CHANTERELLE.

Canton, cap. and seaport of Kwantung prov., China, on Chukiang R., 80 mi. from the sea. Pop. 1,840,000.

Canton and Enderbury Islands, Pacific Is. claimed by US guano companies (1856). Negotiation (1939) led to arrangements for joint Brit.-US use, admin. for 50 yrs. Trans-oceanic air base.

Cantonese *see* CHINESE.

Cantor, Eddie (1892–1964), Amer. comedy actor. Film debut, *Kid Boots* (1926); also starred in Ziegfeld Follies.

Canute or **Cnut II** (*c.* 994–1035),

king of England (1016–35), Denmark (1018–28) and Norway (1028–35). Invaded England (1015) but allowed Edmund Ironside to co-rule until his death (1016) then subdued England. Reign noted for peace, sympathy with Church, codification of laws.

canvasback *see* POCHARD.

canyon, cañon, narrow, deep gorge, usually formed in arid or semi-arid areas by rivers cutting into soft rock. Grand Canyon, NW Arizona, US, cut by Colorado R., with walls up to 6,000 ft. high.

Capablanca, José Raoul (1888–1942), Cuban chess player; became a champion at 12 and won World Championship (1921–7).

cape, headland or pointed piece of land jutting into sea or lake.

Cape Breton Island, NE part of Nova Scotia, Canada. Area: 3,970 sq. mi. Sydney and Glace Bay are coalmining cities. National Park occupies rugged, forested N peninsulas. Pop. (1960 est.) 200,000.

cape buffalo, *Syncerus caffer,* species of wild cattle, Bovidae, of S and E Africa; once numerous, decimated by rinderpest.

cape hunting dog, *Lycaon pictus,* wild dog found on grasslands of S and E Africa, 4 toes on the forefeet. Hunts in packs.

cape jumping hare, *Pedites caper,* large herbivorous leaping, rodent of mouse group with long hind legs. Lives in extensive burrows in grasslands of E and S Africa.

Cape of Good Hope, near Capetown, South Africa, at S end of mountainous Cape Peninsula. Discovered by Bartholomew Diaz searching for sea route to India (15th cent.).

Cape Province, largest prov. in Republic of South Africa. Area: 278,465 sq. mi.; cap. Capetown; main towns, Port Elizabeth, East London and Kimberley. Pop. (1964) 5,308,839.

Cape Verde Islands, Portuguese possession in Atlantic Ocean 350 mi. off Cape Verde most W point of Africa. Ten islands divided into 2 groups, Windward and Leeward. Area: 1,516 sq. mi.; cap. Praia on São Thiago. Pop. 201,549.

Capek, Karel (1890–1938), Czech satirical dramatist, novelist, essayist. Best known play *RUR* [*Rossum's Universal Robots*] (1921).

caper, *Capparis spinosa,* floral bud and young berries of genus of low prickly shrubs growing wild in Med.

Cape Hunting Dog

regions; used as condiment and seasoning.

capercaillie, capercailzie, *Tetrao urogallus,* large woodland grouse of N Europe, reintroduced in Scotland after being extinct in Britain. Weighs 8–12lb.

capercailzie *see* CAPERCAILLIE.

Capetians, royal house of France (987–1328), named for Hugh Capet (*c.* 938–996), crowned (987). Direct descendants ruled until death of Charles IV (1328), when throne passed to the VALOIS.

Capetown, cap. of Cape Province and legislative cap. of Republic of South Africa; large port on Atlantic. Has Parl. buildings and university. Founded (1652) by Dutch, taken (1806) by British. Pop. (1960) 807,000.

capibara *see* CAPYBARA.

capillaries *see* BLOOD VESSELS.

capillarity or capillary attraction *see* SURFACE TENSION.

capital, in economics, orig. interest-bearing money; now all goods, incl. land, yielding income; also raw materials, means of production and created goods. Ownership of capital is both private and public in most modern countries, although in Communist countries, nearly all capital is state-owned.

capital punishment, death inflicted as punishment for crime. Once recognized penalty for, *e.g.* sheep stealing, now reserved for murder or treason. Abolished in several European nations and US states.

Capital Territory *see* CANBERRA.

capitalism *see* CAPITAL.

Capone, Al[fonso] (1899–1947), Amer. gangster, b. Italy. Led notorious crime syndicate in Chicago after Prohibition Act passed (1920). Imprisoned (1932–9).

Capote, Truman (1924–   ), Amer. writer of *Other Voices, Other Rooms* (1948), *In Cold Blood* (1966) 'non-fiction novel'. Other titles include *Breakfast at Tiffany's* (1958).

Capp, Al (1909–   ), Amer. cartoonist. Creator of burlesque, satirical comic strip 'Li'l Abner'.

Capra, Frank (1897–   ), Amer. film director. Films include *It's a Wonderful Life* (1946), *State of the Union* (1948), *Riding High* (1950) and *A Hole in the Head* (1959).

Capri, island resort in Bay of Naples, Italy. Holiday home of Augustus and Tiberius, Roman emperors. Pop. 8,000.

Capricorn, Tropic of *see* TROPIC OF CAPRICORN.

Capricorn beetle, longicorn beetle, insect of Cerambycidae family, with long antennae, longest being found in timbermen, *Laminae.* Larvae are wood-boring.

Caprivi, Georg Leo von (1831–99), Ger. statesman, successor to Bismarck (1890–94). Policies reflected

Cape Buffalo

Capuchin Monkey

William II's conservative attitudes.

capsid bug, insect of family Miridae, plant bugs. Species include common green capsid, *Lygocoris pabulinus,* fruit and vegetable pest, and apple capsid, *Plesiocoris rugicollis.*

capuchin, monkey of genus *Cebus,* of C and S America, with naked forehead and hair resembling a monk's cowl.

capybara, capibara, *Hydrochoerus capybara,* largest rodent; resembles guinea pig. Inhabits margins of rivers and lakes in S America.

car *see* AUTOMOBILE.

caracal, *Felis caracal,* reddish-brown lynx, native to deserts and savannahs of Africa and S Asia.

Caracalla [Marcus Aurelius Antoninus Bassianus] (AD 188–217), Roman emperor (211–17), son of Septimus Severus. Noted for cruelty, oppression and personal extravagance; assassinated.

Caracas, cap. and largest city of Venezuela, founded (1567). Financial and commercial centre (coffee, sugar, cacao) with access to Caribbean Sea. In active earthquake area. Pop. (1964) 787,000.

Caravaggio, Michelangelo Amerighi da (1573–1610), Ital. painter. Founded naturalist school in Rome. Criticized by church for refusing to idealize in religious works, *e.g. Madonna di Loreto.*

caravan, house on wheels, usually towed by horse or motor car; also company travelling together for security, esp. crossing desert.

Capybara

caraway, *Carum carvi,* biennial herb of carrot family native to Asia Minor, yielding pungent, aromatic seeds, used as flavouring. Leaves eaten as vegetables and in soup.

carbohydrate, organic substance, containing hydrogen, carbon and oxygen, naturally occurring as sugar, starch, cotton and vegetable gums. Formed in green plants by PHOTOSYNTHESIS.

carbon (C), element occurring in 3 forms; hard, crystalline diamond, soft-layered graphite and amorphous carbon. Occurs in all living matter; main constituent of coal.

The Flight Into Egypt by Michelangelo Caravaggio

carbon dioxide, gas present in atmosphere, formed in combustion of carbonaceous material, respiration and fermentation. In solution in sea and rain water; converted by PHOTOSYNTHESIS into carbohydrates and oxygen. Used in production of washing soda and preparation of mineral waters. Solid carbon dioxide, known as 'dry ice' or 'Drikold', used as refrigerant in food preservation.

carbon monoxide, colourless odourless gas, found in volcanic and coal gas, and exhaust fumes of motor cars. Produced by burning carbonaceous fuels in deficiency of air or oxygen.

Carbonari ('charcoal burners'), 19th-cent. Ital. political secret society orig. in Naples. Aimed at expulsion of foreign rulers and establishment of democracy. Uprisings (1820 and 1830), later merged with Young Italy movement of Mazzini.

Carboniferous *see* GEOLOGICAL TABLE.

carborundum, silicon carbide (SiC_2) discovered (1891) by Achison. Issued as abrasive or refractory substance. Manufactured in electric furnaces from glass sand (silica) and coke (carbon).

carboxylic acids, series of organic compounds widely distributed in nature. Simplest member, *formic acid,* HCOOH, is irritant in some insect bites and stings, *e.g.* ants, wasps; vinegar is weak solution of *acetic acid,* $CH_3 \cdot COOH$; *citric acid* is chief acid constituent of citrus fruits.

Carcassonne, cap. of Aude department, S France; 13th-cent. walled city restored (19th cent.). Pop. 38,100.

carcinogen, chem. compound producing malignant tumours in man or animals. Isolation of carcinogens started (1915) when Yamagima and Ichikawa showed that repeated application of coal tar to skin of rabbits produces cancer. Aromatic hydrocarbons present in tobacco smoke cause cancer in animals.

cardamom, *Elettaria cardamomum,* spice from seed capsules of E Indian plant, used in curries and pickling.

Cardiff, cap. of Wales and county borough of Glamorgan on R. Taff, S Wales. Chief industries shipping and coal, also flour milling, steel, paper and chem. works. University College of S Wales and administrative offices of University of Wales (founded 1893) are in Cardiff, also cathedral of Llandaff. Three members returned to Parl. Pop. (1967) 289,320.

Cardigan, James Thomas Brudenell, 7th Earl of (1797–1868), Brit. army officer. Led disastrous cavalry charge at Balaklava (1854), immortalized by Tennyson's *The Charge of the Light Brigade.*

Cardiganshire, mountainous county of Wales. Area: 693 sq. mi.; county town, Cardigan; main town, Aberystwyth, site of University of Wales. Main occupations salmon-fishing and sheep-rearing. Pop. (1966) 53,000.

cardinal, any of several N Amer. song birds of S and central US, esp. *Richmondena cardinalis.* Name extended to other birds with red plumage.

cardoon, *Cynara cardunculus,* large thistle-like perennial plant of Med. regions. Leafstalks are blanched and eaten like celery.

Carducci, Giosuè (1835–1907), Ital. poet. Self-styled anti-romantic classicist, patriot, liberal and freemason; works include *Risorgimento* and *The Hymn to Satan* (1863). Awarded Nobel Prize for Literature (1906).

Carib, S Amer. Indians of Caribbean linguistic family inhabiting Lesser Antilles. Named by Columbus, Island Caribs almost exterminated by 17th cent. Some 500 pure-blooded Caribs remain on Dominica.

Caribbean Sea, part of Atlantic Ocean. C and S America lie to W and S, West Indies in N and E.

Cariboo Road, wagon road 400 mi. long, built (1862–5) in Fraser valley, British Columbia. Now a highway.

caribou, *Rangifer arcticus,* deer related to reindeer of N America, incl. barren-ground group, *e.g.* Greenland caribou, and woodland and forest group, *e.g.* Newfoundland caribou.

carillon, set of bells worked by keyboard and pedals or automatically. Carillon in Parl. building in Ottawa comprises 53 bells, installed (1927) as war memorial.

Carinthia, S prov. of Austria bordering on Yugoslavia and Italy. Scenery attracts many tourists.

Carleton, Guy, 1st Baron Dorchester (1724–1808), Brit. army officer. Commander of Brit. forces in America (1782–3). Governor-in-Chief of Brit. N Amer. provinces (1786–98).

carline thistle, *Carlina vulgaris,* spiny biennial of daisy family, native to Britain. Thistle-like leaves and purple and yellow flowers.

Carlow, county of SE Ireland, largely undulating. Area: 346 sq. mi.; county town, Carlow. Pop. (1963) 33,342.

Carlsbad Caverns, Amer. national park, SE New Mexico. Estab. as national monument (1923), as national park (1930); noted for limestone caves.

Carlyle, Thomas (1795–1881), Scot. prose writer. Translated Ger. romantics Goethe and Schiller. Critic of Brit. society in *Sartor Resartus* (1833–34) and *French Revolution* (1837). Expressed belief in hero leadership through *On Heroes, Hero-Worship, and the Heroic in Society* (1841) and biog. of Frederick the Great.

Carman, [William] Bliss (1861–1929), Canadian poet. Collections include *Low Tide on Grand Pré* (1893), *Après Airs* (1916) and *Sanctuary* (1929).

Carmarthenshire, county of S Wales. Area: 919 sq. mi.; county town, Carmarthen. Hilly, wooded, with fertile valleys for farming. Anthracite seams in S. Pop. (1966) 166,000.

Carmel, Mount, mountain (1,791 ft.) in NW Israel. Owing to biblical connections, a place of pilgrimage. Religious order of Carmelites founded by Berthold (c. 1155).

Carnac, village in Brittany, France, site of important group of prehistoric monuments.

Carnap, Rudolf (1891–1970), Ger.-American philosopher, pioneer of LOGICAL POSITIVISM. Rejected almost all traditional philosophy and claimed that only object of philosophy is description and criticism of language of particular sciences.

carnation, *Dianthus caryophyllus,* perennial herbaceous plant with many varieties. Important, scented greenhouse crop, its flowers are popular as buttonholes.

Carnegie, Andrew (1835–1919), Amer. industrialist and philanthro-

Carline Thistle

pist, b. Scotland, became Divisional Superintendent of Pennsylvania Railroad, Pittsburgh, where Carnegie iron works were ultimately estab. Retired (1901) to devote fortune to libraries, scientific institute and endowments, incl. Palace of Peace, the Hague and Carnegie Hall, New York.

Carnegie, Dale (1888–1955), Amer. broadcaster, teacher of public speaking, author of *How to Win Friends and Influence People* (1936), *How to Stop Worrying and Start Living* (1948).

Carnegie Endowment for International Peace, foundation organized to promote peace by publicity and support of interested agencies. Estab. (1910) by ANDREW CARNEGIE.

carnelian, cornelian, variety of chalcedony, generally blood-red in colour, a native silica. Iron oxide is probably source of the colour.

carnivore, mammal of order Carnivora, adapted to catching and eating flesh. Terrestrial carnivores, *Fissipeda,* include dog, cat, otter, badger and weasel groups; marine carnivores, *Pinnipedia,* include seal, sea lion and walrus.

carnotite, yellow earthy hydrous mineral, found in Colorado, US; source of uranium.

Carolina duck, wood duck, *Aix sponsa,* of N America nesting in hollow trees. Male has large head crest.

Carcassonne

Cardinal Bird

Madonna with a Carthusian (*c.* 1450) by Petrus Christus

Caroline Islands (US Trusteeship) *see* MICRONESIA.

Carolingians, dynasty of Frankish rulers (751–987) founded by Pepin the Short (*c.* 714–68); his son CHARLEMAGNE (crowned 800) brought family to its zenith. Treaty of Verdun (843) divided the Empire among his grandsons, who founded dynasties ruling Germany until 911, and France until 987.

Carossa, Hans (1878–1956), Ger. poet, novelist and physician. Works include *The End of Dr. Burger* (1913), *The Star Above the Clearing* (1946), and autobiog. *Childhood* and sequels (1922, 1928, 1941).

carotenoids, large group of natural pigments with 2 sub-groups: carotenes, unsaturated hydrocarbons, and oxygenated compounds, most important being carotenols. Carotene, extracted from carrots and green leaves, is mixture of 3 compounds.

Carothers, Wallace Hume (1896–1937), Amer. chemist. Work on linear polymers laid foundation for production of nylon.

carp, genus *Cyprinus,* of longlived freshwater food fish, orig. in Asia. Ancestor of the goldfish; specimens may weigh up to 40 lb.

Carpathians, mountain range in E Europe extending N from near Bratislava in Czechoslovakia, to Romania (highest peak 8,749 ft.).

Carpentaria, Gulf of, extensive inlet penetrating N coast of Australia.

Carpenter, John Alden (1876–1951), Amer. composer. Music frequently depicts scenes of Amer. life. Works include ballets *Krazy Kat, Sky-scraper.*

carpet, rug, usually floor covering made of woven or felted woollen, worsted or mixed fabrics; orig. used in E countries. France was 1st European country to manufacture them. European industry depended on hand loom until introduction of power loom (1841).

carpet beetle, buffalo bug, *Anthrenus scrophulariae,* small black, white and red beetle. Related pests include hide beetle, genus Trox and larder beetle, *Dermestes lardarius.*

Carpetbagger, Amer. polit. term popularized in period of Reconstruction. Referred to speculators and entrepreneurs who started business in devastated S states with no more than they could carry in a carpet-bag.

Carr, John Dickson (1906–   ), Eng. mystery writer, b. US. Also wrote under name of Carter Dickson. Books include *The Bride of Newgate* (1950), *The Dead Man's Knock* (1958).

Carrantuohill, highest peak in Ireland (3,414 ft.), situated in Macgillicuddy's Reeks, County Kerry, W Ireland.

Carrel, Alexis (1873–1944), Amer. surgeon and biologist. Awarded Nobel Prize for Physiology and Medicine (1912) for research into ligature and grafting of blood vessels.

carriage, non-self-propelling conveyance, esp. of passengers, by road or rail, with 2 or more wheels and of various shapes and sizes. Covered horse or mule-drawn carriage dates from *c.* 15th cent. Much used in 17th and 18th cent. Hansom cab plying to hire introduced in London (1834). Other 2-wheeled carriages include stanhope, tilbury, gig and dog-cart. Private 4-wheeled carriages widely used in 19th cent. included brougham, landau, victoria and 4-in-hand. Open 4-wheeled carriages include phaeton, wagonette and brake. Public vehicles, *e.g.* drag and omnibus, had seats inside and out.

carrion crow *see* CROW.

Carroll, Lewis, orig. Charles Lutwidge Dodgson (1832–98), Eng. writer and mathematician. Fantasy and satire merged in famous works, *Alice's Adventures in Wonderland* (1865) and *Through the Looking Glass and What Alice Found There* (1872).

carrot, *Daucus carota,* widely distributed usually biennial plant with orange-coloured edible roots.

Carson, Sir Edward (1854–1935), Irish barrister and politician. Solicitor General for Ireland (1892) and England (1900–6); opponent of Irish Home Rule, instrumental in formation of (Ulster) Volunteers (1912–14).

Carson, 'Kit' (1809–68), Amer. frontiersman and folk hero. Noted Indian fighter, acted as guide for J. C. Fremont's Western expeditions and led Gen. Kearney's troops from N Mexico to California (1846).

Carson, Rachel Louise (1907–64), Amer. writer. Books include *Under the Sea Wind* (1941), *The Edge of the Sea* (1954) and *Silent Spring* (1962) which points out danger to wild life from artificial fertilizers and pest control.

cart, two-wheeled, springless vehicle used in agriculture and for conveying heavy loads. Dog-cart, two-wheeled with back-to-back seats, used orig. to carry sporting dogs. Tax-cart, light, sprung cart, orig. paying low tax or none for use of highway.

Carter, Howard (1873–1939), Brit. archaeologist. Supervised excavations of Egyptian Valley of Kings and tombs of Thutmose IV and Queen Hatshepsut.

Carthage, Tyrian colony, N Africa, traditionally founded by Phoenicians (*c.* 814 BC) and by 300 BC richest city in W Med. Conflict with Rome resulted in 3 PUNIC WARS (264–146 BC), ending in destruction of Carthage. Site later colonized by Julius Caesar and Augustus; became educ. centre. Captured by Moslems (697).

Carthusians, R.C. order of monks noted for austerity; founded (1084) by St Bruno at Chartreux, France. Chartreuse liqueur first made at their monastery in Grenoble.

Cartier, Sir George-Étienne (1814–73), Canadian statesman. First minister of Lower Canada (1858–62) in Cartier-Macdonald ministry; largely responsible for French-Canadian interest in confederation; defence minister in 1st Canadian govt. Involved in 'PACIFIC SCANDAL' (1873).

Cartier, Jacques (1492–1557), Fr. explorer. Landed in Gaspé area of Canada (1534), proclaiming Fr. sovereignty. Discovered St Lawrence R. (1535) and 1st to navigate it (1539); founded Hochelaga (now Montreal). Colonizing expedition abandoned (1541).

Cartier-Bresson, Henri (1908–), Fr. photographer. Founded Magnum-Photos (1947); works widely exhibited. Compiled books of photographs.

Cartwright, Edmund (1743–1823), Eng. inventor of prototype of modern power-loom and wool-combing machine.

Caruso, Enrico (1873–1921), Ital. operatic tenor. Achieved fame in US (New York debut, 1903). One of first singers to exploit gramophone recording successfully.

Carver, George Washington (1864–1943), Amer. agric. chemist. One of 1st prominent Negro educators, worked to improve economy of South by teaching soil improvement and crop diversity.

Casablanca

Cary, [Arthur] Joyce [Lunel] (1888–1957), Eng. novelist, author of *Mister Johnson* (1939), *Herself Surprised* (1941), *To be a Pilgrim* (1942) and *The Horse's Mouth* (1943).

Casablanca, seaport and largest city of Morocco on NW Atlantic coast, 60 mi. S of Rabat. Exports grains, hides, wool and phosphates and has flourishing tourist trade. Pop. 1,085,000.

Casadesus, Robert (1899–), Fr. pianist. Noted soloist, also formed piano team with wife; composed piano concertos and symphonies.

Casals, [Pao] Pablo (1876–), Sp. cellist and conductor. Musical director of Barcelona orchestra (1919–36). Known for interpretation of Bach's cello pieces.

Casanova de Seingalt, Giovanni Giacomo (1725–1798), Venetian adventurer and author, international gambler, spy and womanizer. Imprisoned in Venice (1755–6), escaped and lived in Paris until 1774. Wrote on subjects ranging from poetry to theology.

Cascade Range, mountain range extending more than 500 mi. from California to Brit. Columbia, yielding timber and, from rivers on Pacific slopes, hydro-electric power. Many national parks.

Casement, Roger David (1864–1916), Irish revolutionary. Brit. consular service (1895–1913). Attempted to obtain Ger. aid for 1916 Irish rebellion. Returned in Ger. submarine, captured and hanged for treason; regarded by Irish as martyr patriot.

Casgrain, Abbé Henri Raymond (1831–1904), Fr.-Canadian writer and historian, a founder of Mouvement Littéraire du Québec. Wrote *Légendes Canadiennes* (1861).

cashmere, natural fibre from wool of goats, from Kashmir prov. of India. Extremely fine and soft.

Caslon, William (1692–1766), Eng. type-setter. Founded 'old-style' type face (1722); facilitated illustrated publications.

Caspian Sea, situated between Europe and Asia, surrounded by land. Area: 170,000 sq. mi. World's largest salt lake, with valuable sturgeon (black caviar) and salmon fisheries. R. Volga and canals connect it with Baltic and White Seas; important Soviet inland transport route. Because of surface evaporation level of lake is steadily dropping.

Cass, Lewis (1782–1866), Amer. statesman. Governor of Michigan territory (1813–31). Unsuccessful Democratic candidate for US presidency (1848). Sec. of State (1857–60).

Persian carpet

Cassandra, in Gk. myth., daughter of Priam of Troy. Prophetess of Apollo who caused her prophecies never to be believed. After fall of Troy, captive of Agamemnon, killed with him by his wife Clytemnestra.

Cassatt, Mary (1845–1926), Amer. painter and etcher associated with Impressionists. Excelled in mother-and-child scenes and figure painting.

Cassin, René (1887–), Fr. jurist. Member of Fr. delegation to League of Nations (1924–36) and later to UN (1946–58), instrumental in estab. UNESCO. Deputy chairman (1946) of UN Commission drafting Declaration of Human Rights. Awarded Nobel Peace Prize (1968).

Cassirer, Ernst (1874–1945), Ger. philosopher, studied relationships of science and philosophy.

cassiterite, tinstone, chief tin ore, occurring in lodes associated with igneous rocks in Malaya, Bolivia, Nigeria and China; largest output from waterborne cassiterite. 'Stream' tin still found on beaches of Cornwall.

Cassius Longinus, Gaius (d. 42 BC), Roman soldier. Quaestor under Crassus; commanded Pompey's fleet in Civil War; a leading conspirator against Caesar (44 BC). Joined Brutus in E provinces, defeated by Octavian and Mark Antony at Philippi (42 BC), and committed suicide.

Casson, Sir Hugh Maxwell (1910–), Brit. architect. Director of Architecture, Festival of Britain

(1948–51). Works include *Homes by the Million* (1945), *An Introduction to Victorian Architecture* (1948).

cassowary, family Casuariidae of solitary, flightless forest-dwelling birds of N Australia, New Guinea and Polynesia. Male incubates eggs.

castanets, 2 shell-shaped percussion instruments joined by string and struck together with finger and thumb. Used by Sp. dancers.

caste, in Hindu population of India, exclusive social grouping. No member of any caste may marry outside it, while its rules may also regulate his occupation and his diet.

Castiglione, Baldassare (1478–1529), Ital. writer and diplomat. Employed by Duke of Urbino as ambassador to Henry VIII in England and Louis XII in France. Wrote *Il Cortegiano*.

Castile, former kingdom of Spain, united with Aragon on marriage of Ferdinand and Isabella (1479). Now 2 provinces; Old Castile in N, main towns Burgos, Santander, Segovia; and New Castile in S, main towns Madrid, Toledo, Cuenca. Main rivers, Douro, Tagus and Guadiana. Few industries, sheep grazing; mineral resources include mercury.

Castle, Barbara Anne (1911–   ), Brit. cabinet member, 1st Sec. of State and Min. of Employment and Productivity (1968–   ). Chairman of Labour Party (1958–9), Min. of Overseas Development (1964–5) and Transport (1965–6).

Castlereagh, Robert Stewart, Viscount, 2nd Marquess of Londonderry (1769–1822), Brit. statesman, War Min. and Foreign Sec. during Napoleonic wars. Helped organize 'Concert of Europe' against Napoleon. Represented Britain at Congress of Vienna (1814).

Castor and Pollux, in Gk. and Roman myth., half-brothers, Castor, son of Tyndareus and Leda, Pollux, son of Zeus and Leda. Identified with constellation Gemini (The Twins) in later legend.

castor bean, seed of castor-oil plant, *Ricinus communis,* widely naturalized in trop. and temp. regions. Oil obtained from castor beans used as purgative but mainly as lubricant in internal combustion engines. India and Brazil produce 55%–65% of world supply.

Castro Ruz, Fidel (1927–   ), Cuban revolutionary; premier (1959–   ). Imprisoned (1953) for opposition to BATISTA dictatorship, later released; launched 26th of July movement (1956). Guerilla campaign deposed Batista régime (Jan. 1959). Proclaimed allegiance to Communist

Cassowary

bloc (1961), supported revolutionary movements throughout Latin America. Collectivized agriculture and expropriated industry.

casuistry, branch of ethics which deals with delicate moral questions. Term also refers to arguing away of ambiguous acts by hair-splitting subtleties.

cat, domestic breed of *Felis catus* derived from African wildcat, *F. libyca*. Short-haired include Siamese, Manx, Maltese, blue Russian and Abyssinian; long-haired include tabby, tortoise-shell, blue and silver Persian or Angora with derivatives chinchilla and smoke.

catacombs, early Christian subterranean cemeteries arranged in vaults and galleries. Those of Rome were built before AD 500. Also underground system of tunnels, found esp. in Paris, Egypt, Rome.

Catalan, Romance Indo-European language, spoken by *c.* 5 million people in NE Spain.

Catalonia, formerly separate prov. of NE Spain. Main towns: Barcelona, Tarragona and Lerida. Produces wine, olive oil and hydro-electric power from Ebro, Segre and Cinca rivers. Languages, Catalan and Spanish. Lost autonomy after Civil War (1936–9).

catalpa, small genus of deciduous Amer. and Asiatic trees of trumpet-creeper family Bignoniaceae, suited to

towns. Indian bean is *Catalpa bignoides*.

catalyst, in bio-chemistry, alters the speed of reactions and is consumed in the process. A physical catalyst does not itself react, but alters conditions to assist reaction.

catamaran, orig. log raft for use in surf by natives of Madras, India. Now any outrigger canoe, and specifically a twin-hulled racing yacht.

catapult, ancient and medieval weapon with retractable arms attached to cords. Arms drawn back and spears, arrows, or stones propelled forward. Apparatus (20th cent.) for propelling aircraft from decks of ships.

cataract, disease of eye in which lens becomes opaque; causes include faulty development, injury, infection and senility. Vision may be restored by removal of lens.

catbird, *Dumetella carolinensis,* solitary grey bird of mocking-bird family of N America with a cat-like mewing call. Also a species of Austral. bower-bird.

caterpillar, larva of butterfly or moth. In storing food for pupae stage, it may moult many times, each time growing larger. Many forms are garden pests.

catfish, group of 9 freshwater and 2 marine families of scaleless food fish, named from the barbels around the mouth, abundant in the New World, some travel overland in dry seasons.

Cathay, medieval European name for China.

Cather, Willa (1876–1947), Amer. novelist. Most famous works include *My Antonia* (1918) and *A Lost Lady* (1923), *Death Comes for the Archbishop* (1927) and *Shadows on the Rock* (1931).

Catherine I, orig. Martha Skavronskaya (*c.* 1683–1727), empress of Russia (1725–7). Servant girl until capture by Russians (1702). Mistress and wife (1711) to Emperor Peter I.

Catherine the Great or **Catherine II** (1729–96), daughter of Pruss. field-marshal, she married future Russ. Emperor Peter III (1745) and succeeded to his throne (1762) after his murder at her instigation. Unfulfilled projects for reforms; despite professed liberalism, fitted well into age of benevolent despots. Chief events of her reign were 3 partitions of Poland, resulting in great territorial gains for Russia, 2 successful wars against Turkey, and war with Sweden.

cathode ray tube, vacuum tube with electron gun which projects a beam of electrons on to a phosphor-coated

Blue Russian Tabby Cat

screen; uses include receiving of television and radar signals.

cathode rays, streams of electrons emitted from a cathode (negative electrode) in gas discharge tube at low pressure. Impingement on to hard surface produces X-rays.

Catiline [Lucius Sergius Catilina] (*c.* 108–62 BC), Roman patrician. Governor of Africa (68–66 BC), excluded from consular elections by impending trial for misgovernment. Defeated in plans to gain consulship and popular support (65–63 BC), organized far-reaching conspiracy, but thwarted by Cicero. Left Rome after Cicero's *In Catilinam,* joined forces in Etruria. Conspirators arrested and executed, Catiline killed in battle.

Catlin, George (1796–1872), Amer. artist and chronicler. Painted Amer. Indian portraits (1829–38). Wrote *Life Among the Indians* (1867).

catmint [UK], **catnip** [US], *Nepeta cavaria* of thyme family native to Britain and Europe. Tea, made of leaves and flowering tips is old medicinal remedy.

catnip *see* CATMINT.

Cato, Marcus Porcius (234–149 BC), Roman statesman, general and writer. Consul (195 BC) with Flaccus, censor (184 BC), legislated against luxury. Enemy of CARTHAGE and wrote *De Re Rustica* on agriculture.

Catt, Carrie Chapman, nee Lane (1859–1947), Amer. suffragette. Pres. of National American Woman Suffrage Association; organized League of Women Voters.

cattail moth *see* OWLET MOTHS.

cattle, *Bos taurus,* domesticated descendants of wild cattle Bovidae. These RUMINANTS are useful to man being draught animals, also yielding dairy products, meat and hides. Milk breeds include Ayrshire, Brown

Friesian Cattle

Swiss, Dairy Shorthorn, Emmenthal, Friesian, Guernsey, Holstein and Jersey; meat producers include Aberdeen Angus, Charollais, Hereford and Shorthorn. Many breeds are dual purpose, *e.g.* the Normandy and Holstein-Friesian.

Catullus, [Gaius Valerius Catullus] (*c.* 87–*c.* 54 BC), Latin lyric poet. Adapted Gk. metres; estab. new form of literature in Rome. Best known poems are those addressed to Lesbia; also many satires and epigrams.

Caucasus Mts., range *c.* 1,000 mi. long from the Black Sea to the Caspian Sea. Highest point Mt. El'brus (18,481 ft.), containing important oil wells.

cauliflower, *Brassica oleracea* var. *botrytis,* edible vegetable of CABBAGE family. Introduced from Cyprus (17th cent.), now grown extensively as commercial or garden crop.

Cavafy, Constantin (1863–1933), modern Gk. poet. Work shows E Roman and Byzantine, rather than classical Gk. influence. *Complete Poems* pub. in English (1961).

Cavaliers, the supporters of Charles II in the English CIVIL WAR.

cavalry, mounted branch of an army, now retained only for ceremonial purposes. Used by Persians, Greeks and Romans; main fighting force of every army at time of Crusades.

Cavan, county of Ireland, low-lying with hills in N. Area: 730 sq. mi.; county town, Cavan. Agriculture is main occupation. Pop. (1963) 56,594.

cave, subterranean hollow space in earth's crust. Sea-cave formed by action of waves and by boulders and pebbles being thrown against cliff. Inland caves often found in limestone regions.

cave paintings *see* ALTAMIRA; LASCAUX.

cave period, term often given to

Catalans dancing the Sardana

Paleolithic period, knowledge of which comes mainly from cave remains.

Cavell, Edith (1865–1915), Brit. nurse. Matron at Brussels hospital in World War 1, she was shot by Germans for aiding escape of Allied prisoners.

Cavendish, Henry (1731–1810), Eng. chemist and physicist. Discovered that air consists of constant proportions of oxygen and nitrogen; also discovered the composition of nitric acid.

Cavy

Cavendish, Spencer Compton, 8th Duke of Devonshire (1833–1908), Brit. statesman. Led Lib. Unionists who broke with Gladstone (1886) over Home Rule for Ireland. Left Unionists (1904) when abandonment of free trade proposed.

Cavendish, Victor Christian William, 9th Duke of Devonshire (1868–1938), Gov.-General of Canada (1916–21), Colonial Sec. (1922–4).

Cavour, Camillo Benso, Conte di (1810–61), Ital. statesman. Premier of Sardinia under Victor Emmanuel. Chief architect of Ital. unification. *See* RISORGIMENTO.

cavy, *Cavia porcellus,* tailless rodent

of S America and ancestor of the GUINEA PIG.

Caxton, William (*c.* 1422–91), 1st Eng. printer, set up press in Bruges (1473) and published fine books starting with his own translation of *Recuyell of the Historyes of Troye.* The 2nd book, also a translation was *Game and Playe of the Chesse.* Returned to England (1476) and set up his press in Westminster. First book to be published there was *Dictes and Sayengis of the Philosophres* (1477). Subsequently published *c.* 90 books, some his own translations.

Cayenne, cap. and seaport of Fr. Guiana in S America; exports gold, balata and rosewood. Pop. 13,000.

Cayenne pepper, condiment prepared from pods of several species of *Capsicum,* native to C and S America.

Cayman Islands *see* WEST INDIES.

Cebu, port on Cebu Is., Philippines; commercial centre. Pop. (1960) 300,000.

Cecchetti, Enrico (1850–1928), Ital. dancer and maître de ballet; dancer and teacher in St Petersburg. Devised system of exercises.

Cecil, Lord David (1902–   ), Eng. critic and biographer, author of urbane studies incl. *Early Victorian Novelists* (1934), *The Young Melbourne* (1939) and *Lord M.* (1954).

Cecil, Edgar Algernon Robert, 1st Viscount Cecil of Chelwood (1864–1958), Eng. statesman; helped draft Covenant of League of Nations. Pres. of League of Nations Union (1923–45). Awarded Nobel Peace Prize (1937).

Cecil, Robert, Earl of Salisbury (*c.* 1563–1612), Eng. statesman, Sec. of State (1596). Became chief adviser to James I after death of Elizabeth I.

Cecil, Robert Arthur Talbot Gascoyne, 3rd Marquis of Salisbury (1830–1903), Brit., statesman. As Disraeli's Foreign Sec. (1878–80), his 'Salisbury Circular' outlined Brit. policy in Near East and led to Congress of Berlin (1878). P.M. (1885, 1886–92, 1895–1902). Supported French over FASHODA INCIDENT (1898) and US over Venezuela Boundary Dispute. Opposed Irish Home Rule.

cecropia moth, *Sauria cecropia,* largest moth in N America. Native of E America; larvae feed on many forest and fruit trees.

cedar, coniferous tree of genus *Cedrus* of pine family, with short needle leaves arranged in close spiral on spine-like branches.

celandine, name of 2 unrelated plants. Lesser celandine, *Ranunculus ficaria*

Cones of Atlas Cedar

of buttercup family is small herb with yellow flowers and heart-shaped leaves. Greater celandine, *Chelidonium majus* of poppy family is erect branched herb with divided leaves and yellow flowers.

Celebes, Sulawesi, volcanic island of E Indian Archipelago between Borneo and Moluccas. Area: 72,080 sq. mi.; cap. Macassar. Part of Republic of Indonesia. Exports coffee, coconuts, sugar, copra and spices; deposits of gold, copper, salt and tin. Pop. (1964) 7,000,000.

celery, *Apium graveolens,* biennial plant of Europe and America. Blanched stem used in salads and as vegetable, dried leaves as flavouring.

celesta, orchestral keyboard instrument invented (1886) by Auguste Mustel in Paris. Hammers strike steel bars attached to wooden resonators.

celestite, translucent mineral, white to faint bluish in colour. Occasionally granular, crystals are of radiating fibres.

Céline, Louis-Ferdinand, orig. Louis Ferdinand Destouches (1894–1961), Fr. novelist and physician. Works include *Journey to the End of the Night* (1932) and *Nord* (1960).

cell, fundamental unit of living matter, performing all functions of life: nutrition, digestion, respiration, reproduction, *etc.* First described (1838–9) by Schieder and Schwann. Cell consists of nucleus which contains CHROMOSOMES, cytoplasm, cell membrane; animal cells lack cell wall ('cellulose') and chloroplast which contains chlorophyll present in plant cell. Transition from unicellular forms, through colonial forms to multicellular organism has occurred through development of specialized

cells. Man has *c.* 1,000 million million. *See* TISSUE.

cell, primary and secondary, in electricity, device in which chem. reaction is made to produce electrical energy. Primary cells produce electrical currents from electrodes (*e.g.* copper and zinc dry cell). Secondary cells, in which exchange between chem. and electrical energy is reversible, are called accumulators.

Cellini, Benvenuto (1500–71), Florentine goldsmith and sculptor. Famous works include the statue 'Perseus with the Head of Medusa' (Florence).

cello, violoncello, lowest member of violin family. Developed in 17th cent., it gradually replaced bass viol as bass line in orchestras and chamber groups, and as solo instrument.

celluloid, solid, highly inflammable substance made by mixing nitrated CELLULOSE with camphor and alcohol. Use as substitute for hard rubber, ivory, bone, largely died out with advent of less inflammable preparations of cellulose treated with acetyl chloride.

cellulose, essential constituent of all vegetable cells. White, opaque carbohydrate insoluble in water, nearly pure in the fibre of cotton, linen and hemp. Boiling with dilute sulphuric acid changes it to dextrose; nitric acid converts it into nitrocellulose, the base of CELLULOID, collodion and guncotton. Used in enamels, explosives and other chem. preparations.

Celtic, declining Indo-European language; 2 sub-groups comprise 1) Irish and Scots Gaelic, and 2) Welsh and Breton. Extinct groups are Manx and Cornish.

celtuce, *Lactuca sativa asparagina,* edible vegetable derived from and combining flavours of lettuce and celery.

Cenozoic, Caenozoic *see* GEOLOGICAL TABLE.

censorship, system under which circulation of printed matter or production of plays or films may be prohibited. In UK, Lord Chamberlain had to approve plays (1843–1968) before presentation. Films must be approved by Brit. Board of Film Censors. Sale of publications may be banned under Obscene Publications Act (1857). In US, some states have official censorship of films.

Centaurs, in Gk. myth., race of beings half human, half equine, living in Thessaly. Defeated in battle by the Lapiths.

centipede, a class, *Chilopoda,* of predatory arthropods. With flat segmented body, distinct head, antennae and 3 pairs of jaws; $1-10\frac{1}{2}$ in. long.

Species include C Amer. *Scoropendra gigantea,* and the cosmopolitan house centipede, *Scutigera forceps.*

Central African Republic, former Fr. colony of Ubangi-Shari between Cameroon and Sudan. Area: 238,000

sq. mi.; cap. Bangui. Savanna in N, rain forest in S. Exports cotton, coffee and diamonds. Independence (1960). Pop. (1963) 1,200,000.

Central America, isthmus connecting N and S America, comprising republics of Guatemala, Costa Rica, Nicaragua, Honduras, El Salvador, Panama and British Honduras.

Central American Common Market (CACM), body estab. (1960) under aegis of ORGANIZATION OF AMERICAN STATES to facilitate economic relations between its members, such as mutual tariff reduction. Comprises Costa Rica, El Salvador, Nicaragua, Guatemala and Honduras.

Central Committee of the Communist Party, highest organ of Soviet Communist Party. Members are elected at party congresses. Appoints Presidium and Secretariat and, between congresses, directs party activity. Power curtailed during Stalinist era, but revived afterwards.

Central Intelligence Agency (CIA), independent executive bureau of US govt. estab. by 1947 National Security Act, given special powers (1949) for purpose of secrecy. Has no domestic police powers. Allen W. Dulles, director (1953–61), strengthened CIA and emboldened tactics. Agency was deeply involved in abortive US invasion of Cuba (1961).

Doric temple of Ceres at Paestum

Persian ceramic wall tile (13th cent.)

Central Treaty Organization, called **CENTO,** defensive military alliance, formed (1955) by Iraq, Iran, Turkey, Pakistan and UK on basis of Baghdad Pact. Iraq withdrew (1958). Known as Middle East Treaty Organization until 1959.

centrifugation, means of separating solid, of which particles are too fine to be filtered, from a liquid. Liquid is spun at high velocity so that 'centrifugal force' moves denser material, *e.g.* suspended solids, to sides of tubes containing liquid. Ultracentrifuge, working at greater speeds (720,000 rpm), is used in determining particle size and molecular weight.

century plant, *Agave americana,* Mexican plant of *Amaryllis* genus. Pulque and Mescal are derived alcoholic beverages also used medicinally. Named for long interval (5–100 yr.) between blooms.

cèpe *see* BOLETUS.

cephalopod, class, Cephalopoda, of marine free-swimming mollusca incl. squid, cuttlefish and octopus. Movement aided by a propulsion organ. Numerous fossil forms.

ceramics, art and science of POTTERY.

Cerberus, in Gk. myth., 3-headed dog which guarded passage to and from Underworld.

cereal, variety of annuals of grass family, cultivated for edible fruit, known as grain. Cereal crops cover *c.* half world's arable land, chief in order of acreage being wheat, rice, millet, sorghum, maize, barley, oats, rye. Some cereals fermented to make alcohol.

Ceres, Roman goddess of the earth and the growing corn, identified with Gk. goddess DEMETER. Worshipped particularly by farmers.

Cerf, Bennett Alfred, (1898–1971), Amer. publisher and writer. Founded Random House (1927). Published humourous books, *e.g. Encyclopaedia of American Humor.*

Cervantes, Miguel de (1547–1616), Sp. author and dramatist, best known for classic picaresque novel *Don Quixote* (1605). Other fiction includes the pastoral romance *Novelas ejemplares* (1613).

cestode, ribbonlike invertebrate of Cestoda class of Platyhelminthes; parasitic in intestinal canals of vertebrates. Species include TAPEWORM.

cetacean, aquatic fish-like mammal of order Cetacea, divided into toothed whales, *e.g.* dolphin and cachalot, and whalebone whales, *e.g.* Greenland whale. Blubber commercially valuable.

Ceuta, free port of Sp. Morocco opposite Gibraltar, on site of Carthaginian colony. Admin. by Spain as part of Cádiz prov. Pop. 67,000.

Cévennes, 300 mi. mountain range

lying along Rhône valley in S France. Highest peaks Mt. Lozère (5,650 ft.) and Mt. Mézenc (5,755 ft.). Coal-mining, wool and silk main industries. Ancient cap. Mende. Pop. (1954) 7,752.

Ceylon [**Sri Lanka**], trop. island in Indian Ocean. Area: 25,332 sq. mi.; cap. Colombo. Dutch settlements captured by British (1795–6), became Brit. colony by Treaty of Amiens

(1802); self-governing dominion of Brit. Commonwealth (1948). Exports tea, rubber, coffee, rice and gems, esp. sapphires and rubies. Pop. (1965) 11,504,000.

Cézanne, Paul (1839–1906), Fr. painter. Subjects mainly still-lifes, bathers and portraits of his mistress. Later work includes *Cardplayers* and *Grandes Baigneuses*.

Chad, Lake, lake on NE boundary of Nigeria. Area varies from rainy to dry season, 20,000 to 7,000 sq. mi.

Chad, Republic of [**République du Tchad**], inland country of N Africa. Area: 496,000 sq. mi.; cap. Fort Lamy. Acquired independent territorial status (1946); repub. since

1960. Semi-arid steppe land. People, mainly Moslem; 10% literate. Main products dates, cattle, cotton and groundnuts, ivory and hides. Pop. (1965) 3,361,000.

Chadic, group of Afro-Asian languages chiefly spoken in Nigeria, Cameroon, Chad and Central African Republic. Most widespread of group is Hausa, *c.* 9 million speakers.

Chadwick, Sir James (1891–), Brit. physicist. Awarded Nobel Prize for Physics (1935) for discovery of the neutron (1932).

chafer, insect of scarab beetle family; clumsy flight and movement. Root-eating larvae are destructive. Species include dive beetle and COCK-CHAFER.

chaffinch, *Fringilla coelebs,* finch of N Europe woodlands. Male has pinkish breast and white bars on wings.

Chagall, Marc (1889–), Russ. painter. Themes were love, marriage

Self-portrait by Paul Cézanne

and pathos of life, *e.g. Lovers Over the Town.* Term 'Surrealist' 1st applied to his work.

Chaillis, Paul Belloni du (1831–1903), Fr. explorer. Made 2 expeditions to Africa and discovered the pygmy races of C Africa.

Chain, Ernst Boris (1906–), Brit. biochemist, b. Berlin. Awarded Nobel Prize for Physiology and Medicine (1945) with Sir Alexander Fleming and Howard Florey, for work on penicillin.

chalcedony, semi-precious stone. Cryptocrystalline variety of quartz; common forms include agate, bloodstone, onyx and chrysoprase.

chalcocite, brittle, lead grey, opaque mineral; source of copper. Crystals found in Cornwall, England.

chalcopyrite, brittle, opaque mineral often mistaken for gold. Brass yellow, sometimes tarnished. Principal source of copper mined in Cornwall, England.

Chaldea, Chaldaea, S part of valley of Tigris and Euphrates; name given to Babylonia from Chaldaeans, Semitic nomads who settled in S Babylonia (*c.* 1200–800 BC).

Chaldeans, OT name for inhabitants of Babylonia, centre of astronomical learning. Term later used loosely to denote magicians or astrologers.

Chaliapin, Feodor Ivanovich (1873–1938), Russ. opera singer. Exponent of Ital. and Russ. opera, esp. title role in Mussorgsky's *Boris Godunov.*

chalk, fine-grained, soft, white limestone of exceptional purity. Composed of remains of calcareous algae and shell debris. Widely worked for agric. use as lime, and for cement.

chalk hill-figures, common in S England, large figures cut in chalk on limestone hills. Few from Iron Age remain. Some, esp. on Salisbury Plain, cut recently.

chamber music, music written for small instrumental ensemble with one player to a part.

Chamberlain, Joseph (1836–1914), Brit. statesman, champion of imperial unity and tariff reform. Reform mayor of Birmingham (1873–6). Pres. of Board of Trade (1880–5) and Colonial Sec. (1895–1903). Resigned (1903). Proposal to abandon England's traditional free trade policies split Lib. Unionist Party and caused defeat (1906).

Chamberlain, Sir [**Joseph**] **Austen** (1863–1937), Brit. statesman. Son of Joseph Chamberlain, entered Parl. (1892). Twice Chanc. of the Exchequer, secured assent to imperial tariff preference. Helped negotiate treaty with Irish Free State after becoming Cons. leader (1921). Prominent in signing LOCARNO PACT (1925) as Foreign Sec. Awarded 1925 Nobel Peace Prize with Charles Dawes.

Chamberlain, Neville (1869–1940), Brit. statesman, son of Joseph Chamberlain. Lord Mayor of Birmingham (1915); Director-General of labour recruiting during World War I. Chanc. of Exchequer and Min. of Health (1920s, 1930s). Succeeded Stanley Baldwin as P.M. (1937). Tried to limit Hitler's activities in Europe by 'appeasement'. Brit. débacle in Norway (April 1940) forced his resignation.

Chamberlain, Owen (1920–), Amer. physicist. Awarded Nobel

Chaffinch

Prize for Physics (1959), with Emilio Segre, for demonstrating existence of anti-proton.

Chambers, Sir William (1726–96), Eng. architect whose chief work was *Somerset House.* His *Treatise on Civil Architecture* became standard work.

chameleon, lizard of Old World family of reptiles, Chamaeleonidae, with long, prehensile tail. Species include common chameleon, *C. chamaeleon,* of Med. coast.

chamois, *Rupicapra rupicapra,* agile ruminant intermediate between antelope and goat of mountains of Europe and SW Asia. Once widely hunted, now protected.

Champagne, NE prov. of France before Revolution, now within Aube, Marne, Haute-Marne, Ardennes and Yonne departments. Chief towns, Rheims and Troyes; famed for sparkling wines.

Champlain, Samuel de (1567–1635), Fr. explorer, sailed up St Lawrence R. (1603), founded Quebec and proclaimed New France (1608). Initiated fur trade with Iroquois and explored St Lawrence region. Regarded as founder of Fr. empire in N America.

Champollion, Jean-François (1790–1832), Fr. pioneer Egyptologist. Published paper (1821) solving riddle of Egyptian hieroglyphic writing.

Chancellorsville, Battle of (May 1863), in US Civil War. Robert E. Lee attacked Union Army near Chancellorsville, Va. Thomas (Stonewall) Jackson surprised and routed Unionists; Lee's last great victory.

Chandler, Raymond [Thornton] (1888–1959), Amer. writer of crime fiction. Created Philip Marlowe, private detective.

Chanel, Gabrielle ('Coco') (1883–1971), Fr. fashion designer. Partly financed Diaghilev's company and designed costumes for Cocteau's *Antigone* and various ballets.

change ringing, ringing of church bells in set patterns called 'peals'.

Changshu, Ch'ang-sha, cap. of Hunan prov., SE China, port on Siang river. Known since 3rd cent. BC as literary and transit centre. Cap. of Chu kingdom in Five Dynasties period (907–960). Silk, coal and lead industries; tea and rice trade; cotton, glass manufacturing. Pop. (1960), *c.* 500,000.

Channel Islands, group of islands off Normandy coast, France, in Eng. Channel. Main isles are Jersey, Guernsey, Alderney, Sark, Jethou; all (but a few Fr. owned) Brit. since Norman Conquest. Area: 75 sq. mi;

Autour d'elle by Marc Chagall.

chief town, St Helier (Jersey). Agric. and pastoral, cattle produce for Eng. markets. Official language, English. Pop. (1965) 115,000.

Chanson de Roland, Fr. *chanson de geste* of *c.* mid-11th cent. Narrative epic poem of Count Roland's adventures during Charlemagne's campaign against Moors.

chanterelle, canterelle, *Cantharellus cibarius,* flat-topped, edible, yellow fungus, with pleasant aroma, found in deciduous woods in Europe.

Chaos, according to Gk. poet Hesiod, formless void from which gods came into being.

Chaplin, Charles Spencer (1889–   ), English-born film actor, director, producer, writer and composer. Helped found United Artists (1920). Portrayals of 'underdog' enabled him to identify with an enormous audience. Films include *The Gold Rush,* *City Lights, The Great Dictator,* and *Limelight.* He left the US (1952) to live in Switzerland.

Chapman, George (*c.* 1559–1634), Eng. poet, scholar, playwright. Notable translations of *Iliad* and *Odyssey.* Plays include the comedy *All Fools* (*c.* 1599).

Chapman, John (1774–1845), nicknamed Johnny Appleseed, Amer. pioneer and folk hero. Led nomadic existence in Pennsylvania and Ohio; preached and distributed apple seeds to promote estab. of orchards.

Chapman, John Jay (1862–1933), Amer. essayist. Wrote on politics, literature and religion. Books include *Emerson and Other Essays* (1898), *New Horizons in American Life* (1932).

char, food fish of genus *Salvelinus* of salmon family inhabiting deep cold

Chameleon

lakes. European species is *S. alpinus*. N Amer. char is called trout.

characin, carnivorous fish of trop. waters, with strong jaws and short, scaly body. Best known species is piranha.

Charcot, Jean-Martin (1825–93), Fr. neurologist, 1st to use hypnosis for medical treatment and with pupil SIGMUND FREUD, diagnosed HYSTERIA.

chariot, 2-wheeled, horse-drawn vehicle used by Egyptians, Persians, Greeks and Romans for war and racing; and later by Britons for war.

Charlemagne [Charles the Great or **Charles I]** (742–814), Frankish king from 768,. emperor of the West (800–814); member of CAROLINGIAN dynasty. Shared kingdom with younger brother Carloman until latter's death (771). Invaded Italy to support pope against Lombardy; crowned Lombard king (774). Conquered Navarre and Sp. March from Moors (788); subjugated Saxons and forced conversion to Christianity after bitter struggle (772–804). Supported Leo III's accession to papal see (800) and crowned emperor by Leo, thus forming basis for HOLY ROMAN EMPIRE. Most powerful and influential figure of his time, created military frontier marches and administered empire through personal representatives (*missi dominici*). Decrees (capitularies) reflected concern for welfare of poor. His palace school at Aachen, founded by Alcuin, became centre of 'Carolingian renaissance' of learning. Source for cycle of medieval romances incl. *Chanson de Roland* (*c.* 1100).

Charles [II] the Bald (823–77), emperor and Frankish king. Became king of W Franks after defeating (841) his brother Louis the German; peace imposed at Treaty of Verdun (843). Crowned emperor (875).

Charles [III] the Fat (839–88), emperor and Frankish king. Emperor (881), king of W Franks (885); deposed (887).

Charles IV (1316–78), Ger. emperor and Bohemian king. Succeeded father to Bohemian throne (1346); crowned emperor (1355). Promulgated Golden Bull (1356), designating elector-princes; added Silesia and Lusatia to family territories. Founded University of Prague (1348).

Charles V (1500–58), Holy Roman Emperor (1519–58), and as Charles I, Sp. king (1516–56); son of Philip I of Castile. Greatest Habsburg emperor, most powerful ruler in Europe. Fought successful campaigns against French (1520s) and consolidated

Caernarvon Castle, scene of the investiture of Prince Charles as Prince of Wales (1969)

influence in Italy over papacy (1529). After attempts to reconcile Reformation movement in Germany, broke power of Ger. Protestant princes (1546–7), but was forced to accept compromise Peace of AUGSBURG. Successfully promoted Catholic Reform (COUNCIL OF TRENT, 1545), and enlarged Sp. Empire in America. From 1530s increasingly delegated powers to his brother, later Ferdinand I; after 1554, began to renounce titles. Retired (1556) to a monastery.

Charles VI (1685–1740), Holy Roman Emperor and as Charles III, king of Hungary. Unsuccessfully claimed Sp. throne, beginning War of SPANISH SUCCESSION before accession to Empire (1711). To circumvent his own succession problem, issued PRAGMATIC SANCTION, by which Habsburg lands were to pass to daughter, Maria Theresa.

Charles VII (1697–1745), Holy Roman Emperor and, as Charles Albert, elector of Bavaria (1726–45). Joined coalition against Maria Theresa in War of AUSTRIAN SUCCESSION, and was elected emperor (1742).

Charles I (1600–49), 2nd Stuart king of Britain (1625–49). Offended Eng. public after succeeding his father, James I, by marriage to Catholic Henrietta Maria of France. Ensuing struggle with Puritan-dominated Parl. over control of money led to PETITION OF RIGHT (1628), after which Charles ruled without parl. (1629–40), greatly restricting civil liberties. Attempts to impose Episcopacy in Scotland brought war and king resorted to parl. Long Parl. of 1640 brought about death of THOMAS WENTWORTH and end of arbitrary taxation. Fear of king and Catholics mounted and Civil War

broke out. Charles surrendered to Scots (1646). Tried by high court of justice controlled by Parliamentarians, convicted of treason and beheaded.

Charles II (1630–85), Stuart king of Britain (1660–85). Fled to France (1646) and, after his father, Charles I's, beheading, crowned king in Scotland (1651). After defeat by Cromwell, escaped to Europe. With aid of GEORGE MONCK and the conciliatory Declaration of Breda, restored as king (1660). Favoured tolerance but Clarendon Code struck at nonconformity. Charles entered 2 Dutch wars (1664–67, 1672–4). Forced to approve Test Act (1673) of religious allegiance. Dissolved parl. (1681) to block Exclusion Act against his brother James, and ruled absolutely thereafter. Reign marked by gradual rise of parl. power and polit. parties, and flourishing of art and literature.

Charles [IV] the Fair (1294–1328), Fr. king from 1322. Last ruler of direct Capetian lineage.

Charles [V] the Wise (1337–80), Fr. king from 1364, regent (1356–60), dealt with popular revolts. During reign, English driven out of France. Strengthened royal power, founded standing army and patronized learning.

Charles [VI] the Mad (1368–1422), Fr. king from 1380. Intermittently insane after 1392. France ruled by members of family, whose rivalries led to civil war (1411) between Armagnacs and Burgundians, which merged with HUNDRED YEARS WAR and ravaged France.

Charles VII (1403–61), king of France (1422–61) when Joan of Arc besieged Orléans (1429). Captured N France from English, which permitted

Charles' coronation at Rheims (1429). Issued Pragmatic Sanction of Bourges (1438) estab. control of church in France.

Charles VIII (1470–98), king of France (1483–98). Invaded Italy (1494) and claimed Naples for France. Distinguished at battle of Fornovo (1495), but forced by Holy League forces to retreat.

Charles I [Charles Robert of Anjou] (1288–1342), king of Hungary. Elected king (1308), crowned (1310); founder of Hungarian branch of ANGEVIN dynasty.

Charles XII (1682–1718), king of Sweden (1697–1718). Challenged by Russ.-Polish-Danish alliance of 1699. Routed Danes, then Peter the Great at Narva (1700), crushed Poland; campaign in Russia ended at Poltava. Failed to push Turkey into war with Russia. Shot during invasion of Norway.

Charles XIV of Sweden see BERNADOTTE.

Charles Albert (1798–1849), king of Sardinia (1831–49). Attempted to free Italy from Metternich's rule. Defeated by Austrians (Novara, 1849), abdicated in favour of his son Victor Emmanuel II. Granted his country a constitution (1848).

Charles Martel (689–741), Frankish ruler. United all Merovingian kingdoms under his rule. Halted Moslem invasion of Europe in decisive battle of Poitiers (732). Father of Pippin the Short; grandfather of Charlemagne.

Charles [Philip Arthur George], Prince of Wales (1948–), heir to Brit. throne. Son of Elizabeth II and Prince Philip; created Prince of Wales (1968).

Charles the Bold (1433–77), last reigning Duke of Burgundy. Led Burgundian resistance (1467–77) to Louis XI of France.

Charles the Great see CHARLEMAGNE.

Charlotte Amalie, cap. of US Virgin Islands Tourist resort. Main products, rum and handicrafts. Pop. *c*. 12,900.

Charlottetown, cap. of Prince Edward Is. Canada; exports island products. Founded (1750) by French, later taken by British. Access to mainland by ferry service. Pop. (1964) 17,956.

Charon, in Gk. myth., boatman of Styx who ferried souls of the dead to Hades; son of Erebus.

Chartism, 19th cent. Eng. polit. movement. In 1833 it submitted charter containing 6 demands for reform (1) abolition of property qualifications for MPs (2) manhood suffrage (3) ballot voting (4) equal electoral districts (5) payment of MPs (6) annual parliaments.

Chartres, cap. of Eure-et-Loire department, NW France, on the Eure. Cathedral of Notre Dame (built 1240) noted for stained glass windows. Light industry. Pop. (1963) 28,750.

chartreuse see CARTHUSIANS.

Charybdis, in Gk. legend, see SCYLLA.

Chase, Lucia (1907–), Amer. dancer. Joined Ballet Theatre (1940), co-director since 1945. Best remembered for character roles.

Chase, Salmon Portland (1803–73), Amer. statesman and opponent of slavery. As US Sec. of Treasury (1861–64), originated national banking system. Chief Justice, US Supreme Court (1864–73).

Chase, Stuart (1888–), Amer. writer and govt. economic adviser. Works include *Men and Machines* (1929), and *The Tyranny of Words* (1938).

chat, insectivorous bird of thrush group of genus *Saxicola*. Whinchat and stonechat inhabit rocky areas in Europe, Australia and N America.

Chataway, Christopher John (1931–), Eng. athlete and politician. Ran world record 5,000 m. in 1954.

Chateaubriand, François René, Vicomte de (1768–1848), Fr. writer and diplomat. Exiled during Revolution, active in politics until 1830. Wrote *The Genius of Christianity* (1802), incl. extracts 'Atala' and 'René'. A founder of Fr. Romanticism.

Chatelier, Henry le (1850–1936), Fr. chemist. Estab. laws of chem. equilibrium and displacement of equilibrium.

Chatham, Earl of see PITT, WILLIAM.

Chattanooga, city in Tenn., US. Manufacturing and transportation centre. Headquarters of TENNESSEE VALLEY AUTHORITY. Pop. (1960) 205,000.

Chattanooga campaign, in US Civil War (Aug.-Nov. 1863). Chattanooga, Tenn., as centre of communications, important Union objective. Con-federates, under Braxton Bragg, besieged town but driven from area by Ulysses S. Grant and retreated to Georgia.

Chaucer, Geoffrey (*c*. 1343–1400), Eng. poet and civil servant, often employed on diplomatic missions. Early work influenced by Fr. models; translated *Roman de la Rose*. Later inspired by Italians incl. Dante and Boccaccio, as in *The House of Fame*, *The Parliament of Fowls* and *Troilus and Criseyde*. Latest work represented by great unfinished cycle of 23 *Canterbury Tales* (*c*. 1387).

chauvinism, aggressive and exaggerated nationalism. Named after Nicholas Chauvin, Napoleonic soldier. Term associated with militarism, imperialism and racism.

Chauviré, Yvette (1917–), Fr. dancer of international standing. Best known for roles in *Istar* and *Giselle*.

Chavez, Carlos (1899–), Mexican composer, conductor and musicologist. Wrote for Mexican native instruments, *e.g.* in *Xochipilli-Macuilxochtl* (Mexican god of music).

Ché Guevara see GUEVARA, ERNESTO.

checkerberry see WINTERGREEN.

checkers see DRAUGHTS.

cheesecloth see MUSLIN.

cheetah, *Acinonyx jubatus*, cat of grasslands and semi-deserts of Africa and SW Asia. Reaches speeds of *c*. 60 m.p.h.; hunts in groups.

Cheever, John (1912–), Amer. short-story writer. Works, featuring ironic understatement, include *The Wapshot Chronicle* (1957).

Chekhov, Anton (1860–1904), Russ. dramatist and short-story writer. Works reflect loneliness and frustration of man and dullness of middle class Russ. life. Plays include *The Cherry Orchard, The Three Sisters, Ivanov* (1887) and *The Seagull* (1896).

Chellean see ABBEVILLIAN.

chemistry, science concerned with

Cheetah

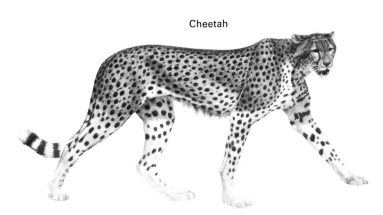

composition of and changes in substances.

chemistry, inorganic, study of properties of elements and their compounds, except most carbon compounds.

chemistry, organic, study of compounds formed from carbon and such elements as hydrogen, oxygen, nitrogen, and to lesser extent, sulphur and phosphorus.

chemistry, physical, application of physical measurements and laws to chem. systems and their changes, covering a range of subjects intermediate to chemistry and physics.

Chemnitz, centre of textile industry in Saxony, E. Germany. Grew in 19th cent. with development of coalfields of Middle Saxony; now manufactures cars, chemicals and food. Heavily bombed in World War 2; few old buildings remain. Renamed Karl Marx-Stadt (1953). Pop. (1964) 250,000.

Chemulpo *see* INCHON.

Chen Po-ta (1904–   ), Chinese Communist leader. Joined Party (1927) and became Political Secretary to MAO TSE-TUNG. Leader in cultural revolution after appointment as rector, Peking University (1967).

Chengtu, Ch'engtu, cap., of Szechwan prov., SW China. Important road junction; produces silk, cotton textiles and matches. US air base in World War 2. Pop. (1964) 1,007,000.

Cheops (Khufu, Khufwey), 2nd Egyptian king of 4th dynasty (*c.* 2700 BC), builder of pyramid at Gizeh.

Chephren (Khafre) (*fl.* 2565 BC), Egyptian king of 4th dynasty, son of Cheops, builder of 2nd pyramid at Gizeh.

Cherbourg, town, prob. of Roman origin, in Manche, N France, with fortified seaports and naval station on Eng. Channel. Taken by English (1758). Harbour extended (1889) and again by Germans during occupation (1940–4). Pop. (1965) 40,000.

Chéret, Jules (1836–1932), Fr. draughtsman and painter whose theatre and opera posters influenced poster artists, notably Toulouse-Lautrec.

Cherokee, largest Indian tribe in SE North America. Settled farmers, frequently fought Iroquois. Estab. (1827) Cherokee nation, with govt. modelled on that of white colonists.

cherry, fruit, wood and tree of genus *Prunus* of rose family. Smooth stone enclosed in fleshy, usually edible, tissue. Native to Asia Minor, most varieties are derived from sweet-cherry, *P. avium.*

Cherubini, [Maria] Luigi Carlo Zeno-

Pyramid of Cheops

bio **Salvatore** (1760–1842), Ital. composer of operas and sacred music, incl. *Medée* (1797). Director of Paris Conservatoire from 1822.

chervil, *Anthriscus cerefolium,* annual herb of parsley family with sweet and aromatic leaves used for flavouring in cookery. Native to Russia, reaching Med. area *c.* 300 BC.

Cherwell, Lord *see* LINDEMANN, FREDERICK ALEXANDER.

Chesapeake Bay, inlet on Atlantic coast of Maryland and Virginia, US, 200 mi. long. Large sea-food industry. Most important port on its shore is Baltimore.

Branch of flowering cherry

Cheshire, county of NW England, largely flat and fertile. Area: 1,015 sq. mi.; county town, Chester; main towns, Crewe, Birkenhead. Famed for dairy produce, particularly cheese. Pop. (1966) 1,472,000.

chess, ancient game, possibly Indian in origin. Played on checkered board with 32 chessmen divided between 2 players, moved according to conventional manoeuvres.

chest *see* THORAX.

Chesterfield, Philip Dormer Stanhope, 4th Earl of (1694–1773), Eng. statesman and author of the worldly *Letters to His Son* (pub. 1774).

Chesterton, G[ilbert] K[eith] (1874–1936), Eng. poet, essayist, novelist. Best-known works are fantasy novels, *The Napoleon of Notting Hill* (1904), *The Man Who Was Thursday* (1908) and 'Father Brown' series of detective stories.

chestnut, tree of genus *Castanea* of beech family found in N temp. regions. Species include sweet or Sp. chestnut, *C. sativa,* Amer. chestnut, *C. dentata,* and Jap. chestnut, *C. crenata.* Fruit is burr-like containing 2–3 nuts. Wood strong and durable.

chevet, in architecture, eastern termination of a church choir, a distinctly Fr. development.

Chevreul, Michael Eugène (1786–1889), Fr. chemist. Discovered margarine, stearin and olein; research work on dyes and soap-making.

chevrotain, mouse deer, Traqulidae, small family of ruminants of SE Asian forests. One of smallest hoofed mammals, without antlers.

Cheyenne, N Amer. Indian tribe. Orig. farmers, became nomadic buffalo hunters when horse introd. (1760). Colorado gold discovery (1858) forced Cheyennes into reservation where govt. neglect provoked raids by Indians, who were then massacred by US army.

Cheyenne, state cap. of Wyoming,

Chickaree

US. Sheep and cattle market. Pop. (1960) 43,505.

Chiang Ching (1915–), wife of Mao Tse-tung. Deputy head of Cultural Revolution, personally directed many RED GUARD activities.

Chiang Kai-shek (1887–), Chinese military and polit. leader. Emerged as head of KUOMINTANG in 1920s; leader (1928–48), ruled with extensive power. Driven from mainland (1948) after Communist triumph in civil war. Continued to challenge current regime from Taiwan-based Nationalist govt. after 1948.

chianti *see* WINE.

Chibcha, S Amer. Indians of Colombia. Most populous and best-organized state between Mexico and Peru at time of Sp. conquest. Defeated, put down by 1541; language almost completely died out and few of their wooden buildings survived.

Chicago, city in Illinois, US, on S shore of L. Michigan. Most important

Horse or Common Chestnut: (a) blossom (b) fruit (c) leaf

communications centre in Amer. midwest. Wheat market and meat packing are major industries. Built on Fort Dearborn site (1803). Pop. (1960) 5,959,000.

Chicago, University of, founded (1891), subsidized privately. Noted for graduate faculties and research programmes.

Chichester, Sir Francis (1901–), Eng. air pioneer and yachtsman. Completed solo voyage round world in ketch *Gypsy Moth IV* (Aug. 1966 to May 1967).

chickadee, common N Amer. tit. In Canada and N US, black capped chickadee, *Parus atricapillus* (willow tit in Europe); in S US smaller Carolina chickadee, *P. carolinensis*.

chickaree, *Tamiasciurus hudsonicus,* Amer. red squirrel, named after its call.

Chickasaw, tribe of N Amer. Indians closely related in culture to the Choctaw, their constant enemies. Occupied the Mississippi until 1834 when moved to an Oklahoma reservation.

chickenpox, infectious epidemic, virus disease. Characterized by eruption of succession of blisters. Incubation 2–3 weeks.

chickweed, low annual or perennial herb of genus *Stellaria* of pink family, native to temp. regions. Small, white flowers. Old World weed, *S. media* is well-known species.

chicle, gumlike substance derived from latex of trop. Amer. trees in Yucatan and Guatemala, *e.g.* Sapodilla, *Achras sapota* of Sapotaceae family. Introduced into US as rubber substitute.

chicory [UK], **Belgian endive** [US], *Cichorium intybus,* European annual plant, also grown in US; leaves used in salads, root ground and roasted as coffee substitute.

Chief Justice (of the Supreme Court), in US, presiding judge over Supreme Court or highest appellate court of each state. Selection and power vary according to different state constitutions. Chief Justice of Supreme Court appointed by Pres. with advice and consent of Senate; 9 nominations have been rejected by Senate.

chiffchaff, *Phylloscopus collybita,* bird of European warbler family. Named after its repetitive song.

chiffon, light, tough fabric made of silk, rayon or cotton; softest and thinnest of woven sheet fabrics.

chigger, larva of certain mites parasitic on vertebrates; causes itch. Amer. variety is *Trombicula irritans.*

Chessmen wearing costumes of the Napoleonic Wars

chigoe, jigger, *Tunga penetrans,* minute, blood-sucking, flea orig. of S America, but now estab. over much of Africa and tropics. Causes serious, sometimes fatal, sores.

Childe, Vere Gordon (1892–1957), Brit. archaeologist. Works include *The Dawn of European Civilization* (1925) and *What Happened in History* (1942).

Santiago, Chile

Chile [**República de Chile**], S Amer. repub. Area: 286,400 sq. mi.; cap. Santiago. W Andes dominate country. Crops include olives, flax, sugar beet. Mineral resources: nitrates, copper, iodine, sulphur, iron

and manganese. Population mostly of Sp. and Indian descent; official language Spanish; possession of Spain until independence (1818). Unit of currency, peso. Pop. (1966) 8,789,389.

Chile pine *see* ARAUCARIA.

chili *see* PEPPER.

Chimaera, in Gk. myth., monster with lion's head, goat's body and snake's tail. Killed by Bellerophon.

chimaera, scaleless fish with incomplete backbone and extended thread-like tail. Grinding plates replace teeth.

Chimborazo, inactive volcano with snow-capped cone, highest peak (20,577 ft.) in Ecuadorean Andes. Explored 1st (1802) by Alexander von Humboldt.

chimes, set of tubular bells which are struck with hammer. Member of orchestral percussion group.

chimpanzee, *Pan troglodytes,* ape of central W African forests. Most

Chimpanzee

Chimpansee

intelligent infra-human primate it possesses high level of curiosity. The pygmy chimp or bonobo, *P. paniscus,* is found S of Congo river.

Chimu, kingdom, ancient S Amer. Indian civilization on N coast of Peru, absorbed by Inca Empire.

China, Great Wall of, Chinese fortifications *c.* 1,500 mi. long from Kansu to Hopeh province, along S edge of Mongolian plain. Present restored form dates from Ming Dynasty (1368–1644).

China, People's Republic of [**Chung-Hua Jen-Min Kung-Ho Kuo**], country occupying most of E Asia, most populous in world. Includes China, Manchuria, Inner Mongolia, Tibet, Yunnan and Sinkiang. Area: *c.* 4,300,000 sq. mi.; cap. Peking; main cities, Shanghai, Canton, Sian, Tientsin. Land slopes SE from Tibetan mountains, drained by 3 great river systems: Hwang-Ho Yangtze-Kiang, and Si-Kiang. Climate varies from temp. to trop., featuring summer monsoons. Largely pastoral and agric., irrigation and crop rotation extensively practised. Major crops rice, sugar and tea, wheat, cotton.

Scanty mineral resources. Emperors of Chinese Dynasties ruled (*c.* 2205 BC–AD 1912) until revolution, when last Manchu emperor abdicated. Dislike of foreign intervention led to Opium War (1839–42), Taiping Rebellion (1848–65) and Boxer Rebellion (1900). Conflict (1894–5) with Japan ended with China's defeat. Civil war (1919) culminated in triumph (1928) of KUOMINTANG under Chiang Kai-shek. Subsequent war with Japan (outbreak 1931) merged with Communist challenge; People's Repub. estab. (1949) under MAO TSE-TUNG. Heavy industry concentrated in Manchuria. Light industries and processing agric. products important in cities. Population concentrated in lowland provinces; 90% population are Han (Chinese). Main religions Confucianism, Buddhism and Taoism. Unit of currency, yuan. Pop. (1963) *c.* 705,000,000.

China, Republic of [**Chung-Hua Min Kuo**], island of Taiwan (Formosa), off SE coast of China, E Asia. Area: 13,886 sq. mi.; cap. Taipei. Ceded (1895) to Japan, but returned to China (1945); now governed by

Chinese Nationalist Party. Lost membership of UN (1971) to mainland China. Rice, sugar and tea are grown. Pop. (1965) 12,791,000.

china clay, rock composed almost entirely of mineral kaolinite; used in pottery and paper-making.

chinch bug, small, elongated plant bug, *Blissus leucopterus* of US. Destructive to grass, wheat and other grains. Related to European *Ischnodemus sabulcti.*

chinchilla, *Chinchilla lanigera,* small grey rodent, of Chilean and Bolivean Andes. It is *c.* 10 in. long, and valued commercially for its pelt.

Chinese, chief language of Sino-Tibetan family. Standard form Mandarin, spoken by 378 million, but many large dialects, incl. Wu (Shanghai, 46 million), Cantonese (Canton 27 million), Min (Foochow, 22 million), Hakka (Kiangsi, 20 million), Hunanese (Changsha, 26 million). Mandarin is basis of new standard language Kuo-yu (official language). Literary language Wênyen is the same in all dialects.

Chinese lantern, winter cherry, *Physalis alkekengi,* plant of Eurasian origin, bearing fruit in inflated orange calyx, dried to form floral decoration.

chinese parsley *see* CORIANDER.

Chinese pheasant, ring-necked pheasant, ornamental, often hybrid, variety of Old World PHEASANT.

Ch'ing or **Manchu,** Chinese ruling dynasty (1644–1712). Forced to grant trading rights to Europeans in 19th cent. Revolution of 1911 marked end of rule.

Chinon, town in Indre-et-Loire department, C France, on Vienne river, where Joan of Arc revealed her mission to the Dauphin (1429). Pop. (1964) 6,100.

Chinook, N Amer. sea-going Indian tribe of Penutian linguistic stock, occupying Columbia valley, W US.

chinook, name for SALMON.

chinook, warm, dry, west wind of E Rocky Mts. Loses moisture as rain on W slopes; brings early spring thaw (sometimes flooding).

chipmunk, genus *Tamias* of squirrel family of N America and Asia. Common N Amer. *T. striatus* is marked with black and yellow stripes and has cheek pouches. Winters in state of partial hibernation.

Chippendale, Thomas (1718–79), Eng. furniture-maker. Style based on Queen Anne and Georgian design but with Fr. Gothic and Chinese elaboration. Used dark mahogany without inlays. Work valued by antique collectors.

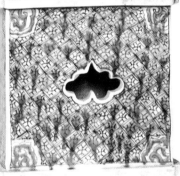

Porcelain Buddhist statue of lion

Chippewyan *see* ATHAPASKAN.
Chirico, Giorgio de (1888–), Ital. painter. Joined Carra (1914) to formulate Metaphysical painting, expressing belief that places and objects possess own spirit. Work influenced Surrealists.
chital, axis deer, *Axis axis,* white-spotted, red-brown deer of India and Ceylon.
chiton, in ancient Greece, tunic worn by both men and women under cloak (*himation*).
chiton, marine mollusc with long, flattened body. Largely vegetarian.
Chittagong, formerly Islamabad, town in E Pakistan, important port 10 mi. from mouth of Karnaphuli. Grown since Indian independence

(1947), now trading in rice, jute, tobacco, sugar cane, tea and coffee. Manufactures paper, woollen textiles, fertilizers and tyres. Pop. (1964) 367,000.
chivalry *see* KNIGHTHOOD.
chives, *Allium schoenoprasum,* perennial plant of onion family; tubular leaves used in salads and as flavouring.
chlamydomonas, genus of freshwater protozoans with 2 flagellae and a pigment spot. Member of animal group nearest plants, has bright green chlorophyll and cell walls of cellulose.
chlorine (Cl), element occurring as sodium chloride (common salt), also found in sea water and rocks. Corrosive greenish-yellow gas with pungent odour. Obtained as by-product in manufacture of caustic soda or, through Downs process of electrolysis, in manufacture of sodium. Used to make hydrochloric acid and non-inflammable solvents, *e.g.* carbon tetrachloride and organic derivatives such as chloroform.
chlorite, green stone, hydrous silicate of aluminium, ferrous iron and magnesium, associated with and resembling micas. Greasy to touch.
chloroform ($CHCl_3$), clear, colourless, non-inflammable, volatile liquid with sweet smell and ANAESTHETIC properties. Manufactured by chlorination of alcohol or acetone in alkaline solution. Importance declined because of potency and deleterious action on heart.
chloromycetin, chloramphenicol, ANTIBIOTIC used in treatment of infectious diseases. Obtained from cultures of *Streptomyces venezuelae.* First identified (1947) by Burkholder.
chlorophyll, complex pigment, existing only in autotrophs. Molecule similar to blood pigment, haemoglobin. Chlorophyll is green, but colour may be masked by other pigments. Absent from all heterotrophs, incl. all ANIMALS.
Cho Oyu, mountain in Himalayas, forming part of Nepal-Tibet border. Sixth highest peak in the world (26,750 ft.). First climbed (1954) by Austrian party.
chocolate *see* COCOA.
Choctaw, N Amer. Indian tribe of Muskogean linguistic stock and similar in culture to Creek and Chickasaw. Formerly occupied C and

Acrobat performing in Chinese park

S Mississippi; friendly with French, moved to reserve in Oklahoma (1832).
cholera, acute infectious disease usually caused by water-borne *Vibrio cholerae* and characterized by severe diarrhoea, muscular cramps and collapse. Formerly occurring in epidemics, now largely controlled.
cholesterol, white crystalline alcohol of steroid group of substances; concentrates in blood of aged animals and contributes to hardening of arteries, coronary conditions and gallstones. Occurs in all tissues of organism, esp. adrenal glands and nervous tissue of spine and brain.
cholla, several spiny, tree-like cacti of SW US and Mexico, esp. *Opontia cholla* and teddy bear cholla, *C. fulgida.*
Chomo Ljari, Jomolhari, formerly Chumalhari, Tibetan sacred mountain, 23,997 ft., in W Assam Himalayas on undefined Bhutan-Tibet border. First climbed (1937).
Chomsky, Noam, Amer. linguist. Published *Syntactic Structures* (1957), which proposed to use transformation as instrument for description of syntax.
chondrite, type of stony meteorite.
Chopin, Frédéric François (1810–49), Fr.-Polish composer and pianist. Taught and composed in Paris from 1831. Wrote some of best work during association with GEORGE SAND (1838–47). Piano works include concertos, sonatas, polonaises and mazurkas.

Chinese Pheasant

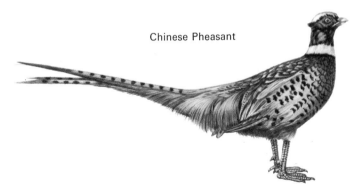

chorale, hymn of Lutheran Church. Tunes often used in Ger. baroque music as themes for larger choral works. Chorale prelude, for organ, is based on chorale tune.

chord, group of 3 or more simultaneously sounded notes in music, and basic material of harmony since 17th cent. Chords may be built up of any intervals, but in traditional tonality, major triad is basic unit. *See* HARMONY.

chordate, animal of phylum Chordata with gills, dorsal nerve chord and supporting skeletal rod (notochord). Includes VERTEBRATE (higher chordates), and tunicate, LANCELET, and HEMICHORDATE (lower chordates).

Chou En-Lai (1898–   ), Chinese Communist leader. Politically active since student days in France, founder of Chinese Communist Party; took part in LONG MARCH. First premier and Foreign Minister (1949–   ) of Chinese People's Republic. Prominent since 1954 Geneva conference on Indo-China.

chough, genus *Pyrrhocorax* of Old World crow family, with black plumage and red feet. Species include Cornish chough, *P. pyrrhocorax,* with long red beak, and Alpine chough, *P. graculus,* frequently scavenging feeder.

Chrétien de Troyes (c. 1135–83), Fr. court poet, author of Arthurian romances, *Yvain, Erec et Enide, Launcelot* and *Perceval* incorporating Grail legends.

Christchurch, 2nd largest city of New Zealand, on R. Avon. Important commercial and industrial city; educ. centre with cathedral. Prosperity depends on rich cornlands and sheep stations of Canterbury Plains. Exports wool and meat from Lyttelton. City founded (1850) by Eng. Anglican colonists. Pop. (1964) 247,000.

Christmas Rose

Christian Science, religion founded by Mary Baker Eddy, after recovery of health (1866) through reading of Christ's healing power in NT. Doctrine was stated in *Science and Health* (1875).

Christianity, religion originating in life and teachings of Jesus Christ. The Bible, containing NT stories of Christ and early apostles and OT Jewish mytho-history, formed basis of Christian faith. Early church tended to be highly organizational and this tendency, coupled with geographic spread of Christianity, soon resulted in variety of churches (*e.g.* R.C., Eastern Orthodox). Subsequent reformed churches (Protestant) were reaction against elaborate ritual and doctrines imposed by traditionalists.

Christie, Agatha Mary Clarissa (1891–   ), prolific Eng. writer of detective fiction, creator of Hercule Poirot and Miss Marple. Books include *The Mysterious Affair at Styles* (1920), *The Murder of Roger Ackroyd* (1926) and *Third Girl* (1966); plays include *The Mousetrap,* on London stage since 1952.

Christmas Island, in Indian Ocean, 250 mi. SW of Java. Area: 60 sq. mi. Annexed by UK (1888). Now territory of Australia. Phosphate deposits and coral. Pop. *c.* 2,000.

Christmas Island, one of Line Is. in Pacific, largest atoll (95 sq. mi.) with guano deposits and coconut plantations. Attached to Gilbert and Ellice Is. (1919), became US strategic air base. Pop. (1963) 300.

Christmas rose, *Helleborus niger,* perennial plant of buttercup family. Blooms at Christmas; evergreen leaves with white or greenish flowers.

Christopher, Saint (*c.* 3rd cent.), Christian martyr of Asia Minor, patron saint of travellers. Feast day, 25 July.

Christy, Henry (1810–65), London

banker and collector of ethnographica. His concept of classification of stratification levels revolutionized knowledge of Paleolithic period.

chromatography, chem. term describing physical methods used to measure components of complex chem. compounds. Used in study of vitamins, hormones, dyestuffs and antibiotics.

chromite, brittle opaque brownish-black mineral compound, *e.g.* sodium chromite, which may be magnetic. Source for chromium.

chromium, silver white, very hard, metallic ELEMENT. Always occurs in compounds, which are highly toxic, particularly as chromite. Prepared by reduction of chromic oxide by aluminium in Thermite Process. Used in manufacture of stainless steel and in electroplating.

chromosome, thread-like structure in CELL nucleus. Controls HEREDITY by transmitting characteristics through genes. Every body cell in each species contains same number of chromosomes; $\frac{1}{2}$ that number are in germ cell, egg or sperm. There are 46 in man's cells, 78 in the dog, hundreds in the paramecium.

Chronicles I and II, OT history books, providing supplement to, and commentary on, *Kings I and II* and follow them in the Bible, but prob. written 300–250 BC.

chrysanthemum, genus of annual or perennial herbs of daisy family, native to Orient, but widely distributed. Late blooming red, yellow, and white flowers. Floral emblem of Japan.

chrysoprase (SiO_2), apple-green CHALCEDONY with nickel oxide impurity; semi-precious gem stone.

Chu Teh (1886–   ), Chinese soldier and politician; commanded Chinese Red Army (1930–54) when made vice-chairman of People's Republic of China.

chub, species of fish of Cyprinidae family. In Europe *Leuciscus cephalus,* freshwater member of carp family. In America, river chub, *Hybopsis kentuckiensis,* and silver chub, *Semotilus corporalis.*

chuckwalla, *Sauromalus obesus,*

Chough

herbivorous lizard of iguana family of W US desert regions. Aestivates below ground during food and water shortages.

Chumash, Santa Barbara Indians, group of almost extinct N Amer. Indian tribes. Lived in California; Sp. missions estab. (18th cent.).

Chungking, city of SW China, in Szechwan prov., cap. of repub. (1937–46). River port *c.* 500 mi. from mouth of Yangtze and commercial cap. of W China. Industries include cotton and silk mills, paper, iron, steel and chem. plants. Pop. (1963) 2,121,000.

Church, Alonzo (1903–), Amer. logician and mathematician, noted for proof that Decision Problem is insoluble.

Church of England *see* ENGLAND, CHURCH OF.

Church of England in Australia *see* ENGLAND, CHURCH OF.

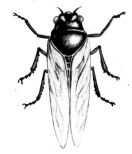

Periodical Cicada of North America

Church of Ireland *see* ENGLAND, CHURCH OF.

Church of Scotland *see* SCOTLAND, CHURCH OF.

Church of the Province of New Zealand *see* ENGLAND, CHURCH OF.

Churchill, river of N Saskatchewan and Manitoba, Canada, *c.* 1,000 mi. long. Flows into Hudson Bay.

Churchill, John, 1st Duke of Marlborough (1650–1722), Eng. general and courtier. Supported James II against Monmouth (1685), William of Orange (who made him Earl of Marlborough 1689) against James II (1688), James again (1692–8), Queen Anne (1702–11) and George I (1714). Famed for victories in War of Spanish Succession at Blenheim (1704), Ramillies (1706), Oudenarde (1708) and Malplaquet (1709). Gained favour under Anne through influence of wife Sarah Jennings (1660–1744) and P. M. Godolphin. Disgraced (1710) but reinstated (1714).

Churchill, Odette *see* SPECIAL OPERATIONS EXECUTIVE.

Churchill, Winston (1871–1947), Amer. novelist. Author of historical novels, *Richard Carvel* (1899) and *The Crisis* (1901) and polit. novels, *e.g. The Inside of the Cup* (1913).

Churchill, Sir Winston Leonard Spencer (1874–1965), Brit. statesman. Fought in India, the Sudan and South Africa. Elected to Parl. (1900). First Lord of the Admiralty (1911–15) until discredited by failure of Dardanelles expedition in World War 1. Returned to office under Lloyd George (1917–21); Cons. Chancellor of Exchequer (1924–9). Out of office during 1930s, regained influence by opposing 'appeasement' of Germany. Replaced Neville Chamberlain (1940) as P.M. and became symbol of Brit. resistance to Nazi Germany in World War 2. Attended series of international conferences prior to end of war incl. Casablanca, Yalta, Teheran and Potsdam. Leader of opposition (1945–51). Cons. victory (1951) returned him to power; retired 1955. Written works include *The Second World War,* 6 vols. (1948–53), for which he won Nobel Prize for Literature (1953).

C.I.A. *see* CENTRAL INTELLIGENCE AGENCY.

cicada, family, Cicadidae, of insects mainly of trop. and sub-trop. areas. Broad body and 2 pairs of transparent wings; noted for loud call.

Cicero, Marcus Tullius (106–43 BC), Roman orator and statesman. Reputation in law-courts estab. (76 BC). Consul (63 BC), responsible for suppression of Catilinarian conspiracy, delivered *In Catilinam.* Opposed Caesar and popular party. Reconciled with Caesar (48 BC), delivered *Philippics* against Antony (44–43 BC). Murdered by Antony's agents. Speeches include *In Verrem* (70 BC), *Pro Caelio* (56 BC); writings, philosophical and literary, *De Oratore* (55 BC), *De Re Publica* (52–45 BC), and 4 collections of letters, *e.g. Ad Atticum.*

Chrysanthemum

cichlid, family Cichlidae, freshwater trop. fish; some predatory. Species of genus *Tilapia* carry their eggs in their mouths.

Cid, El *see* DIAZ DE VIVAR, RODRIGO.

cider, in Europe fermented apple juice containing 4–7% alcohol; in US, unless classified as 'hard cider', is unfermented juice. Brandy made from residue of fermented juice known as applejack.

cigarette beetle, *Lasioderma serricorne,* small brown beetle. Larvae feed on stored tobacco leaves and products.

Cimabue, Giovanni (*c.* 1240 – *c.* 1302), Ital. painter regarded as founder of modern painting and Florentine school. Mosaic *St John* (Pisa Cathedral); *Sta Trinita Madonna* (Uffizi, Florence) and frescoes in Church of St Francis, Assisi.

Cincinnati, city in Ohio, US, on Ohio R. Communications and cultural centre, light industry. Pop. (1960) 994,000.

cineraria, ornamental blooming plants derived from species *Senecio*; 2 main varieties, dusty miller and the greenhouse *S. cruentus* are popular garden plants.

Cinna, Lucius Cornelius (d. 84 BC), Roman democrat and consul

Chrysoprase, showing cut and mounted stones

The Pantheon in Naples by Francesco di Paolo, an outstanding example of 18th cent. classicism in architecture

(87–84 BC) in Sulla's absence. Proposed recall of Marius, expelled from Rome; returned with Marius, and proscribed Sulla's followers. Prepared to resist Sulla's return (84 BC), but killed by mutinous troops at Brundisium.

cinnamon, sweet spice from dried inner bark of E Indian evergreen tree, *Cinnamomum zeylanicum*; used in cookery and medicine.

cinquefoil, plant of genus *Potentilla* of rose family, with yellow flowers. Most species perennial herbs from N temp. and subarctic regions. Species include creeping cinquefoil, *P. reptans,* and silvery cinquefoil, *P. argentea.*

Cintron, Conchita (1925–), Sp. woman bullfighter noted for artistry in arena.

circle, closed curve, equidistant throughout its length from its fixed central point.

cirque, deep rounded hollow with steep sides, found in glaciated mountains, formed by erosion. Also called *corrie* (Scotland) or *cwm* (Wales).

cirripede *see* BARNACLE.

cirrus clouds *see* CLOUD.

Cisalpine Republic *see* CAMPO FORMIO, TREATY OF.

Citizens' Advice Bureau, Brit. state-supported, national organization (estab. 1939), which gives advice to public and acts as mutual 3rd party between govt. and public. Each bureau is self-governing and staffed (c. 70%) by part-time volunteers.

citizenship *see* NATURALIZATION.

Citlaltepetl, volcanic mountain, highest in Mexico (18,700 ft.), in Veracruz state.

citrin, variety of QUARTZ.

citrine, semi-precious yellowish-white gem stone resembling topaz; made by heating black quartz.

City, The, area of London with most of head offices of financial, stock-broking and insurance companies, Bank of England, the Merchant and other banks, Stock Exchange, St Paul's Cathedral, The Tower, The Mansion House, Guildhall and The Temple.

Ciudad Bolívar, city in Venezuela on Orinoco. Independence from Spain declared by Simon Bolivar (1819), hence its name. Trading centre exporting gold, diamonds, hides and skins. Pop, 26,000.

Ciudad Trujillo, cap. of Dominican Republic. Founded by Columbus' brother Bartholomew (1496); Santo Domingo until 1936 when named after dictator Rafael Trujillo. After his death (1961), reverted to orig. name. Pop. (1964) 529,000.

civet, mammal of carnivore family *Viverridae*. Species include African civet, *Civattictus civetta,* and Indian civet, *Viverra zibetta,* with grey coat and erectile manes.

civic universities (UK), term referring to 19th and early 20th cent. universities, founded in industrial cities to supplement older established places of higher learning. Includes Manchester, Birmingham, Liverpool, Leeds, Sheffield, Nottingham, Durham and London.

civil law, codified law governing private affairs in contrast to public and criminal law. Based on Roman law, esp. as formulated in *Corpus Juris Civilis* and revived 11th–12th cent. Adopted by European countries, Latin America and some Asian nations.

civil rights, in US, those rights guaranteed by BILL OF RIGHTS and 'equal protection' clause of 17th Amendment of US Constitution.

Extended to equalize minority group rights in employment. Congress passed 3 Civil Rights Acts (1957, 1960, 1964), last one being in 1875; 1964 Act provided for more effective enforcement of rights. Civil rights movement of 1960s protested illegal practices against Negroes. *See* MARTIN LUTHER KING.

civil service, body of people employed in civil admin. of govt., not incl. military or elected officials. Term 1st applied to Brit. administrators in India, later to Brit. home officials. Entry to Brit. Civil Service by competitive examination since 1855. In US, reform of 'Spoils System' (*i.e.* patronage) began with Pendleton Act (1883).

civil war, conflict between people of same state or community.

Civil War, in Eng. history, struggle (1642–6) between Charles I and Cromwell's Parliamentarians, ending with king's capture (1646). Short 2nd civil war begun with Charles' escape; ended with his recapture (1647).

Civil War, in US (1861–5), conflict between Union (N states) and CON-FEDERACY (S states). Causes included sectional rivalry campaign to abolish slavery and STATES' RIGHTS quarrel. Union forces, under ULYSSES S. GRANT, were ascendant after 1863 and South, led by ROBERT E. LEE, surrendered 1865.

Clackmannanshire, smallest county of Scotland. Area: 54 sq. mi., county town Alloa. Main occupations, sheep-farming, coal-mining, brewing and distilling. Pop. (1966) 43,000.

Clair, René (1898–), Fr. film writer, director and producer; films include *Sous les Toits* (1947), *Les Belles de Nuit* (1952), and *Tout l'Or du Monde* (1961). First film director to be elected to French Academy (1960).

clam, bivalve mollusc, lives in sand. Round clam, *Venus mercenaria,* of NW Atlantic coast and long clam, *Mya arenaria,* are common. Some species are edible.

Clapperton, Hugh (1788–1827), Scot. explorer. Travelled in W Africa and collected much information about Hausa states.

Clare, county of W Ireland. Area: 1,235 sq. mi.; county town, Ennis. Main occupations, agriculture, slate and lead. Pop. (1964) 73,762.

claret *see* WINE.

clarinet, single-reed woodwind instrument with cylindrical bore, invented late 17th cent. Bass or alto extends 1 octave lower.

Clark, Jim (1936–68), Scot. motor-racing driver, World Champion (1963, 1965). Record number of

Grand Prix victories in a year, 7 in 1963.

Clark, [John] Grahame [Douglas] (1907–), Brit. archaeologist. Specializes in prehistoric Europe; wrote *The Mesolithic Settlement of Northern Europe* (1936) and *The Stone Age Hunters* (1967).

Clarke, Ron[ald William] (1937–), Austral. long-distance runner, estab. 6 world records during 1960s in 2–6 mi. events.

Clark, Sir Wilfred Edward Le Gros, (1895–), Brit. anatomist, anthropologist and palaeontologist. Wrote *Early Forerunners of Man* (1934) and *History of Primates* (1949).

clarkia, genus of hardy annual herbs of willow herb family of N America bearing clusters of small flowers.

classicism, concept in literature, art and music; dominance of technical precision over content; clarity, rationality, repression of emotion, and free play of imagination. Opposite of ROMANTICISM.

Claude Lorrain *see* LORRAIN, CLAUDE.

Claudel, Paul (1868–1955), Fr. dramatist, poet, diplomat and R.C. apologian. Work based on profound religious conviction, deals with salvation or destruction of soul. Works include plays: *L'Annonce faite à Marie* (1912), *Le Soulier de Satin* (1929), and poems.

Claudius (10 BC–AD 54), Roman emperor (41–54), nephew of Tiberius, proclaimed emperor on the assassination of CALIGULA. His reign was one of consolidation. His 4th wife was his niece Agrippina, said to have murdered him to ensure throne for her son, NERO.

Clausewitz, Karl von (1780–1831), Pruss. general and military strategist. Wrote *On War* (1832), advocating total destruction of enemy.

clavichord, small keyboard instrument, developed in 15th cent. Small tangents of brass, activated by keys, press against strings.

clavicle *see* COLLAR BONE.

clavier, generic name for stringed keyboard instruments.

claw, pointed horny nail of foot of animal or bird.

clawed frog, amphibian of *Xenopus*

Clawed Frog

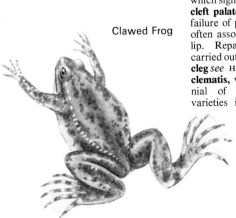

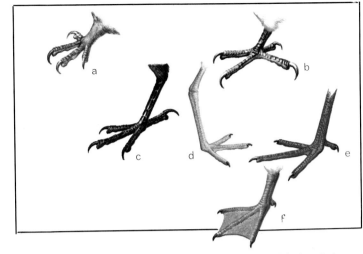

Types of bird claw: (a) swift (b) woodpecker (c) hooded crow (d) plover (e) stork (f) duck

genus, with webbed, clawed feet; found in Africa S of Sahara.

clay, earthy hydrous aluminium silicate. Sticky and plastic when wet, it hardens when dry or fired. Used in making brick, tile, porcelain, china, earthenware and drainage pipes, and for filtration.

Clay, Cassius *see* MUHAMMAD ALI HAJ.

Clay, Henry (1777–1852), Amer. lawyer and politician. Congressman and Senator from Kentucky (1806–52). Sec. of State (1825–9). Unsuccessful National Republican Party presidential candidate (1832) and Whig candidate (1844).

Clay, Lucius D[uBignon] (1897–), Amer. general. Directed operations to overcome Berlin blockade as US Military Gov. (1947–9).

Clayton-Bulwer Treaty (1850), effort to resolve US-Brit. rivalries in C America, particularly over proposed Panama canal. Though unpopular in US, it remained in force until 1901.

clearwing, day-flying moth with scaleless transparent wings and wasp-like body colour. Larvae are woodborers. Currant clearwing, *Sesia tipuliformis* and Amer. peach tree borer, *Sanninoidea exititiosa*, are fruit pests.

clef, sign at beginning of written music which signifies pitch of notes.

cleft palate, congenital defect due to failure of palate to unite before birth, often associated with divided or hare lip. Repair may be successfully carried out in infancy.

cleg *see* HORSEFLY.

clematis, vine or nonclimbing perennial of genus *Clematis*. Garden varieties include Jackman clematis and Jap. clematis. Wild variety, *C. vitalba*.

Clemenceau, Georges (1841–1929), Fr. statesman. Premier (1906–9, 1917–19), called 'Tiger'. Instrumental in Allied victory in World War 1 as coalition premier. Opposed US Pres. Wilson at Peace Conference of Versailles, regarding 1919 treaty as too lenient to Germans.

Clemens, Samuel Langhorne *see* TWAIN, MARK.

Clement, Saint, pope (*c.* 88–97 AD) traditionally a disciple of St Peter.

Clement V, orig. Bertrand de Got (1264–1314), became pope (1305) under auspices of Fr. king, Philip IV. Removed seat of papacy to Avignon (1309); acquiesced in disbanding of Knights Templar. His *Constitutiones Clementinae* (1313), important in canon law.

Clement XI, orig. Giovanni Francesco Albari (1649–1721), became pope (1700). Recognized Charles of Habsburg as Sp. king. Sought to stamp out JANSENISM in the Church, condemning several Jansenist doctrines in his bull *Unigenitus* (1713).

Clement, René (1913–), Fr. film director whose films include *Les Maudits* (1947), *Knave of Hearts* (1954) and *Plein Soleil* (1960).

Clementi, Muzio (1752–1832), Ital. composer and pianist; work includes studies *Gradus ad Parnassum*.

Cleopatra (69–30 BC), queen of Egypt. Joint ruler with brother Ptolemy; consolidated power with support of Julius Caesar, to whom she bore a son. After Caesar's death, she became mistress of Mark Antony, co-ruler of Rome with Octavian and

Lepidus. Octavian defeated Antony and Cleopatra at Actium (31 BC) and both committed suicide.

Cleveland, city in Ohio, US, on S shore of L. Erie. Port for Great Lakes shipping; iron and steel industries. Pop. (1960) 876,000.

Cleveland, [Stephen] Grover (1837–1908), 22nd (1885) and 24th (1893) US Pres., Democrat. Lawyer in Buffalo where able reform programme led to successful campaign for Gov. of New York. Won 1884 election after receiving reform Republican (MUGWUMP) support. As Pres. pushed civil service reform and attacked high tariff rates. Defeated (1888) by Benjamin Harrison. Returned to office (1892). Alienated radical Democrats by upholding gold standard, and protectionists by continuing to advocate low tariffs. Sent troops into Illinois (1898) to break Pullman strike. In foreign affairs firmness caused UK to back down in Venezuela border dispute (1897).

Cliburn, Van (1934–), Amer. pianist. Studied at Juilliard School of Music. Won 1st Tchaikovsky award (1958).

click beetle, insect of family Elateridae, of agric. importance in temp. regions. Larvae, wireworms, feed on roots, stems and tubers of root, grass and cereal crops.

cliff, usually vertical, rock face, either inland or along coastline. Formed often by faulting and wind and water erosion.

climate, av. atmospheric conditions of place or region throughout seasons, which, if regarded individually, constitute weather.

Clivia

Clouded Tiger

Clinton, De Witt (1769–1828), Amer. statesman, nephew of George Clinton. Mayor of New York City (1803–15); sponsored Erie Canal. Unsuccessful presidential candidate (1812). Gov. of New York (1817–21; 1825–8).

Clinton, George (1739–1812), Amer. statesman. First gov. of New York (1777–95). Opposed Federal Constitution. US vice-pres. (1805–12).

Clinton, Sir Henry (1738–95), Eng. general. Commanded Brit. forces during Amer. Revolution, assumed supreme command (1778); captured Charleston (1780).

Clio, in Gk. and Roman myth., Muse of History.

clipper, long, slender sailing vessel, with rectangular sails and 3 backward-sloping masts; renowned for speed. Developed by Americans at Baltimore and Boston (19th cent.) from Fr. principles.

Clive, Robert, Baron Clive of Plassey (1725–74), Eng. general and statesman. Military victories, particularly at Plassey (1757), helped establish power of Britain in India. Gov. of East India Co. (1765–7). On return to England, impeachment proceedings drove him to suicide.

Cliveden, country seat of the ASTOR FAMILY purchased by William Waldorf Astor (1893). Became famous in the 1930s when Nancy Astor entertained the 'Cliveden set', of influential Cons. politicians and newspapermen who favoured appeasement with Germany.

clivia, genus of S African herbs of family Amaryllidaceae with large funnel-shaped flowers.

cloisonné, enamel decoration, esp. in Celtic and Byzantine art, in which solid metal outlines are filled with enamel paste or powder, baked, and finally ground smooth.

closewing moth *see* PYRALID MOTH.

clothes moth, widely known small moth of family Tinacidae. Larvae feed on woollen goods, fur, feathers and other animal materials, Common species include *Tineola biselliella* and *Tinea pellionella*.

Clotho, in Gk. and Roman myth., 'The Spinner', one of the Fates.

cloud, mass of minute water particles condensed from water vapour in cool air, at high altitude; classified according to ht. At c. 30,000 ft. are *Cirrus*,

Coal Tit

resembling feathery wisps or mares' tails, and *Cirro-stratus*, forming a broad thin sheet, 10,000–24,000 ft; *Cirro-cumulus*, fair weather signal, round tufty, smaller than *Alto-cumulus*; *Alto-stratus* heavier than *Cirro-stratus*. Below 7,000 ft: *Strato-cumulus*, grey and heavy, not always rain-producing; *Nimbus*, dark shapeless rain clouds. *Cumulus* (c. 4,500–6,500 ft.) and *Cumulo-nimbus* (c. 4,500–20,500 ft.) produce heavy showers and thunderstorms. *Stratus* (below 3,500 ft.), horizontal and misty.

cloudberry, *Rubus chamaemorus,* small creeping moorland plant of rose family, found in temp. zones. Resembles blackberry, and has edible fruits.

clouded leopard *see* CLOUDED TIGER.

clouded tiger, clouded leopard, *Neofelis nebulosa,* large carnivorous

Strato-Cumulus and Cumulus clouds

mammal of cat family. Length up to 6 ft. Ranges from Nepal to Borneo. Mainly arboreal, preys on birds and small animals.

clove, *Carophyllus aromaticus,* pungent aromatic bud of evergreen shrub found in E Indies; used whole for pickling and flavouring, ground for confectionery; oil used medicinally.

clover, plant genus *Trifolium* of pulse family, but can also be other genera. Low-growing trifoliate plant, of temp. regions. As pasture ingredient, increases output of animal products.

Clovis I (*c.* 466–511), Frankish king, founder of Merovingian dynasty. Wife St Clotilda converted him to Christianity (*c.* 496). United most of Gaul and SW Germany.

club moss, low evergreen plant of genera *Lycopodium* and *Selaginella,* with scale-like leaves. Found in trop. and sub-trop. forests. *L. clavatus* used for manufacture of vegetable sulphur.

Cluj, cap. of Cluj region and 2nd largest town in Romania. Industry includes munitions, car bodies, chemicals and textile industries. Pop. (1964) 205,000.

cluster fly, blow fly, large brown fly related to the BLUEBOTTLE.

Clyde, river of SW Scotland, about 100 mi. long. It rises in S Lanarkshire and flows through Glasgow, before expanding into the Firth of Clyde at Dumbarton. The main commercial shipping route of Scotland, with important shipbuilding yards.

Clytemnestra, in Gk. myth., wife of Agamemnon. Took Aegisthus as paramour during Agamemnon's absence at Trojan War; murdered her husband on his return. Later killed by Orestes, her son.

Cnossus, ancient city of Crete. Site of palace of Minos, excavated by Sir Arthur Evans, revealing evidence of civilization of *c.* 3000 BC. *See* MINOAN CIVILIZATION.

coach, formerly private CARRIAGE, now large, 4-wheeled, horse-drawn carriage, esp. for state occasions; motor coach, char-a-banc, one-decker omnibus or rly. coach.

coach whip snake, *Masticophis flagellum,* long, slender, harmless snake of agric. areas of S US. Long tapering tail and braided-looking scales.

coal, banded material occurring in underground deposits, consisting of carbon and carbon compounds formed by decomposition of vegetable matter for thousands of years. A source of fuel, it also yields gas, coke, benzine, naphthalene, plastics, tar and rayon.

coal tit, *Porus ater,* smallest bird of TIT family.

coast, area where sea meets land. Coastal features *i.e.* cliff, abrasion platform, beach, cave, *etc.* result from interaction of geological, marine and atmospheric factors.

Coast Ranges, mountain belt of W North America from Alaska to Mexico, varying in ht. from 2,000–19,850 ft. (Mt. Logan).

coati, large snouted, omnivorous mammal of raccoon family, of forests of S and C America. Females and young live in groups; adult male, or coatimundi, is solitary.

coatimundi *see* COATI.

cobalt, silvery-white, magnetic, metallic element, occurring with nickel,

Example of Cloisonné work. Metal strips, twisted into a decorative shape are laid against the surface of the vase and filled with coloured enamel

Cobra

sulphur and arsenic. Used in pigments. Chemically active, forms many compounds. Radioactive cobalt 60 used to treat cancer and in detecting flaws in metals.

cobaltite, source of COBALT.

Cobb, Ty[rus] [Raymond] (1886–1961), Amer. baseball player. Highest career batting av. (·367); won batting title 12 times.

Coblenz see KOBLENZ.

cobra, family Elapidae, of very venomous Asiatic and African snakes. When excited neckskin is expanded by movement of ribs into broad hood. Indian cobra is *Naja naja.* King cobra, *N. hannah,* is largest and most dangerous snake and attacks anything. Species include Egyptian cobra, *N. haje.*

cockatoo, easily domesticated crested PARROT of Australia, New Guinea and Philippines.

cockchafer, beetle of scarab family incl. maybugs and junebeetles, genus *Melolantha* in Europe and *Phyllophaga* in N America. Large European *M. vulgaris* destroys vegetables.

Cockchafer

Cockcroft, Sir John Douglas (1897–1967), Brit. physicist. Awarded Nobel Prize (1951), with E. T. S. Walton, for research into atomic nuclei.

cocker spaniel, small dog, popular as pet. Easily trained to the gun.

cockle, edible bivalve mollusc of genus *Cardium* with equal convex shells and scalloped edges.

cockroach, order of flat, thickset, omnivorous widely distributed insects, and most numerous in the tropics, with an unpleasant odour. The cosmopolitan domestic species are *Blatta orientalis* and *Periplaneta americana.*

cocoa, cacao, *Theobroma cacao,* spreading tree of Sterculia family, found in forests of C and S America. Grows to av. ht. of 30 ft., and has large, round fruits each containing 20–40 seeds or cocoa beans, yielding up to 10 lb. of cocoa per tree. Ingredient of chocolate, used for confectionery and as a beverage. Crème de cacao is a liqueur.

coconut palm, *Cocos nucifera,* trop. tree bearing large brown hard-shelled fruit; edible white kernel ('copra') used in confectionery, yields oil used in soap; husk provides fibre for matting, leaves for thatch.

Cocos Keeling, group of 23 coral islands in Indian Ocean, under Austral. authority since 1955. Discovered (1609) by Capt. Keeling.

Cocteau, Jean (1889–1963), Fr. poet, dramatist, film-maker and painter. Taste for fantasy found expression in films. Works include novels *Thomas l'Imposteur* (1923) and *Les Enfants Terribles* (1929), the play *La Machine Infernale* (1934), and films *La Belle et la Bête* (1945) and *Orphée* (1949).

Cocytus, in Gk. legend, one of the 5 rivers of HADES.

cod, food fish of family Gadidae of most cold and Arctic waters, esp. N Atlantic. Atlantic cod, *Gadus morhua,* found chiefly off coast of Newfoundland, weighing 5–25 lb. is commercially important; products include cod liver oil and isinglass.

Code Napoleon, first modern law code, promulgated (1804) by Napoleon I. Replaced local customs in France with series of national compilation of legal rules. Important in development of civil law, it codified much of modern Roman law.

codeine, alkaloid derived from morphine, but less narcotic and addictive. Used medicinally orally or hypodermically as sedative and analgesic.

codling moth, *Carpocapsa pomonella,* small European moth widely distributed elsewhere. Larva stage (apple worm) destroys fruit and vegetables.

coelacanth, order of deep-bodied fish with 3-lobed tail existing 300,000,000 yr. ago and thought extinct until specimen of genus *Latimeria* discovered (1938) near East London, South Africa. Coelacanth of different species have since been caught.

coelenterate, predominantly marine invertebrate animal of phylum Coelenterata comprising CORAL, SEA ANEMONE, JELLYFISH and hydroid.

coffee, *Coffea arabica,* evergreen shrub native to Arabia, grown extensively in Brazil, Africa and Asia. Seeds roasted and ground to make coffee. Unknown in Europe until 17th cent. World production 3,809,000 metric tons.

cognac see BRANDY.

cognition, in philosophy, knowledge of theories. Originated as distinguishable branch of inquiry with Encyclopedic school inaugurated by Christian Wolf. Theories of cognition include EMPIRICISM, REALISM, IDEALISM.

Cocker Spaniel

Cohen, Harriet (1895–1967), Eng. pianist, known for interpretations of Bach and Bax.

Cohen, Leonard (1934–   ), Canadian Jewish author, poet and songwriter. Works include *Flowers for Hitler* (1964), *Beautiful Losers* (1966).

Coke, Sir Edward (1552–1634), Eng. lawyer and judge. Became Attorney General (1593), Chief Justice of common pleas (1606). Championed Parliament against king, upholding common law. Dismissed (1616) for incurring enmity of James I. Helped draft PETITION OF RIGHT (1628).

col, depression in range of hills or mountains. In meteorology, ridge of low pressure between 2 anticyclones.

Colbert, Jean-Baptiste (1619–83), Fr. statesman, chief minister of Louis XIV after 1661. Exponent of MERCANTILISM, protected Fr. industry

Drying coffee on cement floors in Ecuador. Process may take several weeks, the coffee being turned twice a day

through tariffs and subsidies, created navy, developed road and canal building, and colonization.

cold war, economic and polit. rivalry between nations which falls short of military conflict. Popularly used for post-World War 2 struggle between Communist nations and West.

coleoptera, largest order of insects; includes beetles and weevils.

Coleridge, Samuel Taylor (1772–1834), Eng. poet, philosopher and literary critic, prominent in Romantic revival. Collaborated with Wordsworth on *Lyrical Ballads* (1798). Works include 'The Ancient Mariner' and 'Kubla Khan' (pub. 1816), 'Christabel,' *Biographia Literaria* (1817).

Coleridge-Taylor, Samuel (1875–1912). Eng. composer of choral pieces incl. setting of Longfellow's *Hiawatha's Wedding Feast* (1898).

Colette, Sidonie Gabrielle (1873–1954), Fr. author, famous for analytical studies of women. Works include novels *Chéri* (1920) and *La Chatte* (1933). *Claudine* series written with husband (Henri Gauthier-Villars).

Coligny, Gaspard de (1519–72), Fr. admiral, Huguenot leader during Wars of Religion. Influence on King Charles IX and increasing strength of Huguenots alarmed Catherine de Medici and resulted in St Bartholomew's Day Massacre.

collar bone, clavicle, part of shoulder girdle extending from top of shoulder to edge of sternum (chest bone).

collective farming, agric. co-operative system. In USSR Stalin instituted *kolkhoz* in which land, farm equipment, *etc.,* were pooled although workers retained some land and livestock. Chinese commune places greater emphasis on communal living and has wider application, incl. industrial workers. *See* KIBBUTZ.

College of Justice, supreme civil court of Scotland, composed of the lords of council and session (the judges), together with the advocates (barris-

ters) and clerks of session.

Collins, Michael *see* APOLLO PROJECT.

Collins, William (1721–59), Eng. pre-Romantic poet. Works include 'Ode to Evening' (1746) and 'How Sleep the Brave' (1746).

Collins, [William] Wilkie (1824–89), Eng. novelist, associate of Dickens. Works include *The Woman in White* (1860) and *The Moonstone* (1868).

Collodi, Carlo, orig. Carlo Lorenzini (1826–90) Ital. author, wrote *Pinocchio: The Story of a Puppet* (1880–3).

colloid, substance dispersed in solvent as particles too small to be seen, but larger than molecules. Characteristics are adsorption and coagulation.

collotype, method of printing using glass plate coated with gelatine on which image is photographically reproduced.

colobus monkey, genus of slender monkeys living in treetops of forests of Africa. Long tail ends in tuft, fur long and silky. Fur hunting has almost exterminated the guereza, *Colobus abyssinicus.*

Cologne, Köln, river port of Rhine-Westphalia, Germany, Roman route and trade centre; Gothic cathedral. Its metal industries use Ruhr coal. Also famed for perfume, clothing, rubber, glassware and chocolate. Damaged during World War 2. Pop. (1965) 857,000.

Colombia [República de Colombia], S Amer. republic. Area: 439,530 sq.

mi.; cap. Bogotá. Pres., senators and representatives elected by popular vote for 4 yr. term. Valleys yield coffee (70% of exports), sugar, cocoa, tobacco, cereals, cotton; mineral resources, coal, salt, iron ore, plat-

Coconut Palm: (a) male flower (b) female flower (c) section of coconut showing fibre, shell, pulp containing seeds, and milk (d) 2 yr. old shoot which has sprouted from coconut

inum, emeralds. National language, Spanish. Discovered by Spanish (16th cent.). Bolivar created Republic of Colombia (1819). Armed forces seized power (1953). Pop. (1964) 18,068.000.

Colombo, cap. and chief port of Ceylon, with fine artificial harbour. Industry connected with tea processing; exports include cocoa, rubber, tea and copra. Pop. (1963) 511,000.

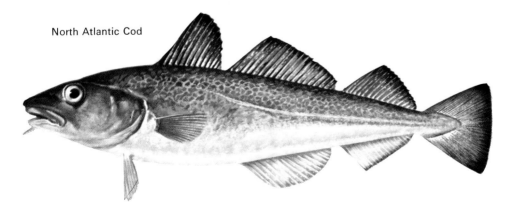

North Atlantic Cod

The Colosseum, Rome

Colombo Plan, organization set up (1951) by Brit. Commonwealth countries to give technical and educ. aid to underdeveloped SE Asian countries. Members are Afghanistan, Bhutan, Burma, Cambodia, Ceylon, India, Indonesia, Korean Republic, Laos, Malaysia, Maldive Is., Nepal, Pakistan, Philippines, Singapore, Thailand and the Vietnamese Republic, and outside the area, Australia, Canada, Japan, New Zealand, UK and US.

Colón, town and seaport in N Panama, at Atlantic entrance to Panama Canal. Pop. (1960) 59,598.

Colorado, 38th state of W US, admitted 1876. Area: 104,200 sq. mi.; cap. Denver; main towns, Pueblo, Colorado Springs and Greeley. NE area was part of (1803) Louisiana Purchase. Gold boom (1858); gold, silver, copper, molybdenum, lead mined. Crops include sugarbeet, wheat and maize. Many national parks in Rocky Mts. with some of finest mt. scenery in world. Pop. (1964) 1,961,000.

Colorado, river 2,000 mi. long, formed by junction of Grand and Green rivers. Flows SW through Utah and Arizona (incl. GRAND CANYON) into Mexico and drains into Gulf of California. Dams (*e.g.* Hoover) and reservoirs have been built for irrigation and generation of hydro-electric power.

colorado or **potato beetle,** *Leptinotarsa decemlineata,* beetle orig. re-

Colorado Beetle

stricted to W North America, now found wherever potatoes cultivated. Causes extensive damage and is very serious pest. Also attacks other garden vegetables, esp. tomatoes.

Colorado Plateau, in the states of Arizona, Utah, Colorado and New Mexico, at a height of 5,000–11,000 ft.; vast arid upland with some of America's most spectacular mountain scenery, incl. the GRAND CANYON.

Colosseum, Coliseum, in Rome, amphitheatre built *c.* 75–80. Vast oval building which held about 45,000, on tiers around the arena.

Colossians, Epistle to the, NT book written by St Paul (*c.* 62 AD) while in prison at Rome, to the Church at Colossae.

Colossus of Rhodes, bronze statue of Helios, in Rhodes, 100 ft. high; took 12 yr. to build. One of SEVEN WONDERS OF THE WORLD.

colour, color, sensation produced in the eye by excitation of the cones in the retina, esp. by LIGHT. Pigmented objects produce colour by absorbing certain wavelengths and reflecting the light of all others; or by diffraction of light rays striking unpigmented surface.

colour bar *see* RACISM.

colour blindness, inability to distinguish certain colours, more common in men than women.

colours *see* diagram below.

Colt, Samuel (1814–62), Amer. inventor of a revolver, patented 1835.

coltsfoot, *Tussilago farfara,* plant of daisy family and common weed of N regions. Hairy scaly stalk, yellow spring flower and large heart-shaped leaves.

Colum, Padraic (1881-1972). Irish poet and dramatist. Associated with Irish Renaissance, plays incl. *The Fiddler's House* (1907) and *Thomas Muskerry* (1910). *Wild Earth* (1907) is collection of poems about rural Irish life.

Columba, Saint (521–597), early Christian missionary, b. Ireland, founder of the monasteries Derry (545), Durrow (553), Kells and Iona, Scotland. Made many journeys to Scot. Highlands to convert Picts.

Columbia, cap. of S Carolina, US. Site chosen (1786); chartered as city (1854). Centre of rich agric. area with large cotton mills. Pop. (1960) 97,433.

Columbia, river of N America (*c.* 1,400 mi. long) rising in Canadian Rockies, and flowing to Amer. Pacific coast in Oregon. Among 1st big dams were Bonneville and Grand Coulee. Kootenay, Spokane and Snake are tributaries.

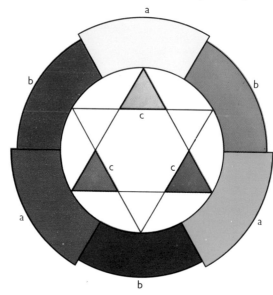

Primary, secondary and tertiary colour chart: (a) Primary colours (unobtainable by mixing other colours), *e.g.* yellow, blue, red (b) Secondary colours (obtainable by mixing 2 primary colours), *e.g.* green, purple, orange (c) Tertiary colours (obtainable by mixing a primary and a secondary colour), *e.g.* fawn, olive, brown. Complementary colours are a pair of colours which turn to white when mixed, *e.g.* the primary and secondary colours opposite each other on this chart

Halley's Comet, photographed in 1910

Columbia University, New York, N.Y., leading US university. Founded (1754) as King's College by charter of George II, renamed Columbia (1784). Scene of student revolt (1968).

columbine, plant of genus *Aquilegia,* of buttercup family, incl. *c.* 70 species found in temp. regions. Native European species, *A. vulgaris,* is purple or white. *A. caerulia,* blue and white variety, is state flower of Colorado.

Columbus, Christopher, Sp: **Christobal Colon** (*c.* 1446–1506), Genoese navigator, discoverer (for Sp. crown) of America. In 1492 landed in Cuba, Bahamas and other W Indian Is. Landed in S America (1498), located mouth of Orinoco River. Died in obscurity in Spain.

column, in architecture, upright cylindrical or polygonal body, used for support or adornment; may bear statue or memorial.

Comanche, tribe of nomadic N Amer. Indians. Formed loose confederation with Kiowa, Cheyenne and Apache tribes. Although orig. fiercely opposed white man, reduced by war and disease to 1,500 (1904) when confined to Oklahoma reserve.

combustion, process of burning, incl. respiration and decomposition, occurring through oxidation, liberating heat and light; leads to formation of carbon dioxide.

comedy, light, amusing play with happy ending; dates from 5th cent. BC. Old Comedy (Aristophanes) was social satire; Middle Comedy (4th cent. BC) was myth. burlesque; New Comedy (from 320 BC, Menander imitated by Terence and Plautus) with love-motive, stock characters and situations. By Middle Ages, any tale of common folk, often in colloquial or dialect form. Eng. Elizabethan Romantic included comedies of Shakespeare. In France, Molière combined classical influence with commedia dell'arte in Comedy of Manners, which developed in England into Restoration Comedy (Congreve) and later in 18th cent. into satirical character comedies of Sheridan and Goldsmith, and of Oscar Wilde in 19th cent. G. B. Shaw, Maugham and Noel Coward produced social comedies in 20th cent.

comet, luminous celestial body moving about Sun, consisting of nucleus, enveloping coma, and tail. Some move in elliptical orbits returning at calculable intervals, *e.g.* Encke's and Halley's; others moving parabolically may never return, *e.g.* Biela's (last seen 1852).

Comfort, Alexander (1920–   ), Brit. medical biologist and writer.

comfrey, *Symphytum officinalis,* rough leaved perennial plant of borage family. Formerly used in medicine.

Cominform (Communist Information Bureau), co-ordinating organ of Communist parties of USSR, its E European allies, France and Italy. Estab. (1947); dissolved (1956).

Comintern (Communist International), association of world Communist parties estab. (1919) by Lenin; dissolved (1934). Zinoviev, Trotsky, Radek and Bukharin were other leading members. Dominated by Russ. Communists.

Comity of Nations, traditional courtesy by which a court recognizes laws and legal decisions of another country, although not required to do so by international law.

commandos, Brit. army raiding unit raised in World War 2, for swift, marauding invasions into enemy-held territory.

commedia dell'arte, Ital. comedy dating from mid 16th cent. Travelling actors improvised the stock character in which they were cast (Harlequin, Pantaloon, etc.). The form derived from PLAUTUS and TERENCE and developed later into PANTOMIME and COMEDY.

commodity, in economics, term for anything which can be traded for something else.

Commodus, Lucius (161–192), Roman emperor (180), son of Marcus Aurelius during whose reign he held proconsular power. Strangled by athlete Narcissus.

common cold, upper respiratory infection, possibly due to as yet unidentified viruses. Highly infectious; complications may arise (*e.g.* SINUSITIS, TONSILITIS).

common law, uniform body of 'unwritten' Eng. law, evolved by judges in the courts from custom and from precedents estab. by previous cases, and is complementary to statute or 'written' law. Has influenced all Eng.-speaking nations.

Common Market *see* EUROPEAN ECONOMIC COMMUNITY.

Commonwealth, term used to describe the Cromwellian regime in Brit. Isles. (1649–60).

Commonwealth of Nations, British, system of fully autonomous nations, formerly within BRITISH EMPIRE, created by Statute of Westminster (1931). Members recognize Brit. leadership in matters of mutual interest. Charter members, Britain, Canada, Australia, New Zealand, Union of South Africa (withdrew 1961) and Irish Free State (withdrew 1949). India and Pakistan (1947) and Ceylon (1948) were 1st repub. members.

Commonwealth Fund, trust, incorporated (1918) in New York, which awards grants for education and research, available to Brit. subjects and, by invitation, to applicants from W European countries, Australia and New Zealand.

Commune of Paris, revolutionary Fr. govt. Overrode National Assembly (1871). After withdrawal of Pruss. troops from city, again tried to assert authority, but was put down with massive bloodshed by Pres. Thiers and army.

communication, transfer of thoughts and messages, esp. through press and other mass media.

communications satellites, used to relay broadcast signals (incl. TV). *See* SATELLITES.

Communion, Holy, participation in sacrament of Lord's Supper (I *Cor.* x) in Christian Churches. R.C. Church and High Anglican believe in doctrine of Real Presence of Christ in bread and wine; to others the Communion is symbolic only.

communism, system of society in which property (esp. real property and means of production) is held in common by all members of society, not by individuals. As theory of govt. and social reform, communism can be attributed to Plato whose *Republic* outlined society with communal

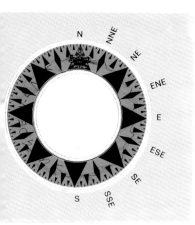

Compass Rose

property. In England, forms of communism manifested in Sir Thomas More's *Utopia* and such groups as the LEVELLERS. Capitalist enterprise, reinforced by industrial revolution, gave rise to modern communism. Protest against appalling labour conditions found early spokesman in JEAN-JACQUES ROUSSEAU.

Communism, modern, international movement advocating state socialism (*see* MARXISM), arising out of Marx and Engels' *Communist Manifesto* (1848). Marxian communism spread through founding of FIRST INTERNATIONAL and rise of Social Democratic parties in Europe. Radical form taken (1903) in Russia when Bolsheviks, under Lenin, urged immediate violent revolution to overthrow capitalism and estab. world socialist state. Bolsheviks triumphed in RUSSIAN REVOLUTION (1917). Leninists urged workers' union for international revolution; stateless, universal Communism would theoretically follow 'dictatorship of proletariat'. Stalin consolidated Communist power in USSR during 1930s. Soviet victory in World War 2 brought addition of E European satellites to Communist bloc. Estab. of Communist state in China (1949) under Mao Tse-tung joined 2 of world's most populous nations but by early 1960s China's accusations of Soviet conciliation with West had brought rift.

Communist Manifesto *see* MARX, KARL.

Communist Party, in US, organized (1919) to become revolutionary successor in US of INDUSTRIAL WORKERS OF THE WORLD. Post-war influence reduced by Truman administration and trials of Alger Hiss (1949–50) and top Communists. Constant govt. attack and scrutiny

continued to isolate Party during 1960s.

Como, lake of N Italy in mountainous region of great beauty. Area: 56 sq. mi.

company, limited [UK], organization, public or private and legal in character, formed to carry out activities (usually on profit basis). Members are liable under 1855 Limited Liability Act to amount of their subscription. Act brought Brit. practice in line with that of Continent. In US, corporations are functionally and legally similar.

Company of Merchant Adventurers *see* CABOT, SEBASTIAN.

comparative philology, the comparative study of languages.

compass, instrument for drawing circles and measuring distances (mathematics), and for determining direction (navigation).

competition, in economics, term for the degree in which the market can be influenced; perfect competition is a theoretical model in which many producers with no control over price produce identical goods which are sold by market exchange or auction.

Compiègne, town of Oise department, N France. World War 1 armistice (Nov. 1918) signed nearby.

Compromise of 1850, measures passed by US Congress balancing interests of slave and free states. Provided California's admission as free state, abolished slavery in District of Columbia, left issue of slavery in W Territories open, provided strict fugitive slave law, and estab. boundary of Texas.

comptometer, arithmetical calculating machine, developed from calculator patented by D. E. Fett (1887).

Compton, Arthur Holly (1892–1962), Amer. physicist. Awarded Nobel Prize (1927) with C. T. R. Wilson for method of perceiving paths of electronically charged particles.

Compton-Burnett, Ivy (1892–1969),

Eng. novelist. Works include *Men and Wives* (1931) and *A God and his Gifts* (1963).

computer, electronic machine widely used in commerce, industry and research to carry out large numbers of calculations at great speed and to store information. Sequence of calculations controlled by programme, *i.e.* series of precisely defined instructions, inserted into machine. Programming languages evolved to describe operations which machine will carry out.

Comte, Isadore Auguste (1798–1857), Fr. philosopher, founder of positivism. Rejected metaphysics and relied entirely on the findings of the positive sciences. Invented the term 'sociology'.

Conacher, Lionel (1901–54), Canadian athlete. Played football, ice hockey, and lacrosse, for which he was named (1955) all-round Canadian athlete of first half of 20th cent.

Conakry, cap. and main port of Republic of Guinea on Tumbo Is. Ships iron ore, coffee, bananas and palm produce. Pop. (1960) 113,000.

Conant, James Bryant (1893–   ), Amer. chemist, author of *On Understanding Science* (1947). Research in reduction and oxidation, haemoglobin, free radicals and chlorophyll.

concentration camp, institution for detention of elements of the population deemed dangerous by polit. regime. First applied to Brit. detention camps in Boer War. Mainly associated with the single-party state, notably Russia (after 1917), Germany (1933–45), Spain (after 1938). Symbolized by Hitler's Nazi state, where several (notably Auschwitz and Treblinka in Poland) were used as extermination camps in which more than 6 million people, mostly Jews and Poles, were killed.

Concepción, city of Chile, cap. of Concepción Prov. on Bío-Bío; outport is Talcahuano, naval base. Major

Concorde supersonic jet airliner

educ. and manufacturing centre, founded (1550). Pop. (1964) 170,000.

concertmaster [US], **leader** [UK], 1st violinist of orchestra, who leads string section.

concerto, music for one or more soloists and orchestra, usually in 3 movements or sections.

conch, marine, carnivorous, mollusc with spiral univalve shell, used as ornament. Species include large *Strombus gigas* of W Indies.

Concorde, supersonic passenger aircraft developed jointly by France and UK. Maiden flight Toulouse (Mar. 1969).

Condé, Fr. family, branch of House of Bourbon. **Louis** [I] **Bourbon** (1530–69), involved in conspiracy of Amboise (1560), killed in Battle of Jarnac. **Louis** [II], **the Great Condé** (1621–86), general, successful in Thirty Years War. During Fronde, sided with court, then Spaniards; pardoned later by Louis XIV and led French against William of Orange in 3rd Dutch War.

condenser, in electricity, device to increase capacity of conductor of electricity, *i.e.* for receiving and holding a greater charge, *e.g.* Leyden Jar.

condenser, in chemistry, device for condensing vapour into liquid, consisting of glass tubes cooled by air or water. Used in industry to collect gases or liquids.

Condillac, Étienne Bonnot de (1715–80), Fr. philosopher, developed theory of sensationalism. Attempted to simplify JOHN LOCKE's theory of knowledge in *Traité des Sensations* (1754).

condor see ANDEAN CONDOR.

Condorcet, [Marie] **Antoine de Caritat, Marquis de** (1743–94), Fr. philosopher and mathematician. Girondist member of Legislative Assembly and of the Convention, outlawed by Jacobins. Wrote *Esquisse d'un Tableau historique de Progrès de l'Esprit humain.*

coneflower, wild flower of N Amer. daisy family. Purple, *Echinaceae,* are grown as garden plants; yellow, *Rudbeckiae,* commonly called Black-eyed Susan.

conenose, name for ASSASSIN BUG.

Conestoga wagon, freight-carrying vehicle drawn by 6 horses, originated by Pennsylvanian farmers (18th cent.), broad wheeled with wide, long, deep wooden base, canvas-covered hoop top. Used by US pioneers.

Confederacy (1861–5), govt. estab. by 7 S US states at Montgomery, Alabama after election of Abraham Lincoln. Lincoln's declaration of war followed by secession of 4 more states. Jefferson Davis elected Pres.; Judah P. Benjamin outstanding cabinet member. Fell after Lee's surrender at end of Civil War.

Confederation, Articles of, early definition of US govt. distribution of power, ratified (1781); superseded by Constitution of US (1789). Unsatisfactory because of central govt.'s subordinate position with Congress dependent upon states for funds and execution of decrees. Most significant achievement was Ordinance of 1787 on the Northwest Territory.

Confederation of the Rhine, league of Ger. princes, formed under Napoleon's protection. Disbanded 1813.

Confession, in R.C., Orthodox and High Anglican Churches, disclosure of sin to priest to obtain absolution. Term also used for specific statement of religious belief, *e.g.* Augsburg Confession.

Confucius (551–479 BC), Chinese philosopher. Teachings developed and altered so that by 2nd cent. BC they dominated Chinese thought. Advocated a rational 'this-world' philosophy, emphasizing humanity, respect for ancient sages, and govt. by personal virtue.

conger, eels of trop. and temp. ocean waters. Conger eel, *Conger conger,*

usually marine, grows to *c.* 6 ft. in length and *c.* 100 lb. in wt.

conglomerate, sedimentary rock made up of rounded, weathered fragments of other rocks, cemented by finer grained material.

Congo, kingdom of, historic W African state, now included in REPUBLIC OF THE CONGO, CONGO REPUBLIC and ANGOLA. Discovered by Portuguese (1482).

Congo, river of C Africa, one of largest (2,900 mi.) in world, draining basin of 1,425,000 sq. mi.

Congo, Belgian see CONGO, REPUBLIC OF THE.

Congo, French see CONGO REPUBLIC.

Congo, Republic of the, [République Démocratique du Congo], formerly Belgian Congo, in C Africa. Renamed Zaire (1971). Area: *c.* 905,000 sq. mi.; cap. Kinshasa (Leopoldville). Agric.

products include palm oil, cocoa, cotton, rubber and coffee. Rich mineral resources, esp. in Katanga Prov., which brought civil war shortly after independence (1960) by attempting to secede. Pop. (1966) 15,986,000.

Congo Republic, formerly Fr. Congo, C Africa. Area:132,000 sq. mi.; cap. Brazzaville. Exports timber, palm oil,

rubber, tobacco and coffee. Independent (1960). Pop. (1964) 900,000.

Congress [US], legislative branch of federal govt. Instituted (1789) under Article 1 of US Constitution. Comprises SENATE and HOUSE OF REPRESENTATIVES. Proceedings recorded in *Congressional Record.*

Congress of Industrial Organizations see AMERICAN FEDERATION OF LABOR AND CONGRESS OF INDUSTRIAL ORGANIZATIONS.

Congress of Racial Equality [CORE], Amer. civil rights group, estab. 1941.

Congreve, William (1670–1729), Eng. dramatist, master of Restoration comedy of manners in such plays as *The Double Dealer* (1693), *Love for Love* (1695), and *The Way of the World* (1700). Also wrote tragedy *The Mourning Bride* (1697).

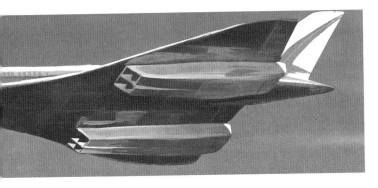

A seascape by John Constable

conifer, class of woody perennials comprising 7 families (about 500 species) mainly trees, ranging from medium to gigantic. Only 4 of 7 families are cone-bearing as name implies. Trees grown for afforestation as well as timber, pulp, resin and turpentine. Includes PINE, CYPRESS, YEW and SEQUOIA.

conifers, mostly evergreen trees of gymnosperm group, commonest in N temp. regions; bear cones and sometimes berries. Include fir, spruce, cedar, *etc.*

Connally, John Bowden (1917–   ), Amer. lawyer and politician. Sec. of the Navy (June–Nov. 1961). Democratic Gov. of Texas (1963–   ).

Connaught, smallest of the 4 Irish provinces, W Ireland. Formerly a kingdom.

Connaught, Arthur William Patrick Albert, Duke of (1850–1942), Gov.-General of Canada (1911–16), 3rd son of Queen Victoria; commander-in-chief in Med. (1907–9).

Connecticut, New England state of US. Area: 4,899 sq. mi.; cap. Hartford; main towns, New Haven and Bridgeport. Settled in 1630s by Dutch and Puritans. Main occupations, tobacco growing, poultry and dairy products, metal working, textiles, printing and publishing. Pop. (1967 est.) 2,925,000.

Connelly, Marc[us Cook] (1890–   ), Amer. playwright. Author of *The Green Pastures* (1930) and *A Story for Strangers* (1948).

Connemara, district of W Galway, Ireland.

Conner, Ralph, orig. Charles William Gordon (1860–1937), Canadian novelist and Presbyterian minister. His novels of pioneer life include *A Tale of the Selkirks* (1898) and *The Foreigner* (1909).

Connolly, James (1870–1916), Irish republican and socialist politician. Placed the nationalist cause before socialism in Ireland. Shot by British.

Connolly, Maureen (1934–69), Amer. tennis player, known as 'Little Mo'. US singles champion (1951, 1952, 1953); Wimbledon champion (1952, 1953, 1954).

Conrad, Joseph (1857–1924), Eng. novelist. Concerned with moral exploitation and personal psychology. Books include *Nostromo* (1904), *Heart of Darkness* (1902), *Lord Jim* (1900), *Victory* (1915) and *The Secret Agent* (1917).

conscription, compulsory enrolment of citizens for military purposes. Recorded in Greece and Rome, 1st modern use was during Fr. Revolutionary Wars; since invoked in most European countries. Introduced in US in Civil War.

Conservative Party, Brit. polit. party whose policy generally includes belief in free enterprise, distrust of state intervention, conservation of established order in Crown and Church and scepticism of value of sweeping changes in national life. Title replaced 'Tory' in time of SIR ROBERT PEEL; title 'Unionist' adopted towards end of 19th cent.; with formation of Liberal-Cons. coalition after World War 1, reverted to 'Conservative'.

Most recent Cons. govts. (1959–64, 1970–   ).

Constable, John (1776–1837), Eng. landscape painter. Depicted meadows, watermills and in particular Suffolk countryside. *The Hay Wain* created sensation at Louvre (1824).

Constance, Lake [Ger: Bodensee], Alpine lake bordered by Switzerland, Austria and Germany. Area: 207 sq. mi.

Constant, Paul Henri Benjamin, Baron D'Estournelles de (1852–1924), Fr. diplomat and politician. Favoured disarmament and was Fr. delegate at Hague conference (1907). Shared Nobel Peace Prize (1909) with Auguste Beernaert.

Constant [de Rebecque], Benjamin (1767–1830), Fr. writer and political theorist; criticized Napoleon and Bourbon monarchy. Notable for psychological novels *Adolphe* (1816) and *Cécile* (1st pub. 1952).

Constantine I (*c.* 280–337), 1st Christian Roman emperor. Became ruler of W empire after battle of Milvian Bridge (306), thereafter tolerating Christianity, and of E after routing Licinius at Adrianople and Sartari (324). Social and military reformer, held 1st Council of Nicaea (325), founded new cap. Constantinople (330).

Constantine IV (648–85), Byzantine emperor (668), campaigned successfully against Sicilians and Arabs, defeated by Bulgars (679).

Constantine V (719–775), Byzantine emperor (741). Enforced support of iconoclastic doctrines throughout empire, resulting in breach with Pope Stephen III.

Constantine VI (770–797), Byzantine emperor. Held 2nd Council of Nicaea, lost territory to Arabs and Bulgars, deposed and blinded by mother Irene.

Constantine XI (1404–53), last Byzantine emperor, unsuccessful in obtaining aid against Mohammed II by proclaiming unity of E and W churches. Killed in storm of Constantinople by Turks.

Constantine II (1940–   ), king of Greece, son of Paul I and Frederika. Married Princess Anne-Marie of Denmark. Son Paul (b. 1967) is present heir to throne. Exiled 1968.

Constantine, Sir Learie [Nicholas] (1901–71), W Indian politician and cricketer. Appointed to Race Relations Board (UK) in 1966. Life peer (1969). Writer of several books on cricket.

Constantinople *see* ISTANBUL.

constellation, in astron. name given to groupings of stars. In N hemisphere names largely mythological *e.g. Andromeda*; in S Hemisphere (mapped 16th–18th cent.) named after animals or scientific equipment, *e.g. Telescopium*. Greeks recognized 48, incl. 12 zodiacal signs. Altogether 88 constellations are recognized.

constitution, body of fundamental rules estab. by sovereign power of state; limits and defines relations of lesgislative, judicial, and executive powers. Codified in US and in continental Europe since late 18th cent. Unwritten Brit. constitution, comprising customary and statutory law, modified and changed by general will, as expressed by parl.

Constitution of United States, document written at Constitutional Convention (1787) establishing federal system of govt., which began 1789. Provided separation of powers with duties delegated to executive, judicial, and legislative branches. Includes 22 amendments, of which first 10 (Bill of Rights) guarantee individual liberties.

Constitutional Act (1791), Brit. act; declared that Quebec was to be divided into 2 prov. Upper and Lower Canada, each having separate govt. based on appointment.

Constitutional Convention, meeting held by Washington at Philadelphia (1787) attended by 12 of 13 states; new US Constitution drawn up.

Constructivism, art movement arising out of Cubism. Aimed at creating works of art existing in their own right unrelated to natural forms. Exponents include Gabo, Pevsner, Nicholson, Hepworth and Mondrian.

Consumers' Association (Canada), body responsible for protection of consumers' interests in all forms of commerce.

Consumers' Union (US), protects consumer interests, investigates consumer complaints, produces *Consumer Reports* on products, for buying public.

consumption *see* TUBERCULOSIS.

continent, large continuous mass of land *i.e.* Asia, Africa, N America, S America, Europe and Australia. Upper level of crust underlying continents composed of SIAL; low level, underlying ocean basins of SIMA. Each continent has a 2,000–4,000 million yr. old central CONTINENTAL SHIELD, to which younger rocks have been added.

Continental Congress (1774–89), convocation of representatives of Thirteen Colonies of N America. First Continental Congress, called to review colonial rights and grievances, abolished trade with Britain. Second Continental Congress issued Declar-

ation of Independence (4 July 1776), conducted Amer. Revolution against Britain, worked out Articles of Confederation (1776–81) and governed provisionally until 1789 when US Constitution was adopted.

continental drift, theory that continents and islands move relative to each other. Alfred Wegener postulated that *c.* 200 million yr. ago all land masses were joined, and moved to present position *c.* 5 million yr. ago. Are still moving apart.

continental shelf, relatively narrow marginal area of continent submerged by oceanic water. Continental features, *e.g.* cliffs, and river valleys may be represented.

continental shield, broad plain underlain by pre-Cambrian rocks, over 600 million yr. old, forming large area of each continent; surrounded by mountain areas and young coastal plains, a few hundred ft. above sea level. European shield underlies Norway, Sweden, Finland, N Germany and Poland; N Amer. shield (Canadian or Laurentian Shield) underlies Greenland and NE Canada.

Continental System, policy devised (1806) by Napoleon I to curtail English power by economic boycott. All trade with Britain forbidden. Its failure was result of Eng. naval superiority.

continuo, basso continuo, thorough bass, bass line of piece of baroque music, realized by at least 1 string player and keyboard player, usually

The harbour at Lindau on Lake Constance, with the German Alps in the background

harpsichordist, who improvises accompaniment.

contour, line along which some property is constant, or its representation in a map or diagram, esp. line joining all points at same height above sea-level.

contrabassoon *see* BASSOON.

contraception, birth control, prevention of conception; 1st successful means emerged mid-19th cent. Use advocated by Annie Besant (1847–1933). Methods used include STERILIZATION, total abstinence or during certain phases of MENSTRUATION, prevention of sperm entry to uterus, the 'PILL', or intra-uterine devices. In under-developed countries, cost of contraception may exceed that of having a baby. Birth control is still

Constructivist painting (1913) by Piet Mondrian

Cooper's Hawk

widely opposed on religious grounds, *e.g.* by R.C. Church and by orthodox Jewry. Many states in US, still have laws forbidding advertisement, sales, or spread of information.

Conway of Allington, William Martin, 1st Baron (1856–1937), Eng. mountaineer. Published with Rev. William Coolridge 1st series of Alpine climbing guidebooks. Led 1st major expedition to Karakoram (1892).

cony, name for rabbit, esp. Syrian rock hyrax, *Procavia capensis.*

Cook, James (1728–79), Eng. navigator. Sailed round the world; explored Pacific and Antarctic. Discoveries include Easter Is., Marquesas, Hawaiian group; charted New Zealand and E coast of Australia. Killed by natives off Hawaii.

Cook, Mount, highest peak in New Zealand (12,349 ft.), in S Alps, South Is. Also mountain (13,760 ft.) in SE Alaska, in St Elias Range.

Cook Island, S Pacific group, comprising 6 large and numerous small islands. Area: 93 sq. mi. Discovered (1777) by Capt. Cook; Brit. protectorate (1888) annexed (1901) by New Zealand; internal self-government introduced (1964). Citrus fruits, tomatoes, copra and arrowroot exported. Pop. (1964) 23,000.

Cooley, Charles Horton (1864–1929), Amer. social philosopher. Influential views concerning individual and society and primary social groups.

Coolidge, [John] Calvin (1872–1933), 30th US Pres. (1923–9), Republican. Massachusetts state Gov. (1919–20), becoming nationally prominent over use of militia to end

Boston police strike (1919). Selected as Repub. vice-presidential candidate (1920), became Pres. upon Warren Harding's death (1923). Elected for full term (1924).

Coolidge, William Augustus Brevoort (1850–1926), Amer. mountaineer. Made a record 1,700 expeditions. Editor of *Alpine Journal* (1880–9).

co-operative, in UK, term applied to movement founded (1821) by Robert Owen. Object was for group of consumers to supply its own material wants, eliminating capitalist (middle man). First co-operative shop opened (1844) by followers of Owen at Rochdale, Lancs., England. By 1961 co-operative movements had 13 million members.

Co-operative Commonwealth Federation (CCF) *see* New Democratic Party.

Co-operative for American Relief Everywhere (CARE), Amer. organization founded (1945) to send food, textiles, books and tools to impoverished peoples; run by amalgamation of religious, labour and nationality groups, supported by voluntary contributions. Incorporated (1958) Medical International Co-operation Organization (MEDICO).

co-operative societies, groups formed voluntarily for members' benefit; worker- or consumer-owned organization. Robert Owen (1771–1858) was founder.

Cooper, Anthony Ashley, 1st Earl of Shaftesbury (1621–83), Eng. politician, main opponent of Charles II's pro-catholic policies.

Cooper, Sir Astley Paston (1768–1841), pioneer Eng. surgeon who removed cyst from head of George IV; 1st to amputate hip joint successfully.

Cooper, Gary (1901–61), Amer. film

actor. Pictures include *A Farewell to Arms, Pride of Yankees, Sergeant York, High Noon.* Often cast as shy, lanky cowboy.

Cooper, James Fenimore (1789–1851), 1st Amer. novelist to acquire international fame; writer of hist. novels and sea stories, but most famous for 'Leather-Stocking Tales', incl. *The Last of the Mohicans* (1826) and *The Deerslayer* (1841).

Cooper, Peter (1791–1883), Amer. inventor, industrialist and philanthropist. Built 'Tom Thumb', 1st Amer. steam locomotive (1830); leader in securing public school system for New York City. Presidential candidate of Greenback Party (1876).

Cooper's hawk, hawk of genus *Accipiter,* N Amer. representative of European sparrow hawk.

coot, bird of rail family, genus *Fulica.* Common *F. atra* of Europe, C and S Asia, NW Africa and Australia. Dark plumage, white bill. Mostly non-migratory. Similar Amer. coot, *F. america,* found from Canada to Peru.

Copenhagen, København, cap. of Denmark since 1443, on island of Zealand. 1st civic charter granted 1254; University founded 1479; occupied by Germans (1940–5). Shipping centre; industries include textiles, watches, porcelain, brewing, distilling and sugar refining. Pop. (1965) 555,019.

Copenhagen, Battle of (1801), naval encounter during Fr. Revolutionary Wars. Brit. fleet, under Sir Hyde Parker and Horatio Nelson, defeated Danish fleet.

Copernicus, Nicholas (1473–1543), Polish astronomer and mathematician. In *De Revolutionibus Orbium* (1530) described Sun as centre of universe, with Earth and planets

European Coot

165

Copenhagen, laid out to a Royal design, uses its canals for travelling and sightseeing

revolving around it. Founder of modern astronomy.

Copland, Aaron (1900–), Amer. composer and conductor. Encouraged contemporary music. Composed symphonies, film music, ballets, *e.g. Appalachian Spring* (1944) and opera, *e.g. The Tender Land* (1959).

copper, (Cu), metallic element. Malleable and ductile, uses include roofing, utensils, coins and electrical wire. Constituent of alloys, *e.g.* bronze, brass. Mainly mined in N and S America, Rhodesia and Congo.

copperhead, *Ancistrodon contortrix,* poisonous snake of pit viper family of E North America and Canada. One of most venomous Austral. snakes, *Denisonia superba, c.* 3 ft. long, with copper-coloured head.

copra *see* COCONUT PALM.

coprolites, fossilized excrements of extinct sauria and fish. True nature estab. from occurrence in remains of Ichthyosauria.

Copt, Egyptian descended from ancient native race, or member of Coptic church.

Coptic, Hamitic language divided into 5 main dialects of Gk. script. Extinct *c.* 1500 but still used in Coptic church liturgy.

copyright, legal right of authors, composers, artists, *etc.* to print, publish and sell their works for given number of yr. and to prevent others from doing so without their given consent. Various Berne conventions and Universal Copyright Convention, sponsored by UNESCO, have been signed by most countries and cover international copyright.

cor anglais *see* OBOE.

coracle, portable, primitive, oval fishing boat, with skin-covered wicker frame.

coral, marine animal of coelenterate class *Anthozoa,* known since Ordovi-

cian times. Calcareous skeleton of red coral, *Corallium nobile,* of Med. Sea, used as jewellery and ornaments. Some species esp. *Madreporia,* are reef-builders. Types of reef include atoll and littoral fringe reef, of which Great Barrier Reef off NE Australia is largest in world.

coral fish, numerous species of fishes inhabiting coral reefs, including Butterfly fish, Damsel fish, Parrot fish

coral reefs *see* ATOLL.

Coral Sea, Battle of, air-sea battle in which Jap. forces defeated by Amer. (May 1942) and forced to withdraw from SW Pacific.

coral snake, harlequin snake, poisonous snake of Mexico, C and S America, related to cobra.

Corbett, James John (1866–1933), Amer. boxer; 1st heavyweight champion (1892–7) after acceptance of QUEENSBURY RULES. Wrote *The Roar of the Crowd* (1925).

Corbusier, le, *see* JEANNERET, CHARLES EDOUARD.

Corday, Charlotte (1768–93), Fr. anti-Jacobin revolutionist. Assassin of Jean-Paul Marat, whom she stabbed in his bath. Guillotined.

Cordillera, parallel ranges of mountains; 1st applied to S Amer. Andes. In W of N America, Rocky Mts. and Sierra Nevada are collectively called The Cordilleras.

Córdoba, city of Argentina, cap. of Córdoba prov. Has 17th cent. Jesuit cathedral and university, founded 1613. Pop. (1960) 589,000.

Córdoba, Córdova, city of Spain on Guadalquivir River, cap. of Córdoba prov. Founded by Carthaginians, developed by Moors who built mosque (now cathedral). Pop. (1965) 215,000.

Cordobés, El, orig. Manuel Benítez (1936–), Sp. bullfighter. Achieved early fame with carefree style. Greatest money-winner in bullfighting history.

corduroy *see* VELVET.

CORE *see* CONGRESS OF RACIAL EQUALITY.

Corelli, Arcangelo (1653–1713), Ital. violinist and composer. Considered creator of *concerto grosso* form.

coreopsis, tickseed, annual or perennial plant of genus *Coreopsis;* yellow or crimson daisylike flowers.

Corfu, northernmost of Ionian Is. off Albanian and Gk. coasts, also name of chief town and port. Olives, pomegranates, figs and grapes grown. Pop. (1964) 27,000.

corgi, small Welsh dog of 2 varieties, Pembrokeshire, short-tailed and red or red and white, Cardiganshire,

Anemone Fish

long-tailed and any colour except white.

Cori, Carl Ferdinand (1896–) and his wife **Gerty Theresa Cori** (1896–1957), Amer. biochemists. For contributions to biochemistry, esp. research on carbohydrate metabolism and enzymes, shared with B. A. Houssay, Nobel Prize for Physiology and Medicine (1947).

coriander, *Coriandrum sativum,* annual herb, native of Med. countries, grown in Morocco and US; seeds used as flavouring, oil used medicinally.

Corinth, city of Greece on isthmus between mainland and Peloponnesus. Founded (*c.* 1000 BC), great trading and cultural centre; rivalry with Athens contributed to PELOPONNESIAN WAR. Destroyed (146 BC) by Romans. New Corinth erected nearby after 1858 earthquake. Famous citadel, Acrocorinth; canal across isthmus opened 1893. Pop. (1960) 15,892.

Corinthian architecture *see* GREEK ARCHITECTURE.

Group of Corals from the Caribbean S

Cormorant

Corinthians I and II, Epistles of NT written by St Paul from Ephesus (c. 55 AD), to church at Corinth which he had founded some 5 yr. before.

Coriolanus, Gnaeus Marcius, Roman general (c. 500–450 BC) named after capture of town Corioli from Volscians. Exiled from Rome for tyrannical aspirations, joined Volscians. Prepared to attack Rome, but dissuaded by mother and wife. Put to death by Volscians.

Cork, largest county of Ireland, noted for fertile soils and dairy produce. Area: 2,876 sq. mi.; county town, Cork; main towns, Cobh, Fermoy and Kinsale. Agriculture main occupation; tourism important. Pop. (1963) 330,443.

Cork, county town and seaport of Cork, SW Republic of Ireland, on R. Lee, 11 mi. from Cork Harbour. Market town for SW; distilling and tanning. Present city founded as trading centre by Danes. Import and export trade with UK, Netherlands, Spain and France. Pop. (1966) 122,066.

cork, outer tissue produced by evergreen cork tree of the Med. to replace epidermis as a protective layer. Impervious, compressible and elastic bark. Trees can be stripped about every 10 yr. for c. 150 yr.

corkwood see BALSA.

corm see BULB.

cormorant, diving-bird of family Phalacrocoracidae. Long bodies; mainly black plumage; poor fliers. Species include white-breasted cormorants, exclusive to S hemisphere, great cormorant, *Phalacrocorax carbo,* of N Atlantic coasts, Asia and Australia, green cormorant or shag, *P. aristotelis,* and N Amer., *P. auritus.*

corn borer, *Ostrinia nubilalis,* larva of European moth now pest in parts of US, boring into ears of grain.

corn ear worm, destructive larva of owlet moth.

Corn Laws, legislation enacted (1815) in UK prohibiting import of corn when domestic price fell below certain level. Anti-Corn Law League formed (1838) and, after Irish famine (1845–6) bringing with it need for cheap food, Corn Laws were repealed by Robert Peel (1846).

corncrake, landrail, *Crex crex,* short-billed European game bird of rail family with tawny plumage. Timid, frequents long grass; harsh call. Numbers diminishing.

Corneille, Pierre (1606–84), Fr. dramatic poet and classical tragedian. His masterpiece, tragi-comedy *Le Cid* (1637) was complete reworking of Sp. play. *Le Menteur* (1643) is a comedy. Tragedies exalt human will and subordinate passion to duty.

cornelian cherry, dogwood, cornel, *Cornus mascula,* shrub of cornel family found in N temp. mountain regions. Edible berries used in preserves and in manufacture of *vin de cornoulle,* French liqueur.

Cornell, Katherine (1898–), Amer. actress appeared in *The Green Hat, The Barretts of Wimpole Street, Candida* and *The Three Sisters, etc.*

Cornell University, Amer. university, founded in Ithaca, NY (1865). Nonsectarian, with land-grant, state and private support. Several schools in New York city.

cornet, brass wind instrument created in France (c. 1880) by adding valves to post horn. Sound softer than trumpet; used mainly in brass bands.

cornflower, *Centaurea cyanus,* hardy annual of daisy family native to Med. regions. Formerly weed in European grainfields, now popular garden flower, esp. blue variety.

Cornish see CELTIC.

cornstarch, cornflour, starch prepared from corn.

Cornucopia (Lat: horn of plenty), in classical myth., horn of goat Amalthea which suckled infant Zeus; had power to produce whatever possessor wished.

Cornwall, county and duchy of SW England, incl. Scilly Is. Area: 1,375 sq. mi.; county town, Truro. Main occupations, tin and copper working, fishing and tourist industry. Pop. (1966) 353,000.

Cornwallis, Charles, 1st Marquess (1738–1805), Eng. general in Amer. War of Independence. Gov.-General of India (1786–93, 1805); viceroy of Ireland (1798–1801).

Cornwallis, Edward (1713–76), Gov. of Nova Scotia and founder of Halifax. Appointed (1749), hoped to strengthen Eng. colony, but disillusionment brought resignation (1752).

coromandel wood, variety of ebony obtained from E Indian tree, *Diospyros melanoxylon.*

corona see ECLIPSE.

Corot, Jean Baptiste Camille (1796–1875), Fr. landscape painter associated with Barbizon school. In Italy (1825) developed treatment of light and tone. Later, portraits and figure studies, esp. of women.

corporation [US], business organization similar to COMPANY, LIMITED.

corpuscles, blood see HAEMOGLOBIN, LEUCOCYTES.

corrie see CIRQUE.

Corsica [Corse], Med. is. and dept. of France, separated from Sardinia by Strait of Boniface. Area: c. 4,000 sq. mi.; cap. Ajaccio. Mountainous areas support sheep farming. Main products, olives, cereals, vines, fruits; small-scale industry and fishing; tourist centre. Pop. (1964) 275,465.

Corte-Real, Gaspar (c. 1450–1501), Portuguese navigator. On 1st and only successful voyage (1500), explored S tip of Greenland.

Cortez, Hernando or **Cortés, Hernán** (1485–1547), Sp. conqueror of Mexico. Went to Hispaniola (1504) and accompanied VELAZQUEZ to Cuba (1511). His conquests extended over most of Mexico and C America.

Cortot, Alfred (1877–1962), Fr. pianist and conductor. Founded

Cork bark being stripped off the tree

Steep cliffs at Land's End, Cornwall, the westernmost point of England

(1918) École Normale de Musique, Paris. Specialized in playing music of Beethoven and Chopin. Wrote *La musique française du piano.*

corundum, mineral aluminium oxide. Purer varieties used as gems, coarser as abrasives (*e.g.* emery). Chief corundum gems are ruby, sapphire, and topaz.

Corunna, La Coruña, seaport and cap. of Corunna prov. NW Spain. Armada set sail (1588) from Corunna to conquer England; sacked by Drake (1589), defended by the British under Sir John Moore against the French (1809).

corvette, full-rigged sloop of war, carrying up to 20 guns on upper deck. A modified trawler, with guns and anti-submarine devices used as escorts in World War 2.

Cos [Kos], Gk. island, Aegean Sea, where Hippocrates laid foundations of medical science (5th cent. BC). Ruins include temple of Asclepius.

Cosgrave, William Thomas (1880– 1965), Irish statesman. After Sinn Fein split (1922), remained loyal to Free State. Pres. of executive council of Ireland (1922–32). Opposition leader until resignation (1944).

cosmic radio waves *see* COSMIC RAYS.

cosmic rays, high speed radio-active particles of extra-terrestrial origin, entering the earth's atmosphere with high velocity, enormous energy and power.

cosmos, autumn-blooming annual plant of thistle family *c.* 2 ft. tall; cultivated varieties derive from Mexican *Cosmos bipinnatus.*

Cosmos, name given to series of satellites launched by USSR for space observation. Cosmos 1 was launched 16 Mar. 1962.

Cossacks, peasant-soldiers of S Russia and Siberia who, until 1918,

held privileges of autonomous govt. in return for military service. Descendants of fugitive serfs settled in Don and Dnieper areas (16th–17th cent.). Activity in peasant revolts (esp. in 18th cent.) cost them much autonomy. Prominent in 19th cent. wars and colonization. Before 1917 number *c.* 8,000,000. After armed resistance in 1930s their communities came under Soviet admin., but retained many customs and traditions.

cossid, moderately large moth family incl. European goat moth, *Cossus cossus,* whose larvae burrow into trees, as does N Amer. species, *Prionoxuystus robiniae.* Austral. cossid, *Xyleures,* has 10 in. wingspan.

cost of living index, measurement of cost of consumer goods and service necessary to maintain definite standard of living. Orig. used to measure incidence of poverty, now used by govt. as guide to fiscal policy, and as basis for wage negotiation. In UK, Index of Retail Prices (1947) compiled by Cost of Living Advisory Committee; in US, Consumer Price Index (1945) compiled by Bureau of Labor Statistics.

Costa Brava, NE Med. coast of Spain from Port Bon on Fr. frontier, to Blanes, 40 mi. N of Barcelona. Tourist centre, containing the resorts, Tossa, Lloret de Mar, Cadaqués, Palamos and Blanes, until recently little-known fishing villages.

Costa del Sol, E coast of Spain stretching 270 mi. from Cabo de Gata S to Tarifa. Fine beaches; resorts, *e.g.* Torremolinos, Marbella and Málaga attract many tourists.

Costa Rica [República de Costa Rica], repub. of Latin America between Pacific and Caribbean. Area: 19,659 sq. mi.; cap. San José.

Cultivated coastal areas; interior high jungle plains with 2 volcanic ranges; central valley, drained by Reventazon and Rio Grande. Coffee, bananas, cocoa, sugar and dairy produce are important. Pop. (1966) 1,154,132.

Côte d'Azur, most W part of Fr. Riviera, incl. Monaco. Main towns of this fashionable resort area are Nice, Antibes, Menton and Cannes.

cotoneaster, genus of shrubs of rose family, most varieties having glossy green leaves, small pink or white flowers and abundant crimson berries. *C. horizontalis* is popular garden variety.

Cotopaxi, world's highest active volcano (19,344 ft.), in C Ecuador.

Cotton, John (1584–1652), Puritan clergyman. Dissatisfied with conditions in Anglican Church, emigrated from England to Boston (1673) where he became one of spiritual leaders of Massachusetts Colony. With Thomas Hooker wrote *Survey of the Sum of Church Discipline* (1648).

cotton, natural fibre produced from plant, genus *Gossypium,* of mallow family, cheapest and most widely used natural fibre. Has been spun, woven and dyed since pre-historic times. Cotton manufacture, huge industry, esp. in UK and US (18th and 19th cent.). USSR, India, China and Mexico are other chief producers.

cotton boll weevil *see* BOLL WEEVIL.

cottonmouth *see* WATER MOCCASIN.

cottontail, mammal of rabbit family, numerous in N America and parts of S America; uses abandoned burrows.

cottonthistle *see* SCOTCH THISTLE.

Cottrell, Leonard (1913–   ), Eng. anthropologist whose books have helped to popularize archaeology and prehistory. They include *The Lost Pharaohs* (1950), *Seeing Roman Britain* (1956), *The Lion Gate* (1965).

Coubertin, Pierre de, Baron (1863–1937), Fr. scholar. Brought about revival of Olympic Games. New series of Games began in Athens (1896).

couch grass, *Agropyron repens,* troublesome perennial weed on arable land, with creeping rhizomes of which each broken piece is capable of reproduction.

cougar *see* AMERICAN LION.

Coughlin, Charles Edward (1891–   ), R.C. priest in US. Bitterly opposed New Deal programme through news media.

Coulomb, Charles Augustin de (1736–1806), Fr. physicist. Formulated Coulomb's law which states the forces existing between charged bodies and

Temple of Asclepius at Cos

the coulomb, a unit of electrical quantity named after him.

council, ecumenical, in Christianity, convocation of duly constituted authorities of whole church. Modern R.C. canonists recognize Ephesus, Nicaea, Basle, Ferrara and Trent among over 20 councils. *See* ECUMENISM.

Council for Mutual Economic Assistance (COMECON), formed (1949) to co-ordinate economic policy within E Europe. Expanded scope to facilitate organization of industrial production under 1959 charter. Albania expelled (1961) from orig. membership of USSR and satellite countries. Mongolian People's Republic joined (1962).

Council of Constance, the *see* GREAT SCHISM.

Council of Europe, founded (1949) to safeguard political and cultural heritage of Europe, and facilitate economic and social progress. Membership comprises nearly 20 nations, primarily from W and N Europe.

counterpoint, in music, melodic decorations built round theme; dominant feature of Renaissance and Baroque music, and fabric of fugal writing.

countertenor, male alto, adult male singer; uses falsetto or head voice with exceptional facility.

county [O.E., shire], in the Brit. Isles, the main polit., social and admin. division. Although a únit of govt. before Norman conquest (1066), modern form estab. by Local Government Act (1888), by transferring admin. duties from magistrates to county councils. There are 40 counties in England, 33 in Scotland, 6 in N Ireland, 26 in Ireland. System adopted with variations in most countries settled by British. In US, county is principal geographic and political subdivision of all states excepting Alaska; called a parish in Louisiana.

Couperin, François (1668–1733), Fr. composer, harpsichordist and organist; famous for harpsichord concertos, organ pieces and church music.

Courbet, Gustave (1819–77), Fr. painter. Rejected idealism in art, *e.g. Funeral at Ornans.* Imprisoned during suppression of Commune (1871). *Studio of the Painter,* visual manifesto of his philosophy.

Courcelle (Courcelles), Daniel de Rémy (1626–98), governor of New France (1669–72). Led expedition (1666) along Richelieu River against Iroquois. Subsequent intrusion into Mohawk's territory brought peace (1667) with Iroquois nation.

courgette, zucchini, *Cucurbita pepo,* small marrow, 2–8 in. long, ridged outer skin; used as vegetable, baked, fried or stuffed.

Cournand, André Frédéric (1895–   ), Fr.-American physician. Shared Nobel Prize for Physiology and Medicine (1956) with D. W. Richards and W. Forssmann, for developing new techniques in treatment of heart diseases.

courser, group of long-legged wading birds related to PLOVER, of arid regions of S Asia and Africa, sometimes migratory.

court, in law, official body charged with judging legal cases. Semi-eccles. courts of Egypt and Babylonia had become secular by Roman era. In UK, High Court of Justice (dating from Judicature Act of 1873) comprises Chancery, Queen's or King's Bench divisions and court of appeal. In US, 2 systems are Federal and state courts. Supreme Court is chief court of Federal system.

Courtenay, Henry (1496–1538), Marquis of Exeter and Earl of Devon, cousin of Henry VIII. Beheaded for alleged aspiration to Eng. throne.

Cousteau, Jacques-Yves (1910–   ), Fr. underwater explorer and writer. Inventor of aqualung and other aids to oceanographic research. Wrote *The Silent World* (1953) and *The Living Sea* (1963).

Covent Garden, Royal Opera House, orig. site of London Theatre; later of Royal Italian Opera House (opened 1732). Present house (opened 1858) home of Royal Opera Co. and Royal Ballet Co.

Coventry, city and county borough of Warwickshire, England. Developed around 11th cent. Benedictine Abbey. Centre of cloth industry in England until 18th cent., now industrial centre producing motor cars and synthetic textiles. City centre, incl. famous cathedral, destroyed in 1940 air-raid. Pop. (1966) 316,000.

cow parsley, wild chervil, *Anthrisus sylvestris,* plant of Umbelliferae family, found in temp. regions. Common hedgerow plant, with white clusters of tiny flowers.

Coward, Sir Noel (1899–   ), Eng. actor, playwright, and composer. Best known for witty comedies incl. *Private Lives* (1930), *Blithe Spirit* (1941), revues, musical comedies, songs and film scripts.

cowbird, N Amer. bird of oriole family with parasitic egg-laying habits. Feeds on insects esp. cow parasites; species include *Molothrus ater.*

Cowell, Henry Dixon (1897–1965), avant garde Amer. composer and pianist. Wrote symphonies, operas; edited *New Musical Quarterly.*

Cowes, seaport of Isle of Wight, England, comprising E and W Cowes. Contains Osborne, Queen Victoria's country house. Home of Royal Yacht Squadron and annual Cowes Regatta.

Cowper, William (1731–1800), Eng. pre-Romantic poet. Writings include intensely religious *Olney Hymns* (1779), *The Task* (1785) and shorter poems incl. 'John Gilpin' (1782).

cowry, marine mollusc, family, Cypraeidae, of periwinkle group abundant in trop. waters. *Cypraea moneta* used as money and decoration in parts of Africa and Asia.

cowslip, *Primula veris,* plant of primrose family; wild flower of temp. zones with yellow bell flowers.

Bonjour, Monsieur Courbet! by Gustave Courbet

Crowned Crane

Cox, James Middleton (1870–1957), Amer. polit. leader and newspaper owner. Gov. of Ohio (1913–15, 1917–21). Unsuccessful Democratic pres. candidate (1920). Autobiog. *Journey Through My Years* (1946).

coyote, prairie wolf, bush wolf, *Canis latrans,* small, nocturnal greyish-brown wolf of plains of W North America.

coypu, *Myocastor coypus,* aquatic rodent of porcupine group. Native of S America.

Cozzens, James Gould (1903–), Amer. novelist. Author of *Guard of Honor* (1948), which won Pulitzer Prize, and *By Love Possessed* (1957).

Detail of *Venus with Cupid as a Honey Thief* (1537) by Lucas Cranach the Elder

crab, mainly marine and carnivorous crustacean of order Decapoda, many of which are edible. Species include dark green shore crab, *Carcinus maenas,* European edible crab, *Cancer pagurus* and Amer. Atlantic blue crab, *Callinectes hastatus.*

crab apple, *Malus pumila,* tree of apple family of Europe and W Asia; small reddish-yellow fruit bitter flavour; valued as ingredient in drinks and preserves.

Crabbe, George (1754–1832), Eng. poet and cleric; best known poems *The Village* (1783), *The Borough* (1810) from which Benjamin Britten took the theme of his opera *Peter Grimes.*

Craigie, Sir William Alexander (1867–1957), Brit. lexicographer. Worked on *Oxford Dictionary* and *A Dictionary of American English on Historical Principles.*

crake, small marsh bird of rail family, short bill and stout body. Species include rare European spotted crake, *Porzana porzana,* and little crake, *P. parva.* Carolina crake is the SORA.

cramp ball, *Daldinia concentrica,* spherical red-brown European fungus.

Cranach, Lucas (1472–1553), Ger. painter, famous as portraitist and animal painter. Portraits included Luther, Charles V and electors of Saxony.

cranberry, *Vaccinium oxycaccys,* vine-like shrub with bitter, crimson berries, native to Europe and US; traditional sauce with game and fowl.

Crane, Stephen (1871–1900), Amer. novelist and war-correspondent who influenced Amer. prose writing. Most famous book *The Red Badge of Courage* (1895).

crane, long-legged, long-necked, omnivorous wading bird found everywhere except S America. Species include grey European common crane, *Grus grus,* and Amer. whooping crane, *G. americana.*

crane fly, daddy-long-legs, slender long-legged fly. Larvae usually live in ground. Some species known as leatherjackets; some, *e.g. Tipula paludosa,* are pests.

cranesbill geranium, flowering plants of geranium family, found in temp. zones. Five-segmented fruits form long pointed beak when ripe.

Cranko, John (1927–), Eng. dancer and choreographer. Best known ballets are *Pineapple Poll, The Lady and the Fool* and *The Prince of the Pagodas.*

Cranmer, Thomas (1489–1556), Eng. prelate, chiefly responsible for reforming Eng. church under Henry VIII and Edward VI. Secured Henry's divorce from Catherine of Aragon, was appointed Archbishop of Canterbury (1533). Supported Act of Supremacy (1534), use of Eng. Bible, revised *Book of Common Prayer* (1552). Accused of treason and heresy at Mary's accession, imprisoned and burned at the stake.

crappie, *Pounoxis annularis,* N Amer. freshwater fish of C regions; belongs to sunfish family.

craps, popular US dice game, played with 2 dice.

crater, hole produced by explosion of established volcano; may be formed on earth's surface by meteoric impact, *e.g.* Meteor Crater, Arizona.

Crater Lake, intensely blue lake in Crater Lake National Park (Oregon, US). Occupies near-circular caldera 6 mi. in diameter with steep walls of up to 2,000 ft.

crawfish *see* CRAYFISH.

Crawford, Isabella Valancy (1850–87). Canadian poet. Her narratives include *Old Spookses' Pass* (1884) and *Malcolm's Katie* (1884).

Crawford, Joan (1908–), Amer. film actress of over 70 films. Won Academy Award for *Mildred Pierce* (1945).

crayfish, crawfish, freshwater crustacean, incl. 2 families, Astacidae and Parastacidae. Many edible, esp. large Tasmanian *Astacopis gouldi.* Term applied to some marine crustaceans of Palinuridae family.

Crécy, small town in N France. Site of battle during Hundred Years War in which Edward III defeated Philip VI of France (26 Aug. 1346).

credit rating, assessment of prospective customer's financial position, undertaken by banks and money lending agencies.

Coyote

View over the flat valley of Mesara, Crete

credit sales *see* HIRE PURCHASE.

credit unions, in Canada, co-operatives chartered by state or federal govt. which give loans only to members.

Cree, tribe of N Amer. Indians, closely related to Ojibwa. Plains Cree lived on the prairies, hunted buffalo by driving them into enclosures; woodland Cree lived around Hudson Bay and Peace, Athabaska and Slave rivers.

Creek, group of N Amer. Indian tribes living in Alabama and Georgia. Settled agriculturalists, allied against N tribes. Rebelled against whites in Creek War (1813–14). Defeated by Andrew Jackson at Horseshoe Bend.

creeping jenny, *Lysimachia nummularia,* plant of primrose family found in moist grass or forest in temp. zones. Common garden flower.

creeping thistle *see* CANADA THISTLE.

crème de menthe, mint-flavoured liqueur.

Cremer, Sir William Randal (1828–1908), Brit. pacifist and trade unionist who helped found the Carpenters and Joiners' Union (1860). Advocate of international arbitration. Awarded Nobel Peace Prize (1903).

Creon, in Gk. myth., king of Thebes. Brother of Jocasta, mother and wife of Oedipus. *See* ANTIGONE.

creosote bush, *Larrea tridentata,* shrub of Zygophyllaceae family of N America growing thickly on Colorado desert fringes.

crêpe, lightweight fabric with wrinkled texture, orig. woven from raw silk.

cress, *Lepidium sativum,* tiny plant native of Persia used as garnish. Watercress, *Nasturtium officinale,* larger leaves and stronger flavour, used in salad and soups.

Cressida, according to medieval romance, daughter of Calchas, seer of Greeks in Trojan War, and beloved of Troilus, son of Priam.

crested grebe, *Podiceps cristatus,* largest GREBE; about the size of gull, with two stiff tufts of black head feathers.

crested tit, Eurasian tit, *Pauus iristatus, c.* $4\frac{1}{2}$ in. long, distinguished by prominent black and whitish crest and distinctive voice.

Cretaceous *see* GEOLOGICAL TABLE.

Crete, island prov. of Greece in Med. Sea. Area: 3,240 sq. mi.; main cities, Candia and Canea. Mt. Ida highest point (8,195 ft.). Mountainous with fertile valleys; site of Minoan or Cretan Bronze Age civilizations, centred on Cnossus. Declined with growth of Gk. city-states, later subject to Roman, Turkish, Saracen and Venetian rule until taken (1699) by Turks who ruled until its return to Greece (1913). Pop. (1964) 483,258.

cretinism *see* HYPOTHYROIDISM.

cribbage, old Eng. card game for 2 players. Scores marked with pegs on a board.

Crick, Francis Harry Compton (1916–), Brit. scientist. Awarded Nobel Prize for Physiology and Medicine (1962) with Maurice Wilkins and James Watson, for work in establishing structure and function of nucleic acid (DNA).

cricket, any of saltatorial orthopherous insects, family Gryllidae, esp. genus *Gryllus.* Chirping notes produced by males by rubbing together parts of forewings.

cricket, Eng. national summer game dating from 13th cent. Marylebone Cricket Club (MCC), now world governing body, formed (1787). County cricket dates from *c.* 1850. Test matches, dating from 1877, are played between England, Australia, New Zealand, West Indies, South Africa, India, Pakistan. *See* ASHES, THE; LORD'S.

Crimea, peninsular prov. of Ukrainian SSR on N coast of Black Sea. Area: 9,945 sq. mi.; cap. Simferopol; main towns Sevastopol, Kerch and Yalta. Steppeland with fertile coastal plain; oil and iron ore deposits in E. Annexed by Russia (1783); autonomous repub. of Russ. federation (1921). Popular tourist area. Pop. (1956) 1,119,000.

Crimean War (1853–56), fought between Russia and Britain, France and Turkey. General causes were conflict between Britain and Russia over control of Dardanelles. Pretext was Russian-French quarrel over guardianship of Palestinian holy places. Turkey's rejection of Russian demands prompted Russia's occupation of Moldavia and Wallachia. Turkey declared war (1853). France and England joined (1854). Main campaign centring on Siege of SEVASTOPOL in Crimea, was marked by futile gallantry (*e.g.* battle of BALAKLAVA) and heavy casualties. Treaty (*see* PARIS, CONGRESS OF) checked Russ. influence in SE Europe.

criminology, study of criminal and his behaviour, pioneered by Lambroso, *L'Uomo Delinquente* (1876); other studies are by S. and E. Glueck, W. Healy, E. H. Sutherland *etc.*

crinoid, fossil animal of phylum ECHINODERMA, sub-phylum Pelmatozoa, 'rooted' into sea floor. Found widely in post-Ordovician rocks.

Cripps, Sir [Richard] Stafford (1899––1952), Brit. politician. Expelled from Lab. Party (1939) for urging united front with communists; re-admitted (1945). Chanc. of Exchequer (1947–50), implemented austere economic measures.

critical constant, properties of substances at CRITICAL POINT.

critical point, in physics and chemistry, point above or below which certain phenomena will not occur.

critical pressure, pressure which will liquefy gas at CRITICAL TEMPERATURE.

critical temperature, temperature above which gas cannot be liquefied.

critical volume, volume occupied by 1 gram-molecule at CRITICAL TEMPERATURE and CRITICAL PRESSURE.

croaker, food fish of N Amer. Atlantic coast; named after sound they make.

Croatia, autonomous republic, N Yugoslavia since 1918; formerly part of Austria-Hungary. Mountainous area; agriculture main occupation.

Croce, Benedetto (1866–1952), Ital. aesthetic philosopher, art critic and historian. *The Philosophy of the Spirit* (1902–17) reflects his idealism. Min. of Education (1920–1).

Crockett, David ('Davy') (1786–1836), Amer. frontiersman, active in W Tennessee. US congressman (1827–31, 1833–5) from Tennessee. Killed at Alamo, Texas.

crocodile, carnivorous occasionally man-eating reptile of Crocodylida family. Species include Nile crocodile, *Crocodylus niloticus, c.* 15 ft. long; Asian marsh crocodile, mugger, *C. palustris;* dangerous estuarine crocodile, *C. porosus,* 20 ft. long; Amer. crocodile, *C. acutus.*

crocodilian, animal related to large mesozoic reptiles, incl. gavial, crocodile, alligator and caiman.

crocus, genus of flowering plants of iris family; over 80 species, native to S Europe and Med. regions. Saffron Crocus, *C. sativus,* cultivated for use as flavouring and for saffron yellow dye.

crofting, system used esp. in highlands and islands of Scotland where tenant rents and cultivates small holding or croft, producing food and raising animals for his own needs.

cromlech, term for prehistoric standing stones, *e.g.* STONEHENGE; orig. used for prehistoric burial chamber of 1 or more upright stone slabs.

Cromwell, Oliver (1599–1658), Lord Protector of England (1653–8). Strong Puritan in Parl. before Civil War. Military ability at Edgehill (1642) and Marston Moor (1644) estab. him in command of anti-royalist forces. Charles I's flight after Naseby (1645) led Cromwell to demand his execution. Declared repub. after king's death (1649) and led punitive expedition to Ireland; defeated royalist Scots under Charles II (1651). Dissolved 'Rump' Parl. (1653); PROTECTORATE estab. with Cromwell as Lord Protector. Declined crown, but new constitution strengthened powers (1657). His Navigation Acts (1651) provoked war with Dutch (1652–4); war with Spain (1655–8) over trade rights. Succeeded by son, Richard (1626–1712) who resigned after 1 year (1659).

Cromwell, Thomas (*c.* 1485–1540), Eng. statesman. Sec. to Cardinal Wolsey (1523), helped suppress monasteries. Succeeded Wolsey as Henry VIII's chief adviser (1529–40); instrumental in separation of Eng. church from Rome. Executed for treason.

Cronus, ancient Gk. god of the harvest (Roman Saturn), son of Uranus and Gaia. His rule was Golden Age, time of peace and happiness. Supplanted by Zeus.

Crookes, Sir William (1832–1919), Eng. chemist and physicist. Discovered thallium, invented Crookes tube, high vacuum tube, important in electricity and ionization.

crops, plants grown for special purpose and harvested.

croquet, outdoor game played with mallets and hard balls on a grass court marked with hoops and pegs.

Crosby, Bing, orig. Harry Lillis Crosby (1904–), Amer. singer and film actor. Popularized many songs, *e.g.* 'White Christmas'; films include *Going My Way, High Society.*

crossbill, bird of the Finch family; the crossed bill enables it to extract seeds from fruit and cones. European

crossbill, *Loxia curvirostra,* inhabits coniferous forests as does Amer. white-winged crossbill, *L. leucoptera.*

crossbow, medieval military weapon consisting of bow set on stock. Used to fire arrows, metal and stones.

croton, trop. plant of Spurge family. Seeds of spurging croton, *Croton tiglium,* native of India, yield powerful purgative extract, croton oil.

croton bug, *Blatta germanica,* small, active, winged species of cockroach common in US.

crow, family, Corvidae, of large gregarious perching birds with a worldwide distribution, characterized by powerful beak, loud call and mainly black plumage. Species include carrion crow, *Corvus corone,* and hooded crow, *C. corone cornix,* of Europe, Amer. crow, *C. tradyrhychus,* RAVEN, ROOK, JAY and MAGPIE.

Crow, tribe of N Amer. Indians of Siouan linguistic stock. Nomadic hunters in Yellowstone river area; allied with whites against Sioux in 1870s.

crowberry, *Empetrum nigrum,* small prostrate trailing shrub of crowberry family, found on moorland in N temp. regions. Black edible berries.

crowfoot, name loosely applied to many species of plants of genus *Ranunculus* of buttercup family, with deeply divided leaves resembling crow's claw. Water crowfoot, *R. aquatitis,* has white flowers.

Crown, the, in UK govt., integral constitutional tenet involving exercise of the royal prerogative, seldom invoked since 18th cent. Also symbol of common allegiance for Brit. Commonwealth.

crown imperial *see* FRITILLARY.

Crown land [UK], crown-owned land. Since reign of George III revenue has been surrendered to parl. which disburses it annually in form of civil list—allotted expenditure for certain members of royal family.

crown of thorns, *Euphorbia splendens,* species of climbing spurge with spiny stems. Native of Madagascar.

crowned pigeon, large pigeon with fanlike erectile crest of head feathers.

crucifixion, death by hanging from wooden cross, used orig. in Near East and adopted by Romans for slaves and criminals. Romans used T-shaped cross until abolition by Constantine.

Cruikshank, George (1792–1878), Eng. caricaturist, illustrator and etcher. Most famous work is *Life in London,* in collaboration with his brother, and etchings for Grimm's *German Popular Stories.*

cruiser, warship capable of high

speed. Used for screening battle fleet, reconnaissance and convoy duties.

Crusades, expeditions sent under banner of cross, particularly by European Christians (11th–14th cent.) to recover Holy Land. First Crusade (1098–99) culminated in capture of Jerusalem (1099). Recapture of Jerusalem by Saladin (1187) necessitated 3rd Crusade (1189–92) of Richard I of England, Frederick Barbarossa and Philip II of France, after which a truce allowed pilgrims to visit Holy Places.

crustacean, animal of the arthropod class, Crustacea, incl. crabs, lobsters, barnacles, shrimps and waterfleas, found sometimes on land and in every type of aquatic habitat; segmented body, often covered by a chitinous carapace, 2 pairs of antennae, 2 pairs of mouth parts and up to 60 pairs of jointed legs.

cryogenics *see* LOW TEMPERATURE PHYSICS.

cryolite, colourless to snow-white mineral resembling ice. A fluoride, it is important in manufacture of aluminium.

crystal, solid body arising from solidification of chem. elements and compounds. Possesses internal structure, the crystal lattice.

Crystal Palace, building erected in Hyde Park, London for Great Exhibition (1851). Moved to Sydenham (1852–3); mostly destroyed by fire (1936). Site of national sports centre.

crystallization, formation of CRYSTALS from vapour, liquid or solution on cooling or evaporation.

crystallography, study of the forms of crystals; involves relationships between crystal faces, axes, inter-facial angles and symmetry.

Cuauhtemoc, Guatemotzin, Quauhtemotzin (Eng: 'Swooping Eagle') (1497–1525), last Aztec emperor of Mexico. Opposed Sp. forces under Cortez, defended Mexico City under siege (1521) until captured. Executed by Cortez.

Cuba [**República de Cuba**], island repub. of W Indies. Area: 44,218 sq.

mi.; cap. Havana. Largest, most densely populated Caribbean island; world's 2nd largest sugar producer. Other main crops, tobacco and fruit. All industry nationalized (1959) and co-operative farms estab. (1960). Mineral resources include iron ore,

Nile Crocodile

Cuckoo

American Cuckoo

manganese and nickel. Discovered by Columbus (1492) and conquered by Spanish (16th cent.). Became independent (1902) during Spanish-American War. Dictatorship of Batista overthrown by revolution led by Fidel Castro (1959). US severed diplomatic relations (1962) and Cuba turned economically and politically to USSR and China. Inhabitants mainly of Sp. descent. Unit of currency, the peso. Pop. (1966) 7,833,000.

Cubism, early form of abstract art developed in Paris (after 1907) by Picasso, Braque, Gris and Léger. Emphasizes rectangular treatment of forms.

cuckoo, family, Cuculidae, of mainly insectivorous birds. Some species are social parasites, laying eggs in other birds' nests. Common cuckoo, *Cuculus canorus*, migrates in summer to Europe and N Asia. N Amer. species include the blackbilled cuckoo, *Coccyzus americanus*, and ROADRUNNER.

cuckoo bee, genus, *Psithymus*, of social insects; parasitic upon bumble bees.

cuckoo pint, *Arum neglectum*, poisonous plant of Arum family, found in S temp. coastal climates. Large triangular leaves and tiny yellow flowers; red berries.

cuckoo spit *see* FROG HOPPER.

cucumber, *Cucumis sativus*, creeping plant of gourd family, with elongated fruit, native of NW India, widely grown in temp. regions; edible gherkin is one of 30 related species.

cucumber beetle *see* LEAF BEETLE.
cucumber tree, name for MAGNOLIA.

cuirass, heavy body armour worn esp. by cavalry in 16th and 17th cent. In Brit. Army, part of ceremonial dress of Life Guards and Royal Horse Guards.

cuisenaire rods, coloured rods of varying lengths, used to teach children fundamental mathematics.

Cukor, George (1899–   ), Amer. film director. Films include *Born Yesterday* (1950), *A Star is Born* (1954) and *My Fair Lady* (1964).

Cullen, Countee (1903–46), Amer. Negro poet. Collections of verse include *Copper Sun* (1927) and *The Black Christ* (1929).

Culloden, moorland near Inverness, Scotland. Site of battle (1746) in which Jacobites under Prince Charles Edward Stuart were totally defeated by Duke of Cumberland's army. Prince escaped to France.

cultured pearl, semi-precious PEARL formed within certain molluscs after

Cushion Moss

artificial introduction of irritant. Mainly produced in Japan. Widely used in jewellery industry.

Cumberland, largely mountainous county of NW England, part of Scotland until 1157. Area: 1,521 sq. mi.; county town, Carlisle. Low fertile land in N; sheep-farming and tourism esp. in LAKE DISTRICT. Industries include coal-mining, iron and steel production. Pop. (1966) 296,000.

cumin, *Cuminum cyminum*, small annual plant grown in Egypt and Syria. Aromatic seeds used to flavour curry and meat dishes, esp. in Oriental cooking.

Cummings, E[ward] E[stlin] (1894–1962), Amer. poet. Lyrics have startling typographical effects (*e.g.* omission of capital letters). Autobiog. *The Enormous Room* (1922) on his imprisonment in World War 1.

Cumulus cloud *see* CLOUD.

Cunard Line, shipping line on the N Atlantic run, founded by Sir Samuel Cunard (1787–1865). Ships included *Lusitania* (1907), *Mauritania*, *Queen Mary* (1936), *Queen Elizabeth I* (1940) and *Queen Elizabeth II* (1969).

cuneiform, form of writing developed in Tigris-Euphrates valley, used by Babylonians and Assyrians. Script has historical parallels with Egyptian hieroglyphics. Important remains found at Nineveh, Lagash and Susa.

Cunningham, Andrew Browne, 1st Viscount of Hyndhope (1883–1963), Brit. admiral, commander in Mediterranean (1939–42).

cup fungus, disc-shaped fungi of Pezizale family. At maturity, spores are discharged from asci (spore sac) in such numbers that they appear as a cloud of smoke.

Cupid, Roman god of love, son of Venus and brother of Amor. Adapted from Gk. Eros. Both represented as winged boys carrying bow and arrow.

cuprite, Cu_2O, reddish brittle mineral found in crystal or massive earthy form. Source of copper.

Curaçao, island of Netherlands Antilles in S Caribbean Sea. Area: 394 sq. mi.; cap. Willemstad. Discovered by Alonso de Ojeda (*c.* 1499), acquired by Dutch (1634). Mainly flat, surrounded by coral reefs. Curaçao liqueur orig. made on island. Pop. (1961) 187,041.

curare, alkaloid, from bark of Strychnos plants. Used by Amazon Indians as arrow poison; paralyses muscles. Limited medicinal use to relax muscles.

curassow, family, Cracidae, of arboreal gamebirds found in Americas. Species include great curassow, *Crax rubra,* and crested curassow, *C. alector.*

curculio, weevil, legless larva which live internally in various parts of plants, esp. plum curculio, *Conotrachelus menupher,* a fruit pest.

Curie, Marie, née Marja Sklodowska (1867–1934), Fr. scientist. With her husband **Pierre Curie** (1859–1906) and Henri Becquerel, awarded Nobel Prize for Physics (1903), for their study of radiation; and Nobel Prize for Chemistry (1911) for discovery of and work on radium and polonium.

curlew, large moorland bird of sandpiper family. N Amer. long-billed curlew, *Numenius americanus,* is largest.

Cup Fungus

Curley, James Michael (1874–1958), Amer. politician. Boston mayor and Mass. gov. (1935–7). Convicted (1946–7) of fraud, but pardoned.

currant, *Ribes sativum,* shrub native to W Europe. Black currant, *R. nigrum,* and Red currant, *R. rubrum,* eaten fresh or made into conserves.

currant, small seedless RAISIN grown mainly in Levant, orig. in Corinth.

current *see* ELECTRICITY.

current, movement of fluid in determined direction. Air currents, or wind, caused by earth's rotation are affected by differences of density and temperature. Winds and other atmospheric forces cause ocean currents. Ocean currents flow clockwise in the N hemisphere, and anti-clockwise in the S hemisphere.

curry, blend of spices and herbs, usually accompanied by boiled rice with base of meat, fish, eggs, vegetables *etc.,* originating in India.

curtain wall, in medieval architecture, outer wall surrounding castle usually carrying towers.

Curzon, George Nathaniel, 1st

Marquess Curzon of Kedleston (1859–1925), Brit. statesman. As viceroy of India (1899–1905) pacified NW border. Foreign Sec., at Lausanne Conference (1922–3).

Cushing, Harvey (1869–1939), Amer. surgeon and medical historian. Technically improved brain surgery and estab. neuro-surgery.

cushion moss, moss of Bryales order. One of the softest textured mosses, widely distributed in N temp. latitudes.

Cushitic, branch of Afro-Asian group of languages, mostly spoken in Ethiopia, Sudan, Somalia, Kenya and Tanzania. Most important member of the group is Somali.

Custer, George Armstrong (1839–76), Amer. army officer. Distinguished career in Civil War and campaigns against Cheyenne and Sioux. 'Custer's Last Stand', in which his regiment was killed by Sioux (1876) at Little Bighorn, has been much debated.

customs *see* TARIFFS.

cuttlebone *see* CUTTLEFISH.

cuttlefish, family of marine cephalopods of shallow waters of most trop. and temp. seas. Calcareous shell, cuttlebone, is internal.

cutworm, larvae of butterfly family Noctuidae. Nocturnal caterpillar feeds on young plants. Some destroy fruit tree buds. Related to armyworm, which destroys grains and cereals.

Cuvier, George Léopold Chrétien Frédéric Dagobert, Baron (1769–1832), Fr. geologist and zoologist. Founder of comparative anatomy and palaeontology; rejected continuous evolution theory.

Willemstad, capital and natural harbour of Curaçao in the Dutch Antilles

Cuzco, [City of the Sun], cap. of Inca Empire of Peru, dating from 13th cent. At time of Sp. conquest (1532) unique gold decorated palaces, temples and public buildings were richest in the world. Spaniards built on Inca foundations. Modern city is tourist centre. Pop. (1965) 78,289.

cwm *see* CIRQUE.

cyanide, hydrogen cyanide (hydrocyanic acid, prussic acid, HCN) and its derivatives, esp. metal salts. Poisonous and characterized by bitter almond smell. Used in steel manufacture, electroplating.

Cybele, mother and fertility goddess of Phrygia, Asia Minor, identified with Gk. Rhea. Worship introduced at Athens (*c.* 430 BC), and at Rome (205 BC).

cybernetics, study of control and communications processes in both animals and machines; theoretical foundations for the computer industry.

Cyclades, *c.* 200 islands of Gk. Archipelago, Aegean Sea. Area: 1,023 sq. mi.; cap., Ermoupolis. Group contains Delos, centre of ancient religion, Andros and Melos, with Hellenic and Roman remains. Products include wine, olive oil, tobacco, and wheat. Pop. (1965) 150,000.

cyclamate, artificial sweetener used particularly in soft drinks. Controversy (1968) over possible cumulative damage to consumers.

cyclamen, genus of plants of primrose family. Native to European and Med. regions. Flowers white to deep

Nicosia, the capital of Cyprus, lying in a wide inland plain

red. Species *C. persicum* is popular houseplant.

cyclamine, synthetic sweetening agent.

cycling, bicycle riding, sport popularized in 1880s. Instituted as racing event at first modern Olympic Games (1896). Tour de France is important annual cycling event.

cyclone, atmospheric area of low pressure and surrounding, rotating winds. Trop. cyclones are violent storms incl. typhoons and hurricanes; extra trop. cyclones are milder areas of depression which cause most rain and snow. *See* WIND.

cyclonic rain *see* RAIN.

Cyclopes, in Gk. myth., 1) sons of Uranus and Gaia; made lightning for Zeus and sided with Olympian gods against Titans. 2) one-eyed sons of Poseidon, lived in Sicily. One, Polyphemus, was blinded by ODYSSEUS.

cyclops, small freshwater crustacean with single median eye. Enlarged antennae are used as oars.

cylindrical projection *see* PROJECTIONS.

cymbals, orchestral untuned percussion intrument, orig. oriental, made of 2 concave metal discs which are clashed together.

Cynics, Gk. school of philosophy founded by Antisthenes (500–400 BC); members met at Cynosarges and considered virtue highest and only good, despised pleasure and worldly goods. Basis of Stoicism.

cypress, family of coniferous trees, Cupressaceae, native to Med. regions, Asia and N America. Tiny needle leaves in overlapping pairs and woody cones. Lawson cypress, *Chamaecypams lawsonia,* grows to 200 ft.

Cyprus, island repub. in Med. Sea. Area: 3,527 sq. mi.; cap. Nicosia. Produces wheat, olives, citrus fruits. Occupied by Greeks, Phoenicians and Romans before Turkish conquest (1571). Brit. colony (1925). Self-rule

granted 1960. Strife between Gk. and Turkish Cypriots after World War 2 ended with UN cease-fire (1964). Pop. (1966) 607,000.

Cyrene, orig. cap. and port of ancient Cyrenaica, one of greatest Gk. colonies. Estab. mid-7th cent. BC and noted for intellectual life and medical school.

Cyrus the Great (*c.* 600–529 BC), consolidated Persian empire. United Medes and Persians, defeated Croesus of Lydia, adding Asia Minor and, later, Babylonia, Assyria, Syria, Palestine and lands E and N of empire. Ruled wisely and tolerantly, regarded by Greeks as ideal ruler.

Cyrus II (424–401 BC), younger son of Darius II, supported Spartans in PELOPONNESIAN WAR, conspired against elder brother Artaxerxes II, pardoned, but raised army (Xenophon enlisted). Reached Babylonia (401 BC), defeated and killed by Artaxerxes at Cunaxa.

czar *see* TSAR.

Czech, Slavic Indo-European language, with 10 million speakers.

Czechoslovakia [Československá Socialistická Republika], repub. of C Europe. Area: 49,700 sq. mi.; cap. Prague; principal cities, Brno, Bratis-

lava, Ostrava. Rich in agric., land, forests, and minerals; well-developed industry. Formerly part of Austro-Hungarian Empire; declared independence (1918), comprising regions BOHEMIA, MORAVIA, SILESIA and SLOVAKIA. Created largely through work of T. G. Masaryk and Benes. Slovakian separatist feeling fostered by Germany; Hitler's rise and Western appeasement resulted in MUNICH PACT (1938) through which Germany obtained Bohemian hinterland. Dissolved (1939) after Ger. occupation; liberated (1945), Communist take-over (1948) and 1960 constitution declared it a socialist repub. Reforms of 1st Sec. Dubcek and Pres. Svoboda curtailed by Soviet occupation (1968).

Czerny, Carl (1791–1857), Austrian pianist and composer. Pupil of Beethoven. Best known for his technical studies which are still in use.

Cypress branch with cones

dab, edible spiny-scaled marine fish of genus *Limanda* of flounder family. Includes lemon sole, *L. limanda.* Lives in shoals in N Atlantic.

dabchick, bird of genus *Podiceps* of grebes. Common species are least grebe, *P. dominicus* of S US and S America and little grebe, *P. ruficollus,* of European Arctic regions.

Dacca, chief city of E Bengal and cap. of E Pakistan. Manufacture and trade centre; remains of 17th cent. Mogul cap. include Bara Katra palace. Pop. (1961) 556,712.

dace, *Leuciscus leuciscus,* small swift freshwater fish of carp family with silver colouring.

dachshund, small Ger. dog with sleek, short-haired coat, drooping ears and short legs. Kept as house pet and for hunting small game.

dada, name of art movement in 1920s, centred on Paris. Led by Tristan Tzara, its basic principle was abandonment of traditional forms and usages.

daddy-long-legs *see* CRANE FLY.

Daedalus, in Gk. myth., Athenian sculptor and architect. Built Labyrinth, prison for Minotaur, in Crete. Imprisoned with son ICARUS.

daffodil, name usually restricted to common yellow daffodil or lent lily, *Narcissus pseudonarcissus* of Amaryllis family, found growing wild in woods and fields of temp. countries.

Daguerre, Louis Jacques Mandé (1789–1851), Fr. painter. Inventor of the daguerreotype, 1st generally available photographic process.

Dahl, Roald (1916–   ), American novelist, b. Wales. Estab. reputation for macabre as in *Kiss Kiss* (1960).

Dahlgren, John Adolphus Bernard (1809–70), Amer. naval officer. Designer of 9 in. and 11 in. guns called

Dabchick

Dahlgrens; wrote widely on naval ordnance.

dahlia, genus of herbaceous tuberous-rooted late-flowering plants of daisy family. Native to Mexico and S America, widely cultivated. Well known species include *Dahlia coccinea, D. pinnata* and *D. juarezii.*

Dahomey, Republic of, in W Africa on Gulf of Guinea. Area: 47,000 sq.

mi.; cap. Porto Novo; chief city and port, Cotonu Little coastline, backed by forested hinterland. Exports palm

Daffodil

kernels and oil. Settled by succession of tribal kingdoms, annexed by France (1892); independent (1960). Pop. (1967) 2,508,000.

Dail Eireann, legislative assembly of Republic of Ireland, 1st assembled (1919) in Dublin. In 1922, after creation of Irish Free State, name was given to chamber of deputies which, with upper house (Seanad Eireann), constitutes state legislature. Dail, or lower house, has 147 elected members.

Daimler, Gottlieb (1834–1900), Ger. engineer and pioneer automobile manufacturer. His improvements in internal combustion engine led to growth of motor-car industry.

daisy, *Bellis perennis,* small perennial herb of Compositae family, native to Europe and W Asia. Among other species, but not of same genus, are *Chrysanthemum leucantheum,* ox-eye daisy, and *Brachycome iberidifolia,* swan river daisy.

daisybush, evergreen trees or small shrubs of daisy family, native to New Zealand. Common garden varieties include *Olearia haastii* and *O. macrodonia.*

Dakar, cap. of Senegal; communication centre on W coast of Africa. Pop. (1966) 450,000.

Dakota Indians *see* SIOUX.

Daladier, Edouard (1884–1970), Fr. statesman, radical socialist deputy (1919–40; 1946–58), premier (1938–40). Signatory of MUNICH PACT. Interned in Germany (1943–5).

Dalai Lama, head of Lamaist religion of Tibet and Mongolia. Considered divine and a reincarnation of his predecessor; 5th Dalai Lama given (1640) temporal rule over all Tibet and built monastery near Lhasa. During 1959 Tibetan revolt against Chinese Communists 14th Dalai Lama fled to India.

Dachshund

Dalberg-Acton, John Emerich Edward, 1st Baron Acton (1834–1902), Eng. historian. Planned *Cambridge Modern History.* Liberal Roman Catholic; writings include *History of Freedom* (1907).

Dale, Sir Henry Hallett. OM (1875–1968), Brit. scientist. Shared Nobel Prize for Physiology and Medicine

Soft Construction with Boiled Beans. Premonition of Civil War 1936 by Salvador Dali

(1936) with Otto Loewi for study of acetylcholine as agent in transmission of nerve impulses.

D'Alembert, Jean le Rond *see* ALEMBERT.

Dalen, Nils Gustaf (1869–1937), Swed. scientist. Awarded Nobel Prize for Physics (1912) for inventing automatic regulator for acetylene gas lights used in signal transmission.

Dali, Salvador (1904–), Sp. surrealist artist. Work influenced by Freudian psychology, expressing irrational dream world, *e.g. Persistence of Memory*. Produced 2 surrealist films with Luis Buñuel, incl. *Le Chien Andalou* (1929).

Dallas, city of N Texas, US. Financial and industrial centre; cotton and oil processing. Scene of assassination (1963) of Pres. John Kennedy. Pop. (1963) 679,690.

Dalmatia, narrow coastal region of Yugoslavia along Adriatic with mountainous interior. Famous for scenic beauty. Chief towns, Split, Dubrovnik. Austrian until 1920; cap. Zadar ceded by Italians (1947).

Dalrymple, James, 1st Viscount Stair (1619–95), Scot. jurist. Prominent lawyer, lost office (1681). Became Lord Advocate under William III.

Dalrymple, John, 1st Earl of Stair (1648–1707), Scot. statesman, son of James Dalrymple. Sec. of State under William III. Promoted Union of Scotland and England.

Dalrymple, John, 2nd Earl of Stair (1673–1747), Scot. army officer and diplomat. Ambassador to Paris (1715–20) where his spies thwarted Jacobite intrigues. Prominent in War of Spanish Succession.

Dalton, [Edward] Hugh [John Neale],

Baron Dalton of Forest and Frith (1887–1962), Brit. politician. Lab. Chanc. of Exchequer (1945–47); instrumental in nationalizing Bank of England.

Dalton, John (1766–1844), Eng. scientist. Revived atomic theory, which he applied to table of atomic weights and in developing Dalton's Law of partial pressures of gases.

dam, stone or concrete structure built across river to store water or regulate its flow for irrigation and to supply power plants. Notable dams include Aswan Dam across Nile R., Boulder Dam on Colorado R. (highest in world, 726 ft.), Grand Coulee and Shasta dams, and Indus barrage in W Pakistan.

Dam, [Carl Peter] Henrik (1895–), Danish biochemist. Awarded Nobel Prize for Physiology and

Medicine (1943) with Edward Doisy for work on vitamins.

Damascus, cap. of Syria. Held by Assyrians, Persians and Romans, later underwent Moslem conversion (7th cent.); Great Mosque built on Christian church, orig. temple of Zeus. Known for sword-making. Sacked by Tamerlane (14th cent.). Ottoman control (1516–1918); became Syrian cap. (1943). Pop. (1963) 545,000.

Damocles, courtier of Dionysius I, tyrant of Syracuse. Declared his patron to be happiest of mortals; was invited to sit on throne of Dionysius, where he observed, above his own head, a naked sword hanging by a single hair.

Dampier, William (1652–1715), Eng. buccaneer and explorer. Fought in Dutch War (1673), plundered Sp. ships (1679–81) in Latin America. Author of hydrographic treatise *Discourse of Trade Winds* (1699). Commanded expedition in S Pacific, discovered Dampier Archipelago and Dampier Strait.

Damrosch, Walter (1862–1950), Amer. conductor and composer, b. Germany. Son of **Leopold Damrosch** (1832–85), composer who founded New York Symphony Soc. (1878). Compositions include operas and choral works.

damsel fly, small delicate predatory insect of dragonfly group.

damson *see* PLUM.

Dana, Charles A[nderson] (1819–97), Amer. newspaper editor. Estab. high standards of writing as editor and part owner of New York *Sun* (1868–97).

Dana, Richard Henry (1815–82), Amer. writer and lawyer. Best known for *Two Years before the Mast* (1840), narrative of voyage around Cape Horn to California as seaman.

Danaë, in Gk. myth., daughter of Acrisius, king of Argos. Mother of PERSEUS by Zeus, who appeared before her as a shower of gold.

The Danube in Yugoslavia

Dallas, Texas

dance, rhythmical steps and movements of the body, primarily spontaneous expression of emotion and known from earliest times. Primitive peoples evolved different styles: Asiatic posturing, Hawaiian hula, Iroquois corn-dance, Austral. corroborees. Music reinforces mood and rhythm. BALLET has evolved as one of the most sophisticated forms of dance. Popular dance forms, incl. jigs and hornpipes, rounds, squares, reels, mazurkas, *etc.*, have evolved from folk dances. Amer. barn dances indicate Negro origins, also evident in much modern dancing, incl. foxtrot, samba, rumba, tango, quickstep. *See* FOLK DANCING.

dandelion, *Taraxacum officinale,* wild, European plant, cultivated in Asia and N America; leaves used in salads and medicine.

Daniel, book of OT, believed written *c.* 168 BC; story of Daniel, a Jew living in 6th cent. BC, who rose to power in Babylon. Historical accuracy is disputed, but its inspirational value is unquestioned.

Daniels, Josephus (1862–1948), Amer. statesman, newspaper editor, and author. US Sec. of the Navy (1913–21); ambassador to Mexico (1933–42). Wrote *The Wilson Era* (1944–6).

Danilova, Alexandra (1900–   ), Russ. ballerina. Joined Diaghilev's Ballets Russes. Noted for interpretation of classical roles.

Danish, Scandinavian Indo-European language in Denmark, Greenland, Iceland and Virgin Is.

D'Annunzio, Gabriele (1863–1938), Ital. writer and nationalist. Most famous work is novel *Il Fuoco* (1900).

Dante [Alighieri] (1265–1321), Ital. poet. Wrote *La Vita Nuova* (1292), prose and poetry narrative about an idealized Beatrice (Portinari). Exiled from Florence (*c.* 1302), he wrote *Divine Comedy*, recording journey through Hell and Purgatory (guided by Vergil) and Paradise (guided by Beatrice) in 100 cantos of *terza rima.*

Danton, George Jacques (1759–94), Fr. revolutionary. Powerful oratory gained him popularity. Leader of leftist Cordeliers, he was instrumental in overthrowing the monarchy (1792). Head of provisional repub. govt. and Min. of Justice, set up 1st Committee of Public Safety (1793). Guillotined after struggle for power with Robespierre.

Danube, European river rising in SW Germany and flowing 1,725 mi. to the Black Sea through S Germany, E Austria, Hungary, NE Yugoslavia and SE Rumania. Always an important waterway (2nd longest in Europe); navigable by ocean-going ships up to Braila. Connected by canal to the Rhine system via the Main. Danubian commission of 1948 excluded non-Danubian countries from use of river.

Daphne, in Gk. myth., nymph loved by Apollo. In trying to flee from him, she was changed into a laurel tree (Gk. *daphne*).

daphne, flowering shrub of Mezereum family native to Europe and Asia. *Daphne mezereum* and *D. laureola,* spurge laurel are found in Britain and Europe. Chinese *D. odora* and *D. retusa* grown in gardens and greenhouses.

daphnia *see* WATERFLEA.

Da Ponte, Lorenzo (1749–1838), Ital. poet and librettist. Author of librettos for Mozart's *Cosi fan tutte, Don Giovanni* and *The Marriage of Figaro.* Helped spread Ital. culture in US.

Dardanelles, strait connecting Sea of Marmara with the Aegean, *c.* 40 mi. long, 1–4 mi. wide. Orig. called the Hellespont, ancient Troy prospered near its W entrance. Importance as strategic zone contributed to Crimean War (1854–6) and GALLIPOLI campaign in World War 1.

Dar-es-Salaam, seaport and cap. of

Griffon mural from the palace of Darius at Susa

Tanzania, E Africa. Sisal hemp, cotton, coffee and minerals are main exports. Pop. (1968 est.) 273,000.

Darien Scheme, Scot. act chartering a trading company (1695). Efforts to estab. colony on Isthmus of Panama (1698–9) failed; heavy loss of life and to investment.

Darius [I] the Great (c. 558–486 BC), king of Persia (521–486 BC). Extended and consolidated power by means of satraps responsible only to him, system later adopted by Alexander the Great. Revolt of Ionian city states (500 BC) led to unsuccessful expeditions against Greeks, 2nd being at Marathon (490 BC).

darkling beetle, family Tenebrionidae of plant-eating terrestrial beetles. Mealworms, larvae of *Tenebrio molitor* are reared for bird food.

Darlan, Jean Louis (1881–1942), Fr. admiral. Advocated collaboration with Germany after appointment to VICHY GOVERNMENT (1940). Went over to Allied side after Allied landing in N Africa (1942). Assassinated.

darnel, poison rye grass, tare, *Lolium temulentum,* weed found in grain fields; if infected with fungus, becomes poisonous to man and livestock.

Darnley, Henry Stuart, Lord (1545–67), Scot. nobleman, 2nd husband of Mary Queen of Scots. Father of James I of England. Joined in murder of David Rizzio (1566); killed, probably at instigation of Earl of Bothwell.

Darrow, Clarence [Seward] (1857-1938), Amer. lawyer. Champion of 'underdog', defended labour leaders (*e.g.* Eugene Debs) and many accused of murder, incl. Leopold and Loeb. Opposed W. J. Bryan in Scopes trial (1925), involving teaching of Darwinian theory.

darter, *Auhinga,* bird of family Auhingidae, related to cormorant. Inhabits inland tropical lakes and swamps. Species *A. auhinga* of S US, African, *A. rufa,* and Indian *A. melanogaster.*

darter, small fish of large genus *Etheostoma* of N Amer. perch. Many species have brilliant colours.

Dartmouth College, Hanover, N.H., US; nonsectarian college for men, founded 1769. Supreme Court ruling (1819) upheld state law to make it a public institution.

Darwin, cap. of Northern Territory, Australia, on inlet of Timor Sea. Orig. called Palmerston (1872), renamed after Charles Darwin. Important air terminal. Pop. (1964) 14,000.

Darwin, Charles Robert (1809–82), Eng. naturalist. Explorations, observations and investigations as official naturalist on the vessel *Beagle* led to theory of EVOLUTION, known as Darwinism, set out in *On the Origin of Species* (1859) and *The Descent of Man* (1871). His theories on man's ancestry and principle of natural selection, were bitterly contested by the church.

Darwin, Erasmus (1731–1802), Eng. scientist and poet. His *Zoonomia* (1794–6) anticipated Lamarck's evolutionary theories. Grandfather of CHARLES DARWIN.

Darwin's sheep, Central Asian wild sheep.

dasyure, terrestrial carnivorous marsupial of family Dasyuridae. Austral. *Dasyurus quok,* noted for savagery and destructiveness.

date line, international, line following 180° meridian of longitude, agreed upon to compensate for date difference caused by standardization of time zones originating at Greenwich, UK; 24 hr. lost when crossing it W to E and gained E to W.

date-palm, *Phoenix dactylifera,* tree grown widely in N Africa and W Asia. Now cultivated in S California and Mexico; nutritious brown fruit eaten raw.

dating, in archaeology, estab. of era in which remains are found. Often estimated by earth layer. Fluorine test, measuring age from bone and teeth and fluorine content, exposed PILTDOWN hoax. Most effective method, Carbon-14, in which degree of radioactivity determines age.

Daudet, Alphonse (1840–97), Fr. author. *Lettres de mon Moulin* (1866) and *Tartarin de Tarascon* (1872) depicted with gentle satire his native Provence. Novels of social criticism include *Fromont Jeune et Risler Aîné* (1874).

Daughters of the American Revolution (DAR), organization open to female descendants of those who fought in Amer. Revolution, founded (1890).

Daumier, Honoré (1808–79), Fr. painter and cartoonist. Created *c.* 4,000 satirical lithographs. Later paintings include *Don Quixote and Sancho Panza* and *The Good Samaritan.*

Dauphiné, region and former prov. of SE France. Chief towns Vienne and Grenoble. Ruled by Counts of Vienne and governed by eldest sons of Fr. kings, who took title of Dauphin. Incorporated by Louis XI into France.

David (d. *c.* 972 BC), shepherd who became king of Hebrews. Hebrew national hero, slayer of GOLIATH, lover of Bath-sheba. Ruled Judah for 40 yr., capturing Jerusalem, and consolidating kingdom. Regarded as founder of royal line of Israel, to which Jesus later belonged. Story told in *Book of Samuel.*

David, Gerard (c. 1450–1523), Dutch painter. Early Flemish master, best known for altarpieces such as 'Baptism of Christ'.

David, Jacques Louis (1748–1825), Fr. hist. painter and court painter to Napoleon. Pictures include *The Rape of the Sabine Women* and *Death of Marat.*

Davie, Alan (1920–   ), Scot. artist. Surrealist paintings often influenced by Celtic art. Won 1963 Sao Paulo prize for 'Best Foreign Painting'.

Davie, Cedric Thorpe (1913–   ), Scot. composer. Works include symphony and music for revival (1949) of *The Three Estates.*

Davies, Joseph Edward (1876–1958), Amer. diplomat. Ambassador to USSR (1937–8), source for his book, *Mission to Moscow* (1941).

Darter Fish

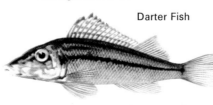

Davies, Robertson (1913–), Canadian writer and newspaper editor. Author of satirical newspaper column, 'The Diary of Samuel Marchbanks'. Also wrote plays and novels.

Davies, [Sarah] Emily (1830–1921), Eng. suffragette. Helped organize 1st woman suffrage petition, presented to Parl. by J. S. Mill.

Da Vinci, Leonardo *see* LEONARDO DA VINCI.

Davis, Bette, orig. Ruth Elizabeth Davis (1908–), Amer. film actress. Won academy awards for *Dangerous* (1935) and *Jezebel* (1938).

Davis, Colin Rex (1927–), Eng. conductor. Musical director of Sadler's Wells (1961–5). Zestful interpreter esp. of Berlioz.

Davis, Jefferson (1808–89), Amer. statesman, Pres. of Confederacy (1861–5). US Sec. of War (1853–7). Senator from Mississippi, resigned at state's secession. As Pres. of South during Civil War, strongly centralized authority brought criticism. Captured and confined until 1867, but never prosecuted.

Davis, John (1550–1605), Eng. navigator. His search for North West Passage, clarified much Arctic geography. Died in E Indies fighting pirates.

Davis, Jr., Sammy (1925–), Amer.

Date-palm (a) the feather-like leaf (b) section through date (c) male flower (d) female flower (e) fruit cluster

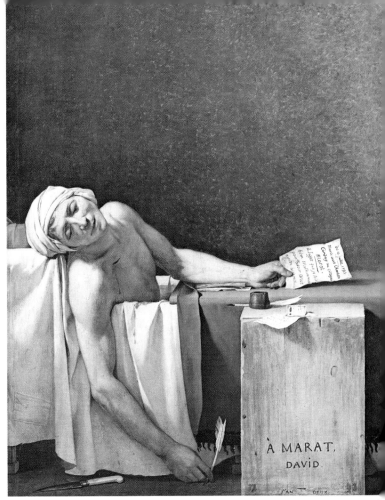

Death of Marat by J. L. David

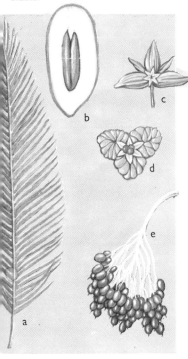

film actor and singer. Noted dancer and impressionist; films include *Oceans 11*.

Davis Cup [Dwight Davis International Bowl], trophy presented to national team winning international lawn tennis championship. Donated by Dwight Filley Davis (1879–1945), Amer. public official.

Davis Strait, Arctic water passage between Greenland and Baffin Is., connecting N Atlantic with Baffin Bay. Discovered (1587) by Eng. navigator John Davis.

Davisson, Clinton Joseph (1881–1958), Amer. physicist. Shared Nobel Prize for Physics (1937) with Sir George Thomson, for confirmation of Louis de Broglie's theory of wave properties of moving electrons.

Davitt, Michael (1846–1906), Irish politician. Imprisoned for Fenian activities. Helped Charles Parnell found National Land League (1879). Instrumental in formation of United Irish League (1898).

Davy, Sir Humphry (1778–1829), Eng. scientist. Isolated sodium and potassium by means of electrical decomposition; estab. elementary nature of chlorine. Invented miner's safety lamp.

Dawes, Charles Gates (1865–1951), Amer. statesman and banker. Vice Pres. of US (1925–9). Promoted Dawes Plan (1924) to Reparations Commission of Allied nations, providing for reduction in payment of REPARATIONS and stabilization of Ger. finances. Awarded Nobel Peace Prize (1925).

Day-Lewis, Cecil *see* LEWIS, CECIL DAY.

daylight saving time (D.S.T.), time reckoned (usually 1 hr.) later than standard time. Adopted in many countries as war-time measure; continued after World War 2 as 'summer' time by turning clocks ahead in spring and back in autumn.

DDT, dichloro-diphenyl-trichloroethane, insecticide invented (1940) for controlling flies, mosquitoes, lice and fleas. Helps control of insect-borne diseases, *e.g.* malaria, typhus, yellow fever. Various insects have developed resistance to DDT.

dead man's finger, *Xylaria hypoxylan,* fungus found on dead wood. *X. polymorpha* is commonly found on stumps of deciduous trees, esp. beech.

dead men's fingers, *Alcyonium digitarum,* soft, pink coral found on coasts of Brit. Isles, sometimes growing 6–9 in. high.

dead-nettle, several annual or perennial herbs of Labiatae family, native of Europe, temp. Asia and N Africa. Leaves resemble NETTLE but have no sting.

Dead Sea, salt lake on Israel-Jordan border, 49 mi. long, 1292 ft. below sea level. Lies in Ghor depression. Far saltier than the oceans.

Dead Sea Scrolls, collection of ancient documents and fragments discovered (1947) in caves 12 km. S of Jericho, in Jordan; date from *c.* 200 BC– AD 100.

deadly nightshade, *Atropa bella-*

Orphan in Graveyard by Delacroix

donna, poisonous plant of genus *Solanum.* Contains atropine which is used medicinally.

deafness, partial or complete loss of hearing caused by illness, injury, or congenital defect. Partial deafness frequently overcome by electrical aids. School for deaf estab. (1755) in Paris by Charles de l'Épée. Many of the deaf can be taught to speak; rest (deaf mutes) use lip reading or manual alphabet.

Death's Head Hawk Moth and Caterpillar

Dean, James (1931– 55), Amer. actor. Films include *East of Eden* and *Rebel Without a Cause.*

death, end of life and cessation of all vital functions in animal or plant. Heart may beat after cessation of breathing and resuscitation is sometimes possible through stimulation of nervous system for a short period after cessation of heartbeat. In humans there is danger of brain damage if period exceeds 20 min.

death cap, genus of toadstool, of which *Amanita phalloides* is most poisonous fungus known.

death penalty *see* CAPITAL PUNISHMENT.

Death Valley, desert in SE California, US. Area: *c.* 3,000 sq. mi. Arid basin 276 ft. below sea level with alkali flats and salt beds; gold and borax mines (19th cent.); now a national monument and tourist attraction. Has highest temperature (134° F.) in US.

death watch beetle, *Xestobium rufovillosum,* beetle which attacks old seasoned wood. Notorious for knocking sound made by pupae.

death's head hawk moth, *Acherontia atropos,* moth with skull-like mark on thorax. Found esp. in Europe and Africa. Larvae feed on potato leaves.

De Bakey, Michael Ellis (1908–   ), Amer. surgeon. Noted for work in cardiac surgery, esp. in late 1960s.

Debrecen, city in E Hungary. Commercial centre. Formerly a stronghold of Hungarian Protestantism. Pop. (1963) 126,000.

Debs, Eugene V[ictor] (1855– 1926), Amer. socialist leader. Pacifist and advocate of industrial unionism; imprisoned (1895) for violating injunction in strike at Pullman, Ill. Pres. candidate 5 times.

Debussy, Claude (1862– 1918), Fr. composer. Works include piano music *e.g. Clair de Lune*; orchestral pieces such as *L'Après-Midi d'un Faune, Nocturnes* and *La Mer*; and opera *Pelléas et Mélisande.* Considered leading Fr. impressionist musician.

Debye, Peter Joseph Wilhelm (1884– 1966), Amer. physicist, b.

Netherlands. Awarded Nobel Prize for Physics (1936) for work on molecular structure.

decathlon, 10 event athletic contest, comprising 100, 400, 1500 metre runs, 110 metre high hurdles, javelin and discus throws, shot put, pole vault, high jump and long jump. Introduced to Olympic Games 1920.

Decca, system of application of radio to marine and air navigation. Maximum range 240 mi. from master station. Each chain has 1 master and 3 slave stations *c.* 120 mi. apart and each about 60 mi. from the master station. Used primarily for direction finding, synchronization and meteorological purposes.

Deccan, triangular region of S India. Chief cities, Bangalore, Mysore, Hyderabad. Includes Carnatic region, scene of 18th cent. British– French struggle for Indian supremacy.

Decembrists, members of military revolt at St Petersburg, Russia, on accession of Nicholas I in Dec. 1825. Conspiracy formed to replace Nicholas with his brother Constantine and obtain constitution. Its failure ended with hanging of some of its leaders.

decimal, in arithmetic, a fraction having 10 or some power of 10 as a denominator. Represented by a point, thus ·4 means 4/10ths and 62·5 means $62\frac{1}{2}$. To divide or multiply by 10 or multiples of 10, point is moved one way or another, thus 33·412 divided by 1000 is ·033412. Coinage in most countries follows decimal system, adopted by Australia (1966), adopted in UK (1971).

decorations, civil and military reward for service; orig. medieval practice of conferring knighthood. Brit. orders of knighthood: Garter, Thistle, Bath. Other orders include Red and Black Eagle (Prussia), Legion of Honour (France); military orders include Iron Cross (Germany), Croix de Guerre (France), Victoria Cross (UK), Purple Heart (US), Red Star (USSR).

De Coster, Charles, Théodore Henri (1827– 79), Belgian author. Chief work *La Legende d'Ulenspiegel*

(1868) based on Germanic folk hero Till Eulenspiegel.

Dedekind, Julius Wilhelm Richard (1831–1916), Ger. mathematician. Known for work on algebraic functions; originated a theory of irrational numbers.

Dee, John (1527–1608), Eng. mathematician and astrologer. Most notable work *Monas Hieroglyphica* (1564). Reputation mainly as a magician. Advocated adoption of Gregorian calendar.

deer, *Cervidae,* large family of mammals of RUMINANT sub-order incl. deer, elks, reindeer, wapitis. Antlers, confined to males except for reindeer and caribou, usually branched and shed annually. Fawns are usually spotted. Heights vary from 13 in., in the Pudu, to over 6 ft., European elk and N American moose.

defence mechanism, unconscious behaviour pattern designed to avert anticipated or imagined criticism or condemnation. Forms include adoption of socially accepted motives, repression of distress, regression to infantile behaviour.

deflation *see* INFLATION.

Defoe, Daniel (1660–1731), Eng. writer. Author of *Robinson Crusoe* (1719), story of a castaway on desert island, *Moll Flanders* (1722), *Roxana* (1724). Influential pamphleteer and journalist.

Degas, Hilaire Germain Edgar (1834–1917), Fr. Impressionist painter. Ballet dancers, modistes, women washing, were among his themes.

De Gaulle, Charles André Joseph Marie (1890–1970), Pres. of France (1958–69). Opposed armistice with Germany (1940) and founded Free French movement in UK during World War 2. Elected interim pres. (1945); resigned (1946). Recalled (1958); made premier then pres. (1958); re-elected (1965). Instrumental in withdrawal of France from Algeria; opposed NORTH ATLANTIC TREATY ORGANIZATION and vetoed Brit. attempts to enter EUROPEAN ECONOMIC COMMUNITY. Policies have been marked by fervent patriotism and a desire for European military and economic self-sufficiency. Resigned after referendum defeat, 1969.

Dekanawideh, Deganawida [The Heavenly Messenger] (*c.* 16th cent.), N Amer. Indian culture hero. Reputed founder of Iroquois Five Nations confederacy in E Canada and US.

Dekker, Thomas (*c.* 1572–1632), Eng. dramatist. Best known for the *Shoemaker's Holiday* (1600). Other works include collaborations.

Delacroix, Ferdinand Victor Eugène

L'hippodrome by Edgar Degas

(1798–1863), Fr. Romantic painter, mainly of historical subjects. Among best known works are *Justice of Trajan, Abduction of Rebecca, Christ on Lake Gennesaret, Christ on the Cross.*

De la Mare, Walter (1873–1956), Eng. poet and novelist. Work characterized by imaginative settings. Poetry includes children's *Peacock Pie* (1912). Best known novel *Memoirs of a Midget* (1921).

Delaware, Atlantic state, US. Area: 2,057 sq. mi.; cap. Dover; main city Wilmington. Industry dominated by DuPont Co. First settled by Dutch (1630s); seized by British (1664). First to ratify US Constitution. Pop. (1964) 446,292.

Delaware, E US river, rising in SE New York, flows into Delaware Bay. Strategically important in Amer. Revolution; known for Gen. Washington's crossing (1776).

Delaware, group of N Amer. Indian tribes of Algonkian linguistic stock. Migrated to the Atlantic from NW. Treaty with William Penn (1682), but Iroquois attacks drove them into Ohio; later settled in Oklahoma reservations. Survivors of Gradenhutten massacre (1782) in Pennsylvania fled to Ontario, where their descendants now live.

Death Watch Beetle

Deledda, Grazia (1875–1936), Ital. novelist, b. Sardinia. Author of *Cenere* (1904; Eng. tr., *Ashes,* 1908). Awarded Nobel Prize for Literature (1926).

De Leon, Daniel (1852–1914), Amer. socialist leader; doctrinaire Marxist who favoured industrial rather than trade unions. Helped found INDUSTRIAL WORKERS OF THE WORLD.

Delft, city in Holland, famous for manufacture of pottery of same name. Industry flourished 1650–1750.

Delhi, city in NW India, Cap. of Delhi state, on the Jumna. Became Mogul cap. (1638) of Shah Jehan. Cap. of India from 1912; replaced (1931) by **New Delhi.** Pop. (1963) 2,228,000. *See* ill. p. 182.

Delian League, union of Gk. states founded at DELOS (478 BC) under Athenian leadership, later developing into Athenian empire. Disbanded at end of PELOPONNESIAN WAR (404 BC). Second confederation founded 378 BC; lasted until defeat by PHILIP OF MACEDON (338 BC).

Delibes, [Clement Philibert] Leo (1836–91), Fr. composer and organist. Famous for ballets *Coppélia* (1870), *Sylvia* (1876) and operas.

Delilah, in OT, Philistine woman loved by SAMSON, whom she betrayed by cutting his hair, which destroyed his physical strength.

Delius, Frederick (1862–1934), Eng. composer. Works, both romantic and impressionist, include operas, choral work, orchestral pieces and some church music.

Deller, Alfred George (1912–   ), Eng. counter-tenor. Contributed to revival of 15th and 16th cent. music.

Delos, Gk. island in Aegean Sea, traditional birthplace of APOLLO and ARTEMIS. Area: 2 sq. mi. Contains ruins of temple to Apollo. Used as port for Confederacy of Delos (478 BC), a Mediterranean defence system against the Persians. Restricted (426 BC) to worship of Apollo.

Temple of Apollo at Delphi

Delphi, ancient Gk. town on Mt. Parnassus, site of oracle dedicated to APOLLO. Chief priestess, called PYTHIA, advised states and individuals, often enigmatically. Became Gk. treasure house until looted and abolished (AD 390) by Romans. Modern name Kastri. Some ruined temples remain and festivals are held.

delta, roughly triangular alluvial plain usually very fertile, formed at a river mouth where sediment is deposited. Name comes from Gk. letter, *delta* (Λ), similar in shape to triangular Nile delta.

dementia praecox *see* SCHIZOPHRENIA.

Demeter, in Gk. myth., earth goddess of corn, harvest and fruitfulness.

Daughter of Cronus and Rhea, mother by Zeus of PERSEPHONE. She and her daughter were leading figures in Eleusinian mysteries, representing seasonal cycle. Her Roman counterpart was Ceres.

De Mille, Cecil B[lount] (1881–1959), Amer. film director, founder of Paramount film company. Directed *Cleopatra, The Greatest Show on Earth, The Ten Commandments, etc.*

democracy (Gk: power of the people), govt. by people as a whole, rather than by a class, group or individual. Democracy in Gk. city states denied to slaves status of citizenship. Roman Repub. initiated popular representation. Modern democracy arose out of demands for polit. and legal equality and, later, economic and social equality; advanced by Puritan, Amer. and Fr. revolutions. Principal theorists, Locke and Rousseau. Modern democratic states based politically on competing party system.

Democratic Party, one of 2 major US polit. parties. Arose as Democratic Republican party under Thomas Jefferson in opposition to Alexander Hamilton's Federalists. Under Andrew Jackson, party name changed to Democratic (1828). Splits, created by slavery issue and Civil War, decimated party. Revived after RECONSTRUCTION era (1876) with emergence of united Southern faction. Radical ascendency (1896) brought wider base of support, appealing to farmer and big-city industrial classes, and, in 20th cent. to Negro and ethnic minorities. Became identified with reform, particularly after F. D. Roosevelt's NEW DEAL (1932).

demography, study of statistics relating to birth, marriage and death in given area, to determine rates of reproduction, death and fertility.

Demoivre, Abraham (1667–1754), Eng. mathematician. Pioneered development of analytic trigonometry and theory of probability.

demonology *see* SATANISM.

Demosthenes (383–322 BC), Athenian orator and statesman. Opposed aggression of PHILIP OF MACEDON, delivering *Philippics* (351, 349, 341 BC), *Olynthiacs* (349 BC) and *On the Chersonese* (341 BC). War finally declared with Philip, Athenians defeated at Chaeronea (338 BC). Also speeches in trials and on public policy, *e.g. On the Crown* (330 BC).

Dempsey, William Harrison ('Jack') (1895–   ), Amer. boxer. World Heavyweight Champion (1919); defended title successfully 5 times. Defeated by Gene Tunney (1926).

Demy, Jacques (1931–   ), Fr. film director of *La Baie des Anges* (1963), *Les Parapluies de Cherbourg* (1964).

Denbighshire, county of N Wales. Area: 666 sq. mi.; county town, Denbigh; admin. centre, Ruthin. Land hilly in S; sheep farming important. Coal, iron, lead, slate and gravels extracted. Agriculture and tourism in N. Pop. (1965) 178,480.

dengue, breakbone fever, acute, infectious disease characterized by fever and muscle pains. Caused by virus transmitted by mosquitoes, esp. in trop. regions.

denim, strong coarse twill-weave cotton fabric, 1st made in Nîmes, France. Name from *Serge de Nîmes*.

The Observatory of Delhi built in 1710 for Raja Jai Singh

17th cent. Frederiksborg castle on the Danish island of Zeeland

Cliffs on the east coast island of Mon, Denmark

Picturesque Danish farm buildings

Denmark [Kongeriget Danmark], kingdom of NW Europe, comprising Jutland Peninsula and Danish Archipelago. Area: 16,619 sq. mi.; cap. Copenhagen; main towns, Aarhus,

Odense. Greenland, Bornholm and The Faeroes are Danish. Largely lowland country. Settled by Germanic tribes, formed kingdom 9th cent. Occupied by Germany 1940–5. Agric. economy, esp. dairying; also fishing. Food processing most important industry. Parliament, *Rigsdag*, comprises one elected house, *Folketing*. High standard of living due to secure economy. State language is Danish; main religion Lutheran. Unit of currency, kroner. Pop. (1965) 4,768,000.

Dennis, Nigel (1912–   ), Eng. novelist and critic; wrote the satire *Cards of Identity* (1955).

density, property of matter defined as measurement of a quantity of matter in a unit volume of a substance. Calculated by dividing mass by volume occupied at standard temperature and pressure.

Dent, Thomas Clinton (1850–1912), Brit. mountaineer known for 1st ascent of Aiguille du Dru (1878) and for originating Alpine Distress Signal.

dentition, arrangement of teeth in vertebrate mammals, varying with different orders. In homodonts (*i.e.* porpoises) teeth are all similar. In heterodonts, divisible according to position and function, into incisors, canines, premolars, molars.

Denver, cap. of Colorado, US, settled (1858), made cap. (1867). Mining booms of 1870s and 1880s and agric. development contributed to its growth; now manufactures mining machinery, aircraft and meat products. Pop. (1968) 494,000.

deodar, *Cedrus deodara*, species of conifer native to Himalayas. Cultivated as ornamental tree because of graceful branches and soft green foliage.

Depew, Chauncey Mitchell (1834–1928), Amer. lawyer and politician, chairman (1898) of Vanderbilt organization, senator for New York (1899–1911).

depression, in general economic terms, a period of crisis characterized by falling prices, restricted credit, bankruptcies, unemployment. The Great Depression followed the 1929 crash of New York stock market.

depression, in psychiatry, type of emotional reaction. Characteristics include loss of physical, intellectual and emotional vigour. May be fleeting or permanent, mild or severe, acute or chronic.

depression, low, cyclone, region of low atmospheric pressure characteristic of temp. latitudes, formed by warm air meeting and rising over cold polar air on land, passage of depression marked by specific sequence of weather phenomena. In N hemisphere moves E across Atlantic affecting Iceland, Brit. Isles, Norway and Med. region.

De Quincey, Thomas (1785–1859), Eng. essayist. Mostly remembered for *Confessions of an English Opium-Eater* (1822); pioneer student of Ger. philosophical and philological writings.

Derain, André (1880–1954), Fr. painter and stage designer. Identified with many art movements of his day, incl. Fauve and Cubist schools and traditions of Picasso and Matisse. Created designs for Diaghilev's ballets.

Derby, 14th Earl of *see* STANLEY, EDWARD GEORGE GEOFFREY SMITH.

Derby, 16th Earl of *see* STANLEY, FREDERICK ARTHUR.

Derby, Eng. horse race instituted by Earl of Derby (1780) run over course $1\frac{1}{2}$ mi. long at Epsom, Surrey in May or June. A Derby also run at Louisville, Ky.

Hills in the Nubian Desert

Desert Oasis

Camels grazing in the desert

Derbyshire, inland county of C England. Area: 1,000 sq. mi.; county town, Derby. Main towns, Buxton and Matlock have warm mineral springs. Arable farming in flat S; mountainous N incl. Peak District and national park, used for sheep pasture and tourism. Coal, iron, lead, zinc, manganese and fluorspar extracted; industry includes ironworks, paper, cotton and brewing. Pop. (1965) 778,030.

De Rojas, Fernando (*c.* 1475–1538), Sp. writer whose classic *La Celestina (The Spanish Bawd)* influenced many contemporary authors.

derrick, framework or tower erected over a deep hole to support drilling or hoisting equipment. Most common form is 3-legged derrick built over oil wells.

Der Spiegel [The Mirror], controversial W German news magazine.

Descartes, René (1596–1650), Fr. mathematician and philosopher, founder of Cartesianism, based on distinction between spirit and matter, summed up in his dictum in *Discourse on Method* (1637), 'I think, therefore I am'. Also regarded as founder of analytic geometry; he greatly influenced writers of 17th cent.

desert, any barren, uninhabitable region where rainfall is insufficient to support vegetation. May be divided into trop. or hot deserts (*e.g.* Sahara) and mid-latitude deserts (*e.g.* Gobi).

Des Moines, cap. city of Iowa, US, at junction of Des Moines and Raccoon rivers. Estab. as military fort (1843), became cap. (1857); now important industrial centre producing machinery and processed farm products. Pop. (1968) 210,000.

Dessalines, Jean-Jacques (1758–1806), Negro leader of successful Haitian revolt against French. Proclaimed himself emperor (1804) but rule was despotic and harsh; assassinated by followers.

destroyer, ship orig. designed (1890s) to destroy torpedo boats. Primary duties to torpedo enemy ships, screen battle fleets, find and destroy enemy submarines, conduct reconnaissance and patrols and escort merchant ships.

detergent, substance aiding cleansing action of water, *e.g.* soap. Specifically synthetic substance acting as cleanser and helping water to penetrate surface of another substance, *e.g.* reduces surface tension between oil and water, and thus water can remove dirt adhering to oil.

determinism, in philosophy, principle that phenomena are conditioned by preceding data, and in turn determine condition of future situations. In psychology, it denies existence of causeless acts, and in ethics opposes belief in freedom of the will.

Detroit, city of Michigan, US, on Detroit R., linking Lakes Erie and St Clair. Orig. Fr. trading station; now major industrial centre; headquarters of US Ford motor industry. Pop. (1965) 1,670,000.

Deucalion, in Gk. myth., son of Prometheus, and with wife Pyrrha only human beings to survive flood sent by Zeus. Commanded by an oracle to throw the bones of their mother (*i.e.* the earth) behind them; from these, new generation arose.

Deuteronomy, 5th Book of Pentateuch. Name means 'second law'; supplements laws given to Moses on Mt. Sinai.

Deuxième Bureau, Fr. Ministry of Defence intelligence dept.

De Valera, Eamon (1883–), Irish statesman. Imprisoned (1916) for part in Easter rebellion, he was pres. of Sinn Féin party (1917) and head of Dáil Éireann's fund-raising campaign in US (1919–20). Re-entered Dáil (1927) with Fianna Fáil govt., became P.M. (1938). Kept Ireland neutral in World War 2. Pres. of Ireland since 1959.

De Valois, Dame Ninette, orig. Edris Stannus (1898–), Eng. dancer and choreographer. Prima ballerina at Covent Garden (1919); danced for Diaghilev's company (1923–6). Formed (1946) Sadler's Wells Ballet and Sadler's Wells Opera Ballet (now Royal Ballet). Productions include *The Haunted Ballroom, Checkmate, The Rake's Progress.*

devaluation, lowering of the value of a currency in terms of gold, so that its exchange rate falls. One result, imports become more expensive as exports become cheaper; intended to check INFLATION and restore foreign confidence in the currency.

devil's apron, species of kelp of genus *Laminaria* with large thallus resembling apron.

devil's coach horse, *Staphylinus olens,* insect of rove beetle family over 1 in. long.

devil's-paintbrush, orange hawkweed, *Hieracium aurianticum,* C European weed with flame-coloured flowers.

devil's shoelace, bootlace weed, mermaid's fishline, *Chorda filum,* common seaweed of the colder N hemisphere with long cord-like fronds up to 20 ft. long.

Devolution, War of (1667–8), conflict between France and Spain, arising out of Louis XIV's claims to Sp.

Netherlands. War ended with Treaty of Aix-la-Chapelle.

Devonian *see* GEOLOGICAL TABLE.

Devonshire, 8th Duke of *see* CAVENDISH, SPENCER COMPTON.

Devonshire, 9th Duke of *see* CAVENDISH, VICTOR CHRISTIAN WILLIAM.

Devonshire, county of SW England. Area: 2,612 sq. mi.; county town, Exeter; main towns, Plymouth, Dartmouth, Torquay. In N, Exmoor National Park; in SW Dartmoor Upland; rich lowland, famous for dairy cattle and cider apple orchards. Also fishing, tourism, and extraction of china clay, tin, slate, ochre. Pop. (1963) 823,000.

De Vries, Peter (1910–   ), Amer. writer and journalist. Works include *The Tunnel of Love* (1954), *Reuben, Reuben* (1964).

dew, moisture deposited on earth's surface at night, when earth's radiation has cooled lower layers of atmosphere and water vapour has condensed into drops.

Dew Line, D[istant] E[arly] W[arning] System, series of radar stations operated by Canada and US along 70th parallel guarding against surprise transpolar nuclear attack.

dew point, temperature at which moisture begins to form; if below freezing point, dew freezes and ice crystals form hoar frost.

Dewar, Sir James (1842–1923), Scot. chemist and physicist who discovered methods of liquefying hydrogen and other gases.

Dewar flask, container for storing liquefied gases for investigation at low temperatures; invented by SIR JAMES DEWAR. Principle used in domestic vacuum flask.

dewberry, trailing bramble of genus *Rubus,* similar to blackberry, but with earlier and larger fruit.

Dewey, George (1837–1917), US admiral who defeated Sp. fleet at Manila Bay (1898).

Dewey, John (1859–1952), Amer. philosopher and educator; philosophy mainly pragmatist. Progressive approach to education based on 'learning by doing'. Works include *The School and Society* (1899), *Art as Experience* (1934), *Logic* (1938).

Dewey, Thomas Edmund (1902–   ), Amer. Republican politician, Gov. of New York state (1942–55). Unexpectedly lost US Pres. election to Harry Truman (1948).

Dhaulagiri, Himalayan peak (26,795 ft.) of W C Nepal. First climbed in 1960.

dhow, single-masted boat with lateen sail, common in Arabian Sea and on E African coast.

Diabelli, Antonio (1781–1858), Austrian composer and music publisher. Composed waltz theme of Beethoven's *Diabelli Variations.*

diabetes, disease characterized by polyuria, excessive secretion of urine. *D. mellitus,* caused by INSULIN deficiency, leads to excess sugar in blood and urine. Treatment by diet and injections of insulin.

diabolists and diabolism *see* SATANISM.

diadem spider, *Aranea diadema,* garden spider commonly found in Europe. Characterized by crown-shaped markings, hence its name.

Diadochi (Gk: successors), generals and administrators of Alexander the

The Big Hole in the Kimberley diamond mines, South Africa

Great whose attempts to take over his empire on his death (323 BC) led to succession of civil wars. Result (281 BC) was splitting of empire.

Diaghilev, Sergei Pavlovich (1872–1929), Russ. art critic and impresario. Formed Ballets Russes which performed in London, Paris and other cities. His dancers included Balanchine and Massine.

dialect, characteristic manner of speech generally peculiar to given geographic locality. Often, though it may utilize a number of words not used in other areas, it is only a matter of pronunciation.

dialysis, separation of solute from colloidal solution by passage through semi-permeable membrane, *e.g.* cellophane, parchment. Examples of solutes are starch, glue, gelatin.

diamond, hardest mineral, crystalline form of carbon found as pebbles, grains and in conglomerates. Used as abrasive. Because of its lustre, has become most prized gemstone. Most gem (colourless) diamonds come from South Africa and the Congo, but diamond-bearing gravels worked in Ghana, Brazil and India. Largest known diamond is Cullinan from South Africa, now contained in Brit. Crown.

Diana, in early Roman myth. goddess of the moon, identified with Gk. Artemis, goddess of hunting; assisted women in childbirth; worshipped esp. at Ephesus.

diastase, amylase, enzyme which converts starch to sugar. Important for digestion and fermentation; present in saliva (as ptyalin), in pancreatic fluids (as amylopsin) and in some plants.

diatom, microscopic plant of algae group with silicone-containing shell, found in fresh or salt water in Arctic and other cold regions. Diatomaceous earth and diatomite formed from shells of dead diatoms. Diatomite, found in parts of US, used industrially, esp. for insulating against heat and sound.

Diaz, Bartholomew (d. 1500), Portuguese navigator. First European to navigate Cape of Good Hope (1486–8) and open up sea route to India.

Diaz, Porfirio (1830–1915), Mexican statesman. Leader of insurrection (1854) and of Mexican army against

Maximilian. Pres. (1877–1911).

Diaz de Vivar, Rodrigo [El Cid] (1040–99), Sp. hero, subject of earliest epic ballad *Poema de Mio Cid.* Captured Valencia from Moors and ruled there till his death.

Diaz del Castillo, Bernal (1492–1581), Sp. conquistador. Wrote *Historia verdaders de la Conquista de la Nueva España* (1632).

dice, small cubes usually of ivory or bone with 6 sides numbered by dots from 1 to 6 so that opposite faces total 7. Antique origin. Several games of chance, incl. craps, poker dice, back-gammon and board games are played with dice.

Dichter, Ernst (1907–), Amer. psychologist, developed application of social science to advertizing, public service and politics (motivational research). Author of *Successful Living* (1947), *Strategy of Desire* (1960) and *Handbook of Consumer Motivations* (1964).

Dickens, Charles John Huffam (1812–70), Eng. writer, began career as journalist. Satirical approach 1st revealed in *Oliver Twist* (1838). Several works appeared serially, incl. *Nicholas Nickleby* (1838–9). After travels in US, satirized Amer. democracy in *Martin Chuzzlewit* (1843–4). Visited Italy and Switzerland. *David Copperfield* (1849–50) is partly autobiog. 'A Christmas Carol' appeared in *Christmas Stories* (1853). *A Tale of Two Cities* (1859) is hist. novel. *Great Expectations* (1861) combines suspense and poignancy. Dickens' satirical work, inclining to caricature, protested against injustice and combined sentimentality with melodrama.

Dickinson, Emily Elizabeth (1830–86), Amer. poet whose short, often cryptic, lyrics were not published until

Dill

1890s and 1950s. Lived in almost complete seclusion.

dicotyledon, dicotyledonae, large class of angiosperms with 2 seed-leaves in embryo plant. Class includes many forest and fruit trees, food plants, *e.g.* potato, bean, and ornamentals, *e.g.* rose, clematis.

Diderot, Denis (1713–84), Fr. encyclopedist and philosopher. Anti-clerical materialist, he strove like Voltaire and Rousseau in cause of reason. Life work was editorship of *Encylopédie* (1751–65). Also wrote *Rameau's Nephew* and *Jacques le Fataliste,* satires of contemporary mores.

Dido, in Roman myth., queen and founder of Carthage. Fell in love with Aeneas and when he left her, killed herself by jumping on to a burning pyre.

Didrikson-Zaharias, Mildred [Babe] (1914–56), Amer. athlete and golfer. World record holder in 3 athletic events. Took up golf (1935) and also excelled in this sport.

Diefenbaker, John G[eorge] (1895–), Canadian statesman and P.M. (1957–63). Trained as lawyer, 1st elected to House of Commons (1940), assumed leadership of Cons. Party (1956). Ousted as head of party in leadership convention of 1967.

Diels, Otto Paul Herman (1876–1954), Ger. chemist. Shared Nobel Prize for Chemistry (1950) with Kurt Alder for developing method of synthesizing benzene ring hydrocarbons.

Diesel, Rudolf (1858–1913), Ger. engineer noted for his work on fuel-oil engine that bears his name.

diesel engine, internal combustion engine, invented by Rudolf Diesel. Air drawn into cylinder is heated by compression, heated air ignites liquid fuel sprayed into cylinder. Though heavier than petrol engines, uses cheaper fuel. Patented 1892.

Dietrich, Marlene, orig. Maria Magdalene von Kosch (1904–), Ger.-American actress and singer. Best known film *The Blue Angel* (1930). Has made many stage and cabaret appearances.

differential calculus, mathematical process concerned with problems of change of function with 1 variable, devised by Isaac Newton and Leibrutz; INTEGRAL CALCULUS is inverse of this.

diffraction of light, bright and dark fringe pattern which forms the blurred edge of a shadow. Caused by wave motion of light taking different passages round an obstruction. Pat-

The Foxglove is a member of the Digitalis genus

tern seen more clearly by use of diffraction grating, an opaque surface punctuated with slits of different widths, used in astronomy.

Digby, Sir Kenelm (1603–65), Eng. author, naval commander and diplomatist. Chancellor to Queen Henrietta Maria. Discovered necessity of oxygen in plant life.

digestion, process by which body converts food into soluble form which can pass into circulation and be used by tissues. In man, starch broken down by saliva in mouth, proteins by gastric juices in stomach, and fats by bile in small intestine. Unabsorbed waste passed out through large intestine and rectum.

digital computer, electronic computing machine, receives and processes numerical information in programmed form; modern machines operate by electrical pulses representing numbers in a binary code.

digitalis, genus of Old World plants of Scrophulariaceae family. Foxglove, *D. purpurea,* is common European species. The leaves yield poisonous alkaloid, digitalin, as well as several other poisonous glucosides.

Dijon, cap. of Côte-d'Or department in SE France. Route centre with important trade in wines and agricultural products. Pop. 112,800.

dill, *Anethum graveolens,* European annual or biennial herb of parsley family. Aromatic seeds used for pickling and flavouring.

Dilthey, Wilhelm (1833–1911), Ger. philosopher. Favoured distinction between natural and social sciences whose analytical methods could be used to reach an understanding of structural unity of individual and social life.

DiMaggio, Joseph Paul (1914–   ), Amer. baseball player known as the 'Yankee Clipper'. Major league record (1941) by hitting safely in 56 consecutive games.

diminishing returns, law of, in economics, the prediction that, after a certain point, an increase in one factor of production, other factors being constant, will yield relatively decreasing returns both in production of commodities and in exploration of land. Relevance is particularly marked in, *e.g.* India and China where the balance of numbers and food supply is vital.

D'Indy, Vincent *see* INDY, VINCENT D'.

Dinesen, Isak, orig. Karen, Baroness Blixen (1885–1962), Danish short-story writer. Works published in English include *Seven Gothic Tales* (1934), *Winter's Tales* (1943).

dingo, *Canis dingo,* medium sized wild dog, only wild carnivore of Australia. Hunts its prey (rabbits, sheep, poultry) chiefly at night.

dinoflagellate, minute animal of order *Dinoflagellata* with 2 flagella. Some species have chlorophyll. Species include *Gymnodinium,* both marine and freshwater, causing fish poisoning 'red tide' that occurs on Florida coast, and *Floctiluca* causing phosphorescence at sea. Parasitic dinoflagellates exist.

dinosaurs, extinct order of land reptiles 2–90 ft. long, some herbivorous, some carnivorous. Flourished during Mesozoic Era; died out by end of Cretaceous period. Numerous fossil remains found esp. in NW America.

Diocletian [Gaius Aurelius Valerius Diocletianus] (245–313), Roman emperor (282–305). Divided empire with Maximian and also with Galerius and Constantius Chlorus. His rule tended to absolutism. His capital was Nicodemia.

Diogenes (*c.* 400–*c.* 325 BC), Gk. cynic philosopher, influenced by Antisthenes. Held that happiness is attained by satisfaction of natural needs in cheapest and easiest way. Said to have lived in an earthenware tub in Athens.

Diomedes, in Gk. myth., Thracian king, son of Ares who fed his horses on human flesh. Killed by Heracles (8th Labour).

Diomedes, in classical myth., son of Tydeus and King of Argos; in Trojan War friend of Odysseus with whom he removed Palladium from Troy.

According to Vergil's *Aeneid,* settled in Italy after Trojan War.

Dionysus, also called **Bacchus,** Gk. god of wine, son of Zeus and Semele. His worship originated in Thrace and Asia Minor, accompanied by wild ecstasy esp. in women, worshippers called Maenads or Bacchantes. In Athens, poetry and drama accompanied Dionysian festivals; in countryside he was worshipped as god of vegetation. Roman counterpart is Liber.

Diophantus, (3rd cent. AD), Gk. mathematician, pioneer in solving type of indeterminate algebraic equations. This work is now called Diophantine analysis.

diopside, mineral of PYROXENE group varying in colour from white to dark green. Found as slender crystals in basic rocks.

Dior, Christian (1905–57), Fr. fashion designer, dominant after World War 2. Introduced 'New Look' (1947) and boosted fashion industry with help of industrialist Marcel Boussac.

diphtheria, infectious disease caused by bacteria. Characterized by fever, disorder of respiratory tract and sometimes slight paralysis. Disease can be prevented or modified by immunization.

dipper, water ouzel, only aquatic perching bird, of family Cinclidae, closely related to wrens. Lives near cold mountain streams. Species include European *Cinclus cinclus* and N Amer. *C. mexicanus.*

Dirac, Paul Adrien Maurice (1902–   ), Brit. physicist. Awarded Nobel Prize for Physics (1933) with Erwin Schrodinger, for work in developing Heisenberg's theory of quantum mechanics. Evolved theory of electron (1928) and predicted existence of positron (1931).

Director of Public Prosecution, in England, official under supervision of Attorney-General, who assists in legal aspects of criminal prosecutions of national importance. Does not investigate but can direct local police forces as to line of inquiry. Criminal cases referred to him by Home Office.

Dingo

Directory, Fr. govt. (1795–9), with executive of 5 directors, chosen by 2 legislative chambers. Sièges and Barras helped Bonaparte (later NAPOLEON I) overthrow Directory by coup d'état of 18 Brumaire.

Dirichlet, Peter Lejeune (1805–59), Ger. mathematician whose chief work was in theory of complex numbers, potential and equations of 5th degree.

Dirksen, Everett McKinley (1896–1969), US Republican senator from Illinois (1950–69). Leader of party since 1959.

disarmament, act of disarming or limiting armed forces and use of certain weapons. UN has concerned itself with problem and has permanent commission now consisting of all UN members. In 1963 US, USSR, UK, concluded treaty prohibiting nuclear testing in atmosphere, space, under water.

disarmament, nuclear, effort, esp. among certain nuclear powers (US, USSR, UK) to halt further proliferation of nuclear skills. Discussed at 1955 Geneva conference, talks on test-ban treaty resumed (1958) with support of UN Disarmament Commission. Progress in 1960s hampered by refusal of France and China to endorse discussions.

discount rate *see* BANK RATE.

discrimination, accordance of differential treatment usually on racial or religious grounds. Practice of social discrimination on racial grounds provoked agitation in US (1960s) for extension of civil rights to Negroes in all aspects of Amer. life, and in UK passing of Race Relations Act.

Disney, Walt[er Elias] (1901–66), Amer. cartoon film producer; creator of Mickey Mouse (1928), Donald Duck, Goofy, *etc.* Feature-length cartoons include *Snow White and the Seven Dwarfs, Fantasia, Bambi;* nature films include *The Living Desert* and *The Vanishing Prairie.*

Disraeli, Benjamin, 1st Earl of Beaconsfield (1804–81), Brit. statesman and writer. Twice Tory P.M. (1868, 1874); responsible for Reform Bill (1867) which benefited Cons. Party. Favourite of Queen Victoria, and had her crowned Empress of India (1876).

Dissenter, in UK, one who adheres to a religion other than that of the Established Church. Applied to those who failed to accept Act of Uniformity (1662). Denotes more popularly the Protestant dissenters referred to in Toleration Act (1689). The name Non-conformist is synonymous.

Distajhil, twin peaks, (25,868 ft. and 25,250 ft.) connected by ridge, in

Great Karakoram, N Kashmir, known by natives as Malungi Dias. First climbed (1960) in 34 days.

Di Stefano (1926–   ), Argentinian footballer; European Footballer of the Year (1957, 1959); capped 7 times by Argentina and 31 times by Spain.

distemper, in veterinary medicine, several infectious diseases, esp. canine distemper, a contagious, catarrhal disease of young dogs.

distillation, vapourization of a liquid followed by condensation back into the liquid form, intended either to separate liquid mixtures into their base components or to purify a liquid contaminated with non-volatile impurities.

district attorney, in US, law officer, responsible for conduct of prosecutions. Federal attorneys appointed by pres. to deputise for attorney-general, one being assigned to each Federal judicial district. At state level, usually elective county officer.

District of Columbia, seat of US govt. containing federal cap., Washington. Area: 70 sq. mi. Ceded to US (1790) by Maryland; Congress 1st met 1800. Pop. (1961) 764,000.

diver, loon, large web-footed bird with sharp, pointed bill of family Gaviidae. Restricted to N hemisphere; frequents fresh water in summer and salt water in winter.

divination, foretelling the future by non-rational, non-scientific methods such as omens, oracles, signs and portents. Originated among Chaldeans, spread to Greece and Rome and is still extant in crystal-gazing, palmistry and astrology.

Divine, Father, orig. George Baker (1882–1965), Amer. Negro leader who estab. religious community in Harlem, New York.

Divine Right, idea that kingship is of divine sanction and cannot be lawfully set aside or challenged. The concept was held in England until 17th cent., when authority of Parl. became supreme.

divining rod, forked branch or Y-shaped metallic rod used by people apparently possessing the power to discover water or minerals beneath earth's surface.

divorce, decree of dissolution of marriage granted by court on proof of matrimonial offence. In UK divorce law is derived mainly from eccles law. Main grounds in US and UK are adultery, desertion and cruelty.

Dix, Dorothea Lynde (1802–87), Amer. humanitarian. Superintendent of Women Nurses during Civil War, she devoted herself to prison reform and improvements in care of insane.

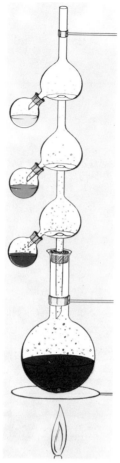

Fractional distillation: the steam from the substance with the highest boiling point condenses last (a), that with the lowest boiling point, first (b). As a result substances can be separated according to the point on the distillation column at which they condense

dixiecrat [Dixie Democrat], in Amer. political history, any of S Democrats who left Democrat party for its support of Civil Rights legislation (1948).

Djakarta, formerly **Batavia,** city of NW Java and cap. of Indonesia. Founded by Dutch (1619); occupied by British (1811–16). Industries include iron foundries, printing and chem. plants. Contains University of Indonesia. Pop. 2,900,000.

Djibouti, Jibuti, port and cap. of Fr. Somaliland in E Africa on Gulf of Aden. Exports Ethiopian products. Pop. 17,000.

Djilas, Milovan (1911–   ), Yugoslav writer and statesman (1945–54). Vice-president to Marshal Tito, ousted and later jailed (1956–61) for over-democratic views and support of Hungarian uprising. His *New Class* (1957) is a critique of Communist bureaucracy.

DNA, abbreviation for dioxyribonucleic acid. *See* NUCLEIC ACID.

Dnieper, river of Ukraine, USSR. Rises in Valdai Hills 150 mi. W of Moscow and after 1100 mi. enters Black Sea.

Dniepropetrovsk, formerly Ekaterinoslav, Russ. river port on Dnieper in Ukraine. Manufactures metal products. Pop. 790,000.

Dniester, river of SE Europe. Rises on N slope of Carpathian Mts. in Poland, runs 150 mi. into Black Sea SW of Odessa.

Dobbs, Mattiwilda (1925–   ), Amer. soprano. First Negro to be internationally acclaimed in opera.

doberman, doberman pinscher, short-haired, smooth-coated, large dog, developed by Ger. breeder Ludwig Dobermann.

Döblin, Alfred (1878–1957), Ger. novelist and physician, best known for expressionistic *Berlin Alexanderplatz* (1929) which shows influence of James Joyce.

dobson fly, aquatic, nocturnal insect, family Corydalidae of order Megaloptera. Species include New Zealand *Archichauliodes dubitatus* and larger N Amer. dobson fly or hellgrammite, *Corydalus cormitus.*

Dobzhansky, Theodosius (1900–   ),

Portrait of *Doge Leonardo Loredano* (c. 1501), by Giovanni Bellini

Amer. geneticist known for study of genetics and evolution. Among his works are *Genetics and the Origin of Species* (1937), *Evolution, Genetics and Man* (1955) and *Mankind Evolving* (1962).

dock, several perennial weeds of genus *Rumex* of Polygonaceae family. Long lance-shaped leaves are popular antidotes to nettle stings.

dodder, several species of *Cuscuta,* a parasitic genus of Convolvulaceae, native to trop. and temp. regions.

Dodge, Joseph Morrell (1890–1964), Amer. banker and statesman prominent as financial adviser on economic policy to US govt.

Dodge, Mary Elizabeth Mapes (1831–1905), Amer. author of children's stories incl. *Hans Brinker* (1865). Edited *St Nicholas* (1873–1905).

dodo, *Rhaphus cucullatus,* large flightless bird of pigeon order. Native to Mauritius, it became extinct in 17th cent.

dog, domestic carnivorous mammal of genus *Canis. C. lupus* (WOLF) and *C. aureus* (JACKAL) are its nearest relatives. Dog thought domesticated since Mesolithic period (*c.* 8,000 BC). Now classed as sporting, non-sporting and toy; breeding has produced specialized varieties.

doge, chief magistrate in extinct repubs. of Venice and Genoa. In 14th cent. held office for life; later reforms made office elective for 2 yr. periods.

dogfish, small shark of several families found mainly in temp. but also in trop. waters. Spiny dogfish, *Squalus acanthias,* of family Squalidae, most common. Lesser spotted dogfish, *Schyliorhinus canicula,* is found in European and Med. waters.

Dogger Bank, sandbank 6–20 fathoms deep in North Sea between Britain and Denmark, famous as fishing ground. Site of naval engagement (1915) between Britain and Germany.

dog's mercury, *Mercurialis perennis,* creeping perennial herb of spurge family, native to Europe and SW Asia. Though poisonous, formerly used in medicine.

dog's-tooth violet, *Erythronium dens canis,* species of lily growing in mild climate. Bulb has toothed appearance.

dogwood, *Cornus sanguinea,* European berry-bearing deciduous shrub with white flowers.

Dohnanyi, Ernö von (1877–1960), Hungarian composer and pianist. Compositions include symphonies, operas and *Variations on a Nursery Song* (1913) for piano and orchestra.

Doisy, Edward Adelbert (1893–), Amer. biochemist. Awarded

Nobel Prize for Physiology and Medicine (1943) with Henrik Dam for work on vitamins.

Dolci, Danilo (1925–), Ital. social worker known as 'Gandhi of Sicily'. Awarded Lenin Peace Prize (1956). Works include *To Feed the Hungry* (Eng. tr. 1959), *Waste* (1963).

doldrums, equatorial low pressure region circling between major trade winds. Area is subject to heavy rains, constant high humidity and lack of winds.

dolerite, igneous rock of basic composition, normally occurring in widespread dykes and sills. Often used for roadstone. Known as diabase in US and Europe.

Dolin, Anton, orig. Patrick Healey-Kay (1904–), Eng. dancer and choreographer who helped found US Ballet Theatre, for which he created *Bluebeard.* Now artistic director of London's Festival Ballet.

Dollard des Ormeaux, Adam, also **Daulac** (1635–60), Fr. adventurer in Canada. Heavily outnumbered, he and small band withstood Iroquois at Long Sault (1660), but eventually were all killed. Ensuing legend was later questioned.

Dollfuss, Engelbert (1892–1934), Austrian statesman, assumed dictatorial powers (1933) to check Social Democrat party backed by Nazis. Reliance on Western support and Italian friendship proved disastrous; assassinated by Austrian Nazis.

dolmen, prehistoric burial chamber, usually consisting of 2 or more upright standing stones, topped by capstone.

Dolmetsch, Carl (1911–), Eng. player of recorder, violin and viola.

dolomite, rock, honey coloured magnesian LIMESTONE, composed of dolomite (mineral), sometimes with calcite.

dolomite, colourless to grey carbonate, usually crystalline, mineral. Pearly crystals often have curved faces.

Dolomites, mountain range in S Tyrol, subdivision of Alps. Among famous skiing resorts is Cortina d' Ampezzo.

dolphin, family of cetaceans, Delphinidae, with communication form akin to human vocalization. Species include common dolphin *Delphinus delphis,* of Atlantic, Indian and N Pacific oceans.

Domagk, Gerhard (1895–1964), Ger. biochemist. Awarded Nobel Prize for Physiology and Medicine (1939) for work on prontosil and sulphanilamides in anti-bacterial treatment. Obliged by Nazi decree to decline award.

Bicycle taxis in Djakarta

General Sudirman Avenue, Djakarta

Domesday Book (1085–6), record of county by county survey of English property values, owners and general population, ordered by William the Conqueror. A basic source in medieval history.

Dominica, one of Windward Is. in Caribbean. Area: 300 sq. mi.; chief town, Roseau. Semi-autonomous (1966). Largely Negro inhabitants, speaking Fr. patois. Pop. (1964) 65,000.

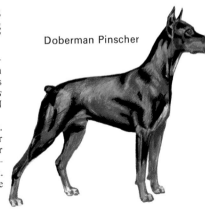

Doberman Pinscher

Dominican, order of preaching friars formed at Toulouse (1215), called Black Friars because of black mantle and scapular worn over white habit. Thomas Aquinas notable Dominican theologian.

Dominican Republic [República Dominicana] on E of Hispaniola Is. in W. Indies. Area: 19,300 sq. mi.; cap. Santo Domingo; other cities, Santiago de los Caballeros and Puerto Plata.

Agriculture main occupation, some gold, copper and iron mined. Independence from Spanish (1821). Pop. (1960) 3,014,000.

Donatello, orig. Donato di Niccolò di Betto Bardi (1388–1466), Ital. sculptor and painter, noted for keen sense of proportion and close adherence to nature. Famous equestrian statue by him in Padua and 'David' in Florence.

Donegal, county of NW Ireland. Area: 1,838 sq. mi. (incl. 39 sq. mi. water); county town, Lifford; other towns, Donegal, Ballyshannon. Offshore islands include Aran. Mountainous, occupations are agriculture, growing flax, potatoes and sheep raising; fishing; quarrying. Pop. (1963) 113,842.

Donen, Stanley (1924–   ), Amer. film director of *Singin' in the Rain* (1952), *Seven Brides for Seven Brothers* (1954), *Charade* (1963).

Dönitz, Karl (1891–   ), Ger. admiral. Chief of state on Hitler's demise (1945), authorized Ger. military capitulation. Sentenced to imprisonment at Nuremberg, released from Spandau (1956).

Donizetti, Gaetano (1797–1848), Ital. composer of over 60 operas, incl. *Lucia di Lammermoor* and *Don Pasquale.*

donkey *see* ASS.

Donne, John (1571–1631), Eng. poet and divine. Born a Catholic, took Anglican orders and became Dean of St Paul's Cathedral, London. Leading exponent of metaphysical school of poetry. Best known poems include Holy Sonnets, *The Ecstasie,* sonnet on death, and *Epithalamium.*

doodlebug, larvae of ANTLION.

Doolittle, Hilda ['HD'] (1886–1961), Amer. poet, translator, novelist. Work identified with Imagism, distinguished by clear and precise visualization of scenes, images, objects. Married Eng. imagist Richard Aldington (1892–1962).

Dorcas gazelle, *Gazella dorcas,* one of the smallest of gazelles. Stands less than 2 ft. at shoulder and has horns up to $13\frac{1}{2}$ in. long.

Dordogne, department of SW France. Area: 3,561 sq. mi.; cap. Périgueux. Contains extensive vineyards and iron, coal and manganese deposits. Grottoes with prehistoric wall-paintings discovered at LASCAUX (1940).

Doré, Paul Gustave (1833–83), Fr. artist of religious and historical works; illustrated standard editions of the Bible, *Paradise Lost, The Inferno, Don Quixote,* also works of Rabelais and Balzac.

Doria, ancient region of Greece. Dorian peoples invaded Greece (c. 1100–1000 BC), settled latterly in Peloponnesian islands. Responsible for Doric architecture.

dormitory town, town which provides for accommodation and recreational needs of population but not employment; this usually obtained in some nearby centre of industry.

dormouse, mammal of European family Muscardinidae. Hibernation lasts half the year. Species include fat dormouse, *Glis glis,* garden dormouse, *Eliomys quercincus,* common dormouse, *Muscardinus ardanarius,* only species native to Britain, and blind dormouse, *Typhlomys cinereus,* of Indo-China.

Dorset, county of S England. Chalk down and heathland and fertile valleys. Area: 821 sq. mi.; county town, Dorchester; main towns, Poole, Weymouth. Agriculture important, esp. dairying. Known for Portland and Purbeck building stone; Maumbury Rings and Maiden Castle prehistoric sites. Tourism important in coastal resorts. Pop. (1964) 319,800.

Dortmund, W Ger. industrial city in Ruhr valley, 36 mi. NE of Dusseldorf. Rly. and canal centre. Iron and steel and brewing are main industries. Pop. (1962) 640,000.

dory, marine fish of family Zeidae, esp. the John dory, *Zeus faber,* weighing up to 20 lb.; common in Mediterranean.

Dos Passos, John (1896–1970), Amer. novelist, essayist. Most famous book is trilogy *USA* (1938); it combines narrative proper with 'Newsreel', 'Biography', and 'Camera Eye'. Other famous books were *Three Soldiers* (1921) and *Manhattan Transfer* (1925).

Dostoyevsky, Feodor Mikhailovich (1821–81), Russ. novelist; works characterized by realistic narrative style and psychological insight. Most famous works are *House of the Dead* (1862), *Crime and Punishment* (1866), *The Idiot* (1868) and *The Brothers Karamazov* (1880).

dotterel, *Eudromias morinellus,* small migratory plover of black, brown and white colouring.

Douala, Duala, chief port of Cameroon Republic, W Africa. Exports palm products. Pop. 50,000.

double bass, 4-stringed instrument, survivor of VIOL family. Played with bow in orchestra and plucked for jazz to supply bass line.

Doughty, Charles Montagu (1843–1926), Eng. writer and traveller in the Middle East; author of *Travels in Arabia Deserta* (1888).

Douglas, powerful Scot. lowland clan in 13th and 14th cent. **Sir James Douglas** (c. 1286–1330) was associate of Robert the Bruce, killed in Spain fighting Moors; **Archibald Douglas** 'Bell the Cat' was opponent of James III. Last Earl of Douglas d. 1488.

Douglas, Norman (1868–1952) Brit. novelist and essayist. Earned fame with *South Wind* (1917) a witty, philosophic idealization of Capri.

Douglas, Stephen Arnold (1813–61) Amer. politician. Democratic Senator from Illinois (1847–61), championed popular sovereignty, as in KANSAS-NEBRASKA BILL. Lincoln-Douglas debates featured 1858 campaign for re-election, during which he asserted territorial rights to exclude slavery. Unsuccessful Democratic pres. nominee (1860) after Southern faction broke away.

Douglas, Thomas, 5th Earl of Selkirk (1771–1820), Scot. philanthropist. Estab. Red River Settlement, W Canada (1812) on land owned by Hudson's Bay Company.

Doric Temple at Segesta, Sicily

Dorcas Gazelle

Douglas, William O[rville] (1898–), Associate Justice of US Supreme Court (1939–). Supported New Deal and was Chairman of Security and Exchange Commission (1937–9).

Douglas fir, *Pseudotsuga taxifolia,* evergreen tree of W N America and Mexico. Timber exported in large quantities as lumber and plywood. State tree of Oregon.

Douglas-Home, Sir Alexander Frederick (1903–), Brit. statesman. Foreign Secretary (1960–3, 1970–), P.M. (1963–4), opposition leader (1964–5). Disclaimed Earldom of Home to become P.M.

douroncouli, *Aotus trivirgatus,* monkey of C and S America. Omnivorous and nocturnal, blinded by daylight.

dove, several small birds of family Columbidae. Collared dove, *Streptopelia decaocto,* found mainly in S central Europe and British Is. Also see PIGEON.

dovekie, little auk, *Plautus alle,* auk of Arctic waters; sometimes breeds in Europe. Incubation of single egg shared by both parent birds.

Dover, cap. of Delaware, US, settled (1683). Situated on St Jones River; shipping and canning centre. Pop. (1968) 7,300.

dowitcher, snipe-like bird of sandpiper family. Species include short-billed dowitcher, *Limnodromus griseus,* of N America and long-billed dowitcher, *L. scotopaceus.*

Dowland, Robert (1586–1641), Eng. court lutanist, published collections of lute music.

Down, county of Northern Ireland, with Mourne Mts. in S, undulating fertile lowland to N. Area: 952 sq. mi.; county town, Downpatrick; other towns, Lisburn, Newry. Main industries, agriculture and linen; fishing and tourism. Pop. (1965) 267,013.

Downing Street, London street off WHITEHALL, in which are located official residences of UK premier and chanc. of exchequer, numbers 10 and 11. All premiers since Walpole (1745) have lived there.

Downs, North and **South,** 2 ranges of chalk hills in SE England separated by the Weald.

Doyle, Sir Arthur Conan (1859–1930), Brit. author and physician, creator of Sherlock Holmes in *The Sign of the Four* (1890), *The Hound of the Baskervilles* (1902), *The Case-book of Sherlock Holmes* (1927); also historical romances, novels and works on spiritualism.

Dracula, VAMPIRE monster created by Bram Stoker in the book *Dracula* (1897); subject of many horror films.

dragon, fabulous monster of Christian, Chinese, Japanese and other folklore. In most cases it was a huge, winged reptilian fire-breathing quadruped, evolved from vague ideas of prehistoric saurians.

dragonfly, carnivorous insect of order Odonata with two pairs of membranous glassy wings, large eyes and long thin body. Species include demoiselle dragonfly, *Agrian virgo;* Austral. *Petalura ingentissima* has wing-span of $6\frac{1}{2}$ in.

dragoon, cavalry soldier trained to fight on foot. Term orig. applied to Fr. horsemen who carried a short musket, called a dragoon.

Douglas Fir: (a) twig with cone (b) male flower (c) female flower (d) seeds

Collared Dove

Drake, Sir Francis (1540–96), Eng. sailor and navigator. Sailed round the world (1577–80) in the *Golden Hind,* 1st Englishman to do so. Achieved fame for raids on Sp. fleet in W Indies and C America (1570–2). Destroyed Sp. fleet at Cádiz (1587) and helped to defeat ARMADA (1588).

Drakensberg, mountain range of South Africa, 700 mi. long, along Natal-Basutoland border reaching over 11,000 ft.

drama, developed literary form in which material is presented in combination of speech and action. Western drama originated in Gk. religious festivals (Dionysia); led to form of classical TRAGEDY of character and situation. Popular COMEDY developed alongside using stock characters. In Middle Ages the Church adopted dramatic representations (MIRACLE PLAYS) for teaching. RENAISSANCE revived classical theories while at popular level in Italy COMMEDIA DELL'ARTE flourished. Fusion of classical and popular traditions gave England ELIZABETHAN and JACOBEAN drama. Classical models were more rigidly observed in France. RESTORATION DRAMA was largely artificial and gave way to Sentimental and then ROMANTIC drama. REALISM introduced in 19th cent. developed alongside poetic drama (Irish dramatic movement). This cent. has seen psychological interest deepening and finding expression in theatre of the absurd, theatre of cruelty, *etc.* Oriental drama has maintained a strong conventional tradition as in Japanese No and Kabuki plays.

Drambuie see WHISKY.

draughts [UK], **checkers** [US], game of skill for 2 persons using 24 round pieces on chequered board with 64 alternate light and dark squares. Aim of game is to take all opponent's pieces or to prevent him from moving.

Dravidian, family of languages, spoken chiefly in S India and Ceylon, incl. Telugu (37 million, India), Tamil (32 million, Ceylon and S India), Kannada (33 million, S India) and Malayalam (c. 20 million, S India).

Drayton, Michael (1563–1631), Eng. poet best known for pastorals and sonnets featuring 'Idea', the object of his adoration. Also wrote hist. poems.

dreams, mental activities pursued in sleep, generally made up of visual images; not usually influenced by sensory impression. Considered important in ancient times and among primitive peoples; until Freud, largely neglected by psychological sciences. Other famous interpreters were Adler and Jung.

Dred Scott Case, brought before US Supreme Court (1856–7). Decision, rejecting a Negro slave's plea for freedom because he had lived in free territory, decreed that Negro 'whose ancestors were sold as slaves' was not entitled to rights of Federal citizen. It declared MISSOURI COMPROMISE unconstitutional and further aggravated North-South dispute.

dredging, underwater excavation to clear or deepen rivers, channels, *etc.* Carried out *e.g.* by series of buckets on belt or suction pipe operating from centrifugal pump.

Dreiser, Theodore (1871–1945), Amer. novelist, a principal exponent of Naturalism. Works include *Sister Carrie* (1900, 1912), *An American Tragedy* (1925); also autobiog. works *Hey-Rub-a-Dub-Dub: A Book of the Mystery and Terror and Wonder of Life* (1919).

Dresden, city of East Germany, cap. of former state of Saxony on Elbe. Dresden china made at Meissen. Most of city destroyed in World War 2, many art treasures removed to Russia. Industries include textiles, machinery and metallurgy. Pop. 468,000.

Dreyfus Affair (1894–1906), scandal arising out of trial of Capt. Alfred Dreyfus (1859–1935) for treason. A Jew accused of selling military secrets to a foreign power, his case divided France into groups of royalists, militarists, Catholics and republicans, socialists, anti-clerics. Efforts (Emile Zola wrote 'J'accuse') to clear Dreyfus were long thwarted before he was freed. Affair discredited monarchists and clericalists and hastened separation of Fr. church and state.

Driesch, Hans (1867–1941), Ger. biologist and philosopher. Viewed basis of life as non-mechanistic vital agency, which he called 'entelechy'

(after Aristotle). Author of *Geschichte des Vitalismus* (1905), *Parapsychologie* (1932).

drill *see* MANDRILL.

Drogheda, urban district and seaport in S Ireland, on the Boyne. Captured in famous battle by Cromwell (1649). Pop. 16,800.

drone fly, *Eristalis tenax,* large flower-haunting hover fly resembling drone honeybee. Larvae are maggot type.

drongo, insectivorous bird of family Dicruridae of Africa, Asia and Australia, with long tail, black irridescent plumage and hook tipped bill. Species include king crow, *Dicrurus macrocercus,* of India.

Church of the Holy Cross, Dresden

dropwort, *Filipendula vulgaris,* perennial European and Asian herb of rose family; fern-like leaves and white flowers. Water-dropwort is common name for poisonous species.

drosophila *see* FRUIT FLY.

Droste-Hülshoff, Annette von (1797–1848), Ger. poetess. Author of religious and nature poems and short novel *Die Judenbuche* (1842).

Drude, Paul Karl Ludwig (1863–1906), Ger. physicist. Studied relationship between optical and electrical phenomena, and electromagnetism.

drug addiction *see* ADDICTION.

drugs, substances used internally or externally to promote changes in physical or mental state, usually taken for prevention or alleviation of disease. Antibiotic drugs, incl. penicil-

lin and streptomycin, used in treating infections. Continued use of certain drugs such as opiates, cocaine, and morphine, can lead to physical addiction, an overpowering craving which if not met results in physical illness.

Druids, ancient religious body of priests and teachers in Celtic Gaul and Britain. Expert astrologers, they taught immortality of the soul. Ceremonies included cutting mistletoe with a gold knife, and perhaps human sacrifice. Druidism died out in Gaul by 1st cent. and soon afterwards in Britain.

drum, oldest form of percussion instrument; consists of a skin stretched over a hollow cylinder, which resonates when the skin is struck. Types in orchestral use are bass drum, snare drum, tenor drum and kettle drum or timpani. Jazz bands use bass and snare drum, and tom-tom.

drumlin, rounded hillock of unsorted glacial material deposited as ice sheet flows over area. Typical shape like inverted bowl of spoon.

Drummond, William Henry (1854–1907), Canadian poet and physician. Humorous poetry includes *The Habitant, and other French-Canadian Poems* (1897), *Johnnie Courteau and Other Poems* (1901).

Drummond of Hawthornden, William (1585–1649), Scot. poet and author. *The Cypress Grove* (1623) was a meditation on death. Visited by Ben Jonson (1619), his notes on their conversations were published (1842).

Drury Lane, London street and theatre district. The Drury Lane Theatre (Theatre Royal) orig. founded (1671). The present (4th) building was opened (1812).

dry dock, incl. graving, slip, and floating docks, can be emptied of water after ship has floated in, facilitating repairs or cleaning.

dry rot, condition of timber in buildings when it becomes soft, cracked and powdered, exuding water. Caused by fungus, in Europe, *Merulius lacrymans,* and America, *Lenzitus saepiaria,* esp. in damp unventilated conditions.

Dryads, in Gk. and Roman myth., nymphs who lived in trees (Gk: *drus,* a tree).

Dryden, John (1631–1700), Eng. poet and man of letters. Poetry includes the lyrical *Song for St. Cecilia's Day* (1687) and longer satirical works *Absalom and Achitophel* (1681) and *The Hind and the Panther* (1687). Works include plays, *e.g. All for Love* (1687); critical essays, incl. *Essay of*

Dramatick Poesie (1668), which introduced a more natural, speech-like prose to the language; and translations, notably the whole of Vergil (1697).

Drysdale, George Russell (1912–), Austral. artist who has exhibited in New York, London and Sydney. Works include *Sofala* and *The Drover's Wife*.

Du Barry, Jeanne *see* BARRY, JEANNE DU.

Du Bois, W[illiam] E[dward] B[urghardt] (1868–1963), Amer. writer on racial equality. Editor (1910–33) of *Crisis*, journal of National Assoc. for Advancement of Colored People.

Du Maurier, Daphne, (1907–), Eng. writer whose works include *Jamaica Inn* (1936) and *Rebecca* (1938), plays and biographies.

Du Maurier, George Louis Palmella Busson (1834–96), Brit. artist and writer; best known for drawings in *Punch* magazine and novel *Trilby* (1894).

Dual Entente (1895), acknowledgement of mutual interests between Russia and France to counter TRIPLE ALLIANCE (1882).

Dubcek, Alexander (1921–), Czech politician. Leader of Czech Liberal movement of 1968 which met with strong opposition from Russia.

Dublin, cap. of Republic of Ireland in Co. Dublin, on R. Liffey and Dublin Bay. Centre of the PALE. Scene of Easter Rebellion (1916). Important docks and shipyards; chief industries brewing, distilling and textile manufacture. University of Dublin, Trinity College, founded (1591). Pop. (1968) 560,000.

Dublin, county of E Ireland. Area 356 sq. mi.; county town, Dublin; other town Dun Laoghaire, steamer port for Dublin. Flat and fertile in N, Wicklow Mts. in S. Coastal fisheries important. Pop. (1964, excluding Dublin city) 180,884.

Dubois, Eugene (1858–1940), Dutch anatomist and palaeontologist. Discovered bones of an animal intermediate between man and existing anthropoid apes, *Pithecanthropus erectus*, in Java.

Dubrovnik, city of Croatia, NW Yugoslavia, formerly Ragusa. Founded by Gk. colonists *c.* 7th cent., became powerful merchant repub. (14th cent.). Retains much medieval architecture; Adriatic port and resort. Pop. (1968) 23,000.

Dubuffet, Jean (1901–), Fr. artist, creator of primitive, child-like and humorous effects, opposed to 'good taste'. Exhibited sculptures *Little Statues of Precarious Life* (1954).

Duchamp, Marcel (1887–1968) Fr. artist, leader of Dadaist movement. Famous works include *Nude Descending a Staircase*.

duck, aquatic bird of family Anatidae with long flat bill, long neck and webbed feet. Plumage waterproofed by oil from gland near tail. Many migrant species.

duckbill, duckbilled platypus, semiaquatic, egg-laying mammal of Australia and Tasmania. Burrows in river banks; stores food in its cheeks. Most reptile-like of the mammals.

duckweed, Brit. name for perennial plants of *Lemna*, genus of family Lemnaceae. Floats freely in ponds and tanks. *L. minor* is commonest species.

Ducommun, Élie (1833–1906), Swiss journalist and pacifist. Commissioned by Congress of Rome to found International Bureau of Peace, with headquarters at Berne (1891). Shared Nobel Peace Prize (1902) with Charles Albert Gobat.

Dudintsev, Vladimir Dmitrievich (1918–), Russ. writer, author of *With Seven Brothers* (1952), *In His Place* (1954), *Not By Bread Alone* (1956) and *Tales* (1963).

Dudley, Robert, Earl of Leicester (*c.* 1532–88), Eng. courtier and favourite of Elizabeth I. Involved in plot to place Lady Jane Grey on throne. Leader of Puritan party at court from *c.* 1564. Commanded unsuccessful expedition to Netherlands (1585–7).

due process of law, Anglo-Amer. concept of law, intended to protect individual from govt.; 14th Amendment to US Constitution forbade states to abridge privileges and immunities of the citizen in favour of arbitrary, capricious or unreasonable govt. action.

O'Connell Street, Dublin, before removal of Nelson's statue and column in 1965

duel, combat usually arranged by challenge and fought under conventional rules, generally to solve personal quarrel or decide point of honour. After duelling became illegal, survivors guilty of murder and liable to execution.

Dufay, Guillaume (*c.* 1400–74), Franco-Flemish composer and singer, leader of Burgundian school. Composed masses, motets, chansons.

Duff Cooper, Alfred, 1st Viscount Norwich (1890–1954), Brit. Cons. leader, war-time Min. of Information (1940), Brit. Ambassador to France (1944–7).

Dufferin and Ava, 1st Marquis of *see*

The walls of Dubrovnik, dating from 14th-16th cent.

Paddock at Ascot (1935) by Raoul Dufy

Dufy, Raoul (1877–1953), Fr. painter. His work is decorative, incl. designs for tapestries, ceramics, textiles.

dugong, *Dugong dugon,* whale-like herbivorous mammal. Found near coast of Indian ocean, Australia and Red Sea, it is now rare.

Duguay-Trouin, René (1673–1736), Fr. naval officer. Notorious privateer, captured Rio de Janeiro (1711).

Duhamel, Georges (1884–1966), Fr. writer. Best known for cyclical novels *Cycle de Salavin* (1920–32), *Chronique des Pasquier* (1933–45).

duiker, small, short-legged antelope of African bush S of Sahara. Hunted for red-brown or grey hide. Common species the grey duiker, *Sylvicapra grimmia.*

Duisburg, city of West Germany, at junction of Rhine and Ruhr rivers. Indust. centre of Ruhr district, manufactures steel, machinery, textiles. Pop. (1964) 492,000.

Dukas, Paul (1865–1935), Fr. composer famous for scherzo *The Sorcerer's Apprentice* and opera *Ariane et Barbe-bleu.*

Duke University, co-educational college, Durham, N Carolina, opened 1838, named Duke University (1924). Noted for tobacco culture and medical research.

Dukhobors, orig. Russ. religious sect. Persecuted, they emigrated in 1890s and settled in W Canada. Clashes with govt. and neighbours (1950s) over social unorthodoxies of sect.

DUKW [duck], code word for military amphibious vehicle used in World War 2.

dulcimer, medieval stringed instrument struck with small hammers.

Dulles, Allen Welsh (1893–1969), Amer. govt. official, Director of CENTRAL INTELLIGENCE AGENCY (1953–62).

Dulles, John Foster (1888–1959), Amer. politician and lawyer. US delegate to UN General Assembly (1945–8, 1950). As Sec. of State (1953–9), emphasized collective security of US and allies and advocated preparedness for 'instant retaliation' as greatest deterrent to war.

Dulong, Pierre Louis (1785–1838), Fr. physicist and chemist, discoverer of nitrogen chloride. With Alexis Petit formulated (1819) Dulong-Petit Law: product of specific heat of an element in solid state, multiplied by its atomic weight, is approximately constant for all elements. Dulong also devised formula for calculating heat value of fuels from their chemical composition.

dulse, *Rhodymenia palmata,* edible seaweed; consists of solitary or tufted red fronds growing on rocks, shellfish or other seaweeds.

Duluth, city at head of L. Superior, NE Minnesota, US. Settlement began 1852 and became leading Great Lakes grain exporter; industries include cement, metal and wood products. Pop. (1968) 110,000.

duma, Russ. house of representatives, granted by Nicholas II after revolution of 1905. Legislative powers curtailed by tsar's prerogative. Last duma (1912–17) terminated by March revolution.

Dumas, Alexandre (1802–70), Fr.

novelist, known as Dumas *père*. Wrote (or accepted responsibility for) numerous hist. novels incl. *The Three Musketeers* (1844), *The Count of Monte Cristo* (1844–5) and *The Black Tulip* (1850).

Dumas, Alexandre (1824–95). Fr. dramatist and novelist, called Dumas *fils*. Author of *La Dame aux Camélias* (1852), basis of Verdi's opera *La Traviata*; *Le Fils Naturel* (1858) and other plays of moral or social theme.

Dumas, Jean Baptiste André (1800–84), Fr. chemist, founder of École Centrale and distinguished for researches on atomic weights, vapour densities and oxidation.

Dumbarton Oaks, Washington DC, meeting place (1944) of UK, US, USSR and Nationalist China where agreement was reached about creation of UNITED NATIONS.

Dumfriesshire, county of SW Scotland bordering Solway Firth. Area: 1,072 sq. mi.; county town, Dumfries; other towns, Moffat, Annan, Sanquhar. Mainly hilly, agriculture and animal rearing important. Hosiery and tweed manufactured. Dumfries, port and royal burgh. Pop. (1964) 27,042. Pop. of county (1964) 88,113.

Dumouriez, Charles François (1739–1823), Fr. revolutionary general, victor of Valmy and Jemappes (1792). Recalled by Convention after Louis XVI's death, fled to Austria and in Napoleonic Wars advised allied cause.

Dunant, Jean Henri (1828–1910), Swiss philanthropist. Urged measures for relief of wounded in war-time. Brought about Geneva Conference (1863) followed by Geneva Convention (1864) and establishment of International Red Cross. Author of *Souvenir de Solferino*. Shared Nobel Peace Prize (1901) with Frederic Passy.

Dunbar, William (*c.* 1460–*c.* 1520), Scot. poet often imitative of Chaucer. A satirist and accomplished versifier, his works include *The Thrissil and the Rois* (1503), *The Golden Targe* (1508), *The Dance of the Sevin Deidly Synnis*.

Dunbartonshire, county of Scotland, mountainous in N between Lochs Lomond and Long, and flat in S. Area: 232 sq. mi.; county town, Dumbarton; other towns, Clydebank, Kirkintilloch, Helensburgh. Sheep-raising in N; market gardening in S to supply Glasgow. Industry includes shipbuilding, engineering, printing and dyeing. Pop. (1964) 202,929.

Duncan, Isadora (1878–1927), Amer. dancer of international renown and teacher influenced by Gk. art. Danced with bare feet and clad in flowing scarves. Esp. advocated freedom of movement and break with convention. Wrote *My Life* (1927) and *The Art of the Dance* (pub. 1928).

Dundee, city port of Angus, Scotland on Firth of Tay. Centre of jute manufacture, other industries include engineering and dyeing. Site of Queen's College, University of Dundee, formerly part of St Andrew's University. Pop. (1968) 184,000.

dune, sandhill in coastal and desert regions formed by transport of sand by wind; up to 600 ft. high in Sahara. Can be anchored, *e.g.* by marram grass, as around Zuider Zee, Netherlands.

dung beetle, insect of Scarab beetle family that rolls balls of dung in which to lay eggs and provide food for larvae.

Dunham, Katherine (1910–), Amer. dancer and choreographer, director of her own school since 1931. Books include *Form and Function in Primitive Dance*.

Dunkirk, Dunkerque, 3rd largest Fr. port, situated in Nord department on Strait of Dover near Belg. frontier. Important for fishing and shipbuilding. In World War 2, over 338,000 Brit. and Allied troops evacuated to Britain from beaches near Dunkirk (26 May–4 June 1940). Pop. (1962) 27,617.

dunlin, *Calidris alpina*, migrant wading bird of sandpiper group with black patch on lower breast plumage.

Dunlop, John Boyd (1840–1921), Irish veterinary surgeon; invented the rubber pneumatic tyre.

Dunn, L.[eslie] C.[larence] (1893–), Amer. geneticist. Among his books are *Heredity, Race and Society* (with T. Dobzhansky, 1952) and *A Short History of Genetics* (1965).

Duns Scotus, John (1270–1308), medieval Scot. scholastic theologian. A Franciscan, he gained title Doctor Subtilis for skill in controversy. He originated Scotism, a metaphysical doctrine opposed to Thomism.

Dunsany, Edward John Moreton Drax Plunkett, 18th Baron (1878–1957), Irish playwright, author of *A Night at an Inn* (1916), *The Glittering Gate* (1914) and other popular satires.

Dunstaffnage Castle, castle on Loch Linnhe, Scotland, built 13th cent. Residence of early Scot. kings. A Campbell stronghold captured from the MacDougalls in 1308.

Duplessis, Maurice le Noblet (1890–1959), Canadian politician, Premier of Quebec (1936–9, 44–59). Founded l'Union Nationale provincial party. Exercised autocratic power, esp. in application of anti-Communist Padlock Law.

du Pré, Jacqueline (1945–), Brit. cellist; soloist with principal Eng. orchestras and on international tours.

Dupré, Marcel (1886–), Fr. organist and recitalist; composed

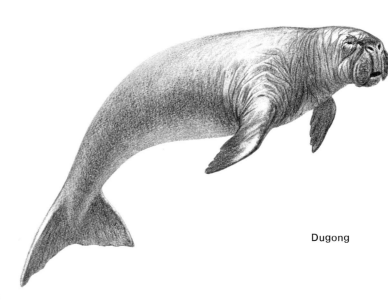

Dugong

Dung Beetle

choral works, noted improvisor. Director of Paris Conservatoire (1954).

Dupuytren, Guillaume, Baron (1777-1835), Fr. surgeon. A fibula fracture and contraction of the hand, described in his writings, are named after him.

Durant, Will[iam James] (1885–), Amer. educator and writer. Works include *Philosophy and the Social Problem* (1917), *The Meaning of Life* (1932) *The Age of Faith* (1950).

Durante, Jimmy (1893–), Amer. actor-comedian. Successful on radio, television and in films; entered films (1929).

Duras, Marguerite (1914–), Fr. writer and scenarist. Screen texts include *Hiroshima Mon Amour, Half Past Ten on a Summer Night*; novels include *Moderato Cantabile* (1958) and *L'Amante anglaise* (1967).

Durban, largest city of Natal prov. of Republic of South Africa founded (1824). Site of University of Natal. Manufacturing centre, and port exporting fruit and coal. Pop. (1968) 682,000.

Dürer, Albrecht (1471–1528), Ger. artist and goldsmith, painted several great altarpieces, created famous engravings on wood and copper. Latterly court painter to Charles V, and friend of Luther. Most celebrated engravings include the 'Apocalypse' series, the 'Great Passion', 'Melancholia', 'The Knight' and 'St Jerome in His Study'.

Durham, city and county town of Co. Durham, England. Situated in loop of Wear R. Cathedral begun in 1093;

Philipsburg on Saint Martin in the Dutch West Indies

castle built by William the Conqueror, now part of university. Pop. (1964) 22,010.

Durham, county of NE England. Area: 1,015 sq. mi.; county town, Durham; main towns, Gateshead, South Shields, Stockton, Sunderland, Hartlepools, Jarrow, Darlington. Pennine moorlands in W; centre and E densely populated industrial area, rich coalmines; industries include ship-building, heavy industries. Pop. (1964) 1,517,000.

Durkheim, Émile (1858–1917), Fr. sociologist. Considered one of the founders of sociology, held that individual behaviour determined by social harms. Works include *Suicide* (1897) and *The Elementary Forms of Religious Life* (1912).

Durrell, Gerald Malcolm (1925–), Eng. zoologist and writer, whose books include *My Family and Other Animals* (1956), *A Zoo in My Luggage* (1960).

Durrell, Lawrence (1912–), Eng. novelist and poet. Most famous works 'The Alexandria Quartet' of *Justine* (1957), *Balthazar* (1958), *Mountolive* (1958) and *Clea* (1960), a portrayal of the same events from 4 people's viewpoints.

Durrenmatt, Friedrich (1921–), Swiss dramatist. Plays, terse and almost grotesque, include *The Visit* (1956) and *The Physicists* (1962).

Duse, Eleanora (1859–1924), Ital. actress and dancer. Combined simplicity with emotional power in such plays as Ibsen's *Lady from the Sea* and Sardou's *Fedora*.

Düsseldorf, Ger. city at junction of Düssel and Rhine rivers. Industries include production of iron and steel goods and chemicals. Pop. 498,300.

dust, particles of solid matter in atmosphere; includes soil and rock particles, minute organisms, pollen, particles from burning fuel and factories, and particles of volcanic and meteoric origin.

dusty miller, *primula auricula,* term referring to several plants with hairy white or grey leaves. *Senecis cineraria* is stiff perennial variety.

Dutch, Germanic Indo-European language, with 17 million speakers in Holland and Belgium. *See* also FLEMISH.

Dutch school, term used to describe Dutch portrait and GENRE painters, most of 17th cent, incl. the VAN EYCKS, HOLBEIN, RUBENS, REMBRANDT, FRANS HALS and others.

Dutch West Indies, Curaçao, autonomous region of Netherlands comprising 2 island groups in Caribbean

Sea: 1) off Venezuela, Curaçao, Bonaire, Aruba. Chief industry oil refining; 2) in NW Leeward Is., St. Martin, St Eustatius, Saba. Popular tourist area. Pop. 203,600.

Dutchman's-breeches, *Dicentra cucullaria,* N Amer. wild flower; yellowwhite flowers resemble a pair of baggy trousers.

Dutchman's-pipe, *Aristolochia macrophylla,* climbing vine native of eastern US; yellow-brown flowers have shape of tobacco pipe.

Dutrochet, René Joachim Henri (1776–1847), Fr. physiologist. Studied plant respiration, demonstrated (1837) necessity of chlorophyll for absorption of carbon dioxide.

Duvalier, Francois ('Papa Doc') (1907–71), dictator pres. of Haiti (1957–71). Govt. supported by indisciplined private army.

Dvořák, Antonin (1841–1904), Czech composer and violinist. His 9 operas little known outside Czechoslovakia but his 7 symphonies incl. *No. 5 (From the New World)* and *1st Cello Concerto* (1865) are concert pieces in W Europe and N America.

dwarf, in plants and animals, term applied to specimens which do not attain normal height.

Dyak, non-Mohammedan Malay peoples of Borneo, incl. Kayan and Sea Dyaks.

dyestuffs, materials used to impart colour to textiles or other substances. Orig. obtained from natural materials *e.g.* plant roots, best known being indigo and alizarin. Synthetic dyes manufactured from distillation products of coal tar and known as aniline colours.

dyke, in geology, result of an intrusion of IGNEOUS ROCK which cuts across the layering of country rocks.

Dylan, Bob (1941–), Amer. folksinger and composer. Works, often containing social criticism, influential in 1960s.

dynamics, branch of physics studying effects of forces not in equilibrium and laws of motion thus produced.

dynamite, powerful explosive invented by Alfred Bernhard Nobel (1833–96). Consists of 75% nitroglycerine held in an absorbent, often kieselguhr [fuller's earth]. Nitrate mixture used as absorbent in US increases explosive force.

dysentery, amoebic, trop. type of dysentery caused by parasitic protozoan, *Entamoeba histalytica.* Usually affects large intestine producing diarrhoea which may contain blood and mucus; associated with fever, malaise, sickness.

E

eagle, many varieties of birds of prey of family Accipitridae. Usually nests on inaccessible cliffs and feeds on rabbits and hares.

eagle-owl, *Bubo bubo,* owl of family Strigidae, found everywhere in world except Australia.

Eakins, Thomas (1844–1916), Amer. portrait and genre painter and sculptor. Paintings include *The Clinic of Professor Agnew* and *The 'Cello Player.*

ear, organ of hearing. In man, consists of outer ear (auricle), middle ear, small space in temporal bone, and inner ear, containing cochlea, organ in which nerve of hearing has its end filaments.

Earhart, Amelia (1898–1937), Amer. aviator, 1st woman to fly solo across the Atlantic (1932). Lost (1937) on flight to Howland Island.

Early English, in history of Eng. architecture the 1st stage (13th cent.) of Gothic period. Examples include parts of Lincoln and Salisbury Cathedrals, Westminster Abbey.

Earth, the, planet of solar system, 3rd in distance from Sun (*c.* 93,000,000 mi.). Rotates on axis, causing day and night; revolves in elliptical orbit around the Sun, taking $365\frac{1}{4}$ days to complete orbit, inclination producing change of seasons. Earth is slightly flattened at poles. Between 2,000 million and 5,500 million yr. old, according to one theory, formed from space-dust; layered structure with magnetic core.

earth tongues, tongue-shaped fungi of genus *Geoglossum*; black, yellow or olive green, found in grassland.

earthball, smokeball, *Scleroderma aurantium,* common fungus of woods and heaths. Rounded fruit body has hard, scaly, olive-yellow wall containing purple-black mass of powdery dry spores.

earthenware, all forms of baked clay, or pottery; usually designates the coarser varieties.

earthnut, pignut, hognut, *Conopodium majus,* perennial S European plant with edible tubers; black with white inside.

earthquake, sudden movement of Earth's crust due to fracture of rock strata or volcanic eruptions. Resulting vibrations may cause changes in surface level, cracks in ground or giant waves (tsunami). Earthquakes are recorded on seismographs. Main zones of activity: 1) Pacific belt including Philippines, Japan, Alaska, W coasts of Americas; 2) belt through Mediterranean, Persia, Himalayas and East Indies; 3) mid-oceanic ridges.

earthstar, common name for several fungi of *Geastrum* genus.

earthworm, annelid worm living in soil. Common species of N hemisphere is *Lumbricus terrestris* with cylindrical segmented body.

earwig, insect of order Dermaptera; conspicuous forceps, cerci, at end of abdomen. Nocturnal and omnivorous; majority are tropical. European earwig, *Forficula auricularia,* has been introduced into America, S Africa and Australasia; genus *Arixemia* of canals of SE Asia.

East Anglia, district of E England, counties of Norfolk, Suffolk, Cambridgeshire, Huntingdon and part of Essex. Was kingdom, *c.* 620–920.

East China Sea, Eastern Sea, arm of Pacific, bounded by China and Japan. Yellow Sea at N, linked with South China Sea by Formosa Strait.

East India Company, Brit. company chartered (1600) by Elizabeth I for monopoly of trade with E. After Clive's victories over Fr. rivals it became virtual ruler of India in 18th cent.; following Indian Mutiny of 1857 Company was abolished (1858).

East Lothian, formerly Haddingtonshire, county of SE Scotland. Area: 267 sq. mi.; county town, Haddington. Largely agricultural with fisheries and collieries. Pop. (1963) 51,814.

East Pakistan, district of PAKISTAN,

Eagle Owl

Diagram of ear (a) auricle (b) cartilaginous part of auditory meatus (c) bony part of auditory meatus (d) tympanic membrane or eardrum, (e), (f), (g) chain of ossicles (hammer, anvil and Sylvius bones) in (h) tympanic cavity, (i) stirrup bone, (j) semicircular duct, (k) oval window, (l) Eustachian tube, (m) utricle and saccule (n) perilymph, (o) endolymphatic duct, (p) auditory nerve (q) cochlear duct

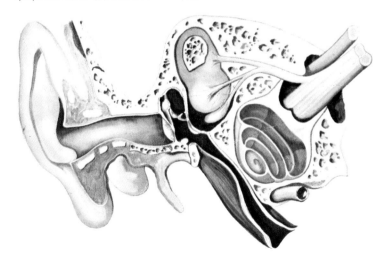

Echeveria vetusa

comprising E territories of former Bengal and Assam areas, bounded by India and Burma. Area: 55,134 sq. mi.; cap. Dacca; ports Chittagong, Chalna. Drained by Ganges and Brahmaputra. Contains *c.* 60% of Pakistan's population. Largely agricultural, chief products include rice, hemp, oilseed, sugar, silk, tea and coal. Pop. (1964) 50,844,000.

Easter, Christian festival commemorating resurrection of Jesus Christ. Instituted *c.* 68 AD, named after Anglo-Saxon goddess of spring. In the W, falls on 1st Sunday after full moon after vernal equinox, between Mar. 22 and Apr. 25. In E, calculated from Julian calendar.

Easter Island, S Pacific island *c.* 2,350 mi. W of Chile, to which it belongs. Area: 46 sq. mi. Volcanic and fertile, famous for monolithic stone heads. Pop. (1968) *c.* 850.

Easter Rebellion, abortive uprising in Dublin against Brit. rule (24—29 Apr. 1916) forcibly suppressed. Led to Anglo-Irish war (1918—20) and establishment of Irish Free State.

Eastman, George (1854—1932), Amer. inventor and philanthropist. Founder of Eastman Kodak Co. Invented dryplate photographic process, devised roll film, and process for colour photography.

Eastman, Max (1883-1969), Amer. author and editor of *The Masses* (1913—17) until its suppression in World War 1. Works include *Enjoyment of Laughter* (1936), autobiog. *Enjoyment of Living* (1948). Translated writings of Leon Trotsky.

Ebbinghaus, Hermann (1850—1909), Ger. experimental psychologist; studied memory and pioneered study of intelligence in school children.

Eberhart, Richard (1904—), Amer. poet who uses short lines and few rhymes. Works include *Selected Poems 1930–1965* (1966) and *Collected Verse Plays* (1962).

ebony, trees or shrubs of genus *Diospyros* of Ebenaceae family; grows in trop. and sub-trop. climates. Black hardwood used for cabinet work; derived largely from *D. ebenum* of S India and Ceylon. *D. kaki* (E Asia) and *D. virginiana* (W America) other well-known species.

Eccles, Sir John Carew, FRS (1903—), Austral. research physiologist. Shared Nobel Prize for Physiology and Medicine (1963) for research on nerve cells.

Ecclesiastes, poetical book of OT, written (*c.* 200 BC) by a man of high station in Jerusalem, contrasting the verities of this world with those of the eternal.

Ecclesiasticus or **The Wisdom of Jesus,** apocryphal book of OT written by Jesus, son of Sirach of Jerusalem (*c.* 200—175 BC). Advises passive submission to the Divine will.

echeveria, genus of Amer. succulent perennials, family Crassulaceae, with ornamental leaves in rosette formation and bell-shaped flowers.

echidna, spiny ant-eater, spiny-backed monotreme found in rocky parts of Australasia. Poisonous glands on hind legs; eggs hatched in pouch. Species include Tasmanian, *Tachyglossus setosus*.

echinoderm, marine animal of phylum Echinodermata, usually of pentagonal shape. Calcareous skeleton is sometimes joined to form shell; *c.* 5,000 species include starfish, sea urchin and sea lily.

echinoid, sea-urchin, invertebrate marine animal of phylum Echinodermata. Skeleton is globular, comprising calcareous plates and spines.

Echo, in Gk. myth., nymph whose speech Hera caused to be limited to the repetition of the last words of others.

echo, in physics, reflection of sound. Ships measure depth of water with an instrument which indicates the length of time it takes for sound to echo off the sea bed.

Eckermann, Johann Peter (1792—1854), Ger. scholar and author, and secretary to Goethe. His *Conversa-*

tions with Goethe (1836—48) provide valuable key to Goethe's thought.

Eckhart, Johannes, 'Meister' (*c.* 1260-1327), Ger. Dominican theologian and mystic who taught in Paris and preached in Frankfurt, Cologne and Strasburg. Charged with heresy (1327); some of his teaching pronounced heretical (1329).

eclecticism [Gk: selection], philosophical term applied to any body of doctrines loosely combined from various distinct systems of thought. Seems characteristic of periods immediately succeeding great creative epochs.

eclipse, in astronomy, partial or complete obscuring of one celestial body by another as viewed from a fixed point. Partial eclipses of both Sun and Moon occur in relation to Earth every yr. Total eclipses occur about once every 2 yr. although most are not visible from Earth.

ecology, study of animals and plants in their natural surroundings (*e.g.* temperature, soil and light). Also interrelation in animal and plant community. In social science, relation of man to natural environment.

economics, study of production, distribution, and consumption of commodities. First attempts at analysis were by ancient Greeks, Plato (*Republic*) and Aristotle. Development of modern economics begun through LAISSEZ-FAIRE, advocated by physiocrats and elaborated upon by classical economists, Adam Smith (*Wealth of Nations*, 1776), David Ricardo and J. S. Mill; founded on belief in inflexible natural laws governing exchange and production of goods. Challenged in 19th cent. by socialists, esp. Karl Marx (*Das Kapital*, 1867), who believed in societal change on moral and social grounds as well as economic, and threw light on weaknesses of classical market economy such as crisis recurrence. Classical form reestablished (1870s) and applied mathematically by Alfred Marshall. J. M. Keynes (*General Theory,*

Lunar Eclipse, showing how the Moon moves into the Earth's shadow. The complete eclipse takes 1-2 hr.

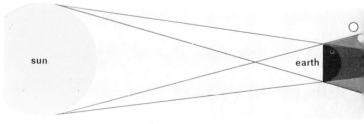

1936) enabled study to incorporate forecasting of economic trends (econometrics).

Ecuador [República de Ecuador] repub. of S America. Area: 119,870 sq. mi.; cap. Quito; chief port, Guayaquil. Comprises C valley, E forest-clad mountains and W low-

lands between Andes and Pacific. Principal exports, incl. bananas, rice, cacao, coffee and cotton, come mainly from E and N. Small quantities of gold, silver and oil are produced. President elected by popular vote, and may not run for 2 consecutive terms. Pres. appoints prov. governors. Unit of currency, the sucre. Pop. (1967) 5,510,000.

ecumenism, term for 20th cent. movement aimed at unification of Christian churches. World Council of Churches (1948) brought together more than 200 Protestant, Orthodox and Old Catholic churches. Since 2nd General Vatican Council (1962), R.C. church has been increasingly involved in quest for church unity.

Eddington, Sir Arthur Stanley (1882-1944), Eng. astronomer and physicist who developed a theory of relativity and gravitation. Discovered mass-luminosity relationship of stars. Books include *The Nature of the Physical World* (1927), *The Expanding Universe* (1933) and *The Philosophy of Physical Science* (1939).

Eddy, Mary Baker (1821-1910), Amer. founder of Christian Science movement. Her *Science and Health* appeared in 1875. Planned *Manual* for conduct of church and all details of its development. Pastor of Mother Church, Boston.

edelweiss, *Ceontropodium alpinum,* small perennial plant of high Alps. Dense woolly white appearance.

Eden, [Robert] Anthony, 1st Earl of Avon (1897-   ), Brit. statesman. Foreign Sec. (1935-8, 1940-5); Cons. P.M. (1955-7). Resigned after SUEZ CRISIS (1956).

Eden, Garden of, in OT, 1st home of man. Created by God, it contained the trees of life and knowledge, and housed Adam and Eve. They were banished after tasting the forbidden fruit [*Gen.* 2:3].

edentata, arboreal or terrestrial order of mammals with no visible teeth, only enamelless molars. Species include anteater, sloth, armadillo.

Edgeworth, Maria (1767-1849), Irish novelist who advocated education of women. Novels about Ireland include *Castle Rackrent, The Absentee, Ormond* and *Belinda.* Daughter of Richard Lovell Edgeworth (1744-1817), an educ. theorist and inventor.

edible frog, *Rana esculenta,* frog found in Europe. Legs eaten, esp. in France.

Edinburgh, cap. of Scotland and county town of Midlothian, near Firth of Forth. Became burgh (1329) and cap. (1437). Importance declined with union of Scot. and Eng. crowns (1603). University of Edinburgh (1583) has noted medical school. Centre of learning and literature (18th-19th cent.). Industries include engineering, tanning, chemicals and brewing. Leith is city's port. Annual International Festival of Music and Drama. Pop. (1965) 475,400.

Edinburgh, Duke of *see* PHILIP, PRINCE.

Edinburgh University, founded (1583), early referred to as College of King James. Renowned for its medical school.

Edirne, Turkish city, formerly Adrianople, near Gk. and Bulgarian borders. Founded by Emperor Hadrian AD 125. Exports silk and tobacco. Pop. 27,200.

Edison, Thomas Alva (1847-1931), Amer. inventor who made important contributions to wireless telegraphy and telephony, the generation and distribution of electricity. Invented phonograph (1878), 1st practicable

electric light bulb (1879) and the kinetoscope (1891) forerunner of ciné camera and projector.

Edmonton, cap. and rly. centre of Alberta, Canada, on N Saskatchewan R. Market centre for agricultural and petroleum products; oil, gas and coalfields. In the 19th cent. it was one of the most prosperous trading stations of W Canada growing from a Hudson's Bay Company post. Pop. (1968) 282,000.

Edmund Ironside (d. 1016) king of part of England, rival of Canute. On Edmund's death, Canute acquired entire Eng. kingdom.

Edomites, inhabitants of S Israel (between Dead Sea and Gulf of Aqaba). Descendants of Esau, often at war with neighbours, esp. Hebrews.

Education Act (1944), Brit. legislation which centralized control of education under Min. of Education. Abolished separate authorities for elementary education and made secondary education mandatory.

Edward [Antony Richard Louis] Prince (1964-   ), 3rd son of Queen Elizabeth II of Great Britain and Northern Ireland.

Edward I (1239-1307), king of England (1272-1307), son of Henry III. Conquered Wales but d. before he could subdue Scotland; carried out legal and admin. reforms such as Statutes of Westminster (1275-90) and summoned the MODEL PARLIAMENT (1295).

Edward II (1284-1327), king of England (1307-27), son of Edward I. Married Isabella of France. An incompetent ruler, dominated by favourites, esp. Despensers and Piers

Princes Street and the Walter Scott Monument, Edinburgh

Egyptian Art: wall painting of Rameses III and his wife. In one of the graves at Biban-el-Harim

Gaveston. Defeated by Scots at Bannockburn (1314); deposed by wife and Roger Mortimer, and murdered at Berkeley Castle.

Edward III (1312–77), king of England (1327–77), son of Edward II. Claimed Fr. throne through his mother Isabella and began HUNDRED YEARS WAR (1337). Defeated French at Crécy and Poitiers with help of son, EDWARD THE BLACK PRINCE. Black Death led to demands for social change; cost of wars strengthened parl. power.

Edward IV (1442–83), king of England (1461–83), son of Richard, Duke of York. Defeated Lancastrians (1461) and became king. EARL OF WARWICK'S attempt to reinstate deposed Henry VI ended with Edward's victory (1471) at Tewkesbury.

Edward V (1470–83), king of England (1483). Confined with brother Richard, Duke of York, in Tower of London by Richard, Duke of Gloucester, who declared them illegitimate and took throne as Richard III. Later believed that Gloucester had princes murdered.

Edward VI (1537–53), king of England (1547–53). Succeeded father, Henry VIII, under Council of Regency controlled by uncle, EDWARD SEYMOUR; reign marked by general liberalization. Duke of Northumberland overthrew Seymour and persuaded king to declare LADY JANE GREY heiress.

Edward VII (1841–1910), Brit. king (1901–10), eldest son of Queen Victoria. Improved international relations through wide travels; promoted Entente Cordiale with France.

Edward VIII (1894–   ), Brit. king (1936), eldest son of George V. As Prince of Wales, attracted attention through interest in social reform. Forced to abdicate after announcing intention to marry divorcée, Mrs. Wallis Simpson. As Duke of Windsor, married her (1937). Gov. of Bahamas (1940–5).

Edward the Black Prince (1330–76), eldest son of Edward III of England. Fought in battle of Crécy and captured John II of France while winning at Poitiers (1356). Created Prince of Aquitaine and Gascony after Treaty of Brétigny (1360), but bad health forced him to resign (1372). Survived by son, later Richard II.

Edward the Confessor (1005–66), king of England (1042–66), son of Ethelred II; succeeded Harthacanute. Probably promised William of Normandy throne, but recognized HAROLD as successor. Dispute resolved by Norman Conquest. Edward canonized (12th cent.).

Edwards, Jonathan (1703–58), Amer. Calvinist theologian. His sermons resulted in religious revival in New England, the 'Great Awakening'.

eel, edible fish of order Apodes; naked skin or minute scales and small gill openings. Most are marine in trop. or sub-trop. areas, esp. Pacific.

eel grass, grass wrack, *Zostera marina,* perennial creeping marine herb. Found in Europe and N America.

eel-pout, *see* BURBOT.

Egbert (d. 839), king of Wessex (802–39). Succeeded Beohtric without opposition; eventually enforced submission of Kent, East Anglia, Mercia and Northumbria, thereby securing rule of all Anglo-Saxon kingdoms.

Egeria, in Roman religion, nymph of a spring, revived as a guardian of children. Legendary wife of King Numa.

egg *see* OVUM.

Eggleston, Edward (1837–1902), Amer. minister and author. Works include *The Hoosier Schoolmaster* (1871) and *The Circuit Rider* (1873).

eggplant, *see* AUBERGINE.

eglantine rose *see* SWEETBRIAR.

Egmont, Lamoral, Count of (1522–68), Flemish statesman and soldier. Protested against Sp. misrule of Netherlands; Alva had him executed. His career is theme of a tragedy by Goethe with music by Beethoven.

Egmont, Mount, extinct volcano (8,260 ft.), North Is., New Zealand. Known by Maoris as Taranaki, forms centre of Egmont National Park.

egret, slender heron-like bird with white plumage. Species include once rare great egret, *Egretta alba*; little egret, *E. garzetta*; cattle egret, *Ardeola ibis*, of Asia, Africa and the Americas.

Egypt, ancient kingdom founded *c.* 3rd millenium BC, rose to great power in Middle East; finally absorbed by Rome 30 BC. Cultural remains include temples, pyramids and tombs, showing development of complex and highly organized society. *See* also UNITED ARAB REPUBLIC.

Egyptian, Afro-Asian language family, preserved only in documents and monuments.

Ehrenberg, Ilya Grigorevich (1891–   ), Russ. novelist and journalist. Satirical works include *The Stormy Life of Lasik Roitschwantz* (1928), *The Thaw* (1954).

Ehrlich, Paul (1854–1915), Ger. bacteriologist. With Elie Metchnikoff shared Nobel Prize for Physiology and Medicine (1908) for work in immunology. Discovered first effective cure for syphilis.

Eichendorff, Josef, Freiherr von (1788–1857), Ger. writer of lyric poetry and prose. Known for verses set to music by Schumann, Mendelssohn and Brahms.

Eichmann, Karl Adolf (1906–62), Ger. Nazi official, head of Jewish Emigration Centre, Berlin (1940), involved in mass extermination and deportation of Jews. Escaped Allies (1945), discovered in Argentina (1960); convicted of crimes against Jews by Israeli court (1962) and executed.

eider duck, *Somateria mollissima,* found in N regions. Male distinguished by black belly and white back. Eider down is commercially valued for stuffing quilts and cushions.

Eifel, plateau in NW Germany, part of Rhenish Slate Mountains; practically barren with deep valleys, extinct volcanoes and crater lakes.

Eiffel, Alexandre Gustave (1832–1923), Fr. engineer. Developed steel lattice beam used in construction. Designed **Eiffel Tower,** erected for Paris Exposition (1889).

Eiger [The Ogre], peak (13,036 ft.) in

Bernese Oberland, Switzerland. First climbed (1858). Notorious N side particularly dangerous.

Eijkman, Christian (1858–1930), Dutch physician. Shared Nobel Prize for Physiology and Medicine (1929) with F. G. Hopkins for work on cause of beri-beri.

Einstein, Albert (1879–1955), Amer. scientist, b. Germany. Developed quantum theory of RELATIVITY (1905), later completing mathematical formula published (1949) as appendix to *The Meaning of Relativity* (1922). Awarded Nobel Prize for Physics (1921) for work on photo-electric effect. Also contributed to study of atom and cause for world peace.

Einthoven, Willem (1860–1927), Dutch physiologist. Awarded Nobel Prize for Physiology and Medicine (1924) for developing electrocardiograph to record heart actions.

Eisenhower, Dwight David (1890–1969), 34th US Pres. (1953–61), Republican. Rapid rise as military commander during World War 2 included posts as chief of Allied Forces in North Africa (1942–3) and Supreme Allied Commander of invasion of Europe (1944). Later, Army Chief of Staff (1945–8) and commanded NATO forces (1950–2) in Europe before nomination as Repub. pres. candidate and election victory (1952). As Pres., pursued moderate domestic policies. Fostered anti-Communist alliances and commitments in SE Asia, the Middle East, and Latin America. Sent troops to enforce integration in schools in Little Rock, Arkansas (1957). Popularity enhanced by general economic prosperity. Published account of Allied victory over Germany, *Crusade in Europe* (1948).

Eisenstein, Sergei Mikhailovitch, (1898–1948), Russ. film director. Pioneer of motion pictures, notable films include *Battleship Potemkin* (1925), *Alexander Nevsky* (1938), and *Ivan the Terrible* (1944).

El Amarna, Tel, Akhenaten's cap. (c. 1574–62 BC) on E bank of Nile, between Cairo and Luxor. Finds of Flinders Petrie excavations included valuable correspondence in Babylonian cuneiform.

eland, *Taurotragus onyx,* large African antelope with spirally twisted horns. Fawn-coloured with slight striping. Easily tamed.

Elba, island off Tuscany, C Italy. Area: 86 sq. mi. Became a principality under the exiled Napoleon (1814–15). Chief town is Portoferraio; iron industry. Pop. (1968) 29,100.

Eiffel Tower

Elbe, river of Europe flowing 725 mi. from Czechoslovakia into North Sea at Cuxhaven, Germany. Major European waterway, navigable for 525 mi.

Elbrus, Mount, twin conical peaks (18,481 and 18,356 ft.), in Caucasus, Georgian SSR; highest mountain in Europe. First climbed 1868.

Elburz, mountain range in Persia, S of Caspian Sea. Mt. Demavend, a dormant volcano, is highest peak (18,000 ft.).

elder, *Sambucus nigra,* deciduous bushy tree of honeysuckle family, common in Europe. Strong smelling flower and black or red berries.

El Dorado, legendary land believed to be in S America and to contain fabulous wealth. Attracted 16th cent. adventurers incl. Pizarro, Raleigh, Coronado. The name is often used to mean any utopian land.

Eleanor of Aquitaine (c. 1122–1204), queen of Henry II of England. Marriage (1137–52) to Louis VII of France annulled. Then married Henry, Duke of Normandy, bore him 2 sons Richard I and John, whom she aided in unsuccessful revolts against Henry. Helped Richard secure throne (1189).

elecampane, *Inula helemium,* tall hairy perennial plant of daisy family with toothed leaves and clusters of yellow flower heads.

election, organized voting to choose representatives or office holders. Used in ancient Greece and Rome. Elections and popular SUFFRAGE evolved with growth of democracy. In England, elections regularized after 1688; secret ballot 1872.

electoral college, in US politics, body of state electors which chooses Pres. and Vice Pres. Number of electors determined by total representation of state in US Congress. Pres. candidate wins by obtaining majority in electoral college (majority of popular vote not necessary). Failure to obtain majority of electors throws vote into House of Representatives (1 vote for each state). Current practice enables party to carry whole state if it achieves plurality of vote.

Electors, in Ger. history, princes with right to elect Holy Roman emperor. By 13th cent. number fixed at 7: archbishops of Mainz, Trier and Cologne, king of Bohemia, duke of Saxony, margrave of Brandenburg and elector of the Palatine. Office disappeared (1806) with dissolution of Empire.

Elderberries

Elk

Electra, in Gk. myth.; daughter of AGAMEMNON and Clytemnestra; helped brother Orestes avenge Agamemnon's death.

electric storm *see* THUNDERSTORM.

electrical engineering, development and application of electrical energy for human use. Branches concern creation of electrical machinery; transmission, distribution and generation of power.

electricity, general term for physical phenomena associated with electrons in movement, esp. as source of power. The atom, regarded as basic unit of matter, is held to be made up of negative charges (electrons), positive charges (protons) and neutral charges (neutrons). Loss of an electron leaves atom positively charged and gain of an electron gives it negative charge. Flow of electric current is movement of electrons and protons. Occurs naturally in lightning and may be induced, *i.e.* a body may be charged. An electric motor transforms electrical into mechanical energy and heat may be produced in the charged body, *e.g.* radiant elements in electric fire, incandescent filaments in light bulbs.

electrocardiogram, instrument used to diagnose disorders of the heart.

electrochemistry, branch of science and technology dealing with the interchange between chem. and electric energy. Includes study of, *e.g.* ELECTROLYTES, IONS.

electrode, term for points of entry and exit of electric current (positive and negative poles) of a voltic or electrolytic cell, thermionic valve, *etc.*

The positive electrode is the *anode*, the negative is the *cathode*.

electroencephalograph, instrument for recording electrical potential of nerve cells in the brain. Used in diagnosing brain disorders, notably epilepsy. Recorded results called EEGs.

electrolysis, production of chem. changes by passage of electric current through an ELECTROLYTE; used for electro-plating.

electrolyte, non-metallic electric conductor in which the ions carrying the current migrate to the electrodes, causing chem. changes.

electron, basic subatomic particle with negative unit charge and negligible mass. Electrons move in orbits around nucleus of atom. Movement of electrons constitutes electric current.

electronics, study of the movement of electrons through a vacuum in gases and semi-conductors, and its practical applications. A branch of electrical engineering.

elegy, reflective poem of regret or lamentation over the dead. Famous Eng. examples are: *Lycidas* by Milton, *Elegy written in a Country Churchyard* by Gray.

element, name for material which cannot be decomposed by chem. process into subsidiary materials; 92 elements occur in nature and 11 more have been made in the laboratory.

elephant, mammal of order Proboscidea incl. African, *Loxodonta africana,* and Indian species, *Elephas maximus.* African larger than Indian reaching *c.* 11 ft. and $4\frac{1}{2}$ tons with larger ears and tusks. Trunk is

very sensitive, flexible and strong. Live in herds with occasional solitary or 'rogue' elephant. One calf born at a time. Lifespan of 50 years in African and 70 in Indian.

Elephant Bill (1897–1958), nickname of James Howard Williams, Brit. author of *Elephant Bill* (1950), *Bandoola* (1953) and other books.

elephantiasis, disease caused, in humans, by entry of filaria worm into body; resulting in blockage of lymph channels and immense enlargement and thickening of affected part.

Eleusis, shrine of Demeter and Persephone near Athens. Mysteries of the 2 goddesses celebrated there annually.

elf cup, toadstool with large cup. Varieties include orange elf cup, *Peziza aurantia,* found on lawns and in woods; scarlet elf cup, *P. coccinea,* found on decaying or dead wood.

Elgar, Sir Edward William (1857–1934), Eng. composer; works include *Enigma Variations* (1899), *Pomp and Circumstance* marches.

Elgin, 7th Earl of, *see* BRUCE, THOMAS.

Elgin, 8th Earl of *see* BRUCE, JAMES.

Elgin Marbles *see* BRUCE, THOMAS, 7th Earl of Elgin.

El Greco [Domenicos Theotocopulis] (*c.* 1547–1614), Gk. painter who spent most of his life in Spain. Blended late Byzantine and late Italian Mannerist with intense emotionalism and spiritual fervour; strong sense of movement and use of light as *e.g.* in *Assumption of the Virgin, View of Toledo.*

Elijah, in OT, Hebrew prophet;

15th cent. Russian icon of the prophet Elias

hallenged Ahab and priests of Baal n Mt. Carmel. Disappeared in fiery hariot. Known as Elias in NT; rominent figure in the Koran.

liot, Charles William (1834–1926), mer. scientist. President of Harvard Jniversity (1869–1909), instrumental n its development.

liot, George, orig. Mary Ann or Marian Evans (1819–80), Eng. writer. Jovels depict middle-class provincial fe; also wrote poems and articles. Works include *The Mill on the Floss* 1860) and *Middlemarch* (1872).

liot, T[homas] S[tearns] (1888– 965), Eng. poet and critic, b. US. arly work such as *Prufrock and Ither Observations* (1917), *The Vaste Land* (1922), characterized by recision of language and variation of orm and rhythm. Poetic dramas nclude *Murder in the Cathedral* 1935). Awarded Nobel Prize for terature (1948).

Elisabethville *see* LUBUMBASHI.

lixir, substance formerly believed in nd sought by alchemists to turn base netals into gold. An elixir to prolong fe was also thought to exist.

Elizabeth [Angela Marguerite] (1900–), widow of King George VI of Great Britain, on whose death (1952) she took the title of Queen Elizabeth he Queen Mother. Before her mar- iage (1923) she was Lady Elizabeth Bowes-Lyon; children, Elizabeth II and Princess Margaret.

Elizabeth I (1533–1603), queen of England (1558–1603), daughter of Henry VIII and Anne Boleyn. Succeeded to throne after perilous early life; showed ability during time of large debts and religious strife. Church of England estab. 1559; Mary Queen of Scots executed (1587); Spanish Armada defeated (1588) and Irish rebellion put down (1603). Elizabeth popular with her subjects. Age regarded as one of greatest in Eng. history.

Elizabeth II (1926–), Queen of Great Britain and Northern Ireland (1952–), of House of Windsor, daughter of George VI. Married Philip Mountbatten, Duke of Edin- burgh (1947). Children are Princes Charles, Andrew, and Edward, and Princess Anne.

Elizabethan drama, name given to works written and produced between c. 1570 and 1600, representing the blending of native tradition in com- edies and chronicle plays with Renais- sance classicism, mostly in blank verse (Marlowe, Shakespeare, Jonson); and in tragedies which explored the heights and depths of human experience and comedies in

African Elephant

which everything from sophisticated word-play to hearty bawdry could find place.

Elizabethan Style, in architecture, a Renaissance art form (16th–17th cent.); particularly characteristic were Eng. country houses of the period (Knole, Penshurst). Incorporated ele- ments of Eng. Gothic.

elk, *Alces alces,* largest DEER of Europe and Asia. Inhabits marsh- lands; disappeared from W Europe (3rd cent.). Amer. variety is WAPITI.

Elk Island National Park, Alberta, Canada. Area: 75 sq. mi.; founded 1913, located near Edmonton. Fenced preserve for wildlife.

Ellesmere Island, mountainous island in Arctic Ocean, W of Greenland. Area: 77,392 sq. mi. Part of Northwest Territories, Canada. Base camp for Robert Peary's 1909 polar expedition.

Ellington, Edward Kennedy ('Duke') (1899–), Amer. jazz musician and composer. Composed major jazz works as well as popular numbers (*e.g. Mood Indigo*), and film scores.

Elliot, Gilbert John Murray Kynynmond, 4th Earl of Minto (1845–1914), Brit. imperial admini- strator. Gov.-General of Canada (1898–1904); facilitated participation in South African War (1899– 1902).

Elliott, Herbert James (1938–), Austral. athlete. Set world record for mile and 1500 metres (1958) and record tally of 17 4-min. miles still holds. Retired 1962.

ellipse, in mathematics, a closed curve, not a circle, of which the sums of the distances between all points on the curve and two fixed points, or foci, are equal.

Ellis, [Henry] Havelock (1859–1939), Eng. psychologist and author. Known for *Studies in the Psychology of Sex* (7 vols., 1897–1928), and other scientific writings in literary style.

Ellison, Ralph (1914–), Amer. writer of short stories and essays. Author of *Invisible Man* (1952) and lecturer on Negro folk culture.

Ellsworth, Lincoln (1880–1951), Amer. explorer. Financed Roald

Amundsen's Arctic aviation ventures. Flew over North Pole (1926); 1st to fly over Antarctica (1935).

elm, family of deciduous trees with rough oval leaves. Wych elm, *Ulnus glabra,* reaches 120 ft. in ht. Species include Eng. elm, *U. procera,* smooth-leaved elm, *U. carpinifolia,* and slippery elm, *U. rubra,* of N America.

Elman, Mischa (1891–1967), Amer. violinist. Toured widely in Europe and America.

El Paso, Texas, Amer. city on Rio Grande River bordering Mexico. Centre for light industry, tourism and trade. Pop. (1960 est.) 277,000.

El Salvador *see* SALVADOR.

Elsevier, Louis (1540–1617), Dutch publisher. Founded Leiden press (1583), continued by descendants until 1712; name still used.

Elsinore, Helsingør, Danish industrial and fishing centre. Ferry port to Sweden. Nearby Kronborg castle built by Frederick II (1580), model for castle in Shakespeare's *Hamlet.* Pop. (1960 est.) 26,700.

Eluard, Paul, orig. Eugène Grindel (1895–1952), Fr. poet, leading sur-realist. Works include *Mourir de ne pas Mourir* (1924) and *Au Rendez-vous Allemand* (1945).

Elyot, Sir Thomas (*c.* 1490–1546), Eng. author of 1st English-Latin

Parts of an Elm Tree: (a) bud (b) twig with leaves (c) winged fruit with one seed

dictionary (1538). Wrote 1st treatise on education written in English, *The Book Named the Governour* (1531).

Élysée Palace, in Paris, residence of Fr. kings until 1848. Now official residence of Fr. pres.

Elysium, Elysian Fields, in Gk. myth., home of blessed after death; land of perpetual peace and sunshine.

Emancipation, Edict of (1861), pro-clamation freeing all Russian serfs ($\frac{1}{3}$ pop.) issued by Tsar Alexander II. Abuse of edict by landlords helped to provoke Russian Revolution.

Emancipation Proclamation, edict freeing slaves in US, effective 1863, issued by Pres. Lincoln (Sept. 1862) during Civil War. Intended to deplete South's reserves and enhance Union cause in Europe.

embalming, artificial preservation of a body after death. Greatest develop-ment and use by ancient Egyptians, who used spices and soda solutions.

embroidery, ancient art of decorating cloth with varied stitches of coloured or metallic thread. Use recorded in Egypt, Babylonia and China. European medieval work mainly concerned with religious and myth. subjects.

embryo, developing organism prior to emergence in animals from egg membranes by hatching or birth, and in plants from seed. In viviparous animals, applied to organism during early stages of intra-uterine develop-ment, in man up to 2nd month. Study called embryology.

emerald, green gem variety of BERYL. Finest clear emeralds come from Colombia and Brazil.

emerald lizard, *Lacerta viridis,* lizard found in temp. regions. Male's throat turns blue during mating season.

Emerson, Ralph Waldo (1803–82) Amer. essayist, poet and transcen-dentalist philosopher. Unitarian min-ister in Boston (1829–32). In *Nature* (1836) set forth belief in mystical unity of nature; also well known for his *Essays* (1841), *Journal* and *The Conduct of Life.*

emery *see* CORUNDUM.

emigration, act of leaving one's native country to settle in another. Period of greatest emigration was 17th–19th cent. when many Europeans emigra-ted to N and S America and Africa.

Emmet, Robert (1778–1803), Irish patriot, sought French aid for Irish independence. Led uprising of 1802; arrested and executed.

Emmett, Daniel Decatur (1815–1904), Amer. song writer famous for *Old Dan Tucker* (1843) and *Dixie* (1859). A founder of Virginia Min-

Room furnished in the Empire style of decor

strels (1843), he appeared as a black-face singer.

emotion, in psychology, response to stimuli which involves physiological changes; leads to further activity.

emperor moth, *Saturnia pavonia,* purple-grey moth with 4 conspicuous eyespots on wings. Eggs laid in bunches round stem of food plant.

emphysema, disease involving abnormal distention of lung tissues by air or other gases, causing breathing and circulatory deficiencies and chest deformity.

Empire State Building, New York City, tallest (1,250 ft.) building in the world, 102 storeys. Built 1930–1; tourist attraction in Manhattan.

Empire style, decoration and costume of early 19th cent. France.

empiricism, philosophical belief, opposed to RATIONALISM, that all knowledge is derived from experience. Refutes innate ideas and *a priori* truth.

Empson, William (1906–), Eng. poet and critic; wrote *Seven Types of Ambiguity* (1930), a critical study. Later works include *Poems* (1935) and *Milton's God* (1961).

Ems dispatch (July 1870), incident

Emu

ading to Franco-Prussian War. William I of Prussia refused to assure French at Ems meeting that no Hohenzollern would seek Sp. throne. Bismarck provoked Fr. govt. by publishing altered text of William's reply.

emu, *Dromaius novaehollandiae,* 2nd largest living bird; flightless; found in Austral. deserts. Dark brown plumage; incubation takes *c.* 2 months with *c.* 15 eggs.

enamel, hard, smooth, resistant coating on metal, pottery, *etc.,* or varnish, paint or lacquer on wood, metal and leather. First method used by Egyptian, Gk., Roman and medieval craftsmen.

encephalitis, sleeping sickness, inflammation of the brain caused by virus, characterized by degeneration of nerve cells; symptoms include fever, lethargy, paralysis of nerves, followed by mental deterioration, personality change, *etc.*

enclosure, practice of fencing off land formerly subject to common rights (open field system). Arose out of demand for wool in UK (*c.* 1400). Landless workers moved to cities, where they were to supply the labour for Indust. Revolution. Enclosure, by encouraging efficient tillage and reclamation of wasteland, enabled England to achieve agric. self-sufficiency to face rapid population growth of late 18th and 19th cent.

Enclosure Acts, in Eng. history, collective term for legislation to enclose common lands. Statutes passed between 1235 and 1869.

Encyclopedists, 18th cent. collaborators in the Fr. *Encyclopédie* of Diderot and d'Alembert. Contributors included Voltaire, Montesquieu, J.–J. Rousseau.

Endecott or **Endicott, John** (*c.* 1588–1665), Gov. of Massachussetts Bay Colony (1628–30). Organized at Salem a Separatist church on Plymouth model. Harshly prosecuted Quakers.

Enderbury Island *see* CANTON AND ENDERBURY ISLANDS.

Enders, John Franklin (1897–   ), Amer. bacteriologist. With T. H. Weller and F. C. Robbins, awarded Nobel Prize for Physiology and Medicine (1954) for research on polio virus.

endive [UK], **chicory** [US], *Cichorium endiva,* plant native to Europe. Leaves used in salads.

endocrine glands, ductless glands, organs secreting substances directly into bloodstream; concerned with body metabolism, growth and reproduction. Principal glands are thyroid, pituitary, parathyroid, adrenals, parts of pancreas, testes and ovaries.

Endymion, in Gk. myth., shepherd of Mt. Latmos. Loved by Selene, moon goddess, who gave him eternal sleep and immortality.

energy, in physics, the ability or capacity to do work. A body may possess potential energy because of its position (*e.g.* coiled spring), kinetic energy because of its motion (*e.g.* thrown stone).

Enesco, Georges (1881–1955) Romanian violinist, composer and teacher. Works include 2 Romanian rhapsodies for orchestra.

Engadine, upper (Swiss) part of Inn valley, *c.* 60 mi. long; contains Swiss National park, 54 sq. mi. (Lower Engadine), and resorts *e.g.* St Moritz, (Upper Engadine).

Engels, Friedrich (1820–95), Ger. socialist philosopher who collaborated with KARL MARX, esp. on *The Communist Manifesto* (1848). His own influential works include *Landmarks of Scientific Socialism* (1878) and *The Origin of the Family, Private Property and the State* (1884).

engineering, science and art of designing and building engines, machines and public works. Field subdivided into aeronautical, chemical, civil, electrical, hydraulic, mining.

England, country of NW Europe, part of United Kingdom of Great Britain and N. Ireland; occupies S part of Brit. Is. Area: 50,000 sq. mi.; cap. London; other main cities Birmingham, Manchester, Liverpool, Newcastle, Bristol. Mountains and highland masses in N, W and SW. Climate temperate, lying within influence of warm moist SW winds. Britain incorporated into Roman Empire (AD 43). Romans left (410) and people reverted to Celtic state system. Saxon invaders (6th cent.) developed Germanic culture; Vikings and Danes also settled in different areas. State became unified monarchy under Ethelred I (d. 871); ruled by different dynasties after Norman conquest, Plantagenet, Lancaster, York, Tudor, Stuart, Orange, Hanover, Windsor. Agriculture in all areas, most important in S and E; dairy and sheep farming, market gardening and fruit growing. Food, however, largely imported. Fishing centred on E coast. Industry more important, esp. around coalfields of Northumberland, Durham, Yorkshire, Midlands and Lancashire; *e.g.* heavy industries, ship-building and textiles. Extensive communication systems. Population descended from Anglo-Saxons and Danes, with Celtic strains in N and

Sheffield in England's industrial North

W; largely urban-dwelling with persistant migration from rural areas. Administration from Parliament in London, and local govt. by county, borough, urban and rural district councils. Main religious denominations are Church of England, Roman Catholic, Congregational, Methodist, Presbyterian and Baptist. Unit of currency, the pound sterling. Pop. (1965) 45,374,000.

England, Church of, estab. church in England. Henry VIII withdrew allegiance to Pope and declared sovereign head of Eng. church; confirmed by Act of Supremacy (1534). Under Mary, England again Roman Catholic, but Elizabeth I restored Protestantism. Act of Supremacy (1559) defined constitutional position of Church and relation to Crown. High Church holds to ritualism and apostolic succession, Low Church emphasises Bible and preaching. Archbishop of Canterbury is chief primate of C. of E. and of unestab. Episcopal Church in Scotland, Church of Ireland, Church in Wales, Anglican Church of Canada, Church of England in Australia and Church of the Province of New Zealand.

English Channel, strait between England and France, 21 mi. across at narrowest point, Dover-Calais. Swum 1st, Dover-Calais, Captain M. Webb, (25 Aug. 1875), 21 hr. 45 min.; 1st woman swimmer: Gertrude Ederle, (6 Aug. 1926), Cap Gris Nez-Dover, 14 hr. 34 min. Record time of 9 hr. 35 min. France-England (16 Aug. 1964), Barry Watson.

English flute *see* RECORDER.

engraver beetle, *Scolytus rugulosus* introduced into N America from

Epidaurus

Remains of the Agora in Ephesus, once the metropolis of Asia Minor

Europe, common orchard pest.

engraving, process by which lines are cut on wood, metal or stone, esp. with an instrument called a burin, for reproduction by printing. *See* ETCHING.

Enlightenment, Age of, Age of Reason (18th cent.) period of rationalist, liberal, humanitarian and scientific trends. Expressed in such works as Diderot's *Encyclopédie,* and the thought of Voltaire, Rousseau, Montesquieu, Hume, Paine, Kant and Lessing; and in the Fr. and Amer. revolutions.

Ensor, James Sydney, Baron (1860–1949), Belgian painter and etcher who broke away from realistic tradition. Works include *The Skate* and *Strange Masks.*

Entebbe, city in S Uganda on NW shore of L. Victoria Nyanza; founded 1893. Pop. (1968) *c.* 11,000.

entente cordiale *see* TRIPLE ALLIANCE and TRIPLE ENTENTE.

enteritis, inflammation of the intestines, particularly small intestine, caused by food poisoning or infection.

entomology, orig. branch of zoology dealing with insects. Now restricted to study of true, *i.e.* 6-legged, insects.

entrepreneur, in economics, person who assumes risk and management of industry or trade. Classical economists of 18th cent. tended to confuse him with capitalist, whose role is often more passive. Joseph Schumpter and other 20th cent. economists identified his competitive drive for innovation and improvement as motive force behind capitalist development.

Enugu, city in SE Nigeria, centre of coal-mining industry of W Africa.

Cap. of secessionist BIAFRA ; outbreak of Nigerian civil war (1967)

Enver Pasha (1881–1922), Turkish general. Leader of YOUNG TUR revolution (1908) and of Turkish forces in World War 1. Defeated exiled to Russia.

enzymes, the catalysts of most c the chemical changes occurring i living cells. Some are found in natura secretions such as digestive juice pepsin and trypsin. Vegetabl enzymes also occur, *e.g.* diastol which converts starch into sugar.

Eocene *see* GEOLOGICAL TABLE.

eohippus, small fossil animal, th earliest horse, found in Eurasia and N America at beginning of Eocene period.

eolithic *see* STONE AGE.

Eos [Gk: dawn], in Gk. myth. goddess of dawn. Her Roman coun terpart was Aurora.

Epaminondas (*c.* 418–362 BC) Theban statesman and general, whose methods influenced Alexander the Great. Defeated Spartans at Leuctra (371 BC) and at Mantinea (362 BC) Founded Megapolis in Arcadia.

Ephesians, epistle of NT, written by St Paul (*c.* AD 62) during his Roman imprisonment. A plea for Christian unity addressed to Eastern Church.

Ephesus, chief of the 12 Ionian towns of Asia Minor in antiquity. Contains ruined Temple of Diana (6th cent. BC).

epic poem, long, narrative poem, orig. in hexameters; subject usually the exploits of the heroes of tradition or history. Examples are *The Iliad* and *The Odyssey* (Gk.); *The Aeneid* (Latin); *Beowulf* (O.E.); *Chanson de Roland* (Fr.); *Paradise Lost* (Eng.); *Gerusalemme Liberate* (Ital.).

Epictetus (*c.* 55–135), Gk. Stoic philosopher. Became a slave in Rome, was later freed and retired to Nicopolis. His teachings advocated the brotherhood of man.

Epicurus (*c.* 341–270 BC), Gk. atheist philosopher and founder of Epicurean school. Believed that life should be happy and that one should avoid pain and seek pleasure.

Epidaurus, temple precinct, *c.* 20 mi. E of Argos, dedicated to healer-god, Asclepius.

epidote, brittle, subtranslucent, hard mineral. Usually pistachio-green and found in calcareous rocks.

epiglottis, flap of mucous membrane and cartilage in mammals at base of tongue which closes the GLOTTIS during swallowing.

epigram, concise and pointed saying, often in verse, orig. Gk.

epilepsy, chronic nervous disorder characterized by fits in which the patient suffers muscular spasms and may lose consciousness for a short period (petit mal) or long period (grand mal).

Epirus, prov. of NW Greece; flourished esp. as kingdom under Pyrrhus (3rd cent. BC).

epistles, in NT, 21 letters, traditionally ascribed to the Apostles, addressed to some of the new churches and individual members of them.

epitaph, lines in verse inscribed on tombstones or other monuments to commemorate the dead, sometimes serious and in literary form, sometimes scurrilous.

Epsom, Eng. town in Surrey, near London, venue of the Oaks, Derby and other famous horse races.

Epstein, Sir Jacob (1880–1959), Brit. sculptor of Russo-Polish descent. Influenced by vorticism and African art.

equal area projections *see* PROJECTIONS.

equation, in chemistry, a statement of a reaction between substances begun with the product: *e.g.* $H_2 + Cl_2 = 2HCl$.

equation, in mathematics, statement of equality of 2 quantities or algebraic expressions: *e.g.* $(x + y)(x + y) = x^2 + 2xy + y^2$.

equator, imaginary line forming a circle drawn around the earth, or a planet, equidistant from the poles, dividing the globe into N and S hemispheres.

equinox, time of year when day and night are equal throughout the world because sun is exactly overhead at the equator at noon and is 12 hr. above and 12 hr. below horizon. Occurs 20 or 21 Mar. (vernal equinox) and 22 or 23 Sept. (autumnal).

equity, principles of justice developed by Court of Chancery in England to supplement Common Law. Fused with Common Law (1875).

Erasmus, Desiderius (1466–1536) Dutch Augustinian monk and humanist philosopher. Published 1st Gk. edition of NT (1516). Lifelong opponent of religious bigotry, his thought influenced Thomas More and Eng. reformers.

Erastianism, doctrine that punitive measures against sin should be left to civil authorities. Named after Thomas Erastus (1524–83) a follower of ZWINGLI.

Erato, in classical myth., Muse of the love lyric.

Eratosthenes of Alexandria (*c.* 275–*c.* 195 BC), Gk. astronomer and mathematician. Measured circumference of the earth to within 50 mi. of present estimates.

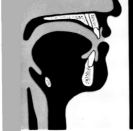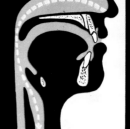

In the pharynx or throat the windpipe and the food passage join. The epiglottis leaves the windpipe free when breathing (blue dots), but closes it when swallowing to allow food (black arrow) to pass freely down the oesophagus.

Erebus and Terror, volcanic peaks (13,202 ft. and 10,750 ft.), on Ross Is., Ross Sea, Antarctica. Discovered (1841) by Sir James C. Ross.

Erfurt, indust. town of E Germany, 64 mi. SW of Leipzig. Market town and rly. junction. Pop. 190,000.

erg, unit of work or energy: 1 erg represents work done when force of 1 dyne acts through distance of 1 cm.

ergosterol, substance found in human skin, which when exposed to ultraviolet radiation (sunlight) becomes vitamin D.

Eric the Red (*fl.* 10th cent.), Norse chieftain. Discovered and colonized Greenland; father of Leif Ericsson.

Ericsson, Leif (*fl. c.* AD 1000), traditional Norse discoverer of America. Son of Eric the Red.

Erie, N Amer. Indian tribe of Iroquoian stock; inhabited area around L. Erie in 17th cent. Traditional enemies of Iroquois league, almost exterminated in 1656 after one of the most destructive Indian wars. A few descendants live on reservations in Oklahoma.

Erie, Lake *see* GREAT LAKES.

Erie Canal, connects Hudson R. with L. Erie. Completed 1825, it was improved (1918). Now called the New York State Barge Canal, it connects industrial cities, *e.g.* Cleveland and New York City.

Erigena, John Scotus (810–*c.* 877) Irish theologian, master of the palace school in Paris. Work includes 1st medieval synthesis of philosophy and theology *De Divisione Naturae.*

Erinnyes *see* EUMENIDES.

Eritrea, prov. of Ethiopia from 1962; Ital. colony (1936–41). Narrow agric. coastal plain on Red Sea. Cap. Asmara; chief port, Massawa.

Erlanger, Joseph (1874–1965), Amer. physiologist. With H. S. Dasser shared Nobel Prize for Physiology and Medicine (1944) for research into functions of nerve threads.

Erlenmeyer, Emil (1825–1909), Ger. chemist, originator of the flask named after him. Discovered formula for naphthalene (1866).

ermine moth, *Hyponomenta malinellus,* moth related to tiger moth, with spotted wings. Caterpillar is very hairy, like small ermine.

ermine, stoat, *Mustela erminea,* fur-yielding mammal of weasel family, *c.* 11 in. long with 5 in. tail. Tawny above and white below, turning white in winter in N countries. Called short-tailed weasel in US.

Ernst, Max (1891–). Ger. surrealist painter and sculptor, a Dadaist in his early years.

Eros, Gk god of love. According to Hesiod's *Theogony* he was 1st of the gods; process of procreation initiated by him. Later he is described as a boy, son of Aphrodite.

erosion, process by which land areas are worn away, including weathering of rock, transport and deposition of subsequent debris, by rivers, oceans, ice and atmospheric action. Erosion of soil (denudation), resulting in removal of fertile topsoil can be a problem in agric. areas.

Erse *see* CELTIC.

Erskine, Thomas, 1st Baron (1750–1823), Scot. lawyer. Made lord chancellor and a peer (1806). Defended Thomas Paine's *The Rights of Man* and revised libel laws.

erythrocyte, red blood corpuscle, formed in red bone marrow which carries HAEMOGLOBIN to combine with oxygen in lungs and return carbon dioxide from the tissues.

Esau, in OT, son of Isaac, cheated of his inheritance by his twin Jacob. Ancestor of the Edomites.

Eschenbach, Wolfram von *see* WOLFRAM VON ESCHENBACH.

Escoffier, Auguste (1847–1935), chef and writer on cookery. Published *Le Livre des Menus* (1912) and *Ma Cuisine* (1934).

Escorial, former royal residence 26 mi. S of Madrid, Spain, built 1563–84. Contains noted library and collection of Sp. paintings.

Esdras I and **II,** apocryphal Books of OT dating from 6th cent. BC; mainly transcripts of EZRA. Esdras II is an account of Ezra's revelations.

Esenin or **Yesenin, Sergei Aleksandrovich** (1895–1925), Russ. Imaginist lyric poet, one of the most popular of the early Revolution.

Eskimo, people of Arctic and Labrador coasts. Pop. (1963) *c.* 55,000. Six main cultural groups: MacKenzie; Copper or Blond Eskimos, thought to be of mixed descent from Norse colonists of Greenland; Caribou; Central; Labrador; East and West Greenlanders. Culture varies from area to area but most build snow or semi-subterranean winter houses and have skin summer tents, hunt seal, bear, walrus and caribou. Social organization is centred on village. Origins thought to be the Barren Lands and Aleutian Islands (1000 BC).

Eskimo-Aleut, group of indigenous N Amer. languages, with a steadily declining number of speakers.

esparto, Spanish grass, halfa, *Stipa tenacissima,* tall perennial grass of S Spain and N Africa. Furnishes tough, tenacious fibre used in papermaking.

Esperanto, artificial international auxiliary language, based on Latin Romance word roots. Invented (1887) by a Pole, Dr. L. Zamenhof.

espionage, spying, clandestine procuring of information, esp. military, about a foreign country; developed by Frederick the Great. By 1900 most nations had a secret service.

Essen, West German indust. city in N Rhine-Westphalia. Centre of Ruhr coal, iron and steel district; Pop. 727,000.

Essenes, sect, possibly referred to in Dead Sea Scrolls, of pre-Christian Jews who rejected sacrificial temple cult.

essential oils, volatile substances of vegetable origin; impart characteristic flavour or odour to the plant of origin. Used as perfumes and flavouring agents.

Essex, maritime county of SE England, incl. Canvey and Mersea Is. Area: 1,419 sq. mi.; county town, Chelmsford; other towns, Southend, Colchester, Clacton. Mainly agric., with oil installations on Thames estuary in S, and tourism around coast. Epping Forest in W. University of Essex opened (1964) near Colchester. Pop. (1965) 1,221,230.

Essex, Robert Devereux, 2nd Earl of (1567–1601), Eng. earl, favourite of Queen Elizabeth I. Fell from favour and executed after failure of Irish expedition (1599) and abortive revolt.

Estates-General, French national assembly (1302–1789), in which chief

estates, comprising clergy, nobility and commons, were separated. First summoned by Philip IV; powers never clearly defined. Did not meet (1614–1789) until Louis XVI called it to solve govt. financial crisis. Dominated by 3rd estate (commons) who tried to transform it from consultative to legislative assembly; defied king declaring itself NATIONAL ASSEMBLY.

ester, organic compound formed by reaction of alcohol and acid. Some fats and vegetable or animal oils are esters of GLYCEROL. Used in making explosives, paints, perfumes.

Esterhazy, [Marie Charles] Ferdinand Walsin (1847–1923), Fr. army officer who confessed (1899) to guilt in DREYFUS AFFAIR. After acquittal by court-martial (1898), he fled to England. Confessed (1899) to selling military secrets to Germany.

Esther, hist. book of OT. Story of Esther, Jewish wife of Ahasuerus (Artaxerxes), King of Persia (485–465 BC), who prevented massacre of Jews.

Estienne, Robert (1503–59), Fr. printer and scholar. Son of founder of family of printers, **Henri Estienne** (d. 1520). Printed and edited many works, specializing in classical authors, dictionaries (esp. Latin thesaurus in 1541), and critical editions of the Bible. Nephew, **Henri Estienne** (1531–98), took over Geneva business; compiled *Thesaurus Graecae Linguae* (1572).

Estonian, Finnic language with 1 million speakers in Soviet Repub. of Estonia.

Estonian SSR, repub. of USSR, with coastline on Gulf of Finland, Baltic and Gulf of Riga. Area: 17,780 sq. mi.; cap. Tallinn. Agric. and dairy farming are main industries. Pop. 1,196,000.

estrogen [US] *see* OESTROGEN.

estrus [US] *see* OESTRUS.

estuary, inlet of sea at mouth of river where fresh and salt water mix as river water meets sea water.

etching, process by which parts of a metal plate are eaten away with acid to produce an original which may be used like an ENGRAVING for printing.

Ethelred [II] the Unready (*c.* 968–1016), king of England (978–1013, 1014–16). His inability to deal with Danish peril earned him name of the Unready. Temporarily deposed (1013) by Danish Swend.

ether, in chemistry, type of organic compound, characterized by linking oxygen atom with 2 alkyl radicals. Popular usage refers to anaesthetic. Einstein finally disproved theory of

ether as transmitter of energy phenomena in physics.

Ethiopia, independent empire of NE Africa, incl. Eritrea. Area: 400,000 sq. mi.; cap. Addis Ababa. Region of high plateaux and mountains, trop. in

valleys, temp. on higher land. Conquered by Italians (1935–6). Liberated by Brit. troops (1941) and Emperor Haile Selassie restored. Mainly pastoral, exporting coffee, hides and skins. Pop. (1965) 23,000,000.

Ethiopic, Semitic Afro-Asian group of languages. *See* AMHARIC.

ethnology, orig. science of distributions of human races, now study of particular cultures.

ethyl, organic radical or group of atoms capable of behaving like an element. Basis of several important compounds incl. ethyl alcohol.

ethylene, colourless, faintly odorous, sweet-tasting gas; with oxygen, forms an explosive mixture. Used as illuminating gas, as anaesthetic, and to bring out colour of citrus fruit.

Etna, in E Sicily, highest active volcano (10,750 ft.) in Europe. Subject of Gk. and Roman legends.

Eton College, Eng. public school for boys founded (1440) by Henry VI.

Etruria, territory of ETRUSCANS in W Central Italy, now parts of Tuscany and W Umbria.

Etruscans (12th cent. BC), ancient people of W Central Italy who came from Asia Minor; at height of their civilization *c.* 500 BC. Wealth based partly on knowledge of metalworking; noted for sculpture, tomb decorations and architecture. Declined in 5th and 4th cent. BC when Romans captured Veii (396 BC) and Gauls invaded N.

etymology, study of derivation of words. It revealed regular phonological relations, firstly in Indo-European languages (as in GRIMM'S LAW).

eucalyptus, evergreen timber tree of myrtle family native to W Australia. Yields gums, resins, oils, tars and useful woods. Common species is blue gum, *Eucalyptus globulus.*

Eucharist, sacrament of Holy Communion in certain Christian churches. Word denotes thanksgiving; applied to consecration of bread and wine.

Eucken, Rudolph Christoph (1846–1926), Ger. philosopher of 'activism',

Mount Etna, near Catania, Sicily

theory based on ethics and idealism. Nobel Prize for Literature (1908).

Euclid (*c.* 300 BC), Gk. mathematician. His treatise, *Elements*, comprising postulates, rules, theorems, problems, formed basis of Euclidean geometry. Writings in astronomy and mechanics attributed to him.

Euclid of Megara (*c.* 450–*c.* 380 BC), Gk. philosopher, disciple of Socrates; held that sole reality is idea of virtue.

Eugene, Prince of Savoy (1663–1736), Fr. soldier. Joined Austrian army, led defeat of Turks at Zenta (1697). Allied leader, with Marlborough in War of Spanish Succesion, at Blenheim (1704), Oudenarde (1708) and Malplaquet (1709). Commanded an army which defeated Turks at Belgrade (1716).

eugenics, study of human genetics, particularly of those factors which could improve future generations.

euglenoids, class of algae common in fresh water, esp. ponds rich in organic substance.

Eulenspiegel, Till, Ger. peasant hero (14th–15th cent.) of satirical tales in which he scores off his social superiors in often coarse and brutal practical jokes. Theme became popular throughout Europe.

Euler, Leonhard (1707–83), Swiss mathematician; one of the founders of modern mathematics; developed new methods of analysis.

Euler-Chelpin, Hans Karl August Simon von (1873–1964), Swedish chemist b. Germany who, with Sir Arthur Harden, was awarded Nobel Prize in Chemistry (1929) for work on enzymes.

Eumenides 'Kindly Ones', in Gk. myth., the Furies who tortured conscience of evil-doers, esp. murderers and traitors. Also called Erinnyes 'Terrible Ones.'

euphonium, brass instrument of the FLUGELHORN type with 4 valves, used in brass bands.

Euphrates, river in SW Asia, *c.* 1,700 mi. long. Rises in E Turkey and merges with the Tigris in Iraq. Mesopotamia on Euphrates, was site of earliest known civilization.

euphuism, literary style named after *Euphues* (1579), a romance by John Lyly. Characteristics are antithesis, use of far-fetched allusions.

eurhythmics, teaching methods developed by Jaques-Dalcroze of expressing harmony through bodily movements.

Euric (*fl.* 5th cent.), king of the Visigoths of Spain (466–*c.* 484). Conquered nearly all Spain and part of Gaul.

Euripides (*c.* 480–406 BC), Gk. tragedian. Plays show lively interest in human character and rational approach to the gods. Surviving plays include *Alcestis, Medea, Ion, Trojan Women* and *Bacchae.*

Europa, in Gk. myth., daughter of Agenor of Phoenicia. Zeus in the shape of a bull abducted her to Crete. Derivation of *Europe.*

Europe, continent comprising *c.* 4,000,000 sq. mi. Forms peninsula of Eurasian land mass projecting into Altantic, separated from Asia by Ural and Caucasus mountains, Black and Caspian seas. Mountain chain, incl. Pyrennees, Alps, Carpathians and Balkans, extends from Iberian Peninsula to Caucasus. Highest point is Mt. Elbrus (18,481 ft.) in Caucasus. Between these young fold mountains and the ancient Scandinavian shield in N, extends mainly fertile agric. land of European plain, drained by Volga, Don, Dnieper, Danube, Elbe, Oder, Rhine, Seine, Meuse, Garonne and Moselle. S of mountain chain are mountainous peninsulas *e.g.* Iberia, Italy, Balkans, and rich agric. basins of the Po and Danube. Europe is subject to the moderating influence of W Atlantic winds; climate varies considerably from the cold N to warm sunny S, precipitation decreases E from humid W coast. In N, TUNDRA and coniferous forest; on fertile European plain, with rich mineral deposits, industrialization has occurred. River valleys are densely populated, esp. in the Danube and Po basins and along the coasts of Italy and Portugal. Politically, Europe is divided into many sovereign states of varying size. Pop. 610,000,000. See map p. 210.

European Atomic Energy Community (EURATOM), created 1958 to promote atomic energy development within EUROPEAN ECONOMIC COMMUNITY. Aims include common market for nuclear raw materials and equipment and joint research.

European bison *see* WISENT.

European Coal and Steel Community (ECSC), formed 1952 by Benelux group, France, W Germany and Italy, to provide its members with unified market for coal and steel products.

European Community, name for merger (1965) of Council of Ministers of EEC, ECSC, and EURATOM. Comprises BENELUX nations, France, W Germany, and Italy. Greece and Turkey have associate status.

European Economic Community (EEC), the Common Market, comprising Belgium, the Netherlands, Luxembourg, France, W Germany

Benedictine Abbey at Melk, on the river Danube in NE Europe

and Italy; Greece became associate member (1962). Founded by Rome Treaty (1957). Created customs union and programmed gradual elimination of tariff barriers between members, and free movement of labour and capital. Member nations achieved rapid economic progress. UK successfully negotiated entry (1971) after 2 bids failed (1963, 1968).

European Free Trade Association (EFTA), customs union and trading group, estab. (1960) by UK, Sweden, Denmark, Norway, Austria, Switzerland and Portugal. Finland became associate member (1961). Provided for gradual reduction of tariff restrictions between members.

European Nuclear Energy Agency *see* ORGANIZATION FOR ECONOMIC CO-OPERATION AND DEVELOPMENT.

Eurydice *see* ORPHEUS.

eurypterid, fossil invertebrate of Paleozoic period, like large aquatic scorpion reaching 7 ft. in length.

Eusebio, Ferreira da Silva, footballer b. Mozambique. Signed for Benfica of Lisbon, Portugal (1961). Footballer of the Year (1965). Capped by Portugal 30 times.

eustachian tube, canal of bone and cartilage connecting pharynx and middle ear in vertebrates.

Euterpe, in Gk. myth., Muse of lyric poetry.

euthanasiä, painless killing; advocated from earliest times for people suffering from incurable and painful diseases.

Evans, Sir Arthur John (1851–1941), Eng. archaeologist. Excavations in Crete led to discovery of remains of a civilization he called Minoan.

Evans, Caradoc (1878–1945), Welsh short-story writer and novelist. Works include *My People* (1915), *My Neighbours* (1919) and *Nothing to Pay* (1930).

Evans, Dame Edith Mary (1888–), Eng. stage and film actress;

successes include Rosalind in *As You Like It* and Lady Bracknell in *The Importance of Being Earnest*.

Evans, Geraint Llewellyn (1922–), Welsh opera singer, principal baritone at Covent Garden, London and Glyndebourne, Sussex.

Evans, Herbert McLean (1882–), Amer. anatomist and embryologist, discoverer of vitamin E (1922).

Evans, Maurice (1901–), Amer. actor; supervisor of the New York City Center Theater (1949–51). Noted for Shakespearian productions.

Evans-Pritchard, Edward Evan (1902–), Brit. social anthropologist. Author of *Essays in Social Anthropology* (1962).

evaporation, conversion of a liquid into a vapour. Rate of evaporation increased with application of heat and by lowering of pressure on the liquid.

Eve, OT wife of Adam; in *Genesis* she precipitated the fall of mankind.

Evelyn, John (1620–1706), Eng. writer, whose Diary covered 1620– 1706 (pub. 1818–19). In London during the Plague and the Great Fire. A founder of the Royal Society.

evening primrose, *Oenothera biennis*

plant native to N America; yellow flowers open in late afternoon.

Everest, Mount, highest point (29,028 ft.) in the world, in Nepal Himalayas. First climbed (1953) by Tensing Norkay and Sir Edmund Hillary.

Everglades, swamp area on S tip of Florida peninsula. Became US National Park (1941).

evergreen, tree or plant which remains in foliage throughout the year. In the tropics many broad-leaved angiosperms are evergreen, whereas in cold areas evergreens are chiefly conifers *e.g.* pines, firs, hemlocks and spruces.

everlasting flowers, flowers that if hung upside down until dried will last for 2–3 yr. Often dyed or bleached white. Includes flowers of *Xerantheum, Helipterum, Waitzia,* etc.

Everyman, medieval morality play in which the hero, Everyman, is summoned by Death to appear before God. Of his friends, only Good Deeds will accompany him.

Evesham, Battle of, fought (1265) near Evesham, Worcestershire, England. Victory for Henry III's forces decisive in struggle against SIMON DE MONTFORT.

Evil Eye, apparent ability to cause ill-luck, injury or death by a glance; once attributed to certain people, esp. witches.

evolution, theory of the gradual shaping of the Earth and of life on Earth. Concept was first defined by Darwin and Lamarck against bitter opposition of most Christian thinkers who believed in a literal 'creation'. Evidence of evolution was first sought and documented in anatomy and embryological data and from comparative study of fossil remains.

Excalibur, in Eng. myth. name of King Arthur's magic sword. It ensured his immunity in battle.

excavator, mechanical device for digging holes, used in preparation of trenches, reservoirs, embankments and in mining operations.

exchange, foreign, rate at which currency of one country is exchanged for that of another. Varies with the state of market balance of payments position and demand for and confidence in given currencies.

excise, duties levied on goods produced within a country, distinct from customs duties imposed on goods entering a country from abroad. Purchase tax, levied in some form on most articles, is included in excise revenue receipts.

excommunication, act of excluding a person from membership of a religious body, usually to punish the person expelled and to protect remaining members from his influence. Used against those condemned of heresy by R.C. Church.

excretion, elimination of useless or harmful metabolic products; organs mainly concerned being kidneys of vertebrates, malpighian tubes of insects, and nephridia of invertebrates.

existentialism, philosophy which tries to explain man's nature solely in the light of his experience, derived from Kierkegaard and Heidegger. Exponents include J.–P. Sartre, Albert Camus, Karl Jaspers.

Exodus [Gk: going out], 2nd book of Pentateuch. Deals with period of Jewish history during which Israelites, under Moses, escaped from captivity in Egypt; Moses received, on Mt. Sinai, the TEN COMMANDMENTS and other laws from God.

expansion, in physics, enlargement of a body in bulk or surface. Rise in temperature causes expansion of volume in solids, liquids and gases. Amount of expansion which a unit volume of any substance undergoes per 1° rise in temperature is called its co-efficient of cubic expansion.

explosives, materials undergoing decomposition or combustion exerting enormous sudden pressure. Commonly known explosives include gunpowder, dynamite and gelignite.

expressionism, term for art which tries to represent an emotional state. In painting Bosch, El Greco and Goya used this approach; 19th and 20th cent. expressionism developed through the work of van Gogh, Kokoschka, Chagall, Rouault, Jack Yeats and Kandinsky, and in the theatre through that of Strindberg, Brecht and Eugene O'Neill.

extrasensory perception [ESP], faculty of perception beyond known sense organs. Belief in the existence of ESP is not widely accepted.

Extreme Unction, sacrament of the R.C. and Orthodox Churches of anointing and giving final Communion to the dying.

extrusive rock, any IGNEOUS ROCK which reaches the earth's surface by volcanic action, incl. lava and pyroclastic material.

Eyck, Jan van, (*c.* 1370–1440) and his brother **Hubert van Eyck** (*c.* 1366–1426), Dutch painters who founded Flemish school. Hubert painted most of altarpiece of Ghent Cathedral, *Adoration of the Lamb.* Jan was court painter to Philip the Good of Burgundy.

eye, organ of sight, consisting of

Panel of Ghent altarpiece by Hubert and Jan v. Eyck

light-sensitive mechanism which transmits stimuli to central nervous system of the body. Human eye consists of ball with transparent cornea in front with iris whose muscles control amount of light received through lens by RETINA at back of ball, for transmission along optic nerves to brain.

eyebright, *Euphrasia officinalis,* annual herb, native to N temperate regions.

Eyre, Edward John (1815–1901), Brit. colonial administrator. Explorer in Australia (1833–45); published *Discoveries in Central Australia* (1845). Appointed Gov. of Jamaica (1864); recalled (1866) for conduct in suppressing a Negro revolt.

Eyre, salt lake in S Australia, discovered by E. J. Eyre (1840). Area: *c.* 3,430 sq. mi. Frequently dry.

Eysenck, Hans Jurgen (1916–   ), Brit. psychologist, author of *Uses and Abuses of Psychology* (1953), *Smoking, Health and Personality* (1965).

Ezekiel, prophetical book of OT, written by priest, Ezekiel (*fl.* 592 BC). Foretells fall of Jerusalem.

Ezra, historical Book of OT, opening with return of Jews from exile in Babylon to Jerusalem (537 BC) and covering 80 yr., during which Temple was rebuilt.

F

Fabergé, Peter Carl, orig. Karl Gustavovich Fabergé (1846–1920), Russ. goldsmith. Work included celebrated Easter eggs commissioned by Tsars.

fable, short moral tale; characters often beasts or inanimate objects. Aesop provided model.

fabliau, popular comic, often bawdy tale, characterized by satiric verse. Popular in medieval France.

Fabre, Jean Henri (1823–1915), Fr. teacher and entomologist. Published popular scientific works incl. *Science élémentaire* (1862–5), *The Life of the Fly* (Eng. tr. 1913).

Factory acts, legislation of Brit. Parl. to regulate conditions and hours of work, safety and sanitary provisions in factories and workshops. Health and Morals of Apprentices Act (1802); Cotton Mills Act (1819) forbade employment of children under 9 and reduced hours of labour for under-16s to 72 per week; further acts (1845, 47). Factory inspectors appointed (1833).

Faeroese, Scandinavian dialect related to Icelandic and medieval Norse. Language of Faeroe Is.

Fahrenheit, Gabriel Daniel (1686–1736), Ger. instrument maker, 1st to recognize superiority of mercury over alcohol for thermometers. Devised Fahrenheit scale on which water freezes at 32°F and boils at 212°F.

faience, various kinds of glazed pottery with decorative designs. Name from Faenza, Italy, where pottery made (15th cent.).

Fairbanks, Douglas, orig. Douglas Elton Ulman (1883–1939), Amer. stage and film actor; appeared in *Mark of Zorro* (1920), *The Three Musketeers* (1921). Co-founder of United Artists.

Fairbanks, Douglas Elton Jr. (1909–   ), Amer. film actor whose roles include *Dawn Patrol, Gunga Din.* Created Honorary KBE [Knight of the British Empire] (1949).

Fairfax, Thomas, 3rd Baron Fairfax of Cameron (1612–71), Brit. soldier, commanded Parliamentary army dur-

Madonna and Child: faience plaque by Della Robbia

ing Civil War. Defeated Charles I at Naseby (1645), but refused to sit as judge in king's trial. Resigned as commander (1650) because of opposition to invasion of Scotland.

fairy, in folklore, supernatural being with magical powers. Concept and description varies; described as demonic, mischievous, loving and bountiful. National variations include Arab djinns, Eng. pixies, Ger. elves, Scandinavian trolls.

Faisal, Malik Faisal bin Abdul Aziz al Saud (1905–   ), king of Saudi Arabia (1964–   ); became viceroy of the Hejaz (1926); declared Crown Prince (1953). P.M. and foreign min. (1957–61).

Falaise, town in Calvados, N France with Norman remains.

Falange, orig. *Falange Española,* fascist movement and party in Spain. Founded (1933) by José Antonio

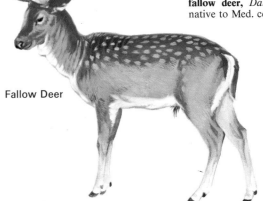

Fallow Deer

Primo de Rivera. At end of Sp. Civil War (1939), programme became basic law of Sp. state under Franco. Party dissolved 1966.

falcon, bird of prey of family Falconidae; large wing span, powerful hooked beak and rapid flight. Often trained for use in hunting. Species include peregrine, merlin and kestrel.

Falkland Islands, group of islands in S Atlantic, *c.* 300 mi. E of Strait of Magellan. Area: 4,700 sq. mi.; cap. Port Stanley. Whaling and sheep rearing main occupations. Ownership disputed by Britain and Argentina. Pop. (1968) 2,200.

fall line, boundary between uplands and coastal plain, where rivers drop in falls or rapids and provide water power for industry. Philadelphia and Washington are fall line cities.

Falla, Manuel de (1876–1946), Sp. composer. Works include ballets *El Amor Brujo* and *The Three-cornered Hat,* and opera *La Vida Breve.*

fall-out, atmospheric, radioactive material resulting from nuclear explosion. May cause various diseases (leukemia, bone cancer) as well as genetic damage. Atmosphere now measured regularly for evidence of radiation.

fallow deer, *Dama dama,* mammal native to Med. countries, rare in wild state. Herds in S Europe are semi-domesticated; in Britain, they are park animals.

Fanfani, Amintore (1908–), Ital. politician. Christian Democrat, 4 times Premier, often in coalition with left-wing parties.

Fangio y Cia, Juan Manuel (1911–), Argentinian racing driver. World Champion 5 times (1951, 1954–7). Retired (1958) after 24 Grand Prix victories.

Fantin-Latour, Ignace Henri Jean Théodore (1836–1904), Fr. painter and lithographer, noted for portrait groups of famous contemporaries.

Faraday, Michael (1791–1867), Eng. physicist and chemist. Liquefied chlorine (1823), discovered benzol (1825). Work in electrolysis laid foundations of electro-chemistry. Showed (1831) that motion of a conductor in magnetic field led to generation of an electric current.

Farjeon, Eleanor (1881–1965), Eng. novelist and dramatist. Best known for children's books incl. *Martin Pippin in the Apple Orchard* (1922), *Over the Garden Wall* (1933).

Farnese, Ital. noble family of Parma. **Alessandro Farnese** (1468–1549) became pope as Paul III (1534). Excommunicated Henry VIII of England (1538), made Parma a duchy (1545), which remained in family until its extinction (1731). Paul III's grandson **Ottavio Farnese** (1520–86) married Margaret of Parma, daughter of Charles V. His son **Alessandro Farnese** (1545–92) became a general under Philip II of Spain. Appointed Sp. gov. of Netherlands (1578); forced Henry of Navarre to raise siege of Paris (1590). **Elizabeth Farnese** (1692–1766), wife of Philip V of Spain, gained duchy for son Philip (1748).

Faroes, Faeroe Islands, group of 21 volcanic islands in N Atlantic. Area: 540 sq. mi.; cap. Thorshavn (on largest island Stromo). Main exports, fish and wool. Became Danish crown possession (1814); achieved virtual autonomy (1848). Pop. (1968) 37,000.

Farouk I (1920–65), king of Egypt (1936–52). Forced to abdicate (1952) by military coup of Mohammed Naguib and Abdel Nasser. Went into exile in Europe.

Farragut, David Glasgow (1801–70), Amer. naval officer noted for victories during Civil War over Confederate navy at New Orleans (1862) and Mobile Bay (1863). Ranks of vice admiral (1864) and admiral (1866) specially created for him by Congress.

Farrell, James T[homas] (1904–),

Amer. novelist, best known as author of 'Studs Lonigan' trilogy (1932–5).

fascism, polit. movement of militant, totalitarian and nationalistic character. Postulates that state is all-powerful; govt. is an OLIGARCHY. Violently opposes communism and tends to isolate minority groups. Name from Latin *fasces,* bundles of rods (carried as symbols of authority). Ital. Fascist party, formed (1919) by Benito Mussolini, orig. republican and socialist in outlook; Fascist govt. in Italy (1922–43). By 1936, there were fascist parties in Germany, Austria, Hungary, Poland, Romania, Bulgaria, Greece and Japan. Ger. NAZISM and Sp. FALANGE strongly influenced by Mussolini. Fascism in UK, *see* SIR OSWALD MOSLEY.

Fashoda Incident, Anglo-French dispute (1898–9) over control of upper Nile region. Fr. forces took Fashoda (now Kodok) but withdrew upon Brit. insistence. Peaceful settlement marked end of Fr. claims in area.

Fates [Gk: *Moirae*; Lat: *Parcae*], in classical myth., daughters of Zeus and Themis; 3 goddesses who presided over course of human life.

Fatimite, Fatimide, Arabian family claiming descent from Fatima, a daughter of Mohammed the Prophet. Ruled Egypt (*c.* 968–1171). Obaidullah claimed caliphate (909) and conquered Cyrenaica and Libya. Successors conquered Sicily, W Arabia, Palestine and Syria. Cairo

became Fatimite cap. (969). Rule officially ended (1171).

fats, naturally occurring substances consisting of glycerides of higher fatty acids found in plants and animals.

Faubus, Orval Eugene (1910–). Democrat Gov. of Arkansas (1955–67). Called out Arkansas National Guard to prevent integration of Central High School, Little Rock (1957).

Faulkner, William (1897–1962), Amer. author. Works, mostly set in Mississippi, depicting decadence of the South, include *The Sound and the Fury* (1929), *Sanctuary* (1931), *Requiem for a Nun* (1951). Awarded Nobel Prize for Literature (1949).

fault, in geology, fracture of strata due to earth movements; may be small or deep and extend a great distance.

Fauré, Gabriel (1845–1924), Fr. composer and teacher. Director of Paris Conservatoire (1905–20). Compositions include opera *Pénélope,* songs and a Requiem (1887).

Faust, medieval Ger. legendary figure. Supposedly a scholar, said to have sold his soul to the devil for 24 yr. Story inspired Marlowe and Goethe, among others.

Fauvism, short-lived modern art movement (*c.* 1905–8). Used bold forms and brilliant colour. Exponents included Matisse, Dufy and Derain.

Fawcett, Dame Millicent, née Garrett

Flower painting by Ignace Fantin-Latour

(1847– 1929), leader of non-militant woman suffrage movement in England. Pres. of National Union of Women's Suffrage Societies (1897– 1918).

Fawkes, Guy (1570– 1606), Eng. conspirator, leader in GUNPOWDER PLOT (1605) to blow up Houses of Parl. Hanged after capture and confession.

feather-star, sea-lily, off-shore marine animal of *Crinoidea* class of Echinodermata; 1 in.– 3 ft. long.

Federal Bureau of Investigation (FBI), branch of US Dept. of Justice, independent of state police forces, estab. (1908) to investigate crimes against federal law. Enforces laws against espionage, white-slave traffic, blackmail, racketeering, *etc.*

Federal Communications Commission (FCC), US govt. agency estab. by Congress (1934) to license and regulate television and radio.

Federal Housing Administration (FHA), US govt. agency created (1934) by Congress to provide home loan insurance. Regulates building through its minimum standards for construction and design.

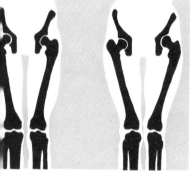

Diagram showing difference between male (left) and female (right) femur

Federal Reserve System, US central banking system (estab. 1913). Each of 12 reserve banks serves Federal Reserve district. National banks maintain reserves on deposit with regional banks. Money supply and credit conditions regulated by Federal Reserve Board.

Federal Trade Commission (FTC), US govt. agency estab. by Congress (1914) to protect fair competition in business. Since 1938 orders of commission have legal validity.

federalism, system of govt. dividing responsible power between central (federal) govt. and sub-divisions (states, provinces, *etc.*). Leading

exponents of system include US, Canada and Australia.

Federalist Papers, series of essays written (1787– 8) by Alexander Hamilton, James Madison and John Jay to promote adoption of US Federal Constitution.

Federalist Party, US political party (*c.* 1791– 1824) whose main spokesman was ALEXANDER HAMILTON. Subsequent Federalist Parties have advocated strong central govt.

Feiffer, Jules (1929–), Amer. cartoonist and writer. Created Munro, 4-year-old drafted by mistake into army. Collections include *Sick, Sick, Sick* (1958).

Feininger, Lyonel (1871– 1956), Amer. painter and graphic artist. Teacher at Bauhaus (1919– 32).

feldspars, felspars, group of minerals composed of potassium-aluminium silicate, sodium-aluminium silicate or calcium-aluminium silicate. Usually white but appear in other colours. Part of earth's crust.

feldspathoids, mineral group related to FELDSPARS, composed of same elements, though in different proportions. Found in some basic rocks.

Fellini, Federico (1920–), Ital. film director. Academy Awards for *La Strada* (1954) and *Nights of Cabiria* (1957). Also noted for *La Dolce Vita* (1960), $8\frac{1}{2}$ (1963).

femur, thigh bone in man.

fen, flat, low-lying land sometimes covered by water. When drained, provides arable land. In England, N Cambridgeshire, W Norfolk and Isle of Ely known as The Fens.

fence lizard, *Sceloporus undulatus,* insectivorous reptile of Iguana family, of pine forests of E US.

fencing, sport in which 2 combatants use light foil, sabre or épée, descendants of old duelling swords. Introduced as Olympic event for men (1890), for women (1924).

Fénelon, François de Salignac de la Mothe (1651– 1715), Fr. theologian and writer. Archbishop of Cambrai (1695– 1715). Author of *Télémaque* (1699). Exponent of QUIETISM.

Fenians, Irish secret revolutionary society formed (*c.* 1858) to secure independence from England. Risings and terrorism suppressed by British, but attracted attention to Irish problems. US Irish emigrants' attempted invasion of Canada, led by John O'Mahony, ended in failure. See SINN FEIN.

fennec, *Fennecus zerda,* nocturnal lightish-coloured fox of desert regions of N Africa and Arabia.

fennel, *Foeniculum dulce,* feathery herb used for fish sauces and salad

dressings. Wild fennel, *Foeniculum vulgare,* used as stuffing.

Ferber, Edna (1887– 1968), Amer. novelist and playwright, author of *So Big* (1924), *Show Boat* (1926; later a musical), *Stage Door* (1936; with G. S. Kaufmann). Later novels include *Giant* (1952).

fer-de-lance, *Bothrops atrox,* poisonous snake *c.* 5– 6 ft. long found in trop. America and W Indies.

Ferdinand I (1503– 64), Holy Roman Emperor (1558– 64). Became king of Bohemia (1526) and of Hungary (1527); succeeded by son Maximilian II. Nephew became Philip II of Spain.

Ferdinand and Isabella of Spain. Ferdinand (1452– 1516) became Ferdinand II of Aragon (1470) and Isabella inherited Castile (1474). He took the title Ferdinand V and ruled the 2 separate kingdoms. Moors and Jews were expelled from Spain, Inquisition set up; New World discovered and divided between Spain and Portugal.

Fermanagh, inland county of N Ireland. Area: 715 sq. mi.; county town, Enniskillen. Agriculture, pottery and linen. Pop. (1963) 52,400.

Fermat, Pierre de (1601– 65), Fr. mathematician. Founded modern theory of numbers. Postulated that a light-ray, traversing different media, follows path of least time.

fermentation, chem. change caused by enzyme action, *e.g.* production of vinegar. Yeast enzyme system causes alcoholic fermentation by producing ethyl alcohol and carbon dioxide from sugar.

Fermi, Enrico (1901– 54), Amer. nuclear physicist. Awarded Nobel Prize for Physics (1938) for work on radioactive substances. Headed group which achieved 1st controlled nuclear reaction (1942).

fern, flowerless perennial plant, order Filicales, of more than 6,000 species. Widely distributed, esp. in tropics. Fossils indicative of many early varieties.

Fennec

Fernandel, orig. Fernand-Joseph-Désiré Contandin (1903–71), Fr. film actor. Among films are *Le Petit Monde de Don Camillo* (1953), *Le Mouton à 5 Pattes.*

Fernando da Noronha, islands in S Atlantic off NE Brazil. Discovered by Portuguese (1503). Used by Brazil as military base.

Fernando Po, island in Gulf of Guinea, part of Equatorial Guinea. Area: 785 sq. mi.; cap. Santa Isabel. Discovered by Portuguese (1471); ceded to Spain (1778). Exports cocoa, timber, coffee. Pop. (1968) 71,000.

Ferrara, city in Emilio, N Italy, on delta of the Po. Cap. for Este family, many works of art remain. Pop. (1965) 138,000.

Ferrer, Jose Vicente (1912–   ), Amer. actor, director and producer. Played Iago in *Othello* (1943–5). Films include *Cyrano de Bergerac* (1950) and *Joan of Arc.*

ferret, domesticated albino variety of polecat, genus *Puturius* of family Mustelidae. Used to hunt rabbits and kill rats.

Ferrier, Kathleen (1912–53), Eng. contralto of international repute. Sang in festivals at Salzburg, Zurich, Vienna, Amsterdam and Edinburgh.

Ferry, Jules François Camille (1832–93), Fr. statesman. Min. of Education (1879–80, 1882); premier (1880–1, 1883–5). Estab. modern Fr. educ. system. Built up Fr. colonial empire in Africa and Indo-China.

Fertile Crescent, historic region of Near East, between Nile and Euphrates and Tigris rivers. Includes part of present-day Israel, Lebanon, Syria, Jordan and Iraq.

fertility rites, orig. festivals celebrating advent of spring, of which the Dionysia and Christian Easter rites were 2 variants.

fertilization, union of female egg cell (ovum) with male sperm cell (spermatozoon). Activation of egg by sperm results in change in substance (cytoplasm) of egg cell.

fertilizer, substances (natural or artificial) used to increase yield of plants. Organic materials include animal manures, bone meals; inorganic include nitrate of soda, superphosphate.

fescue, perennial grass of *Festuca* genus, most important being meadow fescue, *F. elatior.* Valuable as fodder.

feudalism, system by which tenants or vassals worked land belonging to overlord to whom they had to swear allegiance, financial and military support. Hierarchical system ranging from king to serf. Widespread in Europe until 13th cent. Feudal relationship known as fief.

Old Town gate at Fez

fever, higher than normal body temperature, usually symptom of infection or disease.

feverfew, *Chrysanthemum parthenium,* perennial herb of daisy family. Dried leaves and flowers used to make medicinal tea.

Feynman, Richard P[hillips] FRS (1918–   ), Amer. physicist. Staff member of atomic bomb project, Los Alamos (1943–5). With S. Tomonaga and J. S. Schwinger, awarded Nobel Prize for Physics (1965) for research in quantum electrodynamics.

Fez, city in N central Morocco. Consists of old city (founded 808) and new city (founded 1276). Contains *c.* 100 mosques, ancient Moslem university. Noted for native industries. Pop. (1968) 216,000.

fez, brimless cap worn by Mohammedans of Morocco. Name from city of FEZ.

Fibiger, Johannes Andreas Grib (1867–1928), Danish pathologist. Awarded Nobel Prize for Physiology and Medicine (1926) for discovery of a type of cancer.

Fibonacci, Leonardo [also **Leonardo da Pisa**] (*c.* 1180–*c.* 1250), Ital. mathematician whose work on algebra and arithmetic was standard for centuries.

fibre [UK] **fiber** [US], threadlike tissue capable of being spun into yarn. Animal fibres, mainly composed of protein include silk, wool, hair of rabbit, badger, *etc.*; vegetable fibres, mostly of cellulose, include cotton, kapok, hemp. Synthetic fibres are either organic (rayon) or inorganic (nylon).

Fichte, Johann Gottlieb (1762–1814), Ger. philosopher who developed idealism of KANT. Advocated liberal democracy and patriotism. Works include *Critique of all Revelation* (1792), *Science of Knowledge* (1794), *Addresses to the German People* (1808).

fiddler crab, several burrowing crabs of genus *Uca* found in salt marshes and on sandy or muddy shores of N and S America and Indian Ocean.

Field, Eugene (1850–95), Amer. journalist and poet. Children's verses include 'Little Boy Blue' and 'Wynken, Blynken, and Nod'.

Field, John (1782–1837), Irish pianist and composer of nocturnes which influenced Chopin.

Field, Rachel (1894–1942), Amer. writer of children's books, novels and poetry; novel *All This, and Heaven Too* (1938).

Field of Cloth of Gold, place near Calais, France, where Henry VIII of England met Francis I of France (1520) to discuss alliance possibilities. Name given because of lavish display of wealth by both retinues.

fieldfare, *Turdus pilaris,* migrant bird of thrush family. Breeds in higher altitudes of N Europe, nests in colonies.

Fielding, Henry (1707–54), Eng. dramatist, novelist and judge. Wrote successful burlesques for stage, but noted for satirical novels esp. *Joseph Andrews* (1742), *Tom Jones* (1749) and *Amelia* (1752) and for championing law and social justice.

Fields, Gracie (1898–   ), Eng. singer and comedienne; 8 command performances (1928– 57). Best-known songs include 'The Biggest Aspidistra in the World'.

Fields, W[illiam] C[laude] (1879– 1946), Amer. film actor famed for portrayal of comic characters.

Fife, county of E Scotland, between Firths of Tay and Forth; known historically as Kingdom of Fife. Area: 505 sq. mi.; county town, Cupar; other towns, St. Andrews, Dunfermline, Kirkcaldy and new town of Glenrothes. Coalmining, fishing and agriculture important. Pop. (1965) 320,877.

Fifth Column, collaborationist group, native to one country but working for another. Term 1st used in Spanish Civil War to refer to rebels inside Madrid who were expected to join with the 4 attacking columns.

fig, *Ficus carica,* broad-leaved tree bearing soft many-seeded fruit. Prob. grown 1st in Arabia, spread to Med. countries and US.

Figaro, fictional character, witty and resourceful. Orig. barber in Beaumarchais' *Le Barbier de Sévile* (1775) and hero of his *Mariage de Figaro* (1784). Depicted as rebel against abuses of ancien régime.

figwort, perennial plant of family Scrophulariaceae. Species include common figwort, *Scrophularia nodosa.*

Fiji Islands, Brit. colony in S Pacific comprising over 250 islands,

c. 80 of which are inhabited. Area: 7,056 sq. mi.; cap. Suva, Viti Luvu Is. Discovered (1643) by Tasman and annexed 1874. Crops include sugar cane, rice; trop. fruits; gold mines. Pop. (1968) 428,000.

filbert, *corylus maxima,* deciduous tree or shrub of birch family. Orig. in W Asia often cultivated for nut crop.

Filchner, Wilhelm (1877– 1957), Ger. explorer and geophysicist. Led Antarctic expedition (1910– 12), discovered Luitpold Land, SE of Weddell Sea.

film, motion picture synchronized with sound. Series of pictures (24 per sec.) projected on to screen so that eye cannot discern junctions.

filtration, separation of suspended undissolved solids from liquids. Used in chemistry, in filtering solids and bacteria from public water supplies, manufacture of sugar, beet, oils, paints. Filters include absorbent paper, fabrics, sands and charcoal.

finch, bird of family Fringillidae of 125 species. Some migrants, some songsters, *e.g.* canary.

finger-prints, impressions of surface ridges of human finger. As no 2 are exactly alike, used, esp. by police, as means of identification.

Finland, repub. of N Europe between Sweden and USSR. Area: 130,120 sq. mi.; cap. Helsinki. Conquered and Christianized by Sweden (12th cent.),

ceded to Russia (1809), achieved independence (1917); admitted to UN (1955). Half land surface covered by lakes and bogs. Agriculture chief industry. Pop. (1968) 4,650,000.

Finnish, Finnic language, it has 4 million speakers in Finland.

Finno-Ugrian, Indo-European linguistic group consisting of Finnish and Ugrian.

Finsteraarhorn, highest peak (14,032 ft.) of Bernese Oberland, S Switzerland. First climbed (1812); NE wall remains a challenge.

fir, general name for widely distributed tall coniferous evergreen tree Abies. European species include silver fir, *A. alba,* and Norway spruce, *Picea abies.* Others include hemlock, Japanese parasol and Douglas fir.

Firbank, Ronald (1886– 1926), Eng. novelist, portrayer of eccentric characters. Best known work *Prancing Nigger* (1924).

Firdausi, orig. Abul Kasim Mansur (*c.* 940– *c.* 1020), Persian epic poet. Author of classic *Shah Namah.*

fire damp, term applied to methane, or marsh gas, often found in coal mines. Mixed with air explodes violently when in contact with naked flame.

fire salamander, *Salamandra salamandra,* European amphibian with dark skin and yellow markings. Found in damp hilly places.

firearms, weapons discharging projectiles by use of explosives. Developed in Europe (13th cent.) after invention of gunpowder. First weapons were artillery pieces of mortar type. Portable guns developed in next century. Most rapid improvements in 19th cent.

fireball *see* METEORITE.

firecrest, *Regulus ignicapillus,* insectivorous bird similar to goldcrest.

fireworks, preparations of explosives of inflammable nature used for display purposes. Thought to have originated in China, introduced to Europe (14th cent.). Potassium nitrate and chlorate of potash commonly used; manufacture generally supervised.

first aid, name for emergency medical treatment given in cases of sudden illness or accident pending arrival of physician. Service offered esp. by RED CROSS and certain ambulance organizations.

Firth, Raymond (1901–   ), Eng. social anthropologist. Works include

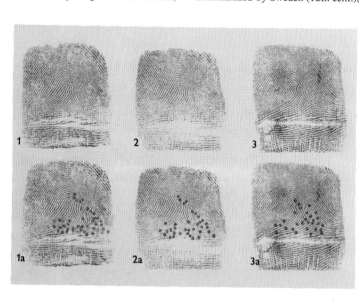

Of the fingerprints shown 1 and 2 are identical. This is proved by the dot pattern (1a and 2a) while 3a is quite different. For the purpose of police identification, a pattern of 12 to 16 dots is sufficient.

Ancient castle near Turku, Finland

Finnish landscape

Primitive Economics of New Zealand Maori (1929) and *Essays on Social Organization and Values* (1964).

firth, arm of the sea, esp. in Scotland, *e.g.* Firth of Forth, Solway Firth; often lower part of river estuary.

Fischer, Emil FRS (1852–1919) Ger. organic chemist. Awarded Nobel Prize for Chemistry (1902) for experimentation in sugar and purine groups.

Fischer, Hans (1881–1945) Ger. organic chemist. Awarded Nobel Prize for Chemistry (1930) for work on chlorophyll and haemin.

Fischer-Dieskau, Dietrich (1925–   ), Ger. baritone, world-wide reputation as operatic singer.

Fish, Hamilton (1803–93), Amer. statesman. Gov. of New York (1849–50), US Senator (1851–7), Sec. of State (1869–77). Negotiated settlement with Great Britain of 'Alabama Claims'.

fish, aquatic animal mainly of class Pisces with over 20,000 species. Gill-breathing vertebrate with scales and fins; eats plankton and aquatic animals and plants. Reproduces mainly by eggs, fertilization occurring after spawning. Largest fish is whale shark, up to 50 ft. long; smallest is goby, $c. \frac{2}{5}$ in. long. Use of fish for food purposes is a large world industry.

fish louse, invertebrate animal of subclass Branchiura. External and gill parasite of fish and other marine animals.

Fisher, Andrew (1862–1928), Austral. statesman, b. Scotland. P.M. (1908–9, 1910–13, 1914–15) and Labour leader. Imposed land taxes to break up large estates; other progressive reforms.

Fisher, James Maxwell McConnell (1912–   ), Brit. ornithologist. Works include *Birds as animals* (1939) and *Adventure of the World* (1954).

Fisher, John (1459–1535), Eng. prelate who denounced (1527) Henry VIII's divorce of Catherine of Aragon. Made cardinal by Pope Paul III while imprisoned (1535). Beheaded (1535) for opposing Act of Supremacy. Canonized (1935).

Fisher, John Arbuthnot, 1st Baron (1841-1920), Brit. admiral. First Sea Lord (1904–10), introduced Dreadnought battleship. Returned to post (1914–15); resigned over Dardanelles policy dispute with Churchill.

fishing, commercial and sporting pastime since ancient times. Fish commercially captured by drift nets, trawls and use of hook and line. Fish caught in salt or freshwater using hook, with live bait or artificial flies made from feathers, at end of rod and line.

fission, nuclear, breaking-up of atomic nucleus by neutron bombardment in uranium and plutonium. Chain reaction causes disappearance of fissile material explosively (as in atomic bomb) or under control (as in the pile).

Fitzgerald, Edward (1809–83), Eng. man of letters known for translation (1859) of *The Rubaiyat of Omar Khayyam.*

Fitzgerald, Ella (1918–   ), Amer. singer. Renowned for jazz, Negro spiritual interpretations and renderings of Cole Porter hit songs.

Fitzgerald, F[rancis] Scott [Key] (1896–1940), Amer. novelist, short-story writer of jazz-age 'lost generation'. Novels include *The Beautiful and the Damned* (1921), *The Great Gatsby* (1925), *Tender is the Night* (1934).

Primitive fishing traps still used in Thailand

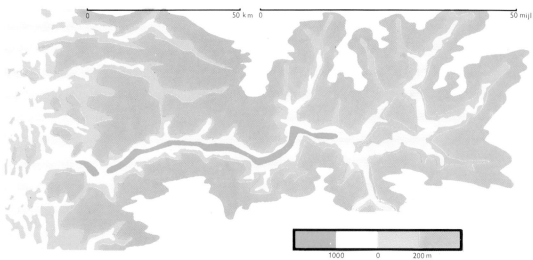

Sognefjord, Norway, showing contours of a typical fjord coastline

Fitzroy, Augustus Henry, 3rd Duke of Grafton (1735–1811), Eng. politician, prominent Unitarian. P.M. 1766-70; resigned over the Amer. tea duty.

Fitzroy, river, Western Australia, important cattle and wool farming area. Rice grown in irrigated areas.

Five, the, group of Russ. composers, founders of national school of music. Included Mili Balakirev (1837–1910), Rimski-Korsakov (1844–1908), Borodin (1833–87), Moussorgsky (1839–81) and César Cui (1835–1918).

Five Year Plan (1928), 1st of series of state programmes introduced by Stalin to impose collectivization of agriculture and speed industrialization. Ruthlessly enforced, it caused much suffering. Other programmes followed and practice has been adopted esp. in Cuba, Egypt, China.

fjord, fiord, long, very narrow, deep, steep-sided indentation of sea. Gouged out by glaciers; esp. well developed along mountainous coasts *e.g.* Norway, Chile, New Zealand, W Canada.

Flaccus, Quintus Horatius *see* HORACE.

flagellate, protozoan animal of class

Common flamingoes in flight

Mastigophora with 1 or more flagellae giving mobility. Small, usually oval, with parasitic and free living plant and animal forms, *e.g.* euglena, volvox.

flageolet, small flute of recorder type with 4 finger holes and 2 thumb holes, popular in 18th cent.

Flagstad, Kirsten (1895–1962), Norwegian soprano, famous for her Wagnerian roles.

Flaherty, Robert Joseph (1884–1951), Amer. film director known for documentaries such as *Nanook of the North* (1922). Other films include *Tabu* (1931), *Elephant Boy* (1936) and *Louisiana Story* (1948).

flame, area where chem. reaction takes place between gases heated above kindling temperature, producing heat and light.

flame flower, N Amer. plant. Species include *Phlox paniculata,* herbaceous form, *P. divaricata,* dwarf alpine form, and *P. drummoundi,* annual native to Texas.

flamenco, dance and music of Sp. gypsies, characterized by abrupt, vigorous movements, and use of castanets, to accompaniment of guitars and hand clapping.

flamingo, gregarious wading bird of family Phoenicopteridae, with long legs. Breeds in colonies. Found in temp. and trop. zones.

Flanders, former county of Netherlands, famous in 13th cent. for cloth industries. France annexed E part (1668); remainder became part of kingdom of Belgium (1830). Scene of heavy fighting in both World Wars. Dunkirk is on coast. Language, Flemish.

flat feet, condition of human foot in

which entire sole rests upon the ground. Caused by muscle weakness and consequent straining of ligaments.

flatfish, species of order Heterosomata with compressed flattened body and both eyes on same side of head. Species include turbot, halibut, flounder, sole, plaice and fluke.

Flathead or **Salish,** tribe of N Amer. Indians of Bitterroot R. valley, W Montana (19th cent.). Wars with Blackfoot, concluded by peace treaty (1872), reduced numbers to *c.* 350. Now settled in Montana.

flatworm, invertebrate worm of *Platyhelminthes* genus, incl. *Turbellaria,* free-living and aquatic, *Trematoda,* parasitic flukes, *Cestoidea,* parasitic tapeworms.

Flaubert, Gustave (1821–80), Fr. author, best known for *Madame Bovary* (1857). Other works include *The Temptation of St Antony* (1874), *Three Tales* (1877).

flea, wingless, leaping insect of order Siphonaptera with 1,500 species. Sucks blood of birds and mammals and transmits disease, esp. bubonic plague and endemic typhus.

fleabane, several herbs of family

Plaice, a gastronomically popular flatfish

Compositae. Certain species formerly used medicinally.

Flecker, James Elroy (1884–1915), Eng. poet. Works include *The Golden Journey to Samarkand* (1913).

Fleet Street, in City of London, associated with journalism and news services; contains offices of most Brit. daily newspapers.

Fleming, Sir Alexander (1881–1955), Scot. bacteriologist who discovered lysozyme (1922) and penicillin (1928). Shared Nobel Prize for Physiology and Medicine (1945) with Sir Howard Florey and Ernst Boris Chain, for work on penicillin.

Fleming, Ian Lancaster (1908–64), Eng. writer. Creator of secret agent James Bond, in such books as *From Russia with Love* (1951), *Casino Royale* (1954), and *Goldfinger* (1959).

Fleming, Sir Sandford (1827–1915), Canadian engineer and surveyor. Co-founder of Royal Canadian Institute at Toronto (1849). Commissioned as surveyor for number of rly. incl. the Intercolonial (1863).

Flemish, Germanic Indo-European language, closely related to Dutch, with 5 million speakers in Flanders region of Belgium.

Flesch, Rudolf (1911–), Amer. author, b. Austria. Writer of *The Art of Readable Writing* (1949), *How to be Brief* (1912) and *The ABC of Style* (1965).

Fletcher, John (1579–1625), Eng. dramatist. Collaborated with Francis Beaumont on about 50 comedies and tragedies.

Fleury, André Hercule de (1653–1743), Fr. statesman and cardinal, tutor of Louis XV and virtual ruler of France (1726–43). Domestic policy successful; involved in foreign wars, became unpopular through persecution of Jansenists.

flicker, woodpecker of N America. Species include yellow-shafted flicker, *Colaptes auratus,* ant eating bird common in E North America; and further W, red-shafted flicker, *C. cafer.*

Flinders, Matthew (1774–1814), Eng. naval captain, hydrographer and explorer. Helped George Bass in survey (1793–1800) of New South Wales, Australia. First to survey part of W Australian coast (1801–3). Author of *Voyage to Terra Australis.*

flint, hard brown mineral often found in chalk and limestone. Consists mainly of silica; breaks with shell-like fracture. Used by primitive man for making tools and weapons.

Flintshire, county of N Wales. Area: 256 sq. mi.; county town, Mold; other

The Ponte Vecchio over the River Arno, Florence

towns, Rhyl, Flint. Mainly lowland and agricultural; coal and lead mined. Pop. (1967) 163,110.

Flodden, area of the Cheviot Hills, England, scene of defeat of James IV of Scotland by Eng. under Earl of Surrey (9 Sept. 1513).

flood, inundation of low-lying land usually river water. Lower Nile valley depends on annual flooding for fertile silt. Flood reclamation, *e.g.* polders of Zuider Zee (Netherlands) requires damming, draining and soil fertilization. Flood control, regulation of rivers by dams, locks and ditches; sea water excluded by dykes.

Florence, Firenze, city of Tuscany, Italy, on Arno R. Founded by Romans (*c.* 185 BC), became independent trading city. Dominated by Medici family (15th cent.) politically and culturally. Included (1860) in Kingdom of Italy; cap. 1865–71. Manufacturing and rly. city, chiefly cultural centre associated with Dante, Boccaccio, Machiavelli, Michelangelo, Leonardo da Vinci and the Medicis. Many museums and churches, remains of Roman amphitheatre and baths; contains Uffizi Gallery and Ponte Vecchio. Periodically subject to floods (as in 1968) which have seriously damaged art treasures. Pop. (1965) 454,000.

Florey, Baron Howard Walter (1898–1968), Brit. pathologist, b. Australia. Awarded Nobel Prize for Physiology and Medicine (1945) with Sir Alexander Fleming for work on penicillin.

Florida, extreme SE state of US. Area: 58,560 sq. mi.; cap. Tallahassee; large towns, Jacksonville, Tampa, St Augustine (oldest city in US) and Miami. Largely low-lying peninsula between Atlantic Ocean and Gulf of Mexico, with swampy Everglades area

in S. Discovered (1513) by Spaniard Juan Ponce de Leon, bought (1819) from Spain by US; became state (1849). Mainly agric., producing sugar, rice, oranges, cotton, tobacco. Cape Kennedy is on E coast. Pop. (1967) 5,996,000.

Flotow, Friedrich, Baron von (1812–83), Ger. composer; operas include *Alessandro Stradella* (1844) and *Martha* (1847).

flounder *see* FLATFISH.

flour, finely ground and sifted meal of cereal, esp. wheat, consisting of starch and gluten. Different grades of flour make bread, pastry, macaroni.

flower, part of seed plant containing reproductive organs.

flowering rush, *Butomus umbellatus,* tall perennial plant of family Butomaceae. Aquatic with long stout grass-like leaves, umbel of rose-pink flowers followed by heads of purple fruit.

flugelhorn, brass instrument similar in shape to bugle, but with 3 pistons, producing fuller tone than cornet. Also alternative name for SAXHORN family.

fluke, parasitic suckerbearing flat worm of class Trematoda, living externally or internally in host. Blood flukes, found in Egypt and trop. America, enter body through drinking water or skin of bathers.

fluorescence, conversion of short wavelength radiation (*e.g.* X-rays, ultra-violet) into radiation of longer wavelengths (such as visible light). Materials displaying fluorescence include barium sulphide, calcium tungstate. Fluorescent screens used in television sets and radiography.

fluorine (F), very active, pale yellow gaseous element, with irritating odour; dangerous to inhale. Discovered (1771) by Scheele. Used as domestic water additive.

Fluorite

fluorite, fluorspar, mineral, calcium fluoride, of various colours. Found in veins cutting, *e.g.* gneiss, slates and limestones. Used in metallurgy and in preparation of hydrofluoric acid, opal glass and enamel.

fluorspar *see* FLUORITE.

flute, woodwind instrument of silver or wood with range of 3 octaves played by blowing across small aperture near one end. Bass [UK] or alto [US] flute is a little longer, giving 4 or 5 extra tones. *See* PICCOLO and RECORDER.

fly, insect of order Diptera comprising 60,000 species. Larvae are soft-skinned maggots or wormlike. Rapid breeding makes several species pests, *e.g.* HORSEFLY; others, *e.g.* MOSQUITO and TSETSE FLY, transmit disease.

fly-agaric, *Amanita muscaria,* poisonous but rarely fatal fungus, found in pine and birch forests.

flycatcher, small insectivorous woodland bird of Muxicapidae family of Europe, Asia, Africa and Australia. Species includes E Asian paradise flycatchers with brilliant plumage.

Flying Doctor Service, Austral. medical service. Covers 2 million sq. mi. of interior, formed 1927.

Flying Dutchman, legendary spectre-ship, believed to haunt Cape of Good

Fly-agaric

Hope area. Subject of opera by Wagner.

flying fish, trop. fish of various families with enlarged pectoral fins. Species include Atlantic flying fish, *Exocoetus volitans* and Catalina flying fish, *Cypselurus heterurus.*

flying fox, animal of fruit bat group, incl. Indian flying fox, *Pteropus giganteus* and kalong, *P. vampyrus c.* 5 ft. in length.

flying lemur, name of 2 species of *Cynocephalus* or *Galeopithicus* found in Australia. Called 'collugo' by natives.

flying saucer *see* UNIDENTIFIED FLYING OBJECTS.

flying squirrel, several species of squirrel of Asia, N America and Europe. Skin folds spread like parachute and animal glides through air.

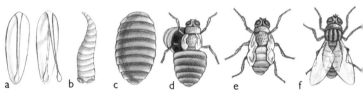

Life cycle of the fly (a) egg (b) larva (c) pupa (d) emerging from pupa (e) newly hatched fly, before wings have hardened (f) mature fly

Foch, Ferdinand (1851–1929), Marshal of France. Took part in battles of the Marne, Ypres and the Somme in World War 1; became chief of Fr. general staff and head of Allied armies on the W Front (1918). Prominent in armistice and peace negotiations.

focus, in optics, point at which converging rays meet, towards which they are directed, or from which diverging rays are directed.

foetus, fetus, unborn young of viviparous animals when still in womb of the mother; and of oviparous species, when young are fully developed inside egg.

fog, low lying cloud or thick mist formed by condensation of water around dust particles in air; white in country and soot-laden in cities. Smog is soot- and smoke-laden fog, found in industrial areas.

Fokine, Michel (1880–1942), Russ. dancer and choreographer for Diaghilev's Ballets Russes. Created *Firebird, Petrouchka* and *Le Spectre de la Rose.*

folk dancing, traditional form of dancing, incl. characteristic country or national dancing in costume, performed to accompaniment of folk tunes; *e.g.* Eng. morris dances,

Bohemian polka, Amer. reel, Scot. Highland fling.

Folketing, house of parliament of Denmark, in Copenhagen.

folklore, term coined 1846 by W. T. Thoms to denote traditions, customs and superstitions of a society. Orig. folk tales and folk heroes, became subject of serious study by 19th cent. to anthropologists.

Follett, Wilson (1887–1963), Amer. writer and critic. Author of *The Modern Novel* (1918), *No More Sea* (1933).

Folsom Man, species of man of *c.* 8,000 BC postulated from spear points found with fossilized bones of extinct bison near Folsom, New Mexico.

Fontaine, Pierre François Léonard (1762–1853), Fr. architect. With Charles Percier, responsible for development of Empire style of architecture in France.

Fontainebleau, town of N France, near Paris. Nearby forest was royal hunting park; palace is one of largest royal residences. Pop. (1960) 18,000.

Fontana, Domenico (1543–1607), Ital. architect and engineer; designed Lateran Palace, Rome (1588) and completed dome of St Peter's with Giacomo della Porta.

Fontane, Theodor (1819–1898), Ger. novelist, poet, journalist and drama critic. Wrote *L'Adultera* (1882) and *Effi Briest* (1895).

Fontanne, Lynne [Mrs Alfred Lunt] (1887–   ), Brit. actress. With her Amer. husband appeared in domestic comedies and with Theatre Guild (1924–9).

Fontenoy, Battle of (1745), engagement near Tournai, Belgium, where Fr. army under Marshall Saxe defeated combined Brit. and Dutch forces under Duke of Cumberland.

Fonteyn, Dame Margot (1919–   ), Eng. dancer, prima ballerina assoluta of Royal Ballet and international star. Pres. of Royal Academy of Dancing (1954–   ); m. Dr. Roberto de Arias, Panamanian diplomat and politician.

Foochow, Fuchow, Fu-chou, city of

China, cap. of Fukien prov. near mouth of Min R. Built in T'ang Dynasty (618–906), became largest tea-exporting centre (19th cent.). Now major and commercial and industrial centre. Pop. (1968) 616,000.

Food and Agriculture Organization (FAO), specialized agency of UN, with 110 member states, estab. (1945). Aim is to help nations to raise standard of living by improving efficiency of farming, forestry and fisheries. Operations include research and development programmes and co-ordination of *Freedom from Hunger* campaign.

food poisoning, condition which may be fatal, caused by eating food contaminated with poison (*e.g.* arsenic), poisonous food (*e.g.* certain toadstools), or food contaminated by pathogenic bacteria, usually staphylococci, streptococci or salmonellae.

fool's parsley, *Aethusa cynapium,* dark green common weed of Europe. Has ribbed stem with small white umbels of flower heads.

foot, in vertebrates, terminal part of leg below ankle joint.

Foot, Hugh Mackintosh, Baron Caradon (1907–), Brit. overseas administrator. Gov. and Commander-in-Chief of Cyprus (1957–60), permanent representative at UN (1964–). His brothers, **Sir Dingle Mackintosh Foot** (1905–) and **Michael Foot** (1913–) are Brit. Lab. politicians.

foot-and-mouth disease, acute contagious virus fever of cloven-footed animals. Characterized by vesicular lesions of mouth and feet. May affect horses, poultry and occasionally humans.

football, ball game played since Middle Ages in Europe, now has various distinct forms. Rugby Union (15 a side) developed (19th cent.) at Eng. public schools, distinctive feature that players run carrying the oval ball (played in UK, France, Romania, Australia, New Zealand, South Africa, Fiji). Rugby League (13 a side), Australian Rules (18 a side) and American football (11 a side) developed from it. Greater mobility is a feature of league, and heavy tackling

American Flying Squirrel

and protective clothing of American. Association (Soccer) follows rules set down by Football Assoc. in UK (1863). Now played all over world under auspices of FIFA (Fédération Internationale de Football Association, 100 member countries) which arranges World Cup Confederation, *etc.*

Forbes, James David (1809–68), Scot. physicist who discovered polarization of radiant heat. Pioneered scientific study of glaciers.

Ford, Ford Madox, orig. Ford Madox Hueffer, (1873–1939), Eng. reviewer; edited *English Review* (1908–11), wrote *The Good Soldier* (1915) and *Parade's End* (1924–8). Collaborated with Joseph Conrad on various works.

Ford, Henry (1863–1947), Amer. industrialist, 1st to mass produce motor cars. Founded (1936) Ford Foundation, philanthropic organization.

Ford, John (1586–c. 1640), Eng. dramatist; co-author with Dekker and Rowley of *Witch of Edmonton* (1621). Own plays include *'Tis Pity She's a Whore* (1633), *The Broken Heart* (1633) and *Perkin Warbeck* (1634).

Ford, John, orig. Sean O' Feeney (1895–), Amer. film director. Films include *The Informer* (1935), *Stagecoach* (1939), *The Grapes of Wrath* (1940), *They Were Expendable* (1945) and *The Quiet Man* (1953).

foreign aid, military, technical and financial assistance, usually given at govt. level. Amer. aid began with Lend-Lease (World War 2), and European Recovery Program (Marshall Plan, 1948). UN, US, Brit. and Fr. programmes aid under-developed nations.

foreign exchange *see* EXCHANGE, FOREIGN.

Foreign Legion, infantry corps of Fr. army composed of Fr. officers and foreign mercenaries. Formed by Louis Philippe (1831), it estab. an outstanding reputation. Orig. HQ in Algeria, but since Algerian independence (1962) HQ in France.

Forester, C[ecil] S[cott] (1899–1966), Eng. novelist. Creator of 'Horatio Hornblower', naval officer of Napoleonic wars. Other novels include *The African Queen* (1935).

forestry, art of planting, tending and managing timber as a crop; 80% of world trade is in soft woods used for paper pulp and construction and supplied by Canada ($\frac{1}{2}$ world's supply for newsprint), Sweden, Finland and USSR. US and Canada grow temp. hardwoods. Africa, Asia and S

America are main sources of hardwoods.

Forestry Commission, UK govt. dept. created (1919) to acquire land for afforestation, promote private forestry by grants and control fellings.

forget-me-not, annual or perennial plant of wide distribution with oval leaves and blue or pink flowers. Species include wild or cultivated common forget-me-not, *Myosotis arvensis* and water forget-me-not, *M. scorpioides.*

formaldehyde, simplest alkalyde. Produced by passing methyl alcohol vapour over heated platinum. Important in manufacture of synthetic resins and plastic substances.

formalin, solution of formaldehyde in water. Formerly used as antiseptic and disinfectant, now used to preserve

Spotted Flycatcher

anatomical specimens and in embalming.

formic acid, simplest of fatty acids. Obtained by distillation of sodium formate with mineral acid. Used in dyeing.

Formosa *see* TAIWAN.

formula, in chemistry, written expression which indicates elements, in proportion by weight, contained in 1 molecule of chem. compound.

Forrest, John, 1st Baron Forrest (1847–1918), Austral. explorer; 1st premier (1890–1901) of Western Australia and 1st Australian to be made a peer (1918).

Forrestal, James Vincent (1892–1949), Amer. naval official; Sec. of the Navy (1944–7), 1st Sec. of Defence (1947–9).

Forssman, Werner (1904–), Ger. physician. Developed technique of heart cathetrization for which he shared Nobel Prize in Physiology and Medicine (1956) with Dickinson W.

Ruins of the Temple of Vesta in the Forum, Rome

Richards Jr., and André Frédéric Cournand.

Forster, E[dward] M[organ] (1879–1970), Eng. novelist and critic. Novels include *Where Angels Fear to Tread* (1905), *Howard's End* (1910) and *A Passage to India* (1924). Best known critical work, *Aspects of the Novel* (1927).

forsythia, *Forsythia suspensa,* deciduous Chinese shrub with olive-brown twigs and yellow flowers which appear before leaves. Hybrids widely cultivated.

Fort Peck, dam in NE Montana on Missouri R.; built 1933–40; one of largest earth-filled dams, 21,026 ft. long, 250 ft. high.

Fort Sumter, island in Charleston harbour, S.C., US, scene of opening conflict (12 Apr. 1861) of US Civil War, in which fort was bombarded by Confederates.

Fort Worth, city of Texas, US. Centre of oil industry; agric. and livestock market. Pop. (1960) 350,000.

Fortaleza, city of NE Brazil, cap. of Ceará state. Founded (1609) as fortress, now an industrial sea- and air-port. Pop. (1968) 525,000.

Fortas, Abe (1910–   ), Amer. jurist. Justice of Supreme Court (1965–69). Helped extend court's concern to social issues. Appointment as Chief Justice (1968) failed to get Senate approval.

Forth, river in C Scotland rising in Stirlingshire and flowing *c.* 45 mi. to Kincardine where it becomes Firth of Forth. Crossed by rail bridge (1890) and road bridge (1964) at Queens-ferry near Edinburgh.

forum, market and meeting-place of Roman towns, usually with basilica, public treasury, curia, prison and shops. Forum at Rome extended from Capitoline Hill almost to Colosseum and contained at least 5 temples, 2 basilicas and 2 triumphal arches.

fossil, remains, representation or impression in rocks, of animal or plant. Study of fossils is called PALAEONTOLOGY. Used for dating and correlating strata, and study of evolution. *See* GEOLOGICAL TABLE. Coal is formed from fossilized plants and amber from fossilized resin.

Foster, William Zebulon (1881–1961), Amer. communist; stood for President (1924, 1928 and 1932); became national chairman of Amer. communist party (1945) and, with others, was charged with conspiring to overthrow US govt. (1948).

Fouché, Joseph, Duke of Otranto (1763–1820), Fr. revolutionary, Min. of Police (1799–1815). Created system which foreshadowed modern police state under Napoleon but intrigued with British and Bourbons and was exiled (1815).

four o' clock, marvel of Peru, *Mirabilis jalapa,* perennial plant of trop. America; tubular flowers up to 2 in. long, red, yellow, orange or striped. Name from habit of flowers opening in afternoon; cultivated as temp. garden plant.

4–H Clubs, service of US Dept. of Agriculture for rural youth between ages of 10 and 19. Founded (1914), aim is to promote good citizenship and to encourage community service through use of 'head, heart, hands, and health.'

four stroke engine, internal combustion engine whose operation consists of 4 phases, injection, compression, combustion and exhaust.

Fourier, [François Marie] Charles (1772–1837), Socialist philosopher who evolved system of Utopian communism based on his *Le nouveau monde industriel* (1829–30). Inspired colonies in America such as Brook Farm and Red Bank, N.J., which flourished until mid-19th cent.

Fourier, Jean Baptiste Joseph, Baron (1768–1830), Fr. mathematician who studied heat and numerical equations. Gave his name to theorem on vibratory motion and to trigonometric series.

Fournier, Henri Alban (1886–1914), Fr. writer known as **Alain-Fournier.** Wrote poetic novel *Le Grand Meaulnes* (1913).

Fournier, Pierre Simon (1712–68), Fr. type founder. Devised 1st point system for measuring type. Wrote *Manuel Typographique* (1764).

Fourteen Points, US Pres. Wilson's idealistic programme for peace, presented 8 Jan. 1918. Included idea of LEAGUE OF NATIONS which materialized. *See* VERSAILLES, TREATY OF.

Fourteenth Amendment, US constitutional amendment (passed 1868). Estab. basis of US citizenship and forbade states to curtail individual privileges, to deprive person of rights without 'due process of law', (broadly interpreted by US Supreme Court), or to deny equal protection of law.

Fowler, Francis George (1870–1918) and his brother **Henry Watson Fowler** (1858–1933), Eng. lexicographers who collaborated on *The King's*

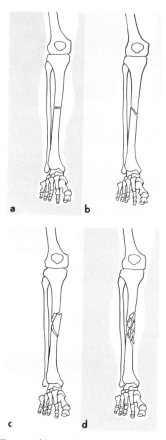

Types of bone fracture (a) simple (b) diagonal (c) impacted (d) compound.

Four o'clock Plant

English (1906), an abridgement of *Oxford English Dictionary* (1911) and *A Dictionary of Modern English Usage* (1926).

Fowler, Sir John (1817–98), Eng. civil engineer, designer of London Underground and joint designer of the Forth Railway Bridge.

Fox, Charles James (1749–1806), Eng. Whig politician and parliamentary reformer. Opposed WILLIAM PITT over Brit. intervention in Fr. revolution. Supported several reform movements such as abolition of slave trade, passed 1807.

Fox, George (1624–91), Eng. religious leader, founder of Society of Friends, called Quakers. Began to preach (1647), several times imprisoned. Made missionary journeys in Europe and America. *Journal* published 1694.

fox, animal of dog family with long body, short legs and long bushy tail. Nocturnal predator living in burrows. European fox, *Vulpes-vulpis,* is 15 in. high, red-brown above and white below. Species include Amer. red black and 'silver tip' fox, *V. fulva,* with longer hair (sometimes bred for fur) and Arctic fox, *Alopex lagopus.*

foxglove, *digitalis purpurea,* perennial of figwort family, native to W and C Europe. Has tapering spikes with purple, pink or white bell-shaped flowers. Popular garden varieties developed. Leaves yield digitalin used in medicine.

fractional distillation, chem. purifying process in preparation of petroleum and other substances.

fracture, breaking of bone, cartilage *etc.,* and resulting condition.

Fragonard, Jean Honoré (1732–1806), Fr. painter of contemporary life and landscapes. Brought individuality to baroque style with free brush technique and rich colouring.

France, Anatole, orig. Jacques Anatole Thibault (1844–1924), Fr. writer. From early ironic charm, *e.g. Thaïs* (1890), novels became noted for polit. satire, *e.g. La Révolte des Anges* (1914). Awarded Nobel Prize for Literature (1921).

France, repub. of W Europe. Area: 212,659 sq. mi.; cap. Paris; principal

cities, Marseille, Bordeaux, and Lyon. Physical features are Massif Central, drained by Seine flowing N and Loire

Mont St Michel, France

flowing W; Pyrenees in S and Alps in E. Self-sufficient agriculture, natural resources include coal, iron, hydro-electric power. Frankish kings emerged as rulers of Roman province of Gaul (5th cent.) and estab. Merovingian and Carolingian dynasties. Powerful Lords disrupted state during Feudal period, further aggravated by HUNDRED YEARS WAR (1337–1453). State centralized under 1st Valois king, Louis XI (1461–83). 16th cent. civil wars of religion ended by 1st Bourbon king, Henry IV. French ascendancy in Europe realized under Louis XIII and Louis XIV. FRENCH REVOLUTION abolished *ancien régime* (1789). State emerged from dictatorship of NAPOLEON as constitutional monarchy (1815–48); Repub. (the 2nd, 1848–52) changed by Napoleon III into 2nd Empire, abandoned after FRANCO-PRUSSIAN WAR. 3rd Repub. (1871–1940) accompanied by prosperity and colonial expansion despite polit. instability. Resources depleted after World War 1 and economic crises of 1920s–30s, France capitulated to Hitler (1940). Occupied in N by Germany and ruled by VICHY regime in S until liberation (1944). 4th Repub. (1946–58) collapsed over Algerian problem and economic inflation. Rise of DE GAULLE brought 5th Repub. (1958), Algerian independence (1961), and independent foreign policy, despite membership in EUROPEAN ECONOMIC COMMUNITY. Religion, predominantly R.C. Unit of currency, the franc. Pop. (1965) 48,700,000.

Francesca, Piero della (*c.* 1420–92), Umbrian painter, renowned for innovations in perspective and in light and atmospheric control. Works include *Flagellation* and *Baptism of*

Christ. Wrote famous geometrical treatise.

Franche-Comté, Free County of Burgundy, former prov. of E France. Cap. Besançon. Named from refusal of some counts to pay homage to Rome. Now departments of Haute-Saône, Doubs and Jura.

Francis of Assisi, Saint (*c.* 1182–1226), founder of Franciscans. Attracted following through piety and devotion, forming brotherhood (papal sanction 1210). Subsequent missionary work included travels throughout Med. countries.

Francis I (1494–1547), king of France (1515–47). Continuous rivalry with Charles V in Italian

Fisherman mending nets at Menton, France

City Hall, Frankfurt am Main

Wars. Captured at Pavia (1525). Dissolute and unscrupulous, also patronized arts and literature.

Francis Ferdinand (1863–1914), Austrian archduke, nephew of Emperor Francis Joseph I. As heir-apparent shot at Sarajevo (1914), an event which precipitated World War 1.

Francis Joseph I (1830–1916), emperor of Austria (1848–1916) king of Hungary (1867–1916). Austrian influence in Germany declined after war with Prussia (1866). Hungary incorporated to form Austro-Hungarian Empire. Wife Elizabeth assassinated (1898). Uncle of Francis Ferdinand.

Francis of Sales, Saint (1567–1622), R.C. preacher. Became bishop of Geneva (1602). Eloquence of sermons converted many Protestants. Treatises include *Treatise on the Love of God.*

Francis Xavier, Saint (1506–52), Basque Jesuit missionary, called the Apostle of the Indies. Helped found Society of Jesus in 1530s with St Ignatius of Loyola. Spent last years of life in Far East.

Franciscans, Grey Friars, religious order founded (1209) by St Francis of Assisi. Includes Conventuals and Capuchins. Began as friars living in absolute poverty, but soon relaxed custom.

Franck, César [Auguste] (1822–90), Belgian composer. Lived in Paris as teacher and organist. Best known for his Symphony in D Minor and his organ works.

Franck, James (1882–1964), Amer.

physicist, b. Germany. Shared Nobel Prize for Physics (1925) with Gustave Hertz for work on atomic theory. Later noted for work on photosynthesis.

Franco Bahamonde, Francisco (1892–), Sp. general and polit. leader (*Caudillo*). Rose to power prior to Spanish Civil War, becoming chief of Insurgent govt. (1936). Dissolved all polit. parties but FALANGE (1937). Kept Spain out of World War 2 despite commitments to Hitler and Mussolini. Restored Sp. monarchy (1947) by law of succession and retained regency post, exercising authoritarian powers.

francolin, several birds of genus *Francolinus* of family Perdicidae, found in Ethiopia, Arabia, Asia Minor, India, S China.

Franconia, lands of E Franks along Main and Rhine rivers. Divided into 2 duchies after 9th cent. Now comprises Bavaria, Württemberg, Baden and Hesse.

Franco-Prussian War (1870–1), conflict between Ger. states and France. Napoleon III provoked into declaring

Francolin

war with disastrous results. After decisive battle of Sedan, Ger. unification achieved by armistice; William I of Prussia created emperor. Germany secured Alsace-Lorraine.

Frank, Anne (1929–45), Dutch Jewish girl. Died in concentration camp after writing diary during flight from Nazis. *The Diary of a Young Girl* (1947) became best-seller. Dramatized as *The Diary of Anne Frank* (1956).

Frank, Ilya Mikhailovich (1908–), Soviet physicist. Awarded Nobel Prize for Physics (1958) with P. A. Cherenkov and I. Y. Tamm for studies of high-energy particles.

Frankau, Pamela (1908–67), Eng. novelist and short-story writer. Works include *Jezebel* (1937) and *The Devil We Know* (1939).

Frankfurt, Frankfurt am Main, city of W Germany, on the Main. Indust., transport and commercial centre. Royal residence of Carolingians; site of Holy Roman Emperors' coronations. Seat of diet of German Confederation (1815–66). Headquarters for US occupying forces after World War 2. Industries include chemicals, electrical goods, machinery. Pop. (1964) 688,100.

Frankfurt, Treaty of, ratification of Treaty of Versailles ending Franco-Prussian War (1871). France ceded most of Alsace and Lorraine and paid large indemnity to victorious Prussia.

Frankfurter, Felix (1882–1965), Amer. judge. Associate Justice of US Supreme Court (1939–62); noted for support of civil liberties.

frankincense, aromatic resin from trees mainly of genus *Boswellia*. Used by ancient Egyptians and Jews as incense in religious rites.

Franklin, Benjamin, FRS (1706–90), Amer. statesman, scientist, printer and writer. Philosophy and wit popularized by *Poor Richard's Almanack* (1732–57). Instrumental in push for independence, helped draft 1776 Declaration of Independence. Popular diplomatic representative in France and Britain, where he negotiated peace after appointment as commissioner (1781). Participated in Federal Constitutional Convention (1787). Invented lightning conductor.

Franklin, Sir John (1786–1847), Brit. explorer and chronicler in N Canada. Led expeditions (1819–22, 1825–7) before 1845 search for North West Passage, during which entire expedition was lost.

Franks, group of European tribes, settled along lower course of Rhine (3rd cent.). Under Clovis, Salian Franks moved into France and made

Market in Freetown, Sierra Leone

him their king (481). E Franks remained in Germany.

Franz Josef Land, archipelago (area 8,000 sq. mi.) in the Arctic Ocean, off Archangel, discovered (1873) and named after Austrian Emperor. Most of 85 islands are ice-covered; there are meteorological observation stations. Area claimed by USSR (1926).

Fraser, Simon (1776–1862), Canadian explorer. Followed Fraser R. to its mouth (1808) while estab. trading posts for North West Co.

Fraser, river in Brit. Columbia, Canada, *c.* 850 mi. long; rises in Rocky Mts. and flows to Pacific, S of Vancouver. Discovered by Alexander Mackenzie (1793), named after Simon Fraser.

Frazer, Sir James George (1854–1941), Brit. classicist. Author of *The Golden Bough* (1890), 1st comprehensive study in comparative religion, folklore and mythology.

Fréchette, Louis Honoré (1839–1908), Fr. Canadian poet and journalist. His poetry (*e.g., Les Fleurs Boréales,* 1879) won him place in French Academy. Major work, *La Légende d'un Peuple* (1887), cyclically celebrated Fr. Canadian history.

Frederick [I] Barbarossa (1124–90), Holy Roman Emperor (1155–90). Succeeded to Ger. kingdom (1152). Crushed powerful Ger. princes, but quarrels with papacy led to defeat by Lombard League at Legnano (1176). Joined Third Crusade.

Frederick II (1194–1250), king of Germans (1212–20), Holy Roman Emperor (1220–50). Invested with Sicilian dominions (1197) by Pope Innocent III. Quarrelled with papacy after crowning as king of Jerusalem (1229), giving rise to long struggle.

Frederick I (1657–1713), elector of Brandenburg (1688–1713). Crowned 1st king of Prussia (1701).

Frederick [II] the Great (1712–86), king of Prussia (1740–86). Opened WAR OF AUSTRIAN SUCCESSION (1740), securing Silesia. Leadership and military genius during SEVEN YEARS WAR (1756–63) made Prussia foremost military power in Europe. Enlarged realm by 1st partition of Poland (1772). Prolific writer, patron of arts and literature. Became symbol for Ger. nationalism.

Frederick [III] the Wise (1463–1525), elector of Saxony (1486–1525). Supported Luther, although remaining Catholic. Founded University of Wittenberg (1502).

Frederick [V] the Winter King (1596–1632), Elector Palatine (1610–20). Chosen king of Bohemia

(1619) after Protestant diet had deposed Ferdinand II. Disastrously defeated at White Mountain (1620), lost all his territories. Ancestor of Hanoverian kings of England.

Frederick VI (1769–1839), king of Denmark (1808–39) and of Norway (1808–14). Alliance with Napoleon after English attacked Copenhagen (1807); Norway transferred to Sweden by Congress of Vienna.

Frederick William (1688–1740), king of Prussia (1713–40). Laid foundations for strong Prussian army.

Fredericksburg, battle (1862) in Amer. Civil War near Fredericksburg, Va., in which Confederates inflicted heavy losses on Union army.

Fredericton, cap. of New Brunswick, Canada, on St John R. in centre of fruit growing and lumbering region. Pop. (1968) 20,000.

Frederiksborg, royal castle in Zeeland, Denmark. Started in 17th cent., it is now a museum.

free port, zone within port where goods can be landed, handled and re-shipped without intervention by customs authorities.

free trade, commerce without restrictive duties. European Economic Community and European Free Trade Assoc. are efforts at international free trade and at abolition of protective tariffs between members.

Freemasonry, doctrine and practices of secret fraternity of Free and Accepted Masons. Derived from medieval masons' guild, but later not restricted to stoneworkers. Order, based on supremacy of custom, has adherents in many countries. European secret societies often formerly involved in politics.

Free-Soil Party, in US history, polit. organization (1847–8), opposed expansion of slavery into territories acquired from Mexico. After COMPROMISE OF 1850 eventually absorbed by new Republican party.

freethinkers, those who arrive at religious convictions through reasoning, rejecting supernatural interpretations and eccles. traditions. Term used in 18th cent. England, esp. to denote deists; in France associated with Voltaire and Encyclopedists.

Freetown, cap. of Sierra Leone founded (1788) for liberated slaves. Cap. of British Africa (1808–74). Exports diamonds, iron-ore, coffee and cocoa; industries include fish processing and soap manufacture. Pop. (1968 est.) 130,000.

Frege, Gottlob (1848–1925), Ger. mathematical logician. Demonstrated mathematics as form of deductive logic.

Fremantle, port of Perth, Western Australia at mouth of Swan R. Exports wheat, fruit and wool. Pop. 25,000.

Frémont, John Charles (1813–90), Amer. soldier, explorer and politician, known as the 'Pathfinder'. Led several expeditions to Amer. West. Republican Pres. candidate (1856). Removed from command in Union army during Civil War. Gov. of Arizona (1878–83).

French, John Denton Pinkstone, 1st Earl of Ypres (1852–1925), Brit. field-marshal who commanded the British Expeditionary Force (1914–15); reorganized home defences (1915–18) and became lord-lieutenant of Ireland (1918).

French, romance Indo-European language, with 42 million speakers in France, approx. 10 million in Belgium, Canada and Switzerland, over 12 million in parts of Africa and Far East, where it is spoken as 2nd language.

French and Indian War (1756–63), N Amer. conflict between French and British. Aided by Iroquois Indians, British attacked Fr. forts and cities, finally winning Quebec on Plains of Abraham (1759) where commanders Montcalm and Wolfe fell. Treaty of Paris (1763) ended Fr. claims to Canada and Amer. West.

Interior of the cathedral at Rheims, an outstanding example of French Gothic Art

French art, earliest important form seen in Roman remains, *e.g.* arena at Arles, aqueduct at Nîmes. Gothic architecture epitomized by cathedrals of Paris, Rheims, Chartres; Renaissance by Loire châteaux; classicism by palace of Versailles. By 18th cent. Fr. sculpture had become prominent through works of Houdon, and later Rodin and Bourdelle, as had Fr. painting, esp. through Delacroix and 19th cent. Impressionists, Manet, Monet, Renoir, Gauguin. 20th cent. artists include Matisse, Braque, Rouault and Bonnard.

French Community, body (estab. 1958) promoting economic and defensive co-operation between France and African nations, formerly Fr. colonies. Orig. set up to replace French Union (1946–58), its governing institutions functioned primarily as consultative organs after 1960, when African member states gained independence.

French Guiana, Fr. possession in N South America. Area 35,135 sq. mi.; cap. and chief port Cayenne. Produces sugar, cocoa and coffee. Hardwoods exported; gold and bauxite mined. Devil's Is. is off coast. Pop. 36,000.

French horn, brass instrument of about 11 ft. of coiled tubing, whose bore widens into a flared bell-shape.

French Polynesia, group of 5 archipelagos comprising *c.* 130 islands in S Pacific, an overseas territory of France. Area: 1,550 sq. mi. Chief industries are copra, vanilla, phosphates and tourism. Chief town is Papeete. Pop. (1956) 80,000.

French Revolution, Fr. polit. uprising, begun 1789. Product of 18th cent. liberalism, oppression of poorer classes, and assertion of capitalist class against outdated system. Immediate cause was state's vast debt; Louis XVI convened ESTATES-GENERAL (May 1789), which declared itself the National Assembly. Louis yielded, but dismissal of Necker led to storming of the BASTILLE. National Guard organized, privileges abolished, and commune estab. as govt. of Paris. King imprisoned (1791) upon attempt to flee and forced to accept new constitution, DECLARATION OF THE RIGHTS OF MAN. PILLNITZ declaration used as pretext for FRENCH REVOLUTIONARY WARS (1792). Formation of National Convention led to abolition of monarchy and estab. of First Republic (Sept. 1792) and Louis' execution for treason (Jan. 1793). *See* REIGN OF TERROR; DIRECTORY.

French Revolutionary calendar, official calendar of France (1793–1805), dividing year into 12 thirty-day months and five holidays. Computed from Sept. 22, 1792, when monarchy was displaced by the Fr. Republic.

French Revolutionary Wars, general European conflict (1792–1802), precipitated by French Revolution. PILLNITZ Declaration used by Fr. govt. as pretext for war with Austria (later Prussia) which led to French successes and brought about series of alliances. Period (1795–7) marked by rise of NAPOLEON through victories in Italy. By beginning of 19th cent., England was alone against France. Short-lived peace (1802) followed by NAPOLEONIC WARS.

French Somaliland *see* AFARS AND THE ISSAS, FRENCH TERRITORY OF THE.

fresco, method of painting on ground of stucco or plaster. Mineral pigments used, which combine quickly with fresh plaster. Notable frescoes include those at St Mark's, Florence by Fra Angelico, and at Vatican by Raphael.

Freud, Anna (1895–   ), Brit. psychoanalyst, daughter of Sigmund Freud; noted for work on child psychoanalysis.

Freud, Sigmund (1856–1939), Austrian psychiatrist, pioneer of PSYCHOANALYSIS. Stated that sexual desires start in infancy, repression of these result in mental abnormality, *e.g.* Oedipus complex; interpretation of dreams important in psychoanalysis, *The Interpretation of Dreams* (1900). Other works include *The Ego and the Id* (1923).

Freudenberg, Karl Johann (1886–   ), Ger. chemist known for work on stereochemistry and organic chemistry.

Freytag, Gustav (1816–95), Ger. playwright and novelist. Among plays *The Journalists* (1855) was most successful.

Fribourg, Freiburg, Swiss Canton (since 1481) and city on Fr.–German linguistic frontier. Cheese, watches, paper and chocolate manufactured. Pop. 158,000 (canton); 20,000 (city).

Fried, Alfred Hermann (1864–1921), Austrian pacifist and publicist. Founded Austrian Peace Society (1892) and 1st German pacifist paper *Die Wappen Nieder!* (1891). Prominent in major international peace movements, shared Nobel Peace Prize (1911) with Tobias Michael Carel Asser.

Friedland, town formerly in E Prussia, since 1945 included in USSR as **Pravdinsk.** Napoleon's victory over Russians at Friedland led to Treaty of Tilsit (1807).

Friedrich, Caspar David (1774–1840), Ger. romantic landscape painter.

Friesland, Frisia, prov. of N Netherlands comprising several of W FRISIAN ISLANDS. Area: 1,325 sq. mi. Subdued by Charles V (1523), who created separate prov. of E Friesland, now part of Germany. Low-lying, fertile, dairy-farming country. Cap. Leeuwarden. Pop. (1968) 480,000.

frigate, orig. long narrow sailing or rowing vessel of Mediterranean. Now denotes warship with raised quarter-deck and forecastle, about same tonnage as a destroyer.

frigate, bird of family Fregatidae. Predatory on young of seabird colonies. Indigenous to trop. S Atlantic, Pacific and Indian oceans.

frilled lizard, *Chlamydosaurus kingi,* arboreal insectivorous reptile of Australia. Named after fold of skin which ruffs in aggressive display.

Friml, Rudolf (1881–   ), Czech composer; light operas include *The Firefly* (1912), *Rose Marie* (1927).

Frisch, Max (1911–   ), Swiss writer. Best known play is *Andorra* (1961); novels include *Stiller* (1954), *Homo Faber* (1957).

Frisian Islands, island chain off coasts of and belonging to the Netherlands, Germany and Denmark. Main occupations: fishing, stock-raising.

fritillary, bulbous plant of lily family native to N hemisphere. Species include crown imperial, *Fritillaria imparialis,* and snake's head, *F. meleagris.*

Frobisher, Sir Martin (*c.* 1539–94), Eng. navigator. Made 3 unsuccessful voyages in search of NW passage to China. Vice-admiral in Drake's expedition to W Indies (1585). Participated in defeat of Armada (1588).

Froebel, Friedrick Wilhelm August (1782–1852), Ger. educ. reformer, founder of kindergarten system (1836). Wrote *The Education of Man* (1826).

frog, tailless, aquatic amphibian of genus *Rana.* Uses sticky tongue to seize prey; young known as tadpoles.

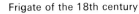

Frigate of the 18th century

Bohemian Landscape by Caspar David Friedrich

Species include common frog, *R. temporaria*, Amer. woodfrog, *R. sylvatica*; hind legs of edible frog, *R. esculenta*, regarded as delicacy in France and S US.

froghopper, cuckoo-spit insect, spittle bug, insect of family Cercopidae. Larvae enveloped in froth often seen on plants. *Philaerus spumarius* is European and N Amer. species.

Frohman, Charles (1860–1915), Amer. theatrical producer. Promoted exchange of plays between London and New York.

Froissart, Jean (*c*. 1337–1410), Fr. chronicler and courtier. Travels in Italy, Scotland and Flanders provided material for *Chroniques* (4 vols.), 1st printed *c*. 1495.

Fromm, Erich (1900–), Ger.-Amer. psychoanalyst. Works, centred on problems of man in western industrial society, include *Escape from Freedom* (1941) and *Beyond the Chains of Illusion* (1962).

Fronde, name given to Fr. civil wars during Louis XIV's minority (1648–53). First, caused by quarrels over taxation, was suppressed by Mazarin and Louis, Prince de Condé. Second occurred after quarrel between Condé and Mazarin, who fled to Germany; peace restored (1653) and royal authority strengthened.

Frontenac, Louis de Buade, Comte de

(*c*. 1622–98), Gov. of New France (1672–82, 1689–98). Collaborated with JEAN TALON in development of W Canada fur trade and exploration. Planned campaign of French and Indian War (1689–97). Chateau Frontenac Hotel Quebec is named after him.

Frost, Robert (1874–1963), Amer. poet. Lyrical, dramatic, and reflective verse best seen in *West-running Brook* (1928) and *A Further Range* (1936). *Complete Poems* (pub. 1949) includes 'The Road not Taken' and 'Mending Wall'.

frost, weather condition occurring when temperature falls to 0°C or below. Gradations include 1) Ground frost, hoar frost, atmospheric water crystallization. 2) Rime, ice crystals formed when water drops are driven against exposed surfaces by wind. 3) Glazed frost, frozen rain. 4) Black frost, sub-freezing temperatures affecting fluids within plants, occurring without crystallized ground frost.

fructose *see* SUGAR.

fruit, fertilized ovary of flower, varying in type from dandelion tufted seed to cultivated apple. Edible fruit classified as tree fruit, *e.g.* apple, orange; bush and small fruit, *e.g.* strawberry, blackcurrant; stone fruit *e.g.* plum; pip fruits *e.g.* grape; berry

e.g. raspberry; and nut fruit *e.g.* walnut.

fruit bat, mainly arboreal mammal of bat family, Megachiroptera, found in trop. and sub-trop. regions of Africa and Asia. Species include flying fox and kalong.

fruit fly, insect pest of citrus fruit, peaches, plums, *etc.* Widespread Med. fruit fly. *Ceratitis capitata*, has been exterminated in US.

Fry, Christopher (1907–), Brit. playwright. Author of *The Lady's Not for Burning* (1948), *A Sleep of Prisoners* (1951). Translated works by Giraudoux and Anouilh.

Fry, Edwin Maxwell (1899–), Brit. architect. Pioneer of modern Eng. architecture in housing, schools and hospitals.

Fry, Elizabeth (1780–1845), Eng. Quaker prison reformer and philanthropist. Worked to improve conditions of Newgate prison, London.

Fry, Roger (1866–1934) Eng. painter and critic. Arranged 1st exhibition of post-impressionist paintings in England (1910); organized Omega Workshops (1913) which applied Cubism to interior decoration, pottery, textiles, etc. Member of Bloomsbury Group, articles and lectures collected in *Vision and Design* (1920) and *Transformations* (1926).

Funicular railway near Zermatt, Switzerland

Helotiale Fungus

Frye, Northrop (1912–   ), Canadian literary critic known for *Anatomy of Criticism* (1957). Author of study of William Blake, *Fearful Symmetry* (1947) and of Shakespeare, *Fools of Time* (1968).

Fuchs, Leonhard (1501–66), Ger. physician whose *De historia stirpium*, a botanical compendium, became a standard work. Genus *Fuchsia* named after him.

Fuchs, Sir Vivian Ernest (1908–   ), Brit. geologist and explorer. Led Commonwealth Antarctic crossing (1957–8).

fuchsia, colourful shrub of willow herb family. Most species native to trop. America. Popular for garden and indoors.

Fugger, Ger. merchant family of Augsburg, in 16th cent., richest in Europe. Highpoint reached by Jacob Fugger II (1459–1525). Fortunes declined with those of Habsburgs, whose wars they financed.

fugue, polyphonic piece of music, based on melody. J. S. Bach achieved highest form of fugue composition.

Fujiyama, or **Mount Fuji**, highest peak (12,389 ft.), of Japan. Shinto sacred mt. is dormant volcano.

Fukien, maritime province of S China; area, 47,500 sq. mi.; cap. Foochow. Mountainous, lumber important resource; tea, esp. flower-scented varieties grown. Has coal, iron, copper, gold, silver resources. Majority of population live on coast. Pop. (1963) 14,650,000.

Fukuoka, city, N Kyushu, Japan, cap. of Fukuoka prefecture, on Hakata Bay. Produces textiles, pottery, paper and metal goods. Pop. (1968) 650,000.

Fulbright, [James] William (1905–   ), Amer. politician. Democratic Senator from Arkansas (1945–   ). Promoted teacher and student exchange in Fulbright Act (1946); chairman of Foreign Relations Committee in 1960s.

Fuller, Melville Weston (1833–1910), Amer. lawyer. US Chief Justice (1888–1910), known for strict interpretation of Constitution.

Fuller, [Richard] Buckminster (1895–   ), Amer. engineer and architect. Designed geodesic dome.

Fuller, [Sarah] Margaret (1810–50), Amer. writer and literary critic. Works include *Woman in the Nineteenth Century* (1845). With husband Marchese Ossoli supported 1848 Revolution in Italy.

Fuller, Thomas (1608–61), Eng. Anglican cleric. Compiled *Worthies of England* (1622); wrote *History of the Holy Warre* (1639).

fulmar, migratory marine bird of

Ocelot fur

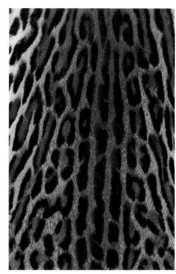

shearwater family. Species include *Macronectes giganteus*, polymorphic giant fulmar.

Fulton, Robert (1765–1815), Amer. inventor, builder of 1st commercially successful steamship in Amer. waters, *Clermont* (1807). Also a canal engineer and landscape painter.

fumitory, animal plant of Fumariaceae family with fern-like foliage. Widely distributed species *Fumaria officinalis*.

function, in mathematics, expression of relation between 2 or more variables. Value of one varies with change in value of other. Any one of variables may be taken as dependent; others being independent. Functional analysis (theory and application) is used in statistics, economics, and social science.

fundamentalism, conservative, mainly Protestant, religious movement of 20th cent. upholding fundamental doctrines of 'revealed' religion in face of scientific 'doctrines' (such as evolution).

Fundy, Bay of, Atlantic inlet between Canada and US. Famous for tides reaching 70 ft.

Fundy National Park, S New Brunswick, Canada, on Bay of Fundy. Area: 79.5 sq. mi.; founded 1948.

fungus, any of several plants of order Thallophyta, mostly parasitic, *e.g.* mushroom, toadstool etc.

funicular, rly. running on cables, esp. in mountainous country; used to transport tourists and skiers.

Funk, Isaac Kaufman (1839–1912), Amer. author and pastor. Founded (1878) publishing firm, later Funk and Wagnalls Co.

fur trade, marketing of valuable animal skins. Encouraged exploration of Asia and N America (17th–19th cent.), esp. Canada, where beaver pelt was responsible for estab. of Hudson's Bay Company and North West Company.

Furies *see* Eumenides.

Furtwängler, Wilhelm (1886–1954), Ger. musician. Conductor of Berlin Philharmonic Orchestra (1922–45).

G

gabbro, coarse-grained, basic, plutonic IGNEOUS ROCK, dark coloured and heavy. Occasionally layered due to settling of crystals from magma.

Gaberones, cap. of Botswana, S Africa. Pop. (1965) 12,000.

Gabin, Jean, orig. Jean-Alexis Moncorgé (1904–), Fr. film actor. Films include *Pépé le Moko* (1937) and *Le Jour se lève* (1939).

Gable, Clark (1901–60), Amer. film actor. Best known for roles in *Gone With the Wind* and *It happened One Night,* for which he won an Oscar (1935).

Gabo, Naum (1890–), Amer. sculptor, b. Russia. Exhibited at Brussels International Exhibition (1958). Noted for use of modern synthetic materials in his sculpture.

Gabon [La République Gabonaise], former Fr. colony of Equatorial

Africa on Gulf of Guinea. Area: 102,089 sq. mi.; cap. Libreville. Became independent republic (1960), remained member of French Community. Pop. (1963) 404,000.

gaboon viper, *Bitis gabonica,* large gaudy African snake of viper family with pair of small horns on end of nose and thick body. Strikes and bites fiercely.

gadfly, *Tabanus borinus,* insect *c.* 1 in. long, black above and reddish beneath; larvae live in damp soil. Female is bloodsucking and troublesome to cattle and horses in hot weather.

Gadsden Purchase (1853), strip of land purchased by US from Mexico to acquire access to most practicable route for S rly. to Pacific.

Gaelic language *see* CELTIC.

Gaelic literature, literature of Gaelic languages. Welsh classics include 12th cent. *Mabinogion* and romances of the Merlin, Aneurin and Taliesin cycles. Irish Gaelic sagas include *Cuchulain* legend. Scot. Gaelic has been separate from Irish since 16th cent. Bardic tradition is common to all branches of Gaelic literature.

Gag, Wanda (1893–1946), Amer. writer, painter and illustrator. Illustrated many children's books, incl. *Millions of Cats* (1928).

Gagarin, Colonel Yuri [Alekseyevich] (1934–68), Russ. cosmonaut; 1st man in space (Apr. 1961) circled earth in 108 min. in spaceship satellite. Killed in air crash.

Gaia, in Gk. myth., goddess of Earth. According to Hesiod's *Theogony,* she was 1st to emerge out of primeval chaos, and gave birth to Uranus, the sky. Their children were Cronus and the Titans.

gaillardia, genus of chiefly W Amer. herbs of daisy family with hairy foliage and flower heads with yellow, purple or variegated rays. Species include the blanket flower, *G. aristata.*

Gainsborough, Thomas (1727–88), Eng. painter. Noted for landscapes and portraits, *e.g. Blue Boy, Harvest Wagon* and *Watering Place.* Chosen as one of 36 members of Royal Academy (1768).

Gaitskell, Hugh Todd Naylor (1906–63), Brit. politician. Labour M.P. (1945–63). Min. of Fuel and Power (1947–50), Chanc. of Exchequer (1950–1), leader of parl. Lab. party (1955–63).

galago *see* BUSHBABY.

Galahad *see* ARTHURIAN LEGEND.

Galapagos, group of volcanic Pacific islands belonging to Ecuador. Area: 3,020 sq. mi.; cap., San Cristobal. Salt and hides exported to Guayaquil. Pop. (1965) 2,000.

Galatea, 1) in Gk. myth., sea nymph who loved Sicilian Acis, slain by Cyclops Polyphemus; 2) ivory statue brought to life by Aphrodite, made by Pygmalion, King of Cyprus.

Galatians, St Paul's Epistle to the, book of NT, believed written *c.* AD 49 at Ephesus. Exposition of how Christianity superseded law of Moses; man justified in sight of God by faith.

galaxy, system containing stars, nebulae, star clusters and interstellar matter. The Milky Way is galaxy

Tree trunks awaiting shipment in Port Gentil, Gabon

containing Solar System. Galaxies are classified according to shape (spherical, elliptical, spiral, amorphous).

Galba (4 BC–69 AD), Roman emperor (68–69), succeeded Nero.

Galbraith, John Kenneth (1908–), Amer. economist and diplomat; US ambassador to India (1961–3). Books include *The Affluent Society* (1958), *The Liberal Hour* (1960) and *The New Industrial State* (1967).

gale, strong WIND, between stiff breeze and hurricane; gale-force starts at Force 8 on Beaufort scale.

Galen (*c.* 130–*c.* 200), Gk. physician. Of his many treatises, 100 survive. Accepted as authoritative till 16th cent., he is regarded as founder of experimental physiology.

galena, chief ore of lead, often found as cubic crystals. It is opaque, lead-grey colour, with metallic lustre. Mined at Broken Hill, Australia, and in Brit. Columbia.

Galicia, district of NW Spain, former kingdom, now incorporated in 4 modern provinces.

Galilee, in NT times, Roman prov. of Palestine, N of Samaria, and W of Jordan R. Cap. Tiberias. Christ's boyhood home.

Galilei, Galileo (1564–1642), Ital. astronomer, mathematician and physicist. Laid basis of modern experimental science. Constructed

Portrait of Mr. and Mrs. Andrews in a Landscape by Thomas Gainsborough

GALL BLADDER

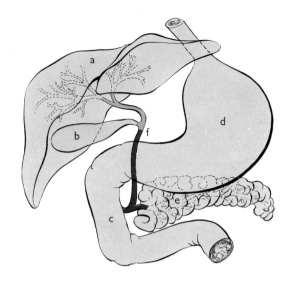

1st astronomical telescope (1609). Published paper (1632) supporting Copernican theory of solar system. Forced by Inquisition to renounce belief that Earth revolved round Sun.

gall bladder, membranous muscular sac present in most vertebrates. Stores bile from liver. In man pear-shaped and situated on underside of right lobe of liver. Opens by cystic duct which joins hepatic duct to form bile duct.

gall wasp, insect of order Hymenoptera. Some are parasitic. Presence of larvae results in plant excrescences or galls from which insect emerges.

Gallatin, Albert (1761–1849), Amer. financier and politician, b. Switzerland. US Sec. of the Treasury (1801–14), he reshaped national financial policy from Federalist to Jeffersonian principles.

galleon, 3-masted, square-rigged warship with 2 decks, used by Europeans to transport treasure from Americas. Vessels of Spanish Armada (1588) against England.

galley, long, narrow vessel fitted with sail, mainly propelled by oars. Rowers were slaves or prisoners-of-war. Used in ancient and medieval times, esp. in Med. area.

Gallic Wars, campaigns of Julius Caesar during proconsulship of Gaul (58–51 BC). Began by quelling aggression of Helvetii, Aedui and Belgae. Invasion of Britain (54 BC). Vercingetorix led revolt of C, E and N Gaul (53 BC), crushed by Caesar.

Gallico, Paul William (1897–   ), Amer. writer. Books include *The Adventures of Hiram Holliday* (1939), *Flowers for Mrs Harris* (1958) and *The Man Who Was Magic* (1968).

Gallipoli, port in European Turkey, overlooking entrance to Aegean Sea from Dardanelles. Scene of intense fighting in Anglo-French siege (1915-16) during World War 1.

Gallup, George Horace (1901–   ), Amer. statistician and public opinion analyst. Founder (1935) of Amer. Institute of Public Opinion (the 'Gallup Poll').

Galois, Evariste (1811–32), Fr. mathematician. Most important work was in theory of equations and groups.

Galsworthy, John (1867–1933), Eng. novelist and dramatist. Works include *The Forsyte Saga* (1922), *A Modern Comedy* (1928) and *The End of the Chapter* (1934). Awarded Nobel Prize for Literature (1932).

Galt, Sir Alexander (1817–93), Canadian politician. Advocate of confederation of Canadian provs.; defended protective tariffs as Finance Min. (1858–62; 1864–6).

Gall bladder and digestive system: *a.* liver, *b.* gall bladder, *c.* duodenum, *d.* stomach, *e.* pancreas, *f.* common bile duct. (Bile flows through the hepatic duct (blue) into the gall bladder, where it is concentrated. It then passes via the common bile duct into the duodenum)

Galt, John (1779–1839), Scot. novelist and founder of Canada Co. (1826). Novels of rural life included *Annals of the Parish* (1821).

Galton, Sir Francis (1822–1911), Eng. scientist, founder of eugenics. Devised system of fingerprint identification. Works include *Hereditary Genius* (1869).

Galvani, Luigi (1737–98), Ital. physician and physicist. From his research on frogs, established relation of animal muscle to electricity and initiated study of electro-physiology. Galvanism and GALVANOMETER are derived from his name.

galvanometer, instrument for measuring electric (galvanic) current in conductor; works by deflection of magnetic needle by current. Ammeter, calibrated galvanometer through which current is made to pass. Voltmeter, calibrated galvanometer in series with a high resistance.

Galway, county town of Co. Galway, Ireland. Remains of Sp. influence in medieval trading in architecture. Centre of Gaelic culture. Pop. (1966) 26,192.

Galway, county of W Ireland. Lowland, rising in W to Connemara Mts. Area: 2,375 sq. mi.; county town Galway. Limestone and marble quarrying, copper and lead mining; stock raising and fishing important. Pop. (1965) 150,886.

Gama, Vasco da (c. 1469–1524), Portuguese navigator; 1st European to reach India by sea (1497–9). Voyage round Africa encouraged growth of Portuguese empire.

Gambetta, Léon (1838–82), Fr. states-man. Played important part in creation of Third Republic. Premier (1881–2).

Gambia, The state of W Africa within British Commonwealth. Area: 4,003 sq. mi.; cap. Bathurst. Gambia R. is main trade artery of the region. Agricultural, relying on peanut crop. Self-governing 1962; native authorities constitute indirect local rule. Pop. (1965) 336,000.

games, theory of, mathematical principle applying statistical logic to choice of strategies when 2 or more are available. Applied to military problems, economics and sociology, card games, *etc.*

gamma globulin, one of several protein fractions of human blood plasma or serum containing most antibodies. Used as immunity measure, esp. for measles and hepatitis.

Gamow, George (1904–   ), Russ.-American physicist. Known for application of nuclear physics to stellar evolution.

Gandhi, Indira (1917–   ), P.M. of India, daughter of Jawaharlal Nehru. She led Indian National Congress (1959–60) and became executive board member of UNESCO (1961). Became 1st Indian woman P.M. (1966) on death of Shastri.

Gandhi, Mohandas Karamchand (1869–1948), Indian leader, known as Mahatma (great souled). Educated in England, began campaign (1915) for Indian independence. Asserted Hindu ethics by abstaining from Western ways of living, but preached Christian and Moslem scriptures as well as Hindu. Imprisoned several times by

Brit. rulers for passive resistance, employing fast as chief weapon. Prominent in conferences leading to independence (1947); disappointed by partition. Shot by Hindu fanatic.

Ganges, Gunga, river of India c. 1,500 mi. long, rising in Himalayas and flowing to Bay of Bengal. Sacred Hindu river, visited by pilgrims. Important for irrigation and as source of hydro-electric power.

ganglion, mass of nerve tissue found either at junction of 2 nerves or within the brain. May denote small cystic tumour containing fluid. Also *see* NERVOUS SYSTEM.

gannet, marine bird of family Sulidae found off all coasts except Antarctica. Nests on cliffs in colonies. Commonest species is northern gannet or Solan goose, *Sula bassana.*

Ganymede, in Gk. myth., son of Tros, king of Troy. Zeus, in form of an eagle, took him to Mount Olympus and made him his cup-bearer.

gar *see* GARPIKE.

Garamond, Claude (d. 1561), Fr. designer and maker of printing types. Brought roman type into general use to replace Gothic (Black letter) type.

Garbo, Greta, orig. Greta Loviso Gustafson (1905–   ), Swedish-born Amer. actress. Famous for her beauty and restrained acting in films such as *Anna Christie, Camille, Ninotchka.*

García Lorca, Federico (1898–1936), Sp. writer. Major poet of his generation. Shot by Falangists at outbreak of Sp. Civil War. Works include *Blood Wedding* (1938).

Garda, Lago di Benaco, largest lake in Italy, Area: 143 sq. mi.; surface 120 ft. above sea level.

Garden City, town built in rural area according to planning principle whereby industries, controlled development, parks and cultural centre are built within town area. First in England planned (1903) at Letchworth; 2nd was Welwyn Garden City. Similar schemes in Europe and US.

garden spider, *Araneaus diadematus,* yellowish brown arachnid with white cross on abdomen. Constructs orb-shaped web.

Gannet

gardenia, genus of evergreen trees and shrubs of bedstraw family with white or yellow flowers. Native to trop. S Africa and Asia. Named after Alexander Garden, Scot. naturalist.

Gardner, Erle Stanley (1889–1970), Amer. detective story writer whose plots turn on a point of law; creator of Perry Mason. Works include *The Case of the Velvet Claws* (1933), *The D.A. Breaks an Egg* (1949). Has also written under pseudonym of A. A. Fair.

Gardner, John William (1912–   ), Amer. govt. official and spokesman on education. US Sec. of Health, Education and Welfare (1965–8).

Garfield, James Abram (1831–81), 20th US Pres. (1881), Republican. Congressman from Ohio (1863–80), nominated as compromise candidate for pres. (1880). Fatally shot by Charles Guiteau.

Garibaldi, Guiseppe (1807–82), Ital. soldier and patriot. Fought with Sardinian forces against Austria (1848). Helped Victor Emmanuel become king of Italy by conquest (1860) of Sicily and Naples with 1,000 volunteer 'Red Shirts'. Twice (1862, 1867), unsuccessful in attempts to conquer papal states.

Garland, Judy, orig. Judy Gumm (1923–69), Amer. actress. Best known for *Broadway Melody* (1938), *The Wizard of Oz* and *A Star is Born* (1954). Starred in cabaret and on TV.

garlic, *Allium sativum,* perennial plant of lily family, native to Asia with pungent, strong-smelling, bulbous root. Used to flavour meat and salad dishes.

Garneau, François Xavier (1809–66), Fr. Canadian historian. His *Histoire du Canada* (1845–8) antagonized clergy with its criticism of church power in Fr. Canada.

garnet, hard, brittle crystalline mineral used as gemstone. Found in gneiss and mica schist. Coarser varieties are used as abrasives.

Garonne, river of SW France, c. 400 mi. long, flowing into Bay of Biscay near Bordeaux.

garpike, gar, *Lepisosteus spatula,* fish of Gulf of Mexico. May reach 20 ft. in length.

Garrick, David (1717–79), Eng. actor and manager. One of the greatest interpreters of Shakespeare. Friend of Samuel Johnson and his circle. Manager of Drury Lane Theatre (1747–76); made important stage reforms.

Garrison, William Lloyd (1805–79),

Garnet in raw and polished state

Amer. printer and abolitionist. Published *Liberator* (1831–65) journal which advocated abolition of slavery in South.

garrote, form of capital punishment, strangulation by tightening neck collar. Form used in Spain and Portugal.

Garter, Order of the [Most Noble Order of the Garter], Brit. order of knighthood, estab. (c. 1344) by Edward III. Orig. limited to 26 members; now unlimited. Motto, *Honi soit qui mal y pense.*

garter snake, widely distributed viviparous harmless American colubrid snake of genus *Thamnophis,* longitudinal stripes on back.

Gary, Romain (1914–   ), Fr. writer and diplomat. Works include *Education Européenne* (1943), *Les Racines du Ciel* (1956) and *Le Manger d'Etoiles* (1966).

gas *see* STATES OF MATTER.

gas grid, in UK, network of pipes for distribution of gas, both coal and natural gas.

gas mask, protective head-gear with absorption system to remove toxic gases from air.

gas plant, *Dictamnus albus,* Eurasian perennial herb. Flowers give off a flammable vapour in hot weather. Formerly reputed to have considerable healing powers.

Gascony, former prov. of SW France. Part of Aquitaine in Middle Ages, was in dowry of Eleanor, who married Henry II of England. Eng. possession until c. 1453. Reformed (1790) as part of 7 departments.

gasoline *see* PETROLEUM.

Gasser, Herbert Spencer (1888–1963), Amer. physiologist. Director Rockefeller Institute (1935–53). With Joseph Erlanger, awarded Nobel Prize for Physiology and Medicine (1944) for work on nerve fibres.

gastroenterology, branch of medical science which deals with diseases of stomach and intestines.

gastropod, snail of class gastropoda, phylum *Mollusca.* Chamberless shell usually coiled in asymmetrical spiral. Lives mostly in water, but some, *e.g.* garden snails, live on land.

gastrotrich, common aquatic roundworm of class gastrotricha. Feeds on protozoans, diatoms and bacteria.

Gates, Horatio (1727–1806), Amer. Revolutionary general, b. England. Forced surrender of Brit. army at Saratoga (1779). Commanded Carolina Campaign but defeated at Camden (1780).

Gatling, Richard Jordan (1818–1903), Amer. inventor of Gatling multiple-firing gun, precursor of machine-gun.

Gaudí y Cornet, Antonio (1852–1926), Sp. architect many of whose structures are in Barcelona. Introduced colour into his façades and improvised designs from rubble, bricks and polychrome tiles.

Gauguin, [Eugène Henri] Paul (1848–1903), Fr. landscape and figure painter and sculptor. Deserted his family (1885) went to Tahiti (1891) and Marquesas Islands (1895) where he remained until his death. Works include *Ta Matete, Portrait of a Breton Woman, Tahitian Landscape.*

Gaul, Roman prov.; divided into Cisalpine (N Italy) and Transalpine (France and areas W of Rhine). Name derived from Celtic settlers of 3rd–4th cent. BC. Conquered by Julius Caesar in GALLIC WARS (58–51 BC).

Gaulle, Charles De *see* DE GAULLE, CHARLES.

gaur, *Bibos gaurus,* largest of wild cattle living in small herds in forested hills of S Asia. Olive-brown coat, dorsal hump-like ridge, strongly curved horns.

Gauss, Karl Friedrich (1777–1855), Ger. mathematician and astronomer. Founded mathematical theory of electricity, did magnetic and electrical

research. The gauss, a magnetic unit is named after him.

Gautier, Théophile (1811–72), Fr. poet, novelist and critic. Leader of the Parnassians. Novels include *Mademoiselle de Maupin* (1835) and *Le Capitaine Fracasse* (1863).

gavial, *Gavialis gangeticus,* animal of crocodilian group with rod-like snout. Feeds on fish; not dangerous to man. Found in certain rivers of India.

Gay, John (1685–1732), Eng. poet and dramatist. Author of *The Begger's Opera* (1728). 1st opera with Eng. libretto. Also wrote ballads, pastoral poems and pamphlets.

gayal, *Bibos frontalis,* species of cattle closely related to and often considered the domesticated version of GAUR. Found in Burma and Assam, lives in semi-wild herds.

Gay-Lussac, Joseph Louis (1778–1850) Fr. chemist and physicist. Discovered cyanogen; isolated boron from boracic acid; invented hydrometer.

Gaza, town in **Gaza strip,** disputed territory, between Egypt and Israel on Med. coast. Pop. (1964) 37,800.

gazelle, sandy-coloured antelope of genus *Gazella.* Remarkable for speed, it lives in herds chiefly in Africa, also in Asia and India. N African dorcas gazelle, *Gazella dorcas,* is one of smallest.

Gazette, London, Edinburgh, Belfast, Ottawa, official govt. publications listing official appointments, proclamations, Orders in Council, *etc.*; also gives notices of bankruptcy,

winding up of partnerships, *etc.*

Gdansk, formerly **Danzig,** city and port of Poland on Vistula. Formerly cap. of E Prussia, became free city (1919). Occupied (1939–45) by Germany; taken by Russia, given to Poland and renamed Gdansk. Pop. (1965) 319,000.

gean *see* PRUNUS.

gecko, reptile of Geckonidae family, native of warm climates. Adhesive padded feet enable vertical or upside down walking in most species. Diet of small animals and insects.

Geddes, Norman Bel (1893–1958), Amer. stage designer, actor and producer. Sets for New York Metropolitan Opera Company included *Pelléas et Mélisande, The Miracle* and *Jeanne d'Arc.*

Geddes, Sir Patrick (1854–1932), Scot. biologist and sociologist. Related knowledge of evolution of sex to town planning and regional development as in *City Devolution* (1904).

Geiger, Hans (1882–1945), Ger. physicist and inventor. Helped develop Geiger counters used in detection of nuclear radiations and particles.

Gelinas, Gratien (1909–   ), Canadian playwright, scriptwriter and comic review star as 'Fridolin'. Author of *Tit-coq* (1950) and *Bousille et les Justes* (1957).

Gemini *see* ZODIAC.

gemsbok, *Oryx gazella,* rare antelope of desert regions of SW Africa. Generally grey with long horns.

gemstone, valued substance of mineral or organic origins, classed according to beauty, rarity and durability. Precious stones include diamond, ruby, sapphire, emerald. Semi-precious stones include amethyst, aquamarine, topaz and jade.

gene, unit of hereditary material in chromosomes of reproductive cells. Reproduced at each cell division and carries hereditarily transmissible characteristics. Common to all groups of animals and plants.

General Agreement on Tariffs and Trade (GATT), international agency under UN auspices, estab. 1948. Organized to facilitate trade by reducing tariff and other barriers and to eliminate discriminatory practices in international commerce. Critical Kennedy round (1964) of negotiations introduced 5 yr. plan to reduce tariffs by one third.

General Assembly, governing bodies of Presbyterian Churches. General Assembly of Church of Scotland, annual meeting of representative ministers and elders, directs church affairs and is its highest court.

Gavial

Women of Tahiti by Gauguin

General Assembly *see* UNITED NATIONS.

Genesis, first book of OT and of the Pentateuch. Describes creation of the world and traces Hebrew history from Abraham to Joseph. Generally thought to have been compiled after the Exile.

Genet, Jean (1910–   ), Fr. novelist, dramatist. Works include plays *The Balcony* (1957) and *The Blacks* (1959) and novels incl. *Our Lady of the Flowers* (1964).

genet, mammal of civet family with long tail. Preys nocturnally on small mammals and birds. Found in Syria, Africa and S Europe.

genetics, study of heredity variation of organisms, tracing reduplication of genes in normal cell division. Environment acts as filter to variations, *i.e.* natural selection, permitting individuals with certain inherited features to survive and reproduce, others to die out. Documented studies on sweet pea by Gregor Mendel (1822–84) was foundation of study.

Geneva, city of W Switzerland on L. Geneva, cap. of Geneva canton. Financial, cultural, and indust. centre. Focus of Reformation under CALVIN, became part of Switzerland (1815). Palais des Nations housed League of Nations; seat of International Red Cross and several UN agencies. Pop. (1965) 291,000.

Geneva, Lake, Lac Léman, between Switzerland and France. Area: *c.* 225 sq. mi.; 1,220 ft. above sea level. Scenery attracts tourists.

Geneva Convention, international agreement (1864) regulating treatment of wounded in war. Later extended to cover treatment of sick and prisoners and protection of civilians in war-time. Revised (1906, 1929, 1949).

Geneva or **'Breeches' Bible** (1560), Version produced in England as Protestant propaganda against Catholic Queen Mary; financed by congregation at Geneva. Divided into chapters, printed in roman type, with marginal notes.

Genghis Khan or **Jenghiz Khan** (*c.* 1162–1227), Mongol chieftain. Completed conquest of Mongolia (1206), captured most of Ch'in empire in China (1213–15). Subjugated (1218–24) Turkistan, Transoxania, Afghanistan, and penetrated SE Europe. Grandfather of Kublai Khan.

genital system *see* SEX ORGANS.

Genoa, Genova, port on Med., cap. of Liguria, NW Italy. Roman seaport, monopolized, with Venice, Med. sea trade during Middle Ages. Industrial and transport centre. Foreign rule before union with Sardinia (1815). Known for Cathedral of San Lorenzo and University of Genoa (founded 1812). Pop. (1965) 848,000.

genre, style of painting concerning everyday life subject-matter. Occasionally found in early art, popular-

Gecko

GEOLOGICAL TABLE; THE TIME SCALE

Estimated ages in millions of years

Period	Epoch	Time	Major Events	Animal and plant life
Quaternary	Recent	c. 1	Ice Ages affect temperature in N hemisphere. Sea retreats.	Rise of modern man: Ice Ages; vegetation Arctic forms to present form.
	Pleistocene	c. 2		
Tertiary	Pliocene	c. 7	Shallow seas in Europe; thick unconsolidated clays. Terrestrial deposits on Great Plains. Alpine-Himalayan mountain building.	Man-apes in Africa. Acme and wane of mammals. Rise of modern mammals. Archaic mammals; snakes. Vegetation of modern type.
	Miocene	26		
	Oligocene	37–38		
	Eocene	53–54		
	Palaeocene	65		
Cretaceous		136	Chalk deposited in deep seas over Europe and Asia. Marginal seas in North America.	Extinction of reptiles e.g. dinosaurs. 1st true birds. 1st angiosperms.
Jurassic		190–195	Deep sea in Europe, large coral limestone deposits. Swamps in North America.	Ammonites, belemnites, dinosaurs abundant. Small primitive mammals.
Triassic		225	Shallow sea in W Europe. Red terrestrial sands in North America.	1st mammals; acme of ammonites. Ferns i.e. gymnosperms, conifers.
Permian		280	Shallow seas; salt and continental deposits. Mountain building.	Last trilobites; rise of ammonites and reptiles.
Carboniferous (Pennsylvanian) (Mississippian)		345	Shallow seas over continents; extensive mountain building in Europe. Coal formation.	Rise of amphibians, sharks, reptiles, insects. Brachiopods, crinoids important. Swamp plants.
Devonian		395	Erosion; depression with large shallow seas. Terrestrial sandstones; thick shales.	Amphibians evolve. Bony fish abundant. Last graptolites. 1st seed plants.
Silurian		430–440	Erosion; low areas resubmerged. Mountain building in North America, Europe and Siberia.	Jawless fishes; acme of eurypterids. Rich coral reefs.
Ordovician		c. 500	Europe and North America mainly submerged. Continental uplift.	Acme of graptolites; 1st jawless fishes; molluscs spread; algae.
Cambrian		c. 570	Europe mainly submerged. North America submerged with large shallow areas.	Trilobites dominant; 1st graptolites, corals, brachiopods. Algae and spores.
Pre Cambrian		c. 4,000	Exposed in cores of continent e.g. Canadian and Scandinavian Shields.	Traces of life rare and only in late Precambrian. Forerunners of trilobites, worms, sponges found. Algae, fungi known.

PHANEROZOIC EON

CAINOZOIC

MESOZOIC

PALAEOZOIC

ARCHAEOZOIC

ced (16th cent.) by Flemish painter
Pieter Brueghel. Later Dutch exponents included Vermeer and Hals.

gentian, low growing plant of family
Gentianaceae, almost cosmopolitan
in distribution. Some species have
blue flowers. Popular in rockgardens.
Some contain a bitter component used
as a tonic.

geodesy, science of measuring shape
and size of the earth incl. weight,
density, *etc.* In geodetic survey of
earth's surface, curvature of earth
must be taken into account.

geology, science of the Earth; its
composition, structure, processes,
and history; includes the disciplines,
petrology, stratigraphy, structural
geology, palaeontology, geophysics,
and geochemistry.

geometry *see* EUCLID, NON-
EUCLIDEAN GEOMETRY.

geomorphology, science of the Earth's
surface features; their character,
origin and evolution.

geophysics, the study of the earth by
physical methods *e.g.* gravity, magnetism, earthquakes.

George, Saint (3rd–4th cent.), patron
saint of England since time of Edward
II. Perhaps a Roman soldier
martyred for the faith in Asia Minor.
Most famous exploit was the slaying
of a dragon.

George I (1660–1727), first Hanoverian king of Great Britain and Ireland
(1714–27). Speaking little English, he
left admin. of govt. to ministers, a
practice which initiated cabinet govt.
in UK.

George II (1683–1760), king of Great
Britain and Ireland (1727–60). Continued father's policy of govt. through
ministers, notably SIR ROBERT
WALPOLE. Last Brit. king to lead
troops in battle (at Dettingen, 1743;
War of Austrian Succession).

George III (1738–1820), king of
Great Britain and Ireland (1760–
1820). Attempted reassertion of royal
authority in govt. through ministers
sympathetic to himself (North, Bute).
Lost Amer. Colonies. Tory ministry
of William Pitt the younger (1783–
1801) terminated royal ambitions.
Insanity led to regency of his son.

George IV (1762–1830), king of
Great Britain and Ireland (1820–30),
and prince regent (1811–20). Personally unpopular, ruled through Tory
ministers.

George V (1865–1936), king of Great
Britain, Ireland and Emperor of India
(1910–36). Changed family name
from Saxe-Coburg-Gotha to Windsor
(1917).

George VI (1895–1952), king of Great
Britain, Ireland and Head of British

Gentian

Commonwealth (1936–52), became
king when brother Edward VIII
abdicated. Father of Elizabeth II.

George, Henry (1839–97), Amer.
economist. Proposed 'single tax' on
land to cover cost of government.
Advocated full free trade, repudiated
socialism (except concerning land
ownership). Wrote *Progress and
Poverty* (1879).

George, Stefan (1868–1933), Ger.
symbolist poet. Refuted Nazism, went
to Switzerland. Poems include
Albagal (1892), *Das Jahr der Seele*
[The Soul's Year] (1892), *Das Neue
Reich* [The New Kingdom] (1928).

Georgetown, cap. and main port of
Guyana. Industrial and shipping
centre; exports bauxite, diamonds,
gold and rum. Pop. (1963) 72,964.

Georgetown University, Washington
DC, US. Founded by Jesuits (1789),
chartered (1815). Notable law and
medical schools.

Georgia, state in SE US. Area: 58,214
sq. mi.; cap. Atlanta. Other principal
cities, Savannah, Augusta, Columbus.
Predominantly lowland. Region discovered by Spanish (1540), claimed
by England (1663). Produces cotton,
maize, tobacco, fruit, timber. Recent
indust. expansion based on textile and
natural resources development. Pop.
(1967) 4,511,000.

Georgian Bay Islands, Canadian
National Park in Ontario. Founded
1929, island group in L. Huron. Area:
54 sq. mi.

Georgian SSR, Georgia, constituent
republic of USSR in Caucasus. Area:
26,911 sq. mi.; cap. Tbilisi [Tiflis].
Ruled by Persia after autonomy as
kingdom (3rd cent.); branch of
Armenian dynasty until 1801, when it
came under Russ. protection. Independent (1917–21), it became
Soviet republic. Predominantly agric.,
produce includes wine; some mineral
deposits and heavy industry. Pop.
(1966) 4,611,000.

Georgian style of architecture, in UK
during reigns of George I, II and III,
(1714–1820) based on revival of
Palladianism introduced by Inigo
Jones and Sir Christopher Wren.
Characterized by classical symmetry
and simplicity. Notable example is St
Martins-in-the-Fields, London, by
James Gibbs.

geranium, widely distributed garden
plant of genus *Pelargonium,* native to
South Africa. Cranesbill geranium
grows wild in Americas.

gerbil, sand rat, mammal and gregarious burrower of rat family of drier
parts of Africa and Asia. Hind legs
used for leaping. Species include fat-
tailed gerbil, *Pachyuromys duprasi.*

gerenuk, *Litocranius walleri,* gazelle
with long thin legs and neck.
Also known as giraffe-necked gazelle.

geriatrics *see* GERONTOLOGY.

German art, in architecture, earliest
notable buildings were Romanesque
churches (Hildesheim, Speier,
Worms, Maintz); this style influenced Gothic art which appeared in
13th cent. (Bamberg, Naumberg,
Limburg). 18th cent. Baroque flourished esp. in Austria and Bavaria.
Modern styles of Behrens and
Gropius arc outstanding. Painting
developed in many centres, incl.
Cologne, Nuremberg, Colmar, *etc.*
In Renaissance the names of Dürer,
Holbein, Altdorfer and Cranach are
outstanding. Also famous was
manufacture of furniture and Dresden
china (esp. in 18th cent.). The 20th
cent. has produced some expressionist
sculpture and painting of repute (*e.g.*
Kokoschka).

Geranium, *Pelargonium radula*

German measles *see* RUBELLA.

germander, *c.* 100 species of plant genus, *Teucrium*, of the mint family, of cosmopolitan distribution. Common N Amer. forms *T. canadense* and *T. occidentale* and Brit. *T. scorodonia* are frequently known as wood sage.

Germanic languages, group of Indo-European languages to which English and German belong. **German** has *c.* 90 million speakers in Germany, Austria and parts of Switzerland.

Germany [**Deutschland**], country of NC Europe bounded on E by Poland and Czechoslovakia, S by Austria, W by France and Low Countries, N by Baltic, North Sea and Denmark. Divisible geographically into N Ger. plain, extensive agric. area; central area of block mountains, important cattle and forestry area; Rhine rift fault where tobacco, grapes and hops are grown; and S Ger. Alpine foreland. Rich coal, iron and copper deposits, esp. in Ruhr, Saar and Saxony. For many cent. a conglomeration of hundreds of states loosely allied to Holy Roman Empire; unification and statehood came primarily as response to Fr. ambitions. With Napoleon's downfall, confederation estab. (1815) in which Prussia gradually attained supremacy. Prussian king became Ger. emperor (1871), and under Bismarck Germany acquired a nationalist outlook. World War 1, in part a response to this, saw overthrow of empire and formation of repub. Between wars deplorable Ger. economy (in part because of Fr. effort to extort war reparations) resulted in political confusion facilitating rise of ADOLF HITLER and NAZI party. In 1933, Hitler became chancellor and estab. Third Reich. Conscription (1935) and other militaristic manifestations were soon followed by Anschluss (Austrian annexation, 1938), invasion of Czechoslovakia (1938) and Poland (Sept. 1939). Last move began World War 2. Following 1945 surrender, considerable territorial adjustment made Oder-Neisse line E (Polish) frontier. Deterioration of E–W relations led to partition of state (1949) into 2 separate repub.

Germany, East [**Deutsche Demokratische Republik**]. Area: 41,659 sq.

Karl Marx-Allee, East Berlin, Germany

mi.; cap. East Berlin; other main cities Leipzig, Dresden. Collectivization of agric. land (1960). Communist puppet govt. until 1955 when USSR recognized East German state. Language German; religion, R.C.; unit of currency, Deutsche Mark. Pop. (1963) 17,135,867.

Germany, West [**Bundesrepublic Deutschland**]. Area: 95,959 sq. mi.; cap. Bonn; main cities Hamburg, Munich, Cologne, Frankfurt. Fore-

most trading European nation, large indust. plants, skilled labour, coal deposits. Language German; religions, Protestant and R.C.; unit of currency, Deutsche Mark. Pop. (1965) 57,485,000.

Gerona, town, cap. of Gerona prov. NE Spain. Resisted French in Peninsular War (1808–9). Notable Gothic cathedral. Pop. (1961) 32,800.

Geronimo (*c.* 1829–1909), Apache leader; led retaliatory raids on Arizona when his band was moved to a New Mexico reservation (1876); finally surrendered (1886).

gerontology, geriatrics, scientific study of old age. Concern is with diseases and the care of the aged.

Gershwin, George (1893–1937), Amer. composer. Treated jazz idiom in symphonic form. Best known works include *Rhapsody in Blue* (1924), *American in Paris* (1928) and Negro opera *Porgy and Bess* (1935).

Gesell, Arnold Lucius (1880–   ), Amer. psychologist and pediatrician. Studied chronological norms in child

development. Best known work *The First Five Years* (1940).

Gestapo, [**Geheime Staatspolizei**], secret police in Nazi Germany (1933–45). Combined with Hitler's SS after 1936 under Himmler. Carried out ruthless policy of investigation, torture and extermination. Indicted as one body at Nuremberg war crimes trials (1945–6).

gestation *see* PREGNANCY.

Gethsemane, Garden of, at foot of the Mount of Olives, near Jerusalem. Christ went there after the Last Supper. Scene of His agony, betrayal and arrest.

Getty, J[**ean**] **Paul** (1892–   ), Amer. business man. Made fortune in oil, and formed Getty Oil Co. Author of several books, incl. *Europe in the 18th cent.* (1947), and *The Joys of Collecting* (1965).

Gettysburg Address (19 Nov. 1863), brief speech by US President Lincoln delivered at dedication of cemetery at site of Battle of Gettysburg (July 1863), containing the famous statement of the principles of Amer. govt. 'of the people, by the people, for the people.'

Gettysburg Campaign, in Amer. Civil War (June-July 1863). Confederate army under R. E. Lee victorious at Chancellorsville, attempted invasion into S Pennsylvania; met Union forces W of Gettysburg, driven to Cemetery Hill, where decisively defeated (July 2); Lee retreated (July 4). Marked turning point of war.

geyser, hot spring from which gushing column of hot water and steam is explosively discharged at intervals. Manifestation of late phase of volcanic activity, *e.g.* Old Faithful, Yellowstone Park, Wyo., and Rotorua, New Zealand.

Ghana, republic of W Africa, former

Brit. colony and protectorate, **Gold Coast,** and former UN Trust Territory of (Brit.) Togoland. Area: 91,843 sq. mi.; cap., Accra. Independent since 1957; republic since 1960. Ghana has equatorial climate with trop. forests in S, dry, hot climate with semi-arid savanna in N; mountains of Togo in E. European slave trade 17–19th cent. Economy dominated by cocoa (30% world total); exports timber, gold, manganese, coffee, rubber, bananas. Pop. (1965) 7,945,000.

Ghats, 2 mountain ranges, Eastern and Western, parallel to coasts of peninsular India; form 2 edges of Indian Plateau, or Deccan. Important teak forests.

Ghent, [Fr: **Gand;** Flemish: **Gent**] city, commercial centre and river port of Belgium, cap. of E Flanders prov., at confluence of Lys and Scheldt; major focus of canals and railways. Important as wool trade centre during 16th cent. Occupied by Germans in World Wars 1 and 2. Industries include glass, cotton and linen. Pop. (1965) 229,000.

gherkin *see* CUCUMBER.

ghetto, formerly section of a city in which Jews lived. Segregation in separate localities was voluntary in early middle ages, but compulsory ghettos were introduced in Spain and Portugal in late 14th cent. and famous

Portrait of a Girl by Ghirlandaio

Frankfurt ghetto estab. by ordinance (1460). Ghettos usually autonomous. Last ghetto in Rome abolished (1870). Term now often used to cover sections of cities characterized by poverty and acute social disorganization and inhabited by members of a minority group (*e.g.* predominantly Negro sections in Amer. cities).

Ghibellines *see* GUELPHS AND GHIBELLINES.

Ghiberti, Lorenzo (1378–1455), Florentine painter, goldsmith and sculptor who designed and made bronze doors of the baptistry in Florence (1401–50).

Ghirlandaio, Domenico (1449–94), Florentine fresco painter. Principal works are lives of Mary and St John the Baptist for Santa Maria Novella (Florence) and *The Calling of the First Apostles* (Sistine Chapel).

ghost moth, *Hepialus humuli*, moth of swift group. White males fly around together at dusk giving a ghostly appearance. Larvae feed on roots and are often pests.

Giacometti, Alberto (1901–66), Swiss surrealist sculptor and painter; Sculptures show elongated, emaciated human figures.

giant panda, *Ailuropoda melanolenca*, large mammal of Tibet, related to raccoon. White above with black underparts.

giants, beings of more than human size, common in folklore. In Gk. myth., they attempted unsuccessfully to conquer the Olympian gods; in Scandinavian myth. were linked with Creation stories. Children's stories and allegories perpetuate the idea.

Giant's Causeway, coastal feature of Antrim, N Ireland, where cooling of basalt resulted in hexagonal jointing. Folklore attributes origin to race of giants making road to W Scotland.

Giauque, William Francis (1895–), Amer. chemist, co-discoverer of 2nd and 3rd isotopes of oxygen. Awarded Nobel Prize for Chemistry (1949) for study of properties of substances at very low temperature.

Gibbon, Edward (1737–94), Eng. historian. Author of *The Decline and Fall of the Roman Empire* (1776–88).

gibbon, smallest anthropoid ape of genera *Hylobates* and *Symphalanga*, found in SE Asia and E Indies. Have slender bodies and long arms.

Gibbons, Orlando (1583–1625), Eng. organist at court of James I. Composed anthems, madrigals (*e.g.* 'Silver Swan') and instrumental works.

Gibbs, Josiah Willard (1839–1903), Amer. physicist who estab. basic

Gravensteen castle in Ghent

theory for physical chemistry. Contributed to knowledge of thermodynamics.

Gibraltar, Brit. colony on promontory S of Andalusia prov., Spain. Lookout on Straits of Gibraltar, W entrance to Med. Sea. Area: 2 sq. mi. A fortress, naval base, free port and tourist centre. Pop. (1964) 26,000. Rock of Gibraltar and Mt. Abyla known as Pillars of Hercules.

Gide, André (1869–1951), Fr. writer. Semi-autobiog. novels of conflict against convention include *Les Nourritures Terrestres* (1897) and *Les Faux-Monnayeurs* (1925). Founded *Nouvelle Revue Française* (1909). Awarded Nobel Prize for Literature (1947).

Gielgud, Sir John (1904–), Eng. actor and director. Known for Shakespearean roles, esp. Hamlet (since 1929). Solo performance in *Ages of Man* (1958–9).

Gieseking, Walter (1895–1956), Ger. pianist. Known as interpreter of Fr. impressionist composers, esp. Debussy and Ravel.

gila monster, *Heloderma suspectum,* venomous lizard of deserts of SW US and Mexico. Can survive months of fasting, on store of surplus fat in tail.

Gilbert, Sir Humphrey (*c.* 1539–83), Eng. soldier, navigator and explorer. Took possession of Newfoundland (1583), and founded settlement. Drowned during voyage home.

Gilbert, Sir William Schwenk (1836–1911), Eng. wit and playwright. Librettist of Sullivan's light operas. Author of *Bab Ballads* (1869 and 1873).

Gilbert, William (1540–1603), Eng. physicist and physician to Elizabeth I. Discovered distinction between frictional electricity and magnetic phenomena.

Gilbert and Ellice Islands, group of Pacific islands. UK crown colony. Area: 369 sq. mi.; cap. Tarawa. Estab. 1915, administered with Brit. Solomon Is. and New Hebrides. Inhabitants: Micronesian in Gilberts, Polynesian in Ellice group. Exports copra and rock phosphates. Pop. 50,000.

Gilbreth, Frank B[unker] (1868–1924), Amer. engineer and efficiency expert. Co-author with his wife, of *Motion Study* (1911), a pioneer work of business management.

gild *see* GUILDS.

Giles, Carl Ronald (1916–   ), 'Giles', Brit. cartoonist. Caricatures elements in Brit. attitudes and customs, often represented through family life.

Gill, Eric Rowland (1882–1940), Eng. sculptor, engraver and typeface designer. Sculptures include 'Stations of the Cross' in Westminster Cathedral.

Gillespie, Dizzy, orig. John Birks (1917–   ), Amer. jazz trumpeter, bandleader and composer.

Gillette, King Camp (1855–1932), Amer. inventor of safety razor.

gills, organs in fish and larval amphibians for absorption of oxygen dissolved in water. Assimilated through thin enclosing membrane. Certain invertebrates have comparable organs, *e.g.* mantle in bivalve molluscs.

Stained glass panel from the church of Chalons-sur-Marne depicting John and Mary at the foot of the cross

Gilman, Charlotte, née Perkins (1860–1935), Amer. writer and lecturer on economics, ethics and sociology. Worked for socialist and female suffrage movements.

gin, spirit distilled from grain and flavoured with juniper berries. Percentage of alcohol varies from 40 to 50.

ginger, *Zingiber officinale,* perennial plant with hot, spicy root. Orig. from S China but known to ancient Greeks, Romans and Indians. Sliced and preserved in syrup, as confection; ground ginger used as spice.

Ginkel, Godert de, 1st Earl of Athlone (1644–1703), Dutch general in service of William III of England. Commander of army in Ireland (1689).

ginkgo, maidenhair tree, *Ginkgo biloba,* deciduous tree, with fan-shaped leaves. Native to China, but widely planted elsewhere. Survived from group of trees existing in prehistoric era.

Ginsberg, Allen (1926–   ), Amer. poet. Spokesman of 'beat' generation. One of his best-known poems is *Howl* (1956).

ginseng, aromatic plant of genus *Panax.* Species include the Chinese *P. schinseng* and *P. quinquefolius* of N Amer. woodlands. Aromatic root has a sweetish taste and is valued medicinally, esp. in China and Korea.

Giorgione, orig. Giorgio Barbarelli (*c.* 1477–1510), one of founders of Venetian school of painting. Style typified by *The Tempest.* Other works include *The Three Philosophers* and the *Castelfranco Madonna.*

Giotto di Bondone (*c.* 1267–1337), Florentine artist. Influenced European painting by adopting naturalist style Frescoes include scenes in life of St Francis, at Assisi and cycle of biblical frescoes (*e.g.* life and passion of Christ, in Padua).

Gipps, Sir George (1790–1847), Gov. of New South Wales, Australia (1838–46). Conservative policies on land grants denounced by squatters and gold miners. Gippsland Lakes and area of Victoria named after him.

Gipsy, Gypsy, Romany, person belonging to nomadic tribe, believed to have originated in India. Entered Europe early 15th cent. Most of them are found in the Balkans, Spain and Italy. Have their own language and customs. Est. numbers, 1 million.

gipsy moth, *Lymantria dispas,* insect of tussoch moth group extinct in Britain *c.* 1850 but a serious pest in N. Amer. forests, having been accidentally introduced. Larvae eat so many leaves that tree dies.

giraffe, hoofed mammal of Africa S Sahara. Tallest of animals (reaches 1 ft. in height), long neck enables it eat leaves of trees. Fast enough outrun most of its enemies.

Giraudoux, Jean (1882–1944), F writer and diplomat. Wrote novel *e.g. Suzanne et le Pacifique* (1921 also plays *Amphitryon 38* (1929), *L Guerre de Troie n'aura pas Lie* (1935).

Girl Guides, organization founded b Lord Baden-Powell to promote worl citizenship, sociability, and outdoc life for girls (7–17 yr. old). In US **Girl Scouts** (founded 1912 by Juliett Low) have similar aims.

Girondins or **Girondists,** Fr. revolu tionary party. Moderate republicans instrumental in estab. of Firs Republic (1792–3) until their over throw by Jacobins.

Gish, Lillian (1896–   ), Amer stage and film actress. Appeared i such films as *Hearts of the World* an *Romola.* Sister, Dorothy Gish (1898–   ) also an actress.

Gissing, George Robert (1857–1903) Eng. novelist. Best known work *New Grub Street* (1891); also wrote *Bor in Exile* (1892).

Giza, El, Gizeh, city of N Egypt on Nile R., opposite Cairo; the Sphinx and pyramids are nearby. Pop. (195 est.) 177,000.

Gjellerup, Karl Adolf (1857–1919) Danish poet and novelist. Early novels biographical, later writing shows Buddhist and Indian influ ences, *e.g. The Pilgrim Kamanitc* (1906). With Henrik Pontoppidan awarded Nobel Prize for Literature (1917).

glacier, tongue of ice flowing down valley from mountain source o accumulated snow. **Glaciology,** study of glacierial distribution, character action and effects.

Glacier National Park, in Brit Columbia, Canada, founded 1886 Area: 521 sq. mi. Alpine region ir Selkirk Mts.

gladiolus, corm rooted plant, *Gladi olus,* native to S Africa. Naturalized ir Europe as garden plant, grows to 4 ft and has long stalks of flowers of various colours.

Gladstone, William Ewart (1809–98), Brit. politician. Tory and Liberal M.P. (1832–95); Chanc. of Ex chequer (1852–5). Joined Liberal party and became P.M. (1868–74). Initiated educational and voting re forms and Irish land acts. Again P.M. (1880–5; 1886; 1892–4), resigning several times over Irish Home Rule question. Great orator and admini strator.

Entry into Jerusalem by Giotto

Glamorganshire, county of S Wales. Welsh Mountains in N; Vale of Glamorgan in S. Area: 813 sq. mi.; county town, Cardiff. Extensive coal-mining at Rhondda, Merthyr Tydfil. Industries include iron-smelting, tin-plating. Pop. (1966) 1,252,000.

gland, organ which builds up chemical compounds for secretion. Most glands discharge through ducts either to outer surface of skin, *e.g.* sweat glands, or to an inner surface, *e.g.* digestive glands secreting into the gut. Ductless or endocrine glands secrete hormones directly into the blood, *e.g.* thyroid gland.

Glaser, Donald Arthur (1926–), Amer. physicist. Awarded Nobel Prize for Physics (1960) for invention of bubble chamber to observe tracks of moving subatomic particles.

Glasgow, port and burgh of Scotland, on R. Clyde. Scotland's largest city, it has extensive shipyards; commercial centre, light and heavy manufacture, distilling. Contains art museums and University of Glasgow (founded 1451). Pop. (1964) 1,049,115.

glass, non-crystalline, usually transparent, inorganic substance. Withstands high temperature; manu-factured by heat fusion, dating from prehistoric times in Egypt and SE Asia. Medieval European countries were skilled in art of glassware making. Also *see* STAINED GLASS.

glass snake, joint snake, lizard of genus *Ophisaurus* of slowworm family. Has rudimentary limbs, feeds on mice, worms, insects. Asia Minor variety, *O. apodus*; 3 known US species.

Glastonbury, town of Somerset, England. Prehistoric lake dwellings found at foot of Glastonbury Tor, site of ruined medieval monastery. Also said to be Isle of Avalon of Arthurian legend. Traditionally site of 1st Eng. Christian Church.

Glauber, Johann Rudolf (1604–68), Ger. scientist. Made contributions to analytical chemistry; Glauber's salt named after him.

glaucoma, group of eye diseases characterized by increasing pressure within eyeball and often resulting in impaired vision or blindness.

Glencoe, valley in N Argyllshire, Scotland. Scene of massacre (1692) of Macdonald clan by Campbells.

Glendower, Owen (*c.* 1359–*c.* 1416), Welsh leader of rebellion against Henry IV (1399). Proclaiming himself Prince of Wales, waged war against English until defeat (1415).

Glenn, John H[erschel], Jr. (1921–), Amer. astronaut; 1st Amer. to orbit earth (3-orbit flight, 1962).

glider, engineless airplane depending on gravity for forward motion and upon upward air currents for attaining altitude. Man's 1st heavier than air flights were made using gliders. The sport is called **gliding.**

Glinka, Mikhail Ivanovich (1804–57), Russ. nationalist composer. Best known works are operas *A Life for the Tsar* (1836), *Ruslan and Ludmilla* (1842).

globe candytuft, *Iberis umbellata,* cultivated annual plant with tufted flowers. Orig. from island of Candia, Greece.

globe fish, found in trop. and subtrop. regions. Swallows air, becoming almost globular. Includes poisonous spined *Tetrodon,* found in Nile and S Amer. and Indian rivers.

Globe Theatre, old playhouse in London. Built 1599, destroyed (1644) by Puritans. Most of Shakespeare's plays first presented at the Globe.

glockenspiel, tuned percussion instrument consisting of set of steel bars of different lengths which player hits with hammers. Produces bell-like sound.

Glorious Revolution (1688–9), in Eng. history, overthrow of Catholic James II. William of Orange petitioned to rule as William III jointly with Mary II, James' Protestant

Glacier showing crevasses

daughter. Their acceptance of BILL OF RIGHTS assured parl. authority in place of 'divine right of kings'.

glory-of-the-snow, *Chionodoxa luciliae,* bulbous plant, of lily family. Native to high altitudes of Crete and Asia Minor.

glossopteris, genus of Permian-Triassic fossil. Fern-like plants, characterized by thick fronds with connecting veins.

glottis, opening between vocal chords of larynx in mammals which controls production of sound.

Gloucester, Eng. dukedom held by several members of royal family.

Gnu

Thomas of Woodstock (1355–97), son of Edward III. Opposed nephew, Richard II, executed for treason. **Humphrey** (1391–1447), son of Henry IV, served as regent (1420–1) of England during brother Henry V's participation in wars with France. **Richard** (1452–85) became king as Richard III.

Gloucestershire, county of W England. Area: 1,259 sq. mi.; county town Gloucester; principal city Bristol. Predominantly agric., sheep raising (Cotswold Hills) in E; dairy farming in Severn valley; Forest of Dean in W. Centre of wool industry in middle ages. Pop. (1966) 1,054,000.

Gluck, Christoph Willibald von (1714–87), Ger. operatic composer whose later works emphasize simplicity and unity of style. They include *Orfeo ed Euridice* (1762), *Alceste* (1767), *Iphigénie en Tauride* (1779).

glucose *see* SUGAR.

Glueck, Nelson (1900–71), Amer. archaeologist famous for discoveries in Palestine, Transjordan and Negev desert. Works include *Explorations in Eastern Palestine* (1934–51), *Deities and Dolphins* (1965).

gluten, elastic protein substance in grain, giving consistency to dough. It remains after starch is extracted.

glutton, *Gulo gulo,* carnivorous mam-mal related to weasel and N Amer. WOLVERINE, found in N temperate regions. Good climber and swimmer *c.* $2\frac{1}{2}$ ft. long. Voracious predator, remorselessly hunted.

glycerol, glycerin[e], colourless, odourless, viscous alcohol, found naturally in form of glycerides, principal constituents of animal and vegetable fats and oils. Many uses include sweetening and medicine.

glycogen, animal starch, form in which carbohydrates are stored in animals, esp. in the liver. A tasteless white powder discovered by Bernard (1857).

Glyn, Elinor née Sutherland (1864–1943), Eng. novelist, scenario and short-story writer. Best-known novel, *Three Weeks* (1907).

Glyndebourne Festival, annual international season of opera, held every summer since 1934 in private opera house near Glynde, Sussex, England. Founded by John Christie, Brit. music patron.

Gmelin, Leopold (1788–1853), Ger. chemist. Discovered potassium ferricyanide (also called Gmelin's salt).

gnat, small fly of mosquito family. Species include European house gnat *Culex pipeus* and Amer. eye gnat. Larvae aquatic.

gnatcatcher, *Polioptila,* genus of small Amer. insectivorous warblers.

Gnosticism, rationalistic doctrine which arose in Christian church in 1st cent. AD. Emphasized knowledge rather than faith. Gnostics attempted to combine Christ's teachings with Gk. and Oriental philosophies. Held that God was unknowable and unapproachable. Influenced early Christianity by forcing it to define its doctrine in declaring Gnosticism heretical.

gnu, antelope of E and S Africa with buffalo-like head. Species include nearly extinct White Tailed Gnu or Black Wildebeest *Connochaetes gnu.*

Goa, former Portuguese colony, W India on Arabian Sea. Area: 1,300 sq. mi.; cap. New Goa or Pangim. Annexed by India (1961).

goanna, monitor, largest Austral. lizard. The perentie, *Varanus giganteus* grows to 7 ft. and is found in desert areas.

goat, hollow-horned ruminant of genus *Capra,* family Bovidae, with narrow head, in males beard on chin, swept back horns and short upturned tail. Wild goats include PASANG, MARKHOR and IBEX. Gives nutritious milk, most important breed being the Swiss or alpine.

goat moth, large moth of cassid family with grey wings and goat-like smell.

Goldcrest

Large pinkish larvae take 3–4 yr. to develop, feed on wood of elm, ash and willow. Species include European *Corsus corsus* and N Amer. *Prionoxystus robiniae.*

Gobat, Charles Albert (1843–1914), Swiss statesman and pacifist. Pres. of Berne International Peace Bureau (1906–14). With Élie Ducommun, awarded Nobel Peace Prize (1902).

Gobbi, Tito (1915–), Ital. baritone opera singer. Has sung in major theatres throughout the world and in films.

Gobelins, Manufacture Nationale des, Fr. tapestry manufacturers. Founded (15th cent.) as dye works; purchased (1662) by Louis XIV. Now state-controlled.

Gobi, desert *c.* 400 mi. from N to S and *c.* 1,000 mi. E to W, partly in Mongolian People's Republic and partly in Inner Mongolia.

goby, small spiny-finned fish of family Gobiidae. Some entirely freshwater, others only enter rivers to spawn. Species include black goby, *Gobius niger.*

go-carting [UK] **karting** [US], modern sport of driving and racing small low internal combustion engined vehicles. Low profile gives driver illusion of great speed and provides stability. Invented in California (1957) by Art Ingels.

God, idolised divinity. Jewish, Christian and Moslem concept is of an infinite, immanent, transcendent being who is all powerful, all good, all creating, all knowing. Often personalized, loves and judges mankind.

Godard, Jean-Luc (1930–), Fr. film producer of the NOUVELLE VAGUE. Films include *A Bout de Souffle* (1959), *Vivre Sa Vie* (1962) and *Les Carabiniers* (1963).

Godavari, river of India, flowing 900 mi. from Western Ghats to Bay of Bengal. Important for hydro-electric power, and irrigation near delta.

Gödel, Kurt (1906–), Amer. mathematical logician, Czech. born. Known for theorem (1931) proving mathematics could not be consistent and axiomatic.

Goderich, Viscount see ROBINSON, FREDERICK JOHN.

godetia, annual plant, *Oenothera*, of California and Chile. Related to evening primrose.

Godunov, Boris (c. 1551–1605), Tsar of Russia (1598–1605). Favourite of Ivan IV; ruled as regent during reign of Feodor I (1584–98) and succeeded him. Re-colonized Siberia and encouraged foreign trade. Died while opposing the false pretender Dmitri.

Godwin, Earl of Wessex (d. 1053), Eng. statesman. Adviser of Canute, exiled by Edward the Confessor (1051).

Godwin, Mary, orig. Mary Wollstonecraft (1759–97), Eng. writer. Author of *Vindication of the Rights of Women* (1792).

Godwin, William (1756–1836), Eng. writer and political philosopher. Chief work *Enquiry Concerning Political Justice* (1793). Materialist and Utopian ideas, popular among Romantic poets.

Godwin Austen, Mt., or **K2,** mountain in Kashmir Himalayas (Karakoram). Second highest peak (28,250 ft.) in the world.

godwit, migrant wader of sandpiper family. European species include bar-tailed godwit, *Limosa lapponica* and black-tailed godwit, *L. limosa*, with rusty brown breast.

Goebbels, Paul Joseph (1897–1945), Ger. Nazi leader. Min. of Propaganda

Glutton

from 1933. Committed suicide during Siege of Berlin.

Goering, Herman (1893–1946), Ger. Nazi leader, founder and leader of the GESTAPO. Committed suicide in prison after sentence of death at Nuremberg.

Goethe, Johann Wolfgang von (1749–1832), Ger. poet, dramatist and novelist of outstanding importance in development of Ger. and European literature. Wrote lyric poetry, which helped mould Ger. language, also novels *Die Leiden des jungen Werthers* (1774), *Wilhelm Meisters Lehrjahre* (1796). Became leader of literary *Sturm und Drang* movement and published plays incl. *Faust* (Part I 1808, Part II 1832).

Gog and Magog, symbolic figures of the OT who have passed into Brit. mythology as survivors of a legendary race of giants. In the Apocalypse, represent enemies of kingdom of God.

Gogarty, Oliver St John (1878–1957), Irish physician and writer, associated with Dublin literary movement. Senator of Irish Free State (1922–36).

Gogh, Vincent van (1853–90), Leading Dutch post-Impressionist painter. Painted only during the last 10 yr. of his life. Noted for dynamic works using brilliant colour.

Gogol, Nikolai Vasilyevich (1809–52), Russ. civil servant and writer of humorous and satirical works, incl. *Taras Bulba* (1834) and *The Government Inspector* (1836).

goitre, chronic enlargement of thyroid gland producing swelling on front of neck; attributed to lack of iodine. In exophthalmic goitre (Graves' disease), enlargement of thyroid gland is accompanied by protrusion of eyeballs, palpitation, *etc.*

gold, ductile and malleable metallic element, chemically inactive. Good conductor of heat and electricity. Occurs naturally or as alloy with other metals. Quest for gold dates from prehistoric times; stimulated European exploration in Americas and figured largely in 19th and 20th cent. economics (see GOLD STANDARD). Chief producers are South Africa, USSR, Canada and US.

Gold Coast see GHANA.

gold standard, system for stabilizing international trade and finance until 20th cent. Technically, it determined unit value of each nation's currency to fixed legal price. System broke down after World War 1 during the Depression, when fixed gold standard helped transmit internal economic crises to world economy. Many currencies now fixed to US dollar, but drain on Amer. gold reserves resulted in questioning of system in 1960s, leading some countries, notably France, to exchange dollars for gold.

Goldberg, Arthur Joseph (1908–), Amer. lawyer. Served as Judge on Supreme Court (1962–5) and as UN Representative (1965–8).

Goldberg, Rube (1883–1970), Amer. cartoonist. Worked on New York *Evening Mail* (1907–21).

goldcrest, *Regulus regulus,* smallest European bird, with golden streak on crown. Common in pine woods.

Golden Bull, name of an important imperial charter. Chief was that composed (1356) by Charles IV providing constitution for Holy Roman Empire.

Golden Calf, in OT, idol made by Aaron and destroyed by Moses on his return from Mt. Sinai (*Exodus* XXXII).

golden eagle, *Aquila chrysaëtos,* rare species of eagle of Europe, Asia and N America. Dark-brown plumage and 6 ft. wingspan; carries prey in talons. Female larger than male.

Golden Fleece, fleece of winged ram which carried Phrixus and Helle from Thebes. Ram sacrificed to Zeus and fleece guarded by dragon at Colchis. Later recovered by JASON.

Golden Gate, suspension bridge over Golden Gate waterway San Francisco, US. Opened 1937 as longest single-span suspension in world, 4,200 ft. between towers; total length, 9,266 ft.

Golden Globe, round the world race (1968–9) for single handed yachtsmen competing for trophy, and £5,000 for fastest time. Sponsored by *Sunday Times*, England.

Golden Horde, orig. the Mongol warriors of Batu Khan. Empire founded mid-13th cent. and comprised most of Russia. Power of

Black-tailed Godwit

Golden Horde khanates finally crushed by IVAN III (1487).

Golden Horn, opening of Bosporus, separating Istanbul from suburbs, forming natural harbour.

Golden Mile, area of W Australia, S of Kalgoorlie, named because of valuable gold claims (£100 million in 50 yr.). Pop. 25,000.

golden pheasant, *Chrysolophus pictus,* multi-coloured pheasant of Tibet and China. Popular as ornamental bird.

goldeneye, *Bucephala clangula,* migrant duck of merganser group with white spot beside the eye.

goldenrod, perennial plant of daisy family with spike of yellow flowers. Native of Europe and N America. Species include *Solidago virgaurea* and *S. canadensis.*

goldfinch, *Carduelis carduelis,* colourful Eurasian finch with red throat, black nape and parts of tail and wings, and yellow back and wings.

goldfish, *Carassius auratus,* small fresh-water fish of carp family of Asiatic origin. Controlled breeding has led to variety of forms.

Golding, William Gerald (1911–), Eng. novelist. Allegorical works include *Lord of the Flies* (1954), *Pincher Martin* (1956) and *Free Fall* (1959).

Goldman, Emma (1869–1940), Amer. anarchist imprisoned for advocating birth control (1916) and obstructing the draft. Deported to Russia but returned to US and denounced Communist bureaucracy.

Goldschmidt, Richard (1878–1958), Amer. zoologist, b. Germany. Did much to unify evolutionary theory.

Goldsmith, Oliver (1728–74), Eng. poet, dramatist and novelist. Unsuccessful as physician, turned to writing. Close friend of Samuel Johnson and his circle. Works include *The Vicar of Wakefield* (novel, 1766), *The Deserted Village* (poem, 1770) and *She Stoops to Conquer* (comedy, 1773).

Goldwater, Barry Morris (1909–), Amer. Republican politician, defeated Pres. candidate (1964). Prominent spokesman for conservatives in US in 1960s.

Goldfinch

golf, game played with specially-made clubs over outdoor course. Aim is to drive a small ball into series of holes in fewest possible strokes. Oldest club, Royal and Ancient Golf Club, St Andrews, Scotland (1764).

Golgi, Camillo (1844–1926), Ital. physician, neurologist, histologist. With S. Ramón, awarded Nobel Prize for Physiology and Medicine (1906) for work on structure of nervous system.

Golgotha [Hebrew: place of the skull], scene of Christ's crucifixion. Also called Calvary.

Goliath, in OT, giant champion of Philistines, enemies of Israel. Killed by David with a stone from his sling. (1 *Sam.* XVII).

Gomes, Estevâo, (c. 1483–1538), Portuguese explorer in the service of Spain. Explored coast of America from Florida to Cape Race (1524–25). Sailed (1535) to Rio de la Plata and trekked across Gran Chaco in search of silver and gold.

Gompers, Samuel (1850–1924), Amer. labour leader. Instrumental in foundation of what was to become (1886) American Federation of Labor, and its pres. (1886–94, 1896–1924). Rejected radical and socialist programmes, supported wage demands and shorter working hours.

Gomulka, Wladyslaw (1905–), Polish politician; Communist party leader (1943–8, 1956–70). Ousted from party (1949), charged with nationalist deviations. Reinstated after Poznan riots (1956). Pursued course of averting Soviet intervention and popular revolt.

Goncharov, Ivan Aleksandrovich (1812–91), Russ. novelist. Wrote *Oblomov* (1858).

Goncourt, Edmond [Huot] de (1822–96) and **Jules [Huot] de** (1830–70) Fr. brothers, writers, collaborators. Works include *Renée Mauperin* (1864), *Journal des Goncourt* (9 vols., 1887–96).

gondola, narrow, flat-bottomed boat used on canals and lagoons of Venice. Traditionally rowed with one oar by gondolier standing in stern.

gong, percussion instrument of Oriental origin, consisting of free-hanging metal disc with turned-in edges; struck with soft drum-stick.

gonorrhea, acute infectious inflammation of genital passages in both male and female, transmitted by sexual intercourse. Symptoms are pain in passing water and a discharge. Penicillin and sulphonamides used in treatment.

Gonzaga, Ital. princely family, ruled

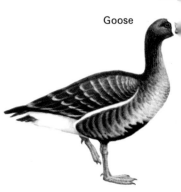
Goose

Mantua. **Luigi** (1267–1360) gained control of Mantua. Isabella D'Este and her son **Federico II** (d. 1540) made it most magnificent court in Europe.

Good Friday, Friday before Easter, observed by Christians as commemoration of day of Christ's Crucifixion.

good king henry, *Chenopodium bonus-henricus,* perennial plant of goose-foot family native to Europe and naturalized in N America. Flowers and seeds in tapering spikes. Formerly collected as pot herb.

Goode, John Paul (1862–1932), Amer. geographer. Known for editions of maps and books on geography, incl. Goode's school atlases.

Goodman, Benjamin David ('Benny') (1909–), Amer. clarinetist and jazz musician. Organized own orchestra (1934) and contributed to development of swing music.

Goodyear, Charles (1800–60), Amer. inventor. Developed vulcanized rubber (1839).

goosander, *Mergus merganser,* mainly marine, diving duck of N Eurasia. Related to merganser and smew.

goose, webfooted bird of duck family, genus *Anser* being grey and *Branta* black. Inhabits N hemisphere; migratory. Wild geese breed only in tundra regions. Species include greylag, bean and barnacle goose. Geese are reared commercially.

gooseberry, shrub *Ribes* of family Saxifragaceae, native to cool, moist climates; berry used in preserves.

goosegrass, *Galium aparine,* straggling annual weed of bedstraw family 1–4 ft. long with whorls of small leaves and small prickles on fruit, stem and leaves causing it to cling to plants, clothing, *etc.*

gopher, small burrowing rodent of squirrel group of N and C America. Called pocket gopher from cheek pouches for carrying food.

goral, *Naemorhedus goral,* goat-like bovine animal of mountains of E Asia. Both sexes have horns.

Gorboduc, legendary early Brit. monarch. By dividing his kingdom between his 2 sons, he created considerable civil strife. Title of 1st Eng. tragedy (by Thomas Norton and Thomas Sackville).

Gordian knot, in Gk. legend, intricate knot tying yoke to the pole of Gordius' wagon. Oracle said that he who loosened knot would rule Asia; Alexander the Great cut it with his sword.

Gordon, Charles George (1833–85), Brit. soldier and administrator. Commander of Chinese army that quelled Taiping Rebellion. Governor of Egyptian Sudan (1877–80). Killed in siege of Khartoum.

Gordon, George, 6th Baron Byron (1788–1824). Eng. poet. Travelled in Greece, Spain and Italy. Died at Missolonghi fighting for Gk. independence against Turks. Wrote *Childe Harold's Pilgrimage* (cantos I and II 1812; III and IV 1816–7); *The Vision of Judgement* (1822); *Don Juan* (1819–24).

Goldeneye Duck

Gordon, George, 1st Earl of Aberdeen (1637–1720), Scot. statesman; Chanc. of Scotland (1682–4). Supported Treaty of Union (1705–6).

Gordon, George Hamilton, 4th Earl of Aberdeen (1784–1860), Brit. statesman; P.M. (1852–5). Resigned after vote of censure on mismanagement of Crimean War.

Gordon, John Campbell Hamilton, 1st Marquis of Aberdeen and Temair (1847–1934), Gov.-General of Canada (1893–8). Conflict with P.M. Sir Charles Tupper over Senate appointments (1896–7).

gorge, deep, narrow valley cut by river. Canyons, *e.g.* Grand Canyon, Ariz., US, are deep gorges.

Gorgons, in Gk. myth., 3 sisters (Euryale, Medusa and Stheno) with snakes instead of hair. Their gaze turned people to stone. Medusa, the only mortal one, slain by Perseus.

gorilla, *Gorilla gorilla,* anthropoid ape found in deep forests of Cameroon, Gabon and Congo. Reaches 6 ft.

tall, weighing 300–600 lb; long arms, uses knuckles in walking; vegetarian and nomadic.

Gorki, Maxim, orig. Alexei Maximovitch Peshkov (1868–1936), Russ. writer. Author of short stories, novels, *Foma Gordeyev* (1899) and drama, *The Lower Depths* (1902), depicting outcasts of society. Lived abroad after 1905 because of Marxist beliefs. Returned 1928; wrote *Life of Klim Samgin* (1927–36), covering revolutionary period (1880–1934).

Gorky, Arshile (1904–48), Armenian-born Amer. painter influenced by Picasso and Miró. Used colour to achieve emotional effect.

Gorky, Gorki, city of Russ. SFSR, known as Nizhni Novgorod before 1932, at confluence of Oka and Volga R.; cap. of Gorky oblast. Founded 1221; site of great annual fairs. Leading indust. and transport centre. Pop. (1967) 1,100,000.

gorse, furze, spiny evergreen bush of pea family; fragrant yellow flowers followed by black hairy seed pods. Species include common *Ulex europaeus.*

Gorton, John Grey (1911–), Austral. premier (1967–71), and Liberal statesman. Various ministries: Interior, Works, Education and Science.

goshawk, *Accipiter gentilis,* hawk of Eurasia and N America. Destructive of poultry and game birds; trained for falconry.

Gospels of Matthew, Mark, Luke and John, first 4 books of the NT; deal with the life, death, resurrection and teachings of Christ.

Göteborg, or **Gothenburg,** 2nd city of Sweden, founded by King Gustavus Adolphus (1619); major port, commercial manufacturing centre. Connected with Baltic near Stockholm by Göta ship canal, using Göta R. and Lakes Venner and Vetter. Pop. (1963) 405,000.

Gothic, style of architecture and art which developed in France (12th cent.). Spread throughout Europe and dominant for 400 yr. revived 19th cent. Characterized by use of flying buttresses and pointed, ribbed arches and spacious windows, esp. in cathedrals, *e.g.* Notre Dame (Paris) Chartres and Milan. Eng. Gothic is divided into Early English (Salisbury Cathedral), Decorated (Exeter Cathedral), and Perpendicular (King's College Chapel, Cambridge).

Gothic Revival, in architecture, imitative 19th cent. style, popularly synonymous with Victorian. In literature, manifested in late 18th cent. 'Gothic Romances', usually set in

Gorilla

pseudo-Gothic surroundings (*e.g.* Horace Walpole's *Castle of Otranto,* 1764; or Mary Shelley's *Frankenstein,* 1818).

Gothic script, type of handwriting developed in 12th cent. France, emulated in print. Present day usage limited to legal documents.

Goths *see* VISIGOTHS.

Gotland, Swedish island in Baltic Sea. Area: *c.* 2,400 sq. mi.; cap. Visby. Site of many Stone Age and Bronze Age remains. Annexed (1654) by Sweden.

Gottfried von Strassburg (*fl.* 13th cent.), Ger. poet, author of *Tristan* (*c.* 1210), basis of Wagner's opera.

Göttingen, city on Leine R., Hanover, West Germany. Manufactures optical and precision instruments. University (1737) became centre for mathematics and physics (late 19th cent.). Pop. 79,000.

Gottsched, Johann Christoph (1700–66), Ger. critic and playwright. Influenced 18th cent. Ger. writers; stressed purity of language and classic construction. Plays include *The Dying Cato* (1732).

Gottwald, Klement (1896–1953), Czech. politician. Premier (1946–8) under Benes, whom he succeeded after Communist coup. Purged party of more liberal elements.

gouache, method of painting which mixes water colours with gum arabic thus rendering them opaque.

Golden Pheasant

Gouda, commercial town of Netherlands famous for its market. Gouda cheese produced in region. Pop. (1960) 43,118.

Goujon, Jean (*c.* 1510–*c.* 1566), Fr. Renaissance sculptor. Famous for bas-relief decoration, esp. on façade of Louvre (1550–62).

Gould, Jay (1836–92), Amer. industrialist. Speculator in railroad shares; owned major interest in 4 lines. Collaboration with James Fish to control gold market caused speculative panic of 1869.

Gounod, Charles (1818–93), Fr. composer. Wrote operas *Faust* (1859) and *Romeo and Juliet* (1867). Later concentrated on religious music.

gourami, *Osphronemus gorami,* large freshwater food fish of SE Asia. Brightly coloured varieties are popular aquarium fish.

gourd, trailing plant with succulent usually edible fruit of pumpkin family of Asian and Mexican origin. Globular yellow gourd derived from *Cucurbila maxima,* weighs up to 240 lb.

gout, metabolic disease confined mainly to males. Characterized by excess of uric acid in blood and deposition of crystals at joints causing painful and tender inflammation. Dietary treatment.

Gower, John (*c.* 1330–1408), Eng. poet, contemporary of Chaucer. Author of *Confessio Amantis,* 34 thousand couplets, containing many tales.

Goya [y Lucientes], Francisco José de (1746–1828), Span. painter noted for scenes of Iberian life, festivals and bullfights. Produced series of savage etchings. *Caprice, The Miseries of War* and *Shooting of the Rebels of May 3* are among his best-known works.

Gozo *see* MALTA.

Gracchi, The, Roman reformers. **Tiberius Sempronius Gracchus** (d. 133 BC), as tribune advocated re-

Diagram showing the triangular method of grafting

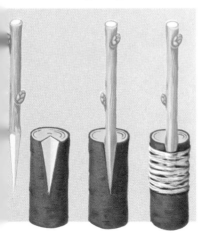

distribution of public land (much had been appropriated by wealthy, thus ruining small-scale farmers). Motion opposed but carried. Tiberius killed in riot while seeking unconstitutional re-election. **Gaius Sempronius Gracchus,** as tribune from 123 BC, re-enacted Tiberius' agrarian law, and among reforms set fixed price for corn and proposed Roman franchise for Latins. Killed in riot after failure to renew office.

Grace, W[illiam] G[ilbert] (1848–1915), Brit. cricketer and physician, scored over 54,000 runs and took over 2,800 wickets in 1st class cricket; captained England in Test matches against Australia.

Graces or **Charites** [Gk: *charis* grace], in Gk. myth., daughters of Zeus, named Aglaea (Splendour), Euphrosyne (Festivity) and Thalia (Rejoicing).

grackle, *Quiscalus quiscala,* commonest Amer. blackbird of blackish-purple colour.

grafting, in horticulture, practice of uniting 2 plants and growing them as one. The stock may be a mature plant or a root. the scion (part to be grafted) may be a bud or a cutting.

Grafton, Duke of *see* FITZROY, AUGUSTUS HENRY.

grafts *see* TRANSPLANTS, ORGAN.

Graham, Martha (1893–   ), Amer. dancer and teacher. Developed new techniques entirely different from those of classical ballet. Runs own company and school.

Graham, Thomas (1805–69), Scot. chemist. Formulated Graham's Law: rate of diffusion of gas is inversely proportional to square root of density. Discovered process of dialysis.

Graham, William Franklin ('Billy') (1918–   ), Amer. evangelist whose campaigns draw large crowds, many conducted on radio and television.

Grahame, Kenneth (1859–1932), Brit. writer. Best known work is children's book *The Wind in the Willows* (1908), an animal fantasy.

Grainger, Percy Aldridge (1882–1961), Austral.-Amer. pianist and composer. Known for adaptations of folk music. Popular pieces include *Molly on the Shore.*

grampus, killer whale, *Orcuius orca,* largest of dolphin family. High dorsal fin, *c.* 50 teeth. Predator on seals, porpoises, fish and birds. Distribution is worldwide.

Gran Chaco, sub-trop. region of C South America, incl. SE Bolivia, NW Paraguay, SW Brazil and N Argentina. Area: *c.* 250,000 sq. mi.

Don Luis, Prince of Parma by Goya

Important for cattle raising and supplying world's tannin.

Granada, cap. of Granada prov. S Spain, built on site of Roman town. Ruled by Moors until 1492, when Spain introduced Christian rule. Growth in modern times due to sugar industry. Pop. (1965) 162,000.

Granada, modern prov. of S Spain, once Moorish kingdom. Area: 4,838 sq. mi. Largely mountainous, with Sierra Nevada in SE. Valleys fertile, producing cotton, tobacco, sugar, grapes and olive oil.

Grand Bank, shallow part of N Atlantic Ocean near Newfoundland; noted as fishing ground. Area: *c.* 500,000 sq. mi.

Grand Canal, oldest and longest (1,000 mi.) canal in world, runs from Peking to Hangchow, China. Started 540 BC, completed over 2,000 yr.; main object to transport tribute rice from Yangtze Valley to Peking. Parts still in use.

Grand Canyon, gorge, *c.* 1 mi. deep, 4–18 mi. wide and 217 mi. long, cut by Colorado River, US, through near-horizontal rocks, reaching those deposited *c.* 2,000 million yr. ago. Tourist attraction; whole area of canyons in Arizona comprises Grand Canyon National Park.

Grand Coulee Dam, on Columbia R., Washington, US; world's largest concrete structure, completed 1941. Leading hydro-electric power source.

Grand National, Eng. steeplechase run annually since 1839 (except 1916–18) in March or April at Aintree, Liverpool. Course *c.* 4½ mi. long. Recognized as world's greatest steeplechase.

Grass Snake

Grand Old Party (GOP), popular term for US REPUBLICAN PARTY.

Grand Prix, title of certain international motor car and motor cycle races.

Grand Prix de Paris, international horse-race for 3 yr. olds held at Longchamps in June; stake highest in Europe.

Grand Remonstrance, list of protests (1641), supplementing PETITION OF RIGHT, against Eng. King Charles I's arbitrary rule. Drawn up by Long Parliament.

Grand Teton, US National Park, Wyoming; founded 1929, named after Grand Teton Mountain (13,766 ft.). Area is classic example of block faulting and glacial erosion.

Grange, Harold Edward ('Red') (1903–), Amer. football player. Star halfback for University of Illinois (1922–5). Played professional football (1926–35).

Granger movement, Amer. agrarian movement (1867–76). Local units, called granges, became political forms of social protest. Instrumental in passing Granger Laws in 4 Midwestern States dealing with railroad and storage rates.

Granit, Ragner Arthur (1900–), Swedish physiologist. Awarded Nobel Prize for Physiology and Medicine (1967) for work on chemical and physiological processes in eye.

granite, coarsely-crystalline, acid IGNEOUS ROCK containing visible quartz, feldspar and mica minerals. Formed below earth's crust and exposed by erosion of overlying rocks.

Granjon, Robert (*fl.* 1545–88), Fr. typesetter and designer. Created *Caractères de civilité,* intended as Fr. equivalent of italics. A later type face is named after him.

Grant, Cary, orig. Archibald Alexander Leach (1904–), Eng. actor. Known for Hollywood films, esp. light romantic comedies, *e.g. Arsenic and Old Lace.*

Grant, Ulysses Simpson, orig. Hiram Ulysses Grant (1822–85), 18th US Pres. (1869–77), Republican. Commander-in-Chief of Union Army in Civil War. Implacable policy of dividing and destroying Confederates ended with ROBERT E. LEE's surrender at Appomattox Courthouse (1865). Republican pres. candidate (1868), won easily. Administrations characterized chiefly by bitter partisan politics and corruption. Made unsuccessful bid for 1880 nomination.

Grant's gazelle, *Gazella granti,* large antelope of E African savannah country. Horns diverge and are ringed.

Granville-Barker, Harley (1877–1946), Eng. actor, manager and playwright. After producing, wrote series of plays incl. *Madras House* (1910) and the critical *Prefaces to Shakespeare* (5 vols. 1923–46).

grape, smooth-skinned juicy berry of vine. Globular or oblong shaped; colours green to white, deep purple to black; grows in clusters. Numerous hybrids and varieties of Old and New World types. Species include *Vitis vinifera,* and *V. rotundifolia.* Since ancient times eaten both fresh and dried as fruit, and fermented to produce wine.

grape hyacinth, *Muscari atlanticum,* hardy bulbous perennial plant, with small blue flowers. Over 40 species native to Europe and Asia Minor.

grapefruit, *Citrus decumana,* fruit widely cultivated in trop. areas. Round in shape with bitter yellow rind and acid juicy pulp.

graphite, allotropic carbon, known also as plumbago or black-lead. Used as lubricant, for polishing and in making pencils.

graphology, art of detecting character from handwriting.

graptolite, extinct floating marine hemichordate thought to be oldest ancestor of man, 1–6 in. long, found in late Cambrian, Ordovician and Silurian shales.

Grass, Günther (1927–), Ger. writer. Author of plays, poetry and novels, best known of which is *The Tin Drum* (1959).

grass, widely distributed plant of Gramineae family. Those with blade-like leaves and jointed stems include hay and pasture grasses and cereals.

grass of parnassus, *Parnassia palustris,* perennial plant with solitary delicate white buttercup-like flower. Found in European marshland.

grass snake, *Natrix natrix,* non-venomous snake common in Europe and found in N Africa and C Asia. N Amer., *Ophiodrys vernalis,* is bright green and also non-venomous.

grass spider, *Agalena nalvia,* common N Amer. arachnid. Spins concave web on grass.

grasshopper, insect of order Orthoptera, with hind legs adapted for leaping. Includes longhorned grasshoppers, *Tettigonioidea,* and short horned grasshoppers, *Acridoidea.* Many are agricultural pests, *e.g.* locust.

grass tree, Australasian tree of Xanthorrhoea species. Woody trunk with tuft of spear-like leaves and protruding spike 5–10 ft. high.

gravel, rock fragments rounded by water, greater than 2 mm. in diameter. Used in road building and in concretes. Quartz is commonest constituent.

Graves, Robert Ranke (1895–), Brit. poet, novelist and critic. Interest in myth., both in fiction and social history. Best known for historical novel, *I Claudius* (1934).

Graves' Disease *see* GOITRE.

gravitation, defined by Newton; every body attracts or tends to approach every other body with force proportional to masses, and inversely as square of distance. Gravitation accounts for orbital movement of planets round sun, and satellites round planets. **Gravity** is force which acts to draw bodies towards Earth; mass of body being an operative factor.

Gray, Thomas (1716–71), Eng. poet.

The famous Alhambra in Granada

The Lion Gate: architecture of the Mycenean culture, Greece

Early poetry classical, *e.g.* 'On a Distant Prospect of Eton College'. Best known work 'Elegy Written in a Country Churchyard'. Later verse approached Romanticism, *e.g.* 'The Descent of Odin'.

grayling, *Thymallus thymallus,* grey-coloured, fresh-water fish of salmon group. Found in Europe and N America. Also a butterfly *Eumenis semale.*

Gray's Inn *see* INNS OF COURT.

Graz, 2nd largest city of Austria, cap. of Styria prov. Gothic cathedral and 16th cent. university. Industries include metallurgy, machine manufacture. Pop. (1961) 237,000.

A fine example of Greek sculpture: 'Hermes with the child Dionysus on his arm' by Praxiteles

Great Australian Bight, shallow bay of Indian Ocean on S coast of Australia (1,450 mi. long). Barren coasts buffeted by Antarctic storms.

Great Barrier Reef, largest area of coral structures in world, 1,250 mi. along continental shelf off coast of Queensland, E Australia. Area: 80,000 sq. mi. Lagoon inshore from barrier reef has 2 navigable channels.

Great Bear Lake, NW Canada, lake at *c.* 400 ft., drained by Great Bear R. Area: 12,000 sq. mi. Discovered *c.* 1800. Noted for uranium ores on E shore.

Great Britain, part of BRITISH ISLES, political term by which England, Scotland and Wales have been known since (1707) Act of Union.

great circle, formed on surface of a sphere by a plane passing through centre of the sphere, dividing it into 2 equal pieces. Referring to Earth, lines of longitude and the Equator are great circles. Lines of latitude which do not pass through the earth centre are small circles.

Great Dividing Range, mountains and plateaus running parallel to E coast of Australia. Highest peak is 7,349 ft.

Great Fire of London (1666), swept through city, devastating almost all of medieval London. In 4 days it destroyed some 13,000 buildings, incl. St Paul's Cathedral. Cleared disease spread by GREAT PLAGUE (1665).

Great Lakes, 5 connected fresh-water lakes, Superior, Michigan, Huron, Erie and Ontario, forming much of E central border between Canada and US. Total area: 94,710 sq. mi. Lakes drain into St Lawrence River and Atlantic Ocean; area drained: 292,000 sq. mi. Much trade carried from interior, *e.g.* wheat, copper, coal, livestock and cars. System closed for 4 months each year by ice and storms.

Great Plague, severe epidemic (1665) of bubonic plague in England; in 1 yr., 15% of London's population perished.

Great Plains, grassland plateau of W US and Canada, E of Rocky Mts., sloping from 6,000–2,000 ft. Subject to extremes of temperature and low rainfall.

Great Rift Valley, geological fault system forming depression stretching from Jordan valley to Mozambique. Marked by Red Sea.

Great Salt Lake, largest salt lake in N America, 2nd saltiest in world. Area: 1,800 sq. mi. In NW Utah, water lost by evaporation. Salt mining and tourism important.

Great Schism, split in R.C. Church (1378–1417), concluded by the Council of Constance. Death of Gregory XI eventually produced 3 rival popes.

Ended when Council elected Martin V as pope. By failing to resolve papal-council dispute over supreme authority, Schism delayed Catholic reform.

Great Slave Lake, joined to Great Bear Lake by Mackenzie R., NW Canada. Rich in fish; gold mined at Yellowknife on N shore.

Great Smoky Mountains, National Park in N Carolina and E Tennessee, part of Appalachian Mts. Area: 800 sq. mi. highest peak 6,642 ft.; 200,000 acres of virgin forest.

great spotted cuckoo, *Clamator glandarius,* crested Eurasian cuckoo with dark white-edged tail and brown upper parts spotted with white.

great spotted woodpecker, *Dendrocopos major,* bird of woodpecker family with black back, white shoulder patches and crimson tail markings. Found in woods and forests of Europe.

great tit, *Parus major,* largest Eurasian tit. Head is blue-black, underparts yellow with black stripe on breast.

Great Trek, mass migration (1835–6) of Boer farmers out of Cape Colony, South Africa to escape Brit. domination. Resulted in foundation of Natal, Transvaal and Orange Free State.

Greater London, county incl. City of London and 32 metropolitan boroughs, created under London Government Act (1963). Pop. (1966) 7,914,000.

grebe, diving bird of order Podicipediformes, with brilliant plumage; world wide distribution. Crested grebe, *Podiceps cristatus,* is largest species. Amer. species include *Aechmophorus occidentalis.*

Greece, country of SE Europe in Med. region. Area: 50,944 sq. mi.; cap. Athens. Mountainous, country split by Isthmus of Corinth on mainland,

also comprises numerous islands in surrounding Aegean and Ionian Seas. Fertile valleys provide agric. subsistence, producing cereals, olives and fruit. Once centre of civilization (1000 BC–146 BC), Greece subsequently part of both Roman and Turkish Empires. Successful struggle for independence led to estab. of kingdom (1833–1924), last of which ended with deposition of Constantine II. Greek is official language; Gk. Orthodox is estab. religion. Unit of currency: drachma. Pop. (1965) 8,612,000.

Greek, Indo-European language. Ancient Greek comprised many regional dialects, *e.g.* Attic-Ionic, Doric and Aeolian. Modern Greek derived from common language (Koine) formed after dissolution of city states.

Greek architecture, earliest known remains include town walls of Tiryns and Mycenae. Subsequent work, highly developed in temples, classed by form of column. Temple of Hera at Olympia early building of Doric style, perfected 5th cent. BC, *e.g.* Parthenon. Ionic order of Asia Minor, found in Greece after 500 BC in such works as Erectheum. Ornate Corinthian (mid–4th cent.) little used. Hellenistic architecture (4th cent. BC) was florid.

Greek art, earliest form expressed in vase painting (*c.* 900–700 BC), geometric designs then representations of men and animals. Attic pottery (6th cent. BC), black-figured, myth. and religious themes; perfection reached in 5th cent. red-figured vases; painters include Douris and Brygos. Ornamentation from 400 BC marked decline of the art. Sculpture developed (7th cent. BC) in Crete, Peloponnese and Ionia, union of latter 2 formed Attic school which used stone, later marble; also bronze, esp. at Argos and Sicyon. Subjects largely religious, though by 5th cent. some, *e.g.* Phidias, depicted athletic victors. Softer expression, simplicity and grandeur in 4th cent. BC, esp. in work of Praxiteles, Scopas. Hellenistic sculpture more dramatic, *e.g.* 'Dying Gaul', 'Laocoon'. After Roman conquest, works largely imitative. Other forms of art included wall-paintings, *e.g.* Mycenae, and frescoes, *e.g.* Cnossos, Crete; declined after 4th cent.

Greek Church, Eastern or **Orthodox Church,** name of branch of Christianity which continued in Eastern Empire after Pope Leo IX excommunicated patriarchs of Constantinople (1054). Under several semi-autonomous patriarchs; religion of USSR, Greece and much of E Europe.

Greek mythology, legend and literature whose subject matter revolved around themes of Gk. religion. Characteristics and stories of gods taken from many sources, some indigenous, others Minoan, Mycenaean, Egyptian and Asian. Cults

also grew up around various mysteries (Eleusinian, Orphic, *etc.*) and Oracles (as at Delphi).

Greeley, Horace (1811–72), Amer. newspaper editor and polit. leader. Founded New York Tribune (1841); coined slogan 'Go West, young man'. Republican party supporter, broke with Grant admin. and ran as pres. candidate (1872) for Liberal Republicans.

Green, Henry, orig. Henry Vincent Yorke (1905–), Eng. novelist. Works include *Living* (1929) and *Nothing* (1950).

Green, Julian (1900–), Fr. writer of psychological novels and plays, incl. *Avarice House* (1926).

green algae, *Chlorophyta,* phylum of plant kingdom, considered ancestral type from which higher green plants evolved. Aquatic, mainly freshwater, or terrestrial in moist areas.

green belt, town and country planning concept, esp. important in UK. Involves preservation of countryside surrounding a town and control of construction.

green laver *see* SEA LETTUCE.

Green Mountain Boys, partisan armed groups from Vermont region, led by Ethan Allen (1737–89) in Amer. Revolution. Formed orig. to defend area against New York land speculators.

green toad, *Bufo viridis,* Eurasian toad with glossy green (occasionally yellow) colouring.

green turtle, *Chelonia mydas,* widely distributed edible turtle of trop.

Silenus with Lyre on Greek vase (5th Cent. BC)

Green Toad

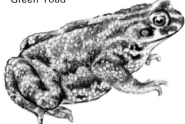

Greylag Goose

waters. Shell is olive-greenish coloured. Eggs are highly nutritious.

Greenaway, Catherine ('Kate') (1846–1901), Eng. painter, illustrator esp. of children's books. Wrote *Under the Window* (1879).

Greenback Party, in US history, organization promoting currency expansion (1874–6). Membership W and S farmers; wanted inflated currency to wipe out farm debts. Dissolved after 1884 election, many members later became Populists.

Greene, Graham (1904–   ), Brit. writer. Earlier works characterized by 'shock' element (*e.g. Brighton Rock,* 1938); later by Catholic themes, as in *The End of the Affair* (1951). Other works include *The Third Man* (1950), plays, and short stories.

Greene, Nathaniel (1742–86), Amer. Revolution general, commander of Carolina campaign (1781–2), finally forcing Brit. evacuation of Charleston (1782).

greenfinch, common European song bird, *Chloris chloris.* N Amer. greenfinch or Texas sparrow is *Arremonops rufivirgatus.*

greengage, small round variety of plum. Sweet and green-coloured when growing. Native of France, introduced to England (18th cent.).

Greenland, world's largest island, NE of N America, belongs to Denmark. Area: 837,627 sq. mi.; cap. Godthaab. Mountainous interior covered by ice-cap; population, comprising Danes and Eskimoes lives mainly on S and W coasts. Occupations centre on fishing industry. World's leading source of cryolite. Pop. (1964) 41,000.

Greenough, Horatio (1805–52).

Whippet, a smaller form of Greyhound

Amer. sculptor. Principal works include statue of George Washington and 'The Rescue'.

greenshank, large slender green-legged wading sandpiper, *Tringa nebularia,* of N Europe. Migrates S in winter.

Greenway, Francis Howard (1777–1837), Austral. architect, b. England (transported 1814 for forgery). Many fine examples of early colonial Austral. architecture around Sydney.

greenweed [UK], **woodwaxen** [US], European plant of pea family. Species include deciduous dyer's greenweed, *Genista tinctoria,* and hairy greenweed *G. pilosa.*

Greenwich, borough of SE London, England. Site of Royal Naval College. Stands on 0° meridian, from which calculations of geographic longitude and Greenwich Mean Time are made.

Greenwich Village, district of Manhattan, New York City. Exclusive residential area (19th cent.), became focal point of 'beat' intellectuals.

Gregorian calendar *see* CALENDAR.

Gregory [I] the Great, Saint Gregory (*c.* 540–604), pope (590–604). Estab. temporal power of papacy by firmness, alienating Rome from Constantinople. Encouraged monasticism, sent missionaries (incl. Augustine) to England. Wrote much and contributed to development of Gregorian chant or PLAINSONG.

Gregory [VII], Saint, orig. Hildebrand (*c.* 1020–85), pope (1073–85). As chief minister under Leo IX and successors campaigned for church reform. Ensuing reaction continued after election as pope, esp. over forbidding investiture of clerics by lay rulers. Leading opponent, Ger. King Henry IV, excommunicated (1076), later set up anti-pope and forced Gregory to flee to S Italy, where he died.

Gregory IX orig. Ugolino di Segni (*c.* 1143–1241), pope (1227–41). Took steps to codify canon law and organized Inquisition. Most of reign occupied by struggles with Emperor Frederick II whom he twice excommunicated.

Gregory XI, orig. Pierre Roger de Beaufort (1331–78), pope (1370–8). Went to Italy (1377) to end Babylonian Captivity at Avignon. Efforts to bring about peace failed; elections after his death began GREAT SCHISM.

Gregory XIII, orig. Ugo Buoncompagni (1502–85), pope (1572–85). Introduced (1582) reformed calendar known as the Gregorian.

Gregory, Lady Isabella Augusta (1852–1932), Irish writer. Helped

found Abbey Theatre, Dublin, which she managed and directed.

Gregory, James (1638–75), Scot. mathematician. Invented reflecting telescope (Gregorian telescope), described in his *Optica Promota* (1663).

Grenada, island in E Caribbean Sea, one of Brit. Windward Is. Area: 120 sq. mi.; cap. St. George's. Became British 1783. Pop. (1963) 92,000.

Grenfell, George (1849–1906), Eng. Baptist missionary. Explored Africa and surveyed Congo basin and effluents of Congo (1884–5).

Grenoble, cap. of Isère department. SE France on R. Isère. Historic cap. of Dauphiné. Paper, electrical goods manufactured. Pop. (1962) 162,764.

Grenville, George (1712–70), Brit. statesman, P.M. (1763–5). Policy of taxing Amer. colonies hastened events leading to Amer. Revolution. Prosecuted JOHN WILKES, thereby provoking polit. reformers.

Grenville, Sir Richard (*c.* 1541–91), Eng. naval officer. Commanded fleet carrying 1st colonists to ROANOKE ISLAND (1585). Mortally wounded aboard *Revenge* in battle with Sp. treasure ships.

Grenville, William Wyndham, Baron Grenville (1759–1834), Brit. statesman, son of George Grenville. William Pitt's Foreign Sec. (1791–1801). As P.M. (1806) formed 'ministry of all the talents' which abolished slave trade. Resigned 1807.

Gretna Green, village of Dumfries, Scotland, near Eng. border. Famous as place for eloping couples from England to be married (1754–1856).

Grew, Nehemiah (1641–1712), Eng. plant physiologist. Prob. 1st to observe sexual nature of plant reproduction. Wrote *The Anatomy of Plants* (4 vols. 1682).

Grey, Albert Henry George, 4th Earl (1851–1917), Brit. statesman, Gov.-General of Canada (1904–11). Lib. member of House of Commons (1880–6); returned to Parl. (1894) in House of Lords. Opposed Home Rule Bill in 1886.

Grey, Beryl (1927–   ), Eng. ballerina, debut 1942 as Odette-Odile in *Swan Lake.* With Royal Ballet until 1956, since when she has made many guest appearances.

Green Turtle

Grey, Charles, 2nd Earl (1764–1845), Brit. statesman. As Whig leader of House of Commons; supported Wilberforce's act to abolish slave trade (1807). During term as P.M. (1830–4) Reform Bill (1832) and Abolition of Slavery in Brit. Colonies (1833) were passed.

Grey, Sir George (1812–98), Brit. colonial governor and author. Explored NW coast of Australia for Royal Geographical Society. Gov. of South Australia (1841–5), New Zealand (1845–53), and Cape Colony (1854–9). P.M. of New Zealand (1877–9). Author of *Polynesian Mythology* (1855).

Grey, Lady Jane (*c.* 1537–54), queen of England. Married against her wish to Lord Guildford Dudley (1553) as part of plot to alter succession in her favour on death of Edward VI. Proclaimed queen (1553), imprisoned after 9 days and beheaded; succeeded by Mary I.

grey heron, *Ardea cinerea,* large grey heron with black crest and reddish bill and legs. Powerful flier.

greyhound racing, derived from coursing in which greyhounds chase hares on sight. Now held on oval enclosed tracks with mechanical hares. Originated in US, 1st Eng. track opened 1925. Popular betting sport.

greylag goose, *Anser anser,* commonest Eurasian wild goose. Breeds from Spain to Japan. Probable ancestor of domestic goose.

Grieg, Edward Hagerup (1843–1907), Norwegian composer with intensely national style. Best known for *Peer Gynt Suite,* piano concerto and short piano pieces.

Grierson, Sir Herbert John Clifford (1866–1960), Brit. historian, critic. Leading authority on Shakespeare, Donne and 17th cent. literature. Author of *Cross-Currents in the Literature of the Seventeenth Century* (1929).

Grieve, Christopher Murray *see* MCDIARMID, HUGH.

griffin, in myth., animal usually represented as half lion and half eagle. Orig. Hittite, in heraldry it represents vigilance.

Griffith, Arthur (1872–1922), Irish statesman, founder of SINN FEIN. Leading propagandist and apologist for Irish ideals. In absence of Eamon de Valera, commanded revolution (1919–20); 1st Pres. of Irish Free State (1922).

Griffith. D[avid] [Lewelyn] W[ark] (1875–1948), Amer. film producer and director. Initiated use of flashback, cross-cutting, fade-outs.

Films include *Birth of a Nation* (1915), *Orphans of the Storm* (1921).

Grignard, Victor (1871–1935), Fr. chemist. With P. Sabatier, awarded Nobel Prize for Chemistry (1912) for discovery of Grignard reagent, a halogen compound.

Grillparzer, Franz (1791–1872), Austrian dramatist; works include *Der Traum: ein Leben* (1817–34), *Des Meeres und der Liebe Wellen* (1831).

Grimaldi, Joseph (1779–1837), Eng. clown and pantomime actor; popularity of songs long outlived him.

Grimm, Jakob Ludwig Karl (1785–1863) and **Wilhelm Karl Grimm** (1786–1859), Ger. brothers best known for collection of folk and fairy tales (1812–15). Jakob also formulated **Grimm's Law,** a theory of relationships in Indo-European languages.

Grimmelshausen, Hans Jakob Christoffel von (1625–76), Ger. writer. Autobiographical-picaresque novel, *Der Abentheurliche Simplicissimus Teutsch* (1669, Eng. tr. 1912) gives contemporary satirical view of Thirty Years War.

Grimond, Joseph ('Jo') (1913–), Brit. politician. Leader of Lib. Party (1956–67).

Grimsby, county borough, Lincs., England, on R. Humber. Largest fishing port in UK. Pop. (1964) 96,700.

Grindelwald, tourist resort and climbing centre in Bernese Alps, Switzerland, at foot of Eiger.

grindle, *Amia calva,* fish of bowfin family of Great Lakes and Mississippi valley. Reaches $2\frac{1}{4}$ ft.; able to live out of water for long periods.

Gris, Juan (1887–1927), Sp. expatriate Cubist painter. Work primarily oil and collage still-lifes; wrote *Les Possibilités de la Peinture* (1924).

Grisons, Graubünden, mountainous canton of E Switzerland. Area: 2,746 sq. mi.; cap. Chur. Tourists attracted to Engadine valley and St Moritz. Became Swiss canton (1803) after Napoleon's mediation. Romansch language still spoken. Pop. (1960) 147,458.

Le Tourangeau by Gris

Grizzly Bear

grizzly bear, *Ursus horribilis* of N American Rocky Mts. Formidable when aroused, some bears weigh 1,400 lb.

Gromyko, Andrei Andreevich (1909–), Soviet diplomat. Ambassador to US (1943–6) and to UK (1952–3); 1st Soviet representative on UN Security Council (1946–8). Chief deputy Foreign Min. (1949–52) and Min. of Foreign Affairs since 1957.

Groningen, city of NW Netherlands, cap. of Groningen prov. Member of Hanseatic League and cultural centre during Middle Ages. Agric. and trade centre. Pop. (1965) 154,000.

Gropius, Walter (1883–1969), Ger.-American architect. Founded BAU-HAUS (1919), for which he designed buildings at Dessau. Leading 'functional' architect.

Gropper, William (1897–), Amer. painter and cartoonist. Satiric style often used as social commentary. Best known works include murals in the Schenley Building (New York).

Gros Ventre, N Amer. Indian tribe of Algonkian linguistic stock. Plains tribe dependent on buffalo-hunting; descendants live on a Montana reservation.

Groseillers, Médart Chouart, Sieur des (1618–*c.* 1696), Fr.-Canadian explorer. With brother-in-law Pierre Radisson, persuaded Brit. to estab. trading company, later known as Hudson's Bay Company.

Grossglockner, highest peak in Austria (12,460 ft.), 1st climbed 1800.

Grosz, George (1893–1959), Ger. artist, associated with Dada, famed

for satirical post-World War 1 drawings. Worked in US from 1933, painted symbolic war pictures during World War 2.

Grotefend, Georg Friedrich (1775–1853), Ger. classical scholar. Gained 1st real success in translating Persian CUNEIFORM script.

Grotewohl, Otto (1894–), E Ger. statesman, since 1945 leading member of Ger. Socialist Party; Chancellor since 1949.

Grotius, Hugo (1583–1645), Dutch jurist and statesman. Author of *De Jure Belli et Pacis* (1625), 1st definition of international law.

Groulx, Lionel-Adolphe, Abbé (1878–1967), Canadian historian. Influenced Fr.-Canadian nationalism in early 20th cent. esp. through book *Si Dollard Revient* (1919).

ground beetle, carnivorous insect. Larvae lie in soil, debris or bark, and adults prey on insects, slugs or snails. *Calosoma sycophanta* of Europe has been introduced to US to combat caterpillar of gipsy moth. The violet ground beetle, *Carabus violaceus,* is commonest species.

ground ivy, *Glechoma hederacea,* low aromatic perennial plant of thyme family. Naturalized in N America. Also known as gill-over-the-ground.

groundnut *see* PEANUT.

groundsel, herbaceous plant, *Senecio vulgaris,* of Compositae family. Found in temperate areas of Europe, with small yellow flowers and deeply cut leaves. *Baccharis halimifolia* is N American variety.

grouper, carnivorous bass of semi-trop. waters. Species include coney and jewfish.

grouse, game bird of N hemisphere. Species includes *Lagopus scoticus,* or Red Grouse, as well as snow (Ptarmigan), sand and Canadian grouse.

Grove, Frederick Philip (1871–1948), Canadian novelist. Works, illustrating struggle of prairie life, include *Settlers of the Marsh* (1925) and *Fruits of the Earth* (1933).

Grove, Sir George (1820–1900), Eng. musicologist, famous for *Dictionary of Music and Musicians* (1878–79), still a standard work.

Gruenther, Alfred Maximilian (1899–), Amer. general. Chief of Staff in World War 2 (1943–5), and of NATO forces in Europe (1951–6).

Grunewald, Mathias (*c.* 1480–1528), Ger. painter mainly of religious subjects. Famous representations of the crucifixion at Colmar, Basle and Karlsruhe.

Gruyère, town in Fribourg canton, Switzerland. Area famous for cheese of this name.

Gryphius, Andreas (1616–64), Ger. dramatist and poet. Sonnets, odes, epigrams and religious lyrics written in Latin, High German and Silesian; best known is 'Vanitas! vanitatum vanitas!'

Guadalajara, 2nd city of Mexico, cap. of Jalisco state, founded (1530) and named after city in Spain. Moderate climate due to high altitude. Many industrial and agric. products; famous for ceramics. Pop. (1960) 580,617.

Guadalcanal, one of Solomon Islands, SW Pacific. Captured by US forces in World War 2 after occupation by Japanese (1942–3).

Guadalquivir, main river of S Spain, draining area of 21,000 sq. mi. Region of Andalusia depends on it for irrigation.

Guadalupe Hidalgo, Treaty of, signed (1848), ended war between US and Mexico. Texas and much of SW US recognized as Amer. territory.

Guadalupe Mountains, US national park in Texas, opened 1966. Area: 121 sq. mi.

Guadarrama, Sierra de, mountain range of C Spain. Average height 5,000 ft.; highest peak Pico de Peñalara, 8,000 ft.

Guadeloupe, Fr. overseas department in Leeward Is., W Indies. Area: 688 sq. mi.; cap. Basse-Terre. Discovered by Columbus (1493); French settled it (1635). Pop. (1965) 319,000.

Guam, NW Pacific island, largest of Mariana group, administered by US as unincorporated territory and military installation. Area: 210 sq. mi.; cap. Agana. Inhabitants are subsistence farmers producing trop.

crops. International airport. Pop. (1966) 79,000.

guanaco, *Llama huanacos,* S Amer. mammal of high altitudes related to the camel. Orig. thought to be wild ancestor of LLAMA and ALPACA.

guano, fertilizer of accumulated excrements of seabirds, collected esp. in Peru and parts of W Africa. Utilized in manure and gunpowder before replacement by synthetic chemicals.

Guarani, S Amer. Indians of Paraguay and S Brazil. Inter-married with early Sp. settlers, and adopted Sp. customs. Until recently a few independent non-Christian groups known as Cainguá remained. Known as Tupi in Brazil.

guards, orig. the elite regiments in an army. English guards 1st appeared in Charles II's reign. Function as royal bodyguard. Brit. Army has 7 regiments of guards: 2 horse, 5 foot. In US each state has national guard, organized like Federal Army, operating on part-time, voluntary basis.

Guareschi, Giovanni (1908–68), Ital. writer. Creator of Don Camillo and Peppone, parish priest and Communist mayor, in novels such as *The Little World of Don Camillo* (1950).

Guarneri, Ital. family of 17th and 18th cent.; violin makers in Cremona.

Guatemala, Republic of, trop. country of C America. Area: 42,042 sq. mi.; cap. Guatemala City; main

towns, Tikal, Petén. Climate varies with altitude and exposure to rain-bearing winds from Caribbean. 75% of pop. directly dependent on agriculture, *e.g.* corn, cocoa, sugar, coffee, bananas. Rich in minerals but limited by transport difficulties. Pop. (1965) 4,575,000.

guava, small tree, *Psidium,* of trop. America. Fruit, a fleshy berry, is used in preserves.

Guayaquil, chief port, largest city of Ecuador, on the Pacific. Founded 1537. Site of historic meeting between Bolivar and San Martin (1822). Pop. (1966) 651,542.

gudgeon, *Gobia fluviatilis,* small European fresh water fish, related to carp.

guelder rose, *Viburnum opulis,* small tree of honeysuckle family of N temperate regions. Grows to 7–8 ft.; creamy flowers in clusters,

Guelphs and Ghibellines, rival parties, orig. in 12th cent. Germany, 13th–14th in Italy. Partisans of houses of Welf (dukes of Bavaria and Saxony) and of Hohenstaufen, struggled for imperial crown after Henry IV's death (1197) until Hohenstaufen line died out (1268). In Italy, struggle continued 13th–14th cent., Guelphs backed papacy and Ghibellines supported imperial claims.

guerilla warfare, harassing action by small bands of men in enemy-occupied territory. Chief contribution of Amer. Revolutionaries to warfare. Widely used by Mao Tse-tung, during Chinese civil war. After World

The Crucifixion (1512-15) by Grünewald

Guillemot

War 2, used extensively in such countries as Cuba and Vietnam.

Guernica, Basque town of Viscaya prov., N Spain. Destruction (1937) by German planes, in Sp. Civil War inspired Picasso's famous painting.

Guest, Edgar Albert (1881–1959), Amer. poet. Verse includes *A Heap o' Livin'* (1916).

Gueux [Fr: beggars], name given to Dutch and Flemish noblemen who signed petition against Sp. oppression (1566). Chartered (1569) by William the Silent, successful in siege of Leiden (1574).

Guevara, Ernesto ('Che') (1928–67), Cuban revolutionary and polit. leader, b. Argentina. Castro's economic adviser until 1965, d. in Bolivia after capture for leading Comm. guerilla activity. His exploits inspired many left-wing revolutionary movements.

Guggenheim, family of Amer. philanthropists, fortune based on smelting and refining metals. Foundations assist artists and scholars. **Meyer Guggenheim** (1828–1905) and son **Daniel Guggenheim** (1856–1930) made greatest contribution.

Guiana, region on NE coast of S America, colonized (19th cent.) by Britain, France and Netherlands. *See* also FRENCH GUIANA; GUYANA; SURINAM.

Guiana, British *see* GUYANA.

Guiana, French, Fr. overseas territory on NE coast of S America. Area: 35,000 sq. mi.; cap. Cayenne. Administers island group incl. St Joseph, Ile Royal and Ile du Diable (former penal settlement). Pop. (1961) 33,000.

guided missile, self-propelled projectile directed to target by remote

radio control; carries explosive warhead. Course may be directed from land or air.

Guildford, Earl of *see* NORTH, FREDERICK.

guilds, gilds, associations of people joined in common employment or causes. Word from Anglo-Saxon *gild,* payment or money. Guilds began (12th cent.), orig. composed of groups of merchants, and then of craftsmen for protection of trading interests. Powerful in Middle Ages; disappeared with industrial revolution.

Guillaume, Charles Édouard (1861–1938), Fr. physicist, known esp. for invention of alloys invar and platinite. Awarded Nobel Prize for Physics (1920).

guillemot, short-tailed, long-billed diving bird, abundant on rocky N Atlantic coasts. Common *Uria aalge* breeds without nesting and lays single egg on open cliff ledge.

Guillotin, Joseph Ignace (1738–1814), Fr. physician. Defended capital punishment, proposed use of beheading machine (1789) named guillotine after him.

guillotine, instrument of execution, consisting of upright frame supporting triangular blade; decapitates victim when blade is released. Notorious symbol of the REIGN OF TERROR.

guinea, Eng. gold coin in use before 1817; 1st minted 1663, worth 20s. Term used now for 21s., value fixed in 1717.

Guinea, Republic of, state of trop. W Africa. Area: 94,924 sq. mi.; cap. Conakry. Formerly French, independent (1958). Portuguese coastal

exploration, 15th cent.; Fr. penetration from mid-19th cent. Main crops, rice, bananas, palm fruits, citrus fruits and rubber. Bauxite worked. Pop. (1966) 3,608,000.

Guinea fowl, *Numida meleagris,* game bird of Med. lands with short bill, fleshy red wattle and casque. Considered delicacy by Greeks and Romans.

guinea pig, domesticated form of CAVY. Common as pet, also bred for laboratory experiments. Variety of colours and hair types has been achieved, *e.g.* angora, with long hair, and Brazil, with a curly coat.

Guinevere *see* ARTHURIAN LEGEND.

Guinness, Sir Alec (1914–), Brit. actor. Achieved international fame

through films such as *Kind Hearts and Coronets, The Lavender Hill Mob* and *The Bridge on the River Kwai.*

Guise family (1496–1675), Fr. ducal family. Founder **Claude de Lorraine, 1st Duke** (1496–1550). Notable members were **François de Lorraine** (1519–63), 2nd Duke, military commander and leader of the Catholics under Francis II, and **Mary de Guise,** mother of Mary Stuart. Title died out 1675.

guitar, 6-stringed, flat-backed instrument with frets on the fingerboard. Popular in 17th-18th cent., renewed interest in guitar music in 20th cent. Electric guitar introduced for sound amplification.

Gujarat, Gujerat, state of W India since 1960. Area: 72,245 sq. mi.; cap. Ahmedabad. Pop. (1961) 20,633,350.

Gulbenkian, Calouste Sarkis (1869–1955), financier, industrialist and diplomat; made a fortune from Middle East oil. Calouste Gulbenkian Foundation was estab. (1956) as an international charitable foundation to aid the visual and performing arts, education and science.

Gulbenkian, Nubar Sarkis (1896–1972), Turkish philanthropist; son of Calouste Gulbenkian. Fortune based on petroleum industry in Middle East. Endowments assist the arts in UK and elsewhere.

Gulf Stream, warm ocean current flowing NE from Caribbean Sea; after passing Florida Straits, broadens into North Atlantic Drift, flowing to Barents Sea and NW Europe.

gull, family of web-footed seabirds, Laridae. White or grey in colour, strong swimmers and powerful fliers.

gullet *see* OESOPHAGUS.

Gullstrand, Allvar (1862–1930), Swedish ophthalmologist. Awarded Nobel Prize for Physiology and Medicine (1911) for study of optical images and of light refraction in eye.

guncotton, nitrocellulose, explosive compound of carbon, hydrogen, oxygen and nitrogen which looks like unrefined cotton. Used in ammunition and blasting.

gunpowder, explosive made from potassium nitrate, sulphur and carbon, used in blasting and formerly in weapons. Believed to have been invented in 9th cent. China; introduced to Europe in 14th cent.

Gunpowder Plot, Eng. Catholic plan to blow up James I and Brit. Houses of Parl. (5 Nov. 1605). Failure due to warning letter dispatched on previous day. GUY FAWKES day celebrated every year in Britain with bonfires and fireworks.

Gunter, Edmund (1581–1626), Eng. mathematician, and astronomer. Invented portable quadrant (1618) and Gunter's Chain, a decimal scale used for surveying.

guppy, rainbow fish, *Lebistes reticulatus,* small fish native to S America. Male, rainbow coloured, 1 in. long; female, greenish-grey, *c.* 1½ in. long. Adults cannibalistic.

Gur, family of W African languages spoken in Mali, Upper Volta, parts of Ghana and Ivory Coast. Includes Moshe and Dagbane.

Gurkha, certain predominantly Hindu tribes of Nepal. Large military contingents formerly recruited for British Indian Army.

gurnard, marine fishes allied to Bullheads with spiny armoured head and 6 finger-like feelers. May weigh up to 5 lb.

Gurney, Sir Goldsworthy (1793–1875), Eng. physician; inventor of oxyhydrogen blowpipe and 'Drummond Light'. Invented high-pressure steam jet (1823).

Gustaf VI, Oscar Fredrik Wilhelm Olaf Gustaf Adolf (1882–   ), king of Sweden. Succeeded to throne 1950.

Gustavus I [Vasa] (1496–1560), king of Sweden (1523–60). Reign marked by estab. of National Protestant Church (1527), freed Sweden from economic subjection to Hanseatic League (1537).

Gustavus II, [Gustavus Adolphus] (1594–1632), king of Sweden (1611–32). Formed alliance with Denmark (1628), France (1629), pledged support to Protestant side in THIRTY YEARS WAR.

Gustavus III (1746–92), king of Sweden (1771–92). By coup d'état

(1772) restored royal prerogatives lost by his predecessors.

Gustavus IV [Gustavus Adolphus] (1778–1837), king of Sweden (1790–1809). Deposed because of anti-French policies and despotic rule.

Gustavus V (1858–1950), king of Sweden (1907–50). Maintained neutrality in both World Wars.

Gustavus VI *see* GUSTAF VI.

Gutenberg, Johann, orig. Johannes Gensfleisch (1400–68), Ger. printer believed by some to have invented printing; also to have printed Mazarin or 42-Line Bible. Most facts about him disputed.

Guthrie, Sir [William] Tyrone (1900–71), Brit. theatrical producer and author. Administrator of Old Vic and Sadler's Wells (1939–45); helped found Shakespeare Festival Theatre in Stratford, Canada (1953).

gutta percha, milky juice obtained from trop. trees of Sapotaceae family. Used in manufacture of golf balls.

Guyana, sovereign democratic state of Brit. Commonwealth on NE coast of S America. Area: 83,000 sq. mi.; cap. Georgetown. Formerly Brit. colony of British Guiana, independent 1966. Plans to become repub. 1970. Low-lying, watered by Demerara, Essequibo and Berbice rivers. Sugar, rice and coconuts grown. Gold, diamonds and bauxite mined. Pop. (1967) 691,000.

Gwalior, city in Madhya Bharat, Union of India, formerly in state of Gwalior. Known for 15th cent. Jain figures and early Hindu antiquities. Leather, pottery and cotton provide main occupations. Pop. (1963) 314,000.

Gwyn or **Gwynne, Eleanor ('Nell')** (1650–87). Eng. comic actress.

Gyrfalcon

Mistress of Charles II, bore him 2 sons.

gymnastics, sport and training by exercises of the body, dating from Gk. Olympic games (8th–4th cent. BC). Modern gymnastics date from early 19th cent. Germany. Competitive gymnastics (instituted at 1896 Olympics) include vaulting horse, parallel and horizontal bars, rope climbing, stationary rings.

gymnosperm, botanical term for seed plants in which ovules are not enclosed in an ovary. They include cycads and conifers.

gynaecology, branch of medicine concerned with ailments peculiar to women, esp. of reproductive system.

gypsophila, gauze plant, chalk flower, plant of family Caryophyllaceae with tiny white flowers on slender stalks; popular in bouquets and decorations.

gypsum, hydrous calcium sulphate mineral. From natural state, plaster of Paris obtained; from processed gypsum, alabaster (used in building industry).

gypsy *see* GIPSY.

gyrfalcon, *Falco rusticulus,* large falcon of N Europe highly valued in Middle Ages for hunting.

gyroscope, instrument invented (1852) by Jean Foucault. Its rotation causes centrifugal force, overcoming gravity. Used for navigation in ships and aircraft.

Herring Gull

H

Haarlem, town and river port of N Holland prov., Netherlands. Centre of bulb growing industry. Pop. (1966) 172,000.

Habakkuk, prophetic book of OT, written *c.* 550 BC. Poems on triumph of justice and divine mercy over evil.

habeas corpus, in law, writ from a judge to custodian of a person directing that the person be brought to a particular place at a particular time. In UK and US, served primarily as safeguard against wrongful imprisonment.

Haber, Fritz (1868–1934), Ger. chemist. Invented Haber process, with Karl Bosch, for preparation of synthetic ammonia. Awarded Nobel Prize for Chemistry (1918).

Gravenstenen Bridge, Haarlem

haboob [Arabic: *habub,* violent wind], violent dust or sand storm of N Africa and India.

Habsburg, Hapsburg, ruling house of Austria (1282–1918). Austria became hereditary possession under Count Rudolf of Germany; by 1438 Ger. imperial office vested in Habsburg house. Status as world power came after acquisition of Low Countries by Maximilian I's marriage (1477); Charles V's accession as emperor added Spain; Hungary and Bohemia incorporated (1526) through later marriage. Weakened by wars of succession during 18th cent. With Francis II's assumption (1804) of title, Emperor of Austria, family history became synonymous with that of Austria (after 1867 Austro-Hungarian Monarchy). After death of Emperor Charles I, who abdicated (1918), claims of dynasty passed to his son, Archduke Otto.

hachures, short lines of shading on a map to represent differences in slope. When thick and close together, slope is steep; if thinner and farther apart, slope is gentle.

hackberry, *Celtis occidentalis,* deciduous tree of elm family. Grows in E US and Europe. Small edible fruit; root contains dye used for linen.

Hadassah, Hebrew name for Esther. Also name of Women's Zionist Movement in US, founded by Henrietta Szold (1912).

haddock, *Gadus aeglefinus,* species of marine carnivorous fish of Gadidae family. Found on N Atlantic coasts and round British Isles. Has black spot behind each pectoral fin. Eaten fresh or smoked.

Hades, in Gk. myth., the Underworld. Home of the dead, situated under the earth and surrounded by R. Styx. Also god of the Underworld. *See* PLUTO.

Hadrian (AD 76–138), Roman emperor of Sp. descent. Patron of learning and architecture. During reign (117–138) abandoned Trajan's conquests in Mesopotamia and adopted defensive policy. Visited Britain and built wall from Solway to the Tyne, known as Hadrian's Wall.

Hadrian's Wall, Roman fortification in Britain, $73\frac{1}{2}$ mi. long from Tyne to Solway. Built *c.* AD 121–127 by Emperor Hadrian. Large sections (6 ft. high, 8 ft. thick) and forts remain.

Haeckel, Ernst Heinrich (1834–1919), Ger. biologist and philosopher. Writings on evolution include *History of Creation* (1862) and *The Riddle of the Universe* (1899).

haematite [UK] **hematite** [US], hard mineral occurring in red earthy masses and dark grey crystals. Oxide of iron; important as an ore.

haemoglobin [UK] **hemoglobin** [US], protein in red blood corpuscles, combined with iron and carrying oxygen.

haemophilia [UK] **hemophilia** [US], hereditary condition characterized by delayed clotting of blood and consequent difficulty in checking haemorrhage. Inherited only by males through mother.

haemorrhage [UK] **hemorrhage** [US], condition characterized by copious escape of blood from vessels.

Hagen, Victor Wolfgang von (1909–), Amer. archaeologist, explorer and naturalist. Among books are *Ecuador the Unknown* (1939), *Highway of the Sun* (1956), *The Roads that led to Rome* (1967).

Hagen, Walter (1892–1969), Amer. golfer. Winner of US Open (1914, 1919) and of US Professional Golfers Association championships (1921, 1924–7).

Hagenbeck, Karl (1844–1913), Ger. circus manager and animal trainer. Estab. Zoological Garden at Hamburg (1907).

hagfish, blind eel-like marine fish less than 2 ft. long, of class Cyclostomata. Several species found in temp. Pacific coastal waters.

Haggai, prophetic book of OT, written *c.* 250 BC in Jerusalem after return from the Captivity.

Haggard, Sir H[enry] Rider (1856–1925), Brit. novelist, writer of romantic adventure stories such as *King Solomon's Mines* (1885), *She* (1887).

Hague, The, admin. centre and seat of govt. of Netherlands, cap. of S Holland prov. Industry includes printing and consumer products. Used by Germans in World War 2 as base for launching flying bombs and rockets. Pop. (1966) 593,000.

Hahn, Otto, FRS (1879–1968), Ger. chemist. Awarded Nobel Prize for Chemistry (1944) for discovery of fission of heavy nuclei.

Hahnemann, Samuel *see* HOMOEO-PATHY.

Haida, tribe of N Amer. Indians inhabiting Queen Charlotte and Prince of Wales Is. Built cedar plank houses and sea-going dugout canoes.

Haifa, main port of Israel on Bay of Acre at foot of Mt. Carmel. Oil refineries using oil piped from Middle East; heavy industries. Pop. (1965) 201,000.

Haig, Douglas, 1st Earl (1861–1928), Brit. field-marshal, commander-in-chief in World War 1 after 1915. Devoted himself to cause of ex-servicemen. Pres. of Brit. Legion and Chairman of United Services Fund.

hail, frozen form of precipitation. Nucleus is carried to cold upper areas and coated with ice before falling to ground.

Haile Selassie (1891–), emperor of Ethiopia. Carried out reforms in educ. system and abolition of slave-trading. Crowned Emperor (1930).

Haddock

Escaped to England (1936) after Italy invaded Ethiopia (1935) and regained his throne (1941).

Hainan, Chinese island, district of Kwangtung prov. Area: 14,000 sq. mi.; cap. Hoihow. Rugged and mountainous with trop. vegetation, crops and climate. Pop. (1963 est.) 3,000,000.

Hainaut, prov. of SW Belgium. Area: 1,436 sq. mi.; cap. Mons; main towns Charleroi, Tournai. Independent in 10th cent. People mainly Walloons. Coal, iron and steel industries. Pop. (1960 est.) 1,264,414.

Haiphong, largest port of North Vietnam, former Fr. naval base. Under Fr. protection (1884) until Jap. occupation in World War 2; became part of North Vietnam (1955). Pop. (1965 est.) 369,000.

hair, filamentous outgrowth of the skin, consisting of modified epidermic tissue. A hair consists of cylindrical shaft and a root, set in a flasklike depression (hair follicle).

hairmoss, pigeon wheat, *Polytrichum* of order Bryales, often used, like carpet moss, in stuffing bedding and in making brooms and dusters.

hairstreak, group of butterflies Lycaenidea found in temp. and trop. regions. Purple hairstreak, *Thecla quercus,* is found throughout Europe.

Haiti, republic on W Hispaniola Is., W Indies. Area: 10,714 sq. mi.; cap. Port-au-Prince. Densely populated. Orig. Spanish, Fr. colonists developed sugar plantation using Negro slaves (17th cent.). Surrendered to France (1697); independent 1804; US naval control until 1934. Population comprises Mulattoes and Negroes (95%); French official language. Produces coffee, sisal, bananas, rubber and sugar; gold, silver, copper and iron. Pop. (1965) 4,485,000.

hake, *Merluccius merluccius,* food fish of Brit. seas and coasts of Europe, Africa and America. Slender voracious, deep water fish, reaching 4 ft. in length.

Hakluyt, Richard (1552–1616), Eng. geographer. Encouraged Eng. discovery and colonization, esp. in N America. Chief work *The Principal Navigations, Voyages, Traffics and Discoveries of the English Nation.*

Halas, George Stanley (1895–   ), coach for 40 yr. of highly successful Chicago Bears. Co-founder of American National Football League.

Haldane, J[ohn] B[urdon] S[anderson] (1892–1964), Brit. scientist, known for application of mathematics to biology. Took Indian citizenship.

The Palace of Peace, The Hague

Hale, Edward Everett (1822–1909), Amer. clergyman and writer. Known for short story *A Man Without a Country* (1863).

Haleakala, mountain (10,023 ft.) on Maui Is., Hawaii. Dormant volcano with crater 3,000 ft. deep, 21 mi. in circumference.

Halévy, Jacques François Fromental Élie (1799–1862), Fr. romantic composer. Most successful opera was *La Juive* (1835).

half uncials cursive, quasi-minuscule writing style used in early MSS. Influenced continental *scriptura libraria* of 7th and 8th cent.

Haliburton, T[homas] C[handler] (1796–1865), Canadian politician and writer. Presented satire through comic creation Sam Slick in *Nova Scotian* and *The Clockmaker* (1836).

halibut, *Hippoglossus vulgaris,* largest flatfish, up to 10 ft. long of N Atlantic and N Pacific. Popular food fish.

Halicarnassus, ancient city of Caria, SW Asia Minor, birthplace of Herodotus and Dionysius. Mausoleum, built in memory of King Mausolus by his wife, was one of Seven Wonders of the World.

Halifax, cap. of Nova Scotia, Canada, and main winter port with ice-free harbour. Founded 1749, terminus of 1st regular steamship trade to Britain (1840). Shipbuilding, oil-refining and fishing. Pop. (1966) 184,000.

Halifax, Edward Frederick Lindley Wood, 1st Earl of (1881–1959), Brit. statesman, Gov.-General of India (1926–31). Helped negotiate MUNICH PACT as Foreign Sec. (1938–40).

halite, geological name for sodium chloride, common or rock salt. Found in cubic crystals or granular masses in beds of limestone, dolomite or shale. Colourless, transparent and soluble.

Hall, Benjamin (1838–65), notorious Austral. bushranger and bandit. Carried out numerous raids and holdups before being tracked down and shot.

Hall, Charles Francis (1821–71), Amer. explorer. Led expeditions to the Arctic and looked for Sir John Franklin's party. Died while trying to reach North Pole in US ship *Polaris*.

Hall, James Norman (1887–1951), Amer. man of letters. Known as collaborator with Charles Nordhoff on trilogy *Mutiny on the Bounty* (1932), *Men Against the Sea* (1933) and *Pitcairn's Island* (1934).

Hall, Peter Reginald Frederick (1930–   ), Brit. theatre producer. Director of Royal Shakespeare Theatre, Stratford-on-Avon (1960); made name with production of *Waiting for Godot* (1955).

hall mark [UK], set of marks stamped on gold and silver articles attesting to authenticity of metal.

Hall of Fame for Great Americans, The, memorial on campus of New York University honouring distinguished citizens of US. Completed (1900).

Hallam, Henry (1777–1859), Eng. historian, one of 1st to use original documents. Best known work *A View of the State of Europe in the Middle Ages* (1818).

Hair Moss

Conference of Officers at the Culveniers Doelen (1663) *by Frans Hals*

Hallé Orchestra, symphony orchestra founded (1857) by Sir Charles Hallé, based in Manchester, England.

Halley, Edmund (1656–1742), Eng. astronomer, 1st (1682) to predict return of a comet. Financed publication of Newton's *Principia* (1686–7).

Halley's comet, named after astronomer, Edmund Halley, who predicted orbit (1682). Verified when seen 75 yr. later, proving comet revolved around sun. Seen 1910, due 1986.

Hallowe'en [All Hallows Eve] Oct. 31, evening vigil before Christian feast celebrating All Saints Day. Superstition and customs associated with witches and ghosts are Celtic in origin.

Hallstrom, Sir Edward John Lees (1886–   ), Austral. philanthropist who has supported cancer research, zoological societies. Established Livestock and Farmers Trust in New Guinea.

hallucination, false sensory impression which invents or misinterprets external phenomena. Psychiatry considers it symptomatic of repressed desires.

hallucinogenic drugs, those which produce hallucinations, *i.e.* promote loss of contact with reality and cause recipient to imagine happenings very real to himself but of no physical reality, *e.g.* LSD.

halogen, in chemistry, group name for fluorine, chlorine, bromine, iodine and astatine. All are non-metallic, monovalent and form negative ions.

Hals, Frans (*c.* 1580–1666), Dutch painter who greatly influenced Dutch school. Noted for his portraits, *e.g. Laughing Cavalier.*

Halsey, William Frederick (1882–1959), Amer. admiral, commander of Amer. 3rd Fleet in World War 2. Naval forces under his command defeated Japanese in Battle of Santa Cruz Is. (Oct. 1942), Guadalcanal (Nov. 1942) and Leyte Gulf.

Halsted, William Stewart (1852–1922), Amer. surgeon. Discovered method of anaesthetising by injecting cocaine into certain nerves. Initiated use of rubber gloves in surgery.

Ham, in OT, one of 3 sons of Noah, ancestor of Ethiopians and Egyptians.

hamadryas baboon, *Papio hamadryas,* baboon of Arabian peninsula with long dark hair covering forequarters and flesh-coloured chest and rump.

Hamburg, city and seaport of W Germany on Elbe estuary. Member of HANSEATIC LEAGUE in Middle Ages, made free city (1510) and joined Ger. Confederation (1815). Extensively damaged in World War 2. Manufactures machinery and chemicals; shipyards. Pop. (1965) 1,854,000.

Hameln, Hamelin, town of Lower Saxony, W Germany. Scene of the exploits of the legendary Pied Piper. Pop. 52,000.

Hamilcar Barca (d. 228 BC), Carthaginian commander during 1st Punic War. Set out (237 BC) to conquer Spain, but killed in battle. Father of Hannibal.

Hamilton, city and lake port, S Ontario, Canada. At head of L. Ontario, it is important rail and air centre. Iron and steel industries; textiles; shipping. Pop. (1966) 431,000.

Hamilton, Scot. noble family. **James Hamilton,** 1st Duke of Hamilton (1606–49), soldier and politician, executed for support of Charles I against Cromwell. **William Hamilton,** 2nd Duke of Hamilton (1616–51), soldier and politician, attempted restoration of Charles I.

Hamilton, Alexander (1755–1804), Amer. statesman. Leading proponent of Constitution through contributions to FEDERALIST PAPERS. First Sec. of the Treasury, estab. Bank of the United States. Leader of centralizing Federalist Party, opposed by Jefferson. Killed in duel with Aaron Burr, whom he had kept from presidency (1800).

Hamilton, Emma, Lady (*c.* 1761–1815), mistress of Sir William Hamilton, Brit. Ambassador at Naples and later his wife (1791). After 1798, mistress of Horatio Nelson, whose daughter she bore (1801).

Hamilton, Sir William Rowan (1805–65), Irish mathematician. Known for discovery of quaternions.

Hammarskjold, Dag (1905–61), Swedish statesman and Sec. General of UN (1953–61). Represented UN in Middle East Crisis (1956) and the Congo (1960–1). Extended UN influence. Posthumously awarded Nobel Peace Prize (1961).

Hammerstein, Oscar (1895–1960), Amer. librettist and lyricist. Collaborated with composer Richard Rogers in successful stage musicals.

Hammett, Dashiell (1894–1961),

Canal in old Hamburg

Hangnest

Amer. writer of detective stories, *e.g. The Maltese Falcon* (1930).

Hammurabi, king of Babylon (reigned *c.* 1792–1750 BC) of Amorite dynasty. Best remembered for legal code.

Hampden, John (1594–1643), Eng. politician famous for his refusal to pay Ship Money to Charles I (1638). Became a hero of Parliamentarians in Civil War.

Hampshire, county of S England incl. Is. of Wight. Area: 1,698 sq. mi.; county town Winchester. Mainly agricultural, incl. forest areas, *e.g.* New Forest. Headquarters of Royal Navy at Portsmouth harbour. Pop. (1966) 1,483,000.

Hampton Court, Eng. palace on R. Thames erected by Cardinal Wolsey (1515), partially rebuilt by Christopher Wren. Site of Conference (1604) authorizing King James Bible.

Hampton Roads, Va., natural harbour at entry of Chesapeake Bay, US, with ports of Newport News, Portsmouth, Norfolk and Hampton. Hampton Roads Peace Conference (3 Feb. 1865), meeting to end Civil War.

hamster, small nocturnal rodent of temp. Europe and W Asia. Has internal cheek pouches to carry food; eats small animals and vegetation. Common hamster, *Cricetus cricetus* is grey or brown. Golden hamster, *Mesocricetus,* a popular pet, is smaller and used for medical research.

Hamsun, Knut (1859–1952), Norwegian novelist best known for *Hunger* (1890), *Pan* (1894) and *The Growth of the Soil* (1917). Awarded Nobel Prize for Literature (1920).

Han (202 BC–*c.* AD 220), dynasty of China. its 400 yr. of expansion and culture broken only by Hsin dynasty (*c.* AD 9–*c.* AD 25). Civil service examinations introduced; 1st encyclopedic history and dictionary produced. Buddhism introduced.

hand, prehensile extremity of fore limb, with skeleton composed of 5 metacarpal bones, 1 for each finger, which articulate with wrist or carpal bones above, and phalanges or finger bones below. Also a unit of length, approx. 4 in. used in measurement of horses.

Handel, George Frederic (1685–1759), Ger.-English baroque composer. Wrote 46 operas, bringing Ital. opera forms and styles to England. Best known for 18 oratorios incl. *Israel in Egypt* (1739) and the *Messiah* (1742).

Handy, W[illiam] C[hristopher] (1873–1958), Amer. Negro blues musician and composer. Wrote 'Memphis Blues' (1912) and 'St Louis Blues' (1914).

Hangchow, Hangchou, cap. of Chekiang prov., China, port on Tsientang R. Founded AD 606. Famous for silk industry. Pop. (1957) 784,000.

Hanging Gardens of Babylon, terraced building planted with gardens, constructed by Nebuchadnezzar. One of Seven Wonders of the World.

hangnest, Baltimore oriole, *Icterus galbula,* black and orange N Amer. bird, genus intermediate between finches and starlings. Almost always gregarious, they nest in hanging constructions.

Hankow, city and port of Hupei prov., China. Forms great commercial and industrial centre with Hanyang and Wuchang. Total pop. (1957) 2,146,000.

Hanna, Marcus Alonzo ('**Mark**') (1837–1904), Amer. capitalist and politician. Republican Party fund-raiser, leader. Party chairman (1896–1900), US Senate (1897–1904).

Hannibal (247–182 BC), Carthaginian general, son of Hamilcar. After journey across Alps, Ital. campaign culminated in victory over Romans at Cannae (216 BC); failed to capture Rome, recalled to defend Carthage (203 BC), defeated by Scipio at Zama (202 BC). Thereafter went into exile and poisoned himself to avoid surrender to Rome.

Hanno (*fl. c.* 470 BC), Carthaginian navigator; explored NE African coast.

Hanno the Great (*fl.* 3rd cent. BC), Carthaginian politician. Advocated peace with Rome during 2nd PUNIC WAR (218–202 BC).

Coin commemorating Hannibal's use of elephants in his Italian campaign

Hanoi, cap. of North Vietnam, formerly cap. of Fr. protectorate of Tonkin in 2 parts, separated by lake. Manufacturing centre, with rice mills, cement, match and machine tool factories. Taken over (1955) by Communist Viet-minh govt. Bombed by South Vietnam-Amer. forces in Vietnam War. Pop. (1960) 414,620.

Hanover, House of, Eng. royal house. Succession claimed through Sophia, granddaughter of James I, wife of Elector Ernest Augustus. Act of Settlement (1701) made their son, George, heir to Queen Anne to exclude Catholic Stuart line. Hanoverian monarchs were George I, George II, George III, George IV and William IV.

Hanover, indust. city, commercial centre of N West Germany, cap. of Lower Saxony. Leading member of HANSEATIC LEAGUE; cap. (1815) of kingdom of Hanover. Manufactures rubber, cars, machinery and consumer goods. Agricultural, with lead, iron, copper in Harz Mts., and coal in SW. Pop. (1965) 553,000.

Hansard, name for official reports of UK Parliamentary proceedings. Thomas Curson Hansard (1776–1833) printed accounts of debates (1803). The London *Times* took over from Hansard family (1895) and from 1908 debates reported by govt. staff.

Hanseatic League, mercantile organization of N Ger. towns for trading.

Common Hamster

Became great confederation by 14th cent. and most seaports of Baltic Sea and E North Sea were members. Provided privileges, and protection by its army; declined (14 ports left by 17th cent.) and ended by 19th cent.

Hansen, Alvin Harvey (1887–   ), Amer. economist; one of 1st to realize fiscal implications of income analysis. Works include *The Dollar and the International Monetary System* (1965).

Hansen's disease, Hansen's bacillus *see* LEPROSY.

Hanson, Howard Harold (1896–   ), Amer. composer, conductor and teacher. Works include *2nd*, or *Romantic, Symphony;* opera *Merrymount*; and cantata *Song of Human Rights.*

Hapsburg *see* HABSBURG.

hara-kiri, Jap. practice of honourable suicide. Once obligatory after disobedience or disloyalty. Still occasionally practised.

Harald Bluetooth (d. *c.* 985), 1st Christian king of Denmark (935–85).

harbour, area of water where ships anchor in safety. Natural harbours exist where sea penetrates land via narrow opening, *e.g.* New York, or river mouths which are liable to

European Hare

silting. Artificial harbours made by construction of breakwater to provide shelter, *e.g.* Southampton, Takoradi, Buenos Aires.

Harden, Sir Arthur (1865–1940), Brit. biochemist. Shared Nobel Prize for Chemistry (1929) with Hans von Euler-Chelpin for research in alcoholic fermentation.

Hardie, [James] Keir (1856–1915), Scot. labour leader, founder of Independent Labour party and supporter of Suffragettes. Wrote *From Serfdom to Socialism* (1907) and *After Twenty Years* (1913).

Harding, John, 1st Baron Harding of Petherton (1896–   ), Brit. field-

marshal and executive who served in both World Wars.

Harding, Warren Gamaliel (1865–1923), 29th US President (1921–3), Republican. Pres. candidate (1920), won easily on non-committal platform. Cabinet mostly inefficient and corrupt; died shortly before revelations of scandal in Interior (*see* TEAPOT DOME) and Justice depts. and in Veterans' Bureau.

hardness, in mineralogy, resistance a substance offers to being scratched. Measured by MOHS scale, ranging from softest (1) to hardest (10).

Hardy, Thomas (1840–1928), Brit. novelist and poet. First success was *Far From the Madding Crowd* (1874). Later works include *The Mayor of Casterbridge* (1886). *Tess of the D'Urbervilles* (1891).

hare, rodent of genus *Lepus,* order Lagomorpha, with longer ears and hind legs than the rabbit. Snowshoe rabbit and jack rabbit, in fact hares, native to N America; arctic hare, circumpolar distribution; blue hare, Eurasian variety; hare of C and W Europe introduced in N America.

Hare, Robert (1781–1858), Amer. chemist. Invented oxyhydrogen blowpipe.

harebell, bluebell, perennial wild flower, *Campanula rotundifolia,* of bellflower family Campanulaceae. Blue bell-shaped blossoms.

harelip, congenital cleft of one or both lips, but usually upper only. Often occurs with associated cleft palate. Early surgery successful.

Hargreaves, James (1745–78), Brit. weaver and inventor, built the 'spinning-jenny' (1764), a great improvement on existing machinery.

Harlan, John Marshall (1899–   ), Amer. jurist, Associate Justice of US Supreme Court (1955–   ). Awarded Croix de Guerre (France and Belgium) for service during World War 2.

Harlem, area of Manhattan, NY, US, estab. 1658. One of largest Negro communities in US, scene of rioting (1960s).

Harlequin, stock character of pantomime and COMMEDIA DELL'ARTE, counterpart to Columbine. An acrobat and wit.

Harlow, Jean, orig. Harlean Carpentier (1911–37), Amer. film actress whose films included *Hell's Angels, Platinum Blonde, Saratoga.*

harmattan, dry, cold NE wind from Sahara desert, affecting NW Africa (Oct.–March). Adverse effects on trop. crops but beneficial to health.

Harmensen, Jacob *see* ARMINIUS, JACOBUS.

harmonica, mouth organ, simple musical instrument; an enclosed box containing tuned metal reeds with holes through which air is blown or sucked.

harmonium, musical instrument; pipeless, reed-vibrated ORGAN. Has 5-octave keyboard. Pedals fill air chamber, providing compression.

harmony, in music, 2 or more notes sounded simultaneously, producing chords; also, relationship of such combinations to each other.

Harmsworth, Alfred Charles William, Viscount Northcliffe (1865–1922), Brit. newspaper proprietor. Founded *Daily Mail* (1896), *Daily Mirror* (1903); acquired *The Times* (1908). Revolutionized Brit. journalism. Pioneered pictorial newspapers.

Harmsworth, Harold Sidney, Lord Rothermere (1868–1940), Brit. newspaper proprietor and politician. Founded *Sunday Pictorial* (1915). Brit. Air Minister (1917–18).

harnessed antelope *see* BUSH BUCK.

Harold, Harald (*c.* 1022–66), king of England (1066). Named by Edward the Confessor to succeed to throne. Opposed by William of Normandy, whose claim he had earlier promised to support. Ensuing conflict decided by Battle of Hastings, in which Harold was killed; William became king.

harp, stringed musical instrument, with triangular frame; player plucks the strings. Modern orchestral harp has range of $6\frac{1}{2}$ octaves and each string can play any of 3 notes at the touch of a pedal.

harp seal, common arctic seal found as far S as Maine coast. Male has black crescent suggesting harp along each side, and black face and throat.

Harpers Ferry, town in NE W Virginia, US; scene of John Brown's raid on US arsenal (1859) and 9 major engagements of Civil War. Pop. (1960) 572.

Harpies, in Gk. myth., birds with the faces of women, believed to embody the souls of the dead which snatched away those of the living.

harpsichord, stringed keyboard musical instrument, popular (16th–18th cent.). Precursor of PIANO.

harrier, bird of prey of genus *Circus,* family Falconidae, usually 17–23 in. long. Poultry is favourite prey. *C. cyaneus,* hen-harrier, was common in Europe, now rare. *C. hudsonius* is N Amer. marsh hawk.

Harriman, [William] Averell (1891–   ), Amer. diplomat and govt. official. Ambassador to USSR (1943–6); Gov. of New York (1953–9); chief US negotiator of Nuclear

Harp Seal

Test Ban Treaty (1963); US ambassador-at-large during 1960s.

Harris, Frank (1856–1931), Amer. journalist and author, b. Ireland. Works include *Oscar Wilde, his Life and Confessions* (1920), *Bernard Shaw* (1931), plays and novels.

Harris, Joel Chandler (1848–1908), Amer. Southern author. His 'Uncle Remus' stories were in Negro dialect; later collected in *Uncle Remus: his Songs and Sayings* (1880).

Harris, Roy Ellsworth (1898–), Amer. composer, pupil of Nadia Boulanger. Work includes 6 symphonies, 3 string quartets, 3 ballets.

Harris tweed, material woven by hand from virgin Scot. wool on Is. of Harris, Outer Hebrides.

Harrison, Benjamin (1833–1901), 23rd US Pres. (1889–93), Republican. Senator from Indiana (1881–7). Equivocal stand on civil service reform displeased reformers and party bosses. Approved highly protective McKinley Tariff Act.

Harrison, Rex Carey (1908–), Eng. stage and film actor; roles include 'Professor Higgins' in *My Fair Lady*.

Harrison, Ross Granville (1870–1959), Amer. biologist. Introduced hanging-drop culture method for study of living tissues.

Harrison, William Henry (1773–1841), 9th US Pres. (1841), Whig Gov. of Indiana Territory (1800–12). Met Indian unrest under Tecumseh at Tippecanoe (1811). Unsuccessful Whig pres. candidate (1836). Renominated (1840), he defeated Martin Van Buren. Died after 1 month in office.

Harrod, Sir [Henry] Roy Forbes (1900–), Brit. economist. Co-editor *Economic Journal* (1945–61). Works include *International Economics* (1933), *Life of Lord Keynes* (1951).

Harrow, borough of Greater London, England. Pop. (1964) 8,963. Includes Harrow Public School, founded 1571, opened 1611.

Hart, Moss (1904–61), Amer. dramatist. Collaborated with George S. Kaufman on *You Can't Take It With You* (1936).

Harte, [Francis] Bret (1836–1902), Amer. writer. His humorous stories of the West included 'The Luck of Roaring Camp' and 'The Outcasts of Poker Flat'.

hartebeest, several African antelopes, S African, esp. *Alcelaphus caama*, reddish-brown in colour, *c.* 4ft. high.

Hartford, cap. of Connecticut, US. Centre of commerce, industry, culture. Settled (1635–6) around Dutch trading post. Famous for insurance business. Pop. (1963) 162,180.

Hartford, Huntington (1911–), Amer. financier and art patron. Founded Huntington Hartford Foundation (1948); annually awards 5,000 dollars to outstanding writer, composer or artist. Author of *Art or Anarchy* (1964).

Hartford Foundation, estab. (1942) by John A. Hartford and George L. Hartford for medical research.

Hartline, Haldan Keffer (1903–), Amer. physiologist. With R.A. Granit and G. Wald, awarded Nobel Prize for Physiology and Medicine (1967) for discoveries concerning primary chem. and physiological processes of the eye.

Hartmann von Aue (*c.* 1170–*c.* 1220), Ger. poet, known for romances *Erec* and *Iwein*. Through *Erec* Arthurian legend entered Ger. literature.

Hartnell, Norman (1901–), Brit. dress designer. Dressmaker to Queen Elizabeth II, and Queen Elizabeth the Queen Mother.

hart's-tongue, *Phyllitis,* genus of ferns, common in Europe and E Asia. Rare *P. americana* found in US and S Canada.

Harun al-Rashid (*c.* 764–809), 5th

Hart's Tongue Fern

Abassid caliph (786–809), made Baghdad centre of Arabic culture. Figures prominently in *Thousand and One Nights*; his reign is depicted as a Golden Age.

Harvard University, privately endowed university for men at Cambridge, Mass., US. Founded (1636) as Harvard College, became university (1780). Affiliated with women's Radcliffe College (founded 1879).

harvest bug [UK] **chigger** [US], mites of family Trombidiidae; the 6-legged larval forms of several species of Trombicula. Swarm in summer and autumn. Cause irritation by piercing the skin.

harvest mouse, *Micromys minutus,* small European fieldmouse. Builds round nest in plant stems.

harvester-spiders, harvest-men, predatory, oval-shaped arachnids of

Hartebeest

order Opiliones. Abound in temp. N hemisphere and in India.

Harvey, William (1578–1657), Eng. physiologist, 1st to understand function of heart as a pump and circulation of the blood.

Haryana, state of India, formed (1966) from S part of former Punjab. Chandigarth, joint cap. of Haryana and Punjab.

Harz Mountains, most N mountain system of Germany, extending *c.* 60 mi. between Elbe and Weser rivers. Rises to 3,745 ft. Richly forested. Total area: *c.* 780 sq. mi. Upper Harz rich in metal and mineral deposits. Timber industry and tourist trade.

Hasdrubal, name of 2 Carthaginian generals. 1) Son-in-law of Hamilcar whom he succeeded (229 BC) as commander in Spain. Founded Cartagena and increased Carthaginian Empire. 2) Son of Hamilcar and brother of Hannibal. Conducted campaign in Spain against the Romans but killed in battle at Metaurus (207 BC).

hashish, hasheesh, various preparations from flower of Indian hemp plant. An intoxicant or narcotic, smoked, chewed or imbibed. Used in medicine as anodyne.

Haskell, Arnold Lionel (1903–), Brit. ballet critic and author. Gov. of Royal Ballet School. Author of *Diaghileff* (1935), *Ballet Retrospect* (1964).

Hastings, Sir Patrick Gardiner (1881–1952), Brit. lawyer and Labour M.P. Attorney-general of 1st Brit. Lab. govt. (1923). Author of *Cases Famous and Infamous* (1950).

Hastings, Warren (1732–1818), Eng. statesman, 1st Gov.-General of India. As Gov. of Bengal (1772–4), introduced reforms in provincial govt. and judicial system. Made Gov.-General 1774. Resigned office and returned to England (1785). Impeached on charges of corruption; acquitted after 7-yr. trial.

Hastings, Battle of (also known as **Senlac**), confrontation between armies of William, Duke of Normandy (William the Conqueror) and Harold II of England (14 Oct. 1066) at Senlac Hill near Hastings, Sussex, England. Harold killed. William's victory initiated Norman conquest of England and he was crowned William I of England (25 Dec. 1066).

Hatshepsut, Hatshepsowet, (d. *c.* 1481 BC), queen of 18th Egyptian dynasty (*c.* 1501– *c.* 1481 BC), daughter of Thutmose I. Reigned with her half-brother Thutmose III. Concentrated on keeping peace and building country's economy. Built temple at Deir el-Bahri.

Hauptmann, Gerhart Johann Robert (1862–1946), Ger. poet, dramatist and novelist; his style was initially naturalistic, *e.g. The Weavers* (1892), later romantic, *e.g. Hannele* (1893), finally realistic, *e.g. Emanuel Quint* (1910). Awarded Nobel Prize for Literature (1912).

Hausa, widely distributed people of N Nigeria numbering over 6 million. Hausa languages are basically Hamitic but people mainly Negroid. Predominantly Moslem.

Haussmann, Georges Eugène, Baron (1809–91), Fr. architect largely responsible for present layout of Paris. Boulevard Haussmann is named after him.

Havana, La Habana, cap. of Cuba; largest city and chief seaport of W Indies (founded *c.* 1515). Exports tobacco, minerals, sugar. Pop. (1966) 982,900.

Havelok the Dane, Danish prince, hero of 14th cent. Anglo-Danish legend, *The Lay of Havelok the Dane.*

Haverford College, founded for men by Quakers (1833) at Haverford, Pa., US.

Havre[-de-Grâce] Le, city and port of Seine-Inférieure department, NW France, at mouth of R. Seine. Chief Fr. transatlantic port (founded 1517) with important docks and shipbuilding yards. Pop. (1966) 223,000.

Hawaii, US state in C Pacific Ocean, consisting of 8 major islands. Area: 6,424 sq. mi.; cap. Honolulu. Islands (formerly Sandwich Is.) mostly fertile; sugar cane and pineapples chief crops, also coffee, fruit and nuts. Tourism and military installations of economic importance. Discovered by James Cook (1778). Annexed by US (1898), became US territory (1900). Bombing of PEARL HARBOR by Japanese

(1941) precipitated US entry into World War II.

Hawaii Volcanoes National Park, in Hawaii, US (formed 1916). Area: 360 sq. mi.

Hawaiian Islands, with Midway, Wake and Johnston Is., group in POLYNESIA (E Pacific Ocean) forming US state of HAWAII.

hawfinch, *Coccothraustes coccothraustes,* stout-billed finch distributed over Eurasia and N Africa. Plumage is deep brown on the back with blue-black wings and white-tipped tail.

hawk, general name for several birds of prey incl. *Accipitridae* kites, buzzards, harriers, and *Falconidae* falcons and caracaras. Many were trained to hunt in falconry; most nest in tree eyries.

hawk moth, lepidoptera of family *Sphingidae,* of more than 100 species. Death's-head hawk moth (*Acherontia atropos*) has skull-like markings on thorax and is a nocturnal flier.

hawkbit, *Leontoden,* genus of biennial or perennial herbs of Compositae family. Found in Europe and Asia. Produce yellow flowers.

Hawkes, Jacquetta (1910–), Brit. archaeologist and journalist. Author of *Early Britain* (1945) and *Journey Down a Rainbow* (1955).

hawking, falconry, sport of hunting game, using trained birds of prey, popular in medieval Europe. Trained hawk carried on gloved wrist of the falconer; unhooded and released on sight of prey; fallen bird retrieved by dogs.

Hawkins or **Hawkyns, Sir John** (1532–95), Eng. mariner and slave trader. Commanded Eng. rear squadron against Sp. Armada (1588).

Hawkins or **Hawkyns, Sir Richard** (*c.* 1562–1622), Eng. naval commander. Served in fleet which defeated Sp. Armada (1588). Captured by Spanish, imprisoned (1597–1602).

hawksbill turtle, *Eretmochelys imbricata,* trop. carnivorous marine turtle. It produces the commercial turtleshell.

Hawley-Smoot Tariff Act (1930), most highly protective tariff legislation in US history. Retaliatory action by foreign govt. led to sharp decline in US foreign trade. Policy reversed by Trade Agreements Act (1934).

Haworth, Sir Walter Norman (1883–1950), Eng. biochemist. With Paul Karrer, awarded Nobel Prize for Chemistry (1937) for work on carbohydrates and vitamin C.

hawthorn, may tree, shrub or small tree, of the rose family of N America

and Eurasia, unknown S of the equator. It bears fragrant clusters of white or red flowers and berries called haws.

Hawthorne, Nathaniel (1804–64), Amer. writer many of whose works investigate the nature of sin and are marked by Puritanism. They include *The Scarlet Letter* (1850), *The House of the Seven Gables* (1851), *The Marble Faun* (1860).

hay fever, inflammation of mucous membrane of nose, caused by sensitivity to foreign substances, usually plant pollen.

Haydn, Franz Joseph (1732–1809), celebrated Austrian composer. While choir leader to Prince Miklós Esterházy in Hungary, he composed most of his symphonies, string quartets, piano sonatas, operas and Masses. Works include *Farewell* (1772) and *Surprise* (1791) symphonies, and oratorios *The Creation* (1798), *The Seasons* (1801).

Hayes, Helen, orig. Helen Hayes Brown (1900–), Amer. actress. Roles include the queen in *Victoria Regina* (1937–8). Appeared in such films as *A Farewell to Arms.*

Hayes, Rutherford B[irchard] (1822–93), 19th US Pres. (1877–81). Gov. of Ohio (1868–72, 1876–7). Chosen as pres. candidate (1876); won subsequent election by 1 electoral vote. Withdrew federal troops from South. Took conservative stand on financial and labour issues. Urged civil service reforms.

Haymarket Square riot, violent anarchist demonstration in Chicago (4 May 1886). Bomb exploded and 11 were killed.

Haywood, William Dudley ('Big Bill') orig. William Richard Haywood (1869–1928), Amer. labour leader, co-founder of INDUSTRIAL WORKERS OF THE WORLD. Imprisoned in World War 1 for sedition, he escaped (1921) to Russia.

hazard, dice game popular in 18th cent. England. Amer. 'craps' prob. derived from it.

hazel, shrubs and nuts of genus *Corylus* of Eurasia. Common variety yields useful elastic wood; cultivated varieties furnish cobs, filberts and Barcelona nuts. Twigs used in water divination.

Hazlitt, Henry (1894–), Amer. journalist; business columnist for *Newsweek* (1946–66). Publications include *The Critics of Keynesian Economics* (1960).

Hazlitt, William (1778–1830), Eng.

Hawksbill Turtle

essayist and critic, champion of Elizabethan drama in *Characters of Shakespeare's Plays* (1817), *Dramatic Literature of the Age of Elizabeth* (1820).

head, part of the body uppermost in humans and foremost in animals. Consists of skull, brain, eyes, mouth, nose; circulation and nerve elements.

Hearn, [Patricio] Lafcadio [Tessima Carlos] (1850–1904), writer, b. Ionian Is. of Irish and Gk. parents. In 1890, went to Japan and became Jap. citizen under name of Yakumo Koizumi. Works include *Some Chinese Ghosts* (1887), *In Ghostly Japan* (1899).

Hearne, Samuel (1745–92) Eng. explorer in N Canada for Hudson's Bay Co. Expeditions to mouth of Coppermine R., and overland to Arctic Ocean (1771–2).

Hearst, William Randolph (1863–1951), Amer. newspaper publisher. Founded newspaper empire incl. *New York Journal-American*. Leading exponent of sensationalist press.

heart, muscular organ which maintains blood circulation in animals. Human heart contains 4 chambers and is located in left side of chest cavity. The functioning of the heart is essential to life.

heart attack [coronary thrombosis], blocking of blood supply to heart caused by blood clot. May be fatal or cause severe damage.

heartburn *see* INDIGESTION.

heartsease, pansy, cultivated garden flower of *Viola* genus, orig. European weed. There are striking variations of size and colour.

heat, form of energy obtained from, or converted into, mechanical, electrical and chem. energy. Radiant heat is electromagnetic vibration, with wavelength longer than that of visible light. Temperature is a measure of quantity of heat in a substance. Melting and boiling are changes in state (solid to liquid, liquid to gas) of a substance on application of heat. Heat required for these changes is **latent heat.**

Heath, Edward Richard George (1916–   ), Brit. politician. Cons. P.M. (1970–   ); President of Board of Trade (1963–4). Elected leader of Cons. Party (1965).

heath, heather, genus *Erica* of Ericaceae, containing over 500 shrubs and trees, common in Africa and Europe. Plants have bell-shaped hanging flowers. *E. cinerea*, bell-heather and *E. ciliaris*, Dorset Heath are common Brit. varieties.

heaven, popularly refers to part of space visible from Earth; also to Utopia or paradise. In Christian and other theistic teaching, Heaven is the abode of God.

Heaviside, Oliver (1850–1925), Eng. scientist. Predicted existence of ionised layer in upper atmosphere (Heaviside layer), which reflects radio waves.

heavy spar *see* BARITES.

Hebbel, Christian Friedrich (1813–63), Ger. poet and dramatist. Noted for tragedies incl. *Judith* (1840) and trilogy *Nibelungs* (1856).

Hebe, in Gk. myth., goddess of youth. Daughter of Zeus and Hera, wife of Heracles after his deification. Identified with Lat. Juventas.

Hebra, Ferdinand von (1816–80), Austrian dermatologist, founder of modern dermatology.

Hebrew, Semitic Afro-Asian language, with *c.* 1 million speakers in Israel. Artificially revived in 20th cent.

Hebrew literature had OLD TESTAMENT, APOCRYPHA and parts of *Pseudepigraphia* among its earliest achievements. *Talmud, Midrash* and *Targum* date between 2nd and 4th cent. *Masora* and Talmudic commentaries date from 6th–7th cent. Diasporic writings of 11th–14th cent. include Cabala's *Zohar* (in Spain). Scattered writers of Middle Ages include Ibn Gabirol, Rashi, Maimonides and Caro. Modern Hebrew literature began with Moses Mendelssohn and includes work of Abramovitch, Sforim, Bialik, S. J. Agnon and Moshe Shamir.

Hebrew University, opened (1925) at Jerusalem. Contains Hadassah Medical School and Weizmann Inst.

Hebrews, epistle of NT, ascribed to St Paul. It proclaims ascendancy of Christ and superiority of the new religion.

Hebrides, Western Isles, group of *c.*

The *Pont de Tancarville* over the Seine at Le Havre

500 islands off W and NW coast of Scotland; *c.* 100 are inhabited. Area: 2,812 sq. mi.; main town Stornoway. Divided into Inner and Outer Hebrides, separated by the Minch and Little Minch. Largely moorland; fishing and sheep and cattle raising are important. Tweeds manufactured. Pop. (1959) 80,000.

Heckel, Erich (1883–1970), Ger. expressionist painter who, with Kirchner and Pechstein, founded *Die Brücke* group (1905).

Hector, in Gk. myth., son of Priam and Hecuba, husband of Andromache. Slain by Achilles in Trojan War.

Hecuba, in Gk. legend, wife of Priam of Troy and mother of Hector, Paris, Cassandra.

hedge sparrow, small Old World bird of Prunellidae family, also called accentors. Common European hedge sparrow, *Prunello modularis,* also called dunnock or shufflewing, has reddish-brown back, grey head and underparts and white-tipped wings. An early breeder, its nest is often chosen by the CUCKOO. There are Siberian, Alpine and other varieties.

hedgehog, insectivorous nocturnal mammal about 10 in. long of Erinaceus family, not found in the New World, remarkable for spiny armature and short tail. When startled, it rolls itself into a protective ball, spines standing out in all directions. Hibernates in winter.

Hedgehog with young

Part of the famous castle at Heidelberg

hedonism, in ethics, theory that pleasure or happiness, of self (egoistic) or others (universal), is object of actions. Exponents have included Epicurus, Hume, J. S. Mill.

Hegel, Georg Wilhelm Friedrich (1770–1831), Ger. philosopher. Formulated concept of historical dialectic: fusion (synthesis) of opposite concepts (thesis and antithesis). Activating principle was *Volksgeist* (world spirit) in universe of perpetual self-creation. Works include *Phenomenology of Mind* (1807) and *Science of Logic* (1812–16). Greatly influenced subsequent philosophies of history, esp. Marx.

Heidegger, Martin (1889–   ), Ger. philosopher who adapted ideas of KIERKEGAARD. Works include *Sein und Zeit* (1927).

Heidelberg, city in West Germany, on Neckar R. Famous for 13th cent. castle and university (founded 1386). Centre of Calvinism during REFORMATION. Pop. (1965) 125,000.

Heifetz, Jascha (1901–   ), Amer. violinist, b. Poland. Has toured US and Europe with great success.

Heilbron, Rose (1914–   ), Eng. barrister (1949). Recorder of Burnley (1956–   ); 1st woman to hold this legal office.

Heilunkiang, N Manchurian prov. of China. Area: *c.* 180,000 sq. mi.; cap. Harbin. Wheat, sugar beet, flax grown and exported. Mineral resources include coal and gold. Pop. (1963) 14,860,000.

Heine, Heinrich (1797–1856), Ger. lyric poet. *Die Harzreise* (1826) is a collection of prose travel sketches. *Buch der Lieder* (1827) contains much of his characteristic verse. Critic of Ger. romanticism.

Heisenberg, Werner Carl (1901–   ), Ger. physicist. Awarded Nobel Prize for Physics (1932) for theory of quantum mechanics and discovery of allotropic forms of hydrogen.

Heister, Lorenz (1683–1758), Ger. surgeon. Wrote *Chirurgie* (1719), widely translated throughout Europe.

Heitler, Walter (1904–   ), Ger. physicist. Among his works are *Theory of Chemical Bond* (1927), *Man and Science* (1963), and papers on cosmic rays, the meson theory and quantum electro-dynamics.

Helen, in Gk. myth., daughter of Zeus and Leda, most beautiful of women. Suitors swore oath to support Helen's husband, Menelaus. When Paris abducted her to Troy, Greeks undertook expedition to Troy, resulting in Trojan War.

Helicon, mountain group in Boeotia, C Greece, highest peak 5,736 ft. Believed by Greeks to be abode of Muses.

helicopter, aircraft with horizontal rotating wings (rotors) which enable it to take off and land vertically, to move in any direction, and to hover.

Heligoland, Helgoland, Ger. North Sea island. Area: *c.* 1 sq. mi. Ancient stronghold, known to Romans; it was captured by Danes (1714); seized by Britain (1807), who ceded it (1890) to Germany in exchange for Zanzibar, and Witu (in Kenya).

Inhabitants of Frisian descent, live by tourism and fishing.

Heliogabalus, Elagabalus (*c.* 205–222), Roman emperor (218–22). Reign notorious for profligacy; killed by Praetorian guards.

Heliopolis *see* BAALBEK.

Helios, in Gk. myth., the Sun, usually represented as charioteer. Later identified with Apollo. Father of Phaethon.

heliotrope, plant that turns to face the sun.

helium, inert, colourless, gaseous element. Although slightly heavier than hydrogen it is non-inflammable and therefore used in airships and balloons.

Hell, place or state of punishment reserved for sinners after death, according to Christian belief. Tendency now to regard Hell as a metaphysical concept. Idea of Hell is also contained in Islam and other great religions.

hellebore, genus of perennial herbs of the buttercup family. Found in Europe and Asia, frequently used as ornamental flowers, esp. black hellebore, *H. niger,* known as Christmas rose.

Hellespont, ancient name for Dardanelles. Natural point for crossing from Europe to Asia, used by Xerxes, 480 BC, Persians and Alexander the Great, 334 BC.

Hellman, Lillian (1905–   ), Amer. playwright. Wrote *The Children's Hour* (1934), *The Little Foxes* (1939), *Toys in the Attic* (1960).

Helmholtz, Hermann Ludwig Ferdinand von FRS (1821–94), Ger. scientist. Formulated principle of conservation of energy (1847). First to measure nerve impulses; invented ophthalmoscope. Works include *Physiological Optics* (1856–67) and *Sensations of Tone* (1863).

Helmont, Jan Baptista van (1577–1644), Flemish chemist. Discovered carbon dioxide; distinguished gases from liquids and solids.

Héloïse, pupil of ABELARD. As result

Helicopter (a) 1. The rotors at rest 2. Tilt of the rotor blades for ascent 3. Tilt of the rotor blades for level forward flight 4. Tilt of the rotor blades for descent (b) Diagram showing how the vertical tail rotor counteracts the torque of the main rotor blades (c) Tilt of the main rotor blades for (top to bottom) vertical ascent; level forward flight; level backward flight; turning to starboard

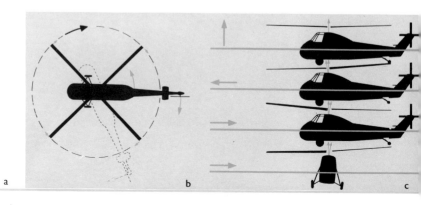

of their secret marriage he was castrated by her uncle, and later wrote autobiog. *Historia Calamitatum.*

Helpmann, Sir Robert Murray (1909–   ), Brit. dancer, actor and choreographer, film and opera director, b. Australia. With Sadler's Wells Ballet Co. (1933–50); also acted in and produced Old Vic and Stratford-on-Avon productions of Shakespeare.

Helsinki, formerly **Helsingfors,** cap., chief commercial centre and largest port of Finland, founded (1550) by Gustavus Vasa of Sweden. Harbour kept open in winter by icebreakers. Pop. (1966) 508,353.

Helvetia, Latin name for Switzerland. The Helvetii were a Celtic race who tried to conquer Gaul (58 BC); defeated by Julius Caesar.

Helvétius, Claude Adrien (1715–71), Fr. philosopher, author of *Essays on the Mind* (1758). Held that all intellectual activity arises from sensation, and regarded self-interest as sole motive for action.

hemichordate, marine animal distinguished by presence of dorsal supporting rod, by gill slits in the wall of the pharynx and by a dorsal tubular nervous system.

Hemingway, Ernest (1899–1961), Amer. novelist, short-story writer. Developed a sparse, clear, laconic style, in *The Sun Also Rises* (1926), *A Farewell to Arms* (1929), *For Whom the Bell Tolls* (1940) and *The Old Man and the Sea* (1952). Awarded Nobel Prize for Literature (1954).

hemlock, biennial umbelliferous herbs of N hemisphere of genus *Conium.* Source of alkaloid poison conium used medicinally.

hemlock spruce, N Amer. coniferous trees of genus *Tsuga.*

Hémon, Louis (1880–1913), Canadian writer, b. France. Author of *Maria Chapdelaine* (pub. 1916), novel of farm life in Quebec.

hemp, *Cannabis sativa,* herb of nettle family. Stems can be treated like flax to produce fibre for twine, rope and coarse cloth. Used in cattle-feeding, in medicine and making marijuana. *See* MANILA HEMP, SISAL.

hen harrier *see* HARRIER.

henbane, *Hyoscyamus niger,* plant of nightshade family indigenous to the Old World. Flowers are source of an alkaloid poison and leaves of hyoscyamine.

Hench, Philip Showalter (1896–1965), Amer. physicist. Awarded Nobel Prize for Physiology and Medicine (1950) for work on adrenal glands.

Henderson, Arthur (1863–1939), Brit. Lab. politician. Awarded Nobel

Peace Prize (1934) for his work as Pres. of World Disarmament Conference (1932).

Hengist and Horsa, Jutish brothers who came to Kent (449) to help fight the Picts; estab. themselves and ruled there until 488.

Henie, Sonja (1913–69), Norwegian ice skater. World champion 10 consecutive times; Olympic gold medallist 3 times (1928, 1932, 1936).

Henley, William Ernest (1849–1903), Eng. poet, editor and critic. Known for poems 'Invictus' and 'England, My England'; collaborated with R. L. Stevenson on *Deacon Brodie* (1892).

henna, *Lawsonia inermis,* small Old World trop. shrub. Leaves yield reddish-brown dye used in Arab countries for colouring hands.

Hennepin, Louis (1640–c. 1701), Fr. Franciscan friar. Explorer of Upper Mississippi valley in N US.

Henrietta Maria (1609–66), queen of England. Daughter of Henry IV of France; m. Charles I (1625). Fears that her influence over Charles would result in restoration of R.C. Church in UK helped provoke Civil War. Exiled by Parl. (1644–60).

Henry I (1068–1135), king of England (1100–35), son of William I. Able administrator, waged war with brother Robert II of Normandy. Succeeded by daughter Matilda.

Henry II (1133–89), Eng. king (1154–89). Son of Matilda and Geoffrey IV of Anjou. Marriage to Eleanor of Aquitaine gave him extensive Fr. possessions. Centralized much power in royal authority, limited ecclesiastical powers (opposed by THOMAS À BECKET).

Henry III (1207–72), Plantagenet Eng. king (1216–72), son of John. Extravagant and absolutist tendencies led to Barons' War (1263) and Simon de Montfort's summoning of parl. From 1267 son Edward was actual ruler of England; succeeded as Edward I.

Henry IV (1367–1413), Eng. king (1399–1413), wrested crown from Richard II. Maintained prerogatives against parliamentary encroachments of previous reign. Persecuted Lollards. Left crown in serious debt.

Henry V (1387–1422), Eng. king (1413–22), son of Henry IV. Reopened Hundred Years War and defeated French at Agincourt (1415). Crushed Lollard Rebellion (1417). Strong rule further indebted crown through foreign involvements.

Henry VI (1421–71), Eng. king (1422–71). Reign marred by Wars of Roses. Insane after 1453, he became a pawn in the York–Lancaster power struggle, was deposed, restored and finally put to death by Edward IV.

Henry VII (1457–1509), 1st Tudor king of England (1485–1509), descendant of John of Gaunt. Took throne from Richard III after victory at Bosworth. Ended Wars of Roses and put down opposition. Strengthened monarchy, esp. financially.

Henry VIII (1491–1547), king of England (1509–47), son of Henry VII. Internal prosperity under Cardinal WOLSEY. First of 6 marriages (to Catherine of Aragon) ended in divorce opposed by papacy which facilitated REFORMATION, to which

Portrait of Henry VIII by Hans Holbein the Younger

ANNO·ÆTATIS·   ·SVÆ·XLIX·

Henry previously hostile. Eng. church estab. with king as head (1534).

Henry II (1519–59), Fr. king (1547–59). Married Catherine de Medici. Recovered Calais from England (1558) and terminated Fr. ambitions in Italy. Killed in a tournament.

Henry III (1551–89), Fr. Valois king (1574–89). Reign disrupted by Wars of Religion and ambitions of GUISE family. Assassinated.

Henry IV (1553–1610), 1st Fr. Bourbon king (1589–1610) and king of Navarre (1572). Led Huguenots (1569), abjured Protestantism to unite kingdom. Estab. religious tolerance through Edict of Nantes (1598). With minister Sully he restored order, industry and finance. Assassinated by Ravaillac.

Henry [I] the Fowler (c. 876–936), Ger. king (919–936). Estab. Ger. boundaries by defeating Fr. and Hungarian armies.

Henry III (1017–56), Ger. emperor (1046). Medieval empire reached zenith during reign. Supported religious reforms and 3 times imposed choice of pope.

Henry IV (1050–1106), Ger. emperor. Church policies condemned by Pope Gregory the Great, who excommunicated him. Forced to travel to Canossa for absolution (1077). Later deposed Gregory (1081). Himself forced to abdicate (1105) by son, Henry V.

Henry, O. orig. William Sydney Porter (1862–1910), Amer. short-story writer. Published collections of stories incl. *Cabbages and Kings* (1904), *The Four Million* (1906).

Henry, Patrick (1736–99), Amer. patriot and orator. Radical supporter of individual liberties and leader of opposition to Brit. rule. Leading spokesman for Bill of Rights.

Henry the Navigator (1394–1460), Portuguese prince, patron of voyagers who explored the west coast of Africa laying foundations of Portuguese colonial empire.

Henryson, Robert (c. 1425–c. 1506), Scot. poet, author of *The Testament of Cressid,* sequel to *Troilus and Criseyde* by Chaucer.

Henschel, Sir George, orig. Isidor George Henschel (1850–1934), Brit. conductor, composer and baritone, b. Germany; 1st conductor of Boston Symphony Orchestra (1881) and of Scottish Orchestra (1893–5).

hepatica, genus of ranunculaceous plants, related to anemone, native to Europe.

hepatitis, inflammation of liver, often symptom of conditions such as catarrhal jaundice.

Hepburn, James, 4th Earl of Bothwell (1536–78), Scot. nobleman and 3rd husband of Mary Stuart (1567). Implicated in assassination of Lord Darnley, fled to Denmark where he died insane.

Hepburn, Katherine (1909–   ), Amer. actress. Stage debut (1928), film debut (1932); won Oscar (1934) for *Morning Glory.* Other films include *Stage Door, The African Queen* and *Summertime.*

Hephaestus, Gk. god of fire, identified with Roman VULCAN.

Hepplewhite, George (d. 1786), Eng. cabinet-maker and furniture designer. Style is graceful and delicately curvilinear.

Hepworth, Dame Barbara (1903–   ), Brit. sculptor. Created mostly massive abstract works in concrete, bronze, wood and stone.

Hera, in Gk. myth., queen of Olympian gods, sister and wife of Zeus. Revered as protectress of women and of married. Identified with Roman JUNO.

Heracles, in Gk. myth., son of Zeus and Alcmene. Strangled snakes sent by Hera to kill him in his cradle. Performed 12 labours to obtain purification of murder of wife and children as result of madness imposed by Hera.

Heraclitus (c. 535–475 BC), Gk. philosopher at Ephesus. Pronounced change the only reality; permanence was illusion. Believed fire to be the underlying universal substance.

herald, orig. official messenger of ruler; later one who supervised court ceremonial, precedence, *etc.*

heraldry, genealogy, precedence and armorial bearing, *i.e.* science of a

or

argent

gules

azure

sable

vert

Heraldic colours with their black-and-white equivalents

HERALD. In Middle Ages, rules for use of personal devices such as coats of arms, badges and crests, were estab. and regularized.

herb robert, *Geranium robertianum,* annual or biennial plant with disagreeable odour. Native to Europe and Asia; pink or white flowers.

Herbert, George (1593–1633), Eng. clergyman, religious poet of Metaphysical school. Poems published posthumously in *The Temple: Sacred Poems and Private Ejaculations.*

Herbert, Victor (1859–1924), Amer. composer, conductor and cellist, b. Ireland. Works include *The Red Mill*

Mosaic of Neptune and Amphitrite found at Herculaneum

Skull of a herbivore (cow) showing teeth

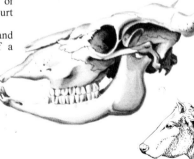

(1906), *Sweethearts* (1913) and *Eileen* (1917).

herbicide, type of PESTICIDE.

herbivores or **herbivora,** in mammalian classification, group almost co-extensive with ungulates, feeding mainly on herbage.

Hercegovina, Herzogovina, now S part of Yugoslavia federal repub. of Bosnia-Hercegovina.

Herculaneum, popular Roman resort near Samnite city of Pompeii at foot of Mt. Vesuvius in S Italy, which were both buried in eruption of 79. Archaeological discoveries 1st made at Herculaneum (1709) and Pompeii (1748).

Hercules, in Roman religion derived from and identified with Gk. HERACLES. Worshipped as god of victory and commercial enterprise.

Hercules beetle, *Dynastes hercules,* lepidopterous genus of giant beetle with formidable pincers. Common in Andean highlands of S America.

Herder, Johann Gottfried von (1744–1803), Ger. philosopher and poet. Pioneer in *Sturm und Drang* literary school and in introduction of Shakespeare and other writers in Germany. Wrote *Outlines of the Philosophy of Man* (1784–91).

heredity, process whereby characteristics of living organisms produced and transmitted from parent to offspring. Characteristics are results of biological make-up and environment. Hereditary factors, genes carried in chromosomes, are constituents of all cells of organism transmitted from generation to generation. Studied scientifically as GENETICS.

Herefordshire, county in W England with Malvern Hills in E and Black Mountains in S. Area: 842 sq. mi.; county town Hereford. Largely agricultural, famed for cider and cattle. Pop. (1966) 140,000.

Hergé, [Georges Remi] (1906–   ), Belgian cartoonist. Creator of 'Tintin' the child reporter who upholds moral values in corrupt and adult world.

Her Majesty's Stationery Office (HMSO), Brit. govt. dept. (estab. 1786) to supply official stationery and supervise printing of govt. publications, books, pamphlets, reports.

hermaphroditism or **hermaphrodism,** condition of double or doubtful sex. Sometimes existence in same individual of internal and external organs of both sexes; or condition in which organs of each side are of different sexes.

Hermes, in Gk. myth., son of Zeus and Maia, messenger of the gods, inventor of lyre and flute. Identified with Roman Mercury.

Hermione, in Gk. myth., daughter of Helen and Menelaus and wife of Neoptolemus.

hermit crab, crustacean decapod with soft asymmetrical abdomen which it protects by living in gastropod mollusc shells.

Hermitage, home of Andrew Jackson, near Nashville, Tennessee, US. National monument.

Hermitage, museum in Leningrad, contains finest collection of paintings in Soviet Union.

Hermite, Charles (1822–1901), Fr. mathematician, known for work on elliptic functions and theory of equations.

Hermon, highest point (9,232 ft.) of Anti-Lebanon range. Snow-capped massif forms part of Syria-Lebanon border famous as site of many ancient ruined temples.

Hero, in Gk. myth., priestess of Aphrodite whose lover Leander was drowned swimming the Hellespont. In despair she drowned herself.

Herod the Great (d. 4 BC), son of Antipater, King of Judaea. Ruled as protégé of Rome in Jerusalem at time of Jesus' birth and according to St Matthew ordered massacre of all male infants in Bethlehem.

Herodotus (*fl.* 5th cent. BC), Gk. historian. Great work is history of Graeco-Persian wars (500–497 BC). Characterized by colourful anecdotal style. Known as 'Father of History'.

heroic couplet, Eng. verse form of 5 (iambic) feet rhyming in alternate lines.

heroin, heroine, diacetylmorphine, white bitterish crystalline powder. Used as anodyne and sedative. Importation to US now illegal because of dangers of addiction.

heron, long-legged, long-necked wading bird, related to bittern. Prey captured by quick thrust of dagger-like bill. Breeds in colonies called heronries.

herpes, inflammatory skin disease, characterized by eruptions of grouped vesicles on reddened base. Includes shingles and cold sores.

Herrick, Robert (1591–1674), Eng. poet and cleric. Known as greatest of Cavalier poets. Works include *Hesperides* (1648).

Herrick, Robert (1868–1938), Amer. realistic novelist. Author of *The Web of Life* (1900), *Clark's Field* (1914).

herring, *Clupea harengus,* plentiful marine fish of cold and temperate waters, allied to sprat, brisling and shad. Moves in vast schools, caught with seines, gill nets, other trawls, *etc.* Fished on large scale in North Sea, N Atlantic, Baltic and N

Grey Heron

Pacific coastal waters (Alaska, Japan).

herring gull, *Larus argentatus,* common marine bird of family Laridae. Large scavenger, feeds on fish. Found in Europe, similar to N Amer. seagull.

Hérriot, Édouard (1872–1957), Fr. statesman, Radical Socialist leader. Premier (1924–5, 1932) and pres. of National Assembly (1947–54).

Herschel, Sir William, orig. Friedrich Wilhelm Herschel (1738–1822), Eng. astronomer, b. Germany. Discovered planet Uranus (1781); 2 satellites of Uranus (1787); 6th and 7th satellites of Saturn (1789). Worked with sister **Carolina Lucretia Herschel** (1750–1848).

Temple of Hephaestus near Athens (built *c.* 400 BC)

Herring

Hibiscus

Hersey, John (1914–), Amer. war correspondent, writer and editor. Early novels include *A Bell For Adano* (1944), and factual *Hiroshima* (1946).

Herstmonceux, village in Sussex, England. Site of Royal Observatory, formerly at Greenwich.

Hertfordshire, one of home counties of S England, partly in greater London. Area: 631 sq. mi.; county town Hertford; other towns St Albans, Letchworth. Agriculture and market gardening important. Pop. (1966) 872,000.

Hertz, Gustav (1887–), Ger. physicist. Awarded Nobel Prize for Physics (1925) for studies of kinetics of electrons.

Hertz, Heinrich Rudolf (1857–94), Ger. physicist. Confirmed existence of electromagnetic waves and proved they follow same laws as light waves.

Herzen, Alexander Ivanovitch (1812–70), influential Russ. revolutionist and writer. Exiled after 1847, attacked tsarist autocracy through émigré periodical *Kolokol* (1857–62).

Hesiod (*c.* 8th cent. BC), Gk. poet. One of 1st to use non-myth. material, *e.g. Works and Days,* a didactic poem on agriculture. Wrote *Theogony,* a myth. history and genealogy of the gods.

Hesperides, in Gk. myth., daughters

Heulandite in its natural state

of Hesperus the Evening Star, and guardians of the APPLES OF THE HESPERIDES

Hess, Dame Myra (1890– 1965), Eng. concert pianist. London performances during World War 2 met with great success.

Hess, Victor Franz (1883– 1964), Austrian physicist. Discovered cosmic rays, shared Nobel Prize for Physics (1936).

Hess, Rudolf (1894–), Ger. Nazi, joined Party 1920. Landed by parachute (May 1941) near Glasgow, Scotland, with peace proposals to Duke of Hamilton and Lord Simon. Prisoner of war until 1945; sentenced to life imprisonment after trial at Nuremberg.

Hesse, Hermann (1877–1962), Ger. writer. Became Swiss citizen (1923); published short stories, poetry and novels. Awarded Nobel Prize for Literature (1946).

Hesse, [Hessen], autonomous state, in W Germany. Area: 7,931 sq. mi.; cap. Wiesbaden. Main cities, Frankfurt-am-Main, Darmstadt. Industry important; products include chemical machinery, textiles, optical equipment. Pop. (1961) 4,814,400.

hessian fly, *Phytophaga destructor,* small Old World fly naturalized in N America, destructive to wheat crops.

Hestia, in Gk. myth., goddess of hearth and domestic life. Daughter of Cronus and Rhea. Identified with Latin VESTA.

heterocyclic compounds, organic compounds containing atoms of carbon and one or more atoms of nitrogen, oxygen or sulphur. Include complex molecules of haemoglobin and chlorophyll as well as many alkaloids, antibiotics, vitamins and carbohydrates.

heulandite, mineral consisting of hydrous calcium and aluminium silicate. Crystals monoclinic and coffin-shaped. Occurs in basaltic rock cavities.

Hevesy, Georg von (1885–1966), Hungarian-Swedish chemist. Awarded Nobel Prize for Chemistry (1943) for research into use of isotopes as chemical indicators. Co-discoverer with Coster of element hafnium (1922).

hexagon, 6-sided figure in plane

geometry. May be regular, with each of the sides equal, or irregular.

Heyer, Georgette (1902–), Brit. novelist. Works include historical novels, *Royal Escape,* Regency romances and detective stories.

Heyer, John Whitefoord (1916–), Austral. film-maker. Produced *The Back of Beyond, The Native Earth, The Overlanders.*

Heyerdahl, Thor (1914–), Norwegian anthropologist famous for voyage, with 5 others, from Peru to Tuamoru Islands in S Pacific, on raft Kon-Tiki. Among books are *Kon-Tiki,* (1948), *American Indians in the Pacific* (1952), *Aku-Aku* (1957).

Heymans, Corneille (1892–1968), Belgian physiologist. Awarded Nobel Prize for Physiology and Medicine (1938) for work on importance of carotid sinus and aortic mechanisms in regulating blood pressure.

Heyrovsky, Jaroslav (1890–1967), Czech chemist. Won Nobel Prize for Chemistry (1959) for devising electrochemical method of analysis (1922).

Heyse, Paul (1830–1914), Ger. writer, leading exponent of the *Novelle* form; best remembered for *Die Kinder der Welt* (1873). Awarded Nobel Prize for Literature (1910).

Heyward, DuBose (1885–1940), Amer. author of *Porgy and Bess,* (dramatized 1935), and other Negro tales such as *Mamba's Daughters,* (dramatized 1939).

Heywood, Thomas (*c.* 1575–1641), Eng. dramatist and actor, author of *An Apology for Actors* (1612), *A Woman Killed with Kindness* (printed 1607), *The English Traveller* (1633).

Hiawatha (*c.* 1500 AD), Amer. Indian Onondaga chieftain. Reconciled warring tribes with his League of Six Nations. In Longfellow's poem, semi-legendary hero.

hibernation, spending of winter in a dormant state, keeping body activities to minimum. Practised by some fish, reptiles and animals, notably bears.

Hibernia, classical and poetic name for Ireland.

hibiscus, ornamental herbaceous plant of mallow (Malvaceae) family, comprising *c.* 150 herbs, shrubs and trees. Found in trop. and warm temp. areas. Some species cultivated for food and fibre products.

hiccough, spasm of the diaphragm,

Benedictine monastery of St Michael at Hildesheim

generally associated with indigestion and stomach irritation.

Hickok, James Butler ('Wild Bill') (1837–1876), Amer. scout, stage driver on Santa Fé and Oregon Trails. Scout in Union army in US Civil War; later toured with Buffalo Bill (1872–3).

hickory, timber and nut-producing tree, of *Carya* genus, of E Canada and US, incl. pecan, *C. illineonsis* and nutmeg, *C. myristicaeformis.*

Hicks, Sir John Richard (1904–   ), Eng. economist. Principal work, *Value and Capital* (1939), chiefly responsible for interest in problems of economic equilibrium and indifference-curve approach.

hide beetle *see* CARPET BEETLE.

hieroglyphs (Gk: sacred carvings), pictorial writing of ancient Egyptians, developed in pre-dynastic times, *i.e.* before *c.* 3100 BC.

High Veld, N Cape of Good Hope Prov. (Cape Prov.), S Africa, central plateau region, 3,000 to 4,000 ft. above sea level. Gentle rolling semi-arid grassland; livestock grazing and mining.

Highland games, sports meetings in N Scotland; events include tossing caber, throwing hammer, Highland dancing.

Highlands, mountainous region N of Central Rift Valley, Scotland. Sparsely populated; activities include subsistence farming, forestry. Gaelic language and Highland costume now little used.

highway, a main road. In Eng. law any road over which a right of way had been estab. by 21 yr. of uninterrupted use. In America, any one of national trunk roads, controlled and partly sponsored by the Federal Govt. The Ital. *autostrada,* Ger. *autobahn,* Amer. turnpike and Brit. MOTORWAYS are highways constructed for rapid motor traffic.

Hilbert, David (1862–1943), Ger. mathematician. Made important contributions to theory of numbers, theory of invariants and integral equations; his book *Grundlagen der Geometrie* (1899) examined foundations of geometry.

Hildebrand *see* SAINT GREGORY [VII].

Hildesheim, ancient Ger. city, in Lower Saxony. 11th cent. cathedral and other hist. churches badly damaged in World War 2. Textiles, machinery and glass manufactured. Pop. 75,000.

Hill, Archibald Vivian (1886–   ), Eng. physiologist. Awarded Nobel Prize for Physiology and Medicine (1922) for discoveries relating to heat production in muscles.

Hieroglyphics on tomb of Nefertiti

The Himalayas

Hill, Joe, orig. Joseph Hillstrom (1822–1915), Amer. leader of IWW (Industrial Workers of the World). Executed (1915) on circumstantial evidence of murder. Became a legend in the Amer. Labour movement.

Hillary, Sir Edmund (1919–   ), New Zealand mountaineer. Reconnoitred Everest with Eric Shipton; joined Sir John Hunt's 1953 expedition and with Tenzing was 1st to reach summit. Co-leader of Commonwealth Antarctic Expedition (1955). Books include *High Adventure, East of Everest* (with George Lowe) and *No Latitude for Error*.

Hilliard, Nicholas (1537–1619), Eng. miniaturist portrait painter; court painter to Elizabeth and James I.

Himachal Pradesh, territory of NW India. Area: 10,885 sq. mi.; cap. Simla. Pop. (1961) 1,351,144.

Himalayan black bear, *Sclenarctos thibetanus,* mammal with pointed snout, black coat and white V-shaped mark on chest. Forest dwelling from Persia to Himalayas.

Himalayas, mountain range of central Asia, extending *c.* 2,000 mi. forming natural barrier between Tibet and India, Nepal, Sikkim and Bhutan. At least 17 peaks over 26,000 ft., incl. Mt. Everest 29,028 ft., world's highest mountain. Highest mountain range, formed at end of Tertiary period by folding of sediment into series of parallel ranges. Climate varies with altitude, though E receives more rain. Sparsely inhabited; agriculture in valleys; lumbering, grazing, hunting and tourism.

Himmler, Heinrich (1900–45), Ger. socialist leader. Head of Nazi SS (1929), Hitler's deputy (1936). Responsible for death of millions of prisoners in World War 2; committed suicide when captured by British.

Hindemith, Paul (1895–1963), Amer.

violinist and composer, b. Germany. Works include symphony from *Mathis der Maler* (1934) and musical settings for Walt Whitman's *When Lilacs Last in the Dooryard Bloom'd* (1946). Became US citizen (1946).

Hindenburg [und Beneckendorff], Paul von (1847–1934), Ger. military and polit. leader. Field marshal during World War 1, commanded forces after 1916. Elected (1925) Pres. of Reich and, with Socialist support, re-elected (1932) over Hitler. After appointing Hitler chancellor (1933), served as figurehead until his death.

Hindi, Indian spoken language of Indo-European family. Also refers to literary languages, Hindi and Urdu.

Hindu Kush, mountain range of Asia. Extends 500 mi. W from Pamir Knot across N Afghanistan; av. ht. 15,000 ft.; Tirach Mir 25,420 ft.

Hinduism, comprehensive term used by W to include social and religious beliefs of loosely related sects which include most of India's population. Use of ancient Veda scriptures, caste system and veneration of animals are unifying features.

hinny *see* ASS.

Hinshelwood, Sir Cyril Norman (1897–1967), Brit. chemist. With Nikolai Semenov, awarded Nobel Prize for Chemistry (1956) for studies in chemical kinetics.

Hipparchus (*c.* 160–*c.* 125 BC), Gk. astronomer. Evolved 1st map projections, calculated longitude. Made 1st known comprehensive sky chart giving positions of 850 stars. Studied equinoxes and apparent orbits of Sun and Moon.

hippeastrum, genus of trop. Amer. bulbous plants of family Amaryllidae. Widely cultivated for showy white to crimson flowers.

Hippias (6th–5th cent. BC), Gk. tyrant, son of Pisistratus. Ruled Athens with brother Hipparchus. Deposed by exiled Alcmaeonids with help of Sparta. Assisted Persians with advice at Marathon (490 BC).

Hippocrates, (*c.* 460–*c.* 377 BC), great Gk. physician, regarded as founder of medicine. Distinguished scientific medicine from philosophy and religion. The 72 books, known as *Corpus Hippocraticum* include some written by Hippocrates and represent collective works of disciples.

Hippocrates of Chios (5th cent. BC), Gk. mathematician. Author of *Elements,* 1st systematic treatise in geometry. Regarded as originator and systematizer of mathematics.

Hippocratic Oath, taken by graduates in medicine; represents HIPPO-

CRATES' ideals of ethical professiona conduct.

Hippolytus, in Gk. myth., son c Theseus. His stepmother, Phaedra caused his death at the hands c Poseidon, after he rejected her love.

hippopotamus, a family of ungulates Hippopotamidae, esp. species *Hippo potamus amphibius.* Large stou mammal weighing up to 4 t. nov confined to certain rivers in trop Africa. Nocturnal and herbivorous lives in small groups.

hire purchase, system whereby good are bought on payment, over a state period, of equal instalments. Pur chaser does not legally own good until agreed terms have been fulfilled.

Hirohito (1901–   ), Emperor o Japan. Became constitutional mon arch (1946) by order of Occupying Powers; renounced war; first Jap crown prince to visit Europe (1921).

Hiroshima, Japanese city on Honshu Is. First city (founded 1594) des troyed by atomic bomb (1945) c 80,000 killed over 4 sq. mi. Precipi tated Jap. surrender at end of Worlc War 2. Rebuilt, now chief commer cial, industrial and cultural centre o its region. Pop. (1965) 504,000.

Hispaniola, island of Greater Antilles West Indies, discovered (1492) by Columbus. Area: *c.* 30,000 sq. mi Includes Haiti and The Dominicar Republic.

Hiss, Alger (1904–   ), Amer. public official. Charged with transmitting confidential documents to USSR (1948). Tried twice, convicted o perjury (1950) and imprisoned; re leased (1954).

histamine, organic compound. Ad ministered by subcutaneous or intra venous injection for treatment of, e.g rheumatoid arthritis.

Himalayan Black Bear

Hobby

Hippeastrum

history, recording and interpretation of the past. Orig. limited to inquiry and statement, post-Renaissance attempted scientific breakdown, by language, religion, documentation, law, *etc.* Further stimulated by 19th cent. evolutionists' discoveries; works of Marx and Weber led to further fragmentation of the discipline (into archaeology, sociology, anthropology, *etc.*). Certain 20th cent. historians (Toynbee, Dilthey, Meinecke) continued to attempt general evaluations of events.

Hitchcock, Alfred Joseph (1899–), Anglo-Amer. film director. Specializes in suspense. Films include *The Lady Vanishes* (1938), *Rebecca* (1940), *Psycho* (1960).

Hitchcock, Frank Harris (1869–1935), Amer. lawyer and govt. official. US Postmaster General (1909–13), estab. parcel post and postal savings banks; promoted air mail service.

Hitchcock, Henry-Russell (1903–), Amer. architectural historian; publications include *The International Style* (1932–66).

Hitler, Adolf (1889–1945), Ger. polit. leader, b. Austria. Helped found NATIONAL SOCIALISM; imprisoned for attempted coup in Bavaria ('beer-hall putsch', 1923) and wrote *Mein Kampf*, documenting Nazi ideology. Depression after 1929 aided rise to power (by 1932 Nazis were largest party in Reichstag), culminated in appointment as chanc. (Jan 1933). Estab. dictatorship (Mar. 1933) by attributing Reichstag fire to Communists. Crushed opposition within party by purges (helped by henchmen such as Goebbels, Himmler), and enacted anti-Semitic legislation. Office of chanc. and pres. united (1934) in person of the Führer. Aggressive foreign policy and Anglo-French appeasement policy (*see* MUNICH PACT) led to World War 2 (1939). Personal leadership of

Russian campaign (1941) had disastrous results; thwarted assassination attempt (1944). Defeated on all fronts, committed suicide (Apr. 1945). Unsubstantiated rumours of escape persisted after end of war.

Hittite civilization (*c.* 2000–1200 BC), ancient people in Asia Minor. Thought to be one of 1st peoples to smelt iron. Most powerful (1400–1200 BC), empire extended over much of Asia Minor.

hives, popular name for urticaria and various other skin diseases.

HMSO *see* HER MAJESTY'S STATIONERY OFFICE.

Ho Chi Minh (1892–1969), North Vietnamese politician. Helped found Fr. Communist Party. Comintern leader, Shanghai, China. Founded Vietnamese Communist Party (1930). Led Viet Minh and Vietnam govt. (1945). Gained control of N Vietnam after war (1946–54) with French. Pursued militant policy in effort to re-unite Vietnam through war with South in 1960s.

Hoban, James (*c.* 1762–1831), Amer. architect. Designed White House, Washington, D.C., built (1792–99); rebuilt by Hoban after fire of 1812.

Hobart, cap. and port of Tasmania, Australia. Founded (1804) as seat of govt. of Brit. colony of Van Diemen's Land. Commercial centre, industries include paper manufacture, flour milling, and fruit preserving. Pop. (1965) 119,415.

Hobbema, Meindert (1638–1709), Dutch landscape painter. Works include *The Avenue, Middelharnis, The Mill,* and *Entrance to a Village.*

Hobbes, Thomas (1588–1679), Eng. philosopher. Best known work, *Leviathan* (1651), held that body politic formed to offset otherwise natural anarchy, and advocated royal absolutism; theory attacked by Locke. Other works include *De Corpore Politico* (1650).

Hobbs, Sir Jack, orig. John Hobbs (1882–1963), Brit. cricketer. Scored 197 centuries and 61,221 runs in first-class cricket; played for Eng. (1907–30), retired 1935.

hobby, *Falco subbuteo,* small grey falcon with long wings and short tail. Feeds on insects and birds such as swallows.

Hobhouse, Leonard Trelawney (1864–1929), Eng. philosopher and sociologist. Editor of the *Sociological Review.* Works include *Principles of Sociology, The Metaphysical Theory of the State* (1918) and *The Rational Good* (1921).

Hobson, John Atkinson (1858–1940), Eng. economist. Held that social

reform should be based on economic theory. Works include *Imperialism* (1902), *Work and Wealth* (1914), *Wealth and Life* (1929).

Hochhuth, Rolf (1933–), Swiss playwright. Controversial plays include *The Deputy* (1962) and *The Soldiers* (1965) which some Englishmen interpreted as attack on Sir Winston Churchill.

hock *see* WINE.

hockey, game played on field or ice. Field hockey originated in England, now played in many countries. Game comprises 2 teams of 11 players competing on pitch (100 by 60 yd.); played by men and women. Ice hockey began in Canada, standardized in 1870s. Played on ice rink (200 by 85 ft.) by 2 teams of 6 players. Professional National Hockey League (Canada and US); annual international competitions.

Hodgkin, Alan Lloyd (1917–), Brit. physiologist, conducted research

Hindu Temple at Somnathpur, India (AD 1050-1300)

Portrait of a Young Lady by William Hogarth

into nerve cells; shared Nobel Prize for Physiology and Medicine (1963) with A. F. Huxley and Sir John Eccles.

Hodgkin, Dorothy Mary Crowfoot (1910–), Brit. biochemist. Awarded Nobel Prize for Chemistry (1964) for determining structure of compounds to combat pernicious anaemia.

Hoffa, James Riddle (1913–), Amer. labour leader. Pres. of International Brotherhood of Teamsters (1957–61). Notorious union 'boss', repeatedly tried (1947–64), finally convicted on charges of jury tampering and mail fraud; imprisoned (1967).

Hoffmann, Ernst Theodor Amadeus (1776–1822), Ger. Romantic composer and novelist. Opera *Undine* (1816) and novels were basis of Offenbach's *Tales of Hoffman.*

Hoffnung, Gerard (1925–59), Eng. humorous illustrator and musician. Creator of Hoffnung Music Festival (1956) and Hoffnung Interplanetary Music Festival (1958, 1959). Published works include *The Hoffnung Companion to Music* (1957) and *Ho Ho Hoffnung* (1959).

Hofmann, August Wilhelm von (1818–92), Ger. chemist, founder of German Chemical Soc. (1868). Identified aniline as dye substance and investigated coal-tar products.

Hofmann, Josef Casimir (1876–1957), Amer. pianist and composer, b Poland. Compositions (several written under name of Michael Dvorsky) include works for piano and a symphony.

Hofmannsthal, Hugo von (1874–1929), Austrian dramatist and poet. Plays include *Der Tor und der Tod* (1893), *Jedermann* (1911), *Ariadne auf Naxos* (1912).

Hofstadter, Robert (1915–), Amer. physicist. Shared Nobel Prize for Physics (1961) with Rudolf Mössbauer for structural investigations of protons and neutrons.

hog *see* PIG.

Hogarth, William (1697–1764), Eng. painter and engraver. Best known for series of satiric studies of Eng. social life, *e.g. Marriage à la Mode* and *The Rake's Progress*. Formal technique influenced by Ital. painters.

Hogben, Lancelot (1895–), Brit. scientist and writer. Author of *Mathematics for the Million* (1936) and *Science for the Citizen* (1938).

Hogg, James (1770–1835), Scot. poet and writer, 'the Ettrick Shepherd'. Verse includes *The Queen's Wake* (1813) and *Madoc of the Moor* (1816).

hogmanay, name given to New Year's Eve in Scotland and N England.

Hohenstaufen, Ger. dynasty, dukes of Swabia from 1079, emperors and Ger. kings (1138–1254), kings of Sicily (1194–1266). Chief rivals were the Guelphs.

Hohenzollern, Ger. princely family. Rulers of Brandenburg (1415) and kings of Prussia (1701–1918), also Ger. emperors (1871–1918).

Hokkaido *see* JAPAN.

Hokusai (1760–1849), Jap. graphic artist. Woodcuts influenced 19th cent. Fr. painters, esp. Degas. Depicted Jap. life and landscape, and studies of birds and animals, *e.g.* the series *Hundred Views of Fuji.*

Holbein, Hans (*c.* 1497–1543), Ger. portrait and religious painter. Court painter to Henry VIII (1536). Portraits include Sir Thomas More, Henry VIII. Designed woodcut illustrations for Luther's Bible.

Hölderlin, Johann Christian Friedrich (1770–1843), Ger. lyric and symbolist poet. Famous works include *Bread and Wine* (1800–03), *The Death of Empedocles* (1800), and novel *Hyperion* (1797–9). Became insane 1806.

Holinshed, Raphael (d. *c.* 1580), Eng. chronicler. Work (pub. 1578) includes *Chronicles* of England, Scotland and

Portrait of Nicolas Kratzner by Hans Holbein the Younger

Ireland, main source for Shakespeare's history plays.

Holland see NETHERLANDS.

Holland, Parts of, admin. county, part of Lincolnshire, E central England. Area: *c.* 419 sq. mi.; county seat, Boston. Agric. fen area. Pop. (1966) 105,000.

holly, *Ilex,* genus of evergreen, smooth-leaved shrubs. Species include Amer. holly, *I. opaca,* and European holly *I. aquifolium* with yellow, red or white berries.

hollyhock, *Althaea rosea,* perennial plant of mallow family, native of China now widely distributed. Grows 8–10 ft. high.

Hollywood, suburb of Los Angeles, Calif. US. Centre of the Amer. film industry since 1911.

Holman, William Arthur (1871–1934), Austral. politician, premier (1913–20). Introduced industrial arbitration and mining regulation acts among important social legislation.

Holmes, Oliver Wendell (1809–94), Amer. writer and physician. Best remembered for prose dialogue collections, *e.g. The Autocrat of the Breakfast Table* (1858). Poetry includes 'Old Ironsides', published in collection, *Poems* (1836). His son, **Oliver Wendell Holmes** (1841–1935), Associate Chief Justice of US Supreme Court (1902–32), known as 'great dissenter' for his forthright, liberal opinions. Writings include *The Common Law* (1881).

holmium, chemical element included in group of rare-earth metals.

Holst, Gustav (1874–1934), Brit. composer of Swedish descent. Works include orchestral suite, *The Planets* (1914–16), and operas, *The Perfect Fool* (1920–22) and *At the Boar's Head* (1924).

Holst, Imogen (1907–), daughter of GUSTAV HOLST, whose biography she wrote (1938); conductor and composer of folk-song arrangements, associated with Benjamin Britten in the Aldeburgh Festivals.

Holt, Harold Edward (1908–67), Austral. Liberal statesman, P.M. (1966–7). Chairman (1960–7) of International Monetary Fund, International Finance Corporation and International Bank for Reconstruction and Development. Accidentally drowned in Bass Strait.

Holy Alliance, treaty signed (1815) between Emperors of Russia, Austria and Prussia. They agreed to work to preserve the status quo in Europe.

Holy Communion see COMMUNION, HOLY.

Holy Ghost, Holy Spirit see TRINITY.

Holy Grail legend, medieval myth surrounding cup used by Jesus at Last Supper. Joseph of Arimathea is supposed to have caught Christ's blood in it. Legend symbolized quest for spiritual regeneration.

Holy Loch, 3 mi. long inlet of Firth of Clyde, Argyllshire, W Scotland. Became (1961) base for US guided missile nuclear submarines.

Holy Orders, degrees to which clergy belong; under which they may carry out duties; in which they are invested in special ceremony.

Holy Rollers, a disparaging term applied to some members of Pentecostal sects because of their ecstatic behaviour during services.

Holy Roman Empire, revival of the ancient Roman empire of the W under Charlemagne and his successors. Rudolph, 1st Habsburg Emperor (elected 1273), thereafter the empire was Ger. institution. Dissolved (1806) by resignation of Francis II, following his unsuccessful struggle against Napoleon.

Holy Week, in Christian religions, week preceding Easter, commemorating Christ's Passion and death.

Holyoake, Keith Jacka (1904–), New Zealand statesman. Deputy P.M. and Min. of Agriculture (1949–57). P.M. for 2 months in succession

Double variety of Hollyhock

Holy Week procession at Seville

to S. G. Holland (1957). Re-elected as P.M. (1960).

Holyrood House, royal palace in Edinburgh, Scotland, on site of 12th cent. abbey built by David I. Palace built by James IV (1501), destroyed by fire (1650), was residence of Scot. kings. Rebuilt and now used by Royal family on official visits.

Home, Earl of see DOUGLAS-HOME, SIR ALEXANDER FREDERICK.

Home Counties, term used to cover counties contiguous to the London Conurbation, *i.e.* Essex, Kent, Surrey, Berkshire and Hertfordshire. Former county of Middlesex absorbed in Greater London (1965).

Home Guard, orig. the Local Defence Volunteers, formed (1940) as a supplement to the regular army, for defence of the British Isles in World War 2. In less than 8 weeks, they numbered over 1 million volunteers.

Home Rule, movement begun in Ireland (1870), arising out of demands for autonomy. Unity achieved by CHARLES PARNELL. Brit. parl. failed to pass Gladstone's 1st Home Rule Bill (1886); 2nd (1893) thwarted by House of Lords; 3rd (1912) never effective because Irish rebellion (1916) led to recognition of Irish Free State (1921). N Ireland governed under 4th Home Rule bill, passed 1920.

Homer, Gk. epic poet (*c.* 9th-7th cent. BC) author of *Iliad* (Trojan War) and *Odyssey* (wanderings of Odysseus after Trojan War) orig. written to be recited or chanted. *Homeric Hymns,* attributed to Homer, are of later date.

Homestead Act, passed by US Congress (1862), permitting settlers

Honey Fungus

on previously unoccupied land (up to 160 acres) to become owners after 5 yr. Encouraged settlement of W US.

homoeopathy, system of therapeutics introduced (1796) by Samuel Hahnemann, who held that cure of disease is effected by minute doses of drugs capable of producing in a healthy individual symptoms of the disease being treated.

homosexuality, sexual attraction and behaviour towards one of the same sex. Causes and treatment are matters of controversy.

Honan, prov. of China along W Hwang Ho delta plain, one of most densely populated. Area: 64,479 sq. mi.; cap. Chengchow. Mountainous with fertile valleys; maize, rice, silk, cotton. Rich coalfields. Pop. (1963) 48,670,000.

Honduras [República de Honduras], 2nd largest C Amer. republic. Area: 43,277 sq. mi.; cap. Tegucigalpa.

Forested highland country, hot and wet at low altitude. Independent (1838); governed by President. Mainly agricultural, producing trop. crops, esp. bananas. Pop. (1965) 2,363,000.

Honegger, Arthur (1892–1955), Swiss composer b. France, one of *Les Six.* Best known works include

Hoopoe

ballets, operas, film scores and oratorios *King David* (1921–23); *Joan of Arc at the Stake* (1935).

honey bees, 4 species of social bees akin to the bumble bees. *Apis mellifera* and *A. indica* are kept by man for honey and beeswax.

honey eater, honey sucker, vari-coloured songbirds of Australasia. With curved bill and protrusible tongue for procuring nectar and insects from flowers. Species include wattlebirds, coldong (four o'clock or friarbird) and the rare stitchbird.

honey fungus, *Armillaria mellea,* yellowish-brown edible fungus with white gills living either on dead tree stumps or as a serious destructive parasite of forest trees.

honey guide, species of *Indicator* and *Protodiscus* piciform birds related to woodpecker. Mostly found in Africa. Conspicuously coloured; nests in holes. Lives on honey and bee larvae.

honey locust, *Gleditsia triacanthos,* N Amer. leguminous tree, 75–140 ft. in ht.; bears pods with edible pulp.

honey-bear, sloth bear, *Melursus ursinus,* bear of Indian subcontinent. Lives on termites.

honeysuckle, *Lonicera,* wild and cultivated erect or climbing shrub of *c.* 175 species of elderberry family, with perfumed flowers; found in warm temp. areas of N hemisphere.

Hong Kong, Brit. crown colony, of great strategic importance, SE China, comprising Hong Kong Is. (cap. Victoria), Kowloon Peninsula, and New Territories. Total area: 391 sq. mi. Ceded to Britain 1842; Kowloon acquired 1860; free port with great entrepôt trade at Victoria. Pop. (1965) 3,716,000.

Honolulu, cap., main port and airline centre of Hawaii, on Oahu Is. Important military and naval base, tourist resort and shipping centre. Pop. (1966) 571,000.

Honshu, largest island of Japan, considered as mainland. Area (with adjacent islands) 87,293 sq. mi.; cap. Tokyo. Important trade and industrial centre. Pop. 55,000,000.

Hooch, Pieter de (*c.* 1629–81), Dutch genre painter. Works centred on interiors, often family domestic scenes.

Hood, Robin *see* ROBIN HOOD.

Hood, Thomas (1799–1845), Eng. poet and humorist, and author of poems of social protest. Works include 'The Song of the Shirt' and 'The Bridge of Sighs'.

hooded crow, species of CROW.

Hook of Holland, port of Netherlands

The harbour of Hong Kong looking towards Kowloon

with steamer services to Harwich, England. Pop. (1963) 2,400.

Hooke, Robert (1635–1703), Eng. scientist. First man to formulate theory of planetary movements as a mechanical problem. Improved astronomical instruments; constructed 1st arithmetical machine and Gregorian telescope, described plant cells.

Hooker, Richard (*c.* 1554–1600), Eng. theologian and political theorist. Chief work *Of the Laws of Ecclesiastical Policy* (1593–7).

Hooker, Sir William Jackson (1785–1865), Eng. botanist. Director of Kew Gardens where he worked with John Henslow in founding a museum of economic botany (1847).

hookworm, parasitic roundworm *Anclysostoma,* common in trop. areas. Causes anaemia in man; larva matures in small intestine.

hoopoe, kakelaar, any of *c.* 7 species of mainly insectivorous Eurasian bird related to roller.

Hoover, Herbert Clark (1874–1964), 31st US President (1929–33), Republican. Headed relief organizations during and after World War 1. Succeeded CALVIN COOLIDGE as presidential nominee (1928). Electoral success was followed by fall of stock market and Great Depression, which he tried unsuccessfully to combat. Overwhelmingly defeated by F. D. Roosevelt (1932).

Hoover, J[ohn] Edgar (1895–   ), Amer. public official. Director of FEDERAL BUREAU OF INVESTIGATION (1924–   ).

Hops

Honey-bear

Hopkins, Harry Lloyd (1890–1946), Amer. politician and administrator. Held various posts as special assistant and close friend of Pres. F. D. Roosevelt.

Hopper, Edward (1882–1967), Amer. painter. Contrasted use of light to depict themes of loneliness and emptiness.

hops, cone-shaped catkins of *Humulus lupulus,* used in flavouring beer. Female catkins grow after flowering and develop glands containing hop.

Horace [Quintus Horatius Flaccus] (65–8 BC), Roman lyric poet and satirist. Introduced by Vergil to Maecenas who became his patron. Works include *Satires, Epodes, Odes, Epistles* and *Ars Poetica.* Verse characterized by perfection of form, sincerity, patriotism and humour. Much influence on Eng. verse.

horehound, hoarhound, *Marrubium vulgare,* herb with bitter aromatic juice. Grows wild in Europe, Asia and US. Used as flavouring and for cough mixtures and lozenges.

hormone, complex organic compound which controls cell metabolism and growth. In animals, produced by secretion of endocrine glands.

horn *see* FRENCH HORN.

horn, bony process in head of certain ungulate mammals, functioning mainly as weapons. Shape varies; may be branched or unbranched. Confined in some species to males, in others found in both sexes.

Horn, Cape, most S point of S America, on Chilean island of Tierra del Fuego, *c.* 1,400 ft. high. First rounded by William Schouten (1616).

hornbeam, tree of birch family, genus *Carpinus,* found in N America and Eurasia. Grows to *c.* 80 ft.; fruit-bearing.

hornbill, fruit-eating mainly trop. bird, remarkable for enormous bill. Grotesque, with noisy flapping flight and loud croaking voice.

hornblende, brittle amphibole mineral, often forming columnar crystals. Colours black, dark green and white.

horned grebe, Slavonian grebe, *Podiceps auritus,* small grebe of N Europe and N America.

horned lizard, common name for 17 species of N Amer. lizards of genus *Phrynosoma,* found in arid regions.

hornet, name given to several species of large WASP, esp. European *Vespula crabro* and N Amer. *V. maculata.*

Horney, Karen (1885–1952), Amer. psychiatrist. Emphasized environmental factors in development of neurosis. Works include *The Neurotic*

Interior by Pieter de Hooch

Personality of Our Time (1937) and *Neurosis and Human Growth* (1950).

horntail, sawfly, woodwasp, hymenopterous family Siricidae of insects. Bore into solid timber.

Hornung, Ernest William (1866–1921), Eng. popular novelist. His gentleman-thief character 'Raffles' first appeared in *The Amateur Cracksman* (1899).

Horowitz, Vladimir (1904–), Amer. pianist. Popular concert pianist of the 1930s.

Horrocks or **Horrox, Jeremiah** (1617–41), Eng. astronomer. Made practical calculations of Moon and Venus orbits.

Wild Honeysuckle

Hoover Dam, in Black Canyon on Colorado R., US; 726 ft. high, 1,244 ft. long arch-gravity structure; forms L. Mead, largest artificial lake in US; formerly Boulder Dam.

hop, *Humulus lupulus,* perennial vine grown for its cone-like flowers, HOPS, used in beer.

Hope, Anthony, orig. Sir Anthony Hope Hawkins (1863–1933), Brit. novelist. Author of *The Prisoner of Zenda* (1894) and *Rupert of Hentzau* (1898).

Hope, Bob, orig. Leslie Townes Hope (1904–), Amer. comedian-actor, b. England. Known for radio shows and film comedies, *e.g. The Road* series, and *Monsieur Beaucaire.*

Hopei, Hopeh, formerly Chihli, prov. of N China, incl. N of Hwang Ho delta plain. Area: 84,942 sq. mi.; cap. Paoting; chief centres Peking and Tientsin. Crops include wheat, millet and soya beans; coal mines. Pop. (1963) 44,720,000.

Hopi *see* PUEBLO INDIANS.

Hopkins, Sir Frederick Gowland (1861–1947), Brit. biochemist. Known for research on muscular energy and oxidation of tissues. Shared Nobel Prize for Physiology and Medicine (1929) with Christian Eijkman.

Hopkins, Gerard Manley (1844–89), Eng. Jesuit and poet. Poems (pub. posthumously) include *The Wreck of the Deutschland.*

Hooded Crow

Houseleek

horse, important herbivorous hoofed mammal, *Equus caballus.* Domesticated since earliest civilization, thought to have been in C Asia. Only wild horse in 20th cent. is *E. przewalski* of Mongolia. Horses are classed as draft, light and ponies. Light horses, such as Arabian and racehorses, used for driving or riding. Horse measured in hands (1 hand = 4 in.).

horse chestnut, *Aesculus hippocastanum,* deciduous tree of soapwort family, native to temp. Eurasia. Its fruit grows in green spiky pods.

horse racing, contest of speed between horses over designated course. Saddle racing includes flat or thoroughbred races or steeplechases. Harness racing performed by horses trained to trot. Famous Eng. events are Epsom Derby, St Leger Stakes, Two Thousand Guineas and Grand National; Amer. 'Triple Crown' comprises Kentucky Derby, Preakness and Belmont Stakes.

horsefly, common name of members of order Diptera, genus *Tabanus.* Bloodsuckers with painful bite. Also called gadfly, cleg, breeze.

horsepower, unit measuring rate of doing work. Now common measure of engine capacity, based on observation by James Watt that 1 horse could carry 100 lb. 330 ft. in 1 minute.

horse-radish, *Armoracia rusticana,*

perennial herb native of C and S Europe, naturalized in N America. Grated pungent root serves as condiment with meats.

horseshoe bat, microchiropterous insectivore, family Rhinolophus, of trop. and temp. latitudes. Characterized by large ears.

horsetail, perennial plant of *Equisetum* genus. Rushlike, related to fern and club moss.

Horsley, Sir Victor Alexander Haden (1857–1916), Eng. physiologist and surgeon; expounded Pasteur method of treating rabies. Made Eng. surgical history (1887) by removing tumour from spinal cord.

horst, mountain resulting from fault movement as opposed to mountain formed by folding of rock.

Horthy de Nagybánya, Nicolaus (1868–1957), Hungarian admiral and statesman. Led Hungarian anti-Communist forces (1919) against govt. of Bela KUN. Regent of Hungary (1920–44).

horticulture, cultivation of fruit, vegetables, flowers and shrubs. First developed in Oriental irrigated regions, ideas transferred to Europe by Crusaders.

Horus, in Egyptian religion, son of Osiris and Isis; sun god and lord of Upper Egypt. Represented as falcon or falcon-headed, often identified with AMMON.

Hosea, prophetic Book of OT written by Hosea (750–735 BC). Foretells doom of N Israel.

Hospitallers, name given to members (knights) of medieval Order of St John of Jerusalem, estab. (1113) to care for pilgrims in Holy Lands. Rivals of Templars; both groups took part in Crusades. Order later moved to Cyprus and Malta.

Hot Springs National Park, SW Arkansas, US, estab. 1921. Area: 1·5 sq. mi. Has rich mineral hot springs.

Hottentot, SW African people, prob. of Bushman linguistic stock. Practise cattle raising and shepherding. Number (1963 est.) 24,000.

Houdini, Harry, orig. Eric Weiss (1874–1926), Amer. escapologist.

Renowned for escapes from bonds also exposed fraudulent mediums.

Houdon, Jean Antoine (1741–1828[), Fr. sculptor. Specialized in portrai[t] sculptures, esp. 'Voltaire' in Comédi[e] Française.

Houphouët-Boigny, Felix (1905– [), Pres. of Ivory Coast (1960– [). Helped draft law (1956), estab. poli[t] autonomy in Fr. overseas depend[-]encies. First African to become Fr[.] min. of state (1957).

House, E[dward] M[andell] (1858–1938), Amer. statesman. Close as[-]sociate of Woodrow Wilson, helpe[d] draft Versailles treaty and Covenan[t] of League of Nations.

house fly, *Musca domestica,* 2-winge[d] insect of order Diptera, of world-wid[e] distribution. Attracted by sugar[y]

Horseshoe Bat

substances; sucker-like feet facilitat[e] walking upside down. Carrier o[f] disease germs.

house mouse, *Mus musculus,* dom[-]estic rodent. Coat usually grey[;] albinos bred in captivity.

House of Commons, representativ[e] assembly, lower house of Bri[t] PARLIAMENT. Members elected b[y] single-ballot system. Presided over b[y] Speaker. Source of all major legisla[-]

How a horse walks (1[)] right back leg is raise[d] when left front leg is i[n] midstep (2) right bac[k] leg touches the groun[d] as soon as right fron[t] leg is lifted. Left bac[k] leg is raised as soon a[s] right front leg is i[n] midstep

tion, institution used by many Commonwealth members, notably Canada and Australia.

House of Lords, upper house of Brit. PARLIAMENT; comprises members of nobility, clergy. Origins in king's council of barons. Presided over by Lord Chanc. Powers curtailed by Parliament Act (1911). Also acts as UK's final court of appeal.

House of Representatives, federal representative assembly, lower house of US CONGRESS. Members elected by populace for 2-yr. periods on proportional basis. Presided over by Speaker. Revenue bills must originate in House; has power to impeach Pres.

houseleek, plant of genus *Sempervivum*. Orig. Eurasian, widely dispersed in Europe and introduced to US. Greyish-green leaves; purple and yellow flowers. Common house-leek, *S. tectorum*.

Housman, A[lfred] E[dward] (1859–1936), Brit. poet and classical scholar. Best known for lyrics (*e.g. 'Bredon Hill'*). Published *A Shropshire Lad* (1896), *Last Poems* (1922).

Houssay, Bernardo Alberto (1887–1971), Argentine physiologist. Shared Nobel Prize for Physiology and Medicine (1947) with C. F. Cori and G. T. Cori for study of pituitary secretions and insulin.

Houston, Sam[uel] (1793–1863), Amer. soldier and statesman. Led Texan capture of Mexican forces at SAN JACINTO (1836). Pres. of Repub. of Texas (1836–8, 1841–4). State Gov. of Texas (1859–61), removed for refusal to join Confederacy.

Houston, port, S Texas, US. Founded 1836, expanded with completion (1914) of ship channel to Gulf of Mexico. Great petroleum depot and exports livestock. Spacecraft development and astronaut training centre. Pop. (1960) 938,000.

hover fly, any member of family Syrphidae of great importance in control of aphids and pollination of flowers.

hovercraft, amphibious vehicle developed (1959) in UK. Supports itself on a cushion of air, allowing it to travel over water, land, small obstacles.

Howard, Brit. noble family, orig. Hereward. After 1483 were earls of Surrey and dukes of Norfolk. **Thomas Howard, 2nd Duke of Norfolk** (1443–1524), Eng. general, defeated Scots at Flodden (1513). **Thomas Howard, 3rd Duke of Norfolk** (1473–1554), uncle of Ann Boleyn, supported her marriage to Henry VIII; influence waned after her death. **Catherine Howard** (*c.* 1521–42), 5th wife of Henry VIII. Beheaded primarily to rid Henry of Howard family influence. **William Howard, 1st Viscount Stafford** (1614–80), beheaded after being falsely implicated in TITUS OATES affair. Present dukes of Norfolk are Earls Marshal of England.

Howard, Sir Ebenezer (1850–1928), Eng. originator of the concept of Garden Cities as independent towns rather than suburbs, set forward in *Tomorrow* (1898); republished as *Garden Cities of Tomorrow* (1902).

Howard, Leland Ossian (1857–1950), Amer. entomologist, leading planner of Amer. programme for curtailing harmful insects and crop pests. Wrote *The Insect Menace* (1931).

Howard, Leslie, orig. Leslie Stainer (1893–1943), Brit. actor. Popular for gentle cynical style in plays (*e.g. Berkeley Square*) and films (*e.g. The Scarlet Pimpernel, Pygmalion*).

Howe, Elias (1819–67), Amer. inventor; obtained 1st patent on lock-stitch sewing machine (1846).

Howe, Gordon (1928–   ), Canadian ice hockey player. Estab. nearly all career records of National Hockey League, incl. goals and total points, while with Detroit team.

Howe, Joseph (1804–73), Canadian statesman and journalist. Agitated for responsible govt., through journals and polit. activity. Premier of Nova Scotia (1860–3), attacked union with Canada, but eventually entered federal cabinet (1869). Appointed prov. Lieutenant-Governor (1873).

Howe, Julia Ward (1819–1910), Amer. author and social reformer. Wrote *The Battle Hymn of the Republic*.

Howe, Richard, 1st Earl Howe (1726–99), Brit. admiral. Commanded Brit. fleet in Amer. Revolution (1776–8). Defeated French (1794).

Howe, Sir William, 5th Viscount Howe (1729–1814), Brit. general. Served under Wolfe at Quebec, commanded at Bunker Hill and became Commander-in-chief of colonies (1775). Defeated patriots at White Plains (1776) and Washington at Brandywine (1777). Resigned for lack of support from Britain (1778).

Howells, William Dean (1837–1920), Amer. novelist and critic. Editor of *Atlantic Monthly* and *Harper's*. Novels include *The Rise of Silas Lapham* (1885).

howling monkey, howler, largest of New World monkeys with prehensile tail and loud voice. Species include red *Alonatta seniculus* and black *A. cavaya*.

Hoyle, Edmond (1672–1769), Eng. writer on card games, esp. whist; his laws of whist were effective for over 100 yr. He also codified laws of backgammon, quadrille, piquet.

Hoyle, Sir Fred (1915–   ), Brit. astronomer and mathematician. Author of *The Nature of the Universe* (1950).

Hrdlička, Aleš (1869–1943), Amer. anthropologist, b. Bohemia. Known for his works on migrations of Amer. Indians. Works include *Physical Anthropology* (1919) and *Old Americans* (1925).

Hubble, Edwin Powell (1899–1953),

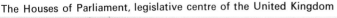

The Houses of Parliament, legislative centre of the United Kingdom

Victor Hugo, the great French Romantic writer

Amer. astronomer. Major contributions through extragalactic nebulae studies.

Huch, Ricarda (1864–1947), Ger.

Riding, Yorks, England. A centre of Eng. woollen industry. Pop. (1966) 132,000.

Hudson, Henry (d. 1611), Eng. explorer and navigator. Explored Hudson R., and later Hudson Bay, while seeking North West Passage. Cut adrift and left to die by mutinous crew in James Bay (1611).

Hudson, William Henry (1841–1922), Eng. author and naturalist, b. Argentina. Best known for *Green Mansions* (1904) and *Far Away and Long Ago* (1918).

Hudson, river in NE US, rising in Adirondack Mts., flows through NY State to Atlantic. Discovered (1524), explored 1609 by Henry Hudson.

Hudson Bay, inland sea of Canada connected to N Atlantic Ocean by Hudson Strait. Explored (1610) by Henry Hudson. Area: *c*. 4,500 sq. mi.

Hudson's Bay Company, organized by Eng. merchants to obtain N Amer. furs for Brit. market (chartered 1670). Rivalled by North West Co., incorporated 1821. After 1869, when land sold to Canada, operated as limited liability company.

Hué, city of South Vietnam, on Hué R., believed founded by Chinese in 3rd cent. Textile centre. Pop. (1964) 104,000.

Huerta, Victoriano (1854–1916), Mexican general and Pres. (1913–14). After serving under Madero, opposed him and became Pres. Despotic rule provoked trouble with US as well as series of local uprisings.

Huggins, Charles Brenton (1901–   ), Amer. scientist. Shared Nobel Prize for Physiology and Medicine (1966) with F. P. Rous for cancer research.

Hughes, Charles Evans (1862–1948), Amer. statesman and judge. Gov. of New York (1907–10) and Associate Justice of US Supreme Court

novelist. Known for hist. novel of Thirty Years War, *Der Grosse Krieg in Deutschland* (1912–14).

huckleberry, N Amer. shrub of genus *Gaylussacia*. Edible black fruit.

Huddersfield, county borough of W

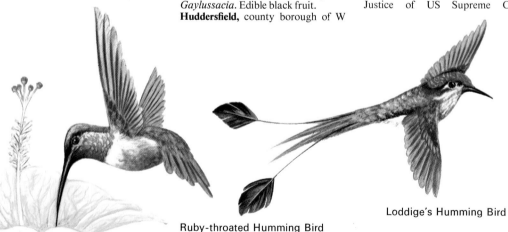

Ruby-throated Humming Bird

Loddige's Humming Bird

(1910–16). Narrowly lost 1916 pres. election to Wilson. Sec. of State (1921–5), Chief Justice of Supreme Court(1930–41).

Hughes, Howard Robard (1905–   ), Amer. industrialist, aviator and film producer. Estab. world flight record (1938), made world's largest aeroplane (1947). Pres. of Hughes Tool Co. and Hughes Aircraft Co. Films include *Hell's Angels, The Outlaw*.

Hughes, [James] Langston (1902–67), Amer. writer. Works (*e.g. The Weary Blues*, 1926) portray Negro life and problems.

Hughes, Richard Arthur Warren (1900–   ), Eng. writer. Best known for *High Wind in Jamaica* (1929).

Hughes, Thomas (1822–96), Eng. writer. Author of *Tom Brown's School Days* (1857).

Hughes, William Morris (1864–1952), Austral. politician, b. Wales. Member of 1st Austral. parliament (1901), held various posts in Labour govts.; supported Britain in World War 1 as P.M. (1915–23). Founded United Australian Party (1929).

Hugo, Victor Marie, Vicomte (1802–85), Fr. writer. Early romantic poetry (*e.g. Les Orientales*, 1829) later became philosophical as in *Les Contemplations* (1856). Drama *Hernani* (1830) brought him prominence. Lived abroad during Napoleon III's rule in France. Greatest of his novels are *Notre Dame de Paris* (1831) and *Les Misérables* (1862).

Huguenots, Calvinist Protestants of France, protagonists in Wars of Religion (16th–17th cent.). Mass emigration after revocation (1685) of EDICT OF NANTES.

Huizinga, Johan (1872–1945), Dutch historian. Best known work *The Waning of the Middle Ages* (1919).

Hull, Cordell (1871–1955), Amer. statesman. As congressman was author of one of 1st Federal income tax laws (1913). Sec. of State (1933–44). Awarded Nobel Peace Prize (1945).

Hull, Robert Marvin (1939–   ), Canadian ice hockey player. Estab. record for most goals, one season (58 in 1968–9) in National Hockey League, while playing for Chicago Black Hawks.

Hull, Kingston-upon-Hull, city and port of E Riding, Yorks., England, on R. Hull at Humber Estuary; 3rd port and chief UK fishing port. Industry includes flour milling. Pop. (1966) 298,000.

hull, term for body framework of ship.

humanism, Renaissance movement in thought, reaction against medieval religious authority; rediscovery of

classical secular (humanistic) attitudes. Included such men as Boccaccio, Sir Thomas More. Later applied to 20th cent. writers such as Babbitt.

Humber, river separating Yorks. and Lincs., E England, estuary of Trent.

Humbert II [Umberto] (1904–   ), king of Italy (1946). Succeeded after father Victor Emmanuel III's abdication; referendum estab. republic, was forced to abdicate.

humble bee, *Bombus,* humble, or bumble bees live in communities mainly in temp. regions. Females and neuters help to build nest, where honey is stored for females, who alone survive winter.

Humboldt, [Friedrich Heinrich] Alexander, Freiherr von (1769–1859), Ger. scientist and explorer. Expeditions to Latin America (1799–1804) advanced use of scientific observation in exploration. Brother **Wilhelm, Freiherr von Humboldt** (1767–1835) was leading educ. reformer and philologist.

Hume, David (1711–76), Scot. philosopher and historian; furthered theories of LOCKE and BERKELEY. Attributed everything in the mind to sensation. Works include *Treatise of Human Nature (1739-40), An Enquiry Concerning the Principles of Morals* (1750) and *Political Discourses* (1752).

Hume, Hamilton (1797–1873), Austral. explorer and bushman. Discovered new routes across Blue Mts., New South Wales.

humidity, climatic state, quantity of water vapour in atmosphere. Precipitation occurs at 100% humidity.

hummingbird, small primarily trop.

insectivorous bird of New World. Name from sound of wing vibration. Colourful species include giant hummer of Andes and Helena's hummingbird of Cuba.

Humperdinck, Engelbert (1854–1921), Ger. composer and teacher. Best known for opera *Hansel and Gretel* (1893).

Humphrey, Hubert Horatio (1911–   ), Amer. politician. Senator from Minnesota; Vice Pres. (1965–9). Unsuccessful Democratic pres. candidate (1968).

Hunan, prov. of C China. Area: 81,081 sq. mi.; cap. Changsha. Predominantly hilly, major producer of tea, rice and minerals (lead, zinc, antimony). Pop. (1963) 36,220,000.

Hundred Days *see* NAPOLEON I.

Shipbuilding: the hull takes shape in dry dock

Hundred Years War (1337–1453), conflict between England and France, result of commercial and territorial rivalries. Eng. monarch, as Duke of Aquitaine, opposed centralizing tendencies of Fr. crown. Eng. successes in 1st phase (Crécy, Poitiers, capture of Calais) were offset in later stages by Joan of Arc and Fr.-Burgundian alliances which ultimately drove Eng. army out of France and Aquitaine. Calais remained in Eng. hands.

Hungarian, branch of Finno-Ugrian group of the Ural-Altaic family of languages.

Hungary [Magyarország] state of E central Europe. Area: 35,918 sq. mi.; cap. Budapest. Primarily agric., industries largely based on metal refining. Conquered (9th cent.) by MAGYARS, predominant people of modern nation. HABSBURG rule (1526–1918); incorporated into

Hyacinth from Asia Minor (*Hyacinthus orientalis*)

16th cent. Hungarian church at Pecs

Austro-Hungarian Empire (1867). Sided with AXIS during World War 2; communist coup resulted in present constitution (1949). Revolution (1956) put down by Soviet troops.

Language Hungarian, religion mainly R.C. Unit of currency, Forint. Pop. (1965) 10,179,000.

Huns, nomadic pastoralists of N Central Asia who appeared in Europe in 4th cent. Highly mobile raiders, under Attila, they forced Emperor Theodosius to pay tribute (432) but invasion of Italy and Gaul (450) resulted in their defeat.

Hunt, Sir John (1910–), Eng. mountaineer. Led 1st ascent of Mt. Everest (1953).

Hunt, William Holman (1827–1910), Eng. painter, one of pre-Raphaelite group. Among best known works, *The Light of the World* and *The Hireling Shepherd*.

Hunter, John (1728–93), Scot. pioneer anatomist and surgeon; made noted anatomical collection. His brother, **William Hunter** (1718–83), was famous obstetrician and head of school of anatomy.

hunting, sport of pursuing animals. Big-game hunting in Africa and elsewhere gained popularity from value of hides, horns, tusks, *etc.* Hunting in Europe, with dogs and horses, is primarily for sport. Foxes, wolves, boars and deer are common prey.

Huntingdonshire, county of E England. Area: 349 sq. mi.; county town Huntingdon. Flat, fertile land; produces wheat, barley. Pop. (1966) 184,000.

Hupei, Hupeh, prov. of C China. Area: 72,587 sq. mi.; cap. Wuhan. Bulk of population lives in rice, wheat and cotton-growing areas. Iron and coal mined. Pop. (1963) 30,790,000.

Huron, confederation of 4 N Amer. Indian tribes of Iroquoian linguistic stock. Lived in Ontario in 17th cent. Numbered about 20,000, depended on agriculture. Competition with Iroquois for fur trade led to their defeat (1648). Eventually settled near Detroit and became known as Wyandot; placed on Oklahoma reservation (1867).

Huron, Lake *see* GREAT LAKES.

hurricane, violent trop. storm, with violent changes in WIND, of velocity over 75 mph. Common along Atlantic seaboard of US. In China Sea, called typhoon.

Hus, Jan (*c.* 1369–1415), Czech. religious reformer. Opposed banning of Wycliffe's doctrines; excommunicated (1410). Fled Prague (1412) and wrote *De Ecclesia*. Burned at stake after being accused of heresy.

hussar, light cavalry soldier. Uniform was usually colourful and included busby and dolman.

Hussein, Ibn Ali (1856–1931), Arab chief. Declared independence from Turkey (1916). After war against Turkey, recognized as king of the Hejaz. Grandson, **Hussein** (1935–) became king of the Hashemite Kingdom of the Jordan (1952).

Husserl, Edmund (1859–1938), Ger. philosopher. Pioneered phenomenology. propounding theories on relationship of conscious mind and external data.

Huston, John (1906–), Amer. film director. Films include *Moby Dick* and *The African Queen*.

Hutson, Don[ald], (1913–), Amer. football player. Pass receiver for Green Bay Packers, estab. 3 all-time National Football League records.

Hutton, James (1726–97), Brit. geologist. Theories of origins of Earth and of atmospheric changes anticipated modern geological science. Wrote *Theory of the Earth* (1795).

Hutton, Sir Leonard (1916–), Brit. cricketer. Captained England in 23 test matches.

Huxley, T[homas] H[enry] (1825–95), Eng. biologist. Wrote in support of Darwinism. Grandson, **Sir Julian Sorell Huxley** (1887–), biologist and writer. Director general of UNESCO (1946–8). Works include *Heredity East and West* (1949). His brother, **Aldous Leonard Huxley** (1894–1963), author of satirical novels *Point Counter Point* (1928) and *Brave New World* (1932), depicting oppressive utopia. Later works reflect interest in mysticism. **Elspeth Josceline Huxley** (1907–), author of *The Walled City* (1948) and *The Mottled Lizard* (1962).

Huygens or **Huyghens, Christian** (1629–95), Dutch physicist, astronomer, mathematician. Improved telescope and clock. Discovered 6th satellite of Saturn (1655). Made 1st pendulum-regulated clock (1657).

Huysmans, Joris Karl (1848–1907), Fr. novelist. Influenced by Edmond and Jules de Goncourt, whose

The important wine-producing town of Tokaj on the southern edge of the Carpathians, Hungary

Académie he joined. Works include *À Rebours* (1884; Eng. tr. *Against the Grain*, 1922).

Hwang-Ho [Yellow River], 2nd longest (*c.* 2,700 mi.) river in China. Known as 'China's Sorrow', because of mass starvation resulting from floods and drought.

hyacinth, popular sweet-smelling flower of genus *Hyacinthus*, native to Med. and S African regions.

Hyde, Edward, 1st Earl of Clarendon (1609–74), Eng. statesman and historian. Became chief adviser of Charles II before Restoration (1660), after which served as Lord Chancellor. Supported religious toleration, but lack of popularity forced him to flee England. Author of *History of the Rebellion*.

Hyderabad, city and cap. of Andhra Pradesh, S India. Founded 1589; cap. of former princely state of Hyderabad. Major commercial centre. Pop. (1966) 1,306,000.

Hydra, in Gk. myth., water serpent which grew 2 heads for each head chopped off: Slain by Heracles.

hydrangea, genus of flowering shrubs of saxifrage family, native to Americas. Pink, white or blue flowers.

hydraulics, applied science of flow of liquids, esp. water. Concerned with momentum, direction and resulting energy. Hydraulic press, invented by Joseph Bramach, comprises 2 liquid-filled cylinders of unequal diameter connected by pipe and fitted with pistons. Used as application of PASCAL's law.

hydrocarbon, compound containing only carbon and hydrogen. Occurs extensively in petroleum and natural gas; also found in plants and coal tar.

hydrochloric acid, corrosive poisonous solution of hydrogen chloride and water. Used in cleaning metals.

hydro-electric power, electrical energy obtained from generators driven by water-turbines. Source of water may be natural (waterfall) or artificial (river-damming).

hydrofoil, in hydrodynamics, wing-like device which produces upward lift when moved through water. Boat or small ship which uses such devices to lift its hull above the water, capable of high speeds.

hydrogen (H), inflammable, colourless gas, lightest of known gases. Forms water when combined with oxygen. Occurs in all organic constituents of plants and animals.

hydrogen bomb, thermonuclear reaction caused by fusion of atomic nuclei of low mass, usually hydrogen isotopes. Explosion yield (measured in megatons) of enormous size; produces fireball and mushroom-shaped cloud. Radio-active fall-out poisons plants and animals, and can cause disease (*e.g.* leukemia). International agreement banning use of nuclear weapons reached (1968).

hydrogen peroxide, heavy, colourless liquid. Used as disinfectant and bleach.

hydrolysis, chem. process in which substance decomposed by reacting with water, involving splitting of hydrogen and hydroxyl ions.

hydrometer, instrument for measuring SPECIFIC GRAVITY of a liquid. Liquid placed in special glass tube and immersed in water.

hydrophobia *see* RABIES.

hydroplane, small, high-powered boat which skims water surface. Primarily of recreational use, also raced.

hydrozoa, class of mainly marine polymorphic animals, of order Coelenterata. Freshwater forms exhibit some primitive characteristics.

hyena, carnivore of family Hyaenidae, adapted to carrion feeding. Jaw muscles powerful for crushing bones; offensive odour. Species include spotted hyena, *crocuta crocuta*.

hygrometer, instrument for measuring water vapour in air (humidity).

Hymen, in Gk. myth., god of marriage, represented as carrying torch and wearing veil.

hymenoptera, large order of insects. Includes ants, bees, wasps.

hymn, religious song of praise used in divine worship. Written in metre and divided into stanzas. A few have survived from early Church, *e.g. Te Deum Laudamus*.

hyoscine, scopolamine, drug obtained from plant group *Solanaceae*. Used as sedative.

hypabyssal, fine-grained igneous rock, intermediate in texture between plutonic and extrusive rocks.

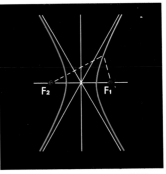

Hyperbola with foci, F1 and F2

hyperbola, in geometry, a plane curve formed by a section of a right circular cone. The cutting plane makes a greater angle with the base than that made by the cone's sides.

hyperopia, defect of eye, in which images focus behind retina. Commonly called long-sightedness.

hypertension, abnormally high blood pressure. Symptom of arterial and heart disease, associated with arteriosclerosis. Cause unknown.

hypnotism, condition of artificially induced sleep, or sleep-like trance. Used to treat and study hysteria, heightens suggestibility. Briefly used by Freud in psychoanalysis; occasionally in modern therapy.

hypothyroidism, cretinism, congenital condition due to absence or insufficiency of secretion of thyroid gland. Causes retarded mental and physical development in infants.

hyrax, tailless quadruped of genus *Procavia* allied to hoofed mammal. Size similar to rabbit, has short fur, clawed forefoot and cleft upper lip. Found in Asia and Africa.

hyssop, small perennial aromatic plant, *Hyssopus officinalis*. Bluish flowers, native to Med. regions.

hysteria, highly emotional and irrational conduct; bodily disturbance is symptom. Defined by psychologists as conversion NEUROSIS. Hypnosis used as cure in late 19th cent.

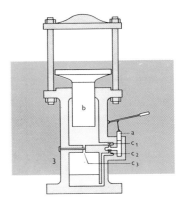

Simple hydraulic press. On the downstroke of the lever the piston (a) compresses the fluid in the lower cylinder forcing it through valve C1 into the upper cylinder, thus raising platten (b). The lever is then raised, sucking up more fluid from the reservoir through valve C2 so that the first stage can be repeated. By opening valve C3 the reservoir is refilled from the upper cylinder

iambus, iamb, metrical foot of 2 syllables, 1st unstressed, 2nd stressed. Usually followed by term denoting number of feet in line, *e.g.* iambic pentameter (5 feet).

Iapetus, in Gk. myth., giant son of Gaia and Uranus, and father of Atlas and Prometheus. Imprisoned in Tartarus for rebelling against Zeus.

Ibadan, largest city of Nigeria, cap. of W region. Exports cacao, palm oil, cotton, rubber. Pop. (1963) 627,000.

Ibáñez, Vicente Blasco (1867–1928), Sp. novelist; spokesman of social reform in *La Cathedral* (1903) and *La Bodega* (1905). Best known for *The Four Horsemen of the Apocalypse* (1916).

Iberian Peninsula, between Atlantic Ocean and Med. Sea, SW Europe, comprising Spain and Portugal. Named after **Iberians**, ancient peoples, believed to have migrated from Africa in Neolithic period.

Ibert, Jacques François Antoine (1890–   ), Fr. composer. Style is light and unpretentious. Has written concertos for flute, saxophone, oboe and cello, also operas and ballets.

Iberville, Pierre Le Moyne, Sieur d' (1661–1706), Fr. Canadian explorer and colonist. Led successful expeditions against British in Hudson Bay area. Located mouth of Mississippi R. (1699). Estab. colonies at Biloxi and Mobile (1702).

ibex, agile wild goat, found in mountains of Europe and Asia. Alpine ibex, *Capra ibex,* saved from extinction.

ibis, wading bird of family Threskiornithidae, related to storks and herons. Occurs in warm regions of the world. Glossy ibis, *Plegadis falcinellus,* is found on all the continents.

Ibiza, Iviza, Sp. Balearic island, Med. Sea. Area: 230 sq. mi.; cap. Ibiza. Main occupations are fishing and growing of olives, citrus fruits, cereals. Popular tourist centre. Pop. (1960) 34,502.

Ibn Batuta, Abu Abdallah Mohammed, (1304–77), Arab traveller in Africa and Far East. His *Travels* was an important medieval geographical source book.

Ibn Khaldun, Abd ar-Rhaman (1332–1406), Arab historian. Among 1st to regard history as a science.

Ibn-Rushd *see* AVERROËS.

Ibn Saud, Abdul Aziz I (1880–1953), founder and 1st king of SAUDI ARABIA. Succeeded his father as sultan of Hejd (1901); conquered surrounding territories (1919–25). Proclaimed king of Hejaz (1926). Changed official title of territories to Kingdom of Saudi Arabia (1932). Promoted Arab nationalism.

ibn-Sina *see* AVICENNA.

Ibo, Eboe, people of W Africa, esp. S Nigeria; number *c.* 4 million, divided into *c.* 500 independent tribes. Main occupation is hoe agriculture. Population of BIAFRA is mostly Ibo.

Ibrahim Pasha (1789–1848), Egyptian viceroy and soldier in Greece and Syria. Early exponent of Arab nationalism, he asserted Egyptian leadership over Arab empire at the expense of Ottoman Turkish pretensions.

Ibsen, Henrik Johan (1828–1906), Norwegian dramatist whose naturalistic work depicts the individual at odds with social convention. Plays include *The Pillars of Society* (1877), *Ghosts* (1881), *Hedda Gabler* (1890), *When We Dead Awaken* (1899).

Icarus, in Gk. myth., son of Daedalus; with his father flew from Crete on wings of feathers and wax. Flew too close to the sun which melted the wax; drowned in that part of Aegean Sea near Crete, now called Icarian Sea.

Ice Age, Pleistocene epoch, in geology, period of extensive glacial conditions. Began *c.* 1 million yr. ago. Ice covered most of N America, Europe and Asia on 4 or 5 occasions.

ice hockey *see* HOCKEY.

ice plant, *Mesembryanthemum crystallinum,* plant of figwort family found in warm dry regions of Old World. Vesicles glisten like ice.

iceberg, mass of floating ice, broken away from glacier or ice-barrier. Usually only $\frac{1}{9}$th visible above surface of water. Often a hazard to shipping.

Iceland [Island], repub. of Europe in Atlantic Ocean, S of Arctic Circle and *c.* 600 mi. W of Norway; comprises Iceland Is. and several smaller islands. Area: 39,707 sq. mi.; cap. Reykjavik. Mountainous and highly glaciated

with volcanoes and hot springs. Settled by Norse (*c.* 850–70); under Norwegian then Danish crown. Declared sovereign state in union with Denmark (1918); independent repub. (1944). Extensive sheep and cattle grazing, limited agriculture. Fishing is main occupation; exports cod, herring. Language, Icelandic. Main religion, Lutheran. Unit of currency, the krona. Pop. (1966) 195,000.

Icelandic, Scandinavian Indo-European language with fewer than 1 million speakers in Iceland.

Icelandic literature, importance of which lies in early works (*c.* 1000–1300), mainly anonymous and closely linked to Old Norse. Notable are sagas, narratives in prose and verse, *e.g.* collection of heathen songs, *Edda*. Recent works have reflected increasing romantic and nationalist trends.

Ichabod [Hebrew: inglorious], in OT, grandson of Eli. So named to commemorate capture of Ark by Philistines at his birth.

I-ching, Book of Changes, one of 5 Chinese classics making up canon of Confucian school of thought. Contains mystical speculation.

ichneumon, *Herpestes ichneumon,* small carnivorous mammal of family Veverridae, native to Africa and S Asia. Regarded as sacred by ancient Egyptians.

ichneumon-fly, parasitic insect of family Ichneumonidae. Several thousand species exist in Europe and N America. Eggs laid in larvae or eggs of other insects, esp. of order Lepidoptera.

Ibis

15th cent. Russian Icon from Novgorod

ichthyology, branch of zoology dealing with the study of fishes.

ichthyosaur, large porpoise-shaped aquatic reptile, abundant during Jurassic period of Mesozoic times. Fish-like in appearance with flipper-like limbs and powerful tail.

Ickes, Harold Le Claire (1874–1952), Amer. politician. Sec. of Interior under Pres. F. D. Roosevelt (1933–46); one of strongest supporters of NEW DEAL programmes.

iconoclasm, [Gk: image breaking], opposition among Christians in Byzantine Empire to worship of ICONS, on grounds that such amounted to image-worship. Came to denote opposition to estab. beliefs and customs in general.

Icons, representations of Christ, an angel or a saint in E Orthodox Church. Painted on flat surface, often embossed with gold or silver.

icterus *see* JAUNDICE.

Ictinus (*fl.* 5th cent. BC), Gk. architect. Designed PARTHENON at Athens, temple of Eleusis, and temple to Apollo at Phigalia in Arcadia.

id, in PSYCHOANALYSIS, subconscious instinctive drive, functioning on principle of pleasure. Developed by Freud as one of 3 motivating forces of human personality, others being ego and superego.

Idaho, Rocky Mountain state of W US. Area: 83,557 sq. mi.; cap. Boise. Mountainous in N, plateau in S. Largely agric., esp. cattle grazing; potatoes, sugar beet grown; produces cheese, butter, wool, wheat; timber industry important. Mineral resources include gold, silver, lead, zinc, copper. Pop. (1965) 699,000.

idealism, in philosophy, theory that nothing outside ideas has any reality. The only reality of objects is in the impression they make on the mind. Developed along different lines by *e.g.* Plato, Descartes, Leibniz, Kant.

identikit, system, evolved by Hugh C. McDonald, used in identification, esp. by police in criminal hunts. Cards bear variant drawings of individual features (eyes, mouth, hair, *etc.*) which witnesses select. Composite likeness made up, photographed and circulated. Adopted Los Angeles (1959); 1st used in UK (1961).

Ides, in Roman calendar, 15th day of Mar., May, July, Oct.; 13th day of other months. Julius Caesar assassinated Ides of March, 44 BC.

idiocy, severe congenital mental deficiency, usually accompanied by heart ailment which, if present, reduces life expectancy to *c.* 14 yr.

idolatry, worship of images or other objects which represent a god or other supernatural power. Extensively practiced among ancient civilizations incl. Egyptians, Chaldeans, Greeks, Romans. Hebrews violently opposed such worship; Christian Church allows images of Christ, Virgin Mary and saints. Opposition in E (6th–7th cent.) led to rise of ICONOCLASM.

Idrisi, Mohammed al- (1100–*c.*1165), Arab geographer, author of *A Description of the World,* or *Book of Roger* (1154). Alternative title acknowledges his patron, Roger II of Sicily.

If, Château d', castle in Marseille harbour, France. Formerly used as polit. prison. Location used by Dumas for *The Count of Monte Cristo.*

Ifni, Sp. prov. of NW Africa on Atlantic coast. Area: 740 sq. mi.; cap. Sidi Ifni. Barren country occupied by Spanish (15th cent.). Ceded to Spain by Morocco (1860). Ownership now disputed by Morocco and Spain. Pop. (1966) 54,000.

Ifugao, people of N Philippines. Use extensive terracing and irrigation system for rice growing. Infrequent contact with outsiders. About 80,000 remain.

Ignatius of Loyola, Saint, orig. Inigo Lopez de Recalde (*c.* 1491–1556), Sp. nobleman who dedicated himself to life of Christian service while recovering from wounds. Founded (1534) Society of Jesus (JESUITS); order approved by Pope Paul III (1540). Author of *Spiritual Exercises* (1522–3).

igneous rocks, rocks which, during their history, have been in a molten state. If cooling has been rapid, volcanic rocks occur with glassy or vitreous material, due to incomplete crystallization. In plutonic rocks, where cooling has been slow, crystallization is almost perfect.

The Parthenon designed by Ictinus, on the Acropolis, Athens. *Right,* ground plan

282

Common Iguana

Igor (1151–1202), Russ. prince, hero of 12th cent. epic *The Lay of the Host of Igor.* Used by Borodin for opera *Prince Igor.*

iguana, family of mostly arboreal trop. Amer. lizards of order Iguanidae. Common species is *Iguana tuberculata.* Prevailing colour is green; eggs and flesh are edible.

iguanodon, 2-legged dinosaur of order Ornithiscia. Fossils found in Cretaceous rocks in Europe. Reached 15–25 ft. in length.

Ijsselmeer, shallow freshwater lake in Netherlands, separated (1932) from N Sea by construction of dyke 19 mi. long. Previously called Zuider Zee. Large areas (polders) reclaimed, thereby increasing amount of arable land.

Île-de-France, ancient prov. of France, bounded by Rivers Seine, Marne, Beuvronne, Thève and Oise. Cap. was Paris. After Revolution, divided into department of the Seine. Fertile, prosperous district with market gardens, orchards, and wine as the principal industry.

Île-de-France, former name of MAURITIUS.

Iliad, Gk. epic poem (*c.* 900–800 BC) in 24 books, attributed to Homer; tells of wrath of Achilles and of Trojan War.

Ilium *see* TROY.

Illinois, group of N Amer. Indian tribes of Algonkian linguistic stock. Scattered over N Illinois and S Wisconsin in 17th cent. Almost wiped out by wars with Iroquois and Sioux.

Illinois, midwestern US state. Area: 55,947 sq. mi.; cap. Springfield; principal city, Chicago. Plains terrain; agric. produce includes livestock, corn; manufacturing, food processing, transportation centred in Chicago. Fr. exploration (begun 1673); passed to British (1763). Won by US during Amer. Revolution; achieved statehood (1818). Great expansion period began after Civil War. Pop. (1965) 10,081,158.

Illuminati [Lat. 'enlightened ones'], mystic sects claiming special knowledge of God, esp. order founded (1776) in Germany. Aims were republican and anti-Catholic. Supported by the Freemasons, it was denounced in Germany as dangerous and suppressed (1784).

illumination of manuscripts, decoration of hand-written books with coloured pictures, esp. initial-letter and marginal decorations. Early Christian examples include Irish *Book of Kells* (8th cent.).

Illyria, former Gk. colony along E coast of Adriatic Sea (estab. 7th or 6th

Initial with portraits of the Four Evangelists from an illuminated gospel manuscript (9th cent. Frankish-Saxon)

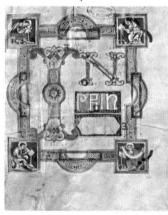

cent. BC). Conquered by Rome (16 BC); became Roman prov. of Illyricum (AD 9). Napoleon estab. Illyrian colonies as part of empire. After Congress of Vienna (1814), became Austrian kingdom of Illyria (until 1849). Territory forms present-day Yugoslavia and Albania.

ilmenite, mineral of basic igneous rocks resembling haematite; black and opaque, composed of oxides of iron and titanium. Used in white paint and alloys.

Ilyushin, Sergei Vladimirovich (1894–), Russ. aircraft designer. Principal designs include the turboprop IL-18 (1957) and turbo-jet IL-62 (1962) passenger aircraft.

image, in optics, visual likeness of object reflected from a mirror or refracted by a lens. A real image is the result of light rays passing through an object; in a virtual image they only appear to do so.

Imagism, literary movement in US and UK (1910–20), part of reaction to Romanticism, stressing clear poetic images. Exponents included Richard Aldington, T. S. Eliot, H. D. (Hilda Doolittle), Amy Lowell and Ezra Pound.

Imhotep (*fl. c.* 2980 BC) physician, vizier and architect of 3rd dynasty King Zoser. Supervised building of step pyramid at Sakkara, Egypt; deified after death, and identified with Asclepius by Greeks.

Immaculate Conception, belief that the Virgin Mary was, from moment of her conception, free from stain of ORIGINAL SIN. Proclaimed dogma by Pope Pius IX (1854), the belief was made binding for Roman Catholics.

Immermann, Karl Lebrecht (1796–1840), Ger. playwright and novelist. His *Die Epigonen* (1836) is one of earliest Ger. social novels. Plays include *Merlin* (1832).

immigration, movement of individuals leaving one country and transferring their homes to another. US receives largest number of immigrants, over 300,000 (1965); Canada over 146,000 (1965); Australia and New Zealand over 226,000 (1965). Unrestricted entry of Commonwealth immigrants to UK was stopped by legislation (1968).

immortality, religious concept of an afterlife current in Assyrian and Egyptian cultures and also held by Plato and the followers of Zarathustra. Hinduism (*see* REINCARNATION) endorses the concept in part; Judaism and Christianity affirm the continuity of man's spiritual existence after physical death.

Impala

Route de Louveciennes (1872) by Pissarro, an example of Impressionist painting

immunity, capacity which a living organism possesses to resist and overcome infection. It can be induced by various processes of immunization. *See* also; INOCULATION.

impala, *Aepyceros melampus,* medium-sized antelope of S and E Africa, with long lyre-shaped horns in the male. Reddish brown back and white underparts.

impeachment, UK judicial parl. procedure against public official. UK House of Lords impeachment of Warren Hastings (1788–95) was one of the last UK cases. US House of Representatives can impeach non-congressional officials, Senate can try cases. Pres. Andrew Johnson was impeached and acquitted.

imperial moth, *Eacles imperialis,* large yellow Amer. moth with purple or brown markings. Larvae feed on maple, oak leaves, *etc.*

imperialism, extension of rule or influence by one country over another by diplomatic, military or economic means; manifested in empire. Refers esp. to denote European expansion (late 19th cent.) into Asia and Africa.

impetigo, inflammatory skin disease, characterized by eruption of isolated pus-filled blisters, usually on the face. Highly infectious.

Impressionism, school of painting. Originated in France (1870), popular in 1890s. Evolved new methods of composition and lighting by using broken colours to depict quick visual impressions, often from nature, *e.g.*

landscapes; technique esp. successful with sunlight. Exponents include Monet, Degas, Renoir, Sisley.

impressment, practice of forcibly seizing recruits for military or naval duty. Mainly used by Prussian army under Frederick II.

Incas, name ordinarily given to the population of Peru before conquest by Pizarro (1533), but restricted to ruling caste, ruler himself being the Inca. Civilization, centred at Cuzco, may go back to 1200 BC. Achieved high level of culture as shown by social system, knowledge of agriculture, roadmaking, ceramics, textiles and buildings, *e.g.* Temple of the Sun at Machu Picchu.

incest, sexual relations between people of close kinship. Incest and marriage of such people are prohibited by law or custom in most societies, though laws on actual kin concerned vary.

Inchon, Chemulpo, ice-free seaport and city of S Korea. Scene of UN military landings (1951). Pop. *c.* 402,000.

inclined plane, a plane placed at an angle other than 90° to its base. In physics it works as a machine reducing the force needed to move a load upward.

income tax, govt. tax on income, 1st developed in Holland, introduced to Britain during Napoleonic wars by Pitt (1799) and in US during Civil War. Major source of revenue.

Incubus, traditionally, demon believed (esp. during Middle Ages) to father witches and deformed children in sleeping women.

incunabula, name given to books of early days of printing (15th cent.). Examples of work by Gutenberg, Jenson and Caxton.

Independence, city of W Missouri, US. Founded 1827; assembly point for wagon trains going W. Pop. (1960) 62,328.

Independence, American War of *see* AMERICAN REVOLUTION.

Independence, Declaration of, formal statement adopted (4 July 1776) by representatives of 13 Amer. colonies announcing separation from Britain and creating US. Almost entirely written by Thomas Jefferson, document sets out principle of govt. under theory of natural rights.

Inca figurines

The Independence Hall in Philadelphia where the Declaration of Independence was signed on July 4th, 1776

Independent Labour Party, Brit. socialist party. Founded (1893) at Bradford; Lab. party emanated from it. Broke with Lab. (1932) and allied with Communists, after which influence declined.

Independent Television Authority (ITA), Brit. company formed (1955) after govt. permitted TV services other than those of British Broadcasting Corporation. Financed by advertising revenue.

Independent Treasury System, estab. (1846) in US out of distrust of banks and bankers after Andrew Jackson's refusal to recharter Bank of the United States. Public revenues placed in Treasury, which distributed its reserves in various banks throughout country; Treasury independent of national banking interests. Inconsistent govt. policy led to termination with enactment of FEDERAL RESERVE SYSTEM (1913).

Index [Librorum Prohibitorum], catalogue of books which Roman Catholics were forbidden to read. First published (1559); put in care of Holy Office (1917). Abolished by Second Vatican Council (1962–5).

India, triangular S subcontinent of Asia; independent repub. within Brit. Commonwealth. Area: 1,228,811 sq. mi.; cap. New Delhi; main cities, Bombay, Calcutta, Madras. Sub-trop. climate, heavy summer monsoon rains, esp. in E. Primarily agric., rice and millet; exports cotton, tea, spices. Industry includes textiles, engineering. Earliest known civilization (Indus valley, *fl. c.* 2500–*c.* 1500 BC). HINDUISM estab. 3rd cent. AD. Moslems penetrated (11th cent.) and

by 16th cent. flourished under Mogul empire. 18th cent. Anglo-French colonial rivalry ended with CLIVE's victories for Brit. East India Co. Sepoy Rebellion (1857) led to transfer of power to Brit. Crown. Drive for independence under GANDHI's leader-

ship achieved 1947, although MOSLEM LEAGUE agitation led to separation of Pakistan. India became (1950) repub. under Nehru. Subsequent problems: overpopulation, underdeveloped economy; foreign policy followed neutral line, despite border disputes with China, struggle with Pakistan over E Bengal. Main languages, Hindi and English; Hindu and Moslem are predominant faiths. Unit of currency, rupee. Pop. (1966) 515,029,000.

India rubber tree, rubber plant, *Ficus elastica,* tall evergreen tree with long leathery leaves, of India and Burma. Grown as pot plant elsewhere.

Indian bean *see* CATALPA.

Indian corn, maize, *Zea mais,* stout annual grass, extensively grown for food in N America and improved by scientific breeding.

Indian crested swift, insectivorous bird of Hemiprocnidae family. Unlike other swifts, is not in constant flight.

Indian literature, vernacular writings of Indian subcontinent. Ancient remains primarily Vedantic (hymns and ritualistic treatises). Pali (Buddhist) and Prakrit (Jainist) predominant before rise of modern literature (16th cent.). Popularizing of Sanskrit encouraged by Hindu pietistic movement, incl. classics *Ramayana, Bhagavad Ghita.* Urdu verse written for Mogul court based on Persian poetry. Modern literature includes work in English and major languages of India and Pakistan.

Indian Mutiny, Sepoy Rebellion (1857–8), uprising against rule of East India Co. by native soldiers (sepoys). Bengalese troops resented 1856 annexation of Oudh, their homeland, and angered by issue of cartridges coated with fat of cows (sacred to Hindus). Revolt (Feb. 1857) spread over N central India, Delhi captured, Lucknow besieged and entire Brit. colony massacred at Cawnpore. Mutiny subdued by Mar., 1858. Resulting reforms included transfer of rule from East India Co. to Brit. Crown.

Procession in honour of the goddess Kali at Tiruvannamalai, India

Victoria Memorial, Calcutta, India

Child bride at Jodhpur, India

Indian National Congress, Indian polit. party, founded (1885) to hasten India's constitutional progress to dominion status. Became more militant after Gandhi's call for complete independence (1917). Pioneered passive resistance and civil disobedience. Outlawed (1942–5) for failure to support British in World War 2. Under Nehru, became ruling party of India (1947).

Indian Ocean, 3rd largest ocean, extends from E Africa to Australia and India to Antarctica. Area: 28,360,000 sq. mi. Deepest known point off Java, *c.* 24,000 ft. Strong seasonal winds (monsoon) bring rain to SE Asia.

Indian paintbrush, herb of genus *Castilleja.* Wyoming state flower.

Indian pipe, *Monotropa uniflora,* leafless saprophylic plant of N Amer. and Asian woodlands. Name comes from use of pithy stems as tobacco by Indians.

Indian shot *see* CANNA.

Indian Territory, name given to reservations set aside for Indian habitation in US. Estab. by Indian Intercourse Act (1834). Such areas included E half of Oklahoma (N of Red R.), ended (1907) when Oklahoma attained statehood.

Indiana, midwestern state of US. Area: 36,291 sq. mi.; cap. Indianapolis. Heavy industry in cities such as Gary, South Bend. First settled by French, taken over by British (1763) and US (1783); admitted as state 1816. Agriculture: livestock, wheat, corn; industry includes steel, motor vehicles and mining. Pop. (1965) 4,999,000.

Indianapolis, cap. of Indiana, US, agric. and transportation centre. First settled (1820), incorporated (1836). Industry: drugs, rubber products. Pop. (1966) 639,000.

Indian Crested Swift

Pueblo Indian of New Mexico

Indianapolis '500', Amer. 500 mi. motor car race held annually on Memorial Day (May 31) at Indianapolis Motor Speedway.

Indians, pre-European inhabitants of Americas, now largely assimilated. S Amer. cultures included Maya, Toltec, Aztec, Inca and Chibcha, some of which reached high cultural level. All fell during Sp. conquest. N Amer. Indian tribes driven back by westward expansion into Indian Territories. Some 400,000 remain in US and Canada.

indictment, formal written charge of crime pronounced by public prosecutor before grand jury. Once approved, accused person sent to trial. Persons suspected of crime brought to trial by presentment (no formal bill of indictment having been offered).

indigestion, dyspepsia, lack or failure of digestive function. Causes vary. Heartburn, a common form, caused by excessive acid in stomach.

indigo, important blue dye, dating from ancient India and Egypt. Obtained from leguminous plants (chiefly *Indigofera tinctoria*) by fermentation, freeing colourless indican, which oxidizes to blue indigo.

indium, metallic element. Silver-white, malleable and ductile, resembles aluminium.

Indo-China, SE Asian peninsula, comprising Cambodia, Laos, North and South Vietnam. Formerly called French Indo-China.

Indo-Chinese War, fought (1946–54) between Vietminh (coalition of nationalist and Communist groups under HO CHI MINH) and French after failure of negotiations for Vietnamese independence. Decisive battle Dien Bien Phu (1954) broke Fr. resistance. Subsequent Geneva Conference divided Indo-China into North and South Vietnam, Laos and Cambodia.

Indo-European languages, family of inflectional languages, originating prob. in C or N Europe or SW Asia before 2000 BC. Include languages of N India, Persia and Europe (except Hungarian, Finnish, Lapp, Estonian, Basque).

Indonesia, republic of Malay archipelago comprising Sumatra, Java, Borneo, Celebes, Moluccas and many smaller islands. Area: 735,893 sq. mi.; cap. Djakarta. Agric. products include rice, rubber, sugar, coffee; major producer of tin, oil, rich mineral deposits. Strong Islamic influence countered by European trading interests, esp. Dutch who ruled area after

Ox-drawn plough in Indonesia

Irrigation is essential for growing rice in paddy fields

1798 as Netherlands E Indies. Repub. estab. (1945), but not consolidated until after UN mediation (1949). Emergence of SUKARNO led to total

repudiation of Dutch (1956). Language, Malayo-Polynesian; main religion, Islam. Unit of currency, rupiah. Pop. (1966) 104,500,000.

Indonesian, national language of Indonesia, although not most commonly spoken. Closely related to Malay.

Indore see MADHYA PRADESH.

indri, *Indri brevicandata,* largest mammal of lemur group. Fur thick and silky; found in Madagascar.

induction, in electricity, electrifying or magnetizing of a neutral body by proximity to a charged body. Achieved by various methods incl. movement of a conductor through a stationary magnetic field.

indulgence, in R.C. Church, total or partial remission of temporal punishment for sin, providing the sin has already been forgiven and sinner is in state of grace. System was once grossly abused, with indulgences being sold; violently opposed by Luther. Practice approved in moderation by Council of Trent (1563).

Indus, river of S Asia, (*c.* 2,000 mi. long). Flows through Kashmir and Pakistan. Major irrigation source for Pakistan.

Indus civilization, earliest known civilization (*fl.* 2500–1500 BC) of India. Resembled Mesopotamian, advanced urban culture. Cotton textiles produced, wheat and barley grown. Remains include brick buildings, pictorial writing on seals.

industrial arbitration, means of settling disputes between employers and workers by seeking decision of external party; either by mutual agreement or by govt. intervention. Implementation in UK, Industrial Court (estab. 1919) and in US, by govt. through TAFT-HARTLEY LABOR ACT (estab. 1947).

Industrial Revolution, process of industrialization (1750–1850) in Britain. Founded on widening overseas markets, development of banking, and invention of machines and new processing methods, expansion of production took place, esp. in iron and steel, coal, cotton and pottery industries. Accompanied by population increase and transportation developments, it turned Britain from predominantly agric. country into leading indust. nation of world. Rapid change spread to Germany, US (after 1850), Japan, USSR and others in 20th cent.

Industrial Workers of the World (IWW), revolutionary organization of labour unions, founded (1905) in Chicago. Leaders included Eugene Debs. Decline set in after 1917.

Indy, [Paul Marie Théodore] Vincent d' (1851–1931), Fr. composer, pupil of Franck and leader of radical school. Works include *Symphony on a*

Indri

French Mountain Air, chamber music.

inert gases see NOBLE GASES.

inertia, in physics, property of matter to resist changes while in motion. Force must be applied to surmount it.

infancy, in medicine, term applied to child from birth to age of *c.* 2 yr. Legal term denotes person under 21 yr. (18 in some US states), though from age 12 (girls) 14 (boys) more commonly known as minors.

infantile paralysis see POLIOMYELITIS.

infantry, branch of army trained, equipped and organized to fight on foot. Orig. body of men collected by *infantes* of Spain.

inferiority complex, psychiatric term for ideas centring on real or imaginary handicaps. Behavioural patterns may be guided by attempts to compensate for it. Term originated by ALFRED ADLER.

infinity, mathematical concept (symbol: ∞) larger than any number. In geometry, position of undefined distance from area considered.

inflation, in economics, situation created by increase in currency beyond needs of trade. As purchasing power falls, prices rise. Large influx of bullion may bring inflation, *e.g.* in Europe after discovery of America. Wars are most common cause: govt. borrows and issues paper money;

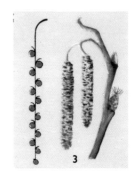

Types of inflorescence: 1. simple ear (vervain), 2. complex ear (rye grass), 3. catkin (hazel), 4. spadix (cuckoo–pint)

domestic supply incapable of meeting consumer demand, causing prices to rise. **Deflation** reflects opposite tendencies: purchasing power rises as prices fall. Characteristic decline in business brings unemployment. Govts. usually resort to devaluation of currency to counteract deflation.

inflorescence, flowering shoot of a plant comprising stem, stalks, bracts and flowers.

influenza, infectious condition characterized by general neuralgic and muscular pains, considerable weakness and fever. Caused by virus. Rarely fatal, except in cases of serious epidemic or onset of pneumonia.

infra-red rays *see* SPECTRUM.

Inge, William (1913–), Amer. playwright. Works portray frustrations of life in small towns and include *Come Back Little Sheba* (1950), *Picnic* (1952), *Bus Stop* (1955) all of which have been made into films.

Inge, William Ralph (1860–1954), Eng. prelate and author. Dean of St. Paul's Cathedral, known as 'the gloomy dean' (1911–34). Wrote works on mysticism, incl. *Personal Idealism and Mysticism* (1907) and contributed many varied articles to the *Evening Standard*.

Ingersoll, Robert Green (1833–99), Amer. orator and lawyer, noted for speech (1876) nominating James G.

Blaine for pres. and lectures incl. *Why I am an Agnostic* (1896).

Ingres, Jean Auguste Dominique (1780–1867), Fr. neo-classical painter, draughtsman and portraitist. Awarded Grand Prix de Rome (1801). Portraits characterized by purity of form and sculptural calm. Works include *Oedipus and the Sphinx, Joan of Arc* and *La Source*.

inhibition, term applied in psychology to state of mind preventing development of certain actions or thoughts. Also applied to sentence passed upon clergymen, preventing exercise of ecclesiastical functions, and to writ, preventing judge from proceeding with a case.

Inisfail, (Irish: *Inis Fáil,* island of destiny), literary name for Ireland.

initiation, in anthropology, magical or religious ceremony among primitive peoples to mark transition from childhood to adult status. Male circumcision is a common rite.

injection, method employed in medicine to introduce liquid into the body, usually administered by means of fine needle and syringe. May be subcutaneous (into skin), intravenous (into vein), intramuscular (into muscle), spinal (into spinal tissues).

injunction, the formal written order of a court commanding or prohibiting a certain act.

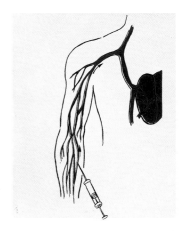

Intravenous injection

ink, coloured liquid used in printing and writing. Known since prehistoric days. Various forms in use; ordinary writing inks, copying ink and Indian ink. Made up from various chemical solutions, mostly aniline dyes.

ink cap, genus of fungi incl. *Coprinus comatus,* shaggy cap or lawyer's wig, with scaly cap and smooth pale yellow centre. *C. atramentarius* has brownish cap and contains a chemical similar to antabuse, a drug used in treatment of alcoholism.

Inkerman, scene of final Fr. and Brit. victory over Russians in Crimean War (1854).

inner ear *see* EAR.

Inner Hebrides *see* HEBRIDES.

Inner Mongolia, autonomous prov. of China. Area: 540,000 sq. mi.; cap. Huhehot (formerly Kweisui). Climate continental. Agriculture limited; irrigation necessary; animal grazing main occupation. Industry, steel, centred in Paotow. Pop. (1957 est.) 9,200,000.

Inner Temple *see* INNS OF COURT.

Innocent I, Saint (d. 417), pope (401–417). Condemned Pelagius and supported St John Chrysostom. During reign Rome sacked by Alaric and Visigoths (410).

Innocent III (1160–1216), pope (1198–1216). Influence helped Otto IV and then Frederick II to become emperor; forced John of England to a humiliating surrender; called 4th Lateran council which proclaimed crusade (1215) and initiated crusade against Albigensians.

Innocent X, orig. Giambattista Pamfili (1574–1655), pope (1644–55). Rejected Treaty of Westphalia (1651); attacked Jansen's *Augustinus* (1653), thus sanctioning opposition to Jansenism in France.

The Stamaty Family (1818), a drawing by Ingres

Innsbruck

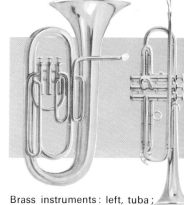

Brass instruments: left, tuba; right, trumpet

Innocent XI, (1611–89), orig. Benedetto Odescalchi, pope (1676–89). Quarrelled with Louis XIV over collection of revenues (1682) and condemned the revocation of Edict of Nantes (1685). Beatified (1956).

Innocents, Holy, children of Bethlehem, put to death by Herod the Great in attempt to kill the infant Jesus.

Inns of Court, 4 legal societies in London, England, responsible for training and subsequent qualification of barristers. They are Lincoln's Inn, Gray's Inn, Inner Temple and Middle Temple.

Innsbruck, cap. of Tyrol prov., W Austria. Orig. Roman city, important in Middle Ages as strategic location. University founded (1677). Alpine tourist centre. Pop. (1964) 108,000.

inoculation, method of immunization against disease. Active inoculation consists of injection of weak strain of infection and consequent production of the body's own immunity to it. Passive inoculation, used when no time for active immunity to be built up, consists of injection of antitoxins from previously infected subject.

Inonu, Ismet (1884–), Turkish soldier and statesman. Succeeded Kemal Ataturk as pres. (1938–50). Returned (1961) after military coup, but forced to resign (1965).

inorganic chemistry *see* CHEMISTRY.

inquest, any inquiry, but primarily that by coroner into cause of person's death. Necessary only in cases where cause of death not apparent or appears to have been result of violence.

Inquisition, instrument of medieval Catholic church intended to facilitate suppression of heresy. Founded (1248) by Innocent IV. Itself suppressed in 19th cent. by Papacy, it was most active in 15th and 16th cent.

Spain. Torquemada was a notorious Inquisitor-General. Victims were tortured and burned.

insanity, lunacy, social and legal term rather than medical, referring to mental derangement or disorder. Indicates condition rendering affected person unfit to enjoy liberty of action because of unreliability of behaviour and concomitant danger to himself and others.

insect, invertebrate of class Insecta, most abundant group of arthropods. Adult has body divided into head, thorax and abdomen, head bearing a pair of antennae, thorax having 3 pairs of legs and usually 2 pairs of wings. Most are terrestrial and breathe air by tracheae. Usually a 3 stage life history involving egg, larva and pupa prior to adulthood. Nearly 1 million known species.

insecticides *see* PESTICIDES.

insectivore, small, nocturnal or diurnal insect-eating mammals, largest being hedgehog. Habitat terrestrial, arboreal or aquatic. Several species hibernate.

insectivorous plants, plants which supplement nitrogen supply by digesting small insects caught in cavities on plant, *e.g.* pitcher plant, by viscidity of leaves, *e.g.* Portuguese fly catcher, or by distinct movements, *e.g.* Venus' flytrap.

insomnia, inability to sleep normally. Causes may be physical, as with respiratory difficulties, but are often thought to be psychological.

instinct, apparently inborn behaviour pattern of animals. Common to all members of species, develops without any learning process, *e.g.* birds' nest-building behaviour, or human instinct of self-preservation, adaptation to environment, *etc.*

Institute of France (Fr: *Institut de*

France), estab. (1795). Composed of 5 academies: *L'Académie Française, L'Académie des Inscriptions et Belles-Lettres, L'Académie des Sciences, L'Académie des Beaux Arts,* and *L'Académie des Sciences Morales et Politiques.*

instruments, musical, divisible into 4 main groups; STRING, WIND, (incl. woodwind and brass), PERCUSSION, and KEYBOARD.

insulation, in electricity, resistance to passage of electric current presented by certain substances (insulators). These include dry air, rubber, paraffin, wax, porcelain, paper and chloride. Plastic fibres used for light current.

insulin, hormone secreted into the bloodstream from the pancreas which controls the body's use of sugar. Diabetics, whose production of insulin is low or non-existent, require insulin obtained from other mammals.

Insull, Samuel (1859–1938), Amer. financier, b. Englan. Ultimately vindicated of charges of embezzlement in connection with his holdings in public utilities.

insurance, method of cover received in

Insectivorous plants: left—the Venus Flytrap, right—the Pitcher Plant

business transactions in return for a stated premium, guaranteeing insured person against loss which might arise from causes beyond his control, *e.g.* fire, theft, accident. First insurance was on foreign trading vessels and their cargoes. Since late 19th cent. the state has been prominent in field of social insurance (*see* SOCIAL SECURITY).

integral calculus, branch of higher mathematics which constructs relationships of variables from rates of change, *e.g.* method of finding area enclosed by curves.

integration, union of 2 groups of people divided on ethnic, religious, economic or social grounds. As a deliberate policy, chief exponent is US where restrictions on Negroes continued to exist after Civil War. Failures by state governments, esp. in the South, to enforce legislation led to birth of CIVIL RIGHTS movement.

intelligence, generally defined as ability to use understanding of past experience to meet new or similar situations. Potential intelligence to certain extent related to heredity, but attainment depends largely upon environment. Intelligence tests, 1st devised by ALFRED BINET (1905), help determine individual learning ability. Mental capacity calculated on result of tests for specific age groups. I.Q. (Intelligence Quotient) based on comparison of mental and chronological age. Aptitude and personality tests have now superseded I.Q. tests in importance.

intelligence, military, information collected and interpreted by Intelligence officers of army, navy and air force regarding actual or potential enemy.

Inter-American conferences *see* PAN-AMERICANISM.

interest, money paid for use of borrowed capital at fixed percentage rate usually yearly, half-yearly or quarterly. May be simple or compound (*i.e.* interest on accumulated interest).

interference, in physics, effect produced by combination of wave motions (2 converging light or sound waves, resulting in, *e.g.* reinforcement or neutralization). Interference occurs only when waves are of similar length and frequency.

Intergovernmental Maritime Consultative Committee (IMCO), set up (1959) to facilitate co-operation among governments in achieving safe and efficient navigation, it seeks to remove restrictions on movement of international shipping. Includes 60 members.

interior decoration, treatment of interior of buildings in style reflecting contemporary architecture. Thus Fr. classical styles in 17th cent. were reflected in 'Louis XIV' interiors. Mid 20th cent. interiors tend towards simplicity using strong colours, plain light wood, large areas of glass and functional furniture.

Interlaken, Swiss tourist centre between Lakes Brienz and Thun. Famed for view of Jungfrau. Pop. (1962) 5,000.

intermezzo, [Ital: 'in the middle'],

Interior of a room decorated in Louis XIV style

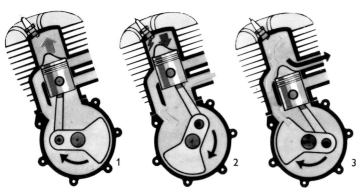

Two-stroke internal-combustion engine: 1. on the upstroke the piston compresses the mixture while keeping both ports closed, 2. mixture is ignited while inlet port is open, 3. next lot of mixture is forced into cylinder and exhaust is expelled through open port

comic opera developed from comic interlude in 17th cent. opera or ballet. Term also applied to free and short instrumental composition.

internal combustion engine, engine with higher thermal efficiency than steam engine, driven by energy from ignition of gas mixtures from fuel injected into cylinder with introduced atmospheric oxygen. Expansion at high temperature drives piston forcibly along cylinder and turns crankshaft. Universally used for road-transport vehicles.

International [Workingmen's Association], called First International, estab. (1864) by Karl Marx in London. Dissolved (1874) after disagreement over policy for achieving workers' unity. Second or Socialist International (estab. 1889), broke up during World War 1 when powerful Ger. group supported nation's war efforts; revived 1919, includes Socialist parties of many countries. Soviet Union dominated Third International (*see* COMINTERN). TROTSKY founded Fourth International (1937).

International Atomic Energy Agency, specialized UN agency, estab. (1957) to promote peaceful uses of atomic energy. Authorized to buy and sell fissionable materials and offer technical assistance to member states.

International Bank for Reconstruction and Development (World Bank), specialized body of UN. Estab. (1945), headquarters Washington, DC. Funded by UN members, serves as loan agency for member states and private investors; aims to facilitate investment, foreign trade, discharge international debts.

International Civil Aviation Organization (ICAO), agency of UN estab. (1947) at Montreal. Aim is promotion

of international safety codes and symbols.

International Court of Justice, chief judicial organ of UN, estab. (1945) to replace Permanent Court of International Justice. Comprises 15 justices; usually sits at The Hague. Renders decisions (binding on all UN members) on matters of international law; also advises when requested by General Assembly.

International Criminal Police Commission (INTERPOL), organization, estab. 1923 (revived after World War 2), to counter international crime. Promotes co-operation of countries in capturing criminals.

International Finance Corporation (IFC), UN agency, founded (1956) as an affiliate of International Bank for Reconstruction and Development. Purpose is to encourage growth of productive enterprise in member states, esp. in under-developed areas.

International Geophysical Year (IGY), programme of international research into natural phenomena over designated period (July 1957 to Dec. 1958). Organized by scientists with govt. co-operation. Included studies of solar system, Earth's magnetic field, weather and climate, oceans. Weather satellites used for research.

international law, law of nations, body of rules applicable to conduct of independent states in their relations with each other. Frequent resort to arbitration of disputes at Hague conferences by late 19th cent.; subsequent need for international settlement led to creation of League of Nations, then UN.

International Monetary Fund (IMF), specialized agency of UN; estab. (1945), headquarters Washington, DC. Facilitates discharge of inter-

national debt by enabling member states to buy foreign currencies.

International Red Cross Committee founded (1863) in Geneva to co-ordinate work of the various national Red Cross committees (88 in 1963), consists of 25 Swiss nationals elected by society members. Directs relief and assistance in times of war, epidemic, famine and other catastrophes.

Awarded Nobel Peace Prize (1917, 1944, 1963).

International Union for Conservation of Nature and Natural Resources, founded (1948) to facilitate international co-operation, promote scientific research, distribute information and conduct educ. programmes for conservation esp. in Africa, Middle East.

Interpol *see* INTERNATIONAL CRIMINAL POLICE COMMISSION.

Interregnum, term used in Eng. history for period between reigns of Charles I and Charles II (1648–60), only time country has been without a monarch.

Interstate Commerce Commission, empowered by US Congress to regulate transportation practices between states. Orig. estab. (1887) because of rly. malpractices, jurisdiction extended (1906) over commerce and express communications; rates and labour disputes also subject to ICC regulations.

intestacy, legal term for state of dying without leaving valid will. Inheritance of property left by intestates is governed by law in most countries, with estate going to spouse or children where possible.

intestine, portion of alimentary canal in vertebrates in which latter stage of digestion and collection of waste products take place. Consists of small intestine, large intestine and rectum; approx. 32 ft. long.

Intolerable Acts, term given by Amer. patriots to 5 laws adopted (1774) by Brit. parl. Included QUEBEC ACT; limited geographical and polit. freedom. Arose out of Boston Tea Party.

introversion and **extroversion,** in

An example of an invertebrate: jellyfish

psychology, terms introduced by C. G. Jung to describe opposing types. Introvert's general activity directed inwards upon himself; extrovert's directed towards external world. Each person has both tendencies, one usually dominating other.

intrusive rocks, any IGNEOUS ROCK forced into rocks of different type while molten.

intuitionism, term for philosophies dependent on theory that man can perceive truth and ethical principles without assistance of intellect or experience. Common among medieval mystics.

Inverness, royal burgh, port on Moray Firth and county town of Inverness-shire, Scotland. A centre of unsuccessful Jacobite uprisings (1715, 1745). Industry includes shipbuilding, tweed manufacture. Pop. (1963) 29,603.

Inverness-shire, largest county of Scotland, in NW. Area: 4,211 sq. mi.; county town, Inverness. Includes Skye and Outer Hebrides, except Lewis; mountainous. Hydro-electric power and fishing important. Pop. (1966) 85,000.

invertebrate, animal without backbone, *i.e.* animals belonging to all phyla except Chordata. Group includes jellyfish, insects, sponges and worms.

Io, in Gk. myth., woman loved by Zeus who disguised her as a white heifer. Discovered by Hera, Zeus' wife, who sent a gadfly to torment her.

iodine, non-metallic element found in marine areas, esp. in seaweed. Dark, shiny crystalline solid, essential to functioning of THYROID gland. Chief source of commercial iodine is Chile saltpetre.

ion, atom or molecule which has gained or lost electrons, producing positive (cation) or negative (anion) electric charge.

Iona, island about $3\frac{1}{2}$ mi. long in Inner Hebrides, Scotland. St Columba landed AD 563, founded monastery which became centre of Celtic church. Cathedral (12th cent.) has been restored by Iona Community. Pop. (1961) 130.

Ionesco, Eugène (1912–), Fr. playwright associated with theatre of the absurd. Best known work *Rhinoceros* (1959) symbolizes conformity.

Ionia, ancient narrow region of W coast of Asia Minor, inhabited in ancient times by Ionian Greeks. Colonies founded (11th cent. BC). Cities became highly developed esp. culturally, *e.g.* Gk. poetry and literature, Ionian philosophy. Area

fell to Lydians (560– 546 BC). Lost prosperity when incorporated in Macedonian, Roman and Turkish Empires.

Ionian Islands, chain of Gk. islands in E Ionian Sea off W coast of Greece, comprising 7 large islands and many islets. Islands include Corfu, Naxos, Leucas, Ithaca, Cephalonia, Zante and Cythera. Total area: 1,117 sq. mi. All mountainous; wheat, olives and grapes grown on lower slopes.

Ionian Sea, part of Med. Sea between SE Italy and Greece.

ionization, process producing an ION. May be induced by passage of charged particles into matter, or by X or gamma rays, in which electron is rejected from atom by proton (photoelectric effect).

ionosphere, region of upper atmosphere of earth 60– 1,000 km. above ground. Gases highly ionized by solar radiation. Divided into layers, *e.g.* Kennelly-Heaviside layer; reflects low frequency radio waves.

Iowa, N Amer. Indian tribe of Siouxan linguistic stock who lived N of the Great Lakes. Subsisted on agriculture and buffalo hunting; semi-nomadic existence. Few descendants live on reservations in Kansas and Oklahoma.

Iowa, N central state of US. Area: 56,290 sq. mi.; cap. Des Moines. Plains climate characterized by marked variations of temperature. Became state (1846). Mainly agric., produces cereals, soya beans, potatoes. Livestock important. Coal deposits. Industries include food

processing, consumer goods. Pop. (1963) 2,780,000.

ipecac, 2 S Amer. shrubs, *Cephaelis ipecacuanha* and *C. acuminata.* Roots yield drug ipecac.

Iphigenia, in Gk. myth., daughter of Agamemnon. Sacrificed to Artemis at Aulis to enable becalmed Gk. fleet to sail to Trojan War. Rescued by Artemis who made her priestess at Tauris.

Iqbal, Mohammed (1873– 1938), Indian Moslem poet and political leader. Early advocate of Hindu-Moslem unity, later supported concept of separate Moslem state.

Iquaçu, Iquazu, river (500 mi.) of S America, tributary of Parana R. Famous for waterfall with single leap of 230 ft.

Iran, kingdom of SW Asia, formerly Persia. Area: 636,300 sq. mi.; cap. Teheran. Mainly agric., sheep and goats reared for wool manufacture.

Chief export crude oil. Centre of ancient PERSIA, ruled by succession of dynasties, ending with Qajar dynasty (1794– 1925) founded by Aga Mohammed Khan. Brit. and Russ. incursions ended (1946). Subsequent problems revolved around oil rights, esp. during MOSSADEGH's premiership (1951–3). Official language, Farsi; main religion, Islam. Unit of currency, rial. Pop. (1966) 26,284,000.

Dome and Minarets of the King's Mosque, Isfahan, Iran

Iranian, branch of Indo-Iranian sub-family of Indo-European languages; includes Baluchi, Persian, Saka.

Iraq [Al Jamhouriyah al Iraquia], repub. in SW Asia. Area: 173,259 sq. mi.; cap. Baghdad; chief port, Basra. Population concentrated around Tigris and Euphrates rivers. Mountainous N rich in oil; dates, cotton grown in SE. Centre of ancient

Mesopotamian civilization. Resisted Turks in 16th cent. Brit. mandate (1920–32), kingdom (1921–58) until military coup led by Kassem (overthrown 1963). Recent policy similar to other Arab nations. Main language, Arabic; religion, Islam. Pop. (1966) 8,338,000.

Ireland, island W of Great Britain divided into 2 states, 27,137 sq. mi. in Republic and 5,237 sq. mi. in NORTHERN IRELAND. Climate mild and damp, with heavy rainfall in extreme W. Restrictions on Catholics up to 1750; UK of Gt. Britain and Ireland formed (1800). R.C. emancipation (1829). Agitation against English, *e.g.* Irish Rebellion (1848). Measure of Home rule granted (1914) to S but suspended by World War 1. Irish Free State of S created 1921; 6 counties of N formed N Ireland to remain with Brit. Republic of Ireland declared sovereign independent state (1949).

Ireland, Republic of, Eire [Poblacht na H'eireann], state occupying 85% of island of IRELAND. Area: 27,137 sq. mi.; cap. Dublin; main towns, Cork, Galway. Consists of 26 counties. Became independent republic (1949). Traditional language Gaelic (Erse), still spoken esp. in W; English predominates. Main religion, R.C. Currency unit, Irish pound (Eng. pound legal tender). Pop. (1966) 2,881,000.

Irene, (*c.* 752–803), empress of Byzantium, wife of Emperor Leo IV. After his death she ruled (780–802) for her son Constantine IV. Regarded as a saint by Gk. Church for her attempts at Council of Nicaea to restore image-worship.

Ireton, Henry (1611–51), Eng. soldier. Became member of Parliamentary forces (1642). Married Cromwell's daughter Bridget (1646). Took part in battles of Edgehill (1642) and Naseby (1645). Elected M.P. (1645). Signed warrant for execution of Charles I.

iridium, rare metallic element. Occurs as an alloy of platinum. One of the heaviest elements; very hard.

Irigoyen, Hipolito (1850–1933), Argentine statesman. Pres. (1916–22, 1928–30). Introduced numerous social reforms.

iris, perennial plant of family Iridaceae, native to temp. regions. Leaves sword-shaped; flowers blue or yellow. Many varieties of bearded irises grown as garden flowers.

Irish elk, *Megaceros giganteus,* large fossil deer of Pleistocene period. Remains found in bogs, esp. near Dublin, Ireland.

Irish Free State *see* IRELAND.

Irish language *see* GAELIC.

Irish moss, carrageen moss, *Chondrus crispus,* reddish-brown perennial seaweed in N Europe and N America. Used in preparation of jellies and for making size and surgical dressings.

Irish National Theatre *see* ABBEY THEATRE.

Irish Republican Army (IRA), unofficial army actively pressing (1920s) for Irish Repub. incl. Northern Ireland. Organized by Michael Collins from rebel units dispersed after Easter Rebellion, trained in guerilla warfare and terrorism. Declared illegal (1936) by Eamon De Valéra.

Irish Sea, part of Atlantic Ocean between Gt. Britain and Ireland; 110 mi. long and 150 mi. at its widest.

iron (Fe), metallic element. Ductile, malleable, magnetic and chemically active. Compounds found in soil, plants and animals. Early iron industry used charcoal to smelt ore; today pig or cast iron made by smelting ore mixed with coal, coke and limestone. Usually converted into wrought iron or steel. Industry 1st developed where coal and iron were easily accessible, *e.g.* Staffordshire, England; W Pennsylvania, US.

Iron Age, period of industrial development using iron for tools, *etc.* Followed Bronze Age. Began *c.* 2500 BC in E, *c.* 1200 BC in Egypt and India, and *c.* 1800 BC in Europe.

Iron Cross *see* DECORATIONS.

iron lung, mechanical device for inducing respiration. Used in asphyxia, *etc.* Effects expansion and contraction of lungs by mechanical changes in air pressure *c.* 12 times per min.

Iron Mask, Man in the, mysterious Fr. prisoner brought to Bastille (1698), d. 1703. Wore black velvet mask to prevent identification. Rumours as to his identity started by Voltaire's *Age of Louis XIV* and Dumas Père's *Le Vicomte de Bragelonne.*

iron pyrites *see* PYRITES.

Ironside, William Edmund, 1st Baron (1880–1959), Brit. soldier in secret service in S Africa. Commanded forces in Archangel (1918–19), later in Persia and India. Inspector-General of Overseas Forces (1939); Commander-in-Chief Home Forces (1940).

ironstone, sedimentary rock containing over 15% iron. Composition varies between iron sulphides, carbonates, silicates and oxides. Over 2 million tons of iron ore yielded by Pre-Cambrian ironstones of L. Superior region. Precipitated in lakes and swamps (*e.g.* bog ore).

ironwood *see* BEEFWOOD.

Iroquois, 5 tribes (Mohawk, Oneida, Onondaga, Cayaga and Seneca) of Iroquois League of N Amer. Indians. Founded (*c.* 1570) by Mohawk Hiawatha and prophet Deganawidah. Struggle with Hurons for control of fur trade dominated military history of New France; also involved in Anglo-French wars. There were *c.* 17,000 Iroquois left in 1963.

Iroquoian, linguistic group of N Amer. Indians. Included Huron confederacy, Wyandot, Susquehanna, Erie and tribes of Iroquois confederacy.

Irrawaddy, largest river in Burma, with delta, *c.* 1,250 mi. long. Provides N–S transportation route and irrigation for rice growing. Most of Burma's population lives in valley. Scene of Jap.-British fighting, World War 2.

irredentism, in 19th cent. Ital. politics, referred to ambition to incorporate Ital. speaking regions left to Austria after 1866 in a united Italy. Main reason for Italy's entry into World War 1.

irrigation, artificial application of water to soils to sustain plant growth in areas of insufficient rainfall. Methods include flooding areas from canals and ditches; check flooding by watering strips of land; farrow method in which water is run between crop rows; and sprinkler systems.

Irish Moss

Islam: mosque of Mohammed Ali, Cairo

Irtysh, river (2,700 mi.) in USSR, tributary of Ob R.
Irving, Sir Henry, orig. John Henry Brodribb (1838–1905), Eng. actor and manager. Acting success in *Eugene Aram* and *Hamlet.*
Irving, Washington (1783–1859), Amer. essayist, historian and biographer. Produced the comic *History of New York* (1809) under pseudonym Diedrich Knickerbocker. Other essays and stories include *The Sketch Book of Geoffrey Crayon, Gent* (1820) and 'Rip Van Winkle' tales.
Isaac, OT Hebrew patriarch. Son of Abraham and Sarah. Husband of Rebecca, father of Esau and Jacob.
Isabella I (1451–1504), queen of Castile *see* FERDINAND AND ISABELLA.
Isabey, Jean Baptiste (1767–1855), Fr. portrait painter. Became court painter to Napoleon. Son Eugène (1803–86) was genre painter.
Isaiah, prophetic book of OT, written (800–700 BC) mainly by Isaiah. Calls Jews to repentance, foretells coming of Christ, the Redemption, and establishment of the Church.
Iseult *see* TRISTAN AND ISOLDE.
Isfahan, Esfahan, city of C Iran, traditionally dated to ancient Persian Empire. Architecturally important. Wheat, rice, tobacco and fruit produced; metal work and textile centre. Pop. (1963) 340,000.
Isherwood, Christopher William Bradshaw (1904–), Eng. writer. *The Berlin Stories* (1946) and *Prater Violet* (1945) are among his novels. Plays include *Dog Beneath the Skin* (with W. H. Auden, 1935).
Ishmael, in OT, son of Abraham and Hagar. Exiled into wilderness with his mother on account of jealousy of Abraham's wife, Sarah. Moslems honour him as Arab forefather.
Ishtar, in Assyrian and Babylonian myth., mother goddess (as such identified with Gk. Aphrodite and Roman Venus) and goddess of love, fertility, sex and war. Story of Ishtar's mourning for beloved Tammuz, her descent to underworld, consequent barrenness of earth and return of vegetation with her return constitutes vegetation myth of Asia Minor and Med. regions.
Isis, nature goddess of Egyptian religion (*c.* 1700–1100 BC). In Egyptian myth., faithful wife and sister of Osiris. Centres of worship were Memphis, Abydos, Philae. Her symbol was the cow.
Islam, Mohammedanism, religion of Moslems. Based on revelations of Mohammed the Prophet, its doctrines are based on the *Koran* (word of God) and the traditions and life (*Sunna*) of the Prophet. Concepts of god, heaven and hell akin to Jewish and Christian notions; all 3 religions having similar histories. Religious duties include sincere profession of the creed, worship 5 times daily, alms-giving, the Ramadan fast, and pilgrimage to Mecca. Moslem sects include Sunnites, Shiites, Khawarij. Faith spread rapidly after foundation (6th cent.) and today includes N Africa, the Middle East, Iran, Pakistan, Indonesia and isolated pockets of SE Europe, USSR, China and the S Pacific. There are *c.* 350 million faithful.
Islamabad *see* CHITTAGONG.
Islamic art, distinctive style in architecture, painting, *etc.*, common to Moslem countries. Mosques faced towards Mecca and were generally domed. Minarets corresponded with Christian campaniles. Horse-shoe arch dates from 8th cent. Decoration followed intricate geometrical patterns. Also evident in applied arts such as metal work, carpets, fabrics and wood carving.
island, land area surrounded by water. Greenland is largest in the world. Continental islands created by submergence of coastal highlands with only summits left above water, *e.g.* Great Britain, Jap. archipelago. Oceanic islands formed by ascent of ocean floor or by coral growth.
Isle Royale, US National Park, NW L. Superior. Comprises large island and 200 small islands. Total area: 843 sq. mi.
Ismail Pasha (1830–95), ruler of Egypt (1863–79), 1st Khedive (viceroy). Schemes, such as Suez Canal, seriously indebted Egypt and forced him to submit (1876) to Anglo-Fr. management of govt. Deposed in favour of son Tewfik Pasha.
isobar, in meteorology, line on map joining places with same atmospheric pressure at stated time. On weather maps, barometric gradient shown by distance between isobars.
Isocrates (436–338 BC), Gk. orator. Influenced by Socrates and Sophists. Polit. writings largely devoted to unity of Greece; greatest work, *Panegyricus* (380 BC) urged Athens and Sparta to unite against Persia.
isogamy, biological term to describe condition in a species where sexual cells (gametes) are alike, in contrast to male/female differentiation in higher organisms. Characterizes certain algae and protozoa.
isohyet, line on map joining places with equal depth of rainfall at any stated time.
Isolde *see* TRISTAN AND ISOLDE.
isomerism, in chemistry, relationship between 2 or more compounds that contain same atoms but differ in properties because structural arrangement differs.
isostasy, state of equilibrium between Earth's high and low land. Continental land mass, lighter in consistency of rock material, thus rises above heavier ocean floor.
isotherm, line on map joining places with same temperatures at given time. Temperature is usually reduced to mean sea level.
isotope, in chemistry, variant forms of elements that have same chem. properties but different masses. Atoms of isotopes have same number of protons in their nuclei but varying number of neutrons.
Israel [Medinat Israel], repub. in Middle East, Jewish national state, founded (1948). Area: 7,993 sq. mi.;

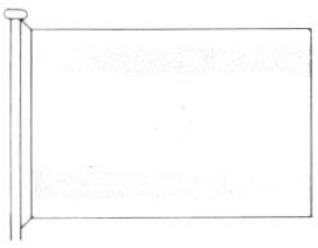

cap., Jerusalem; main cities, Tel Aviv, Jaffa, Haifa. Warm climate, agriculture important, conservation of soil and water resources; fishing widespread. Potash, bromine, phosphates, copper and salt mined; heavy industry around Haifa. Diamond cutting and polishing contributed 40% export value (1959). Threat of Arab invasions led to 1956 and 1967 wars; Israeli victories preceded UN medi-

Gardens of the Palazzo Borromeo on Isola Bella, Lake Maggiore, Northern Italy

ation. Language, Hebrew; main religion, Judaism. Unit of currency, Israeli pound. Pop. (1966) 2,657,000.

Istanbul, city and port, Turkey, built on both sides of Golden Horn, outlet of Bosporus. Name changed from Constantinople (1930). Centre of Byzantine Empire, largest city of medieval Europe. Occupied by Allies (1918–23); replaced by Ankara as cap. (1923). Many masterpieces of Turkish architecture. Pop. (1965) 1,751,000.

Istria, peninsula in Croatia, NW Yugoslavia. Area: *c.* 2,000 sq. mi.; chief town Pula. Acquired (1797) from Venice by Austria. Except for Trieste territory, peninsula given to Yugoslavia by Ital. peace treaty (1947). Produces cereals, oil, livestock; shipyards and bauxite mines.

Italian art, reached its height during ITALIAN RENAISSANCE (14th-16th cent.), moving from religious to humanistic themes and attitudes. Techniques increasingly important; use of perspective (*e.g.* Uccello), experiments with paint (*e.g.* Leonardo da Vinci), frescoes (*e.g.* Fra Angelico). Sculptors included Michelangelo, Ghiberti Donatello. Painters included Botticelli, Raphael, Titian, Tintoretto, Correggio and Veronese. In Baroque period (17th cent.) notable artists were Bernini, Caravaggio and Caracci. Subsequent schools influenced by and based on Renaissance period.

Italian language, Indo-European Romance language with *c.* 55 million speakers, mostly in Italy.

Italian literature, in earl; forms consisted of vernacular writing; by 13th cent. Dante, Petrarch and Boccaccio estab. national language and had many Renaissance imitators

inside and outside Italy. Their poetic forms and devices became common to other European literatures. Ariosto, Boiardo and Tasso were great poetic names of 16th cent., Machiavelli excelled in prose. Later writers included Manzoni and Leopardi.

Italian Renaissance, re-birth of learning, introducing classical form to painting, literature, *etc.* Stimulated by fall of Rome to the Turks (1453) and move of classical scholars to Florence, Venice and other parts of Italy. Notable figures were Leonardo da Vinci, Michelangelo, Raphael, Machiavelli and Ariosto. *See* ITALIAN ART.

italics, form of printed type first used in Venice (1500), said to be imitation of handwriting of Petrarch. Used to distinguish certain sets of words, *e.g.* book titles, foreign language words.

Italy, independent repub. of S Europe, incl. Sicily and Sardinia, excluding Vatican City state and San Marino. Area: 116,246 sq. mi.; cap. Rome; main cities, Milan, Venice, Florence, Naples. Agriculture important, producing Med. crops, mulberries, cotton

and flax; dairying important in N; sulphur from volcanic areas of Sicily, marble from Alps and hydro-electric power important. Industry includes heavy, consumer goods, chemicals. Language, Italian; state religion, R.C.; unit of currency, lira. Pop. (1966) 52,520,000.

Ithaca, one of IONIAN ISLANDS.

Itten, Johannes (1888–1967), Swiss expressionist painter, sculptor and architect. Set out principles of BAUHAUS preliminary course.

Iturbide, Agustín de, (1783–1824), Mexican revolutionary, emperor of Mexico (1822–3). Colonel in Sp. Army in Mexico, proposed that Mexico be ruled by Sp. Bourbon prince; later crowned himself emperor. Opposition headed by Santa Anna deposed him (1823).

Ivan [III] the Great (1440–1505), grand-duke of Moscow. Enlarged Muscovite territory and freed Muscovy from allegiance to GOLDEN HORDE (1480). Under Ivan, govt. became autocratic; 1st Russ. law book compiled.

Ivan [IV] the Terrible (1530–84), grand duke of Moscow (1533). Had himself crowned tsar (1547). Con-

quered Kazan (1552) and Astrakhan (1557). Introduced new code of law and estab. diplomatic and commercial relations with England. Created special corps to combat treason by terror.

Ives, Burl, orig. Icle Ivanhoe Ives (1909–   ), popular Amer. actor and folksinger. Also known as collector of folksongs and ballads.

Ives, Charles (1874–1954), Amer. organist and composer. Won Pulitzer Prize (1947) for his Third Symphony. Also wrote chamber music, suites and songs.

ivory, hard white tooth, found as elephant, walrus, *etc.,* tusks. Used for piano keys, billiard balls and decorative carvings.

Ivory Coast, Republic of the, indep. state of former Fr. West Africa. Area: 124,550 sq. mi.; cap. Abidjan. Climate ranges from semi-arid to trop. First European visit (15th cent.), with trade in gold, ivory, ostrich feathers,

and later, slaves. Independent (1960). Exports wood, coffee, cocoa, bananas, diamonds. French and *c.* 60 African languages; main religion, Animism. Unit of currency, franc. Pop. (1966) 3,920,000.

ivy, *Hedera helix,* evergreen woody shrub of family Araliaceae. Trails on ground or climbs walls and trees by tiny roots. Greenish-yellow flowers secrete much nectar. Poison ivy or poison oak, *Rhus toxicodendron,* native to N America.

Ivy League, mainly athletic association of NE US colleges (Brown, Columbia, Cornell, Dartmouth, Harvard, Pennsylvania, Princeton, Yale). Formalized as athletic group (1946).

Iwo Jima, volcanic island, largest of Volcano Is. Mt. Suribachi, extinct volcano in S. Jap. air base in World War 2, taken by US (1945).

Ixatacihuatl [Aztec: white woman], extinct volcano (17,342 ft.), near Popocatepetl, C Mexico.

Izmir, Smyrna, city and port, W Turkey, on Aegean Sea. One of largest cities in Asia Minor under Roman and Byzantine rule; fell to Ottoman Turks (1424). Gk. population exchanged for Turkish minorities in Greece (1923). Pop. (1965) 417,000.

Izvestia [Russ: news], official daily newspaper of USSR. Founded (1917) after Feb. Revolution.

J

jabiru, *Xenorhynchus asiaticus.* Austral. and E Indian stork; wingspan *c.* 5 ft., frequents swamps and coastal waters. White body, green-brown extremities, red legs; eats frogs, insects, fishes.

jacana, lilytrotter, trop. marsh bird of family Jacanidae of Old and New World with long legs and toes with flat straight claws enabling it to walk on aquatic plants, *e.g.* lily leaves. Male does most of the incubating of eggs and looks after young. Amer. jacana, *Jacana spinosa,* is maroon and black.

jacaranda, *Jacaranda acutifolia,* blue-flowered shrub of S hemisphere, growing to *c.* 20 ft. Native of Brazil; introduced into Australia.

Jackal

jack rabbit, *Lepus,* large N Amer. hare of W plains, having very long ears and long hind legs.

jackal, slender, long-legged wild dog intermediate between fox and wolf. Hunts nocturnally in packs, taking carrion or living prey and is a useful scavenger. Oriental jackal, *Canis aureus,* is found in N Africa and S Asia. Black-backed jackal, *C. mesomelus,* is hunted for its reddish fur.

jack-by-the-hedge, garlic mustard, *Alliaria officinalis,* erect biennial plant related to the cabbage; has heart-shaped leaves, small white flowers and pungent smell.

jackdaw, *Corvus monedula,* bird of family Corvidae, related to crow.

Black and nesting in groups, it is found in Europe and W Asia.

jack-in-the-pulpit, *Arisaema atrorubens,* N Amer. plant of arum family with upright club-shaped spadix and sheathing leaves, and mass of scarlet berries.

Jackson, Andrew (1767–1845), 7th US Pres. (1829–37), Democrat. Emerged as military hero of War of 1812 with victory at battle of New Orleans. Narrowly missed election as Pres. (1824), popularity in W frontier areas led to success (1828). Jacksonian democracy brought SPOILS SYSTEM, strengthening of executive power. Estranged South in conflict with Vice-Pres. John Calhoun over NULLIFICATION crisis. Second admin. dominated by fight against the Bank of the United States; Jackson successfully opposed attempts to re-charter it.

Jackson, Sir Barry Vincent (1879–1961), Brit. theatre manager; founded Malvern Festival (1929); revitalized Shakespeare Memorial Theatre, Stratford-upon-Avon (1946–8).

Jackson, Robert Houghwout (1892–1954), Associate Justice of US Supreme Court (1941–54). Served as negotiator in Allied agreement on trials of war criminals (1945–6).

Jackson, Thomas Jonathan ('Stonewall') (1824–63), Confederate general, most renowned after R. E. Lee. Victor of Shenandoah Valley campaign and 2nd battle of BULL RUN. Mortally wounded at Chancellorsville.

Jacob, Jewish patriarch of OT. Twin of Esau whom he cheated of his birthright; son of Isaac and Rebecca. His 12 sons originated the 12 tribes of Israel.

Jacob, François (1920–), Fr. biologist. With A. Lwoff and J. Monod, awarded Nobel Prize for Physiology and Medicine (1965) for work in genetics.

Jacob, Max (1876–1944), Fr. writer and painter. Forerunner of Surrealism. Works include novel *Saint-Matorél* (1909) and prose poetry *Cornet à dés* (1917).

Jacobean, term applied to architecture and decoration characteristic of reign of James I; basically Perpendicular style with neo-classical (Renaissance) additions. Furniture massive and carved; houses panelled with ornamental plaster-work.

Jacobean drama, plays written in England during reign of James I. Comedies generally either satirical or sentimental; tragedies either tragicomedies or characterized by violent, often unnatural actions and passions;

Jackdaw

much use made of revenge themes. Playwrights included Webster, Ford, Middleton.

Jacobi, Abraham (1830–1919), Amer. physician. With his wife **Mary Putnam Jacobi** (1842–1906), he pioneered pediatrics in New York.

Jacobin, Fr. revolutionary polit. club. In early days, included GIRONDISTS; led by Mirabeau, Sieyès and Lafayette. Became increasingly radical and, under Robespierre, instituted REIGN OF TERROR. Influence ended by Robespierre's fall and execution (1794).

Jacobites, adherents of STUART claimants of Eng. throne after 1688; sought restoration of James II. Instrumental in rebellion of 1715, supporting James Edward Stuart; later defeated at Culloden (1745) supporting Charles Stuart, last serious Jacobite Pretender.

Jacob's ladder, blue-flowered perennial plant of Polemoniaceae family. Species found in Europe and N America.

Jacquard, Joseph Marie (1752–1834), Fr. mechanic. invented Jacquard loom, first to weave figured patterns.

Jacquerie, Fr. peasants' uprising (1358), begun in Normandy. Suppressed by Charles II of Navarre with great brutality.

jade, silicate minerals used as gem, ranging in colour from white to green. Prized in Far East, form either nephrite or jadeite.

jadeite, pyroxene mineral, less common form of jade. Hardness makes it difficult to reshape. Green shades most valuable.

jaeger, Arctic skua, rapacious bird of family Stercorariidae. Pursues weaker birds to make them drop prey.

Jael, OT Jewish heroine, contemporary of Deborah. She killed Canaanite general Sisera.

Jaffa *see* TEL AVIV.

Jack Rabbit

A Jainist temple, Khajurho, Central India

jaguar, S and C Amer. cat, *Panthera onca,* with black spots and yellow coat. Frequents wooded river banks, fiercest S Amer. carnivore.

jai alai, pelota vasca, Sp. Basque game similar to handball in 3-walled auditorium (*fronton*). Popular in other countries.

Jainism, Indian religion, arising (6th cent. BC) with Buddhism as protest against Hinduism. Doctrine based on belief in universal eternity; soul retains identity through transmigration and eventually attains NIRVANA. Adhered to by *c.* 1½ million Indians.

Jaipur, former princely state, part of Rajasthan (since 1949), India. Cattle-raising area; industry includes cotton textiles, pottery. Cap. Jaipur, commercial centre, noted for jewellery.

Jakarta *see* DJAKARTA.

jalop, cathartic drug obtained from tuberous roots of Mexican *Exogonium purga.*

Jamaica, island country in Caribbean Sea, Brit. Commonwealth member. Area: 4,411 sq. mi.; cap. Kingston. Primarily agric. economy, products include fruits, spices, coffee. Tourism important. Discovered by Columbus (1494); settled by Spanish (1509–1670), when ceded to Britain. Population, largely Negro, suffers from overcrowding and unemployment. Agitation led to internal autonomy (1953), independence (1962). Main language, English; unit of currency, pound. Pop. (1965) 1,745,000.

James, NT epistle ascribed to St James. Addressed to all the Christian churches, advocating practical morality.

James I (1394–1437), king of Scotland (1424–37), son of Robert III.

Held by English (1406–24); returned to suppress uprising of Scot. nobles, group of which murdered him.

James II (1430–60), king of Scotland (1437–60), son of James I. Douglas family acted as regents during his minority. Accidentally killed during invasion of England in Wars of the Roses.

James III (1451–88), king of Scotland (1460–88), son of James II. Troubled reign ended in death at hands of rebellious nobles.

James IV (1473–1513), king of Scotland (1488–1513), son of James III. Married Margaret Tudor, through whom later Stuarts claimed Eng. throne. Prosperous rule, invasion of England led to death at Battle of Flodden.

James V (1512–42), king of Scotland (1513–42), son of James IV, father of Mary, Queen of Scots. Died shortly after beginning of war with England.

James I (1566–1625), king of Great Britain (1603–25). Succeeded to Scot. throne (1567) on abdication of mother, MARY, QUEEN OF SCOTS. Allied himself with predecessor, Elizabeth of England; accepted mother's execution (1587). Authorized translation of Bible. Reliance on incompetent favourites (such as VILLIERS), inconsistency of position on Catholic-Protestant conflict and claims of divine right were unpopular. N Amer. colonization begun during his reign.

James II (1633–1701), king of Great Britain (1685–8), brother of Charles II. Converted to Catholicism, exiled (1678–80); Parl. attempts to exclude him from succession failed. Alienated subjects by advocating Catholic faith; birth of heir led to GLORIOUS REVOLUTION of 1688 and flight to France. Defeated in Ireland (1690), trying to regain throne from William III.

James, Henry (1843–1916), Anglo-Amer. novelist. Works, reflecting contrast between sophisticated Europeans and less cultured Americans, include *Daisy Miller* (1879), *The Portrait of a Lady* (1881) and *The Ambassadors* (1903). Best known short story, 'The Turn of the Screw'. Psychological character studies widened scope of novel.

James, Jesse Woodson (1847–82) Amer. outlaw. With brother [**Alexander**] **Frank[lin]** James (1843–1915), led gang of robbers, who terrorized midwest in 1870s.

James, Saint, NT apostle. Son of Zebedee and Salome, brother of St John. Beheaded by Herod Agrippa. Patron saint of Spain.

James, Thomas (*c.* 1593–1635), Eng. explorer and navigator. Explored James Bay, Canada (1631) while searching for North West Passage.

James, William (1842–1910), Amer. psychologist and philosopher, brother of Henry James. Laid foundations for Amer. experimental psychology in *Principles of Psychology* (1890). Philosophical works include *Will to Believe* (1897), *Varieties of Religious Experience* (1902) and *Pragmatism* (1907).

James Bay, large SE extension of Hudson Bay, between Quebec and Ontario Provs., Canada; *c.* 300 mi long [N to S] and up to 150 mi. wide; contains Akimiski Island and many smaller ones; trapping, hunting, fishing in surrounding area; 1st explored by T. James (1631).

Jameson, Sir Leander Starr (1853–1917), Brit. colonial administrator. Led unauthorized Jameson Raid (1895) into Boer colony of Transvaal. Later premier of Cape Colony (1904–8).

Jamestown, 1st permanent Eng. settlement in America. Founded (1607) on peninsula, now an island in James R., Virginia, as trading post. Little remained by late 19th cent.

Jammu and Kashmir *see* KASHMIR.

Jamshedpur, industrial city in Bihar prov., E India. One of largest steel centres of Orient. Pop. (1965) 376,000.

Jan Mayen, island in Arctic Ocean, E of Greenland. Site of dormant volcano. Has meteorological observatory and radio station. Discovered (1607) by Hudson.

Janáček, Leos (1854–1928), Czech. composer. Works include rhapsody, *Taras Bulba,* and operas, incl. *Jenufa.*

Janet, Pierre (1859–1947), Fr. psychologist, founder of automatic psychology. Made important contributions to use of hypnosis and

Jaguar

knowledge of mental pathology. Works include *Les Obsessions et la Psychasthénie* (1903).

Janissaries, élite Ottoman Turkish army corps. Orig. comprised Christian hostages and prisoners. Liquidated by Mahmud II (1826).

Jansenism, doctrine emanating from works of Dutch theologian Cornelius Jansen (1585–1638). Advocated austerity; belief in predestination similar to Calvinists', despite adherence to Catholic Church.

Janus, in Roman religion, orig. one of principal gods. Regarded as god of doorways, looking inward and outward. Thus often represented with 2 faces. Developed into god of beginnings (January named after him). Doors of temple only closed in peace time.

Japan [**Nippon Koku: Land of the Rising Sun**], empire, archipelago off E coast of Asia. Area: 142,741 sq. mi.; cap. Tokyo; other main cities,

Osaka, Kyoto, Yokohama. Principal islands: Honshu, Kyushu, Shikoku, Hokkaido. Unstable mountainous region produces volcanic activity (FUJIYAMA), earthquakes, typhoons. Widespread farming, esp. rice, fruit, raw silk; industry characterized by small consumer enterprise, also heavy, *e.g.* shipbuilding. Empire dates from 7th cent. BC. Heavy Buddhist influence by 9th cent.; SHOGUN (warrior families) dynasties estab. 12th cent. European influence resisted (1630s) to regain polit. stability. Imperial authority restored by civil war (1871) and Westernization begun, abolishing class system and promoting indust. development. Successful wars against China (1894–5) and Russia (1904–5); 2nd Chinese war merged with World War 2 after Jap. attack on PEARL HARBOR (1941); surrendered after atom bombs dropped on Hiroshima and Nagasaki (1945). New constitution curtailed imperial power (1946). Subsequent problems revolved around Amer. influence, esp. presence of US military bases. Language, Japanese; religions, Shinto, Buddhism. Unit of currency, yen. Pop. (1966) 99,180,000.

Japan, Sea of, body of water between Japan and Korea. Connected with E China Sea in S.

Japanese, language of Old World,

Japanese rice fields

only known member of its family, with over 100 million speakers in Japan and Lynkyn Islands.

Japanese beetle, insect, *Popillia japonica*, related to scarab beetle. Discovered in US (1916), destroys fruit.

Japanese drama, lyric genre, *No*, symbolic and restrained, originated at ancient religious festivals. Surviving *No* plays written primarily in 15th cent. Comic interlude, *kyogen*, involving dialogue but not music, was simultaneous development. More popular *kabuki* (17th cent.) allowed freer presentation.

Japanese music, much of it borrowed, esp. from China, scales are 5-toned. Ancient forms of sacred music include *gagaku* and *kagura*; secular music dates from 16th cent. with introduction of *samisen* (type of lute). Other instruments include *koto* (zither). No harmony in Western sense of term; rhythm provided by drums.

Japheth, in OT, son of Noah. Descendants were to occupy 'isles of the Gentiles', usually taken to mean Med. Europe and Asia Minor.

japonica, flowering quince, spiky Asiatic shrub, *Chaenomeles*. Fruit sometimes used in preserves.

jarrah, *Eucalyptus marginata*, large Austral. eucalyptus tree. Wood used extensively in flooring, fencing, *etc.* Resists decay.

Jarvis Bay, coastal Federal Territory of Australia, 123 mi. E of Canberra. Fine natural harbour.

jasmine, genus of scented flowering shrubs of Asia, S America and Australia. Popular garden plant; oil used in perfume manufacture.

Jason, in Gk. myth., leader of the ARGONAUTS, sailed to recover Golden Fleece in order to regain kingdom of Iolcus from Pelias, Secured the fleece from Aeëtes, King of Colchis, whose daughter MEDEA helped Jason and returned with him.

jasper, impure form of an opaque, crypto-crystalline silica, usually red or brown.

Jasper National Park, in Rocky Mts., W Alberta, Canada. Area: 4,200 sq. mi.; founded 1907. Noted for spectacular mountain scenery.

Jaspers, Karl (1883–1969), Ger. philosopher. Existentialist works exalt love as highest expression of life; include *Man in the Modern Age* (1931) and *Reason and Existence* (Eng. tr. 1956).

jaundice, icterus, condition characterized by yellowness of skin and excretions. Caused by bile pigments of blood or diseases of liver. Infectious hepatitis is most common form.

jaunting car, low-set, open, 2-wheeled horse-drawn Irish vehicle, with side seats back-to-back.

Jaurès, Jean Léon (1859–1914), Fr. Socialist politician, journalist and pacifist. Radical deputy (1883–7, 1893–8, 1902–14). Supported Dreyfus. Attempted to avert outbreak of World War 1; assassinated by nationalist. Author of *Histoire Socialiste de la Révolution Française*.

Jasper

Java, Djava, 5th largest island of Malay Archipelago, comprising 9% total area and 70% pop. of Republic of Indonesia. Area *c.* 50,000 sq. mi.; cap, Djakarta. Broad coastal strips with central volcanic mountain range. Hindu traders known from 1st cent. AD; subject to Portugal (16th cent.) and Holland until part of Indonesia (1946). Soil fertile, climate trop. Land forested; sugar, tobacco, tea, coffee, grown. Pop. (1966) 73,150,000.

Java man *see* PITHECANTHROPUS.

Java Sea, shallow, trop. sea of Indonesia with many islands. Scene of Jap. victory over Allied fleets (1942) resulting in Japan's control of E Indian waters.

Javanese, language of Malayo-Polynesian family with *c.* 50 million speakers, mostly on island of Java.

javelin, throwing-spear formerly about 6 ft. long, with range of *c.* 40 yd. Modern javelin is 8 ft. 6 in. long and is thrown as field event at athletic meetings, *e.g.* Olympic Games.

jay, gaily coloured bird of crow family. European jay, *Garrulus glandarius,* has blue-black wings and pinkish-brown body. Blue jay, *Cyanocitta cristata,* of US, and Stellers jay, *C. stelleri,* have blue plumage. Eats nuts and grubs.

Jay's Treaty (1794), Anglo-Amer. treaty authorizing joint commission to settle boundary disputes between Brit. colonies (now Canada) and US.

Signed for US by John Jay, whose name it bears.

jazz, folk music style of Amer. Negro origin. Characteristics include syncopation, beat and improvisation. Spiritual and BLUES music were 1st expression of jazz but later extended to dance music and marches. Has also influenced such composers as Stravinsky and Dvořák. Saxophone became predominant solo instrument.

Jeanne d'Arc *see* JOAN OF ARC.

Jeanneret, Charles Édouard, known as **Le Corbusier** (1887–1965), Swiss architect. Radical approach to aesthetic and technical problems in building, *e.g.* mass-produced housing in Citrohan model (1945). Major works include chapel at Ronchamp and UN building, New York. Writings influenced 20th cent. architecture, *e.g. Towards a New Architecture* (1927).

Jeans, Sir James Hopwood (1877–1946), Brit. philosopher, physicist and mathematician. Developed tidal theory of origin of solar system with H. A. Jeffreys. Works include *The Universe Around Us* (1929) and *Physics and Philosophy* (1942).

Jedda, Jiddah, chief port of Hejaz, Saudi Arabia, on Red Sea. Port of Mecca. Pop. *c.* 200,000.

jeep, 4-wheel drive military motor vehicle; ¼ ton carrying capacity; used for reconnaissance, passengers, light cargo; named after initials G.P., 'General Purpose' vehicle.

Jeffers, Robinson (1887–1962), Amer. poet. Work stressed modern man's introverted alienation from natural world, *e.g. Tamar and Other Poems* (1924). Stage adaptation of *Medea* (1947) successful in New York.

Jefferson, Thomas (1743–1826), 3rd US Pres. (1801–9), Republican. Author of Declaration of Independence (1776), and leader of agrarian Democrats of Virginia. As Sec. of State (1790–3) in Washington's cabinet, opposed centralizing Federalists under ALEXANDER HAMILTON, whose support (1800) gave Jefferson presidency after tie with AARON BURR had sent vote to House of Representatives. Admin. highlighted by LOUISIANA PURCHASE (1803).

Jeffreys, George, 1st Baron Jeffreys of Wem (*c.* 1648–89), Eng. chief justice notorious for harshness at trials after Monmouth's Rebellion (1685), known as Bloody Assizes. Appointed lord chancellor by James II.

Jehoiakim, in OT, king of Judah (*c.* 609–*c.* 597 BC). Re-established idol worship, burned book of Jeremiah's prophecies. Died before capture of Jerusalem by Nebuchadnezzar.

Jehovah's Witnesses, religious sect founded in US (1872) by Charles Taze Russell, orig. known as Russellites. Teachings centre on 2nd coming

The Battle of Jena, Napoleon at the head of his troops, from the famous painting by Thévenin

of Christ. Members refuse to participate in warfare or government. Publish pamphlets *The Watch Tower* and *Awake.*

Jehu, in OT, king of Israel (*c.* 841–*c.* 814 BC). Anointed by Elisha, murdered kings of Israel and Judah. Recklessness with which he drove his chariot is proverbial.

Jellicoe, John Rushworth, 1st Earl (1859–1935), Brit. admiral; commanded Grand Fleet (1914–16), victorious in Battle of JUTLAND (1916); 1st Sea Lord (1916–17); admiral of the fleet (1919); Gov.-General of New Zealand (1920–4).

jellyfish, gelatinous umbrella-shaped, MEDUSA stage of certain marine coelenterates. Tentacles with stinging cells used for capturing victims. Common jellyfish, *Aurelia aurita,* transparent except for light purple markings.

Jena and Auerstadt, Battles of, confrontations between Prussian and Fr. forces (1806). Victories for Napoleon's army were decisive in defeat of Prussia.

Jenghiz Khan *see* GENGHIS KHAN.

Jenkins' Ear, War of (1739–41), struggle between England and Spain which merged into the war of the AUSTRIAN SUCCESSION. Robert Jenkins, a master mariner, claimed to have had his ear cut off by the Spanish (1731) and roused public opinion so that Walpole was forced to declare war.

Jenkinson, Robert Banks, 2nd Earl of Liverpool (1770–1828), Brit. Tory politician. Supported Wellington's campaign in Spain while in War Office (1809–12). As P.M. (1812–27), instrumental in Napoleon's deportation to St Helena. Admin. saw adoption of repressive measures against internal disorders.

Jenner, Edward (1749–1823), Eng. physician. Developed smallpox vaccination (1796), laying foundation of modern immunology.

Jenner, Sir William (1815–98), Eng. physician and anatomist, 1st in England to distinguish between typhus and typhoid fever (1847).

Jensen, Johannes Vilhelm (1873–1950), Danish poet and novelist. Awarded Nobel Prize for Literature (1944) for the epic *Den Lange Rejse* (*The Long Journey*).

Jenson or **Janson, Nicholas** (d. *c.* 1481), Fr. printer. Worked with Gutenberg in Venice; known as introducer of Roman type.

jerboa, fawn-coloured jumping rodent of family Dipodidae of mouse group. Found in sandy semi-desert regions of the Old World. Most common is

Egyptian jerboa, *Jaculus jaculus.*

Jeremiah, prophetic book of OT. Tells story of priest Jeremiah (*fl.* 600 BC), imprisoned for foretelling fall of Jerusalem; released after prophecy fulfilled (586 BC).

Jerez de la Frontera, city in Cádiz prov., Andalusia, SW Spain. Lies on fertile plain of Guadalquivir R.; sherry named after town. Pop. (1960) 130,900.

Jericho, village in disputed territory of Jordan R. valley. Capture by Joshua marked Hebrew arrival in Canaan (the Promised Land); kingdom of Judah fell with capture by Babylonia. Excavations reveal walled city in existence *c.* 7000 BC.

Jeroboam I (*c.* 932–*c.* 915 BC), king of N Israel following breach with Rehoboam, son of Solomon. Fervent supporter of IDOLATRY, set up golden images at Dan and Bethel.

Jerome, Saint, orig. Sophronius Eusebius Hieronymus (*c.* 340–420), Christian scholar (ordained 379) who translated Bible into Latin (*The Vulgate*); 1st to distinguish apocryphal books of Bible.

Jerome, Jerome K[lapka] (1859–1927), Eng. author; best known for *Three Men in a Boat* (1889). Other works include the play *The Passing of the Third Floor Back* (1907).

jersey, machine-knitted or woven stretchy fabric. Orig. hand-knitted in Is. of Jersey, UK, for fishermen's woollen top garment.

Jersey City, port on W bank of Hudson R. in NE New Jersey, US. Access to New York City by tunnel and ferry, important rly. and commercial centre. Industry includes steel, chemicals, food processing. Founded 1836. Pop. (1960) 276,101.

Jerusalem, cap. of modern Israel, ancient city of Palestine. Called the Holy City, site of sacred places of Judaism, Christianity and Islam. Captured by David (*c.* 1000 BC), became national centre for Jews; after Roman occupation, thrived until capture by Arabs (637). Fanatic vandalism led to CRUSADES, but after 1187 fell to Turks. Brit. mandate estab. (1917). Became cap. (1950) of newly-created state of Israel; Old City in Jordanian hands until 1967 Arab-Israeli war, now occupied by Israeli troops. Pop. (1964 est.) 240,000.

Jerusalem artichoke *see* ARTICHOKE.

Jervis, John, 1st Earl of St Vincent (1735–1823), Brit. admiral. Commander of fleet in Med. in 1790s, victorious against Spain off Cape St Vincent with help of Nelson. First Lord of the Admiralty (1801–6).

The Chapel of Ronchamp by Le Corbusier (C. E. Jeanneret)

Jespersen, Otto (1860–1943), Danish linguist. Helped revolutionize language teaching in Europe; distinguished phoneticist.

Jesse, in OT, father of David. Name later symbolized royal line. Represented by medieval artists as source of family tree of Jesus.

Jesuits *see* JESUS, SOCIETY OF.

Jesus [Gk: saviour] **Christ** [Gk: anointed] (*c.* 4 BC–AD 29 or 30), central figure of CHRISTIANITY. According to NT gospels of Matthew, Mark, Luke and John, b. in Bethlehem to Mary, wife of Joseph of Nazareth. A Jew, He lived at a crucial time in Jewish history. People of Galilee and Judaea were eager for deliverance from Roman domination. After baptism by His cousin, John the Baptist, Jesus became a wandering teacher accompanied by band of disciples. Attracted great crowds with His preaching and living of the principles He taught. In Jerusalem for the Passover, He was betrayed by one of disciples, Judas Iscariot. Arrested in Garden of Gethsemane, tried and convicted of blasphemy by eccles. court. Roman gov., yielding to popular opinion, sent Jesus to His death by crucifixion. After 3 days, He rose from the dead. Book of Acts relates how, 40 days later, in the sight of His disciples, He ascended to Heaven.

Jesus, Society of, Jesuits, R.C. religious order founded (*c.* 1534) by IGNATIUS OF LOYOLA. Approved by

Jay

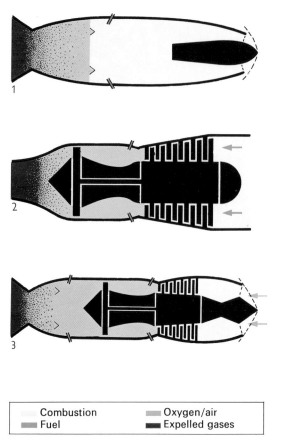

| Combustion | Oxygen/air |
| Fuel | Expelled gases |

Three types of jet engine: 1. Ramjet. The injected fuel burns with the air driven in through the front of the motor. 2. Turbo-jet. A compressor forces the air, by means of the blades on the turbine, into the combustion chamber. 3. Turbo-jet with re-heat. The flow of gas is accelerated still further by an additional injection of fuel in front of the turbine

pope (1540). Original aims were educ. and missionary work and suppression of heresy. Polit. involvement (18th cent.) resulted in expulsion from France, Portugal and Spain and suppression by pope (1773). Revived (1814), it has since been expelled from many countries of Europe and America.

jet, black variety of brown coal, compact in texture. May be polished and used in jewellery.

jet propulsion, forward movement achieved by reaction caused by expanding gases ejected rearwards. Jet aircraft used in World War 2; subsequently greatly developed. Principle also applied to rocket propulsion.

jet stream, high altitude (c. 20,000 ft.) strong, generally W winds concentrated in Earth's upper troposphere. Associated with DEPRESSION fronts.

Jevons, W[illiam] Stanley (1835–82), Eng. economist. Developed theory that value determined by utility in *Theory of Political Economy* (1871). First to apply mathematical reasoning to economics.

jewfish *see* GROUPERS.

Jewish Holy days, traditionally celebrated days in Jewish calendar. Include Day of Atonement (*Yom Kippur*) in Jewish New Year (usually late Sept. in modern calendar), Passover and Pentecost.

Jews, descendants of tribes of Israel and adherents of JUDAISM. In OT, lineage traced from Abraham and 12 tribes of Israel; orig. settled in Egypt; persecution by the Pharaoh prompted Exodus led by Moses. Settled in Canaan under Saul; 1st temple built by Solomon. Kingdom then split into Israel and Judah. Temple destroyed by Babylonians (586 BC), rebuilt (516

BC). Independence regained under Maccabees, Jerusalem destroyed by Romans (AD 70). After fall of Roman Empire, Jews appeared in W Europe but from 12th–19th cent. exiled from many countries. Capitalism and European revolutions improved conditions; emancipation led to cultural assimilation and ZIONISM. Persecution, beginning in Russia (1881) gradually diminished until rise of Nazism when 6 million exterminated before and during World War 2. Refuge sought in Palestine, resulting in formation of Jewish state of Israel (1948) by UN.

Jew's ear, *Auriculoria auricula,* edible fungus with gelatinous fairly tough flesh and translucent appearance. Grows on branches esp. elder.

Jex-Blake, Sophia Louisa (1840–1912), Brit. doctor largely responsible for acceptance of women into medical profession. Secured legal right to practise in Britain (1877). Founded medical school for women in Edinburgh (1886).

Jezebel, in OT, Phoenician wife of Ahab, King of Israel; introduced Baal-worship into Israel. Name used to denote wicked woman.

Jidda *see* JEDDA.

Jim Crow, subject of minstrel act by Thomas D. Rice in Washington, US (1833). Came to be used as disparaging term for Negroes, and to describe laws or practices designed to segregate or discriminate against them.

Jiménez, Juan Ramon (1881–1958), Sp. poet whose works include *Sonetos Espirituales* and *Platero and I.* Awarded Nobel Prize for Literature (1956).

Jinnah, Mohammed Ali (1876–1948), Indian politician and Moslem leader. Pres. of Moslem League (1916, 1920, 1934–48); 1st Gov.-General of newly created state of Pakistan (1947–8).

jiujitsu *see* JU-JITSU.

Jivaro, several S Amer. Indian tribes of E Andes of Ecuador, often known as Montaña area. Renowned for custom of head-hunting. Approx. $\frac{2}{3}$ killed in revolts and tribal wars after contact with Europeans (16th cent.). Spread of Quechua language and 19th cent. rubber boom almost completely destroyed aboriginal culture.

Joab, in OT, nephew of David, whose armies he commanded. Responsible for deaths of Abner, Absalom and Amasa. Executed by Solomon.

Joachim, Joseph (1831–1907), Hungarian violinist; founded Joachim Quartet (1869). Renowned for interpretation, esp. of Beethoven and Brahms.

Joachim, Saint, traditionally father of Virgin Mary and husband of St Anne.

Joan of Arc (*c.* 1412–31), Fr. saint and national heroine. Claimed to hear voices of St Catherine, St Margaret and St Michael urging her to aid Dauphin in his struggle against the English. Dressed in men's clothes, she led army which raised siege of Orléans (1429). This led to coronation of Dauphin as Charles VII at Rheims. Captured at Compiègne (1430); tried and condemned by English as heretic and sorceress; burnt at stake (1431). Canonized (1920); feast day, 30 May.

Joanna the Mad (1479–1555), Sp. queen of Castile and Leon (1504–55), wife of PHILIP I. After king's death, became insane and never ruled.

Job, poetical book of OT. Tells of revelation to Job that man cannot comprehend the wisdom of God.

Jodrell Bank, site in Cheshire, England, of gigantic radio-telescope of great precision, with world's largest fully steerable antenna.

Joel, prophetic book of OT predicting famine and desolation for Judah, but promising forgiveness of God upon repentance of sin.

Joffre, Joseph Jacques Césaire (1852–1931), marshal of France. Commanded Fr. troops on Western Front (1914–16). Chairman of Allied War Council (1916–18).

Johannesburg, city of S Transvaal, largest city of South Africa. Founded (1886) as gold-mining centre. Now centre of commerce, industry, transportation. Pop. (1963) 1,224,000.

John, 3 epistles of NT, ascribed to apostle John; homilies setting forth the nature of Christian fellowship.

Statue of Joan of Arc, Orléans

John XXIII, orig. Angelo Roncalli (1881–1963), pope (1958–63). Became patriarch of Venice and cardinal (1953). As pope, showed deep concern for church reform and promotion of world peace. Convened Second VATICAN COUNCIL (1962–5).

John (1167–1216), king of England (1199–1216); often known as John Lackland. Son of HENRY II, he succeeded Richard I whose throne he had previously attempted to seize. Unsuccessful invasion of France (1214). Forced to sign MAGNA CARTA (1215). Succeeded by son HENRY III.

John [III] Sobieski (1624–96), king of Poland (1674–96). Led successful campaigns against Turks (1673, 1683) briefly restoring national prestige.

John [II] the Perfect (1455–95), king of Portugal (1481–95). With Spain, concluded Treaty of Tordesillas (1494), establishing limits of each country in its colonizing.

John, Augustus Edwin (1878–1961), Eng. painter and etcher, noted for portraiture. Portraits include Queen Elizabeth II, G. B. Shaw, Lloyd George.

John, Gospel according to Saint, book of NT relating events of Jesus' ministry and interpreting truth of His message.

John Birch Society, extremely conservative Amer. anti-Communist organization (founded 1958). Named after John Birch, OSS captain killed by Chinese Communists (1945).

John Bull, used to describe the typical Englishman or the Eng. national character. Name comes from the *History of John Bull* (pub. 1712) by John Arbuthnot.

John Chrysostom, Saint (345–407), saint of E Orthodox Church. Spent 10 yr. in the desert, before being appointed bishop of Constantinople (398). Deposed by Empress Eudoxia and Theophilus, bishop of Alexandria (403), later recalled. Exiled by Arcadius.

John Dory, dory, *Zeus faber,* flat, almost oval-shaped fish of family Zeidae; frequents Med. and Atlantic coasts of Europe. Esteemed in Europe as food.

John Henry, Amer. legendary hero, subject of many Negro ballads.

John of Gaunt, Duke of Lancaster (1340–99), 4th son of Edward III of England. His son by 1st marriage became Henry IV. Fought in Hundred Years War. Married daughter of Pedro the Cruel of Castile. Ruled England for a time as viceroy to Edward III. Fought against John I

Johannesburg

(1386–8) over claim to throne of Castile.

John of Lancaster, Duke of Bedford (1389–1435), regent of England and France. Son of Henry IV of England. Assumed regency on death of Henry V (1422). Administered France until siege of Orléans (1428–9) which marked appearance of JOAN OF ARC and decline of Eng. supremacy.

John of the Cross, Saint, orig. Juan de Yepis y Álvarez (1542–91), Sp. mystic and poet. Entered Carmelite order (1563); ordained (1567). Imprisoned (1577–8) for attempts to reform order. Works include *Ascent of Mount Carmel* and *Cantico Espiritual.*

John o' Groat's, place on N coast of Caithness, Scotland, $1\frac{1}{2}$ mi. W of Duncansby Head. Erroneously said to be most N point of UK.

John the Baptist, Christian saint, cousin of Jesus, son of Zacharias and Elizabeth. Led ascetic life preaching; baptized and recognized Jesus as the Messiah. Imprisoned and executed by Herod (*c.* AD 38).

Johns Hopkins University (1870), Baltimore, Md., US. Privately financed Amer. university which experimentally stressed graduate research from its founding. Founded (1867) by Johns Hopkins.

Johnson, Amy (1904–41), Brit. airwoman, 1st to make a solo flight from England to Australia (1930). Killed when flying as a member of Air Transport Auxiliary.

Johnson, Andrew (1808–75), 17th US Pres. (1865–9), Democrat. One of few party members to support Lincoln; elected Vice-Pres. (1865), becoming Pres. upon Lincoln's death. De-

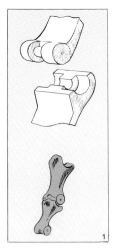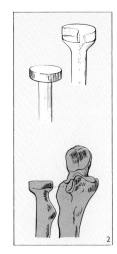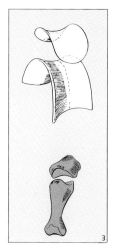

Joints (anatomical) : 1. Hinge joint 2. Pivot joint 3. Saddle joint 4. Ball-and-socket joint

nounced by Republicans for Reconstruction Program; almost impeached by Senate for trying to remove Sec. of War, EDWIN STANTON (1868).

Johnson, Hewlett (1874–1966), Eng. theologian, Dean of Manchester (1924–31); Dean of Canterbury (1931–63). Known as the 'Red Dean'; published books on Communism in Russia and China.

Johnson, James Weldon (1871–1938), Amer. Negro author. A founder of National Association for the Advancement of Colored People. Wrote *Autobiography of an Ex-Coloured Man* (1912).

Johnson, Lyndon Baines (1908–), 35th US Pres. (1963–9), Democrat. Achieved power in US Senate as party's majority leader (1955–60). Elected Vice-Pres. (1960), succeeded

The ruins of Petra, Jordan

to presidency on death of John Kennedy. Legislative record of social reform offset by involvement in Vietnamese war and racial unrest.

Johnson, Martin Elmer (1884–1937), Amer. explorer and author. Photographed wild life on expeditions to South Sea Is., Borneo and Africa.

Johnson, Pauline (1862–1913), Canadian poet, born of Indian-English parentage. Works include *The White Wampum* (1895) and *Flint and Feather* (1912).

Johnson, Samuel (1709–84), Eng. critic, poet and essayist. Wrote *A Dictionary of the English Language* (1755), pamphlets, travel accounts, lives of poets, sermons and prayers. In 1763, met James Boswell who wrote his biography. Tour of Hebrides produced *A Journey to the Western Islands of Scotland* (1775). *Lives of Poets* (1779–81) was his last major work.

Johnson, Walter Perry (1887–1946), Amer. baseball player. Acknowledged as fastest pitcher of all, holds strikeout records. Won 414 games while pitching with Washington Senators.

Johnson, Sir William (1715–74), Brit. colonial official in America and superintendent of Indian affairs. Defeated French at Lake George (1755), thus preventing them gaining N colonies.

Johnston, Joseph Eggleston (1807–1901) US Confederate general. Victor of 1st battle of Bull Run. Lost Vicksburg (1863) and Atlanta campaigns.

Johnston Island, in C Pacific, *c.* 760 mi. SW of Honolulu. Discovered by British (1807); claimed by US (1858). Became US naval base (1941).

Nuclear tests carried out in area (1962).

Johore, state of Malaysia, SE Asia, or S of Malay Peninsula. Area: 7,321 sq mi.; cap. Johore Bahru. Largely low-lying with C upland; produce rubber, palm-oil. Part of Federation o Malaya until 1963; ruled by sultan accepted Brit. protectorate (1914) Pop. (1964) 1,126,000.

joint, place of union between 2 bones esp. one which admits of more or less motion in one or both bones; joints are particularly susceptible to diseases such as arthritis and gout.

joint snake *see* GLASS SNAKE.

joints, in woodwork, the fastening together of pieces of timber in a variety of ways to withstand the stress to which the finished structure will be subjected.

Joliot-Curie, Frédéric (1900–58), Fr. scientist. With his wife **Irène Curie** (1897–1956), daughter of Pierre and Marie Curie, shared Nobel Prize for Chemistry (1935) for work on radioactive elements.

Jolson, Al, orig. Asa Yoelson (1886–1950), Amer. singer. First success (1909) in San Francisco singing 'Mammy' in blackface. Appeared in *The Jazz Singer,* 1st sound film.

Jonah, prophetic book of OT relating fictitious story of Jonah's missionary journey. A parable to remind Jews of their mission to save the Gentiles by proclamation of the truth.

Jonathan, in OT, eldest son of Saul and friend of David. Killed with his father, at battle of Mt. Gilboa against the Philistines.

Jones, Casey, orig. John Luther Jones (1863–1900), Amer. folk hero of many songs and ballads. Locomotive engineer who saved passengers in crash of *Cannon Ball* express (1900), but was himself killed.

Jones, Sir Edward Burne- *see* BURNE-JONES, SIR EDWARD.

Jones, Inigo (1573–1652), Eng. architect. Studied Renaissance buildings of Palladio in Italy and introduced classic architecture of late Renaissance and Georgian periods in England. Finest work, Royal Banqueting Hall in Whitehall, London.

Jones, James (1921–), Amer. novelist. First book was *From Here to Eternity* (1951), later books include *Some Came Running* (1957) and *The Thin Red Line* (1962).

Jones, John Paul (1747–92), Amer. naval pirate and hero. Raided Brit. coasts (1778–9) in *Ranger.* Later served as admiral in Russian navy.

Jones, Sir William (1746–94), Eng. jurist and philologist. Translated from Gk. and Oriental sources. First man to suggest common origin of Sanskrit, Gk. and Latin languages.

Jongkind, Johann Barthold (1819–91), Dutch landscape painter and etcher. Precursor of Impressionist movement.

jonquil *see* NARCISSUS.

Jonson, Ben (1573–1637), Eng. dramatist and poet. Author of many comedies incl. *Volpone, The Alchemist* and *Bartholomew Fair,* as well as poetry and 30 court masques.

Jordaens, Jacob (1593–1678), Flemish painter. After Rubens' death, recognized as leader of Antwerp school. Painted humorous scenes and religious pictures, such as *The Last Supper, Christ and the Doctors.*

Jordan, David Starr (1851–1931), Amer. zoologist and philosopher. Chief director of World Peace Foundation. Apostle of Puritanism and Nordic superiority, also defended progressive social reforms.

Jordan, Hashemite Kingdom of The, kingdom of Middle East, NW Arabian peninsula. Area: 37,291 sq. mi.; cap. Amman. Formerly called Transjordan or Transjordania. Bordered on E by Saudi Arabia, on W by Israel.

Fruits, vegetables, wheat grown, phosphates, potash mined in mainly arid mountainous country. Under Ottoman Empire from 16th cent. until 1918; part of Brit. mandate of PALESTINE; became semi-independent emirate (1923); kingdom proclaimed

View of Grenoble by Jongkind

(1946). Lost old city of Jerusalem and territory W of Jordan R. in Arab-Israeli war (June 1967). Population mainly Arab. Language, Arabic. Official religion, Islam. Unit of currency, Jordanian dinar. Pop. (1967 est.) 2,071,000.

Jordan, river flowing *c.* 230 mi. from Anti-Lebanon Mts. S to Dead Sea. Marks parts of Israel-Jordan and Israel-Syria borders and flows through Jordan's Rift Valley. In Israel, irrigates Negev Desert. In Bible, scene of baptism of Jesus.

Jorn, Asger, orig. Asger Oluf Jørgensen (1914–), Danish expressionist painter. Published a *Sketch of a Methodology of the Arts* (1958).

Joseph, in OT, favourite son of Jacob and Rachel, sold into slavery by brothers. Became vizier to Pharaoh and helped father and brothers in a famine. Sons Ephraim and Manasseh gave their names to 2 of the 12 tribes of Israel.

Joseph, chief of Nez Percé Indians [Hinmaton-Yalaktit] (*c.* 1840–1904). Led tribe in rejection of US land

The Bridge (1958) by Asger Jorn

Juneberry

cessions and consequent retreat to Canada. Defeated Custer at Battle of Big Hole (1876), but surrendered to US forces under General Miles (1877).

Joseph, Saint, in NT, husband of Virgin Mary and foster-father of Jesus. Carpenter at Nazareth, descended from David, king of Israel.

Joseph II (1741–90), Holy Roman emperor, son of Francis I and Maria Theresa. Liberal-minded monarch, he cut feudal power of nobles (1781) by abolishing serfdom, curtailed Church power, extended education. Attempt to annex Bavaria thwarted by War of Bavarian Succession (1778–9).

Joseph of Arimathea, in NT, influential Jew, member of the Sanhedrin, who obtained body of Jesus from Pilate for burial in a new tomb. Connections with Glastonbury and Holy Grail are probably later inventions of Middle Ages.

Josephine [Marie Josèphe Tascher de la Pagerie] (1763–1814), wife of Napoleon Bonaparte. He had married

age annulled (1809) because of her alleged sterility.

Joshua, historical book of OT, describing invasion and conquest of Palestine by the Hebrews.

Joshua tree, *Yucca brevifolia,* tree of desert regions of SW US. It has short leaves, greenish flowers and extended branches.

Jostedalsbreen, glacier of W Norway, largest in Europe. Area 340 sq. mi. Highest point rises to 6,700 ft.

Jotunheim, mountain range of S central Norway, highest in N Europe; Galdhøpiggen rises to 8,400 ft. Bordered by JOSTEDALSBREEN glacier.

Jouhaux, Léon (1879–1954), Fr. trade union leader. Head of Confédération Générale du Travail (1909–47); organized International Confederation of Free Trade Unions (1949). Founded Popular Front (1935) and was deported to Germany after fall of France. Awarded Nobel Peace Prize (1951).

Joule, James Prescott (1818–89), Eng. physicist. Estab. fundamental principle of relation between heat and mechanical energy. Electrical unit, the joule, is named after him.

Jove *see* JUPITER.

Jowett, Benjamin (1817–93), Eng. scholar. Master of Balliol, Oxford (1870). Noted for university reform and translations of Plato, Aristotle and Thucydides.

Joyce, James (1882–1941), Irish writer. Main works, *Portrait of the Artist as a Young Man* (1917), *Ulysses* (1922) and *Finnegan's Wake* (1939), exercised a strong influence on subsequent literature.

Joyce, William ('Lord Haw Haw') (1906–46), Anglo-Amer. Nazi radio propagandist during World War 2. Hanged by British for treason.

Juan Carlos (1938–   ), Pretender to Sp. throne. Favoured ahead of father, Don Juan, by Franco to succeed in event of BOURBON restoration.

Juan Fernández, group of 3 volcanic islands on Pacific Ocean, 400 mi. SW of Valparaiso belonging to Chile. Pop. *c.* 300.

Juarez, Benito Pablo (1806–72), Mexican politician and national hero. Acted as Pres. during War of the Reform (1858–61). Captured Maximilian of Habsburg, the French-supported emperor of Mexico and overthrew Fr. rule in the country.

Judaea, Judea, Greco-Roman name for S Palestine. Orig. occupied by tribe of Judah in OT.

Judah, 4th son of Jacob and Leah in OT. One of Israel's 12 tribes named after him, since it claimed to be descended from him. Also name of one of 2 kingdoms into which Palestine was divided after Solomon's death.

Judaism, religious beliefs and observances of the JEWS; oldest monotheistic religion and the one from which Christianity and Mohammedanism are derived. Based primarily on scriptures of OT, the TALMUD and the TORAH, distinctive observances include male circumcision, daily services in Hebrew, observance of Sabbath (7th day of week) and 3 principal festivals, Passover, Pentecost and Tabernacles. Movements in Judaism have included Pharisees, Sadducees and Essenes of NT times, Karaites (8th cent.), Chasidism (18th cent.), Reform movement in Germany (begun 1810) and Liberal Judaism in US. Festivals celebrated in SYNAGOGUE or in the home. Priest known as Rabbi. *See* ZIONISM.

Judas Iscariot, one of the 12 disciples of Jesus, whom he betrayed. Only non-Galilean apostle; acted as treasurer.

Judas Maccabeus *see* MACCABEES.

Judas tree, redbud, N Amer. leguminous trees and shrubs of genus *Cercis,* with rose or white flowers. Common redbud *C. canadensis* is native to E N America.

Jude, Judas, in Bible, one of the 12 apostles of Jesus; possibly also called Thaddeus and Lebbaeus. Distinguished by St Luke as son or brother of James; also identified as brother of Jesus and author of Epistle of St Jude.

Jude, epistle of NT. Traditionally written by St Jude, brother of James the Less, between AD 65 and 80, warning against false prophets and heresy.

Queen Juliana of the Netherlands and her husband, Prince Bernhard

Judo: throwing techniques, 1. leg throw, 2. hip throw, 3. shoulder throw, 4. arm throw. Groundwork, 5. sacrifice throw, 6. locking technique, 7. strangling technique, 8. arm lock

judge, one empowered to hear civil and criminal cases and pronounce sentence. In UK, judges appointed by Lord Chancellor on govt. nomination and must be barristers of several years' standing. In US, judges mostly chosen by popular election, but also appointed by governor or elected by legislature.

Judges, historical book of OT describing govt. of the judges who ruled Israel before union of the tribes, and the many wars fought in defence of Palestine.

Judith, Apocryphal book of OT relating fictitious events of reign of Nebuchadnezzar. Not in accord with Jewish history.

judo, sport developed (1882) by Jigor Kano, based on less dangerous practices of JU-JITSU. A coloured belt indicates level of skill (black being highest).

Juggernaut, in Hindu religion, form of KRISHNA, an incarnation of VISHNU. Said that devotees threw themselves in front of vehicles carrying his image in religious processions. Has come to denote any mighty force crushing all in its path.

ju-jitsu, jujutsu, method of weaponless self-defence, from which JUDO is derived, developed in ancient Japan. Requires extensive training and detailed knowledge of anatomy.

juke box, coin operated, automatically selecting phonograph. Dates from early 1900s.

Julian calendar *see* CALENDAR.

Julian the Apostate (*c.* 331–63), Roman emperor (361–3); despite unsuccessful attempt to restore paganism, displayed tolerance towards Christians.

Juliana (1909–), queen of Netherlands (1948–), daughter of Queen Wilhelmina and Prince Henry of Mecklenburg-Schwerin. Married Prince Bernhard of Lippe-Biesterfeld (1937). They have 4 daughters.

Julius Caesar *see* CAESAR, JULIUS.

July Revolution or **Revolution of 1830,** Fr. coup d'état which deposed Charles X and created bourgeois monarchy of Louis Philippe. Led by Thiers against repressive and reactionary measures of Charles' ministries.

Jumna, Indian river, 850 mi. long, main trib. of Ganges. Rises in Himalayas through Uttar Pradesh, joining Ganges at Allahabad.

jumping hare, *Pedetes cafer,* S African nocturnal rodent of Pedetidae family. Can leap up to 30 ft.

jumping mouse, *Zapus hudsonius,* rodent of Dipodidae family, native to N America.

juncobird, snowbird, slate-coloured bird of finch family. Winters in E US and Canada.

June bug, May beetle, brown nocturnal scarab beetle of genus *Phyllophaga.*

Juneau, cap. of Alaska, US, with ice-free harbour. At foot of Mt. Juneau and Mt. Roberts, connected by bridge with Douglas on Gastineau Channel. Founded (1881) by gold prospectors; cap. since 1906. Trading, fishing and lumbering centre. Pop. (1960) 6,797.

Juneberry, N Amer. shrubs of genus *Amelanchier* of Rose family. White flowers; edible berries.

Jung, Carl Gustav (1875–1961), Swiss psychologist and psychiatrist who with FREUD made important contributions to analytic psychology. Later diverged from Freud's emphasis on sex in neurosis. Postulated concepts of extroversion and introversion as general classification of character.

Jungfrau [Ger: maiden], peak (13,653 ft.) in Bernese Oberland, Switzerland. Has highest point reached by railway in Europe (11,412 ft.). First climbed, 1811.

jungle fowl, birds of *Gallus* genus, of Phasianidae family native mostly to Far East. Considered origin of domestic fowls.

junior, in Eng. law *see* BARRISTER.

juniper, coniferous evergreen shrub of genus *Juniperus,* with dark berries. Grows in N hemisphere. Oil from berries used in medicine and gin.

Junius, Letters of, series of letters (1769–71), written under pseudonym, attacking some well-known people, incl. George III. Appeared in *Public Advertiser,* a London newspaper. Possibly written by Sir Philip Francis.

Chinese Junks at Singapore

junk, large Chinese sea-going vessel with 3 masts, square sails of matting and a high poop.

Juno, in Roman religion, wife of Jupiter, later identified with Gk. Hera. Primarily goddess of women, with several names indicating attributes, *e.g.* Juno Lucina, goddess of child-birth.

Jupiter, Jove, in Roman religion, orig. a sky-spirit. Later the protector in battle; in peace-time associated with morality and justice. Chief of Roman gods, husband of Juno. Identified with Gk. Zeus.

Jupiter, largest planet in solar system, *c.* 483,900,000 mi. from Sun; diameter *c.* 88,770 mi.; rotates on axis in *c.* 9 hr. 55 min., circles sun in 11 yr. 315 days; 12 known satellites. Surface temperature $-140°C$; shrouded in clouds, only permanent feature is oval marking 'the Great Red Spot'. Largely or entirely composed of gases (hydrogen, helium, ammonia and methane).

Jura, mountain range in E France and W Switzerland. Made up of parallel ridges; limestone and sandstone with numerous caves and fossils. Pine-forested with grazing. Watchmaking and pipemaking in several towns.

Jura, Scot. island of Inner Hebrides, separated from mainland by Sound of Jura. Area: 147 sq. mi.

Jurassic era *see* GEOLOGICAL TABLE.

jurisprudence, study of general nature of law, its principles, functions and concepts, and of theory of justice.

jury, from Anglo Norman times in England, body of men assembled to decide from presented evidence verdict in important trials. Custom gradually institutionalized by 18th cent. when it began to be copied elsewhere (incorporated in US constitution). Jurors are now selected from voters' roll.

Justice of the Peace (JP), in UK, local magistrate appointed by special commission. Normally unpaid, they are responsible for initiation of criminal proceedings. In US, office is usually elective and officers may only try misdemeanours.

Justinian I (483–565), Byzantine emperor. Consolidated empire by recovering Italy and N Africa. Advocated supremacy of emperor over Church. Codified Roman law (Justinian Code), the basis of modern European jurisprudence.

jute, natural fibre from tropical annual plant, genus *Corchorus*. Main sources are 2 species grown in E Pakistan. Known in W since *c.* 1830. Coarse fibre used for sacking, rope and carpet backing, *etc.*

Jutes *see* ANGLO-SAXONS.

Jutland [**Jylland**], peninsula of N Europe comprising mainland of Denmark and part of Ger. Schleswig. E coast fertile; dairying and cattle-raising. Site of major naval battle of World War 1 (1916); resulted in Ger. fleet returning to base though with fewer losses than British.

Juvenal [Decimus Junius Juvenalis] (*c.* AD 60–140), Roman satirical poet (*fl.* AD 98–128). The 16 Satires, violent attacks on follies and vices of Roman life, are characterized by bitter ironical humour, pessimism and sympathy with the poor.

juvenile courts, separate courts set up in US (1899), UK (1908) to deal with juvenile delinquents. In UK, probation system figures prominently in proceedings.

juvenile delinquency, term for offences committed by minors which would be judged criminal in adults. Frequently found in bad family and environmental situations; factors now recognized by rehabilitation programmes. Punitive measures, passed through juvenile court, include approved schools and probation.

Mosaic portrait of the Emperor Justinian I, Ravenna

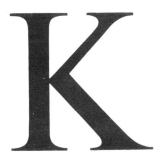

K

K 2 *see* GODWIN-AUSTEN.

Ka, in Egyptian religion, vital force in each individual during life, and preceding him into next world to prepare his welcome. May also mean 'soul'.

Kabalevsky, Dmitri Borisovich (1904–), Soviet composer. Works include 4 symphonies, 3 piano concertos, and film music.

Kabuki *see* JAPANESE DRAMA.

Kabul, cap. of Afghanistan. Situated on both sides of Kabul R. at 6,000 ft. Important trade centre for centuries, commanding Khyber Pass. Caravan trade in carpets, silks and cotton. Pop. (1964) 450,000.

Kachin, Mongol people of mountains of Assam and N Burma. Mainly agricultural; tribal social structure; animistic religion. Language, Kachin, one of Tibetan-Burman group of Indo-Chinese languages.

Kadar, Janos (1912–), Hungarian politician. Head of secret police (1948–51); imprisoned (1951–4). Premier of Soviet-backed govt. (1956–8, 1961–5).

kaffir corn, *Sorghum vulgare caffrorum,* grass native to S Africa, with short-jointed leafy stalks. Red, white and blackhull kaffirs are leading varieties.

Kaffirs, Kafirs, name applied by Europeans in S Africa to Bantu-speaking Negroes. First used by Arab slave traders referring to Africans.

Kafka, Franz (1883–1924), Ger. writer, b. Prague. Work deals with futility of escape for man in modern society. Best known novels are *The Trial* (1925) and *The Castle* (1926).

Kagawa, Toyohiko (1888–1960), Jap. pacifist and social worker. Arrested in World War 2 for pacifism. Wrote poetry, fiction and religious (Christian) studies.

kagu, *Rhynochetus jubatus,* bird of New Caledonia, now close to extinction. Long orange legs and greyish plumage.

Kailas, mountain (22,028 ft.) in Kailas Range, SW Tibet. Tradition-ally abode of Hindu god Siva; focus of Buddhist and Hindu pilgrimage.

Kairouan, sacred Islamic town in Tunisia, founded 670. Famous 9th cent. mosque. Carpet industry important. Pop. *c.* 40,000.

Kaiser, Georg (1848–1945), Ger. dramatist whose expressionist dramas include trilogy *The Corals* (1917).

kakapo, nocturnal New Zealand parrot, *Strigops habroptilus.* Almost flightless; lives in burrows.

Kalahari, hot DESERT of S Africa, centred in Botswana (formerly Bechuanaland). Area: *c.* 120,000 sq. mi. Wide transition area between arid and semi-arid; rainfall fluctuates. Sparsely populated by Hottentots and Bushmen.

kalanchoe, genus of trop. African and Austral. shrubs of family Crassulaceae. Numerous forms are cultivated as ornamental plants.

kale, kail, cole, cole wort, *brassica oleracea acephala,* variety of cabbage with curly leaves, grown as winter vegetable. Jersey kale grows to 7 ft.; often used for cattle fodder.

kaleidoscope, optical device composed of tube containing 3 mirrors set at angle of 60°, reflecting chips of coloured glass enclosed in one end. Rotation changes the colourful, symmetrical pattern.

Kalgoorlie, town of Western Australia, *c.* 350 mi. E of Perth. Since discovery of Gold Mile gold-field (1893), gold-mining centre of Australia. Pop. (1961) *c.* 21,770.

Kali, in Hindu myth., black goddess of evil and death, consort of Siva. Personifies mother goddess devouring life she has produced.

Kaliningrad, formerly **Königsberg,** seaport of Russ. SFSR on Bay of Danzig. Cap. of E Prussia until ceded to Russia at Potsdam Conference (1945). Centre of Teutonic culture.

Kalanchoe blossfeldiana

Kabul

Products include chemicals, amber. Pop. (1967) 261,000.

kalmia, New York laurel, N Amer. shrub of heath family with clusters of showy flowers.

Kalmuck, autonomous repub. of Russ. SFSR, estab. 1958. Existed earlier (1935–44), but dissolved because inhabitants allegedly collaborated with Germans during World War 2. Pop. (1961 est.) 193,000.

Kamchatka, peninsula and prov. of Russ. SFSR, NE Siberia. Area: 215,914 sq. mi. Active volcanic region. Produces wood, coal, petroleum. Sparsely populated.

Kamenev, Lev Borisovich, orig. Rosenfeld (1883–1936), Russ. revolutionary and politician. One of triumvirate (with Stalin and Zinoviev) who succeeded Lenin (1924). Brother-in-law of Trotsky; expelled from Communist Party (1927 and 1932); executed as Trotskyist (1936).

Kamerlingh Onnes, Heike (1853–1926), Dutch physicist. Awarded Nobel Prize for Physics (1913) for study of properties of helium.

Kamet, 1st Himalayan mountain over 25,000 ft. to be climbed (1931). Height 25,447 ft.

kamikaze [Jap: divine wind], name for Jap. suicide pilots, who during World War 2, intentionally crashed bomb-laden planes on their targets.

Kampala, cap. city of Uganda, 10 mi. from L. Victoria. Commercial centre; seat of Makerere University. Pop. *c.* 50,000.

Kanchenjunga, Himalayan mountain (28,146 ft.) 3rd highest in the world; 1st climbed (1955) by Brit. expedition.

Kandahar, prov. of SE Afghanistan. Area: *c.* 50,000 sq. mi.; cap. Kandahar. Pop. *c.* 100,000. Mountainous with fertile land in N and S.

Landscape with Tower by Kandinsky

Kandinsky, Wassily (1866–1944), Russ. painter. One of founders of abstract painting and of Blaue Reiter group.

Kandy, city of C Ceylon. Ancient cap., founded *c.* 500–400 BC. Trade centre for tea, rice, cocoa, rubber. Famed for Buddhist Temple of the Tooth. Pop. (1963) 70,400.

Kang Hsi (1656–1722), outstanding Chinese emperor. Consolidated administration of empire, subjugated Tibet, halted Russian penetration in Manchuria.

Kang Sheng (*c.* 1904–), vice-chairman of Chinese National People's Congress Standing Committee (1965–), member of Mao Tse-tung's inner circle.

kangaroo, several herbivorous marsupials of Australasia. Great grey kangaroo, *Macropus giganteus,* reaches 8 ft. in ht. Young remain in mother's pouch for 1st 10 months.

Part of the old town of Kano

Hunted for fur or because of damage to crops; numbers decreasing, thus in some areas protected by law.

kangaroo rat, rodent with long hind legs and tail. Desert kangaroo rat, *Dipodomys deserti,* of SW US is nocturnal.

Kannada *see* DRAVIDIAN.

Kano, city of Kano prov., N Nigeria. Flourished as caravan centre (19th cent.), now communications and transport centre. Peanut industry, cotton spinning, metal and leather handicrafts. Pop. (1963) 295,000.

Kanpur, formerly **Cawnpore,** manufacturing city of Pradesh, N India. Railway centre at bridging point of Ganges. Cotton, woollen and jute mills. Pop. (1965) 1,086,000.

Kansas, state of C US. Area: 82,264 sq. mi.; cap. Topeka; main cities Wichita, Kansas City. Prairie state, producing largest US wheat crop with sorghum, oats, soy beans.

Minerals include petroleum, natural gas, coal. Manufacturing associated with transportation, food, chemicals, petroleum, printing and consumer goods. Pop. (1960) 2,178,611.

Kansas City, 2 adjacent cities of same name, one in Kansas, one in Missouri. Commercial, industrial, transportation and cultural centre. Total pop. (1965) 921,000.

Kansas-Nebraska Bill (1854) introduced by Stephen A. Douglas, estab. territories of Kansas and Nebraska out of that part of Louisiana Purchase closed to slavery by MISSOURI COMPROMISE (1820). Territories had right of self-determination on slavery which intensified conflict between North and South.

Kansu, sparsely-populated prov. of NW China. Area: 141,506 sq. mi.; cap. Lanchow. Agriculture in river valleys; oil fields in N. Pop. (1963) 12,800,000.

Kant, Immanuel (1724–1804), Ger. philosopher. Author of *Critique of Pure Reason* (1781), *Foundations of the Metaphysics of Ethics* (1785) and other works, in which he argued knowledge should be subordinated to faith. Central thesis based on distinction between phenomena (things of experience) and noumena (things-in-themselves). Knowledge of noumena impossible, but knowledge of their existence forms basis of ethics. Moral conduct guided by categorical imperative (creation of universal law through self-willed action). Ultimately, faith, not knowledge, justifies belief in freedom of the will. His theories profoundly influenced 19th cent. philosophy.

Kanuir, a Nilo-Saharan language, with over 1 million speakers in Nigeria.

kaolin, fine-textured, soft, whitish clay, consisting chiefly of kaolinite. Used in manufacture of porcelain; purified for medicinal use.

kaolinite, clay mineral, main constituent of KAOLIN. Formed from decomposition of aluminous minerals.

kapok tree, trop. tree of Bombacacae family with palmate leaves and fleshy fruit. Silky fibres used as filling for insulation, sleeping bags, *etc.*

Karachi, former cap. (1947–59), largest city and port of Pakistan on W edge of Indus delta. Founded 1729; 18th cent. trading centre; developed rapidly on annexation (1843) to Brit. Indian Empire. Pop. (1961) 1,913,000.

Karajan, Herbert von (1908–), Austrian conductor of the Berlin Philharmonic Orchestra (1955). Artistic director of Vienna State Opera (1957–64).

Karakoram, mountain range of Kashmir, NW India, and Tibet. Includes Mt. Godwin-Austen (28,250 ft.), 2nd highest peak in world.

Kara-Kum, 2 deserts in S USSR. Caspian Kara-Kum is in SE Turkmen SSR. Contains Merv oasis; sulphur mines. Aral Kara-Kum is in Kazakh SSR. Total area: 131,270 sq. mi.

Karamanlis, Constantine (1907–), Gk. statesman and lawyer. P.M. (1955–63). Agreement with UK and Turkey (1959) led to estab. of repub. of Cyprus.

karate, method of unarmed self-defence developed in Japan. Involves use of hands, elbows, knees and feet for blows to vulnerable parts of the body, *e.g.* temple, throat, groin.

Karelian Autonomous Soviet Socialist Republic, formerly **Karelo-Finnish SSR,** territorial admin. subdivision of Russ. SFSR. Area: 66,700 sq. mi.; cap. Petrozavodsk. Covered by thousands of lakes, heavily forested.

The baroque palace at Karlsruhe

Main occupations in timber industry, marble and quartzite quarrying, and iron and magnetite mining. Main languages, Russian and Finnish. Pop. (1965 est.) 696,000.

Kariba, gorge on Zambesi R., on Zambia-Rhodesia border. Site of dam (enclosing world's largest man-made lake, 175 mi. long; 40 mi. wide) constructed (1955–60) to provide hydro-electric power. Dam designed by Fr. engineer André Coyne.

Karl-Marx-Stadt *see* CHEMNITZ.

Karloff, Boris, orig. William Henry Pratt (1887–1969), Eng. stage and film actor; best known roles were in horror films, esp. as Frankenstein's monster.

Karlsruhe, Ger. indust. city, in Baden-Württemberg. Founded (1715) on semi-circular plan, now cultural and admin. centre. Pop. 224,000.

karma, in Indian religion and philosophy, sum of a man's actions which are carried forward from one existence to the next, determining it for good or bad. Differing interpretations of karma are found in Jainism, Hinduism and Buddhism.

Karnak, village of C Egypt on E bank of Nile R. Ancient city of Thebes built round temple of Ammon, ruins of which remain.

Karrer, Paul (1889–), Swiss chemist. With Sir Walter N. Haworth, awarded Nobel Prize for Chemistry (1937) for work on vitamins, flavins and carotinoids.

karri, Austral. gumtree, *Eucalyptus diversicolor,* found in SW of Western Australia. Timber used in building.

Karroo, 2 areas (Great Karroo and Little Karroo) of semi-desert in W Cape Province, South Africa. Total area: 100,000 sq. mi. Partly irrigated, providing grazing for sheep and goats and fruit growing.

Karsh, Yousuf (1908–), Canadian photographer, famous for portraits of leading 20th cent. artists and statesmen, *e.g.* Sir Winston Churchill.

Flower vase of Chinese porcelain, Kang Hsi period (1662-1722)

Kasbah near Ouarzazate, Morocco

karst, orig. barren limestone region along NE coast of Adriatic Sea. Now used to refer to similar scenery, characterized by potholes, underground fissures and arid topsoil.

Kasai, former prov. of Repub. of the Congo. Agriculture important, also industrial diamond mines. Gained independence (1960), S region renamed Mining State of South Kasai. Reconstituted as 2 provinces (1966).

Kasavubu, Joseph (1917–69), Congolese polit. leader. Imprisoned after 1959 revolt, but became 1st Pres. of Repub. of the Congo (1960). Deposed (1965) by Col. Joseph Mobutu.

kasbah, casbah [Arabic: a castle or fortification], in N Africa term for native section of city, or that part surrounding a castle or fortress.

Kashmir, Jammu and Kashmir, state in NW India and NE Pakistan. Area: 86,023 sq. mi.; comprising Indian Kashmir and Azad (or Free) Kashmir. Mainly mountainous with densely populated Vale of Kashmir producing wheat and rice. Sovereignty disputed by India and Pakistan. Repeated UN attempts at settlement have failed. Annexed by India (1957) but Pakistan continues to occupy N and W. Pop. *c.* 5,000,000.

Kastler, Alfred (1902–), Fr. physicist. Awarded Nobel Prize for Physics (1966) for work on energy levels of atoms, leading to further development of lasers and extremely accurate atomic chronometers.

Kästner, Erich (1899–), Ger. poet, novelist and children's writer, *e.g. Emil und die Detektive* (1929). *Fabian* (1931), a novel, concerned with nihilism and polit. violence.

katabolism, biological term for physical and chemical changes occurring in the body in production of energy during assimilation of food particles.

Katanga, former prov. of SE Repub. of the Congo, cap. Elisabethville. Withdrew from central govt. after independence of Congo (1960) under Pres. Tshombe; secession ended by UN intervention (1963). Rich in copper, uranium, diamonds.

Katchen, Julius (1926–69), Amer. concert pianist. International fame esp. for interpretation of works of Brahms.

Katmandu, cap. of Nepal, founded 723. Orig. ruled by Newars; independent 15th cent.; captured by Gurkhas (1768). Centre of economic, political and social activity. Pop. (1964) 220,000.

Kattegat, Cattegat, broad arm of North Sea, 137 mi. long, between Sweden and Jutland, Denmark. Joins Skaggerak and Baltic Sea.

katydid, insect of long-horned grasshopper family with auditory organs on legs. Makes sound by rubbing forewings together. Eggs laid in soil or in plant tissue. European *Tettigomia viridissima* is bright green.

Kauffman, Angelica (1741–1807), Swiss artist, successful in England and Italy. Known for portraits and decorative painting. One of original members of Royal Academy.

Kaufman, George S, (1889–1961), Amer. playwright and stage director. Works include *You Can't Take it with You* and *The Man who came to Dinner* (both written in collaboration with Moss Hart).

Kaufmann, Mount *see* LENIN PEAK.

Kaunas, Kovno, city of C Lithuania, river port on Niemen R. Cap. (1918–40). Food and textile manufacture. Pop. *c.* 250,000.

Kaunda, Kenneth David (1924–), African politician, founder of United National Independence Party (1960). First Pres. of Zambia (1964).

kauri gum, pine tree of New Zealand. Straight trunk reaches *c.* 100 ft. Valued for timber and gum. Latter used in varnish preparations.

Kautsky, Karl Johann (1854–1938), Ger. Socialist. Helped found Independent Social Democratic party in Germany, leading spokesman for orthodox Marxism in Second International. Opposed Lenin and the Bolshevists.

kayak, Eskimo canoe, usually holding 1 person. Wooden frame, *c.* 18 ft. long, 2 ft. wide, covered with skins. Also cover top around canoist, to keep water out.

Kaye, Danny, orig. David Daniel Kominsky (1913–), Amer. comedy actor. Film debut in *Lady in the Dark*

(1944); others include *The Secret Life of Walter Mitty.* Devoted much time to promoting UNICEF.

Kay-Shuttleworth, Sir James Phillips (1804–77), Eng. educationalist. Founded teacher training college (1839) at Battersea.

Kazakh, Turkic language of Altaic family, with over 3 million speakers in USSR.

Kazakh Soviet Socialist Republic (SSR), Kazakhstan, 2nd largest constituent repub. of USSR. Area: 1,057,900 sq. mi.; cap. Alma-Ata. Mainly steppeland, with Altai and Tien Shan Mts. in E; climate continental. Became Union repub. (1936). Agriculture has been mechanized and industrialized. Pop. (1967) 12,413,000.

Kazan, Elia (1909–), Amer. stage, film director. On stage, directed *Skin of our Teeth, Death of a Salesman, After the Fall.* Films include *A Streetcar Named Desire, On the Waterfront, East of Eden.* Author of novels, *America, America* and *The Arrangement.*

Kazan, city and cap. of Tatar SSR, Russ. SFSR. Founded (1401) on present site by Khan of Tatar. Industrial and commercial centre. Pop. (1967) 804,000.

Kazantzakis, Nikos (1883–1957), Gk. writer and politician. Wrote *The Odyssey, a Modern Sequel* (1938) in which he examined popular philosophies.

Kazin, Alfred (1915–), Amer. literary critic. Works include *On Native Grounds* (1942), autobiog. *A Walker in the City* (1951), *Contemporaries* (1962).

kea, *Nestor notabilis,* brownish green

St Basil's cathedral, Moscow, commemorates the conquest of Kazan

Typical karst terrain

parrot with long sickle shaped upper mandible. Found in S New Zealand; feeds on carrion, insects, berries and honey.

Kean, Edmund (1787–1833), Eng. actor who excelled in portrayals of Shakespearean characters. Esp. remembered for his Shylock (1814).

Keaton, Joseph Frank ('Buster') (1896–1966), Amer. film actor; appeared in *The General*, *Limelight* (1953), *Round the World in 80 Days* (1957).

Keats, John (1795–1821), Eng. Romantic poet. One of finest Eng. lyricists, his verse includes poems such as 'Ode to a Nightingale', 'Ode on a Grecian Urn' and unfinished epic 'Hyperion'. Also wrote sonnets and romantic medieval works, *e.g.* 'The Eve of St Agnes' and 'La Belle Dame sans Merci'. Died in Italy, where he had gone because of poor health.

Keble, John (1792–1866), Eng. cleric and poet; a founder of OXFORD MOVEMENT. Author of *The Christian Year* (1827) devotional poems based on Book of Common Prayer.

Kedah, state of Federation of Malaya (1946). Area: 3,660 sq. mi.; cap. Alor Star. Chief products, rice, tin, rubber. Pop. (1961) 794,086.

Keita, Modibo (1915–), African political leader. First Pres. of Repub. of Mali (1959–). Led Mali into union with Ghana and Guinea (1962) to establish Union of African States.

Keith, Minor Cooper (1848–1929), Amer. capitalist and rly. builder. Developed United Fruit Co. Directed construction of rly. in Costa Rica from Caribbean coast to San José (completed 1890). Pres. of International Railways of Central America (1912–28).

Kekulé von Stradonitz, Friedrich August, FRS (1829–96), Ger. chemist who developed ring theory for molecular structure of benzene.

Kelantan, state of Malaya, Federation of MALAYSIA. Area: 5,750 sq. mi.; cap. Kota Bahru. Ceded by Siam to Britain (1909); unfederated Malay state until formation of Federation of Malaya (1948). Products include rice, rubber, copra, tin and gold. Pop. (1961) 579,246.

Keller, Gottfried (1819–90), Swiss novelist, leading Ger. literary figure. Works include autobiog. *Der grüne Heinrich* (1854–5).

Keller, Helen Adams (1880–1968), Amer. author and lecturer. Blind and deaf from age of 2, she was taught to read and write by Anne Sullivan Macy. Graduated from Radcliffe College (1904); spent much of her life aiding the handicapped. Author of *Teacher, Anne Sullivan Macy* (1956).

Kellogg, Frank Billings (1856–1937), Amer. lawyer and statesman. As US Sec. of State (1925–9), promoted KELLOGG-BRIAND PACT (1928). Senator (1917–23); ambassador to UK (1924–5). Awarded Nobel Peace Prize (1929).

Kellogg-Briand Pact, Pact of Paris, agreement (signed Aug. 1928) condemning war and advocating peaceful settlement of international disagreements. Promoted by ARISTIDE BRIAND of France and F. B. KELLOGG of US.

Kells, Book of, early illuminated Ms of Latin gospels, prob. written 8th–9th cent. Found at Kells, Co. Meath, Ireland; now in library of Trinity College, Dublin.

Kelly, Edward ('Ned') (1855–80), Austral. bushranger; with brother **Daniel Kelly** and 2 confederates, carried out bank-robberies on the Victoria-New South Wales border (1878–80). Captured and hanged (1880).

Kelly, Grace Patricia, now **Grace, Princess of Monaco** (1929–), Amer. actress whose films include *High Society, Dial M for Murder.*

Married Prince RAINIER of Monaco (1956).

Kelly, Hugh (1739–77), Irish dramatist, critic and journalist. Plays include *A Word for the Wise* (1770), *The School for Wives* (1773).

Kelly, Walt (1913–), Amer. cartoonist best known for his satirical comic strip 'Pogo'.

kelp, general term for large seaweeds, some of which may have fronds up to 200 ft. long. Fan kelp or TANGLE is used as cattle food; red kelp in the alginate industry.

kelpie, Austral. breed of short-coated sheep-dog developed from collie (imported from UK) or dingo-collie cross.

Kelvin, Lord *see* THOMSON, WILLIAM.

Kemal, Pasha, Mustafa, later **Ataturk** (1881–1938), Turkish leader; 1st pres. of Turkish repub. (1922–38). Ruling as a dictator, carried out drastic programme of westernization.

Kemble, Roger (1721–1802), Eng. actor and manager. His son **John Philip Kemble** (1757–1823) managed Drury Lane (1788–1803) and Covent Garden (1803–8); distinguished tragedy actor playing opposite his sister SARAH KEMBLE SIDDONS. Their brother **Charles Kemble** (1775–1854) excelled in comedy esp. with his daughter **Fanny Kemble** (1809–93) whose greatest roles included Juliet and Lady Macbeth.

Kempis, Thomas à *see* THOMAS À KEMPIS.

Ken, Thomas (1637–1711), Eng. prelate and hymn writer. Deprived of his see (1691) for refusing to swear allegiance to William [III] of Orange.

Kendall, Edward Calvin (1886–), Amer. biochemist. With P. S. Hench and Tadeus Reichstein, awarded Nobel Prize for Physiology and Medicine (1950) for work on hormones of cortex of adrenal glands.

Kea

The Kenyan plateau south-west of Nairobi. The valley continues into Tanzania

Kendrew, John Cowdery (1917–), Eng. chemist. With M. F. Perutz, awarded Nobel Prize for Chemistry (1962) for determining structure of myoglobin.

Kennedy, John Fitzgerald (1917–63), 34th or 35th US Pres. (1961–3), Democrat. Elected to House of Representatives (1946); US Senator from Massachusetts (1952). New Frontier programme called for new support for social security, civil rights, urban renewal, and accelerated space programme. Foreign policy manifested in formation of ALLIANCE FOR PROGRESS with Latin America and the PEACE CORPS. Criticized for ill-fated Cuban invasion of 1961, but firm stand forced Soviet withdrawal of nuclear weapons from Cuba (1962). Expanded US military role in Vietnam (1963). Assassinated (Nov. 1963) allegedly by Lee Harvey Oswald. Among his written works are *Profiles in Courage* (1957).

Kennedy, Joseph Patrick (1888–1969), Amer. diplomat; US ambassador to UK (1937–40). His eldest son JOHN FITZGERALD KENNEDY (1917–63) became 34th or 35th Pres. of US. John's brother, **Robert Francis Kennedy** (1925–68) was US Attorney General (1961–4); US Senator from New York (1965–8); pres. candidate (1968); assassinated in Los Angeles. **Edward Moore Kennedy** (1932–) became US Senator from Massachusetts (1962).

Kennedy, Cape, formerly **Cape Canaveral,** in Florida, US. Missile-testing centre and rocket-firing range since 1950. Renamed (1963) after Pres. John F. Kennedy.

Kennelly, Arthur Edwin (1861–1939), Amer. electrical engineer; worked with THOMAS EDISON. Verified existence of ionized layer in upper

atmosphere (1902) in same year it was postulated by OLIVER HEAVISIDE.

Kenneth [I] MacAlpine (d. *c.* 860), king of Scots. In 843, estab. rule over Alban (united kingdom of Picts and Scots); made Scone, Perthshire, his capital.

Kenny, Elizabeth (1886–1952), Austral. nurse; developed method of treating infantile paralysis by means of hot moist applications and passive exercise.

Kensington and Chelsea, Royal Borough of, borough of London, England, since 1965, comprising former boroughs of Kensington and Chelsea. Contains Kensington Palace, former royal residence, and Victoria and Albert Museum.

Kent, William (1684–1748), Eng. landscape gardener, architect and painter. Early user of informality in landscape gardening.

Kent, maritime county of SE England. Area: 1,440 sq. mi.; county town Maidstone; main towns, Dover, Canterbury, Rochester. Undulating, mainly agric. land on which cereals, root crops, fruit and hops are grown. Pop. (1966) 1,325,000.

Kentigern, Saint *see* MUNGO, SAINT.

Kentucky, S central state of US. Area: 40,395 sq. mi.; cap. Frankfort; main cities, Lexington, Louisville; Covington. Appalachian Mts. in E, Ohio R. in N, Mississippi R. in SW. Agric. products include tobacco, corn, potatoes; chief industries, food-processing, manufacture of electrical and metal goods. Famous for horse-breeding. Known as Blue Grass State. Pop. (1960) 3,038,156.

Kentucky and Virginia Resolutions, passed 1798 and 1799. Kentucky Resolution, written by Thomas Jefferson, denied to Federal govt. powers not delegated to it by Constitution. Virginia Resolution, written by James Madison, similar, though milder. Regarded as 1st clear statement of STATES' RIGHTS theory.

Kentucky coffee tree, Kentucky mahogany, *Gymnocladus dioica,* N Amer. tree of family Leguminosae. Pods contain large seeds formerly used as coffee substitute.

Kentucky Derby, annual horse race held at Churchill Downs, Ky., US.

Kenya, repub. of E Africa on Indian

Ocean. Area: 224,960 sq. mi.; cap. Nairobi. Arid region in N, L. Victoria

in SW. Temp. climate on inland plateau. Crops include coffee, tea, maize. Mineral resources, gold, copper, asbestos. Game hunting and tourism important. Settled (7th cent.) by Arab and Persian slave traders; controlled by Portugal (16th–17th cent.). Made Brit. protectorate (1895). Outbreak of MAU MAU terrorism (1952). Independence (1963); became a repub. (1964). Main languages, English, Swahili; religions, animism, Christianity. Unit of currency, E African shilling. Pop. (1966) 9,643,000.

Kenya, Mount, extinct volcano (17,058 ft.) in national park of C Kenya. Tea grown on slopes. First climbed (1899).

Kenyatta, Jomo (Johnstone), orig. Kamau Ngengi (*c.* 1889–), African statesman. Pres. Kenya African Union (1947); accused of MAU MAU leadership, imprisoned (1953–9). Pres. Kenya African National Union (KANU) (1961). P.M. of Kenya (1963–4); 1st Pres. (1964–). Author of *Facing Mount Kenya* (1938).

Kepler, Johannes (1571–1630), Ger. astronomer. Discovered 3 laws of planetary motion (Kepler's laws). A founder of modern astronomy.

Kerala, state of SW India on Arabian Sea. Area: 15,000 sq. mi.; cap. Trivandrum. Crops include tea, spices, coconuts, rice. Extensive mineral deposits of graphite and lignite. Created (1956) from former princely states of Travancore and Cochin. Pop. (1961) 16,903,715.

Kerensky, Alexander Fedorovich (1881–1970), Russ. revolutionary politician. Became premier of 2nd provisional govt. (1917). Overthrown by Lenin (Nov. 1917) during Bolshevik revolution. Has lived in US since 1940.

Kerguelen Is., Desolation Is., largest island of archipelago in S Indian Ocean; a whaling station. In Fr. possession (1893–1960); dependency of Malagasy Repub. (created 1960).

Kern, Jerome David (1885–1945), Amer. composer of light operas and film scores. Most popular songs include 'Ol' Man River', from *Showboat* (1927) and 'Smoke Gets in Your Eyes' from *Roberta* (1933).

kerosene, mineral oil derived from petroleum, coal or wood; used as illuminant, insecticide or fuel.

Kerouac, Jean-Louis ('Jack') (1922–69), Amer. writer of 'beat generation'. Works include *On the Road* (1957), *Big Sur* (1963).

kerria, beauty bush, deciduous Chinese shrub with yellow flower, widely cultivated in gardens.

Kerry [Ciarri], maritime county of Republic of Ireland. Area: 1,859 sq. mi.; county town Tralee. Chief occupations, farming, dairying, fishing. Popular tourist area. Macgillycuddy's Reeks (3,414 ft.) highest mountains in Ireland. Pop. (1966) 112,642.

Kersh, Gerald (1911–), Brit. author of short-stories, film and television scripts and novels, incl. *Night and the City* (1937), *They Die with their Boots Clean* (1941), *Fowler's End* (1958).

Kesteven, Parts of, admin. area of SW Lincolnshire, England. Area: 724 sq. mi. Formed (1888) with county offices at Sleaford. Pop. (1966) 226,000.

kestrel, *Falco tinnunculus,* small European bird of family Falconidae. Hovers before swooping on prey, usually rodents and insects.

Ketcham, Hank (1920–), Amer. cartoonist. Created Dennis the Menace. Collections include *I Wanna Go Home* (1965).

ketone, organic compound related to aldehydes, containing groups united to carbonyls. Simplest ketone is ACETONE.

Kett, Robert (c. 1500–49), Eng. tradesman. Led unsuccessful revolt (1549), against enclosure of common land; executed.

kettledrums *see* TIMPANI.

Kew Gardens, site of Royal Botanic Gardens, Kew, Surrey, England. Area: c. $\frac{1}{2}$ sq. mi.; estab. (1841), also has botanical research centre.

Key, Francis Scott (1779–1843), Amer. poet. Author of 'Star-spangled Banner', US national anthem.

key *see* SCALE.

keyboard instruments, musical instruments which produce sound when player depresses levers set in a row at front. Group includes pipe and reed organs, harpsichord (virginals and spinet), clavichord, pianoforte and celesta.

Keyes, Roger John Brownlow, 1st Baron (1872–1945), Brit. admiral. Commanded raids on Zeebrugge and Ostend at end of World War 1. Organized commando forces early in World War 2.

Keynes, John Maynard, 1st Baron (1883–1946), Eng. economist and govt. official. Attended Versailles conference (1919) as member of Brit. delegation; disagreement with settlement expressed in *Economic Consequences of the Peace* (1919). Classical theorist until Depression (1929), after which he favoured large-scale govt. planning and spending to promote employment; *The General Theory of Employment, Interest, and Money* (1936) revolutionized economic analysis and profoundly affected policy in Western democratic nations.

Kestrel

Khachaturian, Aram Ilich (1903–), Russ. composer. Influenced by Russ. folk music. Works include ballet *Gayane* and suite *Masquerade,* piano and violin concertos.

Khama, Sir Seretse (1921–), Pres. of Botswana (1966–). Renounced tribal inheritance. Became premier (1965) before assuming presidency.

Khan, Mohammed Ayub *see* AYUB KHAN, MOHAMMED.

Khan, Yahya (1917–), Pakistani army officer and polit. leader. Commander-in-chief of army after 1966, became president (1969), resigned after India defeated Pakistan (1971).

Kharkov, city, SE Ukraine, USSR. Transport and indust. (mainly heavy) centre. Cap. of Ukraine (1919–34). Pop. (1964) 1,048,000.

Khartoum, cap. and commercial centre of Sudan. Founded (1823); besieged (1885) by Mahdists, who killed Gen. CHARLES GORDON. Pop. (1965) 173,500.

Khayyam, Omar (d. 1123), Persian poet. Author of *Rubáiyát,* epigrammatic verse, popularized after Edward Fitzgerald's translations (1859). Also known as a mathematician and astronomer.

Khmer, civilization of Cambodia and Laos (began 6th cent.). Highly developed architecture (Angkor Wat) and sculpture. Decline (1350) after wars with Annamese, Chams and Siamese.

Khoisan, language family of S and E Africa, including Hottentot, Bushman, Hatsa and Sandawe.

Khrushchev, Nikita Sergeyevich (1894–), Soviet polit. leader.

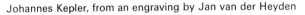

Johannes Kepler, from an engraving by Jan van der Heyden

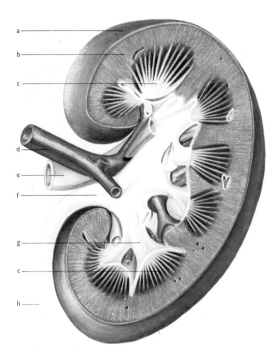

Cross-section of Kidney: (a) capsule (b) cortex (c) papilla (d) artery (e) vein (f) pelvis (g) calyx (h) ureter

Rose in Communist party to Politburo (1939) and succeeded Stalin (1953) as 1st Sec. of Party. Consolidated power by becoming premier (1958). Denounced Stalin (1956) and adopted policy of 'peaceful co-existence' with West. However, protested US espionage at Paris summit meeting (1960) and withdrew missiles from Cuba (1962) when challenged by US Pres. JOHN KENNEDY. Policies embittered Communist China. Deposed (1964) over economic difficulties and aggrandizement of power.

Khyber Pass, on border of W Pakistan and Afghanistan. Trade route; strategic importance for Brit. forces in 19th cent. Afghan wars.

kiang, *Equus hemonius,* wild ass of Tibet and Central Asia, with reddish back and sides, white underparts, and stripe along the spine.

Kiangsi, prov. of SE China. Area: 63,630 sq. mi.; cap. Nanchang. Hilly, fertile land; leading producer of rice and tungsten. Pop. (1963) 17,900,000.

Kiangsu, prov. of E China, on Yellow Sea. Rich agric. region and most densely populated prov. Pop. (1963) 45,230,000.

kibbutz [Hebrew: commune], type of COLLECTIVE FARMING used in Israel. Ownership of property and earnings is communal. Work crews live on farm, run by elected foremen.

Kicking Horse Pass, in Rocky Mts., Canada. Highest point (5,340 ft.) of Canadian Pacific Rly. route.

Kidd, William (*c.* 1645–1701), Brit. privateer. Arrested (1699) on piracy charges, tried and hanged. Became subject of legend as cruel captain, alleged to have buried huge treasure.

kidnapping, unlawful removal of person by force, usually with intention of claiming ransom. Differs from abduction, which requires intent of sexual intercourse to be actionable.

kidney vetch, greyish perennial plant, *Anthyllis vulneraria,* related to pea. Found in Europe and Asia; formerly used as medicine for kidney diseases.

kidneys, in vertebrates, 2 bean-shaped, reddish-brown organs lying in abdomen near spine. Function as urine filter.

Kidron, valley separating Mount of Olives from Jerusalem.

Kiel, city of West Germany, Baltic seaport. Naval base dismantled after World War 2. City incorporated by Prussia (1866). Pop. (1965) 270,000.

Kiel Canal, artificial waterway connecting Kiel, West Germany, with North Sea. 61 mi. long; opened 1895. Also called Kaiser Wilhelm Canal.

Kierkegaard, Soren Aabye (1813–55), Danish philosopher. Held that man's search for truth was personal; works characterized by intensity and mysticism. Wrote *Either/Or* (1843), *Stages on Life's Way* (1845) and more specifically religious *Training in Christianity* (1850). His ideas influenced Existentialism of 20th cent.

Kiesinger, Kurt Georg (1904–), Ger. polit. leader. Min.-Pres. of Baden Württemberg (1958–66), Chanc. of West Germany (1966–69).

Kiev, cap. of Ukrainian SSR. Indust. and transport centre. Cap. of medieval Russia, finally incorporated with Ukraine (1654). Cathedral and monastery remain as city's link with Byzantium. Pop. (1967) 1,371,000.

Kikuyu, Bantu people of E Africa. Agriculturalists, many joined polit. movements, such as MAU MAU, after losing land in Kenya.

Kikuyu, Bantic language of Niger-Congo group, with over 1 million speakers in S parts of Africa.

Kilanea, active volcano on slope of MAUNA LOA, Hawaii. Crater is 3,646 ft. high.

Kildare, inland county, S Repub. of Ireland. Area: 654 sq. mi.; county town, Kildare. Largely flat, arable land. Headquarters of Irish horse racing at the Curragh. Pop. (1966) 66,486.

Kiang or Wild Ass

Kilimanjaro, mountain (19,565 ft.) highest in Africa, NE Tanzania. Comprises 2 peaks, Kibo and Mawenzi. First climbed 1848.

Kilkenny, inland county, SE Repub. of Ireland. Area: 800 sq. mi.; county town, Kilkenny. Largely agric. region. Pop. (1966) 60,472.

killdeer, large plover of N America, *Charadrius vociferus*. Penetrating cry.

Killiecrankie, pass in Perthshire, Scotland. Scene of battle (1689) to restore James II to Eng. throne.

killifish, fish of *Fundulus* genus, related to guppy. Species include African, *F. guloris*.

kilt, in Scotland, wrap-over skirt developed (17th cent.) from wearing of belted plaid. Usually tartan, pleated at back, about knee-length. Regarded as national dress of Scotsmen, esp. Highlanders; worn by Highland and Lowland regiments in Brit. army, and some Irish regiments.

Kimberley, city of Cape Prov., South Africa. Centre of great diamond mining region. Pop. (1963) 79,031.

Kinabalu, Mount, peak of N Borneo (13,455 ft., highest on island). Feared by natives as abode of spirits.

Kincardineshire, county of E Scotland. Area: 382 sq. mi.; county town, Stonehaven. Mountainous, sheep grazing and quarrying; fishing. Pop. (1966) 25,000.

kindergarten [Ger: children's garden], educational system, often emphasizing play, for children at informal, pre-elementary school level. Developed (1837) by Friedrich Froebel.

kinetics, in physics, study of forces that produce or change motion. Governed by principles, *e.g.* Newton's Laws of Motion, of MECHANICS. In chemistry, study of rates of reactions. Factors include temperature, pressure, concentration and composition of reactants.

King, Martin Luther (1929–68), Amer. clergyman and civil rights leader. Founded Southern Christian Leadership Council. Chief advocate of non-violent action in resistance to segregation of Negroes; awarded Nobel Peace Prize (1964). Wrote *Where Do We Go from Here* (1967). Assassinated in Memphis, Tenn.

King, William Lyon Mackenzie (1874–1950), Canadian P.M. (1921–6, 1926–30, 1935–48). His request for dissolution of parl. (1926) provoked constitutional crisis when Gov.-General BYNG refused and appointed Arthur Meighen as P.M.; returned to power by subsequent election. Instrumental in elaborating STATUTE OF WESTMINSTER (1931).

Led Canada's participation in World War 2.

King Charles spaniel, variety of Eng. toy spaniel with black and tan coat. Favourite of Charles II, after whom it was named.

king cobra, largest of venomous snakes, *Naja hannah,* of SE Asia and East Indies. Grows to more than 15 ft. in length.

king snake, non-poisonous constrictor snake of N America. Species include eastern king snake, *Lampropeltis getulus,* which eats rodents.

kingbird, bird of genus, *Tyrannus,* with grey-black plumage and white tail. Species of E N America called tyrant flycatcher and bee martin.

kingcrab, edible species, *Paralithodes camtschatica,* of stone crab. Found off N Pacific coasts.

kingfisher, any bird of family Alcedinidae, of world-wide distribution, esp. SE Asia. Feeds on fish and insects. Usually crested, has bright plumage.

Kings, books of OT, called 1st and 2nd Kings. Relate history of Hebrews from death of David until fall of Judah. Include reign of Solomon, division of kingdom into Israel and Judah, and lives of prophets, Elijah and Elisha.

Kingbird (of Paradise)

Kings Canyon, National Park, E California, US. Area: 719 sq. mi.; estab. 1940. Dominated by 2 river canyons.

King's Counsel *see* QUEEN'S COUNSEL.

Kingsley, Charles (1819–75), Eng. clergyman and writer. Opponent of J. H. NEWMAN. Best known for novels

Sofia Cathedral, Kiev, the oldest church in the Soviet Union

Kinkajou

Westward Ho! (1855) and *The Water Babies* (1863).

Kingston, cap. and port of Jamaica. Founded (1692); became cap. (1872). Exports sugar, rum, bananas, bauxite. Pop. (1964) 126,000.

Kingston-upon-Hull *see* HULL.

King William's War *see* FRENCH AND INDIAN WARS.

kinkajou, nocturnal mammal, *Potos caudivolvulus,* related to raccoon. Found in C and S Amer. forests; has prehensile tail.

Kinross-shire, county of Scotland. Area: 82 sq. mi.; county town, Kinross. Comprises level plain, where cereals grown, surrounded by hills. Pop. (1966) 6,000.

Kinsangani, formerly Stanleyville, city of Zaire (Congo) on the Congo at head of navigation from Kinshasa. Cotton and rice exported. Scene of much fighting in Congolese war (1964). Pop. 126,500.

Kinsey, Alfred Charles (1894–1956), Amer. biologist. Known for his work, *Sexual Behaviour in the Human Male* (1948), popularly known as *The Kinsey Report.*

Kinshasa, formerly Leopoldville, cap. of Zaire (Congo); river port of the Congo. Commercial and transport centre. Founded (1887); became cap. of Belgian Congo (1929). Pop. (1960) 403,000.

Kiowa, tribe of N Amer., orig. of Montana area (17th cent.), later spreading throughout W US. Typical nomadic Plains culture. Allied with Comanche, waged wars against both whites and other tribes.

Kipling, Rudyard (1865–1936), Eng. writer, b. India. Author of popular poems such as 'Mandalay' and 'Gunga Din', stories in *Plain Tales from the Hills* (1888), and children's stories such as *The Jungle Book* (1894), *Just So Stories* (1902); works shed light on India, army life and Brit. imperialism. Awarded Nobel Prize for Literature (1907).

Kirchner, Ernst (1880–1938), Ger. expressionist painter. Early work uses harsh colours; later work abstract.

Kirghiz, Turkic language of Altaic family, with 1 million speakers in USSR.

Kirghizia, constituent repub. of USSR, in C Asia. Area: 78,000 sq. mi.; cap. Frunze. Mountainous Tien Shan system dominates; primarily pastoral people. Pop. (1965 est.) 2,609,000.

Kirin, Chilin, prov. of E Manchuria, China. Area, 70,000 sq. mi.; cap. Changchun; main city, Kirin. Mountainous, forested; agriculture, grazing and lumbering important; lead, iron, gold, coal mined. Contains Yenpien Korean Autonomous district. Pop. (1957) 12,550,000.

Kirkcudbrightshire, maritime county of SW Scotland. Area: 899 sq. mi.; county town, Kirkcudbright. Hilly in NW; undulating agric. land with cattle-grazing in SE. Pop. (1966) 29,000.

Kirov, oblast of Russ. SFSR. Area: *c.* 40,735 sq. mi.; admin. centre Kirov (orig. Vyatka). Large phosphorite deposits; textiles, tyres and machinery manufacture. Pop. (1959) 1,919,000.

kirsch *see* BRANDY.

Kiruna, mining town of N Sweden. Centre of Lappland iron-mining district. Iron ore (60–70% pure) shipped to Lulea (Baltic Sea) and Narvik. Pop. 27,000.

kitchen, part of house assigned to cooking and cleaning. In the 20th cent., labour-saving appliances have been introduced.

Kitchener, Horatio Herbert, 1st Earl Kitchener of Khartoum and of Broome (1850–1916), Brit. army officer. Defeated Khalifa's army at Omdurman (1898), then appointed Gov.-General of Sudan. Organized tactics against Boers (1900–2); Sec. of State for war (1914–16). Drowned off Orkney Is. on way to Russia.

Bathing Women by Kirchner

kite, bird of vulture group. Feeds on small reptiles and insects. Species include red kite, *Milvus milvus,* and black kite, *M. migrans,* of Europe, Asia, Africa and Australia.

kithara, U-shaped musical instrument of the ancient Greeks, with 5 to 7 strings stretched between a crossbar at the top and a sound box at the bottom. Played by plucking.

kittiwake, *Rissa tridactyla,* small white gull of N Atlantic with yellow bill. Other species found in N Pacific and Bering Sea.

Kittredge, George Lyman (1860–1941), Amer. teacher and literary historian. Edited *English and Scottish Popular Ballads* (1904; with H. C. Sargent) and *The Complete Works of Shakespeare* (1936). Also published books on aspects of Chaucer, *Sir Gawain,* and Malory.

kiwi, rare nocturnal flightless insectivorous bird of New Zealand, with no tail and short wings hidden beneath brown plumage. Species include common brown kiwi, *Apteryx australis* and great spotted kiwi, *A. haasti.*

Klee, Paul (1879–1940), Swiss artist. Influenced by primitive African sculpture. Works, noted for piquancy of design, include *Twittering Machine, Musical Dinner Party.* Taught at BAUHAUS. Worked both as painter and graphic artist.

Klein, Abraham Moses (1909–), Canadian poet. Edited *Canadian Zionist* (1936–7). Zionism found expression in *Hath Not a Jew* (1940) and *The Hitleriad* (1944). *The Second Scroll* (1951) is parable in form of pilgrimage to Israel.

Klein, Felix, FRS (1849–1925), Ger. mathematician. Noted for research in geometrics and theory of functions.

Kleist, Heinrich Bernt Wilhelm von (1777–1811), Ger. Romantic poet and playwright. Works include the comedy *Der Zerbrochene Krug* (1806), and *Das Käthchen von Heilbronn* (1810), *Der Prinz von Homburg* (pub. 1821).

Klinger, Friedrich Maximilian von (1752–1831), Ger. dramatist whose play *Sturm und Drang* (1776) gave STURM UND DRANG literary period its name.

klipspringer, *Oreotragus oreotragus*, small African antelope found in mountainous regions from Cape of Good Hope to Sahara Desert.

Klondike, region of W Yukon Territory, Canada. Gold strike on Bonanza Creek (1896) followed by gold rush (1897–8). Dawson, centre of rush, has declined in population from *c.* 20,000 to under 1,000.

Klopstock, Friedrich Gottlieb (1724–1803), Ger. poet. Greatest work is unfinished epic *Der Messias* (1748–83).

knapweed, hardhead, Spanish button, perennial plant of daisy family allied to thistle. Species include greater knapweed, *Centaurea scabiosa*, and N Amer. brown knapweed, *C. jacea*.

knee, joint formed by lower end of femur and upper end of tibia and by the patella or kneecap. Powerful ligaments and muscles maintain stability.

Kneller, Sir Godfrey (1646–1723), Eng. portrait painter, b. Germany. Court painter to Charles II, William III and George I. Painted portraits of fellow-members of Whig Kit-Kat Club.

Knickerbocker, Dutch family name which came to refer to US Dutch settlers in general. Pseudonym of WASHINGTON IRVING was Diedrich Knickerbocker.

Knight, Dame Laura, née Johnson (1877–1970), Eng. painter. Best known for studies of circus and theatrical life.

knighthood, orig. system of conferring royal favour as reward for religious or military service. Religious orders included TEMPLARS; military, Knights of St John. 9 Brit. orders still exist. They include The Order of the Garter (founded *c.* 1347), the Thistle (1687), the Bath (1725), the British Empire (1917).

Knights Hospitallers *see* HOSPITALLERS.

Knights of Columbus (K.C. or K. of C.), US society for R.C. men over age of 18 founded (1882) at New Haven, Conn. Publishes monthly *Columbia*. 1968 membership totalled 1,183,896.

Knights Templars *see* TEMPLARS.

knitting *see* TEXTILES.

knives, among the oldest tools and weapons, known to primitive man. Stone knives were used in paleolithic times. They were shaped by flaking, battering, or later, grinding. Modern knives have hardened steel blades attached to some form of holding part, usually of wood, metal, ceramic or bone. Sheffield (in England) and Solingen (in Germany) have, and Toledo had, a reputation for making fine knives.

Knossos *see* CNOSSUS.

knot, *Calidris canatus*, small wading bird of sandpiper family, abundant on European shores; breeds in Arctic regions.

knotweed, several hardy perennial plants, genus *Polygonum*, with knotty stems and broad, oval leaves.

Know-Nothing movement, in US history, popular name for American Party (*fl.* 1850s) which sought exclusion of Catholics and foreigners from public office. Name from members' habit of answering questions with 'I don't know'.

Knox, John (*c.* 1510–72), founder of Scot. Presbyterianism. Converted from Catholicism, went to Geneva during Mary I of England's reign. Returned (1558) and estab. Presbyterian movement in Scotland. Tried to abolish papal authority. After abdication of Catholic Mary, Queen of Scots, set up Church of Scotland.

koala, *Phascolarctos cinereus*, small, tailless Austral. marsupial, *c.* 2 ft. long, with grey fur. Eats eucalyptus leaves and flowers. Protected since 1936.

Kobe, largest port of Japan, on Honshu Is. Handles *c.* 37% Japan's foreign trade. Industries include ship-building, machinery and metal, and food processing plants. Educational centre. Pop. (1965) 1,217,000.

Koblenz, cap. of Rhineland-Palatinate, West Germany, at confluence of Rhine and Moselle rivers. Important wine centre, also manufactures machinery, pianos. Pop. (1963) 95,000.

Koch, Ludwig, (1881–), Ger. author and naturalist. Famous for recordings and interpretations of bird-song.

Koch, Robert (1843–1910), Ger. physician and bacteriologist. Discovered nature of germs causing anthrax, tuberculosis and cholera. Awarded Nobel Prize for Physiology and Medicine (1905) for developing tuberculin test.

Kocher, Emil Theodor (1841–1917), Swiss surgeon. Awarded Nobel Prize

Knapweed

for Physiology and Medicine (1909) for research on thyroid gland.

Kodály, Zoltán (1882–1967), Hungarian composer. Collaborated with Bartók on collections of folk melodies. Compositions, largely nationalistic, include *Summer Evening* (1906), *Háry János* (1927) *Dances of Galánta* (1933).

Kodiak, largest island in Gulf of Alaska. Area: 3,465 sq. mi.; cap. Kodiak. Salmon fishing chief industry. Habitat of Kodiak bear.

Kodok, formerly Fashoda, village on the White Nile in W central Sudan. Scene of FASHODA INCIDENT.

Koestler, Arthur (1905–), Hungarian novelist and journalist. Works, mainly anti-Communist, include *Spanish Testament* (1937), *Darkness at Noon* (1941) and *The God that Failed* (1950).

Koh-i-noor [Persian: mountain of light], large diamond found at Golconda, India. Acquired by Queen Victoria (1850), re-cut and placed among Brit. crown jewels.

kohlrabi, *Brassica oleracea gongylodes*, edible plant of cabbage family. Grown mostly for cattle fodder.

Koko Nor, Chinghai, Tsinghai, salt lake in NE Tsinghai prov., China, 350 sq. mi. at 10,500 ft. above sea level.

Kokoschka, Oskar (1886–), Austrian artist; noted for portraits and landscapes. *See* illus. p. 318.

kola, tree of W trop. Africa, West Indies and Brazil. Extract of leaves used in flavouring soft drinks.

Koldewey, Robert (1855–1925), Ger. architect and archaeologist. Discoveries at Babylon (1899–1917)

The Crab by Kokoschka

revealed massive fortifications and complex streets.

Kolyma, river, 1,550 mi. long, of NE Siberia, USSR; drains area of 250,000 sq. mi. Upper basin rich in gold mines.

Komodo dragon, dragon lizard, *Varanus komodoensis,* world's largest lizard, may reach 10 ft. in length. Discovered (1912) on Komodo and adjacent Indonesian islands. Relic of extinct order of giant reptiles.

Königsberg *see* KALININGRAD.

kookaburra, *Dacelo noraeguinaea,* laughing jackass; arboreal kingfisher of Australasia with bill hooked at end. Named from its cry.

Kooning, William De (1904–   ), Dutch-Amer. painter. Exponent of abstract expressionism, best known for paintings of women, characterized by erotic style and colour.

Kootenay National Park, SE Brit. Columbia, Canada. Area: 543 sq. mi.; estab. 1920. Predominantly mountainous; has hot mineral springs.

Koran [Arabic: *quran,* reading], Islam bible, sacred book of Muslims. Regarded as Word of God revealed to Mohammed by angel Gabriel. Historically of Jewish and, to some extent, Christian origin.

Korda, Sir Alexander (1893–1956), Hungarian film director. His films include *Private Life of Henry VIII* (1932), *Rembrandt* (1936), *Lady Hamilton* (1941), *Perfect Strangers* (1945).

Kordofanian, little-known Niger-Congo language family.

Korea [**Cho-son**], peninsular region of NE Asia, divided since 1948 into North Korea and South Korea. Area: 85,286 sq. mi. Mountainous in E, fertile soil; diverse climate. People of Mongolian extraction, history heavily influenced by Chinese; Confucianism made official religion under Yi dynasty (1392–1910); annexed by Japan. Independent after World War 2, then divided. Uneasy truce remained after Korean War (1950–3).

Korea, Democratic People's Republic of [**North Korea**], country of N region

of KOREA. Area: 46,540 sq. mi.; cap. Pyongyang. Agric. and indust. production improved after estab. of Communist govt. (1948). Pop. (1964) 12,100,000.

Korea, Republic of [**South Korea**], country of S region of KOREA. Area:

38,031 sq. mi.; cap. Seoul. Main occupations: grain farming, fishing. Republican govt. interrupted by coup

which estab. military regime (1961–3). Pop. (1964) 29,375,000.

Korean, the only known language of its family, it has 34 million speakers in Korea and part of Manchuria; in structure very similar to Japanese.

Korean War, conflict fought between Communist and non-Communist forces (1950–3) in Korea. Invasion by North Korean troops (soon backed by Chinese) led to UN authorization to support South Korea with an international military operation. Fighting centred around 38th parallel. Ceasefire negotiations (begun 1951 at Panmunjom) led to 1953 agreement ending war.

Kosali, Eastern Hindi, Indic Indo-European language, with 30 million speakers in N parts of India.

Kosciusko, Thaddeus (1746–1817), Polish military officer. Fought for colonials against Britain in Amer. Revolution. Leader of unsuccessful rebellion (1794) against Prussian and Russ. control of Poland.

Kosciusko, Mount, peak, SE New South Wales, Australia. Highest (7,305 ft.) in Australia.

kosher [Hebrew: fit for use], term for food, esp. meat, complying with Jewish dietary laws. Meat must be killed according to Mosaic law and drained of blood.

Kossuth, Louis (1802–94), Hungarian revolutionary. Instrumental in Hungarian uprising against Austria (Mar. 1848); Pres. of short-lived repub. (1849), fled abroad after Russ. troops moved in to aid Austria.

Kosygin, Alexei Nikolayevich (1904–), Soviet polit. leader. Economics and indust. expert under Khrushchev, whom he succeeded (1964) as premier and chairman of council of ministers.

koumiss, popular Tartar and Arab drink, derived from mare's or camel's milk. Used as a diuretic.

Koussevitzky, Serge Alexandrovich (1874–1951), Amer. conductor, b. Russia. Led Boston Symphony Orchestra (1924–49).

Kowloon, city and port of Hong Kong, on mainland of China. Ceded to Britain (1861); strategic importance; source of metal deposits. Pop. (1961) 1,580,000.

Kozhikode, formerly Calicut (1956), seaport of Kerala, SW India; famous spice centre; exports ginger, pepper, cinnamon. Plundered for spices (16th cent.). Pop. (1960) 127,000.

Krafft-Ebing, Richard von (1840–1902), Ger. neurologist, recognized authority on psychology of mental disorders. Most famous work is *Psychopathia Sexualis* (1886, Eng. tr. 1892).

krait, several venomous snakes, genus *Bungarus,* of SE Asia and Malay Archipelago.

Krak, El Kerak, city in S central Jordan, formerly walled citadel of Moabites. Captured by Saladin (1188); Christians expelled by Turks (1910). Modern trade centre. Pop. c. 10,000.

Krakatoa, Krakatau, volcanic island in Sunda Strait, Indonesia. Major eruption (1883) almost destroyed island. Resultant tidal waves killed c. 36,000 people. Volcanic action again reported (1950).

Krakow, Cracow, city of Poland, on Vistula R. Cap. from 14th cent. until 1595. Became Austrian in partition of Poland (1795); under protection of Austria, Russia and Prussia (1815); reverted to Poland (1919). Cultural centre with Jagellonian University

(founded 1364). Iron and steel industries. Pop. (1965) 517,000.

Krebs, Sir Hans Adolf (1900–), Ger.-British biochemist. With F. A. Lipmann, awarded Nobel Prize for Physiology and Medicine (1953) for studying conversion of food to energy.

Kreisler, Fritz (1875–1962), Austrian violinist. Won Vienna Conservatoire Gold Medal aged 10; became world famous.

Kremlin, triangular walled citadel (dating from 12th cent.) at centre of city of Moscow. Contains Uspenski and Arkhangelski Cathedrals, govt. offices. Grand Palace, built 19th cent., now houses Soviet Supreme Council.

Krenek, Ernst (1900–), Austrian-Amer. composer. Noted for jazz opera *Johnny Strikes Up* (1927). Also composed chamber, orchestral and choral music.

Kreutzer, Rodolphe (1766–1831), Fr. violinist and composer. Beethoven dedicated to him *Kreutzer Sonata.* Best known for 40 études for violin. Composed operas, concertos and sonatas.

Krishna, in Hindu religion, 8th incarnation of VISHNU. Krishna cult currently very popular.

Krivoy Rog, city of Ukrainian SSR, USSR, on Ingulets R. Centre of iron mining industries. Captured by Nazis in World War 2, suffered heavy damages. Pop. (1967) 498,000.

Kronstadt, city and port of USSR, on Kotlin Is., Gulf of Finland. Founded (1703) by Peter I. Centre of revolutionary activity (1825, 1905, 1917); defended Leningrad in World War 2. Now base of Soviet Baltic fleet.

Kropotkin, Piotr Alexeievich (1842–1921), Russ. anarchist prince. Became interested in peasants and renounced title. Fled from Russia after arrest for political views; imprisoned in France, after revolution of 1917.

Kruger, [Stephanus Johannes] Paul (1825–1904), South African statesman. Secured independence of Transvaal (1881) by negotiating Pretoria Agreement with British. Pres. of Transvaal (1883–1900), opposed policies of Cecil Rhodes.

Kruger National Park, game reserve in Transvaal, South Africa. Area: 8,400 sq. mi. Founded (1898) by Pres. Paul Kruger.

Krupp, Ger. family of armament manufacturers. **Friedrich Krupp** (1787–1826) estab. steel plant in Essen. His son **Alfred Krupp** ('The Cannon King') (1812–87) specialized in armaments and his son **Friedrich Alfred ('Fritz') Krupp** (1854–1902)

expanded the business. Armament manufacture carried on by **Gustav Krupp von Bohlen und Halbach** (1870–1950) and **Alfried Krupp von Bohlen und Halbach** (1907–67) who was imprisoned for war crimes (1948–51).

Krutch, Joseph Wood (1893–1970), Amer. author and literary critic. Wrote *The Modern Temper* (1929) and *The Measure of Man* (1954) as well as books on Thoreau and Samuel Johnson.

krypton *see* NOBLE GASES.

Ku Klux Klan, in US history, 2 distinct secret societies; original Ku Klux Klan founded (1866) to maintain white supremacy in South. Disbandment ordered (1869), but local organizations continued. Second Ku Klux Klan (founded 1915) added to white supremacy, intense hatred of foreigners, anti-Catholicism and anti-Semitism. Spread in North and South during 1920s. After World War 2 several states barred the order.

Kuala Lumpur, town, SW Malaya, cap. of Selangor and Federation of Malaya. Economy based on rubber and tin. Pop. (1957) 316,000.

kuass, Russ. mildly alcoholic beverage. Made by fermenting rye meal, dough of wheat and adding sugar and fruit.

Kubelik, Rafael (1914–), Czech conductor at Prague and later Chicago (1950), Covent Garden (1955–8), Bayerischer Rundfunk, Munich, from 1961.

Kublai Khan (1216–94), Mongol emperor. Became khan (1260) of empire founded by grandfather, Genghis Khan. Defeated Sun dynasty of China (1279). Founded Yüan dynasty. Favoured Buddhism but tolerated other religions.

Kubrick, Stanley (1928–), Amer. film director. Films include *Paths of Glory, Dr. Strangelove, 2001: A Space Odyssey.*

Kuchuk Kainarji, Treaty of (1774), peace treaty between Russia and

A fine hand-written and illuminated Koran from Atjeh, Sumatra

Turkey. Ceded certain Black Sea ports to Russia, thus facilitating annexation of the Crimea (1783) and gave Russia rights as protector of Christians in Ottoman Empire.

kudu, *Strepsiceros strepsiceros,* antelope of E and S Africa. Male has long spiral horns.

Kuibyshev, formerly Samara, city of RSFSR, on Volga R. Industrial centre, with metallurgical and chemical industries. Founded (1586) as Muscovite stronghold. Pop. (1967) 969,000.

kulan, *Equus hemionus,* rare wild ass of Mongolia.

Kulturkampf, struggle in Germany to restrict power of Catholic Church in politics, as represented through Centre party. Govt. under Chancellor Bismarck passed series of laws (1873–87), incl. measures to break down school system. Ceased when Bismarck, fearing rise of Socialism, rescinded anti-Catholic policies.

kumquat [Chinese: golden orange], shrub native to China and Japan, producing a small orange-like fruit often candied as a sweetmeat.

Kun, Bela (1886–*c.* 1937), Hungarian polit. leader. Head of short-lived Communist dictatorship (1919–20); forced to withdraw troops from Slovakia after overrunning region. Thought to have died in Communist purges of Russia.

Kung-fu-tzu *see* CONFUCIUS.

Kuomintang, Chinese nationalist movement, organized (1912) in accordance with principles of SUN YAT-SEN. Strengthened (1922–4) with help of Communists, later purged. Estab. Nanking govt. (1928) under CHIANG KAI-SHEK after gaining military control of country. Authori-

tarian rule lasted until 1947, when Civil War forced Chiang and Nationalists to flee (1950) to Taiwan.

Kurdish, Iranian Indo-European language, with *c.* 5 million speakers in parts of Turkey, Iraq, Iran and USSR.

Kurdistan, plateau and mountainous region (area: *c.* 74,000 sq. mi.) occupying parts of NE Iraq, NW Iran, E Turkey and Soviet Armenia. Inhabited by several million **Kurds,** nomadic pastoral people; warlike, fanatic Sunnite Moslems.

Kuril Islands, chain of volcanic islands of RSFSR, in NW Pacific Ocean between Kamchatka and Hokkaido. Total area: 6,159 sq. mi. Sulphur mining, fishing, hunting. Became Japanese possession (1875); annexed (1945) by USSR.

Kurosawa, Akira (1910–), Jap. film director. Films include *Rashomon, The Seven Samurai, High and Low.*

Kusch, Polycarp (1911–), Amer. physicist. Shared Nobel Prize for Physics (1955) with W. E. Lamb, Jr. for work on electron properties.

Kutch, Ranns of, extensive mud and salt flats between India and W Pakistan. Flooded in monsoon season, soil is infertile. Boundary disputed by India and Pakistan.

Kutenai, N Amer. Indians of Kutenai language group. Driven W by Blackfoot, apparently settled near Kootenay R., Oregon from which they take their name. Later settled on Flathead Reservation, Montana.

Kutusov, Mikhail Ilarionovitch (1745–1813), Russ. field-marshal. Commanded forces against Napoleon's invasion (1812); after battle of Borodino, retreated and defeated French at Smolensk after their withdrawal from Moscow (1812).

Kuwait [Al-Kuwait], independent Arab sheikdom, NE Arabia, near

head of Persian Gulf. Area: 5,800 sq. mi.; cap. Kuwait. Mainly desert with 20% of world's known oil reserves.

Brit. protectorate (estab. 1897), terminated 1961 with proviso for military aid if requested. Pop. (1966) 467,000.

Kuwait City, cap. and chief port of Kuwait; industry based on oil. Pop. (1961) 152,000.

Kwa, group of Niger-Congo languages, incl. Ibo and Yoruba, spoken in W Africa.

Kwakiutl, North Amer. Indian tribe of Wakashan linguistic stock. Inhabit N Vancouver Is. and adjacent mainland. Dependent on seafood and berries.

Kwangsi-Chuang, inland prov., S China, until 1958 Kwangsi prov. Area: 85,868 sq. mi.; cap. Nanning. Chief products are rice, sugar cane, timber, coal, iron ore. Pop. (1963) 19,390,000.

Kwangtung, maritime prov. of S China on South China Sea. Area: 89,344 sq. mi.; cap. Canton. MACAO and HONG KONG on coast. Sub-trop. climate with heavy rainfall. Agriculture in river valleys and delta lowlands. Silk industry important. Mineral resources include manganese, coal, tungsten. Pop. (1963) 37,640,000.

Kweichow, prov. of SW China. Area: 67,142 sq. mi.; cap. Kweiyang. Rice, wheat, beans in lowland; plantations and forests in highland. Pop. (1963) 16,890,000.

kyanite, metamorphic mineral found under conditions of high stress and moderate temperature. Occurs as long blue or white crystals; insoluble in acid. Hardness varies.

Kyd, Thomas (*c.* 1557–95), Eng. dramatist, contemporary of Shakespeare. Best remembered for play *The Spanish Tragedy* (1589).

kymograph, instrument for recording pressure of fluids, esp. of blood in blood-vessel.

Kyoto, city and cultural centre of S Honshu, Japan. Wood-carving, embroidery and bronze handicraft exported. Many ancient Buddhist temples. Founded 8th cent.; cap. of Japan (794–1868). Pop. (1965) 1,365,000.

Kyrie eleison [Gk: Lord have mercy], in R.C. Church, invocation incorporated in Mass. Also used in High Church of England.

Kyushu *see* JAPAN.

Kudu

L

labour, in economics, factor of production. In perfect competition, price of labour (wages) is elastic and depends on demand.

Labour Party, in UK, polit. party pledged to implement socialist policies (see SOCIALISM). Known, until 1906, as Labour Representation Committee; adopted programme (1918) and set up local branches of party to which individual members were admitted. Official opposition by 1922, formed minority govt. (1924, 1929). Took office as majority govt. (1945–51, 1964–70). Strongly supported by TRADE UNIONS. Prominent Labour Party figures have included Ramsay Macdonald, Aneurin Bevan, Clement Attlee and Harold Wilson.

Ladybird

Labrador, part of prov. of NEW-FOUNDLAND, NE Canada at mouth of Gulf of St Lawrence. Area: 110,000 sq. mi.; cap. Battle Harbour. Mountainous terrain has discouraged settlement. Fishing, iron mining and timber chief occupations. Pop. (1961) 13,534.

Labrador Current, cold ocean current flowing S from Baffin Bay to Newfoundland and into Gulf of St Lawrence. Causes semi-permanent belt of fog; floating ice constitutes continuous hazard to shipping.

labradorite, feldspar blue-greenish mineral. Popular semi-precious stone.

laburnum, *Laburnum anagyroides*, deciduous tree native to S and C Europe, widely grown in US. Has clusters of yellow flowers and poisonous seeds.

lac insect, scale insect of genus *Laccifer lacca*, of India and SE Asia. Female secretes waxy material, a source of lacquer and shellac.

Laccadive, Minicoy and Amindivi Islands, group of 19 islands of India, in Arabian Sea. Area: 11 sq. mi. Pop. (1961) 24,108.

lace, hand or machine patterned fabric. Types of hand-made laces include crochet, bobbin and needle-point (buttonhole stitch). Finest lace made from linen. Lace-making developed 16th cent., reached height of production (18th cent.) in Flanders. Machine-made lace 1st appeared *c.* 1760. Chief modern centres: France, Belgium, England, Ireland, Italy.

lace bug, insect of family Tingidae with lacy pattern on head, thorax and wings. Feeds on leaves of trees.

Lacedaemon, Laconia, in ancient history, part of S Peloponnesus, Greece. Region named after myth. ruler, Lacedaemon, son of Zeus. Cap. Sparta, named after his wife.

lacewing, any of several insects of family Chrysopidae, with delicate wings. Larvae prey on aphids.

Lachesis, in Gk. myth., 1 of 3 Fates who controlled lives of men. Charged with measuring length of life.

Laclos, [Pierre] Choderlos de (1741–1803), Fr. writer and army officer. Wrote novel *Les Liaisons Dangereuses* (1782).

Lady Fern

lacrosse, outdoor field sport originated by N Amer. Indians, now Canada's national game. Played by 2 teams of 10 players; women's lacrosse team has 12 players. Popular in E US.

lactic acid see LACTOSE.

lactose, sugar occurring in milk, less sweet than cane sugar. Found in mammalian milk. Bacterial fermentation with glucose produces lactic acid.

Ladoga, Lake, largest European fresh-water body of water, NW Russ. SFSR. Area: 7,100 sq. mi. Provides link for Volga R., Black and White Seas.

Lady Amherst's pheasant, *Chrisolophus amherstiae*, colourful pheasant of China and Tibet. Crown is green, crest red, breast and abdomen white, and cape barred.

Lady Day see ANNUNCIATION.

lady fern, *Athyrium filixfemina*, large fern with delicate fronds. Found in damp regions of N and W Europe.

Lace Ruff. Detail from a portrait by Moreelse

ladybird, ladybug, small beetle of family Coccinellidae. Red or yellow with black spots; most species feed on aphids. *See* illus. p. 321.

lady's bedstraw, *Gallium verum,* perennial plant with small yellow flowers. Common in dry grassy areas of Europe.

lady's ear drop *see* FUCHSIA.

lady's smock, cuckoo flower, *Cardamine pratensis,* perennial plant related to cabbage. Has white and lilac flowers.

lady's tresses, any orchid of genus *Spiranthes.* Species include *S. autumnalis* and *S. romanzoffiana.*

Ladysmith, town in Natal, South Africa. Brit. garrison besieged (1899–1900) by Boers during South African War. Pop. (1965 est.) 28,000.

Lafayette, Marie Joseph Paul Yves Roch Gilbert du Motier, Marquis de (1757–1834), Fr. general and statesman. Fought in Amer. Revolution against Britain, negotiated for Fr. aid (1780). Active in Fr. Revolution, commanded National Guard (1789). Opposed Jacobins, imprisoned in Austria (1792–7) after deserting army.

La Follette, Robert Marion (1855–1925), Amer. statesman. Initiated reform legislation as Gov. of Wisconsin (1901–6). Senator (1906–25), opposed business interests and US entry into World War 1. Pres. candidate (1924) for Progressive party. Won nearly 5 million votes.

La Fontaine, Henri (1854–1943), Belgian lawyer. Headed International Peace Bureau after 1907. Awarded Nobel Peace Prize (1913).

La Fontaine, Jean de (1621–95), Fr. poet. Author of *Fables Choisies* (1668–94) based on AESOP and other classical sources. Instrumental in re-estab. of fable as poetic form.

lager, a light beer. Most European 'beers' are lagers. Contains more unfermented malt extract and carbonic acid and less alcohol than beer.

Lancer

Lagerkvist, Pär Fabian (1891–), Swedish writer. Novels include *The Dwarf* (1944), *Barabbas* (1950); plays collected in *Dramatik* (3 vols., 1956). Awarded Nobel Prize for Literature (1951).

Lagerlöf, Selma Ottiliana Lovisa (1858–1940), Swedish novelist. Works include *The Saga of Gösta Berling* (1891) and children's classic *The Wonderful Adventures of Nils* (1906). Awarded Nobel Prize for Literature (1909).

Lagos, federal cap. and chief port, W Nigeria. Partially built on offshore islands. Exports palm oil, peanuts; communication centre. Formerly centre of slave-trade market; annexed (1861) by Britain. Pop. (1963) 675,000.

Lagrange, Joseph Louis, Comte (1736–1813), Fr. mathematician and astronomer. Did important studies of sound vibration and Moon and Jupiter. Instrumental in France's adoption of metric system of weights and measures.

La Guardia, Fiorello Henry (1882–1947), Amer. polit. leader. As mayor of New York City (1934–45), instituted large-scale reform.

Lahore, city in West Pakistan. Has notable Moslem art remains, Punjab University and museum. Financial centre. Pop. (1961) 1,297,000.

laissez-faire, in economics, doctrine that economic system functions best without govt. interference; unregulated by artificial means, economic order tends to favour maximum good for individual and community as a whole. First formulated by PHYSIOCRATS in reaction against MERCANTILISM; later adapted by Adam Smith, founder of classical ECONOMICS, who stated that national wealth could be better achieved through competition than state regulation. Guide to polit. and economic action in 19th cent., competition's tendency to foster monopoly led to govt. regulation by beginning of 20th cent.

lake [Scot: *loch;* Irish: *lough*], inland body of water occupying basin. Formed by filling of glacial or volcanic depression, or by interference in river system, often by artificial means, *e.g.* damming.

Lake District, region of NW England, mountainous with 16 lakes, in Cumberland, Westmorland, Lancashire. Largest lake is Windermere and highest mountain, Scafell Pike (3,210 ft.).

lake dwelling, habitation built on artificial island, usually made of tree trunks; preserved by waterlogging.

The Pearl Mosque, Lahore

First found in Switzerland, remains date from Neolithic era.

lalique, art nouveau style glassware, decorated with figures in relief. Introduced by René Lalique (1860–1945), Fr. jeweller.

Lally, Thomas Arthur, Baron de Tollendal, Comte de (1702–66), Fr. army officer of Irish parentage. Gov. of Fr. India (1758–61). Executed for alleged treason after surrender to British at Pondicherry.

Lalo, [Victor Antoine] Édouard (1823–92), Fr. composer. Author of opera *Le Roi d'Ys* and orchestral violin work *Symphonie Espagnole.*

Lamaism, form of Buddhism prevalent in Tibet, Nepal and Mongolia. Introduced into Tibet in 7th cent., monastery estab. near Lhasa (749). Spiritual head, DALAI LAMA, ruled in Tibet until 1959.

Lamarck, Jean Baptiste Pierre Antoine de Monet, Chevalier de (1744–1829), Fr. naturalist. Pioneered work on invertebrate paleontology with classification system. Author of *Flore française* (1778). His theory of evolution, forerunner of Darwinism, based inherited characteristics on environmental need.

Lamartine, Alphonse de (1790–1869), Fr. writer and polit. leader. Romantic poetry best seen in *Les Méditations Poétiques* (1820). Other works include *Histoire de Girondins* (1847). Headed provisional govt. after 1848 Revolution; his moderation led to loss in support.

Lamb, Charles (1775–1834), Eng. writer. Friend of Coleridge, master of critical essays as in *Specimens of English Poets* (1808) and *Essays of Elia* (1823).

Lamb, William, 2nd Viscount Mel-

bourne (1779–1848), Eng. statesman. Whig P.M. (1834, 1835–41) during period of much social reform. Trusted adviser of young Queen Victoria. His wife, **Caroline Lamb, Viscountess Melbourne** (1785–1828), known for her affair with Lord Byron.

Lambert, Constant (1905–51), Eng. composer and conductor. Best known for musical score *Rio Grande* (1929).

Lambert, Johann Heinrich (1728–77), Ger. mathematician and scientist. Helped develop concept of hyperbolic functions in trigonometry; also did studies of light, heat and colour.

Lambeth Conference, assembly of all diocesan bishops of Anglican Communion. Held every 10 yr. (since 1867) at Lambeth Palace, chief residence of Archbishop of Canterbury.

Lambton, John George, 1st Earl of Durham (1792–1840), Brit. statesman. Promoted liberal measures, incl. Reform Bill of 1832. As Gov.-General of Canada, prepared *Report on the Affairs of British North America* (1839), advocating self-govt., but opposing Fr. nationalism in Canada. Document instrumental in drive for independence.

Lamentations, prophetic book of OT, attributed to Jeremiah. Series of poems mourning fallen Jerusalem. Stanzas in Chapters 1–4 form Hebrew alphabetical acrostic.

Lammas Day [orig. 'loaf-mass'], Eng. harvest holiday. Formerly 1 Aug.

lammergeier, *Gypaëtus barbatus,* largest European bird of prey; has 9–10 ft. wingspan. Also called bearded vulture.

lamp shell, any Brachiopod with body enclosed by valvular shells. Fossils date from Cambrian period.

lamprey, primitive eel-like fish of group Hyperoartia. Has horny teeth for feeding on blood of other fish. Great Lakes fishing industry has been hindered by presence of lampreys.

Lanarkshire, county, S central Scotland. Area: 892 sq. mi.; county town, Lanark. Textile and shipbuilding industries extensive in and near Glasgow. Sheep and cattle raising in S. Pop. (1966) 1,577,000.

Lancashire, county, NW England. Area: 1,866 sq. mi.; county town, Lancaster. Rich in coal and iron deposits in W and S, great indust. region around Liverpool and Manchester; cotton textiles, shipyards. Pop. (1966) 5,189,000.

Lancaster, House of, Eng. royal family. Founded by Edmund ('Crouchback'), 1st Earl of Lancaster (1245–96), son of Henry III, who was granted title in 1267. John of Gaunt,

son of Edward III became duke (1362), through marriage into Lancaster family and his son became 1st Lancastrian king as Henry IV. Others were Henry V and Henry VI. Rivalry with House of York led to WARS OF THE ROSES.

lancelet, small fish-like animal of group Cephalochordata. Feeds on plankton. One of most primitive chordates, probable link between vertebrates and invertebrates.

Lancelot *see* ARTHURIAN LEGEND.

lancer, orig. a light cavalry soldier who carried a lance. Name survives in certain regiments, *e.g.* 16th Queen's Lancers in UK.

Lanchow, cap of Kansu prov., NW China, on the Hwang-Ho. Destroyed (1920) by earthquake. Recent indust. expansion; major oil refining and transport centre. Pop. (1957) 699,000.

Land, Edwin Herbert (1909–), Amer. scientist. Invented 'polaroid' camera (1947) enabling immediate film processing.

Landau, Lev Davidovich, FRS (1908–68), Russ. physicist. Awarded Nobel Prize for Physics (1962) for work on theory of state of helium gas at temperature near absolute zero.

Landes, region of SW France. Area: 3,604 sq. mi. Drainage and forestation have reclaimed parts of marshy, sandy Atlantic coast region; sheep grazing. Pop. (1962) 260,495.

landing craft, vessel designed to land personnel, equipment and stores necessary for sustained occupation of enemy territory. Variety of types, *e.g.* amphibious, transport vehicles.

Landor, Walter Savage (1775–1864), Eng. writer. Poetry, incl. *Pericles and Aspasia* (1836), reflects classical and historical interests.

Landowska, Wanda (1877–1959), Fr.-Polish musician. Helped revive interest in harpsichord music.

landrail *see* CORNCRAKE.

Land's End, promontory, Cornwall,

A Lamaist priest in Tibet

SW England; most W point in England. Has 60 ft. granite cliffs.

Landseer, Sir Edwin Henry (1802–73), Eng. painter. Popular pictures of animals include *The Monarch of the Glen.*

landslide, mass movement of earth and rock sliding down a slope. Chief cause is loosening of material by rainfall or earth movements, *e.g.* earthquakes; or by avalanches of snow *etc.*

Landsteiner, Karl (1868–1943), Amer. pathologist, b. Vienna. Awarded Nobel Prize for Physiology and Medicine (1930) for discovering human blood groups. Helped identify Rh blood factor (1940).

Landy, John (1930–), Austral. athlete. Rivalled Roger Bannister and became (1954) 2nd man to run mile in under 4 min.

Lane, Sir Allen Lane Williams (1902–70), Brit. publisher. Founder of Penguin Books Ltd. (1936), leader in 'paperback book' industry.

Lanfranc (*c.* 1005–89), Ital. prelate, Archbishop of Canterbury (1070–89). Reformer of abuses in Eng. Church, also a scholar and author of treatise on transubstantiation. Friend and adviser of William the Conqueror.

Lang, Andrew (1844–1912), Scot.

The weight of snow and ice in an avalanche such as this can cause a landslide

Lapis Lazuli

man of letters. Best known for translations, incl. those of *Iliad* and *Odyssey*. Also wrote poetry; theory of myth in *Myths, Literature, and Religion* (2 vols., 1887).

Lange, Christian Louis (1869–1938), Norwegian diplomat, pacifist and historian. Delegate to League of Nations after 1920. Awarded Nobel Peace Prize (1921) with Hjalmar Branting.

Langer, Susanne K. (1895–   ), Amer. philosopher. Focusing her work on aesthetics, major contribution is distinction between symbolic function-making in science and art.

Langland, William (*c.* 1332–1400), Eng. poet. Allegorical account of clerical life, *The Vision Concerning Piers Plowman,* is attributed to him.

Langley, Samuel Pierpont (1834–1906), Amer. scientist. Experimented in aircraft design; full-scale model reconstructed, flown successfully (1914) after his death.

Langmuir, Irving (1881–1957), Amer. chemist. Helped develop radio vacuum tube. Awarded Nobel Prize for Chemistry (1932) for studies contributing to immunology. Devised cloud-seeding method to produce precipitation.

Langton, Stephen (*c.* 1150–1228), Eng. prelate. Elected Archbishop of Canterbury (1207), but prevented by King John from assuming see until 1213. Supported barons in struggle with John, culminating in MAGNA CARTA.

Langtry, Lily (1852–1929), Eng. actress, known as the 'Jersey Lily'. Wilde wrote *Lady Windermere's Fan* for her.

language, developed and systematic form of communication used by man. *See* LINGUISTICS; PHILOLOGY; SEMANTICS.

Languedoc, former prov., S France; cap. Toulouse. Centre of wine industry. Incorporated by France (1271).

Lanier, Sidney (1842–81), Amer. poet. Interest in music-poetry relationship reflected in poetry, *e.g.* 'The Marshes of Glynn'. Popular shorter verse includes 'The Song of the Chattahoochee'.

Lansbury, George (1859–1940), Brit. polit. leader. Founded (1912) and edited *Daily Herald.* Reformer and pacifist, headed Labour Party in Parl. (1931–5).

Lansdowne, 5th Marquis of *see* PETTY-FITZMAURICE, HENRY KEITH.

Lansing, cap. of Michigan, US. Settled 1837; expansion came with automobile industry. Pop. (1963) 169,000.

Laoighis, Leix, inland county, S central Republic of Ireland. Area: 664 sq. mi.; county town, Port Laoighise. Mountainous in N; agriculture and dairying are chief occupations. Pop. (1966) 44,662.

Laos, kingdom of SE Asia. Area: 91,428 sq. mi.; cap. Vientiane; royal

residence, Luang Prabang. Mountainous terrain with trop. forests. Chief crop is rice; exports coffee, opium. Lao people descended from Chinese immigrants (13th cent.), after which became part of KHMER Empire. Fr. protectorate (1893–1940). Autonomous kingdom of Indo-China (1947–54), fully independent after Geneva Conference. Main religion, Buddhism. Unit of currency, kip. Pop. (1964) 2,700,000.

Lao-tse *see* TAOISM.

La Paz, admin. cap. and largest city of Bolivia, 12,000 ft. above sea level.

Founded 1548; centre of Sp.-Indian struggles. Pop. (1965) 461,000.

lapis lazuli, gemstone composed mainly of lazurite, usually blue in colour. Found in Afghanistan, Chile, Burma, US. Formerly used in ornamental furniture manufacture.

Laplace, Pierre Simon, Marquis de (1749–1827), Fr. astronomer and mathematician. Evolved form of nebular hypothesis. Helped develop theory of mathematical probability.

Lapland, region of N Europe, comprising parts of Finland, Sweden, Norway, USSR. Characterized by forests, lakes. Rich mineral resources. Main port, Murmansk. Inhabited by LAPPS.

La Plata, cap. of Buenos Aires prov., E Argentina. Chief industry is preparation of meat for export. Called Perón (1952–5). Pop. (1966) 406,000.

Lapps, N Scandinavian people, concentrated largely in Norway (called Finns). Semi-nomadic, hunt reindeer, fish. Origins believed to be C Asian, then pushed N. Speak Finno-Ugric language. Pop. *c.* 30,000.

lapwing, *Vanellus vanellus,* large plover, with erratic flight and shrill cry. Found in Europe and C Asia.

lar gibbon, *Hylobates lar,* white-handed gibbon of Asia. Expert climber living in family groups.

larch, tall deciduous coniferous tree related to pine, found mainly in N hemisphere. European, *Larix deciduo,* and Amer., *L. occidentalis,* used in building.

larder beetle *see* CARPET BEETLE.

Lardner, Ring [gold Wilmer] (1885–1933), Amer. humorist and writer.

Lapp

Works include *You Know Me Al* (1916), *The Love Nest and other Stories* (1926).

Lares and Penates, household gods of Roman religion. Lares represented ancestral spirits; Penates were guardians of the store-cupboard.

Larionov, Mikhail Fëdorovich (1881–1964), Russ. abstract artist. Initiated short-lived Rayonist movement.

lark, insectivorous bird of family Alaudidae; skylark is noted for its song. Found primarily in Europe and Asia. Amer. species include horned lark.

larkspur, hardy plant of genus *Delphinium,* related to buttercup. Colourful flowers stand on tall spikes. Widely distributed in N hemisphere.

La Rochefoucauld, François, Duc de (1613–80), Fr. writer. Best known for his maxims which appeared in *Réflexions ou Sentences et Maximes Morales* (1665); human behaviour ascribed to selfishness.

Larrey, Dominique Jean (1766–1842), Fr. surgeon. While in Napoleon's army, introduced forerunner of modern ambulance.

Lars Porsena, Etruscan king (end of 6th cent. BC). According to tradition, repulsed in attempt to restore Tarquin kings to Roman throne; subsequently made peace with Rome.

Lartet, Édouard (1801–71), Fr. archaeologist. Found evidence of man's contemporaneous existence with extinct mammals. Classified Stone Age cultures.

larva, 1st form of insect; emerges from egg as grub, maggot, or caterpillar. Adult insect appears after metamorphosis.

larynx, organ lying above windpipe containing vocal cords. Consists chiefly of cartilage and muscle. Inflammation of lining causes laryngitis; often accompanied by loss of capacity to speak.

La Salle, Robert Cavelier, Sieur de (1643–87), Fr. explorer. Developed trade in central N America through command at Fort Frontenac. Claimed Mississippi valley after descending river (1682); subsequent attempt to reach its mouth by sea ended in murder by his own men.

lascar, seaman of E Indies. Orig. an inferior class of sepoy.

Las Casas, Bartolomé de (1474–1566), Sp. Dominican missionary and historian, called 'Apostle of the Indians'. Work in Sp. America culminated in greater legal protection for Indians.

Lascaux caves, group of caverns near Montignac, SW France. Discovered

The famous cave paintings at Lascaux, France

(1940) by chance. Contain paintings (*c.* 18,000 BC) depicting animals and hunting scenes.

laser, abbrev. for 'light amplification by stimulated emission of radiation', instrument producing coherent light in intense focused beam. Used for transmission of energy in physics and accelerating chem. reactions.

Laski, Harold Joseph (1893–1950), Eng. polit. scientist and economist. Member of Fabian Soc., professor at University of London after 1926. Works include *Democracy in Crisis* (1933), *The American Democracy* (1948) and *Liberty in the Modern State* (1930, rev. 1948).

Las Palmas, major city and port of Canary Is. Tourist resort. Pop. (1965) 239,000.

Lassalle, Ferdinand (1825–64), Ger. socialist and political writer. Instrumental in estab. 1st Ger. workers' political party (1863).

Lassen Peak, only active volcano (10,453 ft.) in US, apart from Hawaii and Alaska. Located in Lassen Volcanic National Park, N California.

Last Supper, in NT, celebration of Passover feast by Jesus and disciples shortly before His arrest. Marked by institution of HOLY COMMUNION.

Las Vegas, city of S Nevada, US. Growth began with rly. link (1905).

Resort, renowned for opulence and gambling casinos. Pop. (1960) 64,405.

Latakia, Ladhiqiyah, Med. port of Syria. Phoenician and Roman (known as Laodicea) town. Distribution (esp. tobacco) centre. Pop. (1960) 67,600.

La Tène, shallows of L. Neuchâtel, Switzerland. Site of Celtic remains from 2nd Iron Age, prob. dating from 4th–1st cent. BC.

Lateran Treaty, agreement (signed 1929) between Church and state in Italy. Confined papal sovereignty to newly-created Vatican City and specified extra-territorial buildings.

Lark

laterite, reddish soil formed in trop. regions by decomposition of underlying rocks, such as basalts, granites, shales. Usually soft; impregnated with ferric hydroxide.

latex, milky fluid found in several plants consisting of an emulsion of various substances. Exuded from Pará rubber tree and worked into rubber.

Latimer, Hugh (*c.* 1485–1555), Eng. Protestant reformer. Converted to Protestantism (1524); imprisoned several times. Bishop of Worcester (1535–9); condemned for heresy (1553) and burned at stake.

Latin, Indo-European dead language of Rome, *lingua franca* of Roman Empire and R.C. Church. Precursor of Romance languages.

Latin America, those countries of S and C America, West Indies and Mexican N America in which Spanish, Portuguese and French are spoken.

Latin American Free Trade Association (LAFTA), partnership formed (1960) by Argentina, Brazil, Chile, Colombia, Ecuador, Mexico, Paraguay, Peru, Uruguay and Venezuela, to create a free trade area. Tariff and trade barriers gradually being reduced over a 12-yr. period under programme agreed at Punta del Este (1967).

latitude and **longitude,** in geography, angular distances of a place from the equator (0° lat.) and first meridian (0°

Lavender

long., Greenwich, England) respectively. *See* PROJECTION.

Latium, Lazio, ancient region of C Italy, orig. territory of Latini. Modern region covers provinces of Viterbo, Rieti, Rome, Frosinone and Latina. Area: 6,635 sq. mi.; cap. Rome. Pop. (1961) 3,922,783.

La Trappe *see* TRAPPISTS.

Latrobe, Benjamin Henry (1764–1820), Amer. architect; contributed to classical revival in US building. His Bank of the US (Philadelphia Custom House) is based on the PARTHENON. Built 1st Amer. cathedral at Baltimore, Md. (1805–18).

Latter Day Saints *see* MORMONS.

Latvia, constituent repub. of Soviet Union, on Baltic. Area: 24,840 sq. mi.; cap. Riga. Incorporated with Russia (1721). Became independent after World War 1; forced into mutual assistance pact by Russia (1939). Agriculture and forestry basic industries, also shipbuilding and food processing based on imported materials. Pop. (1961) 2,190,000.

Latvian *see* LETTISH.

Laud, William (1573–1645), Eng. High Churchman. Archbishop of Canterbury from 1633. Supported Charles I; tried to eradicate Calvinism in England and Presbyterianism in Scotland. LONG PARLIAMENT impeached him; executed 1645.

laudanum, tincture of OPIUM.

Lauder, Sir Harry, orig. Henry MacLennan (1870–1950), Scot. comedian and singer, esp. of own compositions, *e.g.* 'I love a Lassie'.

Lauderdale, John Maitland, Duke of (1616–82), Scot. politician. A Covenanter who changed sides, supported Charles II and became member of the CABAL.

laughing gas (N_2O), nitrous oxide, colourless, transparent gas with sweet taste. Formerly used as an anaesthetic.

laughing jackass *see* KOOKABURRA.

Laughton, Charles (1899–1962), Eng. stage and film actor. Films include *The Private life of Henry VIII, The Barretts of Wimpole Street, Mutiny on the Bounty.*

laurel, name of various shrubs and small trees, incl. cherry laurel, *Prunus laurocerasus;* bay or sweet laurel, *Laurus nobilis,* used as a spice; spurge laurel, *Daphne laureola.* Also name of certain trop. Amer. trees of Rhododendron and Magnolia families and Austral. Cryptocarpa.

Laurentian Shield, rocks forming ancient core of N America, covering area of NW Canada and part of Greenland.

Laurier, Sir Wilfrid (1841–1919),

Lapwing

Canadian statesman, Liberal P.M. (1896–1911). Helped define party doctrine. Estab. practice of choosing regionally representative cabinet. Supported Brit. position in South African War.

Lausanne, cap. of Vaud canton, SW Switzerland. Port on L. Geneva. Pop. (1965) 204,000.

Lausanne Conference, peace treaty (1922–3) between Allies and Turkey resolving problems raised by TREATY OF SÈVRES, not recognized by new Turkish govt. under Ataturk.

lava, material composed of molten silicates extruded on the earth's surface from volcanic craters. Basic lava may flow for miles forming shield-like volcanoes *e.g.* MAUNA LOA, Hawaii. Magma is lava before exposure to air.

Laval, Pierre (1883–1945), Fr. politician. Premier and Foreign Sec. (1931–2, 1935–6). Vice-premier of Pétain's govt. (1940). Made premier by Hitler (1942). For collaboration with Germany, executed for treason at end of World War 2.

lavender, *Lavandula officinalis,* sweet-smelling herb of Labiatae family, native of W Med. countries. Oil of flowers used extensively in pharmacy and cosmetics.

laver, several edible seaweeds, esp. of genus *Porphyra.* Valued as food in China, Japan and parts of England.

Laveran, [Charles Louis] Alphonse (1845–1922), Fr. physician and bacteriologist. Discovered cause of malaria (1880). Awarded Nobel Prize for Physiology and Medicine (1907) for work on the causes of disease.

Lavoisier, Antoine Laurent (1743–94), Fr. chemist; founder of modern chemistry. Conducted quantitative experiments; explained combustion. Devised chem. nomenclature which serves as basis of modern system.

law *see* ROMAN LAW; COMMON LAW.

Law, Andrew Bonar (1858–1923), Brit. statesman, b. Canada. Made fortune in Scotland as banker and iron-merchant. Entered parl. as Cons. M.P. (1900); elected leader of Opposition (1911); Colonial Sec. (1915–16); Chanc. of Exchequer (1916–19); Lord Privy Seal (1919–21). Became P.M. (1922); resigned following year.

Law, John (1671–1729), Scot. financier in France. Founded Banque générale (1716); acquired monopoly of trade with Louisiana (1717). Excessive speculation led to collapse of venture.

law of nations *see* INTERNATIONAL LAW.

lawn tennis *see* TENNIS.

Purple Laver

Lawrence, D[avid] H[erbert] (1885–1930), Eng. writer of novels, essays and poems which show man's natural and instinctive passions. They include *Sons and Lovers* (1913), *Women in Love* (1920), *Lady Chatterley's Lover* (1928).

Lawrence, Ernest Orlando (1901–58), Amer. physicist; invented cyclotron (1931). Awarded Nobel Prize for Physics (1939) for research on atomic structure.

Lawrence, Gertrude (1902–52), Eng. actress and singer. Appeared in musicals incl. *The King and I*. Worked with NOEL COWARD in *e.g. Private Lives*.

Lawrence, Saint (d. 258), early Christian martyr, believed to have been burned to death. Feast day, 10 Aug.

Lawrence, T[homas] E[dward] (1888–1935), Brit. soldier, adventurer and writer, b. Wales. During World War 1 helped Arab revolt against Turks, gaining name 'Lawrence of Arabia'. Wrote *The Seven Pillars of Wisdom* (1935).

Laxness, Halldór [Kiljan] (1902–   ),

Icelandic novelist. Cycles of novels include *Salka Valka* (1931–2), *Independent People* (1934–5). Awarded Nobel Prize for Literature (1955).

lay, short lyric or narrative poem intended to be sung. Orig. applied specifically to historical or heroic narrative poems, sung by minstrels.

Layamon (*fl.* 12th cent.), Eng. poet, author of *Brut*, alliterative chronicle of Brit. history giving earliest version in English of the ARTHURIAN LEGEND.

Layard, Austen Henry (1817–94), Brit. archaeologist, writer and diplomat. Excavated at Nimrud, Nineveh and Babylon; presented his collection of Assyrian antiquities to British Museum.

lay reader, layman licensed in some churches to conduct certain services, to officiate at funerals, and to preach.

Lazarists, R.C. teaching order founded by St Vincent de Paul (1625). Named from 1st priory St Lazare, Paris.

Lazarus, in NT, brother of Mary and Martha of Bethany, raised from the dead by Jesus.

lazurite, mineral of the feldspathoid group, found in massive form or as cubic crystals. Occurs in varying shades of blue and is a constituent of lapis-lazuli.

lead (Pb), soft metallic element occasionally occurring naturally as free metal; chief ore is galena. Easily pressed into sheets, used for roofing, type metal, piping and protection against radio-activity, *etc.*

Leadbelly, orig. Huddie Ledbetter (1888–1949), Amer. folk and blues singer, composer of 'Goodnight Irene', 'Cumberland Gap', 'Rock Island Line' and other songs.

leader *see* CONCERTMASTER.

leaf, outgrowth of stem of plant. Functions include assimilation of carbon, absorption of light and breathing. Chlorophyll gives green colour. Evergreen leaves are termed

Lava stream from Mauna Loa, Hawaii

persistent, those which fall annually, deciduous.

leafbeetle, insect of family Chrysomelidae with bright coloured shiny appearance and short antennae. Larvae are stem borers, root feeders or leaf miners and include pests COLORADO POTATO BEETLE and cucumber beetle.

leaf-cutting bee, solitary insect of carpenter bee group, found all over the world. Egg cells are built in a burrow with circular pieces cut from leaves.

leafhopper, long-bodied hopping and flying insect of Cicadellidae family with worldwide distribution. Damages plants by sucking sap, and transmits virus disease.

leaf insect, predominantly arboreal trop. herbivorous insect with leaf-like shape. Eggs are hard-shelled like seeds.

leaf-nosed bat, insectivorous member of bat family Phyllostomatidae. Found in C and S America. Once thought to be blood-sucking, often called vampire bat.

leaf roller, any larva or caterpillar which twists leaf over itself to form a protective case for feeding and pupation.

League of Nations, 1st major organization of world's countries dedicated

Leaf Insect

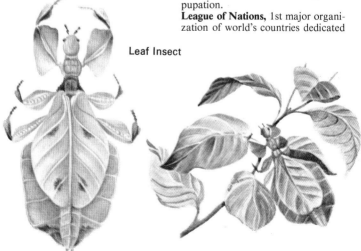

to preservation of peace and international co-operation. Founded (1920) as part of TREATY OF VERSAILLES after World War 1; headquarters at Geneva. Members included (at some time) all major nations except US and Saudi Arabia. Abandoned after failure to hold members together in action against aggressor nations, *e.g.* Japan (1931), Italy (1935), and those members' withdrawal. Dissolved itself (1946) and transferred services and property to UNO.

Leakey, Louis Seymour Bazett (1903–   ), Brit. archaeologist. Discovered (1958, 1959, 1961–3), fossil remains in E Africa incl. those of Zinjanthropus, proto-man living *c.* 1,750,000 yr. ago. Author of *The Stone-Age Culture of Kenya* (1931), *Olduvai Gorge* (1952).

Lean, David (1908–   ), Eng. film director. Films include *Great Expectations* (1946), *Lawrence of Arabia* (1962), *Dr. Zhivago* (1965).

Lear, Edward (1812–88), Eng. writer and humorist. Best known for his illustrated limericks and poems incl. *A Book of Nonsense* (1846).

leather, durable material prepared from hide or skin of animals, fish and reptiles. Prepared by curing, and removal of flesh, hair and salts.

leatherback *see* LEATHERY TURTLE.

leatherjacket *see* CRANEFLY.

leatherwood, moosewood, *Dirca palustris,* Amer. shrub with tough pliant stems and small yellow flowers. Tough inner bark used by Amer. Indians for fibrous thongs.

leathery turtle, luth, leatherback [US], *Dermochelys coriacea,* largest marine turtle, 6 ft. in length and weighing 1,000 lb. Brown leather appearance; heartshaped from above. Eyes exude secretion which protects them from sea water.

Leavis, Frank Raymond (1895–   ), Eng. literary critic. Founder and editor of literary quarterly *Scrutiny* (1932–53). Works include *New Bearings in English Poetry* (1932), *The Common Pursuit* (1952).

Lebanon [Al-Jumhouriya al-Lubnaniya], Arab repub. between Med., Israel and Syria. Area: 4,000 sq. mi.;

cap. Beirut; main towns, Tripoli, Sidon. Narrow strip of land with Lebanon Mts. Centre of Phoenician culture; part of Ottoman Turkish Empire (16th–early 20th cent.); part

of Fr. mandate with Syria from 1918; independent (1944). Agric. products include fruit, tobacco, silk and cotton. Languages, French and Arabic. Main religions, Islam and Christianity. Pop (1965) 2,366,000.

Leblanc, Nicholas (1742–1806), Fr. physician and chemist. invented Leblanc process for manufacturing sodium carbonate which was used in 19th cent. textile and glass industries.

Lebrun, Charles (1619–90), Fr. painter. Studied under Poussin, became court painter to Louis XIV. Responsible for much of the decoration of the Louvre and Versailles palaces.

Leconte de Lisle, Charles Marie René (1818–94), Fr. poet, leading Parnassian. Works include *Poèmes Antiques* (1852), *Poèmes Tragiques* (1884).

Leathery Turtle

Le Corbusier *see* JEANNERET, CHARLES ÉDOUARD.

Leda, in Gk. myth., wife of Tyndareus of Sparta. Visited by Zeus in form of swan; bore Castor and Pollux, Helen and Clytemnestra.

Lederberg, Joshua (1925–   ), Amer. geneticist. With G. W. Beadle and E. L. Tatum, awarded Nobel Prize for Physiology and Medicine (1958) for work on genetics of bacteria.

Lee, Robert Edward (1807–70), Amer. army officer, commander of Confederate forces (1865) in Civil War. Victor at 2nd Battle of Bull Run (Aug. 1862) and at Chancellorsville (May, 1863), but failed in attempts to penetrate N, *e.g.* in GETTYSBURG CAMPAIGN. In WILDERNESS CAMPAIGN, withstood Union attacks under Grant, to whom he surrendered (Apr. 1865) at Appomattox Courthouse. Became symbol of Southern resistance.

Lee, Tsung Dao (1926–   ), Amer. physicist, b. China. Shared Nobel Prize for Physics (1957) with C. N. Yang, for disproving principle of conservation of parity.

leech, aquatic worm of annelid group Flattened body with sucker at both ends. Most are blood-suckers. Found chiefly in fresh water of temp. and trop. regions. Leech of genus *Hirudo* formerly used in medicine to bleed patients.

leechee *see* LITCHI.

Leeds, city of West Riding of Yorkshire, England. Centre of coal, iron and wool industries since 17th cent. Also has printing works and leather manufacturing. Pop. (1966) 508,000.

leek, *Allium porrum,* biennial plant related to onion, with cylindrical bulb and flat leaves. Vegetable used in soups. National emblem of Wales.

Leeuwenhoek, Antony van (1632–1723), Dutch naturalist. Made simple microscopes, with which he was 1st to see protozoa and bacteria. Gave 1st complete description of red blood cells.

Leeward Islands, group of islands in N Lesser Antilles of West Indies extending from Puerto Rico SE to Martinique. Area: 1,273 sq. mi. Discovered (1493) by Columbus, colonized (17th cent.) by English, French, Danes and Dutch.

Legendre, Adrien Marie (1752–1833), Fr. mathematician. Noted for research on theory of elliptic functions and theory of numbers; invented method of least squares. Collaborated on compilation of logarithmic and trigonometric tables.

Léger, Alexis Saint-Léger, orig. St. John Perse (1887–   ), Fr. poet and statesman. Poetry includes *Eloge* (1911), *Anabase* (1924), *Amer* (1957). Awarded Nobel Prize for Literature (1960).

Léger, Fernand (1881–1955), Fr. painter. Modified cubist style manifested in his cylindrical and machine-like forms. Executed several ballet sets and decorative murals.

legion, Roman army unit, orig. comprising 1,000 infantrymen; later increased to 3,000–6,000, divided into 10 cohorts. Adopted the eagle as a standard.

Legion of Honour *see* DECORATIONS.

Legros, Alphonse (1837–1911), Fr. historical and portrait painter. Noted also for etchings and sculpture.

Lehár, Franz (1870–1948), Hungarian composer. Works, mostly operettas, include *The Merry Widow* (1905).

Lehmann, Lotte (1888–　　), Amer. soprano, b. Germany. Made debut as Sieglinde in *Die Walküre* (1930). Known as concert artist and singer of Lieder.

Leibniz or **Leibnitz, Gottfried Wilhelm, Baron von,** FRS (1646–1716), Ger. philosopher and mathematician. Devised new form of differential and integral calculus. In *Systema Theologicum* (1686), sought to promote union of Catholic and Protestant Churches. In philosophical works, expounds view of universe as having a number of monads in harmony with each other and with God; thus faith and reason are not in conflict.

Leicester, city and county town of Leicestershire, England. Roman town (AD 50). Manufactures hosiery, shoes, elastic fibres and typewriters; agric. market. University of Leicester founded (1921), chartered (1957). Pop. (1966) 284,000.

Leicester, Earl of *see* DUDLEY, ROBERT.

Leicestershire, inland county, C England. Area: 832 sq. mi.; county town, Leicester. Mainly agric., dairy produce (Stilton cheese); important coal and iron deposits. Fox-hunting, *e.g.* Melton Mowbray. Pop. (1966) 716,000.

Leichardt, [Friedrich Wilhelm] Ludwig (1813–48), Ger. explorer in Australia. Walked 600 mi. through New South Wales to Moreton Bay, Queensland (1843). Never returned from expedition attempting to cross Continent (1848).

Leiden, Leyden, city of South Holland prov., W Netherlands. Manufactures textiles and machinery. University founded 1575. Pop. (1966 est.) 100,000.

Leif Ericsson (*fl.* 1000), Norse discoverer of America, son of ERIC THE RED. Believed to have reached America between Newfoundland and Virginia when blown off course on return to Greenland.

Leigh, Vivien (1913–67), Eng. stage and film actress. Awarded 'Oscars' for *Gone With the Wind* (1939) and *A Street-car Named Desire* (1951).

Leinster, fertile prov. of Republic of Ireland. Area: 7,624 sq. mi. Comprises much of SE Ireland, incl. Dublin. Pop. (1966) 1,412,465.

Leipzig, leading commercial city, East Germany. Industries include textiles, machinery, chemicals and steel works; educ. and music centre. University founded (1409). Site of Battle of Leipzig (Battle of Nations), decisive victory by Russ., Austrian and Prussian forces over Napoleon (1813). Pop. (1965) 596,000.

Leitrim, county in N Republic of Ireland. Area: 589 sq. mi.; county town, Carrick-on-Shannon. Iron, lead, coal mined; coarse linen and woollens manufactured; fishing in R. Shannon. Pop (1966) 30,532.

Lely, Sir Peter, orig. Pieter van der Faes (1618–80), Dutch portrait painter. Court painter to Charles II of England.

Lemaître, Georges, Abbé (1894–　　), Belgian astrophysicist, mathematician. Helped to develop theory of expanding universe.

Le Mans, cap. of Sarthe department, NW France. Industries include machinery, chemicals, textiles. Scene of annual 24-hr. sports car race. Pop. (1963) 142,000.

Le May, Curtis Emerson (1906–　　), Amer. air force officer and politician. Headed bomber commands during World War 2; vice-chief of staff (1957–61). Vice-pres. candidate (1968) on George Wallace's Independent ticket.

Lemelin, Roger (1919–　　), Fr. Canadian novelist. *Au Pied de la Pente Douce* (1944) satirizes contemporary life in working-class Quebec City. *Les Plouffe* (1948) continues in same vein.

lemming, nocturnal rodent related to vole. Norway lemming, *Lemmus*

Painting by Charles Lebrun of the founding of the Académie des Sciences in the library of Louis XIV, 1666

lemmus, of mountains of N Norway and Lapland is noted for mass migration during periods of overpopulation. Lemming mouse, *Synaptomys,* is N Amer. variety.

Lemnos, Gk. island in Aegean Sea. Area: 180 sq. mi.; cap. Kastron; chief port, Moudros. Fishing, agriculture are main occupations. Pop. (1961 est.) 22,800.

lemon, fruit of evergreen tree, *Citrus medica,* grown in Med. regions, Florida, California and South Africa. Juice used medicinally and in cooking, rind in candied peel.

lemon sole *see* DAB.

lemur, mammal of family Lemuridae, intermediate between insectivores and monkeys. Nocturnal and arboreal, eats fruit and insects. Species include

Lemming

Lemur

black and white ruffled lemur, *Lemur variegatus* and ring-tailed lemur, *L. calta.*

Lena-Kirenga, river of Siberia, USSR, flowing N into Arctic Ocean; *c.* 3,000 mi. long. Rich in tungsten, molybdenum, zinc, tin, gold.

Lenau, Nikolaus, orig. Nikolaus Niembsch von Strehlenau (1802– 50), Ger. Romantic poet. Best known for *Faust* (1836) and lyrics, characterized by melancholy and pessimism.

Lend-Lease Act, passed (1941) by US Congress, empowering Pres. to sell, lend or lease US supplies to Allies during World War 2. Countries such as Britain provided reciprocal programmes. Act ended 1945.

L'Enfant, Pierre Charles (1754– 1825), Fr. architect. Plans for Washington DC (1792) were not implemented until 1901.

Lenin, Vladimir Ilyich, orig. V. I. Ulyanov (1870– 1924), Russ. revolutionary, founder of the Soviet Union. Exiled twice for anti-govt. activity, engineered split of Russian Social Democratic Party between Bolshevists and Menshevists (1903). Differed from orthodox Marxism in his advocacy of violent revolution to achieve overthrow of capitalism. Returned to Russia to overthrow Kerensky govt. (Nov. 1917) and estab. Council of People's Commissars. Civil war (1918– 20) ended with founding of USSR; Lenin exercised dictatorial powers through positions as Chairman of Council and Chairman of Communist Party. COMINTERN largely his creation.

Lenin Peak, 3rd highest mountain (23,382 ft.) of USSR, on Kirghiz-Ladszhik SSR border. Orig. Kaufmann Peak; 1st climbed 1928.

Leningrad, port and city of USSR, cap. of Leningrad oblast. Founded as St Petersburg by Peter the Great; cap. of Russ. Empire (1709– 27, 1730– 1918); became Petrograd (1914), and Leningrad (1924); withstood Nazi siege (1941– 43). Exports grain, timber, hemp, hides, caviar. Industries include heavy machines, clothing, consumer goods. Pop (1967) 3,665,000.

lens, portion of transparent medium such as glass, with 2 polished surfaces, which may be either convex or concave.

Lent, Christian period of 40 days of penance before Easter (Ash Wednesday to Easter Sunday). Commemorates Christ's sojourn in the Wilderness.

lentil, *Lens esculenta,* small branching plant. Cultivated for its round flat seeds which are dried and used in cooking. Native to S Europe.

Leo *see* ZODIAC.

Leo IX, Saint (1002– 54), pope (1049– 54). Reforms of clergy largely implemented by Hildebrand (later GREGORY VII). Began formal schism of E and W by excommunication of Michael Cerularius (1054).

Leo X (1475– 1521), pope (1513– 21), son of Lorenzo de Medici. Failure of 5th Lateran Council (1512– 17) to achieve desired reforms led to beginning of Protestant Reformation under Luther.

Leo XIII, orig. Gioacchino Vincenzo Rafaele Luigi Pecci (1810– 1903), pope (1878– 1903). Leader of eccles. and social reform. His encyclical, *Rerum Novarum* (1891) set out condition of the working classes.

Leo Africanus (*c.* 1483– 1554), Moorish traveller in Africa and Near East. Description of African journeys for many years the only source of information on Sudan.

León, Luis Ponce de (1528– 1591), Sp. scholar, poet and mystic. Imprisoned by Inquisition (1572– 76). Works include *Los Nombres de Cristo* (1583– 85) and *La Perfecta Casada* (1583).

León, region and former kingdom of NW Spain. United with Castile by Ferdinand III. Area: 5,433 sq. mi.; cap. León; main towns include Salamanca, Zamora, Valladolid. Mountainous and forested; agriculture and minerals.

Leonardo da Vinci (1452– 1519), Ital. artist, scientist, engineer and mathematician, b. Florence. His paintings include *The Last Supper* and *Mona Lisa*. One of the first to understand laws of inertia and leverage. Appears to have anticipated Harvey's discovery of circulation of the blood.

Leoncavallo, Ruggiero (1858– 1919), Ital. operatic composer. Works include *I Pagliacci* (1892), *La Bohème* (1897), *Zaza* (1900).

Leonidas (d. 480 BC), Spartan king. Defended pass of Thermopylae with small force of Spartans (also some Thebans and Thespians) against Persians (480 BC), but defeated and killed.

leopard, *Panthera pardus,* mammal of cat family, found in Africa and Asia. Has yellow-buff coat with black

Leonardo da Vinci, a self-portrait

markings. Prey includes monkeys, birds and reptiles.

leopard moth, *Zeuzera pyrina,* medium-sized moth, grey with black spots. Found in Europe. Larvae are woodboring.

Leopardi, Giacomo, Conte (1798–1837), Ital. poet. Lyrics, characterized by pessimism and patriotism include *Versi* (1824) and *Canti* (1831). Also published *Operette Morali* (1826–7), philosophical work in prose.

Leopold I (1640–1705), emperor of Holy Roman Empire (1658–1705). Engaged in wars with Turkey (1661–4, 1682–99); supported Netherlands against France (1672); became involved in War of Spanish Succession.

Leopold II (1747–92), emperor of Holy Roman Empire (1790–2). Formed alliance with Prussia against revolutionary France (1792). Died before hostilities began.

Leopold I (1790–1865), first king of independent Belgium (1831–65). Served with Russ. army against French (1813–14). Elected to throne on independence of Belgium.

Leopold II (1835–1909), king of Belgium (1865–1909). His reign was one of indust. and colonial expansion. Financed STANLEY's expedition to the Congo (1879–84).

Leopold III (1901–), king of Belgium (1934–51). Led Belgian resistance to German occupation in World War 2, but surrendered (May 1940). Imprisoned by Germans. Abdicated in favour of son Baudouin.

Leopoldville *see* KINSHASA.

Lepanto, Battle of, naval engagement between fleet of Holy League and Turkish fleet (1571). Turks defeated and 10,000 Christian slaves released. Ended threat of Turkish naval supremacy in Med.

lepidoptera, insect order of *c.* 100,000 species of butterflies and moths, with 4 wings, 3 pairs of legs and sucking mouth parts. Eggs become larvae of caterpillar type which feed on plants.

Lepidus, Marcus Aemilius (d. *c.* 77 BC), Roman politician. Consul (78 BC) despite Sulla's opposition. Proposed various measures, *e.g.* restoration of public lands, but defeated by Catulus and Pompey. His son, **Marcus Aemilius Lepidus** (d. *c.* 12 BC), supported Antony after murder of Julius Caesar; member of 2nd triumvirate with Antony and Octavian. Gov. of Africa after Philippi, later deprived of office by Octavian.

leprosy, Hansen's disease, mildly infectious disease caused by bacteria. Symptoms include ulcers, tubercular nodules, loss of fingers, toes. Most prevalent in trop. regions. Treated with sulfa drugs.

Lepsius, Karl Richard (1810–84), Ger. Egyptologist. Led Pruss. expedition to Egypt (1842–6); discovered the Canopus Decree (1866), like ROSETTA STONE, bilingual inscription. Works include *Denkmäler aus Ägypten und Äthiopien* (1849–59).

lepus, large N Amer. hare of W plains with very long ears and long hind legs.

Lermontov, Mikhail Yurevich (1814–41), Russ. lyric poet. Influenced by Byron and Pushkin. Works include *The Demon* (1829–41, Eng. tr. 1930), autobiographical poem, and a novel *A Hero of Our Time* (1840, Eng. tr. 1928).

Lerner, Alan Jay (1918–), Amer. theatrical writer and producer. Best known stage productions include *My Fair Lady* (1956) and *Camelot* (1960).

lesbianism, sexual attraction between women, *i.e.* female HOMOSEXUALITY.

Lesotho, formerly **Basutoland,** enclave of Republic of South Africa. Area: 11,716 sq. mi.; cap. Maseru.

Mountainous country; maize and wheat grown; cattle, sheep and goats reared. Became Brit. protectorate (1868); achieved self-govt. (1965) under King Moshoeshoe II. Pop. *c.* 1,000,000.

Lesseps, Ferdinand Marie, Vicomte de (1805–94), Fr. diplomat and engineer. Ambassador to Madrid (1848–9). Directed construction of SUEZ CANAL (1859–69). Began work on PANAMA CANAL (1881); company bankrupt (1888).

Lessing, Gotthold Ephraim (1729–81), Ger. dramatist and critic; attacked imitation of Fr. classicism

The Winter Palace, Leningrad

and upheld Shakespeare as model for Ger. playwrights. Works include *Miss Sara Sampson* (1755), *Minna von Barnhelm* (1767), *Nathan der Weise* (1779).

Lethe, in Gk. myth., one of rivers of HADES. Water drunk by souls of the dead to convey forgetfulness of previous existence.

Lettish, Latvian, Baltic Indo-European language with *c.* 2 million speakers in Soviet Repub. of Latvia.

lettre de cachet, in Fr. law under *ancien régime,* official, sealed communication from king to individual or group; usually gave notice of imprisonment or exile. Abolished during Fr. Revolution.

lettuce, *Lactuca sativa,* vegetable widely grown for use raw in salads. Varieties include asparagus (var. *angustana*), cabbage (var. *capitata*) and cos (var. *longifolia*).

leucite, white or grey mineral often found in volcanic rock of recent origin. Occurs as octagonal crystal, usually opaque.

Leuckart, Karl Georg Friedrich Rudolf (1823–98), Ger. zoologist. Pioneer in parasitology, animal physiology and developed a classification of invertebrates.

Leopard

Detail from *The Last Judgment* by Lucas van Leyden

leucocyte, white blood cells. Blood contains *c*. 11,000 leucocytes per cub. mm., or one to every 500 red cells. Broadly, function is to combat bacteria and repair injury.

leukemia, cancer-like disease of the blood, marked by an increase in the white blood cells. Incurable, but may be relieved or controlled by X-rays and drugs.

Levant, former name for E Med. area, esp. coastal regions of Turkey, Lebanon, Syria and Israel.

levanter, hot dry dusty E wind experienced in LEVANT region of E Med.

Levellers, extreme Protestant sect of Eng. Civil War period. Advocated religious and social equality. Suppressed by Cromwell.

Lever, William Hesketh, 1st Baron Leverhulme (1851– 1925), Eng. industrialist. Built 'garden city' for employees at Port Sunlight, Cheshire (1881).

Levites, descendants of Levi, son of Jacob and Leah, and in OT times the bearers of the Ark of the Covenant. In NT times, the Levites were the 'lawyers'; they could preach, but were not allowed to offer the holy sacrifice.

Leviticus, 3rd book of Pentateuch,

detailing offices, ministries and ceremonies of the priests and Levites.

Lewes, Battle of, fought (1264) near Lewes, Sussex, in which Eng. king, Henry III, was defeated by barons under SIMON DE MONTFORT.

Lewis, largest island of Outer Hebrides, W Scotland. Area: 859 sq. mi.; cap. Stornoway. Mountainous moorland; fishing and crofting important. Pop. *c*. 19,900.

Lewis, C[ecil] Day (1904–   ), Eng. poet whose collections of verse include *The Magnetic Mountain* (1933), *Word Over All* (1943), *Collected Poems* (1954). Author of detective novels (under pseudonym of Nicholas Blake). Poet Laureate since 1968.

Lewis, C[live] S[taples] (1898– 1963), Eng. writer and literary critic. His books for children include *The Lion, the Witch and the Wardrobe*; works of popular theology include *The Screw-Tape Letters.*

Lewis, Gilbert Newton (1875– 1946), Amer. chemist. With HAROLD C. UREY, discovered heavy water (1932). Noted for his work on thermodynamics and atomic structure.

Lewis, [Harry] Sinclair (1885– 1951), Amer. novelist and playwright. His

works depict satirically but sympathetically, Amer. middle-class life They include *Main Street* (1920) *Elmer Gantry* (1927), *The God Seeker* (1949). Awarded Nobel Prize for Literature (1930).

Lewis, John L[lewellyn] (1880– –1969), Amer. labour leader, Pres. of United Mine Workers (1920–60). Founded and headed (1935–40) CIO.

Lewis, Matthew Gregory (1775– 1818), Eng. author of melodramatic novels, plays. Best known for *The Monk* (1796), a 'Gothic' novel.

Lewis, [Percy] Wyndham (1882– 1957), Eng. painter and writer Founded Vorticism, 1st Eng. abstract movement, and published its journal *Blast* (1914– 15).

Lewis and Clark Expedition (1803– 6), military exploring expedition across N America financed by US Congress and led by Meriwether Lewis (1774– 1809) and William Clark (1770– 1838). Contributed valuable information about Amer. Far West and strengthened US claims to Oregon territory.

Lexington and Concord, Battles of, 1st engagements (Apr. 1775) of Amer. Revolution. Brit. infantry withdrew to Boston after meeting with armed resistance at these 2 Massachusetts towns.

Leyden, Lucas van, orig. Lucas Jacobsz (1494– 1533), Dutch painter and engraver; an originator of Dutch genre painting. Noted for woodcuts. incl. *Ecce Homo* (1510).

Leyte, 8th largest of PHILIPPINE ISLANDS. Area: 2,785 sq. mi.; cap. Tacloban. Produces hemp, sugar, rice and tobacco. Battle of Leyte Gulf, decisive victory for Amer. forces over Japanese (1944).

Lhasa, cap. of Tibet, 12,000 ft. above sea level. Centre of Lamaism until Chinese conquest of Tibet (1950). Pop. (est.) 50,000.

Lhotse, mountain joined to Everest on Tibet-Nepal border, 4th highest in world, 27,890 ft.; 1st climbed 1956.

liana, term for climbing and twining trop. forest plants.

Liaoning, prov. of S Manchuria, China. Area: 58,300 sq. mi.; cap. Shenyang. Chief manufacturing region of China. Pop. (1963) 24,090,000.

Libby, Willard Frank (1908–   ), Amer. chemist. Awarded Nobel Prize for Chemistry (1960) for development of radio-active dating method of measuring age of materials.

Liberal Party, Brit. polit. organization; developed from WHIG PARTY in early 19th cent. Dominant in 50 yr. after 1832 Reform Bill, prominent leaders included Palmerston and Gladstone; split over imperialist issue. Lloyd George central figure in early 20th cent., but party declined with rise of Labour Party.

Liberal Party, Canadian polit. organization; formed in 1850s to campaign for 'Representation by population'. Did not gain extended period in office until 20th cent. under Laurier and later Mackenzie King. Shared major party status with PROGRESSIVE CONSERVATIVE PARTY in 1950s and 1960s.

Liberia, Republic of, country of tropical W Africa. Area: 43,000 sq. mi.; cap. Monrovia. Formed (1837)

by settlement of freed Negro Amer. slaves by American Colonization Society; constitution modelled on that of US. Exports agric. products incl. rubber, gold and palm oil. Religions animism and Christianity. Unit of currency, dollar. Pop. (1964) 1,090,000.

Liberty, Statue of, landmark dominating harbour of New York City. Presented (1884) by Franco-American Union to commemorate alliance during Amer. Revolution. Designed by F. A. Bartholdi, 152 ft. statue depicts woman, whose raised arm holds a torch.

Liberty Bell, rung (July, 1776) to proclaim Declaration of Independence by Amer. colonists. Remains as exhibit in Independence Hall, Philadelphia.

Libra see ZODIAC.

libretto [Ital.: little book], text or book of words of an opera, oratorio, *etc.*

Libreville, city and cap. of Gabon Republic, W Africa. Founded 1840. Exports timber. Pop. (1964) 46,000.

Libya [**Libiyya**], country of N Africa, on Med. Sea. Area: 679,362

sq. mi.; caps. Tripoli and Benghazi; other main cities, Beida, Tobruk. Primarily desert, coastal products include dates, olives. Chief export, oil, discovered 1957. Mainly Arab population. Under Ottoman rule (1551–1911), seized by Italy. Important World War 2 battleground. Inde-

pendence (1951); joined (1953) Arab League. Original federal structure centralized by 1963 constitutional changes. Unit of currency, Libyan pound. Pop. (1966) 1,682,000.

lichen, plant form, grey, green, red or brown, composed of algae and fungi living together. Grows on rocks and trees from polar regions to tropics.

lichi see LITCHI.

Lichtenstein, Roy (1923–   ), Amer. artist, leading exponent of 'Pop art'. Uses comic strip and advertisement copy in his work. Experiments with plastics, brass and enamelled metals.

Liddell Hart, Sir Basil Henry (1895–1970), Eng. author and military strategist. Early advocate of mechanized warfare; writings were influential in World War 2. Works include *The Future of Infantry* (1933), *The Tanks* (1959).

Lidice, village, C Bohemia, Czechoslovakia. Completely destroyed by Nazis (1942), as reprisal for assassination of Heydrich.

Liebig, Justus, Baron von, FRS (1803–73), Ger. chemist. Compiled a dictionary of chemical knowledge (begun 1837). Contributed to agricultural chemistry incl. development of artificial fertilizers.

Liebknecht, Wilhelm (1826–1900), Ger. polit. leader. Marxian socialist, founded Ger. Social Democratic Party (1869). His son, **Karl Liebknecht** (1871–1919), killed after arrest for leading Spartacist revolt.

Liechtenstein, sovereign principality of Europe in Alps between Austria and Switzerland. Area: 65 sq. mi.; cap. Vaduz. Primarily agric. produce.

Created (1719) by union of 2 dukedoms. Adopted Swiss currency; joined (1924) customs union with Switzerland. Main language, German; religion, Roman Catholicism. Pop. (1966) 20,000.

Liège, Luik, city of E Belgium, on Meuse R., cap. of Liège prov. Commercial, indust. and communication centre; manufactures arms, machinery, beer, flour. Trading centre from 10th cent. Fell to Germans (1914, 1940). Pop. (1965) 452,000.

Lifar, Serge (1905–   ), Russ. ballet dancer and choreographer, who danced in Diaghilev's Ballets Russes. Premier danseur and then maître de ballet at the Opéra in Paris (1929–58). *Icare* (1935) was 1st of his highly individual ballets.

ligaments, short bands of tough fibrous tissue connecting 2 bones at a joint, or holding an organ, *e.g.* liver or uterus, in position.

ligature, thread used in surgery, usually of catgut, silk or thin wire, to tie off bloodvessels, tumours, *etc.,* thus preventing passage of blood or other fluid.

light, certain electro-magnetic vibrations which have the power of exciting the organs of sight and which are transformed in the brain into visible colours and shapes.

light year (ly), distance travelled by light in 1 terrestrial year, *i.e.* 6 million million mi.; used to express distance of stars from Earth.

Leptis Magna, Libya, an important harbour in Roman times

The oldest lighthouse on the Dutch coast, on Terschelling

lighter, large open flat-bottomed boat for loading and unloading ships in port, and for carrying goods short distances.

lighthouse, structure in or adjacent to navigable waters, equipped to give optical or radio-electrical guidance to ships. Identified by characteristic light flashes, fog sirens, radio signals.

lightning *see* THUNDERSTORM.

lignin, substance resembling cellulose which lines wood fibre and incorporates lignose, lignone and lignin.

lignite, brownish-black, low-grade coal with woody texture. Contains high percentage of hydrocarbons.

Limoges Porcelain

Smoky flame; low heating power. In brown coal, a variety of lignite, wood tissue is obscure.

lignum vitae, hard heavy wood of 2 species of guaiacum, *Guaiacum officinale* or *G. sanctum.* Used for making rulers, *etc.*; formerly thought to have medicinal value.

Liguria, orig. region of Europe stretching from lower Rhône valley to W Alps and upper Po area, inhabited by the Ligures. Modern region covers provinces of Genoa, Imperia, La Spezia and Savona. Area: 2,097 sq. mi. Pop. (1968 est.) 1,720,000.

lilac, *Syringa vulgaris,* common flowering deciduous shrub of olive family, native to Europe and Asia. Cone-shaped clusters of fragrant blue, lilac, pink or white flowers; very hard wood.

Lille, cap. of Nord department, N France. Commercial and cultural centre; buildings include Flemish exchange (17th cent.) and Vaubin's citadel. Industries such as textiles, brewing, food processing and metallurgy. Pop. (1962) 431,000.

lily, perennial bulbous plant of genus *Lilium,* native to N temp. zones. Showy, bell-shaped flowers. White madonna lily reputed to be one of the oldest in cultivation.

lily-of-the-valley, *Convallaria majalis,* perennial plant of lily family, native to Europe, Asia and SE US. Dark green leaves with bell-shaped, fragrant, white flowers.

lilytrotter *see* JACANA.

Lima, cap. and largest city of Peru, on coast. Commercial, political and cultural centre; imports raw materials

The valley of the Po, Liguria, Italy

to supply industries. Founded (1535) by Francisco Pizarro. Pop. (1964) 1,657,000.

lima bean, *Phaseolus lunatus,* annual, fast-climbing plant, native to S America, Cultivated for broad, flat, edible seed; used as vegetable in salads and soups.

lime, linden, tall deciduous tree native to N temp. regions. Yellowish white fragrant flowers; heart-shaped leaves. Common lime, *Tilia europaea,* gives white wood used in furniture.

Limerick, county in Munster, SW Republic of Ireland. Area: 1,037 sq. mi.; county town, Limerick. Dairy farming and fishing are chief occupations; hydro-electric plant on Shannon R. Pop. 143,000.

limestone, sedimentary rock composed wholly or partly of calcium carbonate. Usually white, but impurities give it variety of colours. Formed by consolidation of marine organisms, *e.g.* shells or corals, or from chem. precipitation. Used as building stone. Varieties include chalk, marble, dolomite.

limited company *see* COMPANY, LIMITED.

Limoges, city and cap. of Haute-Vienne department, S central France, on Vienne R. Famous for ceramics and porcelain, based on local clay. Cattle market. Pop. (1962) 120,000.

limonite, brown haematite, bog iron, iron ore, a hydrated ferric oxide. Colour varies from yellow to dark brown.

limpet, marine gastropod mollusc with flat cone-shaped shell. Adheres to rocks, feeding on seaweed. Found on most coasts free from winter ice

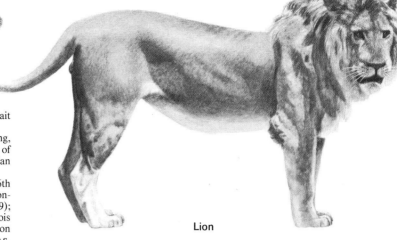

Lion

esp. in S hemisphere. Used for bait and food.

Limpopo, river, *c.* 1,000 mi. long, rising in Transvaal prov., Republic of South Africa and flowing to Indian Ocean.

Lincoln, Abraham (1809–65), 16th US Pres. (1861–5), Republican. Congressman from Illinois (1847–9); gained prominence (1858) in Illinois senatorial campaign debates on slavery with STEPHEN DOUGLAS. Successful pres. candidate (1860), directed Northern cause, using near-dictatorial powers after outbreak of CIVIL WAR; morally justified Union cause through EMANCIPATION PROCLAMATION and GETTYSBURG ADDRESS. Opposed by Republican radicals at outset of 2nd term for policy seeming to favour leniency towards South. Assassinated (Apr. 14, 1865) by JOHN WILKES BOOTH.

Lincoln's Inn *see* INNS OF COURT.

Lincolnshire, county of E England, divided into administrative districts of Parts of Holland in SE, Parts of Kesteven in SW and Parts of Lindsey in N. Total area: 2,665 sq. mi.; county town, Lincoln; main towns, Grimsby, Boston, Sleaford. Land flat and low; reclaimed fen in SE, wooded in SW and marshy in N. Agric., with shipbuilding, fishing and net manufacture. Pop. (1966) 784,000.

Lind, Jenny (1820–87), Swedish soprano, called 'The Swedish Nightingale'. Debut (1838) as Agathe in Weber's *Der Freischütz.* Toured Europe and US.

Lindau, tourist resort on L. Constance, Baden-Württemburg, West Germany. Pop. (1968 est.) 25,000.

Lindbergh, Charles Augustus (1902–), Amer. aviator. Made 1st trans-

Lily

atlantic, solo, nonstop flight (1927) in his monoplane. Avoided public appearances after kidnap and death of son (1932). With Alexis Carrel invented a 'mechanical heart' (1936).

Lindemann, Frederick Alexander, 1st Viscount Cherwell (1886–1957), Eng. physicist. Wrote *The Physical Significance of the Quantum Theory* (1932).

linden *see* LIME.

Lindisfarne, Holy Island, small island off coast of Northumberland, England. Former religious and missionary centre, with ruins of monastery built (AD 635) by St Aidan. Pop. (1961) 190.

Lindsay, Sir David (1490–1555), Scot. poet whose poems satirize eccles. and polit. abuses. Works include *Ane Pleasant Satyre of the Three Estaitis* (1540).

Lindsay, John Vliet (1921–), Amer. polit. leader. Republican-Independent Mayor of New York City (1966–), considered a leading moderate urban reformer.

Lindsay, Nicholas Vachel (1879–1931), Amer. poet. Books of verse include *General William Booth enters into Heaven* (1913), *The Golden Whales of California* (1920).

Lindsey, Parts of, administrative county, part of LINCOLNSHIRE, England. Centre, Lincoln. Pop. (1966) 453,000.

Line Islands, Equatorial Islands, coral group of 10 islands in C and S Pacific Ocean. Includes Fanning, Christmas and Washington (Brit.); Kingman, Palmyra and Jarvis islands (US); rest claimed by both countries.

linen, fabric made from fibre of flax plant, *Linum usitatissimum,* prepared by retting. Uneven texture, durable and crisp. Introduced to N Europe by Romans, flourished in Middle Ages. Ireland is chief producer of fabric; Belgium produces finest fibre.

ling *see* BURBOT.

lingua franca, spoken language allowing limited communication between people of mutually unintelligible languages. Orig. applied to language used by traders in E Med. region. Modern examples include use of Latin in R.C. Church, and of French by diplomats.

linguistics, the science of language, concerned both with its nature and historical development.

Linnaeus, Carolus, orig. Karl von Linné (1707–78), Swedish botanist, founder of modern systematic botany. Estab. binomial method of designating plants and animals. Linnaean nomenclature comes from 1758 edition of his *Systema naturae* (1735).

linnet, *Carduelis cannabina,* small partly migratory finch, found in open bushy countryside of Europe and W Asia.

linotype, in printing, type-setting machine, patented (1884) by Ottmar Mergenthaler. Operated by keyboard, it carries and makes cast of plate of a line.

Lin Piao (1908–), Chinese polit. leader, Min. of Defence (1959–). Helped found Chinese Red Army. Ranked behind Mao Tse-tung in Communist Party hierarchy.

linseed, seed of common flax plant which yields an oil used in paint, varnish and linoleum. After oil extraction, residue used in cattle-feeding as linseed cake.

Linz, city of Upper Austria, on R. Danube, known in Roman times as Lentia. Iron and steel centre with chem. and manufacturing industries. Pop. (1964) 202,000.

lion, *Panthera leo,* mammal of cat family native to Africa, SW Asia and W India. Yellow to brown in colour; male usually has black or tawny mane. Hunts antelope, zebra, *etc.* and lives in group called pride.

Lipchitz, Jacques (1891–), Amer. sculptor, b. Lithuania. Early cubist style gave way to concern with movement and myth. themes.

Lipmann, Fritz Albert FRS (1889–), Amer. biochemist. With H. A. Krebs, awarded Nobel Prize for Physiology and Medicine (1953) for discovery of coenzyme A.

Lippi, Fra Filippo (c. 1406–69), Florentine painter. Works include *Coronation of the Virgin,* and the choir of Prato Cathedral.

Lipton, Sir Thomas Johnstone (1850–1931), Brit. yachtsman. Unsuccessful 5 times in attempts to win America's Cup yachting trophy.

liqueur, strong, sweet, highly flavoured alcoholic beverage. Contains 27%–80% alcohol. Varieties include benedictine, chartreuse, crème de menthe.

liquid *see* STATES OF MATTER.

liquorice, sweet-tasting, dried root of leguminous plant, *Glycyrrhiza glabra,* of Europe and Asia. Used in confectionery and medicine.

Lisbon, Lisboa, cap. and Atlantic port of Portugal, at mouth of Tagus R. Important transport and commercial centre. Founded by Phoenicians, grew after 12th cent. Has university, many famous medieval buildings. Pop. (1964) 1,397,000.

Lisgar, 1st Baron *see* YOUNG, JOHN.

Lister, Joseph Lister, 1st Baron (1827–1912), Brit. surgeon. Used carbolic acid to prevent septic infection, founder of antiseptic surgery. Introduced absorbable ligature and drainage tube.

Liszt, Franz (1811–86), Hungarian Romantic composer, musician. Leading pianist of his time, protégés include Wagner, Strauss. Among works are symphonic poem *Les Préludes, Hungarian Rhapsodies,* Dante and Faust symphonies.

litany, form of prayer consisting of a series of supplications, used in Christian worship from earliest times.

litchi, lychee, lichi, *Litchi litchi,* Chinese tree, now grown in S Florida and California. Cultivated for fruit, sweet jelly-like pulp and single seed enclosed in thin brittle shell.

Llama

lithium, soft white element, the lightest known metal. Discovered 1817.

lithography, process of surface printing taken from stone, zinc or aluminium; invented (c. 1798) by Aloys Senefelder in Munich.

lithosphere, outer shell, crust, of Earth extending up to c. 30 mi. into mantle and composed mainly of silicate rocks.

Lithuanian, Baltic Indo-European language, with 3 million speakers in Soviet Republic of Lithuania.

Lithuanian SSR, constituent repub. of USSR on Baltic Sea. Area: 25,200 sq. mi.; cap. Vilna. Flat, often marshy, land; agriculture is main occupation; industry centres on processing consumer goods. Settled by Liths (c. 1500 BC). Withstood series of invasions, remaining independent until 1386 merger with Poland. Incorporated by USSR (1940). Main religion, Roman Catholicism. Pop. (1963) 3,026,000.

litmus, colouring matter obtained from various lichens. Used as indicator to test acidic or alkaline nature of aqueous solutions. Blue colour is turned red by acids and restored by alkalis.

little auk [UK], **dovekie** [US], *Plautus alle,* sea bird with black upper and white underparts and short beak. Feeds on plankton. Mainly breeds in Greenland and Spitzbergen.

Little Bighorn, Battle of (1876), also known as 'Custer's Last Stand', battle fought near Little Bighorn R., Montana, US. Scene of defeat and death of GEORGE CUSTER and his men by Sioux Indians.

Little Rock, cap. and main agric. market of Arkansas, US. Founded as trading post (1772); became state cap. (1836). Industries include concrete manufacture, prefabricated housing and insecticides. Pop. (1963) 185,000.

Littré, Maximilien Paul Émile (1801–81), Fr. scholar and lexicographer; advocate of doctrine of

Adoration of the Child by Fra Filippo Lippi

positivism. Best known for his *Dictionnaire de la Langue Française* (1863–72).

liturgy, orig. term for celebration of Eucharist in Christian Church; now used for any service of public worship.

Liu Shao-ch'i (1898–   ), Chinese polit. leader. High-ranking trade unionist; elected to succeed Mao Tse-tung, influence in Communist regime subsequently declined.

liver, large gland of vertebrates, in man lying below diaphragm on right side. Functions include secretion of bile, storage of carbohydrates as glycogen, regulation of blood composition (esp. iron content), destruction of unnecessary red corpuscles and synthesis of blood proteins.

Liverpool, 2nd Earl of *see* JENKINSON, ROBERT BANKS.

Liverpool, seaport, Lancashire, England, on R. Mersey. Great trade centre, extensive docks; formerly leading market for cotton. Connected with Birkenhead by tunnel. Founded *c.* 1207. Has 2 cathedrals. Pop. (1966) 712,000.

liverwort, flowerless, moss-like plant of class Hepaticae. Grows in water and moist ground or on tree-trunks. *Marchantia* and *Riccia* are 2 common genera.

livingrock cactus, *Ariocarpus fissuratus,* cactus of SW US and adjacent Mexico.

Livingstone, David (1813–73), Scot. missionary doctor and explorer in Africa, medical missionary in Bechuanaland (1841–52). Discovered Zambesi R. (1851), Victoria Falls (1855) and Lakes Ngami, Shirwa and Nyasa. Disappeared while exploring upper Nile region; found by HENRY STANLEY (1871).

Livius, Titus *see* LIVY.

Livonia, medieval country on E shore of Baltic Sea. Area: 45,000 sq. mi. Comprises what became LATVIA and ESTONIA.

Livy [**Titus Livius**] (59 BC–AD 17), Roman historian. Life work was *History of Rome,* started (*c.* 25 BC); orig. 142 books, 35 survive.

lizard, reptile of suborder Lacertilia (Sauria), incl. gecko, iguana, chameleon, monitor and slow-worm. Found in temp. and trop. regions. Terrestrial, fossorial, arboreal and aquatic species with long body (few in. to 10 ft.), tapering tail and 2 pairs of legs.

Ljubljana, Laibach, city and cap. of Slovenia, NW Yugoslavia, on Sava R. Political, economic and cultural

Praca do Rocio, Lisbon

centre; industries include tanning, textiles, brewing. Pop. (1964) 178,000.

llama, S Amer. hoofed ruminant of genus *Lama* of camel family. Believed to be descended from guanaco. Valued by Incas as pack animal and for providing fur, flesh and tallow.

llanos, Sp.-American term for extensive grassy plains of Orinoco basin, Venezuela, and E Colombia. Famous for cattle-breeding and rare orchids.

Llewellyn, Richard, orig. Richard Lloyd (1907–   ), Welsh novelist. Author of *How Green Was My Valley* (1939), *None but the Lonely Heart* (1943), *Sweet Morn of Judas Day* (1964).

Lloyd George, David, 1st Earl Lloyd George of Dwyfor (1863–1945), Brit. statesman, b. Wales; P.M. (1916–22). Entered Parl. 1890; Liberal anti-imperialist. Chanc. of Exchequer under Asquith, used budget to force election (1910) and curtail House of Lords' veto power. Headed World War 1 coalition govt., attended Paris Peace Conference (1919).

Lloyd's, association of Eng. insurance underwriters orig. covering marine risks only, now issuing most types of insurance policies. Name derived from the coffee house kept by Edward Lloyd in 18th cent.

loach, small freshwater fish of family Cobitidae, found in Europe, Asia and N Africa. Body elongated and cylindrical; 3–6 pairs barbels present. Feeds on insects and worms. Species include stone loach, *Nemacheitus barbatula.*

loam, soil composed of humus, sand, silt and clay particles. Gritty and plastic when moist.

Lobachevsky, Nikolai Ivanovich (1793–1856), Russ. mathematician, pioneer in non-Euclidean geometry. Wrote *Principles of Geometry* (1829–30), *Imaginary Geometry* (1835).

lobelia, annual or perennial plant of genus *Lobelia,* native to temp. regions. Leaves small and rounded; blue, red, yellow or white flowers.

lobster, large edible marine crustacean of family Homaridae found on rocky coasts. Has 5 pairs of jointed

Lobelia

Lizard

Lobster

legs, 1st pair having pincer-like claws. Is green alive, but red when cooked. Species include Amer. *Homarus americanus* and European *H. vulgaris*.

lobworm, lugworm, segmented marine worm found in sand and mud. Used as angler's bait.

local government, admin. of public affairs in localized areas. Jurisdiction usually encompasses residual powers, *i.e.* those not delegated to national or state govts.

Locarno Pact, series of treaties concluded among European nations (1925) at Locarno, Switzerland, guaranteeing Ger. borders in W, as designated by Treaty of Versailles (1919). Germany also agreed to demilitarize Rhineland and was promised League of Nations membership. Chief architects of Pact were Stresemann, Briand and Austen Chamberlain.

loch *see* LAKE.

lock, artificial enclosure of water within river or canal system facilitating transfer of vessel from 1 level to another. Constructed at points where land slopes sharply.

Locke, John (1632–1704), leading Brit. exponent of empiricist philosophy. In *Essay concerning Human Understanding* (1690), contradicted Hobbes by asserting initial good in man; experience basis of knowledge. Defended constitutional monarchy in *Two Treatises on Government* (1689); his work influenced framers of US Constitution.

lockjaw *see* TETANUS.

locomotive, rly. engine developed early 19th cent. (*e.g.* Stephenson's 'Rocket', Cooper's 'Tom Thumb') with use of steam as driving force. Electric locomotives (*c.* 1895) obtain power from 3rd rail or overhead wire. Diesel electric trains (*c.* 1925), in which electric generator is driven by Diesel engine, have extensively replaced steam engines on most rly. systems.

locust, short-horned grasshopper, in-

sect of family Acrididae, with short antennae. Commonly migrates in swarms, devastating large areas of crops. Species include desert locust, *Schistoarca gregaria,* migratory locust, *Locusta migratoria.*

lodestone, variety of magnetite, a black magnetic iron oxide, occurring in crystals, masses and loose sand.

Lodge, Henry Cabot (1850–1924), Amer. polit. leader. Republican Senator from Massachusetts (1893–1924), led attack on Pres. Wilson's role in formulation of Treaty of Versailles and estab. of League of Nations. His son, **Henry Cabot Lodge, Jr** (1902–), served on various US diplomatic missions incl. UN (1953–61) and Vietnam (1963–5). Unsuccessful Republican vice-pres. candidate (1960).

Lodge, Sir Oliver Joseph (1851–1940), Brit. physicist. Helped develop radio telegraphy; did important work in ether studies.

Lodz, city, C Poland. Industrial centre; textile manufacturing. Chartered (1423); passed to Prussia (1793), to Russia (1875); reverted to Poland (1919). Pop. (1965) 743,000.

loess, wind-deposited silt or dust originating from glacial deposits. In N China, a fine yellow loam, rich in lime; mixed with humus, forms Black Earth of USSR; also deposits in C Europe and C US. Forms fertile soils.

Loewi, Otto (1873–1961), Amer. physiologist, pharmacologist, b. Germany. Shared Nobel Prize for Physiology and Medicine (1936) with Sir Henry Hallet Dale for study of chemical transmission of nerve impulses.

Lofoten Islands, group of 4 main and several small islands off NW coast of Norway. Area: 474 sq. mi. Heavily glaciated; fishing main industry. Used as Ger. base in World War 2.

Logan, Mount, highest peak (19,850 ft.) in Canada and 2nd highest in North America, in SW Yukon. Central peak 1st ascended (1925); named after Sir William Logan.

loganberry, hardy plant of genus *Rubus,* found on Pacific coast of US. Cross between raspberry and Amer. blackberry; red-purple fruit.

logarithms, mathematical tabular system devised by John Napier (1614) to simplify arithmetical computations. By converting numbers to their equivalent expressed in bases and exponential powers, operations of multiplication, division, and finding square roots can be done by addition, subtraction and division respectively.

loggerhead, *Caretta caretta,* carni-

vorous turtle of trop. and sub-trop. seas, with large head.

logic, study and discipline dealing with principles of valid inference. Aristotle founded systematic logic, using SYLLOGISM and deductive method (reasoning from general to particular). Inductive logic develops from particular to general.

logical positivism, school of modern philosophy which attempts to apply mathematical methodology to philosophy. In theory, empirical test is only means of verifying proposition.

logistics, branch of military operations concerned with supply and maintenance of equipment. Strategic implications involve personnel movement, evacuation and hospitalization.

Logos [Gk: word], term for Gk. and Hebrew metaphysical concept of a link between God and man. According to Gospel of St John the identification of Christ as the Second Person of the Trinity, the Word of God made flesh; the manifestation of God in a finite, created being.

Loire, principal Fr. river system. R. Loire is 670 mi. long and with its tribs., Mayenne, Sarthe, Loir, Allier, Cher, Vienne and Sèvres, drains more than one-fifth of France. Rises in Massif Central, flows N and W.

Lollards, followers of JOHN WYCLIFFE (14th–15th cent.). Sect in England who anticipated some reformation doctrines esp. use of vernacular Bible, but also attacked eccles. wealth, denied doctrine of Transubstantiation and attacked the monastic system. Declined after Wycliffe's death.

Lombards, Teutonic people who invaded N Italy (568), estab. kingdom of Lombardy. Attacked Rome and were conquered by Charlemagne (774) who adopted the Iron Crown of the Lombard kings.

Lombardy, densely populated region of N Italy incl. basin of R Po; named from kingdom of LOMBARDS. Area: 9,191 sq. mi. Main industries, textiles (esp. silk), iron and steel. Pop. (1961) 7,406,152.

Lombardy poplar *see* POPLAR.

Lomé, cap. and port of Togo Republic on Gulf of Guinea. Exports cocoa, coffee and copra. Pop. (1962) 90,000.

Lomond, Loch, largest freshwater loch of Scotland, *c.* 24 mi. long with maximum width of 5 mi.

Loggerhead Turtle

Long-tailed Tit

Mts. in S. Crops include flax, oats, potatoes. Linen manufactured. Pop. (1966) 118,664.

Long, Huey Pierce (1893–1935), Amer. polit. leader. Gov. of Louisiana (1928–31), US Senator (1932–5), ruthlessly pursued 'Share the wealth' policies and built strong polit. 'machine'. Assassinated at Baton Rouge.

Long Island, island E of New York Bay, US. Area: 1,682 sq. mi.; connected to Manhattan, New York City by bridges and tunnels. Industrial, manufacturing and tourist centre.

Long March, journey from Kiansi prov. to Shensi prov. (*c.* 6,000 mi.) made (1934–5) by approx. 9,000 Chinese Communist troops; under constant threat of attack from Nationalist forces. Their leaders included Mao Tse-tung and Lin Piao.

Long Parliament, name given to Eng. Parl. (1640–60) whose opposition to Charles II led to Civil War; after expulsion of Presbyterian members (1648), known as Rump Parliament. Expelled by Cromwell; reassembled (1659) and finally dissolved at the RESTORATION (1660).

long-eared bat, most common mammal of bat family found in temperate and tropical regions of both hemispheres. Common long-eared bat, *Plecotus auritus,* has ears almost as long as the body. It is the only bat that can walk and climb.

long-eared owl, *Asia otus,* woodland bird, common in N latitudes of America and Eurasia. Named from erectile tufts on side of head.

Longfellow, Henry Wadsworth (1807–82), Amer. poet, esp. known for sentimental lyrics and narrative poems, *e.g. Evangeline* (1847) and *The Song of Hiawatha* (1855).

Longford, county of Leinster prov., Republic of Ireland. Area: 421 sq. mi.; county town, Longford. Industries mainly agricultural. Pop. (1966) 28,943.

longhorn beetle, longicorn, beetle of family Cerambycidae with long antennae. Larvae are wood-boring and a forest pest.

Longinus, Cassius (*c.* AD 220–273), Gk. writer on philosophy and rhetoric. As counsellor to Zenobia of Palmyra, executed by Aurelian for rebellion. *On the Sublime* has been mistakenly attributed to him.

longitude *see* LATITUDE.

longsightedness [UK] *see* HYPEROPIA.

Big Ben clock tower, London

Longstreet, James (1821–1904), Amer. Confederate general. His delay in carrying out LEE's orders to attack at Gettysburg (1863) has been held responsible for Confederate defeat.

long-tailed duck [UK], **old squaw** [US], *Clangula hyemalis,* sea duck with small round head, short bill and long pointed tail feathers, white body and black wings.

long-tailed tit, *Aegithalos caudatus* small bird with black, white and pink plumage and long graduated tail. Native of Europe and N Asia.

loom, frame machine used for weaving cloth. Power loom introduced (1785–87) by Cartwright. Joseph Marie Jacquard perfected (1804) automatic action, making it possible to weave intricate designs.

loon *see* DIVER.

looper, measuring worm, inchworm, spanworm, caterpillar of geometrid moth, moves with looping action of the body.

loosestrife, *Lysimachia vulgaris,* downy perennial plant with yellow flowers. Marsh loosestrife, *L. salicaria,* has purple flowers.

Lorca, Federico García (1898–1936), Sp. poet and dramatist. His poems include *Poema de Cante Jondo* (1931). Among powerful tragedies are the trilogy *Bodas de Sangre* (1933), *Yerma* (1934) and *La Casa de Bernarda Alba* (1936).

Long-eared Bat

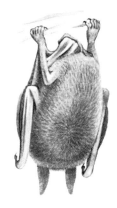

Lomonosov, Mikhail Vasilyevich (1711–65), Russ. scientist and writer. Made important contributions to chemistry and physics and wrote grammar which reformed Russ. lang.

London, Jack, orig. John Griffith London (1876–1916), Amer. novelist and short-story writer. *The Call of the Wild* (1903) and *White Fang* (1906) are adventure stories set in Alaska.

London, cap., chief port, industrial, cultural and transport centre of England, of United Kingdom of Great Britain and Northern Ireland, and of British Commonwealth of Nations, on R. Thames, on site of Roman town, *Londinium.* Greater London comprises THE CITY and 32 metropolitan boroughs (County of London). Buildings of tourist interest include St Paul's Cathedral, Westminster Abbey, Houses of Parliament and Big Ben, Buckingham Palace, Tower of London and Tower Bridge. Parks include Hyde Park, Kensington Gardens, Hampstead Heath. Pop. (1966): City of London, 4,600; Greater London, 7,914,000.

London, University of, non-sectarian co-educational institution in London, founded (1836).

London Bridge, bridge in City of London over R. Thames, removed, block by block (1968), to be rebuilt in Arizona, US.

London pride, *Saxifraga umbrosa,* perennial W European plant with small pink flowers on long stems.

Londonderry, city and port of Northern Ireland with linen manufactures and shipbuilding. On site of monastery founded by St Columba (546). Centre of social and polit. unrest (1969). Pop. (1966) 55,681.

Londonderry, county of NE Northern Ireland. Area: 813 sq. mi.; county town, Londonderry. Flat, with Sperrin

Lord Chamberlain, officer in Royal Household of UK. Duties formerly included censorship of plays.

Lord Chancellor, head of the judiciary in England; nominates and appoints Eng. judges and magistrates. Speaker of the House of Lords and a member of the Cabinet.

Lord Chief Justice, Pres. of Queen's Bench Division of High Court of Justice; ranks next to Lord Chancellor in England.

Lord Lieutenant, representative of sovereign in each of the counties of England, Scotland, Wales and Northern Ireland.

Lord of the Isles, title formerly given to rulers of W Isles of Scotland; 1st conferred on Somerled of Argyll (1135) by David I.

Lord's, cricket ground, NW London, England; home of Marylebone Cricket Club (MCC) and regarded as world centre of the game.

lords and ladies, cuckoo pint, *Arum maculatum,* perennial plant of arum family with dark green arrow-shaped leaves, often spotted; bright red poisonous berries.

Lords, House of *see* HOUSE OF LORDS.

Lord's Prayer, Our Father, Pater Noster, most widely known and used Christian prayer. Taught by Jesus to his disciples; part of Sermon on the Mount (*Matt.* vi 9–13).

Lorentz, Hendrick Antoon, FRS (1853–1928), Dutch physicist; for-

Portrait of a young man by Lorenzo Lotto

mulated relations between electricity, magnetism and light. With Pieter Zeeman, awarded Nobel Prize for Physics (1902) for studies of influence of magnetism on radiation.

Lorenz, Konrad Zacharias, FRS (1903–), Austrian ethnologist. Popularly known for his studies of animal behaviour. Works include *King Solomon's Ring* (1952) and *On Aggression* (1966).

loris, tailless animal of family Lorisidae; found in SE Asia, India and Ceylon. Species include slender loris, *Loris tardigradus,* and slow loris, *Nycticebus coucang.*

Lorrain, Claude, orig. Claude Gellée (1600–82), Fr. landscape painter. Estab. himself in Rome where he executed several pictures for Pope Urban VIII. Works include *Fête Villageoise, Un Port de Mer au Soleil Couchant.*

Lorraine *see* ALSACE.

lory, small gregarious parrot found in Australia, New Guinea, Malaya and Polynesia. Brilliantly coloured with brush-tipped tongue used to gather nectar and pollen.

Los Angeles, city and seaport of S California, US, founded 1781. Shipping, indust., communications and transport centre. Industries include food-processing, manufacturing of aircraft, missiles, electronic equipment. Trade centre for citrus fruit. Area includes Hollywood, motion picture and television centre. Pop. (1960) 2,479,075.

Lot, in OT, son of Haran, nephew of Abraham. Warned by angel to leave Sodom. Wife turned into pillar of salt for looking back.

Lotharingia, historic empire formed (893) under Treaty of Verdun with Lothair I as emperor, from part of Carolingian empire. Covered present-day Moselle, Meurthe, Meuse and Vosges departments of France.

Loti, Pierre, orig. Louis Marie Julien Viaud (1850–1923), Fr. novelist noted for his exotic works incl. *Pêcheur d'Islande* (1886; Eng. tr., *An Iceland Fisherman*),*Vers Ispahan* (1904).

Lotto, Lorenzo (*c.* 1480–1556), Venetian painter; celebrated for portraits and altar pieces.

lotus, various water lilies. Species include Egyptian lotus, *Nymphaea,* with blue or white flowers, and Amer. lotus, *Nelumbo lutea,* with yellow flowers. Lotus blossom symbolic in Indian art and religion, Indian lotus, *Nelumbo nucifera.*

lough *see* LAKE.

Louis [I] the Pious (778–840), emperor of Holy Roman Empire (814–40), son of CHARLEMAGNE.

Louis [VI] the Fat (1081–1137), king of France (1108–37). Devoted himself to consolidating power of monarch. Defeated armies of Henry I of England and Emperor Henry V (1116–20).

Louis [IX], Saint (1214–70), king of France (1226–70). Defeated Eng. invasion under Henry III; led Crusade to Egypt (1248) but defeated (1250). Returned to France (1254); died during Crusade against Tunis. Reign brought peace and prosperity to France.

Louis XI (1423–83), king of France (1461–83), m. Margaret of Scotland. Attempts to consolidate monarchy (*e.g.* by excessive taxation) led to feudal revolt (1464–5). Tried to offset power of barons by improving position of lower classes.

Louis XII, Father of the People (1462–1515), king of France (1498–1515). Took possession of Milan (1499), conquered Naples (1501). Defeated by Henry VIII of England and Emperor Maximilian I in the 'Battle of the Spurs' (1513).

Louis [XIV] the Great, also known as the **Sun King** (1638–1715), king of France (1643–1715). During early years of his reign, France ruled by MAZARIN. Louis assumed absolute control of affairs after 1661, declaring *L'état, c'est moi* (I am the state). His reign was marked by indust. and territorial expansion. Fr. army was most powerful military organization in Europe. Engaged in numerous wars, esp. with Spain, Holland and England. These wars and his fiscal policy brought economic ruin to France and prepared the way for the FRENCH REVOLUTION.

Louis XV (1710–74), king of France (1715–74). Left govt. to Duke of Bourbon and Cardinal Fleury. Dominated by mistresses incl. Madame de Pompadour and Madame Du Barry. Personal extravagance and expenditure on wars in Europe brought France to verge of bankruptcy and revolution.

Louis XVI (1754–93) Dauphin (1765), m. MARIE ANTOINETTE (1770); king of France (1774–92). FRENCH REVOLUTION began (1789);

Slow Loris

Example of the ornate furniture of the Louis XIV period

escaped to Varennes from Paris (1791) but captured and brought back. Ruled as constitutional king until Sept. 1792, when he was deposed, tried for treason and guillotined.

Louis [XVIII] le Désiré (1755–1824), king of France (1814–24). Assumed royal title on death of Louis XVII. On fall of Napoleon (1814), ascended throne. Expelled by Napoleon (Mar. 1815) during Hundred Days; restored by allied armies (June 1815).

Louis, Joe, orig. Joseph Louis Barrow, (1914–　　), Amer. boxer. World heavyweight champion (1937–49). Defended title 24 times.

Louisbourg, Fr. fortress built (1713) SE Cape Breton Is. Capture (July 1758) by Brit. forces under Amherst and Wolfe instrumental in subsequent defeat of French at Quebec (1759) during Seven Years War in N America.

Louisiana, state of S central US, on Gulf of Mexico. Area: 48,523 sq. mi.; cap. Baton Rouge; main cities, New Orleans, Shreveport, Lake Charles. Low country on Gulf coastal plains; low hills in N. Drained by Mississippi R. and tribs. Crops include rice, sugar cane, cotton; mineral resources, salt, petroleum, natural gas, sulphur. Industries include oil-refining, chemical processing, aluminium smelting. Fr. territory (1682). Area W of Mississippi ceded to Spain (1762); E to Britain (1763). Sold to US by France

(1803) in LOUISIANA PURCHASE. Pop. (1960) 3,257,022.

Louisiana Purchase, transfer of Louisiana Territory from Fr. to Amer. possession. Negotiated for America by Robert R. Livingston and James Monroe. Price, c. 15,000,000 dollars. Ratified Oct. 1803. More than doubled size of US.

Louis-Napoleon see NAPOLEON III.

Louis-Philippe [the Citizen King] (1773–1850), king of France (1830–48). Became member of Jacobin club (1790) and fought with revolutionary army. On deposition of Charles X (1830), chosen as King of the French. Moved from liberal to absolute monarchy; in face of Bonapartist intrigues and rise of socialistic movement, abdicated in 1848.

Louisville, largest city of Kentucky, US; indust., commercial and communications centre. Manufactures tobacco, household appliances, farm machinery. Founded (1778). Pop. (1960) 607,000.

loup-cervier see LYNX.

Lourdes, town of Hautes-Pyrénées department, SW France. Nearby grotto, where Virgin Mary appeared to BERNADETTE OF LOURDES, visited by many thousands of pilgrims every year. Pop. (1962) 16,023.

Lourenço Marques, chief port and cap. of Mozambique, on Delagoa Bay. Founded (1544) by Portuguese; became cap. (1907). Exports gold, chrome, coal and grains. Pop. (1960) 184,000.

louse, small, wingless insect. Sucking louse, order Anoplura, parasitic on man and other mammals, *e.g. Pediculus humanus,* louse of human head and body. Biting louse or chewing louse, order Mallophaga, is parasitic on birds, incl. poultry, and mammals.

lousewort, large, mainly perennial herb, genus *Pedicularis,* of N temp. latitudes. Vari-coloured flowers.

Louth, Lubhaidh, smallest county of Republic of Ireland. Area: 317 sq. mi.; county town, Dundalk. Coarse linens, fish, esp. oysters, dairy produce. Pop. (1966) 69,162.

Louvain, Leuven, city of Brabant prov., Belgium. Cap. of Brabant until 15th cent. Weaving centre (14th cent.). Industries include tanning, brewing, food processing. Pop. (1961) 32,524.

Louvois, François Michel le Tellier, Marquis de (1639–91), Fr. politician.

Portrait of Marie Antoinette, wife of Louis XVI, by Salbreux

Lovebirds

War minister to Louis XIV, responsible, through military reorganization, for supremacy of Fr. army. Enforced revocation of Edict of Nantes (1685).

Louvre, the, former Fr. royal palace converted by Napoleon I into art museum. Contains one of finest collections in world, incl. the 'Venus de Milo' and Leonardo da Vinci's *Mona Lisa.*

lovage, *Levisticum officinale,* European herb with peppery leaf, used in soups and stews.

love bird, small short-tailed parrot of genus *Agopornis* of Africa and *Psittacula* of India. The Austral. love bird or budgerigar, *Melopsittacus undulatrus* also a popular cage bird.

love-in-a-mist, *Nigella damascena,* annual garden plant with blue or white flowers and feathery leaves.

Lovelace, Richard (1618– 57), Eng.

Lake Lugano, with Monte Bré in the background

poet imprisoned for royalist sympathies (1648). Works collected in *Lucasta* (1649).

Lovell, Sir [Alfred Charles] Bernard (1913–), Brit. astronomer. Director since 1951 of Jodrell Bank Observatories.

lover fly, any member of family Syrphidae of order Diptera; important in control of aphids and pollination of flowers.

Low, Sir David (1891– 1963), Brit. polit. cartoonist, b. New Zealand. Created Colonel Blimp, caricature of ultra-conservative Englishman. Collections include *Low on the War* (1941), *Years of Wrath* (1946).

Low Countries, name, referring to physical features, of districts constituting Belgium and the Netherlands.

low temperature physics, cryogenics, term for production, and effects of, very low temperatures (–200° or less).

Lowell, James Russell (1819– 91), Amer. poet and diplomat. US minister to Spain (1877– 80), to UK (1880– 5). Works include *The Vision of Sir Launfal* (1848), *Three Memorial Poems* (1876), *Political Essays* (1888).

Lowell, Robert (1917–), Amer. poet whose highly symbolic verse includes *Lord Weary's Castle* (1946), *The Mills of the Kavanaughs* (1951) and autobiog. *Life Studies* (1959).

Lower Canada *see* QUEBEC.

Lower Saxony [Niedersachsen], state of West Germany. Area: 18,226 sq. mi.; cap. Hanover. Formed (1946) in British-occupied zone; joined Federal Republic of West Germany (1949). Low-lying flat land in SE rises to Harz Mts. Agriculture and mineral deposits important. industries include heavy machinery, textiles. Pop. (1960) 6,641,000.

Lowry, Malcolm Boden (1909– 57), Canadian novelist, b. England. His works describe the absence of human contact; they include *Ultramarine* (1933), *Under the Volcano* (1947), *Hear Us O Lord From Heaven Thy Dwelling Place* (1961).

Loyalists, in Amer. Revolution, those who supported Brit. cause. Many emigrated to Brit. colonies in Canada, where they became known as United Empire Loyalists.

Loyola, Ignatius *see* IGNATIUS OF LOYOLA.

LSD *see* LYSERGIC ACID DIETHYLAMIDE.

Luanda, Loanda, cap. and Atlantic port of Angola. Founded (1575); centre of slave traffic to Brazil (17th– 19th cent.). Exports sugar, coffee, cotton, sisal. Pop. (1960) 225,000.

Lübeck, city of Schleswig-Holstein, West Germany, port on Baltic Sea. Produces machinery and textiles. leading city of HANSEATIC LEAGUE; joined Ger. Confederation as free Hanseatic city (1815); incorporated into prov. of Schleswig-Holstein (1937). Noted for its Gothic buildings. Pop. (1965) 240,000.

Lübke, Heinrich (1894–), Ger. politician. Member of Pruss. *Landtag* (1931– 3); imprisoned (1933– 5). Member of Federal Parl. (1949– 50, 1953– 9); Pres. German Federal Republic (1959– 69).

Lublin, city of SE Poland. Trade centre, 1 of oldest Polish towns. Seat of 1918 Socialist govt. and provisional govt. after liberation (1944) of Poland by Soviet troops. Pop. (1964) 194,000.

Lubumbashi, formerly **Elisabethville,** city of Republic of the Congo, cap. of prov. of S Katanga. Centre of copper and uranium mining region. Renamed 1966. Pop. (1959) 184,000.

Lucan [Marcus Annaeus Lucianus] (AD 39– 65), Roman poet and rhetorician. Gained Nero's favour, later ordered to commit suicide. Only surviving poem is *Bellum Civile* (10 books), erroneously known as *Pharsalia,* on war between Caesar and Pompey.

Luce, Henry Robinson (1898– 1967), Amer. publisher. Founded *Time* (1923), *Fortune* (1930); bought *Life* (1936). His wife, **Clare Boothe Luce** (1903–), edited *Vanity Fair* (1933– 4). US Representative from Connecticut (1943– 7); ambassador to Italy (1953– 7).

Lucerne, cap. of Lucerne canton, Switzerland, on L. Lucerne. Machine and printing industries; examples of 8th cent. and 14th– 15th cent. architecture. Popular summer resort. Pop. (1964) 73,000.

Lucerne, Luzern, German-speaking canton of Switzerland. Area: 576 sq. mi.; cap. Lucerne. Agriculture main occupation. Population mostly R.C. Pop. 253,500.

lucerne *see* ALFALFA.

Lucerne, Lake, Vierwaldstättersee, Swiss lake. Area: 44 sq. mi. Borders cantons of Lucerne, Uri, Schwyz, Unterwalden. Popular tourist area.

Lucian [Gk: Loukianos] (*c.* AD 120–200), Gk. rhetorician and satirist. Best known for satirical dialogues, *e.g.* on mythology, *Dialogues of the Gods* and *Dialogues of the Dead*, and on philosophy, *e.g. Menippus*.

Lucknow, Lakhnau, cap. of Uttar Pradesh, N India. Cultural and educ. centre. Suffered 5-month siege during Sepoy Rebellion (1857–8). Pop. (1965) 725,000.

Lucretius [Titus Lucretius Carus] (*c.* 96–55 BC), Roman philosophical poet. Ardent believer in philosophy of EPICURUS. Poem, *De Rerum Natura* (6 books), written at time of religious scepticism, attempted to dispel current fears and superstitions.

Lucullus, Lucius Licinius (*c.* 114–57 BC), Roman general and statesman. Served under Sulla in Asia (87 BC). Consul (74 BC), distinguished service in 3rd Mithridatic War. Recalled to Rome (67 BC). Library became centre for literary Greeks in Rome.

Luddites, in Eng. history, name given to those taking part in machine-wrecking riots (1811–16). Revolt against unemployment caused by introduction of industrial machinery.

Ludendorff, Erich (1865–1937), Ger. general and chief of staff to Hindenburg. Supported Hitler's Munich 'beer-hall *Putsch*' (1923).

Ludwigshafen-am-Rhein, river port and industrial city on Rhine, twin city

The Market Place, Lubeck

Lucerne

of Mannheim, West Germany. Trade centre with heavy industry. Pop. (1965) 176,000.

Luftwaffe, Ger. air force reorganized (1933) by Hermann Goering. Massive bombing attacks led Germany to victory in Poland, Low Countries and France.

Lugano, lake of Switzerland and N Italy. Area: 20 sq. mi. Town of Lugano, in Ticino Canton, S Switzerland, is a spa. Pop. 20,000.

Lugones, Leopoldo (1874–1938), Argentinian realist poet.

lugworm, lobworm, tube-dwelling, greenish-yellow bristle worm. Inhabits muddy sand between the tide marks. Species include the common European lugworm, *Arenicola morina*.

Luini, Bernardino (*c.* 1480–1532), Italian figure painter.

Lukács, György (1885–1971), Hungarian philosopher and critic. Works include *Existentialisme ou Marxisme* and *The Destruction of Reason*.

Luke, third of NT gospels, attributed to St Luke. Recounts life and teachings of Jesus.

Luke, Saint, prob. author of 3rd Gospel of NT, and of *Acts of the Apostles*. St Paul refers to him as the 'beloved physician'.

Lully, Jean-Baptiste (1632–87), Fr. composer b. Italy. Became leader of Louis XIV's orchestra and court composer.

Lumière, Louis Jean (1864–1948), Fr. cinema pioneer, who, with brother, **Auguste Marie Louis Nicholas Lumière,** invented the cinematograph for projecting moving pictures.

lumpsucker, *Cyclopterus lumpus,* dark-coloured N European marine fish. Eggs are laid above low water mark and guarded by male.

Lumumba, Patrice (1925–61), 1st premier of Republic of the Congo upon independence (June 1960). Dismissed by Pres. Kasavubu (Sep. 1960) and placed under house arrest. Killed in Katanga.

luna moth, *Actias luna,* pale green moth with purple brown markings and eyespots on wings.

lunacy *see* INSANITY.

lunar eclipse *see* ECLIPSE.

Lundy Island, island off Devon, England. Area: *c.* 1½ sq. mi. Pop. (1959 est.) 20.

Lüneburg Heath, large area of heathland in N Germany. Scene of German surrender at end of World War 2.

lungfish, fish of the order Dipneusti: breathes with lunglike structure. Hibernates in dry season, some species in burrows. Possibly transitional between fish and amphibian.

lungs, in mammals organs of respiration in which outgoing carbon dioxide is exchanged for oxygen. Man's 2 lungs are situated in the chest.

Luo, Nilo-Saharan language, with almost 1 million speakers in Kenya.

lupin, perennial plant of pea family, native to Med. region and N America. Flowers a variety of colours borne in long spike. Russell lupin is popular garden hybrid.

Lusaka, cap. of Northern Rhodesia from 1935; of Zambia since 1964. Agriculture and trade centre. Pop. (1964) 122,000.

lute, 6-stringed instrument shaped like half pear, with fretted finger-board, whose strings are plucked. Popular-domestic musical instrument (15th–16th cents.).

luth *see* LEATHERY TURTLE.

Luther, Martin (1483–1546), leader of Protestant Reformation in Germany. Augustinian monk of R.C. Church, prominent after campaign (1517) against sale of INDULGENCES in which he nailed 95 theses to

Esch-sur-Sûre, Luxembourg

Wittenberg church door. Excommunicated (1521); translated NT into German and drew up AUGSBURG CONFESSION, formulating basis for Lutheranism.

Lutheranism, sect of Protestant Church, founded on teachings of Luther and stated in Book of Concord (1580). Doctrinal justification founded on faith. Distinguished by absence of ritual; flourishes primarily in Germany, Scandinavia.

Luthuli, Albert John (1899–1967), African chief and polit. leader in Repub. of South Africa. Openly opposed apartheid laws; deposed from chieftaincy (1952); kept under restriction for rest of his life. Author of *Let My People Go* (1962). Awarded Nobel Peace Prize (1960).

Lutyens, Sir Edwin Landseer (1869–1944), Eng. architect. Works include govt. buildings, New Delhi, India and Cenotaph memorial, London.

Luxembourg, cap. of Luxembourg. Financial centre and industrial centre. Pop. (1964) 77,000.

Luxembourg, duchy and state of Europe. Area: 998 sq. mi.; cap. Luxembourg. Economy based on

steel production, iron mining. Raised to duchy status while under Holy Roman Empire. Member of Ger. Confederation, now constitutional monarchy. Joined (1947) BENELUX union. Official language, French; main religion, Roman Catholicism. Unit of currency, Luxembourg franc. Pop. (1964) 333,000.

Luxemburg, Rosa (1870–1919), Ger.

Lyons

revolutionary, b. Poland. Leading figure in Social Democratic Party, but broke away and, with Karl Liebknecht, founded Spartacus Party during World War 1. Arrested and shot after leading Spartacist revolt.

Luxor, town in Upper Egypt, with remains of ancient Thebes, incl. temple built by Amenhotep III. Pop. *c.* 35,000.

Luzon, largest island of Phillipines. Area: 40,420 sq. mi.; main city, Manila. Mountainous E contains active volcanoes. Agric. products include rice, sugar, hemp, tobacco; manganese, chromite among chief resources. Pop. 12,526,459.

Lvov, city in W Ukrainian SSR. Transport and textile manufacturing centre. Founded 1526; Polish possession (1919–39). Pop. (1967) 502,000.

lycanthropy, human adoption of wolf-forms, associated with witchcraft. Also name of mental disease when patient imagines himself an animal.

lychee *see* LITCHI.

Lycurgus (*c.* 396–*c.* 324 BC), Athenian orator. Pupil of Isocrates. Only 1 of 15 speeches survives. Financial administrator in Athens (338–326 BC); reconstructed theatre of Dionysus.

Lycurgus, legendary founder of unique Spartan constitution. Archaeological evidence dates legislation ascribed to Lycurgus at *c.* 600 BC. mentioned by Herodotus and Xenophon; biography by Plutarch.

Lydia, ancient kingdom of W Asia Minor, cap. Sardis. Empire attained

Lupin

Lyre Bird

peak of power and wealth under Croesus (560–546 BC); conquered by Cyrus of Persia (546 BC). Invention of coinage attributed to Lydians.

Lyell, Sir Charles (1797–1875), Brit. geologist who originated terms Eocene, Miocene and Pliocene. Wrote *Principles of Geology* (1830–3).

lymph, clear, saline body fluid which carries nourishment to tissue cells and waste matter from them.

lymphocytes, white blood cells formed in LYMPH nodes.

Lynen, Feodor (1911–), Ger. biochemist. With K. E. Bloch, awarded Nobel Prize for Physiology and Medicine (1964) for work on cholestorol and fatty acid metabolism.

lynx, member of cat family with short tail and tufted ears. Rare European lynx, *Lynx lynx,* is found in N Europe and Siberia. The Canadian lynx or loup-cervier, *L. canadensis* is the largest N Amer. lynx. *See* BOBCAT.

Lyonesse, fertile, prosperous kingdom widely thought to be submerged between Cornwall and Scilly Isles, UK. Referred to in Arthurian legends.

Lyons, city of SE France at junction of Rhône and Saône rivers. Commercial, communications and financial centre with silk, plastics and pharmaceutical industries. Pop. (1962) 886,000.

lyre, ancient Gk. stringed musical instrument, played with a plectrum.

lyrebird, Austral. bird of *Menura* family. The pheasant-like superb lyrebird, *M. novae-hollandiae,* dis-

plays its lyre-shaped tail in courtship ritual.

lyric, orig. song set to lyre music, now used generally to denote any short poem expressing emotion.

Lysander (d. 395 BC), Spartan naval commander in Peloponnesian War. Defeated Athenians at Aegospotami (405 BC). Powerful after fall of Athens, but deposed by Spartans on grounds of misgovernment. Killed at Haliartus in battle against Boeotians.

Lysenko, Trofim Denis (1898–), Russ. agronomist; supporter of non-Mendelian genetic theory stating that environmental changes can be inherited.

lysergic acid, diethylamide [LSD] hallucinatory (prob. non-addictive) drug, capable of inducing emotional disturbance. Occasionally used in treatment of alcoholism.

Lyskamm, Alpine peak (14,888 ft.), in the Monte Rosa massif. Source of a sizable glacier.

Lytton, Edward George Earle Lytton Bulwer, 1st Baron Lytton of Knebworth (1803–73), Eng. politician and writer. Works include hist. novels *The Last Days of Pompeii* (1834), *Rienzi* (1835) and *Harold* (1848).

Lynx

M

Maastricht, cap. of Limburg prov., SE Netherlands, on Meuse canal section. Important glass and ceramic industries. Has 6th cent. cathedral. Pop. (1965 est.) 94,939.

Mabinogion, collection of medieval Welsh tales, composed for oral recitation, from manuscripts of *White Book of Rhydderch.* Tales prob. became part of ARTHURIAN LEGEND.

Mabuse, Jan de, orig. Jan Gossaert (*c.* 1478–1533), Flemish painter, influenced by Ital. artists. Works include *Man with a Rosary.*

McAdam, John Loudon (1756–1836), Scot. engineer. Introduced (*c.* 1815) improved roads, made of crushed stone, known as 'macadam roads'.

McAdoo, William Gibbs (1863–1941), Amer. polit. leader. Sec. of Treasury (1913–18). Contested Democratic pres. nomination (1920, 1924).

Macan, village of C Asiatic Turkey, near Kayseri, having relics of distinctive turf huts.

Macao, Macau, Portuguese possession, estab. 1557, SE China. Status confirmed under 1887 treaty with China. Area: 6 sq. mi.; cap. Macao, free port, distribution centre. Pop. (1960) 174,000.

macaque, thickset omnivorous monkey. Often lives at high altitudes, esp. SE Asia. Species include BARBARY APE and RHESUS MONKEY.

MacArthur, Douglas (1880–1964), Amer. army officer. Chief of staff (1930–5). Commanded Far East US forces during World War 2; directed post-war Allied occupation of Japan. Later recalled (1951) by Pres. Truman while heading UN force in Korean war.

Macassar, port and chief town, SW Celebes, Indonesia. Exports timber, coffee, copra and rubber produced on islands. Pop. (1963) 450,000.

Macauley, Thomas Babington, Baron Macauley of Rothley (1800–59), Eng. writer. Best known for Whig interpretation of history in *The History of England From the Accession of James the Second* (5 vols., 1849–61). Also wrote poetry, as in *Lays of Ancient Rome* (1842).

macaw, brightly coloured, long-tailed parrot, found in trop. rain forests of Central and S America. Species include large scarlet macaw, *Ara macao.*

Macbeth (d. 1057), Scot. king. Killed Duncan and took crown (1040). Defeated and killed by Malcolm III. Basis of Shakespeare's *Macbeth.*

Maccabees, Jewish family (*fl.* 2nd cent. BC). Founded by **Mattathias** (d. 166 BC). He and his sons led opposition against Syrians. **Judas Maccabeus** (d. 161 BC) reconquered Jerusalem; **Simon Maccabeus** (d. 135 BC) estab. Jewish independence (142 BC).

Maccabees, last 2 books of OT.

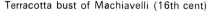
Terracotta bust of Machiavelli (16th cent)

Sheep-farming in Macedonia

Covers history of MACCABEES family.

McCarthy, Joseph Raymond (1908–57), Amer. politician. Republican Senator from Wisconsin (1947–57), conducted controversial investigations of persons, incl. many with Communist sympathies, suspected of subversive activities.

McCarthy, Mary (1912–), Amer. writer and critic. Author of novel *The Group* (1963).

Macchu Picchu, ancient Peruvian city. Rebuilt by Incas, who abandoned it. Remains discovered 1911.

McClellan, George Brinton (1826–85), Amer. army officer. Union general in Civil War. Thwarted Lee in Antietam campaign. Relieved of command (1862). Democratic opponent of Lincoln in 1864 pres. election.

McClintock, Sir Francis Leopold (1819–1907), Brit. explorer. Discovered (1857–9) fate of Sir JOHN FRANKLIN after several expeditions to Arctic regions.

McCormack, John (1884–1945), Irish concert tenor. Popular singer of sentimental songs.

McCormick, Cyrus Hall (1809–84), Amer. inventor of reaper (patented 1834). Built (1847) factory in Chicago to process its manufacture.

McCrae, John (1872–1918), Canadian poet. Author of 'In Flanders Fields' written during World War 1.

McCullers, Carson (1917–67), Amer. novelist. Works, usually set in South, include *The Heart Is a Lonely Hunter* (1940), *The Ballad of the Sad Café* (1951).

McCulloch v. Maryland, case (1819) decided by US Supreme Court involving federal-state dispute over control of currency. Decision upheld federal govt. supremacy over states.

McDiarmid, Hugh, orig. Christopher Murray Grieve (1892–), Scot.

poet. Works are nationalist (*e.g.* 'A Drunk Man Looks at the Thistle'), sometimes Marxist (*e.g.* 'Hymns to Lenin').

Macdonald, Flora, Scot. heroine. Helped Charles Edward Stuart escape to France after 1746 defeat at Culloden.

Macdonald, [James] Ramsay (1866–1937), Brit. statesman. Helped found Labour Party, lost leadership when discredited for pacifism during World War 1. Became (1924) 1st Labour P.M., defeated over issue of ZINOVIEV LETTER. Again P.M. (1929), repudiated by Party after heading Conservative dominated National govt. (1931–5).

Macdonald, Sir John Alexander (1815–91), Canadian statesman, 1st P.M. of Dominion, Conservative. Dominated negotiations for Confederation, achieved 1867. 'PACIFIC SCANDAL' forced his resignation (1873). Again P.M. (1878–91).

McDougall, William (1871–1938), Amer. psychologist, b. England. Used biological approach to study of psychology. Wrote *Introduction to Social Psychology* (1908).

MacDowell, Edward Alexander (1861–1908), Amer. composer. Works include piano sonata, for orchestra, *Indian Suite*, and popular *Woodland Sketches*.

McDowell, Ephraim (1771–1830), Amer. surgeon. Performed 1st ovariotomy (1809).

mace *see* NUTMEG.

Macedonia, region of S Balkan Peninsula, SE Europe, extending over parts of Yugoslavia, Bulgaria and

The ancient village of Macan, near Kayseri (Caesarea), Turkey

Greece. Area: *c.* 26,000 sq. mi.; predominantly mountainous and agric. Roughly corresponds to ancient kingdom of **Macedon** at its height under Phillip II and Alexander the Great (4th cent. BC).

MacEwen, Sir William (1848–1924), Scot. surgeon. Pioneered work in bone surgery, esp. of brain and spinal chord.

McGee, [Thomas] D'Arcy (1825–68), Irish journalist, instrumental in estab. Dominion of Canada. Promoted union with speeches (1858–67). Assassinated for anti-Fenian views.

McGill University, predominantly Eng.-speaking, non-sectarian university in Montreal, Canada, opened 1829. Noted for schools of medicine and physical sciences.

Macgillicuddy's Reeks, mountain range, Co. Kerry, Ireland, incl. Carrantuohill (3,414 ft.).

Mach number, unit of high-speed flight, expressing ratio between speed of object and speed of sound in particular environment in which object is moving. Named after Austrian physicist, Ernst Mach (1838–1916).

Blue and Yellow Macaw (left) and Red, Blue and Yellow Macaw (right)

Machado de Assis, Joaquim María (1839–1908), Brazilian novelist. Works depict social conditions in Brazil, notable for ironical insights; include *Epitaph for a Small Winner* (1881), *Don Casmurro* (1900).

Machado [y Ruiz], Antonio (1875–1939), Sp. lyric poet. Author of

Soledades (1903), series of evocative poems.

Machiavelli, Niccolò (1469–1527), Ital. polit. leader and writer, b. Florence. Prominent during republican era (1492–1512), ruined by restoration of the Medici. Author of *The Prince* (1513), an objective analysis of means to achieve power; had enormous influence.

machine gun, firearm with automatic mechanism for rapid and continuous discharge of rifle bullets. Developed primarily by Gatling and Browning. First used *c.* 1870.

Mack, Connie, orig. Cornelius McGillicuddy (1862–1956), Amer. baseball manager of Philadelphia Athletics (1901–50). His teams won 5 World Series.

Macke, August (1887–1914), Ger. Expressionist painter. Exponent of bright colour; member of Munich group, Blaue Reiter.

Mackenzie, Alexander (1822–92), Canadian statesman, b. Scotland. First Liberal P.M. (1873–8) of Canada.

Mackenzie, Sir Alexander (1764–1820), Canadian fur trader and explorer, b. Scotland. Traded in Athabaska region for North West Co. Reached Arctic Ocean (1789) by following then unknown Mackenzie R. to its mouth. Made 1st overland journey to Pacific Ocean (1793).

Mackenzie, Sir Compton Edward Montague (1883–), Brit. novelist. Author of *Sinister Street* (1914)

Madonna and Child
by Parmigianino

and farces *Whisky Galore* (1947) and *Thin Ice* (1956).

Mackenzie, William Lyon (1795–1861), Canadian journalist and secessionist, b. Scotland. Publisher of *Colonial Advocate* (1824–34), advocated free trade and agric. economy. Organized short-lived REBELLION OF 1837; failed in attempt to seize Toronto. Escaped to US, later imprisoned for estab. govt. on Navy Is. Niagara. Returned to Canada 1849.

Mackenzie, river (1,120 mi. long) of NW Canada. Once important fur trade route, oil and mineral deposits discovered. Named after SIR ALEXANDER MACKENZIE.

Mackenzie King, William Lyon *see* KING, WILLIAM LYON MACKENZIE.

mackerel, *Scomber scombrus,* marine fish, related to tuna and blue-fish. Spiny-finned, travels in schools and migrates to deep water in winter. Commercially important.

Mackinac *see* MICHILIMACKINAC.

McKinley, Mount, peak (20,270 ft.), S central Alaska, highest mountain in N America. Located in Mt. McKinley National Park; 1st climbed 1913.

McKinley, William (1843–1901), 24th US Pres. (1897–1901), Republican. Congressman from Ohio, sponsored protective McKinley Tariff Act (1890). Elected Pres. (1896) over WILLIAM JENNINGS BRYAN, aided by MARCUS HANNA and gold standard platform. Admin. dominated by expansionism and acquisition of Philippine Is. Fatally shot at Buffalo, N.Y.

Mackintosh, Charles Rennie (1868–1928), Scot. architect and artist. Imaginative building designer *e.g.* Glasgow School of Art. Graphic and decorative work are leading examples of *art nouveau*.

McLachlan, Alexander (1818–96), Canadian poet, b. Scotland. Works include *The Spirit of Love and Other Poems* (1846) and *Lyrics* (1858).

MacLeish, Archibald (1892–), Amer. poet. Early lyrics include personal *The Pot of Earth* (1925). Later works: verse dramas *The Fall of the City* (1937), *J.B.* (1958); *Collected Poems, 1917–52* (1952).

MacLennan, Hugh (1907–), Canadian novelist. Works, often depicting conflict of dual heritage, include *Two Solitudes* (1945), *Each Man's Son* (1951) and *The Watch That Ends the Night* (1959).

Macleod, John James Rickard (1876–1935), Scot. physiologist. Shared Nobel Prize for Physiology and Medicine (1923) with Sir Frederick Banting for insulin treatment of diabetes.

McLuhan, [Herbert] Marshall (1911–), Canadian writer. Developed provocative theory of communications. Works include *The Gutenberg Galaxy; The Making of Typographical Man* (1962) and *Understanding Media: the Extensions of Man* (1964).

MacMahon, Marie Edmé Patrice Maurice, Comte de, Duc de Magenta (1808–93), Fr. marshal, Pres. of France (1873–9). Victor at Magenta (1859); defeated by Prussians at Sadowa (1870). Headed govt. with royalist support; failed to restore Bourbon dynasty in France. Forced to resign by republican majority.

McMillan, Edwin Mattison (1907–), Amer. scientist. Awarded Nobel Prize for Chemistry (1951) with Glenn Seaborg for discovering elements neptunium and plutonium.

Macmillan, [Maurice] Harold (1894–), Brit. statesman, Conservative P.M. (1957–63). Before heading govt. held series of high cabinet posts (1951–7). As P.M. worked for improving East-West relations and UK's entry into European Economic Community.

McNamara, Robert Strange (1916–), Amer. public official. As Sec. of Defense (1961–8), supervised unification of armed forces. Pres. of World Bank (1968–).

McNaughton, Andrew George Latta (1887–1966), Canadian army officer, diplomat. Commanded Canadian forces in Britain during World War 2. Delegate (1948) to UN Security Council.

MacNeice, Louis (1907–63), Brit. poet, b. Ireland. Associated with Auden, Spender in poetry of social protest (*e.g. Blind Fireworks,* 1929). Ironic later works include *The Earth Compels* (1938), *Solstices* (1961).

Macpherson, James (1736–96), Scot. poet. Author of disputed epics *Fingal* (1761) and *Temora* (1763), which he claimed to have transcribed from Gaelic bard, Ossian; works influenced Romantic movement.

macrophage, large amoeba-like blood cell, capable of destroying bacteria; found in animal tissue. Smaller infection-destroying cells are called microphages.

Madagascar *see* MALAGASY REPUBLIC.

Madariaga [y Rojo], Salvador de (1886–), Sp. writer. Author of essays, *e.g. The Genius of Spain* (1923); hist. works include *Spain: A Modern History* (1958).

madder, name for variety of perennial herbs of genus *Rubia*. Eurasian *R. tinctorum* cultivated for madder dye.

Mackerel

Madeira Islands, archipelago off NW African coast, forming Funchal district of Portugal. Area: 300 sq. mi.; cap. Funchal. Largest of islands is **Madeira,** scenery and climate of which make it tourist resort. Noted for wine, embroidery. Pop. (1963) 283,000.

Madero, Francisco Indalecio (1873–1913), Mexican statesman, Pres. (1911–13). Advocate of democracy and social reform, led revolution against Díaz regime (1910). Shot during insurrection.

Madhya Pradesh, largest state of India. Area: 171,217 sq. mi.; cap. Bhopal; main city Indore. Rich agric. region; large coal and manganese deposits. Pop. (1961) 32,372,408.

Madison, James (1751–1836), 4th US Pres. (1809–17), Democratic-Republican. Drafted (1787) much of Amer. Constitution, contributed to FEDERALIST PAPERS. Prepared Virginia resolutions protesting ALIEN AND SEDITION ACTS. Sec. of State (1801–9), succeeded Jefferson as Pres. WAR OF 1812 dominated admin.

Madonna, [Ital: my lady] name given to Virgin Mary. Widely used to denote pictures or statues representing her.

Madras, main port and state cap. of Madras (now Tamizhagam), SE India. Founded (1639) by British. Chief industry, textile milling; has university. Pop. (1965) 1,865,000.

Madrid, cap. of Madrid prov. and Spain. Communications, indust. and commercial centre. Became Sp. cap. 1561; under siege for 29 months in Civil War (1936–9). Notable buildings include Bourbon palace, Prado Museum. Pop. (1965) 2,793,000.

madrigal, musical composition (*fl.* 14th–16th cent. in Italy) written for 2 or more singers. Based on poetic form consisting of 1–4 stanzas.

madroño, *Arbutus menziesii,* evergreen tree or shrub of West N America. White flowers and orange-red berries; brown dye obtained from bark.

Maecenas, [Caius] (d. 8 BC), Roman patron of literature. Horace and Virgil were members of his literary circle.

Maelstrom, narrow sound between 2 islands of Lofoten group, NW Norway. Opposing tidal currents create dangerous whirlpool. Name is applied to all fatal whirlpools.

Maes, Nicolaes (1632–93), Dutch painter, pupil of Rembrandt, influenced by Van Dyck. Works include *Old Woman Praying.*

Maeterlinck, Maurice Polydore Marie Bernard, Comte de (1862–1949),

Belgian writer. Influenced by Fr. Symbolists. Works include dramas *Pelléas et Mélisande* (1892) and *The Blue Bird* (1909). Awarded Nobel Prize for Literature (1911).

Mafeking, town, NE Cape Prov., South Africa. Scene of 7 month siege of Brit. garrison by Boers during South African War. Pop. (1967 est.) 8,200.

Mafia, name of organized gangs (*fl.* 19th–20th cent.) of brigands in Sicily and S Italy. Gained polit. influence until suppressed by Mussolini. Mafia organizations brought to US by emigrants. Organizations periodically suspected of controlling many illegal operations, both in Italy and US.

Magdalena, river *c.* 1,000 mi. from source in SW Colombia to Caribbean Sea near Barranquilla.

Magdalenian, in geology, last Upper Paleolithic culture (*c.* 10,000–8000 BC). Data based on remains found in Pyrenees region, esp. cave paintings of Lascaux, France and Altamira, Spain.

Magdeburg, city of East Germany, port on Elbe R., fortified cap. of former Prussian prov. of Saxony. Self-ruling city (1188) within Holy Roman Empire, member of Hanseatic League; destroyed (1631) during Thirty Years War. Severely damaged in World War 2. Pop. (1965) 268,000.

Magellan, Ferdinand (*c.* 1480–1521) Portuguese navigator. Died during

The *Calle de Alcala,* Madrid

Sp.-financed expedition (1519–22), 1st to circumnavigate world.

Magellan, Strait of, narrow passage between S America and Tierra del Fuego, *c.* 350 mi. long. Discovered (1520) by Magellan.

Magi, caste of ancient Persia, reputed to possess supernatural powers. Magian priests spread Zoroastrian doctrine after Zoroaster's death. Also refers to Wise Men of the East in NT (Caspar, Melchior, Balthazar) who brought gifts to Jesus at His birth.

magic, attempt to control events by supernatural means. Word derived from Persian Magi, priests. Its practice depends on correct use of ritual and spell. Black magic associ-

Magic: African tribal dance to cast out evil spirits

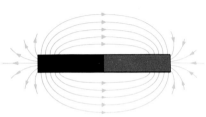

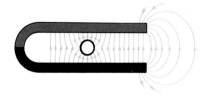

Magnetism: examples of magnetic fields. Top, simple bar magnet. Bottom, Horseshoe magnet, showing deflection when iron bar is introduced into the field (black is North pole; purple is South pole)

ated with powers of evil. Also *see* WITCHCRAFT.

Maginot Line, fortification system along Fr. frontier, begun by André Maginot (1877–1932), Fr. Min. of War. Failed to deter Ger. flanking action (1940) in World War 2.

magistrate, in Eng. jurisprudence, official responsible for admin. of justice. Powers similar to those of US JUDGE.

magma, material composed of molten rock, formed within Earth's interior. Source of igneous and sulphide rocks. Becomes lava upon reaching surface.

Magna Carta, in Eng. history, charter estab. areas over which king had no jurisdiction, sealed (1215) by King John of England at Runnymede in face of demands by barons. Prob. most important document in evolution of Eng. constitution, became symbol of legal supremacy.

magnesia *see* MAGNESIUM.

magnesite, magnesium carbonate mineral, usually white, rarely found in crystal form. Used in manufacture of cement, firebrick.

magnesium (Mg), silver white metallic element. Ductile, malleable, burns brilliantly. Used in signal lighting, photography. Oxidizes to form magnesia, used as insulation because of high melting point.

magnetic poles, points on Earth's surface at which magnetic force is vertically downwards (horizontal compass renders no result). Both N

and S magnetic poles change position constantly.

magnetism, iron-attracting property. Prob. 1st observed in lodestone (*see* MAGNETITE). Artificial magnetism involves transfer or induction of property to other materials. Electric current producing magnetism creates electro-magnet. Freely-suspended magnet (or magnetized body) turns so that its S pole points towards N magnetic pole; principle used in compass.

magnetite, black mineral with metallic lustre, consisting of magnetic oxides of iron. Lodestone variety is natural magnet.

magneto, generator which converts mechanical into electrical energy. Equipped with spark coil to ignite petrol vapour in internal combustion engine.

magnitude, in astronomy, brightness of celestial objects. Measurement standardized from Ptolemy's scale of 6 gradations.

magnolia, deciduous or evergreen tree or shrub of genus *Magnolia*. Native to N America and Asia. Species include southern magnolia or bull bay, *M. grandiflora*, with large white flowers.

Magnus [I] the Good (1024–47), king of Norway (1035–47), son of St Olaf. Succeeded to Danish throne (1042).

Magnus [VI] the Law Mender (1238–80), king of Norway (1263–80). Ceded Hebrides to Scotland. Reformed legal system, estab. royal succession.

Magnus VII (1316–73), king of Norway (1319–43), and Sweden (1319–64). Forced to abdicate Norwegian throne; deposed in Sweden because of unpopular alliance with Denmark.

magot *see* BARBARY APE.

magpie, long-tailed bird of crow family. Known as collector of shiny objects. Species include black-billed magpie, *Pica pica*.

maguey, Mexican name for various species of genus *Agave,* esp. *A. cantala.* Source of liquors mescal and pulque.

Magyars, main people of Hungary. Orig. nomadic, migrated (5th cent.) from Urals to Caucasia; forced W, settled in Hungary (9th cent.). Christianity introduced by ST STEPHEN. Magyar language belongs to Finno-Ugric family.

Mahábhárata, sacred book of Hindu India, compiled (200 BC–AD 200) by bards, later revised by priests. Sanskrit epics include poem *Bhagavad-Gita.*

Maharashtra, state of W India. Area: 118,717 sq. mi.; cap. Bombay.

Formerly part of Bombay prov. Fertile Deccan plateau yields cotton. Chief crop, rice; deposits include manganese, iron ore. Pop. (1961) 39,553,718.

Mahdi [Arab: divine guide], in Islam, man who will lead faithful at end of world. Most prominent claimant to title was **Mohamed Ahmed** (1848–85), leader of rebellion in Anglo-Egyptian Sudan; captured Khartoum (1881). His followers were defeated (1898) by army under Lord Kitchener at Omdurman.

Mahler, Gustav (1860–1911), Austrian composer. Works include cycle of songs *Das Lied von der Erde,* and 9 symphonies. Conducted Imperial Opera, Vienna (1897–1907).

Mahmud II (1784–1839) Ottoman sultan of Turkey (1808–39); introduced reforms, incl. suppression of Janizaries (1826). Bessarabia was ceded to Russia, and Greece achieved independence.

mahogany, hard red-brown wood of various trees of Meliaceae family, esp. *Swietenia mahogani*; found in trop. America. Used for making furniture.

Mahrattas, Marathas, people of W central India. Cap. Poona. Supplanted Moguls (18th cent.), under Sivaji, as chief power in India. Subjugated (1818) by British.

Maiden Castle, ancient fort near Dorchester, England. Ramparts enclose 45 acres. Inhabited *c.* 2000 BC.

maidenhair, fern of genus *Adiantum,* native to trop. and warm temp. areas, with small thin delicate leaves.

maidenhair tree, gingko, *Gingko biloba,* deciduous tree native to E China with fan-shaped leaves, fleshy fruit and edible nuts.

Maidstone, market town, county borough of Kent, England. Hospital (estab. 1260) for pilgrims to Canterbury. Pop. (1961) 59,800.

Mailer, Norman (1923–), Amer. writer. Wrote *The Naked and the Dead* (1948), novel on World War 2. Other works include *Barbary Shore* (1951), *An American Dream* (1964);

Maidenhair Fern

Magpie

autobiog. *Advertisements for Myself* (1959); also poetry.

Maillol, Aristide Joseph Bonaventure (1861–1944), Fr. sculptor. Best known for massive female nudes. Works include 'Fame'.

Maimonides, Moses (1135–1204), Jewish philosopher and physician, b. Spain. In *Mishna Torah,* attempted to codify Jewish oral law. Also wrote influential *Moreh Nebukim* ['Guide for the Perplexed'], treatise on religious and metaphysical problems.

Maine, largest New England state of NE US. Area: 33,215 sq. mi.; cap. Augusta; principal cities Portland, Lewiston. Rocky coast, hilly terrain. Agriculture, fishing, timber, main occupations. Industries include shipbuilding, papermaking. Pop. (1960) 969,265.

Maintenon, Françoise d'Aubigné, Marquise de (1635–1719), 2nd wife of Louis XIV of France. Had considerable influence at court. Founded school of St-Cyr for daughters of poor noblemen.

Mainz [Fr: **Mayence**], indust. and commercial city of West Germany, on R. Rhine; cap. of Rhineland-Palatinate. Important river port, trade centre; manufactures chemicals, machinery. Contains Johannes Gutenberg University. Pop. (1965) 144,000.

Maisonneuve, Paul de Chomedey, Sieur de (1612–76), founder and 1st Gov. of Montreal, Canada.

maize, *Zea mays,* leading Amer. grain crop, naturalized in S Africa, India, China, S Europe and Australia. Grain may be roasted or boiled. When coarsely milled, called hominy or polenta; with gluten removed becomes cornflour.

majolica, maiolica, Ital. or Sp. enamelled pottery manufactured since 13th cent. Characterized by background of rich blue on which decoration is painted.

Majorca, Mallorca, Sp. island, largest of BALEARIC group in Med. Sea. Area: 1,350 sq. mi.; cap. Palma [de Mallorca]. Mountainous terrain with farming and fishing as main occupations. Makes brandies, embroidery, wickerwork and MAJOLICA ware. Tourism important. Pop. (1960) 363,199.

majority, in law, age at which a person may become responsible for his own affairs. In UK, 18; in US, 18–21 according to state.

Makalu, 5th highest mountain (27,824 ft.) in the world, in NE Nepal Himalayas. First climbed 1955.

Makarios III, orig. Michael Christedoulos Mouskos (1913–), Gk. Orthodox Archbishop of Cyprus, leader (1950–) of union with Greece movement in Cyprus. Pres. of Repub. of Cyprus (1959–).

Malabar Coast, term applied to S part of W coast of India. Sandy, low coastal strip, with mangrove lagoons; narrow cultivated lowland; steep, forested slopes of Western Ghats. Densely populated, esp. in S cities, Mangalere, Kozhikode.

Malacca, SW area of Malayan peninsula. Area: 640 sq. mi.; cap. Malacca. Exports rubber. Rich trade centre in 15th cent. Declined in importance with rise of SINGAPORE. Pop. *c.* 300,000.

Malachi, prophetical book of OT, attributed to Ezra. Foretells retribution awaiting people and priests who had grown lax.

malachite, green mineral, carbonate of copper. Occurs as crystals or in masses. Used as gemstone, and as basis for pigment.

malacostracan, crustacean of subclass Malacostraca, incl. lobster, crab, shrimp.

Málaga, city of S Spain, cap. of Málaga prov. Med. port and winter resort. Exports wine, fruit, fish. Pop. (1965) 322,000.

Malagasy Republic, formerly **Madagascar,** state on Madagascar Is., Indian Ocean. Member of Fr. Community. Area: 228,000 sq. mi.;

cap. Tananarive; chief port, Tamatave. Narrow coastal strip in E; central highlands; broad lowland in W. Agriculture and timber main occupations. Exports gold, cattle, bark. People mainly of African and Indian descent. Unit of currency, Malagasy franc. Pop. (1967) 6,750,000.

Malamud, Bernard (1914–), Amer. Jewish author. Works include *The Assistant* (1957), *The Fixer* (1966).

Malan, Daniel F[rançois] (1874–1959), P.M. and leader of Nationalist party of Union of South Africa (1948–54). Advocated apartheid and white supremacy, laid foundation for segregationist legislation passed by succeeding Nationalist govts.

malaria, intermittent fever caused by

Maize plant showing: (a) male flower, (b) female flower (c) root system

parasite living in red blood cells. Carried by female mosquito of Anopheles group. Now found only in trop. and sub-trop. areas. Before 1925, treated with quinine, now by synthetic drugs, *e.g.* paludrine.

Malawi, formerly **Nyasaland,** repub. of E Africa, member of Brit. Commonwealth. Area: 45,411 sq. mi.; cap. Zomba; main city of S

region, Blantyre. Borders Zambia, Mozambique, Tanzania. Produces tea, tobacco, cotton, groundnuts. Population African, Asian, European. Pop. (1966), 4,042,412.

Malawi, Lake *see* LAKE NYASA.

Malay, a Malayo-Polynesian language, with *c.* 10 million speakers in Malaya and Straits Settlements.

Malaya, region of S Malay Peninsula, SE Asia. Area: 50,700 sq. mi.; cap. Kuala Lumpur. Became Federation (1948); independent 1957; joined FEDERATION OF MALAYSIA (1963). Largely mountainous with dense forests, equatorial climate. Tin and rubber, important. Pop. (1964) 8,272,000.

Malayan bear *see* SUN BEAR.

Malayo-Polynesian, widespread language family, covering a vast area incl. Madagascar, Formosa, New Zealand and Hawaii.

Malaysia, Federation of, federation of SE Asia, formed 1963 by union of Federation of Malaya (11 states incl. Singapore), Sabah (N Borneo) and

Sarawak; member of British Commonwealth of Nations. Area: 128,655 sq. mi.; cap. Kuala Lumpur. Singapore seceded (1965). Main languages, Malay, English, Chinese; religion,

Section of the Penang to Kuala Lumpur railway, Malaya

Islam, currency Malaysian dollar. Pop. (1962) 10,365,000.

Malcolm [III] Canmore (d. 1093), king of Scotland (1059–93), succeeded his father Duncan I after defeat of MACBETH. He married Margaret, sister of Edgar Atheling.

Malcolm X, orig. Malcolm Little (1925–65), Amer. Negro leader. Founded (1964) Black Nationalist movement after leaving Black Muslims. Assassinated 1965.

Maldive Islands, Brit. protected sultanate; large group of coral islands

400 mi. SW of Ceylon. Area: *c.* 115 sq. mi.; cap. Malé. Pop. (1963) 93,000.

Malenkov, Georgi Maximilianovich (1902–), Russ. statesman. Made full member of Politburo and a deputy premier in 1946; succeeded Stalin as premier (1953). Introduced more conciliatory foreign policy. In 1955 he resigned; succeeded by BULGANIN. Expelled from Communist party (1961).

Malherbe, François de (1555–1628), Fr. poet and critic. Influential in regularizing Fr. language.

Mali, republic, formerly **French Sudan,** of W Africa; indep. 1960. Area: 464,874 sq. mi.; cap. Bamako. Moslem state of Mali (13th–15th

cent.); conquered by French (1880–95); became repub. within Fr. community (1958). Economy now based on agriculture. Main languages tribal and French; religions Islam and animism. Pop. (1965) 4,654,000.

Malinowski, Bronislaw (1884–1942), Polish anthropologist. Did important study of Andaman Islanders in W Pacific. One of 1st to apply functionalism to social anthropology.

mallard, *Anas platyrhynchos,* wild duck of N hemisphere. Commonest Brit. duck and origin of most domestic ducks.

Mallarmé, Etienne Stéphane (1842–98), Symbolist poet. Works include *L'Après-midi d'un Faune* (1876) on which Debussy based his orchestral prelude.

Mallard

mallee, shrubs mostly of eucalypt species having numerous spreading trunks, ability to withstand arid conditions and to regenerate after bush fire, *e.g.* peppermint box, *Eucalyptus odorata,* blue mallee, *E. fruticetorum,* green mallee, *E. viridis.*

Mallorca *see* MAJORCA.

mallow, annual or perennial herb of genus *Malva*; native to N temp. regions. Large dissected leaves and purple, pink or white flowers.

Malmö, indust. city and seaport on S tip of Sweden. Industries include metal manufacturing, shipbuilding, textiles, chemicals. Administered by Denmark until annexation by Sweden (1658). Pop. (1965) 249,000.

Malmsey, Malvoisie, sweet wine produced (Middle Ages) in Aegean area. Similar wines come from Cyprus, Sicily, the Canaries.

malnutrition, impaired bodily health, with loss of vitality of the tissues; a consequence of inadequate food, or inability, due to disease, to utilize the food.

Malone, Edmond (1741–1812), Eng. scholar. Published chronology of Shakespeare's plays (1778). Exposed Shakespeare forgeries of William Ireland.

Malory, Sir Thomas (*fl. c.* 1470), Eng. writer. Compiled prose version of Arthurian stories based on Fr. romances; pub. by Caxton as *Morte d'Arthur* (1484).

Malpighi, Marcello, FRS (1628–94), Ital. anatomist and physiologist. Discovered capillaries in the human lung; made anatomical studies of chick embryo and of silkworms.

Malplaquet, village of Nord department, France, near Mons; site of battle in which British and Austrians under Marlborough and Prince Eugene, defeated French in War of Spanish Succession (1709).

Malraux, André (1901–), Fr. politician and author, concerned mainly with revolution and freedom. Took part in Chinese civil war (1925–7), and Sp. civil war (1936–9). Works include *La Condition Humaine* (1933), *L'Espoir* (1937). Abandoned Communism to become De Gaulle's Min. of Information (1945–6, 1958); Min. of Cultural Affairs (1959–).

malt, partially germinated grain of

various cereals, chiefly barley, used as flavouring, and fermented with yeast to produce alcohol.

Malta, group of islands comprising Malta, Gozo and Comino in Med. Sea. Area: 122 sq. mi.; cap. Valletta.

Member of Brit. Commonwealth (1964). Ruled by Phoenicians, Greeks, Carthaginians, Romans and Saracens. Annexed by British (1814). Economic dependence on Britain reduced after withdrawal of military forces (1972). Local sterling currency and UK pound legal tender. Pop. (1963) 325,000.

Malta fever *see* UNDULANT FEVER.

Malthus, Thomas Robert (1766– 1834), Eng. economist. Initiated modern population study. Predicted in *An Essay on the Principle of Population* (1798) that population would increase more rapidly than food supply; regarded war, famine and disease as normal checks to population growth.

mamba, long, slender arboreal snake of genus *Dendroaspis*. Found in S and C Africa. Poisonous bite can cause death. Black mamba, *D. polylepis*, is common species.

Mamelukes, orig. slaves brought to Egypt, trained as soldiers by Ayyubite sultans. Siezed power (1250) forming 2 dynasties, Turkish (1250–1382) and Circassian (1382–1517). Ousted by Turks (1517); rebelled against Turks (1769); Napoleon I helped put down rebellion, Mamelukes massacred (1811) by MOHAMMED ALI.

mammal, most advanced group of vertebrate animals showing highest development in animal kingdom. It has hair on body, with secreting glands, diaphragm used in respiration and teeth rooted in sockets in bone. The heart is 4-chambered. It is warm blooded and air-breathing. Except for MONOTREMES, the mammal is viviparous and suckles young. Foetus undergoes gestation period during which it is nourished by an organic connection or placenta to uterine wall. Brain is well developed and intelligence is shown.

mammary gland, or **breast,** in human male, a rudimentary structure; in the female, develops with onset of puberty, increasing in size and altering in shape. After parturition secretes milk.

mammillaria, genus of cacti, chiefly native to Mexico. Flowers appear in a ring round top of plant; red fruit.

mammoth, extinct very large elephant of Eurasia and N America with long slender tusks curved upwards and outwards. Woolly mammoth developed in cold climates. Known from fossil remains of Pleistocene period, frozen corpses from the Siberian tundra and cave paintings.

man, biped mammal of primate order. Differs from apes and monkeys in having opposable thumbs, erect posture, shorter arms, longer legs, broader soles to feet, brain larger and more complex with greater capacity for learning. Modern man is regarded as a single species, *Homo sapiens*.

Man, Isle of, mountainous island off NW coast of England, in Irish Sea. Area: 221 sq. mi.; cap. Douglas. Internal self-govt.; UK responsible for external affairs, *e.g.* defence. Fishing, tourism important. Manx language still spoken. Pop. (1961) 48,200.

man o' war bird, frigate bird, sea bird of genus *Fregata*. Noted for powers of flight.

Managua, cap. of Nicaragua on S shore of Lake Managua. Destroyed (1931) by earthquake and fire. Now commercial, manufacturing and polit. centre; industries include cotton ginning, textiles, pharmaceuticals. Pop. (1964) 275,000.

Manáos *see* MANAUS.

Manasseh, Prayer of, apocryphal book of OT, *c.* 7th cent. BC.

manatee, aquatic mammal of genus *Trichechus*, with rounded tail and 2 front flippers. Found in W Africa (*T. senegalensis*), Florida and W Indies. Hunting has greatly reduced numbers.

Manaus, formerly **Manáos,** cap. of Amazonas state, NW Brazil, on Rio Negro. Important inland port; economic and commercial centre of Amazon area. Founded 17th cent., thrived during rubber boom. Exports timber and furs. Pop. (1965) 175,340.

Mancha, La, high plateau in central Spain, setting of Cervantes' *Don Quixote.*

Manchester, indust. city and inland port of N Midlands of England, on Manchester Ship Canal. Prospered with growth of cotton industry. Modern industries include vehicle building, dyeing, rubber goods. Contains Victoria University (founded 1846). Pop. (1966) 625,000.

Manchester Ship Canal, canal 35 mi. long, joining Manchester with Mersey estuary and Irish Sea; opened 1894.

Manchuria, major region of NE China, comprising Heilungkiang,

Manatee

Kirin and Liaoning provs. Area: 300,000 sq. mi.; main towns, Shenyang, Harbin; ice-free ports Port Arthur and Dairen. Since 1949, W area included in Inner Mongolia Autonomous Region. Ruled by Japan 1905–45; returned to China and lost autonomy. Forests with fur-bearing animals important. Coal, iron and oil resources. Pop. (1957) 51,500,000.

Manchu-Tungus, minor branch of Altaic languages, spoken in China and the USSR.

Mammillaria occidentalis

Mandarin Duck

Mandalay, city of Mandalay prov., Burma, on Irriwaddy R. Religious, cultural and trade centre. Industries include jade cutting, gold and silver work, silk weaving. Pop. (1964) 322,000.

Mandarin *see* CHINESE.

mandarin duck, *Aix galericulata,* fresh-water, crested Asian duck. Variegated purple, green, chestnut and white plumage.

Mande, Mandingo, branch of Niger-Congo language family; spoken in Upper Niger and Senegal regions.

Mandeville, Bernard (1670–1733), Eng. satirical writer whose *Fable of the Bees* (1714) attacks social restraint and defends self-interest in ethics.

Mandeville or **Maundevyle, Sir John,** reputed author of 14th cent. book of travels intended as guide for pilgrims to Holy Land. Orig. written in French; Eng. tr. 15th cent.

mandoline, musical instrument of lute family, with 4 or 5 pairs of strings, each pair tuned to 1 note. Plucked with a plectrum.

mandrake, *Mandragora officinarum,* narcotic, short-stemmed European herb. Fleshy, often forked, root thought to resemble a human form.

mandrill, *Papio sphinx,* large ferocious-looking baboon of W Africa. Blue and scarlet markings on hairy face.

Déjeuner sur l'Herbe by Manet

maned wolf, *Chrysocyon jubatus,* large wild dog of wooded central S America. Pointed muzzle, large erect ears, reddish-brown coat and long legs.

Manet, Édouard (1832–83), Fr. impressionist painter. Early works incl. *Olympia* (1865), *Déjeuner sur l'Herbe* (1863) vehemently rejected. His work in oils (*peinture claire*) influenced other painters.

mangabey, slender long-tailed monkey of genus *Cercocebus,* found in forests of Africa. *C. albigena* has long hair on its head.

manganese (Mn), hard and brittle metal, discovered (1774) by Gahn. Chiefly used as constituent of alloys.

mangel-wurzel, mangold, mangold-wurzel, variety of beet, *Beta vulgaris,* cultivated as vegetable and cattle food. Native to Europe.

mango, *Mangifera indica,* tree bearing fleshy yellowish-red fruit, native of Malaya and W Indies. Eaten ripe, preserved or pickled.

mangosteen, *Garcinia mangostana,* evergreen tree of Malaya and E Indies. Edible fruit has white or reddish pulp enclosed in thick purplish rind.

mangrove, various trop. evergreen trees found in swamp areas. Amer. mangrove, *Rhizophora mangle,* common in Florida and Mexico.

Manhattan, borough of New York City, mainly on Manhattan Is. Founded (1626) by Dutch. Leading financial, commercial, entertainment and cultural centre.

Manhattan Project, development of atomic energy leading to atom bomb. *See* J. ROBERT OPPENHEIMER.

Mani (*c.* 216–276), Persian founder of

MANICHAEISM. Claimed to be apostle of Jesus; crucified. Followers centred at Babylon and Samarkand.

mania, symptom of insanity characterized by loquacity, instability of movement and emotion. Movements are purposeless, speech becomes incoherent, will-power disappears.

Manichaeism, dualist religion which sought to combine some elements of Mithraism with Christianity, taught by Persian Mani (*c.* AD 216–276).

Manila, chief city of SW Luzon, Philippine Is., on Manila Bay. Commercial, educ. centre. Processing of agric. produce. Founded 1571 by Spanish. Former cap. of Philippines. Pop. (1965) 1,145,730.

Manila hemp, strong, cord-like fibre obtained from abacá or Manila hemp plant, *Musa textilis*; used in muslin, paper, *etc.*

Manilius, Marcus, Latin poet; author of didactic poem on astronomy, *Astronomica* (5 books extant), written during reigns of Augustus and Tiberius.

Manipur, state of NE India. Area: 8,628 sq. mi.; cap. Imphal. Largely jungle with hills in N. People farm river valleys. Pop. (1961) 780,037.

Manitoba, easternmost Prairie prov., W central Canada. Area: 251,000 sq. mi.; cap. Winnipeg. Uninhabited tundra in N, borders on Hudson Bay in NE, further S are lakes and farmlands. Agric. produce, primarily wheat; industries include lumber, mining (esp. copper). Hydro-electric power and oil reserves being developed. Region chartered as part of Rupert's Land to Hudson's Bay Co. (1670). Prov. created 1870; enlarged (1881, 1912). Pop. (1961) 921,686.

Manlius Capitolinus, Marcus (d. *c.* 384 BC), Roman consul (392 BC). Repulsed invasion by Gauls (*c.* 389 BC).

Mann, Thomas (1875–1955), Ger. writer and essayist; lived in US (1936–52). Works include *Buddenbrooks* (1900), *The Magic Mountain* (1924), *Doctor Faustus* (1948). Awarded Nobel Prize for Literature (1929).

manna, in OT, substance eaten by Israelites in wilderness; may have been an edible lichen, *Lecanora esculenta,* or sweet, gummy substance from tamarisk tree, *Tamarix mannifera.*

Mannerheim, Baron Carl Gustav Emil (1867–1951), Finnish army officer and statesman. Regent of New Finnish repub. (1919). Pres. of Finland (1944–6).

Mannheim, indust. city and seaport of Baden-Württemburg, West Germany, on R. Rhine. Chartered 1606; became residence of Palatine electors. Industries include manufacture of machinery, precision instruments, chemicals. Pop. (1965) 328,000.

Mannheim, Karl (1893–1947), Austrian historian and sociologist. Author of *Ideology and Utopia* (1929), study of social beliefs.

Manning, Henry Edward (1808–92), Eng. cardinal, initially Anglican. Under influence of OXFORD MOVEMENT, became Catholic (1857). Worked for social and prison reform, and improved labour conditions. Archbishop of Westminster (1865–92).

Manolete, orig. Manuel Rodriguez y Sánchez (1917–47), Sp. matador; gored at height of career.

manometer, instrument used to measure pressure of gases; consists of U-shaped tube partially filled with liquid.

manorial or **seignorial system,** medieval European economic and social system, allied to FEUDALISM, under which peasants held lands they worked in return for fixed dues to landlords. Declined with growth of towns and capitalist commerce.

mansard, type of roof named after Fr. architect, François Mansard (1598–1666). Slope from eaves to ridge forms 2 portions and gives higher interior space.

Mansfield, Katherine, orig. Kathleen Beauchamp (1888–1923), Brit. writer b. New Zealand. Works include *Bliss* (1920), *The Garden Party* (1922).

Mantegna, Andrea (1431–1506), Ital. painter of Paduan school, influenced by antiquity. Works include *Holy Family,* and *Parnassus.*

mantis, mantid, orthopterous insect of family Mantidae. Species include praying mantis, *Mantis religiosa,* of W Europe and E US. Preys on flies, grasshoppers, caterpillars.

mantis fly, widely distributed insect of family Mantisidae. Larvae feed on wasps' and spiders' eggs.

mantis shrimp, *Squilla mantis,* marine crustacean with pair of appendages modified for grasping prey. Lives in burrows on sea bottom of warmer oceans; feeds on smaller crustaceans.

Manu, Laws of, code supposedly promulgated by Manu Vaivasvata, in Hindu myth., founder of human race. Laws reflect Hindu thought in the Buddhist period.

manure *see* FERTILIZER.

Manx *see* GAELIC.

Manx cat, short-haired tailless variety of domestic cat.

manzanita, *Arctostaphylos manzanita,* evergreen shrub with white or pink flowers native to N America.

Manzoni, Alessandro Francesco Tommaso Antonio (1785–1873), Ital. novelist and poet. An advocate of a united Italy. Became famous with publication of the historical novel *I Promessi Sposi* (1825–7).

Mao Tse-tung (1893–   ), Chinese polit. leader and theorist. Helped found Chinese Communist Party, consolidating authority after LONG MARCH (1934–5). Prolonged civil war of 1930s and 1940s culminated in triumph over Chiang Kai-shek's Nationalists and estab. of People's Repub. of China (1949) with Mao as Chairman (1949–59). Retained post as Party Chairman in 1960s, instigating purges of leadership through 'cultural revolution' after 1966. Widely influential as exponent of active revolution and guerilla warfare.

Maori, aboriginal inhabitants of New Zealand, of Polynesian stock. Discovered by Dutch (17th cent.) but were not subdued until 19th cent. when they were granted possession of their lands under British sovereignty (Treaty of Waitangi, 1840).

Maori Wars, in New Zealand history, sporadic clashes between Brit. and New Zealand troops and MAORI forces (1840s–80s). Arose out of official purchase and settlement of Maori land.

Maned Wolf

map, representation on 2-dimensional surface of the Earth or part of it.

maple, deciduous tree or shrub of genus *Acer,* native to N temp. regions. Species planted as ornamental trees, for valuable timber or for sap.

maquis, Fr. underground resistance movement during World War 2. Co-ordinated with Allies, later organized as Fr. Forces of the Interior (FFI). Instrumental in liberation of France (1944).

Mar, John, Earl of (1675–1732), Scot. nobleman, orig. a Whig, later became Jacobite, but changed allegiance so often that he was nicknamed 'Bobbing John'. Headed Jacobite rebellion of 1715 and died in exile.

marabou, long-legged bird of stork family with large bill. Native to Africa, related to Indian adjutant bird.

Maracaibo, port and city of Venezuela on channel connecting L. Maracaibo with Gulf of Venezuela. Major S Amer. petroleum export centre; also exports coffee, hides and cacao. Pop. (1964) 503,000.

Marat, Jean Paul (1743–93), Fr. revolutionary leader. Founded (1789) journal *L'Ami du Peuple.* Leader of Cordeliers. Stabbed to death in his bath by anti-Jacobin Charlotte Corday.

Marathi, Indic Indo-European language, it has 20 million speakers in W India (Bombay region).

Marathon, Battle of, decisive encounter in which Persian invaders defeated (490 BC) by Athenians, under Miltiades, NE of Athens. A runner was sent bearing news of victory to Athens; origin of the MARATHON RACE.

marathon race, long distance race derived from run of Gk. Pheidippides

Manx Cat

from Marathon to Athens to announce defeat of Persians (490 BC). Became modern Olympic Games event (1896); distance standardized to 26 mi. 385 yd. (1908).

marble, limestone in crystallized state. Variety of colours. Used in sculpture and architecture; capable of taking on high polish.

Marbury v. Madison, case (1803) decided by US Supreme Court under Chief Justice John Marshall involving official appointment by Pres. John Adams, subsequently unsanctioned by Jefferson admin. Decision estab. precedent of Court's right to review constitutionality of legislation.

Marc, Franz (1880–1916), Ger. painter, member of Blaue Reiter expressionist group. Evolved colourful, patterned style.

marcasite, pale coloured brittle mineral of stalactitic-crystal form.

Marcel, Gabriel Honoré (1889–), Fr. existentialist philosopher and dramatist. Works include *L'Homme de Dieu* (1925), *Mystery of Being* (1951–2).

Marciano, Rocky, orig. Rocco Francis Marchegiano (1924–69), Amer. boxer. Became heavyweight champion 1952; retired (1956).

Marco Polo *see* POLO, MARCO.

Marconi, Guglielmo, Marchese (1874–1937), Ital. physicist. Best known for development of wireless telegraphy. Transmitted long-wave signals (1895), trans-Atlantic signals (1901). With Carl Braun, awarded Nobel Prize for Physics (1909).

Marcos, Ferdinand Edralin (1917–), Philippine lawyer and statesman. Elected pres. 1965.

Marcus Aurelius Antoninus, orig. Marcus Annius Verus (121–180), Roman emperor (161–180). Successfully defended empire in series of border troubles. Best known as Stoic philosopher, author of *Meditations*.

A type of Italian marble called *Vert des Alpes*

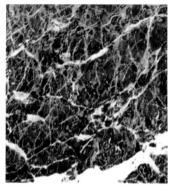

Mardi Gras [Fr: Shrove Tuesday], last day before Lent, celebrations date from Middle Ages. Famous carnivals held in New Orleans, Rio de Janeiro, Nice.

Marengo, Battle of, victory (1800) for Fr. forces, under Napoleon, against Austrians in Piedmont, NW Italy.

mare's tail, *Hippuris vulgaris,* aquatic perennial herb with whorls of slender leaves and minute green flowers. Native to Europe, Asia and N Africa.

Margaret, Saint (c. 1045–93), queen of Scotland, wife of Malcolm III. Founded monasteries, promoted church reform, esp. links between England and Scotland.

Margaret (1353–1412), queen of Denmark, Norway and Sweden. Daughter of Waldemar IV of Denmark, m. (1363) Haakon VI of Norway, succeeding to throne on his death (1380). Ruled Denmark as regent (1375–87) for her son Olaf, who died 1387. Defeated Albert of Mecklenburg of Sweden (1389) and ruled autocratically through grandnephew, Eric of Pomerania, who became king of the 3 nations (1397).

Margaret of Angoulême (1492–1549), sister of Francis I of France, queen of Navarre through marriage to Henri d'Albret. Patronized Renaissance literature, wrote classic *Heptameron.*

Margaret of Anjou (c. 1429–82), wife of Henry VI of England, through whom she ruled autocratically. Opposed by Richard, Duke of York; struggle led to WARS OF THE ROSES (1455). Captured (1471) at Tewkesbury; returned to France.

Margaret of Valois (1553–1615), daughter of Henry II, queen of France when husband Henry of Navarre became Henry IV. Banished from Paris (1583) for intrigues; marriage annulled (1599).

Margaret Rose, Countess of Snowdon (1930–), Brit. princess, 2nd daughter of George VI. Married (1960) Antony Armstrong-Jones.

Margaret Tudor (1489–1541), daughter of Henry VII; wife of James IV of Scotland, estab. Scot. claim to Eng. throne.

margarine, artificial butter, made from liquid mixture of edible vegetable oils or animal fats. Legally designated as oleomargarine in US.

margin, money given to broker for speculation in securities. Forms only percentage of cash involved; broker supplies balance. In US, Federal Reserve Board can fix percentage of margin to control speculation.

marguerite, any of several daisy-like

European Marmot

flowers, esp. *Chrysanthemum leucanthemum.*

Mari, autonomous repub., Russ. SFSR in Volga valley. Area: 9,000 sq. mi.; cap. Yoshkar-Ola. Largely forested; timber industry. Conquered by Ivan IV (1552). Pop. (1965) 651,000.

Maria Theresa (1717–80), daughter of Emperor Charles VI, empress of Austria (1745–65) through marriage to Francis I, co-ruler (1765–80) with son Joseph II. Succeeded to Habsburg lands under PRAGMATIC SANCTION, challenged WAR OF THE AUSTRIAN SUCCESSION (1740–8) and SEVEN YEARS WAR (1756–63). Participated in Polish partition of 1772. Popular and able ruler in prosperous era.

Marianas Islands, volcanic chain of islands in W Pacific. Area: c. 406 sq. mi.; main islands, Guam, Saipan, Tinian. Produce coffee, sugar cane. Discovered (1521) by Magellan; Sp.-controlled until 1898. Guam ceded to US; rest now under UN trusteeship. Population mainly Japanese and Micronesian. Pop. (1963) 75,500.

Marie Antoinette (1755–93), daughter of Francis I and Maria Theresa of Austria, queen of France through marriage to Louis XVI (1770). Extravagance, involvement in series of scandals made her unpopular. Opposed economic measures of Necker; phrase 'Let them eat cake' as solution to bread famine attributed to her. Attempted to negotiate with Fr. revolutionaries (1791–2), guillo-

Markhor

tined after enduring harsh treatment during imprisonment.

Marie de France, (*fl. c.* 1150–1215), Fr. poet, author of *Lais,* based on Celtic fables, with love as main theme.

Marie de' Medici (1573–1642), queen of France, daughter of Francesco de' Medici.

Mariette Pasha, Auguste Edouard (1821–81), Fr. archaeologist. Directed excavations of Egyptian pyramids in 1850s. Founded Cairo's Egyptian Museum.

marigold, several plants of genus *Calendula* with orange or yellow flowers. *C. officinalis* is pot marigold. So-called African marigold, *Tagetes erecta,* is unrelated species, native of Mexico.

marijuana *see* CANNABIS.

Marin, John (1870–1953), Amer. painter of landscapes. Best known for semi-abstract water-colours.

Marini, Marino (1901–   ), Ital. sculptor. Works include 'Horse and Rider', other statues of horses and horsemen.

Maritain, Jacques (1882–   ), Fr. neo-Thomist philosopher. Elaborated upon doctrines of St Thomas Aquinas as in *Art and Scholasticism* (1920), *True Humanism* (1936), *Man and the State* (1951).

maritime law, system of law governing navigation and overseas commerce. Evolution of international agreements on shipping dates from ancient times; collected in works such as *Consolato del Mare* and Eng. *Black Book of the Admiralty.*

Maritime Provinces, Atlantic seaboard provs. of Canada. Comprise New Brunswick, Nova Scotia and Prince Edward Is.

Marius, Caius (*c.* 155–86 BC), Roman general, 7 times consul. Gained renown against Ger. invaders in N Italy. Headed popular party, rivalled SULLA in civil war; seized Rome (87 BC) in alliance with Cinna, ruthlessly destroying opposition.

Marivaux, Pierre Carlet de Chamblain de (1688–1763), Fr. playwright. Author of comedies and romances characterized by keen insights and subtle affected style as in *Le Jeu de l'Amour et du Hasard* (1730) and *Les Fausses Confidences* (1737).

marjoram, several mints of genera *Origanum* or *Marjorana,* known as pot marjoram and sweet marjoram.

Mark, Gospel according to Saint, book (2nd Gospel) of NT. Short and terse, narrates life of Jesus from His Baptism to the Passion and Resurrection.

Mark, Saint, orig. John Mark, reputed author of Gospel according to St Mark. Martyred in Venice.

Mark Antony *see* ANTONIUS, MARCUS.

markhor, *Capra falconeri,* largest of wild goats found in Afghanistan and Himalayas. Spiral horns and long shaggy coat.

Markiewicz, Constance Georgine Gore-Booth, Countess (1868–1927), Irish patriot. First woman elected to Brit. Parliament, refused to take her seat. Active in 1916 Easter Rebellion, later served in Irish parliaments (1918–27).

Markova, Dame Alicia, orig. Lilian Alicia Marks (1910–   ), Eng. ballerina. Danced with Diaghilev's Ballet Russe (1925–9); Rambert Ballet (1931–3); many guest appearances. Roles include 'Giselle'. Co-founder of Festival Ballet.

Marlborough, 1st Duke of *see* CHURCHILL, JOHN.

Marlborough, Sarah, Duchess of, orig. Sarah Jennings (1660–1744), Eng. noblewoman at court of Queen Anne; m. John Churchill, 1st Duke of Marlborough. For several yr. entirely dominated Anne.

marlin, large oceanic game fish of genus *Makaira.* Upper jaw elongated into spearlike structure.

Marlowe, Christopher (1564–93), Eng. dramatist and poet. Among his works are *Tamburlaine* (*c.* 1587), *Dr Faustus* (*c.* 1588), *The Jew of Malta* (*c.* 1589), *Edward II* (*c.* 1592).

Marmora or **Marmara, Sea of,** body of water (*c.* 4,300 sq. mi.) separating Europe and Asia. Lies between Bosphorus and Dardanelles.

marmoset, small squirrel-like monkey of family Callithricidae, found in SE Brazil and Amazon forests. Species include common marmoset, *Callithrix jacchus,* and pygmy marmoset, *Cebuella pygmaeus,* the smallest monkey.

marmot, plant-eating rodent of genus *Marmota;* found in temp. regions. Short legs, heavy body and dull, coarse, thick fur. N Amer. marmots include woodchuck.

Marne, department of NE France. Area: 442,195 sq. mi.; cap. Châlons-sur-Marne; main city, Rheims. Named after Marne R. (328 mi.). Scene of 2 crucial battles during World War 1. Ger. advance (Sept. 1914) stalled when William II called it off; 2nd battle representing last major Ger. offensive, was turned back.

Marprelate Controversy, Eng. religious argument (16th cent.). Seven Puritan-inspired pamphlets, published (1588–9) under pseudonym Martin Marprelate, attacked authoritarianism of Church of England.

Marquand, J[ohn] P[hillips] (1894–1960), Amer. novelist, journalist and critic. Creator of Jap. detective Mr

African Marigold

Moto. Novels include *The Late George Apley* (1937), *Point of No Return* (1949).

Marquesas, group of 11 volcanic islands of French Polynesia, NE of Tahiti. Chief islands, Naku Hiva and Hiva Oa. Exports copra, tobacco, vanilla. Total area: 480 sq. mi. Pop. (1956) 3,936.

marquetry, in decoration, use of variously coloured wood and mother-of-pearl as inlay, esp. in furniture. Characteristic of Oriental and Louis XIV period in Europe.

Marquette, Jacques (1637–75), Fr. Jesuit missionary, explorer in N America. Estab. several missions before descent of Mississippi R. with Louis Jolliet.

Marrakech, Marrakesh, town of Morocco, one of traditional capitals, founded 1062. Market centre, known for metal and leather works. Pop. (1964) 264,000.

marram grass, coarse perennial grass of genus *Ammophila*, grown on sandy shores to bind sand. Species include Amer. *A. arenaria* and European *A. baltica*.

marriage, union, sanctioned by custom and religion, of persons of the opposite sex as husband and wife. In most countries accompanied by rite, ceremony or sacrament (matrimony). Marriage laws and customs may vary considerably from one country to another.

marrow, soft tissue in interior cavities of bones. Red marrow occurs in spongy bones, *e.g.* ribs, vertebrae, skull; yellow marrow, containing fat, fills cavities of long bones, *e.g.* femurs.

Marryat, Frederick (1792–1848), Eng. naval officer and author. Books include *Frank Mildmay* (1829), *Mr. Midshipman Easy* (1836), *The Children of the New Forest* (1847).

Mars, Roman god of war, orig. an agricultural deity. His Gk. equivalent was ARES; both are represented as warriors.

Mars, 4th known planet in order of

Marseille

House Martin

distance from the Sun (*c.* 141,700,000 mi.); diameter *c.* 4,220 mi.; mass one-tenth that of Earth. Its solar orbit takes *c.* 687 days, its period of axial rotation is *c.* 24 hr. 37 min. 23 sec., and it has 2 small satellites. Its atmosphere contains nitrogen.

Marsala, seaport of Trapani prov., Sicily; orig. fortified by Carthaginians. Main industry, production of sweet wine, Marsala. Pop. (1961 est.) 79,000.

Marseillaise, Fr. national anthem written and composed by Rouget de Lisle. Known as *Marseillaise* because it was sung by soldiers from Marseille who stormed Tuileries (1792).

Marseille, main seaport, 2nd city of France on Med. Sea; founded *c.* 600 BC by Gk. settlers as Massalia; major Roman city of S Gaul. Industries include flour-milling, sugar and sulphur refineries, engineering, shipbuilding. Pop. (1962) 783,738.

Marsh, Dame [Edith] Ngaio (1899–), New Zealand author and theatrical producer. Creator of Chief-Inspector Roderick Alleyn of Scotland Yard. Works include *A Man Lay Dead* (1934), *Surfeit of Lampreys* (1941), *Off With His Head* (1957), and autobiog. *Black Beech and Honey Dew* (1966).

marsh fern, *Dryopteris thelypteris,* fern found in marshes and fens. Almost universal distribution.

marsh gas *see* METHANE.

marsh mallow, *Althaea officinalis,* perennial herb with pink flowers, native to Europe, Asia and N Africa. Found in marshes. Root yields mucilage used in confectionery.

marsh marigold, kingcup, *Caltha palustris,* perennial herb with yellow flowers and heart-shaped leaves native to Europe, Asia and N America.

marshal, medieval officer of state,

orig. one in charge of horses. Revived as military title of honour in Fr. by Louis XIV.

Marshall, Alfred (1842–1924), Eng. economist, taught at Cambridge (1885–1908). Systemized classical economics, his analytical contributions laying foundations of neo-classical school. Developed marginal utility theory. Main work: *Principles of Economics* (1890).

Marshall, George Catlett (1880–1959), Amer. army officer and diplomat, US Sec. of State (1947–9) and Sec. of Defence (1950–1). Army Chief of Staff in World War 2. With DEAN ACHESON developed European Recovery Program (known as Marshall Plan) for US aid to devastated European countries (1947). Awarded Nobel Peace Prize (1953).

Marshall, John (1755–1835), Chief Justice of US Supreme Court (1801–35). A Federalist, he was opposed by Jefferson and other presidents, but broadened Supreme Court's role by enabling it to review constitutionality of legislation by fairness of his decisions. Viewed Federal govt. powers as being subject to broad constitutional interpretation.

Marshall Islands, 2 chains of coral atolls, Micronesia, C Pacific Ocean; part of US Trust Territory of Pacific Islands. Total area: 70 sq. mi. Discovered 16th cent. Micronesian population self-governing. Pop. (1960) 14,163.

Marshall Plan *see* MARSHALL, GEORGE CATLETT.

Marsilius of Padua (d. 1340), Ital. political theorist. His *Defensor Pacis* (1324) set out theory that eccles. power should be subordinate to secular. Created Archbishop of Milan.

Marston, John (1575–1634), Eng. dramatist and satirist. Plays include *The Malcontent* (1604), *The Dutch Courtesan* (1605) and, with Jonson and Chapman, *Eastward Ho* (1605).

Marston Moor, Battle of (1644), fought in W Riding of Yorkshire, during Eng. Civil War. Decisive victory for Parliamentarians over Royalists.

marsupial, several viviparous, non-placental mammals of order Marsupialia. Most have a pouch containing mammary gland and serving as receptacle for young. Species include kangaroo, wombat, bandicoot, opossum.

marsupial mole, *Notoryctes typhlops,* burrowing Austral. marsupial resembling common MOLE.

Martello Tower, round fort built on Eng. coast and in Channel Is. at time of threatened invasion by Napoleon I.

marten, chiefly arboreal carnivore with long body and short legs of genus *Martes,* found in N forests. European variety is *Martes martes*; Amer. variety, *M. americana,* has brown pelt known as Amer. sable.

Martha, in NT, sister of Mary and Lazarus who, when Jesus visited their house at Bethany (*Luke* X, 38; *John* XI, 2), prepared the meal, while Mary listened to Jesus.

Martí, José (1853–95), Cuban scholar and patriot. Exiled for anti-Spanish revolutionary activities. In New York published journal *La Patria* advocating Cuban independence. Landed in Cuba (1895) but was killed in battle of Dos Rios.

Martial [Marcus Valerius Martialus] (*c.* AD 40–104), Latin poet, b. Spain. Worked under patronage of Emperors Titus and Domitian. Epigrams (14 books extant) are short poems expressing single idea concisely and pointedly, providing sharp picture of contemporary Roman life.

Martin, Archer John Porter (1910–), Eng. biochemist. With Richard Synge, awarded Nobel Prize for Chemistry (1952) for discovery of partition chromatography (method of separating and identifying chem. substances for analysis).

martin, small European swallow with short, fanned tail. Species include house martin, *Delechon urbica,* and sand martin, *Riparia riparia.*

Martin du Gard, Roger (1881–1958), Fr. novelist. Author of *Les Thibault* (8 vols., 1922–40), an analysis of Fr. bourgeois society. Awarded Nobel Prize for Literature (1937).

Part of portrait of Guidoriccio da Fogliano by Simone Martini

Virgin with St Anne by Masaccio and Masolino

Martineau, Harriet (1802–76), Eng. economist and novelist. She was a feminist, absolutionist and philosophic atheist. Works include *Poor Law and Paupers Illustrated* (1833), *Illustrations of Political Economy* (9 vols., 1834) and *Society in America* (1837).

Martini, Simone (*c.* 1284–1344), Sienese painter. Work characterized by rich colour and earthy realism.

Martinique, overseas department of France, in Windward Is., W Indies. Area: 425 sq. mi.; cap. Fort-de-France. Rugged, mountainous, dominated by volcano Mont Pelée (4,799 ft.). Discovered (1502) by Columbus; colonized by French (1635). Economy depends on sugar cane, rum and bananas. Pop. (1965) 321,000.

martyr (Gk: a witness), in Christian church one who gives his life for the Christian faith; 1st recorded Christian martyr is Stephen (*Acts* VI, VII).

Marvell, Andrew (1621–78), Eng. Metaphysical poet, satirist and politician. Poems, published posthumously, include 'Bermudas', 'To His Coy Mistress'.

Marx, Karl Heinrich (1818–83), Ger. philosopher and radical leader, chief theorist of modern socialism. Published (1848) *Communist Manifesto* with Friedrich Engels, document founding MODERN COMMUNISM. Spent rest of life in London; organized (1864) International Workingmen's Assoc., later First INTERNATIONAL. Then wrote *Das Kapital* (Vol. I, 1867; Vols. II, III, ed. by Engels, 1885–94), basis for much of subsequent communist and socialist doctrine. Adapted Hegel's dialectic to produce theory of dialectic materialism, by which social change results from conflict between economic classes, composition of which is determined by control of means of production. Also *see* MARXISM.

Marx brothers, Amer. film actors; Leonard (**Chico**) (1891–1961), Arthur (**Harpo**) (1893–1964), Julius (**Groucho**) (1895–), Herbert (**Zeppo**) (1901–). Films include *A Night at the Opera* (1936), *A Day at the Races* (1937), *A Night in Casablanca* (1946).

Marxism, polit. and economic system of thought, originating in philosophy of KARL MARX. Also known as economic determinism, method of analysis being dialectical materialism. Based on assertion that social change results from class struggle over control of means of production. Final stage of struggle is between capitalist class and proletariat; predicted triumph (with use of violent revolution if necessary) of working class would end in classless society. Mixed economies and improved labour conditions in 20th cent. have discredited some of Marx's predictions.

Mary, the **Virgin Mary,** in NT, mother of Jesus, wife of Joseph of Nazareth. Most highly exalted in R.C. and Greek Churches; belief in Her IMMACULATE CONCEPTION and virginity at Jesus' birth is fundamental. In art, often represented as the Madonna.

Mary [**I**] **Tudor** (1516–58), queen of England (1553–8). Daughter of Henry VIII and Catherine of Aragon, she remained Roman Catholic and opposed Reformation. On her accession re-introduced Catholicism and persecuted Protestants. In 1554 married Philip II of Spain, became

Peter and John Distributing Alms by Masaccio

involved in war with France and lost Calais, last Eng. possession in France.

Mary II (1662–94) queen of England (1689–94). Protestant daughter of James II of England and Anne Hyde; married her cousin, William of Orange (William III of England), ruled jointly with him until her death. Her sister, Anne, became queen on William's death.

Mary Magdalen, in NT, woman of Magdala, near Tiberius, healed by Jesus (*Luke* VIII, 2). She became his devoted follower, was present at his Crucifixion, and was the first to see the risen Christ (*John* XX).

Mary [Stuart], Queen of Scots (1542–87), queen of Scotland (1542–67), and as consort of Francis II, queen of France (1559–60); daughter of James V of Scotland. Married Dauphin and, after his death, returned to Scotland (1561) which was torn by religious civil war. Married (1565) her cousin Lord Darnley who was murdered 2 yr. later. Mary then married Earl of Bothwell, suspected of being

Darnley's murderer. Ensuing civil war forced her abdication in favour of son, James VI and I. Fled to England; imprisoned by Elizabeth I. After 19 yr. in prison, executed for treason.

Maryland, state of SE US. Area: 10,577 sq. mi.; cap. Annapolis; main cities, Baltimore, Cumberland. Agriculture important (tobacco, poultry). Manufacturing main occupation (shipbuilding, food products, transport equipment). Mineral resources include iron, copper, lead, gold. Pop. (1963) 3,315,700.

Marylebone Cricket Club (MCC), London cricket club founded 1787; now at LORD'S cricket ground.

Masaccio, orig. Tommaso di Simone Guidi (*c.* 1401–28), Florentine painter, leading artist of early Renaissance, among 1st to apply laws of perspective. Surviving paintings include frescoes in Brancacci Chapel in Florence.

Masai, nomadic E African people of Nilo-Hamitic stock, noted for physical courage. Livelihood depends largely on cattle-rearing.

Masaryk, Thomas Garrigue (1850–1937), founder and 1st Pres. of Czechoslovakia (1918–35). Enjoyed great popularity as liberal democrat. His son, **Jan Masaryk** (1886–1948), was foreign minister of exile Czech govt. in London during World War 2 and later in Prague. Said to have committed suicide after Russian coup d'etat (1948).

Mascagni, Pietro (1863–1945), Ital. opera composer and conductor. Best known for *Cavalleria Rusticana* (1890).

Masefield, John Edward (1878–1967), Eng. poet and playwright. Appointed Poet Laureate (1930). First poems *Salt Water Ballads* (1902) include 'Sea Fever' and 'Cargoes'. Among other works is *Reynard the Fox* (1919), a narrative poem.

mason wasp, small black and yellow solitary wasp. Builds nest in hollow stems.

Mason-Dixon Line, boundary between Maryland and Pennsylvania, US, fixed (1763–7) by Charles Mason and Jeremiah Dixon to resolve border disputes. Came to represent boundary between North and South.

Masons *see* FREEMASONRY.

Mass, liturgical service of R.C. Church, incl. celebration of EUCHARIST in which bread and wine are changed into body and blood of Christ, re-enacting Christ's sacrifice on the cross. Low Mass is read; High Mass is more elaborate ritual, chanted and sung.

Massachusetts, New England, maritime state, NE US. Area: 8,257 sq. mi.; cap. Boston; principal cities, Springfield, Worcester, Fall River. Manufactures chemicals, textiles, electrical machinery, paper and wood products. Agriculture and tourism important. Settled (1620) by PILGRIM FATHERS. Pop. (1962) 5,161,000.

Massachusetts Institute of Technology (MIT), scientific school (chartered 1861) at Cambridge, Mass., US. Leading technical college.

massage, manipulation of muscles, *e.g.* by rubbing, kneading, to increase blood supply and thus relieve pain. Used in treatment of rheumatism, fibrositis, *etc.*

Masséna, André (1756–1817), Fr. army officer. Distinguished himself at Rivoli (1799), Essling (1809) and Wagram (1809). Created marshal (1804), Duke of Rivoli (1808) and Prince of Essling (1809). Sent to Spain (1810), failed to dislodge Wellington and recalled by Napoleon. Transferred allegiance to Bourbons at Restoration.

Massenet, Jules Emile Frederic (1842–1912), Fr. composer and teacher at the Paris Conservatoire. Wrote many operas and songs.

Massey, William Ferguson (1856–1925), New Zealand Conservative politician, b. Ireland. Entered parl. 1894; P.M. (1912–23).

Massif Central, mountainous plateau covering most of C France. Contains Auvergne Mts., Cévennes limestone area, Limousin Plateau. Drains into several large rivers, incl. the Seine. Agric. area with several centres of industry incl. Clermont-Ferrand, Saint-Étienne.

Massine, Léonide (1896–), Russ. dancer and choreographer. Appeared with Diaghilev's Ballet Russe (1914–20); with Ballet de Monte Carlo (1932–41). Choreographed *La Boutique Fantasque* (1919), *The Three-Cornered Hat* (1919). Films include *Red Shoes* (1948).

Massys, Matsys, Messys or **Metsys, Quentin** (*c.* 1466–1530), Flemish painter. Influenced by Ital. Renaissance. Painted traditional portraits with religious or moral significance. Works include *Banker and his Wife* (1514).

mastaba, ancient Egyptian rectangular tomb. Low, flat-topped structure with sloping sides, serving as a burial place for pharaohs and nobles in the Old Kingdom.

Masters, Edgar Lee (1868–1950), Amer. poet best known for his *Spoon River Anthology* (1915).

masterwort, *Astrantia major,* perennial herb native to Europe. Pink or white flower clusters.

mastic, gum resin obtained from bark of small tree, *Pistacia lentiscus,* common in S Europe. Used for making protective varnishes, *e.g.* for oil paintings.

mastiff, large powerful short-haired dog, with apricot, fawn or brindled coat. Bred as watchdog.

mastiff bat, thickset, snubnosed bat mainly of America. When wings are folded, forearms can be used for walking. Californian mastiff bat, *Eurnops californicus,* largest US bat.

mastodon, extinct elephant of primitive type. Flourished in Pleistocene period in Europe, Asia and N and S America. Shorter legs and longer body than present species.

Mata Hari, orig. Margaretha Geertruida Zelle (1876–1917), Dutch-Indonesian dancer who acted as Ger. spy during World War 1. Executed by the French.

Matabele, Bantu tribe of W Southern Rhodesia, Africa. Colonization by

Magdalena by Massys

Boers and British produced conflicts; Matabele revolts (1893–1896) suppressed by British; natives were permitted to have a part in the govt.

Matadi, chief port of Congo Repub., on Congo R. Exports include cotton, coffee, copper. Pop. *c.* 60,000.

matamata, *Chelus fimbriata,* reptile of turtle family Chelidae found in rivers of Brazil and Venezuela. Rough shell and long neck. Eggs yield edible oil.

Matapan, Cape [Gk: Tainaron], S extremity of Peloponnesos, Greece. Site of Brit. naval victory (1941) over Italians in World War 2.

maté, Yerba maté, Paraguay tea, aromatic bitter tea brewed from leaves of evergreen tree, *Ilex paraguariensis*; popular in South America.

mathematics, systematic and logical study of relationships between quantities and magnitudes expressed in numbers and symbols.

Mather, Cotton (1663–1728), Amer. theologian and writer. His works include *The Wonders of the Invisible World* (1693) containing an account of the Salem witch trials in which he took part.

Mathewson, Christopher (1880–1925), Amer. baseball player. Won

Docks at Matadi on the Congo River

Nomads at watering place in the Mauritanian desert

373 games as pitcher for New York Giants; 3 shutout victories in 1905 World Series.

Matilda or **Maud** (1102–67), queen of England (1141–8), daughter of Henry I. Married Emperor Henry V; after his death, married Geoffrey Plantagenet, Count of Anjou. Her cousin, Stephen seized throne but was challenged (1139) by Matilda and her half-brother Robert, Earl of Gloucester. She was made queen, but 7 yr. later, withdrew in favour of son, Henry II.

Matisse, Henri (1869–1954), Fr. painter. Simple colourful style. Leading contributor to Fauve movement, and associated with Cubism. Works include *Still Life with a Red Carpet* (1906), *The Pink Nude* (1935), *Large Red Interior* (1948).

Mato Grosso, state of Brazil with Bolivia on W and Araguaia R. on E. Area: 485,549 sq. mi.; cap. Cuiabá. Rubber, timber, maté, quebracho from extensive forests. Cattle rearing; sugar and tobacco grown; manganese, diamonds and gold mined. Pop. (1960) 910,300.

matrimony *see* MARRIAGE.

Matteotti, Giacomo (1885–1924), Ital. polit. leader. Leading socialist opponent of Mussolini and Fascists. Murder by Fascists marked beginning of dominance of Mussolini.

matter, in physics, that which has mass and weight and occupies space. Composed of atoms, there are 3 states—solid, liquid or gas.

Matterhorn, peak (14,701 ft.) on Swiss-Ital. border. First climbed (1865) by Edward Whymper.

Matthew, Gospel according to Saint, first gospel of NT, written by the Apostle Matthew. Recounts Jesus' birth, life, ministry and ends with the Passion and the Resurrection.

Matthew, Saint, orig. Levi, tax-gatherer chosen by Jesus as one of 12 disciples.

Matthews, Sir Stanley (1915–), Eng. footballer; capped by England 56 times.

Maugham, [William] Somerset (1874–1965), Eng. novelist, playwright and short-story writer. Among his novels are *Of Human Bondage* (1915), *The Moon and Sixpence* (1919), *The Razor's Edge* (1944). Plays include *Home and Beauty* (1909), *The Circle* (1921).

Mauldin, William Henry (1921–), Amer. polit. cartoonist. Collections include *Up Front* (1945), *Bill Mauldin in Korea* (1952).

Mau-Mau, secret semi-religious anti-European terrorist organization of Kikuyu tribe of Kenya (c. 1940–60). Attacked esp. European settlers but also any who opposed Mau-Mau. Finally offered free pardon by Kenya govt. (1963).

Mauna Kea, mountain (13,825 ft.) on N central Hawaii. Dormant volcano; world's highest island mountain.

Mauna Loa, mountain (13,796 ft.) on S central Hawaii. Very active volcano, craters include Kilanea; located in Hawaii Volcanoes National Park.

Maundy Thursday, Thursday before Easter when sovereign distributes Maundy money to the poor. Relic of ceremony commemorating Christ washing Apostles' feet.

Maupassant, Guy de (1850–93), Fr. writer, esp. of short stories noted for psychological realism. They include 'Miss Harriet', The Necklace'.

Mauriac, François Charles (1885–1970), Fr. biographer, novelist and essayist. Works include *Thérèse Desqueyroux* (1927), *Nouveaux Mémoires Intérieurs* (1965). Awarded Nobel Prize for Literature (1952).

Mauritania, Islamic Republic of, maritime state of NW Africa. Area: 419,000 sq. mi.; cap. Nouakchott. Became autonomous repub. within Fr. Community (1958); full independence 1960. Economy based on

copper and iron ore. Main languages, Arabic, French. Pop. (1965 est.) 900,000.

Mauritius, island group in Indian Ocean, member of Brit. Commonwealth. Area (with dependencies): 805 sq. mi.; cap. Port Louis. Main islands, Mauritius, Rodriguez. Dutch colony (1638–1710); Fr. possession until taken by British (1810); independence 1968. Economy based on sugar cane, fish, copra. Official language, French. Unit of currency, rupee. Pop. (1966) 802,644.

Maurois, André (1885–1967), Fr. novelist and essayist. Works include *The Silence of Colonel Bramble* (1918; Eng. tr. 1920), *Le Peseur d'Ames* (1931), biographies of Shelley, Chateaubriand, Disraeli, George Sand, etc., as well as hist. works incl. *A History of the USA from Wilson to Kennedy* (1964).

Maximilian I (1459–1519), elected Holy Roman Emperor (1493). Reign occupied with fighting against Louis XI of France, the Hungarians and Turks in Austria. Acquired Spain for the Habsburgs by marriage of son Philip to Joanna, daughter of Ferdinand and Isabella.

Maximilian I (1832–67), emperor of Mexico, younger brother of Emperor Francis Joseph I of Austria. Offered crown of Mexico (1863) by Fr.-controlled Mexican Assembly. In 1866 declared war on ex-president Benito Juárez, and in 1867 was betrayed and shot.

Maxwell, James Clerk (1831–1879), Scot. physicist. Investigated colour perception and colour blindness, and kinetic theory of gases. Developed theory of electromagnetic field on mathematical basis. The maxwell, unit of magnetic flux, is named after him.

May beetle *see* JUNE BUG.

may tree *see* HAWTHORN.

Maya, pre-Columban S Amer. civilization of S Mexico, Guatemala and Honduras. Relics of Classic period (c. AD 317–889) include magnificent decorated stone-buildings. Hieroglyphic inscriptions indicate knowledge of mathematics and astronomy. Culture declined after 9th cent. and Sp. conquest (1697) completed its destruction.

Mayakovski, Vladimir Vladimirovich (1893–1930), Russ. poet. Leader of Russ. futurist movement, after Revolution supported Bolshevism and published much propagandist poetry.

Mayer, Maria Goeppert (1906–), Amer. physicist, b. Germany. Awarded Nobel Prize for Physics

Marie de Medici by Rubens

(1963) with Eugene P. Wigner and Hans D. Jensen, for work on structure of the atom and its nucleus.

Mayflower, ship which carried the Pilgrim Fathers from England to America (1620). Settlement estab. at Plymouth, Mass. Agreement for govt. of colony known as **Mayflower Compact.**

mayflower, name of several spring-blooming plants. Species include hepatica, herb with purplish, pink or white flowers, and trailing arbutus, *Epigaea repens,* creeping evergreen shrub with pink or white fragrant flowers native to America.

mayfly, insect of order Ephemeroptera. Delicate membranous wings and long cerci on abdomen. Aquatic nymph, found in freshwater, has burrowing forelegs and fish-like mandibles. Provides food for fish.

Mayo, Muigheo, maritime county of NW Republic of Ireland. Area: 2,084 sq. mi.; county town, Castlebar. Largely wild and mountainous with lakes. Linens and woollens manufactured. Pop. (1966) 115,588.

Mayon, Mount, volcano peak (8,077 ft.) in the Philippines, in SE Luzon Is.

Mays, Willie Howard (1931–), Amer. baseball player. Versatile outfielder, 2nd to 'Babe' Ruth for home runs hit during career.

mayweed, *Matricaria inodora,* annual or perennial scentless herb with white and yellow daisy-like flowers. Native to Europe and Asia. European chamomile, *Anthemis cotula,* has malodorous juice.

Mazarin, Jules (1602–61), Fr. cardinal and statesman. In papal diplomatic service, sent to France; created cardinal (1641); succeeded Richelieu as chief minister (1642). Attempts to suppress power of nobility provoked FRONDE. Influential at Fr. court as favourite of regent Anne of Austria. Negotiated Peace of Westphalia (1648), concluding Thirty Years War.

Mazeppa (c. 1644–1709), Cossack chieftain. Helped Peter the Great against Charles XII of Sweden; later transferred his allegiance (1708) to Peter's enemy Charles XII; driven into exile in Turkey.

mazurka, lively round dance in 3/4 time. Originally from Poland, it became popular in the 1860s. Chopin composed over 50 mazurkas.

Mboya, Thomas Joseph ('Tom') (1930–69). African polit. leader. Pres. of All-African People's Conference (1958). Kenyan Min. of Economic Development and Planning (1964–69). Author of *Freedom and After* (1963).

Mayan hieroglyphic statue at Copan, West Honduras

mead, an alcoholic beverage known since early times. Made of honey and spices, fermented with yeast.

Mead, Margaret (1901–), Amer. anthropologist. Enlarged scope of anthropology by relating culture to personality. Works include *Coming of Age in Samoa* (1928) and *Sex and Temperament in Three Primitive Societies* (1935).

meadow grass, perennial hay and pasture grasses of genus *Poa,* of wet, cold and temp. regions. Species include Kentucky bluegrass, *P. pratensis* and European wood meadow grass, *P. nemorensis.*

meadow rue, large genus of perennial herbs of buttercup family, native to N temp. regions.

meadow saffron, autumn crocus, *Colchicum autumnale,* purple-flowered garden plant of N Europe and N Africa. Corms and seeds yield drug colchicine used in genetic experiments.

meadowsweet, queen-of-the-meadow, *Filipendula ulmaria,* perennial herb of Rosaceae family, native to Europe and Asia, with pink or white flowers. Also common name for several species of *Spiraea.*

mealworm, larva of hard-back beetle. Feeds on grain products, *e.g.* flour. Bred as food for insectivorous birds and mammals.

mealybug, small insect, injurious to vegetable crops, citrus fruit and plants.

meander, curve in course of a river which flows from side to side in wide loops over flat land. Name from R. Meander in Asia Minor. Ox-bow lake is formed when meandering river cuts across one of its own loops. Common beside banks of Mississippi R., US.

measles, infectious, childhood, viral disease, occurring commonly in epidemics. Characterized by blotchy body rash preceded by running nose, watery eyes and fever. Incubation period 10–14 days.

Meath, An Mhidhe, maritime county of NE Republic of Ireland. Area: 903 sq. mi.; county town, Trim. Undulating fertile land; cattle raising, racehorse breeding and agriculture main occupations. Pop. (1966) 67,279.

Mecca, cap. of Hejaz, W Saudi Arabia. Holy city of Islam, birthplace of MOHAMMED. Place of pilgrimage, esp. Great Mosque enclosing the Kaaba and sacred Black Stone. Pop. (1963) 159,000.

mechanics, branch of physics which deals with effects of forces acting on bodies, primarily those in motion. Subdivided into kinetics and kinematics (solids); hydrostatics and hydrodynamics (liquids); pneumatics (gases).

Mecklenburg, Baltic region of East Germany. Area: 6,068 sq. mi.; hist. cap. Schwerin. Primarily agric. Titular rulers became dukes (1348) within Holy Roman Empire. Joined German Empire 1871.

meconopsis, genus of annual and perennial chiefly Asiatic herbs of family Papaveraceae. Flowers with stigmas form globular mass.

Medawar, Sir Peter Brian (1915–), Eng. zoologist. With Sir Macfarlane Burnet, awarded Nobel Prize for Physiology and Medicine (1960) for work on immunology.

Medea, in Gk. myth., enchantress and daughter of Aeëtes of Colchis. Helped Jason secure Golden Fleece, later bore him 2 children. Abandoned by Jason, contrived death of his new bride, Glauce, and killed her own children; fled to Aegeus of Athens.

Medellín, city of W central Colombia, founded 1675. Situated near extensive gold and silver mines; industrial and mining centre; exports coffee. Pop. (1964) 718,000.

Medes, ancient people of W Asia, in area now NW Iran. Reputedly learned in astronomy. After c. 560 BC Medes ceased to be distinguished from Persians.

Media, former nation of W Asia, approx. covering area occupied by present-day W Iran and S Azerbaijan SSR. Inhabited by the MEDES.

Medici, Ital. family, bankers and rulers of Florence (15th–18th cent.); best known as patrons of Renaissance. **Cosimo de' Medici** (1389–1464), 1st member of family to rule

Florence; expanded business, patronized arts. **Lorenzo de' Medici** (1449–92), called 'Il Magnifico'; generous patron. Averted attempt (1478) by Pazzi family to displace him. His son, **Giovanni de' Medici** (1475–1521), became pope as Leo X (1513–21). **Guilio de' Medici** (1478–1534), became pope as Clement VII (1523–34); defeated by Emperor Charles V, made peace (1529) with him. **Alessandro de' Medici** (1511–37), created hereditary duke of Florence, tyrannical rule ended in his assassination. Succeeded by **Cosimo de' Medici** (1519–74), who became grand duke of Tuscany. **Catherine de' Medici** (1519–89), queen of Henry II of France; instigated (1572) SAINT BARTHOLOMEW'S DAY MASSACRE. **Marie de' Medici** (1573–1642), queen of Henry IV of France; acted as regent for her son upon king's death (1610), ultimately exiled (1630) by Cardinal Richelieu.

medicine, art and science of treatment and prevention of disease. HIPPOCRATES (*c.* 460 BC) known as Father of Medicine. Galen (2nd cent.) chief medical authority for 1,000 yr. Discovery by William Harvey (1628) of circulation of the blood of great importance. Medicine revolutionized in 19th cent. with introduction of antiseptics and microscopy, *etc.* Advances in 20th cent. treatment and control of disease due to use of antibiotics, innoculation with vaccines, nationwide blood-transfusion services. Much reliance now placed on scientific analysis.

Medicine Hat, city of E Alberta, Canada, on S Saskatchewan R. Founded 1883. Trade and transportation centre; industries include grain mills, metal work, fertilizers and meat-packing. Pop. (1961) 24,484.

medicine man, in primitive cultures, sorcerer supposed to possess healing powers, *e.g.* witch doctor.

medick, medic, plant of genus *Medicago* of pulse family. Includes lucern or alfalfa, *M. sativa*, black medick, *M. lupulina* and common, or yellow medick, *M. falcata*.

medieval art and architecture, term applied to works produced in Europe (*c.* 400–1500), during Middle Ages. Architecture utilized stone, most widely used in building churches, culminating in the great GOTHIC cathedrals. Art generally anonymous and executed under the auspices of the Church. Detailed ornamental patterns, often borrowed from Barbaric nations, highly developed in manuscript illumination (*e.g.* BOOK OF KELLS), stone and wood carvings, and metalwork. Artisans generally organized into guilds.

Medina, Al Madinah, city of Hejaz, W Saudi Arabia. Holy city of Islam. Goal of Mohammed's flight from Mecca (622). Great Mosque contains Mohammed's tomb. Pop. (1961 est.) 60,000.

mediterranean, term denoting climate conditions of land areas bordering Med. Sea. Characterized by short, warm, wet winters and long, hot, dry summers; typical vegetation includes olives, grapes and citrus fruits. Also found in California, Chile, South Africa and SW areas of Australia.

Mediterranean Sea, large inland sea, enclosed by Europe, Africa and Asia. Area: *c.* 1,145,000 sq. mi. Connected with Atlantic Ocean by Strait of Gibraltar, with Black Sea by Dardanelles, with Red Sea by Suez Canal. Notably small tidal variation; shores mainly mountainous. Many popular resort areas, *e.g.* Fr. Riviera.

medium *see* SPIRITUALISM.

medlar, *Mespilus germanica,* deciduous sometimes thorny tree native to Europe and Asia. Apple-shaped fruit eaten when partly decayed.

Médoc, region of Gironde department, SW France. Produces wine, esp. red Bordeaux, *e.g.* Château Lafite and Château Margaux.

Medusa, in Gk. myth., one of the 3 GORGONS. Head of Medusa turned anything that met its gaze into stone. Slain by Perseus.

medusa, free-swimming stage of jellyfish, resembling bell or parachute. Stage in development of most marine coelenterates.

meerkat, *Suricata tetradactyla,* small slender mongoose of dry open grasslands of S Africa. Lives in burrows; yellowish brown fur.

meerschaum, absorbent hydrous magnesium silicate resembling white clay, found chiefly in Asia Minor. Used for pipes, cigar-holders, *etc.*

Megalithic Age, archaeological term for period characterized by the building of massive structures and monuments, *e.g.* Stonehenge in England.

megalomania, form of mental illness whose main symptom is delusions of grandeur, wealth, *etc.*

megalosaurus, carnivorous dinosaur up to 20 ft. long with strong, heavy hind limbs and tail. Fossil remains found in W Europe.

megatherium, genus of extinct, herbi-

Medieval Art: reliquary made by the goldsmith Fridericus van Keulen *c.* 1170

Mediterranean coastline near Portofino, Italy

Typical Mediterranean harbour, Peñiscola, Spain

vorous ground sloths of Pleistocene age, found in N and S America. Up to 20 ft. long, with weight centred in tail, hind legs and lower body.

Meighen, Arthur (1874–1960), Canadian statesman. Rebuilt Conservative Party in early 1920s; P.M. (1920–1; 1926).

Meir, Golda (1898–   ), P.M. of Israel (1969–   ).

Meissen, industrial town of Saxony, East Germany, founded 930. Centre, since 1710, of fine porcelain manufacture. Pop. (1959 est.) 48,300.

Meistersingers, members of Ger. guilds of poets and musicians (14th–16th cent.); aimed to preserve medieval traditions of MIN-NESINGERS.

Meitner, Lise, FRS (1878–1968), Austrian-Swedish physicist. Research on nuclear physics and radioactivity aided early development of atom bombs. Discovered element protoactinium (1917).

Mekong, river of S Asia, 2,500 mi. long; rises in Himalayas, flows through Thailand and Laos to South China Sea in South Vietnam.

Melanchthon, orig Philipp Schwarzerd (1497–1560), Ger. humanist and reformer. Strong supporter of LUTHER, ranking 2nd to him in Reformation. His *Loci communes* (1521) set out Protestant dogma. Wrote Augsburg Confession (1530) of Lutheran faith. Developed Ger. schools system.

Melanesia, island region of SW Pacific, N and NE of Australia. Includes New Hebrides, New Caledonia, Bismarck Archipelago, Solomon Is. and Fiji Is. Languages are of Malayo-Polynesian family.

Melanesians, peoples of S Pacific islands from Malaysia to Fiji, of Negroid extraction. Main groups are the Papuans and the taller, finer-featured 'true' Melanesians.

Melbourne, manufacturing and market centre, leading seaport and cap. of Victoria, Australia, on narrow coastal lowland; founded 1835. Growth resulted from nearby gold discoveries (1851). Cap. of Australia until 1927. Pop. (1966) 2,108,499.

Melbourne, 2nd Viscount *see* LAMB, WILLIAM.

Meleager, in Gk. myth., son of Oeneus king of Calydon. Led hunt of boar sent by Artemis to ravage Calydon. Loved Atalanta, to whom he gave the boar's head.

Melilla, Sp. enclave in Morocco. Commercial city and fishing port. Administered as part of Malaga prov. Pop. (1965 est.) 81,182.

Mellon, Andrew William (1855–1937), Amer. financier and public official. Held large interests in many industries, esp. aluminium. Sec. of the Treasury (1921–31). Chief benefactor of National Gallery of Art, Washington, DC.

melodrama, play consisting of sensational action and sentimental appeal. Orig. spoken text with background of music (*e.g.* Greek drama). Most popular during 18th cent., musical aspects gradually declined in importance.

melody, succession or arrangement of musical notes. May be used as harmonic material (*see* POLYPHONY) or as principal element in piece of music.

melon, *Cucumis melo,* sweet, juicy, edible fruit of gourd family, native to S Asia. Important commercially in trop. and sub-trop. countries. Varieties include musk melon, honeydew and cantaloupe, a hard-shelled Med. variety. *See* WATERMELON.

Melville, Herman (1819–91), Amer. author. Novels, mostly concerned with life at sea, include *Typee* (1846), *Moby Dick* (1851) and *Billy Budd* (pub. 1924).

Memlinc or **Memling, Hans** (*c.* 1430–1494), Flemish religious painter. Best known for the *Shrine of St Ursula* (1489).

Memnon, in Gk. myth., son of Eos, the Dawn, and leader of the Ethiopians in Trojan War. Supported Trojans, slain by Achilles.

memory, term for capacity to retain and recall past experiences. Experiments have shown that speed of learning can be correlated with ability to retain; bias and emotional needs also determine content of memory. Experiences affecting personality can often only be recalled through psychoanalytic methods.

Memphis, city of SW Tennessee, US, overlooking Mississippi R. Fort built (1797) by US; city planned 1819. Cotton market and manufacturing centre. Pop. (1963) 545,000.

Memphis, cap. of ancient Egypt on W bank of Nile. Situated at borders of Upper and Lower Egypt. Founded by Menes, 1st king of 1st dynasty (*c.* 3,100 BC); abandoned after Mohammedan conquest (525 BC).

Menander (*c.* 342–291 BC), Gk. New Comedy poet. Influenced Plautus and Terence. Only complete extant work, *The Curmudgeon.*

Menangkabau, Malay people of coasts and highlands of Sumatra. Well-developed social organization, matrilineal clan villages and family ownership of property; mostly orthodox Mohammedans. Language closely related to Malay.

Fishing village on the Mekong river, Cambodia

Metalwork: Merovingian clasps found near Anderlecht

Mencken, H[enry] L[ouis] (1880–1956), Amer. journalist and writer. Collaborated with George Jean Nathan on *Smart Set* (1914–23). Founder and editor of *American Mercury* (1925–33), a satire on contemporary Amer. life. Compiled *The American Language* (1919, supplements 1945, 1948).

Mendel, Gregor Johann (1822–1884), Austrian botanist and priest. Conducted experiments on hybridity in plants and hereditary factors in vegetable matter which provided basis for his theory of heredity.

Mendeleyev, Dmitri Ivanovich (1834–1907), Russ. chemist. Discovered relationship between properties of elements and their atomic weights (periodic law).

Mendelson, Erich (1887–1953), Ger.-American expressionist architect. Buildings include Einstein Tower (1919–20) and Potsdam Observatory (1927).

Mendelssohn, Moses (1729–86), Ger.-Jewish philosopher. In *Jerusalem* (1783), rationalized Judaism. By translating the Pentateuch and the Psalms into German, helped to promote Gentile understanding of Jewish culture.

Mendelssohn-Bartholdy, Jakob Ludwig Felix (1809–47), Ger. composer and conductor. Works include *A Midsummer Night's Dream* (1843, overture written 1826), oratorios *St Paul* (1836) and *Elijah* (1846), *Songs Without Words* for piano, *Hebrides* concert overture.

Mendès-France, Pierre (1907–), Fr. polit. leader. Radical Socialist premier (1954–5), negotiated Fr. withdrawal from Indo-China. Gave up party leadership (1957). Anti-Gaullist leader during Fifth Repub.

Mendicant Orders [Lat: *mendicare*, to beg], collective name for religious orders which subsist mainly on alms, *e.g.* Carmelites, Franciscans, *etc.*

Mendip Hills, range of hills in Somerset, England, reaching 1,068 ft. Caves show evidence of prehistoric occupation.

Mendoza, Diego Hurtado de (*c.* 1503–75), Sp. statesman, novelist and poet. Represented Charles V at Council of Trent (1545–7). Writings include *Guerra de Granada* and poems.

Menelaus, in Gk. myth., brother of Agamemnon. Husband of Helen whom Paris carried off to Troy, causing Trojan War. Recovered Helen at end of war.

menhir, tall, upright standing stone, of Neolithic period, whose purpose is not known; found singly and in groups in Europe, Africa and Asia.

meningitis, inflammation of meninges, membranes surrounding brain and spinal chord. Usually bacterial, may be viral.

Mennonites, fundamentalist, pacifist Protestant sect, orig. Swiss, developed under leadership of Dutchman, Menno Simons (1496–1561). Found chiefly in Kansas and Minnesota, US. Amish are branch of Mennonites.

Menomini, Menominee, tribe of Algonkian N Amer. Indians who inhabited the Upper Great Lakes region; generally peaceful towards settlers.

menopause *see* MENSTRUATION.

Menotti, Gian-Carlo (1911–), Amer. composer. Operas include *The Medium* (1946), *Amahl and the Night Visitors* (1951).

Mensheviks, right wing of Russ. Social-Democratic Party, formed minority (*mensheviki*) party at 1903 congress, opposed to majority (*bolsheviki*) under Lenin. Ousted by Bolsheviks (1917) in final stage of Russ. Revolution.

Menshikov, Alexander Danilovich (1660–1729), Russ. marshal and statesman. Under Peter the Great carried on war with Charles XII of Sweden and implemented reforms. Helped place Catherine I on throne and acted as her chief minister.

menstruation, discharge of cells and blood from female womb. Occurs approximately every 28 days from its beginning at puberty to its ending (menopause), except during pregnancy.

Menuhin, Yehudi (1916–), Amer. violinist. Noted esp. for interpretations of Elgar and Beethoven concertos.

Menzies, Sir Robert Gordon (1894–), Austral. statesman. Attorney-Gen. (1934–9); P.M. (1939–41, 1949–66). Warden of the Cinque Ports (1965–).

Mephistopheles, in Ger. legend, evil spirit to whom FAUST sold his soul; Goethe made him the personification of all evil.

mercantilism, economic policy founded on principle that national wealth is measured in bullion reserves. Acquisition of gold achieved through encouraging exports and levying high duties on imports. Practised (1500–1800) by W European nations; chief exponent JEAN COLBERT. Supplanted during Indust. Revolution by LAISSEZ-FAIRE theories.

Mercator, Gerardus, orig. Gerhard Kremer (1512–94), Flemish mathematician and cartographer. Made 1st map using PROJECTIONS (1568); maps published (1595).

mercerizing, treating of cotton with sodium hydroxide and drying under tension to give silky appearance and greater strength. Developed (mid-19th cent.) by Eng. chemist John Mercer.

Mercia, Anglo-Saxon kingdom of England. In 7th cent. extended from

Merlin

R. Humber to Thames and from Welsh border to East Anglia. Absorbed by Wessex *c.* 825, E part included in Danelaw from 886.

Mercury, planet nearest to the Sun and smallest in Solar System. (*c.* 3,000 mi. in diameter). Rotates annually on axis, and has period of revolution of 88 days.

mercury, quicksilver, only metal liquid below 25°C (72°F); chief source is mineral cinnabar. Very heavy and silvery white, it forms amalgams with most metals. Used in barometers to measure pressure and thermometers to measure temperature.

Meredith, George (1828–1909), Brit. novelist and poet. Among his novels are *The Ordeal of Richard Feverel* (1859), *The Egoist* (1879). Verse includes 'Modern Love' (1862).

merganser, diving sea duck of N hemisphere. Species include N Amer. and European common merganser or goosander, *Mergus merganser,* and N Amer. hooded merganser, *Lophodytes cucullatus.*

Mergenthaler, Ottmar (1854–1899), Ger. born Amer. inventor; developed 1st LINOTYPE typesetting machine, patented 1884.

meridian, circle drawn on Earth's surface passing through N and S Poles. Prime Meridian, estab. by international agreement (1884), passes through Greenwich, England, longitude 0°. *See* LATITUDE.

Merimée, Prosper (1803–70), Fr. author. Short novels include *Colomba* (1841), *Carmen* (1845). His *Lettres à une Inconnue* depict Fr. society in days of 2nd Empire.

merino, Sp. breed of sheep, developed esp. in Australia and New Zealand, to produce fine wool and to withstand extremes of climate.

Merionethshire, maritime county of W Wales. Area: 660 sq. mi.; county town Dolgelley. Mountainous with sheep rearing and slate quarrying as main occupations. Tourism important. Pop. (1966) 38,000.

Merlin, in ARTHURIAN LEGEND, magician and prophet, friend of Arthur.

merlin, *Falco columbarius,* small falcon of mountain regions of N hemisphere; winters on coasts of S Europe. Related to N Amer. pigeon hawk.

Merovingians, Frankish dynasty (5th–6th cent.). Clovis I (466–511) became king of Franks (481), estab. Fr. monarchy, embraced Christianity (496) and made Paris his capital. Kingdom divided after his death. Childeric III, last Merovingian king, deposed (751) by PEPIN THE SHORT.

The Meseta Plateau in Spain

Mersey, river of NW England, 70 mi. long. Important in indust. development of Lancashire by providing water and power for cotton industry. Connected to Manchester by Manchester Ship Canal. Estuary now site of Liverpool port and docks.

Merthyr Tydfil, mining and industrial town of Glamorganshire, S Wales, on major coal field. Pop. (1965) 59,000.

mescal, intoxicating drink prepared from juice of certain species of AGAVE, esp. in Mexico.

mescal, 2 species of cactus *Lophophora williamsii* and *L. lewinni* of C America. Dried tops are used by Indians as stimulant, and hallucinatory drug mescaline is made from them.

mescaline *see* MESCAL.

mesembryanthemum, genus of mostly succulent plants native to hot arid areas, esp. S Africa. Garden varieties include *M. crystallinum,* ice plant.

meseta, geog. term for an extensive upland or plateau, usually with uneven surface, named from area of inland Spain.

Meshed, Mashhad, city of NE Iran at 3,100 ft.; centre of Shiite religion and place of pilgrimage, near borders with USSR and Afghanistan. Pop. (1963) 312,000.

Mesmer, Franz Anton (1734–1815), Austrian physician, developed theory of animal magnetism known as mesmerism (1772). His cures created brief contemporary sensation, but were largely discredited.

Mesolithic *see* STONE AGE.

Mesopotamia, region of W Asia, now in Iraq, on Tigris and Euphrates rivers; contains relics of earliest civilizations, Ur, Lagash, Akkad and early empires of Babylonia and Assyria.

Mesozoic *see* GEOLOGICAL TABLE.

mesquite, leguminous shrubs of *Prosopis* genus ranging from S America to southern US. Roots may reach depths of 70 ft. Flowers resemble catkins.

Messiaen, Olivier (1908–), Fr. composer and organist; influenced by Hindu music; composed works for organ, orchestra and for voices, incl. *Turangalila Symphony* and *Le Banquet Céleste.*

Messiah, 'the Anointed', in Judaism, the leader promised by God to restore the kingdom of David; Christians regard Jesus Christ as this Messiah.

Messina, cap. and port of Messina prov., NE Sicily, Italy. Founded by Greeks *c.* 700 BC. In earthquake region. Pop. (1965) 265,000.

The 12th century Romanesque cathedral of Messina

Mayan ruins at Tula, Mexico

The modern library building of the University of Mexico

The 16th cent. cathedral of Puebla, Mexico

metabolism, chem. processes in a living organism that convert food and oxygen into tissues and energy, largely controlled by ENZYMES.

metal, an element distinguished from a non-metal by lustre, high specific gravity, conduction of heat and of electricity. Characteristics of a metal also include malleability, ductility and crystal formation.

metal fatigue, structural change in metals caused by stress, important esp. in aircraft building.

metallurgy, science of extraction of metals from their ores, and of freeing them from impurities. Also includes study of structure and properties of metals and their use.

metamorphic rock, igneous or sedimentary rock which has been completely transformed by heat or stress; *e.g.* sandstone changes to quartzite, limestone to marble.

metamorphosis, period of change in form and structure when animal is transformed from larva to adult form, *e.g.* caterpillar into chrysalis and later into perfect insect.

Metaxas, Ioannes (or **Tanni**) (1871–1941), Gk. general and royalist politician; estab. military dictatorship in Greece (1936–41). Directed resistance against Ital. invasion (1940–1).

Metchnikoff, Élie, orig. Ilya Ilyich Mechnikov (1845–1916), Russ. biologist. With Paul Ehrlich, awarded Nobel Prize for Physiology and Medicine (1908) for work on immunology.

meteor, shooting star, small object from outside Earth's atmosphere, becomes incandescent entering it. Most are consumed, but some, called meteorites reach surface of Earth.

Meteor Crater, hole *c.* $\frac{3}{4}$ mi. across, in Arizona US, caused by METEORITE impact.

meteorite, object reaching Earth's surface from outer space. Most are pebble-sized but some of 36 ft. and upwards have been recorded.

meteorology, science of phenomena of Earth's atmosphere; encompasses weather, physics and chemistry of atmosphere, and direct effects of atmosphere on life. Based on regular and systematic observations throughout the world.

methane, colourless, odourless, inflammable gas; given off by decaying vegetable matter (marsh gas) and found in mines (firedamp).

methanol, methyl alcohol, wood alcohol, colourless, poisonous liquid, orig. obtained from wood; used as solvent, antifreeze, *etc.*

Methodism, Protestant religious denomination. Originated as part of Church of England revival (*c.* 1729) by JOHN and CHARLES WESLEY. Evangelism and lay preaching are fundamental. Separated from C. of E. (1791); now has *c.* 13 million members, mainly in UK and US.

Methuselah, oldest man in OT; believed to have lived for 969 yr. Son of Enoch and grandfather of Noah. (*Gen.* V).

methyl, group of atoms always found in combination with other atoms, forming many important compounds.

methyl alcohol *see* METHANOL.

methylated spirit, type of spirit, consisting of mixture of methyl alcohol and petroleum.

metric system, system of weights and measurements devised in France and based on the metre. Adopted by many nations.

metronome, clockwork mechanism used to indicate the exact pace of music. Consists of a pendulum with a sliding weight.

Metropolitan Museum of Art, The, civic museum, New York, US. Founded 1870; supported by private endowment and membership fees. Contains European and Amer. paintings and sculpture, also Gk., Egyptian, Medieval and Oriental works of art.

Metropolitan Opera House, principal Amer. opera house, in New York City. Home of Metropolitan Opera Assoc. Inc. Accommodated (1966) in Lincoln Center.

Metternich-Winneburg, Clemens Wenzel Lothar, Prince (1773–1859), Austrian statesman, b. Germany. Min. of foreign affairs (1809–48), negotiated Napoleon's marriage to Marie Louise of Austria, and Fr. alliance (1812); joined Allies against Napoleon, emerged as chief figure at CONGRESS OF VIENNA (1814–15) and of HOLY ALLIANCE. Advocated maintenance of 'balance of power' to preserve *status quo* in Europe. His repressive measures within Austria forced him to abdicate power during Revolution of 1848.

Metz, cap. of Moselle department in Alsace-Lorraine region, formerly frontier fortress town, centre of agric. area. Part of Germany (1871–1918). Pop. (1962) 147,000.

Meuse [Dutch: Maas], European river of France, Belgium and Netherlands, *c.* 575 mi. long.

Mewar *see* UDAIPUR.

Mexican War, conflict (1846–8) between US and Mexico. Immediate cause was annexation of Texas (1845); war declared when Mexico declined to negotiate over border dispute and US claims in California. Mexican forces led by SANTA ANNA failed to thwart Amer. drive towards Mexico City, culminating in entry (1847). Settlement reached under Treaty of GUADALUPE HIDALGO.

Mexico [Estados Unidos Mexicanos], repub. of Amer. continent, between US and Central America. Area: 758,000 sq. mi.; cap. Mexico City;

main cities Guadalajara, Monterrey, Puebla. Mountainous with narrow, hot coastal plains and high central plateau. Most of N is desert. Oil industry and mining important. Crops include trop. fruits, rubber, sugar cane, tobacco, cotton, wheat. Early civilizations included MAYA, AZTEC. Sp. conquest under Cortés (1519); rebellion achieved independence (1821). MEXICAN WAR followed by civil wars. Constitution drawn up (1917) is basis of present-day constitution. Pop. (1967 est.) 45,671,000.

Mexico, Gulf of, part of Atlantic Ocean bounded to N by US and SW by Mexico. It feeds the GULF STREAM.

Mexico City, cap. of Mexico, on site of Aztec city of Tenochtitlán on L. Texcoco, 7,400 ft. above sea level. Founded c. 1325. Important buildings include 16th cent. cathedral. Pop. (1967) 6,285,334.

Meyer, Conrad Ferdinand (1825– 98), Swiss novelist and poet. Works include *Balladen* (1867), *Jürg Jenatsch* (1876), *Der Heilige* (1880).

Meyerbeer, Giacomo (1791– 1864), Ger. composer; worked in Italy and Paris. Operas include *Jephtha's Vow* (1813), *Robert le Diable* (1831) and *L'Africaine* (1865).

Meyerhof, Otto (1884– 1951), Ger. physiologist. With A. V. Hill, awarded Nobel Prize for Physiology and Medicine (1922) for work on cellular oxidation and transformation of lactic acid in muscles.

Meynell, Alice Christina Gertrude (1847– 1922), Eng. poet and essayist. Her works include *Preludes* (1875), *Rhythm of Life* (1893).

Mézy, or **Mésy, Augustin Saffray, Chevalier de** (d. 1665), Fr. administrator in Canada; 1st royal gov. of New France.

mezzotint, ENGRAVING process in which design is worked from a dark background into highlights.

Miami, city and port, S Florida, US; popular winter resort with subtrop. climate. Founded (c. 1870) at Fort Dallas. Important transport terminal. Pop. (1960) 291,688.

Miami, N Amer. Algonkian Indian tribe of the Upper Great Lakes region.

Miami Beach, resort, Florida, US, connected with MIAMI by causeway. Pop. (1960) 63,145.

Miaskovsky, Nicolai Yokovlevich (1881– 1950), Russ. composer. Works include oratorio *Kirov is with us,* 27 symphonies, symphonic poems and piano works.

mica, group of minerals all of which can be split into thin plates with pearly lustre; silicates of aluminium and potassium. Examples are muscovite, biotite and lepidolite.

Micah, prophetic book of OT, attributed to prophet Micah (c. 700 BC); denounces social injustice and hypocrisy but foretells Messianic deliverance.

Michael I (1921–), king of Romania (1927– 30; 1940– 7). Overthrew dictatorship of Ion Antonescu (1944); abdicated in favour of communist repub. (1947).

michaelmas daisy, various species of the *Aster* genus of flowering plants mostly native to N America. Garden varieties include *A. novi-belgii.*

Michaux, Henri (1899–), Belgian surrealist painter. Works express tortured dream-like cynicism.

Michelangelo, orig. Michelagniolo di Lodovico Buonarroti Simoni (1475– 1564), Florentine artist, architect and poet. Leading artist of Ital. Renaissance. Masterpieces include sculptures, *Pietà, David* and *Moses*; painted ceiling of Sistine chapel. Designed Medici chapel, Florence and dome of St Peter's, Rome.

Michelet, Jules (1798– 1874), Fr. historian and novelist. Main historical works *Histoire de France* (1867) and the *Histoire de la Révolution* (1853).

Michelson, Albert Abraham, FRS (1852– 1931), Amer. physicist. Awarded Nobel Prize for Physics (1907) for studies of light and its measurement. Also contributed to relativity studies.

Michigan, N state of US in Great Lakes region. Area: 58,216 sq. mi.; cap. Lansing; other cities Detroit, Bay City, Jackson. Settled by Fr. fur traders (c. 1618), growth of state in 20th cent. due to automobile industry, centred on Detroit. Major manufacturing region with some agriculture and tourism. Pop. (1960) 7,823,194.

Michigan, Lake *see* GREAT LAKES.

Michilimackinac, Mackinac, straits connecting L. Michigan and L. Huron.

N shore was site of Jesuit mission (1671); S shore of fortified post built (1679) by La Salle; later became trading post, ceded to US in JAY'S TREATY (1796). Captured by British (1812); Treaty of Ghent (1814) confirmed US ownership.

Mickiewitz, Adam (1798– 1855), Polish Romantic poet and patriot. Works include *Pan Tadeusz* (1834).

Micmac, Canadian Algonkian Indian tribe; c. 4,000 on reserves in Quebec and Newfoundland (1967).

microbe, microscopic living organism capable of reproduction. Term

View of Metz with the Gothic cathedral of St Étienne in the background

usually applied to BACTERIA causing disease or fermentation.

micrometer, scientific instrument for making measurements with greatest degree of accuracy to within one thousandth of an inch or less.

Micronesia, island group in W Pacific. Includes Marianas, Marshalls, Carolines and Gilbert Is. Natives primarily of Polynesian and Australoid stock; language is Malayo-Polynesian.

Micronesian, people of Micronesia. Pacific islands N of Melanesia, speaking Malayo-Polynesian dialects.

microphone, instrument for converting sound waves into electric impulses; used to record, amplify and broadcast sound.

microscope, optical instrument of 1 or more lenses used for magnifying small objects. Louis de Broglie developed (1942) electron microscope in which electromagnetic fields replace light waves and glass lenses.

Midas, in Gk. myth., king of Phrygia, given by Bacchus power of turning everything he touched to gold. Later

The Middle Ages: top, procession of monks with reliquary; bottom, citizens leading ox in an Easter parade

given ass's ears as punishment for preferring Pan's flute to Apollo's lyre.

Middle Ages, period in W European history considered to have begun with fall of Roman Empire (5th cent.) and to have ended with REFORMATION and RENAISSANCE (15th cent.). Period marked by unity of W Europe within R.C. Church, feudalism, and height of GOTHIC architecture.

Middle East, geographic region defined by history and culture; comprises area where Asia, Africa and Europe converge, bounded by Sahara, Black and Caspian Seas, Indian subcontinent, and Aegean Sea. Countries include Egypt, Israel, Turkey, Iran, Iraq, Syria, Libya.

Middle East Treaty Organization see CENTRAL TREATY ORGANIZATION.

Middle English, period (c. 1100– 1450) when inflected O.E. language was modified and vocabulary augmented by borrowings from French. Important literary works include *Gawayne and the Greene Knight* and poetry of Chaucer.

Middle Temple see INNS OF COURT.

Middlesex, former county of SE England, adjoining London. Area: 232 sq. mi. Ceased to exist as admin. and geog. entity (1965) being absorbed by Greater London, Hertfordshire and Surrey.

Middleton, Thomas (1580–1627), Eng. Jacobean dramatist; wrote realistic comedies *e.g. The Roaring Girl* (1611); and tragedies incl. *The Changeling* (with Rowley, 1653) and *Women beware Women* (1657).

midge, small 2-winged insect esp. of family Chironomidae. Some species have biting mouthparts.

Midlands, region of C England usually taken to include Birmingham and its environs, or counties of Nottingham, Derby, Stafford, Leicester, Rutland, Northampton, Warwick and Worcester.

Midlothian, lowland county of Scotland. Area: 3,662 sq. mi., county town, Edinburgh. Main occupations, fishing, market gardening, fruit growing, dairying, mining, brewing, paper making, shipbuilding. Pop. (1966) 589,000.

midnight sun, name given to the Sun, when visible at midnight, in midsummer, in Arctic and Antarctic regions.

Midway Islands, 3 small islands, N Pacific, NW of Hawaii. Area: *c.* 2 sq. mi. **Battle of Midway** (1942), battle in which Japanese were defeated by Allies. Pop. (1958 est.) 200.

Midwest, Middle West, C region of US incl. plains states of Illinois, Indiana, Ohio, Iowa, Kansas, Nebraska, Minnesota, Wisconsin, N and S Dakota, and E Montana. Mainly agric. with some large cities.

midwife toad, *Alytes obstetricans,* small dark burrowing toad of Europe. After female spawns, male fastens string of eggs round his hind legs and carries them until they hatch.

midwifery, practice of assisting childbirth by trained persons, usually women. *See* OBSTETRICS.

Mies van der Rohe, Ludwig (1886–1969), Amer. architect, b. Germany. Director of Bauhaus (1929–33). Developed logically functional style in US, *e.g.* Seagram building, NY.

M.I.5., secret service division of the British Joint Intelligence Bureau, department of the Foreign Office.

mignonette, annual or perennial herb native to Med. regions and E Africa. Garden variety *Reseda odorata* has small fragrant flowers.

migraine, extremely severe prolonged headache; may be accompanied by nausea and disturbed vision. Affects women more than men.

migration, movement of animals from one area to another for the purpose of breeding or finding fresh food supplies. This occurs seasonally in the case of certain birds and fish.

Mikhailovich, Draja or **Dragoliub** (1893–1946), Yugoslav military leader. War min. and commander-in-chief of exiled Yugoslav govt. in 1941. Began guerilla warfare against Germans but opposed Tito, lost Allied support and was shot for treason.

Milan, Milano, 2nd city, indust., commercial and financial centre of Italy. Centre of Mussolini's Fascist polit. movement after World War I. Industries include silk, chemicals, printing and heavy industries. Cathedral outstanding example of Ital. Gothic. Pop. (1965) 1,673,000.

mildew, destructive growth of parasitic fungi on plants and also similar growth on cotton, linen fabrics, leather, paper. Characterized by whitish, powdery coating on surface.

milfoil, yarrow, *Achillea millefolium,* strongly scented perennial

Midnight sun on the Norwegian coast

Eurasian herb, with white, pink or purple flowers; has been used medicinally from early times. Name water milfoil is given to aquatic plant of unrelated *Myriophyllum* genus.

Milhaud, Darius (1892–), Fr. composer; member of Les Six; works include operas, ballets, orchestral and chamber works, and experiments with polytonality.

militia, organized military force of civilians called upon in national emergency. Known in Europe before formation of regular armies; again raised in UK when Napoleonic invasions threatened, later merged with TERRITORIAL ARMY; in US merged with NATIONAL GUARD.

milk, white fluid produced by female mammals for nourishment of young. Contains protein, fat and carbohydrates. Cow's milk is widely used as human beverage and for production of butter, *etc.*

milk adder *see* MILK SNAKE.

The world famous opera house La Scala, in Milan

milk cap, milky cap, genus of fungi. *Lactarius torminosus,* non-edible flesh-coloured woolly milk cap, yields white acrid milk and *L. deliciosus,* edible saffron milk cap, has mild orange milk.

milk snake, milk adder, *Lampropeltis triangulum,* common, harmless, brightly marked snake of E North America.

milkweed butterfly *see* MONARCH BUTTERFLY.

milkwort, widespread herbs of Polygalaceae family. Common European milkwort is *Polygala vulgaris*; N Amer. *P. senega* was reputed cure for snakebite.

Milky Way, broad belt of *c.* 100,000 million stars, which, viewed from Earth, stretches E–W across sky; the Galaxy of which SOLAR SYSTEM is a part.

Mill, James (1773–1836), Brit. philosopher. Associate of Bentham and advocate of utilitarian theory. Also wrote *History of India* (1817). His son, **John Stuart Mill** (1806–73), became leading exponent of 19th cent. Eng. liberal thought. Author of *Essay on Liberty* (1859), supplemented utilitarianism with humanitarian principles; pleasure (motivating force) should be measured by quality as well as quantity. Other works include *Principles of Political Economy* (1848), *Utilitarianism* (1863).

Millais, Sir John Everett (1829–96), Brit. painter. Orig. associated with PRE-RAPHAELITE BROTHERHOOD, later painted in traditional genres of portraits and medieval history. Works include *Christ in the Carpenter's Shop* (1850).

Millay, Edna St Vincent (1892–1950), Amer. poet. Influenced esp. by Shakespeare, Keats and Hopkins. Works include *The Harp-Weaver and Other Poems* (1923), verse plays, *e.g. Aria da Capo* (1920), and *The King's Henchman* (1927).

Miller, Arthur (1915–), Amer. dramatist. Works include *Death of a Salesman* (1949), *A View from the Bridge* (1955), *Incident at Vichy* (1965).

Miller, Henry (1891–), Amer. novelist. Works include *Tropic of Cancer, Tropic of Capricorn, Black Spring.*

Miller, Joaquin, orig. Cincinnatus Heine Miller (1837–1913), Amer. poet. Noted for *Songs of the Sierras* (1871), group of frontier poems.

miller's thumb *see* BULLHEAD.

millet, name for several cereal and forage grasses, *e.g.* common millet, *Panicum milleaceum.* Grown in Asia, N Africa and S Europe. N Amer. foxtail millet, *Setaria italica,* used for fodder.

Millet, Jean Francois (1814–75), Fr. painter of Barbizon school. Work characterized by large, linear human figures. Paintings include *The Reapers* (1854), *The Gleaners* (1857).

Millikan, Robert Andrew (1868–1953), Amer. physicist and teacher. Awarded Nobel Prize for Physics (1923) for measurement of charge of electron and study of photo-electric phenomena.

millipede, terrestrial arthropod of class Diplopoda. Cylindrical body composed of between 20 and 100 segments, each with 2 pairs of legs. Many species, *e.g. Glomeris marginata,* roll into a ball.

Mills, Robert (1781–1855), Amer. architect. Best known for Washington Monument (1836).

Milk Cap Fungus

Milne, A[lan] A[lexander] (1882–1956), Eng. author and playwright. Children's books include *When We Were Very Young* (1924), *Winnie-the-Pooh* (1926). Plays include *Mr. Pim Passes By* (1919).

Miltiades (d. 489 BC), Athenian general. Defeated Persians at BATTLE OF MARATHON (490 BC).

Milton, John (1608–74), Eng. poet. Early works include 'L'Allegro' and elegy 'Lycidas'. Sided with Puritans during Civil War, served as Cromwell's sec. during Protectorate. Became blind, wrote sonnet 'On His Blindness'. Later wrote blank verse epics *Paradise Lost* (1667), story of Satan's rebellion against God, *Paradise Regained* (1671) and drama *Samson Agonistes* (1671).

Milwaukee, largest city in Wisconsin,

Water Milfoil

15th cent. Flemish miniature depicting assembly of the Order of the Golden Fleece

US, on L. Michigan. Trading post (1795); site of Ger. refugee settlement (1848). Industries include brewing, heavy electrical machinery, diesel and petrol engines. Pop. (1960) 741,000.

mimosa, genus of leguminous trees, shrubs or herbs mostly native to trop. and subtrop. America. Several species respond to light and touch esp. *M. pudica,* the sensitive plant. Related species include ACACIA of Africa and Australia.

mimulus, monkey flower, genus of herbs or shrubs, mostly of temperate N America. Species include common monkey flower, *Mimulus guttatus,* and common musk, *M. moschatus.*

Min *see* CHINESE.

minaret, tower on corner of Islamic mosque from which muezzin calls the faithful to prayer. Common in Middle East countries.

Minch, The, sea channel between Outer Hebrides and mainland of Scotland.

Mindanao, 2nd largest island of S Philippines. Area: 36,540 sq. mi.; chief town, Zamboanga. Pop. (1960) 5,359,000.

Mindszenty, Joseph (1892–   ), Hungarian cardinal. Catholic primate of Hungary, arrested and sentenced for life (1948) for opposing Communist regime. Freed during 1956 revolt, took refuge in US legation, Budapest. Left for Rome (1971).

mine, explosive weapon used in warfare; land mine is buried charge of high explosive; discharged by pressure or by electrical means; naval mines comprise explosive charge in metal case secured to sea bottom by cable.

mine, excavation for extraction of metallic ores and other minerals (*e.g.* coal) from earth's crust; may be surface quarries, sub-surface or sub-marine system of shafts and galleries.

mineral, naturally occurring substance of definite chemical composition forming earth's crust.

mineralogy, the science and study of minerals.

Minerva, orig. Ital. goddess of craftsmen and trade guilds, introduced to Rome from Etruria. Regarded by Romans as daughter of Jupiter and one of principal deities; later identified with Gk. Pallas Athene, whose warlike characteristics she assimilated.

Ming, Chinese dynasty (1368–1644), Ruled China after defeating Mongols; founder, Chu Yüan-chang, estab. cap. at Peking. Empire extended from Korea to Burma at its height. Period marked by literary excellence, fine porcelain. Supplanted by Manchu dynasty.

miniature, art form of small paintings, frequently portraits. Early miniatures on card or vellum developed from manuscript illuminations; form flourished in Persia and India in medieval period. During 18th and 19th cent., ivory and porcelain used and miniatures worn as jewellery.

mining engineering, art and science of extracting metallic ores and minerals of economic value from the earth.

mink, slender semi-aquatic mammal of genus *Mustela* of weasel family. Thick, soft coat of N Amer. mink, *M. vison* is popular fur.

Minkowski, Hermann (1864–1909),

Miniature from a 15th cent. breviary

Miniature: *Adoration of the Wise Men* in an 11th cent. gospel of the School of Echternach

Russ. mathematician. Evolved 4-dimensional geometry, basis of mathematical formulation of theory of relativity.

Minneapolis, city of E Minnesota, US, on Mississippi R., Twin City of St Paul. Indust. and commercial centre of rich mineral region and power supply. City begun 1847; early timber depot. Seat of University of Minnesota, opened 1869. Pop. (1960) 483,000.

Minnesingers, Ger. lyric poets of 12th–13th cent. Sang of love, religion, politics. Influenced by TROUBADOURS; succeeded by MEISTERSINGERS. Included Walther von der Vogelweide, Wolfram von Eschenbach.

Minnesota, N state of US. Area: 84,068 sq. mi.; cap. St Paul; large cities Minneapolis, Duluth. Settled orig. by Fr. fur traders (1679); became British after Seven Years War; ceded to US 1783; became state, 1858. Economy depends largely on agriculture; largest US producer of iron ore. Pop. (1960) 3,413,864.

minnow, *Phoxinus phoxinus,* smallest fish of carp family, common in fresh waters in Europe and Asia. Male is brightly coloured at breeding time. Used as bait by anglers.

Minoan Civilization, ancient civilization of Crete (3000–2100 BC), revealed by excavations at palace of Minos, Cnossus. Pictographic scripts, known as Linear A, and modified version, Linear B (deciphered by Michael Ventris in 1952), discovered largely through work of Sir Arthur Evans.

Minorca [**Menorca**], 2nd largest of Sp. BALEARIC ISLANDS in Med. sea. Area: 271 sq. mi.; cap. Mahon. Fruit and wine produced; tourism important. Pop. *c.* 45,000.

Minnow

Minos, in Gk. myth., king of Crete. Demanded tribute of 7 youths and 7 maidens from Athens to avenge death of son, Androgeus. Built Labyrinth to house Minotaur, offspring of wife Paiphae and bull he had refused to sacrifice to Poseidon; Minotaur slain by Theseus. Became a judge in the Underworld after his death.

Minot, George Richards (1885–1950), Amer. physician and pathologist. With G. H. Whipple and W. P. Murphy, awarded Nobel Prize for Physiology and Medicine (1934) for research on liver treatment of pernicious anaemia.

Minotaur see MINOS.

Minsk, cap. of Byelorussian SSR, W USSR, near Polish border. Occupied by Lithuanians, Poles, Germans, Russians. Key point in Russ. Revolution (1917). Manufactures machinery, shoes, chemicals. Pop. (1967) 717,000.

minster, orig. in England, church belonging to a monastery, e.g. York Cathedral, often called York Minster.

mint, Mentha, aromatic plant, native of Med. area, now widespread. Garden mint, M. rotundifolia, used for sauces and jellies. Peppermint, M. piperita, used in confectionery, soap and medicines. Spearmint, M. spicata, used in chewing gum and sauces.

Minto, 4th Earl of see ELLIOT, GILBERT JOHN MURRAY KYNYNMOND.

minuet, Fr. dance, introduced at the court of Louis XIV (c. 1650). Popular throughout Europe (17th–18th cent.).

Minute man, Amer. long-distance rocket with nuclear warhead; orig. had range (1962) of c. 14,000 km. More recent types have more extensive range.

Miocene see GEOLOGICAL TABLE.

Miquelon and Saint Pierre, group of islands lying off S coast of Newfoundland, Canada. Overseas territory of French Community. Area: 93 sq. mi. (Miquelon 83 sq. mi., St Pierre 10 sq. mi.); cap. St Pierre. Settled (c. 1660) by French. Cod fishing and processing main industry. Pop. 5,500.

Mirabeau, Honoré Gabriel Riqueti, Comte de (1749–91), Fr. nobleman. Elected to States-General as representative of 3rd estate, and became leader of National Assembly. Pres. of Jacobin club (1790) but lost favour because of attempt to establish constitutional monarchy.

miracle plays, medieval religious dramas presenting miracles of the Virgin Mary or the saints; Fr., Eng. and Ger. plays have survived. See PASSION PLAY.

Types of guided missile : 1. air-to-air passive target-seeker which is guided by heat or sound from target aircraft, 2. air-to-air target-seeker which emits its own radar beam to keep it on target, 3. air-to-air semi-active target-seeker, guided by radar signals from ground unit, which are reflected off the target aircraft, 4. beam-riding ground-to-air missile. One radar unit locates the target and informs the second unit which emits a continuous beam, directed at target, in which the missile 'rides'.

mirage, atmospheric optical phenomenon; arises from reflection and refraction of light in calm, extremely hot or cold air. Mainly seen in deserts, and at sea.

Miró, Joan (1893–), Sp. painter, with Dali originator of Surrealist movement. Works include Carnival of Harlequin and the ceramic Walls of the Sun and Moon in the UNESCO buildings, Paris.

Mises, Ludwig Edler von (1881–), Austrian-American economist. Author of standard text The Theory of Money and Credit (1912; Eng. tr. 1934).

Miskolc, city in NE Hungary, on Sajo R. Industrial centre with large metallurgical works. Pop. (1966) 171,000.

missile, general term for weapons of war (esp. rockets) which are directed at target from a distance. See GUIDED MISSILE.

Mississippi, state of S central US, W boundary formed by Mississippi R. Area: 47,716 sq. mi.; cap. Jackson; main cities, Natchez, Vicksburg. Sub-trop. climate. First settlement estab. by French (1699); W part became state (1817); seceded from Union (1861), readmitted (1870) after Civil War. Main crops, cotton, tung-oil, corn. Pop. 2,178,141.

Mississippi, main river (2,350 mi. long) of US. Rises in N Minn., flows S through central states to Gulf of Mexico, forming delta in Louisiana. Navigable S of Falls of St Anthony at Minneapolis. Chief tributaries are Ohio, Missouri, Arkansas and Red rivers; St Louis largest city on river.

Mississippian see GEOLOGICAL TABLE.

Missolonghi, Mesolongion, port on Gulf of Patras, W Greece. Besieged and captured by Turks (1825–6), retaken by Greeks (1829). Death place of Lord Byron (1824).

Missouri, C state of US. Area: 69,686 sq. mi.; cap. Jefferson City; major cities, Independence, St Louis. Prairie land in N and W, fertile lowlands, Mississippi alluvial plain in SE, Ozark Mts. in S. Part of LOUISIANA PURCHASE; entered Union (1821); remained in Union during Civil War, but strong sympathy for South. Agriculture, esp. livestock, important; chief US lead producer. Pop. (1960) 4,319,813.

Missouri Compromise, legislation (1820–1) passed by US Congress, providing for Missouri's entry into Union as slave state. Repealed under 1854 KANSAS-NEBRASKA BILL.

Missouri River, longest river of US (2,466 mi.), flowing SE through Missouri joining Mississippi 17 mi. above St Louis; drains area of 580,000 sq. mi. Main tributaries are Jefferson, Madison and Gallatin rivers.

mistle thrush, *Turdus viscivorus,* large European thrush. Feeds on mistletoe berries.

mistletoe, *Viscum album,* European evergreen, bushy plant. Yellowish flowers and white poisonous berries; parasitic on trees. Used as Christmas decoration.

mistral, cold, dry, powerful, N wind of Fr. Med. provinces.

Mistral, Frédéric (1830–1914), Provençal poet. Led Félibrige movement (1904), formed to promote Provençal as literary language. Works include *Mirèio* (1859, Eng. tr. 1867). Shared Nobel Prize for Literature (1904) with José Echegaray.

Mistral, Gabriela, orig. Lucila Godoy Alcayaga (1889–1957), Chilean poetess and educationalist. Works include *Desolación* (1922) and *Rondas para niños.* Awarded Nobel Prize for Literature (1945).

Mitchell, Margaret (1900–49), Amer. novelist and journalist. Author of *Gone with the Wind* (1936).

Mitchell, Sir Thomas (1792–1855), Austral. explorer and surveyor. Built many roads and bridges in New South

Dutch Interior (1928) by Miró

Wales. Later explored Victoria and the C region of the continent.

Mitchell, W[illiam] O[rmond] (1914–) Canadian author of novels and short stories. They include *Canadian Short Stories* (1960), *Jake and the Kid* (1962).

Mithras, in ancient Persian myth., god of light and truth. In some respects rites of Mithras similar to Christianity. Worshipped in Rome throughout imperial era, esp. by army, and in 2nd cent. more prevalent than Christianity.

Mithridates VI, Eupator (*c.* 132–63 BC), king of Pontus. Expansion of power brought conflict with Rome resulting in Mithridatic Wars, First (88–84 BC), Second (83–81 BC), Third (74–63 BC); finally defeated by Lucullus and Pompey.

Mitterand, François Maurice (1916–), Fr. polit. leader. Unsuccessful Pres. candidate against De Gaulle (1965). His unification of the Left almost resulted in defeat of Gaullists in 1967 election.

moa, extinct flightless bird related to kiwi formerly abundant in New Zealand and still extant when Maoris arrived. Remains include bones, skin, feathers, *etc.* Giant moa, *Dinornis maximus* was *c.* 12 ft. tall.

Moabites, Semitic and Hebrew people of OT, living E of Dead Sea.

moccasin, cottonmouth, poisonous semi-aquatic snake, genus *Agkistrodon,* of N and C America. Some reach 5 ft. in length.

Mochica, S Amer. Indians of N coast of Peru. Advanced civilization at its height *c.* AD 450. Language allied to Yunca and Chimu. Some pure Mochica still live in Peru.

mock heroic, satirical poem in which insignificant people and events are treated in an epic framework. A leading example is Alexander Pope's *The Rape of the Lock.*

The Mississippi river

Lolotte (1917) by Modigliani

mock orange, syringa, deciduous shrub of genus *Philadelphus,* native to N America, Asia and Europe. Flowers similar to orange blossom.

mockingbird, N and S Amer. bird, allied to thrush and wren families. Noted for melodious song and as mimic. Species include common mockingbird, *Mimus polyglottos.*

Model Parliament, summoned 1295 by Edward I of England. Estab. precedent by formalizing representative principle; important stage in development of Eng. government.

moderator, presiding minister in the courts of the Presbyterian Church, *i.e.* presbytery, synod and the annual GENERAL ASSEMBLY.

modern art, term used loosely for painting and sculpture of late 19th and 20th cent. Taken to include in painting IMPRESSIONISM, FAUVISM, CUBISM and non-figurative art, which has wholly replaced objective with subjective representation.

Modigliani, Amedeo (1884–1920), Ital. painter and sculptor; influenced by African primitive art. Known for strangely elongated portraits.

Mogadishu, Mogadiscio, seaport and cap. of Repub. of Somalia. Taken by British (1941) in World War 2. Pop. (1965) 142,000.

Mogul, Mughal, Moslem empire of India. Dynasty founded (1526) by Baber, descendant of Tamerlane. Weakened (18th cent.) by Sikhs and Mahrattas, empire maintained by British until 1857.

mohair, fabric made from smooth glossy hair of Angora goat. Used by itself or combined with wool, silk, *etc.*

Mohammed, Muhammed, Mahomet (*c.* 570–632), founder of Islam, b. Mecca of Koreish tribe. His visions (*c.* 610), recorded in KORAN formed basis of new religion. Plot to kill him led to flight (Hegira) in 622 from Mecca to Medina, where he estab. basis of Mohammedan empire. Captured Mecca (630). Islamic law based on his sayings and on Koran.

Mohammed Ali (1769–1849), Egyptian pasha [governor] (1805–49), founder of royal house ended by estab. of repub. (1953). Military success led to subjugation of Cairo (1805); defence of Arabia and Greece until defeated at Navarino (1827). Denied Syrian governorship by Ottoman sultan, occupied Syria (1833). European intervention thwarted his revolt of 1839 in Asia Minor.

Mohammedanism, alternative name for ISLAM, religion of Moslems.

Mohave, N Amer. Indians of Yuman linguistic stock. Inhabited Colorado river region (18th cent.). Some 1,000 survive.

Mohawk *see* IROQUOIS.

Mohawk Trail, route of Mohawk Indians between Hudson and Connecticut rivers, now followed by State highway 2. Formerly used by settlers emigrating W.

Mohegan, Mohican, N Amer. Indians of Algonkian linguistic stock of SW Connecticut. Broke from Pequot rule and, supported by British, became one of most powerful tribes of S New England. Increase of white settlement led to virtual extinction by 19th cent.

Mohican *see* MOHEGAN.

Moholy-Nagy, László or **Ladislaus** (1895–1946), Hungarian painter, designer, writer. Experimented with new materials, *e.g.* plexiglass. Taught at BAUHAUS; founded Institute of Design, Chicago (1937). Influenced by CONSTRUCTIVISM.

Mohorovicic discontinuity, boundary between Earth's crust and denser mantle beneath. Discovered by Andrija Mohorovicic (1857–1936), Croatian geologist.

Mohs, Friedrich (1773–1839), Ger. mineralogist. Developed Mohs' scale of HARDNESS.

Moiseiwitsch, Benno (1890–1963), Eng. pianist, b. Russia. Noted for interpretations of Romantic works.

Moissan, Henri (1852–1907), Fr. chemist. Devised electric arc furnace (1892) and produced 1st artificial diamonds (1897). Awarded Nobel Prize for Chemistry (1906) for isolating fluorine.

molasses, thick brown syrup obtained from refining of cane and beet sugar. Used in making rum and treacle.

Moldavia, region of E Romania. Area: 14,694 sq. mi.; cap. Jassy. Comprises Carpathians in W; fertile plain in E is major wheat source. After death of Prince Stephen the Great (1504), came under Turkish control. Romanian rights estab. 1859. Pop. (1967 est.) 3,150,000.

Moldavian SSR, constituent repub. of USSR. Area: 13,017 sq. mi.; cap. Kishinev. Separated from Romania by Pruth R. Formerly Bessarabia, incorporated (1940) after Romania had ceded Bessarabia back to Russia. Pop. (1966) 3,425,000.

mole, small insectivore of Europe, Asia and N America. European common mole, *Talpa europaea* has black velvety fur; food mainly earthworms. Excavates underground passages with spade-like feet. Species include E Amer. common mole, *Scalapus aquaticus,* which has webbed feet.

mole cricket, burrowing cricket of Gryllotalpidae family with spade-like forelegs. Feeds mainly on plant roots.

molecular weight, the sum of the relative weights of the atoms of which a molecule is composed. Used as basic measure of substance.

molecule, smallest portion of a substance able to exist independently and retain properties of original substance.

Molière, orig. Jean Baptiste Poquelin

The *Mona Lisa* by Leonardo da Vinci

(1622– 73), Fr. playwright and actor. Joined company of players which, in 1680, became the Comédie Française. Under patronage of Louis XIV, wrote his great comedies of character, ridiculing a vice or trait of character. His plays, which have been performed all over the world, include *Tartuffe* (1664), *Don Juan* (1665), *Le Misanthrope* (1666), *Le Bourgeois Gentilhomme* (1670).

mollusc, invertebrate of phylum Mollusca. Calcareous shell of one, two or more pieces, enclosing soft unsegmented body. Includes snail, bivalve, squid, *etc.*

Moloch, pagan fire god, worshipped by the Ammonites and Phoenicians in ancient Palestine. Children were burned as a sacrifice to him.

Molotov, Vyacheslav Mikhailovich, orig. V. M. Skriabin (1890–   ), Soviet polit. leader. Foreign min. (1939–49; 1953– 7), negotiated non-aggression pact (1939) with Germany. Influence within Communist party declined with Khrushchev's rise; expelled 1964.

Moltke, Helmuth Karl Bernhard, Graf von (1800–91), Prussian field marshal. With support of Bismarck effected large-scale reorganization of Prussian army (1858–63). Largely responsible for Prussian victories against Austria and France.

Moluccas, Maluku, formerly **Spice Islands,** group of islands in Indonesia between Celebes and New Guinea, incl. Ternate, Halmahera, Ceram and Amboina. Discovered by Portuguese

(*c.* 1512), taken by Dutch (17th cent.).

molybdenite, soft opaque mineral occurring in foliated masses or scales; resembles graphite.

molybdenum, white, high-melting point metal element used as alloy with iron in manufacture of hard high-speed cutting tools.

Mombasa, city and seaport of Kenya, on Indian ocean. With harbour at Kilindini, centre of foreign trade. Exports coffee, cotton, sisal, tea. Pop. (1962) 180,000.

Mon Khmer, language family of SE Asia, comprising Mon, of Burma, and Khmer, of Cambodia.

Mona Lisa [Ital: **La Giaconda**], world-famous painting by Leonardo da Vinci; in Louvre, Paris.

Saltwater Molluscs: 1. Common Whelk 2. Common Cockle 3. Common Limpet 4. Common Periwinkle 5. Common Wentletrap 6. American Piddock 7. Sword Razor Shell 8. Wavy Venus 9. Baltic Tellin 10. Banded Wedge Shell 11. Thin Tellin 12. Rusty Montacute. Freshwater Molluscs: 1. Great Pond Snail 2. Great Ramshorn 3. Painter's Mussel 4. Zebra-Mussel

Monaco, [**Principauté de Monaco**], principality on Med. Sea surrounded by France. Area: 0·6 sq. mi.; cap. Monaco-Ville. Comprises old town of

Monaco, La Condamine and Monte Carlo to E. Ruled by Phoenicians, Greeks, Romans, Lombards, Spain, France, Sardinia, and Princes of House of Grimaldi, assisted by Fr. minister of state since 1911. Economy depends on tourism. Unit of currency, Fr. franc. Pop. (1964) 23,000.

Monaghan, inland county of Repub. of Ireland. Area: 499 sq. mi.; county town, Monaghan. Mainly agric., also linen and lace manufacture. Pop. (1966) 45,726.

monarch butterfly, milkweed butterfly, *Danaus plexippus,* black-veined, brown butterfly, common in North, Central and South America. Feeds on milkweeds.

monarchy, form of govt. in which executive authority is exercised by 1 person. Flourished (16th–18th cent.) in Europe when monarch was invested with absolute, indisputable powers. Impetus supplied by democratic ideas and rise of modern indust. state reduced, in most cases, role of monarch to that of symbolic figurehead.

monasticism, organized community life for religious purposes. Feature of Christianity from 1st cent.; also a feature of Buddhism, Jainism, Islam. Middle Ages in Europe saw rise of great monastic orders, *e.g.* Benedictines, Carthusians, Franciscans, Dominicans, *etc.,* who made contributions to architecture and learning as well as religion.

monazite, yellowish-brown mineral, phosphate of cerium and other metals. Only commercial source of rare-earth elements.

Monarch Butterfly

Mönch, peak (13,468 ft.) of Bernese Oberland, Switzerland. Climbed by Christian Almar and S. Porges (1857).

Monck, Charles Stanley, 4th Viscount Monck (1819–94), Gov.-general of Brit. N America (1861–7); 1st Gov.-general of Dominion of Canada (1867–8).

Monck or **Monk, George, 1st Duke of Albemarle** (1608–70), Eng. army commander and politician. Defeated Scots (1651) at head of Cromwellian army. After Cromwell's death, raised forces in support of Stuarts and effected RESTORATION of Charles II.

Mondrian, Piet (1872–1944), Dutch abstract painter. Works characterized by straight black lines, primary colours and rectangles.

Monet, Claude (1840–1926), leading Fr. Impressionist painter noted for

Monaco

works conveying atmospheric effects; as in series on Rouen Cathedral (1892–5), country landscapes, *etc.*

Moneta, Ernesto Teodoro (1833–1918), Ital. journalist and pacifist. Worked with Garibaldi for unification of Italy. Became interested in the cause of international peace. Awarded Nobel Peace Prize (1907) with Louis Renault.

money, in economics, unit of value or means of payment. Cattle often used as standard of value in ancient societies. Precious metals, durable and intrinsically valuable, became both unit of value and means of payment; govt. coinage instituted after 7th cent. BC. Paper currency (widely in use since 1650) usually based on valuable commodity, for which it can be exchanged upon demand. Also *see* GOLD STANDARD.

moneywort, creeping Jenny, creeping Charlie, *Lysimachia nummularia,* yellow-flowered creeping herb of European origin.

Mongolia, region of NE Asia, lying between Chinese and Russ. borders. Area: *c.* 906,000 sq. mi. Gobi Desert lies in middle of high plateau land. Exports include wool and hides. Conquered by Genghis Khan (1205). Incorporated by China; broke away (1921) became MONGOLIAN. PEOPLE'S REPUBLIC. Inner Mongolian Autonomous Region estab. by Chinese Communists (1949–56).

Mongolian, branch of Altaic language family. Has *c.* 3 million speakers inhabiting Mongolian People's Republic, China and USSR.

Mongolian People's Republic, in-

dependent Asian state comprising most of MONGOLIA. Area: 558,094 sq. mi.; cap. Ulan Bator. Repub. estab. 1924, closely allied itself with USSR. Main religion, Lamaist Buddhism. Unit of currency, tugrik. Pop. (1966 est.) 1,050,000.

mongolism, type of mental deficiency, form of idiocy; so-called because afflicted person has mongoloid appearance, with slanting eyes and flattened nose.

Mongols, nomadic Asiatic tribe from plains E of L. Baikal; under Genghis Khan, Tamerlane and Baber, empire extended over Asia to China and India and into C Europe (12th–16th cent.). Expelled from China (1368); from Russia (1480).

mongoose, small, slender carnivorous mammal of genus *Herpestes*; feeds on rodents, birds' eggs, *etc.*; noted for snake-killing powers. Species include crab-eating mongoose, *H. urba,* and common Indian mongoose, *H. edwardsi.*

The Gare St Lazare by Monet

Monitor, naval vessel designed for coastal bombardment; named after Union turret-ship *Monitor* in American Civil War. Involved in drawn battle in Hampton Roads (1862) with Confederate frigate *Merrimac*.

monitor lizard, large long-bodied trop. lizard of genus *Varanus*. Long forked tongue; aquatic and terrestrial. Species include African lizard, *V. niloticus*.

Moniz, Egas (1874–1955), Portuguese physician. With W. R. Hess, awarded Nobel Prize for Physiology and Medicine (1949) for development of brain surgery as treatment for certain mental diseases.

monkey, mammal of order Primates, incl. guenons, macaques, langurs, capuchins, *etc*. Found in trop. parts of Africa, S America and Asia.

monkey flower *see* MIMULUS.

monkey puzzle, Chile pine, *Araucaria*

Apple Tree by Mondrian

Monkey: white-handed gibbon

View of the Mont Blanc massif

imbricata, S Amer. evergreen tree. Branches in tiers with spirals of stiff leaves; edible nuts.

monkfish, *Squatina squatina,* small sea-bottom dwelling shark. Large pectoral and ventral fins; feeds on molluscs and crustaceans.

monkshood, perennial herb of genus *Aconitum,* esp. *A. napellus,* native to N temp. regions, with hood-shaped flowers. All species are poisonous.

Monmouth, James Scott, Duke of (1649–85), natural son of Charles II of England and Lucy Walters; created Duke of Monmouth (1663) A Protestant, Shaftesbury and Whigs failed to secure succession for him by Exclusion Bill. Led rebellion against Catholic James II; defeated at Sedgemoor (1685) and beheaded.

Monmouthshlre, county of W England, on border with Wales. Area: 546 sq. mi.; county town, Monmouth; other towns, Newport, Abergavenny. Hilly in N and NW. Sheep farming, coal mining and associated industries important. Pop. (1966) 463,000.

Monnet, Jean (1888–), Fr. political economist. Sec.-General of League of Nations (1918). Produced Monnet Plan for revival of Fr. industry and agriculture (1947). Advocated European polit. unification and common market; Pres. of European Coal and Steel Community (1952–5).

monocotyledon, plant of subclass Monocotyledoneae with 1 seed-leaf (cotyledon). Stems usually hollow or soft, *e.g.* palms, bamboos, grains, cereal plants; foliage leaves parallel-veined.

monopoly, in economics, virtual control of supply, enabling owner to fix price at which consumer must purchase product. Legislation places restraints on monopolistic tendencies; in US, Sherman Anti-Trust Act (1890), subsequently reinforced; in UK, Monopolies Commission set up 1948. Govt. monopolies (*e.g.* postal system) operated to facilitate public services, socialist doctrine extends monopoly principle to all basic industries, *e.g.* Brit. Labour govt.'s nationalization of steel.

monosodium glutamate, white crystalline salt extracted from grains or beets. Soluble in water; intensifies flavours, used widely in tinned food.

monotheism, belief in one god as ruler of the universe. Christian, Jewish and Mohammedan religions are monotheistic.

monotreme, egg-laying animal of mammalian subclass Monotremata, comprising only duckbill and echidnas of Australia. Reptilian features and no teeth; secrete milk.

monotype, form of typesetting in which each letter is a separate unit. Machine, with separate keyboard and casting units, invented by Tolbert Lanston (1887).

Monroe, James (1758–1831), 5th US Pres. (1817–25) Democratic-Republican. Sec. of State (1811–17), his 2 term admin. was known as the 'era of good feeling'. Acquired Florida, signed MISSOURI COMPROMISE and promulgated MONROE DOCTRINE.

Monroe, Marilyn, orig. Norma Jean Mortenson (1926–62), Amer. film actress and comedienne. Her films included *Asphalt Jungle, All About Eve, Bus Stop, Some Like it Hot, The Misfits.*

Monroe Doctrine, Amer. foreign policy statement, enunciated in Pres.

The Mont Blanc massif

Monroe's 1823 speech to Congress. Result of disagreement with Russia over NW North Amer. boundaries and fear of European attempts to regain Latin Amer. colonies, which had recently become independent. Opposed to all forms of European interference in the Americas. Provided basis for much subsequent Amer. foreign policy.

Monrovia, cap. and chief port of Liberia, founded (1821) by Amer. Colonization Society for freed slaves. Economy depends on rubber exports to US. Pop. (1962) 81,000.

monsoon, seasonal wind of Pacific and Indian oceans bringing rain to E and SE Asia, India and NE Australia.

monstera, several evergreen climbing plants of order Aroideae, with ornamental foliage. Species include *M. deliciosa* of Mexico.

Mont Blanc, highest peak (15,781 ft.) of the Alps, on France-Italy border. First climbed (1786); highway tunnel through mountain opened 1965.

Montagnais, tribe of Algonkian N Amer. Indians, inhabiting E Mackenzie area. Hunted caribou, small game and fish.

Montagu, Lady Mary Wortley (1689–1762), Eng. author. Wrote *Turkish Letters* when husband was ambassador to Turkey, published with later letters to Lady Bute (her daughter) in 1763. On her return to Britain she introduced smallpox inoculation.

Montagu, Mrs. Elizabeth (1720–1800), Eng. essayist and wit, well-known as one of the leaders of the BLUESTOCKING coterie.

Montaigne, Michel Eyquem de (1533–92), Fr. essayist and moralist. Lived at court of Francis II. From 1571 wrote essays which made him famous. Prophet of tolerance, prudence, urbane scepticism and commonsense.

Montana, state of NW US. Area: 147,138 sq. mi.; cap. Helena; main cities, Great Falls, Billings. Rolling agric. plains in E; mountains in W. Drained by Missouri, Yellowstone, Kootenai rivers. Wheat, barley, sugar beet grown. Mineral resources include petroleum, copper, zinc. Timber and tourism important. Pop. (1960) 674,767.

montbretia, common name for *Tritonia* genus of S African flowering plants. Naturalized in Europe, garden varieties include orange-crimson *T. crocosmiflora*.

Montcalm de Saint-Servan, Louis-Joseph de Montcalm-Gazon, Marquis de (1712–59), Fr. army officer. Sent to Canada (1756) to command Fr.

forces during French and Indian War. Captured Oswego (1756), Fort William (1757) and defended Ticonderoga against larger Brit. force (1758). Died while defending Quebec on PLAINS OF ABRAHAM against British under James Wolfe.

Monte Carlo, resort and port of MONACO, on Côte d'Azur, France. Once known mainly for Casino, founded 1858. Pop. (1956) 9,038.

Monte Carlo Rally, yearly long-distance car speed and endurance trial. Originated 1911; starting points throughout Europe, finish in Monte Carlo.

Monte Cassino, mountain of Campania, S Italy; site of abbey founded (529) by St Benedict; scene of heavy fighting in World War 2; abbey damaged, rebuilt (1956).

Monte Cristo, Ital. island of Tuscan Archipelago. Area: *c.* 4 sq. mi. Mountainous terrain.

Montenegro, federal repub. of Yugoslavia. Area: 5,333 sq. mi.; cap. Titograd. Part of Serbia; became independent 14th cent.; voted to join Yugoslavia (1918). Economy based on agriculture, salt processing and bauxite. Pop. (1961) 471,000.

Monterrey, 3rd city of Mexico, founded as León (1560); named Monterrey (1599). Pop. (1967) 901,000.

Montesquieu, Charles Louis de Secondat, Baron de la Brède et de (1689–1755), Fr. political philosopher, magistrate at Bordeaux. Wrote *Lettres Persanes* (1721) satirizing contemporary Fr. life and institutions. His analysis of the state and law in *L'Esprit des Lois* (1740) had considerable influence, esp. on US constitution and on projected reforms

The Casino, Monte Carlo

to Constituent Assembly in France.

Montessori, Maria (1870–1952), Ital. educ. theorist; originated system of spontaneous education for young children; described in *Montessori Method* (1912).

Monteux, Pierre (1875–1964), Fr. conductor. Conducted several Diaghilev productions in Europe and US; also symphony orchestras incl. Boston and London Symphony Orchestras.

Monteverdi, Claudio (1567–1643), Ital. composer of church music, madrigals and opera. Operas include *Orfeo* (1607) and *Arianna* (1608).

Montevideo, cap. of Uruguay, on Rio de la Plata; a major port of S America. Founded (1726) as military port. Now transport, govt., indust., commercial centre. Contains national university. Pop. (1964) 1,203,700.

Monstera deliciosa, popularly known as the Swiss Cheese plant

Moorhen

Montezuma II (*c.* 1480–1520), Aztec emperor of Mexico. Taken prisoner by CORTEZ at Sp. conquest; restored to throne but killed by former subjects.

Montfort, Simon de, Earl of Leicester (*c.* 1208–65), leader of revolt of barons against Henry III. Revocation (1261) of PROVISIONS OF OXFORD, which Montfort had helped draw up, led to Baron's War (1263–7). Victory at Lewes was followed by summoning

Montreal: American pavilion at Expo' '67

St Joseph's Oratory, Montreal

of Great Parliament, estab. precedent of representation in Eng. Parl. Defeated and killed at Evesham.

Montgolfier, Joseph Michel (1740–1810), Fr. inventor, with brother **Jacques Etienne Montgolfier,** of hot air balloon, which made 1st manned flight (1783).

Montgomery, cap. of Alabama, US; 1st settled 1817. Scene of formation of Confederate States (1861); known as 'Cradle of Confederacy'. Manufacturing and transport centre. Pop. (1963) 143,000.

Montgomery, Bernard Law, 1st Viscount Montgomery of Alamein (1887–), Eng. army officer, commanded Brit. 8th Army in World War 2. Routed Ger. forces in N Africa (1942). Led land forces in invasion of Normandy (1944) and 21st army group in reconquest of Europe. Received Ger. surrender (1945).

Montgomery, L[ucy] M[aud] (1876–1942), Canadian author. Wrote novels, incl. *Anne of Green Gables* (1908), and poetry *The Watchmen, and Other Poems* (1917).

Montgomeryshire, county of N Wales. Area: 797 sq. mi.; county town, Montgomery. Mountainous (Plynlimmon 2,468 ft.), with fertile valleys in E. Slate, lead, limestone quarried. Pop. (1966) 44,000.

Montherlant, Henry Millon de (1896–), Fr. novelist, playwright and poet. Novels include *Les Célibataires* (1934), *Le Chaos et la Nuit* (1963).

Montmartre, area of N Paris on right bank of Seine; includes Sacré-Coeur Church. Centre for artists since 19th cent., now famous for night clubs, *etc.*

montmorillonite, clay mineral which expands on absorbing large quantities of water.

Montpellier, University of, founded (1289) at Montpellier, S France; orig. a medical school. Renowned since Middle Ages.

Montreal, largest city of Canada, Montreal Island, Quebec, on St Lawrence R. Large inland port; chief commercial and indust. centre. Founded, then settled (1642) by French. Cap. of Canadian provs. (1844–9). Advent of World Exhibition (Expo '67) brought increased tourist interest. Pop. (1964) 2,260,000.

Montreal, University of, co-educational, Fr. language university. Founded 1878 as Montreal branch of Laval Univ.

Montrose, James Graham, 5th Earl and 1st Marquis of (1612–50), Scot. soldier. Led Covenanters against Charles I, invaded England (1640).

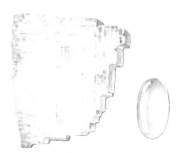

Moonstone in its raw and polished state

Later supported Charles and defeated Presbyterians with Highland army. After Charles' defeat at Naseby and his own at Philiphaugh (1645) fled to Norway. Attempted to raise rebellion in Edinburgh (1650), captured and hanged by Parliament.

Monts, Pierre de Gua, Sieur de (1558–1628), Fr. founder of 1st permanent settlement in Canada. Estab. Port Royal (1605) and sent Champlain to found Quebec (1608).

Mont-Saint-Michel, rocky, fortified island off coast of Brittany, NW France. Connected to mainland by causeway. Contains Benedictine abbey, founded 708.

Montserrat, volcanic island, British Leeward group, W Indies. Area: 32 sq. mi.; cap. and port Plymouth. Discovered (1493) by Columbus; exports cotton, tomatoes and lime products. Pop. (1960) 12,157.

Montserrat, mountain (4,054 ft.), NE Spain, NW of Barcelona. Benedictine monastery built at 2,910 ft.

Moon, only natural satellite of Earth; diameter 2,162 mi. Revolves around earth each month (27 days, 7 hr., 43 min.) at mean distance of 238,857 mi. always showing same face. Other side 1st photographed by Russ. rocket vehicle Lunik III (1959). Shines by reflected light from Sun; said to be full when opposite Sun and new when between Earth and Sun and partly visible. *See* also ECLIPSE.

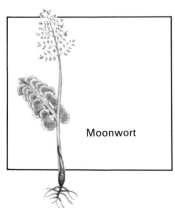

Moonwort

moonfish, horsefish, horsehead, silvery, marine fish of genus *Vomer* with compressed body. Also the opah, *Lampris luna,* edible fish with scarlet fins.

moonstone, translucent, semi-precious pearly form of feldspar. Used as a gem.

moonwort, *Botrychium lunaria,* fern of cold and temp. regions.

Moore, George (1852–1933), Irish novelist and poet. Works include *Esther Waters* (1894), *The Brook Kerith* (1916), *Héloïse and Abélard* (1921).

Moore, Henry (1898–   ), Eng. sculptor. Works in wood, stone, concrete and bronze characterized by organic shape and holes. Executed 'Reclining Figure' for UNESCO building, Paris.

Moore, Sir John (1761–1809), Scot. general, in command of Brit. army sent to Portugal to help Spaniards against Napoleon. Killed in retreat at Corunna.

Moore, Marianne (1887–   ), Amer. poet. Works include *Poems* (1921), *What Are Years* (1941), *O to be a Dragon* (1959).

Moore, Thomas (1779–1852), Irish poet. Works include *Irish Melodies* (1808–34), *Lalla Rookh* (1817).

moorhen, waterhen [UK], **gallinule** [US], *Gallinula chloropus,* common water bird of rail family, frequenting small ponds.

moorland, tract of untilled high ground usually having poor, peaty soil. Often heather-covered; used for sheep-grazing and as source of peat.

Moors, nomadic people of N Africa. Became Moslem *c.* 8th cent.; conquered Spain (711); founded a kingdom which lasted until reconquered by Ferdinand and Isabella (1492). Influenced W European art, architecture, medicine and science.

moose, *Alces americanus,* large animal of deer family. Inhabits Canada and N US. Heavy body, long legs and branching antlers.

moraine, rock debris, carried by glacier or ice sheet. Large angular boulders and rock fragments transported, forming lateral, medial, ground or terminal moraines.

Moral Re-Armament, movement started (1938) by Dr. Frank N. D. Buchman, Amer. anti-Communist evangelist.

morality plays, didactic medieval verse dramas in which Biblical characters of the earlier MYSTERY PLAYS give place to abstractions of vice and virtue. They include *Ane Pleasant Satyre of the Three Estaits,* and *Everyman.*

Moravia, forested district of Czecho-

Photograph of the Moon's surface made by an American satellite

slovakia, E of Bohemian plateau. Agric. and mining area. Chief towns Brno and Ostrava.

Moravia, Alberto (1907–   ), Ital. writer and journalist. Works include *The Woman of Rome* (1947; Eng. tr. 1949), *Conjugal Love* (1949; Eng. tr. 1951), *Two Women* (1957; Eng. tr. 1958).

Moravians, Protestant episcopal sect founded in Bohemia (15th cent.) as offshoot of Hussites; revived in Saxony (18th cent.). Missionary work continues.

Moraviantown, Battle of, encounter (Oct. 1813) near Thames R., S Ontario, during War of 1812. Amer. forces defeated retreating Brit. and Indian troops. Indian leader, Tecumseh, was killed. Also known as Battle of the Thames.

Moray, Earl of *see* STUART, JAMES.

moray eel, marine eel of family Muraenidae, with narrow jaws, strong teeth and no tongue. In Med. region, *Muraena helena,* valued as food fish.

Morayshire, formerly Elginshire, county of NE Scotland. Area: 467 sq. mi.; county town, Elgin; other towns, Kinloss, Lossiemouth. Mountainous in S, lowland in N; agriculture, salmon fishing, whisky distilling. Pop. (1966) 51,000.

More, Sir Thomas (1478–1535), Eng. scholar and lawyer. Lord Chancellor of England (1529–32). Accused of high treason (1534) for refusing to recognize the king (Henry VIII) as head of the Church, and executed. His most famous work is *Utopia.* Canonized 1935.

Moreau, Gustave (1826–98), Fr. painter. Subjects chiefly classical or religious, *e.g. Athenians with the*

Minotaur (1855), *Moses on the Nile* (1878).

morel, edible mushroom of genus *Marchella. M. esculenta,* the commonest, is found in deciduous woods and pastures.

Morenz, Howie (1900–37), Canadian ice hockey player, known as the 'Stratford Streak'. Scored 270 goals, most of them while playing with Montreal Canadiens.

Morgan, J[ohn] P[ierpont] (1837–1913), Amer. financier and philanthropist. Enlarged family fortune, built indust. empire, esp. in rly. holdings. Formed (1901) US Steel Corporation, became symbol of wealth. Renowned art collector.

Morgan, Thomas Hunt (1866–1945), Amer. zoologist. Awarded Nobel Prize for Physiology and Medicine (1933) for research into genetics.

Mörike, Eduard (1804–75), Ger. poet of the Swabian School. Wrote love and nature poems, also short stories.

Moriscos, name given to Sp. Mohammedans baptised as Christians; 1568 edict demanded abandonment of all remaining Moorish customs, leading to revolt and persecution of Moriscos. Finally expelled from Spain (1609).

Morison, Samuel Eliot (1887–   ), Amer. historian; works include *Admiral of the Ocean Sea* (1942), *John Paul Jones* (1959).

Morisot, Berthe (1841–95), Fr. impressionist painter, influenced by Manet and Monet. Works include *La Toilette.*

Morley, Thomas (1557–1602), Eng. composer and organist of St Paul's Cathedral, London. Composed church music, madrigals, lute songs and instrumental music. Published *A*

Plaine and Easie Introduction to Practicall Musick (1597).

mormon cricket, *Anabrus simplex,* wingless, long-horned grasshopper of W US. Destructive to crops.

Mormons, Church of Jesus Christ of Latter-Day Saints, evangelical religious sect founded (1830) by Joseph Smith who claimed to have received divine revelations incl. alleged pre-Columban history of the Amer. people to AD 60. After death of Smith, BRIGHAM YOUNG became leader, transferred centre of movement to Salt Lake City, Utah.

morning glory, common name for various flowering bindweeds of genera *Ipomoea* and *Argyreia.* Amer. variety, *I. purfurea,* annual purple-flowered vine; *A. splendeus,* silver morning glory, native to trop. Asia.

Morocco, [**El Maghreb el Aqsa**], Arab monarchy of NW Africa on Med. and Atlantic. Area: 170,382 sq.

mi.; cap. Rabat; traditional caps. Fez, Marrakesh. Ruled by Romans, Vandals, Byzantines, Arabs, Spaniards and French; independence recognized by France and Spain (1956). Main activities, agriculture, producing Med. crops, and mining. Industry concentrated in Casablanca. Main language, Arabic; main religion, Islam. Unit of currency, dirham. Pop. (1964) 13,451,000.

morphine, bitter crystalline alkaloid derived from opium. Isolated (1806) by A. Sertürner. Used in medicine to relieve pain, induce sleep, and as a sedative.

Morphy, Paul Charles (1837–84), Amer. chess player. Recognized as World Champion (1858–9) at the age of 21; gave up chess 8 yr. later.

Morrice, James Wilson (1865–1924), Canadian landscape painter, influenced by Fauvism. Works include *Venice Night* and *Dieppe: The Beach.*

Morris, William (1834–96), Brit. artist, writer and socialist. Founder of Art and Crafts social and artistic movement. Noted for standards of design in house furnishings and in printing at Kelmscott Press, founded 1890. Works include *The Earthly Paradise* (1868–70), *Socialism: Its Growth and Outcome* (1893).

morris dancing, Eng. country dancing of great age and possibly Moorish origin.

Morrison, Herbert Stanley, Baron Morrison of Lambeth (1888–1965), Brit. statesman. Home Sec. and Min. of Home Security (1940–5). Leader of House of Commons (1945–51) under Labour govt.; Foreign Sec. (1951). Deputy Leader of opposition (1951–55).

Morse, Samuel F[inley] B[reese] (1791–1872), Amer. painter and inventor. A founder of National Academy of Design (1825). Invented electric telegraph, devised MORSE CODE and experimented with submarine cable and telegraphy.

Morse Code, system of communication devised (1837) by Samuel Morse and Alfred Vail. In telegraphy, combinations of dots and dashes (short and long taps) represent letters of alphabet and numerals.

mortar, cannon of muzzle-loading type, of 15th cent. Ital. origin, used for projecting shells short distances at steep angles. Modern mortar fires smoke bombs, flares and high explosives.

mortgage, conveyance of property (usually house or land) as security for loan.

Mortillet [Louis Laurent Marie] Gabriel de (1821–98), Fr. archaeologist. First to divide prehistoric epochs by chronological classification. Investigated Swiss lake dwellings.

Mortimer, Roger de, 1st Earl of March (c. 1287–1330), Eng. soldier. Opposed Edward II in baronial wars (1321–2) and fled to France, where Queen Isabella became his mistress. Their invasion of England led to Edward's abdication (1326). Virtually ruled England until Edward III had him executed.

mortmain, term used, orig. in Middle Ages, for land held by church or other body, never liable for death duties.

Morton, Jelly Roll, orig. Ferdinand Joseph La Menthe (1885–1941), Amer. jazz pianist, composer, band leader. Figured in Creole-influenced New Orleans jazz. Compositions include *Jelly Roll Blues* and *Sidewalk Blues.*

mosaic, surface ornamentation by inlaying small pieces of stone, tile, metal or glass. Used principally for decoration of floors and walls. The art was perfected by Byzantines (6th cent.); revived by Italians (13th cent.) but declined with introduction of frescoes (14th cent.).

Mosaic Law, laws by which the Jewish people were governed, contained in the Pentateuch (first 5 books of OT), chiefly in *Leviticus* and *Deuteronomy* based on 10 Commandments given to Moses on Mt. Sinai.

moschatel, *Adoxa moschatellina,* small herbaceous plant, native to temp. regions. Greenish flowers and musky odour.

Moscow, Moskva, cap. of USSR, on Moskva R. Indust., transport, communications, govt. centre. Produces chemicals textiles, aircraft, rolling stock, precision instruments, machinery, steel. Contains KREMLIN, University of Lomonosov (founded 1755), Moscow Art Theatre, Bolshoi Theatre. Superseded by St Petersburg as cap. (1713–1922). Entire city destroyed by fire (1812), forcing Napoleon to retreat. Pop. (1965) 6,443,000.

Moscow M. V. Lomonosov State University, oldest Russ. university. Founded (1755); dedicated to memory of 18th cent. scientist, Mikhail Vasilyevich Lomonosov.

Moscow-Volga Canal, waterway connecting Volga and Moscow rivers.

Moselle, Mosel, European river. Rises in Vosges Mts., NE France, flowing 320 mi. NE to join the Rhine at Koblenz. Area known for Moselle wine.

Moses, OT Jewish lawgiver, prophet and judge. Led Jews out of captivity in Egypt; received 10 commandments

Mosaic from a Roman villa at Piazza Armerina in Sicily

Mountain Goat

on Mt. Sinai; estab. organized Jewish religion. After leading tribes 40 yr., died before reaching Promised Land.

Moses, Anna Mary Robertson (1860–1961), Amer. primitive painter, known as 'Grandma Moses'. Began painting in her 70s; depicted scenes of farm life.

Moslem League, polit. organization, estab. (1906) to safeguard rights of Moslems in India and Pakistan. Demanded creation of separate Moslem state in 1940s; achieved in founding (1947) of Pakistan.

Moslem religion see ISLAM.

Mosley, Sir Oswald Ernald (1896–   ), Brit. politician, fascist leader. Organized (1932) British Union of Fascists. Wrote polit. and autobiog. works. Detained 1940–3; attempted to revive movement after World War 2.

mosque, building for Moslem worship. Main features are the *maksoura* (prayer hall), with its *mihrab* or prayer niche, indicating direction of Mecca, and the *dikka* (platform for services). First mosque built at Medina, Arabia, by Mohammed (622).

mosquito, insect of family Culicidae. Female sucks blood of animals and man; male is harmless. Malaria is transmitted by genus *Anopheles*; yellow fever by *Aedes aegypti*.

moss, small primitive plant of Musci class, of world-wide distribution. Grows in tufts on moist ground, tree trunks, rocks, *etc.* Sphagnum moss is a source of peat.

Moss, Stirling (1929–   ), Brit. motor racing driver. Brit. National Champion (1950–2, 1954–9); won European Grand Prix (1961).

moss animals, small moss-like animal of phylum Bryozoa, living mainly in the sea, attached to rocks, seaweeds or shells.

moss campion, cushion pink, *Silene acaulis,* perennial herb of Europe and N America. Deep pink flowers.

Mossadegh, Mohammed (1880–1967), Iranian statesman P.M. (1951–3). Nationalized Brit.-owned oil industry (1951). Attempt to overthrow Shah resulted in imprisonment (1953–6).

Mössbauer, Rudolf (1929–   ), Ger. physicist. Awarded Nobel Prize for Physics (1961) with Robert Hofstadter for method of producing and measuring recoil-free gamma-rays.

Mosul, 2nd city of Iraq. Administrative and strategic centre of N, on Tigris R. Probably built on site of ancient Assyrian fortress. Industries include cement, sugar beet and asphalt refining, cotton. Pop. (1965) 388,000.

motet, relatively short, freely contrapuntal piece of vocal music, usually unaccompanied, with Biblical or similar prose text.

moth, insect of order Lepidoptera, distinguished from butterfly by antennae of various types and nocturnal habits. Species include *Tinea pellionella,* clothes moth.

mother-of-pearl, hard iridescent pearly lining of various shells, esp. pearl oysters and mussels. Used for decorative work, jewellery, *etc.*

Motherwell, Robert (1915–   ), Amer. painter and writer. A leading US abstract Expressionist. Edited the *Documents of Modern Art* series (1944–57).

motion sickness, nausea and vomiting caused by effect of motion on labyrinth of ear; experienced on ships, motor vehicles, aircraft, *etc.*

motor car see AUTOMOBILE.

motor-cycling, use of motor cycle for recreation and organized competition. Races include [US] National Jack Pine 500 mi. championship, [UK] TT race, Isle of Man; Grand Prix races in Italy, Holland, France, Germany.

motor-racing, competitive sport for motor-vehicles, estab. 1894 in France. Present day events include Le Mans 24-hr., France; Mille Miglia, Italy; Indianapolis 500, US; annual Grand Prix races in 10 countries of the world, and Monte Carlo Rally.

motorway [UK], road designed to link centres of population; regulation of speed and use facilitate speed and obviate congestion. Modelled on Ital. autostrada, Ger. autobahn. US equivalent: Interstate Highway System.

Mott, John Raleigh (1865–1955), Amer. authority on foreign mission work. Chairman of World's Committee of YMCA from 1926. Awarded Nobel Peace Prize (1946) with Emily Balch.

moufflon, *Ovis musimon,* wild sheep of Corsica and Sardinia. White muzzle and rusty short wool. Male has long curved horns.

mould, name for minute fungi forming furry coating mostly on dead organic matter. Common forms are black bread mould, *Rhizopus nigricans,* and blue mould, *Penicillium.*

Mount Desert Island, island of Atlantic Ocean off NE Maine, US. Area: *c.* 100 sq. mi. Discovered (1604) by France. Became Amer. summer resort from 1868.

Mount Holyoake College, privately controlled college of arts and sciences for women, in South Hadley, Mass., US. Founded (1837) by Mary Lyon.

Mount McKinley National Park, reserve of S Alaska, US, incl. Mt. McKinley. Area: 3,034 sq. mi. Estab. 1917. Known for glaciers, forested valleys and wildlife.

Mount Pelée, active volcano (4,428 ft.) N Martinique, French West Indies. Erupted (1902) destroying St Pierre by gas clouds and killing over 30,000 people.

Mount Rainier National Park, in W Washington, US. Area: 379 sq. mi. Estab. 1899. Centred on Mt. Rainier, conical, ice-covered dormant volcano (14,410 ft.).

Mount Rushmore National Memorial, reserve of Black Hills, South Dakota, US. Area: *c.* 2 sq. mi. Estab. 1925. Faces of George Washington, Thomas Jefferson, Abraham Lincoln and Theodore Roosevelt carved on its face under supervision of Gutzon Borglum (1867–1941).

Mount Strombo, observatory at Australian National University.

Mount Vernon, home in Virginia of George Washington, now US national shrine.

Mount Wilson, peak (5,710 ft.) Sierra Madre, S Calif., US. Site of observatory housing tower telescope, reflecting telescope and spectro-heliograph; founded (1904) by G. E. Hale, supervised by Carnegie Institute.

mountain, elevation of Earth's crust in which summit area is small in proportion to base area. Formed by accumulation (*e.g.* volcanic), earth movement, giving rise to block mountains (*e.g.* Harz Mts.), folding (*e.g.* Jura Mts.) uplift, or combination of all factors (*e.g.* Himalayas, Andes).

mountain ash, species of deciduous trees and shrubs of genus *Sorbus.* Native to N temp. regions; white flowers and orange or red berries. *S. aucuparia,* European species; *S. americana,* Amer. species.

mountain beaver see SEWELLEL.

mountain-building, production of fold-mountain ranges by extreme compression of earth's crust with consequent movements and deformations.

mountain goat, Rocky mountain goat, *Oreamnos montanus,* goat-like mammal related to chamois. Sparsely distributed in mountains of W N America. Thick white coat; short black horns.

mountaineering, sport of climbing mountains. Developed (19th cent.) as French and British began to climb Alpine peaks. Alpine Club founded 1857. Highest known peak, Mt. Everest, 29,145 ft., climbed (1953) by Brit. expedition.

Mountbatten, Viscount Louis [Francis Albert Victor Nicholas] 1st Earl Mountbatten of Burma (1900–   ), Brit. naval officer and administrator. In World War 2, chief of combined operations (1942–3), Supreme Allied Commander SE Asia (1943–6). Last Viceroy of India (1947) and, after partition, last Gov.-General (until independence, 1948). Created Admiral of the Fleet, 1956.

mouse, small omnivorous rodent of family Muridae, esp. of genus *Mus*. Widely distributed. House mouse, *Mus musculus*, believed to be evolved from wild mice of C Asia. Field mouse burrows and hoards food.

mouse deer *see* CHEVROTAIN.

Moustier, Le, cave in SW France which gives its name to the Mousterian culture of the Middle Paleolithic period, where remains of flint weapons and tools used by Neanderthal man were found.

mouth, in anatomy, facial cavity at beginning of gastro-intestinal tract. Functions are ingestion, mastication, lubrication and partial digestion of food. In humans, also one of speech organs.

mouth organ *see* HARMONICA.

Mozambique, Moçambique, overseas prov. of Portugal on SE coast of Africa. Area: 297,731 sq. mi.; cap. Laurenço Marques. Fertile with trop. and sub-trop. climate, rivers Limpopo and Zambesi. Discovered (1498) by Vasco da Gama; Portuguese colony until 1951. Economy based on agriculture; tourism, esp. for game hunting, important. Languages, native, Portuguese; religion mainly ancestor-worship. Pop. (1963) 6,998,000.

Mozart, Wolfgang Amadeus (1756–91), Austrian composer. Toured Europe as child prodigy, performing with sister **Maria Anna Mozart** (1751–1829). In Vienna struggled to make living as composer and teacher. Operas include *The Marriage of Figaro, Don Giovanni* and *The Magic Flute.*

mucous membrane, epithelial layer lining all body cavities and organs. Several cells thick, producing mucus or similar substance, which has protective and lubricating function.

mud dauber, wasp of family Sphecidae. Builds nests of mud cells in which female places eggs.

mudfish *see* BOWFIN.

mudhen, *Fulica americana,* bird of coot family of N America. Inhabits marshes.

mudpuppy, *Necturus maculosus,* amphibian of streams of N America. Reaches 1 ft. in length; bushy, red gills and well-developed limbs.

mudskipper, mudspringer, fish of genera *Periophthalmus* and *Boleophthalmus* found in tropics. Spends long periods of time out of water.

Mueller, Paul Herman (1899–1965), Swiss research chemist. Awarded Nobel Prize for Physiology and Medicine (1948) for discovering insect-killing properties of DDT.

muezzin, Moslem official who calls Mohammedans to prayer by chanting from minaret or from roof of a house.

mufti, Moslem legal adviser consulted in applying religious laws.

mugger *see* CROCODILE.

mugwort, several species of plants of family Compositae, esp. *Artemisia vulgaris.* Perennial aromatic herb with red-brown flowers from temp. Eurasia.

Mugwump, in US polit. history, term applied to Republicans who deserted party to vote Democrat in 1884 pres. election.

Muhammad Ali Haj, orig. Cassius Marcellus Clay (1942–   ), Amer. boxer and Black Muslim minister. Olympic Heavyweight Champion (1960); World Heavyweight Champion (1964–   ), defended title 9 times; deprived of title (1967) for refusing draft into US army.

Muir, Edwin (1887–1959), Scot. poet. Author of *Collected Poems* (1921–51; pub. 1964). Also translator of novels of Franz Kafka.

Mukden, Shenyang, cap. of Liaoning prov., Manchuria, China. Polit. and economic centre of Manchuria; machinery-building, aircraft plants, textile mills. Highly-developed by Japanese before World War 2. Pop. (1957) 2,411,000.

mulatto, Sp. term denoting offspring of one Caucasian and one Negro parent.

mulberry, deciduous trees and shrubs of genus *Morus,* native to N temp. and sub-trop. regions. Leaves of *M. alba,* white mulberry, and *M. nigra,* black mulberry, used for feeding silkworms.

mule *see* ASS.

European Mouse

Moufflon

mule deer, *Odocoileus hemionus,* deer with large ears, of W N America.

Mull, 2nd largest island of Inner Hebrides, Argyllshire, Scotland. Area: *c.* 370 sq. mi.; chief town, Tobermory. Largely mountainous, rising 3,169 ft. to Ben More; soil fertile. Main occupations: livestock raising, fishing, quarrying; tourist industry.

mullein, biennial herb of genus *Verbascum,* found in Europe and Asia. *V. thapsus* has densely woolly leaves and spike of yellow flowers; *V. phoenicium* is purple mullein.

Muller, Hermann Joseph, FRS (1890–1967), Amer. geneticist. Awarded Nobel Prize for Physiology and Medicine (1946) for discoveries concerning hereditary changes or mutations produced by X-rays.

mullet, marine or freshwater fish of Mugilidae family. Grey, with almost cylindrical body. Red varieties also found.

Mulliken, Robert Sanderson, FRS (1896–   ), Amer. chemist and physicist. Awarded Nobel Prize for Chemistry (1966) for work on chemical bonds and electronic structure of molecules.

mullion, in architecture, a vertical division in a window. Usually built of stone or wood. Characteristic of Gothic architecture.

Mumford, Lewis (1895–   ), Amer. writer and critic. Specialist in town-planning. Works include *The Brown Decades* (1931; rev. ed. 1955), *The Culture of Cities* (1938), *The City in History* (1961).

mummichog, several varieties of KILLIFISH.

mummy, corpse embalmed for burial, esp. in ancient Egypt.

mumps, infectious viral disease causing malaise and swelling of parotid salivary glands. Usually childhood disease; in adults complications may affect ovaries, testes, brain.

Munch, Edvard (1863–1944), Norwegian painter, a forerunner of

Expressionist movement. Best known work *Frieze of Life.*

Münchhausen, Karl Friedrich Hieronymus, Baron von (1720–97), Ger. cavalry officer. Far-fetched tales of adventures in Russia became classics. Written and published (1785) in English by Rudolf Erich Raspe.

Mungo, Saint or **Saint Kentigern** (518–603), Scot. saint, Bishop of Glasgow. Patron saint of Glasgow.

Munich, München, city, West Germany, on Isar R. Cap. of Bavaria and Upper Bavaria. Founded 1158; became religious and art centre. Headquarters of Nazi Movement; scene of MUNICH PACT. Transport centre; industries include beer, woodwork, chemicals, leather. Pop. (1965) 1,215,000.

Munich Pact, agreement (Sept. 1938) signed by Germany, Italy, Gt. Britain and France sanctioning Hitler's annexation of Sudetenland, Czechoslovakia. Represented height of Western appeasement policy towards Nazi Germany; agreement thought then to have averted world war.

Munro, Hector Hugh (1870–1916), Brit. author. Wrote short stories under pseudonym Saki, *e.g. Reginald* (1904), *The Chronicles of Clovis* (1911).

Munster, ancient kingdom of Ireland. Area: 9,316 sq. mi. Largest of the 4 provinces; comprises counties Clare, Cork, Kerry, Limerick, Tipperary and Waterford. Pop. (1966) 969,902.

Münster, industrial and commercial city, North Rhine-Westphalia, West Germany. Port on Dortmund-Ems Canal. Formerly cap. of Westphalia. Industries include flour milling, brewing, porcelain manufacture. Pop. (1964) 194,000.

muntjac, muntjak, barking deer, small deer with short antlers of genus *Muntiacus.* Found in S and E Asia and adjacent islands, *e.g. M. muntjac* of Java.

Murat, Joachim (1767–1815), Fr. soldier and king of Naples (1808–15). Played major part in Napoleonic campaigns. Led Sp. invasion (1808), prominent in Battle of Leipzig (1813). Made king by Napoleon I, whose sister he married.

Murdoch, Iris (1919–), Brit. novelist. Works include *The Sandcastle* (1957), *The Time of the Angels* (1966).

muriatic acid, name for HYDROCHLORIC ACID.

Murillo, Bartolomé Esteban (1617–82), Sp. painter. Known for sentimental studies of street urchins and religious paintings. Founder of academy at Seville (1660).

Murmansk, city and ice-free port, N European RSFSR, on NW Kola Peninsula. Largest city in Arctic Circle; developed after World War 1. Base of N fleet of Soviet navy; fishing centre, with canning industries. Pop. (1967) 279,000.

Murphy, William Parry (1892–), Amer. physician. Awarded Nobel Prize for Physiology and Medicine (1934) with George Hoyt Whipple and George Richards Minot, for discovering liver therapy against anaemia.

Murray, George Gilbert Aimé (1866–1957), Brit. classical scholar. Known for verse translations of Euripides and Sophocles.

Murray, James (1721–94), Brit. army officer. Appointed military gov. of Quebec (1760) and became 1st civil gov. of Brit. colony (1764).

Murray, main river of Australia, *c.* 1,200 mi. long. Rises in Snowy Mts., flowing SW into Indian Ocean. Main 19th and early 20th cent. artery of travel and trade in interior; now supplies irrigation water.

Murrumbidgee, river (*c.* 1,000 mi. long), SE Australia. Flows W through New South Wales to Murray R.

Muscat and Oman [Sultanat Masqat wa Oman], independent sultanate of SE Arabia. Area: 82,000 sq. mi.; cap. Muscat. Ruled by Portuguese

(1508–*c.* 1648); close treaty relations with Britain, dating from 1798 when sultan granted commercial rights to East India Co. Economy depends on agriculture; produces tropical crops, esp. fruits, tea, coffee for export; industry includes weaving, leather work and gold and silver filigree work; some pearl-diving. Pop. (1964) 565,000.

muscid fly, *Musca domesticus,* 2-winged fly of temperate regions, related to house-fly.

muscle, contractile fibrous tissue which produces movement in an animal body.

muscovite, common light-coloured mineral of mica group. Found in scaly, massive or foliated form.

Muscovy duck, musk duck, *Cairina moschata,* large crested wild duck native to S America. Dark green and white plumage; widely domesticated.

muscular dystrophy, condition which produces progressive muscular deterioration and wasting esp. in males. Cause unknown.

Muses, in Gk. myth., 9 daughters of Zeus and Mnemosyne, and goddesses of the arts and literature. Orig. worshipped at Pieria and Mt. Helicon.

mushroom, edible fungi of family Agaricaceae. Species include field mushroom, *Agaricus campestris,* horse mushroom, *A. arvensis,* and wood mushroom, *A. silvicola.*

music, deliberate combination of sounds, made by musical instrument or human voice singing. In Europe, 10th–16th cent., music for voices was most significant form (*see* MOTET; MASS). In 17th cent. instrumental music developed independent style; in 18th cent. solo song (ARIA), with instrumental accompaniment, developed. End of 18th cent. produced SONATA style of purely instrumental music (*see* SYMPHONY and CONCERTO). During 19th cent. orchestral music and music for solo piano became most popular medium. In this century, composers have tended to treat voice as an instrument, and to write for small groups of instruments. *See* HARMONY.

musicology, scientific study of music, *e.g.* history, analysis, criticism, music appreciation and music education, *etc.*

musk, *Mimulus moschatus,* perennial plant of figwort family with yellow flowers, popular house plant.

musk ox, *Ovibos moschatus,* mammal intermediate between ox and sheep found in tundra of Canada and Greenland. Short neck and broad head with downward curving horns; thick brown fur has musky odour.

musk rat, musquash, *Ondatra zibethica,* aquatic rodent of vole group, native to N America. Has musky odour. Soft shiny brown fur used for coats, *etc.*

musk rose, *Rosa moschata,* rose native to Med. regions. White musk-scented flowers.

musk thistle, *Carduus nutans,* thistle found in damp localities. Crimson-purple flowers.

Musk Rose

Traditional windmill, Mykonos

musk turtle, stinkpot, N Amer. fresh-water turtle with strong musky odour, of genus *Sternothaerus*.

muskellunge, *Esox masquinongy*, large game fish of pike family. Found in N America, esp. in Great Lakes. Brownish-green body with black spots; reaches over 6 ft. in length and 60 lb. in weight.

musket, heavy, large-calibre hand gun for infantry soldiers. Introduced in 16th cent; predecessor of modern rifle.

muslin, group of woven cotton fabrics, named after Mosul, Iraq. Introduced to Europe from India (18th cent.).

musquash *see* MUSK RAT.

mussel, marine bivalve mollusc. Several species edible as common mussel, *Mytilus edulis*, of N Atlantic coasts and Mediterranean. Freshwater pearl mussel, includes *Unio margaritiferus*, of N Amer. and European rivers.

Musset, Louis Charles Alfred de (1810–57), Fr. romantic poet and dramatist. Published love lyrics *Les Nuits* (1835–40). Plays include *On ne badine pas avec l'amour* (1836).

Mussolini, Benito (1883–1945), Ital. polit. leader, founder of FASCISM. Began as Socialist, but left to organize aggressively nationalist Fascist party after World War 1. As 'Duce', built party by capitalizing on labour unrest. Famous march on Rome (Oct. 1922) led to appointment as premier. Estab. dictatorship; power consolidation completed after murder of MATTEOTTI (1924). Suspended (1928) parl. govt. Conquered Ethiopia (1935–6),

annexed Albania (1939). Joined Hitler and entered World War 2 (1940) in AXIS alliance. Resigned 1943 after Allied invasion of Italy. Shot by partisans.

Mussorgsky, Modest Petrovich (1839–81), Russ. composer. Member of the Five (Russian Nationalist group of composers). Greatest work is opera *Boris Godunov*; other works include orchestral piece *Night on the Bare Mountain,* piano suite *Pictures at an Exhibition* (orchestrated by Ravel). Also wrote songs.

mustard, annual plant of genus *Brassica*. Main types black mustard, *B. nigra*, and white mustard, *B. hirta*, both used in condiment mustard, and Indian mustard *B. juncea*.

mustelid, any of numerous carnivorous mammals of family Mustelidae, comprising weasel, marten, skunk, badger, otter, *etc.*

mute swan, *Cygnus olor*, white swan with black-knobbed orange bill. Found in Europe and Asia.

muttonbird, several Australasian sea-birds of shearwater family caught for their meat, oil and feathers. Includes the short-tailed shearwater, *Puffinus tenuirostris*.

Mycenae, ancient city of NE Peloponnesus, Greece, according to legend, founded by Perseus. Centre of MYCENAEAN CIVILIZATION; conquered in Dorian invasion.

Mycenaean civilization, ancient Gk. civilization discovered esp. by excavations of Heinrich Schliemann at Mycenae. Area inhabited *c.* 3000 BC, possibly by Cretan settlers as culture represented modified form of Minoan civilization. Principal features are city walls of large stone blocks (Cyclopean masonry), and beehive tombs, some 50 ft. high.

Mykonos, island of Cyclades group, Aegean Sea, part of Cyclades department, Greece. Area: 35 sq. mi.; main village, Mykonos. Pop. (1963) *c.* 5,000.

mynah, Asiatic starling of genera *Acridotheres, Gracula*, and *Sturnus*. Talking mynah, *Gracula religiosa*, has black plumage with white wing patches.

myopia, nearsightedness, short-sightedness, condition in which objects are only seen distinctly when near to the eye. Occurs when image is focused in front of retina.

myosotis, plant of genus *Myosotis*, esp. *M palustris*, forget-me-not.

Myrdal Gunnar (1898–   ), Swedish economist and sociologist. Wrote *The American Dilemma*. Sec. of Commerce of Sweden (1945–7). Executive Sec. of UN Economic Commission for Europe (1947–57).

myriapod, obsolescent term for arthropod of group *Myriapoda* with long segmented body and numerous paired, jointed legs. Includes centipedes and millipedes.

Myrmidons, Gk. warrior tribe of Thessaly. According to Homer, descendants of ants changed by Zeus into fighting men.

myrrh, name of small tree of genus *Commiphora*, and of its gum resins. Grown in Arabia and Abyssinia.

myrtle, shrub of tree of genus *Myrtus*, of Asiatic origin. White fragrant flowers, aromatic berries and thick leaves. Used to make perfume.

Mysore, state of S Deccan Plateau, India. Area: 74,210 sq. mi.; cap. Mysore. Major coffee producer. Gold, iron, asbestos and chromite mined. Industry centred on Bangalore and Mysore, incl. military equipment, aircraft, sugar and gold refining. Joined free state of India (1947). Pop. (1961) 23,586,772.

mystery plays, dramatic representations (15th-16th cent.) based on sacred history or on legends of the saints. Eng. collections of plays are know as York, Chester, Coventry and Wakefield cycles.

mysticism, belief that man can apprehend spiritual truths beyond the understanding of the intellect. Christian mysticism is the supernatural unity of man with God through Christ.

myth, traditional story, usually relating supernatural events and actions of gods. Closely associated with religion, myth often recited as part of religious rite. Modern myth interpretation began with Max Müller, who classified them according to purpose; Sir James Frazer's *The Golden Bough* linked myth with idea of fertility in nature. Psychological explanations centre on expression of unconscious needs.

myxomatosis, infectious viral disease of rabbits characterized by growth of soft tumours (myxoma) in connective tissue. Artificially introduced into Brit. Isles and Australia to reduce rabbit population.

Muskrat

nabob, nawab, high-ranking official of the Mogul Empire of India. Name applied in the 18th cent. to any European who made large fortune in India.

Nabokov, Vladimir (1899–   ), Amer. novelist, b. Russia. Early works written in Russian; those in English include *Lolita* (1955), *Pnin* (1957), *Pale Fire* (1962).

Naboth, in OT, owner of vineyard coveted by King Ahab. On refusal to sell, stoned to death. Curse put on Ahab's family by Elijah. (1 *Kings* XXI).

nacre, mother-of-pearl, hard, iridescent substance forming inner layer of certain shells, *e.g.* pearl oyster.

Na-Dene, group of indigenous N Amer. languages, incl. Athapaskan, Eyak, Haida and Tlingit stocks. Number of speakers steadily declining.

nadir, in astronomy, point directly opposite ZENITH, *i.e.* vertically below observer.

Nafud Desert, NW Saudi Arabia. Area: 80,000 sq. mi. Largely red sand, with long dunes.

Nagaland, state of NE India. Area: 6,350 sq. mi.; admin. centre, Kohima. Mountainous region; populace relies on subsistence farming. Agitation for independence during 1960s. Pop. (1961 est.) 369,200.

Nagasaki, city of W Kyushu, Japan, on Nagasaki Bay. Indust. centre with shipyards and fisheries. Early Christian centre; 1st Jap. port visited by W traders. Target (1945) of 2nd atomic bomb which devastated much of the city. Pop. (1965) 406,000.

Nagoya, city, transport centre, C Honshu, Japan. Industries include engineering, chemicals, textiles. Seat of Nagoya University and Shinto shrine (founded 2nd cent.). Pop. (1965) 1,935,000.

Nagpur, city and former cap. of Madhya Pradesh, C India. Transport, indust. and commercial centre. Pop. (1965) 779,000.

Nagy, Imre (1896–1958), Hungarian polit. leader, premier (1953–5, 1956).

Oyster shell showing nacre

Led 1956 revolt against Soviet domination. Fled during Russ. re-occupation; later captured and shot.

Nahas Pasha, Mustapha (1877–1965), Egyptian statesman. P.M. (1936–52); helped negotiate Anglo-Egyptian treaty (1936) giving Egypt independence.

Nahum, prophetic book of OT, written *c.* 650 BC. Foretells fall of Nineveh.

Naiads, in Gk. myth., nymphs of springs, lakes and rivers. *See* NYMPHS.

Naidu, Sarojini (1879–1949), Indian poet and politician. First woman pres. of Indian National Congress (1925). Her poetry, in English, deals with Indian themes.

nail, modified epidermis resulting in horny layer growing at tips of fingers and toes. Produced in nail bed in lower germinal layer of the skin.

nainsook, light cotton fabric of plain calico weave. Usually bleached and used for lingerie.

Naipaul, V[idiadhar] S[urajprasad] (1932–   ), Indian writer, b. Trinidad. Works, written in English, and mainly about Caribbean life, include *The Mystic Masseur* (1957), *The Mimic Men* (1967).

Nairnshire, coastal county, N Scotland. Area: 163 sq. mi.; county town, Nairn. Cattle-raising, fishing, main occupations. Pop. (1966) 8,000.

Nairobi, cap. of Kenya. Commercial centre; ships coffee and sisal through port at Mombasa. Founded 1899. Wildlife reserve at nearby Nairobi National Park. Pop. (1962) 315,000.

Namier, Sir Lewis Bernstein (1888–1960), Brit. historian. His influential *Structure of Politics at the Accession of George III* (1929) examined shifting allegiances of 18th cent. politicians.

Namur, prov., S Belgium. Area: 1,413 sq. mi.; cap. Namur. Mining, cutlery manufacturing. People mainly Fr. speaking. Pop. (1964) 375,634.

Nancy, cap. of Meurthe-et-Moselle department, NE France, on Marne-Rhine canal. Historic cap. of Lorraine. Cultural and commercial centre. Pop. (1962) 209,000.

Nanda Devi, mountain (25,645 ft.) in Himalayas, Uttar Pradesh, N India. Hindu holy place. First climbed 1936.

Nandi, African tribal people of Kenya highlands. Mainly cattle raisers, have resisted external influence.

nandu, *Rhea americana,* 3-toed Amer. flightless ostrich-like bird. Smaller than African ostrich; found

Nandu

in S. Amer. pampas. Eggs are laid on ground and hatched by male.

Nanga Parbat, mountain (26,660 ft.) in Himalayas of NE Pakistan. First ascended (1953) by Austrian-German expedition.

nankeen, firm, durable yellow or buff fabric. Orig. made at Nanking from natural coloured cotton; now widely imitated.

Nanking, city of Kiangsu prov., China, on Yangtze R. Cultural and shipping centre. Treaty of Nanking (1842) ended Opium War. Nationalist cap. of China (1928–37, 1945–9). Pop. (1957) 1,419,000.

nannyberry, *Viburnum lentago,* N Amer. shrub of honeysuckle family. Bears small white flowers and oval bluish-black edible fruit.

Nansen, Fridtjof (1861–1930), Norwegian zoologist and arctic explorer. In 1893 allowed his ship the *Fram* to drift N with an iceflow. With aid of sledges reached further N than any previous expedition. Norwegian ambassador to UK (1905–8). Awarded Nobel Peace Prize (1922) for efforts on behalf of refugees.

Nantes, cap. of Loire-Inférieure department, W France, port on Loire R. Shipbuilding, transport centre. Pop. (1962) 328,000.

Nantes, Edict of, issued (1598) by Fr. King Henry IV granting religious freedom to Huguenots (Fr. Protestants). Anti-Huguenot measures of 17th cent. culminated in Edict's revocation (1685).

Nantucket, island of Massachusetts, *c.* 30 mi. off Cape Cod. Centre of whaling industry until *c.* 1850; later a resort and artists' colony.

Naomi, in OT, left Judah during famine, lived in Moab. Returned to Bethlehem accompanied by daughter-in-law Ruth.

naphtha, liquid obtained from distillation of petroleum, coal tar or wood. Colourless and volatile, used as cleaning solvent and in making varnish.

naphthalene, colourless, crystalline solid with penetrating smell. Obtained from coal tar distillation. Used in making dyes and insecticides.

naphtol, either of 2 hydrocarbon derivatives of naphthalene. Antiseptic properties.

Napier, Sir Charles James (1782–1853), Brit. soldier and statesman. Conquered Sind and Baluchistan.

Napier, John (1550–1617), Scot. mathematician. Invented logarithm, developed 1st logarithmic table. Introduced numerical decimal point.

Napier, Robert Cornelis, 1st Baron Napier of Magdala (1810–90), Brit. army officer. Served in relief of Lucknow (1857); commanded Abyssinian expedition and captured Magdala (1868), forcing release of Brit. prisoners.

Naples, Napoli, cap. of Campania, S Italy. Important seaport, scenic location backed by Mt. Vesuvius. Cap. (1282–1860) of Kingdom of Naples (after 1815 Kingdom of Two Sicilies). Pop. (1963) 1,205,000.

Naples, Kingdom of, former state of S Italy, part (11th-13th cent.) of kingdom of Sicily. Under Sp. rule (1505–1707), period of harsh exploitation. Passed to Austria by Peace of Utrecht (1713). With Sicily, formed Kingdom of the Two Sicilies until 1860.

Napoleon I, orig. Napoleone Buonaparte (1769–1821), Fr. military and polit. leader, emperor (1804–14), b. Corsica. Prominent after quelling Paris insurrection (1795), successful campaign in Italy (1796–7) ended in TREATY OF CAMPO FORMIO with Austria. Egyptian expedition (1798) followed by coup d'état (1799) estab. Napoleon as First Consul. Reorganized state, promulgated CODE NAPOLEON. Crowned emperor by pope. Thwarted European alliance by defeating Austria at Austerlitz (1805), Prussia at Jena (1806), Russia at Friedland (1807). TILSIT peace treaty left only Britain in opposition; CONTINENTAL SYSTEM failed after naval defeat at TRAFALGAR. Virtually ruled entire Continent (1808–12), decline beginning with inconclusive campaign in Spain (*see* PENINSULAR WAR) and invasion of Russia (1812), ending with disastrous retreat from

Moscow. New alliance defeated him at Leipzig (1813), pursued him into France. Napoleon abdicated (1814) and was exiled to Elba. Returned to France (1815), but Hundred Days rule ended at WATERLOO. Exiled to St Helena. Settlement of Napoleonic Wars negotiated at CONGRESS OF VIENNA.

Napoleon II (1811–32), son of Napoleon I and Marie Louise. His father abdicated (1815) in his favour. Never ruled, detained at Vienna for rest of his life.

Napoleon III, orig. Louis Napoleon Bonaparte (1808–73), emperor of France (1852–70), nephew of Napoleon I. After failing in bids (1836, 1840) to become emperor, elected pres. after Revolution of 1848 had estab. repub. Dissolved legislature (1851), assumed dictatorial powers and became emperor. His rule was marked by indust. expansion and succession of military ventures, incl. CRIMEAN WAR. Manoeuvred by Bismarck into Franco-Prussian War (1870), decisively defeated and later deposed.

Napoleonic Wars see NAPOLEON I.

Narbada, Nerbudda, river of C India. Rises in Madhya Pradesh and flows 801 mi. to sea N of Bombay. Sacred to Hindus.

Narbonne, city of S France. Commercial importance in Middle Ages declined after silting up of port. Pop. (1962) 33,691.

narcissism, in psychology, incapacity of individual to have emotional relationship with others. Term derived from Gk. myth. of Narcissus. Normal stage in child development; called secondary narcissism when occurring after puberty.

Narcissus, in Gk. myth., beautiful youth who rejected love of the nymph Echo. Caused by Aphrodite to become enamoured of his own image in a fountain. Finally changed into flower bearing his name.

narcissus, genus of bulbous perennial herbs of genus *Narcissus* of family Amaryllidaceae, found in Europe, Asia and N America. Erect linear leaves; yellow, white or bicolour

Narvik

flowers, often with trumpet-shaped corolla. Species include jonquil, *N. jonquilla*.

narcolepsy, condition characterized by frequent tendency to attacks of deep sleep. Usually of unknown cause.

narcotics, substances acting on nervous system which reduce sensibility. Used medicinally, but large doses induce coma and may be fatal. Main narcotics are opium and its derivatives. Some are addictive. Distribution

Narcissus family, (1) and (2) daffodils (3) polyanthus narcissus (4) pheasants' eye narcissus

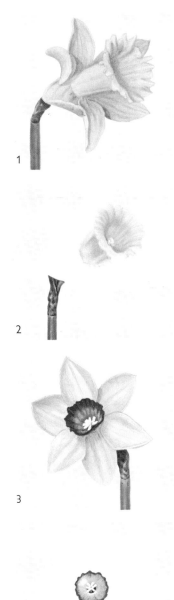

controlled by govt. agencies in many countries.

Narva, city, NE Estonia, on Narva R. Textile and machinery manufacturing; saw-mills. Scene of Swedish victory over Russians (1700). Pop. 25,000.

Narvik, town on NW coast of Norway. Ice-free port (founded 1887) operates as export terminus for Swedish iron-ore. Pop. (1967 est.) 13,000.

narwhal, narwal, narwhale, *Monodon monoceros,* arctic cetacean related to dolphin. Male has long spirally twisted tusk extending forward from upper jaw. Hunted for oil.

Naseby, Battle of, encounter (1645) near Naseby, Northamptonshire between Parliamentarians and Royalists in Eng. Civil War. Decisive victory for Cromwell's forces preceded Charles I's surrender.

Nash, John (1752–1835), Eng. architect and town planner. Designed Regent Street, London; also Marble Arch, after enlarging Buckingham Palace.

Nash, Ogden (1902–71), Amer. poet. Humorous verse collections include *I'm a Stranger Here Myself* (1938) and *Everyone but Thee and Me* (1962).

Nash, Paul (1889–1946), Brit. artist. Best known for landscapes of Western Front and pictures of World War 2, incl. *The Battle of Britain.*

Nash, Richard ('Beau') (1674–1762), Eng. social figure. Fashion leader at Bath.

Nash, Sir Walter (1882–1968), New Zealand statesman. P.M. in Labour govt. (1957–60).

Nashe or **Nash, Thomas** (1567–1601), Eng. satirical pamphleteer and writer. Attacked Puritans in Marprelate Controversy. Began scurrilous pamphlet battle with Richard Harvey (1592). Works include *The Unfortunate Traveller, or The Life of Jack Wilton* (1594). Thought to have finished Marlowe's *Dido, Queen of Carthage.*

Nashville, cap. of Tennessee, US. Founded 1780. Occupied by Union forces after 1862 during Civil War. Grew as cotton distributing, now manufacturing and transport centre. Pop. (1963) 347,000.

Naskapi, tribe of N Amer. Indians of Algonkian linguistic stock. Inhabit E Mackenzie area of N Canada; hunted caribou.

Nasmyth, Alexander (1758–1840), Scot. painter. Best known for portrait of Robert Burns. His son **James Nasmyth** (1808–90) invented (1839) steam hammer to forge paddle-wheel shafts for steamships.

Nasturtium

Nassau, cap. of Bahamas, port on New Providence Is. Tourist resort, commercial centre of Brit. colony. Pop. (1966 est.) 55,000.

Nassau, former duchy, W Germany. Formed Hesse-Nassau prov. of Prussia (1866–1945); contained in Hesse since 1945. Agric. and forested area, noted for Rhine wines.

Nasser, Gamal Abdel (1918–70), Egyptian polit. and military leader. Instrumental in coup estab. Egyptian repub., became pres. (1954) by ousting Mohammed Neguib. Forced (1956) Brit. troops out of Suez Canal area. Pres. of United Arab Repub. (1958–), advocate of Arab unity in 1960s. Defeated in 1967 war against Israel, resigned as pres. Resignation rejected by legislature.

Nast, Thomas (1840–1902), Amer. cartoonist. Best known for caricature attacks on WILLIAM TWEED. Creator of Republican 'elephant', Democratic 'donkey'.

nasturtium, genus of perennial aquatic temp. cruciferous herbs, commonly called watercress. Creeping or freely rooting stems and edible leaves.

nasturtium, name of popular garden plant of geranium order Tropaeolum with rounded flat leaves and varicoloured blossoms.

Natal, E prov. of Republic of South Africa. Area: 35,280 sq. mi.; cap. Pietermaritzburg; main city, Durban. Great inland coal deposits; sugar, tobacco are coastal produce. Founded by Boers as repub. (1838); annexed by British (1843); joined South Africa (1910). Pop. (1960) 2,979,000.

Natal, port on NE coast of Brazil, cap. of Rio Grande do Norte state. Transport and navy centre. Pop. (1960) 154,276.

Natchez, tribe of N Amer. Indians of Natchez-Muskogean linguistic stock. Lived in SW Mississippi during 17th cent. Scattered during wars with French.

Nathan, Israelite prophet in OT, trusted adviser of David and Solomon. Rebuked David for adultery with Bathsheba.

Nathan, George Jean (1882–1958), Amer. editor and drama critic. Worked with H. L. Mencken of *Smart Set* and *American Mercury;* cynical and exacting critic.

Nathanael, one of Twelve Apostles, mentioned only in Gospel of St John. Identified with Bartholomew, missionary in India and Armenia.

National Aeronautics and Space Administration (NASA), US govt. agency (estab. 1958) responsible for space exploration. Supervises construction of equipment and research on flights within and without Earth's atmosphere.

national anthem, patriotic hymn sung on ceremonial occasions. Some countries have had compositions created specifically to serve as anthems.

National Assembly, name adopted by ESTATES-GENERAL of France in 1789, marking its defiance of the king.

national debt, public debt, indebtedness of govt. expressed in monetary terms, usually resulting from revenue deficits, public expenses, or wars. Loan raised through govt. bonds or treasury notes.

National Gallery, London, Brit. art collection. Building, in Trafalgar Square, dates from 1830s. Well known selections of 15th-16th cent. Ital. paintings.

National Gallery of Art, Washington DC, part of Smithsonian Institution, estab. 1937. Noted for Ital. and Fr. paintings.

National Guard, in US, body estab. 1903 to replace state militias. Subject to state jurisdiction in peace-time; responsible to pres. in national emergencies.

National Insurance, in UK, govt. legislation (1946–9) enabling individuals to receive benefits for sickness, unemployment, or retirement. Industrial Injuries Acts cover risks of disablement at work.

National Labor Relations Board, US govt. agency, set up (1935) to affirm labour's right to collective organization and bargaining. Extended (1947) to cover employers' complaints against unions.

National League, US professional baseball league, estab. 1876. Comprises 8 charter members; 4 teams subsequently added. San Francisco (formerly New York) Giants have won 18 league pennants.

national parks, areas of beauty, geog. or hist. interest set aside and preserved for public use. Practice common in many countries, areas officially designated as National Parks in US, Canada, South Africa and UK.

National Recovery Administration (NRA), US admin. bureau estab. by Congress to encourage indust. employment and fairness. Adopted fair practice codes but Supreme Court decided them unenforceable in Schechter Poultry Case (1935). Subsequently abandoned. Symbolized by blue eagle.

national service, in UK, compulsory enrolment of personnel for service in armed forces. Adopted during both World Wars. Also *see* CONSCRIPTION.

National Socialism, Nazism, ideology of National Socialist German Workers' Party (Nazi Party). Programme formulated by ADOLF HITLER in *Mein Kampf* (1923), drawn from sources ranging from Lassallean socialism to Ital. FASCISM. Founded on principles of Aryan 'master race', led by *Führer* [leader], Ger. expansion and eradication of Communists and Jews, 'Germany's greatest enemies'. As sole legal party after Hitler's rise, acted (1933–45) with brutality in consolidating power within Germany and forced outbreak of World War 2 through aggressive external policies.

National Theatre Company, theatre company opened 1963 in London

Natrolite

under direction of Sir Laurence Olivier. Plans exist for expansion and theatre building.

National Trust, non-profitmaking Brit. organization estab. by Act of Parliament (1895) for promoting permanent preservation of lands and buildings of historic interest or natural beauty.

nationalism, polit. and social creed expressing common heritage and culture through unification of an ethnic group. Driving force behind nation-building in 19th cent. Europe and in 20th cent. Asia and Africa. In estab. nations may take extreme form, as in Nazi Germany.

nationalization, state policy involving public ownership of essential services and industries. Adhered to by all Socialists, incl. Brit. Labour Party. Term also refers to acquisition by state of foreign-owned assets.

native cat, Austral. species of weasel-like, carnivorous marsupial of genus *Dasyurus.*

Nativity, The, birth of Jesus Christ celebrated on 25 December in W Churches. Name also given to works of art depicting Christ as a baby.

NATO *see* NORTH ATLANTIC TREATY ORGANIZATION.

natrolite, white silicate of the zeolite group, found in igneous rocks.

Natta, Giulio (1903–   ), Ital. chem. engineer. With Karl Ziegler, awarded Nobel Prize for Chemistry (1963) for evolving system of uniting simple hydrocarbons into large molecule substances.

natterjack, *Bufo calamita,* small toad of W Europe. Brownish yellow in colour; short hind legs.

natural gas, mixture of various gases, usually incl. methane, occurring naturally as deposits in porous rock, often with petroleum. Non-toxic methane, used as domestic fuel has twice calorific value of coal gas.

natural law, in physics and chemistry formulation of some uniform character or correlation of things or events. Frequently used to describe character of phenomena themselves.

natural rights, polit. theory based on premise that all men are born with inalienable rights. Leading exponent, John Locke; argument developed prior to and during Amer. and Fr. Revolutions.

natural selection, tendency of certain members of a species to 'survive', *i.e.* live and perpetuate themselves in a specific environment. Basis of Darwin's principle of evolution described by him and by A. R. Wallace (1858).

naturalization, formal and legal process whereby an individual becomes a national of a country other than that to which he formerly owed allegiance.

Nauplia, seaport of Argolis, Greece, 25 mi. S of Corinth. Cap. of Greece (1830– 4). Pop. (1961) 9,102.

Nauru, C Pacific coral island near Gilbert and Ellice group. Area: 8 sq. mi. Became republic 1968. Administered by Australia (1920– 68). Important phosphate deposits. Pop. (1966) 6,056.

nausea, [Gk: *naus*, ship], feeling of a desire to vomit. May be a symptom of many diseases and nerve affections.

Nausicaa, in Gk. myth., daughter of Alcinous, king of Phaeacea. Welcomed Odysseus when shipwrecked during wanderings after Trojan War.

nautical mile, unit of distance used in sea and air travel; equivalent to 1 min. of great circle of Earth *i.e.* one sixtieth of degree of latitude, UK 6080 ft., 1853·18 km; US and international 6076·1033 ft.

nautilus, carnivorous mollusc of cephalopod group, found in W Pacific and E Indian Ocean. Coiled or straight external shell.

Navaho, Navajo, tribe of N Amer. Indians of Athapaskan linguistic stock, inhabiting NE Arizona. Nomadic hunters and farmers (17th cent.), they raided Pueblo settlements in New Mexico. Settled on reservations in SW US; one of largest surviving tribes.

Navarino, Battle of (1827), decisive action in Greek war of liberation. Combined fleets of England, France

Nauplia, on the Peloponnese, Greece

and Russia defeated Egyptians. Navarino now Gk. seaport of Pylos.

Navarre, mountainous Basque prov. of N Spain, on Bay of Biscay. Area: 4,056 sq. mi. Major portion of former Navarre kingdom which existed separately from France and Spain (1328– 1512).

nave, in architecture, central aisle of a church. Term used to mean the area from the altar to main door, incl. side aisles, intended for use of the laity.

navel, umbilicus, in anatomy, depression in abdomen. Indicates point where mammal foetus was connected by umbilical cord to mother's uterine wall for purpose of obtaining nourishment.

Navigation Acts, Eng. legislation, orig. medieval, re-enacted (1650– 1) to combat Dutch competition in trade with E and W Indies. Later Acts restricted colonial trade to Eng. ports and were among causes of Amer. Revolution. Finally repealed 1849.

Naxos, Gk. island in Cyclades group, Aegean Sea. Formerly centre of Bacchus worship. In Gk. myth. Theseus deserted Ariadne here. Now produces white wine.

Nazareth, town of N Israel where Jesus spent His early years. Place of pilgrimage with many churches and shrines. Pop. (1960 est.) 25,500.

Nazarites, in Bible, those dedicated to service of God. Took vows not to cut their hair and to abstain from wine. They included Samson.

Nazi Party *see* NATIONAL SOCIALISM.

Nazism *see* NATIONAL SOCIALISM.

Nazi-Soviet Pact *see* NON-AGGRESSION PACT.

Neanderthal man, *Homo neanderthalis*, extinct late Paleolithic species

of man. Remains 1st found (1856) in cave in Neanderthal valley near Düsseldorf, Germany.

nearsightedness [US] *see* MYOPIA.

Nebraska, state of central US. Area: 77,227 sq. mi.; cap. Lincoln; main cities include Omaha. Plains with tableland in W. Predominantly agricultural with corn and wheat as main crops. Industries include food processing, machinery and chemical manufacturing. Orig. under Sp. control; part of LOUISIANA PURCHASE. Pop. (1960) 1,411,330.

Nebuchadnezzar II (d. 562 BC), Chaldean ruler of Babylonia (*c.* 605– 562 BC). Conquered Syria and Palestine; captured Jerusalem (597) taking many Jews into captivity. Built Hanging Gardens of Babylon.

nebula, in astronomy, faintly glowing patches in the heavens. Some are star systems (galaxies); others are areas of gas (diffuse nebulae) either illuminated by near stars, or dark.

neck, portion of human or animal body joining head to trunk.

Necker, Jacques (1732– 1804), Fr. statesman and financial reformer. Opposed Court extravagances; made public grave state of nation's finances, and suggested calling of Estates-General. His dismissal (1789) led to storming of the Bastille.

necromancy, practice of foretelling the future by communication with the dead. Practised in OT and classical period. Practice continues in certain primitive cultures.

necropolis [Gk: city of the dead], cemetery, usually in or near large city; also an old or prehistoric burying ground.

necrosis, in medicine, death of a

Nebula Andromeda

particular area of tissue. May be caused by cessation of blood supply, toxic agents or bacteria.

nectar *see* AMBROSIA.

nectarine, *Prunus persica nectarina,* small tree, bearing smooth-skinned edible fruit, smaller and firmer than peach. Used for jams, jellies and in confectionery.

needlefish, garfish, family of long slender fish with beak-like, sharply-toothed jaw. Of *c.* 50 species, some reach 5 ft. in length, incl. European *Belone belone* and Amer. *Tylosurus.*

Needles, The, scenic pointed chalk rocks with lighthouse, off W tip of Isle of Wight, England.

Nefertiti, Nofretete, Egyptian queen, wife of Amenhotep IV. Thought to have exerted strong influence over her husband. A coloured limestone bust of Nefertiti is one of best-known Egyptian antiquities.

negative, in intermediate stages of photography, developed film on which light and dark areas are interchanged. Light is directed through the negative on to sensitive paper to produce positive image.

Negev, Negeb, desert region in S Israel, bordered by Egypt, Jordan, Gulf of Aqaba. Area: 5,140 sq. mi. Major portion is Israeli territory, site of co-operative farming.

negotiable instrument, document conveying legal right to property or money. Cheques and promissory notes are examples.

Negri Sembilan, state of Federation of Malaysia, on W coast of peninsula. Area: 2,550 sq. mi. Federated 1895. Chief products, rubber, rice, tungsten and quartz. Pop. (1961 est.) 422,700.

Negrito, member of various dwarfish Negroid peoples of the Philippines, Malay Peninsula, Andaman Is. and S India.

Negro, member of Negroid race, one of 3 main anthropological divisions of human race (others being Caucasoid and Mongoloid). Characteristics include wiry hair and dark pigmentation.

Neguib, Mohammed (1901–), Egyptian army officer and polit. leader. Led coup d'état deposing King Farouk (1952). Pres. of Egyptian repub. until deposed by Nasser (1954).

Nehemiah, historical book of OT. Relates story of Nehemiah, cupbearer to Artaxerxes I, king of Persia, who later governed Jerusalem (445– 433 BC). Rebuilt city walls and reformed temple worship.

Nehru, Jawaharlal (1889– 1964), Indian statesman. Headed Indian National Congress 4 times during struggle (1919– 47) for independence. Jailed for participation in civil disobedience campaigns in 1930s. First P.M. of independent Indian state (1947– 64), maintained influential neutral stand in foreign affairs.

Neisse, two tributaries of Oder R. Lusatian Neisse (length 140 mi.) forms part of East Ger.– Polish border. Silesian Neisse (length 120 mi.) flows through Poland, joining Oder at Brieg.

Neisser, Albert Ludwig Siegmund (1855– 1916), Ger. physician and dermatologist. Discovered gonococcus bacterium and successfully treated venereal diseases.

Nejd, high plateau in C Saudi Arabia. Former kingdom and home of Arabian horses. Now produces dates and oil.

Nekrasov, Nikolai Alekseyevich (1821– 77), Russ. poet. Among most famous works are *The Red-Nosed Frost* (1863) and the satirical *Who can be Happy and Free in Russia?* (1863– 77; Eng. tr. 1917).

Nelligan, Émile (1879– 1941), Fr. Canadian poet. Romantic poetry includes 'Vaisseau d'Or' and 'La Romance de Vin', both written before he became insane (1899).

Nelson, Horatio, Viscount Nelson (1758– 1805), Eng. naval officer. Incapacitated Fr. fleet at Aboukir Bay (1798), ending Napoleon's campaign in Egypt. Helped in Sicilian attempt to gain Neapolitan throne; prolonged stay in Naples with his mistress, Lady Hamilton. Defeated Danes at Copenhagen (1801). Killed in action at Cape TRAFALGAR (1805) after destroying combined Fr. and Sp. fleets.

Nelson, Robert (1794– 1873), Canadian insurgent. Led abortive invasions of Lower Canada (1838–9), estab. short-lived repub. With Cyrille Côté invaded Lower Canada (1838), proclaimed himself pres. of Canadian republic. Movement lacked support, Nelson retired to US (1839).

nematoda, phylum of unsegmented round-worms, *e.g.* threadworms, eel-worms, of various lengths up to 1 m. Universal distribution; soil, aquatic and parasitic species.

Nemean Lion, in Gk. myth., invulnerable monster, offspring of Typhon and Echidna; strangled by Heracles (1st labour).

nemertina, phylum of unsegmented,

Neontetra

Watering hole in Negev desert

contractile worms of varying length up to 4 m. Mostly marine or littoral. Commonly called ribbon worms; *c.* 600 species.

nemesia, genus of African annual plants of figwort family. Variously coloured, irregular flowers.

Nemesis, in Gk. myth., daughter of Night and personification of retribution, esp. in cases of human presumption towards the gods.

Nemi, Lake, crater lake of C Italy, SE of Rome in Alban Hills. Drained (1928– 32), allowing recovery of 2 ancient Roman pleasure barges.

nemophyla, genus of *c.* 20 species of N Amer. herbs of waterleaf family. Diffuse annuals with blue or white blossoms. Several grown as border plants, incl. baby blue eyes, *N. menziesi.*

Nennius (*fl.* 796), Welsh writer. Credited with compilation of *Historia Brittonum,* early history of England in time of Anglo-Saxon invasions.

neoclassical, dominant style in 18th– 19th cent. in art and architecture. Based on Classical models, Madeleine in Paris, facade of British Museum, London, Lincoln Memorial in Washington, DC, are architectural examples.

Neolithic *see* STONE AGE.

neon *see* NOBLE GASES.

neontetra, *Hyphessobrycon innesi,* small, coloured fish found in Amazon R., S America. Popular aquarium fish.

neophyte [Gk: *neophutos,* newly planted], name given by early Christians to new converts. Term now applied to beginners in general.

neoplatonism, philosophy derived from doctrines of Plato and Oriental religious beliefs, expounded (3rd cent.) by Plotinus. Held that all existence, material and spiritual, emanates from transcendent One; purification obtained by self-discipline. Exponents include Porphyry and Iamblichus; supported by Emperor Julian. Pagan philosophy banned by Justinian (529), but influence continued through Middle Ages.

Neoptolemus or **Pyrrhus**, in Gk. myth., son of Achilles. Summoned to Trojan War after death of Achilles; killed Priam; awarded Andromache, Hector's widow, as captive. Married Hermione, daughter of Menelaus and Helen; slain by Orestes.

Nepal, kingdom of S central Asia, between India and Tibet. Area: 54,362 sq. mi.; cap. Katmandu. Mountainous (contains Mt. Everest)

with fertile valleys and jungle swamps. Agriculture consists mainly of rice, tobacco, cotton and jute crops. Exports timber. Main religions, Hinduism, Buddhism. Unit of currency, Nepalese rupee. Pop. (1966) 10,294,000.

nepheline, rock-forming mineral composed of sodium potassium aluminium silicate. When coloured by other minerals its crystals used as gems.

nephrite, massive, tough, fibrous form of tremolite-actinolite group of minerals. Varies from white to dark green; obtained mainly from boulders in river gravels. Common form of jade.

nephritis, inflammation of the kidneys, esp. in Bright's disease. Acute or chronic; caused by infection, degenerative process or vascular disease.

Nepomuk, Saint John of (*fl.* 14th cent.), Bohemian martyr; in history vicar-general to archbishop of Prague (1393). According to legend confessor of wife of Wenceslaus IV of Bohemia.

Nepos, Cornelius (*c.* 100–*c.* 25 BC), Roman poet and writer. Friend of Catullus and Atticus. Extant works include parts of *De Viris Illustribus* (*c.* 34 BC), a collection of Gk. and Roman biography. *Love Poems* and *Life of Cato* among lost works.

Neptune, 8th planet of solar system, 27,700 mi. in diam. and 2,794,000,000 mi. from Sun. Has 2 satellites. Discovered by Galle and H. d'Arrest (1846).

Neptune, orig. an Ital. god associated with water, in Roman religion god of the sea; identified with Gk. POSEIDON, whose attributes he assimilated.

neptunium, synthetic element, at. no. 93, discovered (1940) by E. M. McMillan and P. H. Abelson of the University of California.

nereid, elongated, segmented, predaceous worm of family Nereidae, both burrowing and free-swimming, *e.g.* ragworm.

Nereids *see* NEREUS.

Nereus, in Gk. myth., wise and kindly sea deity. Father of the **Nereids**, sea maidens (*e.g.* Thetis, Galatea); had power to change himself into any shape.

Neri, San Filippo de', orig. Filippo Romolo Neri (1515–95), Ital. ecclesiastic. Founded Congregation of the Oratory (1564). Much social work and non-ascetic religious teaching led to revival of religion in Rome. Canonized 1622.

Nerina, Nadia, orig. Nadine Judd (1927–   ), Brit. ballerina, b. South Africa. With Sadler's Wells, now Royal Ballet, since 1947.

Nernst, Walther, FRS (1864–1941), Ger. scientist. Awarded Nobel Prize for Chemistry (1920) for studies in thermochemistry.

Nero [Claudius Caesar] orig. Lucius Domitius Ahenobarbus (AD 37–68), Roman emperor (AD 54–68), last of Julio-Claudian family. Adopted by Claudius. Reign characterized by crime and brutality, incl. murder of mother and wife. Blamed Christians for fire in Rome (AD 64) and began their persecution. Fled from Rome and committed suicide after revolt in Gaul became widespread.

Neruda, Pablo, orig. Naftali Reyes (1904–   ), Chilean poet. Works include *Residencia en la Tierra* (1933), *Odas Elementales* (1954). Nobel Prize for Literature (1971).

Nerval, Gérard de (1808–55), orig.

Gérard Labrunie, Fr. writer. Works include *Aurelia, ou le Rève et la Vie* (1855) an autobiography of his eccentric life, and short stories in *Contes et Facéties* (1852).

Nervi, Pier Luigi (1891–   ), Ital. architect and designer. Noted for buildings of reinforced concrete, *e.g.* the Memorial Stadium at Florence (1932), and Palace of Sport, Rome (1950).

nervous system, network of nerves and nerve tissue of animals, concerned with co-ordination and control of other systems and organs. In humans, consists of central nervous system (brain and spinal cord); peripheral nervous system (nerve fibres incl. ganglions connecting sense organs with muscles and glands); and autonomic nervous system.

Nesbit, Edith (1858–1924), Eng. writer of children's books. They include *The Treasure-Seekers* (1899), *Five Children and It* (1902) and *The Enchanted Castle* (1907).

Ness, Loch, Inverness-shire, Scotland. One of deepest lakes in Britain (*c.* 24 mi. long), and supposedly inhabited by monster.

Nessus, in Gk. myth., a Centaur, carried travellers over R. Evenus. Slain by Heracles for attempt to abduct his wife, Deianeira. The poisoned blood of Nessus, smeared on a robe by Deianeira to regain Heracles' love, caused his death.

nest, receptacle prepared by birds and certain mammals, reptiles, fishes and insects for eggs or newborn young. Bird's nests vary from elaborate hangnests of Baltimore orioles and

Terraced fields in Nepal

felt cotton-down nest of Austral. flowerpeckers, to simpler twig, straw or leaf arrangements in tree hollows or on the ground.

Nestor, in Gk. myth., son of Neleus and Chloris, and king of Pylos. Took part in Trojan War; renowned for wisdom.

Nestorians, Christian followers of NESTORIUS. Driven into Persia after the Council of Ephesus (AD 431), they suffered persecution from Kurds and Turks. Nestorians uphold Nestorius' doctrines only on the position of the Virgin Mary.

Nestorius, (*fl.* 5th cent.), Syrian divine, patriarch of Constantinople (428–431). Held that the human and divine natures were not united in Jesus Christ and that Mary could not be called Mother of God. Condemned as a heretic at the Council of Ephesus (431) and banished.

netball, game played by women, popular in UK. Sport played on court by 2 teams of 7 players. Rules and objectives resemble those of BASKET-BALL.

Netherlands, The [Koninkrijk der Nederlanden], constitutional monarchy of W Europe, known unofficially as Holland. Area: 13,202 sq.

mi.; cap. Amsterdam, seat of govt. The Hague; cities, Rotterdam, Utrecht, Haarlem. Rivers, Scheldt, Meuse, Waal, Rhine. In 15th cent. part of Duchy of Burgundy, and later of Habsburg Empire. Repression and persecution of Protestants by Philip II of Spain led to Union of 7 provs. (1579) and independence (1609). Now 11 provs. and 2 autonomous overseas states, SURINAM and CURAÇAO. Joined Luxembourg and Belgium in economic union (Benelux) in 1958. Heavy industry, tourism, agriculture and horticulture important. Language, Dutch; religions Protestantism and Roman Catholicism. Unit of currency, guilder. Pop. (1964) 12,523,000.

Netherlands Antilles, Dutch overseas territory, comprising 4 communities, Netherlands Leeward Is., ARUBA, CURAÇAO and Bonaire. Total area: 371 sq. mi.; cap., Willemstad. All islands of volcanic origin, semiarid. Economy based on oil of Curaçao and Aruba. Pop. (1964) 210,000.

Netherlands Guiana *see* SURINAM.

Tulip fields in the Netherlands

Netherlands New Guinea, W half of New Guinea. *See* WEST IRIAN.

nettle, plant of genus *Urtica,* with stinging hairs. Common stinging nettle, *U. dioica,* found in Europe and N America.

nettle rash *see* URTICARIA.

nettle tree, tree of genus *Celtis* of elm family. Rapid-growing, 30–40 ft. high. Species include *C. australis,* common in Europe and *C. occidentalis,* the N Amer. hackberry.

Neuchâtel, Neuenberg, cap. of Neuchâtel canton W Switzerland, on N shore of L. Neuchâtel. Centre of watchmaking industry. Pop. (1960) 33,430.

Neuchâtel, Lake, largest lake wholly in Switzerland. Area: 93 sq. mi. S of Jura Mts., wine producing area.

Neumann, Johann Balthasar (1687–1753), Ger. baroque architect. Designed rococo church of Vierzehnheiligen, Germany, and palace at Würzburg.

neuralgia, pain felt along the track of a nerve, but not due to any organic disease of the nervous system, *e.g.* sciatica.

neuron, in medicine, a nerve cell with its accompanying processes.

neurosis, disorder of emotional or intellectual functioning, not amounting to insanity. Common disorders are states of anxiety and depression, phobias and obsessions.

Neustria, Merovingian Frankish kingdom of 6th–8th cent. Included most of France N of R. Loire.

neutrality, condition of a state abstaining from participation in a war

between other states, and maintaining an impartial attitude in dealing with belligerent states.

neutralization, in chemistry, process of forming a salt from reaction of an acid with a base.

neutron, elementary nuclear particle having no electric charge, found in NUCLEUS of atoms. Outside nucleus, neutron disintegrates, forming proton, electron and anti-neutrino.

Nevada, one of largest of US states. Area: 110,540 sq. mi.; cap. Carson City; main cities, Las Vegas, Reno. Desert basins used as nuclear weapon testing grounds. Main industry tourism, due to liberal divorce and gaming

Summer house on the river Vecht, Netherlands

laws. Copper, sand and gravel, gold and manganese extensively mined. Agriculture (livestock, wheat, cotton) still important. Ceded to US by Mexico (1848); 1st settled by Mormons, became state (1864). Pop. (1960) 285,278.

Nevis, volcanic island of British Leeward Is., West Indies. Area: 50 sq. mi.; cap. Charlestown. Exports sugar, coconuts, cotton, pottery. Pop. (1956 est.) 15,000.

Nevis, Ben, Inverness-shire, Scotland. Highest peak (4,406 ft.) in UK.

New Britain, volcanic island of Bismarck Archipelago, SW Pacific Ocean. Area: 14,100 sq. mi.; main town, Rabaul. Part of Trust Territory of New Guinea; formerly part of German New Guinea. Pop. (1960) 107,400.

New Brunswick, maritime prov. of E Canada; 1 of 4 orig. provs. Area: 28,354 sq. mi.; cap. Fredericton; cities, St John, Moncton. Part of ACADIA in 17th cent.; orig. Fr. settlers expelled by British (1714); became colony after settlement by UNITED EMPIRE LOYALISTS; joined Dominion of Canada (1867). Occupations include lumbering, mining, agriculture, fishing. Pop. (1961) 597,936.

New Caledonia [Nouvelle Calédonie], volcanic island of Melanesia, SW Pacific; with offshore islands forms Fr. overseas territory. Area: 8,848 sq. mi.; cap. Noumea. Discovered (1774) by Captain Cook, annexed by France (1853). Pop. (1964) 93,000.

New Deal, US domestic reform programme enacted during admin. of Pres. F. D. Roosevelt. Sought recovery from the Depression by centralizing under federal govt. unprecedented amount of economic and social reform. Estab. numerous emergency organizations (e.g. NATIONAL RECOVERY ADMINISTRATION); passed Social Security Act. Long-term projects included TENNESSEE VALLEY AUTHORITY.

New Delhi see DELHI.

New Democratic Party, polit. organization, founded (1961) as union of Co-operative Commonwealth Federation party of Canada and Canadian Labour Congress. CCF estab. 1932 to represent agrarian, labour and socialist aims. First leader J. S. Woodsworth. Party formed provincial govt. in Saskatchewan (1944–64).

New Economic Policy (NEP), official economic policy of USSR (1921–8), introd. by Lenin to counter unrest. Abolished forced labour, requisition of grain, provided open market with fixed prices.

New England, name given to NE region of US, comprising Maine, New Hampshire, Vermont, Massachusetts, Rhode Island and Connecticut. First settled (1620), remained Eng. controlled until Amer. Revolution.

New Forest, region of Hampshire, England. Largest woodland (144 sq. mi.) in UK, enclosed by William I. Inhabited by unique breed of ponies.

New France, Fr. N Amer. colony, mostly modern Quebec. Claimed (1534) by Jacques Cartier, 1st settlement at Quebec under Champlain. Centre of Fr. fur-trading,

Bishop's Palace, Würzburg, designed by Balthasar Neumann

missionary and exploration ventures until Brit. rule estab. by Treaty of Paris (1763).

New Guinea, Territory of see PAPUA AND NEW GUINEA, TERRITORY OF.

New Guinea or **Papua,** world's 2nd largest island, in SW Pacific between Indonesia and Australia. Area: 314,000 sq. mi. Mountain ranges surrounded by trop. jungle. Chief product, copra. Comprises West Irian, Territory of Papua and New Guinea.

New Hampshire, New England state, US; 1 of orig. 13, was 9th to ratify Constitution thereby making it operative. Area: 9,304 sq. mi.; cap. Concord; cities, Manchester, Nashua,

Portsmouth (only port). Mainly hilly, well wooded, highly industrialized; machinery, electrical and electronic products, instruments, wood and paper products. Textile and shoe industries and declining agriculture. Pop. (1960) 606,921.

New Haven, city and port of Connecticut, US (founded 1637–8); site of Yale University (founded 1718); joint cap. of Connecticut with Hartford (1701–1875). Pop. 163,300.

New Hebrides, group of volcanic islands in S Pacific, W of Samoa. Area: 5,700 sq. mi.; cap. Vila. Produces coffee, copra, cocoa. Dis-

covered (1606) by Pedro Queiros. Since 1887, jointly administered by UK and France. Pop. (1963) 68,000.

New Ireland, volcanic island of Bismarck Archipelago, SW Pacific. Area: 3,820 sq. mi.; cap. Kavieng. Formerly part of German New Guinea. Exports copra. Pop. (1960) 39,700.

New Jersey, US state, E coast, 1 of orig. 13. Area: 7,836 sq. mi.; cap. Trenton; cities, Newark, Jersey City, Camden, Paterson, Atlantic City. Mainly low lying with uplands in N. Industries, chemicals, electric machinery, food processing, printing and publishing. Poultry and dairy farming. Pop. (1960) 6,066,782.

New Mexico, SW state of US. Area: 121,666 sq. mi.; cap. Santa Fé; cities, Albuquerque, Roswell, Carlsbad. Contains parts of Great Plains, Rocky Mts., Colorado Plateau. Climate semi-arid, sunny. Resources, petroleum, uranium, potash, copper, timber. Agriculture includes wheat growing, stock raising, cotton. Sp. colony, US territory (1850), 47th US state (1912). Pop. (1960) 951,023.

New Orleans, largest city and chief port of Louisiana, US. Orig. cap. of Fr. Louisiana, transferred to Spain (1763), returned to France (1801), passed to US as part of LOUISIANA PURCHASE (1803). Centre of Dixieland jazz. Mardi Gras festival held annually. Largest US cotton market; industries, sugar refining, shipping, textiles. Pop. (1963) 971,000.

New South Wales, state of SE Australia. Area: 309,433 sq. mi.; cap. Sydney. Exports wool, meat, wheat; iron, copper and gold are among rich mineral resources. Brit. sovereignty proclaimed (1770) by James Cook over most of E Australia. Territory of New South Wales demarcated in 19th cent. Pop. (1966) 4,235,030.

New Testament, 2nd part of the Christian Bible which deals with life and teachings of Jesus Christ (4 Gospels); growth of the Church (*Acts of the Apostles*); letters to individuals and newly-formed Christian communities (Epistles); vision of the

The skyscrapers of New York

struggle between the Church and her enemies (*Revelation*).

new towns, in UK, satellites of older conurbations built to decentralize heavy industries and rehouse population. There are now 18 such towns in England and Wales and 5 in Scotland.

New Year's Day, 1st day of year; Julian and later Gregorian Calendar (1582) fixed it as 1 Jan. The ancients frequently began New Year celebrations at autumnal (21 Sept.) or winter (21 Dec.) solstice.

New York, Atlantic state of E US. Area: 49,576 sq. mi.; cap. Albany; main cities, New York City, Buffalo, Rochester. Orig. Dutch colony, seized by British, held until end of War of Independence. One of the orig. 13 states (1788). Manufacturing and agriculture important. Pop. (1964) 17,915,000.

New York, city, SE NY, largest city, financial, commercial, cultural centre of US. Comprises boroughs of Manhattan, the Bronx, Brooklyn, Queens and Richmond (Staten Island). Large harbour at mouth of Hudson R. makes city leading port. Contains many landmarks, *e.g.* Empire State Building, Statue of Liberty, Broadway and Wall Street. First settled by Dutch (1625), seized by English (1664). Cap. of US (1789–90). Seat of UN H.Q. Pop. (1960) 7,782,000.

New York fern, *Dryopteris novebora-censis,* fern with pale green fronds. Native to E America.

New York laurel *see* KALMIA.

New Zealand, dominion of Brit. Commonwealth, chiefly comprising

NORTH and SOUTH ISLANDS in S Pacific. Area: 103,736 sq. mi.; cap. Wellington; other main cities, Christchurch, Auckland, Dunedin. Mountainous with varied scenery, noted for beauty. Exports dairy products, meat, wool. Islands discovered (1642) by Tasman. Missionaries 1st arrived 1815, native Maoris accepted Brit. sovereignty (1840); bloody subjugation of subsequent Maori uprisings. Separated from New South Wales colony (1841). Achieved dominion status (1907). Unit of currency, New Zealand dollar. Pop. (1966) 2,677,000.

Newark, largest city of New Jersey, US. Major transport, commercial and industrial centre of Greater New York

Metropolitan Area. Puritan settlement (1666). Pop. (1960) 405,220.

Newcastle, city and port of New South Wales, Australia. Vast reserves of coal; large iron and steel industry. Pop. (1966) 233,967.

Newcastle-under-Lyme, borough and market town of Staffordshire, England. Industries include chemicals, pottery and clothing. Pop. (1962) 76,000.

Newcastle-upon-Tyne, city, port and county town of Northumberland, England. Heavy industries include shipbuilding on Tyne R. Pop. (1966) 254,000.

Newcomen, Thomas (1663–1729), Eng. engineer. With Thomas Savery developed atmospheric steam engine.

newel, in architecture, orig. central shaft of spiral staircase. Term now used also to denote intersection of stair with landing.

Newfoundland, most E prov. of Canada, comprises Newfoundland and Labrador. Area: 156,185 sq. mi.; cap. St John's. Lumbering, fishing and mining are chief occupations. Discovered (1497) by Cabot. Brit. jurisdiction retained until union with Canada (1949). Pop. (1961) 457,853.

Newfoundland, breed of large, powerful dog orig. raised in Newfoundland. Coat is dense and oily; stands *c.* 28 in. at shoulders. Noted for sagacity, gentleness, swimming prowess.

Newman, John Henry (1801–90), Eng. churchman. As vicar in Church of England published 1st of *Tracts for the Times* (1833) which gave name to Tractarian Movement. Received into R.C. Church (1845). Wrote spiritual autobiog. *Apologia pro Vita Sua* (1864), epic poem *Dream of Gerontius* (1866), hymns, *etc.* Created cardinal, 1879.

Newport, county borough and seaport of Monmouthshire, Wales. Iron, steel, chem., and heavy engineering industries. Pop. (1965) 107,000.

news agency *see* NEWSPAPER.

newspaper, publication usually intended to convey news. Issued regularly, esp. daily or weekly. Development began 17th cent. with greater use of printing; by late 19th cent. newspapers had achieved mass appeal, giving rise to sensationalism in tabloid reporting. London *Times* and *New York Times* are leading exponents of 'hard news' approach. News gathering supplemented by news agencies, *e.g.* Associated Press, Reuters.

newt, small lizard-like amphibian of genus *Triturus,* related to salamander. Found in N America, Europe and Asia. Crested newt, *Triturus cristatus,* is largest European species.

Newton, Sir Isaac (1642– 1727), Eng. mathematician. In *Principia Mathematica* (1687, Eng. tr. 1729) set out system of universe based on physical laws; formulated laws of gravitation and motion. Founded differential and integral calculus, discovered binomial theorem, composition of light, developed telescope. Reformed coinage while Master of the Mint. Pres. of Royal Society (1705– 27).

Ney, Michel (1769– 1815), Fr. army officer. Served in Napoleon's Russ. campaign (1812). Supported Louis XVIII after Napoleon's abdication; sent to arrest Napoleon on his return from Elba, changed sides and fought at Waterloo (1815). Shot for treason.

Nez Percé, Indian tribe, occupying parts of NW US; noted horse-breeders. During 1870s, under Chief JOSEPH, resisted white settlement. Majority now live on reservation in Idaho.

Niagara Falls, waterfalls of Niagara R. on US-Canadian border; Amer. Falls (ht. *c.* 165 ft.; width *c.* 1,000 ft.) Canadian Falls or Horseshoe Falls (ht. *c.* 155 ft.; width *c.* 2,500 ft.). Tourist centre and hydro-electric power source.

Nibelungenlied, Middle High German

Port Nicholson, harbour of Wellington, New Zealand

epic written *c.* 1160. Inspired Wagner's operatic tetralogy *Der Ring des Nibelungen.*

Nicaea, ancient city of Asia Minor, founded 316 BC. Trading centre under Romans. Site of 2 church councils (325 and 787).

Nicaragua [República de Nicaragua], repub. of Central America. Area: 57,145 sq. mi.; cap. Managua. Mainly agric. with cotton, coffee, sugar and

bananas as main crops. Mineral resources include gold, silver. Sp. possession until independence (1821). Official language, Spanish. Pop. (1968 est.) 1,800,000.

Nicaragua, Lake, freshwater lake in S Nicaragua. Area: 3,100 sq. mi. Proposed as part of much debated canal project.

Nice, resort on Côte d'Azur, SE France. Famous resort of Fr. Riviera. Noted also for perfumes. Pop. (1957) 277,000.

Nicene Creed, statement of Christian belief formulated by Council of Nicaea (325); modified by 1st Council of Constantinople (381) giving orthodox doctrine of the Trinity. Christ, as Son of God, is of the same substance as the Father.

Nicholas, Saint (d. *c.* 350), bishop of Myra, Asia Minor. Patron saint of Russia, children, sailors. In Europe, his feast day (6 Dec.) is observed by exchange of gifts. In Eng.-speaking countries, identified with Santa Claus.

Nicholas [I], Saint, (*c.* 825– 867), pope (858– 67). Upheld right of bishops to appeal directly to Rome without resorting to their superiors.

Nicholas I (1796– 1855), emperor and tsar of Russia (1825– 55). Main achievements were codification of existing laws, banning of the sale of serfs without their families, and considerable improvement in the position of Crown peasants. Fought successful wars with Persia (1826– 8) and Turkey (1827– 9); brutally suppressed Polish uprising (1849); led Russia into disastrous Crimean War (1853– 6).

Nicholas II (1868– 1918), tsar of Russia (1894– 1917). Although intent on preserving autocracy, defeat of Russia by Japan and subsequent revolution (1905) compelled him to allow representative govt. In World War 1, took charge of armed forces leaving govt. to empress under

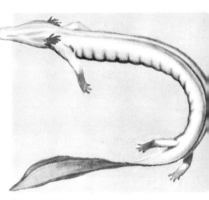

Smooth Newt

influence of RASPUTIN. Abdicated (1917) and executed with his family by Bolsheviks.

Nicholas of Cusa (*c.* 1401– 64), Ger. Catholic cardinal. As papal legate (1451– 2), preached, travelled widely, reformed monasteries.

Nicholson, Ben (1894–), Eng. painter, known for semi-abstract, geometric still-lifes and landscapes. Son of painter Sir William Nicholson.

Nicias (d. 413 BC), Athenian statesman. Negotiated Peace of Nicias (421 BC) by which Peloponnesian War was temporarily suspended. Appointed commander of Sicilian expedition (415 BC), captured and put to death on surrender of Athenian army.

nickel (Ni), white metallic element, at. no. 28. Malleable, ductile, magnetic; resists corrosion. Used in coinage, food industries, electro-plating and stainless steel manufacture.

Nicobar Islands *see* ANDAMAN AND NICOBAR ISLANDS.

Nicodemus, in NT, Pharisee who pleaded that Jesus be given a fair trial. Aided by Joseph of Arimathea, provided for His burial.

Nicolai, Carl Otto Ehrenfried (1810– 49), Ger. composer. Operas include *Merry Wives of Windsor* (1849). Founded Vienna Philharmonic Soc.

Nicholls, Richard (1624– 72), Eng. colonial administrator. Became gov. of New Netherlands colony after Dutch surrender, renaming it New York (1664).

Nicolson, Sir Harold George (1886– 1968), Brit. politician, diplomat, writer. M.P. (1935– 45). Works include biographies of Tennyson (1923), Byron (1924), Swinburne (1926) and his own *Diaries and Letters (1930– 9)* pub. 1966.

Nicosia, cap. of Cyprus. Connected by rail to port of Famagusta. Existing city walls built by Venetians in 16th cent. Pop. (1967) 87,000.

nicotiana, genus of Amer. and Asiatic herbs or shrubs of nightshade family. Large leaves, whitish or purple flowers. Possesses narcotic poisonous properties. *N. tabacum* is source of commercial tobacco.

nicotine, colourless, volatile, liquid alkaloid obtained from leaves of tobacco plant. Up to 2·7% present in tobacco. If injected, causes paralysis of certain parts of nervous system.

Niebuhr, Reinhold (1892–1971), Amer. theologian and historian. Author of *Moral Man and Immoral Society* (1932) and *The Irony of American History* (1952).

Niemeyer, Oscar (1907–   ), Brazilian architect. Designed main buildings in Brasilia, helped plan UN building in New York.

Nietzsche, Friedrich Wilhelm (1844-1900), Ger. philosopher. Most influential work, *Thus Spake Zarathustra* (1883), calls for race of 'supermen' to initiate new morality to replace traditional Christianity. Other works include *The Birth of Tragedy* (1872) and *Beyond Good and Evil* (1886).

nigella, genus of erect, annual European plants of buttercup family. Leaves dissected; flowers blue and white. Species include love-in-a-mist, a popular garden variety.

Niger, river of W Africa, 2,600 mi. long. Rises on border of Sierra Leone and Guinea, flows past Timbuktu, through Nigeria, forms large delta in Gulf of Guinea.

Niger, Republic of, state of W central Africa. Area: *c.* 484,000 sq. mi.; cap. Niamey. Vast, semi-arid plateau with mountains in N. Economy depends on rearing of livestock and export of food

crops and peanuts. Until 1958, part of Fr. West Africa; independent 1960. Pop. (1965 est.) 4,033,500.

Niger-Congo, a major language group with over 30 distinct families, spread over a vast area of C Africa.

Nigeria, Republic of, maritime state of W Africa, member of Brit. Commonwealth. Area: 356,669 sq. mi.; cap. Lagos; main cities, Ibadan, Kano,

Iwo. Semi-desert in N; trop. rain forests; mangrove swamp forest on coastline. Mainly agric. with palm oil, cocoa, cotton, ground nuts exported. Mineral resources include oil, coal, tin, columbite. Became independent (1960), repub. (1963). Federation threatened by secession of BIAFRA. Unit of currency, Nigerian pound. Pop. (1965) 58,600,000.

night ape *see* BUSHBABY.

night heron, nocturnal bird of genus *Nycticorax*. Species include *N. nycticorax,* black-crowned night heron of Old and New Worlds and *Nyctanassa violacea,* yellow-crowned night heron.

nighthawk, long-winged Amer. bird of nightjar family of genus *Chordeiles.* Species include common nighthawk, *C. minor* of N America, and lesser nighthawk, *C. pennis,* of N and trop. S America.

Nightingale, Florence (1820–1910), Eng. nurse and hospital reformer. Prominent after heading hospital in London (1853), took 38 nurses to Crimea (1854) and estab. hospital units at Scutari and Balaklava. Founded (1860) nurses' training institution at St Thomas' Hospital, London.

nightingale, *Luscinia megarhyncha,* small migratory songbird of thrush family. Found in wooded areas of Europe, Asia and N Africa. Plumage reddish-brown; sings at night and during day.

nightjar, goatsucker, nocturnal bird of family Caprimulgidae. Short bill and wide mouth; feeds on insects captured in the air. European nightjar, *Caprimulgus europaeus,* is camouflaged with mottled plumage.

nightshade, any plant of genera *Solanum* and *Atropa.* Black nightshade, *S. nigrum,* has white flowers followed by black berries. Woody nightshade (bittersweet), *S. dulcamara,* has red berries. Extremely poisonous deadly nightshade *A. belladonna* has black berries.

nihilism, rejection of estab. laws, institutions and attitudes. Term first used by Turgenev to apply to 19th cent. revolutionary movement in Russia.

Nightingale

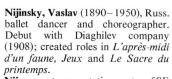

Nilgai

Nijinsky, Vaslav (1890– 1950), Russ. ballet dancer and choreographer. Debut with Diaghilev company (1908); created roles in *L'après-midi d'un faune, Jeux* and *Le Sacre du printemps.*

Nijmegen, transportation centre of SE Netherlands. Dates from Roman colony. Remains from Charlemagne's imperial residence still stand. Industries include ceramics, asphalt, furniture. Pop. (1966) 142,000.

Nike, in Gk. religion, goddess of victory, daughter of Pallas and Styx, usually represented as winged. Presided over all contests, athletic and military; esp. popular after Persian Wars. Worshipped by Romans as Victoria.

Nikolaev, Nikolayev, Ukrainian river port on Black Sea. Naval base and grain centre. Pop. (1965) 280,000.

Nile, river in Africa. Length *c.* 4,150 mi., by some calculations world's longest river. Nile proper fed by Blue and White Niles. Latter rises in L. Victoria, central E Africa, and flows N to Med. Sea. Fertile silt-laden flood waters basis of ancient Egyptian economy; now Sudan and United Arab Repub. heavily dependent on planned use of waters.

Nile, Battle of the, naval engagement fought in Aboukir Bay (1798). Victory by British under Nelson over French ended Napoleon's campaign in Egypt.

nilgai, blue bull, *Boselaphus tragocamelus,* largest Indian antelope. Male bluish-grey with small, curled horns; female tawny and hornless. Extensively hunted.

Nilo-Sahara, group of several African language families.

Nilotic, group of languages of NE Africa, spoken in Sudan, N Uganda; also in parts of Ethiopia, Congo, Kenya and Tanzania.

nimbostratus cloud *see* CLOUD.

nimbus, dark, grey, rain CLOUD. Also, term in art for halo above a divine personage or saint's head.

Nîmes, city and cap. of Gard department, S France. Market centre;

trades in fruit and wine. Roman remains include the Temple of Diana (2nd cent.). Pop. (1961) 99,802.

Nimitz, Chester William (1885– 1966), US navy commander in Pacific during World War 2. Made Admiral of Fleet (1944), head of naval operations (1945– 7).

Nimrod, in OT, mighty hunter (*Gen.* X 8, I *Chron.* I 10). Name came to refer, often ironically, to any would-be hunter.

ninebark, *Physocarpus opulifolius,* Amer. rosaceous shrub with white flowers. Bark separates into many thin layers.

Nineveh, ancient Assyrian cap. Greatest development 7th cent. BC under Sennacherib and Assurbanipal. Its fall (612 BC) to Medes and allies ended Assyrian Empire. Modern excavations began mid-19th cent.

Ninghsia, autonomous region of NW China. Area: 90,000 sq. mi.; cap. Yinchwan. Industries, agriculture (valley of Yellow R.) and mining. Pop. (1963) 1,810,000.

Ningpo, port of Chekiang prov., China, on Yung Kiang R. Chief product fish; industry centres on handicrafts, furniture manufacture. Pop. (1957) 238,000.

Ninian, Saint (*c.* 360– 432), Scot. missionary. Made pilgrimage to Rome, later named Bishop of S Picts. Founded church at Whithorn, Wigtownshire, Scotland (397).

Niobe, in Gk. myth., daughter of Tantalus. Boasted about her many children to Leto, whereupon Artemis and Apollo (children of Leto), killed them all. Turned into a stone column which continued to shed tears.

Nippur, ancient Sumerian city on Euphrates R.; centre of worship of earth-god Enlil. Archaeologists have found thousands of clay tablets.

Nirvana, in BUDDHISM and other religions, a state of supreme bliss or 'annihilation' [Sanskrit] of those desires causing suffering inseparable from existence.

nitrates, salts or esters of nitric acid, most of the salts being soluble in water. Nitrates in soil are source of nitrogen, needed by plants for growth. Metallic nitrates used to make explosives, as fertilizers and in medicine.

nitre *see* SALTPETRE.

nitric acid (HNO₃), colourless or yellow, corrosive liquid. Good conductor of electricity, strong oxidizing agent; reacts with metals, oxides and hydroxides to form nitrates. Used for making explosives and dyestuffs.

nitrification, in chemistry, process of

combining a substance with nitrogen. Combining atmospheric nitrogen with organic compounds, by nitrogen-fixing bacteria, produces NITRATES.

nitro compounds, organic compounds in which 1 or more hydrogen atoms are replaced by the nitro group. Aromatic compounds are derived from benzene and aliphatic from methane.

nitrobenzene, mirbane oil, poisonous, oily liquid which sheds water but absorbs many other liquids. Reduction yields ANILINE. Used in shoe polishes.

nitrocellulose, cellulose nitrate *see* GUNCOTTON.

nitrogen (N), colourless, tasteless, relatively inactive, gaseous element Forms *c.* $\frac{4}{5}$ of atmosphere and occurs in all living material. Isolated in a pure state by Rutherford (1772).

nitrogen-fixing bacteria, bacteria that convert nitrogen in the atmosphere into forms that can be utilized by plants in protein formation. Bacteria can be either in the soil or in roots of leguminous plants.

nitroglycerine, powerful explosive compound produced by action of nitric and sulphuric acids on glycerine. Used in preparation of dynamite, cordite and other high explosives.

Niue Island, S Pacific island. Area: *c.* 100 sq. mi. Discovered by Capt. Cook (1774), became part of New Zealand (1901). Products include copra, bananas. Pop. (1963) 5,000.

Nixon, Richard Milhous (1913–), 37th US Pres. (1969–), Republican. Served in US Congress (1947– 53), gaining prominence in ALGER HISS trials. Vice-Pres. (1953– 61) in Eisenhower admin. Narrowly defeated in 1960 pres. election by John Kennedy. Polit. comeback culminated in 1968 election victory over Hubert Humphrey.

Nkrumah, Kwame (1909–), Ghanaian political leader under whose premiership Gold Coast became independent repub. of Ghana. First P.M. (1957– 60); 1st pres. (1960– 6); deposed by army coup d'état. Exiled to Guinea.

No plays *see* JAPANESE DRAMA.

Noah, in OT, builder of the ark that saved human and animal life from the Flood. According to OT, his sons Shem, Ham, and Japheth are ancestors of the races of mankind.

Nobel, Alfred Bernhard (1833– 96), Swedish chemist and inventor. Patented mixture of nitroglycerine and gunpowder (1863), and dynamite (1866). Bequeathed a fund from

Temple of Nike, Athens

which annual prizes were to be awarded for work in physics, chemistry, physiology and medicine, literature, and for work in the cause of international peace. Awards made annually since 1901 on anniversary of Nobel's death.

nobelium, radio-active chemical element, at. no. 102. Discovered 1957 at Nobel Institute, Sweden.

Nobile, Umberto (1885–), Ital. aeronautical engineer. Designed and piloted airship *Norge* over N Pole in Amundsen-Ellsworth flight (1926). Commanded flight of *Italia* over N Pole (1928); airship crashed on return.

noble gases, inert gases, rare gases, name applied to elements neon, argon, krypton, helium, xenon and radon; characterized by lack of chemical affinity.

noctiluca, non-cellular marine animal of genus *Noctiluca* with phosphorescent granules. Responsible for much of the phosphorescence in the sea.

noctule, *Nyctalus noctula,* large reddish insectivorous bat, common in Africa, Europe, Asia.

nocturne, short lyrical piece usually for piano; favourite form of Chopin's.

noddy, tern of tropical distribution. Species include common noddy or Amer. noddy tern, *Anous stolidus,* with dark brown plumage, and white fairy tern, *A. albus,* the smallest.

Noel-Baker, Philip J[ohn] (1889–), Brit. Labour politician. Elected to Parliament (1929); Min. of State (1945– 6); Sec. of State for Com-

Nightjar

Nomads in Persia (above) and Mauritania (below)

monwealth Relations (1947–50). Publications include *The Arms Race* (1958). Awarded Nobel Peace Prize (1959).

Noguchi, Hideyo (1876–1928), Jap. bacteriologist. Pioneer in diagnosis and treatment of syphilis; discoverer of virus causing oroya fever.

Nolan, Sidney Robert (1917–), Austral. artist. Several paintings deal with Austral. legends, incl. Ned Kelly, the explorers Burke and Swan, and the Gallipoli landings.

Nolde, Emil, orig. Emil Hansen (1867–1956), Ger. Expressionist painter. Work condemned by Nazi regime as degenerate. Includes *Christ Among the Children* and *Ripe Sunflowers.*

nomad, member of race or tribe without fixed location, continually migrating in search of food or pasturage. Characteristic of C Asian herdsmen, Austral. aborigines, African bushmen, European gypsies.

Non-aggression Pact (23–24 Aug. 1939), secret agreement between USSR and Germany to divide Poland and E Europe into spheres of influence, and to foil Anglo-French moves to involve USSR in containing German aggression.

Noncomformist *see* DISSENTER; NON-CONFORMITY.

nonconformity, refusal to comply with certain rules or policies, often those of the estab. church. In 17th cent. applied to those who, while adhering to the doctrine of the Anglican Church, refused to conform to certain of its practices.

non-Euclidean geometry, branch of geometry which studies properties of various types of congruence groups, defined in Euclid's axioms of geometry. Originated with attempt to verify (or refute) certain Euclidean statements, such as the axiom that parallels met at infinity.

Non-jurors, Eng. and Scot. clergymen and schoolmasters who, after Revolution of 1688, refused to take oath of allegiance to William and Mary. Included Archbishop of Canterbury, 7 bishops, and many others.

nonpareil, painted bunting, *Passerina ciris,* small colourful Amer. finch. Head is blue, back green-yellow, body scarlet and wings and tail black. Winters in C America.

Nootka, N Amer. tribe of Mosan linguistic family living on W coast of Vancouver Is. in long communal wooden houses. Depend largely on fishing and whaling. Name is often given to the Aht Confederacy of more than 20 tribes of Northwest Coast area.

Nordau, Max [Simon] (1848–1923), Jewish-Hungarian writer and physician. His once influential novel *Degeneracy* (1892–3) tried to relate genius and degeneracy.

Nordenskjöld, Nils Adolf Erik, Baron (1832–1901), Swedish geologist and explorer. Crossed Arctic Ocean along Siberian coast through Bering Strait thus navigating North East Passage (1879). Commanded mapping and scientific expeditions to Spitsbergen and Greenland.

Nordic Council, advisory organization inaugurated (1953). Members are Denmark, Iceland, Norway, Sweden, Finland (joined 1956). Aims are to improve commercial and cultural links.

Nore, the, sandbank at mouth of Thames R., England. At E end is Nore light-vessel. Famous for mutiny of Royal Navy (1797).

Norfolk, city and port of SE Virginia, US. Natural harbours; largest US drydocks; US navy base and H.Q. of Supreme Allied Command, Atlantic. Shipbuilding, processed sea foods. Pop. (1963) 508,000.

Norfolk, maritime county of E England, part of EAST ANGLIA. Area: 2,054 sq. mi.; county town, Norwich. Agriculture and fishing important. Popular tourist area. Pop. (1966) 586,000.

Norfolk, Dukes of *see* HOWARD.

Norfolk Island, small volcanic Austral. island in S Pacific Ocean. Area: 13 sq. mi.; cap. Kingston. Discovered by Cook (1774). Subtrop., fertile soil; citrus fruits, bananas, coffee grown. Tourist centre. Pop. (1961) 844.

Norkay, Tensing (1914–), Nepalese mountaineer. With Sir Edmund Hillary, first to reach summit of Mt. Everest (1953).

Norman, variety of French spoken by Northmen (NORMANS) who settled in France. As Anglo-Norman (or Anglo-French), official language of England for 300 yr. after Norman Conquest.

Norman architecture, form of ROMANESQUE developed in Normandy and England (11th–12th cent.). Characterized by massive construction, barrel vaults, semi-circular arches. Ely and Durham Cathedrals, Keep (White Tower) of Tower of London are examples.

Normandy [Normandie], district and former prov. of N France. Covers departments of Seine-Inférieure, Eure, Orne, Calvados and Manche. Hist. cap. Rouen; main towns Dieppe, Le Havre, Caen. Agric. region with cattle-raising, apple orchards. Named after Normans who conquered area (10th cent.).

Normans, descendants of Viking settlers in N France (Normandy); under Duke William conquered England (1066).

Norris, [Benjamin] Frank[lin] (1870–1902), Amer. novelist and journalist. Known for *Epic of Wheat,* a trilogy incl. *The Octopus* (1901), *The Pit* (1903) and *The Wolf* (unfinished).

Norrish, Ronald George Wreyford (1897–), Eng. chemist. Noted for work on extremely fast chem. reactions. Awarded Nobel Prize for Chemistry (1967).

Norse language, N Germanic European language, spoken in Scandinavia and Iceland.

Norsemen *see* VIKINGS.

North, Frederick, 2nd Earl of Guildford and 8th Baron North (1732–92), Eng. statesman; P.M. (1770–82) during period leading to and during Amer. Revolution. Carried out policies of George III regarding taxing of colonies, which led directly to rebellion in America.

North African campaign, prolonged conflict (1940–3) during World War 2 along Egypt-Libya coastal area for control of Med. Precipitated by Italy's entry (June 1940). Brit. troops pushed back to ALAMEIN after Ger. reinforcements under Rommel had arrived (1941–2). Ger. and

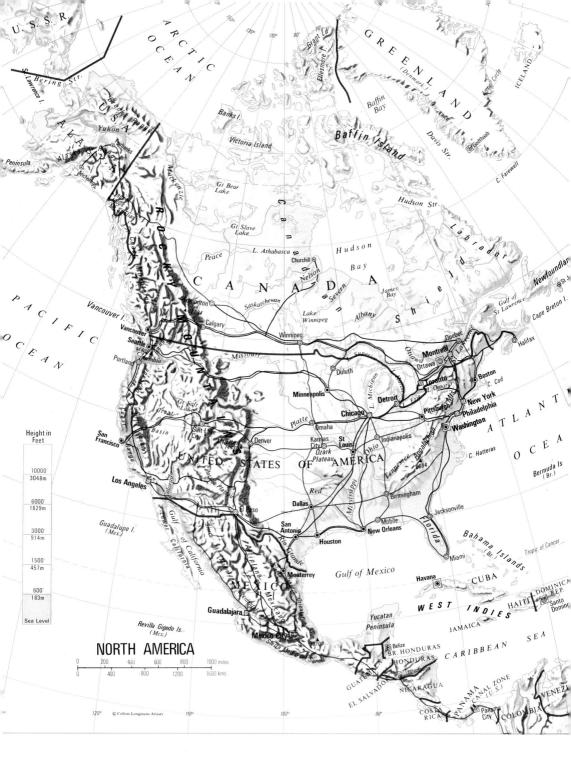

NORTH AMERICA

Ital. troops, trapped after arrival of Allies in Algeria, surrendered May 1943.

North America, 3rd largest continent, N landmass of W Hemisphere; comprises CANADA, UNITED STATES, MEXICO. Area: *c.* 8,000,000 sq. mi.

Extends from Greenland to Alaska in N, separated from S America by Central Amer. countries. Central plain (*c.* 1,500 mi. wide) separates E mountain ranges (Laurentian, Appalachian and Adirondacks) from W Rocky Mts. and drains great river

systems, incl. Mississippi and St Lawrence-Great Lakes. Highest point, Mt. McKinley in Alaska; lowest point, Death Valley, California. Climate varies, temperatures extreme. Rainfall abundant along much of coasts; forested in mountain

The Giant's Causeway, a basalt rock formation on the coast of Antrim, Northern Ireland

ranges, agric. (esp. wheat) in plains, deserts in SW. Extensive mineral resources, those in barren N as yet largely unexploited. Population consists of European descendants, as well as Negroes, Indians and Asiatics. Pop. *c.* 260,000,000.

North Atlantic Treaty Organization (NATO), international defence organization, signed 1949. Charter members: Belgium, Canada, Denmark,

France, Iceland, Italy, Luxembourg, the Netherlands, Norway, Portugal, UK and US; Greece, Turkey and West Germany joined later. Military H.Q., transferred from Paris to Brussels (1967), oversees NATO forces and strategy. Nuclear arms control and Fr. threats to withdraw jeopardized NATO's future in late 1960s.

North Carolina, Atlantic state of SE US. Area: 52,712 sq. mi.; cap. Raleigh; main cities, Charlotte, Greensboro. One of 13 original states. Coastal plains on E rising to Blue Ridge and Great Smoky Mts. in W. Chief products are tobacco, cotton, peanuts and corn. Pop. (1960) 4,556,155.

North Dakota, state of N central US. Area: 70,665 sq. mi.; cap. Bismarck; main cities, Fargo, Grand Forks. Lowland in E, hills in W. Crops include cereals; dairy cattle raised. Mineral resources include petroleum, coal. Population scattered. Pop. (1960) 632,446.

North East Passage, route through

Arctic Ocean from North Sea to Pacific Ocean. First navigated by Swedish explorer Nils Adolf Erik Nordenskjöld (1878–9). Lost importance with development of airways.

North Island, one of 2 main islands of NEW ZEALAND, separated from SOUTH ISLAND by Cook Strait. Area: 44,281 sq. mi. Cities are Wellington (cap. of New Zealand) and Auckland. Geysers and hot springs at Rotorua; natural steam used to generate electricity at Wairakei. Pop. (1966) 1,893,326.

North Pole, N terminus of rotational axis of earth, latitude 90° and longitude 0°. First reached by Robert E. Peary (1909).

North Rhine-Westphalia, state of West Germany formed 1946, incl. Ruhr and Rhine indust. areas. Area: 13,111 sq. mi.; cap. Düsseldorf; cities, Bonn, Cologne, Essen, Duisburg. Pop. (1961) 15,902,000.

North Riding, one of 3 administrative divisions of Yorkshire, England, constituting separate county. Area: 2,127 sq. mi.; county town, Northallerton. Iron-smelting and shipbuilding. Pop. (1965) 581,000.

North Sea, narrow extension of Atlantic between British Isles and NW central Europe; S end forms English Channel. Important fishing area esp. shallows, *e.g.* Dogger Bank. Extension of N Ger. natural gas fields located 1965.

North Star *see* POLE STAR.

North West Company, organization of Montreal merchants and fur traders to compete with Hudson's Bay Co. Territory exploited included Athabasca region, Arctic coast and N Pacific coast. Merged with Hudson's Bay Co. (1821).

North West Mounted Police *see* ROYAL CANADIAN MOUNTED POLICE.

North West Passage, route from Atlantic to Pacific round N coast of Canada, sought by Brit. and Fr. expeditions (15th–16th cent.); 1st navigated by Amundsen (1903–5).

Northampton, county borough and county town of Northamptonshire, England. Industries include shoe manufacturing, tanning, textiles, brewing. Pop. (1966) 122,000.

Northampton, Treaty of (1328), treaty which recognized independence of Scotland following Battle of Bannockburn (1314).

Northamptonshire, county of C England. Area: 914 sq. mi.; county town, Northampton. Iron ore mining, boot and shoe manufacture, and agriculture. Interesting church architecture, *e.g.* Peterborough Cathedral. Pop. (1965) 423,000.

Northcliffe, Alfred Charles William Harmsworth, Viscount (1865–1922), Eng. journalist. Founded weekly paper *Answers to Correspondents* (1888) and *Daily Mail* (1896). Took over *The Times* (1908) and with brother Harold (later Viscount Rothermere) formed Amalgamated Press, largest newspaper combine in world.

North-East Frontier Agency, territory in E Himalayan foothills in Assam State, NE India. Area: *c.* 31,436 sq. mi. Chinese briefly invaded area (1962). Pop. *c.* 450,000.

Northern Ireland, part of United Kingdom, estab. by Govt. of Ireland Act (1920). Consists of 6 Ulster counties of NE Ireland. Area: 5,240 sq. mi.; cap. Belfast; other cities, Londonderry, Lisburn. Largely hilly, with bogs and moors; Mourne, Antrim and Sperrin Mountains surround C fertile lowland around Lough Neagh. Agriculture important on low ground. Irish Republican Army insurgents countered by presence of British troops after 1969. Pop. (1966) 1,478,000

Waterfall from a melting glacier, Jostedalsbre, Norway

Sandefjord, centre of the Norwegian whaling industry

Norwich Canary

Northern Territory, territory of Commonwealth of Australia, between Western Australia and Queensland, mainly in tropics. Area: 523,620 sq. mi.; cap. Darwin. Orig. part of New South Wales, became territory 1911. Economy based on cattle-raising (dependent on artesian water), and mining for gold, mica, tin, uranium. Pop. (1961, excluding Aborigines) 27,095.

Northrop, John Howard (1891–   ), Amer. biochemist. With J. B. Sumner and W. M. Stanley, awarded Nobel Prize for Chemistry (1946) for work on isolation of enzymes and viruses.

Northumberland, John Dudley, Duke of (c. 1502–53), Eng. statesman. Tried to place his daughter-in-law Lady Jane Grey on throne, but was forced to surrender to Mary Tudor and was beheaded for high treason.

Northumberland, border county of N England. Area: 2,018 sq. mi.; county town Newcastle-upon-Tyne. Low-lying, rising inland to Cheviot Hills. Main crops, oats and barley; sheep reared. Rich coal deposits in SE; associated industries include iron founding, shipbuilding, machinery manufacturing. Pop. (1966) 890,000.

Northumbria, kingdom of N England, c. AD 600–900, made up of kingdoms of Bernicia and Deira. Under influence of Irish missionaries became centre of European culture (8th cent.).

Northwest Territories, NW part of Canada, area E of Yukon. Area: 1,304,903 sq. mi. Administered by Min. of Northwest Affairs based in Ottawa. Largely underdeveloped and unpopulated. Products include furs, lumber; rich mineral deposits as yet unexploited. Pop. (1961) 22,998.

Norway [Norge], kingdom of N Europe, occupying N and W portion of Scandinavian peninsula. Area: 125,181 sq. mi.; cap. Oslo; main cities, Trondheim, Bergen. Mountainous with coastal lowlands; coastline deeply indented by fiords. Agriculture confined to scarce cultivated area. Fishing, forestry and mining import-

ant. Industry of increasing importance. Norway has world's 3rd largest merchant navy. Several kingdoms united (9th cent.) by VIKINGS. United with Denmark (1397–1814); with Sweden from 1815 until late 19th cent. Occupied by Germany during World War 2. Unit of currency, the krone. Pop. (1965) 3,753,000.

Norwegian, a Scandinavian Indo-European language; 3 million speakers in Norway.

Norwich, city, county borough and county town of Norfolk, England. Industries include manufacture of textiles, boots, shoes, mustard and starch; foundries and breweries. Cathedral (11th cent.). Pop. (1965) 119,000.

Norwich canary, one of chief varieties of domesticated canary. Very hardy; richly coloured plumage.

nose, facial prominence in man and higher apes above mouth. Divided by plate of cartilage into 2 passages, it passes backwards and downwards to become naso-pharynx. Contains organ of smell.

nostoc, fresh-water blue-green alga of genus *Nostocaceae*. Often found in jelly-like colonies in moist places.

Nostradamus, orig. Michel de Nostredam (1503–66), Fr. astrologer. *Centuries* (1555) contains obscure and symbolic prophecies in rhyme.

Notary Public, public official appointed to administer oaths and draw up and certify certain documents.

notation, in music, signs used to indicate pitch and duration of sounds.

notification, lawful act of giving notice of certain diseases, *e.g.* diphtheria, typhoid fever and tuberculosis, to enable local health authorities to prevent further spread and to compile statistics.

Notre Dame de Paris, Gothic cathedral on island in R. Seine. Dedicated to the Virgin Mary; begun 1163.

Nottingham, city of C England, county town of Nottinghamshire, on R. Trent. Danish borough in 9th cent. Contains Nottingham University. Manufacturing includes cotton and silk goods. Pop. (1966) 310,000.

Nottinghamshire, inland county of C England. Area: 844 sq. mi.; county town, Nottingham. Upland moors border on low-lying fertile land. Cereal crops grown; dairy cattle reared. Coal mining in W. Manufactures lace, hosiery, textiles, bicycles. Contains Sherwood Forest, home of ROBIN HOOD. Pop. (1961) 903,000.

nouvelle vague, style of film-making, esp. in France; chief exponent, Jean-Luc Godard. Techniques include breaking of time sequence and jump-cutting. Aims to involve audience through emotional reaction rather than narrative.

nova, VARIABLE STAR which assumes brightness many times greater than normal at times.

Nova Scotia, maritime prov. of E Canada, original prov. of Confeder-

Norwegian wooden stave church of 12th century

ation (1867). Includes Cape Breton Is. Area: 21,425 sq. mi.; cap. Halifax. Economy based on natural resources: agriculture, mining, processing, fishing, shipbuilding. Pop. (1961), 737,007.

Novalis, orig. Friedrich Leopold Freiherr von Hardenberg (1772–1801), Ger. novelist and Romantic poet. His unfinished novel *Heinrich von Ofterdingen* treats the youth and education of a poet in medieval Europe. Other works include *Hymns to the Night* (1800; Eng. tr. 1889).

Novaya Zemlya, Russ. archipelago in Arctic Ocean, between Barents and Kara seas. Area: 31,892 sq. mi. Used by USSR for nuclear tests. Pop. (1950 est.) 400.

novel, fictional prose narrative of no set length. Techniques vary, tone may be comic, tragic, romantic, realistic. Samuel Richardson's *Pamela* (1740) was 1st modern novel.

Novgorod, historic and commercial city of Russ. SFSR, USSR. In 12th cent. cap. of Russia; key city of Hanseatic League (13th–14th cent.). Cathedral and Kremlin destroyed in World War 2. Pop. (1959) 61,000.

Novi Sad, city of N Yugoslavia in Vojvodina prov., on Danube R. Flour-milling. Centre of Serbian cultural revival in 18th and early 19th cent. Pop. (1963) 82,200.

Novorossisk, leading seaport of Russ. SFSR, on NE coast of Black Sea. Exports wheat and petroleum. Pop. (1959) 93,000.

Novosibirsk, industrial, cultural and communications centre of Siberia. Founded 1893 on Ob R. and Trans-Siberian Rly. Pop. (1967) 1,049,000.

Noyes, Alfred (1880–1958), Eng. poet. Verse, mostly narrative or lyrical, includes *The Torch Bearers* (1922–30) and well known poems 'The Barrel Organ' and 'The Highwayman'.

Nubia, historic region of NE Africa, conquered 19th cent. by Mohammed Ali of Egypt. Now part of Sudan.

Nubian Desert, desert in NE Sudan, between Nile R. and Red Sea.

nuclear energy, energy given out by fission or fusion of atomic nuclei; includes heat which may be used to produce electricity. *See* NUCLEAR FORCES.

nuclear forces, electro-magnetic forces binding protons and neutrons of the atomic nucleus; released when atom is 'split' (atomic fission takes place), destructively with production of great heat and energy in nuclear weapons and usefully in controlled fission within reactor.

nuclear physics, study of nucleus of atom, especially of forces holding together neutrons and protons, and of particles emitted from radioactive nuclei.

nucleic acids, complex organic acids made up of molecular chains. DNA (deoxyribonucleic acid) and RNA (ribonucleic acids). Carry out synthesis of proteins and transfer of genetic code.

nucleus, central part of the atom; containing most of its mass and bearing a positive electrical charge magnitude of which is characteristic of the ELEMENT and determined by number of protons in nucleus; protons and neutrons are bound together by NUCLEAR FORCES.

nucleus, in biology, *see* CELL; CHROMOSOMES.

Nuffield, William Richard Morris, 1st Viscount (1877–1963), Eng. industrialist and philanthropist. From 1912 built Morris Motors Ltd. into a huge combine. Founded Nuffield College, Oxford (1937) and NUFFIELD FOUNDATION for research (1943).

Nuffield Foundation, Brit. and Commonwealth foundation for medical and sociological research. Estab. (1943) by Lord Nuffield with £10 million capital.

Nullarbor Plain [Lat: no trees], vast arid, limestone tableland of S Australia, *c.* 251 mi. wide. Riddled with subterranean caves and passages; crossed by world's longest stretch of straight rly. track.

nullification, doctrine, adhered to by exponents of STATES' RIGHTS in US, that state is not bound to enforce federal legislation. Leading advocate,

Old buildings in Nürnberg

John Calhoun, encouraged South Carolina to nullify federal tariff acts (1832), but state rescinded (1833) after Pres. Jackson had been empowered to use army to enforce tariffs.

nullity, in Eng. law, judicial declaration of invalidity of a marriage.

numbat, banded anteater, *Myrmecobius fasciatus,* small Austral. marsupial about the size of a large rat. Long sticky tongue for clearing termite nests, strong claws and unusual number of teeth (50–52).

Numbers, 4th book of OT, containing 2 censuses of Israelites (hence title) and continuing history of journey to

Rock Nuthatch (left) and Corsican Nuthatch (right)

Promised Land and rise of Joshua as leader.

numerals, figures used to express a number. Letters were used by Greeks and Romans. In 12th cent., Europe adopted Arabic system, still in use.

Numidia, name given by Romans to territory of N Africa. Now E part of Algeria.

numismatics, study of coins and medals, dealing with history and art of coinage among ancient and modern nations. Invention of coinage attributed to Chinese; in W, first coins struck by Lydians of Asia Minor in 750 BC.

nun, member of a religious community of women, esp. one living under vows of poverty, chastity and obedience in a convent.

nun moth, *Lymantria monacha,* European moth; larvae often damage coniferous trees.

Nunc Dimittis, Latin canticle based on words uttered by Simeon when he saw Jesus (*Luke* II 29). Used in R.C. and Anglican churches.

nuncio, papal representative sent on diplomatic missions, having status of ambassador.

Nupé, district of Repub. of Nigeria, W Africa. Area: 6,400 sq. mi.; cap. Bida. Part of Fulani empire before becoming British (1901).

Nuremberg Trials, trial of Nazi leaders and military commanders who survived World War 2, by Allied Tribunal under charter agreed upon by US, UK, USSR and France. All but 3 found guilty of war crimes and crimes against humanity; sentenced (1946) to death or long terms of imprisonment.

Nureyev, Rudolf (1939–), Russ. ballet dancer. Appeared with Kirov Ballet before seeking polit. asylum in Paris (1961). Principal dancer with Royal Ballet, London.

Nurmi, Paavo (1897–), Finnish athlete. Won 6 Olympic titles (1920–32) in 1,500 to 10,000 m. races, and set 20 world records.

Nürnberg, Nuremberg, commercial city of Bavaria, West Germany. Centre of art and literature in Middle Ages, imperial city 1219. After 1937 a Nazi centre; virtually destroyed, World War 2. Scene of trial of Nazi leaders (1945–6). Pop. (1965) 472,000.

nut, hard-shelled dry fruit or seed. More or less distinct separable rind or shell and interior kernel or meat.

nutcracker, *Nucifraga caryocatactes,* bird of crow family of coniferous forests in N Europe and Asia. Brown and white plumage; long straight beak.

nuthatch, small short-tailed sharp-beaked bird of family Sittidae. Creeps up and down trees; feeds on insects and nuts. Species include European nuthatch, *Sitta europaea;* and N Amer. varieties, white-breasted nuthatch, *S. carolinensis,* and red-breasted nuthatch, *S. canadensis.*

nutmeg, hard aromatic seed of fruit of E Indian nutmeg tree, *Myristica fragrans.* Mace, also a spice, derived from seed covering. Oil from seed and covering used in medicine and cosmetics.

nutria; name for COYPU.

nutrition, science that deals with the composition of foods, their use by plants and animals and their effect on health.

nux vomica, poisonous disc-shaped seed of deciduous tree, *Strychnos nux vomica,* of India, Thailand, Indo-China and N Australia. Yields bitter, alkaloid poisons incl. strychnine and derivatives.

nyala, *Tragelaphus angasii,* mammal of Bovidae family closely related to the antelope. Found in S and E Africa. Whitish stripes on dark mane; males have horns.

Nyasa, Lake, former name for L. Malawi, E Africa. Bounded by Malawi, Tanzania, Mozambique. Important African trade artery. Re-named after Malawi independence (1966).

Nyasaland *see* MALAWI.

Nyerere, Julius Kambarage (1922–), African statesman. Formed Tanganyika African National Union (1954); became P.M. (1961), and 1st Pres. of independent repub. (1962). Negotiated union with Zanzibar (1963) and became Pres. of Tanzania.

Nylon, generic name for group of synthetic polyamide fibres, developed in US (1930). Strong, durable, elastic, non-inflammable, easily washed and dried.

nymph, in zoology, immature stages of incompletely metamorphosed insects after quitting egg. Nymph succeeded by perfect insect at its last moult.

Nymphs, in Gk. myth., generic name for large number of female divinities. Associated with water, fertility and superior gods, *e.g.* Nereids, Naiads, Oreads, Dryads and Hamadryads.

Groundnut plant (left). Insets show fruit and how it grows from runners

O

oak, tree or shrub of genus *Quercus,* bearing acorn as fruit. Widely distributed in N temp. regions. Hard, durable wood used in furniture making. Bark of cork oak, *Q. suber,* used commercially in manufacture of cork.

oak apple, reddish spongy apple-shaped gall. Formed on oak trees by larva of gall wasp.

Oakley, Annie, orig. Phoebe Anne Moses (1860–1926), Amer. markswoman and theatrical performer. Appeared in Buffalo Bill's Wild West Show (1885–1902).

oakum, fibre obtained from untwisting ropes. Used in caulking the seams

Oak: Leaves (left) and Acorns (right) of (a) common European Brown Oak (b) Sessile or Durmast Oak (c) American Oak

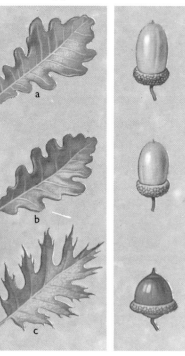

of wooden vessels and deck-planking of steel ships.

oarfish, deep-sea fish with jelly-like transparent body, up to 30ft. long. Often pale blue in colour.

oarweed, tangle, *Laminaria digitata,* large brown seaweed growing below low tide level. Used as cattle food.

oasis, fertile area in a desert, caused either by subterranean waters or sinking of artesian wells.

oat, *Avena sativa,* hardy cereal yielding grain. Native of Asia, also grown in cool climates. Cultivated as food for man, *e.g.* oatmeal, and for animals.

Oates, Lawrence Edward Grace (1880–1912), Eng. explorer, member of expedition to South Pole led by ROBERT SCOTT. Died on return journey.

Oates, Titus (1649–1705), Eng. conspirator. With Israel Tonge invented Popish Plot (1678) against Charles II, resulting in widespread persecution of Catholics. Imprisoned but released (1688).

Obadiah or **Abdias,** prophetic book of OT. Foretells destruction of Edomites, and triumph of Israel. Prob. written 600–550 BC.

obbligato, musical term orig. denoting essential part of composition. Subsequent misunderstanding has reversed meaning.

obelisk, in ancient Egypt, square, monolithic shaft, tapering towards top, with pyramidal apex. First erected (*c.* 2700 BC), in honour of sun god Ra.

Oberammergau, Ger. tourist centre in Bavarian Alps. Famous for *Passion Play* produced every 10 years.

obesity, pathological condition resulting in over-accumulation of fat. Caused by malfunctioning of endocrine glands (*e.g.* thyroid), and over-eating.

oboe, woodwind instrument with double reed and conical bore, developed from medieval shawm or pommer. Oldest member of orchestral woodwind. Cor anglais or English horn is similar, but a fifth lower in pitch.

observatory, building designed for observation of astronomical or meteorological phenomena, *e.g.* Mt. Palomar Observatory, California, and Jodrell Bank, Cheshire, England.

obsidian, volcanic glass, usually black and glossy. Used by prehistoric man for arrowheads.

obstetrics, branch of medicine concerned with childbirth and treatment of mother before and after delivery.

ocarina, musical instrument, elongated oval in shape, with 5 finger holes

The famous marble stairway which leads down to the harbour at Odessa

and mouth-piece. Produces flute-like sound.

O'Casey, Sean (1884–1964), Irish playwright. Early work *Juno and the Paycock* (1925) portrayed Dublin slum life. Later works include *The Plough and the Stars* (1926), *Within the Gates* (1934), *The Drums of Father Ned* (1960).

Occam or **Ockham, William of** see WILLIAM OF OCCAM.

Occleve or **Hoccleve, Thomas** (*c.* 1370–1450), Eng. poet; wrote in Latin, French and English. Main works, *e.g. De Regimine Principium, La Male Règle,* illustrate poverty of post-Chaucerian Eng. literature.

occultism, practice or study of sciences involving supernatural, such as alchemy, astrology, theosophy, magic, spiritualism.

occupational therapy, provision of stimulating activities, both light manual and mental, used in treatment of long-term patients and those suffering from mental disorders. First used in ancient Greece and Egypt.

ocean, geographical name for largest expanses of salt water which cover almost $\frac{1}{4}$ of Earth's surface. Largest is Pacific.

Oceania, collective name for islands in Pacific Ocean incl. Micronesia, Melanesia and Polynesia groups, and sometimes, Australasia and Malay Archipelago.

Ocelot

ocelot, *Felis pardalis,* wild cat found in Texas and S America; valued for its fur. Coat is tawny yellow with black spots or streaks.

Ochoa, Severo, FRS (1905–), Amer. biochemist, b. Spain. Awarded Nobel Prize for Physiology and Medicine (1959) with Arthur Kornberg for research on natural synthesis and composition of nucleic acids.

ochre, ocher, natural earth, mixture of hydrated oxide of iron with, *e.g.* clay, ranging in colour from yellow to brown and red. Used as pigment for colouring paint.

O'Connell, Daniel (1775–1847), Irish polit. leader; founded (1823) Catholic Assoc. Pressure from Assoc. led to Catholic Emancipation Act (1829). Advocated severing union with Britain.

O'Connor, Flannery (1925–65), Amer. novelist and short-story writer. Author of *Wise Blood* (1952), *A Good Man is Hard to Find* (1955).

ocotillo, *Fouqueria splendens,* thorny desert shrub of SW US and Mexico.

octave flute *see* PICCOLO.

Octavian *see* AUGUSTUS.

octopus, *Octopus vulgaris,* marine creature with 4 pairs of sucker-bearing arms and soft, oval body. Lives mostly on sea-bed; black, grape-like eggs.

ode, orig. Gk. poem sung to musical accompaniment, either for single voice, *e.g.* odes of Sappho, Alcaeus, Anacreon, or choral, *e.g.* Pindar. Odes of Horace largely influenced 17th cent. Eng. poets. Revived in France (16th cent.) esp. by Ronsard. Odes of Romantics and later poets less restrained in subject matter and style.

Odense, port on N Fyn Is., Denmark. Industries include machinery, glass, shipbuilding. Site of shrine to Odin. Pop. (1963) 110,000.

Oder [Polish: **Odra**], river (*c.* 550 mi. long) rising in Moravia, Czechoslovakia. Flows NW through Poland into Baltic at Stettin.

Odessa, important seaport, SW Ukrainian SSR, on Black Sea. Commercial and industrial (flour, machinery, chemicals) centre. Scene of mutiny (1905) aboard battleship *Potemkin.* Pop. (1967) 753,000.

Odets, Clifford (1906–63), Amer. playwright. Dramas, centring on capitalist corruption, include *Waiting for Lefty* (1935) and *Golden Boy* (1937).

Odin, in Norse myth., chief god, identified with Ger. WODEN. God of war and learning.

Odysseus [Lat: **Ulysses**], in Gk. myth., king of Ithaca, husband of

An Oasis

Penelope and father of Telemachus. Gk. leader during Trojan War, devised Wooden Horse scheme, enabling Greeks to enter Troy and complete conquest. Hero of Homer's ODYSSEY.

Odyssey, Gk. verse epic of 24 books attributed to Homer. Story of Odysseus' wanderings after Trojan War, during which he encountered series of obstacles before regaining his kingdom, Ithaca.

Oedipus, in Gk. myth., king of Thebes. Abandoned on Mt. Cithaeron when it was prophesied after his birth that he would kill his father Laius and marry his mother, Jocasta. Brought up in Corinth ignorant of his true parentage; fled upon learning of prophecy. Killed Laius on his way to Thebes and married Jocasta after answering riddle of SPHINX. Later learned truth, blinded himself; Jocasta committed suicide. Succeeded by Creon; died at Colonus. Children were Polyneices, Eteocles, Antigone and Ismene.

Oedipus complex, in psychoanalysis, theory that sons love their mothers and hate their fathers. Esp. evident in children of ages 4–5, may affect adult relationships. Concept developed by Freud, draws name from Oedipus legend.

Oersted, Hans Christian (1777–1851), Danish scientist. Pioneered work in electro-magnetism. First to isolate aluminium.

oesophagus, esophagus, tube of alimentary canal connecting mouth with stomach. Also called gullet.

oestrogen, estrogen, any one of group of female hormones inducing OESTRUS.

oestrus, estrus, period of heat (maxi-

mum sexual receptivity) of female animal.

Offa (d. 796), king of Mercia (757–96). Signed with Charlemagne 1st recorded Eng. commercial treaty (796). Built Offa's Dyke, entrenchment along Eng.-Welsh border.

Offaly, county of C Ireland, formerly called King's. Area: 771 sq. mi.; county town, Tullamore. Flat, marshy land, agriculture is main occupation. Pop. (1961) 51,532.

Offenbach, Jacques (1819–80), Fr. composer, b. Germany. Many operettas include *La Belle Hélène*; wrote opera *Les Contes de Hoffmann.*

Office of Strategic Services (OSS), Amer. intelligence agency (estab. 1942) to gain information about enemy nations and undermine war potential. Headed by William Donovan, incorporated after World War 2 by State and War departments.

offset lithography, form of printing in which the image is transferred from a metal plate to a rubber cylinder, then to the paper.

O'Hara, John Henry (1905–70), Amer. novelist and short-story writer.

Part of an oil refinery in Saudi-Arabia

Works include *Butterfield 8* (1935), *Pal Joey* (1940).

O'Higgins, Bernardo (1776–1842), Chilean revolutionary and statesman. A leader of Chile's struggle (1810–17) for independence from Sp. rule. Headed 1st national govt. (1817–23). Exiled to Peru.

Ohio, river (980 mi. long) of E central US. Forms several state boundaries.

Cities on its course include Pittsburgh, Cincinnati, Louisville. Important freight transport route.

Ohio, state of N central US. Area: 41,222 sq. mi.; cap. Columbus; main cities Cleveland, Cincinnati. Industry includes iron and steel mills, manufacture of machinery, foodstuffs, chemicals. Coal, oil, natural gas important. Development aided by opening of SAINT LAWRENCE SEAWAY. Pop. (1960) 9,706,397.

Ohm, Georg Simon (1787–1854), Ger. physicist. Promulgated **Ohm's Law**; the steady current in a metallic circuit is directly proportional to the constant total electro-motive force in the circuit. The **ohm**, named after him, is used as unit of measurement of resistance.

oil, viscous, combustible, unctuous substance, liquid at normal temperature, soluble in alcohol or ether, but not in water. Used in lubricating, lighting, heating, *etc.*; PETROLEUM and its products known as mineral oils. Main oil-producing areas include US, Canada, Persian Gulf. Term also includes animal, vegetable and plant oils, used in perfumery, medicine, cooking, *etc.*

oil beetle, wingless hardskinned beetle of genus *Meloe*. Discharges evil-smelling oily substance from leg joints as defence mechanism.

oil bird, guacharo, *Steatornis caripensis,* nocturnal cave-dwelling, fruit-eating bird of N South America and Trinidad. Oil derived from fat of young.

Oistrakh, David Fyodorovich (1908–), Russ. violinist. His playing, often with his son **Igor Oistrakh** (1931–), has earned him international fame.

Ojibwa, Chippewa, group of N Amer. Indian tribes of Algonkian linguistic stock. Inhabited L. Superior region (17th cent.). Survivors dispersed among other tribes.

okapi, *Okapia johnstoni,* nocturnal mammal of giraffe family of Congo forests. Red-brown in colour with horizontal stripes on legs.

Okhotsk, Sea of, part of NW Pacific Ocean, W of Kamchatka Peninsula. Icebound from Nov. to June.

Okinawa, volcanic island of SW Pacific. Area: 467 sq. mi.; chief port Naha. Produces sugar cane. Scene of US amphibious campaign (April–June 1945).

Oklahoma, state of SW US. Area: 69,919 sq. mi.; cap. Oklahoma City; other main city Tulsa. Enormous deposits of oil, natural gas, lead, zinc. Wheat and cotton grown on prairies in E. Became Indian territory in LOUISIANA PURCHASE; white settlement relatively late. Pop. 2,350,000.

Oklahoma City, cap. and commercial centre of Oklahoma state, SW US, on North Canadian R. Indust. centre with major livestock market and extensive system of oil wells. Contains Oklahoma City University. Pop. (1963) 429,000.

okra, gumbo, *Hibiscus esculentus,* aromatic bean, native to W Indies and Africa, supposedly known to Ancient Egyptians. Grown extensively in southern US. Used as vegetable and in soups and curries.

Old Bailey, street in City of London. Name popularly refers to Central Criminal Court, situated in the street.

Old Catholics, members of R.C. Church originating in Holland in 17th cent.; set up (1870) own organization refusing to accept certain dogma, esp. papal infallibility. Survives in Germany, Netherlands, Austria, Czechoslovakia, Switzerland. Priests permitted to marry.

Old English, stage in development of Eng. language (*c.* 600–1100). West

Okapi

Germanic branch of Indo-European. *See* ANGLO-SAXON LITERATURE.

old man cactus, *Cephalocereus senilis,* columnar, ribbed, usually unbranched cactus with mass of white hairs encircling top. Native to Mexico, attains ht. of 30–40 ft.

old man's beard, *Usnea barbata,* species of lichen of temp. regions. Grey-green in colour. Also common name for European wild clematis.

Old Testament, Hebrew part of the Christian Bible. Relates story of the Jews from time of Moses to year immediately preceding birth of Christ. Based on 3rd cent. BC Gk. translation. W Churches adopted the Latin version, the *Vulgate.*

Old Vic, theatre in London, England; opened (1818) as the Coburg. Renamed (1880) as Royal Victoria Hall (popularly, 'Old Vic'). With appointment (1912) of Lilian Baylis as manager, became renowned for Shakespearean productions.

Oldcastle, Sir John (*c.* 1378–1417), Eng. religious leader of LOLLARDS. Condemned (1413) as heretic; hanged 4 yr. later.

old-squaw *see* LONG-TAILED DUCK.

Olduvai Gorge, in Tanzania, site of discovery (1958–9) by LOUIS LEAKEY of human remains, *c.* 500,000 yr. old.

oleander, *Nerium oleander,* evergreen shrub with lance-shaped leathery leaves and large pink flowers. Native of Old World.

oleaster, *Elaeagnus angustifolia,* ornamental shrub, native of S Europe and W Asia. Yellow flowers and olive-like fruit.

oligarchy [Gk: govt. by few], form of govt. in which power is vested in small group of rulers. Classified by Aristotle in *Politics.* Refers also to group in power.

Oligocene *see* GEOLOGICAL TABLE.

oligochaete, segmented worm of annelid class Oligochaeta. Mainly freshwater species but some terrestrial, incl. earthworm.

olive, *Olea europaea* European evergreen tree, native to Med. regions. Cultivated since ancient times for oil and black or green fruit. Wood prized for ornamental work.

Olives, Mount of, Olivet, ridge E of Jerusalem, visited many times by Jesus. Garden of Gethsemane on W slope. Now site of churches and convents.

Olivier, Laurence Kerr, Lord Olivier of Brighton (1907–   ), Eng. actor, director. Roles include Henry V, Hamlet. Co-director of Old Vic; 1st director of NATIONAL THEATRE COMPANY (1962–   ).

olivine, green, usually transparent,

Opening ceremony of the Olympic Games at Tokyo in 1964

brittle mineral (magnesium iron silicate). Gem form known as peridot.

Olympia, ancient Gk. centre of worship and site of Olympic games, near Alpheus R. in Peloponnesus. Remains reveal existence of temple with statue of Zeus by Pheidias.

Olympic games, athletic meeting of ancient Greece, in honour of Zeus, held every 4 yr. at Olympia (776

BC–AD 394). At first, simply running contest, later extended to boxing, chariot racing and other sports. Games were revived (1896) by Pierre de Coubertin; women included 1912. Winter sports competed for in Winter Olympics (estab. 1924).

Olympus, mountain range of N Greece, between Thessaly and Macedonia, highest of which (9,570 ft.) lies near Aegean coast. Considered by Greeks as home of Olympian gods; later, name Olympus referred to gods' heavenly palace.

Omaha, city and port of Nebraska, US, on Missouri R. Expanded with construction of Union Pacific Railroad. Major transport and shipping centre, with food-processing plants. Pop. (1963) 390,000.

Oman, Sultanate of *see* MUSCAT AND OMAN.

Omar [ibn Ibrahim al-] **Khayyam** [**Giyat ed-din Abu'l Fath**] (*c.* 1044–1123), Persian poet, philosopher, astronomer, mathematician. Best known as author of the *Rubáiyát,* epigrammatic verse quatrains, popularized in Eng. translation (1859) by Edward Fitzgerald.

Wild clematis, known as old man's beard

ombudsman, commissioner appointed to protect individual against govt. or official encroachment on his rights. Introduced in Sweden (1809); appointed by New Zealand (1962), UK (1966), Hawaii (1967).

Omdurman, largest city and trading, cultural and religious centre of Sudan. Orig. cap. of Dervishes who were finally defeated nearby by Kitchener (1898). Pop. 171,000.

Omei Shan, mountain (9,957 ft.) near Kiating, SW Szechwan, China. Held sacred by Buddhists, visited by many pilgrims.

Omsk, city of W Siberia, Russ. SFSR on Trans-Siberian rly. Industries include chemicals, oil-refining, agricultural machinery, textiles, food processing. Pop. (1967) 746,000.

Ona, Indian tribe of Tierra del Fuego, now diminishing in numbers.

onager, *Equus hemionis onager,* rare wild ass of C Asia.

Onassis, Aristotle Socrates (1906–), Gk.-Argentinian shipping magnate. Founded Olympic Airways 1957.

Onega, Lake, 2nd largest European Lake, in USSR. Canal constructed along S shore major link in canal route between Baltic and White Seas.

O'Neill, Eugene Gladstone (1888–1953), Amer. tragic dramatist. Plays, noted for experimental techniques and fatalistic emotional power, include trilogy *Mourning Becomes Electra* (1931), *The Iceman Cometh* (1946) and the partly autobiographical *Long Day's Journey into Night* (c. 1940, pub. 1956). Awarded Nobel Prize for Literature (1936).

O'Neill, Terence Marne (1914–), Irish politician, PM of Northern Ireland (1963– 9). Gradualist policies, aimed at liberalizing Ulster's political and social structure, alienated part of his own Protestant Unionist party without enlisting appreciable Catholic enthusiasm. Created Peer (1970).

onion, *Allium cepa,* biennial plant with edible bulb of pungent smell and flavour. Red, yellow and white varieties, used as culinary vegetable since earliest times.

onion fly, *Delia cepetorium,* two-winged fly. Larvae are pests of onions.

Onyx: left, flat polished stone; right, cut and polished gem stone

Ontario, province of C Canada. Area: 344,092 sq. mi.; cap. Toronto; main cities, Ottawa, Hamilton. Resources include forests, nickel, copper, hydro-electric power. Explored by Champlain (1615), fur trading centre (1680– 1750), joined with Quebec (1774– 1867), one of original provinces of Confederation (1867).

Ontario, Lake *see* GREAT LAKES.

onyx, variety of chalcedony with straight, parallel, alternating bands of colour (white and black or white and brown). Used esp. in making cameos.

oolite, sedimentary rock, usually limestone or ironstone with texture like fish-roe caused by concentrically layered grains.

opah *see* MOONFISH.

opal, non-crystalline form of silica. Impurities determine colour; gem opals usually milky white or pearly with rich play of flashing colours. Richest opal fields found in Australia and Mexico.

opera, stage drama where singing takes place of speech, orig. Ital. court entertainment (16th cent.). Developed formal structure and forms (ARIA, RECITATIVE, *etc.*) *e.g.* in works of Purcell, Handel. Mozart placed more emphasis on drama, further developed by Beethoven, Verdi. In 19th cent., Wagner used continuous music with full orchestral accompaniment. Lyricism practically abandoned in 20th cent. (*e.g.* Berg, Menotti).

operetta, short light OPERA, usually with spoken dialogue, esp. works of Offenbach, Johann Strauss, Gilbert and Sullivan.

ophthalmia, inflammation of the eye, esp. of eyeball.

ophthalmology, branch of medicine concerning structure, function and diseases of the eye.

opium, narcotic drug obtained from unripe capsules of OPIUM POPPY. Source of morphine, heroin, codeine. Opium and derivatives used medically as sedative, but use strictly controlled as they are addictive.

opium poppy, *Papaver somniferum,* perennial plant, native of Europe and Asia. Cultivated as source of OPIUM and for its oily seeds. Also grown as ornamental plant.

Opium Poppy

Opium Wars (1839– 42, 1856– 58), wars between China and Britain, resulting from Chinese refusal to allow importation of opium from India. Hong Kong ceded by China (1842). Brit.-French victory in 2nd war estab. free trade in Chinese ports.

Oporto, city of Portugal on R. Douro from which Port wine takes its name. Exports wine, cork, olive oil. Pop. 310,500.

opossum, prehensile-tailed marsupial of family Didelphidae of E US and S America. Mostly arboreal, though some terrestrial and one aquatic species. Noted for habit of feigning death when in danger. Species include rat-like *Didelphis virginiana.*

opossum shrimp, shrimp-like crustacean of order Mysidaceae. Carries developing young in pouch under thorax. Freshwater species include *Mysis relicta* of Europe and N America.

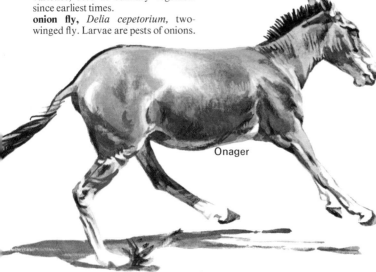

Onager

Opals in raw and polished state

Oppenheimer, J[ohn] Robert (1904–67), Amer. physicist. Directed atomic research (1942–5) leading to production of 1st atomic bomb. Opposed US development of hydrogen bomb.

optics, science of light and the principles underlying phenomena of light and vision, divided into physical and geometrical optics. The former studies light and the phenomena of colour, the latter studies laws governing these phenomena.

oracle, in Gk. religion, answer given by particular gods, usually through priest or priestess, to those who consulted them. Name also applied to shrine where such responses were given. Most famous were shrines of Zeus at Dodona, and of Apollo at Delphi. Apart from SIBYLLINE BOOKS, oracles at Rome were much less important than those in Greece.

Oran, city of Algeria, port on Med. Sea. Founded 10th cent. Occupied by French (1831). Exports wheat, meat, wine. Fr. naval installations evacuated 1962. Pop. (1963) 430,000.

orange, evergreen tree of genus *Citrus,* bearing round, reddish-yellow fruit. Species include *C. sinensis,* common sweet orange, esp. used in production of orange juice, and *C. aurantium,* bitter or Seville orange, used in marmalade making. Oranges rich in vitamins, esp. vitamin C.

Orange Free State, prov. of E central South Africa. Area: 49,838 sq. mi.; cap. Bloemfontein. Wheat, corn grown; diamonds, gold, coal mined. Joined Union of South Africa (1910). Pop. (1960) 1,386,547.

orange-peel fungus, *Aleuria aurantia,* orange cup fungus with hairy outer surface. Common in short grass and on soil in autumn.

Orange Society, militant Irish Protestant organization, named for William of Orange. Formed (1795) to combat Roman Catholic UNITED IRISHMEN.

orange tip, *Anthocaris cardamines,* small pierid butterfly. Male and female have conspicuous orange blotch on tip of forewing.

orangutan, *Pongo pygmaeus,* large ape of low-lying forests of Sumatra and Borneo. Long arms, short legs and reddish brown hair; mainly arboreal, feeding on buds and fruit.

oratorio, musical setting of sacred text for soloists, chorus and orchestra, 1st introduced by St Philip Neri. Examples are Handel's *Messiah* and Britten's *A War Requiem.*

oratory, art of eloquent speaking. Cultivated in Greece and Rome as the branch of rhetoric concerned with effective delivery of speeches. Noted classical orators include Demosthenes, Cicero. Classical models influenced medieval sermons and 18th cent. polit. speeches. Modern speechmaking tends towards informality and term public speaking is now used.

orbit, in astronomy, path described by one body round a heavenly body. In zoology, bony cavity containing the eye in vertebrate animals.

orchestra, group of players of musical instruments under direction of a conductor. Divisible into 4 sections: strings, woodwind, brass and percussion. Except in string section, players are given one part each.

orchid, perennial flowering plant of Orchidaceae family of trop. and temp. regions. Flowers usually showy and of all colours.

Orczy, Baroness Emmusca (1865–1947), Eng. writer, b. Hungary, best remembered for *The Scarlet Pimpernel* (1905). Other works include *I Will Repay* (1906), *Mam'zelle Guillotine* (1940).

Orders, Holy *see* HOLY ORDERS.

Orangutan

ordination, sacrament by which one is appointed to the ministry of the Christian Church.

Ordnance Survey, official topographical mapping of UK for defence purposes at scale of 1 in. to 1 mi. Orig. undertaken by Board of Ordnance 1791, now carried out by Ministry of Housing and Local Government.

Ordovician *see* GEOLOGICAL TABLE.

ore, mineral or rock, producing metal valuable enough to be mined.

Oreads, in Gk. myth., NYMPHS of the mountains.

Oregon, Pacific state of NW US. Area: 96,981 sq. mi.; cap. Salem; cities, Portland, Eugene. Leading industries are manufacture of timber and wood products, also printing and publishing, food processing, electrochemicals and electronics. Became state (1859). Pop. 1,768,687.

Female Opossum carrying young on her back

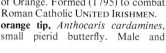
Orange Tip Butterfly

Oregon grape, *Mahonia aquifolium,* evergreen shrub, native to N America. Prickly leaves and yellow flowers, edible blue berries. Popular ornamental shrub.

Orellana, Francisco de (*c.* 1490–1546), Sp. explorer. As member of Pizarro's S Amer. expedition (begun 1538), headed party which reached mouth of Amazon (1541). River received name from his tales of female warriors.

Orestes, in Gk. myth., son of AGAMEMNON and Clytemnestra. Avenged father's murder by killing Clytemnestra and her lover, Aegisthus, with aid of sister Electra. Pursued by Eumenides (Furies), finally acquitted of matricide at court of Areopagus. Married Hermione, daughter of Menelaus and Helen.

Orff, Carl (1895–), Ger. composer of cantatas and operas. Best known work *Carmina Burana* (1937). Devised an approach to teaching music based on improvisation.

organ, keyboard instrument whose sound is produced by air forced through a pipe or past a metal reed (*see* HARMONIUM). Pipe organ dates from medieval times, though it was known to the ancient Greeks and Romans. Modern instruments generally have 2 or 3 keyboards (Great, Swell and Choir) controlling different sets or ranks of pipes and a set of foot pedals.

organic chemistry *see* CHEMISTRY, ORGANIC.

Organization for African Unity (OAU), group of 30 African States, estab. 1963, to promote unity and co-operation. H.Q. at Addis Ababa.

Organization for Economic Co-operation and Development (OECD), founded 1961. Its aims are to promote the economic growth of the 19 member countries, to co-ordinate and improve development aid and to expand world trade. Agencies of OECD are the European Nuclear Energy Agency and European Monetary Agreement.

Organization of American States (OAS), body (estab. 1948) to promote peace and economic development in W hemisphere; H.Q. at Washington. Resisted Communist penetration in hemisphere; excluded Communist Cuba (1962) from council.

organ-pipe cactus, *Pachycereus marginatus,* tree-like cactus of Mexico. Brownish-purple flowers.

organ-pipe coral, *Tubipora musica,* dull red coral generally found on coral reefs. Forms long upright tubes resembling set of organ pipes.

Orient, the East, geographic region E

Golden Oriole

and SE of Europe, incl. Turkey, Iran, India, China, Japan.

orienteering, sport combining Ordnance Survey map reading and cross-country running.

Origen (*c.* 186–254), Christian writer, b. Alexandria. Taught there and in Caesarea. Torture under Decian persecution led to his death. Works include Greek and Hebrew editions of the Bible and the apology *Contra Celsum.*

original sin, in theology, tendency to evil. Considered innate in mankind and transmitted from Adam in consequence of his sin.

Orinoco, river (*c.* 1500 mi. long) of S America. Rises in Guiana Highlands, flows NW to Colombia, then E through Venezuela to Atlantic. Chief port is Ciudad Bolivar, Venezuela. Discovered prob. by Columbus (1498).

oriole, brightly coloured bird of Oriolidae family of Old World, *e.g.* golden oriole. In US, family known as Icteridae, best known species being Baltimore oriole. *See* HANGNEST.

Orion, in Gk. myth., giant and hunter of Boeotia. According to some, he pursued Pleiades and was transformed into a constellation, part of which is Orion's Belt.

Orissa, state of E India. Area: 60,165 sq. mi.; cap. Bhubaneswar. Agric. fertile coastal region. Iron, coal deposits in N. Pop. (1961) 17,548,846.

Orkney, county of NE Scotland comprising Orkney Islands. Area: 376 sq. mi.; county town, Kirkwall, on Pomona (or Mainland), largest of 70 islands. Main occupations: fishing, farming. Occupied by Norway (865–1468). Pop. (1965) 18,000.

Orlando, Vittorio Emmanuele (1860–1952), Ital. polit. leader, premier (1917–19). Attended Paris Peace Conference (1919), but left after failing to secure territorial gains for Italy.

Orléans, name of Fr. royal house of Bourbon-Orléans. **Philippe II, Duc d'Orléans** (1674–1723), acted as regent (1715–23) for Louis XV. Headed luxurious and debauched court, sponsored schemes of JOHN LAW. **Louis Philippe Joseph, Duc d'Orléans** (1747–93), supported Jacobin cause in Fr. Revolution, voted for Louis XVI's execution, but was guillotined on charges of royal aspirations. His son became LOUIS-PHILIPPE, king of the French.

Orléans, cap. of Loiret department, N central France. Clothes manufacturing centre. Besieged by English (1429) until arrival of JOAN OF ARC during Hundred Years War. Pop. (1962) 126,000.

Orlon, trade name for synthetic lightweight acrylic fibre, hard-wearing and wrinkle resistant, manufactured by Du Pont (US).

ormer, large gastropod mollusc related to limpet, found in Channel Is. Common ormer or ear-shell, *Haliotis lamellosa,* is edible.

ormolu, copper and zinc alloy used as imitation of gold. Formerly employed to decorate furniture and clocks.

ornithology, branch of zoology dealing with bird life.

Orpheus, in Gk. myth., poet and musician, son of muse Calliope. Music charmed animals, trees and rocks. Accompanied Argonauts. Went to Hades to recover wife Eurydice; the gods, persuaded by his music released her, but Orpheus broke their condition and Eurydice vanished. Orpheus later torn to pieces by Thracian Maenads; head floated down R. Hebrus and reached Lesbos.

Orr, John Boyd, 1st Baron Boyd Orr (1880–1971), Brit. agric. scientist; 1st director-general (1945–8) of UN Food and Agriculture Organization. Awarded Nobel Peace Prize (1949).

orris root, orrice, *Iris florentina,* fragrant root of iris plant. Powdered and used in perfumery and medicine. Grown in Europe.

Ortega y Gasset, José (1883–1955), Sp. writer. Author of *Revolt of the Masses* (1930), expounding theory of govt. by intellectual minority. Founder of review *Revista de Occidente.*

Ortelius, Abraham (1527–98), Flemish cartographer. Compiled atlas *Theatrum orbis terrarum* (1570).

orthoclase, common potassium pink mineral of feldspar group. Has 2 right-angled cleavages. Used in porcelain manufacture. Some varieties called moonstone used as gems.

Orthodox Church, Eastern, collective name for independent Christian churches of E Europe and W Asia. Originated in split (1054) with Roman Catholic Church under Pope Leo IX. Authority vested in patriarch of Constantinople, rejecting papacy.

orthopaedic surgery, branch of surgery concerning diagnosis and treatment of injuries, deformities, and diseases of bones, joints, ligaments, muscles and nerves, esp. of children.

ortolan, *Emberiza hortulana,* bird of bunting family of Europe and W Asia, wintering in Africa. Eaten as a delicacy in Europe.

Orwell, George, orig. Eric Arthur Blair (1903–50), Eng. writer. Satirical novels, *Animal Farm* (1945) and *1984* (1949) display love of liberty and anger at corruptions in society. Latter depicts ultimate state control.

oryx, *Oryx gazella,* African antelope with long straight horns in both sexes. The pure white Arabian oryx is almost extinct.

Osage, N Amer. Indian tribe of Siouan linguistic stock. Orig. warlike

nomads, they moved from central US plains to Oklahoma reservation. Oil discoveries have made them wealthiest tribe in US.

Osaka, city of S Honshu, Japan, port on Osaka Bay; 2nd largest city of Japan. Commercial and indust. centre. Contains Osaka University. Pop. (1965) 3,166,000.

Osborne, John James (1929–), Eng. dramatist and actor, one of group of 'angry young men' of 1950s. Works include *Look Back in Anger* (1956), *The Entertainer* (1957), *Inadmissible Evidence* (1964).

Oscar *see* ACADEMY AWARDS.

Oscar I (1799–1859), king of Sweden and Norway (1844–59). Succeeded by his son Charles XV, followed by **Oscar II** (1829–1907) who became an international diplomat. Relinquished Norwegian throne at splitting of union with Sweden (1905).

oscillograph, electrical instrument for recording form of waves of alternating currents and high frequency oscillations, *e.g.* sound waves.

osier, variety of willow with flexible twigs or branches used in basket work. Common species is *Salix viminalis,* native to Europe.

Osiris, Egyptian god of underworld, important deity linked with wife, Isis, and son, Horus. Slain by brother Set (Night). Identified with fertility and immortality.

Osler, Sir William (1849–1919), Canadian physician and medical historian. Author of *The Principles and Practice of Medicine* (1892).

Oslo, cap. of Norway, at head of Oslo Fjord. Indust., commercial, cultural centre. Manufactures metal, chemicals, paper. Called Christiania (1624–1925) after Christian IV, who

Royal palace in Oslo (1825-48)

rebuilt city after disastrous fire (1624). Contains university (founded 1811). Pop. (1965) 483,000.

Osman I or **Othman I** (1259–1326), sultan of Turkey, founder of Ottoman dynasty. Conquered large area of Asia Minor.

osmium, hard metallic element, used in alloys and electric light filaments.

osmosis, process in animals and plants in which selective fluids pass through semi-permeable membranes. Makes possible absorption of water by plant roots and passage of digested foods into blood stream.

osprey, fish hawk, *Pandion haliactus,* variety of hawk of Europe, Asia and N America. Brown plumage with white underparts; feeds on fish. Protected in Scotland.

O.S.S. *see* OFFICE OF STRATEGIC SERVICES.

Ossian, Oisin, Irish literary figure, credited with poetry by Scot. author JAMES MACPHERSON.

Ossietzky, Carl von (1898–1938), Ger. pacifist. While imprisoned for denouncing secret Ger. rearmament, awarded Nobel Peace Prize (1935). As a result, Hitler govt. prohibited acceptance of Nobel prizes by Germans.

Ostend [Flemish: **Oostende**] city of W Flanders prov., N Belgium; port and resort of North Sea. Fishing and transportation centre. Pop. (1961) 56,494.

Map of the World (1564) by Ortelius

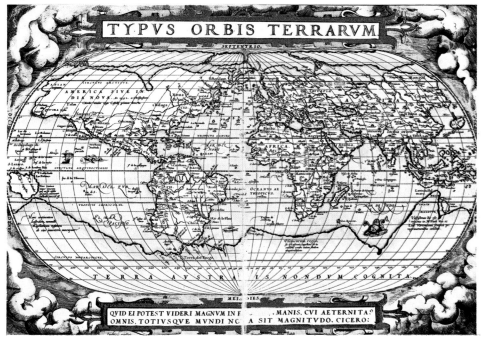

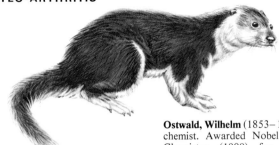

Otter

osteo-arthritis, pathological condition of joints, esp. those bearing weight, usually occurring in elderly people. Characterized by swelling, pain and restriction of movement.

osteopathy, medical practice based on theory that restoration or preservation of health is achieved by manipulation of muscles, *etc.* Pioneered by Andrew Still (1874).

ostracod, tiny marine and freshwater crustacean of sub-class Ostracoda. Body enclosed in hinged bivalve shell.

ostrich, *Struthio camelus,* large, long-legged and 2-toed flightless bird *c.* 8ft. high, native of Africa and Arabia. Male is black with white wing and tail feathers. Plumage formerly valued in millinery.

Ostrogoths, East Goths, branch of Goths, after 4th cent. split, who settled in Hungary. Kingdom (estab. 493) fell to Emperor Justinian I (552). *See* VISIGOTHS.

Rideau Canal, Ottawa, connecting Lake Ontario with the river Ottawa

Ostwald, Wilhelm (1853–1932), Ger. chemist. Awarded Nobel Prize for Chemistry (1909) for work on catalysis. Invented process for manufacture of nitric acid by oxidation of ammonia.

Oswald (*c.* 605–42), king of Northumbria (635–42). Became a Christian, gave Lindisfarne to St Aidan and was killed in battle against pagan Penda, king of Mercia.

Otis, Elisha Graves (1811–61), Amer. inventor of the passenger lift (1857) which facilitated the development of skyscrapers.

Ottawa, city and cap. of Canada, on Ottawa R., SE Ontario. Founded 1827, became cap. of country 1867. Settlement developed after canal built (1826–32) from Chaudière Falls, Ottawa R. to L. Ontario, for fur and timber trade. Industries include paper making, woodworking, watchmaking, electronics. Pop. (1962) 446,000.

Ottawa, N Amer. Indian tribe of Algonkian linguistic stock. Occupied Ottawa R. region in 17th cent., but driven N by Iroquois. In Fr. Indian Wars led by Chief Pontiac, allied with French defeated by British. Majority now settled in Michigan.

otter, *Lutra lutra,* aquatic carnivorous fur-bearing mammal of Europe, N Africa, N Asia. Weighs *c.* 25 lb. and is *c.* 4ft. long; feeds on fish, eels, *etc.,* and can remain underwater for considerable time. Prized for hard-wearing fur.

otter hound, Eng. breed of water dog with thick, shaggy, oily coat, *c.* 23 in. high at shoulder. Trained to hunt otters.

Otto, name of 4 Holy Roman emperors. **Otto I** (912–73) became Ger. king (936). Restored imperial authority, routed Magyars (955), crowned emperor (962). **Otto IV** (*c.* 1182–1218) elected emperor (1198) defeated by Philip of France at Bouvines (1214).

Otto I (1815–67) king of Greece (1832–62), son of Louis I of Bavaria, elected by European powers to rule independent Greece. The Crimean War and military revolts weakened his authority and he was deposed.

Ottoman Empire, Islamic empire estab. in Asia Minor by Turkish tribes on dissolution of Byzantine Empire

(13th cent.). Under Suleiman the Magnificent reached zenith; included Turkey, Syria, Hungary, Egypt, Persia, Arabia, most of Greece and Balkans. Declined, and forced out of existence by Russia and European powers (19th– early 20th cent.).

Otway, Thomas (1652–85), Eng. Restoration dramatist. Noted for his tragedies *Don Carlos* (1676), *The Orphan* (1680), *Venice Preserved* (1682).

ouija board, game named from Fr. *oui* and Ger. *ja* (both meaning 'yes'). The indicator, touched lightly by 2 peoples' fingers, points to letters giving messages believed by some to be from spirits.

ounce *see* SNOW LEOPARD.

Ouspensky, Peter Demianovitch (1878–1947), Russ. philosopher; author of *The Fourth Dimension* (1909), *Tertium Organum* (1920) and *A New Model of the Universe* (1931).

Outram, Sir James (1803–63), Eng. general in Indian Army. With Havelock helped besiege Lucknow during Indian Mutiny (1857).

ouzel *see* DIPPER.

ovary, one of 2 female reproductive glands. Produces germ cells or ova and controls female sex characteristics.

ovenbird, *Seiurus aurocapillus,* N Amer. migratory bird of wood warbler family. Builds oven-shaped grass nest on the ground. Also several S Amer. birds of Furnariidae family.

overture, prelude for orchestra before opera or choral work, or independent orchestral work in similar style, *e.g.* Brahms' *Tragic Overture.*

Ovid [Publius Ovidius Naso] (43 BC–AD 18), Roman poet. Writings, witty and less serious than those of Vergil, include mythological poems, notably *Metamorphoses,* erotic poetry, *Ars Amatoria* (*Art of Love*), poems of exile, *Tristia.* Exiled (AD 8).

ovum, in biology, germ cell produced by female reproductive glands (ovaries). Once fertilized by male, develops into an embryo and later into complete animal or human form.

Owen, Robert (1771–1858), Brit. social reformer. Estab. model indust. town at New Lanark, Scotland (1800). Instigated Factory Act of 1819.

Owen, Wilfred (1893–1918), Brit. poet whose works express anger at cruelty of war. Benjamin Britten's *War Requiem* based on some of Owen's posthumously published *Poems.*

Owens, Jessie (1913–), Amer. athlete. At 1936 Olympic games in

Berlin tied 100 m. record, set records in 200 m. race and long jump.

owl, widely distributed chiefly nocturnal bird of prey of order Strigiformes. Broad head with large forward-facing eyes, noiseless flight. Feeds on rodents and small birds, regurgitating pellets of fur and feathers.

owlet moth, dull-coloured moth of Noctuidae family, commonly attracted to lights. Larvae include cutworms and armyworms, injurious to plants.

ox, adult castrated male of genus *Bos,* used for food and as draft animal. In zoology term includes bison, buffalo and sub-family Bovidae.

oxalic acid, organic, poisonous acid occurring in small quantities in sorrel and rhubarb leaves. Prepared from reaction of carbon monoxide and sodium hydroxide. Used as cleanser, bleach and laboratory reagent.

oxalis, wood sorrel, widely distributed plant of genus *Oxalis.* Tubers used for food in S America. European wood sorrel, *O. acetosella,* is sometimes shamrock.

ox-bow lake *see* MEANDER.

Oxenstierna, Count Axel Gustafsson (1583–1654), Swedish statesman. Chancellor to Gustavus II, after whose death he became virtual ruler of Sweden while regent (1632–44). Initiated widespread reform and centralization.

oxeye daisy, *Chrysanthemum leucanthemum,* large perennial daisy with single yellow-centred white flowers.

Oxfam, name given in 1965 to the Oxford Committee for Famine Relief. Founded (1942) in Oxford, England. Aims to raise funds for the relief of poverty and suffering in underdeveloped areas of the world.

Oxford, city of S central England, county borough of Oxfordshire. Contains OXFORD UNIVERSITY. Motor car manufacturing at Cowley. Pop. (1966) 110,000.

Oxford, Earl of *see* WALPOLE, SIR ROBERT.

Oxford, Provisions of, programme of polit. reform, drawn up (1258) by Simon de Montfort, forced upon Henry III of England. Provided for advisory council and attempted to limit taxation powers. Repudiation (1261) by Henry precipitated Barons' War (1263–7).

Oxford and Asquith, Earl of *see* ASQUITH, HERBERT HENRY.

Oxford Movement, attempt from 1833 to find common ground between Catholicism and Evangelicalism. First led by Newman, who wrote *Tracts for*

College buildings, Oxford University

the Times (1833–41), Keble, Froude and Pusey, who emphasized ritualism. Movement lost ground with conversion to Roman Catholicism of Newman and others.

Oxford University, oldest residential university in UK; now 27 men's colleges, 2 mixed and 5 women's. Centre of learning from 12th cent; University College founded 1249.

Oxfordshire, inland county of S central England. Area: 751 sq. mi.; county borough, Oxford. Largely agric.; motor car manufacturing. Pop. (1966) 349,000.

oxidation, in chemistry, process by which substances combine with oxygen to form oxides. Rust (iron oxide), frequent cause of metal corrosion, occurs when iron is exposed to the atmosphere.

oxide, compound formed by the combination of an element with oxygen. Water is the oxide of hydrogen; carbon dioxide of carbon.

Oxus *see* AMU-DARYA.

oxygen (O), colourless gas, necessary in respiration and most combustion. Discovered by Priestley, and independently by Scheele (1774). Forms 46·5% of the earth's crust, and combines with all other elements except the inert gases and fluorine.

oyster, edible marine bivalve mollusc of Ostreidae family, with rough, irregular shaped shell. Lives on sea-bed or adheres to rocks in shallow water. Pearl bearing oyster found in sub-trop. waters is of genus *Meleagrina.*

oystercatcher, long-billed wading bird of genus *Haematopus* of Europe and N and S America. Feeds on limpets, oysters, *etc.* Black and white plumage.

Ozarks, broken plateau of mountains in S central US. Area: 50,000 sq. mi. Altitude ranges from 1,000–2,500 ft. Tourist centre, source of lead and zinc.

ozone, form of oxygen with 3 atoms in the molecule rather than usual 2. Rarely found in atmosphere. Used in bleaches and disinfectants.

Long-eared Owl

P

paca, *Cuniculus,* large rodent of swampy areas of C and S America, with large head and no tail.

Pacher, Michael (*fl.* 1465–98), Austrian woodcarver and painter. Chief work is altarpiece of St Wolfgang church near Salzburg.

Pacific, War of the, conflict (1879–84) between Chile and Bolivia, aided by Peru. Precipitated by rescinding of Chilean mining contract in Bolivian prov. of Atacama. War declared after Chile took port of Antofagasta. Separate treaties with Peru (1883) and Bolivia (1904) gave victorious Chile provs. of Tacna and Atacama.

Pacific Islands, Trust Territory of the, group of islands in C and W Pacific administered by US under UN trusteeship. Includes Caroline, Marshall and Mariana islands. Ger. colonies before World War I.

Pacific Ocean, world's largest and deepest ocean. Area: 68,634,000 sq. mi. Av. depth, *c.* 14,000 ft., greatest known depth (35,800 ft.) is in Marianas Trench.

'Pacific Scandal' (1873), Canadian political issue which hastened end of Cons. govt. of Sir John Macdonald. Charge was made that Macdonald accepted campaign funds for awarding Hugh Allan's syndicate a contract to build Canadian Pacific Rly.

pacifism, individual or collective opposition to war as means of settling disputes. Some groups, such as religious sects (*e.g.* Quakers), oppose all violence. Teachings of Gandhi have been influential. Nobel Peace Prize recognizes pacifist thought. 20th cent. organizations, esp. UN, seek peace through international cooperation.

Packard, Vance Oakley (1914–   ), Amer. writer. Works, mainly social criticisms, include *The Hidden Persuaders* (1957) and *The Status Seekers* (1959).

pack-rat, *Neotoma cinerea,* large, bushy-tailed rodent of N America. Well-developed cheek pouches in which it carries food and miscellaneous articles it tends to hoard.

paddle-boat, water vehicle propelled by wheels with oar-like appendages. Early forms used by Romans and Egyptians; widely utilized after introduction of steam-driven wheels (1783). Paddle-steamers were a major mode of transportation on Mississippi R. during 19th cent.

paddlefish, *Polyodon spathula,* large Amer. fish, related to sturgeon, with long flat paddle-shaped snout. Found in Mississippi R. and its tributaries.

paddy-field, heavily irrigated or lightly flooded piece of land in which rice is grown. Unhusked rice known as paddy.

Paderewski, [Ignace] Jan (1860–1941), Polish musician and statesman. Popular and noted pianist, compositions include *Minuet in G* for piano. First premier (1919–20) of new repub.

Padua, Padova, city of Venezia, NE Italy. Commercial and transport centre since Roman times, famous for university (founded 13th cent.). Pop. (1964) 212,000.

Paestum, ancient Gk. city in S Italy, formerly Poseidonia, now Pesto. Gk. colony founded (*c.* 600 BC); site of temple ruins. In 273 BC became Roman colony.

Paganini, Niccolò (1782–1840), Ital. virtuoso violinist and composer. Compositions include 24 caprices for solo violin and *Perpetual Motion.*

Page, Ruth (1903–   ), Amer. dancer and choreographer. Toured with Pavlova; devised many ballets, incl. *Frankie and Johnnie* and *Billy Sunday.*

Page, Walter Hines (1855–1918), Amer. journalist, diplomat. Edited *Atlantic Monthly* (1895–8). US ambassador to Britain (1913–18).

Pago Pago, Pangopango, cap. of

Painted Lady Butterfly

Shwe Dagon pagoda, Rangoon

Amer. Samoa, on Tutuila island. Important naval station and harbour. Ceded to US (1872). Pop. (1960) 1,300

pagoda, name for sacred building in Burma, Japan, China, *etc.* Often incorporates distinctive tower with pyramidal upward-curving roofs.

pagoda tree, *Sophora japonica,* deciduous tree of China and Korea.

Pahang, state in SE Malay Peninsula, Malaysia. Area: 13,820 sq. mi.; cap. Kuala Lipis. Mountainous with dense jungle. Pop. (1962 est.) 371,600.

pain, sensation usually caused by excessive stimulation of sensory nerve ends. Tissue damage stimulates responses in consciousness of brain.

Paine, Thomas (1737–1809), Amer. polit. writer, b. England. Contributed to patriot cause in Amer. Revolution with pamphlets *Common Sense* (1776) and *The American Crisis* series. Defended Fr. Revolution in *The Rights of Man* (2 parts, 1791–2). Imprisoned (1793) in Paris for anti-Jacobinism.

paint, pigment of animal, vegetable or mineral origin, prepared in suspension. Also made synthetically.

Painted Desert, vividly coloured region on E bank of Little Colorado R., N Arizona, US. Area: 4,000 sq. mi. Extends SE from Grand Canyon to Petrified Forest.

painted lady, *Vanessa cardui,* migratory butterfly. Brownish-black and orange wings; hind wings each with 4 eyespots. Amer. painted lady is *V. virginiensis.*

painting, one of the fine arts developed by man from earliest times. Examples of Palaeolithic animal paintings have survived and painted Greek vases from 7th cent. BC. FRESCOES were important in art of Ancient Egypt and Rome. Middle Ages saw development of oil colours and portraiture. Renaissance introduced concept of perspective. 18th-19th cent. brought use of water-colour; 19th–20th cent. concept of non-representational art.

paisley, fine wool fabric with scroll designs. Orig. used for shawls made in Paisley, Scotland.

Paiute, Piute, N Amer. Indian tribes of Uto-Aztecan linguistic family. N Paiute opposed (1860s) white settlement in Utah and Idaho.

Pakistan, repub. of S Asia, formerly comprising East and West Pakistan. Area: 365,907 sq. mi.; cap. Rawalpindi; main cities, Karachi, Lahore.

W region, largely mountainous, primarily agric., esp. grains. E region, formerly East Bengal, arable rice-producing land, irrigated by Ganges and other rivers. Achieved nationhood (1947) as Moslem state by separation from India; became repub. (1956). Disputes with India culminated in independence (1971) of East as Bangla-desh. Main languages, Urdu, Bengali; religion Islam. Unit of currency, rupee. Pop. (1961) 102,885,000.

palaeobotany or **palaeophytology,** study of fossil or extinct plants.

Palaeocene *see* GEOLOGICAL TABLE.

palaeography, study of ancient writing. Concerned with deciphering and dating of scripts.

Palaeolithic *see* STONE AGE.

Palaeologus, last dynasty (1260–1453) to rule Byzantine Empire. Last emperor, Constantine XI (1448–53), killed in defence of Constantinople when it fell to the Turks.

palaeontology, study of past geological time, based on fossil remains. Most important method of correlating ages of rock strata.

Palaeozoic *see* GEOLOGICAL TABLE.

Palafox, José de, Duke of Saragossa (*c.* 1776–1847), Sp. army officer. Leader of heroic defence of Saragossa (1808–9) against French during Peninsular War.

palate, term for roof of human mouth. Front portion, hard palate, joins tooth ridge; back portion, soft palate, forms opening of throat with tonsils and uvula.

Palatinate, 2 hist. regions of Germany, RHINELAND PALATINATE and UPPER PALATINATE.

Pale, hist. term for a restricted region within a country, inhabited by non-nationals. In Irish history, denotes region around Dublin where Eng. rule and law was enforced (12th–17th cent.).

Palembang, city of SE Sumatra, Indonesia, on Musi R. Important oil refining and shipping centre; exports rubber, coffee and coal. Pop. (1961) 475,000.

Palermo, cap. and seaport of NW Sicily. Founded by Phoenicians. Varied architecture reflects succession of influences, incl. Byzantine and Norman; 19th cent. university. Pop. (1963) 614,000.

Palestine, orig. Canaan, Holy Land of Jews, Christians and Moslems by SE Med. Sea. Subject region for centuries, fell to Ottoman Turks (1516). Taken by British (1917), became Mandated Territory until partitioned by UN (1948) between Israel and Jordan.

Palestrina, Giovanni Pierluigi da (1525–94), Ital. musician. Conducted choirs of Vatican. Compositions, mainly Masses and motets, include *Missa Papae Marcelli.*

Palgrave, Francis Turner (1824–97), Eng. poet and anthologist. Edited anthology *The Golden Treasury of English Songs and Lyrics* (1861).

Pali, language of sacred Buddhist literature. *See* INDIAN LITERATURE.

palladian architecture, style founded by ANDREA PALLADIO, introduced to England in 17th cent. by Inigo Jones, then spread into Europe. Features include temple fronts.

Byzantine ruins at Mistra, Turkey. On the top of the hill are the remains of the palace of the Palaeologi

Palladio, Andrea (1518–80), Ital. architect, founder of Palladian style in architecture. His masterpiece is Church of the Redeemer, Venice.

palladium (Pd), white metallic element. Used as catalyst for plating and in alloys with gold and platinum.

Pallas, one of the minor planets, or asteroids, revolving round the Sun between Mars and Jupiter. Discovered (1802) by Olbers in Germany.

Pallas Athene *see* ATHENA.

palm, trop. tree or shrub with tall columnar trunk with crown of very

Wooden altarpiece, *St Wolfgang* (1481), by Michael Pacher

Panama Canal

large leaves. Economically important, species include date, coconut, raffia and sago palms.

palm oil, fatty, orange-red oil obtained from fruit of palm tree. Used in manufacture of soap, candles, cosmetics, *etc.*

Palm Sunday, Christian holy day commemorating Jesus' entry into Jerusalem. Celebrated on Sunday before Easter.

Palma or **Palma de Mallorca,** seaport and cap. of Majorca, in Balearic Is., Spain. Roman colony, important under Moors. Has Gothic cathedral, begun 1229. Pop. (1965) 171,000.

Palme, Sven Olof (1927–), P.M. of Sweden (1969–).

Palmer, Arnold (1924–), Amer. golfer. Winner on several occasions of US Open, Brit. Open and US Masters tournaments.

Palmerston, 3rd Viscount *see* TEMPLE, HENRY JOHN.

palmtree moss, *Mnium undulatum,* moss of temp. woodland areas. Large leaves form rosette at end of stalk.

Palmyra, oasis and once great caravan city of Syrian Desert (OT Tadmor).

Palomar Observatory, Mount, observatory located at Mt. Palomar, Calif., US. Has telescope with 200 in. mirror.

paloverde, thorny desert shrub of SW US and Mexico of family Leguminosae. Smooth green bark, bright yellow flowers.

Pamirs, mountain region of C Asia where several of highest mountain ranges of the world meet. These include the Himalayas, Kunlun, Tien Shan and Hindu Kush.

Pampas, plains of Argentina, extending from Andes Mts. to Paraná R. and Atlantic Ocean. Area: *c.* 250,000 sq.

mi. Important cattle-raising region. Modernized agriculture has largely supplanted 19th cent. cowboys.

pampas deer, *Ozotoceras bezoarticus,* deer of S America with small, branched antlers. Coat reddish above and white beneath.

pampas grass, *Cortaderia,* tall, ornamental, perennial grass. Native of S America.

Pamplona, city of N Spain, cap. of Sp. Navarre. Ancient Basque city at base of Pyrenees Mts. Market centre with chem. and textile industries. Each July, feast of San Fermin celebrated by running of the bulls. Pop. (1965) 115,000.

Pan, in Gk. myth., god of flocks and shepherds. Represented as partly goatlike in form. Invented 7-reeded musical pipe. Worshipped orig. in Arcadia, believed to inspire lonely travellers with terror. Identified with Faunus by Romans.

Pan-Africanism, term for polit. movement of 20th cent. Africa aiming at self-determination. Activity increased in 1950s, esp. after Kwame Nkrumah organized Accra conference (1958). Subsequent rival groups of independent nations disbanded with estab. (1963) of ORGANIZATION FOR AFRICAN UNITY.

Panama, repub. of C America; gained independence from Colombia (1903).

Area: 31,890 sq. mi.; cap. Panama City. Exports bananas, cacao, coffee, rice, shrimps and mahogany. Pop. (1967 est.) 1,372,200.

Panama Canal, artificial waterway in C America, 50 mi. long, connecting Pacific and Atlantic Oceans. Opened 1914; has 12 locks and minimum depth of 41 ft.

Panama Canal Zone, strip of land extending 5 mi. on either side of Panama Canal. Total area: 553 sq. mi.; administered since 1903 by US.

Panama City, cap. and seaport of Repub. of Panama. Industries, food processing, textiles, furniture and pottery manufacturing. Pop. 359,000.

Pan-Americanism, movement of economic and polit. co-operation among countries of N and S America. Sporadic 19th cent. attempts frustrated by suspicions of US imperialism. Series of 20th cent. meetings culminated in formation of ORGANIZATION OF AMERICAN STATES and ALLIANCE FOR PROGRESS.

Panathenaea, Athenian festival held in honour of goddess Athena. Procession on last day of festival depicted on frieze on Parthenon.

Pancras, Saint, Christian from Phrygia, martyred in Rome at age of 14. Cult esp. widespread in Europe during Middle Ages.

pancreas, digestive organ of most vertebrates. Cell groups (islands of langerhans) produce insulin.

Palmtree Moss

panda, giant panda, *Ailuropoda melanoleuca,* large bear-like carnivore of Tibet and S China. White with black limbs, shoulders and ears and black rings round eyes. **Lesser panda,** *Ailurus fulgens,* carnivore of Himalayas. Reddish-brown with white markings on face; long bushy tail.

Pandit, Vijaya Lakshmi (1900–), Indian diplomat, sister of Jawaharlal Nehru. Held several ambassadorial posts, served at UN; Pres. of General Assembly (1953–4).

Pandora, in Gk. myth., woman fashioned out of clay by Hephaestus at command of Zeus to avenge wrong done to him by Prometheus. Given life by Athena. Sent to Epimetheus, brother of Prometheus, carrying box which she opened, releasing all evils, while Hope remained in box.

pandora moth, *Coloradia pandora,* moth of W US. Larva is serious pest of pine trees.

Pampas Deer

Pangolin

pangolin, scaly anteater, toothless mammal of Africa and trop. Asia. Back, head, tail and sides protected by scales with sharp points and edges. Species include giant pangolin, *Manis gigantea*, and tree pangolin, *M. tricuspis*.

Pankhurst, Emmeline, (1857–1928), Eng. women's suffrage leader. Founded (1903) Women's Social and Political Union. Militant methods brought frequent arrests; aided by daughters Christabel (1880–1958) and Sylvia (1882–1960).

Panneton, Philippe (1895–1960), Fr. Canadian writer. Novels include *Trente Arpents* (1938) of rural life in Quebec. Also wrote under name of Ringuet.

Pan-Slavism, doctrine of 19th cent. urging polit. and cultural unity of all Slavs. Orig. anti-Russian after Crimean War. Contributed to outbreak of Russo-Turkish War (1877–8); intensified Russ.-Austrian rivalry prior to World War I.

pansy, *Viola,* several species of wild and garden flowers native to Eurasia and N America. Garden pansy or heartsease is *V. tricolor*; mountain pansy *V. lutea.*

pantheism, philosophy that identifies God in all things. Found at all periods, and notably in Chinese and Egyptian religions.

pantheon, orig. building for worship of all gods. Pantheon at Rome built by Agrippa (27 BC, rebuilt by Hadrian *c.* AD 120). Term also denotes building in which great men are buried, *e.g.* Panthéon, Paris.

panther, name denoting genus of cat family incl. leopards. Sometimes applied also to pumas and cougars.

pantomime, orig. type of drama without speech. In 18th cent. term used for mimed wordless scenes and narrative ballets based on 16th cent. Ital. Commedia dell' Arte. Now a typically Brit. Christmas entertainment, containing comedy, songs and dancing.

Panzer [Ger: armour], description of mechanized unit of Ger. army. Organized for rapid attack, Panzer divisions were highly successful in World War 2, esp. in N Africa.

Paoli, Pasquale (1725–1807), Corsican nationalist. Led insurrection (1755) against Genoa. Pres. of Corsica (1755–69). Defeated by French, fled to England. Appointed as Fr. gov. of Corsica (1791), headed short-lived independent state of Corsica.

papacy, office of the pope as bishop of Rome and head of R.C. Church. Estab. as leader of Christian church when, according to R.C. doctrine, Jesus gave Peter primacy of Church.

Papandreou, George (1888–1968), Gk. polit. leader, P.M. (1944, 1963–5). Dispute (1965) with King Constantine II led to prolonged crisis.

Papanicolaou, George Nicholas (1883–1962), Amer. pathologist. Devised method (Pap Smear) for detection of cervical cancer.

papaw, *Asimina triloba,* N Amer. tree. Large leaves, purple flowers; large edible fruit.

papaya, *Carica papaya,* Amer. trop. tree. Large melon-like fruit.

Papen, Franz von (1879–1969), Ger. politician. Chancellor (May-Nov. 1932). Instrumental in securing Hitler's appointment as Chancellor. Acquitted (1946) of war crimes.

paper, thin sheets of matted fibres. Invented in China (2nd cent.), spread to Europe 13th–14th cent. Most paper made from wood pulp or old paper, higher grade from cotton.

Paphos, ancient city of SW Cyprus where Aphrodite, according to legend, emerged from the sea.

Papin, Denis, FRS (*c.* 1674–1714), Fr. physicist. Discovered siphon principle. Considered 1st to raise a piston by steam.

Papineau, Louis-Joseph (1786–1871), Fr. Canadian polit. leader. Speaker of Assembly of Lower Canada (1814–37). Founded Patriot group in split with Reform party and instigated REBELLION OF 1837. Lived in US (1837–45).

paprika, red powdery substance derived from dried sweet peppers. Used in cookery as seasoning.

Papua *see* PAPUA AND NEW GUINEA, TERRITORY OF.

Papua and New Guinea, Territory of, E region, island of New Guinea. Area: 183,600 sq. mi.; cap. Port Moresby. Administered by Australia since 1949, following merger of territories of Papua and New Guinea. Pop. (1965) 2,183,000.

Papuan, Malayo-Polynesian language spoken in New Guinea and adjacent islands.

papyrus, *Cyperus papyrus,* tall sedge, of Africa and Asia. Ancient Egyptians used stem for boats, cloth and sheets of writing material.

parable, term used in Bible for brief narrative illustrating moral. Majority are in NT. Jesus' teachings are often in parables.

parabola, in mathematics, conical section of a cone and a plane parallel to one side.

Paracelsus, Philippus Aureolus, orig. Theophrastus Bombastus von Hohenheim (*c.* 1493–1541), Swiss physician, alchemist and mystic. Maintained each disease had its specific cause; used drugs in treating some ailments.

parachute, umbrella-shaped nylon or silk canopy (developed 18th cent.) reducing speed of falling body through air. Used in military and sporting activity; also as brake for aircraft and spacecraft in landing.

Paradise [Gk: *paradeisos* park or garden], term denoting Garden of Eden; also used to mean heaven or intermediate stage for righteous souls between death and final judgement.

paraffin, hydrocarbon substance resembling wax; used in waterproofing, sealing and sizing and in manufacture of electrical insulators, candles *etc.* Also paraffin oil. *See* KEROSENE.

Paraguay, republic of C South America. Area: 157,000 sq. mi.; cap. Asunción; cities, Concepción, En-

Panda

carnación. Mainly agricultural; cotton, sugar cane, maize, yerba maté, cattle raising. Sp. possession

(1537); Paraguay declared its independence (1811); war with Bolivia (1932–5) left country exhausted. Unit of currency, guarani. Pop. (1967 est.) 2,161,000.

Paraguay River, tributary of Paraná R., rises in Brazil and flows through repub. of Paraguay. Length, 1,300 mi.

parakeet, any of several small, brightly coloured birds of parrot family, noted for ability to mimic human speech. Most common species is budgerigar.

parallax, apparent change in position of a distant object when viewed from different positions, caused by Earth's rotation and revolution. Used in astronomy to measure distance from Earth to celestial objects.

paralysis, loss of muscular movement. May be caused by brain or muscle damage, spinal injury, disease or poison.

Paramaribo, cap. and port of Surinam. Founded (1650) by Eng. colonists. Exports rum, coffee, bauxite. Pop. (1961) 123,000.

Paraná, S Amer. river (c. 2,000 mi. long). Formed by junction of Paranaíba and Río Grande, S Brazil, flows S into Argentina at head of Río de la Plata.

paranoia, in psychoanalysis, mental disorder characterized by persistent, rational delusions, esp. of persecution and grandeur. Often caused by schizophrenia.

parapsychology, study of non-scientific mental phenomena.

parasite, plant or animal which obtains nourishment from another living organism, called its host. Includes insects, protozoans, worms, disease-causing bacteria, fungi.

parchment, writing material prepared from stretched, untanned animal skins. First used in Pergamum (c. 150 BC).

pardon, legal and eccles. term for remission of punishment for a particular case. Pardons sometimes extended by executive or royal prerogative, or in R.C. Church by the pope.

Paré, Ambroise (1510–90), Fr. surgeon. Initiated humane methods in treatment of wounds.

Parent, Étienne (1802–74), Canadian writer. Edited *Le Canadien* (1822–5, 1831–42). Advocated constitutional reform, not extreme action. Urged participation of Fr. Canadians in commercial development and of clergy in social problems.

Pareto, Vilfredo (1848–1923), Ital. sociologist and economist. Influential forerunner of Fascism; wrote *Mind and Society* (1916, Eng. tr. 1935), attacking democratic institutions.

pariah, Indian of low caste, sometimes called untouchable. Term now usually applied only to the ownerless scavenger dogs found in E cities.

Paricutín, volcano (8,200 ft. high) of W central Mexico. Created by 1943 eruption, subsequently grew c. 800 ft.

Paris, cap. and seat of govt. of France, on R. Seine. Indust., transport and communication centre of W Europe. Became cap. (987), medieval commercial and scholastic centre; focus of resistance in revolutions of 1789, 1830, 1848. Culturally predominant (17th–19th cent.). Many historic places remain, incl. Louvre, Cathedral of Notre Dame, Champs Élysées, Hôtel des Invalides, Eiffel Tower and Sorbonne. New city planned (19th cent.) by Haussmann. Pop. (1962) 2,790,000.

Paris, in Gk. myth., son of Priam of Troy. At marriage of Peleus and Thetis called upon to award apple inscribed 'to the fairest' to Aphrodite, Hera or Athena. Chose Aphrodite, with whose help he carried off HELEN, thus causing TROJAN WAR.

paris, genus of Eurasian perennial herbs of family Liliaceae. Whorled

Street in Montmartre, Paris

Paris and the River Seine

leaves; root-stocks bear single yellow-green flower with fetid smell.

Paris, Congress of, conference held (1856) to negotiate settlement of CRIMEAN WAR. Russ.-Turkish boundary in Asia restored to pre-war status.

Paris, Treaty of, name of several treaties signed in Paris. SEVEN YEARS WAR concluded (1763); signatories, England, France and Spain. AMERICAN REVOLUTION negotiated (1783), signed by England and newly-independent US. Settlement (1814–15) of problems arising from abdication by NAPOLEON I and CONGRESS OF VIENNA.

Paris, University of see SORBONNE.

Paris Peace Conference see VERSAILLES, TREATY OF.

Park, Chung Hee (1917–), South Korean polit. leader. Pres. since 1961, when he seized power by military coup.

Park, Mungo (1771–1806), Scot. explorer of Africa. Explored course of Niger R. Drowned in ambush by natives.

Parkinson's disease, disorder of central nervous system, 1st described by Brit. neurologist James Parkinson (1755–1824). Characterized by trembling and rigidity of muscles.

parliament, legislative branch of govt. in UK, widely imitated in other states. UK Parl. comprises HOUSE OF LORDS and HOUSE OF COMMONS. Real executive power vested in PRIME MINISTER and CABINET. Modern development began 13th cent. with series of irregular assemblies, *e.g.* MODEL PARLIAMENT. Issue of parl. sovereignty, result of transfer of taxation powers from king to legislature, led to CIVIL WAR, supremacy affirmed by Glorious Revolution (1688). Development of parties brought parl. control of ministries. Evolution of suffrage (19th–20th cent.) took power away from propertied classes. Supremacy of Commons finalized by PARLIAMENT ACT.

Parliament Act (1911), legislation restricting veto power of House of Lords. Upper chamber given right to delay bill for limited period, but not to reject it.

Parma, city of Emilia-Romagna, N Italy. Agric. market, industries include silk. Area known for Parmesan cheese. Pop. (1965) 163,000.

Parmenides (b. *c.* 510), Gk. philosopher, founder of Eleatic School. Held that real universe is single indivisible whole, and only object of knowledge; change an illusion about which we can only conjecture.

Parmigianino or **Parmigiano,** orig.

Parrot: Swainson's Lorikeet

Francesco Mazzola (1503–40), Ital. painter. Works include *Madonna with St Margaret.* Credited with introduction of etching into Italy.

Parnassus, mountain (8,062 ft.) of C Greece, dedicated, in myth. times, to Apollo, Dionysus and the Muses.

Parnell, Charles Stewart (1846–91), Irish nationalist. United disparate Irish elements in Parl. Agitation for reform led to Land Act (1881). Estab. alliance with Gladstone based on promise of Irish Home Rule. Involved in divorce scandal (1889), lost polit. power.

Parnell, Thomas (1679–1718), Irish poet. Associate of Alexander Pope and Jonathan Swift; verse includes 'The Hermit'.

parotid gland, main salivary gland located in front of and below the ear.

Parr, Catherine (1512–48), queen consort, 6th wife of Henry VIII of England. Acted as queen regent in 1544.

Parrington, Vernon Louis (1871–1929), Amer. literary critic. Author of *Main Currents in American Thought* (3 vols., 1927–30).

parrot, hook-billed, often brilliantly coloured bird of order Psittaciformes. World-wide distribution esp. Australasia and S America. Has ability

to mimic speech; often kept as pet. Species include cockatoo, lory, macaw, parakeet.

parrotbill, thick-billed Asiatic songbird of genus *Paradoxornis.*

Parry, Sir Charles Hubert Hastings (1848–1918), Brit. composer. Best known for choral works; also wrote symphonies, chamber music.

Parry, Sir William Edward (1790–1855), Brit. arctic explorer. Commanded expeditions in search of North West Passage during 1820s.

Parseeism see ZOROASTRIANISM.

Parsifal, figure of ARTHURIAN LEGEND, often identified with Gawain. Provided basis of medieval poem *Parzival* by Wolfram von Eschenbach.

parsley, *Petroselinum crispum,* aromatic herb used as garnish.

parsnip, *Pastinaca sativa,* European vegetable plant with long fleshy edible roots.

Parsons, Sir Charles Algernon (1854–1931), Brit. engineer and industrialist. Invented Parsons steam turbine engine (1889).

Parsons, Talcott (1902–), Amer. sociologist. Works include *Towards a General Theory of Action* (1951) and *Theories of Society* (2 vols., 1961).

Parthenon, temple of Athena on Acropolis, Athens. Built in Doric style under admin. of Pericles (447–438 BC); architects were Ictinus and Callicrates, work supervised by PHEIDIAS. Part of outside frieze acquired (1799–1803) by Lord Elgin, now in British Museum.

Donna di Santa Margherita
by Parmigianino

parthenogenesis, biological reproduction from unfertilized eggs. Occurs naturally in some organisms *e.g.* starfish, bees, dandelions. Can be artificially induced in rabbits, frogs, but resulting offspring rarely reach maturity.

Parthia, ancient region SE of Caspian Sea. Under Seleucid rule (250 BC) until empire estab. (by 1st cent. BC reaching India). Parthians, esp. noted for skill in archery, defeated Romans under Crassus (53 BC). Defeated by Romans (39–38 BC), finally overthrown by Ardashir I (AD 226).

partridge, medium sized Eurasian game bird of Perdicinae family. Plump body, short tail; ground nesting. Grey partridge, *Perdix perdix,* mottled brown above with grey speckled breast, is known as Hungarian partridge in N America. French partridge, *Alectoris rufa,* has red legs, bill and eyelids.

pasang, *Capra hircus aegagrus,* species of wild goat found in Med. regions and Asia Minor.

Pascal, Blaise (1623–62), Fr. mathematician, scientist, religious philosopher. Contributed to differential calculus; propounded law of probability. Defended Jansenism in *Lettres Provinciales* (1656). His *Pensées* (1670) is an apology for the Christian religion.

pasha or **pacha,** title formerly used in Turkey and N Africa for military leaders and provincial governors. Abolished in Turkey (1934), in Egypt (1952).

Pashto or **Pushtu,** Iranian language of Indo-European family. Over 12 million speakers in Afghanistan and Pakistan.

pasque flower, *Anemone patens,* wild flower of N Amer. prairies with bluish-purple flowers. European counterpart, *A. pulsatilla* is spring garden flower.

passacaglia, type of musical composition in slow 3/4 time, orig. Sp. or Ital. court dance. Form used esp. for slow movements by Bach.

Passarowitz, Treaty of, signed (1718) in Yugoslavia at end of 1714–18 war between Turkey, Holy Roman Empire and Venice. Turkey, defeated by Charles VI in Balkans, ceded Yugoslav territory, but gained Venetian possessions in Greece.

Passchendaele, ridge in W Flanders near Ypres. Scene of Allied offensive (1917); heavy losses incurred by both sides.

passenger pigeon, *Ectopistes migratorius,* extinct N Amer. wild pigeon. Numerous until late 19th cent.

Passion, The, in Christian religions, the sufferings of Jesus, esp. His agony in the Garden of Gethsemane, His arrest, trial and Crucifixion. Remembered by Christians during Passiontide, final weeks of LENT.

Passion play, dramatic representation of the PASSION of Christ, a form of miracle play. Most famous staged at Oberammergau, Bavaria every 10 yr.

passion-flower, trop. Amer. vine of genus *Passiflora.* Species include *P. incarnata* which has edible fruits.

passive resistance, refusal on moral or religious grounds to obey regulations; implies willingness to undergo penalties. Gandhi was life-long exponent of policy, also used by some US civil rights advocates.

Passover, Jewish religious festival commemorating deliverance of Israelites from Egypt. Celebrated late March or early April, lasts 7 days. Meals of 1st 2 evenings known as Seders, observed by traditional foods and ceremonies.

Passy, Frédéric (1822–1912), Fr. economist and politician. Helped found International Peace League (1868) and Inter-parliamentary Peace Union (1888). With Jean Henri Dunant awarded 1st Nobel Peace Prize (1901).

Pasternak, Boris Leonidovitch (1890–1960), Russ. novelist and poet. His novel *Dr. Zhivago* (1958) won international fame. Awarded Nobel Prize for Literature (1958) but refused it under Communist pressure.

Pasteur, Louis, FRS (1822–95), Fr. chemist. Proved fermentation caused by bacteria, not spontaneous generation. Developed pasteurization process to kill bacteria by heat. Initiated use of vaccine for anthrax and hydrophobia.

Paston Letters, collection (1422–1509) of correspondence of Paston family of Norfolk. Provide hist. material on customs of England towards end of Middle Ages.

pastoral, in literature, a work idealizing rustic life. The supposedly simple life of a shepherd is contrasted with complexity, hypocrisy of court or city life. Form developed by Theocritus and Vergil, used by others esp. Milton, Spenser, Shelley.

Patagonia, vast semi-arid plateau region of S Argentina and Chile. Sparsely populated; area primarily used for sheep and cattle grazing.

patas, *Erythrocebus patas,* reddish, long-tailed monkey of W Africa.

patent, document conferring exclusive rights on person to manufacture, use and sell invention over specified period. Known in UK as Letters Patent. Patent rights safeguarded outside original country by International Convention (1883).

Pater, Walter Horatio (1839–94), Brit. literary critic. Advocated 'art for art's sake'; works include *Studies in the History of the Renaissance* (1873).

Pater Noster see LORD'S PRAYER.

Pathan, member of semi-nomadic, mainly Moslem, race living in W Pakistan and Afghanistan.

pathology, branch of medical science concerned with structural and functional changes in parts of body, their causes and effects.

patience [UK], **solitaire** [US], general name for large number of card games for 1 player.

Patmos, Gk. island of Dodecanese group, SE Aegean Sea. Area: 13 sq. mi.; main port, Patmos. St John traditionally wrote Revelation here.

Paton, Alan Stewart (1903–), South African novelist and political reformer. Helped form Liberal Association. Novels include *Cry the Beloved Country* (1948).

patriarch [Gk: *patriarches,* head of family], term applied to OT and other progenitors of human race (*e.g.* Noah, Abraham). Also, bishops of certain metropolitan sees of Gk. Orthodox Church.

Patrick, Saint (*c.* 385–461), missionary called 'Apostle of Ireland'; patron

Grey Partridge

saint of Ireland. Studied in Gaul, evangelized in Ireland before going to Rome (441). Created bishop of Armagh. Subject of many legends.

Patroclus, in Gk. myth. intimate friend of Achilles. In Trojan War slain by Hector, thus causing Achilles to be reconciled with Agamemnon and return to the war.

Patterson, Joseph Medill (1879–1946), Amer. journalist. Co-editor of *Chicago Tribune* (1914–25). Founded (1919) tabloid New York *Daily News.* His sister, **Eleanor Medill Patterson** (1884–1948), became exponent of spectacular news presentation.

Patton, George S[mith], Jr. (1885–1945), Amer. army officer. As Commander of 3rd Army in World War 2, directed advance of US forces through Europe (1944–5).

Paul, Saint, orig. Saul of Tarsus (d. *c.* AD 62), leader of early Christian Church. Most widely travelled of the early missionaries; called Apostle of the Gentiles. Set up churches in Asia Minor, Greece and Rome. Martyred in persecution initiated by Nero.

Paul III, orig. Alessandro Farnese (1468–1549), pope (1534–49). Encouraged Society of Jesus and introduced Inquisition to Italy. Commissioned Michelangelo to paint Sistine Chapel frescoes.

Paul VI, orig. Giovanni Battista Montini (1897–), pope (1963–). First pope to leave Italy in 150 yr., visited Holy Land, UN General Assembly; met (1967) Orthodox Patriarch Athenagoras in Turkey.

Paul I (1754–1801), emperor and tsar of Russia (1796–1801). Joined coalitions against France (1799) and Britain (1800). Assassinated upon refusal to abdicate.

Pauline Letters, 14 epistles of NT, attributed to St Paul, of which those to Timothy, Titus and the Hebrews are prob. not his.

Pauling, Linus Carl, FRS (1901–). Amer. chemist. Awarded Nobel Prize for Chemistry (1954) for studies of complex protein molecules. Awarded Nobel Peace Prize (1962). First person to receive 2 Nobel prizes.

Pausanias (d. *c.* 470 BC), Spartan general, victor at battle of Plataea (479 BC) in Persian Wars. Accused twice of treason, took refuge in a temple and starved to death.

Pausanias (*fl.* AD 174), Gk. traveller and geographer. His *Description of Greece* was source for ancient Gk. topography, legends and monuments.

Pavese, Cesare (1908–50), Ital. novelist and critic. Works include *Il Mestiere di Vivere.*

Pavia, town of N Italy, cap. of

Monastery of Certosa di Pavia

Lombard kingdom. Scene of battle in which Emperor Charles V defeated and took prisoner Francis I of France (1525). Pop. (1961) 73,500.

Pavlov, Ivan Petrovich, FRS (1849–1936), Russ. physiologist. Pioneered study of conditioned reflexes with experiments using dogs. Awarded Nobel Prize for Physiology and Medicine (1904) for study of digestive glands.

Pavlova, Anna (1882–1931), Russ. ballerina. Made debut at St Petersburg; danced with Diaghilev's Ballet Russe. After 1910 toured widely, performing solos, esp. *The Dying Swan,* created for her by Fokine.

pawn, pledge, handing over of article to broker as security for loan. If loan not repaid within given time, broker may sell article.

Pawnee, tribe of Caddoan N Amer. Indians; lived in Nebraska. Moved to reservation in Oklahoma (1876).

Paxton, Sir Joseph (1801–65), Eng. architect and landscape gardener. Designed Crystal Palace, London, for 1851 Exhibition.

Paz, Octavio (1914–), Mexican poet and critic. Works include *El Laberinto de la Soledad* (1950) and poems, incl. *Piedra de Sol* (1957).

pea, *Pisum sativum,* annual climbing leguminous herb, widely cultivated for edible pod-borne seeds, used as vegetable. Chickpea, *Cicer arietinum,* also grown for edible seeds in Europe, Asia and S America. *See* SWEET-PEA.

Peace Corps, agency (estab. 1961 by US govt.) to provide trained personnel for work overseas. Provides skilled help in spheres of education, health, agric. and technical development.

Peace River, river of W Canada, major link in Mackenzie R. system, joining Parsnip and Finlay R. with Great Slave R.; length 800 mi.

peach, *Prunus persica,* fruit-tree with decorative pink blossom and sweet stone-fruit. Orig. Chinese, now naturalized throughout warm temperate regions.

Purple Passion-flower of Peru

Peacock

Peacock, Thomas Love (1785–1866), Eng. satirical novelist and poet, largely self-educated. Wrote *Headlong Hall* (1815), *Nightmare Abbey* (1818), *Crotchet Castle* (1831).

peacock, *Pavo,* male game bird native to India and SE Asia, naturalized elsewhere as ornamental bird. In breeding season train-like tail develops beautiful colours and iridescent spots.

peacock butterfly, *Nymphalis io,* European butterfly with eye-mark on each wing like peacock's tail.

Peak District, high plateau S of Pennine Mts. in Derbyshire, England, reaching 2,088 ft. in Kinder Scout.

peanut, groundnut, *Arachis hypogaea,* Brazilian leguminous plant extensively cultivated in sub-trop. countries for its seeds. Eaten raw, roasted and salted, and used to make oil, peanut butter, *etc.*

pear, *Pyrus,* tree and its fruit of European *P. communis* and Oriental *P. pyrifolia,* widely cultivated in temperate regions.

pearl, secretion of mother-of-pearl or nacre, formed in shellfish, esp. pearl-oyster and pearl-mussel. Thin layers of calcium carbonate deposited round foreign body in shell. May be white, pink or black.

pearl gourami, *Trichogaster,* freshwater trop. fish, native to Asia.

Pearl Harbor, US naval base in Hawaii. Japanese attack (7 Dec. 1941), destroying bulk of Pacific fleet, caused US to enter World War 2.

Pears, Peter (1910–), Brit. tenor. Co-founder of Aldeburgh Festival (1948) with Benjamin Britten, whose works he was often 1st to perform.

Pearson, Lester Bowles (1897–), Canadian statesman. Sec. of State for External Affairs (1948–57). Awarded Nobel Peace Prize (1957) for contributing to UN mediation in Suez crisis. Leader of Liberal Party after 1958; PM (1963–8) of minority govt.

Peary, Robert Edwin (1856–1920), Amer. Arctic explorer. Leader of scientific expeditions to Greenland and 1st man to reach N Pole (1909).

Peasants' Revolt (1381), rising of Eng. peasants, led by Wat Tyler and John Ball, resulting from low wages, heavy taxes and breakdown of feudal system. Rebels entered London, seized the Tower. After meeting Richard II, Tyler was killed by Lord Mayor and rebellion then quickly suppressed.

Peasants' War (1524–6), rising of Ger. peasants against oppressive treatment by and extortionate demands of feudal lords. Inspired partly by preaching of MARTIN LUTHER, who, however, violently condemned the rebellion. Rising ruthlessly suppressed. Peasants' defeat contributed to delay of democratic development in Germany.

peat, vegetable matter, carbonised and partially decomposed, found in marshy lands in temperate zone; one of early stages in formation of coal. Used as fuel, mainly in Ireland and N Scotland.

pecan, *Carya illinoensis,* hickory tree of S and central US, producing edible nut.

peccary, pig-like hoofed mammal of genus *Tayassu* of N and S America. Collared peccary, *T. angulatus* has dark grey coat with white collar.

Pechora, river of Russ. SFSR flowing into Barents Sea. Length 1,133 mi.

Pecock, Reginald (*c.* 1395–1460), Brit. bishop and theologian. Writings, models of 15th cent. English, attacked Lollard teachings. Denied authenticity of Apostles' Creed; found guilty of heresy (1458).

pediatrics, branch of medicine which deals with children, their diseases and treatment.

pediculosis, phthiriasis, infectious disease of the body hair and skin, occurring by direct contact and caused by lice, whose eggs can be found in the hair. Treatment effective with use of DDT.

pediment, in architecture, triangular gable-end on building of classical type. Used extensively in Amer. colonial style architecture.

Pedro II, orig. Dom Pedro (1825–91), emperor of Brazil; ended slavery (1888), but forced to abdicate by landowners (1889).

Peeblesshire, inland county of SE Scotland. Area: 347 sq. mi.; county town, Peebles. Mountainous, important for forestry, sheep farming, wool production. Pop. (1967) 13,502.

Peel, Sir Robert (1788–1850), Eng. statesman. As Home Sec., secured passage of Catholic Emancipation Bill (1829), set up London Police Force. P.M. (1834–5); his Tamworth Manifesto (1834) fashioned modern Cons. party. As reforming P.M. (1841–6) Peel promoted Free Trade, introduced Income Tax; repeal of Corn Laws split and brought down his govt. (1846).

peelers, colloq. name for police forces estab. in Ireland (1812–18) and London (1829) by SIR ROBERT PEEL; later denoted also London police (or 'bobbies').

peeper, *Hyla crucifer,* tree frog of E North America.

peerage, body of nobles, esp. Brit. nobility, members of HOUSE OF LORDS. Act of 1963 enabled them to renounce titles.

peewee, pewee, small flycatcher of N America, esp. wood pewee, *Contropus virens.*

peewit *see* LAPWING.

Pegasus, in Gk. myth., winged horse, sprung from blood of Medusa when slain by Perseus. Helped Bellerophon slay Chimaera.

pegmatite, coarse-grained igneous or

Peacock Butterfly

The Temple of Heaven, Peking

metamorphic rock. Frequently contains ore minerals, though seldom in quantity.

Péguy, Charles (1873–1914), Fr. writer and publisher. Opposed social injustice; helped defend Dreyfus. Later became leading Catholic mystic, esp. in poetry incl. *Le Mystère de la Charité de Jeanne d'Arc* (1910).

Peiping *see* PEKING.

Peisistratus or **Pisistratus** (*c.* 605–527 BC), tyrant of Athens. Gained popularity by liberal laws, extended influence of Athenian hegemony to Ionian cities. Exiled twice, nevertheless left strong state to sons Hippias and Hipparchus.

pekan, fisher, *Martes pennanti*, large carnivorous arboreal mammal of weasel family. Native to N America.

Pekinese, Pekingese, Chinese breed of small dog introduced to Europe (1860). Broad skull, small hindquarters, long silky coat.

Peking, cap. of Chinese People's Republic, known as Peiping (1928–49), in Hopei prov. Made cap. (1264) by Kublai Khan. Contains former imperial precinct, now seat of govt., People's University (1912), industries. Pop. (1967) 5,420,000.

Peking man, extinct species of man, related to PITHECANTHROPUS. Remains found near Peking.

Pelagianism, theory which affirms the freedom of the will to choose between good and evil, and denies original sin. Orig. formed by Pelagius (*c.* 360–420 AD), Brit. monk, opponent of Augustinian theory of predestination.

pelargonium, S African plant of genus *Pelargonium*. Cultivated for showy red, pink and white flowers; commonly called geranium.

Pelham, Henry (1696–1754), Brit. statesman. Whig P.M. (1743–54); maintained naval strength whilst reducing national debt.

Pelham-Holles, Thomas, 1st Duke of Newcastle (1693–1768), Eng. Whig statesman. As P.M. (1754–62), left strategy of Seven Years War to Pitt.

pelican, water fowl of genus *Pelecanus*. Very large bill has pouch suspended underneath in which fish are caught. Species include Amer. white pelican, *P. erythrorhynchos* with wingspan of 10 ft.

pelican's foot, *Aporrhais pespelicani*, European marine mollusc found in offshore gravels. Pale brown shell.

pellagra, disease caused by lack of nicotinamide, a B vitamin. Symptoms include sore tongue, skin rash, digestive difficulties and, in extreme cases, mental disorders.

Pellaprat, Henri (1869–1950), Fr. chef and teacher at Cordon Bleu School, Paris. Wrote *L'Art Culinaire Moderne* (1935).

Peloponnesian War (431–404 BC), struggle between Athens and most Peloponnesian states (and Boeotia) led by Sparta. Chief events in 1st 10 years were Athenian successes at Pylos and Sphacteria (425 BC) and Spartan victory at Amphipolis (424 BC). Peace of Nicias (421 BC) only partially observed. Spartans victori-

Pear: left, twig with blossom; right, twig with buds

Pele (1940–), Brazilian football player. Most prominent player in Brazil's team which won World Soccer Cup (1958, 1962).

Pelée, volcano (4,429 ft.), N Martinique, W Indies.

Peleus, in Gk. myth., king of the Myrmidons; father of Achilles by nymph Thetis. All the gods were invited to his wedding except Eris, who in revenge, sent him the APPLE OF DISCORD.

ous at Mantinea (418 BC). Athenian expedition against Sicily (415 BC), urged by ALCIBIADES, ended in destruction of fleet and army (413 BC). Spartans occupied Decelea (413 BC) and ravaged Attica. Athenians rebuilt fleet and despite desertion of allies and Spartan alliance with Persia, gained naval victories (411, 410, 406 BC); finally defeated at Aegospotami (405 BC), obliged to accept terms of Sparta (404 BC).

Peccary

King Penguin (left) and Adelie Penguin (right)

flippers. Species include emperor penguin, *Aptenodytes forsteri,* king penguin, *A. patogonica* and Adelie penguin, *Pygoscelis adeliae.*

penicillin, antibiotic substances produced by *Penicillium* moulds, esp. *P. chrysogenum* and *P. notatum.* Antibacterial effect noted by A. Fleming (1928). E. B. Chain and H. W. Florey prepared drug penicillin (1939).

peninsula, piece of land almost surrounded by water, *e.g.* Iberian peninsula.

Peninsular War (1808–14), fought against French in Iberian peninsula by Britain, Spain and Portugal. Supreme commander, SIR ARTHUR WELLESLEY (later Duke of Wellington), won victories at Vimeiro (1808), Talavera (1809), Salamanca (1812); invaded France (1814) before war ended on Napoleon's abdication.

penis, in males of higher vertebrates, organ which emits sperm in copulation. In mammals also provides a urinary outlet.

Penn, William (1644–1718), Eng. Quaker, founder of Pennsylvania. Joined Quakers (1667), estab. Quaker Colony (1681) of Pennsylvania.

Penney, William, Baron (1909–), Brit. physicist. Designed 1st Brit. atomic bomb; chairman UK Atomic Energy Authority (1963–).

Pennine Alps, mountains of Valais, Switzerland, forming boundary between Switzerland and Italy; contains highest Swiss peaks, *e.g.* Monte Rosa (15,200 ft.), Matterhorn (14,685 ft.).

Pennine Chain, mountain system of N England, 150 mi. long from Scot. border to PEAK DISTRICT, Derbyshire. Poor soil, used for sheep grazing; coal, limestone, lead, iron, fluorspar mined.

Pennsylvania, E state of US, 1 of 13 orig. states. Area: 45,333 sq. mi.; cap. Harrisburg; cities, Philadelphia, Pittsburgh, Erie, Scranton, Allen-

Peony

Peloponnese [**Peloponnēsos**], S peninsula of Greece; chief cities Patras, Corinth; mountainous, mainly sheep-raising area adjoining mainland at Isthmus of Corinth. Ancient Spartan influence crushed by Theban invasion (4th cent. BC). Known for ruins at Sparta, Mycenae, Olympia. Pop. (1961) 1,095,823.

Pelops, in Gk. myth, son of Tantalus. Won Hippodameia in marriage by defeating her father Oenomaus in chariot race. Bribed and murdered Oenomaus' charioteer who cursed house of Pelops. Curse manifested in his sons ATREUS and THYESTES.

pelota *see* JAI ALAI.

pelvis, bony framework for portion of the body below abdomen. Contains bowel, bladder and sex organs. Female pelvis tends to be larger, for child bearing.

Pembrokeshire, county of SW Wales. Area: 615 sq. mi.; county town, Haverfordwest; other towns, Milford Haven, Tenby. Agriculture main occupation; coal, lead and iron mined; tourism developing. Pop. (1961) 93,080.

pemmican, orig. N Amer. Indian food made of dried buffalo or venison meat pounded to a paste and packed with fat into rawhide bags.

Penal Laws, legislation (1st enacted

1559) banning Roman Catholics from civil office and penalizing them for not conforming to Church of England. Ended by Catholic Emancipation Act (1829).

penal servitude, type of punishment used in UK (1853–1949). Minimum length of imprisonment was 3 yr. with hard labour.

Penang, state of Malaysia in W Malaya incl. Penang Is. Area: 400 sq. mi.; cap. George Town. Joined Federation of Malaya (1948) and of Malaysia (1963).

Penates, in Roman religion, household gods, and with Lares regarded as protectors of the house. Also state Penates, guardians of the commonwealth.

Penelope, in Gk. myth., wife of ODYSSEUS. Remained faithful during Odysseus' absence by postponing selection from suitors until completion of a tapestry which she unpicked each night. Finally reunited with Odysseus after 20 yr.

Penfield, Wilder [**Graves**] (1891–). Canadian neurosurgeon. Founded Montreal Neurological Institute (1934). Novels include *No Other Gods* (1954).

penguin, flightless aquatic bird of family Spheniscidae of S hemisphere. Short legs, wings forming strong

town. Major industries produce metal and machinery, food, chemicals, *etc*. Rich agricultural land and extensive forests. Mineral resources include coal, natural gas. First settled by William Penn and Quakers (1681). Pop. (1960) 11,319,366.

Pennsylvanian *see* GEOLOGICAL TABLE.

pennyroyal, small perennial plant of mint family, European *Mentha pulegium* and America *Hedeoma pulegioides*. Bluish flowers; yields aromatic oil.

pennywort, wild plant with roundish leaves and greenish yellow flowers. Species include wall pennywort or navelwort, *Umbilicus rupestris*, found on rocks and walls.

Penobscot, tribe of Algonkian N Amer. Indians. Largest tribe of the Abenaki Confederacy. Lived in Maine.

Pentateuch, name given to first five books of the OT. Known in Judaism as the TORAH.

pentathlon, Olympic athletic event in which participants demonstrate skill in 5 events.

Pentecost [Gk: *pentekoste* 50th], Jewish religious festival celebrating end of grain harvest which takes place 50 days after Passover. Also Christian festival celebrating descent of the Holy Ghost upon the Apostles on the 50th day after Christ's Resurrection. *See* WHIT SUNDAY.

Pentland Firth, strait, 14 mi. long, between Caithness and Orkney Is., N Scotland.

pentstamen, penstemon, N Amer. perennial plant of genus *Pentstemon*. Some grown for showy flowers.

penumbra, shadow cast where light is partially cut off by intervening body. Occurrence exemplified by eclipse.

peony, paeony, perennial herb or shrub of genus *Paionia*. Native to Europe, Asia and NW America. Large white, pink or scarlet flowers.

Pepin or **Pippin of Landen** (d. 639), Frankish mayor under Dagobert I. Daughter's marriage initiated Carolingian dynasty. Grandfather of Pepin the Short.

Pepin the Short (*c*. 714– 768), king of the Franks; 1st of the Carolingians, having seized throne from Childeric III, last of Merovingian kings. Father of Charlemagne.

pepper, fruit of various species of genus *Capsicum* incl. pimento. Eaten as vegetable, pickled or used as seasoning. Spicy varieties include cayenne, paprika, chili, *etc*.

pepper, *Piper nigrum*, trop. plant yielding seeds dried as condiment;

Shooting of the Rebels of May 3, 1808 painted by Goya, to show the horrors of the Peninsular War

ground as black pepper or (without seed cover) as white pepper.

pepper tree, trop. Amer. evergreen tree of genus *Schinus*. Aromatic berries.

peppermint, *Mentha piperita*, perennial herb of temp. N latitudes. Cultivated for aromatic oil.

pepsin, enzyme produced in the stomach. In combination with hydrochloric acid, acts on proteins, changing them to peptons.

peptic ulcer, corrosion of wall of stomach or duodenum. Aggravated by action of gastric juices. Cause unknown; possibly related to stress.

Pepys, Samuel (1633– 1703), Eng. public official and diarist; Sec. of Admiralty (1672– 9, 1684– 9). His secret, shorthand diary (1660– 9) is detailed record of his personal and public life.

Perak, state of Malaysia. Area: 8,030 sq. mi.; cap. Ipoh. Rich in tin, rubber, gold and coal. Pop. (1966 est.) 1,613,728.

perch, spiny-finned freshwater food fish of genus *Perca*. Species include yellow perch, *P. flavescens* of US and *P. fluviatilis* of Europe.

percussion instruments, musical instruments struck to produce sound, as distinct from string or wind instruments. Function is chiefly rhythmic, *e.g.* drum, triangle, cymbals, though

some set up regular vibrations producing sound of definite pitch, *e.g.* xylophone, timpani, glockenspiel.

Percy, Eng. noble family. **Henry Percy, 1st Earl of Northumberland** (1342– 1408) helped secure throne for Henry IV, then took part in plot by son, **Sir Henry Percy** (1366– 1403), called Hotspur, to overthrow king. Plan to crown Edmund de Mortimer ended with Hotspur's death at Shrewsbury. **Thomas Percy, 7th Earl of Northumberland** (1528– 72), planned (1569) release of Mary, Queen of Scots; beheaded after leading unsuccessful revolt against Elizabeth I.

Père David's deer, *Elaphurus davidianus*, species of deer discovered (1865) in China by Fr. missionary Father Armand David.

peregrine falcon, *Falco peregrinus*, swift bird of prey of falcon family, much used in falconry. Found in Europe, Asia and N America. European birds migrate to equatorial Africa; duck hawk is Amer. variety.

Perelman, Sidney Joseph (1904–), Amer. humorist. Wrote scripts for films by Marx Brothers. Books include *Look Who's Talking* (1940).

European Perch

Pérez de Ayala, Ramón (1880–1962), Sp. writer. Works include novel *Belarmino y Apolonio* (1921) and poetry collected in *La Paz del Sendero* (1903).

Perez Galdos, Benito (1843–1920), Sp. writer. Author of 46-novel cycle about 19th cent. Spain, *Episodios nacionales* (1873–1912).

Perez Jimenez, Marco (1914–), Venezuelan military and polit, leader. Member of junta that ousted (1948) Romulo Gallagos. Exercised dictatorial powers until his removal (1957).

perfume, substance prepared from the oils of plants, gums, animal products and synthetic compounds, often dissolved in alcohol. Highly valued as cosmetic preparation.

Pergamum, orig. hill-fortress in NW Asia Minor. Cap. of Attalid dynasty (3rd cent. BC). Literary centre (2nd cent. BC) with 1st extensive use of parchment for books.

Pergolesi, Giovanni Battista (1710–36), Ital. composer. Works include operas *La Serva Padrona* and *Stabat Mater.*

pericardium, 2-layered membrane surrounding the heart. Pericardial fluid between layers protects heart and prevents friction.

Pericles (c. 500–429 BC), Athenian statesman under whose admin. Athens achieved political and cultural zenith. Reformed constitution into well developed democracy; created Athenian empire out of DELIAN LEAGUE resulting in war with neighbouring states and Sparta (459–446 BC), and contributing to Peloponnesian War (431–404 BC). War policy and plague in Athens led to his deposition, but re-elected (430 BC).

peridot, rare gem, transparent variety of olivine.

peridotite, ultrabasic igneous rock composed of olivine and other ferromagnesian minerals.

perigee, in astronomy, point nearest Earth of celestial bodies in orbit around it, *i.e.* Moon and artificial satellites.

Périgord, region of C France now included in Dordogne and Lot-et-Garonne. Famed for its truffles. Important prehistoric remains esp. painted caves of Lascaux.

perihelion, in astronomy, point nearest Sun of celestial bodies in orbit around it, *i.e.* planets, comets.

periodic table, classification of elements arranged by atomic weight. Formulated (c. 1870) by MENDELEYEV.

periscope, optical instrument, which enables observer to see objects not discernible from his position. The image is reflected from an upper

The ruins of Pergamum

mirror or prism to a lower one, then to the eye. Used in submarines.

peritoneum, layered membrane lining abdominal cavity and enclosing in its folds the internal organs. Largest membrane in the body. Contains blood and lymph vessels.

periwinkle, mollusc of world-wide distribution. Species include common or edible periwinkle, *Littorina littorea* and viviparous rough periwinkle, *L. saxatilis.*

periwinkle, perennial trailing evergreen plant of genus *Vinca,* native to Europe. Species include greater periwinkle, *V. major* and lesser periwinkle, *V. minor.*

Perlis, smallest state of Malaysia. Area: 310 sq. mi.; cap. Kangar. Produces rice, rubber, tin. Pop. (1966 est.) 116,393.

Perm, formerly Molotov, city of Russ. SFSR. Commercial and transport centre; industries include machine tools, ship-building, chemicals. Pop. (1967) 785,000.

Permian *see* GEOLOGICAL TABLE.

Perón, Juan Domingo (1895–), Argentinian statesman. Pres. of Argentina (1946–55). Estab. virtual dictatorship aiming at national economic self-sufficiency. Widely popular at first; re-elected 1952; deposed by army coup (1955).

perpendicular, Gothic style in Eng. architecture of 14th–16th cent. Characterized by vertical lines in window tracery and wall panelling.

Perrault, Charles (1628–1703), Fr. writer. His work *Histoires ou Contes du Temps Passé* (1697) contains best

known versions of 'Cinderella' and 'Sleeping Beauty'.

Perrin, Jean Baptiste (1870–1942), Fr. physicist. Awarded Nobel Prize for Physics (1926) for work on structure of matter.

Perse, St-John, orig. Alexis Saint-Léger Léger (1887–), Fr. poet. Works include lyric poems *Anabase* (1924), translated by T. S. Eliot, and *Chroniques* (1960). Awarded Nobel Prize for Literature (1960).

Persephone, Core, in Gk. myth., daughter of DEMETER. Carried off by Hades, made queen of Underworld. Through lamentations of Demeter, granted by Zeus 8 (or 6) months each year on earth, the remainder to be spent in Underworld. Known by Romans as Proserpina.

Persepolis, city of ancient Persian Empire, estab. as ceremonial cap. by Darius I (c. 500 BC); captured and partially destroyed by Alexander the Great.

Perseus, in Gk. myth., son of Zeus and Danaë. Slew Medusa, married Andromeda. Later became king of Argos.

Perseus (c. 212–166 BC), last king of Macedon (179–168 BC); engaged in 3rd Macedonian War against Rome (171 BC), defeated at Pydna (168); taken as prisoner to Rome (167 BC).

Persia, old name for country of SW Asia, now IRAN. Overrun c. 1600 BC by Aryan tribes incl. Medes and Persians. In 6th cent. BC, Cyrus II of Persia defeated Medes and estab. Persian empire; conquered (334 BC) by Alexander the Great; on his death

Persian Cat

passed to the Seleucids until overrun in mid-3rd cent. by Parthians whose rule lasted until AD 226, when 400 yr. reign of Sassanian dynasty began. In 7th cent., Persia conquered for Islam by the Arabs and in 11th cent. came under Turkish rule, followed by Mongol conquest in 13th cent. Mongol rule ended in mid 14th cent. by Tamerlane. From 15th cent. until modern times the 2 main ruling dynasties were the Sasfavi (1502– 1736) and the Qajars (1779– 1926).

Persian or **Iranian,** language forming sub-division of Indo-Iranian, a sub-division of Indo-European.

Persian carpets, most celebrated and magnificent of Asian carpets, from 6th– 7th cent.

Persian cat, small long-haired, domestic cat of genus *Felis.* Orig. raised in Persia and Afghanistan.

Persian Gulf, extension (nearly landlocked) of Arabian Sea. Lies between Iran and Arabia. Area: 90,000 sq. mi.

Persian Wars, struggles (500– 449 BC) between Gk. city states and Persian Empire. Persian expeditions under Darius I (492, 490 BC) unsuccessful; 3rd expedition, undertaken by Darius' son Xerxes I succeeded, but army left in Greece crushed (479 BC). Wars dragged on, but Gk. cities had estab. their freedom.

persimmon, tree of genus *Diospyros.* Species include N Amer. *D. virginiana,* with sweet edible plum-like fruit; and Jap. or Chinese *D. kaki.*

Persian carpet from Isfahan (*c.* 1800)

Perspex [UK] **Plexiglass** [US], trademark for clear, synthetic plastic material made from acetone.

perspiration, secretion of sweat glands on to the skin's surface, where it evaporates, cooling the body.

Perth, city, cap., and commercial centre of Western Australia. Pop. (1965) 465,000.

Perthshire, county of C Scotland. Area: 2,494 sq. mi.; county town Perth. Mainly agricultural; tourist area of great scenic beauty with fishing, shooting and mountaineering.

Peru [**República del Perú**], country of W South America. Area: 496,222 sq. mi.; cap. Lima; chief port, Callao.

Volcanic Andean range on Pacific coast; rain forests of Amazon basin in E. Agric. occupations; mining (gold, silver, zinc) is leading industry. Sp. colonization initiated after Pizarro's conquest (1532) of INCA empire. Independence proclaimed 1821. Defeated in War of the Pacific (1879– 83) by Chile. Main language, Spanish. Pop. (1966) 12,385,000.

Perugia, city of Umbria, C Italy. Cultural centre and market town; important Etruscan and medieval remains. Pop. (1965) 121,000.

Perugino, orig. Pietro di Cristoforo Vannucci (*c.* 1446– 1527), Ital. religious painter. Works include *Christ Giving the Keys to St Peter* in Sistine chapel. Teacher of Raphael.

Perutz, Max Ferdinand (1914–), Brit. chemist, b. Austria. Shared Nobel Prize for Chemistry (1962) with John Cowdery Kendrew, for discovery of molecular structure of haemoglobin and myoglobin.

Peruvian bark, bark of various trees and shrubs of genus *Cinchona. C. calisaya* native to the Andes, also cultivated in Java and India. Yields quinine and other alkaloids.

Peshawar, city of West Pakistan at entrance of Khyber Pass. Important road and rail town; ancient Buddhist centre. Pop. 219,000.

Pestalozzi, Johann Heinrich (1746– 1827), Swiss educational reformer. Urged that educational methods correspond with child's natural development.

pesticide, poison used to destroy insects, fungus or rodents. Insecticides usually arsenic and phosphorus compounds; fungicides include sulphur; rodenticides made from phosphorus and strychnine compounds.

Pétain, Henri Philippe (1856– 1951), Fr. soldier and politician; halted Germans at Verdun in World War 1; created Marshal of France (1918). Premier at time of France's collapse in World War 2, concluded armistice with Germans. Headed VICHY GOVERNMENT. Sentenced to death after the war for collaboration with the enemy, this sentence later commuted to life imprisonment.

Peter, Saint (d. *c.* AD 64) leading member of 12 Apostles. Orig. called Simon, Jesus named him Cephas (Aramaic: a rock; Gk: *petros*). Denied being follower of Christ on night of His arrest; leader of early Christian church; by tradition martyred on Vatican Hill in time of Nero.

Peter I and II, epistles of NT traditionally ascribed to St Peter.

Peter [**I**] **the Great** (1672– 1725), emperor and tsar of Russia (1682– 1725). Co-ruler under regency until 1689, when he consolidated power. Founded modern Russ. state, centring policies on 'westernization' and expansion. Gained access to Baltic in war with Sweden and built (1713) cap. at St Petersburg. Introduced ruthless reform of industry and education, reorganized military and civil service.

Peterborough, city in county of Huntingdon and Peterborough, England. Important rly. and market centre; industries, engineering, brick making. Cathedral dating from Norman times. Pop. (1967 est.) 66,100.

Peterloo Massacre, incident at St Peter's Field, Manchester, England (1819). Large meeting, petitioning for parl. reform and repeal of CORN LAWS dispersed by troops; 11 people killed and over 500 injured. Resulting indignation accelerated reform movement.

Petunia, a member of the Night-shade family

Peter's Pence, ecclesiastical tax imposed in early Middle Ages on landowners for upkeep of the Holy See. Discontinued in England at Reformation, now paid as voluntary offering by Roman Catholics throughout the world.

Petit, Alexis Thérèse (1791–1820), Fr. physicist, who with PIERRE DULONG developed methods for measuring thermal expansion and specific heat of solid bodies.

Petition of Right (1628), document containing constitutional demands presented by Eng. Parliament to Charles I.

Petra, ancient ruined city of Jordan. Contains over 750 tombs and temples; also site of 12th cent. Crusaders' citadel.

Petrarch [Francesca Petrarca] (1304–74), Ital. poet and humanist, inspired by classical literature and civilization. Important influence on European love poetry; main works, in Italian, the sonnets *Canzoniere* and the allegorical work *Trionfi*; in Latin, the epic *Africa*.

petrel, sea bird of family Procellariidae. Species include storm petrel, family Hydrobatidae, of E North Atlantic and Med.; diving petrel, family Pelecanoididae, of Antarctic and S oceans.

Petrie, Sir William Matthew Flinders (1853–1942), Eng. archaeologist and Egyptologist. Surveyed Giza pyramids, excavated great temple at Tanis and Gk. city of Naucratis; founder of Brit. School of Archaeology in Egypt.

Petrified Forest, National Park in Arizona, US, preserving 1 of world's most famous areas of petrified wood dating from Triassic period. Area: 147 sq. mi.

Petrograd *see* LENINGRAD.

petroleum, crude, inflammable mineral oil formed millions of years ago from remains of marine organisms buried and compressed in sea-bed, and transformed by chemical or bacterial reaction into oil. Main oil producing areas are the Middle East, US, the Caribbean and USSR. Crude oil refined by FRACTIONAL DISTILLATION, producing motor spirit (UK petrol, US gasoline), kerosenes (paraffins and vaporizing oils), diesel oils, heavy fuel oils and bitumens, *etc.*

petrology, branch of geology. Studies origin, structure and properties of rocks.

Petronius Arbiter, Gaius (d. AD 65), Roman satirist. Chosen by Nero to be arbiter of taste. Prob. author of satirical picaresque novel, *Satyricon,* which depicts Ital. life under Nero. Principal extant episode is *Banquet of Trimalchio.*

Petty, Sir William (1623–87), Eng. polit. economist. Critic of MERCANTILISM.

Petty, William, 2nd Earl of Shelburne (1737–1805), Brit. statesman, P.M. (1782–3). Whig. Sec. of State under both Pitts. Headed coalition govt. that gave US independence.

Petty-Fitzmaurice, Henry Charles Keith, 5th Marquis of Lansdowne (1845–1927), Brit. statesman. Gov.-General of Canada (1883–8); as Foreign Sec. (1900–6) in Cons. govt., formed alliance with Japan and France, abandoning Brit. isolationist policy.

petunia, perennial herb of genus *Petunia* native to trop. America. Cultivated widely in temp. regions as garden flower.

pewter, any of several alloys of tin with lead, antimony or copper. Malleable, and since Roman times shaped into ornaments and utensils.

peyote, *Lophophora williamsii,* Mexican cactus containing drug mescaline.

Phaedra, in Gk. myth., daughter of Minos and wife of Theseus. Fell in love with step-son Hippolytus, but rejected by him and hanged herself.

Phaedrus or **Phaeder, Gaius Julius** (*c.* 15 BC—*c.* AD 50), Roman fabulist. Fables (5 books), based on works of Aesop, are mostly serious or satirical, expressing attitude of the oppressed under Tiberius and Caligula.

Phaethon, in Gk. myth., son of Helios (the Sun). Attempted to drive Helios' chariot, but unable to control horses. Killed by Zeus' thunderbolt.

phalanger, marsupial mammal of family Phalangeridae. Thick fur, long prehensile tail; nocturnal, arboreal; eats fruit and insects.

phalarope, small aquatic bird of family Phalarapodidae. Resembles sand-piper but has lobate toes. Species include northern phalarope, *Lobipes lobatus,* red phalarope, *Phalaropus fulicarius* and Wilson's phalarope *Steganopus tricolor.*

phallicism or **phallism,** worship of image of male reproductive organ.

Phanerozoic *see* GEOLOGICAL TABLE.

Pharaoh, title of kings of ancient Egypt, from Egyptian Per-'O, Great House or royal palace. Gradually adopted to refer to king himself.

Pharisees, one of 2 main Jewish sects which originated in Maccabean age. Insisted on strictest observance of Mosaic Law. Main opponents were Sadducees.

pharmacopoeia, list of properties, dosage, preparation methods and standards of strength and purity of drugs. First known in 16th cent.; now published by medical councils and shows the recognized legal standards.

pharmacy, preparation and dispensing of medicines and drugs. Carried out by priests and monks in former times. Now on a scientific basis, all drugs being tested before use.

Pharos of Alexandria, lighthouse (480 ft. high) outside Alexandria. One of Seven Wonders of the World, destroyed (14th cent.) by earthquake.

pharyngitis, inflammation of mucous membrane of PHARYNX.

pharynx, cavity at back of mouth and extending upward to nose and downwards to oesophagus, passage for food and air.

pheasant, game bird of *Phasianus* and related genera. Long tapering tail; brilliantly coloured. Common pheasant, ring necked *P. colchicus* of Europe has been introduced successfully to US. Golden pheasant, *Chrysolophus pictus,* is native to China and Tibet. Amherst's pheasant, *Chrysolophus amherstiae,* is of Chinese origin, now well known in aviaries.

Pheidias or **Phidias** (b. *c.* 500 BC), Athenian sculptor, architect and painter. Supervised adornment of PARTHENON. Principal works were gold and ivory statue of Athena Parthenon, and colossal statue of Zeus at Olympia.

phenols, chemical compounds having hydroxyl group OH attached to

Common Pheasant

carbon in the nucleus. Most common is carbolic acid.

Philadelphia, largest city and main port of Pennsylvania; founded (1682) by William Penn, Eng. Quaker. Industries include textile, steel and chemical manufacturing, printing and publishing. Pop. (1963) 2,050,000.

Philae, small island in Nile R., Egypt; ancient religious centre; submerged in construction of Aswan High Dam; important remains (*e.g.* Great Temple of Isis) removed to prevent inundation.

philately, collection or study of postage stamps. Largest and most valuable private collection owned by Queen Elizabeth II; other important collections in British Museum, and Smithsonian Institute, Washington. British National Postal Museum (1969) displays outstanding General Post Office collection.

Philemon, Epistle to, NT epistle written by St Paul to Philemon, influential Christian of Colossae.

Philip, Saint, one of 12 Apostles. Also name of deacon, one of 7 appointed by Apostles, who baptised Ethiopian eunuch.

Philip [II] Augustus (1165–1223), king of France who greatly strengthened the monarchy and crushed rebellious nobles. By defeating King John of England he gained possession of Normandy, Anjou and parts of Poitou and Saintonge.

Philip [IV] the Fair (1268–1314), Fr. king involved in struggle with Pope Boniface VIII, culminating in abduction of the Pope and, after his death, election of Philip's candidate Clement V and establishment of Pope's residence in Avignon.

Philip VI (1328–50), Fr. king under whom the HUNDRED YEARS' WAR with England began.

Philip [I] the Handsome (1478–1506), king of Castile (1506). Son of Emperor Maximilian I. First Habsburg ruler in Spain. Married Joanna of Castile.

Philip II (1527-98), Sp. Habsburg king after abdication of his father Charles V; 2nd wife Mary Tudor of England. Made Spain chief European power; in attempting to restore supremacy of R.C. Church, he increased powers of INQUISITION and lost Spain its Dutch Provinces. Defeat of his ARMADA marked turning point in Spain's position as great power.

Philip V (1683–1746), 1st Bourbon king of Spain, and 2nd son of Fr. Dauphin. His succession, by combining Sp. and Fr. thrones in one family, threatened European balance of

Giant Fulmar, one of the Petrel family

power and resulted in WAR OF SPANISH SUCCESSION.

Philip, Prince, Duke of Edinburgh (1921–), husband of Queen Elizabeth II of Britain; b. Greece, son of Prince and Princess Andrew of Greece; great-great-grandson of Queen Victoria. Accorded title of Prince (1957).

Philip of Macedon (382–336 BC), king of Macedon, seized throne (359 BC) and ruled all Greece by 338 BC. Against his ambition DEMOSTHENES directed his famous orations, the *Philippics.* Assassinated, succeeded by his son ALEXANDER THE GREAT.

Philippi, Battle of, military encounter (42 BC) in Macedon in which republican forces under Brutus and Cassius defeated by Antony and Octavian. Victory consolidated rule of 2nd Triumvirate.

Philippians, Epistle of NT addressed by St Paul to church at Philippi, Macedonia.

Philippines, Republic of, state of SE Asia consisting of *c.* 7,000 islands.

Area: 114,834 sq. mi.; cap. Quezon City; main city Manila, islands, Luzon, Mindanao, Samar. Chief exports, sugar, coconuts, timber, hemp, tobacco. Discovered (1521) by Portuguese explorer Magellan; became Sp. possession; ceded to US 1898; independent repub. 1946. In World War 2 overrun by Japanese, scene of heavy fighting, esp. defence of Corregidor by General MacArthur. Pop. (1965) 33,477,000.

Philistines, ancient people, probably of Cretan origin, who inhabited S Palestinian coast *c.* 1150 BC. Constantly at war with Israelites; conquered by David, and under Solomon incorporated into kingdom of Israel. Regained independence, finally accepted Assyrian domination 8th cent. BC.

Philo Judaeus (*c.* 20 BC–AD 50), Alexandrian philosopher. Attempted to reconcile Bible with works of Gk. philosophers, esp. Plato.

philology, orig. comprehensive study of language and literature. Later applied to study of language families esp. Indo-European. Largely replaced by LINGUISTICS.

philosopher's stone, substance sought by alchemists, who believed it would turn base metals into gold.

philosophy [Gk: love of wisdom], search for ultimate principles of being and knowledge. As discipline, philosophy includes ethics, metaphysics, logic and related fields. Other disciplines are critically examined for basic principles and concepts, philosophy of science, philosophy of history, *etc.*

phlebitis, inflammation of a vein. Most common in varicose veins of the leg. May cause formation of blood clots (thromboses), which may disintegrate and be carried by blood-

Dream of Philip II by El Greco

stream to lodge within an organ, *e.g.* lung.

Phlegethon, in Gk. myth., one of the 5 rivers of Hades. It was of liquid fire, and flowed into Acheron.

phlogiston theory, proposition advanced by Becher and Stahl (17th cent.), that phlogiston, said to be present in all inflammable substances, was given off in burning; theory disproved by LAVOISIER's discovery of oxygen.

phlox, herb of genus *Phlox,* native to N America. Cultivated for showy flowers of various colours. *P. drummondi* has deep purple flowers.

Phnom-Penh, cap. and trading centre of Cambodia on Mekong R. Pop. (1962) 404,000.

phobia, an irrational fear or abhorrence of a particular thing or situation. Creates states of anxiety, panic or even temporary insanity.

phoebe, small Amer. flycatcher of genus *Sayornis,* esp. *S. phoebe* of E North America.

Phoenicia, ancient region occupied by Semitic race (Phoenicians), now mostly in Lebanon. Great traders; developed city states Tyre, Sidon and Byblos. Centre in Crete *c.* 2000–1200 BC. Founded cities on Med. coast, notably Carthage.

phoenix, legendary bird which rises renewed from ashes of its own funeral pyre.

Phoenix Islands, group of 8 coral islands of C Pacific. Area: 11 sq. mi. Includes Canton, Enderbury, Gilbert and Ellice islands. Chief produce: copra.

phonetics, study of speech and sounds

of language. System of phonetic writing aims at accurate transcription of speech sounds.

phonograph or **gramophone,** instrument for reproducing sound prerecorded on cylinder or disc. First phonograph built (1877) by Thomas Edison. Use of discs introduced (1887) by Emil Berliner.

phosphates, compounds of phosphoric acid and various bases. Phosphate of lime used in fertilizers; phosphate of sodium in baking powder and detergents.

phosphorescence, emission of light without heat; released by stored light or other radiation. Causes certain organisms and minerals, *e.g.* fireflies, glow-worms, zinc sulphide, to shine in the dark.

phosphorus (P), non-metallic element. Occurs in red, black, or white forms. Component of protoplasm, hence essential to life. Used in fertilizers, detergents. Discovered (1669) by Henning Brand.

Photius (*c.* 820–891), Gk. churchman. Patriarch of Constantinople (858–867 and 878–886). Champion of independence of Eastern Church against power of Rome; excommunicated by Pope Nicholas I and Pope John VIII.

photography, process of reproducing an optical image on light-sensitive substance exposed to light under controlled conditions in a CAMERA. Pioneers include Daguerre (oxidized silver plates, 1829); Eastman and Kodak (paper-based roll film, 1884); Edison (celluloid film, 1889). Recent developments include production of

Viol (1912) by Picasso

Crowned Pigeon

colour print inside camera 50 sec after exposure.

photon, fundamental unit of RADIATION.

photosynthesis, process by which plants make food involving transformation of carbon dioxide and water into carbohydrates. Occurs in green part of plants and utilizes energy from sunlight. Essential to plant life.

photo-typesetting, automatic method of typesetting, combining mechanical with photographic methods. Type set on sensitized paper or film, making metal type unnecessary. Commercial use began 1948.

phrenology, theory that each mental faculty is housed in a particular part of the brain and an individual's development of any faculty can be determined by his head shape. Disproven by modern research.

Phrygia, ancient region of C Asia Minor, settled (*c.* 1200 BC). Dominated by Lydia after 700 BC, later by Gauls and Romans. Centre of cult of Cybele.

phylloxera, plant lice of genus *Phylloxera.* Grape phylloxera, *P. vitifoliae,* attacks leaves and roots of grape vines in US and Europe.

physical anthropology, branch of anthropology concerned with physical characteristics of peoples. Studies evolution of body types and development of racial groups.

physics, science concerned with fundamental relationship between matter and energy. Major objective is rational explanation of natural phenomena. Branches include mechanics, heat, electricity, magnetism, sound, and atomic theory. Chemistry, although closely related, is not considered part of physics.

physiocrats, group of 18th cent. Fr. economic theoreticians headed by FRANÇOIS QUESNAY. Among 1st to study economic factors, saw land and agriculture as basis of wealth. Influenced Adam Smith and other laissez-faire economists.

physiognomy, art of discerning personality from physical (esp. facial) characteristics; attempts to relate features to criminal tendencies have proved unsuccessful.

physiology, study of process and activities of living organisms. May be either plant or animal physiology.

physiotherapy, method of treating disease and injury by physical means, as opposed to surgery or drugs. Massage, exercise, heat and electrical treatment are used.

pi (π), symbol used to denote ratio of circumference of circle to its diameter; $\pi = 3 \cdot 14159$.

Piaf, Edith, orig. Edith Giovanna Gassion (1915–63), Fr. singer. Known for emotion with which she expressed impoverished people's troubles in songs.

Piaget, Jean (1896–   ), Swiss child psychologist. Pioneer of intelligence testing. Author of *The Language and Thought of the Child.*

piano, pianoforte, musical keyboard percussion instrument having compass of 7 octaves, whose keys operate hammers which strike the strings. First appeared mid-18th cent. Many 19th cent. composers were also virtuoso pianists (*e.g.* Beethoven, Liszt, Grieg and Brahms).

Picardy, former prov. of N France. Cap. was Amiens. Corresponds to modern departments of Somme, and parts of Pas de Calais, Oise, Aisne.

Picasso, Pablo [y Ruiz] (1881–   ), Sp. painter. Associated at start of his Cubist period with Braque in Paris; has developed through Expressionism, Abstractionism, Romanticism, also ceramics and sculpture. Produced ballet sets for Diaghilev's *Parade* (1917); illustrated Ovid's *Metamorphoses.*

piccolo, small woodwind instrument; pitched an octave higher than FLUTE.

Pickford, Mary, orig. Gladys Mary Smith (1893–   ), Amer. film actress, m. Douglas Fairbanks. Starred in sentimental roles, as in *Poor Little Rich Girl.*

picquet, piquet, 2-handed game played with the 32 highest cards of an ordinary deck of cards. Points scored both for holding certain combinations and for winning tricks.

Picts, warlike pre-Celtic tribes of Scotland and NE Ireland. Resisted Roman conquest of N Britain, esp. (AD 296, 306).

pidgin English, business jargon in Chinese idiom, of English and native words. Used by traders esp. in Far East for simple transactions.

Piedmont, region of N Italy watered by Po R. Produce includes fruit, olives, rice and wine. Chief town and cap. is Turin.

Pierce, Franklin (1804–69), 14th US Pres. (1853–7), Democrat. Congressman (1833–42) from New Hampshire. Nominated and elected pres. (1852) on policy of appeasement towards South; subsequently alienated North by authorizing KANSAS-NEBRASKA BILL. Supported GADSDEN PURCHASE.

Pieta [Ital: pity], in art, representation of dead Christ held by Virgin Mary, *e.g.* 'Pieta' by Michelangelo.

pig, mainly herbivorous mammal of family Suidae. Domesticated European and N Amer. breeds developed from European wild boar, esp. for meat (pork) and lard. Has barrel-shaped body and hide covered with short stiff hair.

pig iron, impure iron from blast furnace. So called because cast in moulds called pigs.

pigeon, small bird of family Columbidae of temp. and trop. regions. Largest pigeons are of *Goura* genus. *G. victoria,* crowned pigeon, of New Guinea, has large, lacy head-crest. *Columba palambus,* wood-pigeon or ring dove with greyish plumage is largest European variety. Domesticated breeds are derived from common pigeon or rock dove *C. livia.* Amer. species include mourning dove.

Pigmy *see* PYGMY.

pigweed, plant of genus *Amaranthus.* Edible seeds, small greenish flowers; sometimes used as pot-herbs. Species include *A. retroflexus* and *A. hybridus.*

pika, mouse hare, rabbit-like mammal of family Ochotonidae found in high mountains of Asia and N America. Small ears, short hind legs.

Pike, Zebulon M[ontgomery] (1779–1813), Amer. army officer and explorer. Led expedition into Colorado, sighted peak named after him (PIKE'S PEAK). Killed at siege of York (now Toronto).

pike, *Esox lucius,* ferocious freshwater fish of N temp. regions. Elongated snout; reaches 30–40 lb. in weight. Feeds on other fish, water voles, water birds, *etc.* Valued as food.

pike, obsolete weapon. Usually consisted of long wooden shaft and

Phlox drummondi

pointed steel head. Superseded by bayonet.

pike perch, fish of family Percidae of Eurasia and N America. Species include blue pike perch or blue walleye, *Stilzostedion vitreum.*

Pike's Peak, mountain in S Rockies, Colo., US (14,110 ft.). Discovered (1806) by Zebulon Pike's expedition.

Pilate, Pontius (*fl.* AD 26) Roman procurator of Judaea. Under pressure from Jewish eccles. authorities, ordered execution of Christ.

pilchard, *Sardina pilchardus,* small marine food fish related to herring. Found in S Europe.

pilewort, lesser celandine, *Ranunculus ficaria,* perennial herb of Old World with bright yellow flowers.

Pilgrim Fathers, founders of Plymouth Colony, Massachusetts, US (1620). Group included migrants orig. from England (*c.* 1607–8).

Pilgrimage of Grace (1536), rising of

Palace in Phnom-Penh, Cambodia: now the official residence of the head of state

Eng. Roman Catholics, esp. in Yorkshire, protesting against abolition of papal supremacy and suppression of monasteries by Henry VIII. Leaders arrested and executed (1537).

Pilgrims' Way, route (*c.* 120 mi.) from Winchester to Canterbury, England, taken by pilgrims to shrine of Thomas à Becket. Still traceable in parts.

Pill, The, popular name for oral contraceptive which interferes with human menstrual cycle, preventing ovulation.

Pillars of Hercules, mountains at each side of E end of strait of Gibraltar, Europe. Said to have been erected by Hercules to secure oxen of Geryon.

pillbug, small terrestrial crustacean of genus *Armedillo* of woodlouse family. Rolls into pill-shaped ball.

Pillnitz, Declaration of, statement (1791) calling on European powers to restore Louis XVI to Fr. throne, issued by Emperor Leopold II and Frederick William of Prussia. Resulted in eventual execution of Louis.

pillwort, widely distributed Eurasian water fern of genus *Pilularia*.

pilot fish, *Naucrates ductor,* sub-trop. oceanic fish related to horse mackerel. Found around sharks.

Pilsen, Plzen, indust., commercial and communication centre of Bohemia, Czechoslovakia. Famous brewery and Skoda engineering works. Pop. (1966) 141,000.

Pilsudski, Joseph (1867–1935), Polish military and polit. leader. Commanded Polish forces in World War 1. Proclaimed independent repub. (1918), which he headed until 1922. Successfully campaigned against Russia to restore E frontier. Exercised dictatorial powers (1926–35) after seizing power in coup.

Piltdown Man, skull, jaw and tooth found at Piltdown, Sussex, England (1912) assumed to be *c.* 500,000 yr. old. Later proved to be hoax.

pimento, *Pimenta officinalis,* tree of trop. America. Dried fruits used as spice.

pimpernel, annual herb of genus *Anagallis*. Scarlet, purplish or white flowers. Species include *A. artensis,* scarlet pimpernel.

pinchbeck, alloy of copper and zinc with appearance of gold, invented by Christopher Pinchbeck (*c.* 1670–1732). Used for cheap jewellery.

Pindar [Pindaros] (522–442 BC), Gk. lyric poet. Wrote in literary Doric dialect. *Epinicia,* divided into 4 books, deals respectively with Olympian,

Pythian, Nemean, Isthmian games. Developed triumphal ode (epinicion). Poetry includes chief forms of choral lyrics. Pindaric ode imitated by *e.g.* Cowley, Dryden, Gray and Swift.

Pindus, mountain range running from N Greece to SE Albania.

pine, evergreen conifer of genus *Pinus,* widely distributed in N hemisphere. Long, needle-shaped leaves. Certain varieties yield timber, turpentine, tar, pitch, *etc.* Species include stone pine, *Pinus pinea;* Australian pine, *P. nigra;* pitch pine, *P. rigida;* and Scots pine, *P. sylvestris,* of Europe. Related species include cedar, *Cedrus.*

pine marten, *Martes martes,* mammal found in woods and forests of N Europe and W Asia. Fierce predator living on small mammals and birds.

pine nut, seed of pine tree. Eaten roasted or salted, or used in confectionery.

pineal gland, small gland in head. Co-ordinated with eye, aware of daylight, influences body's awareness of time.

pineapple, *Ananas comosus,* plant native of trop. America, now grown chiefly in Hawaii. Edible, juicy fruit develops from flower spike.

Pinero, Sir Arthur Wing (1855–1934), Eng. dramatist. Wrote farces incl. *Dandy Dick* (1887); initiated realistic movement into plays like *The Second Mrs. Tanqueray* (1893), *Trelawney of the Wells* (1898).

pink, annual or perennial plant of genus *Dianthus* found in temp. regions. *D. caryophyllus* is progenitor of carnations, *D. plumarius,* of garden pinks. Other species include maiden pink, *D. deltoides* and Indian or Chinese pink, *D. chinensis.*

Pinkerton, Allan (1819–84), Amer. detective. Founded Pinkerton National Detective Agency which was active in labour disputes and spied for Union in Civil War.

Pinkie, Battle of, Scot. defeat by Eng. force under Somerset. Caused Scots to send Mary (later Mary, Queen of Scots) to France to avoid marriage to Edward VI of England.

pinochle, Amer. card game for 2–4 players with pack of 48 cards. Prob. originated (19th cent.) in Europe.

pintail, *Anas acuta,* long-necked river duck with long tail feathers.

Pinter, Harold (1930–), Brit. dramatist and actor. One-act plays include *The Room* (1957), *The Dumb Waiter* (1957); among his full-length plays are *The Caretaker* (1960), *The Homecoming* (1964).

Pine : (a) male flowers (b) female flower with young cone (c) cone (d) seed (e) pollen (greatly magnified)

pipe fish, small elongated marine fish of family Syngnathidae. Long tubular snout; body covered with bony plates.

Piper, John (1903–), Eng. artist and designer. Official war artist in World War 2. Since experimented with abstracts, architectural compositions, stage settings, stained glass designs *e.g.* for Coventry Cathedral.

pipistrelle, small insectivorous bat of genus *Pipistrellus* with rapid flight. Species include *P. subflavus,* smallest Amer. bat, and *P. pipistrellus* of Europe and Asia.

pipit, small songbird of genus *Anthus* of family Motacillidae. Black-speckled brown plumage; diet insectivorous. Species include European meadow pipit or titlark, *A. pratensis,* and Amer. water pipit.

Piraeus, Piraieus, port of ancient and modern Athens (founded 5th cent. BC). Largest port and leading indust. centre of Greece. Industries, flour-milling, carpet making, chemicals and shipbuilding. Pop. (1961) 183,877.

Pirandello, Luigi (1867–1936), Ital. dramatist and novelist. Plays include *Six Characters in Search of an Author* (1921), *Henry IV* (1922). Novels include *the Late Mattia Pascal* (1923). Awarded Nobel Prize for Literature (1934).

Piranesi, Giovanni Battista (1720–

Pine Marten

78), Ital. neo-classical engraver and architect. Works include series of engravings of ancient buildings of Rome and *Carceri* (1750) scenes of imaginery prisons.

piranha *see* CHARACIN.

Pire, George Henri (1910–69), Belgian Dominican priest. Founded (1949) international relief organization. Awarded Nobel Peace Prize (1958).

Pisa, Historic city of C Italy on Arno R. Cathedral dates from 1063, with campanile (Leaning Tower) 1174; university founded 1338. Industries include glass, textiles and ceramics. Pop. (1965) 100,000.

Pisa, Council of, council summoned (1409) in attempt to end GREAT SCHISM. Supporters of Gregory XII and Benedict XIII agreed to depose them both and 3rd pope was elected.

Pisano, Andrea, orig. Andrea da Pontaderra (*c.* 1270–1348), Ital. sculptor and architect. Carried on work of Giotto on Florence cathedral campanile and designed bronze doors of baptistery.

Pisano, Nicola (*c.* 1220–87), Ital. architect and sculptor. Works include pulpits in baptistery at Pisa and Siena cathedral.

Pisces *see* ZODIAC.

Pissarro, Camille (1831–1903), Fr. Impressionist painter. Influenced by Barbizon school and Pointillism. Used broken colour to achieve effects of light, esp. in landscapes.

pistachio, *Pistacia vera,* small tree of S Europe and Asia. Large fruit contains greenish edible nut used in cookery and confectionery.

pistil, ovule-bearing organ of a seed plant. Usually consists of ovary, style and stigma.

pistol, small firearm held in one hand. Orig. made in Italy (16th cent.); REVOLVER made in 19th cent. and 'automatic' pistol in 20th cent.

pit viper, venomous snake of family Crotalidae of New World and Asia. Species include bushmaster, rattlesnake, sidewinder, *etc.*

Pitcairn, Pacific island NE of New Zealand, Brit. colony. Area: *c.* 2 sq. mi. Discovered 1767; occupied 1790 by *Bounty* mutineers. Pop. (1961) 88.

pitch, quality of a musical sound dependent on speed of vibrations producing it. The greater the number of vibrations per sec. the higher the note.

pitch, resinous, dark, sticky substance, liquid when heated, solid when cold. Occurs naturally as asphalt. Also residue from distillation of tar, turpentine or fatty oils.

pitchblende, mineral ore containing 50–80% uranium and small amounts

of radioactive salt of radium, 1st separated (1898) by Pierre and Marie Curie. Main deposits, US, Canada, Czechoslovakia and the Congo.

pitcher plant, *Sarracenia purpurea,* insectivorous bog herb of NE US. Leaves modified into form of pitcher.

Pithecanthropus, member of extinct genus of apelike men, alive a million years ago. Known from skeletal remains found in Java, they had apelike profile, small brain and an almost erect posture.

Pitman, Sir Isaac (1813–97), Eng. inventor. Developed an improved system of phonetic shorthand, adapted for use in many languages. His grandson, **Sir [Isaac] James Pitman** (1901–) devised Initial Teaching Alphabet, widely used in teaching of reading.

Pitt, William, 1st Earl of Chatham (1708–78), Eng. statesman, known as 'Great Commoner' for championing constitutional rights. Critic of Walpole and Newcastle; P.M. (1757–68) at head of coalition govt., engineered policy during Seven Years War leading to Brit. victories in Canada and India. Split with Whigs over Amer. colonies. His son, **William Pitt** (1759–1806), P.M. (1783–1801, 1804–6). Headed Tory reform govt., instituting general elections, new taxes to reduce national debt. Policies, esp. economic, curtailed by prolonged wars with France. Enacted (1800) union with Ireland, but resigned after George III's veto of Catholic emancipation.

Pitt-Rivers, Augustus Henry, orig. Lane-Fox (1827–1900), Eng. archaeologist; 1st to employ scientific methods in excavations, esp. stratum classification.

Pittsburgh, city of Pennsylvania, US. Major industrial centre; leading US companies based here include United States Steel, Aluminum Company of America, Gulf Oil, Westinghouse Electric and H. J. Heinz. Important centre of scientific research. Pop. (1960) 604,332.

pituitary gland, small gland situated at the base of the brain and enclosed in a hollow in the skull called pituitary fossa. Its secretions control important body functions incl. activity of sex organs, blood pressure, regulation of hormone production of thyroid gland.

Pius II, orig. Enea Silvio de Piccolomini (1405–64), pope (1458–64). Distinguished humanist poet and author; tried unsuccessfully to organize a crusade against the Turks.

Pius VII (1740–1823), pope (1800–23). Concordat of 1801 with Napoleon restored R.C. Church in

France. Crowned Napoleon I (1804), prisoner of Fr. army (1809–14). Restored Jesuits (1814).

Pius XII, orig. Eugenio Pacelli (1876–1958), pope (1939–58). Controversy over his attitude to Nazism. Opposed military use of atomic energy.

Piute *see* PAIUTE.

Pizarro, Francisco (*c.* 1476–1541), Sp. conquistador. Deceived and killed Inca leader Atahualpa. With partner Diego d'Almagro conquered Peru and founded several settlements, incl. Lima. Assassinated by followers of Almagro.

pizzicato, in music, plucking of strings instead of using a bow with stringed instruments. Also, direction to play (*e.g.* piano) giving this effect.

placenta, organ consisting of material and embryonic tissue by which the embryo of viviparous animals is nourished.

plague, epidemic, highly infectious often fatal disease caused by *Pasteurella pestis* carried by fleas. Symptoms include headache, fever and sores. Occurred sporadically in Europe, notably in Black Death (14th cent.) and Great Plague (esp. London 1665).

plaice, shallow water marine flatfish of flounder family. European plaice, *Pleuronectes platessa,* important commercially.

Plaid Cymru *see* WELSH NATIONALIST PARTY.

plain, large area of relatively flat land. Chiefly caused by glaciation (North European Plain), uplift of sea bed (Atlantic-Gulf Coastal Plain), sediment deposition (W Siberian Plain).

Plains of Abraham, heights outside Quebec, Canada, where Brit. forces, led by Wolfe, defeated Fr. forces under Montcalm (1759).

plainsong, system of church music; non-metrical and unisonal; originated in 5th cent.; 2 main families, Gregorian and Ambrosian chants.

Planck, Max (1858–1947), Ger. physicist. Won Nobel Prize for

Water Pipit

The planet Saturn

Physics (1918) for developing QUAN-TUM THEORY in thermodynamics.

plane, deciduous tree of genus *Platanus* of temp. regions. Pendulous burr-like fruit. Species include Oriental plane, *P. orientalis,* London plane, *P. acerifolia,* with 3-lobed leaves and Amer. plane or button-wood, *P. occidentalis.*

plane geometry, branch of geometry dealing with plane figures, all of which lie on one flat surface of no thickness.

planet, spherical body in orbit round the Sun and shining by its reflected light. *See* SOLAR SYSTEM.

planetarium, instruments or buildings used in model reproduction of celestial bodies and their movements, achieved by projecting points of light on to a domed ceiling. *See* SOLAR SYSTEM.

planetoid *see* SOLAR SYSTEM.

plankton, minute organism which floats in fresh and salt water. Provides food for many marine animals.

plant, member of vegetable group of living organisms. Generally manu-factures own food by process of photosynthesis; has an unlimited growth (*i.e.* old tissue remains in place and new tissue grows away from it); has cells with more or less rigid walls; has no means of independent locomotion. Plants divided into 4 main groups: thallophyta (algae, lichens, fungi); bryophyta (mosses, liverworts); pteridophyta (ferns, club mosses, horse tails); spermophyta (conifers and flowering plants).

plant bug, insect of family Miridae. Mainly feeds on low vegetation.

plant louse, aphid, small insect of family Aphididae. Lives on juices of plants.

Plantagenet, surname applied to Royal house of England, including Henry II, Richard I, John, Henry III, Edward I, II, III, Richard II, Henry IV, V, VI, Edward IV, V and Richard III. Richard II abdicated (1399); house divided into Lancaster and York.

plantain, *Musa paradisiaca,* trop. herbaceous plant. Produces long yellow-green fruit like banana.

plantain lily, plant of genus *Hosta* of lily family, native to China and Japan. Large leaves and spikes of white, lilac or blue flowers.

Plantin, Christophe (1514–89), Fr. bookbinder, printer and publisher. Settled in Antwerp (1549), became foremost publisher in N Europe; produced books renowned for their typographic excellence.

plasma, clear fluid forming 55% of human BLOOD. Mostly water, con-tains also plasma proteins.

plasma, in physics, state of matter in which most of the atoms are split into free electrons and positive ions.

Plassey, Battle of, victory (1757) of ROBERT CLIVE against the Nawab of Bengal which aided estab. of Brit. rule in NE India.

plaster, substance consisting of mix-ture of lime, sand, water, used for protective wall covering and in making casts. *See* PLASTER OF PARIS.

plaster of Paris, fine white powder produced by heating gypsum. Used for casts, wall boards and moulds.

plastics, mouldable, synthetic mater-ials manufactured from POLYMERS. The 2 main groups are thermoplastic materials which can be melted and reset many times, and thermosetting materials which cannot be remoulded.

plastic surgery, surgical alteration of body parts. Usually a transfer of tissue to improve appearance of deformity or after injury, or to make cosmetic improvements.

Plate [Río de la Plata], estuary on E coast of S America formed by Uruguay and Paraná rivers. It is 200 mi. long, 140 mi. wide at mouth.

plateau, term applied to elevated land with relatively level surface.

platinum, greyish-white, valuable metallic element. Resists corrosion. Used for electrical wiring, jewellery and dental alloys.

Plato (*c.* 427–347 BC), Gk. philos-opher, disciple of SOCRATES. Author of *Republic* (written in dialogue form), in which ideal state based on rational order and ruled by philosopher kings. The Idea (ideal form) is reality of appearance, achieving essence in Idea of the Good. Knowledge of

Idea attained by man when reason governs his behaviour. Other extant works (all dialogues) include *Apology, Crito, Phaedo, Timaeus* and *Laws.* Founded (387 BC) Academy in Athens; students in-cluded ARISTOTLE.

Plattsburg, Battle of, encounter (Sept. 1814) in NE New York state, in which outnumbered Amer. troops defeated Brit. forces during War of 1812.

platypus, duckbill, duckmole, *Orni-thorhynchus anatinus,* small aquatic mammal of Tasmania and S and E Australia. Fleshy bill, clawed webbed feet, flattened tail, dense blackish brown fur. Expert swimmer and diver; lives in burrows near water; female lays 2 eggs.

Plautus, Titus Maccius or **Maccus** (*c.* 254–184 BC), Roman playwright. Works, adapted from 3rd and 4th cent. Athenian comedies, reproduce Gk. life and exaggerated Gk. char-acter; lively dialogue and much intrigue, *e.g. Amphitruo, Captivi, Miles Gloriosus.*

Player, Gary (1935–), South African golfer. One of few to win all major international tournaments.

plebiscite [Lat: popular decree], vote of people on particular question, as in referendum. Issue may result from ordinary legislation or decision on national constitution or allegiance.

Pléiade, group of 16th cent. Fr. poets led by Ronsard and du Bellay. Aimed to enrich and purify the Fr. language and create national literature, esp. through classical and sonnet forms.

Pleiades, in Gk. myth., 7 daughters of Atlas and Pleione. Pursued by Orion and turned into constellation which bears their name.

Pleistocene *see* GEOLOGICAL TABLE.

Plekhanov, Georgi Valentinovitch (1857–1918), Russ. revolutionary and Marxist philosopher. Broke with Lenin (1903), taking view that Russia was not ready for socialism, adopted by more moderate Mensheviks.

plesiosaurus, marine reptile of extinct genus from Jurassic and Cretaceous periods. Small head, long neck.

pleurisy, inflammation of pleura, the membrane enclosing the lung. Often occurs with pneumonia and other conditions. Characterized by pain in side on breathing, cough and fever.

Plimsoll, Samuel (1824–98), Brit. politician and reformer. Instrumental in passing Merchant Shipping Act (1878) which standardized maximum load to be carried by Brit.-owned vessels. Legal load designated by line on hull known as **Plimsoll line.**

Pliny the Elder [Gaius Plinius Secund-us] (*c.* AD 23–79), Roman writer.

Author of extant encyclopedic work on natural sciences *Naturalis Historia* (37 books) mostly pub. posthumously. Other works on *e.g.* history, oratory, are lost.

Pliny the Younger [Gaius Plinius Caecilius Secundus] (*c.* AD 61–*c.* 113), Roman orator. Best known for *Letters,* 9 books published before 111; 10th book, correspondence with Trajan, published posthumously.

Pliocene *see* GEOLOGICAL TABLE.

Plisetskaya, Maiya Mikhailovna (1925–   ), Soviet ballerina. Principal dancer of Bolshoi Ballet, renowned for beauty and technique.

Ploesti, city in S Romania, 35 mi. N of Bucharest. Centre of petroleum industry in oil well region. Pop. (1957) 100,000.

Plotinus (b. *c.* AD 205), philosopher, born Egypt, settled in Rome (244). Essence of philosophy is desire to escape from material world. Chief exponent of NEOPLATONISM.

plough, one of earliest of agricultural implements. At first a wooden wedge tipped with iron, pushed or pulled by men or oxen. Modern plough has coulter for cutting, ploughshare for breaking and mould-board for turning over the soil.

plover, gregarious, migratory bird of family Charadriidae. Long legs, short bill; large pointed wings which give rapid flight.

plum, any of various trees and shrubs of genus *Prunus.* Round to oval smooth-skinned fruit. Cultivated for fruit or ornamental flowers.

Plutarch [Ploutarchos] (*c.* AD 46–*c.* 120), Gk. biographer and philosopher. Great work is *Parallel Lives,* 46 paired Gk. and Roman biographies and 4 single biographies. His *Moralia* are dialogues on ethical, historical, literary subjects.

Pluto [Plouton], **Hades,** in Gk. myth., god of the Underworld, son of Cronus and Rhea. Ruled over Underworld with Persephone, daughter of Demeter, whom he carried off from upper world. Known as Dis (Dives) by Romans.

Pluto, planet 9th from Sun, *c.* 3,600 mi. in diameter. Period of rotation round Sun, 248 yr. Discovered 1930.

plutonic rock, igneous rock of holocrystalline granular texture.

plutonium, artificial fissionable metallic radio-active element. First pro-

Plane tree: left, leaf and fruit: right, silhouette and characteristic bark

duced (1940) by Seaborg, McMillan, Kennedy and Wahl. Used as nuclear fuel.

Plymouth Brethren, evangelical sect founded in Dublin by John Nelson Darby (1827). Spread to Europe and esp. N America. Movement follows literal interpretation of Bible and has no ordained ministers.

Plymouth Colony, Pilgrim settlement on Massachusetts coast, US, estab. (1620) by colonists who sailed from England aboard *Mayflower.* United with Mass. Bay colony (1691).

pneumonia, acute lung infection, usually bacterial but may be viral. Characterized by cough, fever, chill, blood-stained spit. Bronchial pneumonia is confined to bronchial tubes, lobar pneumonia affects whole lobe.

Po, longest river in Italy (*c.* 415 mi.) rises near Fr. border. Crosses Plain of Lombardy to Adriatic Sea. Liable to serious flooding.

Pocahontas (*c.* 1595–1617), daughter of Amer. Indian chief Powhatan. Taken prisoner by English (1612), converted to Christianity. Marriage (1614) to John Rolfe helped make peace with Eng. settlers.

pochard, diving duck of world-wide distribution but mainly N hemisphere.

Species include red-chested *Aythya ferina* of N America and *Netta rufina* of Europe with red head and beak.

pocket borough, term used to refer to Eng. parliamentary constituency controlled by 1 man or family. Abolished, together with ROTTEN BOROUGHS, by 1832 Reform Bill.

pocket mouse, nocturnal N Amer. burrowing rodent of *Perognathus* genus. Long hind legs and fur-lined cheek pouches.

Podolia, agric. region of Ukrainian SSR, USSR; cap. Kamenets-Podolsk. Produces sugar beet, wheat, tobacco. Annexed from Poland by Soviet Union (1939).

Poe, Edgar Allan (1809–49), Amer. author, journalist and poet. Influenced Baudelaire and other Fr. writers. Best remembered for *Tales of Mystery and Imagination* (1845).

Poet Laureate, office of court poet in England. Ben Jonson 1st held the laureateship although Dryden 1st held the title. Poets laureate include Wordsworth, Tennyson, Robert Bridges, John Masefield C. Day Lewis.

poetry, in literature, term for imaginative and concentrated writing esp. using metrical and figurative language. Verse may be rhymed or un-rhymed (blank).

pogrom, Russ. word, orig. denoting a riot; later meant attacks on Jews in Russia. Tsarist govt. attempted to direct mass discontent against Jews. Esp. serious 1881–2 and 1903–21.

Duck-billed Platypus

Poher, Alain (1909–   ), Fr. politician. Interim Pres. of France after resignation of Charles de Gaulle (1969).

Poincaré, Jules Henri (1854–1912), Fr. mathematician, physicist. Among numerous contributions to mathematical physics, researched into theory of functions, differential equations and theory of orbits.

Poincaré, Raymond (1860–1934), Fr. statesman. Pres. of repub. (1913–20); Premier (1912, 1922–4, 1926–9). After World War 1, ordered occupation of Ruhr (1923); stabilized currency (1928).

poinsettia, *Euphorbia (Poinsettia) pulcherrima,* plant native to Mexico and C America. Small greenish flowers with scarlet, pink or white bracts.

Point Pelee National Park, in Ontario, Canada. Area: 6 sq. mi. Estab. 1918, resting place for migratory birds. Bathing beaches on shores of Lake Erie, unusual flora.

pointer, hunting dog so called because it hunts by scent and will 'point' to game with tail and muzzle outstretched. Developed in England (17th cent.) from cross of hounds and spaniels. Usually parti-coloured, short-haired and about 24 in. high.

Pointillism, post-Impressionist school of painting, also called divisionism by Neo-impressionists. Technique of painting in points of primary colours to produce livelier secondary colours.

poison, substance having a dangerous or fatal effect on living things. May be corrosive, irritant, hypnotic or metabolic.

poison gas, substance of corrosive or poisonous nature. First employed in World War I. Includes chlorine which affects lung, mustard gas which affects skin, and nerve gases which attack central nervous system.

poison ivy, shrub of genus *Rhus* found in temp. latitudes. Green flowers, white berries and trifoliate leaves, poisonous to touch. *R. radicans* is a climbing species.

Poitiers, Battle of (1356), engagement in Hundred Years War in which Edward the Black Prince defeated the French under John II.

Poitou, former Atlantic province of W France, now included in Vendée, Deux-Sèvres and Vienne departments; cap. Poitiers.

poker, card game, with 2 basic variations, draw and stud poker; usually played for financial stakes. First played in US on Mississippi steamboats.

pokeweed, *Phytolacca americana,* tall, coarse perennial herb of N

America. Dark purple berries contain poisonous seeds and yield emetic and purgative extracts.

Poland [**Polska Rzeczpospolita Ludowa**] repub. of E Europe. Area: 119,800 sq. mi.; cap. Warsaw; other cities Lodz, Krakow, Danzig. Largely forested; major rivers are Vistula and Oder; agriculture and mining are main occupations. Industry centres on metallurgy and textiles. Slavic Poland created 10th cent.; merged 1569 with

Lithuania. Dissolved by Austria, Prussia and Russia in Partitions (1772, 1793, 1795). Independence proclaimed 1918. Occupation by Germans precipitated World War 2. Came under Soviet influence after War. Constitution adopted 1952. Language Polish; main religion, Roman Catholicism. Unit of currency, zloty. Pop. (1964) 31,551,000.

polar bear, *Thalarctos maritimus* or *Ursus maritimus,* large creamy-white, long-necked bear of arctic regions of both hemispheres.

polar hare, arctic hare, *Lepus arcturus,* hare of Arctic regions which turns white in winter.

Polar Regions, areas of N and S extremities of globe centred about poles. *See* ARCTIC REGIONS; ANTARCTICA. *See* map opposite.

polarization of light, light whose transverse vibrational pattern is restricted to a single plane. Polarizing agents include nicol prisms and crystals.

Polaroid, commercial trade name for light polarizing material developed by Edwin H. Land (1932).

Pole, Reginald (1500–58), Eng. churchman; archbishop of Canterbury (1556–8), a cardinal. Failed to restore Catholicism in England after Henry VIII.

pole, extremity of Earth's axis of rotation.

Pole Star, North Star, conspicuous star nearest to N celestial pole; one of earliest reference points in navigation.

polecat, *Putorius putorius,* mammal of Europe and Asia, related to ferret, weasel, marten. Scent glands emit fetid odour; fur of European polecat called fitch. Destroys poultry.

Poliakoff, Serge (1906–69), Russ. abstract artist living in Paris. Work characterized by areas of flat colour in mosaic patterns.

police, civil organization whose func-

The Palace of Culture, Warsaw, Poland

tions are crime prevention, detection, and keeping public order. Eng. and US police forces under local control.

police court, court of summary jurisdiction, known in UK as a Magistrates' court, London excepted. Presided over by stipendiary magistrates or unpaid Justices of the Peace.

poliomyelitis, infantile paralysis, acute, contagious viral infection characterized by fever, headache, muscle pain and, if attacking central nervous system, paralysis. Immunity became possible with Salk vaccine (1955) and Sabin vaccine (1961).

Polish, Slavic Indo-European language, with *c.* 32 million speakers in Poland.

Polish Succession, War of the (1733–5), on death of Augustus II of Poland, France (with Spain and Sardinia) supported deposed Stanislaus I against Augustus' son, Augustus III (supported by Emperor Charles VI and Russia). By Treaty of Vienna, Augustus III kept Poland, Stanislaus received Lorraine, Austria ceded Naples and Sicily to Spain.

Politburo, policy committee of Russ. Communist party (1917–52). Replaced by presidium of Central Committee.

Polk, James K[nox] (1795–1849), 11th US Pres. (1845–9), Democrat. US Representative from Tennessee (1825–39). Admin. distinguished by

Polar Hare

westward expansion, successful handling of Mexican War, and re-estab. of Independent Treasury System.

polka, Bohemian dance, originating *c.* 1830. Popular in Europe for about 50 years.

poll tax, obsolete tax of fixed amount levied on adults, 1st imposed in England (1380). In US, tax to be paid before one can vote, used to disenfranchise sections of population. Practice prohibited by 24th Amendment (1964).

pollack, blue fish, coalfish, saithe, *Pollachius virens,* marine food fish of N Atlantic coasts.

Pollaiuolo, Antonio (*c.* 1429–98), Florentine artist, son of goldsmith **Jacopo Pollaiuolo**; regarded as 1st to study anatomy by dissection, sculpted

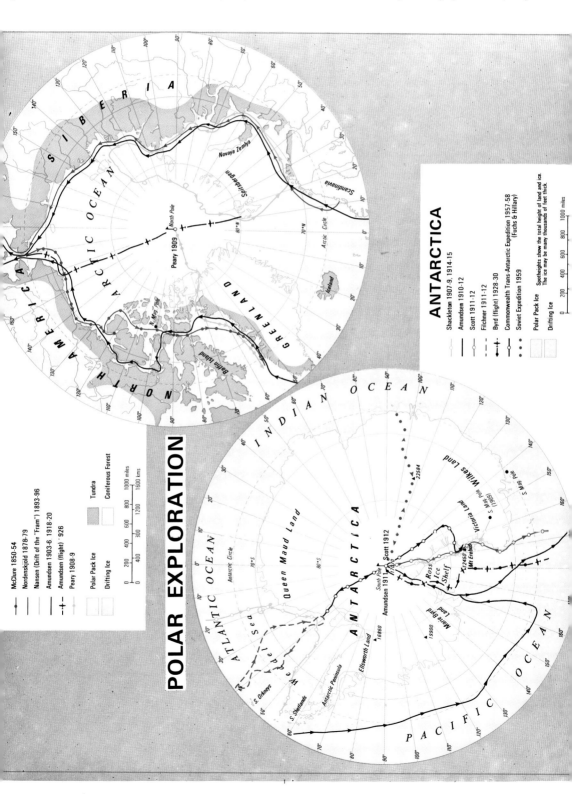

POLAR EXPLORATION

McClure 1850-54
Nordenskjold 1878-79
Nansen (Drift of the "Fram") 1893-96
Amundsen 1903-6 1918-20
Amundsen (flight) 1926
Peary 1908-9

Polar Pack Ice
Drifting Ice
Tundra
Coniferous Forest

ANTARCTICA

Shackleton 1907-9, 1914-15
Amundsen 1910-12
Scott 1911-12
Filchner 1911-12
Byrd (flight) 1928-30
Commonwealth Trans-Antarctic Expedition 1957-58 (Fuchs & Hillary)
Soviet Expedition 1959

Polar Pack Ice
Drifting Ice

Spotheights show the total height of land and ice. The ice may be many thousands of feet thick.

'Labours of Hercules'. With brother **Piero Pollaiuolo** (1443– 96) produced many paintings, designed bronze tomb of Sixtus IV in Rome.

pollen, fine, yellowish dust, produced in anthers of flowering plants. Mature grains containing male element unite with female element in ovule to produce embryo which becomes SEED.

pollination, fertilization in seed plants. Pollen, produced in stamens, is transferred to stigma by wind, bees or other insects.

Pollock, Jackson (1912– 56), Amer. abstract painter. Originator of action painting.

Polo, Marco (*c*. 1254–*c*. 1324), Venetian merchant. With father and uncle reached China (1271), became favourite of Kublai Khan and travelled widely in Asia. Returned to Venice (1295).

polo, orig. Persian outdoor game played between teams of 4 on horseback. Long-handled sticks are used to hit wooden ball into the opponents' goal. Brought from India to England by Brit. army officers (1869).

poltergeist, name given to unexplained force which produces knockings or movement of furniture in a house. Sometimes supposed to have a supernatural origin.

polyandry, custom of a woman having several husbands at the same time.

polyanthus, *Primula polyantha*, hardy perennial herb of primrose family. Cultivated as garden plant.

Polybius (*c*. 202– 120 BC), Gk. historian. Author of *History*, orig. a record of rise of Roman supremacy (220– 168 BC), later extended to cover 1st Punic War (264 BC) and destruction of Carthage (146 BC). Of 40 books, 5 survive.

polygamy, practice of having more than one husband or wife at the same time.

polygon, in geometry, a closed plane figure bounded by 5 or more straight sides. Designated as a regular polygon if all the sides and angles connecting them are equal.

polymer, natural or synthetic substance or mixture made up of molecules in linked chains of identical chem. units. Cellulose is a natural polymer; nylon and rayon are synthetic.

Polyneices, Polynices, in Gk. myth., son of Oedipus, brother of Eteocles and Antigone. Leader of Seven against Thebes, killed by Eteocles.

Polynesia, E division of Oceania, incl. Fr. Polynesia, Hawaiian Is., Samoa, Tonga, Line Is., Cook Is., Ellice Is., Easter Is.

Polynesians, people of Pacific islands between Hawaii, New Zealand and Easter Is. May have come from Malaysia or S America.

polyp, in zoology, name for the hydroid stage of various coelenterates esp. CORAL.

Polyphemus, in Gk. myth., one-eyed Cyclops, son of Poseidon. Lived in cave in Sicily; blinded by Odysseus.

polyphemus moth *Telea polyphemus*, large Amer. silkworm moth with large eyespot on each hind wing.

polyphony, style of musical composition where harmony is made of interwoven melodic strands.

polypus, cyst-like formation of mucous membrane sometimes found in nose, bladder, uterus, *etc*. Removed if malignant, or an obstruction, or if bleeding excessively.

polyvinyl chloride (PVC), colourless thermoplastic material formed by polymerization of vinyl chloride. Resistant to water, acid, alcohol. Used for flooring, coated fabrics, cable covering, *etc*.

polyzoan, member of group of aquatic animals resembling COELENTERATES.

Pombal, Sebastião José de Carvalho e Melo, Marquês de (1699– 1782), Portuguese statesman. Built strong absolutist govt. Ruthlessly suppressed opposition and introduced important reforms, incl. abolition of slavery.

pomegranate, *Purica granatum*, tree found in Med. and similar sub-trop. areas. Scarlet flowers; edible fruit.

Pomerania, historic region of N central Europe on Baltic Sea. Prussian province before World War 1. By Treaty of Versailles divided among Poland, Germany and free city of Danzig. Potsdam Conference (1945) assigned Pomerania E of Oder R. to Poland, Pomerania W of Oder R. becoming part of East German state of Mecklenburg.

Pomeranian, small, strongly-built dog of spitz type. Thick coat, erect ears, tail curved over back.

Pompadour, Jeanne Antoinette Poisson, Marquise de (1721– 64), mistress of Louis XV of France. She exerted great influence, encouraged Fr. alliance with Austria involving France in SEVEN YEARS WAR. Patronized the arts and founded royal porcelain factory at Sèvres.

pompano, *Trachinotus carolinus*, marine fish with scales of blue, silver and gold lustre. Food fish in S Atlantic and Gulf Coast of N America.

Pompeii, ruined Roman port, near Naples, S Italy, at foot of Mt.

Part of the excavations at Pompeii

Vesuvius. Wealthy resort, damaged by earthquake (AD 63); buried after eruption of Vesuvius (AD 79). Ruins, preserved by volcanic ash, discovered (1748); much subsequent excavation.

Pompey [Gnaeus Pompeius Maximus] (106– 48 BC), Roman general, consul and statesman. Fought successfully in Spain, against Spartacus, and in Pontus. Formed 1st Triumvirate with Crassus and Julius Caesar (60 BC). Opposition to Caesar's plans for retaining office led to Civil War (49 BC); defeated at Pharsalus (48 BC) fled to Egypt where he was assassinated.

Pompidou, Georges Jean Raymond (1911–), Fr. polit. leader, P.M. (1962– 8). Supported policies of Pres. De Gaulle; elected President of France (1969).

Pondicherry, Pondichéry, union territory of India. Formerly Fr. India. Area: 196 sq. mi.; cap. Pondicherry, founded 1683. Exports cotton goods, peanut oil. Pop. (1962) 369,079.

pondskater, waterskater, waterstrider, slender, elongated, surface water bug of family Gerridae.

pondweed, aquatic plant of genus *Potamogeton*, growing in ponds and streams. Species include Canadian *Elodea canadensis* and *P. crispus* of the US.

Ponsonby, Vere Brabazon, 9th Earl of Bessborough, Viscount Duncannon (1880– 1956), M.P. (1913– 20); Gov.-General of Canada (1931– 5).

Pontiac (*fl*. 1760– 6), Ottawa Indian chief. Led rebellion (1763– 6) against British take-over of Indian lands. Besieged Detroit, destroyed outposts before Brit. counter-offensive led to peace treaties.

Pontine Marshes, swampy, coastal area SE of Rome, Italy. Formerly malarial, now reclaimed for agricultural use.

Pope Fish

Pontius Pilate *see* PILATE, PONTIUS.

Pontus, region of NE Asia Minor, adjoining Black Sea. Centre of empire of Mithridates VI (*c.* 115–63 BC), annexed by Romans.

pony, small horse, usually not more than 14 hands high.

pony express, mail service (1860–1), 2,000 mi. from St Joseph, Missouri, to Sacramento, California, US, by pony riders taking 8 days.

poodle, breed of dog noted for its intelligence. Thought to have been developed in Germany. Thick frizzy or curly coat usually trimmed in standard style (1st introduced in France). Normally up to 18 in. high; miniature poodles are under 15 in. and toy poodles under 12 in.

Poole, Ernest (1880–1950), Amer. journalist and novelist, best known for *The Harbor* (1915). *The Bridge* (1940) is autobiog.

Poona, city of Maharashtra state W India. Educational centre; industries include cotton and paper, distilling, brass and copper work. Pop. (1965) 797,000.

poor law, legislation administering relief for poor. Eng. act (1601) made

Poplar (a) male catkins (b) leaf of Italian Poplar (c) leaf of Aspen (d) leaf of White Poplar (e) leaf of Siberian Balsam Poplar

public assistance parish responsibility. Poor houses organized for aged, sick and insane; provision of work for able-bodied instituted by 18th cent. Poor Law Amendment (1834) centralized supervision of relief. Eng. practice provided basis for Amer. statutes. Adoption of more uniform system on national scale developed in 20th cent. *See* SOCIAL SECURITY.

Pope, Alexander (1688–1744), Eng. Augustan poet and critic. Published *Essay on Criticism* (1711), mock-heroic epic *The Rape of the Lock* (1712, 1714) and highly successful translations of *Iliad* (1715–20), *Odyssey* (1725–6). Satires on contemporary literary figures include *The Dunciad* (1728, 1742).

Pope, The, official head of Roman Catholic Church. *See* PAPACY.

pope, *Acerina cornua,* small perch-like fish with undivided dorsal fin.

Popish Plot, name given to story, fabricated by TITUS OATES, of Jesuit-inspired plan to assassinate Charles II of England.

poplar, deciduous tree of N temp. regions, genus *Populus.* Lombardy poplar is *P. nigra*; N Amer. cotton-wood, *P. deltoides.*

poplin, finely corded fabric of cotton, rayon, silk or wool.

Popocatepetl, volcanic mountain (17,540 ft.) of Mexico. Permanently snow-capped, dormant since 1702.

poppy, plant of genus *Papaver.* Red, violet, yellow or white flowers. Most commercially important is opium poppy, *P. somniferum,* of Europe and Asia. Corn poppy, *P. rhoeas* found in *Europe;* Californian poppy, *P. californium,* state flower of California.

poppy seed, *Papaver phoeas,* seed of poppy plant. Roasted or steamed and used in bread, rolls, cakes.

Populism, Amer. agrarian polit. movement of late 19th cent. Discontent among mid-western farmers led to formation (1891) of Populist Party. Demands included govt.-owned rlys., free coinage of silver and graduated income tax. Majority of populists had joined Democrats under W. J. BRYAN by 1896.

porcelain, term applied generally to fine glazed pottery, esp. Chinese of Sung and Ming periods. Also European varieties made at Sèvres and Limoges (France), Chelsea, Bow and Staffordshire (England), Meissen and Dresden (Germany).

porcupine, rodent covered with sharp, erectile spines or quills in addition to hair. Common or crested porcupine, *Hystrix cristata,* of S Europe, N Africa and Asia Minor is solitary and terrestrial. *Erethizon dorsatum* of US

Portrait of a Woman by Antonio Pollaiuolo

and Canada has short spines partially concealed by hair.

porcupine grass, *Stipa spartea,* tall stout grass of W US. Grains have long awns; good forage and hay.

porgy, several fish of Sparidae family. Found in warm coastal seas of Americas and Europe.

porifera, phylum of animal kingdom comprising the sponges. Aquatic protozoan animals, usually attached to the sea bed. Classified according to type of skeleton secreted by jelly-like body. Skeleton of genera *Spongia* or *Hippospongia* used commercially esp. as bath sponge.

pork, flesh of domestic pig. Prepared as food, either fresh or cured (ham, bacon).

porphyry, igneous rock consisting of large crystals embedded in ground-mass. Red porphyry valued esp. by ancient Egyptians.

porpoise, small gregarious cetacean of genus *Phocaena.* Blackish above and paler beneath with blunt rounded snout; *c.* 5–8 ft. long. Common porpoise *P. phocaena* found in N Atlantic and Pacific.

Port Arthur, former city and port of Canada on NW L. Superior, Ontario. Combined (1970) with Fort William, renamed **Thunder Bay.** Exports grain. Total pop. (1970) 106,000.

Port-au-Prince, seaport and cap. of Haiti, W Indies. Exports include coffee and cocoa. Pop. (1964) 250,000.

Port Elizabeth, city and port of Cape Prov., South Africa; founded by Brit. settlers (1820). Agric. and indust. centre. Pop. (1963) 291,000.

Port Harcourt, city and port of Niger delta, Nigeria; founded 1915. Terminus for rly. from tin and coal mining areas. Exports palm products, peanuts. Pop. (1961) 75,000.

Port Louis, cap. and only seaport of Mauritius, founded 1735. Exports sugar and sugar products. Pop. (1966) 134,000.

Port of Spain, cap. and seaport of Trinidad and Tobago in W Indies. Major port of Caribbean Sea. Pop. (1957) 95,000.

Port Said, port of United Arab Republic, on Med. entrance of Suez Canal. Founded (1899) during canal construction. Free trade zone estab. 1966. Pop. (1967 est.) 256,000.

Port Sunlight *see* LEVER, WILLIAM HESKETH.

Port Talbot, town and port of Glamorganshire, Wales. Copper, iron and steel production important. Pop. (1963 est.) 51,500.

portcullis, defensive grating suspended in gateway of fortress; can be lowered in case of need.

Porter, Cole (1893–1964), Amer. composer esp. of musicals. Lyrics include 'Night and Day', 'Anything Goes', 'Begin the Beguine'.

Porter, George (1920–   ), Eng. chemist. Known for work on fast chemical reactions, photochemistry, photosynthesis. With M. Eigen and R. Norrish, awarded Nobel Prize for Chemistry (1967).

Porter, Katherine Anne (1894–   ), Amer. writer. Stylistic works include short stories (*e.g. Pale Horse, Pale Rider,* 1939) and novels such as *Ship of Fools* (1962).

Porter, Noah (1811–92), Amer. educationalist and philosopher. Editor-in-chief of *Webster's International Dictionary of the English Language* (1890).

Portland, 3rd Duke of *see* BENTINCK, WILLIAM HENRY CAVENDISH.

Portland, port of Oregon, US. Settled (1845) by New Englanders. Financial, commercial and industrial centre of Columbia R. basin; wool and agric. market. Pop. (1964) 652,000.

Porto Novo, cap. of Dahomey, connected by rly. with Cotonou; important market for palm-oil, cotton, kapok. Pop. (1964) 69,000.

Portsmouth, city of New Hampshire, US. Settled *c.* 1624. Naval and air base. Pop. 25,833.

Portsmouth, port and county borough of Hampshire, England, chief UK naval station. Pop. (1966) 218,000.

Portsmouth, Treaty of, signed (1905) at Portsmouth, N.H., US. Ended Russo-Japanese War.

Portugal, repub. of W Iberian Peninsula, SW Europe. Area: 35,340 sq. mi., incl. MADEIRA IS. and AZORES; cap. Lisbon; main cities Oporto,

Setubal. Largely mountainous with deep valleys. Economy dependent on agriculture and tourism. Wines exported. Industries include ceramics and cork. Language, Portuguese; main religion, Roman Catholicism; unit of currency, escudo. Pop. (1964) 9,228,000.

Portuguese, Romance Indo-European language, with over 75 million speakers in Portugal, Brazil and Portugal's overseas possessions.

Portuguese man-of-war, oceanic animal of genus *Physalia.* Floats on surface of sea. Has long, trailing tentacles with powerful, poisonous stinging organs. Dangerous to man.

Portuguese Guinea, overseas prov. of Portugal, on W coast of Africa between Senegal and Fr. Guinea, incl. Bissagos Is. Area: 14,400 sq. mi.; cap. Bissau. Pop. (1957) 511,000.

Portuguese Timor *see* TIMOR.

Poseidon, in Gk. myth., brother of Zeus, and god of the sea, carrying a trident. Also god of earthquakes and horses. Competed unsuccessfully against Athena for possession of Attica. Identified by Romans with water god Neptune.

positron, particle having identical mass as electron but opposite (positive) charge, produced *e.g.* by decay of certain artificial radio-active elements.

possum *see* OPOSSUM.

Post, George Brown (1837–1913), Amer. architect. Built College of the City of New York, the New York World Building.

postal services, public utility covering delivery of mail. In Britain, govt. control dates from 1657; introduction of penny post (1840). In US, postage stamps first used 1847.

Post-impressionism, movement esp. in Fr. painting. Reaction against IMPRESSIONISM. Most notable exponents VAN GOGH, GAUGUIN, CÉZANNE.

potash, potassium carbonate, compound of POTASSIUM used esp. as fertilizer. Name also applied loosely to various potassium salts.

potassium (K), metallic element. Soft, silver, highly reactive alkali metal; occurs in wide variety of silicate rocks and minerals; essential to life process of all plant and animal cells.

potato, *Solanum tuberosum,* plant with edible tubers. Native of S America but widely grown in temp. countries as staple food.

Potemkin Mutiny *see* RUSSIAN REVOLUTION.

Potomac, river (285 mi. long) rises W Virginia, US, reaches sea at Chesapeake Bay. Navigable by large ships to Washington D.C.

Potosi, city of Bolivia. Most important silver-producing centre of 16th and 17th cent.; now one of Bolivia's leading tin-producing areas. Pop. (1965 est.) 57,000.

Potsdam Conference, meeting (July, 1945) of Allied leaders to implement YALTA CONFERENCE agreement. Estab. US, UK, Fr. and Soviet occupation zones in Germany and Berlin, to be supervised by Allied Control Council and laid economic and polit. basis for post-World War 2 Germany.

Potter, [Helen] Beatrix (1866–1943), Eng. writer and illustrator of books for children. Characters created by her include Peter Rabbit, Jemima Puddle-Duck and Mrs. Tiggy-Winkle.

potter wasp, black and yellow solitary wasp, esp. of genus *Eumenes.* Found in temp. regions.

Potteries, The, region of N Staffordshire, England. Centre of china and earthenware industry; Minton and Wedgewood china manufactured.

pottery, general term for objects made of clay and baked hard. Earliest examples found on Mesolithic sites; orig. hand-made until invention, in Mesopotamia, of potter's wheel (*c.* 4,000 BC), kiln firing also originated in Mesopotamia at this time. Lustrous glazing introduced from Persia in Middle Ages.

Waterfall on the Potomac River, Maryland

Orpheus and Eurydice by Poussin

Poulenc, Francis (1899–1963), Fr. composer, pianist. Works include ballet *Les Biches* (1924) and piano works, *Mouvements Perpetuels* (1918).

poultry, domesticated fowl which serve as source of eggs and meat. Include chickens, turkeys, ducks, geese, pheasants.

Pound, Ezra Loomis (1885–), Amer. poet resident in Europe after 1907; detained (1945–58) for pro-Fascist sympathies in World War 2. Leader of Vorticist and Imagist movements; influenced by Ital., Fr. and Chinese poetry. Writings include *Hugh Selwyn Mawberly* (1920) and the *Cantos* (begun 1919).

Poussin, Nicholas (1594–1665), Fr. classical painter. Themes mainly historical and religious.

Powell, Cecil Frank (1903–69), Brit. physicist. Awarded Nobel Prize for Physics (1950) for development of photographic method for study of nuclear particles.

Powell, [John] Enoch (1912–), Eng. politician. As Cons. M.P. is most outspoken opponent of UK policies on coloured immigration.

power, in physics, capability of doing work. Term usually refers to energy necessary to operate all types of machinery. Sources of power include: the Sun, fuel, nuclear fission, electricity and water power.

Powers, Francis Gary (1929–), US pilot. Tried and imprisoned in USSR after capture (1960) while on U–2 reconnaissance mission. Subsequent exchange (1962) for Soviet spy marked US recognition of necessity of some espionage as part of foreign policy.

Powhatan, group of Algonkian N Amer. Indian tribes inhabiting Virginia. Achieved wide-spread confederacy under chief Powhatan. Scattered after treaty with Iroquois (1722).

Poynings Law, act of Irish Parl. (1494). Stated that approval of Eng. legislature was required for summoning of Irish Parl. and for passing of any legislation. Repealed 1782.

Poznan, Posen, city of Poland. Major river port and industrial centre; agricultural machinery, chemicals, textiles, food-processing. Rising of Poznan factory workers in 1956 set off sequence of events leading to Poland's anti-Stalinist 'October Revolution'. Pop. (1965) 436,000.

praetor, at Rome, orig. holders of executive power, later known as consuls. Subsequently appointed to administer justice among Roman citizens and foreigners, and govern provinces.

Praetorians, body guard of Roman emperors, replacing personal bodyguards of generals of republic. Important part in history of Empire. Disbanded by Constantine I.

Pragmatic Sanction, 1) decree issued (1438) by Charles VII of France, limiting papal authority over church in France; 2) decree issued (1713) by Emperor Charles VI, extending right of succession in Austrian Empire to female line. On death of Charles, led to War of the Austrian Succession.

Pragmatism, system of philosophy which states that the truth of any proposition is judged by its practical results and that only through empirical methods can truth be sought. First formulated by C. S. Peirce; developed by William James and John Dewey.

Prague, Praha, cap. of Czechoslovakia, on Vltava R. Financial, industrial centre; products include machinery, motor-cars *etc.* Settled before 10th cent.; buildings of old town include Gothic cathedral of St Vitus (1344), university (1348). Pop. (1966) 1,025,000.

prairie, tract of grassy, treeless, undulating land; term applies esp. to area of Canada and US extending from Rocky Mountains to Great Lakes.

prairie chicken, prairie fowl, prairie grouse, N Amer. grouse with booming mating call. Popular game bird. Species include greater prairie chicken, *Tympanuchus cupide*, and lesser prairie chicken, *T. pallidicinctus*.

prairie dog, gregarious, burrowing rodent of genus *Cynomys*, of N Amer. prairies. Stout and squat; reddish-grey in colour; barks like a dog.

prairie schooner, long, covered wagon drawn by 2 horses. Used by pioneers crossing plains and prairies of North America.

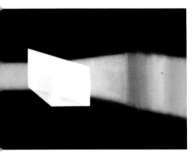

The use of a prism shows that light is made up of seven colours

prairie squirrel, various ground squirrels; *e.g. Citellus franklini* and *C. tridecemlineatus,* of prairies of N America. Vegetarian, stores food in cheek pouches.

prairie wolf *see* COYOTE.

Prandtl, Ludwig, FRS (1875–1953), Ger. physicist. Helped establish physical basis of practical aerodynamics.

Prasad, Rajendra (1884–1963), Indian statesman, 1st Pres. of Repub. of India (1950–62). Helped draft Indian constitution (1948–9).

pratincole, brownish tern-like shore bird of genus *Glareola.* Short bill; long, narrow, pointed wings; forked tail. Common pratincole, *Glareola pratincola* of S Europe, Africa and S Asia, known as locust bird in S Africa.

Pratt, E[dwin] J[ohn] (1882–1964), Canadian poet. Narrative poetry includes *The Witches Brew* (1925), *Dunkirk* (1941).

Pravda [Russ: truth], Russ. daily newspaper; founded 1912. Serves as organ of official Communist line.

prawn, edible crustacean widely distributed in fresh and salt waters of warm and temp. regions. Slender legs, long antennae. Common prawn, *palaemon serratus* is 3–4 in. long.

Praxiteles (b. *c.* 390 BC), Athenian sculptor. Only surviving original work is statue of Hermes carrying infant Dionysus, found at Olympia (1877).

Pre-Cambrian *see* GEOLOGICAL TABLE.

precession of the equinoxes, movement of imaginary line of intersection of celestial equator (equinoctial) and ecliptic; causes positions of Sun at EQUINOX (Mar. 21–22; Sept. 21–22) to move W at rate of 50·26 sec. per yr.

precious stone *see* GEMSTONE.

predestination, Augustinian theological doctrine that God predetermines some souls to salvation. Calvin (1509–64) taught eternal damnation of others.

pregnancy, period of development of the fertilized ovum in the uterus.

Gestation period, time a mother carries her young, varies from species to species but in humans averages 274 to 280 days.

prehistoric man, human being in transitional stage (Pleistocene period) between ape-like form and contemporary man. Includes primitive *Pithecanthropus* and *Sinanthropus* of E Asia and Neanderthaloid man of Eurasia and Africa. Cro-Magnon was prob. 1st *Homo sapiens.* E African fossil remains place man's origin as early as 1,750,000 yr. ago.

Preminger, Otto Ludwig (1906–   ), Amer. film producer-director, b. Austria. Films include *Forever Amber* (1947), *Porgy and Bess* (1959), *Advise and Consent* (1961), *Bunny Lake is Missing* (1965).

Pre-Raphaelite Brotherhood, group of 3 Eng. artists, D. G. Rossetti, John Millais and Holman Hunt, formed (1848) to revive the natural techniques used before 1500. Other artists joined the movement, supported by Ruskin against critical attacks.

Presbyterianism, in Christian Church, system of govt. by elders (presbyters) rather than by bishops. Instituted at the REFORMATION by JOHN CALVIN. Church of Scotland is Presbyterian.

Prescott, William Hickling (1796–1859) Amer. historian. Author of *Conquest of Mexico* (1843) and *Conquest of Peru* (1847).

president, elected head of republic; functions vary from equivalent of constitutional monarch to dictatorship. In US, powers are wide but precisely defined in constitution.

Presidium, in USSR, chief policy-making body of Communist Party's Central Committee. Replaced Politburo, abolished by Stalin. Also refers to presiding govt. council, Presidium of Supreme Soviet.

Presley, Elvis (1935–   ), Amer. singer. Helped popularize 'rock and roll'. Also appeared in films.

press, freedom of the, absence of official restraint on written publications. Right to impose restraint (censorship) usually govt. prerogative. During national emergencies, states may curtail right to freedom of press, as US and UK did during World Wars.

Pressburg, Treaty of, agreement between France and Austria after Napoleon I's victory at Austerlitz.

press-gang, team formerly empowered to recruit men by force for army or navy. Compulsory term was limited (1835) to 5 yr.

pressure, in physics, force applied to unit area of surface of body; distinct from total force exerted on body. Variations in pressure affect boiling and melting points of materials.

Prester John, legendary priest-king reported from 12th cent. as monarch of Asiatic or Abyssinian empire.

Preston, county borough of Lancashire, England. Cotton manufacture and shipping centre. Pop. (1966) 107,000.

Prestonpans, village of East Lothian, Scotland. Site of Jacobite victory (1745) over royalist forces.

Pretender, Old *see* STUART, JAMES FRANCIS EDWARD.

Pretender, Young *see* STUART, JAMES FRANCIS EDWARD.

Pretoria, city and cap. of Transvaal province and administrative cap. of Republic of South Africa. Centre of steel industry and the gold producing area. Pop. 423,000.

Prévost d'Exiles, Antoine François (1697–1763) Fr. novelist and priest, known as Abbé Prévost. Author of *Manon Lescaut,* short novel which served as basis for operas by Massenet and Puccini.

Priam, in Gk. myth., king of Troy during Trojan War. Husband of Hecuba; among 50 sons and many daughters were Hector, Paris, Cassandra. Slain by Neoptolemus at fall of Troy.

price control, regulation of commodity prices to prevent rise in cost of living. Govt. control necessary when economic competition fails to curtail excessive price increase.

prickly pear, common name for various species of the *Opuntia* genus of cacti with flattened, jointed spiny stems. Native to Mexico, Chile; the pear-shaped fruits of several species are edible.

Priestley, J[ohn] B[oynton] (1894–   ), Brit. novelist and dramatist. Novels include *The Good Companions* (1929), *Angel Pavement* (1930), *Lost*

Prickly Pear

Empires (1965). Critical works include, *Literature and Western Man* (1960).

Priestley, Joseph (1733–1804), Eng. theologian, scientist. Attacked orthodox tenets, sympathized with Fr. revolutionaries. His *History of Electricity* (1767) explained rings (Priestley's rings) formed on metal surfaces by electrical discharge.

primate, orig. senior bishop superior to archbishop or metropolitan. Now in R.C. Church purely honorific title. In C. of E. title given to archbishops of Canterbury and York.

primate, members of highest mammalian order. Simian sub-group includes lemurs, galagos; anthropoid composed of monkeys, apes and man. Characterized by flat finger nails and full placental development.

prime minister, premier, chief minister of cabinet, as in Brit. model. As party leader, responsible for appointment of cabinet and for govt. policy.

prime number, in mathematics a number that can be evenly divided only by itself and 1. Euclid proved there is an infinite number of prime numbers.

Primitive Methodist Church, sect which broke with Wesleyan Church in England; founded (1810) by William Clowes and Hugh Bourne. Re-united with Methodists (1932). US branch has held separate General Conferences since *c*. 1830.

Primo de Rivera, Miguel (1870–1930), Sp. military and polit. leader. Ruled (1923–30) with dictatorial powers under Alfonso XIII. Overthrown after army party joined opposition.

Primrose, Archibald Philip, 5th Earl of Rosebery (1847–1929), Brit. Liberal statesman; P.M. (1894–5). Resigned after party split over his imperialist policies.

primrose, *Primula vulgaris,* common European spring-flowering plant usually with pale yellow flowers. Brit. *P. veris* known as cowslip. Himalayan primrose, *P. denticulata,* has lilac-coloured flowers and long stem.

primula, large genus of perennial herbs with white, yellow and pink flowers, found in temp. and mountainous parts of N hemisphere. Main Brit. varieties are common primrose, cowslip and oxlip; cultivated polyanthus are derived from hybrid of primrose and cowslip. *P. auricula* bears several small yellow flowers to a single stem.

Prince Albert National Park, in C Saskatchewan, Canada. Area: 1,496 sq. mi.; founded 1927.

The Union Buildings in Pretoria, South Africa

Prince Edward Island, province off E coast of Canada, in Gulf of St Lawrence. Area: 2,184 sq. mi.; cap. Charlottetown. Economy largely dependent on farming and stock raising; fishing, fur trade, tourism important. Pop. (1961) 104,629.

Prince Edward National Park, on N shore of Prince Edward Is., E Canada. Area: 7 sq. mi.; founded 1936.

Prince of Wales, title created by Edward I for his eldest son after conquest of Wales; since conferred on eldest son of sovereign. The badge is a plume of 3 ostrich feathers enfiled by a coronet.

princess of the night, *Selenicereus pteranthus,* common night-blooming cactus of Mexico. Has green and purple stem, large white flowers.

Princeton, borough of New Jersey, US. Settled (1696) by Quakers. Contains Princeton University and buildings of hist. interest. Pop. (1960) 11,890.

printing, method of reproducing words or illustrations in ink on paper or other material by mechanical means. Used by Chinese from *c*. 11th cent., and from mid 15th cent. in Germany by JOHANN GUTENBERG. In England, WILLIAM CAXTON set up 1st printing press at Westminster, London (1476).

prism, in optics, transparent solid used to change direction of light passing through it. Triangular prisms disperse white light into rainbow band of colours known as SPECTRUM.

privateers, privately owned war vessels having govt. commission to seize enemy shipping (1589–1815). System subject to much abuse as cover for piracy; abolished by Declaration of Paris (1856).

privet, genus of shrubs of olive family. Widely cultivated for hedges, esp. common *Ligustrum vulgare.*

privet hawk moth, *Sphinx ligustri,* Eurasian moth. Larvae feed on privet and lilac leaves.

Privy Council, in UK, royal advisory body. Orig. comprised chief royal officials, Tudors used it as chief governing body. Became honorary with advent of cabinet govt. Membership includes cabinet ministers and other high-ranking officials in UK and Commonwealth.

probate, official establishing of validity of will. In England, registered by Probate division of High Court; in Scotland, called confirmation, responsibility of Sheriff Court; in US normally by courts set up specifically for this function.

probation, judicial system under which offenders, instead of being fined or committed to prison, are placed under supervision of a probation officer for a specified period.

Prochorov, Aleksandr M[ikhaylovich] (1916–), Russ. physicist. With Charles Hard Townes and Nikolai Basov, awarded Nobel Prize

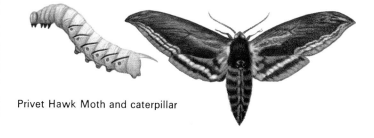

Privet Hawk Moth and caterpillar

The village of Les Baux, north-east of Arles in Provence

for Physics (1964) for work on the maser-laser principle.

Proconsul, extinct primate of Miocene period, fossil remains found in Kenya. Possible ancestor of *Homo sapiens.*

procurator fiscal, in Scot. law, officer whose duties include inquiring into cases of sudden death.

profit, in economics, percentage of return on capital. Separation of management and ownership in modern corporate enterprise has invalidated theory of profit as incentive for production.

programme music, setting of a story or series of events in music without words. Examples include Berlioz' *Symphonie Fantastique.*

programming, computer, preparation of instructions in machine language of a series of operations to be performed by COMPUTER.

Progressive Conservative Party, Canadian polit. organization estab. (1942) out of Conservative Party. Latter formed (1854) by J. A. Macdonald. Since Confederation (1867), remained 1 of 2 major parties in Canada.

Progressive Party, name of 3 different Amer. polit. organizations. 1) Formed (1912) as 'Bull Moose' party by supporters of THEODORE ROOSEVELT after Republican Party had nominated W. H. TAFT. 2) Reform group (1924–46), estab. under Robert La Follette, support lying mainly in Wisconsin. 3) Faction which split (1948) with Democratic Party, nominating HENRY WALLACE for Pres.

prohibition, legal means of controlling manufacture and sale of alcoholic beverages. Militant agitation for prohibition in US led to adoption through 18th Amendment (1919).

Controls repealed by 21st Amendment (1933) after enforcement had failed to curb widespread illegal distribution.

projections, in cartography, parallels of latitude and meridians on which flat map of world may be drawn; none of which represent spherical earth without distortion. Types include 1) azimuthal, where original projection is on to plane, 2) conical, where projection is from globe to cone to plane, 3) cylindrical, where earth is projected on to surrounding cylinder which is unrolled.

Prokofiev, Serge (1891–1953), Russ. composer. Works include operas (*e.g. Love for Three oranges*), Symphonies (*e.g. Symphonie Classique*), an orchestral fairy tale: *Peter and the Wolf,* ballet, (*e.g. Romeo and Juliet*) and concertos for piano and violin.

proletariat, class of wage earners existing on their own labour. Proletariat of ancient Rome was propertyless class. Marxist theory views proletariat as exploited by capitalist class, from which it must take power to achieve classless society.

promethea moth *Callosamia promethea,* large, brown Amer. moth. Larvae feed on trees.

Prometheus, in Gk. myth., gave mankind fire stolen from Hephaestus. Chained by Zeus to rock in Caucasus where his liver was devoured by eagle for refusing to divulge secret about marriage of Peleus and Thetis. Finally, either released by Heracles or submitted to Zeus.

prominent moth, large moth of family *Notodontidae* with erect tuft of scales on each forewing. Species include puss moth, *Cerula vinula.*

promontory, term for projecting headland or high cape.

pronghorn, prongbuck, N Amer. mammal. Only surviving member of family Antilocapridae, between cattle and deer. Stands 3 ft. high, male has forked horns, cast annually.

propaganda, science of moulding opinion by spreading information (or rumour) through any channels to gain political, religious or cultural ends. Important psychological weapon of modern warfare.

Propertius, Sextus (*c.* 50–*c.* 16 BC), Roman elegiac poet. Principal subject of poetry, 1st published (*c.* 26 BC), is his mistress, Cynthia.

Propylaea, portal and entrance to Acropolis, Athens. Erected on W end of Acropolis under admin. of Pericles; begun (437–6 BC) completed in 5 yr.

prose, ordinary form of spoken or

Protea bolusii

written language, without metrical structure, as opposed to poetry or verse. Earliest European surviving literary form is Herodotus' *History of the Persian Wars*.

Proserpina *see* PERSEPHONE.

prostate gland, partially muscular gland, accessory to male reproductive organs. It secretes part of spermatic fluid.

proteaceae, family of flowering shrubs and trees, mostly of S Africa and Australia. *Protea bolusii,* with cone-shaped flower heads, is popular garden plant.

Protectorate govt. of England (1653–9) estab. by OLIVER CROMWELL after Eng. Civil War. Period marked by puritan regime and military administration. Preceded RESTORATION.

proteins, very large group of complex naturally occurring compounds essential to living organisms. Made up of over 20 amino acids.

Protestantism, all Christian churches except R.C. and Eastern Orthodox, most of which originated during REFORMATION. Stresses individual responsibility to God rather than to eccles. authorities.

Proteus, in Gk. myth., wise old man of the sea with power of assuming various forms to escape questioning. In later legend an early king of Egypt, subsequently worshipped as a god.

protococcus, genus of green algae which are common constituents of LICHENS.

protocol, in diplomacy, term for written document recording informal agreements. Code of courtesy governing conduct of diplomatic service.

protoplasm, living material of plant and animal cells; carries out essential processes of respiration, reproduction and waste excretion. Occurs in cell form as basic unit of tissue formation. Composed mostly of oxygen, hydrogen, carbon, nitrogen; *c.* 90% water.

protozoa, unicellular animal phylum. Most members are microscopic, solitary and aquatic. Many are parasitic.

Proudhon, Pierre Joseph (1809–65), Fr. social theorist and journalist. In pamphlet *What Is Property?,* advocated abolition of private ownership, system of communal govt.

Proust, Joseph Louis (1754–1826), Fr. chemist. Established law stating that proportion of elements in any compound is fixed by weight.

Proust, Marcel (1871–1922), Fr. novelist. Withdrew almost completely from society (1906) to write his series of novels *À la Recherche du Temps Perdu* (16 vols., 1913–27), in which he attempted to recall the minutest details of his childhood. This work greatly influenced subsequent novelists.

Provençal, dialect form of French surviving from Romance language (*langue d'oc*) used in S France until 16th cent. Medium of 12th cent. TROUBADOURS' poetry. Revived as literary medium (19th cent.).

Provence, former prov. of SE France bordering Med. Sea; cap. Aix. Main towns, Marseille, Nice, Toulon, Avignon, Arles.

Proverbs, poetic book of OT, collection of moral sayings, mainly attributed to Solomon.

Providence, cap. of Rhode Island, US; terminal port for petroleum; founded 1636; site of John Brown House (1786). Pop. (1965) 187,061.

prune, PLUM that has been dried without fermentation taking place.

Prussia, former Ger. state. Estab. as kingdom with union (1701) of Brandenburg and Prussia under Hohenzollern dynasty; comprised much of NE Germany, cap. Berlin. Threatened Austrian supremacy in 18th cent., acquiring Silesia and W parts of Poland under FREDERICK THE GREAT. Prussian military gains promulgated by BISMARCK during 19th cent. resulted in Ger. unification (1866) and creation of empire (1871). Dominant state in subsequent Ger. history. Reduced after World War 1; dissolved (1947) after World War 2.

Przewalski's horse *see* TARPAN.

Psalms, poetical book of OT, formerly attributed to David, now recognized as the work of various authors between 500 and 63 BC.

psoriasis, chronic skin eruption most often affecting elbows and knees. Cause unknown.

Psyche, in Gk. and Roman myth., beautiful girl loved by Cupid, but forbidden to look at him. She disobeyed and he left her. Later became immortal and was united with him forever.

psychiatry, medical study of human mind in states of ill-health or disease, incl. psychosis, neurosis, criminal behaviour and other mental abnormalities.

psychoanalysis, method of treating disturbed mental states by giving patient insight into conscious and unconscious processes of mind. Pioneer of method was SIGMUND FREUD.

psychology, science of behaviour. Studies conscious and subconscious mental processes (cognition, perception, reason, memory, will, *etc.*) in relation to individuals and their environment.

Pronghorn Antelope

psychosis, name given to certain serious mental disorders most of which satisfy legal criteria of INSANITY in that the patient cannot take care of himself, or is a danger to others, or both.

psychotherapy, treatment of functional aspects of general body disease and of psycho-neurosis by application of psychological methods, esp. suggestion, hypnosis and psychoanalysis.

Ptah, ancient Egyptian god; believed to be creator of the universe; worshipped esp. at Memphis.

ptarmigan, bird of grouse family found in mountains of N hemisphere, having feathered feet. Winter plumage is white. Species include rock ptarmigan, *Lagopus mutus,* and willow ptarmigan, *L. lagopus.*

pterodactyl, extinct order of flying reptiles. Fossils found in Mesozoic rocks in Europe and N America.

pterodophyta, phylum of plants comprising FERN, HORSETAIL and CLUB MOSS groups.

Ptolemy, ancient Egyptian dynasty. Estab. (305 BC) by **Ptolemy I** (Soter, 305–283 BC), a general of Alexander the Great. Early Ptolemies engaged in extension of dominions in Syria, Asia Minor, Greece; control of territories outside Egypt largely due to naval supremacy. Estab. Alexandria as cap. and centre of Hellenistic culture; Library founded by Ptolemy I, Museum by **Ptolemy II**. Period of civil

Ptarmigan

The cathedral of Puebla, one of the oldest towns in Mexico, dates from the 16th century

Puff Adder

war and mob rule occurred under later Ptolemies, esp. after accession of CLEOPATRA [VII] and **Ptolemy XII**. Dynasty ended after defeat of MARCUS ANTONIUS and Cleopatra at Actium (31 BC) and Cleopatra's suicide.

Ptolemy [Claudius Ptolemaeus] (*fl.* 2nd cent.), Gk.-Egyptian astronomer and mathematician. Author of *Almagest*, in which spherical Earth is centre of astronomical system; influential until superseded by works of Copernicus.

puberty, stage when a child's development towards sexual maturity begins. Generally age 11–14 in girls and 13–16 in boys. Secretions of sex hormones cause physical changes *e.g.* growth in penis and production of living sperm in boys; enlargement of hips and breasts, beginning of menstruation in girls.

public prosecutor *see* DIRECTOR OF PUBLIC PROSECUTION.

publishing, trade concerned with the creation and distribution of books and other reading matter. Closely allied to printing and bookselling. Narrowly defined, involves preparation of author's work for chosen market. Introduction of movable type (15th cent.) facilitated large-scale distribution of printed matter.

Pucci, Emilio, Marchese di Barsento (1914–   ), Ital. fashion designer. Esp. known for use of printed silks.

Puccini, Giacomo (1858–1924), Ital. composer. Esp. known for operas incl. *Manon Lescaut* (1893), *La Bohème* (1896), *La Tosca* (1900), *Madame Butterfly* (1904) and unfinished *Turandot* (1st performed 1926).

Puebla, city of C Mexico. Industries, ceramics, textiles, food processing. Pop. (1967) 360,000.

Pueblo, N Amer. Indian tribe of SW US, living in adobe communities. Ancestors were cliff-dwellers until 14th cent. Sp. colonization resisted (17th cent.) by which time tribe had reached high level of civilization. Groups included Hopi and Zuni Indians.

Puerto Rico, smallest island of the Greater Antilles, in West Indies, US possession. Area: 3,435 sq. mi.; cap. San Juan; cities, Ponce, Mayaguez. One of the world's most densely populated regions; after World War 2 heavy emigration to US. Exports sugar, rum, tobacco, cotton, needlework. Sp. possession for 400 years; ceded to US (1898) after Spanish-American War; established commonwealth with full powers of local self-government (1952). Unit of currency, US dollar. Pop. (1963 est.) 2,529,000.

puff adder, *Bitis arietans,* large deadly poisonous viper found throughout Africa. Has short tail and yellow markings on body; inflates upper part of body when excited.

puff-ball, spherical fungus which breaks open when ripe to emit spores. Common puff-ball is *Lycoperdon perlatum.*

puffer, trop. fish of Odontidae family. Body becomes almost circular with erectile spines when air sac is filled.

puffin, *Alcidae fratercula* or *A. lunda,* small marine bird with brightly coloured bill. Nests in colonies on Atlantic coasts. Pacific varieties include horned and tufted puffins.

pug, small breed of dog, orig. Chinese. Broad flat nose, smooth coat and short curled tail.

Pugachev, Yemelyan Ivanovich (d. 1775), Russ. Cossack rebel leader. Claiming to be Peter III murdered by Catherine III, he led peasant revolt. Betrayed and executed.

Pugin, Augustus Charles, Eng. writer on medieval architecture, b. France. His son, **Augustus Welby Northmore Pugin** (1812–52), was leader of Gothic revival. Designed churches, assisted with Houses of Parliament, London.

Pugnani, Gaetano (1731–98), Ital. violinist and classical composer.

Pulitzer, Joseph (1847–1911), Amer. newspaper proprietor, b. Hungary. Became owner (1883) of New York *World* and *Evening World* (1887). Founded (1903) School of Journalism at Columbia University; **Pulitzer Prizes** awarded annually for achievements in Amer. journalism and letters.

pulse, beating of heart, causing changes in volume of blood in arteries.

Normal rate in adults is *c.* 70–80 pulsations per min.

puma *see* AMERICAN LION.

pumice, light, porous igneous rock used as abrasive. Formed by escape of gas through molten lava.

pump, machine for raising water or other fluids. In ancient times the screw type was used for irrigation purposes. Various types exist now, incl. reciprocating, gear and rotary pumps.

pumpkin, *Cucurbita pepo,* vine-like annual plant with large round edible fruit. Native of America, widely cultivated. Also known as squash.

Punch and Judy, puppet play introduced to England (17th cent.) prob. derived from Ital. COMMEDIA DELL' ARTE. Characters include hunchback Punch and his wife Judy.

Punic Wars, series of conflicts between Rome and Carthage for dominance of Med. First Punic War (264–241 BC) resulted in acquisition of Sicily by Rome. During Second Punic War (218–201 BC), Hannibal invaded Italy, but had to return to Carthage, where he was defeated (202 BC) at Zama by Scipio Africanus Major. Third Punic War (149–146 BC) led to destruction of Carthage by Scipio Africanus Minor.

Punjab, region of N India and W Pakistan. Extensively irrigated; chief crop, wheat. Centre of ancient Indus civilization. Annexed (1849) by British, divided between India and Pakistan (1947). **Punjab** state formed 1956. Area: 47,080 sq. mi. Subdivided 1966.

Punjabi, Indic Indo-European language, with 20 million speakers in N India.

pupa, 3rd stage in development of insects which undergo METAMORPHOSIS. First 2 stages are egg and larva.

Gear pump, usually used as an oil pump

pupil, round opening in centre of the eye. Through it light is admitted and focused on the retina. Size of pupil varies with the amount of light in the environment and is affected by drugs.

Purbeck, peninsula of Dorset, England; 12 mi. long. Gives name to Purbeck beds of S England; limestone used for building stone.

Purcell, Henry (1659–95), Eng. composer and organist. Works include church music, notably *Te Deum* and *Jubilate* (1694); compositions for public occasions; operas *Dido and Aeneas* (1689), *The Fairy Queen* (1693).

purchase tax, in UK, tax levied on majority of products. Introduced (1940) as wartime measure. Similar to sales tax of other countries.

pure food laws, legislation against debasement of food quality. In UK, 1st law passed in consumer's interest in 1860; in US, controversy preceded Pure Food and Drugs Act (1906). Regulations govern content, handling, labelling and advertising.

purgatory, state or place where souls are purified from unatoned sin, according to R.C. and E. Orthodox Church. Their suffering can be lessened by prayers of the living. Protestants reject this doctrine.

Purim, Jewish secular festival commemorating rescue of Persian Jews from extermination ordered by Haman.

Puritan Revolution, conflict (1603–49) between Eng. kings James I and Charles I and Puritan Parl. party. Arose out of kings' advocacy of govt. by 'divine right', disputed by Parl. Culminated in CIVIL WAR, execution of Charles and estab. of PROTECTORATE.

Puritanism, social and theological doctrine of Protestantism in Britain and US. Estab. (16th cent.) as reform movement, influenced by Calvinist theory, aiming at less ritualistic worship forms. By 17th cent. had separated from Church of England and opposed Charles I, precipitating Civil War (1642–9). Puritanism taken by colonists to New England, where it survived into 19th cent. as dominant ethic.

purple heron, *Ardea purpurea,* Eurasian heron. Has dark crest, maroon and fawn plumage.

Purple Heron

African pygmies outside mud and leaf hut

purslane, *Portulaca oleracea,* annual herb; fleshy, succulent leaves, sometimes used as salad or pot herb.

pus, thick yellowish-white substance produced as reaction to bacterial inflammation. Composed of white blood cells, bacteria and dead tissue cells.

Pusan, Fusan, city of S Korea. Chief port; industries, ironworks, textiles, food-processing, shipbuilding, rubber. Pop. (1966) 1,425,703.

Pusey, Edward Bouverie (1800–82), Eng. clergyman, a leader of OXFORD MOVEMENT. Regarded as founder or restorer of High Church movement in Church of England. Worked with J. H. NEWMAN on *Tracts for the Times.*

Pushkin, Alexander Sergeyevitch (1799–1837), Russ. poet and novelist. Influenced by Byron and Shakespeare. Works include fairy tale *Russlan and Ludmilla* (1820); poetry *The Bronze Horseman* (1834); autobiog. verse novel *Eugene Onegin* (1831); play *Boris Godunov* (1825).

Pushtu *see* PASHTO.

puss moth *see* PROMINENT MOTH.

Putumaye, river of Colombia, *c.* 1,000 mi. long trib. of R Amazon. Forms boundary of Colombia with Ecuador and Peru.

Pygmy, diminutive Negroid people, sometimes called Negritos or Negrillos, of Africa, Malaysia and New Guinea. Generally hunters living in small nomadic bands in forests and scrub regions.

pygmy hippopotamus, *Choeropsis*

Cirque or corrie of Gavarnie in the Pyrenees

Wave action has eroded the cliffs where the Pyrenees meet the sea

liberiensis, rare hippopotamus of rivers in W Africa *c.* 1/10th size of common HIPPOPOTAMUS.

Pym, John (1584–1643), Eng. polit. leader. Led Puritan opposition to Charles I in Short and Long Parl.; moved impeachment of Stafford. Negotiated alliance (1642) between Parl. and Scots.

Pyongyang, cap. and industrial centre of North Korea. Centre of Buddhist culture from 1st cent. BC. Pop. (1963) 940,000.

pyorrhea, infection of gums and tooth sockets resulting in inflammation and pus formation.

pyralid moth, small or medium sized, slender-bodied moth of largely trop.

Pyrites

group, Pyralididae. Species include cactus moth and closewing moth.

Pyramids, in ancient Egypt, monumental stone structures with square base and triangular sides, meeting at an apex. Erected as tombs for kings of Egypt (*c.* 2700–*c.* 1900 BC). Mostly situated near Memphis, Egypt.

Pyramids, Battle of, Fr. victory (July, 1798) over Mameluke rebels in Egypt. Encounter gave Napoleon control of Egypt until Nelson destroyed his fleet at Aboukir (Aug. 1798).

Pyrenees, mountain range forming natural barrier and boundary between France and Spain. Highest point Aneto (Fr: Néthon) 11,168 ft. Famous waterfall in Cirque de Gavarnie, source of hydro-electric power. Republic of ANDORRA is in E Pyrenees.

Pyrenees, Peace of the, treaty between France and Spain (1659). Louis XIV was to marry daughter of Philip IV of Spain; Spain gave Roussillon and parts of Flanders to France. Franco-Span. border estab. at Pyrenees.

pyrethrum, *Chrysanthemum coccineum,* perennial plant native to Persia and Caucasus. Widely cultivated in temp. regions for red, pink or white flowers and commercially for insecticide pyrethrum powder.

pyrites, iron pyrites, common ore of iron, brass-yellow in colour, with about 46% iron content. Often mistaken for gold (fool's gold).

pyrotechnics, art of making and using fireworks. Highly developed by Chinese. Used today esp. for signalling and for displays.

pyroxenes, group of rock-forming minerals, important constituents of basic igneous and metamorphic rocks. Silicates of calcium, magnesium, iron, *etc.*

Pyrrhus I (*c.* 318–272 BC), king of Epirus and military commander. Attempted to revive empire of Alexander the Great. Defeated Romans at Asculum (279 BC), but with heavy losses, (hence 'Pyrrhic victory'). Failed to establish any influence in Italy.

Pythagoras (*c.* 582–507 BC), Gk. philosopher, b. Samos. Founded religious brotherhood at Crotona. Thought centred on concept that all relationships could be expressed in numbers. Made discoveries in musical intonations and helped develop Euclidean geometry. Believed Earth revolved around fixed point ('hearth') of universe.

Pythia, in Gk. religion, priestess and oracular prophetess of Apollo at Delphi.

python, non-venomous snake of trop. zones of Old World and Australia. Can be up to 30 ft. long. Crushes prey in coils of body.

Python

'Q' *see* QUILLER-COUCH, SIR ARTHUR THOMAS.

Qatar, independent Arab sheikdom, with treaty relations with UK, peninsula on W Persian Gulf. Area: *c.* 4,000 sq. mi.; cap. Doha. Largely barren land; fishing and oil important. Pop. (1967 est.) 80,000.

Qattara, depression of Sahara Desert, in United Arab Repub. Has very soft sand up to *c.* 450 ft. below sea level. Provided protection for Allied forces in World War 2.

Q-boat, ship used by British in World War I to destroy Ger. submarines (U-boats). Disguised as merchant or fishing vessels; armed with hidden guns.

Quadruple Alliance, 1) league formed (1718) by England, France, Austria, Netherlands; forced Spain to give up Sicily and Sardinia (1720). 2) alliance formed (1814) by Austria, England, Prussia, Russia to strengthen coalition against Napoleon I.

quaestor, Roman magistrate, next in rank to consul, primarily concerned with public finances.

Quarrel

quagga, extinct African mammal related to zebra. Excessively hunted for hide in 19th cent.

quail, *Coturnix coturnix,* small migratory game-bird of pheasant family. Netted for food in Med. countries. Chinese dwarf quail, *Excalfactoria chinensis,* is one of smallest Galliformes.

quake grass, dodder grass, *Bromus brizaeformis,* Eurasian grass, naturalized in US.

Quakers, Society of Friends, Christian sect founded (17th cent.) in England by GEORGE FOX. Hold that understanding and guidance comes directly from Holy Spirit. Refuse to worship in estab. Church or to fight in war. Colony estab. (1681) in Pennsylvania, US, by WILLIAM PENN. American Friends Service Committee and Service Council of the British Soc. of Friends awarded Nobel Peace Prize (1947).

quamash, *Camassia quamash,* perennial herb of western N America, related to the lily. Has edible bulbs.

quantum theory, in physics, postulation (1900) by MAX PLANCK that radiant energy does not exist in continuous distribution but in multiples of a small unit (quantum). Theory, developed by Einstein, Niels Bohr and P. A. M. Dirac, is basis of atomic physics.

quarantine, restriction of movement imposed on people or animals who may have been exposed to infectious disease. Originated in 14th cent. Venice.

quarrel, large headed bolt or arrow for use with crossbows and arbalests.

quarter days, those which, in law and commerce, begin each quarter of the year. In England, 25 Mar., 24 June, 29 Sept., 25 Dec.; in Scotland, 2 Feb., 15 May, 1 Aug., 11 Nov.; in US, 1 Jan., 1 April, 1 July, 1 Oct. Days on which it is usually contracted that rents and interest become due for payment.

quartz, the commonest mineral, an oxide of silicon. Many varieties, incl. amethyst, onyx, agate. Pure quartz, colourless and transparent, is used for jewellery and in glassmaking.

quartzite, sandstone metamorphosed into a solid QUARTZ rock; composed of *c.* 90% quartz.

quasars, in astronomy, sources of intense radio activity; 1st detected 1961. Travel at high velocity into space. Exact nature unknown.

Quasimodo, Salvatore (1901–68), Ital. lyric poet. Works include *The Promised Land and Other Poems* (1958). Awarded Nobel Prize for Literature (1959).

Quartz

quassia, *Quassia amara,* trop. shrub or small tree of Surinam. Superseded in medicine by *Picrasma excelsa* of West Indies. Infusion of wood produces bitter tonic.

Quebec, maritime prov. of E Canada. Area: 594,000 sq. mi.; cap. Quebec; main cities, Montreal, Laval. Laurentian Mts. in E, Appalachian Mts. in SE, St Lawrence Valley in S. Extensive timber and mineral resources. Industry includes metal smelting, manufacture of indust. equipment, consumer goods. Tourist trade important. Early Fr. colony based on fur trade (17th cent.) Brit. control estab. (1763). Quebec (as Lower Canada) joined with Ontario (Upper Canada) in 1849. With estab. of Canadian federation, again became prov. (1867). Population 80% French; main religion, Roman Catholicism. Pop. (1961) 5,259,211.

Quebec, cap. of Quebec prov., Canada, port on St Lawrence R. Cultural and tourist centre. Exports wheat and fur. Manufacturing includes paper, metal products. Founded (1608) by French; became

Chinese Dwarf Quail

Château Frontenac in Quebec

cap. of New France (1663); captured by British under Wolfe at Battle of Plains of Abraham (1759). Cap. of Canadian federation (1851–5, 1859–65). Contains Laval University. Population mainly of Fr. descent. Pop. (1967 est.) 164,190.

Quebec Act, one of INTOLERABLE ACTS; passed (1774) by Brit. parl. extending boundaries of Quebec, allowing polit and legal concessions and religious freedom to Fr. Canadians. Intended to estab. permanent Brit. admin. in Canada.

Quechua, Kechua, Quichua, S Amer. group of languages incl. those spoken in parts of Peru, Ecuador, Bolivia, Argentina. Language of the Incas was member of this group.

Queen Anne's lace, wild carrot, *Daucus carota,* annual or biennial plant, common form of cultivated carrot.

Queen Anne's War *see* SPANISH SUCCESSION, WAR OF.

Queen Charlotte Islands, Canadian archipelago, off coast of British Columbia, in Pacific Ocean. Area: 3,780 sq. mi. Largest islands, Graham and Moresby. Lumbering, fishing, cattle-raising are chief occupations.

Qumran

Queen Elizabeth Islands, Arctic archipelago off the coast of northern Canada. Includes Ellesmere, Devon, Bathurst. Has valuable oil deposits.

Queens, borough of New York City, US. Settled by Dutch (1635); became N.Y. borough 1898. Indust. area. Contains La Guardia and John F. Kennedy International airports. Pop. (1960) 1,809,578.

Queen's Counsel, King's Counsel, in Brit. law, senior barrister [England] or advocate [Scotland] appointed by Lord Chancellor. Takes precedence over junior barristers. Wears silk gown, hence expression 'take silk'.

Queen's Evidence [UK], **State's Evidence** [US], in law, evidence given by accomplice in crime on behalf of the prosecution. If verified may be accompanied by witness's acquittal.

Queensberry, John Sholto Douglas, 8th Marquess of (1844–1900), Scot. nobleman and sportsman whose **Queensberry Rules** (1865) govern modern boxing.

Queensland, state of NE Australia. Area: 667,000 sq. mi.; cap. Brisbane. Great Dividing Range separates coastal strip and central plains. Economy based on agriculture; crops include sugar, fruit, cotton, wheat. Mineral resources, copper, bauxite and oil. Became Brit. colony (1859); joined Commonwealth of Australia (1901). Pop. (1967) 1,701,623.

Queenston Heights, Battle of, decisive confrontation in War of 1812 in which the Americans were defeated by British at Queenston Heights, S Ontario, Canada.

Quemoy and **Matsu,** islands off coast of China, in E China Sea. Held by Chinese Nationalists since 1949.

Queneau, Raymond (1903–), Fr. novelist and poet. Works include novels *Le Chiendent* (1933), *Zazie dans le Métro* (1959) and poems *Cent mille milliards de Poèmes* (1961).

Quesnay, François (1694–1774), Fr. economist and physician. Chief work, *Tableau Économique* (1758), advocated govt. according to natural order. *See* PHYSIOCRATS.

quetzal, quezal, *Pharomacrus mocino,* brilliantly plumaged bird of SE Mexico and C America. National emblem of Guatemala.

Quezon, Manuel Luis (1878–1944), Filipino statesman. Crusaded for independence while Pres. of Philippine senate (1916–35); 1st Pres. of Commonwealth of the Philippines (1935–44).

Quezon City, cap. of the Repub. of the Philippines, on Luzon Island. Replaced Manila as cap. (1948). Named

after Pres. Manuel Quezon. Pop. (1965) 482,400.

Quiberon, peninsula of Brittany, NW France, on Bay of Biscay. Scene of Brit. naval victory over France (1759) in Seven Years War, and abortive Royalist invasion (1795).

quicksand, bed of loose, fine sand particles made unstable by saturation with water; found near river mouths, along sea shores and in some glacial deposits.

quicksilver *see* MERCURY.

Quidde, Ludwig (1858–1941), Ger. pacifist and historian. Imprisoned after publication of *Caligula* (1894), portrait of Emperor William II. With F. E. Buisson, awarded Nobel Peace Prize (1927).

quietism, form of Christian mysticism which holds that union with God is achieved through complete passivity of the soul. Founded (1675) by Sp. priest Molinos. Condemned by Pope Innocent XI (1687).

Quiller-Couch, Sir Arthur Thomas (1863–1944), Eng. writer. Edited *Oxford Book of English Verse* (1900). Under Pseudonym 'Q', wrote novels, *Splendid Spur* (1889), *Hetty Wesley* (1903).

quillwort, any of several aquatic plants of genus *Isoëtes*. Has clustered quill-like leaves.

quince, *Cydonia vulgaris,* small tree or shrub. Bears bitter, yellow, pear-shaped fruit used as a preserve.

quinine, alkaloid substance obtained from cinchona bark. Introduced to Europe from Peru (1639); formerly used in treatment of malaria.

quinsy, acute inflammation of the tonsils, accompanied by formation of abscesses.

Quintilian [Marcus Fabius Quintilianus] (*c.* AD 35–95), Roman rhetorician and teacher. Author of 12-vol. treatise on public speaking *De Institutione oratoria.*

Quirinal, one of 7 hills on which ancient Rome was built. Named after god Quirinus.

Quisling, Vidkun (1887–1945), Norwegian politician. Led Norwegian Fascist Party. Aided Nazi invasion of Norway (1940); made premier by Hitler (1942); shot for treason. Name came to refer to any traitor.

Quito, cap. of Ecuador, at 9,350 ft. in the Cordillera. Educ., cultural and polit. centre. Manufactures textiles, chemicals, metal goods. Has university and cathedral. Pop. (1968 est.) 630,000.

Qumran, region of Jordan, on NW shore of Dead Sea. Site of caves in which 1st DEAD SEA SCROLLS were discovered.

R

Rabat, seaport and cap. of Morocco, admin. centre and king's residence; on Atlantic Ocean 60 mi. N of Casablanca. Pop. (1967) 355,000.

rabbi [Hebrew: master, teacher], Jewish religious leader. Now usually refers to those professionally trained and ordained by other rabbis.

rabbit, *Oryctolagus cuniculus,* burrowing, gregarious European rodent. Naturalized in Australia and N America. A prolific and serious pest of farmland. Domestic varieties include long-haired angora. Some bred for fur. Name also applied to native N Amer. cottontail, *Sylvilagus.*

Rabelais, François (*c.* 1490–1553), Fr. writer, monk and teacher of medicine. *La Vie Inestimable de Gargantua* (1532) and *Faits et Dits Héroiques du Grand Pantagruel* (1533) are satiric allegories full of ribald humour and philosophy.

Rabi, Isidor Isaac (1898–   ), Amer. physicist, b. Austria. Awarded Nobel Prize for Physics (1944) for work on magnetic properties of atomic nuclei.

rabies, hydrophobia, fatal disease of animals causing paralysis of muscles, incl. throat, diaphragm and heart. Transferred to man by bite from infected animal, esp. dog.

raccoon, racoon, Amer. nocturnal, omnivorous mammal of genus *Procyon.* Immerses all food in water before eating. Species include common racoon, *P. lotor,* and crab-eating racoon, *P. cancrivorous.*

race, in anthropology, botany and zoology, term for groups of persons, plants or animals having related characteristic physical qualities.

racerunner, *Cnemidophorus sexlineatus,* N Amer. whiptail lizard; noted for its speed.

Rachel, in OT, younger daughter of Laban, and favourite wife of Jacob. Mother of 2 of Jacob's sons, Joseph and Benjamin.

Rachmaninov, Sergei Vassilievich (1873–1943), Russ. pianist and composer. Left Russia (1917) and lived mainly in America. Composed esp.

for piano; also operas, symphonies and songs.

racial discrimination, individual or collective prejudice based on doctrine asserting superiority of one race over another. Its practice as national policy by South Africa and Rhodesia has brought much criticism, resulting in measures such as UN-sponsored economic sanctions.

Racine, Jean Baptiste (1639–99), Fr. classical dramatist. His tragedies include *Andromaque* (1668); *Iphigénie* (1674) and *Phèdre* (1677); religious plays include *Athalie* (1691).

racism, basis of ideology of RACIAL DISCRIMINATION. Manifested in practice of segregation, *e.g.* colour bar, discrimination by whites against other groups in employment, housing, *etc.*

rackets, racquets, game played on enclosed courts by 2 or 4 persons. Ball is struck against end-wall. Squash rackets is a variant.

radar, process of locating distant objects by radio waves. Sir Robert Watson-Watt developed military applications leading to use for marine and aerial navigation, weather forecasting, *etc.*

Radcliffe, Ann (1764–1823), Eng. novelist. Books in 'Gothic' pseudohist. style include *The Mysteries of Udolpho* (1794), *The Italian* (1797).

Radcliffe-Brown, Alfred Reginald (1881–1955), pioneer Eng. anthropologist. Carried out fieldwork in Andaman Is. and Western Australia.

Raddall, Thomas Head (1903–   ), Canadian author. Hist. novels, esp. about Nova Scotia, include *His Majesty's Yankees* (1942), *Roger Sudden* (1944).

Radek, Karl (1885–1939), Soviet polit. leader and journalist. Active in Ger. Socialist politics, joined (1914) Communist party. Became (1920) Sec. of Comintern, leading advocate of world revolution. Imprisoned during Stalin's 1936 purges.

Radetzky von Radetz, Joseph Wenzel, Count (1766–1858), Austrian army officer. Commanded army which defeated Sardinians (1848, 1849) and captured Venice (1849).

Radhakrishnan, Sir Sarvepalli (1888–   ), Indian philosopher and statesman. Leader of the Indian delegation to UNESCO (1946–52). Indian ambassador to the USSR (1949–52). President of Republic of India (1962–7).

radiation, emission and transmission

Raccoon

Radar: high frequency radio pulses transmitted through an antenna echo back from any object in their path and are picked up again by the antenna. A receiver then converts the pulses into a visible image on the radar screen. 1. antenna 2. receiver 3. screen 4. transmitter 5. object 6. reflected impulses

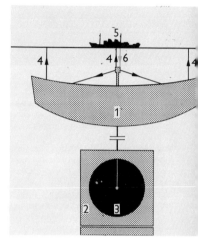

of energy in wave form. Visible light, ultra-violet rays, X-RAYS, radio waves and gamma rays are all forms of electro-magnetic radiation travelling on different wave lengths through space. Term also applied to emission of particles from radioactive substances. *See* RADIOACTIVITY.

radiation sickness, disease resulting from exposure to uncontrolled RADIATION esp. from nuclear weapon. Effects include serious blood damage and genetic impairment.

radicals, in chemistry, group formed of 2 or more elements which maintain identity in chem. changes but cannot exist independently.

Radiguet, Raymond (1903–23), Fr. novelist. Wrote *The Devil in the Flesh* (1923) and *Le Bal du Comte d'Orgel* (1924).

radio, transmission of signals by means of electro-magnetic radio waves. Maxwell postulated their existence (1873); Hertz demonstrated them (*c.* 1886). Marconi 1st demonstrated method of communication (1895).

radioactivity, disintegration of atomic nuclei of certain chemical elements, said to be radioactive, *e.g.* radium, uranium, thorium, actinium, into alpha or beta particles with or without emission of electro-magnetic radiation (gamma or X-RAYS). In nuclear

Rain clouds

Water Rail

reactors any element may be made radioactive. These artificial elements, isotopes, are used in medicine, metallurgy, *etc.*

radioastronomy, branch of astronomy dealing with long-wave radio emissions from outer space. Noted 1st by Jansky (1932). Emission sources include bodies too distant for optical observation as well as non-luminous or dark stars, and larger bodies in solar system incl. Sun, Jupiter, *etc.*

radiolarian, minute marine protozoan of order Radiolaria. Silicate skeleton important in formation of flint on ocean bed.

radiology, use of RADIATION in diagnosis and treatment of disease. X-rays are used to photograph living bone and tissue and also to destroy abnormal (*e.g.* cancer) cells.

radish, *Raphanus sativus,* plant native to Europe and Asia. Fleshy root eaten raw as relish.

radium, naturally occurring radioactive element; product of URANIUM decay. Identified as source of radiation, and 1st isolated as pure salt by Marie Curie (1902). Formerly used to treat cancer, now replaced by radiocobalt.

Radnorshire, county of E central Wales. Area: 471 sq. mi.; county town, New Radnor. Largely mountainous, includes Radnor Forest, moorland where sheep and cattle are raised. Pop. (1966) 18,000.

Raeburn, Sir Henry (1756–1823), Scot. painter. Works mainly portraits of contemporaries.

Raffles, Sir [Thomas] Stamford (1781–1826), Eng. colonial administrator. Instrumental in capture of Java from Dutch (1811). Lieutenant-Gov. (1811–15) of Java, consolidated East India Co. holdings. Secured Singapore (1819).

ragged robin, cuckoo flower, *Lychnis*

flos-cuculi, slender perennial herb native to Europe and N Asia. Has pink flowers, ragged-looking petals.

Raglan, FitzRoy James Henry Somerset, 1st Baron (1788–1855), Brit. army officer, commanded forces during Crimean War. Victorious at Inkerman (1854), subsequently criticized for failure at Sevastopol.

ragtime, style of dance music using syncopated rhythms, introduced *c.* 1910. Originated by Amer. Negroes as forerunner of jazz.

ragweed, any plant of genus *Ambrosia* native to N America. Pollen of common ragweed or hogweed, *A. artemisifolia,* and great ragweed, *A. trifida,* causes asthma, hay fever.

ragworm, anglers' term for various aquatic worms. Widely used as bait.

ragwort, any species of genus *Senecio. S. jacobaea,* weed of Eurasia and W Africa, often poisonous to livestock.

Rahman, Tunku Abdul (1903–), P.M. of Malaysia (1963–70).

Raikes, Robert (1735–1811), Eng. philanthropist. Estab. 1st Sunday School at Bristol (1780).

rail, bird of Ralidae family, found in most regions. Nocturnal marsh bird, species include corncrake, water rail, coot and moorhen.

railway [UK], **railroad** [US], transport system running on fixed rails. Rolling stock orig. horse-drawn until development of steam LOCOMOTIVE. Stockton-Darlington line 1st to regularly carry passengers in England. In US, 1st transcontinental railroad was Union Pacific (completed 1869). In 20th cent., steam has given way to electric and diesel power.

Leo X with Two Cardinals by Raphael

In most countries railways have played important part in making large areas accessible. Faster and safer trains continually being developed to counter increasing popularity and availability of air travel.

Raimu, Jules, orig. Jules Muraire (1883–1946), Fr. comedian and actor. Films include *Marius* and *Un Carnet de Bal.*

rain, drops of condensed water vapour in clouds, heavy enough to fall. Cyclonic rain is associated with passage of CYCLONE. Artificial production of rain has been achieved by sprinkling clouds with silver iodide particles.

rainbow, arch of colours seen in sky. Occurs when sunlight through raindrops separates white light into spectrum colours (as in PRISM).

Raine, Kathleen (1908–), Eng. poet. Converted to Roman Catholicism (1944). Poetry includes *Stone and Flower* (1943), *The Pythoness* (1949).

rainfall zones, climatological areas tabulated according to annual rainfall. Desert is usually defined as having less than 10 in. Monsoon-type rainfall yields over 100 in. annually in parts of Indonesia and SE Asia.

Rainier III, Prince Louis Maxence Bertrand (1923–), Prince of Monaco. Succeeded his grandfather (1949).

Rainier, Mount, peak (14,408 ft.) of Cascade Range, Washington, US. Has 26 glaciers and is centre of Mt. Rainier National Park.

raised beach, strip of level land, formerly beach, now well above sea level due to land rising or sea level falling.

raisin, dried, ripe fruit of certain

varieties of white grape used for dessert, cooking or wine-making. *See* CURRANT.

Rajasthan, state of India with desert in NE, and mountains to SE. Area: 132,152 sq. mi.; cap. Jaipur. Occupations agriculture, cattle raising. Formed 1948; small areas added 1956. Pop. (1961) 20,155,602.

Rajputs, Hindu land-owning warrior caste of N India. Dominant from 7th cent., conquered by British, 19th cent. Since independence of India, Rajput principalities merged in RAJASTHAN state.

Rakaposhi, peak (25,550 ft.) and range of Kashmir, N India.

Rakoczy, noble Hungarian family, princes of Transylvania. **George I** (reigned 1630–48) allied himself with Swedes and French in invading Austria; **Francis II** (1676–1735) led Hungarian uprising against Habsburgs (1703); defeated and exiled (1708).

Raleigh, Sir Walter (*c.* 1552–1618), Eng. courtier, explorer and writer. Favourite of Elizabeth I; attempted (1584–7) to estab. colony 'Virginia' on ROANOKE ISLAND. Introduced potato and tobacco to Europe. On accession of James I, condemned to death for treason; reprieved, wrote *History of the World* while prisoner in Tower of London. After failure of expedition to Orinoco R., executed.

Ramadan, in Moslem calendar, fasting month. Commemorates 1st revelation of the Koran. Devout Moslems abstain from food and drink during daylight hours.

Ramakrishna (1836–86), Hindu mystic. Rejected quietism and preached active benevolence. Followers included SWAMI VIVEKANANDA.

Raman, Sir Chandrasekhara Venkata, FRS (1888–1970), Indian physicist. Awarded Nobel Prize for Physics (1930) for discovery of Raman effect. Investigated molecular diffraction of light and physics of crystals.

Rambert, Dame Marie, orig. Myriam Ramberg (1888–   ), Eng. dancer and ballet mistress, b. Poland. Member of Diaghilev's Russian Ballet Co. (1912–13); founder and director of Rambert Ballet School, London (1920–   ).

Rambouillet, Catherine de Vivonne-Pisani, Marquise de (1588–1665), Fr. society hostess. Presided over literary gatherings of distinguished authors incl. Mme de Sévigné, Descartes and Bossuet.

Rameau, Jean Philippe (1683–1764), Fr. composer and organist. Works include ballets and operas. His *Traité de l'Harmonie* (1722) is basis of modern musical theory.

Rameses or **Ramses [II] the Great** (d. 1225 BC), king of Egypt (1292–1225 BC). Reign marked by protracted war against the Hittites and impressive building programme, incl. temple at Abu Simbel, Ramesseum at Thebes. **Rameses III** (d. 1167 BC) waged wars in Syria and N Africa; reign marked by excessive luxury.

ramie, China grass, *Boehmeria nivea,* perennial plant of nettle family, of SE Asia. Cultivated for strong, silky fibre.

Ramillies, Battle of, victory (1706) in C Belgium, for Eng. and Austrian forces under Duke of Marlborough over French and Bavarians under Villeroi. Led to Allied capture of Fr. strongholds in Low Countries.

Ramón y Cajal, Santiago (1852–1934), Sp. histologist. With Camillo Golgi, awarded Nobel Prize for Physiology and Medicine (1906) for work on nervous system.

rampion, *Campanula rapunculus,* European plant with white, edible roots used in salads.

Ramsay, Allan (1686–1758), Scot. poet. Best known work is pastoral comedy *The Gentle Shepherd* (1725).

Ramsay, Sir William (1852–1916), Scot chemist. Awarded Nobel Prize for Chemistry (1904) for discovery of helium and other inert gases.

ramsons, *Allium ursinum,* garlic with broad leaves. Bulbous root used as seasoning.

Randolph, Edmund (1753–1813), Amer. statesman. Advocated large states. US Attorney General (1789–94), Sec. of State (1794–5).

Rangoon, cap. and major port of Burma, on Rangoon R. Centre of rice-producing region. Exports rice, oil, teak. Industries include dyeing, shipbuilding. University founded 1920. Pop. (1964) 1,530,000.

Ranke, Leopold von (1795–1886), Ger. historian, pioneer of modern, objective approach to history. His survey of world history, *Weltgeschichte* (1881–8) completed after his death.

Ransom, John Crowe (1888–   ), Amer. poet and critic. Founder and editor of *Kenyon Review*. Published *Selected Poems* (1945).

Rapallo, Treaty of, agreement (1922) between Germany and USSR, estab. trade agreements and cancelling war claims. Enabled Germany to develop weapons secretly in Russia.

rape, several plants of genus *Brassica,* esp. *B. napus* and *B. campestris* of Europe, Asia and America. Grown extensively for forage. Seeds yield edible oil.

Raphael [Raffaello Santi or **Sanzio]** (1483–1520), Ital. Renaissance painter and architect. Early works include *The Three Graces.* In Florence, painted *The Entombment* and several Madonnas (for which he is esp. noted), showing influence of Leonardo. Later worked in Rome where he executed tapestries, murals and portraits. Considered one of most influential painters in history of art.

Raphael, in OT, an archangel. Appears in the *Book of Tobit.*

rare earths, rare mineral substances,

Madonna del Granduca by Raphael

oxides of certain metals, orig. thought to be elements.

Rasmussen, Knud Johan Viktor (1879–1933), Danish explorer and ethnologist. Propounded theory that Greenland Eskimos and N Amer. Indians were of same Asian stock.

raspberry, perennial or biennial herb of genus *Rubus* of rose family. Grown in temp. regions for fruit. European *R. idaeus* and N Amer. and Asian *R. strigosus* yield red fruit; black raspberries from *R. occidentalis*.

Rasputin, Grigori Yefimovich (1872–1916), Russ. monk. Exerted great polit. influence at court of Nicholas II, whose haemophilic son he allegedly cured. Assassinated (1916) by group of noblemen.

rat, rodent of almost world-wide distribution, esp. brown rat, *Rattus norvegicus,* and black rat, *R. rattus.* Spreads disease and causes damage to crops, property, *etc.*

ratel, nocturnal carnivorous mammal of genus *Mellivora.* Grey pelt above and black below. Species include S African *M. capensis* and Indian *M. indica.*

rationalism, in philosophy, any theory which rejects faith, intuition, *etc.* in favour of reason. Term esp. used to refer to 17th–18th cent. philosophical movement led by Descartes, Spinoza, Locke.

rat-tail cactus, *Aporocactus flagelliformis,* common trop. Amer. cactus. Slender stems; crimson flowers.

rattan, climbing palms of genera *Calamus* and *Daemonothops* of trop. Asia. Long stems from which rattan (malacca) cane is obtained; used for baskets, chairs, walking sticks.

Rattigan, Terence Mervyn (1911–), Eng. dramatist. Works include *The Browning Version* (1948), *Separate Tables* (1954).

rattle, annual plant of genus *Rhinanthus*; when ripe, seeds rattle in their inflated capsule. Yellow rattle, *R. crista-galli,* of N temp. regions has yellow purple-spotted flowers. Red rattle, or European lousewort, *Pedicularis palustris,* has pink flowers.

rattlesnake, venomous Amer. snake of pit viper group; loose, horny tail segments 'rattle' when shaken. Produces living young. Diamondback,

Crotalus adamanteus, is largest and most dangerous.

Rauschenberg, Robert (1925–), Amer. 'pop' artist. Leading exponent of movement using popular imagery and strip-cartoon material.

Ravel, Maurice Joseph (1875–1937), Fr. composer. Piano pieces include *Valses Nobles et Sentimentales*; for orchestra *Bolero*; ballet *Daphnis and Chloe.*

raven, *Corvus corax,* large black bird of crow family of N hemisphere. Glossy black plumage and sharp pointed bill; hoarse croaking call.

Ravenna, city of Emilia, N Italy, a Roman port; cap. of W Roman Empire (AD 404–493). Has Byzantine mosaics in mausoleum of Galla Placidia and church of San Vitale. Pop. (1957) 90,800.

Rawalpindi, industrial city of NE West Pakistan. Interim cap. of Repub. of Pakistan while Islamabad (new cap.) being built. Pop. (1961) 340,000.

Rawlinson, Sir Henry Creswicke (1810–95), Eng. army officer, administrator and linguist. Deciphered cuneiform inscription of Darius from Behistun.

Rawsthorne, Alan (1905–71), Eng. composer. Works include *Variations for 2 Violins* (1938), piano and violin concertos, symphonies and ballet *Madame Chrysanthème.*

ray, marine disc-shaped fish related to shark. Atlantic electric ray, *Tetranarce occidentalis,* up to 6 ft. long, can inflict severe electric shock. Species include common sting ray, *Dasyatis pastinaca,* and devil ray, *Manta birostris,* found esp. in Gulf of Mexico.

ray, in physics, straight line along which light or other RADIATION is propagated from its source. Also

applied to streams of particles such as electrons emitted from cathode or substance exhibiting RADIOACTIVITY.

Rayleigh, John William Strutt, 3rd Baron (1842–1919), Brit. physicist. Discoverer, with Sir William Ramsay, of gas argon (1894). Awarded Nobel Prize for Physics (1904) for work on sound and light.

rayon, synthetic fibre made of cellulose or fabric woven from it. First made (1889) by Fr. scientist Hilaire de Chardonnet.

Razin, Stenka (d. 1671), Cossack leader and folk hero. Rebelled against tsar. After brief successes, was defeated and executed.

razorbill, razor-billed auk, *Alca torda,* seabird of auk family, of N Atlantic coasts. Plumage black above and white below; sharp black bill with white band.

razorshell, marine bivalve mollusc of family Solenidae. Has long, narrow, curved, thin shell.

Read, Sir Herbert (1893–1968), Eng. art historian, literary critic and poet. Author of *The Meaning of Art* (1931) and *The Philosophy of Modern Art* (1952).

Reade, Charles (1814–84), Eng. novelist and dramatist. Wrote series of propagandist novels, incl. *It's Never Too Late to Mend* (1856). Best known for medieval romance *The Cloister and the Hearth* (1861).

realgar, orange-red crystalline mineral, source of arsenic. Found esp. around hot springs and volcanoes.

realism 1) in philosophy, claim that universal concepts exist independently of individual objects; leading exponent Thomas Aquinas. 2) in painting, the representation of accurate detail (as in work of Rembrandt). 3) in literature, the presentation of

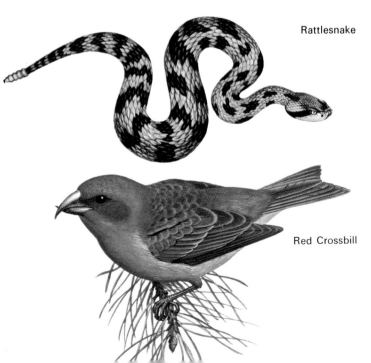

Rattlesnake

Red Crossbill

Electric Ray

things as they are, without abandoning symbolism (*e.g.* Galsworthy, Chekhov).

Reaney, James (1926–), Canadian poet. Works include *The Red Heart* (1949), *A Suit of Nettles* (1958).

Réaumur, René Antoine Ferchault de (1683–1757), Fr. physicist and zoologist. Inventor of thermometer (1731) and improved method of iron manufacture. Author of 6 vol. study of insects (1734–42).

Rebecca, Rebekah, in OT, wife of Isaac, mother of Esau and Jacob. Helped Jacob to secure Esau's birthright (*Gen.* xxiv; xxvii).

Rebellion of 1837, short-lived uprising in Upper and Lower Canada protesting Brit. admin. policies in Canada. Insurgents advocated office holders be elected rather than appointed by Crown. Most of leaders, incl. W. L. MACKENZIE and L. J. PAPINEAU, escaped to US; returned safely under Amnesty Act, 1849.

Recife, formerly Pernambuco, port and cap. of Pernambuco prov., Brazil, founded 1548. University founded 1946. Exports sugar, coffee, cotton, rum. Pop. (1960) 797,000.

recitative, musical declamation intermediate between singing and ordinary speech. Used with simple orchestral accompaniment in opera and oratorio and in church music.

reclamation, process whereby land is won for cultivation. Methods include drainage, *e.g.* Netherlands; irrigation and hill-terracing, *e.g.* Mediterranean areas and SE Asia.

Reconstruction, term applied to US post-Civil War era, during which programme adopted to reorganize defeated states. Congressional Republicans opposed pres. plan to restore civil govt. To enforce Negro

enfranchisement in South, Reconstruction Act passed (1867) by Congress estab. 5 military districts. Structure broke down as South overrun by CARPETBAGGERS. Civil govt. restored by 1876.

recorder, in England, barrister of 5-yr. standing, appointed by Crown in certain cities and boroughs as judge of quarter sessions. In most US states county recorders elected to record deeds, *etc.*

recorder, wind instrument of flute type. Blown from end through whistle mouthpiece; usual sizes are soprano, tenor and bass.

rector, in Church of England, formerly clergyman who received parish tithes. In Protestant Episcopal Church and Scot. Episcopal Church minister in charge of parish.

rectum, in anatomy, terminal part of intestine opening to exterior by anus.

red algae, *Rhodophra,* group of reddish marine plants. Mostly found in depths of warm oceans.

red ant, several large European and Amer. ants.

Red Army [**Worker-Peasant Red Army**], official name (1918–46) of Soviet Army. Set up to combat White Armies of royalist forces after Bolshevik seizure of power (1917).

red bug, cotton stainer, stout red insect of India and US. Feeds on plants, esp. cotton, staining the cotton bolls.

red campion, *Melandrium dioicum,* herb of family Caryophyllaceae with clusters of large rose-pink flowers. Common in Britain, Europe and Asia.

red cardinal, *Richmondena cardinalis,* N Amer. tufted song bird of finch family. Brilliant red underparts, dark red back, black around beak.

red cardinal, brilliant red flower of N Amer. herb, *Lobelia cardinalis.*

Red Cross *see* INTERNATIONAL RED CROSS COMMITTEE.

red crossbill, *Loxia curvirostra,* gregarious woodland bird of N Europe. Upper and lower beak mandibles cross one another. Feeds on pine cones which it shreds.

red deer, *Cervus elaphus,* large red deer of temp. Europe and Asia. Branched antlers, reddish coat with light tail patch.

Red Guard, Chinese Communist youth organization, mobilized (Aug. 1966) by Mao Tse-tung to enforce 'cultural revolution'. Violent methods used in subsequent purge of Mao's opponents led to indust. strikes (1966–7) and decline in Red Guard's importance.

red letter days, main festivals in church calendar. Some calendars denote holy days in red script.

red panda, lesser panda, *Ailurus fulgens,* rare arboreal, herbivorous mammal of E Himalayas. Reddish-brown, with black and white face, long bushy tail.

Red River, important W trib. (1,300 mi. long) of Mississippi R., US. Upper reaches form Texas-Oklahoma boundary.

Red River Rebellion (1869–70), revolt by Métis (Fr. half-breeds) led by LOUIS RIEL after transfer of Red R. Settlement from Hudson's Bay Co. to

Red Deer

Red-necked Grebe

Redshank

Red-breasted Goose

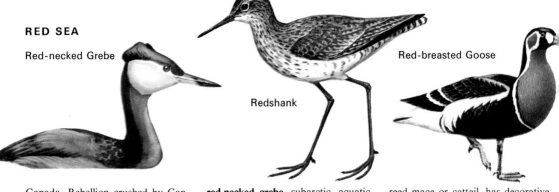

Reindeer

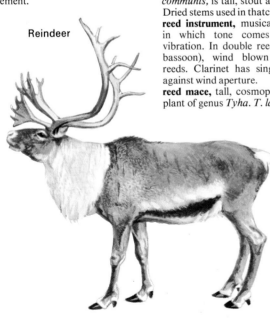

Canada. Rebellion crushed by Canadian troops.

Red Sea, narrow sea, almost landlocked, between Africa and Arabia, *c.* 1,400 mi. long. Linked with Med. Sea by Suez Canal since 1869.

red underwing, *Catocala nupta,* large moth with 2 red bars on underwings. Caterpillars feed on willows, poplars.

red-backed sandpiper, dunlin, *Caladris alpina,* common European and N Amer. shore wading bird. Nests in sub-Arctic marsh and moorland.

redbreasted goose, *Branta ruficollis,* Siberian goose with chestnut front. Inhabits coastal tundra regions.

Redgrave, Sir Michael Scudamore (1908–), Eng. stage and film actor. Noted for interpretations of Shakespeare and Chekhov. Films include *The Lady Vanishes, The Quiet American, Oh What a Lovely War.*

red-hot poker, herb of genus *Kniphofia,* native to S Africa. Bright red or orange poker-shaped flowers. *K. uvaria* is garden species.

Redi, Francesco (*c.* 1626–97), Ital. scientist. Helped disprove Aristotelian theory of spontaneous generation of living organisms.

Redmond, John Edward (1856– 1918), Irish politician. Moderate advocate of Home Rule, led post-Parnell Nationalists in Brit. Parl. Lost support with rise of Sinn Fein movement.

red-necked grebe, subarctic, aquatic bird of Europe and America, incl. Holboell's grebe and European grebe. Reddish neck and underparts.

Redon, Odilon (1840–1916), Fr. painter. Later surrealist artists influenced by his symbolic and mystical themes.

redpoll, *Acanthis flammea,* small grey-brown songbird related to finch. Male has red crown, rosy breast.

redshank, *Tringa totanus,* wading bird, related to sandpiper, of Eurasia and N Africa. Long red legs.

redstart, small, brightly coloured songbird of Eurasia and Americas. Species include *Phoenicurus phoenicurus,* related to thrush, and *Setophaga ruticilla,* flycatcher related to wood warbler.

reduction, chem. reaction opposite to oxidation. Orig. denoted removal of oxygen content of substance; now includes reactions adding one or more electrons to molecule or atom, increasing negative VALENCE.

redwing, *Turdus musicus,* smallest European thrush. Rust-red flanks, whitish eye-bands.

redwood *see* SEQUOIA.

Reed, Walter (1851–1902), Amer. army surgeon, proved (1900) that mosquito germs cause yellow fever. Army hospital, Washington D.C., named after him.

reed, any of several grasses. Cosmopolitan common reed, *Phragmites communis,* is tall, stout aquatic grass. Dried stems used in thatching.

reed instrument, musical instrument in which tone comes from reed vibration. In double reed (*e.g.* oboe, bassoon), wind blown between 2 reeds. Clarinet has single reed laid against wind aperture.

reed mace, tall, cosmopolitan marsh plant of genus *Tyha. T. latifolia,* great

reed mace or cattail, has decorative, spiky flowers.

reed warbler, small European songbird, *Acrocephalus scirpaceus.* Inhabits reed beds, *etc.*

reedbuck, *Redunca redunca,* yellowish-red African antelope. Male has black curving horns.

reel, traditional Scot., Irish and Scandinavian dance using set figures.

referendum *see* PLEBISCITE.

refinery, establishment where products (*e.g.* metals, petroleum, sugar) are refined.

reflexes, actions not under voluntary control. Result from stimulation of a sensory nerve. Conditioned reflexes, formed through association of particular stimulus with specific result, are basis of habit formation and learning.

Reform Bill of 1832, in Eng. history, passed by Earl Grey's Whig govt.; redistributed seats in interest of larger communities; gave franchise to middle-class men.

Reformation, religious revolution in W Europe in 16th cent. Began as reform movement in R.C. Church, evolved into doctrines of Protestantism. Begun in Germany by MARTIN LUTHER and in Geneva by JOHN CALVIN. JOHN KNOX introduced Calvinism to Scotland. Spread of Reformation also furthered by church-state polit. conflict and rise of middle class and commerce. In England, Henry VIII rejected papal control and formed Church of England.

refraction, in physics, change in direction of a ray of light passing from one medium to another. Thus a stick partially immersed in water appears bent at point of immersion.

refrigeration, reduction of temperature below that of atmosphere. Process involves alternative expansion (heating) and contraction (cooling) of air, ammonia, sulphur dioxide or carbon dioxide. Important for food preservation and in surgery.

Regency, in Brit. history, last 9 yr. (1811–20) of reign of George III. Because of king's periodic insanity, govt. conducted in name of Prince of

Wales, later George IV. Period of much literary and artistic activity.

regeneration, regrowth or restoration of damaged tissue. In higher mammals, incl. man, healing of wounds. In crabs, lizards *etc.* entire new shells or skins can grow.

Regensburg, Ratisbon, city of Bavaria, Germany, on R. Danube. River port and communications centre. Cathedral (12th cent.) and notable medieval churches. Pop. 125,000.

Regina, provincial cap., S Saskatchewan, Canada, founded 1882. Cap. of North West Territories (1883–1905). Trade and rly. centre; industries include oil refining, motor car assembly, meat packing, steel works, printing. Pop. (1961) 112,141.

Regulus, Marcus Atilius (d. *c.* 250 BC), Roman soldier. One of commanders in First Punic War, captured by Carthaginians. Sent to Rome to propose peace, but advised continuation of war; returned as promised to Carthage, put to death.

Rehoboam, Hebrew king (*c.* 932–913 BC), son of SOLOMON, under whom N tribes rebelled, forming new kingdom of Israel under Jeroboam I. Judah and part of Benjamin remaining loyal to Rehoboam, formed S kingdom of Judah.

Reichstag, formerly lower chamber of federal Ger. parl. (1871–1945). Under Hitler regime only National Socialist party represented; function being ratification of govt. decisions. Replaced (1949) by Bundestag.

Reichstein, Tadeus (1897–   ), Swiss chemist. Shared Nobel Prize for Physiology and Medicine (1950) with P. S. Hench and E. C. Kendall for work on adrenal functions and on chemistry of cortisone.

Reign of Terror (1793–4), final period of Fr. Revolution. Committee of Public Safety, led by ROBESPIERRE, controlled France; effected ruthless elimination of counter-revolutionaries (*c.* 2,500 guillotined). Ended by Convention, 27 July (9 Thermidor).

Reims *see* RHEIMS.

reincarnation, metempsychosis, belief common to many Eastern religions that after death, soul of a human being enters another body, human or animal.

reindeer, large deer of genus *Rangifer* of Arctic regions of Europe, N America and Asia. Both sexes have long branched antlers. Valued for milk, flesh and skins. Caribou is related species.

reindeer moss, lichen of genus *Cladonia*. Grey, tufted *C. rangiferina*

of Arctic and N regions eaten by reindeer and caribou.

Reinhardt, Max (1873–1943), Austrian theatrical producer and innovator. Made Salzburg Festival world theatrical festival after World War 1. Produced plays in Germany, Vienna, London and New York.

relativity, theory formulated (1905) by EINSTEIN to systematize concepts of space and time. Postulated that all laws of nature are independent of the uniform relative motion of the observers, and that light has the same velocity for all observers in uniform motion. Further, mass and energy are equivalent and interchangeable, and physical realities can be represented mathematically but not visualized. Led to concept of 4-dimensional space-time continuum.

religion, expression of belief in powers higher than man; held to deliberately influence course of human life. Often takes form of attempt to explain origin and nature of universe, and purpose of life. Also practice of rites based on such beliefs. Nature of rites determined by structure of society. Ethical concepts introduced by BUDDHISM, JUDAISM, CHRISTIANITY, ISLAM.

The Cyclops by Redon

Religion, Wars of, general term for series of civil wars (1562–98) in France. Orig. struggle between Protestants (Huguenots) and Catholics; developed into struggle for power between Henry IV and nobility and among the nobles themselves. Peace estab. (1598) by Edict of Nantes.

reliquary, container for keeping or exhibiting relics. Frequently a casket or shrine.

relocation camps, in US history, 10 centres in W states, to which people of Jap. ancestry were moved during World War 2.

Remarque, Erich Maria, orig. Erich Paul Remarck (1897–1970), Amer. novelist and critic, b. Germany.

Redwing

Portrait of Jan Six by Rembrandt

Works include *All Quiet on the Western Front* (1929), *The Night in Lisbon* (1964).

Rembrandt, orig. Rembrandt Harmenszoon van Rijn (1607– 69), Dutch painter. Became popular portrait painter in Amsterdam. Led reaction against Ital. classicism; developed interest in realism, esp. portraits and scenes from life, *e.g. Anatomy Lesson of Dr Tulp* (1632), *Portrait of an Old Woman.* Religious works include *The Woman Taken in Adultery.*

Remus *see* ROMULUS.

Renaissance [Fr: rebirth], period (14th– 16th cent.) of cultural and intellectual revival, originating in Italy, and spreading throughout Europe. Strong classical influence combined with original artistic, literary, and scientific work. Marked end of medieval church dominance. Among the important figures were Leonardo da Vinci, Michaelangelo, Machiavelli, Erasmus, Shakespeare, Cervantes, Rabelais.

Renaissance art, characteristic styles esp. in painting, sculpture and architecture, associated with Renaissance humanist thought and classical inspiration. In Italy, epitomized in work of Masaccio, Brunelleschi, Donatello, Michaelangelo, Raphael, Leonardo da Vinci and Titian.

Renault, Jean Louis (1843– 1918), Fr. jurist. Member of International Court of Arbitration at The Hague (1907). With E. T. Moneta, awarded Nobel Peace Prize (1907).

Renfrewshire, maritime county of SW Scotland, on estuary of R. Clyde. Area: 236 sq. mi.; county town, Renfrew; main towns, Paisley, Greenock. Agric. area; shipbuilding, sugar refining, thread and cotton manufacturing. Pop. (1966) 355,000.

rennet, substance containing gastric juices, incl. rennin which curdles milk; obtained from stomach of unweaned calf. Mainly used in cheese-making.

Renoir, Jean (1894–), Fr. film producer and writer, son of Auguste Renoir. Films include *La Grande Illusion, La Règle du Jeu, Le Déjeuner sur l'Herbe.* Author of *Renoir, my Father* (1962).

Renoir, [Pierre] Auguste (1841– 1919), Fr. impressionist painter and sculptor. Work includes café scenes, bathers and nudes.

rent, in law, payment required of a tenant for use of another's property. In economics, incorporates income and yields from possessions capable of producing profit (*e.g.* tools, machinery, land).

reparations, payment made by defeated nation to victorious, to compensate for material losses incurred in war. After World War 1, Dawes Plan (1924) awarded loan to Germany which had fallen behind in payments to Allies. Young Plan (1929) sought to ensure payment by mortgaging Ger. rlys. and estab. Bank for International Settlements. After World War 2, payment by Germany to Allies was to be effected by confiscation of assets and equipment.

Representatives, House of *see* HOUSE OF REPRESENTATIVES.

reproduction, process by which living things perpetuate own species by production of new individuals. May be sexual or asexual. Asexual reproduction found in plants and lower animals; simplest form is by division of single cell. Sexual reproduction involves union of 2 cells.

reptile, cold-blooded terrestrial or aquatic vertebrate with scaly skin. Oviparous and generally carnivorous. Dominant animal group in Mesozoic period. Groups include turtles, tortoises, tuatara, lizards, snakes and crocodiles.

republic, state in which sovereignty vested in electorate through representatives. Gk. and Roman republics had smaller electorates than modern republics. Govt. of repub. may be centralized (*e.g.* France) or federated (*e.g.* US).

Republican Party, one of 2 major US polit. organizations. Founded (1854) in opposition to slavery, consolidated with election (1860) of Abraham Lincoln. Held power during RECONSTRUCTION. Championed business interests during late 19th cent. Split (1912) when T. ROOSEVELT left party. Blamed for 1929 Depression, Party out of office (except for Eisenhower admin., 1953–61) until 1968 election of Richard Nixon as Pres.

requiem, in R.C. Church, Mass (Dies Irae) sung for the souls of the dead. Mozart, Verdi and others have set requiems to music but the Gregorian setting is most often used in churches.

resin, substance exuded from various plants, esp. pines and firs; used in varnish, shellac, lacquer and medicines. Synthetic resins used extensively in plastics industry.

resistance, partisan guerilla movements formed in occupied countries. Aim to embarrass conquerors by

Detail from *Le Moulin de la Galette* by Renoir

sabotaging indust. production, communications, *etc.*

Resnais, Alain (1922–), Fr. film director associated with NOUVELLE VAGUE. Films include *Hiroshima, mon amour* (1959) and *Last Year at Marienbad* (1961).

Respighi, Ottorino (1879–1936), Ital. composer, pianist and conductor. Works include operas, ballets and orchestral suites, incl. *Fontane di Roma.*

respiration, process by which living organism takes in air or dissolved gases, uses them to produce energy and expels by-products and unused portion. Both animals and plants use oxygen and expel carbon dioxide. In sunlight green plants form starch from carbon dioxide and expel oxygen by photosynthesis.

restharrow, *Ononis spinosa,* leguminous Eurasian shrub with pink flowers. Strong roots hinder plough or harrow.

Restif de la Bretonne, Nicolas Edmé (1734–1806), Fr. writer. Works include novel *Le Paysan Perverti* (1755), autobiog. *Monsieur Nicolas* and *Les Nuits de Paris* (1786–93).

Restoration, in Eng. history, re-estab. of monarchy on accession of Charles II (1660).

Restoration, in Fr. history, period of Bourbon rule, reigns of Louis XVIII and Charles X, from abdication of Napoleon I (1814) to July Revolution (1830). Excluded return of Napoleon I (Hundred Days).

Restoration drama, name given to 2 types of play popular in England in 17th cent. The heroic play, partly inspired by Fr. classical tragedy (Dryden *Conquest of Granada*) and witty, often immoral comedies of manners (Wycherley *The Country Wife*; Congreve *The Way of the World*).

resurrection, rising from death to life again. Used esp. for rising of Christ after crucifixion and for the rising of all the dead at end of world.

Retail Price Maintenance, effort of Brit. govt. to curb rise of cost of living index by regulation of retail prices. Introduced 1964.

retina, membrane lining cavity of eyeball, acting as receiving surface for light rays. Nerve endings (rods and cones) transmit impulses to visual centre of brain through optic nerve.

retriever, any of several breeds of dog, trained to retrieve game, with coarse, thick and oily coat. Common breeds include golden retriever and labrador.

Retz or **Rais, Gilles de Laval, Seigneur de** (1404–40), Breton marshal of France in Hundred Years War. Executed after confessing to kidnapping and torture of children.

Réunion, formerly Bourbon, island in Indian Ocean. Overseas department of France. Area: 969 sq. mi.; cap. St Denis. Pop. (1960 est.) 330,000.

Reuter, Paul Julius de, Baron, orig. Israel Beer Josaphat (1816–99), Ger. news agency pioneer. Founded

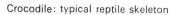

Crocodile: typical reptile skeleton

The 15th century Street of the Knights in Rhodes

Reykjavik

Agency 1849. Now world service for news collection and propagation with reputation of unbiased accuracy.

Reuther, Walter Philip (1907–70), Amer. labour leader. Top posts included vice-pres. Amer. Federation of Labor-Congress of Indust. Organizations (1955–67).

Revelation, apocalyptic book of NT, possibly written by St John the Evangelist. Describes struggle in which Christ and the Church are finally victorious over evil.

Revelstoke, Mount, national park in British Columbia, Canada. Area: 100 sq. mi.

Revere, Paul (1735–1818), Amer. silversmith and patriot. Famous for ride (Apr. 1775) into Massachusetts to warn of advance of Brit. troops at outbreak of Revolution.

Revolution of 1848, series of revolts in W and C Europe, provoked by Feb. Revolution in France. Caused by economic effects of crop failures (1846–7) and liberal, nationalist and socialist discontent. Louis-Philippe overthrown, 2nd Repub. estab. In Germany, popular uprising quelled by Prussian army. Metternich ousted in Austria, but order restored. Initial success of Risorgimento in Italy ended in failure.

revolver, small firearm developed by Samuel Colt (1835) from pistol. Cartridges, contained in revolving chambered cylinder, may be discharged without reloading.

Reykjavik, cap., chief port and trade centre of Iceland. Built near hot springs producing natural heat and hot water supplies. Exports fish products. Pop. (1964) 87,000.

Reynolds, Sir Joshua (1723–92), Brit. portrait and historical painter. A founder and 1st Pres. (1768) of Royal Academy. Published *Discourses* (annual addresses to Royal Academy) influential in art criticism.

Rhadamanthus, in Gk. myth., son of Zeus and Europa. Became judge of the dead in Underworld.

rhapsody, in music, single movement instrumental piece, often based on existing themes.

rhea, large flightless gregarious S Amer. bird, similar to ostrich. Species include common rhea, *R. americana.*

Rheims, Reims, city of Marne department, N France. Founded in pre-Roman times; scene of coronation of Fr. kings from 496. Cathedral dates from 13th cent. Modern centre of champagne trade and woollen industry. Pop. (1962) 144,000.

rheostat, instrument introduced into electrical circuit to vary resistance and control flow of current.

rhesus factor (Rh factor), inherited sex-linked ingredient of human blood. Identified (1940) in blood of rhesus monkey. Union between one partner with Rh factor and one without tends to produce antibodies which can cause obstetric complications.

rhesus monkey, *Macaca mulata,* light brown, stockily built SE Asian monkey. Sacred in parts of India, a pest in others. Used in medical research.

rhetoric, formal discipline or art of communication in words, based on organization of accumulated knowledge. Based on doctrine formulated by Aristotle.

rheumatic fever, acute rheumatoid condition causing migratory arthritis and often involving heart.

rheumatoid arthritis, condition of unknown cause, characterized by extreme pain affecting fingers and wrists, swelling of joints. Tends to be progressive, causing deformities in affected limbs.

Rhine, major European river system. Flows from Swiss Alps through West Germany. Navigable to Basle. Linked by canal with Danube, Rhone, Marne, Ems, Weser, Elbe. Ports include Strasbourg, Mannheim, Cologne, Duisburg, Rotterdam. Enters North Sea through distributaries Waal, Lek.

Rhine, Confederation of the, union of Ger. princes (1806–13) set up by Napoleon. Members disavowed allegiance to Holy Roman Emperor. States included Bavaria, Saxony, Westphalia.

Rhine Province, former Prussian prov. of SW Germany. Included Saar, Rhine and Moselle valley vineyards. Chief city was Cologne. Now divided into RHINELAND–PALATINATE and NORTH RHINE-WESTPHALIA.

Rhineland-Palatinate [**Rheinland-Pfalz**], state of West Germany orig. organized (1946) under Fr. occupation. Formerly known as Rhenish or Lower Palatinate. Area: 7,656 sq. mi.; cap. Mainz; other cities, Coblenz, Ludwigshaven, Trier. Agriculture (esp. wine) and tourism important. Pop. (1961) 3,417,000.

rhinestone, colourless artificial stone usually cut to resemble diamond.

rhinitis, inflammation of mucous membrane of nose. Dust, fumes or bacteria are common causes.

rhinoceros, massive herbivorous thick-skinned ungulate mammal with 1 or 2 horns composed of matted hair. Largest is African white rhino, *Rhinoceros simus.*

rhinoceros beetle, *Dynastes tityus,* scarab beetle of E US. Male has rhinoceros-like horn on head.

rhizopod, minute animal of protozoa group incl. AMOEBA.

Rhode Island, New England state, one of 13 orig. states of US. Area: 1,214 sq. mi.; cap. Providence. Founded (1636) by religious dissenters from Massachusetts, became state 1790. Highly industrialized. Pop. (1960) 859,488.

Rhodes, Cecil John (1853–1902), Brit. administrator and financier. Made fortune from diamond and gold mining (Kimberley and Transvaal). P.M. of Cape Colony (1890–6).

Organized Brit. annexation of Bechuanaland and obtained mining concessions in Mashonaland and Matabeleland (nucleus of Rhodesia). Criticism of Jameson raid forced resignation as P.M. Left endowment for scholarships to Oxford.

Rhodes [Rhodos], largest island of Gk. Dodecanese group. Area: 537 sq. mi.; cap. Rhodes. Settled by Dorians (1000 BC). Site of Colossus (built 280 BC). After conquests by Romans, Seljuk Turks, Crusaders, Ottoman Turks, finally ceded to Greece (1947). Pop. (1961) 63,951.

Rhodesia, self-governing Brit. colony of C Africa. Area: 150,333 sq. mi.; cap. Salisbury; towns, Bulawayo, Umtali. Formerly Southern Rhodesia, part of FEDERATION OF RHODESIA AND NYASALAND (1953–63). After dissolution, Rhodesia made Unilateral Declaration of Independence (1965), regarded as illegal by UK. Population of African Negro descent ruled by European minority. Predominantly agric., exports tobacco and grain. Pop. (1965) 4,330,000.

Rhodesia, Northern see ZAMBIA.

Rhodesia and Nyasaland, Federation of (also called **Central African Federation**), union of former Brit. colony Southern Rhodesia and protectorates of Northern Rhodesia and Nyasaland (1953–63). On dissolution Southern Rhodesia reverted to colonial status as Rhodesia; Northern Rhodesia became Zambia (1964), and Nyasaland Malawi (1966).

Rice Plant

rhodium (Rh), silvery metallic element. Resists corrosion, used in making thermocouples and in electroplating. Discovered (1807).

rhododendron, genus of evergreen shrubs native to temp. regions of N hemisphere. Cultivated for red, pink, purple and white flowers.

Rhodope Mountains, wooded mountain range of Greek-Bulgarian border. Highest peak, Musala (9,595 ft.).

Rhône, river (505 mi. long) rising in Switzerland, flows through L. Geneva to S France. Joined at Lyon by Saône, enters Med. Sea through delta.

rhubarb, *Rheum hybridum,* perennial plant cultivated for edible reddish stalks. Leaves contain poison.

rhyme, rime, identity or similarity of speech sounds. Used in poetry esp. at line endings to form audible patterns.

Rhymer, Thomas the or **Thomas of Erceldoune** (fl. c. 1220) Scot. poet and seer. Said to have predicted death of Alexander III, and Battle of Bannockburn. Reputed author of a poem on the Tristram story.

rhythm, pattern produced by relative stress and duration of sounds in music and language.

rib, 1 of paired curved bones forming bony cage in vertebrates protecting thoracic cavity.

Ribbentrop, Joachim von (1893–1946), Ger. Nazi leader. Foreign Min. (1938–45), influential in forming German-Soviet pact (1939). Tried as war criminal and executed.

ribbon snake, *Thamnophis sauritus,* viviparous snake of N America, with yellow or orange stripes.

ribbon worm, carnivorous worm with elongated body. Mostly found in shallow water.

ribbonfish, common name for deep-sea fish of family Trachipteridae. Long laterally compressed bodies, dorsal fin extends the whole length of the back.

Ribera, Jusepe (c. 1590–c. 1652), Sp. painter. Depicted austere subjects realistically, *e.g. Martyrdom of St Bartholomew.*

riboflavin, lactoflavin, vitamin B present in respiratory enzymes. Occurs in milk, yeast. Deficiency causes skin lesions and corneal damage to eyes. Sources include green vegetables, milk, eggs and liver.

ribonucleic acid (RNA) see NUCLEIC ACID.

Ricardo, David (1772–1823), Brit. economist. Founded 19th cent. school of classical political economy and set out theory correlating rent, profit, wages and taxation, in *The Principles of Political Economy and Taxation* (1817).

African Rhinoceros in a nature reserve

Rice, Elmer (1892–1967), Amer. playwright and novelist. Among works are *On Trial* (1914), *Counsellor-at-Law* (1931).

rice, dressed grain of the cereal grass *Oryza sativa.* Grown extensively in trop. and sub-trop. climates in Asia as staple food, also cultivated in America, Europe and Africa.

rice paper, smooth, white paper used by Chinese artists for painting. Made from rice-straw or other plants.

Rich, Claudius James (1787–1820), Brit. antiquarian. Travelled widely in Asia, had mastery of many Eastern languages. Oriental collections now in British Museum.

Richard [I] Lion Heart (1157–99), king of England (1189–99). Rebelled against Henry II. Went on Third Crusade (1190) with Philip II of France. Imprisoned in Germany 1192, ransomed 1194. Fought Philip in France, killed at Châlus.

Richard II (1366–1400), king of England (1377–99), son of Edward the Black Prince. Reign marked by heavy taxation and uprisings, esp. Peasants' Revolt (1381). Estab. absolute power of monarchy after murder of Thomas Woodstock, Duke of Gloucester, leader of baronial party (1397). Forced to abdicate by cousin, Henry of Bolingbroke, later Henry IV.

Richard III (1452–85), king of England (1483–5), brother of Edward IV. Usurped throne from nephew Edward V; defeated and killed at battle of Bosworth Field (1485) by Duke of Richmond, later Henry VII. Death of Richard ended WARS OF THE ROSES.

Rhinoceros Beetle

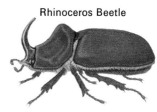

Rio de Janeiro

Richard, [Joseph Henri] Maurice (1921–), Canadian ice hockey player, known as 'Rocket' Richard. Estab. many goal-scoring records while with Montreal Canadians team (1942–60).

Richards, I[vor] A[rmstrong] (1893–), Eng. literary critic. Author of *The Meaning of Meaning* (with C. K. Ogden, 1923), *Principles of Literary Criticism* (1924).

Richardson, Dorothy Miller (1873–1957), Eng. novelist. Author of *Pilgrimage* (12 vols., 1915–38). Pioneer of 'inner monologue' narrative method.

Richardson, John (1796–1852), Canadian author. Works, largely historical, include poems and frontier romances.

Richardson, Sir Owen Willans (1879–1959), Brit. physicist. Awarded Nobel Prize for Physics (1928) for formulation of Richardson's Law of motions of electrons emanating from hot bodies.

Richardson, Sir Ralph David (1902–), Eng. stage and film actor. Roles include Henry IV, Cyrano de Bergerac. Among his films are *Anna Karenina, Long Day's Journey Into Night, The Looking Glass War*.

Richardson, Samuel (1689–1761), Eng. writer. Master of epistolary narrative and one of founders of novel form. Most notable works are *Pamela* (1740) and *Clarissa* (1748).

Richelieu, Armand Jean du Plessis, Duc de (1585–1642), Fr. cardinal and statesman. Created (1624) chief min. to Louis XIII with help of Marie de Medici, whom he had exiled (1630). Gave Fr. monarchy absolute basis, suppressed Huguenots, capturing La Rochelle (1628). Intrigued in THIRTY YEARS WAR to thwart Habsburg ambitions in Germany. Founded Fr. Academy.

Richler, Mordecai (1931–), Canadian writer. Novels reflect ironic view of society's 'outsiders'. Best known novel is *The Apprenticeship of Duddy Kravitz* (1959).

Richmond, Sir Ian Archibald (1902–65), Brit. archaeologist. Known for work on Roman Britain, *e.g.* excavation of Hadrian's Wall. Among works are *The City Wall of Imperial Rome* (1930) and *Roman Britain* (1955).

Richmond, state cap. and river port of Virginia, US; laid out 1737. Was confederate cap. (1861–5). Large tobacco marketing and processing centre; manufactures cottons, fertilizers, foods. Pop. (1963) 333,438.

Richter, Johann Paul Friedrich (1763-1825), Ger. writer. Wrote under name Jean Paul. Novels deeply philosophical in character, *e.g. Quintus Fixlein, Siebenkäs, The Titan*. Influenced Ger. Romantic School.

Richthofen, Manfred von (1892–1918), Ger. ace fighter pilot of World War 1 (known as the Red Baron). Brought down more Fr. and Brit. aircraft than any other aviator. Killed over the Somme.

Rickenbacker, Edward Vernon (1890–), Amer. aviator, hero of World War 1. Chairman of Eastern Air Lines (1953–63).

rickets, rachitis, disease caused by vitamin D deficiency, affecting calcium metabolism and causing softening of bones. Treated with vitamin D.

Rickover, Hyman G[eorge] (1900–), Amer. naval officer. Instrumental in production of 1st atomic powered vessel, submarine *Nautilus*.

rickshaw, light, two-wheeled hooded vehicle drawn by 1 or 2 men.

Ridgway, Matthew B[unker] (1895–), Amer. army officer. Commander in World War 2 (1942–4) and Korea (1950–1); US and UN commander in Far East (1951–2), led Allied powers in Europe (1952–3), chief of staff (1953–5).

Riding Mountain National Park, recreation area and game reserve of Manitoba, Canada. Area: 1,148 sq. mi. Estab. 1929.

Ridley, Nicholas (*c.* 1500–55), Eng. priest and Protestant martyr. Participated (1548) in compilation of Book of Common Prayer. Excommunicated as heretic by Mary Tudor (1553); convicted at 2nd trial (1555), burned at stake with Latimer.

Riel, Louis (1844–85), Canadian revolutionary. Led revolt of Métis (half-breeds) after Canada's acquisition of Red River Settlement, culminating in RED RIVER REBELLION (1869–70). Led unsuccessful North West Rebellion (1884–5).

Riemann, Georg Friedrich Bernhard (1826–66), Ger. mathematician. Noted for discoveries in non-Euclidean geometry and work on theory of complex variables.

Rienzi or **Rienzo, Cola di** (*c.* 1313–54), Roman leader. Papal notary for Clement VI at Avignon, returned to Rome assuming title of tribune (1347). Aimed at Ital. state unified under Roman leadership. Violent and arbitrary rule resulted in assassination.

Riesman, David, Jr. (1909–), Amer. writer and sociologist. Author with others of *The Lonely Crowd* (1950).

Rif, Er Rif, mountain range of N Morocco extending *c.* 180 mi. along Med. coast. Berber inhabitants revolted (1921) against Spain, but suppressed by Sp. and Fr. forces (1926).

rifle, firearm with grooved barrel fired from shoulder level.

rift, in geography, valley formed by sinking of land between 2 more or less parallel faults. Examples include Rhine valley above Wiesbaden and Great Rift Valley of E Africa and Near East, extending over 3,000 mi.

Riga, major sea port and cap. of Latvian SSR in W Soviet Union on W Dvina R. Belonged to Poland (1582,

Sweden (1621), incorporated into Russ. empire (1710). Exports flax, timber, dairy produce; industries include food processing, timber, textiles, metal goods, chemicals. Pop. (1967) 666,000.

Rigaud, Hyacinthe François (1659–1743), Fr. portrait painter. From 1688 official court painter.

right of way, right of public under certain circumstances to pass over private property. In US also refers to land over which public utility, *e.g.* electric power line, passes.

right whale, whalebone whale of genera *Balaena* and *Eubalaena* of polar waters. Grey to black in colour; may reach 50–60 ft. in length, *e.g.* Greenland right whale, *B. mysticetus.*

Rights, Bill of (1689), in Brit. history important stage in constitutional development. Gave inviolable civil and political rights to the people, political supremacy to Parliament, and made it impossible for an R.C. sovereign to succeed to Brit. throne.

Rights, Bill of see CONSTITUTION OF UNITED STATES.

Rights of Man, Declaration of the, historic Fr. document, drafted by Sieyès (1789), became preamble of Fr. constitution of 1791. Influenced by Rousseau, it asserted equality of all men, sovereignty of the people, inalienable rights of the individual to 'liberty, property, security'.

rigor mortis [Lat: stiffness of death], rigidity of muscles and body occurring (depending on atmospheric conditions and state of body) usually 1 or 2 hr. after death. Ended by beginning of decomposition after *c.* 24 hr.

Rig-Veda, oldest of the 4 collections of the Veda, or Hindu scriptures. Consists of 1,028 hymns in Sanskrit.

Riis, Jacob August (1849–1914), Danish-Amer. writer and pioneer sociologist. Author of *How the Other Half Lives* (1890), a study of New York's working classes.

Rijeka, Rieka, seaport of N Yugoslavia, also known as Fiume. Manufacturing centre. Claimed by both Yugoslavia and Italy (1918–47),

ceded to Yugoslavia 1947. Pop. (1967 est.) 100,400.

Rijks or **Ryks Museum,** state gallery in Amsterdam, estab. 1808. Noted for collections of 17th cent. Dutch painters, esp. Rembrandt.

Rilke, Rainer Maria (1875–1926), Austrian mystic poet and novelist. Works include lyrical prayer-book *Stundenbuch* (1905), semi-autobiog. novel *Notebooks of Malte Laurids Brigge* (1910).

Rimbaud, [Jean Nicholas] Arthur (1854–91), Fr. symbolist poet. Stopped writing at 19 at end of close relationship with VERLAINE. Best known poem 'Le Bateau Ivre'. *Une Saison en Enfer* (1873) recalls his adolescence.

Rimini, seaport of C Italy, on Adriatic Sea. Popular summer resort. Orig. site of Roman town. Pop. (1967 est.) 81,000.

Rimsky-Korsakov, Nicolai Andreyevich (1844–1908), Russ. musician, member of nationalist group of composers 'the Five'. Most popular works *Flight of the Bumblebee* and orchestral suite *Scheherezade.*

rinderpest, cattle plague, acute, infectious disease of cattle, sheep, *etc.* Symptoms, high fever and lesions of skin and mucous membrane.

ring dove, *Columba palumbus,* European pigeon with whitish patch on each side of neck. Also Old World dove, *Streptopelia risoria,* with black half ring round nape of neck.

ring ouzel, *Turdus torquatus,* European thrush. Black plumage with white chest.

ring-necked pheasant, *Phasianus colchicus,* Chinese variety of the common pheasant with white neck ring.

ring-necked snake, small non-venomous N Amer. snake of genus *Diadophis.* Usually has yellow or orange neck ring.

ringworm, contagious disease of the skin, hair or nails of man and domestic animals. Caused by fungi of genera *Microsporon* and *Trichoplyton;* characterized by formation of

River Hog

ring-shaped eruptive patches. Between fingers and toes often called athlete's foot.

Rio de Janeiro, major port and industrial centre of Brazil, cap. of Tuanabara state. Cap. of Brazil (1763–1960). Industries include textiles, meat processing, tourism. Explored by Portuguese (1502), Fr. Huguenot colony (1555–67). Harbour dominated by Sugar Loaf Mt. Pop. (1965) 3,800,000.

Rio Grande, river of N America. 1,800 mi. long. Rises in Rocky Mts., flows into Gulf of Mexico. Part of it forms Mexico-Texas border. Known as Rio Bravo del Norte in Mexico.

Rio Muni see SPANISH GUINEA.

Ripon, Earl of see ROBINSON, FREDERICK JOHN, VISCOUNT GODERICH.

Risorgimento [Ital: resurgence], period of Ital. unification in 19th cent. Nationalist hopes disappointed by Congress of Vienna (1814–15), secret societies organized against Austrian domination; group sponsored by Sardinian royal house ultimately successful under Cavour. Despite failure of 1848–9 insurrections, Sardinia conquered most of Italy (1859–60), aided by GARIBALDI. Kingdom of Italy proclaimed 1861. Unification completed (1870) with annexation of Papal States.

river, large natural stream of fresh water draining supply water from land into lakes or seas via natural channel.

river hog, African wild pig of genus *Potamochoerus.* Inhabits trop. forests; brownish red with black markings on face and legs.

Rivera, Diego (1886–1957), Mexican artist. Influenced by Cézanne, Picasso

The Tempio Malatestiano, Rimini

La Conquista by Diego Rivera

and Communist ideology while in Europe. Designed Anahuacalli Museum in Mexico City.

Riverina, fertile district of New South Wales, Australia. Extensively irrigated.

Rivers, Larry (1923–), Amer. painter. Contributor to 'pop' art movement, esp. with work *George Washington crossing the Delaware.*

Riviera, coastal strip of land in France, Italy and Spain, bordering Med. Sea. Noted for coastal scenery, hot, dry climate and beach resorts.

Riyadh, Riad, cap. of Saudi Arabia, in an oasis in C Arabian plateau. Centre of desert transportation and trade. Pop. (1963) 170,000.

Rizzio, David (*c.* 1533–66), Ital.

Rocket Larkspur

musician, secretary to Mary Queen of Scots. Murdered, as suspected lover of queen, by Lord Darnley.

RNA *see* NUCLEIC ACIDS.

roach, *Rutilus rutilus,* silver white freshwater fish of carp family common in N Europe. Similar fish, golden shiner, *Notemigonus cryoleucas,* found in E North America.

road, man-made semi-permanent route-way for wheeled vehicles; 1st developed by Romans. Constructed by building solid foundation with hardwearing surface of packed earth, stones, cobbles, concrete, *etc.*

roadrunner, chaparral cock, *Geococcyx californianus,* bird resembling the cuckoo, of SW US. Poor flier; runs with great speed.

Roanoke Island, small island near Albemarle Sound, North Carolina, US. First Eng. colony in America, estab. (1587) by Sir Walter Raleigh.

Roaring Forties, areas of oceans 40°–50° N or S of equator, named from typical strong W winds.

Rob Roy, orig. Robert Macgregor (1671–1734), Scot. outlaw who lived by cattle-stealing. Imprisoned 1717. After pardon (1727) became lawful citizen.

Robbe-Grillet, Alain (1922–), Fr. novelist and film script writer. Works observe events, but avoid psychological analysis; include novel *Dans le Labyrinth* (1959) and film *L'Année dernière à Marienbad* (1961).

robber crab, purse crab, *Birgus latro,* large coconut-eating land crab of trop. islands of Indian and Pacific Oceans.

robber fly, large hairy predaceous fly of family Asilidae. Austral. *Phallus glaucus* (2 in. long) largest species.

Robbia, Luca della (1400–82), Florentine sculptor, founder of a workshop continued by his sons. Famous for *faience* or *terra-cotta* madonnas.

Robert [I] the Bruce (1274–1329), king of Scotland (1306–29). Led Scots in struggle for independence. Defeated Edward II at Bannockburn (1314). In legend, learnt courage and hope in hiding by watching spider spinning its web.

Roberts, Sir Charles George Douglas (1860–1943), Canadian writer. His poetry, esp. *Orion and Other Poems* (1880) influenced younger writers. Also known for nature stories.

Roberts, Frederick Sleigh, 1st Earl Roberts of Kandahar (1832–1914), Brit. army officer. Conducted successful campaign (1879) against Afghans, subsequently commanded Indian army (1885–93). Commander-in-chief (1899–1900) during South African War.

Robertson, Sir William Robert (1860-1933), Brit. soldier. First to rise from the ranks to field marshal (1920).

Roberval, Jean François de la Rocque, Sieur de (*c.* 1500–60), Fr. noble. Sent by Francis I to colonize E Canada with courtiers and ex-prisoners (1542). Venture failed, returned to France.

Robeson, Paul (1898–), Amer. singer and actor. Leading interpreter of Negro spirituals; stage roles include Othello. Denied US passport (1950–8) for left-wing polit. affiliation.

Robespierre, Maximilien Marie Isidore (1758–94), Fr. revolutionary. Jacobin leader, member of Committee of Public Safety (1793–4). Chief instigator of REIGN OF TERROR, ousted rivals Hébert and Danton. Exercised dictatorial powers after estab. supremacy of Revolutionary Tribunal, but overthrown by Convention; tried and guillotined.

robin, *Erithacus rubecula,* songbird of

thrush family found in Europe and W Asia. Brownish black plumage with orange-red face and breast. Amer. robin, *Turdus migratorius,* is larger, with white-streaked throat and cinnamon coloured breast.

Robin Hood, legendary hero of medieval England. A chivalrous outlaw, he lived in Sherwood Forest with Little John, Friar Tuck, Maid Marion and his band, robbing the rich to help the poor.

Robinson, E[dwin] A[rlington] (1869–1935), Amer. poet. Known for portraits of New England characters (*e.g.* 'Miniver Cheevy') and long narrative *The Man against the Sky* (1916).

Robinson, Frederick John, Viscount Goderich (1782–1859), Eng. statesman. Tory Chanc. of the Exchequer (1823–7), P.M. (1827–8) after Canning's death. Created (1833) Earl of Ripon.

Robinson, Jack Roosevelt (1919–), Amer. baseball player. Joined Brooklyn Dodgers (1947), becoming 1st Negro to play major league baseball.

Robinson, ('Sugar') Ray, orig. Walker Smith (1921–), Amer. boxer. Welterweight champion (1946–51); middleweight champion (1951–2, 1955–7, 1958–60).

Robinson, [William] Heath (1872–1944), Brit. cartoonist. Noted for comic drawings illustrating impracticable machinery.

robot, mechanical device constructed to perform human tasks. Term 1st used by Karel Capek in play *RUR* (*Rossum's Universal Robots*). Examples include automatic steering devices, electronic calculators.

Robsart, Amy (1532–60), maiden name of wife of Robert Dudley, Earl of Leicester. Her mysterious death rumoured to have been arranged by Dudley, a favourite of Elizabeth I.

Robson, Mount, highest peak (12,972 ft.) in Canadian Rocky Mts. Part of Mt. Robson Prov. Park, E Brit. Columbia.

Rochambeau, Jean Baptiste Donatien de Vimeur, Comte de (1725–1807), Fr. army officer. Joined (1780) patriots in Amer. Revolution, helped Washington plan Yorktown campaign (1781). Resigned (1792) command of Northern Army during Fr. Revolutionary Wars.

Rochelle, La, city and cap. of Charente-Maritime department, W France. Huguenots' final stronghold, fell to Richelieu after siege (1627–8). Prospered as Atlantic port (17th cent.) for Canada. Pop. (1962) 66,190.

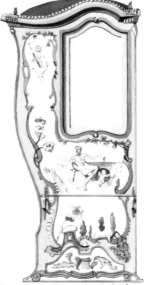

Rococo style section of 18th century carriage

Rochester, 2nd Earl of see WILMOT, JOHN.

Rochester, city of NW New York, US, port on Barge Canal. Manufactures photographic equipment. Settled 1812. Pop. (1960) 493,000.

rock, solid mass of mineral materials forming Earth's crust. Major classifications: 1) igneous, formed from cooling of molten matter (*e.g.* granite); 2) sedimentary, comprises breakdown products of older rock, as in sandstone, shale (also see STRATIFICATION); 3) metamorphic, formed by heat or pressure change (*e.g.* slate, gneiss, marble).

rock crystal, variety of coarsely crystalline quartz, transparent and colourless.

rock dove, *Columba livia,* European pigeon from which most domestic pigeons have been developed.

rock salt see HALITE.

Rockefeller, John Davison (1839– 1937), Amer. industrialist. Built family enterprise, controlled US oil-refining industry through ownership of Standard Oil Co. Philanthropic endeavours included founding of University of Chicago (1892) and estab. of Rockefeller Foundation. His grandson, **Nelson Aldrich Rockefeller** (1908–), held series of top govt. posts before election (1958) as Republican Gov. of New York.

Rockefeller Foundation, trust (estab. 1913) by John D. Rockefeller to subsidize scientific research and promote public health.

rocket, projectile powered by engine ejecting stream of hot gases. Fuel process does not require oxygen from Earth's atmosphere, making possible use in outer space. Forerunner of modern rocket developed (11th cent.) by Chinese.

rocket, rocket salad, biennial or perennial plant of genus *Hesperis,* native to Med. region and Asia. White or purple flowers. Species include dame's rocket, *H. matronalis.*

rocket larkspur, *Delphinium ajacis,* cultivated annual larkspur of S Europe. Flowers range from blue to pink.

Rockingham, 2nd Marquis of see WATSON-WENTWORTH, CHARLES.

Rockne, Knute Kenneth (1888– 1931), Amer. football coach. Led University of Notre Dame to five undefeated seasons.

Rocky Mountain National Park, mountainous region in N Colorado US. Area: 406 sq. mi. Estab. 1915 as national park.

Rocky Mountain sheep see BIGHORN.

Rocky Mountain spotted fever, disease caused by *Rickettsia* transmitted by ticks. Characterized by high fever, pains in joints and muscles, and rash. First found in Rocky Mountain area, now more widely distributed.

Rocky Mountains, range of mountains of W North America, extending from Alaska through Canada to SW US. Many peaks exceed 14,000 ft. in height. Forms continental watershed. Separated from coastal ranges by depressions. Many National Parks (*e.g.* Glacier, Yellowstone).

rococo, ornamental architectural and decorative style. Originated in early 18th cent. France. Characterized by heavy ornamentation, esp. use of curves and scrolls.

Rocroi, orig. Croix-de-Rau, town of Ardennes department, N France. Scene of defeat of Sp. troops by French under Louis II de Condé.

rodent, gnawing mammal of order Rodentia, incl. mouse, rat, squirrel, beaver, porcupine, guinea pig. Mainly terrestrial or burrowing.

Rodgers, Richard Charles (1902–), Amer. composer of musicals. Collaborated with Lorenz Hart (*Pal Joey*) and Oscar Hammerstein (*The King and I, The Sound of Music*).

Rodin, Auguste (1840–1917), Fr. sculptor. Noted for bronze portrayals of human form, or portions of it. Best known sculptures *The Thinker, The Kiss, The Burghers of Calais.*

Rodney, George Brydges, 1st Baron (1719–92), Brit. naval officer. Defeated Sp. squadron at Cape St Vincent (1780). Drove Fr. fleet from the Atlantic (1782).

roedeer, *Capreolus capreolus,* Eurasian deer. Greyish brown; male has 3-pointed antlers. Mainly nocturnal, inhabiting woodlands.

Roethke, Theodore (1908–63), Amer. poet. Wrote poems of simple but strict form, others of more surrealistic form. Volumes of poetry include *Open House* (1941).

Rogation Days, 4 days in R.C. Calendar (25 Apr. and 3 days

Robespierre by Jean Michel Moreau

The Rocky Mountains, Glacier National Park

Baths in villa at Volubilis, showing Roman domestic architecture

preceding Ascension Day) observed by processions asking God's mercy. Custom is adaptation of Roman pagan ceremony seeking blessing for crops.

Roget, Peter Mark (1779– 1869), Eng. philologist. His *Thesaurus of English Words and Phrases* (1852), remains standard reference book.

Rohan, Henri, Duc de (1579– 1638), Fr. army officer. Led (1627– 9) Huguenot opposition to Richelieu, who later chose him to command Fr. army in Grisons (1635). Killed while fighting for Protestants in Germany.

Roland (d. 778), Fr. hero of medieval legend and of 11th cent. epic *Chanson de Roland*, oldest extant *chanson de geste*. In history, soldier of Charlemagne's army, killed in Pyrenees.

Rolland, Romain (1866– 1944), Fr. author and musicologist. Works include 10-vol. novel *Jean Christophe* (1904– 12), drama *Les Loups* (1898), and biography *Beethoven* (1903).

Renaissance: *Tempietto*, San Pietro in Montorio by Bramante

Awarded Nobel Prize for Literature (1915).

roller, *Coracias garrulus,* European bird related to kingfisher. Noted for aerial acrobatic ability. Also name of canary with trilling song.

Rolls-Royce, Eng. automobile manufacturing company. Founded (1906) by Charles Rolls and Sir Henry Royce. Developed motor car of same name. Also builds aircraft engines.

Romagna, region of N Italy, now part of Emilia-Romagna prov. Incorporated (16th cent.) with Papal States, annexed (1860) by Sardinia. Contains repub. of San Marino.

Romains, Jules, orig. Louis Henri Jean Farigoule (1885–   ), Fr. novelist, a founder of UNANIMISME. Author of satirical farce *Knock* (1923) and cycle of novels *Men of Good Will* (1932– 46).

Roman architecture, orig. modelled on Gk. building, incorporated new types, *e.g.* aqueducts, baths, amphitheatres, with individual features, arch, vault, dome. Greatest period 100 BC– AD 300. Public buildings constructed on principle of splendour and utility; marked by unity of design, solidity and grandeur of decoration, *e.g.* Pantheon (built by Agrippa 27 BC), Colosseum, Baths of Caracalla. Triumphal arches elaborately ornamented. Influence on subsequent architecture largely due to Ital. Renaissance use.

Roman art, in earliest forms influenced by archaic Gk. art, but retained native characteristics, *e.g.* strong colour effects. From 400 BC modelled on classical Gk. art, but with new freshness and vigour, and from 300– 100 BC on Etruscan and Greek. Sculpture at peak 1st– 2nd cent. AD, esp. in portrait busts, bas-reliefs and arches, *e.g.* arch of Titus. Painting mostly used in decoration of interior walls of houses, usually mythological scenes. Gem-engraving, both cameo and intaglio, popular in later republic, developed in empire.

Roman Catholic Church, major division of Christian Church. Main tenets include recognition of pope as spiritual leader of the church, belief in apostolic tradition, conveyance of God's grace through the sacraments. Largest Christian denomination with hundreds of millions of adherents throughout the world. Centre of the Catholic community is the Vatican City, Rome.

Roman law, legal system originating in ancient Rome. First formulated (*c.* 450 BC) as Twelve Tables, codified (AD 529– 35) in *Corpus Juris Civilis* by Tribonian under Justinian I. Its

clarity and comprehensiveness led to incorporation in CODE NAPOLEON and modern European and US legal systems.

Romance, in Middle Ages, narrative poem, orig. Fr. or Provençal, dealing with tales of chivalrous love and adventure.

Romance languages, branch of Italic group of INDO-EUROPEAN LANGUAGES; includes French, Italian, Spanish, Portuguese.

Romanesque, style of architecture and art prevalent (11th– 13th cent.) in Europe. Buildings characterized by thick walls, round arches and, in churches, by *basilica* (Gk: cross) floor plan. Religious art shows Byzantine influence.

Romania, Rumania [Republica Socialistâ România], Balkan state of SE Europe. Area: 91,600 sq. mi.; cap.

Bucharest. Crossed by Transylvanian Alps, Carpathians; chief river, Danube. Agric. products include cereals, beef. Major resources, natural gas, oil, timber, minerals. Recent development of steel and chemicals industries. Orig. populated by Thracian tribe, later under Roman rule. Invaded by Goths, Huns, Turks. Independence from Turkey (1856), kingdom estab. 1881. Annexed (1918) Bessarabia. Entered World War 2 against Russia. Communist take-over of govt. (1947). Main language, Romanian. Unit of currency, lev. Pop. (1963) 19,027,000.

Romanian, Rumanian, Romance Indo-European language, with *c.* 19 million speakers in and around Romania.

Romanov, ruling house of Russia (1613– 1917). Dynasty estab. (1613) by Michael, descendant of Ivan IV. Later tsars (after 1730) were descended through female line. Ceased to rule with execution of Nicholas II during Russ. Revolution.

Romans, epistle of NT, written by St Paul to Christians at Rome (*c.* AD 57). Fundamental statement of Pauline theology; stresses justification by faith and universality of divine love.

Romansch, minor Romance Indo-European language. Approx. half a million speakers in SE Switzerland.

Romanticism, 19th cent. movement in the arts, begun in Europe largely as reaction to late 18th cent. neoclassicism. Characterized by emphasis on imagination, emotion, and

Romanesque fresco of Christ in the church of St Clement at Lérida. Spain

artistic freedom; idealized nature and the past. In literature, led to hist. and Gothic novels, and poetry of *e.g.* Wordsworth, Coleridge, Keats. In painting, brought colourful and sentimental approach. In music, stressed feeling rather than form.

Romany or **Gipsy languages,** group of Indic Indo-European languages, used by gipsies.

Rome, city on Tiber R., C Italy, cap. of Italy. Includes VATICAN CITY. Transport, cultural, tourist centre.

Believed founded (753 BC) by ROMULUS, became centre of Roman Empire. Remains of ancient Rome include Colosseum, Forum; Renaissance churches and palaces, such as St Peter's, Villa Borghese. Incorporated by Italy and became cap. (1871). Pop. (1964) 2,455,000.

Rome, ancient, traditionally founded (753 BC) by Romulus, ruled by Etruscans until *c.* 500 BC, when Repub. founded. Ruled by patrician class, electoral franchise gradually

widened; power vested in consuls and senate. Asserted hegemony over rivals in Italy and successfully challenged (3rd cent. BC) Carthage in PUNIC WARS for Med. domination. Internal discontent countered by territorial gains, culminating (1st cent. BC) in victories of POMPEY and JULIUS CAESAR. Empire, estab. 31 BC by AUGUSTUS, marked by flourishing of arts; remarkable engineering projects; comprehensive admin. to govern extensive dominions, stretching from

The Romanesque cathedral at Pisa. The Leaning Tower of Pisa is in the background

Romanesque cathedral, Worms

Britain to Middle East. Rome rebuilt after great fire (AD 64), many beautiful remains still stand. Decline began late 2nd cent., division between West and East grew with emergence of BYZANTINE EMPIRE. Rome's empire ended (476) with deposition of last emperor.

Rommel, Erwin Eugen Johannes (1891–1944), Ger. army officer, prominent member of Nazi party. Commanded Afrika Korps in Libya (1941–2) where known as 'the desert fox'. Involved in generals' unsuccessful attempt to assassinate Hitler (20 July 1944); committed suicide.

Romney, George (1734–1802), Eng. portrait painter, best known subject being Lady Hamilton.

Romney Marsh, drained marshland on Kent coast, SE England. Area: *c.* 69 sq. mi. Sheep-raising region; historic smuggling centre.

Romulus, legendary founder of Rome (*c.* 753 BC). Son of Mars and Rhea Silvia, daughter of Numitor, king of Alba Longa. With twin brother Remus cast into R. Tiber by Amulius, usurper of Numitor's throne; survived and suckled by she-wolf. Killed Remus in quarrel when building walls of Rome. Procured wives for Roman citizens by rape of Sabine women. Vanished in thunderstorm, worshipped as god Quirinus.

Romulus, Augustulus, last West Roman emperor (AD 475–6); deposed by Odoacer. Assassinated by barbarian mercenaries.

Ronga, Bantic Niger-Congo language. Over 1 million speakers in S Africa.

Ronsard, Pierre de (*c.* 1524–85), Fr. court poet, a founder of the PLÉIADE. Best known for love poetry, incl. *Sonnets pour Hélène* (1578).

Röntgen, Wilhelm Conrad (1843–1923), Ger. physicist. Discoverer of the Röntgen ray or X-RAY (1895). Awarded 1st Nobel Prize for Physics (1901).

rook, *Corvus frugilegus,* gregarious European bird of crow family. Black plumage; nests in colonies.

Rooke, Sir George (1650–1709), Brit. naval officer. Destroyed (1702) Fr. and Sp. fleets at Vigo, helped in defeat of French at Malaga (1704).

Roosevelt, [Anna] Eleanor (1884–1962), Amer. public official and writer, wife of Franklin D. Roosevelt. Strongly supported her husband in his polit. career; worked for social reform. US delegate to UN General Assembly (1945–53, 1961); chairman of UN Commission on Human Rights (1946).

Roosevelt, Franklin D[elano] (1882–1945), 32nd US Pres. (1933–45), Democrat. Unsuccessful Vice Pres. candidate (1920). Stricken with poliomyelitis (1921), achieved partial recovery. Gov. of New York (1929–33), nominated and elected Pres. (1932). Instituted NEW DEAL programme to counteract Depression crisis. Sweeping legislation characterized by greater benefits for labour, agriculture and unemployed. Opposition to policies increased after re-election (1936), failed to reorganize Supreme Court, which had invalidated several New Deal measures. Elected for unprecedented 3rd term (1940), kept US out of World War 2 until Japanese attack on PEARL HARBOR. Meetings with Churchill and Stalin laid basis for post-war Europe. Died shortly after election for 4th term of office.

Roosevelt, Theodore (1858–1919),

26th US Pres. (1901–9), Republican. Popular hero after exploits in Cuba (1898) during Sp.-American War, elected Gov. of New York. Vice Pres. nominee (1900), became Pres. on McKinley's death (1901). Vigorously regulated big business by 'trust busting' under terms of Sherman Anti-Trust Act. Militant Latin Amer. policy aroused opposition. Re-elected Pres. (1904), awarded Nobel Peace Prize (1906) after mediating to end Russo-Japanese War. Picked W. H. TAFT as successor, but ran against him as Progressive Pres. candidate (1912) after splitting with Party.

Roosevelt Dam, hydro-electric power dam, part of Salt R. irrigation project in Arizona, US. Completed 1911.

Root, Elihu (1845–1937), Amer. statesman. Sec. of State (1905–9); worked for peaceful relations with Latin America and Japan. Awarded Nobel Peace Prize (1912).

root, that part of a plant which absorbs moisture and food, provides anchorage and support, and may store food. Usually penetrates soil but may grow in air or in water.

Röpke, Wilhelm (1899–1965), Ger. economist. Adviser in post-World War 2 Ger. govts. Works include *Civitas Humana* (1948) and *The Social Crisis of Our Time* (1950).

rorqual, whalebone whale of genus *Balaenoptera.* Hunted in Arctic and Antarctic. Small sickle-shaped dorsal fin and small head. Species include blue whale *Sibbaldus musculus.*

Rorschach test, in psychoanalysis, device consisting of 10 standardized ink blot designs, introduced by Hermann Rorschach. Subject's interpretations indicate underlying personality structure.

Rosa, Salvator (1615–73), Ital. painter and satiric poet, b. Naples. Known for landscapes and hist. scenes, *e.g. Conspiracy of Catiline.*

Rosa, Monte, Alpine mountain group on Swiss-Ital. border. Highest peak is Dufourspitze (15,203 ft.).

Rosario, port of Santa Fé prov., E central Argentina, on Paraná R. Important transport and processing centre. Pop. (1960) 672,000.

rosary, in R.C. Church, a series of prayers, counted as they are said on a string of beads, divided into decades. The prayers used are the Our Father, Gloria and the Hail Mary.

Roscommon, county of Connaught, N central Ireland. Area: 982 sq. mi.; county town Roscommon. Lake district with fertile land. Pop. (1966) 56,130.

rose, flowering plant of genus *Rosa,* comprising over 300 species and over 7,000 varieties. World-wide cultivation; main types are bush, rambler, miniature and climbing varieties.

rose of Jericho, resurrection plant, *Anastatica hierochuntica,* Asiatic desert shrub. Rolls up when dry and expands when moist.

rose of Sharon, *Hibiscus syriacus,* Asian ornamental shrub, and *Hypericum calycinum,* evergreen European shrub. White, rose or purple flowers.

rose quartz, variety of coarsely crystalline QUARTZ, rose-red or pink in colour.

rosebay willowherb, fireweed, *Chamaenerion angustifolium,* perennial plant with spike of pink-purple flowers. Grows on waste ground.

Rosebery, 5th Earl of *see* PRIMROSE, ARCHIBALD PHILIP.

rosella, large colourful parakeet of genus *Platycerus* of Australia and New Zealand.

rosemary, *Rosmarinus officinalis,* evergreen shrub of thyme family of S Europe and Asia Minor; used as culinary herb and in cosmetics.

Rosenberg, Alfred (1893–1946), Ger. 'polit. leader, b. Estonia. Author of work on Nazi racist doctrine *Der Mythus des 20 Jahrhunderts* (1930). Hanged after Nuremberg trials.

Rosenberg Case, trial (1951) in US, of Julius and Ethel Rosenberg, who were found guilty of passing atom bomb secrets to USSR during World War 2. Executed (1953) at Sing Sing, New York.

rose-root, perennial mountain plant, *Sedum rosa,* of N hemisphere. Greenish-yellow flowers; roots have rose-like smell.

Roses, Wars of the, civil struggle (1455–85) for Eng. throne between Houses of Lancaster (red rose) and York (white rose). Lancastrian Henry VI's crown threatened by rise of York claimants, culminating in Edward IV's rule (1461–70, 1471–83); Henry briefly restored (1470–1). Wars ended when Henry Tudor assumed power as Henry VII after defeating Richard III at Bosworth (1485).

Rosetta Stone, ancient Egyptian stone dating from *c.* 197 BC. Discovered (1797) near Rosetta, on Nile R.; now in British Museum. Inscription appears in 3 scripts, hieroglyphic, demotic and Greek; deciphering has led to understanding of Egyptian hieroglyphics.

rose-window, in eccles. architecture, circular window divided by mullions radiating from centre or filled with tracery, suggesting rose-forms.

rosewood, dark red wood obtained from various trop. trees, esp. Brazilian rosewood, jacaranda, *Dalbergia nigra.* Used for cabinet-making, veneering.

Rosicrucians, secret, occult groups claiming ancient Egyptian origins for their movement. Symbols include swastika, pyramid. Modern US movement follows theosophical writings of Johan Andreä.

rosin, residue from distillation of turpentine. Hard, brittle and translucent; used in sealing-wax, for treating violin bows and in powdered form, on ballet shoes.

Ross, Sir John (1777–1856), Brit. naval officer and explorer. Attempted (1818) to find Northwest Passage. Discovered Boothia Peninsula and King William Is.

Ross, Sir Ronald (1857–1932), Brit. physician, b. India. Awarded Nobel Prize for Physiology and Medicine (1902) for work on the malaria-carrying mosquito.

Ross, W[illiam] W[rightson] E[ustace] (1897–1966), Canadian poet. Often called the first modern Canadian poet, his works are terse,

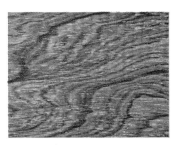

Rosewood

Laconics (1930) and philosophical, *Sonnets* (1932).

Ross and Cromarty, county of N Scotland, incl. some of Outer Hebridean islands. Area: 3,089 sq. mi.; county town, Dingwall. Mountainous with many lochs; whisky distilleries, sheep raising. Pop. (1965) 58,000.

Ross Sea, Antarctic sea discovered (1839) by Sir James Clark Ross.

Rossellini, Roberto (1906–), Ital. film director. Films include *Open City* (1945), key film in neo-realist movement, *Stromboli* (1950), *General della Rovere* (1960).

Rossetti, Christina Georgina (1830–94), Eng. poet; sister of Dante Gabriel Rossetti. Lyric poetry with strong mystical and religious element includes *Goblin Market* (1862), *Time Flies* (1885).

Rossetti, Dante Gabriel (1828–82), Eng. poet and painter; dominant figure of pre-Raphaelite movement. Best known poems 'The Blessed Damozel' and 'Sister Helen' included in *Ballads and Sonnets* (1881). Paintings include *Beata Beatrix* (1863), *Dante's Dream* (1871).

Rossini, Gioacchino Antonio (1792–1868), Ital. composer. Best known for operas *The Barber of Seville* (1816), *William Tell* (1829).

Rostand, Edmond (1868–1918), Fr. poet and playwright. Best known plays *Cyrano de Bergerac* (1897), *L'Aiglon* (1900).

Rostov [-on-Don], city and major port of European RSFSR, on Don R. Indust. and communications centre. Produces machinery, ships, textiles, chemicals. Pop. (1967) 737,000.

Rostow, Walt Whitman (1916–), Amer. govt. economic adviser in 1960s. Author of *The Stages of Economic Growth* (1960).

Rostropovich, Mstislav Leopoldovich (1927–), Russ. cellist. Enjoys international reputation through concert tours in USSR and abroad.

rosy pastor, *Sturnus roseus,* locust-eating starling of Asia and Europe.

Climbing Rose (Paul's Scarlet Climber)

Rothenburg

Glossy black head and wings, pink body.

Rotary International, organization founded 1905 [US], 1914 [UK]. Aims to promote high standards of practice in business and the professions. Supports charities.

Roth, Philip (1933–), Amer. writer whose works mostly deal with contemporary Jewish life in US. Include *Goodbye, Columbus* (1959), *Letting Go* (1962), *Portnoy's Complaint* (1969).

Rothenburg ob der Tauber, ancient walled town in Bavaria, Germany. Medieval aspect preserved. Pop. 11,000.

Rothenstein, Sir William (1872–1945), Eng. portrait painter. Official war artist in both World Wars. Author of *English Portraits* (1898).

Rothschild, international Jewish family of bankers. Foundations of family fortune laid by Frankfurt banker **Meyer Amschel Rothschild** (1743–1812) whose sons opened branches in London, Naples, Paris, Vienna. **Nathan Meyer Rothschild** (1777–1836) supplied Brit. govt. with finances in struggle against Napoleon. Later members of family were philanthropists and patrons of the arts.

Rotorua, town of North Island, New Zealand. Volcanic hot springs are tourist attraction. Pop. (1962) 20,000.

rotten boroughs, in Eng. history, boroughs which continued to return Members of Parl. despite disappearance of electorate. Abolished by 1832 Reform Act.

Rotterdam, city of W Netherlands, world's largest seaport; serves West Germany, Switzerland, Belgium,

France. Industries include ship-building, chemicals, food-processing. Pop. (1965) 731,564.

Rouault, Georges (1871–1958), Fr. expressionist painter. Many of his works draw on the Bible and circus life. They include *Baptism of Christ, The Three Clowns.*

Rouen, city and port of NW France, cap. of Seine-Maritime department. Centre of wine trade; industries include engineering, textiles, chemicals. Has famous Gothic cathedral. Pop. (1962) 123,474.

roulette, game of chance, common feature of gambling casinos. Played under supervision of a croupier.

Round Table *see* ARTHURIAN LEGEND.

rounders, Eng. game similar to baseball which is prob. derived from it.

Roundheads, name given to members of Parliamentarian Party during Eng. Civil War. So called because of their close-cropped hair.

roundworm *see* NEMATODA.

Rousseau, Henri (1844–1910), Fr. primitive painter, known as Le Douanier. Works, incl. *The Sleeping Gipsy* and *The Dream,* were important influence on Cubism.

Rousseau, Jean Jacques (1712–78), Fr. philosopher, b. Geneva. Regarded as founder of Romanticism, theories based on contention that man is good by nature, corrupted by civilization. Aim of govt., primarily expressed in *Le Contrat Social* (1762), is to offset society's institutions, but not to contravene inalienable sovereignty of people. Other works include novel on education *Émile* (1762) and autobiog. *Confessions.*

Rousseau, Théodore (1812–67), Fr. landscape painter. One of leaders of Barbizon School.

rowan, mountain ash, *Sorbus aucuparia,* slender European tree with red berries. *S. americana* and *S. sambucifolia* are Amer. varieties.

rowing, method of propelling boat by means of oars. Orig. used in trade and war, now popular sport. Amateur rowing began (1829) with 1st University Boat Race between Oxford and Cambridge; other main events, UK Henley Regatta; US Yale-Harvard Race.

Roxana (d. 311 BC), Persian wife of Alexander the Great. After his death, imprisoned and killed by Cassander in Wars of the Diadochi.

Roxburghshire, border county of Southern Uplands, Scotland. Area: 665 sq. mi.; county town, Jedburgh. Mainly hilly (Cheviots), drained by Teviot and Tweed rivers. Main

occupations, sheep raising, woollen and tweed manufacturing. Ruined abbeys at Melrose, Kelso, Jedburgh. Pop. (1966) 43,000.

Roy, Camille (1870–1943), Fr. Canadian literary historian and critic. Author of standard *Manuel d'Histoire de la Littérature Canadienne-Française* (1918).

Roy, Gabrielle (1909–), Fr. Canadian novelist. Her works include *Bonheur d'Occasion* (1945), *Alexandre Chenevert, Caissier* (1954).

Royal Academy [of Arts], founded (1768) in London by George III. Stages 2 annual exhibitions, one of old masters, one of contemporary art.

Royal Air Force (RAF), independent Brit. fighting service; amalgamation (1918) of Royal Flying Corps and Royal Naval Air Service; controlled by Min. of Defence. Vital role in Battle of Britain (1940) brought recognition of RAF as essential part of UK armed forces.

Royal Automobile Club (RAC), Brit. organization founded (1897) to protect interests of the motorist. Provides information, technical and legal services. Sponsors rallies and exhibitions.

Royal Canadian Mounted Police, federal law-enforcing organization of Canada. Estab. (1873) as North West Mounted Police, early duties included protecting settlers and preventing Indian disorders. Renamed 1920.

royal fern, royal osmund, *Osmunda regalis,* fern of temp. and trop. regions. Grows to height of *c.* 8 ft.

Royal Gorge, canyon of Arkansas R., Colorado, US. Sheer walls (1,100 ft. high) cut from red granite.

Royal Navy, Brit. fighting ships and their admin. Took permanent form under Cromwell. Dominance helped shape UK foreign policy (19th and early 20th cent.). Now controlled by Min. of Defence.

Royal Society [Royal Society of London for Improving Natural Knowledge], UK scientific society, founded 1660. Eminent scientists elected as fellows (FRS).

Royal Society for the Prevention of Cruelty to Animals (RSPCA), Brit. organization founded (1824) in London to promote humane treatment of animals and provide free veterinary treatment.

Royal Fern with detail of the leaf

War by Henri (le Douanier) Rousseau

Ruanda, Bantic Niger-Congo language. Over 2 million speakers in C Africa.

Ruanda-Urundi *see* RWANDA; BURUNDI.

Ruapehu, dormant volcano (9,175 ft.) in Tongariro National Park, C North Island, New Zealand. Island's highest mountain.

Rub al-Khali, unexplored desert of S Arabia. Area: 250,000 sq. mi.

rubber, general term applied to range of natural and synthetic elastic substances. Natural rubber, caoutchouc, is tough, impermeable, and electrically resistant and obtained from milky latex, mainly from Para rubber tree. Used as adhesive, or for tough products, *e.g.* tyres.

rubber plant, India rubber plant, *Ficus elastica,* house plant. Native to trop. forests of Asia where it grows to 100 ft. Grown indoors, reaching 8–10 ft.; large, shiny, leathery leaves.

rubber tree, various trop. and sub-trop. trees producing milky juice, called latex, from which rubber is derived. Chief source is *Hevea brasiliensis,* native to the Amazon but cultivated in SE Asia; latex collected from cuts made in bark.

rubella, German measles, contagious viral disease characterized by fever, sore throat and skin rash. During pregnancy may cause damage to unborn child.

Rubens, Sir Peter Paul (1577–1640), Flemish painter. Popularity obliged him to employ skilled apprentices to execute areas of his larger works, esp. altar-pieces. Paintings, mostly hist. and sacred, include *Descent from the Cross, Venus and Adonis.*

Rubicon, former river boundary between Gaul and Italy. Crossed (49 BC) by Julius Caesar, in defiance of Senate; initiated civil war. To 'cross the Rubicon' has come to mean to take an irrevocable step.

Rubinstein, Anton Gregorovich (1829–94), Russ. pianist and composer. Founded (1862) St Petersburg Conservatory of Music. Best known work *Kamenoi-Ostrov.*

Rubinstein, Artur (1889–), Polish pianist. Noted esp. for interpretation of Chopin and Sp. composers.

ruby, deep red, transparent gem variety of mineral corundum. Finest rubies come from Burma; occur in crystalline limestone.

ruby-throated hummingbird *Archilochus colubris,* migrant hummingbird of N America. Bright brown-green back with whitish underparts.

rudd, *Scardinius erythorphthalmus,* small European fresh-water fish of carp family. Red fins and eyes.

Rudolf I (1218–91), Habsburg count, elected Ger. king (1273). Defeated Ottocar II, gained Austria, Styria and estab. Habsburg dynasty.

rue, herb of grace, *Ruta graveolens,* European strong-scented perennial herb. Yellow flowers and blue-green leaves with bitter taste.

ruff, common sandpiper of Europe and Asia. During breeding season male has ruff of erectile feathers on neck. Female called reeve.

ruffed lemur, *Lemur variegatus,* primate, largest of the true lemurs. Fringe of hair on the sides of head and neck; varies greatly in colour.

rugby football, team game (15 or 7 a side) developed from football. First systematized at Rugby School, England. Ball is oval and is handled by players; tries scored by touch-down of ball over goal line. In UK, rules differ between Rugby Union (amateur) estab. 1871, and Rugby League (professional).

rugged grouse, *Bonasa umbellus,* N Amer. grouse of family Tetraonidae. Tuft of feathers on each side of neck.

Ruhr, concentrated indust. region of West Germany. Area: *c.* 1,770 sq. mi. Provides coal for extensive steel, machinery and chem. plants. Cities include Essen, Dortmund, Duisburg. After World War 1, occupied by Fr. and Belgian troops until 1925. Devastated in World War 2.

Ruisdael or **Ruysdael, Jacob van** (*c.* 1628–82), Dutch landscape painter and etcher.

Rum [Rhum], small mountainous island of Inner Hebrides, Scotland. Made nature reserve 1957.

rum, spirit distilled from fermented cane sugar by-products, chiefly molasses. Originated in West Indies, most rums for export still produced in the area.

Rumania *see* ROMANIA.

Rumanian *see* ROMANIAN.

ruminant, cloven-hoofed, cud-chewing mammal of order Artiodactyla, incl. cow, sheep, goat, deer, giraffe, camel.

rummy, card game played by 2 or 4 players. Variations include gin rummy and CANASTA.

Rump Parliament, name given to members of LONG PARLIAMENT remaining after withdrawal of Royalists (1642) and exclusion of Presbyterians (1648). Ruled England until expelled by Cromwell (1658).

Rundi, Bantic Niger-Congo language. Over 2 million speakers in C Africa.

runes, oldest Germanic alphabet dating from *c.* AD 300; orig. used by E Goths. The letters consist of straight lines with few curved lines. Used esp. for inscriptions.

Runnymede, meadow of S bank of Thames R., Surrey, England; 3 mi. S of Windsor. Reputedly where MAGNA CARTA was signed (1215).

Runyon, Damon (1884–1946), Amer. short-story writer and journalist. Best known work *Guys and Dolls* (1931).

Rupert (1619–82), Ger. prince and cavalry officer. Grandson of James I. Defeated by Cromwell at Marston Moor (1644). Sponsored colonization of Rupert's Land area of Canada named after him.

rush, various plants, esp. of genera *Juncus* and *Scirpus,* of temp. and cold regions. Cylindrical, often hollow stems used for making mats, baskets, *etc.*

Rush-Bagot Convention, settlement (1817) of Canadian border negotiated by US Sec. of State, Richard Rush, and Brit. Min. in Washington, Charles Bagot. Limited armaments, and estab. precedent of peaceful relations between US and Canada.

Rusk, [David] Dean (1909–), Amer. public official. Sec. of State (1961–9).

Ruskin, John (1819–1900), Eng. essayist and critic. Wrote widely on art, architecture and literature; lec-

Grass huts in the Savannah of Rwanda

tured also on economic and social topics. Publications include *Stones of Venice, Sesame and Lilies,* and autobiog. *Praeterita* (1885–9).

Russell, Bertrand *see* RUSSELL, JOHN, 1ST EARL RUSSELL.

Russell, George William (1867–1935), Irish poet. With W. B. Yeats, one of leaders of Irish literary revival. Main works (published under pseudonym AE) *Homeward: Songs by the Way* (1894), *The Divine Vision* (1904), *Enchantment and Other Poems* (1930).

Russell, John, 1st Earl Russell (1792–1878), Brit. statesman, Liberal P.M. (1846–52, 1865–6). Helped introduce REFORM BILL OF 1832. Forced Foreign Sec. Palmerston's resignation (1851). As Foreign Sec. (1860–5), advocated Brit. neutrality during Amer. Civil War. His grandson, **Bertrand Arthur William Russell, 3rd Earl Russell** (1872–1970), philosopher and mathematician, collaborated with A. N. Whitehead on *Principia Mathematica* (1910–13), major work on symbolic logic. Works attempt to give philosophy scientific basis. Awarded Nobel Prize for Literature (1950). Leading pacifist spokesman.

Russia *see* UNION OF SOVIET SOCIALIST REPUBLICS.

Russian, chief language of USSR. One of the Balto-Slavonic branch of Indo-European languages.

Russian Orthodox Church, branch of Eastern ORTHODOX CHURCH. Orig. headed by patriarch of Constantinople; patriarchate of Moscow estab. 1589. Power and influence declined after Russian Revolution, esp. between 1925 and 1943 (when new patriarch appointed).

Russian Revolution, national up-

risings (1905, 1917) against tsarist autocracy. Discontent over agric. and indust. conditions resulted in series (1905) of strikes, mutinies (*e.g.* battleship *Potemkin* at Odessa); led to limited concessions, such as estab. of *duma* [parl.]. Opposition arose after continued Russ. losses during World War 1. Feb. Revolution (1917) led to estab. of provisional govt. in defiance of tsar, who then abdicated. Socialist opposition to War, led by LENIN, culminated in Oct. Revolution. Communist Party estab.; private ownership abolished, Russia withdrew from War. Ensuing civil war (1918–20) between Red Army, organized by TROTSKY, and White Army, supported by European nations, ended with Communist consolidation of power and founding (1921) of USSR.

Russian Soviet Federated Socialist Republic (RSFSR), largest constituent repub. of USSR, occupying much of W and central regions, incl. Siberia. Area: 6,641,700 sq. mi.; cap. Moscow. Centre of industry and mining. Pop. (1967) 127,312,000.

Russo-Japanese War (1904–5), conflict provoked by Jap. retaliation to Russ. penetration of Manchuria and Korea. Japan's military successes at Mukden and Tsushima resulted in peace settlement reducing Russia's role in E Asia.

Russo-Turkish Wars, series of wars (18th–19th cent.) in which Russ. expansionist ambitions in Med. realized at expense of Ottoman Empire. Final settlement achieved at TREATY OF SAN STEFANO (1878).

rust, corrosive film which forms on iron and metals exposed to air and moisture; caused by oxidation.

rust, disease of various plants caused by parasitic fungi whose spores have appearance of rust.

rutabaga, swede, Swedish turnip, *Brassica napobrassica,* smooth-skinned, biennial plant, similar to turnip. Large edible yellowish root.

Ruth, book of OT. Relates story of Ruth, the Moabite, who accompanied her mother-in-law to Bethlehem and married Boaz. Ancestress of David.

Ruth, George Herman ('Babe') (1895––1948), Amer. baseball player. Played (1914–35) mainly with New York Yankees, estab. many slugging records, incl. 714 home runs (60 in 1927).

Ruthenes or **Ruthenians** (Lat: Russians), name applied to Ukrainians in Middle Ages, then to W Ukrainians of Austro-Hungary. Used for Carpathian Ukrainians only after 1918. Absorbed into USSR when Ruthenia was ceded by Czechoslovakia (1945).

Rutherford, Ernest, 1st Baron Rutherford of Nelson (1871–1937), Brit. physicist, b. New Zealand. Awarded Nobel Prize for Chemistry (1908) for work on radioactivity. Works include *The Electrical Structure of Matter* (1926), *The Newer Alchemy* (1937).

rutile, titanium dioxide mineral. Reddish-brown, occurring in prismatic crystals and granular masses. Found in igneous and metamorphic rocks. Used in welding-rod coatings.

Rutland, smallest county of England. Area: 152 sq. mi.; county town, Oakham. Agric. area; cereals, livestock, cheese. Pop. (1966) 28,000.

Ruwenzori, mountain range, C Africa, on Uganda-Congo border. Highest peaks Margherita (16,795 ft.), Alexandra (16,750 ft.).

Ruyter, Michael Adriaanszoon de (1607–76), Dutch naval officer. Destroyed Eng. fleet in the Medway (1667); with TROMP, led fleet in 3rd Dutch War (1672–8).

Rwanda, Republic of, state of C Africa. Area: 10,169 sq. mi.; cap. Kigali. Largely mountainous and forested. Exports coffee, cotton,

tobacco. Part of Belgian trusteeship Ruanda-Urundi until independence (1962). Pop. (1965 est.) 3,018,000.

rye, *Secale cereale,* tall Eurasian annual grass grown extensively in Eurasia and N America. Black grain used in making black rye bread, rye whisky and for livestock feed.

Rye House Plot, conspiracy (1683) to assassinate Eng. King Charles II and brother James on London road in Hertfordshire. Plot uncovered.

Ryerson, [Adolphus] Egerton (1803-82), Canadian clergyman. Opposed church control of education. Founded (1841) Victoria College, Toronto.

Ryswick, Treaty of, settlement of War of Grand Alliance (1688–97) thwarting Fr. ambitions; signed (1697) at Ryswick, Netherlands. Dutch gained commercial concessions. Savoy's independence and William III's rule of England acknowledged.

Ryukyu Islands, W Pacific archipelago of *c.* 55 islands. Total area: 1,803 sq. mi.; main city, Naha, on Okinawa. Part of Japan (1879–1945); occupied by US forces at end of World War 2. Sovereignty restored to Japan (1953); US forces left 1972. Exports sugar, pineapples. Pop. (1963) 931,000.

S

Saar, The, Saarland, state of West Germany. Area: 991 sq. mi.; cap. Saarbrucken. Intensely industrialized, with important coal mines; industries include steel, ceramics, chemicals. Became polit. unit 1919; since 1957 state of West Germany. Pop. (1961) 1,072,600.

Saavedra Lamas, Carlos, (1880–1959), Argentinian statesman. Foreign Min. (1932–8). Pres. of the Assembly of League of Nations (1936). Helped to end Chaco war between Paraguay and Bolivia. Awarded Nobel Peace Prize (1936).

Sabah, state of NE Borneo, part of Federation of Malaysia. Area: 29,387 sq. mi.; cap. Kota Kinabalu (formerly Jesselton). Predominantly mountainous with dense forests. Produces rubber, timber. British North Borneo until 1963. Pop. (1965) 551,000.

Sabatier, Paul (1854–1941), Fr. chemist. With Victor Grignard, awarded Nobel Prize for Chemistry (1912) for developing method of hydrogenating organic compounds.

Sabbatarians, advocates of strict observance of the Sabbath. Includes Amer. Lord's Day Alliance group and Brit. Lord's Day Observance Society.

Sabbath [Hebrew: rest], religious holy day, 7th day of week, celebrated by services and regarded as day of rest. Observed by Jews from sunset on Friday to sunset on Saturday, by Christians on Sunday, by Moslems on Friday.

Sabines, ancient tribe of C Italy, from earliest times connected with Rome. According to tradition wives for Romulus' citizens taken from Sabines. Constantly warred with Rome, finally amalgamated (3rd cent. BC).

sable, *Martes zibellina,* rare carnivore of weasel family found in N Asia. Reared in Russia in state farms. Blue-black fur with silver tips is most valuable.

sable antelope, *Hippotragus niger,* large dark-coloured antelope of S Africa, closely related to the oryx. Stout, vertical, thinly-ringed horns.

sabre-toothed tiger, extinct mammal of genus *Machairodontidae.* Existed in Pliocene and Pleistocene eras in Europe, India and N and S America. Tusk-like upper teeth.

saccharin, white, crystalline powder produced synthetically. Slightly soluble in water; in dilute solution 500 times as sweet as sugar. Used as non-caloric sugar substitute in manufacture of foods and beverages.

Sacco-Vanzetti Case, in US legal history, controversial trial and conviction (1921) in Massachusetts, of Nicola Sacco and Bartolomeo Vanzetti for robbery and murder. Many believed verdict due to radical polit. views of accused. Retrial upheld previous decision; men executed.

Sacheverell, Henry (1674–1724), Eng. clergyman. In 2 sermons (1709) attacked Whig govt. esp. concerning toleration of dissenters. Charged with libel and sentenced to 3 yr. suspension from preaching.

Sachs, Hans (1494–1576), Ger. poet and dramatist. Prolific writer (*c.* 4,000 poems) best-known works include allegorical poem *Die Wittenbergische Nachtigall;* verse anecdote *Schwank* and 1-act play, *Fastnachtsspiele.*

Sachs, Nelly (1891–1970), Swedish poet and dramatist. Works, incl. *In den Wohnungen des Todes* (1947), relate sufferings of the Jewish people. Awarded Nobel Prize for Literature (1966).

sacrament, religious act or ceremony considered esp. sacred and distinct from other rites, through institution by Jesus Christ. In R.C. and Orthodox Eastern Churches, 7 sacraments (Eucharist, baptism, penance, confirmation, ordination, matrimony, Extreme Unction) held to bestow God's grace on man. Most Protestant denominations observe Holy Communion and baptism, but only as symbols of God's grace.

Sacramento, cap. of California, US, on junction of Sacramento and American rivers. Founded (1839) as New Helvetia; expanded rapidly with discovery (1849) of gold. Industries include missile development, food processing. Pop. (1964) 237,712.

sacred ibis, *Threskiornis aethiopica,* ibis of Nile basin, *c.* 2 ft. long, black and white in colour. Venerated by ancient Egyptians.

sacrilege, profaning of anything held

Sable

to be sacred, particularly the debasing or stealing of religious objects.

Sadducees, Jewish religious and polit. sect (*fl.* 2nd cent. BC—AD 1st cent.). Opposed Pharisees and religious doctrines not taught in Torah, *e.g.* resurrection and immortality. Advocated strict observance of the Law.

Sade, Donatien Alphonse François, Comte de (1740–1814), Fr. author, known as the Marquis de Sade. Imprisoned in Bastille, later confined to lunatic asylum. Novels, incl. *Justine* (1791), *Histoire de Juliette* (6 vols., 1797), deal largely with sexual cruelty and violence; influenced later writers. **Sadism** is derivation of sexual satisfaction through inflicting pain.

Sadi, orig. Musdih-uddin (*c.* 1184–1291), Persian writer. Author of classic poem *Bustan* (1257) and prose work *Gulistan* (1258).

Sadler's Wells, London theatre, built (1931) on site of various previous structures, incl. original 'Musick House' (*c.* 1638), where Grimaldi performed. Closed (1968) after serving as home of Sadler's Wells Opera and Ballet Co. since 1931.

safety lamp, lamp for use in mines designed not to explode firedamp or marsh gas. First successful type invented by George Stephenson and Humphrey Davy.

safflower, *Carthamus tinctorius,* plant of SW Asia and NE Africa. Large orange-red flowers. Oil from seeds used in cooking and as vehicle for medicines, paints, varnishes, *etc.*

saffron, vegetable gold, *Crocus sativus,* crocus with purple flowers. Orange coloured condiment consisting of its dried stigmas used to colour confectionery, *etc.*

saga [Old Norse: story], narrative written 11th–13th cent., relating

Sable Antelope

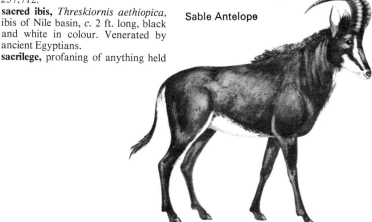

St Moritz, Switzerland

legends of Icelandic or Norse heroes, *e.g. Sturlunga Saga, Njala.*

Sagan, Françoise, orig. Françoise Quoirez (1936–), Fr. novelist and dramatist. Works include *Bonjour Tristesse* (1954), *Un Certain Sourire* (1956), *Aimez-vous Brahms . . .* (1959).

sage, *Salvia officinalis,* aromatic herb of world-wide distribution. Grey-green leaves used as seasoning in cookery.

sage grouse, sage hen, *Centrocercus urophasianus,* long-tailed grouse of sagebrush regions of W N America.

sagebrush, bushy deciduous plant of genus *Artemisia* of W US. *A. tridentata,* common sagebrush, is a silvery grey aromatic shrub.

Sagittarius *see* ZODIAC.

sago, *Cycas revoluta,* palm tree producing an edible starch from ground pith of the stem. Found mainly in Far East; important food item.

saguaro, *Carnegiea gigantea,* tall cactus of Arizona with edible fruit.

Saguenay, river of S Quebec, Canada.

St Bernard dog

Flows into St Lawrence R. Rapid falls provide power for Isle Maligne and Shipshaw hydro-electric plants.

Sagunto, city of E Spain in Valencia prov. Capture by Carthaginians under Hannibal (219 BC) led to Second Punic War. Conquered by Rome (214 BC). Roman remains include amphitheatre. Pop. *c.* 30,000.

Sahara, desert region of N Africa. Area: *c.* 3,500,000 sq. mi.; low plateau with depressions (*e.g.* Qattara) and mountains up to 11,000 ft. Mineral resources include oil, gas, copper, phosphates. Orig. inhabited by Sudanese Negroes invaded by Berbers and Arabs. Pop. *c.* $3\frac{1}{2}$ million.

saiga, *Saiga tartarica,* heavy goat-like antelope of E Russia and W Asia.

Saigon, cap. of South Vietnam and port on Saigon R. Industries largely concentrated in Chinese suburb of Cholon; shipbuilding, food (esp. rice, sugar) and rubber processing, textiles. Scene of riots, military coups and Vietcong terrorism. Pop. (1963) 1,794,000.

sail, area of canvas or other fabric hung from ship's mast and spars to harness force of the wind as means of propulsion. Sails of papyrus used by ancient Egyptians: flax and cotton, formerly used in sailmaking, have been replaced by synthetics. Two main types of sail arrangement are square-rig and fore-and-aft rig.

sailfish, tropical marine fish of genus

Istiophorus. Related to swordfish, it has sail-shaped dorsal fin and spear-like upper jaw. *I. orientalis* of S America reaches 20 ft. in length. Caught commercially and as game.

sailing *see* YACHTING.

sailing ships, wind-propelled vessels prob. 1st used by ancient Egyptians, later by Greeks and Romans. With invention of mariner's compass (14th cent.), use of sails in place of oars became general. Rivalry between Britain and America in Chinese and Indian tea trade led to construction of the clippers—most famous being the Brit. *Cutty Sark* and the Amer. *Ann McKim.* Introduction of steamship (19th cent.) led to gradual disappearance of sailing ships, both as commercial and naval vessels.

Saimaa, large system of connected lakes and largest lake in S Finland with outlet into L. Ladoga.

sainfoin, *Onobrychis sativa viciae folia,* pink-flowered Eurasian leguminous plant. Widely cultivated in Europe as a forage crop.

saint, person whose exceptional holiness in life, attested by miracles after his death, has been formally recognized by Catholic Church as worthy of veneration and to receive prayers of intercession.

Saint Andrews, University of, oldest university of Scotland, founded (1411) in St Andrews, Fife. Women students admitted 1892. One of its 3 colleges, Queen's College, Dundee, estab. (1967) as separate University of Dundee.

Saint Bartholomew's Day Massacre, massacre of Fr. Huguenots, instigated by Catherine de'Medici, which began in Paris on 27 Aug. 1572. Number killed est. at 50,000, incl. Huguenot leader Admiral Coligny. Led to resumption of Fr. Wars of Religion.

Saint Bernard Passes, two Alpine passes. Great Saint Bernard (8,110 ft.) links Val d'Aosta (Italy) with Rhône Valley (Switzerland). Famous hospice founded 10th cent.; Augustinian friars breed Saint Bernard dogs. Little Saint Bernard (7,177 ft.) connects Val d'Aosta with French Savoy.

Sainte Chapelle, Gothic chapel in Paris, France, built (1245–8) by Louis IX to house relics from Holy Land. Noted for stained glass windows.

Saint Christopher, Saint Kitts, island of West Indies. Area: 65 sq. mi.; cap. Basseterre. Intensively cultivated; exports sugar and cotton. First Brit. West Indian possession to be settled (1623). United (1967) with islands of Nevis and Anguilla; latter rebelled (1969). Pop. (1960) 38,113.

Saint Elias Mountains, range in SW

Yukon and SE Alaska, Canada. Highest peaks are Logan (19,850 ft.) and St Elias (18,008 ft.). Area noted for vast glaciers.

Saint Elmo's fire, brushlike jets of light seen round tips of elevated objects (*e.g.* church spires, ships' masts) during thunderstorms. Caused by discharge of electricity into atmosphere.

Saint Gall, canton of NE Switzerland. Area: 777 sq. mi.; cap. St Gallen. Ger. speaking. Mining and textile industries, esp. silk, lace and embroidery. Pop. 340,000.

Saint Gallen, town of NE Switzerland. Benedictine monastery built here (8th cent.). Centre of medieval learning; its library houses world famous collection of early manuscripts. Manufactures lace and embroidery. Pop. (1966 est.) 78,000.

Saint Helena, volcanic island in S Atlantic Ocean, belonging to Britain. Area: 47 sq. mi. Discovered by Portuguese (1501); became Brit. possession (1651). Jamestown is only town. Place of Napoleon's exile from 1815 until his death in 1821. Pop. (1963) 4,802.

Saint John's, cap. of Newfoundland, Canada. Permanent settlement estab. 17th cent. Port for Atlantic and coastal trade; headquarters of large fishing fleets. Industries, fish packing and processing, whale and seal-oil refineries, shipbuilding. Pop. (1961) 63,633.

Saint John's wort, herb or shrub of genus *Hypericum* of temp. and trop. regions with yellow flowers. *H. calycinum,* rose of Sharon or Aaron's beard, is a Eurasian variety.

Saint Kitts see SAINT CHRISTOPHER.

St Laurent, Louis Stephen (1882–), Canadian statesman. Trained as lawyer, entered cabinet (1941). Liberal P.M. (1948–57).

Saint Lawrence, Gulf of, bay of N Atlantic Ocean in SE Canada, at mouth of St Lawrence R. Area: 100,000 sq. mi.; max. depth: 3,275 ft. Important fishing ground.

Saint Lawrence Islands National Park, S Ontario, Canada, in the Thousand Islands. Area: 172 acres. Founded 1914. Located on both shores of St Lawrence R., incl. 13 Canadian islands. Popular camping centre.

Saint Lawrence River, principal N Amer. river draining into Atlantic, 750 mi. long. Flows NE out of L. Ontario into Gulf of St Lawrence. Main cities on it are Kingston, Montreal and Quebec.

Saint Lawrence Seaway, waterway and hydro-electric complex connecting Great Lakes of N America with Gulf of St Lawrence. Constructed (1954–9) jointly by US and Canada. Project, involving construction of locks, dams and canals, opened up important trading area (esp. in grain and minerals) of N Amer. interior to ocean-going ships and greatly increased hydro-electric capacity.

Saint Louis, largest city of Missouri, US. Founded (1764) by French as fur-trading station; ceded (1803) to US in LOUISIANA PURCHASE. Important rail centre and market for furs, grain, hides. Industries, heavy-engineering, automobiles, shoes, chemicals. Pop. (1963) 2,180,000.

Saint Lucia, island in E Caribbean Sea, one of Brit. Windward Is. Area: 233 sq. mi.; chief town, Castries. Discovered (1502) by Columbus; became British 1803. Exports bananas, sugar, coconut oil, cocoa. Pop. (1963) 86,194.

Saint Martin, Fr.-Dutch island in E Caribbean Sea, one of Leeward Is. Area: 37 sq. mi.; chief Fr. town, Marigot, chief Dutch town, Philipsburg. Pop. *c.* 6,000.

Saint Moritz, winter sports and health resort of SE Switzerland. Situated on Inn R., in Upper Engadine valley at height of 6,080 ft. Pop. (1963) 3,750.

Saint Paul, cap. of Minnesota, US, forming with Minneapolis, 'Twin Cities'. Important rail and market centre. Industries, meat packing, machinery, printing and publishing, abrasives. Pop. (1960) 313,411.

Saint Paul's Cathedral, London, England. Designed by Sir Christopher Wren (1675–1710) on site of Old St Paul's which had been badly damaged in Great Fire (1666). Renaissance style with Classical details.

Saint Peter's, Rome, the Patriarchal Basilica of St Peter, in VATICAN CITY. Largest church in the world; replaced 4th cent. basilica built by Constantine on site of 2nd cent. chapel over tomb of St Peter. Building consecrated 1626. Designed chiefly by Bramante and Michelangelo, with piazza by Bernini.

Saint Pierre see MIQUELON.

Saint Valentine's Day, 14 Feb.; possible relic of Roman Lupercalian festival; survives with exchange of gifts and cards between lovers.

Saint Vincent, island of E Caribbean Sea, one of Brit. Windward Is. Area: 150 sq. mi.; cap. Kingstown. Discovered (1498) by Columbus. British and French contested ownership; restored to British (1783). Subject to earthquakes. Exports include arrowroot, cotton, bananas, copra. Pop. (1962) 87,000.

St Vincent, 1st Earl of see JERVIS, JOHN.

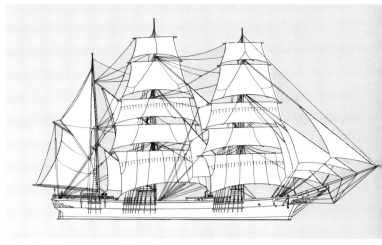

Bark, a 19th century sailing ship

Pagoda in Saigon

Salisbury Cathedral, England

Saint Vitus' dance, chorea, condition characterized by irregular involuntary movements of any part of the body. Most common among children. Cause unknown, but closely associated with acute rheumatic heart disease.

Saint-Cloud, town of N central France, W suburb of Paris. Former residence of Fr. monarchs. Sèvres porcelain manufactured. Site of famous racecourse. Pop. *c.* 30,000.

Saint-Cyr-L'École, town in N France. Gave its name to Fr. military academy, now at Coëtquidan in Brittany.

Saint-Denis, town of N central France, N surburb of Paris. Abbey of St Denis founded here (626). Present 12th cent. Gothic church contains tombs of many Fr. monarchs. Industries, heavy-engineering, chemicals, soap, glue and dye manufacturing. Pop. 94,264.

Sainte-Beuve, Charles Augustin (1804–69), Fr. poet and literary critic. Collected works appeared as *Portraits Littéraires* (1832–9, 1844). Among his hist. works *L'Histoire de Port-Royal* (1840–2).

Saint-Evremond, Charles de Marquetel de Saint-Denis (1610–1703), Fr. writer and soldier. Lived in exile in England from 1660. Influenced by Montaigne; an adherent of school of freethinkers. Works include *Conversations du Maréchal d'Hocquincourt avec le Père Canaye* and *Comédie des Academistes.*

Saint-Gaudens, Augustus (1848–1907), Amer. sculptor, b. Ireland. Public monuments include statues of General Sherman, Lincoln and Parnell.

Saint-Germain, Treaty of, post-World War 1 settlement (1919) between Austria and Allies. Dissolved Austro-Hungarian monarchy, divided empire among new E European states. Reduced Austria to present size and forbade union with Germany. Treaty contained Covenant of League of Nations.

Saint-Just, Antoine Léon de Richebourg de (1767–94), Fr. revolutionary. Believed by means justifiable to achieve the perfect state. Responsible for denunciation of Danton. With Robespierre organized REIGN OF TERROR (1793–4). Guillotined after being ousted with Robespierre.

Saint-Pierre, Jacques Henri Bernardin de (1737–1814), Fr. writer. Author of *Paul et Virginie* (1787), Romantic novel based on voyage to Mauritius.

Saint-Saëns, [Charles] Camille (1835–1921), Fr. composer. Works include the opera *Samson et Dalila,* the tone-poems *Danse Macabre* and *La Jeunesse d'Hercule* and the *Introduction* and *Rondo Capriccioso* for violin and orchestra.

Saint-Simon, Claude Henri de Rouvroy, Comte de (1760–1825), Fr. social philosopher and pioneer socialist; advocated indust. state governed by scientists and technologists. Wrote *Du Système Industriel* (1821), *Nouveau Christianisme* (1825).

Saint-Simon, Louis de Rouvroy, Duc de (1675–1755), Fr. diplomat and writer. Memoirs contain vivid descriptions of court life under Louis XIV and Louis XV.

Sajama, volcano (*c.* 21,000 ft.), in W Bolivia, NW of L. Poopo.

Sakai, Senoi, primitive people of Malay peninsula, probably of Vedda extraction.

Sakhalin, Saghalin, island of N Pacific. Area: 24,560 sq. mi. Ceded to Russia (1875), returned to Japan (1905). At end of World War 2 returned to Russia. Forms Sakhalin region with Kurile Is. Pop. (1965 est.) 638,000.

saké, saki, beer made from fermented rice. National beverage of Japan. High alcoholic content (11%–18%). Served warm.

Saki *see* MUNRO, HECTOR HUGH.

saki, monkey of genus *Pithecia* of trop. S America. Brown to black thick coat and long, bushy nonprehensile tail.

Saladin (1139–93), ruler of Egypt and Syria. United Moslems in military, polit. and economic spheres. His capture (1187) of Jerusalem led to Third Crusade. In spite of various victories by crusaders (esp. at Acre), final outcome resulted in Saladin's controlling all formerly contested territory (incl. Jerusalem) with exception of narrow coastal strip in Syria.

Salamanca, city of W Spain; cap. of Salamanca prov. University (founded *c.* 1230) helped spread Arabic philosophy in Europe. City has beautiful medieval and Renaissance buildings. Pop. (1960) 90,498.

salamander, amphibian of order Caudata. Superficially resembles the lizard but is scaleless with soft, moist, brightly coloured skin. Adults terrestrial and many are viviparous. Species include European *Salamandra maculosa* and N Amer. varieties of genus *Ambystoma.*

Salamis, Battle of (480 BC), sea engagement off island of Salamis in Aegean Sea. Gk. fleet decisively defeated larger Persian fleet.

Salazar, Antonio de Oliveira (1889–1970), Portuguese statesman. Min. of Finance (1926, 1928–40), he stabilized country's economic position. P.M. (1932) until removed from office (1968) after suffering severe stroke. Responsible for new constitution of 1933, by which, in practice, absolute power was accorded to P.M.

Salcantay, peak (20,550 ft.) in Cordillera Oriental, Peru, NW of Cuzco.

Salem, cap. of Oregon, US. Centre of rich agricultural area. Industries include food-processing, paper and sawmills. Pop. (1960) 49,142.

Salem, city of Massachusetts, US. World famous 19th cent. port, esp. for China trade. Scene of preliminary examinations in infamous witchcraft trials (1692) of Salem village (now Danvers). Industries, textiles, leather and electrical goods. Pop. (1960) 39,211.

Salic law, law adopted in Middle Ages by certain noble and royal European families, excluding female succession to offices and titles. Erroneously attributed to Salian Franks. Its application in Hanover at time of Queen Victoria's accession (1837) led to separation of Britain and Hanover.

salicylic acid, white crystalline solid obtained from willow-bark or synthetically from phenol. Used in many medicinal preparations and in food preservation.

Salinger, J[erome] D[avid] (1919–), Amer. writer, best known for picaresque *The Catcher in the Rye* (1951). Other works include *Franny and Zooey* (1961).

Salisbury, 1st Earl of *see* CECIL, ROBERT.

Salisbury, 3rd Marquis of *see*

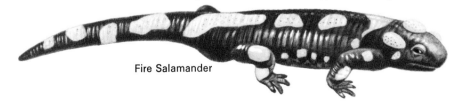

Fire Salamander

Triumphal Arch of the emperor Galerius (160-311) in Salonika

Cecil, Robert Arthur Talbot Gascoyne.

Salisbury, New Sarum, municipal borough and county town of Wiltshire, England. Near site of Old Sarum, seat of bishopric before building of New Sarum (13th cent.). Cathedral, with 404 ft. spire, built 1220–60; 13th cent. churches and bishop's palace. Pop. (1961) 35,500.

Salisbury, cap. of Rhodesia and of Federation of Rhodesia and Nyasaland (1953–63). Founded 1890. Transportation and indust. centre; tobacco market. Gold and chrome mined nearby. Pop. (1965) 327,000.

Salisbury Plain, chalk plateau, Wiltshire, England. Area: 300 sq. mi. Site of prehistoric monuments of Stonehenge and Avebury. Now training ground for Brit. army.

Salish, N Amer. Indian tribe of Pacific Coast area.

saliva, secretion of 3 pairs of salivary glands situated around mouth. Saliva moistens and lubricates food and mouth; helps to digest starch.

Salk, Jonas Edward (1914–   ), Amer. virologist; developed (1954) vaccine used against poliomyelitis.

sallow, shrubby willow of genus *Salix,* esp. great sallow, *S. caprea.* Used in making charcoal for gunpowder.

Sallust [Gaius Sallustius Crispus] (86–35 BC), Roman historian. Expelled from Senate (50 BC), later governor of Numidia. Extant works, modelled on Thucydides, are *Bellum Catilinae, Bellum Jugurthinum* and parts of *Historiae* (covering years 78–67 BC).

salmon, large food and game fish of genera *Salmo* and *Oncorhynchus.* Normal colour silvery blue-grey with dark spots. Atlantic salmon, *Salmo salar,* lives in coastal waters from Arctic southwards to latitude 40°. Migrates upstream to fresh water to spawn then returns to sea. Pacific salmon, *Oncorhynchus,* also migrates to fresh water at spawning time but usually dies after eggs are laid and fertilized.

salmonella, genus of bacteria which inhabits intestinal tract of man and animals. *S. typhi* causes typhoid fever and many other species cause food poisoning in man, and enteritis in rodents and domestic animals.

Salome, in NT, niece of Herod Antipas who, at instigation of her mother, Herodias, asked for head of John the Baptist as a reward for dancing for her royal uncle.

Salonika, Thessalonika, sea port and major city of Macedonia, NE Greece. Founded *c.* 315 BC. Famous churches include Hagia Sophia. University founded 1926. Industrial centre. Pop. (1961) 378,000.

salsify, vegetable oyster, oyster plant, *Tragopogon porrifolius,* plant native to Med. region, grown in N America. Purple flowers; white roots with oyster-like flavour used as vegetable.

salt, mineral crystalline compound, chiefly sodium chloride. Constituent of sea water. Used as food preservative and, when refined, in flavouring. Most of world's supply comes from UK, US, China, India, France.

Salt Lake City, city and cap., N central Utah, US. Founded (1847) by Brigham Young and a group of Mormon pioneers seeking refuge from persecution; now their headquarters. Site of Mormon Temple (built 1853–93) and the Tabernacle (completed 1867). Communications and market centre; industries include metallurgy, meat packing, food processing. Pop. (1963) 349,000.

saltbush, mainly Austral. plants of genus *Atriplex,* inhabiting arid, saline soils and cultivated for forage. *A. semibaccato* has been introduced commercially into California.

salt-dome, dome-like rock structure formed beneath earth's surface by upward movement of a mass of salt. Often associated with oil and gas pools.

saltpetre, nitre, form of potassium nitrate. Chile saltpetre is sodium nitrate. Used in manufacture of gunpowder, fireworks, fluxes, *etc.*

Salvador, El, repub. of C America. Area: 8,000 sq. mi.; cap. San Salvador; other towns, Santa Ana, San Miguel. Mountainous and volcanic with fertile valleys producing coffee, cotton, rice and sugar. Unit of currency, colone. Pop. *c.* 3,000,000.

salvage, in maritime law, term for compensation owner must pay to those who save his ship or cargo from destruction at sea. High salvage rates both encourage others to risk life and property in rescue operations and prevent theft of salvaged property.

Salvation Army, international evangelical and philanthropic movement, founded (1865) in London, England, by William Booth (1829–1912). Organized on military lines, operates many forms of social services.

Salt beds in Thailand where salt is made by salt water evaporation

protein structure. Identified components of insulin molecule.

Sanger, Margaret Higgins (1883–1966), Amer. nurse, pioneer in birth control movement. Organized 1st Amer. conference (1921), international conference (1925).

Sanhedrin [Gk: *synedrion*, assembly], highest Jewish legislative and judicial court of Rabbinic law. Estab. in Jerusalem *c.* 141 BC, dissolved AD 66.

sanicle, cosmopolitan perennial herb of genus *Sanicula*. Roots formerly used medicinally.

Sanpoil, N Amer. Salishan Indian plateau tribe. Lived in Columbia R. region.

sans-culottes, term applied during Fr. Revolution to poorer classes, who wore trousers instead of knee breeches worn by aristocracy and bourgeoisie.

Sanskrit, Indo-European language of ancient India from which many modern Indic languages evolved. In use in India since *c.* 1,500 BC. Sacred, literary and court language was distinct from Prakrit, native language. Main forms are Vedic Sanskrit (mainly religious) from *c.* 1,500 BC and Classical Sanskrit (after *c.* 400 BC). Comparison of Sanskrit with European languages initiated scientific study of languages (19th cent.).

Santa Anna, Antonio Lopez de (*c.* 1794–1876), Mexican politician and revolutionary. Fought in Mexican struggle for independence. Pres. of Mexico (1833–6, 1841–4, 1846–7, 1853–5).

Santa Claus, corruption of *Sinterk-*

Dam on the Tirso River, Sardinia

Greek vase (*c.* 480 BC) depicting the poetess Sappho being praised by Alcaeus

laas, Dutch form of SAINT NICHOLAS. Originated among Dutch colonists in New York, now used throughout English-speaking world.

Santa Cruz de Tenerife, city and port on Tenerife Is., Canary Is., cap. of Tenerife prov. of Spain. Fuelling station for ships, tourist resort. Pop. (1963) 82,620.

Santa Fe, cap. of New Mexico, US. Health resort and tourist centre. Exports Mexican and Indian wares (jewellery, rugs, blankets), agric. products and minerals. Founded (*c.* 1610) by Spaniards; captured (1846) by US. Pop. (1963) 33,394.

Santa Fé, city of E Argentina. Important river port for shipment of grain, livestock and timber products. Pop. (1963) 169,000.

Santander, city and cap. of Santander prov., N Spain. Port on Bay of Biscay; iron works and shipyards. Buildings include a 13th cent. cathedral and castle. Pop. (1965) 126,000.

Santayana, George (1863–1952), Amer. philosopher and poet, b. Spain. Stressed importance of spiritual faith in material world. Wrote *The Life of Reason* (5 vols., 1905–6), novel *The Last Puritan* (1935), and sonnets.

Santiago, cap. and indust. centre of Chile. Founded (1541) by Spaniard, Pedro de Valdivia. Industries include textiles, electrical goods, food processing, chemicals and tobacco. Pop. (1964) 2,314,000.

Santiago de Compostela, city of La Coruña prov., NW Spain. Shrine of Christian pilgrimage since 9th cent.; believed to contain tomb of St James. Contains university (founded 1501). Pop. (1963) 57,165.

Santo Domingo, cap. of Dominican Republic. Oldest extant European inhabited settlement (1496) in Americas. Renamed (1936) Trujillo after ruling dictator; original name restored (1961) on his assassination. Exports sugar, coffee, rum, timber. Pop. 462,492.

São Paulo, cap. of São Paulo prov;

largest city, commercial, industrial and cultural centre of Brazil, founded 1554 by Jesuits. Industries, heavy machinery, textiles, pharmaceuticals. Pop. (1960) 3,825,000.

São Tomé and **Principe,** volcanic islands in Gulf of Guinea, off coast of Africa. Area: 330 sq. mi. and 40 sq. mi.; cap. São Tomé. First settled by Portuguese (1483); formed Portuguese prov. (1522). Exports cacao, coffee, copra, palm oil. Pop. (1961) 64,000.

sap, water solution of inorganic salts (originating in the soil) found in plants. Also the water solution of carbohydrates, manufactured by the plant.

sapele, *Entandrophragma cylindricum,* trop. tree of Africa. Its mahogany-like wood is used in furniture making.

Sapir, Edward (1884–1939), Amer. anthropologist and linguist, b. Germany. Noted esp. for work on Indo-European and American Indian languages.

sapphire, precious gemstone; form of CORUNDUM. Found in Upper Burma, Ceylon, Kashmir, Montana and Queensland. Also produced artificially for use in jewellery and precision machinery.

Sappho (b. *c.* mid 7th cent. BC), Gk. poetess from Lesbos, contemporary of Alcaeus. Principal subject of poems is love, expressed with tender and passionate simplicity, and written in variety of metres. Only fragments of works survive.

saprophytes, any organism which lives on dead organic matter, *e.g.* certain fungi, bacteria, *etc.*

saraband, stately court dance of 17th and 18th cent., evolved from lively Spanish castanet dance.

Saracens, orig. peoples inhabiting frontier land between Roman and Persian Empires. Later referred to Arabs of Syria and Palestine and Mohammedans generally. During crusades applied to peoples of all infidel nations, incl. Turks and Seljuks.

Saragossa, Zaragoza, city and cap. of Saragossa prov., Spain. Communications and commercial centre; trades in wheat, flour, fruit; mechanical and electrical engineering industries. Two cathedrals, La Seo (12th cent. Gothic) and El Pilar (17th cent.). University founded 1474. Pop. (1963) 295,000.

Sarah, in OT, wife of Abraham, to whom, in her old age, a son Isaac was born.

Sarajevo, city of C Yugoslavia, cap. of Bosnia and Hercegovina. Trade and railroad centre. Mosques (16th cent.),

Sarcophagus in the catacomb of St Calixtus in Rome

old Moslem quarters. Assassination (28 June 1914) of Archduke Francis Ferdinand precipitated World War 1. Tobacco and carpet manufacturing, food processing. Pop. *c.* 218,000.

Saratoga, Battle of, encounter (Oct. 1777) during Amer. Revolution, in E N.Y. state, climax of successful colonial defence against Brit. forces under John Burgoyne. Amer. troops commanded by Horatio Gates.

Saratov, city of Russ. SFSR on R. Volga, founded 1590. Major indust. centre with local natural gas source; produces refined oil, machinery, chemicals, textiles, lumber. Pop. (1967) 699,000.

Sarawak, state of Federation of Malaysia since 1963. Area: 48,250 sq. mi.; cap. Kuching. Mountainous with broad coastal plain; large areas of jungle. Crops include rubber, sago, rice, pepper. Petroleum and gold also important. Unit of currency, Malaysian dollar. Pop. (1963) 852,000.

sarcoma, malignant tumour arising in connective tissue and esp. in bone or cartilage. Spreads by extension into neighbouring tissue or by way of bloodstream.

sarcophagus, stone coffin, usually ornamented with sculpture. Used esp. in ancient Greece and Egypt. That of Tutankhamen (*c.* 1550 BC) one of most famous.

Sardanapalus, king of Assyria. Set fire to himself and his palace when besieged in Nineveh by Medes. Identification with Assur-bani-pal unsubstantiated.

sardine, young fish of European pilchard, *Sardinia pilchardus*; found in Mediterranean area and warm coastal waters of Atlantic. Usually preserved in oil or sauce.

Sardinia, Ital. island in W Med. Sea, S of Corsica. Area: 9,302 sq. mi.; cap. Cagliari. Chiefly mountainous with some stock-raising. Zinc, lead and lignite mined. Valuable fisheries. Island under Sp. viceroys (1470–1713) until union with Savoy. 19th cent. kingdom of Sardinia had leading role in Ital. RISORGIMENTO and estab. of united Italy (1861). Pop. 1,500,000.

Sardis, ancient city of Lydia, Asia Minor. Dates from *c.* 8th cent. BC. Captured by Persians, formed part of Roman and Byzantine Empire, ceded (1300) to Seljuk Turks. Probably destroyed by Tamerlane. Site of early Christian church. Coins probably first minted here.

sardonyx, variety of onyx with layers of orange-red sard and white chalcedony. Used as a gem.

Sardou, Victorien (1831–1908), Fr. dramatist, author of many popular comedies, incl. *Les Pattes de Mouche* (1861). More serious works include polit. satire *Rabagas* (1871); *Madame Sans-Gêne* (1893), *Robespierre* (1899).

Sargasso Sea, area of N Atlantic between 40° and 80° W, 25° and 30° N, *i.e.* between West Indies and Azores. Noted for abundance of seaweed.

sargassum weed, gulfweed, seaweed of genus *Sargassum* found in subtrop. waters. *S. bacciferum* is the common gulfweed.

Sargent, Sir Harold Malcolm Watts (1895–1967), Brit. conductor and organist. Conducted BBC Symphony Orchestra (1950–7); conductor-in-chief of Promenade Concerts (1957–67), and Huddersfield Choral Society from 1932.

São Paulo

Sargent, John Singer (1856–1925), Amer. painter, resident in London after 1884. Painted portraits and water colour landscapes.

Sargon II (772–705 BC), king of Assyria (722–705 BC). Consolidated empire, often by removing large numbers of people from an area and replacing them with others less rebellious. Conquered Samaria and Babylon. Estab. city of Dur Sharrukin.

Sark [Fr: Sercq], island in English Channel, one of CHANNEL ISLANDS. Area: 2 sq. mi. Retains feudal ruler, Dame of Sark. Pop. (1961) 560.

Saroyan, William (1908–), Amer. short-story writer and dramatist. Collections include *The Daring Young Man on the Flying Trapeze* (1934); among his plays *The Time of Your Life* (1939).

sarsaparilla, climbing or trailing trop. Amer. plant of genus *Smilax*. Dried roots used as flavouring or olefactory agent.

Sarsi, small tribe of N Amer. Indians of Athapaskan linguistic stock. After attacks by Cree and other tribes, moved from upper Saskatchewan R. and allied with Blackfoot Indians. Customs modified by association with plains culture. Ceded lands to Canada (1877) and moved to a reservation near Calgary, Alberta (1880).

Sarto, Andrea del, orig. Andrea Domenico d'Agnolo di Francesco Vannucchi (1486–1531), Florentine Renaissance artist. Famous frescoes include *Adoration of the Kings* (cloisters of Sant' Annunziata, Florence). Paintings include *Pietà* and *Descent from the Cross*.

Sartre, Jean-Paul (1905–), Fr.

philosopher and writer, exponent of EXISTENTIALISM. Stresses individual's responsibility in midst of meaninglessness. Works include novel *Nausea* (1938), plays *The Flies* (1947), *No Exit* (1945) and philosophical work *Being and Nothingness* (1943).

Saskatchewan, Prairie prov. of W Canada. Area: 251,700 sq. mi.; cap. Regina; other main city, Saskatoon. Rich in mineral resources, esp. uranium; plentiful timber supplies. Abundant wheat produced on flat land suited to large-scale mechanized farming. First European exploration (17th cent.); acquired by Canada 1869, became prov. 1905. Pop. (1961) 925,181.

sassafras, *Sassafras albidum,* N Amer. and Asian tree with yellow flowers, dark blue fruits and aromatic bark and foliage. Various parts of the tree used in manufacture of medicines, foods, drinks and perfume.

Sassanidae, Sassanids, Sassanians, dynasty of Persian kings (AD *c.* 226 – *c.* 641). Cap. Ctesiphon. Founded by chieftain Ardashir who overthrew kingdom of Parthia (*c.* 226). Wars esp. with Rome and Byzantium. Conquered by Arabs (*c.* 641).

Sassoon, Siegfried Lorraine (1886 – 1967), Eng. poet and novelist. Experiences in World War 1 inspired anti-war poems in *Counter-Attack* (1918). *Memoirs of a Foxhunting Man* (1929) is autobiog. novel.

Satan, in Christian teaching, personification of the powers of evil, adversary of God and man.

Satanism, general term for worship of the powers of evil, *e.g.* devils or demons. Specific practices include devil worship, diabolism (sorcery or witchcraft), demonology. Worship may involve desecration of the Christian sacraments, *e.g.* Black or Satanic Mass is Christian Mass said backwards.

satellites, in astronomy, smaller celestial bodies revolving about a planet or star. All planets in solar system except Venus and Mercury have satellites. Russians placed 1st artificial satellite in orbit round Earth (1957). Many have been launched since for scientific and communications purposes.

Satie, Erik (1866 – 1925), Fr. composer. Wrote ballet and film music, and piano pieces incl. *Gymnopédies*.

satin, silk or rayon fabric, sometimes with cotton filling. One side smooth and glossy, other side matt. First made in China; spread to Europe in Middle Ages.

satinwood, close-grained, hard, yellow wood of E Indian tree, *Chlor-*

oxylum swietenia. Used for making furniture.

satire, literary form, in prose or poetry, which ridicules individuals, situations or ideas. Uses mockery, wit, parody or irony; may be humorous or serious.

Saturn, in Roman religion, god of agriculture, later identified with Gk. Cronus, and regarded as father of Jupiter, Juno, Ceres, Pluto, Neptune. Thought to have been early king of Rome, reign known as Golden Age.

Saturn, in astronomy, 6th planet from the Sun (*c.* 887,100,000 mi.) and 2nd largest in Solar System. Revolves about the Sun with sidereal period of 29 yr. 167 days. Has system of 3 concentric rings of dust particles lying in its equatorial plane.

Saturnalia, in Roman religion, festival celebrated (17 – 19 Dec.) in honour of Saturn and the sowing of crops. Period of general festivity, licence for slaves, presents, *etc.*; prototype, possibly origin of Christmas festivities.

Satyrs, in Gk. myth., attendants of Dionysus and spirits of hills and woods. Represented as partly human in form, partly bestial. Identified with Roman Fauni.

Saudi Arabia [Al Mamlaka al Arabiya as-Sa'udiya], independent kingdom of SW Asia. Area: *c.* 927,000 sq. mi.; cap. Riyadh. Pri-

marily agric. and pastoral, with important revenue from oil reserves.

In S are holy cities of Mecca and Medina. Country comprises Nejd, Hejaz, united (1925) by IBN SAUD. Present ruler Feisal dethroned brother (1964). Arab population's religion, Islam. Unit of currency, riyal. Pop. (1963) 6,750,000.

Sauerbruch, Ferdinand (1875 – 1951), Ger. surgeon, initiator of modern thoracic surgery; invented pneumatic chamber to prevent operative pneumothorax (1903 – 4).

sauerkraut, Ger. dish, consisting of shredded cabbage, salt and spices, left until fermented.

Saul, first king of Israel (1030 BC – 1010 BC). Fought successfully against Philistines. Developed insane jealousy of David, former protégé and eventual successor. Reign ended with his suicide after defeat by Philistines on Mt. Gilboa.

savanna, savannah, trop. or sub-trop. grassland with scattered trees or bushes. Vegetation grows rapidly in rainy season. Examples include llanos of Venezuela, campos of Brazil and downs of Australia; most extensive savanna land is in Africa.

Savonarola, Girolamo (1452 – 98), Ital. Dominican and reformer. In Florence gained great influence through preaching. After expulsion of MEDICI family from Florence, set up a Puritan republic. Charged with heresy and excommunicated (1497). Convicted of heresy and burned.

savory, aromatic, menthaceous herb of genus *Satureia.* Summer savory, *S. hortensis,* and winter savory, *S. montana,* used in cooking.

Savoy, House of, European royal family, rulers of Savoy from 11th cent., sometime rulers of Piedmont

Landscape of the Savannah grasslands of Africa

(now Italy), Valois, Bresse, Nice (now France). Acquired Sicily under Peace of Utrecht (1714), exchanged it for Sardinia (1720). **Charles Albert,** King of Sardinia, fought in wars of the RISORGIMENTO, and his son **Victor Emmanuel II** was 1st king of united Italy. Dynasty lasted from 1861 until abdication of Humbert II (1946).

Savoy, Savoie, Alpine region of E France forming departments of Savoie and Haute-Savoie. Includes Mont Blanc (15,781 ft.). Historic cap. Chambéry. Independent county (11th cent.) then a duchy (1416); annexed by France (1792–1815), finally ceded 1860. Dairy farming, forestry with industry based on hydro-electricity; popular tourist area.

sawbelly see ALEWIFE.

sawfish, large ray of genus *Pristis.* Found in warm shallow seas and river mouths of trop. America and Africa. Has flattened elongated snout with row of tooth-like structures along each edge.

sawfly, insect of order Hymenoptera. Female has saw-like ovipositors for laying eggs on twigs and leaves. Caterpillar-like larvae. Some species are gall producing, others are garden pests.

Sax, [**Antoine Joseph**] **Adolphe** (1814–94), Belgian musical instrument maker. Designer of saxophone; produced saxhorn family of brass wind instruments for Fr. military bands.

Saxe, Maurice, Comte de (1696–1750), Fr. army officer; created Marshal of France for success in War of Austrian Succession. Defeated Cumberland at Fontenoy (1745). Wrote *Mes Rêveries* (pub. 1757) on art of war.

Saxe-Coburg, former duchy of C Germany. In 1826 Ernest III of Saxe-Coburg gave Saalfeld to Saxe-Meiningen, obtained Saxe-Gotha and became Grand Duke Ernest I of Saxe-Coburg-Gotha. Prince Albert, his younger son, m. Queen Victoria of England (1840). Last holder of title abdicated 1918.

saxhorn, family of conical bore brass instruments with valves. Designed in 1840s in Belgium, by Adolphe Sax. Includes tuba and euphonium.

saxifrage, herb of genus *Saxifraga* of N temp. and arctic regions. Some species grow wild in clefts of rocks; other species cultivated as garden plants, *e.g.* London pride, *S. umbrosa* and *S. aizoon,* which is rockery variety.

Saxons, Teutonic people, 1st mentioned (2nd cent.) as living in Holstein. Spread S and E, some settling (6th cent.) in SE England and with Angles establishing Anglo-Saxon kingdoms. Charlemagne attempted (8th cent.) their conquest and forcible conversion to Christianity. Final defeat (803) by Franks, incorporated Saxony in Frankish empire and in Catholic Church.

Saxony [Ger: **Sachsen**], area of N Germany, formerly kingdom, later state (cap. Dresden). Orig. inhabited by Saxons, conquered (8th cent.) by Charlemagne. Electorate during Middle Ages, became kingdom (1806), joined (1871) Ger. Empire. W region became LOWER SAXONY with formation of West Germany (1946); E region incorporated by East Germany and dissolved 1952.

Saxony-Anhalt, former state of East Germany, now part of administrative districts of Halle and Magdeburg. Formed from small state of Anhalt and Prussian state of Saxony (region gained from Saxony in 1815 after Napoleonic Wars). Minerals, lignite, salt and potash (world's biggest deposits).

saxophone, family of musical wind instruments, varying in range and size but all having single reed and conical tube of brass. Used in military bands, jazz groups and orchestras. Developed by Adolphe Sax in 1840's.

Say, Jean Baptiste (1767–1832), Fr. economist. Developed and popularized doctrines of Adam Smith. Theory of markets (supply creates demand) contained in *Treatise on Political Economy* (1803).

Sayers, Dorothy L[**eigh**] (1893–1957), Eng. detective fiction writer, creator of Lord Peter Wimsey. Works include *Murder Must Advertise* (1933), *The Nine Tailors* (1934); radio series on life of Christ, *The Man Born to be King* (1943), translation of Dante's *Inferno* (1949).

scab, fungal plant disease character-

Saxifraga aizoon

Saudi Arabia: Civil Service Ministry at Riyadh

ized by hyperplastic scab-like lesions on leaves and fruits. Apple scab is caused by *Venturia inaequalis* and pear scab by *V. pirina.*

scabies, skin disease caused by parasitic infection, *Sarcoptes scabei.* Disease spread only by direct contact of skin to skin; main symptom is intense itch aggravated by warmth.

scabious, annual or perennial herb of genus *Scabiosa* of Europe, Asia and Africa. Species include sweet scabious, *S. atropurpurea,* with white, pink or purple flowers and *S. arvensis,* field scabious, with purple flowers.

Scafell, peak (3,162 ft.), Cumberland, highest in England. Under the jurisdiction of National Trust since 1919.

Scala, Teatro alla, famous opera house in Milan, Italy. Opened 1778; built on site of church Santa Maria della Scala.

Scalawags, term used in South after US Civil War to refer to white Southerners who aided RECONSTRUCTION programme.

scale, in music, arrangement in ascending or descending order of related groups of notes. Forms key of given piece based on tonic or key note.

Scaliger, Julius Caesar (1484–1558), Ital. philologist and physician. Analyzed works of Cicero in *De Causis Linguae Latinae* (1540); advocated improved classification of plants. His son **Joseph Justus Scaliger** (1540–1609) was eminent scholar; founded modern chronology in *De Emendatione Temporum* (1583) and *Thesaurus Temporum* (1606). Pioneered criticism of classical authors.

scallop, bivalve mollusc of genus *Pecten,* of world-wide distribution. Fan-shaped, radially ribbed shell with wavy outer edge. Species include *P. canerinus,* Pacific scallop, and Atlantic bay scallop, *Aequipecten irradians.*

Portrait of Agatha van Schoonhoven by Jan van Scorel

scalp, covering of cranium, top of head from skin to bone incl. many hair follicles. Outermost is the skin; next a fibrous layer connecting skin to underlying muscle, which in turn covers a layer of loose tissue.

scalytail, flying squirrel of genus *Anomalrus* of high forests of trop. Africa. Horny scales under base of tail.

Scandinavia, region of N Europe comprising Sweden, Norway, Finland and Denmark. Culturally and racially term also includes people of Iceland.

Scandinavian, division of Germanic branch of Indo-European languages. Includes Danish, Norwegian, Swedish and Icelandic. Has *c.* 18 million speakers.

Scapa Flow, sea-basin in Orkney Is., Scotland. Brit. naval base in World Wars 1 and 2; scene of scuttling of surrendered Ger. fleet (1919).

scaphopoda, class of marine invertebrate mollusc animals, comprising the tooth shells. Curved tapering shell open at both ends.

scarab, representation or image of

Schnauzer

Egyptian sacred dung-beetle, *Scarabaeus sacer.* Much used by ancient Egyptians as symbol, seal or amulet.

scarab beetle, any of *c.* 30,000 species of beetles of family Scarabaeidae. World-wide distribution; oval bodies characterized by club-ended antennae. Species include dung beetle, June bug, cockchafer, *etc.*

Scaramouche, stock character in Ital. COMMEDIA DELL'ARTE, a cowardly boaster, easily frightened.

Scarborough, municipal borough and resort of N Riding of Yorkshire, England. Developed as spa from 1620. Heavily bombed in World War 2. Pop. (1961) 42,600.

Scarlatti, Alessandro (1659– 1725), Ital. composer. Pioneer of Ital. opera. Composed over 100 operas, masses, cantatas, oratorios, *etc.* His son [Guiseppe] **Domenico Scarlatti** (1685– 1757) composed esp. for harpsichord.

scarlet fever, scarlatina, contagious, febrile disease caused by *Streptococcus pyogenes.* Characterized by sore throat, fever and punctate rash.

scarlet pimpernel, *Anagallis arvensis,* flowering herb. Scarlet, white or purplish blossoms close in wet weather.

Scarron, Paul (1610– 60), Fr. comic poet, novelist and dramatist. Exponent of satirical picaresque novel, *e.g. Roman Comique* (1651).

scaup, diving duck of genus *Aythya. A. marila,* greater scaup, of N hemisphere has bluish-grey bill.

scavenger beetle, beetle which feeds on decomposing vegetable matter, on land or under water.

scepticism, skepticism, in philosophy, theory contending that range of knowledge is limited by capacity of mind or inaccessibility of object. Doctrine originated among ancient Greeks, *e.g.* Democritus. Greatest modern sceptic Kant, exponent of agnostic system.

Schacht, Hjalmar [Horace Greeley] (1877–1970), Ger. financier, pres. of Reichsbank (1923– 30, 1933–9). Attempted to stabilize Ger. mark, opposed payment of REPARATIONS and helped finance rearmament under Hitler. Involved in anti-Hitler plot (1944), imprisoned by Nazis. Acquitted at Nuremberg trials (1946).

Scharnhorst, air and naval action of World War 2. Brit. planes and destroyers inflicted severe damage on Ger. battle-ships *Scharnhorst, Gneisenau,* and *Prinz Eugen* in Eng. Channel, but failed to sink them.

Scheele, Karl Wilhelm, (1742– 86), Swedish chemist, discovered oxygen (1774) independently of Joseph Priestley. Isolated important organic acids; investigated compounds of manganese, barium, arsenic and other metals; discovered chlorine.

Scheldt, Schelde, river (270 mi.) rising in NE France, flowing across W Belgium through a double estuary in SW Netherlands to North Sea. Navigable for 200 mi.

Schelling, Friedrich Wilhelm Joseph von (1775– 1854), Ger. philosopher, associated with Romanticism. Advocated unity of mind and nature. Works include *Philosophy of Nature* (1799), *Transcendental Idealism* (1800).

scherzo, sprightly humorous instrumental musical composition. Usually in quick triple time and in ternary form.

Schiaparelli, Giovanni Virginio (1835– 1910), Ital. astronomer. Discovered asteroid Hesperia (1861); observed markings on Mars which he called canals (1877).

Schick, Bela (1877–   ), Amer. pediatrician, b. Hungary. Devised (1913) Schick test to determine susceptibility to diphtheria.

Schiller, Ferdinand Canning Scott (1864– 1937), Brit. philosopher. A pragmatist, he called his philosophy humanism. Author of *Humanism* (1903), *Problems of Belief* (1924).

Schiller, [Johann Christoph] Friedrich von (1759– 1805), Ger. dramatist, poet and historian, associated with GOETHE and STURM UND DRANG movement. Plays, noted for dramatic action, include *Die Räuber* (1781), *Wallenstein* (1791–3), *Maria Stuart* (1800). Historical works include *The History of the Thirty Years War* (1791–3).

Schism, Great *see* GREAT SCHISM.

schist, metamorphic rock easily split into thin plates. Formed by intense heat and pressure. Includes mica schist, chlorite schist, talc schist. Abundant in Precambrian rocks.

schistosomiasis, bilharzia, parasitic disease caused by infestation of veins by blood flukes of genus *Schistosoma*. Affects man and other mammals in much of Asia, Africa and S America.

schizophrenia, mental disorder formerly called dementia praecox. Characterized by distorted mental processes, withdrawal from external world, sometimes hallucinations and 'split personality'. Treatment includes SHOCK THERAPY.

Schlegel, August Wilhelm von (1767––1845), Ger. author and scholar, noted for translations of Shakespeare. With brother **Friedrich von Schlegel** (1772–1829), edited periodical *Athenaeum*. Both contributed to Ger. Romantic movement.

Schlesinger, Arthur Meier (1888–1965), Amer. historian, with D. R. Fox edited *A History of American Life* (1927–48). His son **Arthur Meier Schlesinger, Jr.** (1917–), also Amer. historian, author of *The Age of Jackson* (1945), *A Thousand Days* (1965). Special assistant to Pres. Kennedy (1961–3).

Schleswig-Holstein, northernmost state of West Germany forming neck of Jutland peninsula. Area: 6,057 sq. mi.; cap. Kiel. Agric. region with heavy industry; shipbuilding, mechanical engineering, textiles, fishing. Duchies Schleswig and Holstein Danish possessions until 19th cent. Schleswig incorporated in Prussia (1864), Holstein (1866). Became state of Federal Republic of Germany (1949). Pop. (1961) 2,316,000.

Schlieffen, Alfred, Graf von (1833–1913), Ger. army officer. Chief of general staff (1891–1906). Originated Schlieffen plan by which strong right wing would outflank Fr. defences. Adopted successfully in World War 2.

Schliemann, Heinrich (1822–90), Ger. archaeologist. Famous for excavations of Troy at Hissarlik in Turkey. Later discovery at Mycenae of shaft tombs with vast burial treasure estab. the character of a great pre-Hellenic civilization.

Schmidt-Rottluff, Karl (1884–), Ger. expressionist painter, engraver and sculptor. Helped found the Brücke group (1905). Works include landscapes and portraits, designs for tapestries, mosaics, *etc.*

schnauzer, short-haired Ger. terrier. Giant, standard and miniature varieties. Long head, blunt nose, small erect ears; coat black or salt-and-pepper. Standard, oldest schnauzer breed, used as guard dog.

Schnitzler, Arthur (1862–1931), Austrian writer. Psychological dramas include *Anatol* (1893), *Liebelei* (1895); also wrote novels and short stories.

Schoenbein, Christian Friedrich (1799–1868), Ger. chemist. Discovered ozone (1840) and developed gun-cotton and collodion (1846).

Schoenberg, Arnold (1874–1951), Amer. composer, b. Austria. Early work romantic (*e.g. Verklärte Nacht*, 1899). Later used ATONALITY in *Pierrot Lunaire* (1912) and in 1920s established 12 note serial method, as in *Suite for Piano* (1923).

scholasticism, philosophy of medieval European theologians, esp. Robert Grosseteste, Thomas Aquinas and Albertus Magnus. Constituted synthesis of philosophy of Aristotle and Christian revelation; esp. influenced by Neo-platonism. Attempted to solve conflict between realism and nominalism and estab. proof of God's existence. Developed from teachings of Abelard, esp. through work of Anselm.

schooner, fore and aft-rigged vessel with 2 or more masts. Developed in early 18th cent. America.

Schopenhauer, Arthur (1788–1860), Ger. philosopher. Believed man's irrational will to be the only reality. Demands of this force are, in essence, insatiable, hence individual is doomed to perpetual suffering. Conflict of wills between individuals, of necessity causes strife and mutual destruction. Release from suffering and discord achieved only by total self abnegation. Works include *The World as Will and Idea* (1818), *Will in Nature* (1836).

Schreiner, Olive Emile Albertina (1855–1920), South African writer. Best known work *The Story of an African Farm* (1883) written under pseudonym of **Ralph Iron**. Other works include *Woman and Labour* (1911).

Schrödinger, Erwin (1887–1961), Austrian physicist, esp. concerned with the physics of the atom. With P. A. M. Dirac, awarded Nobel Prize for

Scaup

Physics (1933) for the mathematical formulation of wave mechanics.

Schubert, Franz Peter (1797–1828), Austrian composer. One of 1st great romantic composers, representing link between Viennese classical school and Ger. romanticism. Genius revealed esp. as creator of Ger. *lieder*, solo songs in which poet's images and mood were recreated to perfection for voice and piano; most noted examples *Der Erlkönig* and *Gretchen am Spinnrade*. Influenced by Beethoven, esp. in symphonies and string quartets. Greatest works include song cycles *Die schöne Müllerin* and *Winterreise*, chamber works Quartet in D Minor (*Death and the Maiden*) and Quintet in A (*The Trout*), and Symphony in C Major and Symphony in B Minor (the *Unfinished*).

Schulz, Charles Monroe (1922–), Amer. cartoonist. Creator of popular 'Peanuts' comic strip.

Schuman, Robert (1886–1963), Fr. statesman. Premier (1947–8); foreign min. (1948–53), worked out plan (1950) for EUROPEAN COAL AND STEEL COMMUNITY.

Schumann, Robert Alexander (1810–56), Ger. composer. Like Chopin and Mendelssohn regarded as a leading representative of refined romanticism. Inspired by writings of Ger. contemporary poets Hoffmann and Jean Paul Richter; musical style shows influence of Bach, Schubert and Beethoven. Works include collections of piano pieces, *Carnaval* and *Kreisleriana, Piano Concerto in A minor*, and *Spring Symphony* and *Rhenish Symphony*. A noted music critic, encouraged appreciation of other composers esp. Chopin.

Schuschnigg, Kurt von (1897–), Austrian statesman. Succeeded as Chancellor (1934) after assassination of Dollfuss. Virtual dictator (1936–8). Attempted to preserve Austrian independence in face of Nazi pressure, but gave way to Hitler. Interned on Ger. invasion.

Schutz, Heinrich (1585–1672), Ger. composer esp. of church music; wrote 1st Ger. opera *Daphne* (1627).

Schweitzer, Albert (1875–1965), Fr. philosopher, musician and medical missionary. Used proceeds from European organ recitals of Bach's

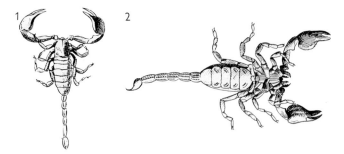

Scorpions: 1. House Scorpion 2. Field Scorpion

work, to finance hospital founded (1913) at Lambarene, Fr. Equatorial Africa. Works include *The Quest of the Historical Jesus* (1906), *Out of My Life and Thought* (1932). Awarded Nobel Peace Prize (1952).

Schwinger, Julian Seymour (1918–), Amer. physicist. With S. Tomonaga and R. P. Feynman, awarded Nobel Prize for Physics (1965) for work on quantum electrodynamics.

sciatica, pain along the course of the sciatic nerve, esp. affecting thigh and leg. Caused by compression and inflammation.

science fiction, literary genre drawing on scientific knowledge or pseudoscience to present fantasy. Early exponents included H. G. Wells and Jules Verne. Genre developed by, *e.g.* George Orwell, Isaac Asimov, Ray Bradbury.

Scilly Islands, archipelago of *c.* 140 small islands off SW England, 5 of which are inhabited. Area: 6½ sq. mi.; cap. Hugh Town; part of Cornwall. Produces early fruit, vegetables, flowers. Pop. (1961) 2,273.

Scipio Africanus Major [Publius Cornelius Scipio] (*c.* 236–*c.* 183 BC), Roman soldier. Appointed commander in Spain (210 BC), during Second Punic War, routed Carthaginians and proceeded to Africa (204 BC). Ended war by defeating Hannibal at Zama (202 BC). Later commanded forces against Antiochus of Syria.

Scipio Africanus Minor [Publius Cornelius Scipio Aemilianus] (*c.* 185–129 BC), Roman soldier, adopted by son of Scipio Africanus Major. Elected consul during Third Punic War, besieged Carthage and destroyed it (146 BC). Ended war against Numantia, Spain (133 BC). Noted as orator and patron of Latin and Gk. letters. Sudden death aroused suspicion of assassination.

sclerosis, in pathology, an invasion of tissue by small cells and fibrous tissue

in response to some irritative or degenerative process.

Scofield, [David] Paul (1922–), Brit. stage and film actor. Noted for Shakespearean roles. Other plays include *Ring Round the Moon* and *Venice Preserved.* Awarded an Oscar for his role in *A Man for All Seasons.*

Scone, parish in Perthshire, Scotland. Near modern village is Old Scone, cap. (8th cent.) of Kingdom of the Picts; in its abbey Scottish kings were crowned on Stone of Destiny until its removal (1296) to Westminster Abbey by Edward I of England.

Scopes trial, in US legal history, trial (1925) of school teacher John T. Scopes for teaching Darwinian theory of evolution, then contrary to Tennessee state law. He was convicted, but was later released on a technicality.

Scorel, Jan van (1495–1562), Dutch painter. Much influenced by Ital. Renaissance styles. Best known for portraits and religious compositions.

Scorpio *see* ZODIAC.

scorpion, carnivorous, nocturnal, arachnid of order Scorpionidae of warm and trop. regions. Long narrow, segmented tail with venomous sting, rarely fatal to man.

scorpion fish, widely distributed marine fish of genus *Scorpaena.* Poisonous dorsal spines.

scorpion fly, harmless insect of order Mecoptera. Males of some species have structure at rear of abdomen resembling scorpion's tail.

scotch fir, scots pine, *Pinus sylvestris,* evergreen tree of Europe and temp. Asia. Spreading branches with short rigid needles; hard yellow wood, valued as timber.

scotch thistle, cotton thistle, *Onopordon acanthium,* biennial prickly European herb with pale purple flowers. Naturalized in N America.

scoter, *Oidemia nigra,* blackish coloured diving duck found off-shore in

Europe in winter. American variety is *O. americana.*

Scotland, N part of UK incl. neighbouring Hebrides, Orkney, Shetland islands. Area: 30,405 sq. mi.; cap. Edinburgh; other main cities, Glasgow, Aberdeen, Dundee. Mountainous Highlands in N include Ben Nevis; central Lowlands region (esp. Glasgow) is manufacturing and indust. centre. Orig. inhabited by Gaelic clans from Ireland; united (884) as kingdom. Repeatedly at war with England until James VI became (1603) James I of England. Act of Union (1707) joined 2 parliaments. Scotland retains cultural and legal entity. Pop. (1966) 5,191,000.

Scotland, Church of, estab. Presbyterian Church of Scotland. 1560 act, inspired by JOHN KNOX, sanctioned and reformed church, based on self-governing units after Geneva models. Two *Books of Discipline* (1560, 1577) laid out church organization. History of C. of S. complicated by relation with crown and establishment. In 17th cent. Scot. establishment was officially episcopal; high-handed efforts to impose nonpresbyterian system on C. of S. led to National Covenant (1638), and closed anti-episcopal ranks. C. of S. consolidated during Commonwealth, again proscribed (1661 Rescissory Act) at Restoration. After 1689 Episcopal Church associated with Jacobite cause; Hanoverians supported C. of S. which had been estab. by act of parl. (1690).

Scotland Yard, headquarters in London, England, of Metropolitan Police. Orig. housed in building on site of palace used by visiting Scottish royalty. Term properly applied only to Criminal Investigation Dept. (CID).

Scots, language of Lowlands and NE Scotland evolved from Northumbrian O.E. Supplanted Gaelic (7th-8th cent.) and estab. as distinct literary and spoken form by 15th cent. alongside Scot. Gaelic (Highlands and W Isles). Inhibited development led to adoption of standard English, esp. as written language.

Scott, Francis Reginald (1899–), Canadian constitutional lawyer and poet. Active in Canadian left-wing politics. Poetry, usually satirical, includes *Events and Signals* (1954) and *Signature* (1964).

Scott, Sir George Gilbert (1811–78), Eng. architect. Active in 19th cent. neo-Gothic revival. Designed Albert Memorial, London; carried out controversial restoration work on Westminster Abbey.

Scott, Michael (*c.* 1175–*c.* 1234), Scot. astrologer and physician at Emperor Frederick II's court. With others translated works of Aristotle from Arabic into Latin. Attained posthumous fame as magician.

Scott, Robert Falcon (1868–1912), Eng. naval officer and Antarctic explorer. Surveyed Ross Sea (1901–4). Reached South Pole 1 month after AMUNDSEN (1912) with 4 companions. All died on return journey. His son **Peter Markham Scott** (1909–   ) is naturalist and artist. Founded Severn Wildfowl Trust (1948).

Scott, Sheila Christine (1927–   ), British aviator and holder of 35 world records.

Scott, Sir Walter (1771–1832), Scot. lawyer, romantic poet and novelist. Interested in Scot. folklore and history. Published ballads *Minstrelsy of the Scottish Border* (1802) and narrative poems incl. *The Lay of the Last Minstrel* (1805), *Lady of the Lake* (1810). Historical novel *Waverley* (1814) began successful series incl. *The Heart of Midlothian* (1818), *Quentin Durward* (1823) and *Redgauntlet* (1824).

Scott, Winfield (1786–1866), Amer. army officer. Successful in War of 1812. Supreme commander 1841–61. In Mexican War headed S expedition, routed Santa Ana and took Mexico City (1847). Unsuccessful pres. candidate (1852).

Scottish Nationalist Party (SNP), polit. party evolved from Scottish Home Rule Association (formed 1886). Advocates self-govt. for Scotland.

Scouts Association (until 1967 Boy

Scotch Thistle

Scouts Association), non-polit., non-military organization founded (1907) by Sir Robert Baden-Powell, to encourage moral, physical and mental development of boys. Incorporated by Royal Charter (1912). Now worldwide movement. Corresponding organization for girls is Girl Guides [UK], Girl Scouts [US].

scree, talus, mass of boulders and broken rocks which accumulate at foot of cliff or mountain. Broken from main rocks by weathering and rolled down by pull of gravity.

screech owl, small Amer. owl of genus *Otus*. Reddish-brown or grey with ear-tufts; wailing cry. Species include N Amer. *O. asio*.

Scriabin, Aleksandr Nikolayevich (1872–1915), Russ. composer and pianist. Developed theories of harmony to express theosophical beliefs. Wrote 10 piano sonatas; orchestral works include *Divine Poem* and *Prometheus*.

scrofula, type of tuberculosis, due to a deposit of tubercle in the skin.

Results in severe scarring, esp. of face.

scrubland, tracts of semi-arid land, covered by undergrowth and stunted trees. Forms maquis in Med. area, mallee and mulga scrub in Australia, cacti scrub in East Africa.

Scudéry, Madeleine de (1607–1701), Fr. author of romances. Best known for *Artamène; ou, le Grand Cyrus* (10 vols., 1649–53), *Clélie* (1654–60).

sculling, art of propelling a boat by means of one or more pairs of sculls, shorter and lighter than oars. First competitive race estab. 1715. Single and double sculling included in Olympic Games, world and European regatta championships.

sculpin, Atlantic sea fish of family Cottidae. Usually scaleless with scanty bony flesh.

scurvy, scorbutus, disease now seen mainly in infancy and old age. Characterized by multiple spontaneous haemorrhages; caused by vitamin C deficiency.

Scylla, in Gk. myth., daughter of Hecate, loved by Poseidon and turned into monster by Amphitrite. Devoured sailors who passed near her cave in Straits of Messina, S Italy, opposite dangerous whirlpool Charybdis, on coast of Sicily.

Scythians, nomadic tribe from Asia. Earliest known horsemen. Settled (7th cent. BC) in S Russia between Don and Dnieper rivers. Expanded S and W; repulsed (*c.* 512 BC) by Persian king, Darius. By 4th cent. BC, a declining power and by 2nd cent. BC, had been overwhelmed by Sarmatians.

sea anemone, sedentary marine animal of phylum Coelenterata.

Scotland: Edinburgh Castle

Glencoe: Typical scenery in the Highlands of Scotland

Sea Grass

Columnar body with one or more circles of tentacles surrounding mouth.

sea campion, *Silene maritima,* wild perennial plant of pink carnation family, common in Europe and Asia. Pink or white flowers; greyish-green foliage.

sea cow, rare, herbivorous, aquatic mammal of trop. coastal waters. Fish-like in shape with hairless body. Species include dugong, manatee.

sea cucumber, marine animal of class Holothuroidea. Long, leathery body with tentacles around anterior end.

sea grass, *Enteromorpha compressa,* common green algae of N European shores. Plants tubular, may reach *c.* 15 in.

Sea Islands, chain of low sandy islands off Atlantic coast of Florida, Georgia and South Carolina, US. Main city, Beaufort, Port Royal Is. Long-fibred sea-island cotton grown in 19th cent.

sea lavender, maritime plant of genus *Limonium* with spikes of white, pink or yellow flowers. Grown in gardens and greenhouses. Purple flowered *L. vulgare* is found on dunes and muddy sea-shores.

sea lettuce, green laver, seaweed of genus *Ulva.* Flat, crinkly, green fronds sometimes eaten as salad.

sea lily, lily-like marine animal of Crinoidae class.

sea lion, large-eared seal. California sea lion, *Zalophus californicus* with dark brown coat and shrill barking voice is commonest and frequently trained; found in N Pacific. Largest is Steller's sea lion, *Eumetopias jubatus,* of Pacific coast of N America; up to 13 ft. in length.

sea otter, *Enhydra lutris,* marine carnivore of shores of N Pacific. Larger than common otter, with long tail; dense, dark brown fur, highly valued commercially.

sea perch, *Serranus scriba,* fish related to sea bass with black-banded,

yellowish body. Found mainly in Med. and Red Sea.

sea pink, thrift, perennial alpine or maritime herb of genus *Armeria,* esp. *A. maritima.* Pink or white flowers. Many species popular as garden plants.

sea robin, gurnard, esp. Amer. gurnard of genus *Prionotus.* Scorpion-like fish with red or brown body.

sea snake, venomous marine snake of family Hydrophidae of coastal waters and estuaries of Indian and Pacific oceans. Long flexible body with fin-like tail.

sea squirt, tunicate marine animal, which contracts its body and ejects water when disturbed.

sea trout, *Salmo trutta trutta,* trout of Salmon family, of northern waters, up to 4 ft. long. Spawns in rivers.

sea urchin, spiny marine animal with calcareous rounded shell of class Echinoidea. Uses spines for walking; lives on rocky sea-shores.

sea wolf, wolffish, *Anarrhichas lupus,* large N Atlantic fish, related to the blenny. Heavy jaw with strong conical teeth.

seabees, popular name for US naval construction battalions in World War 2. Responsible for building and maintaining overseas naval bases, air fields and repair facilities.

Seaborg, Glenn Theodore (1912–   ), Amer. chemist and physicist. With E. M. McMillan, awarded Nobel Prize for Chemistry (1951) for discovery of several elements with atomic numbers greater than that of uranium.

seagull, common name for many species of GULL, esp. marine varieties.

sea-horse, small fish of genus *Hippocampus* of pipefish family. Elongated snout and prehensile tail; mainly found in trop. seas. Species include *H. hudsonius* of N Amer. Atlantic coast.

seal, marine carnivorous mammal of suborder Pinnipedia. Species include eared (family Phocidae) and earless (family Otariidae). Thick smooth coat and flipper-like limbs adapted for swimming. Hunted for skins and oil-yielding blubber.

seance *see* SPIRITUALISM.

seaplane, aircraft designed to take off from land or water. May be fitted with small floats attached to wing-tips (float-planes) or specially shaped hull (flying-boats).

Searle, Ronald (1920–   ), Brit. artist and cartoonist. Creator of the 'Girls of St Trinian's'. Illustrated *A Phoenix too Frequent* by Christopher Fry.

sea-sickness, form of motion sickness caused by rolling of a ship. Character-

Sea Lettuce

ized by nausea, dizziness and often vomiting.

Seattle, principal city, route centre and port of Washington, US; first settled 1851. University of Washington founded 1861. Considerable development resulted from opening of Panama Canal (1914). Industries include timber, aircraft and ship building, chemicals. Pop. (1963) 864,000.

seaweed, common name for all types of marine ALGAE. Usually grows on sea bed from high water mark to a depth of 600 ft.

Sebastian, Saint (d. AD 288), Roman martyr. Killed by Diocletian on revelation of his Christian faith.

Sebastopol *see* SEVASTOPOL.

Second Empire, (1852–70), period in Fr. history when Louis Napoleon, after overthrowing Second Republic, ruled as emperor NAPOLEON III. Terminated by Franco-Prussian War.

secret police, branch of police specifically operating without making presence known. Concerned with internal national security and hence politics. In non-democratic states used as powerful instrument to crush opposition to govt. (*e.g.* Nazi Gestapo, Soviet KGB).

secretary bird, *Sagittarius serpentarius,* S African long-legged hawk with head crest resembling quill pens. Sometimes kept captive to catch snakes and rodents.

Secretary of State, title given to cabinet ministers in charge of certain Brit. govt. depts.; in US, to head of State Department.

securities, evidence of property, *e.g.* bonds or certificates of stock.

Securities and Exchange Commission (SEC), US govt. agency created 1934. Supervises stock exchanges and administers govt. regulations on investment in securities.

Security Council *see* UNITED NATIONS ORGANIZATION.

Sedan, city of Ardennes, France, scene of Fr. defeat in Franco-Prussian

Common Seal

Series of pictures showing how a seagull moves in flight

War and personal surrender of Napoleon III. Now centre for manufacture of wool, metal plate and mirrors. Pop. (1962) 20,336.

Sedan chair, in 17th–18th cent., enclosed chair for 1 person, carried by 2 bearers. Said to have been 1st made at Sedan, France.

sedative, drug administered to allay anxiety, excitement or irritability. Among widely used types are barbiturates, benzodiazepines and phenothiazines.

sedge, grass and rush-like plants, common to swampy areas of trop. and temp. regions. Species include *Carex, Cyperus* and *Scirpus,* used in making paper.

sedimentary rocks, rocks covering greater part of earth's crust. Formed by consolidation of sediment: clay, sandstone, limestone. Vary considerably in texture according to conditions prevailing since deposition.

sedition, in UK broad legal term incl. offences ranging from libel to treason which intend to bring into hatred or contempt, or to incite disaffection against the Sovereign, govt., Parl. or administration of justice. In US also includes attempts to interfere with recruitment of armed forces.

sedum, genus of plants of Crassulaceae family. Mostly perennial herbs with succulent leaves. Includes *S. acre,* wall pepper, *S. sexangulare,* insipid stonecrop, and *S. dasyphyllum,* thick-leaved stonecrop.

seed, fertilized ovule which forms reproductive structure of seed plants. Consists of embryo, stored food and covering.

seed ferns, fossilized remains of fernlike plants found in coal deposits. May be ancestors of seed-bearing plants.

Seeger, Pete (1919–), Amer. folk singer, collector and writer of songs. Best known song, 'Where Have All the Flowers Gone?'

seersucker, orig. thin linen or cotton fabric of Indian manufacture, striped and with ribbed surface.

Segal, George (1924–), Amer. sculptor associated with 'Pop' art movement. Known for life-size plaster casts of people used to emphasize contrast between art and reality.

Segovia, Sp. city of Old Castile; cap. of Segovia prov. Known for Moorish Alcázar. 16th cent. cathedral.

Roman aqueduct still used. Pop. (1960) 33,360.

Segovia, Andrés (1893–), Sp. guitarist. Pioneered use of guitar as concert instrument. Author of many arrangements of classical pieces for guitar.

Segre, Emilio Gino (1905–), Amer. nuclear physicist, b. Italy. Discovered element technetium, assisted in discovery of plutonium. Shared Nobel Prize for Physics (1959) with Owen Chamberlain for detection of antiproton.

segregation, division of activities of 2 groups of people on grounds of ethnic, religious, economic, or social differences. Official policy in South Africa under APARTHEID system.

Seine, river of N France (482 mi.). Serves ports of Rouen and Paris, enters English Channel through estuary at Le Havre.

seismograph, instrument for studying earth tremors. Used in measurement and prediction of earthquakes.

seismology, study of earthquakes and their effects.

Sekondi-Takoradi *see* TAKORADI.

selachians, fish-like vertebrate group, including sharks, skates and rays.

Selangor, state of Malaysia on S Malay peninsula. Area: 3,160 sq. mi.; cap. Kuala Lumpur; towns Klang, Port Swettenham. Under Brit. protection from 1874; joined Federated Malay States (1886) and Federation of Malaysia (1963). Main product rubber. Pop. (1964) 1,258,894.

Selden, John (1584– 1654), Eng. jurist and politician. Opposed Charles I esp. on principle of DIVINE RIGHT; helped frame PETITION OF RIGHT and was committed to the Tower. Works include *England's Epinomis, Jani Anglorum* (1610) and *Analecton Anglo-Britannicon* (1615).

Selene, in Gk. myth., goddess of the Moon, daughter of Hyperion and Theia and sister of Helios (the Sun). Sometimes identified with Artemis.

selenium (Se), non-metallic element. Grey form has property of altering its electrical resistance according to intensity of light falling on it. Used in photocells and rectifiers.

Seleucus I (*c.* 358 BC– 280 BC), one of Alexander the Great's generals who became ruler of Babylonia (312 BC) after Alexander's death and founder of Seleucid dynasty. Extended his

empire to include much of Asia Minor, Syria and Bactria.

self-heal, *Prunella vulgaris,* perennial herb with purple, white or crimson flowers native to N temp. regions.

Selim I (1467– 1520), sultan of Turkey (1512– 20). Extended empire by conquests in Persia, annexed Syria, Palestine and Egypt.

Seljuks, Turkish ruling dynasty. Conquered and controlled most of Near East 11th– 13th cent.

Selkirk or **Selcraig, Alexander** (1676– 1721), Scot. sailor. Spent 4 yr. alone on Juan Fernandez Is. Account of adventure said to have formed basis of *Robinson Crusoe* by Daniel Defoe.

Selkirkshire, hilly, inland border county of SE Scotland. Area: 267 sq. mi.; county town Selkirk; main town, Galashiels. Sheep rearing and woollen manufacture main occupations. Pop. (1966) 20,000.

Sellers, Peter Richard Henry (1925–), Brit. comedy film actor. Appeared in radio series *The Goon Show.* Films include *The Ladykillers, I'm Alright Jack, Dr Strangelove, The Pink Panther.*

selvas, dense equatorial forests of Amazon basin, S America.

Selznick, David Oliver (1902– 65), Amer. film producer. Films include *Gone with the Wind* (1939), *A Farewell to Arms* (1957), *Tender is the Night* (1962).

Semang, pygmy people of N Malay peninsula. Nomadic forest hunters; only about 2,000 remain.

Sedum spectabile

semantics, study of the meaning, and changes in meaning, of language. Concerned esp. with relationship and significance of signs and symbols.

semaphore, signalling apparatus consisting of an upright post with 2 arms turned on pivots to different positions indicating letters of alphabet. System may also be used by a signaller holding a flag in each hand.

Sembrich, Marcella, orig. Praxede Marcelline Kochánska (1858–1935), Polish operatic soprano. Taught in US after retirement (1916).

Semele, in Gk. myth., daughter of Cadmus and Harmonia and mother of Dionysus by Zeus.

Semenov, Nikolai Nicolaevich, FRS, (1896–   ), Soviet chemist. Awarded Nobel Prize for Chemistry (1956) with C. N. Hinshelwood for investigations of chemical reactions.

Seminole, N Amer. Indian tribe of Muskogean linguistic stock. Agriculturists and fishermen, they settled in Florida in 18th cent. Majority now live on Oklahoma reservation, the rest remaining on reservation in Florida Everglades.

semi-precious stones *see* GEMSTONE.

Semiramis, in Gk. legend, daughter of Syrian goddess Derceto, and queen of Assyria. Renowned in war and as builder of Babylon. After death, changed into dove.

Semite, orig. descendant of Shem, in OT, son of Noah. Term now used as linguistic classification; includes Jews, Arabs, Ethiopians, Syrians; in ancient times, peoples of Babylon, Assyria, Chaldea, Canaan, Phoenicia.

Semitic, a branch of Hamito-Semitic languages, widespread in Africa and Asia. Includes Hebrew, Arabic.

Semmelweis, Ignaz Philipp (1818–65), Hungarian physician. First to develop antiseptic method in obstetric surgery; greatly reduced number of deaths from puerperal fever.

semolina, cereal food made from coarse particles of wheat produced during grinding. Used in manufacture of paste foods such as macaroni and as pudding.

Sénancour, Étienne Pivert de (1770–1846), Fr. essayist, disciple of Rousseau. Wrote autobiog. novel *Obermann* (1804).

Senate [Senatus], governing body in ancient Rome. During republic, patrician body controlling finances, foreign affairs, the army and new territory. Power 1st challenged through reforms of the Gracchi, resulting in senatorial and popular parties and control of senate by victorious generals, *e.g.* Sulla, Pompey, Julius Caesar. Authority of Senate diminished after murder of Julius Caesar, lessening still further during empire. Orig. 100 in number, reached 900 in late republic, reduced to 600 by Augustus.

Senate, United States, upper house of US Congress. Senate approval required for treaties and major presidential appointments. Enaction of legislation requires passage by both Senate and House of Representatives. Senators chosen by state legislatures until 1913, when 17th Amendment estab. direct popular election. 2 senators chosen from each state for 6 yr. terms. US vice-pres. presides, voting only in case of a deadlock.

Seneca [Lucius Annaeus Seneca] (*c.* 4 BC–AD 65), Roman philosopher and dramatist, son of Lucius Annaeus Seneca, the rhetorician. Banished from Rome by Claudius (AD 41) recalled (AD 49) as tutor to Nero. Later ordered to commit suicide. Philosophy, influenced by Stoic school, survives in 12 *Dialogi*, 124 *Epistles* and various moral treatises. Also author of 9 tragedies adapted from Gk. models, incl. *Medea, Phaedra, Agamemnon, Oedipus, Thyestes*; influential in Renaissance and later drama.

Seneca, member tribe of closely knit N Amer. Indian IROQUOIS Confederacy.

Senegal, repub. on Atlantic coast of W Africa. Area: 76,124 sq. mi.; cap. Dakar. Coast explored by Portuguese

15th cent. French estab. fort 17th cent. Achieved autonomy in Fr. community (1958); joined Sudanese Republic in Federation of Mali (1959), withdrew and became independent (1960). Economy based on agriculture, esp. millet and ground-nuts. Fishing and mining important. Languages, French and Wolof; religion, Islam. Pop. (1961) 2,980,000.

senna, any species of *Cassia* genus of trop. herbs, shrubs or trees. Dried leaves of *C. acutifolia* and *C. angustifolia* are used as laxatives. *C. marilandica* is found in N America.

Sennacherib (d. 681 BC), king of Assyria (705–681 BC), son of Sargon. Defeated Egyptians (701 BC), destroyed Babylon (*c.* 689 BC). Built magnificent palace at Nineveh.

Sennett, Mack, orig. Michael Sinnott (1884–1960), Amer. film director.

Peanuts awaiting processing at Kaolach, Senegal

Keystone Cops, Buster Keaton and Chaplin featured in his 1920s slapstick comedies.

sensationalism, in philosophy, theory that all knowledge is recording of physical experience.

sensitive plant, humble plant, *Mimosa pudica,* trop. Amer. plant grown in greenhouses. Leaflets fold together when touched.

sensory organs, those parts of an animal whose function, in co-operation with the nervous system, is to detect what goes on outside it, *i.e.* to receive stimuli of all kinds.

Senussi, Moslem reforming sect formed by Sidi Mohammed ben Ali es Senussi (*c.* 1796–1860). Settled in Cyrenaica, opposed Italians in World War 2. Head of sect, Mohammed Sayed Idris el-Senussi, became 1st king of independent Libya (1951).

Seoul, Kyongsong, cap. and commercial centre of Repub. of Korea; founded 1392; cap. of Korean kingdom, headquarters of invading Japanese (1910–45) and of US occupation forces (1945–8). Pop. (1966) 3,376,000.

separation of powers, fundamental principle of constitutional govt. States that legislative, executive and judicial authorities should be separate and totally independent of each other.

Sephardim, Ashkenazim and **Oriental Jews,** 3 major divisions of Jewry. Sephardim are Spanish and Portuguese Jews, now settled in France, Holland, England. Ashkenazim are German Jews living in US, USSR, and E Europe. Oriental Jews live in Africa and Asia.

Gordon setter

sepia, generic name of CUTTLEFISH. Also name of brown pigment orig. derived from ink-like secretion of cuttlefish.

Sepoy Rebellion *see* INDIAN MUTINY.

septicaemia, condition usually characterized by fever, due to invasion of bloodstream by disease-producing bacteria. Sometimes called blood-poisoning.

Septuagint [Lat: seventy], most ancient and celebrated Gk. version of the Hebrew Scriptures. Named after its 70 translators, employed by Ptolemy II. Written in 1st half of 3rd cent. BC.

Sepulchre, Holy, site NW of Calvary, Jerusalem, where body of Christ was laid after the crucifixion. Traditional site now covered by Church of the Holy Redeemer, shared by Orthodox, Coptic, Syrian, Armenian and R.C. churches.

sequoia, 2 species of large coniferous trees of W US coast. Grow to height of 300 ft. Redwood is of genus *Sequoia*; big tree, formerly genus *Sequoia*, now classified in genus *Sequoiadendron.*

Serbia, constituent repub., E Yugoslavia. Area: 34,107 sq. mi.; cap. Belgrade. Primarily mountainous, inhabitants mainly agriculturalists. Distinctive character through link with E Orthodox Church. Kingdom annexed (1459) by Turkey, peasant unrest resulted in drive for independence (achieved 1878). Territorial ambitions led to conflict with neighbours, culminating in BALKAN WARS and World War 1. United with Croatia, Slovenia and Montenegro to form kingdom, ultimately Yugoslavia. Pop. (1961) 7,629,000.

Serbo-Croat, S Slavic Indo-European language with 12 million speakers in Yugoslavia, Dalmatia and surrounding areas.

serenade, in music, movements for chamber orchestra or wind instruments, lighter than orchestral suite.

Serengeti National Park, game conservation area, 1st national park proclaimed in Tanzania. Area: 5,000 sq. mi. Mainly grassy plain inhabited by lion, zebra, types of antelope, gazelle, *etc.*

serfdom, condition of hereditary semi-bondage characteristic of most peasants (serfs) under FEUDALISM. Widespread practice developed throughout Europe during Middle Ages. Disappeared in England before end of Middle Ages; abolished in France by Fr. Revolution; remained in Russia until Edict of Emancipation (1861).

serotine bat, *Eptesicus serotinus,* large-bodied, long-eared bat of wide distribution. Wingspan is *c.* 16 in.

serpent, common name for SNAKE.

serpent, ancient bass wooden musical instrument shaped like coiled snake.

serpentine, a mineral, hydrated magnesium silicate. Found in fibrous form as chrysolite (ASBESTOS) and in massive form. Coloured green, red or mottled, used for ornaments.

serum, thin, transparent, straw-coloured component of blood. Contains antibodies, proteins, fats and sugars. Name also applied to fluid containing bacteria cultures, used in treatment of disease.

Servetus, Michael (1511–53), Sp. theologian and physician. His *Restoration of Christianity* (1553) led to arrest by Inquisition. Ultimately burned in Geneva at Calvin's instigation.

Service, Robert William (1874–1958), Canadian poet. His ballads of Yukon gold rush include 'The Shooting of Dan McGrew'.

service tree, *Sorbus domestica,* tree of Med. countries. Fruit has acid taste.

sesame seed, seed of annual Asiatic plant, benne, *Sesame indicum,* used as flavouring and for oil.

Session, Court of, in Scotland, the supreme civil court, estab. 1532.

Set, Seth, in Egyptian religion, personification of the desert, night and evil. Brother and murderer of OSIRIS.

Seton, Elizabeth Ann (1774–1821), Amer. religious leader. After husband's death (1803), became Roman Catholic and founded Order of Sisters of Charity (1809), serving as 1st superior (1809–21).

Seton, Ernest Thompson, orig. Ernest Seton Thompson (1860–1946), Canadian writer. Author of animal books, *e.g. Wild Animals I Have Known* (1898).

setter, large gun dog. Orig. 2 species, pure white Eng. setter and chestnut-brown Irish setter, from which others, incl. Gordon setter have evolved.

Settlement, Act of, act of Eng. parl. (1701) providing that only Protestant could succeed to throne. Hence if William III and Anne died without heir, succession should pass to House of Hanover.

Seurat, Georges Pierre (1859–91), Fr. painter. Known for use of POINTILLISM technique. Best known work *Un Dimanche à la Grande Jatte* (1886).

Sevastopol, Sebastopol, city and port of S Crimea, Ukrainian SSR.

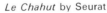

Le Chahut by Seurat

Founded (1784) by Catherine II. Resisted 10-month siege in CRIMEAN WAR (1854–5); fell to Germans 1942; recaptured 1944. Pop. (1967 est.) 200,000.

Seven Deadly Sins, in R. C. theology, mortal sins incl. pride, covetousness, lust, envy, gluttony, anger, sloth. Classification dates from early Christian period. Frequently portrayed by artists.

Seven Weeks War, name for AUSTRO-PRUSSIAN WAR.

Seven Wonders of the World, in antiquity, held to be: Pyramids of Egypt, Hanging Gardens of Babylon, Statue of Zeus at Olympia, Temple of Artemis at Ephesus, Mausoleum at Halicarnassus, Colossus of Rhodes, Pharos (lighthouse) at Alexandria.

Seven Years War, conflict (1756–63) fought in Europe, N America and India between France, Austria, Russia (and allies) and Britain, Prussia (and allies). Involved Fr.-British colonial struggle (*see* FRENCH AND INDIAN WAR) and Austro-Prussian rivalry in Germany. Campaigns by Frederick II in Bohemia and Silesia thwarted by Austria and Russia, but asserted Prussia's rank as power. Britain's colonial supremacy settled by Treaty of Paris after victories over French in N America (PLAINS OF ABRAHAM) and India (PLASSEY).

Seventh Day Adventists, evangelical Protestant Amer. sect. Formally organized 1863. Observe 7th day as Sabbath and live in expectation of imminent 2nd coming of Christ.

Severn, longest river (*c.* 215 mi.) in Britain. Rises in C Wales, flows in estuary to Bristol Channel, SW England. Noted for tidal bore.

Severus, Alexander *see* ALEXANDER SEVERUS.

Severus, Lucius Septimius (AD 146–211). Roman emperor, b. Africa.

After distinguished military service, became consul AD 190. As emperor dismissed Praetorian guard, forming new guard open to all legionaries, quelled opponents and achieved peace in Mesopotamia, Gaul and Britain.

Sévigné, Marie de Rabutin-Chantal, Marquise de (1626–96), Fr. writer. Remembered for her *Letters,* mostly written to her daughter.

Seville, Sevilla, city and port of Andalusia, SW Spain, cap. of Seville prov., on Guadalquivir R. Manufactures tobacco, perfume, textiles. Contains university (founded 1502). Under Phoenician, Roman and Moorish rule. Monopolized trade with New World until 1718. Pop. (1966) 532,000.

seville orange, sour orange, *Citrus aurantium,* bitter type of ORANGE, orig. Indian. Used esp. for marmalade.

Sèvres, town of N France, near Paris. Centre of manufacture of Sèvres porcelain estab. by Louis XV. Pop. (1962) 20,129.

Sèvres, Treaty of, peace settlement (1920) signed at Sèvres, N France, between Turkey and Allies. Abolished Ottoman Empire, reducing Turkey to present boundaries. Rejection of treaty by Kemal Ataturk led to LAUSANNE CONFERENCE.

Sewell, Jonathan (1766–1839), Chief Justice of Lower Canada (1809–38). Laid down procedural law for settlement of suits between Eng. and Fr. Canadians.

sewellel, mountain beaver, *Aplodontia rufa,* primitive rodent of coastal regions of W US. Lives in extensive burrows in which it stores green food for winter.

sex, gender of a plant or animal; structural and functional differences which distinguish male and female, and enable reproduction of the

Shaggymane Mushroom

species. In man, testes of male produce sperm cell which unites with egg cell produced in female by ovaries (*see* TESTIS; OVARY); these cells known as gametes. Sex of resultant embryo determined by structure of chromosomes.

sex organs, genital system, in animals and plants, organs whose function is to reproduce the species.

sexagesima, 2nd Sunday before Lent and the 60th day before Easter in Christian year.

sextant, instrument used in surveying and navigation for measuring altitudes of celestial bodies and their angular distances. Invented by John Hadley in England and Thomas Godfrey in US during 18th cent.

sexton beetle, *Necrophorus humator,* bluish-black carrion-eating beetle. Sometimes called burying beetle.

Seychelles, Brit. crown colony comprising archipelago of 92 islands in Indian Ocean. Total land area: 156 sq. mi.; cap. Victoria. Annexed by French (1744); ceded to Britain (1814). Economy based on export of copra, vanilla, cinnamon. Language, French; religion, Christianity. Currency based on Indian rupee. Pop. (1965) 48,000.

Seymour, Eng. noble family. **Jane Seymour** (*c.* 1509–37) was Henry VIII's 3rd wife and mother of Edward VI. Her brother was **Edward Seymour, Duke of Somerset** (*c.* 1506–52) guardian of Edward VI and Protector of the Kingdom. Supported Reformation, introduced Cranmer's Book of Common Prayer (1549). Supplanted by Duke of Northumberland and executed. His brother **Thomas Seymour, Baron Seymour of Sudeley,** Lord High Admiral of England,

Sharks: 1) Blue Shark 2) Dog Fish 3) Basking Shark 4) Hammer-head Shark

secretly married Catherine Parr, Henry VIII's widow.

Sforza, Count Carlo (1873–1952), Ital. statesman. Led anti-fascist opposition until exiled (1927). Foreign Minister (1947–51).

Sforza, Ludovico, Duke of Milan (c. 1451–1508), one of most lavish of Renaissance princes, patron of Leonardo da Vinci and Bramante.

Shackleton, Sir Ernest Henry (1874–1922), Brit. Antarctic explorer. Member of Scott's 1901–4 expedition. Led expeditions (1907–9, 1914–17, 1921–2). Located and visited South Magnetic Pole (1909).

shad, *Alosa sapidissima,* smallish food fish of herring group of Europe and N America. Spawns in rivers or estuaries.

shaddock, *Citrus grandis,* small citrus tree native to SE Asia and Polynesian Islands. In cultivation replaced by GRAPEFRUIT. Named after Captain Shaddock who introduced seeds to Barbados in 17th cent.

Shaftesbury, 1st Earl of *see* COOPER, ANTHONY ASHLEY.

shag, *Phalacrocorax aristotelis,* green-black seabird of Europe and N Africa related to the cormorant; has crest in breeding season. Nests on cliffs in colonies.

shaggymane mushroom, shaggy cap, *Coprinus comatus,* edible fungus. White and bulbous in appearance.

shagreen, untanned leather with rough granular surface made from shark or ray skins.

Shah Jehan or **Jahan** (1592–1666), Mogul conqueror and emperor (1628–58). Founded modern city of Delhi (1639–48) and built many fine buildings, incl. Taj Mahal near Agra.

Shakers, name for ecstatic sect, United Society of Believers in Christ's Second Appearing. Founded in England c. 1747, taken to US (1774) by group under Ann Lee. Lived in groups, with property communally owned.

Shakespeare, William (1564–1616), Eng. dramatist and poet. Gained knowledge of stage as actor and manager. Reworked esp. historical plays before writing own, covering Eng. history from King John to Henry VIII. Developed form of comedy using prose and blank verse with plots from various literary sources (*As You Like It,* 1599; *The Tempest,* 1611). Tragedies include those with classical background (*Julius Caesar,* 1600; *Antony and Cleopatra,* 1607) and others using historical and legendary material (*Romeo and Juliet,* 1595; *Hamlet,* 1600; *Othello,* 1602; *King Lear,* 1605; *Macbeth,* 1606). Poetry includes sonnets and narrative poems.

shale, common example of SEDIMENTARY ROCKS, soft, fine-grained, layered. Some types are source of oil, esp. in Scotland.

shallot, *Allium ascalonicum,* onion-like plant with small violet-coloured roots and green leaves, used as flavouring. Common shallot is form of *A. cepa.*

Shamanism, orig. religious beliefs and practices of Siberian tribes of N Asia. Based on belief in Shaman, priest-magician, who made contact with good and evil spirits on behalf of tribe. By extension terms applied to similar beliefs and practices among N Amer. Indians.

shamrock, common name for several trifoliate plants, esp. *Trifolium dubium.* National emblem of Ireland and symbol of Trinity in Christianity.

Shan, Thai-speaking, chiefly Buddhist, people of Shan state, E Burma. Rice farming is main occupation.

Shanghai, city and seaport in Kiangsu prov., China. Developed after Treaty of Nanking (1842) permitted foreign trade. Important financial, industrial and educ. centre. Pop. (1957) 6,900,000.

Shannon, longest river of Ireland (224 mi.). Flows through Loughs Allen and Ree to enter Atlantic below Limerick. Source of hydro-electricity. Popular salmon-fishing centre.

Shansi, inland prov. of N China. Area: 60,000 sq. mi.; cap. Taiyuan. Partly surrounded by early part of Great Wall. Major coal mining area, also has iron ore deposits. Pop. (1967 est.) 15,960,000.

Shantung, prov. of NE China on Yellow sea. Area: 55,560 sq. mi.; cap. Tsinan. Crossed by Hwang-Ho R. Agriculture and fishing important. Also formerly silk manufacture. Pop. (1967 est.) 54,030,000.

shanty, chantey, work song of sailors dating from days of sailing ships. Verse sung by shantyman gave rhythm, chorus was sung by group hauling on rope, or performing other task.

Shapiro, Karl (1913–   ), Amer. poet particularly known for his war poems, *e.g. V-Letter* (1944).

shares, in finance, capital holdings in business enterprise, ownership of which certified by possession of stocks. Payments guaranteed by bonds.

shark, cosmopolitan group of carnivorous marine fish. Numerous species include dogfish of temp. waters, Pacific grey shark, *Carcharinus menisorrah* and man-eating shark,

Seville from the clocktower of the cathedral

Carchardon rondeleti of trop. waters, which may be up to 50 ft. long.

sharp-tailed grouse, *Pedioecetes phasianellus,* large grouse with buff-coloured plumage, black mottling, slightly crested head and elongated tail feathers. Found in prairies and open forests of W North America.

Shasta, Mount, volcanic peak (14,162 ft.) of Cascade Range, N California, US. Noted for glaciers and hot springs.

Shastri, Lal Bahadur (1904–66), Indian statesman. P.M. (1964–6). Died after signing peace treaty with Pakistan.

Shaw, George Bernard (1856–1950), Irish dramatist and critic. Fellow-member with Webbs of Fabian Society. Early plays include *Candida*

Shakespeare's birthplace, Stratford-on-Avon (a museum since 1847)

and *Arms and the Man* (1898); major plays include *The Devil's Disciple* (1896), *Caesar and Cleopatra* (1899), *Man and Superman* (1903), *Major Barbara* (1905), *The Doctor's Dilemma* (1906), *Pygmalion* (1912), *Saint Joan* (1924). Also wrote *The Quintessence of Ibsenism* (1891) and important prefaces to major plays. Awarded Nobel Prize for Literature (1925).

Shawnee, N Amer. Algonkian Indian tribe. Lived in parts of Ohio in 18th cent. Later settled on reservations in Oklahoma.

Shays' Rebellion, unsuccessful uprising in Massachusetts, US, of farmers against merchants (1786–7), led by Daniel Shays, Amer. soldier. Shays escaped, later pardoned.

shearwater, migratory long-winged marine bird of several genera, esp. genus *Puffinus,* related to petrel.

sheathbill, antarctic terrestrial bird; bill encased in a horny sheath. Feeds on seabird's eggs and chicks, seaweed, mussels and crustaceans.

Sheba, in OT, region of S Arabia incl. the Yemen and the Hadramaut. Inhabitants, Sabaeans, estab. ancient culture.

sheep, wild and domestic ruminant mammal of genus *Ovis.* Reared domestically for its wool, leather, mutton and milk. Breeds include long-woolled *e.g.* Cotswold, Kentish, Devon and Wensleydale, short-woolled *e.g.* Dorset, Hampshire and Suffolk, mountain breeds *e.g.* Blackface, Cheviot and Exmoor. Its young are lambs.

sheepdog, dog trained to herd and guard sheep. Popular breeds include the short-tailed old English sheepdog with shaggy blue-grey and white coat; and the Scottish collie (long-haired and the less common short-haired varieties) with long pointed muzzle.

Sheffield, city and county borough of Yorkshire, England. Main UK steel manufacturing city. Centre of cutlery production since 14th cent. Pop. (1966) 487,000.

Shelburne, 2nd Earl of *see* PETTY, WILLIAM.

sheldrake, duck of genus *Tadorna* of Old World. Species include European *T. tadorna,* chiefly black and white; frequents coastal regions, nesting in burrows. Female called shelduck.

shelf fungus *see* BRACKET FUNGUS.

shell, hard, outer protective covering of many animals, particularly molluscs; outer covering of eggs of birds.

shellac, refined, melted form of seedlac, obtained from resinous deposits secreted by insects on certain Eastern trees. Used as spirit varnish,

Shield Fern with detail of frond (right)

for surface coating and in electrical insulation.

Shelley, Mary Wollstonecraft (1797–1851), Eng. writer, 2nd wife of PERCY BYSSHE SHELLEY. Wrote 'horror' novel *Frankenstein* (1818) and poetry.

Shelley, Percy Bysshe (1792–1822), Eng. Romantic poet. Expelled (1811) from Oxford for atheistic tract; advocated freedom from social restrictions. Works include *Queen Mab* (1813), *Prometheus Unbound* (1820), *Adonais* (1821) and well known lyrics 'Ozymandias', 'Ode to West Wind', 'To a Skylark'.

shellfish, aquatic animal with hard protective shell covering, *e.g.* oysters, mussels, and other crustacea, used for food. Term also includes cockles, lobsters, crabs, shrimps, *etc.*

Shenandoah, river (*c.* 170 mi. long) rising in Virginia and flowing to Potomac, West Virginia. In US Civil War, its valley was major Confederate grain supply, ravaged (1864–5) by Sheridan.

Shenandoah National Park, estab. 1935, in N Virginia, US. Area: 332 sq. mi. Part of Blue Ridge Mts. in Appalachian system.

Shensi, province of N China. Area: 73,000 sq. mi.; cap. Sian. Population mostly farmers, many living in caves carved from loess. Products include silk, cotton, petroleum, oil, coal, gold. Pop. *c.* 18,130,000.

Shenstone, William (1714–63), Eng. poet and landscape gardener. Works include *The Schoolmistress* (1742), *Pastoral Ballad* (1755).

Shenyang, formerly Mukden, walled cap. city of Liaoning prov., China. Important Manchurian indust. trading centre. Scene of Jap. victory over Russia (1905). Pop. *c.* 2,411,000.

Shepard, Alan Bartlett, Jr. (1923–   ), Amer. naval officer. His 16 min. suborbital space flight (1961) played major part in development of US space programme.

Sheppard, Hugh Richard Lawrie ('Dick') (1883–1937), Eng. cleric and pacifist. Became Dean of Canterbury 1929. A founder of Peace Pledge Union. Author of *The Human Parson* (1924).

Sheraton, Thomas (1751–1806), Eng. cabinet-maker. Published influential *Cabinetmaker's and Upholsterer's Drawing-Book* (1791).

sherbet [Arabic: *sharbat,* a drink], beverage consisting of fruit juices sweetened and diluted with water. Used in Moslem countries. In US, term also used for frozen fruit mixture containing milk, egg-white and gelatine.

Sheridan, Philip Henry (1831–88), Amer. army officer in Civil War. Became commander of Union cavalry corps (1864). After victory at Five Forks (1865) cut off Lee's retreat at Appomattox Court House and forced Confederate surrender.

Sheridan, Richard Brinsley Butler (1751–1816), Brit. dramatist and politician, b. Ireland. Works include *The Rivals* (1775), *The School for Scandal* (1777). As Whig M.P., influential in impeachment of WARREN HASTINGS. Defended Fr. Revolution.

sheriff, public official appointed annually by the Crown in a county (also in London and certain ancient boroughs). In England an honorary appointment. In Scotland a legal official with administrative and judicial duties. In US an elected official, concerned with prison administration and supervision of court processes.

Sheriffmuir, battlefield on Ochil Hills, Perthshire, Scotland, scene of battle (1715) between Jacobites and Hanoverians. Both sides claimed victory.

Sherman, William Tecumseh (1820–91), Amer. army officer. Rose to rank of general in Civil War, commanded (1864) march on Atlanta; devastated

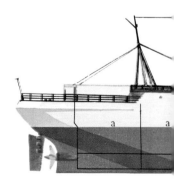

Georgia countryside, believing total destruction of enemy necessary in modern warfare.

Sherman Anti-Trust Act, legislation (1890) regulating restraints in US on interstate and foreign trade. Sponsored by Senator John Sherman (1823–1900) of Ohio. First effectively enforced by Theodore Roosevelt in campaign against monopolies. Powers supplemented 1914, 1936.

sherry *see* WINE.

Sherwood, Robert Emmet (1896–1955), Amer. playwright. Plays include *The Petrified Forest* (1935) and *There Shall Be No Night* (1940).

Sherwood Forest, former Eng. royal forest; orig. covering parts of Nottinghamshire, Derbyshire, Yorkshire. In legend, haunt of ROBIN HOOD.

Shetland Islands, group of *c.* 100 islands comprising county of Zetland, off N Scotland. Total area: 550 sq. mi.; county town Lerwick (on Mainland). Main islands Mainland, Yell, Unst, Foula. Agriculture, esp. sheep raising, and fishing important. Tweed and woollen industry. Pop. (1966) 17,000.

Shetland pony, small active breed of pony from Shetland Is., smallest in Britain. Has thick, shaggy coat, mane and forelock, and great strength and endurance.

Shibboleth, in OT, password by which Jephthah's Gileadites detected their enemies, the Ephraimites, who could not pronounce it properly. Now means watchword or party phrase.

shield fern, common name for various cosmopolitan ferns of *Polystichum* and *Dryopteris* genera.

shieldbug, stinkbug, flattened shield-shaped bug of Pentatomidae family with large triangular thoracic plate. Several species are pests.

Shiites, Shiahs, smaller of 2 main Moslem sects. Predominates in Iran and India. Differed from SUNNITES in proclaiming Ali, cousin of Mohammed, as his legitimate successor.

Shikoku *see* JAPAN.

Shiloh, Battle of, US Civil War encounter (Apr. 1862), fought in S Tennessee. Estab. Union supremacy in subsequent western campaigns. Heavy loss of life.

shiner, N Amer. freshwater fish of carp family. Species include common shiner, *Notropis cornutus* and red fin, *N. umbratilis*.

shingle, shore deposit consisting of pebbles formed by wave action on base of a cliff. Finally becomes SAND.

shingles, virus disease affecting nerve-endings. *See* HERPES.

Shinto, term used for Japanese native religious beliefs and practices. Developed as patriotic State Shinto (stressing divinity of emperor, disavowed 1946) and Cult Shinto (stressing veneration of ancestors).

shinty, form of hockey played in Ireland and in Scot. Highlands. A leather-covered cork ball is used, and the goals, 12 ft. wide and 10 ft. high, are called hails.

Shinwell, Emanuel (1884–   ), Eng. Labour politician and trade union leader. Amalgamated Marine Workers Union (1920); elected M.P. 1922. As Min. of Fuel and Power (1945–7) carried through nationalization of mines. Chairman Parl. Lab. Party (1964–7).

ship, orig. term for sailing vessel with 3 or more masts furnished with square-rigging; now generally used for all sea-going vessels.

ship money, in Eng. history, tax for upkeep of navy and coastal defences. Writs issued by Charles I (1634, 1635), levying ship money in peacetime and on inland as well as maritime counties, opposed by JOHN HAMPDEN. Declared illegal 1641.

shipworm, worm-like marine bivalve mollusc which bores into submerged

Collie sheepdog

timber; a pest to boats and piers. Largest species is common shipworm, *Teredo navalis*.

Shiraz, industrial and commercial city of SW Iran, containing country's largest mosque. Noted esp. for manufacture of rugs and textiles. Pop. (1963) 230,000.

shire, name for administrative divisions into which England, Wales and Scotland are divided. Synonymous with COUNTY.

shire horse, breed of horse descended from English great horse. Orig. bred in Middle Ages to carry knight in full plate armour.

shittim, name applied to various woods, incl. shittah, *Acacia seyal* (used in OT for Ark of Covenant); cascara buckthorn, *Rhamnus purshiana*; false buckthorn, *Bumelia lanuginosa*.

Shiva *see* SIVA.

shock, condition characterized by low blood pressure, shallow breathing, coldness, *etc.* Causes may be injury or severe burn, electric shock, emotional disturbance, *etc.*

shock absorber, hydraulic device for controlling motion of elastic suspension system such as that of a vehicle. Reduces sudden and rapid motion and restores equilibrium.

shock therapy, in psychiatry, treatment involving electricity or chemical agents. Used in treatment of melancholia and depressive disorders.

Diagram of the American nuclear powered cargo/passenger ship *Savannah* showing (a) holds (b) machine room (c) reactor (d) lounge and promenade deck

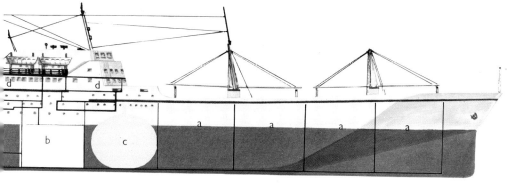

Shorthorn cattle: beef shorthorn (below) has stockier build than dairy shorthorn (above)

Shockley, William Bradford (1910–), Amer. physicist. Shared Nobel Prize for Physics (1956) with John Bardeen and W. H. Brattain for contributions to development of transistors.

shoe-bill, *Balaeniceps rex,* large African bird related to heron. Grey plumage; broad flattened bill.

Shogun, title of Jap. military rulers (12th–19th cent.). Held real power under nominal rule of emperors. Shogunate system of govt. displaced by Meiji restoration (1868).

Sholokhov, Mikhail Aleksandrovich (1905–), Russ. novelist. Many works set in his native Don region, *e.g. The Don Stories* (1926), *And Quiet Flows the Don* (4 vols., 1928–40). Awarded Nobel Prize for Literature (1965).

shooting star, in meteorology, *see* METEOR.

shooting star, N Amer. herb of genus *Dodecatheon* of primrose family. *D. meadia* is common garden species.

shore lark, *Eremophila alpestris,* migrant bird of temperate Eurasia. Striking head markings include 4 long feathers resembling horns.

short circuit, connection, either accidental or deliberate, between 2 points in electrical circuit by path of low resistance instead of circuit of high

Red-backed Shrike

resistance, designed to take current in normal operation.

Shorter Catechism, statement of doctrine set out in form of questions and answers. Prepared by Protestant Westminster Assembly (1643–8). Widely used in religious education in Scotland.

shorthand, method of rapid handwriting using strokes, abbreviations or symbols to denote letters, words, phrases. The main types are phonetic (*e.g.* Pitman's) and orthographic.

shorthorn cattle, Durham cattle, Eng. breed of red, white or roan beef cattle with short horns. Valued for milk and beef.

shortsightedness *see* MYOPIA.

Shoshone, N Amer. Indian tribe orig. of W central US, speaking an Uto-Aztecan language. Now live on reservations in California, Idaho, and Wyoming.

Shostakovich, Dmitri Dmitriyevich (1906–), Russ. composer. Works include symphonies: *First* (1925); *Fifth,* on 20th anniversary of October Revolution (1937); *Seventh,* composed during siege of Leningrad (1942); *Ninth* (1945); operas, *The Nose* (1929), *Lady Macbeth of Mtsensk* (1934); ballets, incl. *The Golden Age.*

shoulder, in man, top part of trunk at each side of neck, extending from base of neck to joint of arm and trunk.

shoveller, river duck of genus *Anas* with large, broad bill. Widely distributed in N hemisphere. Male *A. clypeata* has dark green neck and head, white and chestnut underparts; female is brown.

shrapnel, shell or bullet designed to explode before reaching target and release shower of missiles. Named after inventor, H. Shrapnel, Eng. army officer.

shrew, small widely distributed in-

Common Shrew

sectivorous mammal of genus *Sorex.* Long snout, longish tail and musk glands. Species include common shrew, *S. araneus,* of Europe and Asia, and several pygmy shrews.

Shrewsbury, municipal borough, county town of Shropshire, England. Ancient Saxon and Norman stronghold. Shrewsbury School founded 1552. Pop. (1961) 49,700.

Shrewsbury, Duke of *see* TALBOT, CHARLES.

shrike, songbird of family Laniidae. Strong hooked bill; feeds chiefly on insects often impaling catch on thorns. Species include great grey shrike, *Lanius excubitor,* of Europe and America and African helmet shrike with stiff feathers projecting over nostrils. Eurasian red-backed shrike, *L. collurio,* has chestnut-coloured back, pinkish underparts, blue-grey crown and rump.

shrimp, small edible marine crustacean of suborder Natantia. Slender elongated segmented body with 5 pairs of legs. Species include common brown shrimp, *Crangon vulgaris,* and Amer. shrimp, *Crago septemspinus.*

shrimp plant, *Beloperone guttata,* widely cultivated trop. Amer. shrubby plant. Reddish brown bracts and white flowers.

Shriners, name for members of N Amer. masonic organization called the Ancient Arabic Order of Nobles of the Mystic Shrine.

Shropshire, Salop, county of W England on Welsh border. Area: 1,345 sq. mi.; county town, Shrewsbury. Largely agric. with resources of coal, iron, limestone: lead and iron manufactures. Pop. (1966) 322,000.

Shrove Tuesday [Fr: Mardi Gras], in Christian calendar, day before Lent begins. Named after practice of receiving absolution (shriving). In England, celebrated by eating pancakes.

shrub, low, perennial woody plant, smaller than tree and mostly with permanent stems branching from or near ground. Usually less than 20 ft. high at maturity.

Shuswap, N Amer. Salishan Indian tribe. Previously in Fraser R. area, now live on reservations in British Columbia.

sial, in geology, layer of comparatively light rocks, rich in silica and alumina, occurring beneath surface rocks of continents.

Siam *see* THAILAND.

Siamese cat, short-haired domestic variety of genus *Felis.* Fawn-coloured

with grey or brown face and legs. Originated in Thailand.

Siamese twins, twins joined by tissue. Term derived from male twins, Chang and Eng, b. 1811 in Siam.

Sian, cap. of Shensi prov., N China. Important trade and transport centre. Cap. (as Changan) of Western Han dynasty (202 BC–AD 220), cap. (as Siking) of T'ang dynasty (618–906). Pop. (1957) 1,310,000.

Sibelius, Jean Julius Christian (1865–1957), Finnish composer. Music often inspired by legends and scenery of Finland. Works include tone poems *Finlandia* (1900), *The Swan of Tuonela* (1893); *Valse Triste*; violin concerto (1903); 7 symphonies (1899–1924).

Siberia, Asian region of Russ. SFSR, lying E of Ural Mts. Area: 4,924,100 sq. mi.; chief cities, Vladivostok, Khabarovsk. Agriculture (esp. grain) main occupation of population, most of which lives along Trans-Siberian Rly. (built 1892–1905). Cossacks aided in Russ. conquest (begun 16th cent.); penal colony since 17th cent.

Sibylline Books, collection of oracular utterances, written in Gk. hexameters, thought to have been brought from Greece to Cumae then to Rome. According to tradition 3 volumes bought by Tarquinius Superbus from Sibyl of Cumae. Consulted by Romans in cases of calamities *e.g.* earthquakes, *etc.* Destroyed in burning of Capitol (83 BC).

Sibyls, name given by Greeks and Romans to prophetesses inspired by a god, usually Apollo. Most important Sibyls were Erythraean Sibyl, Ionia, and Sibyl of Cumae, Italy.

Sica, Vittorio de (1901–   ), Ital. film director. Films include *Shoeshine, Bicycle Thieves, Umberto D.*

Sicilian Vespers, rebellion (1282) in Sicily against French rule of Charles of Anjou. Massacre began Easter Monday. Resulted in estab. of Peter III of Aragon as king of Sicily.

Sicily [Sicilia], Med. island off S Italy, separated from mainland by Straits of Messina. Area: 9,930 sq. mi.; cap. Palermo. Mountainous (includes Mt. Etna) except for fertile Catania plain. Exports sulphur, fish, wine. Settled by Phoenicians, Greeks, Romans before Arabs (9th cent.). Kingdom estab. (1130) under Normans, passed to Sp. rule (1282–1713). United (1816) with Naples (*see* TWO SICILIES, KINGDOM OF THE); joined Italy after its conquest (1860) by Garibaldi. Pop. (1967 est.) 4,712,000.

sickener, *Russula emetica,* poisonous red-capped fungus with white gills and stem. Commonly found in meadows

Shore lark

and conifer woods; strong persistent acrid taste.

Sickert, Walter Richard (1860–1942), Brit. Impressionist painter. Studied under Whistler. Works include *Baccarat at Dieppe* and *The Area Steps*.

Sickingen, Franz von (1481–1523), Ger. knight. Supported Emperor Charles V. Sympathized with Reformation, was outlawed and died of wounds after being besieged.

Siddons, Sarah (1755–1831), Eng. actress, daughter of ROGER KEMBLE. Particularly successful in tragic Shakespearean roles, esp. Lady Macbeth.

siderite, chalybite ($FeCO_3$), common mineral iron carbonate found in yellowish brown masses. Valuable ore of iron.

sidewinder, *Crotalus cerastres,* rattle snake of pit viper group of N America. Moves by sideways spiralling action.

Sidgwick, Henry (1838–1900), Brit. utilitarian philosopher. Known for comparative analysis of moral philosophy: *Methods of Ethics* (1874). Founded Society for Psychical Research.

Sidmouth, Viscount *see* ADDINGTON, HENRY.

Sidney, Sir Philip (1554–86), Eng. poet and soldier. His chief works are unfinished pastoral romance *Arcadia* (1590), sonnet sequence *Astrophel and Stella* (1591) and essay *Apologie for Poetry* (1595). Killed in battle at Zutphen, Netherlands.

Sidon, ancient Phoenician port on Med. Sea, now Saida, Lebanon. In Roman times, noted for glass-blowing and purple dyes.

Siegbahn, Karl Manne Georg (1886–   ), Swedish physicist. Awarded Nobel Prize for Physics (1924) for work on X-ray spectroscopy.

Palermo Cathedral, Sicily

The Piazza del Campo in Siena

Siegfried [Norse: Sigurd], hero of N European mythology. Appears orig. in Norse *Volsungasaga*, and in Ger. (13th cent.) *Nibelungenlied*.

Siemens, Ernst Werner von (1816–92), Ger. electrical engineer. Founded firm Siemens and Halske and developed wireless telegraphy. His brother, **Wilhelm von Siemens** (1823–83), worked in England, esp. on dynamo and methods of steel production.

Siena, city of C Italy, cap. of Tuscany. Reached peak as artistic centre (13th–14th cent.). Produces wine, marble. Contains university (founded 13th cent.) and Gothic cathedral. Pop. (1963) 62,215.

Sienkiewicz, Henryk (1846–1916), Polish historical novelist. *Quo Vadis?* (1895) deals with early Christians in Rome; also wrote trilogy on Polish struggle for independence. Awarded Nobel Prize for Literature (1905).

Sierra Leone, peninsular state of W Africa, member of Brit. Commonwealth. Area: 27,925 sq. mi.; cap. Freetown. Wooded hills, grassland

plateau with coastal swamps. Agriculture main occupation. Exports diamonds, iron ore, coffee. Brit. protectorate estab. 1896; independent 1961. Military junta seized power 1967. Main languages, English, Krio. Unit of currency, leone. Pop. (1968 est.) 2,439,000.

Sierra Madre, mountain range of Mexico. Highest peak (Orizaba) 18,700 ft. Divided into Oriental Sierra Madre and Occidental Sierra Madre.

Sierra Morena, mountain range in SW Spain, divided into Sierra de Alcaraz in E, Sierra de Aracena in W. Highest peak *c.* 4,500 ft. Rich mineral resources.

Sierra Nevada, mountain range *c.* 60 mi. long, Andalusia, S Spain. Highest peak is Cerro de Mulhacén (11,411 ft.).

Sierra Nevada, mountain range, E California, US, extending *c.* 430 mi. Highest peak Mt. Whitney (14,495 ft.). East face steep and rugged, W slopes into Sacramento and San Joaquin valleys. Streams on W used for water power and irrigation.

Sierra Nevada de Mérida, mountain range in NW Venezuela extending 200 mi. from Colombian border to Caribbean Sea. Several snow-capped peaks over 15,000 ft.

Sieyès, Emmanuel-Joseph (1748–1836), Fr. revolutionary politician and pamphleteer. Important figure in Estates-General of 1789. Helped draft *Declaration of Rights of Man* (1791). Supported Napoleon Bonaparte in coup d'état (1799).

sight, sense which permits perception of light as form and colour. Impressions are received through lens on retina of eye and transmitted to brain by optic nerve.

Sigismund (1368–1437), Ger. king. Holy Roman Emperor (1411–37), king of Hungary (1387–1437). To end GREAT SCHISM summoned Council of Constance. Succession to throne of Bohemia opposed by Hussites.

Signac, Paul (1863–1935), Fr. painter associated with Georges Seurat in neo-Impressionist movement.

Signorelli, Luca (*c.* 1445–1523), Ital. painter. Early exponent of nude figures. Frescoes in chapel of San Brizio, Orvieto contain some of his finest work.

Sigurd *see* SIEGFRIED.

sika deer, *Cervus nippon,* deer of Japan and E Asia with chestnut brown coat, white-spotted in summer. Found mainly in parks and reservations.

Sikh Wars, conflicts (1845–6, 1848–9) arising out of Indian Sikhs' fear of Brit. encroachment. After defeat in 2nd war, British annexed all Sikh territory.

Sikhs, Indian community, orig. religious, mostly found in Punjab. Founded 15th cent. by Nanak and estab. by teachers incl. Govind. Aim was to unite Hindus and Moslems.

Today Akali Dal movement seeks to estab. Sikh state in NW India.

Sikiang, river of S China. Rises in E Yunnan prov., flowing *c.* 1,250 mi. through Kwangsi and Kwangtung provs. to South China Sea. Forms Canton river delta. Navigable most of its length.

Sikkim, Himalayan protectorate of India. Area: 2,745 sq. mi.; cap. Gangtok. Inhabitants are pastoral nomads. Brit. protectorate (1890–1947), became independent, but passed to India (1950). Main religion, Hindu, although officially Buddhist. Pop. (1966) 183,000.

Sikorski, Wladyslaw (1881–1943), Polish army officer and statesman. Organized nationalist military group. Commanded army (1920) against Russia. P.M. (1922–3), later of exiled govt. after 1939.

Sikorsky, Igor Ivanovich (1889–), Amer. aeronautical designer, b. Russia. Built 1st multi-engined aeroplane (1913). Best known for design and manufacture of helicopters.

Silenus, in Gk. myth., a satyr and companion of Dionysus. Granted King Midas' wish that everything he touched might turn to gold. Represented as inspired and musical or as elderly and drunken.

Silesia, industrial region of C Europe with rich mineral desposits. Divided

Silver Fir: a) female bloom b) male bloom c) needle-like leaves d) cone e) central axis of cone f) single seed

Silver pheasant

between Poland and Czechoslovakia after World War 2. Major towns are Wroclaw (Breslau), Katowice, Bytom (Beuthen), Opava.

silica, common name for silicon dioxide, widely distributed in earth's crust in sand, quartz, granite, *etc.* Used as abrasive, in glass manufacture, ceramics and carborundum.

silicate, widely distributed compound of silica and oxygen, combined with metals, *e.g.* aluminium, barium, iron, *etc.* Silicates include asbestos, clay, emerald.

silicon (Si), non-metallic chemical element, commonly available in silicate form. Used in glass manufacture and as a hardener in steel alloys.

silicones, synthetic chemical products, orig. hydrocarbon radicals. Now term for silicon and oxygen polymers, characterized by chemical inertness, good electrical properties and ability to repel water.

silicosis, occupational disease caused by inhalation of dust particles rich in silica. Causes lung inflammation and growth of fibrous tissues.

silk, natural fibre produced by silkworms, used in fabrics. Usually obtained from cocoon spun by larva of *Bombyx mori* which feeds on mulberry tree. Silk production begun in ancient China, now spread throughout Asia into Europe. Shantung (pongee) silk produced by tussah worm is particularly esteemed.

silkworm, larva of Chinese silkworm moth, *Bombyx mori.* Spins cocoon of commercially valuable silk.

sill, in geology, intrusion of igneous rocks between sedimentary or volcanic beds or along splits in metamorphic rocks.

Sillanpää, Frans Eemil (1888–1964), Finnish writer. Lyrical impressionist novels include *Meek Heritage* (1919) and *The Maid Silja* (1931). Awarded Nobel Prize for Literature (1939).

Silliman, Benjamin (1779–1864), Amer. chemist and geologist. Founded *American Journal of Science* (1818).

Sillitoe, Alan (1928–), Eng. novelist. Described Eng. working class life in *Saturday Night and Sunday Morning* (1958), *The Loneliness of the Long Distance Runner* (1959).

Silone, Ignazio, orig. Secondo Tranquilli (1900–), Ital. novelist. Opposed Fascism. Published novels *Fontamara* (1933), *Pane e Vino* (1937).

silt, mineral particles produced by erosion. Finer than sand but coarser than clay, becomes shale when consolidated into rock.

Silures, powerful tribe of ancient Britain, occupying SE Wales. Resisted Roman conquest but finally subdued by Frontinus (AD 74–8).

Silurian period *see* GEOLOGICAL TABLE.

Silvanus, in Roman religion, spirit of woodlands. Mentioned by Vergil in association with Pan. Cult regarded as very ancient.

silver (Ag), soft, lustrous metallic element. Good conductor of heat and electricity; used in inks, mirrors, photography, metal processing. Highly valued, used in coins, jewellery and utensils.

silver fir, *Abies alba,* evergreen tree, native to mountains of C and S Europe, growing to 150 ft. Greyish bark; erect cones up to 6 in. long.

silver pheasant, *Gennaeus nicthemerus,* large Chinese pheasant with silver back and tail, purple underparts. Well-known in aviaries.

silverfish, fishmoth, *Lepisma saccharina,* primitive insect with elongated, silver-scaled body. Found indoors, feeds on *e.g.* glue in bookbindings.

silverside, small fish of Atherinidae family with silvery stripe along each side of body, esp. *Menidia notata* of Atlantic coast of America. Name also applied to freshwater minnows of *Notropsis* genus.

silver-studded blue, *Plebejus argus,* European butterfly of mountainous and moorland terrain. Azure wings acquire rusty shade at edges. Larvae feed on clover.

Cypresses by Signac

Siskin

silverweed, *Potentilla anserina,* low creeping perennial herb of rose family, of N temperate zone. Silvery silky down on underside of leaves. Also related species, *P. argentea,* of N America.

Sim, Alastair (1900–), Scot. actor-producer. Noted esp. for productions of plays of James Bridie, incl. *The Anatomist, Dr Angelus.*

sima, in geology, layer of rocks consisting of silica and magnesium, occurring beneath ocean floor and continental sial.

Simcoe, John Graves (1752–1806), 1st Lieutenant-Gov. of Upper Canada Prov. Founded (1793) city of York (now Toronto) as provincial cap. and organized road system connecting it with settlement areas.

Simenon, Georges (1903–), Belgian novelist. Works, written in French, include detective fiction (featuring Inspector Maigret) and psychological novels.

Simeon, in NT, devout Jew who recognized infant Jesus in Temple as Messiah. Spoke thanksgiving prayer known as 'Nunc Dimittis'.

Simla, city of NW India, cap. of Himachal Pradesh Territory. Summer cap. during Brit. administration. Pop. (1961) 42,597.

Simnel, Lambert (d. *c.* 1535), Eng. impostor. Claimed to be Edward, Earl of Warwick. Crowned in Dublin as Edward VI. Defeated by Henry VII at Stoke (1487).

Simon, Saint, one of 12 apostles. Also called Simon Zelotes. Son of Mary of Cleophas. Traditionally martyred with St Jude.

Simon of Cyrene, in NT, bystander made to help carry cross of Jesus on way to Calvary.

Simonides (*c.* 556–*c.* 468 BC), Gk. lyric poet from Ceos. Wrote choral lyrics, epinicia, dirges, *etc.,* few of which survive. Also elegiac poems on Persian Wars, incl. epigram on those who fell at Thermopylae.

simoom, simoon, hot desert sandstorm common in N Africa. Heated air rises drawing clouds of dust and sand upwards.

Simplon Pass, Swiss Alpine pass, at 6,589 ft. Hospice founded (1802) by Napoleon. Simplon Tunnel ($12\frac{1}{4}$ mi. long), world's longest rly. tunnel (opened 1905).

Simpson, George Gaylord, FRS (1902–), Amer. palaeontologist and zoologist. Discovered migratory patterns of prehistoric fauna. Works include *Evolution and Geography* (1953), *The Major Features of Evolution* (1953).

Simpson, Sir James Young (1811–70), Scot. obstetrician. First to use general anaesthetic in childbirth (1847).

sin, in religious beliefs, any transgression of the will of God (*see* ORIGINAL SIN). Has come to refer loosely to a serious violation of a moral code.

Sinai, triangular peninsula of NE United Arab Republic; occupied by Israelis in 1967 Arab-Israeli conflict. Arid, mountainous terrain inhabited by Bedouins. Mt. Sinai (where, in OT, Moses received Ten Commandments from God) is in S.

Sinatra, Francis Albert ('Frank') (1917–), Amer. singer and film actor. Films include *From Here to Eternity, The Detective.*

Sinclair, Upton Beall (1878–1968), Amer. novelist and politician. His works, dealing with social and economic problems, include *The Jungle* (1906), *Boston* (1928).

Sind, hot, dry plain of SE West Pakistan, location of ancient INDUS CIVILIZATION. Now well irrigated and used for agriculture esp. rice and wheat. Main city, Karachi.

Singapore, Republic of, sovereign state off S Malay peninsula, member of Brit. Commonwealth. Consists of Singapore Is. and several smaller islands. Total area: 225 sq. mi.; cap. Singapore. Estab. as trading post under East India Co. (1819); with Penang and Malacca, formed Straits

Settlements (1826). Became separate colony (1946). Accorded internal self-govt. 1959. Constituent state of Malaysia (1963–5). Wide range of heavy and light industries; air and naval base with extensive dockyards. Population predominantly Chinese. Pop. (1967 est.) 1,955,600.

Singhalese, Indic Indo-European language with *c.* 7 million speakers in Ceylon.

singing, controlled use of human voice for production of melodious sounds with musical inflections and modulations. Aptitude normally present in human beings. Voices range from female or boy soprano, mezzo soprano, contralto, to male countertenor, tenor, baritone and bass.

single tax, in economics, doctrine advanced by PHYSIOCRATS, advocating collection of revenue based only on land tax. Most successful exponent, HENRY GEORGE.

Sinkiang or **Chinese Turkestan,** prov. of NW China. Area; *c.* 650,000 sq. mi.; cap. Urumchi. Mountainous with plateau in N, desert in S. Cotton, grain and silk grown. Mineral resources, esp. oil. Known as Uigur autonomous region since 1955. Pop. 5,640,000.

sinking fund, sum of govt. or business income set aside; its accumulation allows repayment of outstanding debts. First estab. in Britain (1786).

Sinn Fein [Irish: ourselves alone], Irish separatist national movement founded late 19th cent. Aimed at complete polit. separation from UK. Began with passive resistance to Brit. rule, developed into militant organized opposition culminating in EASTER REBELLION (1916). Continued to oppose compromise with Brit. govt. until estab. of Irish Free State.

Sistine Chapel: scene showing the creation of Adam, from a ceiling by Michelangelo

Sino-Japanese War, First (1894–5), struggle between China and Japan for control of Korea. Jap. victory consolidated by Treaty of Shimonoseki by which China ceded Taiwan and other islands and Liaotung peninsula; Korea awarded nominal independence.

Sino-Japanese War, Second (1931–45), struggle prompted by Jap. desire to dominate E Asia. Annexed Manchuria (1931) setting up state of Manchukuo. Captured Peiping, Shanghai, Nanking (1937); had occupied E coast by 1940. Chinese, forced into W, based at Chungking. With Jap. entry into World War 2, China declared war on Axis powers; Allied aid failed to achieve Chinese victory. Japan surrendered (1945); Cairo Declaration restored Taiwan, Pescadores Is. and Manchuria to China.

Sino-Tibetan, widely-spoken family of languages. Comprises 2 branches, Tibeto-Burman and Chinese.

sinus, name given to numerous air spaces in bones of skull. Communicate with nasal cavity through narrow channels.

sinusitis, inflammation of SINUS. Affects esp. sinuses of nose, ear, forehead and jaw.

Sioux or **Dakota,** largest group in Siouan family of N Amer. Indians. Gradually driven W, they settled (late 18th cent.) W of Missouri R. Invasion of their reservation by gold prospectors in 1874 led to uprising in which General Custer perished.

siphon, bent tube or pipe by which liquid can be transferred by atmospheric pressure from one receptacle to another.

Siqueiros, David Alfaro (1898–), Mexican mural painter. Identified himself with revolutionary socialism. Polit. prisoner (1930, 1960–5). Works include murals at Mexico City Polytechnic Institute.

siren, aquatic eel-like salamander of family Sirenidae of US. Permanent external gills, small forelimbs and no hind limbs.

Sirius, Dog Star, star in constellation Canis Major of N hemisphere. Brightest star in sky. In 1862 observed to have companion, Sirius B, making it a binary or double star.

sirocco, hot, dry S wind from Sahara Desert, affecting N Africa, Sicily and N Med. regions. Known as Khamsin in Egypt. Dries up vegetation.

sisal, sisal hemp, fibre used for making ropes, rugs, *etc.* Obtained from *Agave sisalana* and *A. fourcroydes.*

siskin, *Carduelis spinus,* small, yellow, singing finch of Europe and N America. Formerly a popular cage bird.

Sisley, Alfred (1839–99), Fr. Impressionist painter, noted esp. for landscapes. Influenced by Monet and Renoir.

Sisters of Charity, Fr. Roman Catholic order of nuns founded mid-16th cent., by St Vincent de Paul (d. 1660).

Sistine Chapel, private chapel of the Pope in the Vatican, renowned for frescoes of the Creation, Deluge and Last Judgment, by Michelangelo.

Sisyphus, in Gk. myth., king of Corinth. For misdeeds on earth, condemned in Hades to roll large stone to top of a hill; when stone reached the top, it rolled down again, thus making Sisyphus' punishment eternal.

Sitter, Willem de (1872–1934), Dutch astronomer and mathematician. Applied theory of relativity to astronomy and pioneered theory of expanding universe.

Sitting Bull (*c.* 1831–90), Amer. Indian chief. Leader of Sioux in Battle of Little Bighorn, in which Custer and his troops were killed after famous 'last stand'.

Sitwell, Sir Osbert (1892–1969), Brit. novelist, poet and critic. Works include *Selected Poems* (1943), and series of memoirs. His sister, **Dame Edith Sitwell** (1887–1964), poet and critic, published *Collected Poems* (1954), *A Poet's Notebook* (1934). Her brother, **Sacheverell Sitwell** (1897–), poet and art critic, also wrote biographies, essays and travel books.

Siva, Shiva, 3rd god of Hindu Trinity. Often considered as god of destruction; development, in part, of Vedic storm god. Name means 'the auspicious one'.

Skagerrak, strait 80–90 mi. wide between Norway and Denmark. Connects North Sea with Kattegat and Baltic Sea.

skate, carnivorous ray of genus *Raja* found in coastal waters. Flattened body, long tail, pointed snout with mouth on underside. Food fish. Species include common ray, *R. batis.*

skating, sport of gliding on ice by means of specially designed metal blades fitted to boots. Ice skating includes figure and speed skating, both events in Winter Olympic games, and practised outdoors or on indoor ice rinks. Roller skating, gliding on smooth surface, uses specially constructed metal skates with 4 small roller wheels.

skeleton, in animals, solid framework of body, internal or external and composed of bone and cartilage.

Skiers using chairlift in the Alps

Functions are protection and support of soft tissue, protection of internal organs, storage of calcium and phosphorous.

skepticism *see* SCEPTICISM.

skiing, sport and method of travelling on packed snow. Great speed and mobility achieved with use of polished wooden (or metal) slats attached to soles of boots. Introduced to Winter Olympics (1924).

skimmer, trop. wading bird of family Rynchopidae. Skims water with elongated lower mandible immersed while in search of food. Species include black skimmer, *Rynchops nigra* and African skimmer, *R. flavirostris.*

skin, flexible external covering of body. In humans, consists of outer epidermis and inner dermis. Latter contains blood vessels, nerve endings, hair follicles, sweat and sebaceous glands. Main functions are to protect, to regulate body temperature and to serve as organ of sense and excretion.

skink, lizard of family Scincidae found in desert regions. Long scaled body; terrestrial, arboreal or fossorial. Species include five-lined skink, *Eumeces fasciatus,* of US and common skink, *Scincus scincus,* of African desert.

Skinner, B[urrhus] F[rederic] (1904–), Amer. psychologist. Author of *Science and Human Behaviour* (1953).

skipper, quick-flying insect of family Hesperiidae, related to butterfly.

skittles, games resembling ninepins. A cheese-shaped bowl of *c.* 10 lb. is hurled from a distance of 21 ft. at 9 skittles set up in a diamond pattern, with object of knocking them over. *See* TENPIN BOWLING.

Skopje, historic city, cap. of Macedonia prov., Yugoslavia. Extensively damaged by earthquake (1963). Pop. (1964) 212,000.

Skriabin, Alexander Nicholaevich *see* SCRIABIN, ALEKSANDR NIKOLAYEVICH.

skua, large brown predatory bird of genus *Catharacta* related to jaeger. Found in cold waters of N and S seas. Species include great skua *C. skua* of Polar regions.

skull, bony framework of the head comprising cranium or brain case, and facial skeleton. Contains 22 bones. Protects brain and sense organs, *i.e.* nose, eyes and ears.

skunk, *Mephitis mephitis,* small black N Amer. mammal of weasel family. Long white stripe on back; 2 glands at back of tail eject fetid odour when alarmed or attacked.

skunk cabbage, *Symplocarpus foetidus,* low fetid broad-leaved plant of N America and NE Asia. Grows in moist ground.

Skye, Isle of, largest island of Inner Hebrides, off W Scotland, part of Inverness-shire. Area: 670 sq. mi.; main town, Portree. Largely mountainous, attracts tourists, climbers. Pop. (1963 est.) 7,600.

Skye terrier, type of dog orig. bred in Skye, for hunting work. It has long, silky coat of a silvery blue-grey, short legs and a long, low body.

skylark, *Alauda arvensis,* brown and black bird of Europe and Asia. Feeds on insects and seeds. Noted for its song in flight.

skyscraper, type of building, orig. designed in the US in order to save ground space, consisting of many storeys. Now largely modified and adopted throughout the world. Tallest is Empire State Building, New York, with 102 storeys.

slander, form of defamation against which law may be invoked, consisting of malicious and untrue statements, differing from libel as it is spoken and not written. The words must have been spoken before 3rd party; slandered person must have received damage to finances or reputation.

slate, metamorphic rock, composed mainly of aluminium silicate. Splits readily into thin leaves, used for roofing houses, *etc.*

Slaughter, Frank G|ill| (1908–), Amer. novelist and surgeon. Works include *A Touch of Glory* (1945) and *Epidemic* (1961).

Slave Coast, term formerly applied to W coast of Africa, now Upper Guinea, Nigeria, Dahomey and Togo. Region from which most slaves taken by European traders 16th–19th cent.

slavery, ownership by one human being of another. Fundamental to social system of Gk. city states and Roman empire. Largely replaced in Europe by serfdom under feudal system, but reintroduced after discovery of Americas. Attempts at abolition on humanitarian grounds date from early 19th cent. (slave trade banned by UK 1807; slavery in Brit. West Indies abolished 1833). Major issue in US Civil War, being basis of South's plantation economy. Lincoln's Emancipation Proclamation (1863) and the North's victory abolished slavery in principle.

Slavic, branch of the Balto-Slavic Indo-European languages. Has total of approx. 280 million speakers.

Slavonian grebe, *Podiceps auritus,* bird of grebe family. Glossy black head has broad golden stripe forming short 'horns'.

Slavs, Indo-European racial group, orig. from N Carpathian region. Includes Russians, Poles, Czechs, Slovaks, Bulgars, Slovenes and Serbo-Croats.

sledge, sleigh, sled, carriage with runners for gliding on snow, sometimes horse-drawn. Name is also given to a framework without wheels for dragging goods along.

sleep, bodily state of rest, when conscious mental activities are at a minimum and physical activities drop to similar low level essential to all higher animals. Individual human sleep needs vary, but a certain amount is needed for physical rest and dreaming.

sleeping sickness *see* ENCEPHALITIS.

slide rule, mathematical calculating device, consisting in simplest form of ruler and medial slide. Each graduated with similar logarithmic scales labelled with corresponding antilogarithms.

Sligo, Sligeach, county of Connaught prov., Repub. of Ireland. Area: 712 sq. mi.; county town Sligo. Low coastal land rises to central mountains. Main occupations, fishing, dairying, tourism. Pop. (1966) 62,300.

Slim, William Joseph, 1st Viscount (1891–1970), Brit. army officer. Played leading strategic role as commander of 14th Army in Burma in World War 2. Chief of Imperial General Staff (1948–52). Gov.-General of Australia (1953–60).

slime, mould, fungus of *Myxomycetes* class. Widely distributed, living in moist places on wood or other plant material undergoing decomposition.

Sloan, John (1871–1951), Amer. painter and illustrator. Orig. news-

Skylark

paper illustrator in Philadelphia. From 1905, leader of 'The Eight', group of realistic painters, esp. of New York city scenes; forerunner of 'modern art'. Best known works include *McSorley's Bar* (1912), *Backyards* (1914).

Sloane, Sir Hans (1660–1753), Brit. naturalist and physician, b. Ireland. Bequeathed his 50,000 books, 3,000 manuscripts to form nucleus of British Museum library, London.

Slocum, Joshua (1844–1909), Canadian navigator. Made single-handed voyage round the world (1895–8) in the *Spray*. In 1909, disappeared on voyage to Orinoco R.

sloe, small sour fruit of blackthorn, *Prunus spinosa.* Used to flavour cordials or liqueurs, *e.g.* sloe gin. Also various shrubs of genus *Prunus, e.g. P. alleghheniensis* with dark purple fruit.

sloop, single-masted boat with fore and aft rigging, single headsail jib connected to masthead by jibstay. Until mid 19th cent. used as small warship.

sloth, nocturnal, sluggish, arboreal mammal of family Bradypodidae of trop. America. Long coarse hair; hangs upside down from tree branches and moves along them by means of hooked claws. Species include 2-toed sloth *Choloepus didactylus* and 3-toed *Bradypus.*

sloth bear, *Melursus ursinus,* long-snouted, coarse-haired bear of India and SE Asia. Length *c.* 5 ft., height at shoulder *c.* 2 ft.

Slovak, Slavic Indo-European language, with *c.* 4 million speakers in E Czechoslovakia and parts of Hungary.

Slovakia, SE region of Czechoslovakia. Area: *c.* 18,900 sq. mi.; cap. Bratislava. Mainly agricultural hill country, with increasing industrialization. Part of Hungary from 10th cent. until 1918. People are W Slavs, ethnically akin to Czechs. Pop. (1961) 4,175,017.

Skunk

Slovene, S Slavic Indo-European language with *c.* 2 million speakers, mostly in N Yugoslavia.

Slovenia, autonomous repub. of NW Yugoslavia. Area: 7,900 sq. mi.; cap. Ljubljana. Predominantly hilly with important forestry and agriculture. Pop. (1961) 1,584,400.

slow worm, *Anguis fragilis,* small, legless lizard of Europe, W Asia and Algeria. Also known as blindworm because eyes close after death.

slug, terrestrial mollusc widely distributed in temp. and trop. regions. Oval, much reduced shell; lower surface is the creeping organ. Herbivorous and often destructive to plants. Species include black slug, *Arion atater,* garden slug, *A. hortensis,* and Amer. field slug, *Devoceras agreste.*

Sluys, Battle of (1340), Eng. naval victory over French off coast of SW Netherlands, in Hundred Years War.

small white, cabbage butterfly, *Pieris rapae,* cosmopolitan butterfly whose larvae are cabbage worms.

smallpox, variola, dangerous infectious disease. Characterized by fever and rash which may leave permanent scarring of skin. Protection is afforded by VACCINATION.

smell, one of 5 senses, less developed in humans than sight, touch, hearing. Sensation is produced by stimulation of mucous membrane of mouth, throat and nose.

smelt, small food fish of genus *Osmerus* resembling the salmon. Found in N hemisphere. Species include common smelt, *O. eperlanus.*

smelting, process of obtaining metals from ores by action of chemicals in presence of heat and air.

Smersh, special division of Soviet security organization (1942–6), charged with elimination of opponents to regime. Name from initial letters of Russ. words meaning 'death to the spies'.

Smetana, Bedrich or **Friedrich** (1824–84), Czech composer, pianist and conductor. Regarded as founder of modern Czech music. Helped found National Theatre, Prague (1862). Wrote operas, incl. *The Bartered Bride* (1866).

Smirke, Sir Robert (1781–1867), Eng. architect. Neo-classical style epitomized in façade of British Museum, London.

Smith, Adam (1723–90), Scot. economist. Author of influential work, *An Inquiry into the Nature and Causes of the Wealth of Nations* (1776), 1st systematic formulation of principles of polit. economy. Advocated free trade and gold circulation as basis of national prosperity.

Smith, Bessie (*c.* 1898–1937), Amer. blues singer. Remembered for performance of 'Jailhouse Blues'.

Smith, Donald Alexander, 1st Baron Strathcona and Mount Royal (1820–1914), Canadian politician, b. Scotland. Became governor of Hudson's Bay Co. Played leading part in building of Canadian Pacific Railway and was appointed High Commissioner for Canada in London (1896).

Smith, George (1840–76), Eng. Assyriologist. Translated Gilgamesh epic and conducted excavations at Nineveh.

Smith, Sir Grafton Elliot (1871–1937), Austral. anatomist and anthropologist. Led several expeditions in Nile valley (1900–9). Works include *The Search for Man's Ancestors* (1931).

Smith, Ian Douglas (1919–), Rhodesian politician, P.M. (1964–5). In 1965 declared Rhodesia independent of UK (considered illegal act by UK govt.); became leader of Rhodesia Front. Established republic under constitution perpetuating white minority rule (1969).

Smith, Jedediah Strong (1799–1831), Amer. explorer. Helped open up trapping and trading W of Mississippi. Led small force from Great Salt Lake to San Diego, Calif., then back across Sierra Nevada and Great Salt Desert (1828).

Smith, John (1580–1631), Eng. colonizer in N America. A founder of Virginia colony and later its governor. Captured by Indians (1607) and saved by chief's daughter Pocahontas.

Smith, Joseph (1805–44), Amer. founder of Mormon religion. Led members of his sect from New York to Ohio, Missouri and Illinois. Found tablets (1827), translated as *Book of Mormon,* which with his visions constitute basis of Mormon theology.

Smith, Matthew (1879–1960), Eng. artist. Style derived from Fauvism. Works included landscapes, nudes, still lifes.

Smith, Sydney (1771–1845), Eng. clergyman, essayist and wit. A founder of literary journal *Edinburgh Review* (1802).

Smith, Theobald, FRS (1859–1934),

Slate

Amer. pathologist. With F. L. Kilbourne found (1893) cause of Texas cattle fever. Used neutral bacteria cultures for immunization against diphtheria (1909).

Smith, Thorne (1892–1934), Amer. humorous writer. Works include *Topper* (1926), *The Night Life of the Gods* (1931), *Topper Takes a Trip* (1932).

Smith, William (1769–1839), Eng. geologist. Known for studies of rock strata in Geological Map of England (1815).

Smith, William Robertson (1846–1894), Scot. theologian. His articles on the Bible for *Encyclopaedia Britannica* resulted in an unsuccessful prosecution for heresy.

Smithsonian Institution, US scientific institution set up by act of Congress (1846) under will of James Smithson (1765–1829). Controls national galleries of art, museums of history and natural history. Conducts research into all aspects of science and superintends national meteorological departments, *etc.*

smog, mixture of smoke and fog, commonest in industrial and urban areas. Irritates eyes and respiratory system.

Ai, one of the three-toed Sloth family

Slavonian Grebe

Snow Goose

Snow Crystal (magnified many times)

smoke, volatile matter in atmosphere comprising particles of carbon and hydrocarbon. Considered health risk, therefore controlled by govt. measures advocating clean air and smokeless zones. When combined with fog, forms SMOG.

smoke tree, *Cotinus coggygria,* Eurasian shrub with feathery, usually purple, flowers resembling smoke. Also Amer. smoke tree, *C. americanus.*

Smoky Mountains *see* GREAT SMOKY MOUNTAINS.

Smolensk, city of W Russ. SFSR, founded AD 882. Important trading centre in Middle Ages. Now rly. junction and manufacturing centre. Pop. (1967) 189,000.

Smollett, Tobias George (1721–71), Scot. novelist. Wrote picaresque novels *Roderick Random* (1748), *Peregrine Pickle* (1751) and *Humphry Clinker* (1771). Thought to have influenced Dickens.

smooth snake, *Coronella austriaca,* harmless European snake with smooth, glossy scales. Up to 30 in. long; feeds on lizards and insects.

smuggling, offence of importing or exporting prohibited goods, or other goods, without paying legal duties.

Smuts, Jan Christian (1870–1950), South African soldier and statesman, P.M. (1919–24; 1939–48). Commanded Boer forces in Cape Colony war, sought (1902) reconciliation with British, influential in forming country's Union (1910).

Smyrna *see* IZMIR.

Smyth, Dame Ethel Mary (1858–1944), Brit. composer. Works include opera *The Wreckers* (1906), chamber, orchestral and choral music.

Smythe, Francis Sydney (1900–49), Eng. mountaineer. Took part in expeditions to Kanchenjunga (1930) and Everest (1933, 1936, 1938).

snail, mollusc of class Gastropoda with spiral protective shell. Marine, fresh water and terrestrial varieties. Species include common garden snail, *Helix aspersa* of almost world-wide distribution and *Succinea ovalis* of US. Some edible species.

snake, limbless elongated reptile of suborder Ophidia. Scaly cylindrical body with forked tongue. Mostly found in trop. regions. Venomous and non-venomous species.

Snake River, largest tributary of Columbia River, US. 1,038 mi. long. Provides irrigation over large area; important source of hydro-electric power. Navigation project (begun 1955) will allow navigation from confluence of rivers 140 mi. upstream. Flows through Hell's Canyon, one of deepest river gorges, maximum depth 7,900 ft.

snakeroot, Amer. plant formerly reputed as remedy for snakebites. Species include button snakeroot, *Liatris spicata,* and white snakeroot, *Eupatorium migosum.*

snapdragon, garden plant of genus *Antirrhinum,* esp. *A. majus,* with white, crimson or yellow flowers.

snapper, large marine fish of family Lutjanidae. Mutton snapper, *Lutjanus analis,* of W Indies is favoured food. Also bluefish, *Pomatomus saltatrix.*

snapping turtle, large predaceous aquatic turtle of family Chelydridae, esp. *Chelydra serpentina,* with powerful jaws. Found in fresh waters of N and S America. Alligator snapper, *Macrochelys temminckii,* is a voracious snapping turtle of US Gulf States.

snare drum, percussion instrument. Consists of side drum with catgut strings to produce rattling sound.

Snead, Sam[uel Jackson] (1912–), Amer. golfer. Won P.G.A. Championship (1942, 1949, 1951); British Open (1946).

sneeze, reflex action consisting of brief indrawn breath followed by forcible expulsion of air through nose. Initiated by irritation of lining of nose.

sneezewort, *Achillea ptarmica,* strong-scented, flowering perennial herb, found in N temp. regions.

snipe, brown wading bird of genus *Capella* related to woodcock. Found in New and Old Worlds. Long tail, slender bill; zig-zag flight. Species include common snipe, *C. gallinago,* of Europe and parts of Asia and Africa; Wilson's snipe *C. gallinago delicata* of US.

snipe fly, predatory insect of family Rhagionidae.

snooker, game developed from BILLIARDS, combining pool and pyramids. Form adopted in UK (1951) for professional championships.

Snorri Sturluson *see* STURLUSON, SNORRI.

Snow, Charles Percy, Baron Snow (1905–), Eng. scientist, writer and public official. Parl. Sec., Min. of Technology (1964–6). Author of *Strangers and Brothers,* 11-vol. sequence of novels incl. *Time of Hope* (1949), *The Masters* (1951), *Corridors of Power* (1964), *The Sleep of Reason* (1968).

snow, atmospheric vapour frozen into ice crystals and falling to earth in white flakes of complex structure. Near equator snow lies permanently above 16,000 ft. and at poles from sea-level upwards.

Anatomy of female snakes (a) Windpipe (b) Lung (c) Left aorta (d) Heart (e) Gullet (f) Liver (g) Stomach (h) Fat (i) Gall bladder (j) Intestine (k) Eggs (l) Kidneys

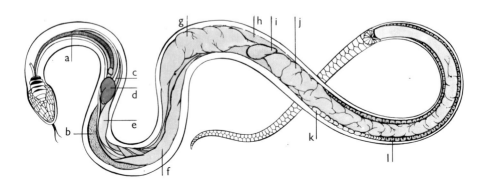

snow bunting, *Plectrophenax nivalis,* small finch of N regions with mainly white plumage. Breeds in Arctic; migrates to Europe and US in winter.

snow finch, *Montifringilla nivalis,* alpine sparrow of Europe and Asia.

snow goose, *Chen hyperborea,* N Amer. white wild goose with black tipped wings and light pink bill and legs. Breeds in tundra regions and migrates S.

snow leopard, ounce, *Panthera uncia,* large cat of mountains of C Asia, Coat whitish with brownish black blotches in summer, almost pure white in winter.

snowberry, ornamental deciduous shrub of genus *Symphoricarpos.* N Amer. *S. allus* bears pink flowers with white berries.

Snowdon, mountain range in Caernarvonshire, NW Wales. Divided by passes into 5 peaks, principal being Y Wyddfa (3,560 ft.), highest summit in Wales. Surrounding area made national park (1951).

snowdrop, bulbous plant of genus *Galanthus* with solitary white pendulous bell-shaped flowers. Species include common snowdrop, *G. nivalis,* cultivated in UK and US and giant snowdrop, *G. elwesii,* native of Med. region.

snowdrop tree, deciduous tree or shrub of genus *Halesia,* native to N America. Silver bell tree, *H. carolina,* of SE US has white bell-shaped flowers.

snowflake, small, hardy, bulbous plant of genus *Leucojum,* native to C Europe and Med. region. White-tipped green or red flowers. Species include spring snowflake, *L. vernum,* and summer snowflake, *L. aestivum.*

snow-in-summer, *Cerastium tomentosum,* low creeping perennial garden plant of Europe. Greyish leaves and white flowers.

snowshoes, webbed frames attached to feet for travel over snow, esp. used in Arctic regions.

Snowy, Austral. river rising in Snowy Mts. Important source of hydro-electric power. Dams also improved flow of Murray R. and aided irrigation.

Snowy Mountains, range in SE Australia. Highest peak Mt. Kosciusko (7,328 ft.). Winter sports centre.

snowy owl, *Nyctea scandiaca,* diurnal, arctic and sub-arctic owl. White plumage with dark brown markings.

snuff, powdered tobacco taken by sniffing as stimulant or sedative.

soap, chemical compound of potash and soda with animal and vegetable oils. Soluble in water and used for detergent or cleansing purposes. Known in variety of forms since 6th cent. BC.

soapberry, trop. tree or shrub of genus *Sapindus* grown for ornament. Fruit formerly used as a soap.

soapstone, steatite, massive, structureless mineral, form of TALC. Comprises complex magnesium silicates. Used for ornamental carvings.

soapwort, European annual or perennial herb of genus *Saponaria,* widely naturalized in US. Juice of some varieties lathers in water; several species are grown in rockeries and borders. Bouncing Bet, *S. officinalis,* has pink or white flowers.

Sobers, Garfield St Aubrun ('Gary') (1936–), West Indian cricketer from Barbados. Holder of many records as batsman and bowler.

Sobieski, John *see* JOHN [III] SOBIESKI.

soccer *see* ASSOCIATION FOOTBALL.

social contract, in philosophy, theory that society originated out of voluntary association, bringing with it mutual obligations. Formulated by Hobbes and Locke, expanded by Rousseau, had great influence on subsequent development of responsible govt. in democracies.

Social Credit, economic programme, developed from theories of Eng. economist, Clifford Douglas. Scheme calls for redistribution of purchasing power by issuing dividends to all persons to counter depression. Adopted by Social Credit Party of Alberta, Canada, elected (1935) under William Aberhart; also achieved power in Brit. Columbia.

social security, in US term for freedom from want secured by govt. allowances, pensions, *etc.* Principle 1st estab. in Germany (1883), in UK replacing Poor Law (1909), in US by Act of Congress (1935).

socialism, economic and polit. doctrine advocating reorganization of society, transferring ownership of property from private interests to state for use as public welfare. Influence marked in 19th-20th cent., esp. with growth of MARXISM, which became distinct from communism after triumph of LENIN and Bolsheviks. Other European 19th cent. exponents included Owen, Blanc, Lassalle.

Society Islands, volcanic islands, main group of Fr. Polynesia, of C Pacific Ocean. Chain (450 mi.) comprises Windward group (incl. Tahiti) and Leeward group. Cradle of Polynesian culture; discovered 1767. Pop. (1956), 54, 450.

Society of Friends *see* QUAKERS.

Snowdrops

Society of Jesus *see* JESUS, SOCIETY OF.

sociology, study of human behaviour in society; helps man to understand his social environment. Systematic discipline since 19th cent., largely through work of Auguste Comte.

Socotra, Soqotra, island in Indian Ocean. Became part of People's Republic of Southern Yemen (1967), formerly in Brit. Protectorate of South Arabia. Area: *c.* 1,584 sq. mi. Pop. (1960 est.) 12,000.

Socrates (469– 399 BC), Gk. philosopher whose disciples included Plato and Xenophon. Believed knowledge obtained by question-and-answer sequence (Socratic method); wisdom based on recognition of one's ignorance. Novel ideas and perceptions on weakness of democratic govt. unpopular in Athens. Assembly, citing misdeeds of his pupil Alcibiades, tried and condemned him on charge of corrupting youth. Died by drinking poison. Teachings preserved in writings of Plato, Aristotle.

soda, sodium carbonate, compound found in certain lakes in US, Canada

Snowy Owl

Salt hills in Jordan near site of Biblical Sodom

and Kenya. Manufactured on large scale from common salt for use in making of glass, soap, *etc.* Sodium bicarbonate is used as baking powder and in medicine.

Soddy, Frederick (1877–1956), Brit. chemist. Awarded Nobel Prize for Chemistry (1921) for studies of isotopes.

Soderblom, Nathan (1866–1931), Swedish Protestant theologian. Became Archbishop of Uppsala (1914). Pioneer of movement for unity of Christian churches. Awarded Nobel Peace Prize (1930).

sodium, soft, silvery-white metallic element. Tarnishes quickly in damp air and reacts violently with water to form sodium hydroxide. Found abundantly in compounds in nature, and widely used in preparations such as soap.

Sodom and **Gomorrah,** in OT, 2 cities, prob. situated N of Dead Sea. Destroyed by God because of their wickedness. Term **sodomy** is applied to unnatural intercourse with other humans or animals.

Sodor and Man, Anglican diocese, orig. of Norse creation. Now confined to Isle of Man, once included (1154–1334) Scot. Inner Hebrides. [Norse: *Sudrey-jar,* Southern isles].

Soest, Konrad von (1394–1425), Ger. artist. Painted altar-pieces for the Marienkirche, Dortmund and elsewhere. Influenced by Burgundian style.

Sofia, cap. of Bulgaria since 1878, on site of ancient Sardica. An important trading centre, held by Turks (1382–1878). Manufacturing industries. Pop. (1965) 801,000.

soft-shelled turtle, aquatic reptile of family Trionychidae, of Africa, Asia and N America. Shell is of bony plates covered with skin. Has long beak with soft lips.

Sogne Fjord, largest Norwegian fjord. Extends 136 mi. inland from Atlantic Ocean, with mountainous sides up to 5,000 ft. high.

soil, loose topmost layer of earth's crust, supporting vegetation. Contains mainly inorganic material (silt, sands, clay, rock fragments), small quantities of organic matter (humus, decaying animal and vegetable remains) and some air and water.

solan goose *see* GANNET.

solar energy, radiation from thermonuclear reactions inside Sun. Emitted as light, radio waves and hard (X-ray) radiations.

Solar System, name for Sun and collection of bodies in orbit round it. Comprises Sun, 9 major planets, their satellites, minor planets (asteroids or planetoids), comets and meteorites.

solder, alloy used in joining metals. Soft solders, which have low melting point, contain lead and tin in varying proportions with some antimony.

soldier fly, 2-winged insect of family Statiomyiidae. Characterized by coloured abdominal stripes; aquatic or terrestrial larvae.

sole, edible flatfish of genus *Solea.* Long body, small mouth, eyes close together. European *S. solea* most important commercially.

solicitor, term in UK for member of legal profession whose business is conducted out of court. Advises clients and engages barristers to represent them in high court, if necessary.

solid *see* STATES OF MATTER.

solitaire *see* PATIENCE.

Solomon (d. *c.* 932 BC), 3rd king of Israel (reigned 970–932 BC). Son and successor of David, renowned for wisdom and riches. Built 1st Temple at Jerusalem (*I Kings* i-xii). In OT books of *Proverbs, Ecclesiastes, Wisdom* and *Song of Solomon* are attributed to him.

Solomon Islands, group of Melanesian islands in W Pacific, discovered 1567. Bougainville and Buka Is. part of Trust Territory of New Guinea. Remainder constitute **British Solomon Islands Protectorate,** 6 large volcanic islands and several islets. Area: 12,780 sq. mi.; cap., Honiara. Exports copra and timber. Pop. (1963 est.) 124,000.

Solomon's seal, flowering plant of N temp. regions. Hybrids of *Polygonatum multiflorum* and *P. odoratum* are garden varieties. In N America species of Smilacina are called false Solomon's seal.

Solon (*c.* 640–559 BC), Athenian statesman, legislator and poet. Gained influence after success of proposed reconquest of Salamis from Megara, named Archon (594 BC). Introduced new constitution with solidarity of various classes and just treatment for all as objectives. Among reforms were cancellation of debt, institution of Heliaea (final court of appeal) and important economic measures. First Attic poet, wrote in elegiacs and iambics, only fragments of which survive.

Solovetski Islands, archipelago, N European Russ. SFSR, in White Sea. Largest island, Solovetsk, has 15th cent. monastery. Since 1917 island has been political prison.

solstice, time when Sun is at greatest possible distance from celestial equator. Sun reaches northernmost point of celestial sphere *c.* 21 June (summer solstice), and southernmost point *c.* 22 Dec. (winter solstice).

solution, in chemistry, homogeneous mixture of solids, liquids or gases effected without chemical change.

Solvay, Ernest (1838–1922), Belgian chemist. Originated Solvay process for preparing washing soda (sodium carbonate); estab. (1863) 1st plant for making soda by this process.

Solzhenitsyn, Aleksander Isayevich (1918–), Russ. novelist. Works include *Cancer Ward* and *The First Circle.* Awarded Nobel Prize for Literature (1970).

Somali, Cushitic Afro-Asian language. Has approx. 2 million speakers in E parts of N Africa.

Somali Republic, Somalia, independent repub. of E Africa, formed (1960) by union of UN Trust

Territory of Ital. Somalia and Brit. Somaliland. Area: *c.* 250,000 sq. mi.; cap. Mogadishu. Under Ital. and Brit. influence from 1880s. Border areas disputed with Ethiopia and Kenya. Economy based on nomadic livestock herding, cultivation of sugar cane and bananas, and leather-work. Lan-

Lenin Square, Sofia

guage, Somali; main religion, Islam. Unit of currency, somalo. Pop. (1964) 2,500,000

Somaliland, French *see* AFARS AND THE ISSAS, FRENCH TERRITORY OF THE.

Somers Islands *see* BERMUDA.

Somerset, maritime county of SW England. Area: 1,620 sq. mi.; county town, Taunton. Towns include Bath, Wells, Glastonbury. Extensive Roman remains at Bath, 12th–13th cent. Wells Cathedral, famous caves of Cheddar Gorge. Mainly agricultural, resorts on coast. Pop. (1966) 638,000.

Somerset, Dukes of *see* SEYMOUR.

Somerset House, UK govt. building in London. Contains General Register of Births, Marriages and Deaths for England and Wales, Inland Revenue Valuation Office, Probate and Divorce Registry, *etc.* E wing houses King's College of University of London.

Somervell, Sir Arthur (1863–1937), Eng. composer. Works include masses, oratorio *The Passion of Christ,* a symphony, settings of lyrics from Tennyson's *Maud* and Housman's *A Shropshire Lad.*

Somme, Battle of the, encounter (July-Nov. 1916) in World War 1, when Britain and France used tanks against Germans for 1st time, making slight gains at heavy cost. Second battle following Ger. offensive (Mar. 1918) resulted in Allied advance over Somme area (Aug. 1918).

Sommerfeld, Arnold Johannes Wilhelm, FRS (1868–1951), Ger. physicist. Did important research in electromagnetic theory, esp. X-rays. Wrote standard work on theoretical spectroscopy *Atomben und Spektrallinien* (1919).

sonar, asdic, method of detecting and locating underwater objects, esp. submarines or shoals of fish, by soundwaves they produce or reflect.

sonata, piece of instrumental music orig. for small groups of instruments, as opposed to cantata for voices and instruments.

song, vocal form of musical expression, normally setting of lyric. May or may not be accompanied by instrumental music. European song developed ballads from troubadour and meistersinger, through lute songs of 17th cent. and reached peak as vehicle of romantic expression in work of Schubert, Schumann and Brahms.

Song of Solomon, poetical book of OT, attributed to Solomon. Primarily a glorification of pure love. Prob. written *c.* 250 BC.

Song of the Three Holy Children,

Deathbed of Mary, part of an altarpiece by Konrad von Soest in the Marienkirche at Dortmund

apocryphal addition to OT *Book of Daniel.* Includes prayer of Azarias, part of which has been used as a hymn since 4th cent.

songthrush, mavis, *Turdus philomelos,* common European songbird with brown plumage and spotted breast.

sonnet, poem of 14 lines, expressing single complete thought or idea and generally written in iambic pentameter. Most common rhyme schemes are the Ital. form with 8 lines (octave) followed by group of 6 lines (sextet), and Eng. form with 3 quatrains followed by couplet.

Sophia, Electress of Hanover (1630–1714), youngest child of Elizabeth, daughter of James I, and Frederick V, Elector Palatine. Her son succeeded to throne of Great Britain and Ireland (1714), as George I.

Sophists, term applied in Athens (middle 5th cent. BC) to persons giving lessons in rhetoric, politics and mathematics for money. Later emphasized rhetoric rather than substance of knowledge, becoming known as quibblers; condemned by Socrates and Plato. Leading Sophists were Protagoras and Gorgias.

Sophocles (496–406 BC), Athenian tragedian. Author of over 100 plays of which 7 survive, incl. *Antigone* (441 BC), *Oedipus Tyrannus, Electra, Oedipus at Colonus.* Introd. 3rd actor on stage, developed scenery and

increased number of chorus from 12 to 15. Wrote each play as artistic entity in itself rather than part of connected tetralogy. Man's will plays greater part, that of the gods a lesser one, than in work of AESCHYLUS.

Sophonisba (3rd cent. BC), daughter of Hasdrubal of Carthage. Betrothed to Masinissa, her father married her to Syphax of Numidea, who became ally of Carthage but was defeated by Masinissa (203 BC).

soprano, highest singing voice in women and boys, latter also known as trebles. Term sometimes applied to

City hall, Mogadishu, Somalia

instruments, *e.g.* soprano saxophone.

sora, *Porzana carolina,* N Amer. short-billed rail with brownish plumage and black cap, mask and bib.

Sorbonne, unofficial alternative name for University of Paris, France. Orig. college, founded (1253) by Robert de Sorbon, obtained reputation as centre of theological study.

Sorel, Charles (1597–1674), Fr. novelist. Works include *Vraie Histoire Comique de Francion* (1622), *Le Berger Extravagant* (1627), early examples of reaction against idealist romances.

Sorel, Georges see SYNDICALISM.

sorghum, *Sorghum vulgare,* important cereal and forage plant native to Africa. Widely cultivated elsewhere under names of Kaffir corn, dhurra, Guinea corn, Indian millet.

sorrel, various species of herbs of temp. regions. Common sorrel, *Rumex acetosa,* is used as flavouring and in salads.

sorrel tree, sourwood, *Oxydendrum arboreum,* deciduous tree from N America, with long leaves and white flowers. Grows to ht. of 60 ft.

Sotho, Bantic language of Niger-Congo group, with over 2 million speakers in parts of SE Africa.

Soto, Hernando de (*c.* 1496–1542), Sp. explorer. Led expedition (1539–42) through Florida, Georgia and Mississippi.

soul, concept of non-material, immortal life-essence or spiritual identity of individual. Mind and body conceived as its vehicle.

Soulages, Pierre (1919–   ), Fr. abstract painter. Works include paintings, engravings, ballet and theatre decor.

sound, wave motion of air or other medium perceptible by ear. Travels at *c.* 764 m.p.h. depending on temperature of medium. Pitch of sound depends on number of vibrations per second, lowest normally audible to human ear *c.* 20 and highest *c.* 20,000.

sound barrier, name for imaginary barrier at which sound waves reach peak, submitting structure passing through them to maximum turbulence. After speed of sound has been passed turbulence is left behind. Sonic boom is explosion caused by passage from sub-sonic to supersonic speed (at 40,000 ft. equals 660 m.p.h.).

Sousa, John Philip (1854–1932), Amer. composer. Led US Marine band from 1880; formed own band (1892). Marches include *Washington Post* (1889), *Stars and Stripes* (1897). Devised sousaphone, tuba-like brass instrument which encircles player's body.

souslik, suslik, *Citellus citellus,* large species of burrowing ground squirrel of C Europe and Russia.

Sousse, Susa, city and port, NE Tunisia. Exports olive oil, phosphates. Founded 9th cent. BC. Pop. *c.* 52,000.

South Africa [Republiek van Suid-Afrika], repub. occupying S part of Africa. Area: 472,359 sq. mi.; admin. cap. Pretoria, legislative cap. Cape-town. Principal cities, Johannesburg,

Durban, Port Elizabeth. Admin. divisions, Cape Province, Natal, Transvaal, Orange Free State. Mainly plateau with dry climate. Crops include maize, cereals, fruits. Rich in mineral deposits, esp. gold, diamonds. First European settlement (1652) by Dutch on Cape. Brit. control assumed 1841. Boer settlements in N challenged by great gold and diamond rushes in late 19th cent., led to BOER WAR. Union of South Africa estab. 1910. Hostility towards black inhabitants resulted in adoption of APARTHEID (segregation) policy. External criticism forced withdrawal from Brit. Commonwealth and estab. as repub. (1961). Official languages, English, Afrikaans; main religions, Protestantism, Animism. Unit of currency, rand. Pop. (1967) 18,733,000.

South African War see BOER WAR.

South America, S continent of W hemisphere. Area: *c.* 6,880,000 sq. mi. Comprises repubs. of Colombia, Venezuela, Ecuador, Peru, Brazil, Bolivia, Paraguay, Chile, Argentina and Uruguay; colonies of Surinam and Fr. Guiana; Guyana, member of Brit. Commonwealth. West dominated by Andean cordillera; central highlands include Mato Grosso and Pampas; drained by Amazon, Plata and Orinoco river systems. Highly developed Indian civilizations (esp. Inca) flourished before Spanish and Portuguese exploration and colonization began in 16th cent. Pop. *c.* 200,000,000.

South American ostrich see RHEA.

South Arabia, Federation of, former protectorate formed (1962) of Arab states in Aden Peninsula, Arabia. See YEMEN, SOUTHERN.

South Australia, state of S Australia. Area: 380,070 sq. mi.; cap. Adelaide. Main occupations, pastoralism, mining (esp. iron ore, salt). Discovered 1802, became Brit. prov. (1836); achieved statehood with Austral. independence (1901). Pop. (1966) 1,090,723.

South Carolina, state of SE US, on Atlantic coast. Area: 31,055 sq. mi.; cap. Columbia. Chief crops tobacco, cotton; textiles manufactured. First explored by Spanish; English estab. permanent settlement (1670). One of 13 original US states; seceded (1860) from Union, re-admitted 1868. Pop. (1960) 2,382,594.

South China Sea, extension of Pacific Ocean off SE Asia. Separated from East China Sea by Formosa Strait. Violent typhoon region.

South Dakota, state of N central US. Area: 77,047 sq. mi.; cap. Pierre; main city, Sioux Falls. Region mainly semi-arid plain, chief produce grains; mineral resources include gold. European exploration (early 18th cent.), purchased by US (1803). Indian uprisings occurred throughout 19th cent. Admitted to US (1889) along

The Iguaçu Waterfalls on the River Iguaçu on the boundary between Brazil and Argentina, South America

with North Dakota. Pop. (1960) 680,514.

South Georgia, island of S Atlantic Ocean, one of Falkland Is. Area: *c.* 1,600 sq. mi.; main town, Grytviken Harbour. Whaling station. Ownership disputed by Argentina and UK.

South Island, larger of 2 principal islands of New Zealand. Area: 58,100 sq. mi.; separated from NORTH ISLAND by Cook Strait. Almost unbroken coastline and large areas of flat grassland incl. Canterbury Plains, famous for sheep and wheat. Chief

cities, Christchurch, Dunedin. Pop. 743,680.

South Orkney Islands, group in S Atlantic Ocean. Contains meteorological station. Ownership disputed by Argentina and UK.

South Pole, S terminus of rotational

SOUTH AMERICA

axis of earth, latitude 90°S, longitude 0°. First reached by Roald Amundsen (1911).

South Sea Bubble, in England, popular name for financial scheme in which South Sea Company (founded 1711) took on UK national debt in return for annual govt. payments and trade concessions. After widespread speculation, company became bankrupt (1720).

South Seas, literary name for parts of Pacific Ocean; South Sea Is. include Melanesia, Micronesia, Polynesia.

South Shetland Islands, group of barren islands in S Atlantic Ocean. Base for Antarctic expeditions and whaling. Ownership disputed by UK, Argentina, Chile.

Southampton, city and seaport of Hampshire, SE England; main transatlantic passenger port. Industries include shipbuilding, aircraft, oil refining. Pop. (1966) 209,000.

Southeast Asia Treaty Organization (SEATO), defence alliance, estab. 1954 at Manila, Philippines. Charter members: Australia, France, New Zealand, UK and US; formed to guarantee peace in SE Asia.

Southern Alps, mountain range of South Is., New Zealand. Highest peak Mt. Cook (12,349 ft.).

Le groom by Soutine

Southern Cross [**Crux**], constellation of 4 principal stars prominently visible in S hemisphere.

Southern Rhodesia *see* RHODESIA.

Southey, Robert (1774–1843), Eng. poet; one of 'Lake Poets'. Works include poems, *e.g.* 'After Blenheim', biographies, *e.g. Life of Nelson* (1813). Poet Laureate (1813–43).

South-West Africa, territory of Africa, on S Atlantic coast. Area: 317,725 sq. mi.; cap. Windhoek. Largely arid plateau, inhabitants chiefly employed with sheep and cattle raising, fishing, mining, esp. diamonds. Annexed (1892) by Germany, governed after World War 1 by South Africa under League of Nations mandate, revoked (1966) by UN.

Soutine, Chaim or **Haim** (1894–1943), Fr. Expressionist painter, b. Lithuania. Works include *The Old Actress* (1924).

sovereignty, term for status, power and authority of sovereign. By transference, supreme power and authority in govt., held by state or community, governing body such as parl., *etc.*

soviet [Russ: council], primary unit of govt. of USSR, with elected members. Under constitution, forms hierarchical chain from rural committees to Supreme Soviet. Orig. organized by workers, peasants, soviets were instrumental in Bolshevik triumph during 1917 Russ. Revolution.

sowbread, *Cyclamen europaeum,* common wild cyclamen of C Europe. Leaves dark green with white spots; crimson or white flowers.

sowbug, woodlouse, slater, small terrestrial crustacean of genus *Oniscus.* Flattened elliptical body; often capable of being rolled into a ball.

Sowerby, James (1757–1822), Eng. natural history artist. Illustrated book called *English Botany* (1792–1807), text by J. E. Smith.

sow-thistle, annual or perennial weedy herb of genus *Sonchus.* Thistle-like leaves, yellow flowers and milky juice. *S. arvensis,* corn sow-thistle, is from Eurasia.

soybean, soya bean, soja bean, *Glycine max,* leguminous annual plant native to Asia. Cultivated in China, Japan, US, Africa, Australia. Grown for forage, made into meal, curds or cake; seeds yield oil, used in glycerine and rubber substitutes.

spa, site of mineral springs supposed to have medicinal properties.

Spaak, Paul-Henri (1899–   ), Belgian statesman, 1st Pres. of UN General Assembly (1946) and of 1st Council of Europe session (1949). Sec. General of NATO (1957–61).

space exploration, navigation in manned spacecraft in regions beyond Earth's atmosphere, region considered to begin at altitude of 100 mi. Unmanned artificial satellites carried out 1st explorations relaying to Earth information about atmos. conditions. Orbital flight by manned vehicle 1st achieved by Yuri Gagarin of USSR (Apr. 1961). Extended flights since have included unmanned probes to Venus and Mars, manned landing by *Apollo 11* on Moon (1969).

spacecraft, vehicle designed for travelling in outer space. Pioneered by USSR and US. Early craft were artificial satellites put into orbit round Earth. Manned vehicles powered by rocket motors, capable of being steered by ASTRONAUT.

space-time, in physics, concept of 4th dimension. Necessitated by Einstein's proof in his theory of relativity that space and time are interdependent.

spaghetti, cord-like wheaten pasta orig. Ital., now consumed throughout Europe and America.

spahis, Moslem cavalry of Ottoman army. Employed by Sultan Mahmud II (1826) to crush JANISSARIES. Name also refers to native Algerian cavalrymen in Fr. army.

Space exploration: An American space rocket on the launching pad

Interior of an American *Apollo* spacecraft

Space exploration: picture of the American *Gemini* VII spacecraft taken from *Gemini* VI shortly before their link-up in space (15 Dec. 1965)

American astronaut E. H. White making his historic 'space walk' in June 1965

The old fishing village of Tossa del Mar, Spain

The Monastery of Montserrat near Barcelona, Spain

The Calle de Alcalá in Madrid, capital of Spain

Spain [Estado Español], state of SW Europe, occupying greater part of IBERIAN PENINSULA. Area: 196,700 sq. mi.; cap. Madrid; main cities, Barcelona, Valencia, Seville. Elevated tableland surrounded and crossed by mountain ranges incl. the Pyrenees, Sierra Nevada, the Cantabrians.

Predominantly agric. (wheat, barley, fruit, vines) with deposits of iron, lead, copper. Fishing important in NW; industries include textiles, light engineering, chemicals. Principal exports fruit, wine, iron ore. Tourism important. Repub. 1931–47 (*see* SPANISH CIVIL WAR). Language, Spanish; main religion, Roman Catholicism. Unit of currency, peseta. Pop. (1968) 32,411,407.

Spallanzani, Lazaro, FRS (1729–99), Ital. scientist. Studied blood circulation, human digestive processes and respiration. Disproved theory of spontaneous generation.

Spanish, a Romance Indo-European language, with over 140 million speakers in Spain and most of the countries of Central and South America.

Spanish Armada *see* ARMADA, SPANISH.

Spanish bayonet, plant of genus *Yucca*, esp. *Y. aloifolia*, native to Mexico, N America and W Indies. Spiky sword-like leaves.

Spanish Civil War, conflict (1936–9) precipitated by military opposition to radical govt. of Sp. repub. (proclaimed 1931). Conservative interests, merged under FRANCO, won early victories over Republican (or loyalist) forces. International non-intervention pact (signed 1936) broken; Germany and Italy supplied arms to Franco's Insurgents, USSR supported Republicans. Triumph by Insurgents (Madrid captured, Mar. 1939) led to estab. of Franco's dictatorship.

Spanish Guinea, former name of **Equatorial Guinea** (created 1968), repub. of W Africa. Area: *c.* 10,000 sq. mi.; cap. Santa Isabel, on Fernando Po Is. Mainland is Rio Muni. Exports cocoa. Pop. (1960 est.) 246,000.

Spanish Main, mainland of Sp. America from Panama to mouth of Orinoco R. Term now refers to Caribbean area, associated with piracy.

Spanish Sahara, Sp. overseas prov. of W Africa. Area: 103,000 sq. mi.; cap. El Aiun. Two regions are Seguia el Hamra, Rio de Oro. Main port Villa Cisneros. Fishing main occupation. Pop. (1968) 48,000.

Spanish Succession, Wars of the (1701–14), European struggle over succession to Sp. throne, after death of Charles II. Claimants, Philip, grandson of Louis XIV of France and Charles, son of Emperor Leopold I. England and Austria allied against France and Bavaria. Hostilities ended by treaties of Utrecht, Rastadt and Baden. In America, war known as Queen Anne's War.

Spanish-American War (1898), struggle for Cuban independence from Spain. Immediate causes included mysterious sinking of US battleship *Maine* in Havana harbour. Sp. forces surrendered after defeat at Santiago de Cuba. Treaty of Paris (Dec. 1898) granted Cuban independence and certain intervention rights to US.

Spark, Muriel Sarah (1918–   ), Brit. novelist, poet and critic, b. Edinburgh. Critical and biographical works include *Tribute to Wordsworth* (1950), *The Brontë Letters* (1954). Among her novels, *The Ballad of Peckham Rye* (1960), *The Prime of Miss Jean Brodie* (1961), *The Mandelbaum Gate* (1965).

sparking plug, spark plug, part used in internal combustion engine to ignite fuel-air mixture. Consists of 2 electrodes between which current from the battery discharges an electric spark.

The Alcázar of Segovia, Spain

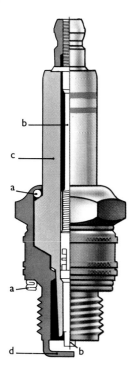

Sparking plug a) compression sealing rings b) centre electrode c) porcelain insulator, d) earth electrode

sparrow, bird of genus *Passer* of finch family with streaked brown and grey plumage. House sparrow, *P. domesticus,* is related to weaverbird; native to N Europe and Asia, naturalized in N America, Australia and New Zealand. Tree sparrow, *P. montanus,* less common in Britain, found in parts of Europe and in China.

sparrow hawk, *Accipiter nisus,* small Old World hawk. Bird of prey with long tail and broad rounded wings. Amer. sparrow hawk, *Falco sparverius,* is a falcon; preys on insects and small mammals.

Sparta [**Sparte**] or **Lacedaemon** [**Lakedaimon**], cap. of Laconia, SE Peloponnese, founded by Dorians. Art and industry highly developed by 7th cent. BC, military skill dominant in 6th cent. BC. Inhabitants divided into Spartiates (ruling class), who alone held civil and legal rights, perioeci (artisans and tradesmen) and helots (slaves). Constitution traditionally founded by Lycurgus (c. 600 BC) transformed monarchical govt. into oligarchy; retained 2 kings, although more governing power held by ephors. Participated in Persian Wars, esp. at

Thermopylae, Salamis and Plataea. Organized Peloponnesian league before 500 BC, but without imperial ambition. Rivalry with Athens culminated in Peloponnesian War (431–404 BC). Sparta victorious; later defeated by Thebans at Leuctra (371 BC). Declined after invasion of Philip of Macedon, and submerged by Roman domination.

Spartacists, radical German Socialist group, founded 1916. Led by Karl Liebknecht and Rosa Luxemburg. Became (1918) German Communist Party. Uprising (Jan. 1919) ruthlessly suppressed by Berlin govt.

Spartacus (d. 71 BC), Thracian gladiator. Escaped from gladiatorial school at Capua and led slave rebellion (73–71 BC) against Rome. Defeated and slain by Crassus.

spastic paralysis, condition in which control of muscles is impaired, leading to involuntary and uncoordinated movements. Caused by brain damage. Physical defects may be accompanied by mental abnormality.

Special Operations Executive (SOE), semi-official Brit. organization in World War 2. Initial task of agents to sabotage Ger. arms manufacture, esp. in occupied France. Later co-ordinated resistance groups in preparation for Allied invasion (1944). Head of Fr. section Maurice Buckmaster; agents included Violette Szabot, Odette Churchill.

specific gravity, ratio of a material's DENSITY to density of water at 4° C.

spectroscope, instrument which disperses electromagnetic radiation into a SPECTRUM. Light is introduced through a slit, its rays made parallel by a lens, diffracted by a prism, and viewed through a telescope eyepiece.

spectroscopy, study of radiant energy phenomena from entire range of electromagnetic wavelengths. Used esp. in analysis of light from stars to determine their motion and composition.

spectrum, in physics, orig. term for colours produced by white light passing through a prism. Rays produced range from infra-red to ultra-violet. Now refers to whole range of electromagnetic radiation, visible and invisible, arranged in order of frequency.

Spee, Maximilian, Graf von (1861–1914), Ger. naval officer. Commanded Ger. fleet in battle of Falkland Is. in World War 1. Defeated; died when flagship *Scharnhorst* sank.

speedwell, herb or shrub of genus *Veronica* found in temp. regions.

Sparrow

Several garden species incl. blue-flowered speedwell, *V. persica.*

speleology, scientific study of caves, their structure, flora and fauna.

Spellman, Francis Joseph (1889–1968), Amer. churchman. Created Archbishop of New York (1939) and cardinal (1946).

Spemann, Hans (1869–1941), Ger. embryologist. Awarded Nobel Prize for Physiology and Medicine (1935) for discovering 'organizer effect' in embryonic development.

Spence, Sir Basil Urwin (1907–   ), Brit. architect. Work includes design for Coventry Cathedral, buildings for University of Sussex, Brit. pavilion for Expo '67 in Montreal.

Spencer, Herbert (1820–1903), Eng. philosopher. Applied scientific doctrines of evolution to philosophy, using 'persistence of force' as unifying principle of knowledge. Works include *The Principles of Psychology* (1855), *First Principles* (1862) and *The Principles of Sociology* (1876–96).

Sparrowhawk

Spider monkey

Spender, Stephen Harold (1909–), Eng. poet and critic. Wrote poems of social protest and later of autobiographical material. Published as *Collected Poems* (1954).

Spengler, Oswald (1880–1936), Ger. philosopher of history. Proposed theory that each civilization has life cycle similar to that of human beings; glorified primitive cultures.

Spenser, Edmund (1552–99), Eng.

Diadem spider on web

poet. Works include *The Shepheardes Calendar* (1579), and poems written during courtship and marriage (*Amoretti* and *Epithalamion*). Used archaic language and developed Spenserian stanza of 9 lines for allegorical epic *The Faerie Queene*.

sperm whale *see* CACHALOT.

spermatophyta, in botany, term for seed-bearing plants. Subdivided into GYMNOSPERM and ANGIOSPERM.

sphagnum, bog moss, peat moss, soft moss of genus *Sphagnum*. Found chiefly in surface of bogs. Used for potting and packing plants.

sphalerite, zincblende, zinc sulphide mineral usually containing iron, manganese or other elements. Occurs in yellow, brown or black crystals or cleavable masses.

sphere, solid geometrical figure with all surface points equidistant from centre; shape of a ball. Volume is 4/3 pi multiplied by radius cubed. Surface is 4 pi multiplied by radius squared.

sphinx, in Egyptian art, lion with human head, often male. Sometimes portrait. Most famous is near Gizeh, United Arab Repub. In Gk. myth., monster represented as winged woman with body of lion or dog, offspring of Echidna and Typhon.

spice, aromatic vegetable product, *e.g.* pepper, ginger, nutmeg, cinnamon, clove, *etc.,* used in cookery to season or flavour food.

spicebush, *Lindera benzoin,* yellow flowered aromatic shrub of N America. Also name for *Calycanthus occidentalis,* N Amer. shrub with fragrant light-brown flowers.

spider, animal of order Araneida. Eight legs, segmented abdomen and 4 pairs of compound eyes. Fine thread from spinnerets is woven into a web which traps flying insects.

spider crab, crustacean esp. of family Majidae, with triangular body and long thin legs.

spider monkey, black or brown monkey of *Ateles* or related genus found in forests of S America. Long slender limbs and prehensile tail.

spider wasp, solitary long-legged wasp. Kills spiders by stinging and injects larvae into them. Larvae later feed on corpses.

spikenard, *Nardostachys jatamansi,* E Indian perennial aromatic herb. Rhizomes formerly used to make ointment.

Spillane, Mickey (1918–), Amer. writer of detective stories, creator of character Mike Hammer. Best known book *I, The Jury* (1947).

spina bifida, rachischisis, abnormality in human infants caused by defective closure of spine.

spinach, *Spinacia oleracea,* widely cultivated annual plant, native to SW Asia. Edible leaves used as vegetable.

spinal column, bony structure peculiar to vertebrates. Consists of numerous small bones called vertebrae held in position by ligaments, skull attached to one end and pelvis through sacrum to other. Through centre runs spinal cord.

spindle tree, shrub or tree of genus *Euonymus*. Orange fruit; white wood formerly used to make spindles. Species include *E. europaeus* of Eurasia.

spinel, very hard mineral consisting of an oxide of magnesium and aluminium. Forms crystals varying from colourless to ruby-red or black. Used as gemstone. It can be produced synthetically.

spinet, small triangular-shaped HARPSICHORD, popular in 17th cent. The virginals, a rectangular spinet, had been popular in previous cent.

spinnaker, large triangular yacht sail. Used for running before wind.

spinning, process of making FIBRE into continuous thread or yarn. Household industry from ancient times. Spinning wheel was replaced (16th cent.) by wheel and treadle. Further revolutionized in 18th cent. by mechanical LOOM.

Spinoza, Baruch or **Benedict** (1632–77), Dutch philosopher. Influenced by Descartes, developed pantheist system (chiefly contained in *Ethics*, 1677), in which all existence embraced by infinite essence (God). Excommunicated (1656) from native Jewish sect for unorthodoxy of thought.

spiny ant-eater *see* ECHIDNA.

spiny lizard, thorny devil, *Moloch horridus,* spine-covered reptile of Austral. deserts. Feeds on ants caught with the tongue. Also name given to iguanid lizard of genus *Sceloporus* of N and C America.

spiraea, shrub of genus *Spiraea* of Rosaceae family found in temp. regions. Small pink or white flowers. Species include Eurasian willow spiraea, *S. salicifolia*.

spiritual, orig. religious folk music of 19th cent. N Amer. revivalist meetings. Now generally refers to Negro songs.

spiritualism, belief in the possibility of communication with the dead. Originated in 19th cent. US, now widespread. Professional medium acts as intermediary, summoning spirits of the dead on behalf of interested parties. Meeting for these purposes known as **seance** [Fr: sitting]. Aims to demonstrate reality

Yacht with red spinnaker set

of apparently paranormal mental and physical phenomena.

spirogyra, widely distributed freshwater green alga of genus *Spirogyra.* Appears as green scum on water.

Spitsbergen, Svalbard, Arctic archipelago, 400 mi. N of Norway. Area: 23,658 sq. mi. Mountainous, with coal mining as main occupation. Ceded to Norway 1920. Pop. (1963) 3,654.

Spitteler, Carl (1845–1924), Ger. Swiss poet and essayist. Works, written under pseudonym Felix Tandem, include *Olympischer Fruhling* (1905–10), *Prometheus der Dulder* (1924). Awarded Nobel Prize for Literature (1919).

spittle bug *see* FROGHOPPER.

spleen, organ in abdominal cavity on left side of body. Total function uncertain, but acts as reserve blood supply, forms white cells, destroys old red cells. Removable without risk.

spleenwort, cosmopolitan genus of ferns. European species are small tufted plants growing esp. on rocks.

Split, city and port of Yugoslavia, on Adriatic Sea. Orig. Roman Spalato, which grew around Emperor DIOCLETIAN's palace. Pop. (1963) 99,614.

Spock, Benjamin McLane (1903–), Amer. doctor and authority on child care. Author of best-selling *Common Sense Book of Baby and Child Care* (1946).

Spode, Josiah (1754–1827), Eng. potter at Stoke-on-Trent. Used crushed bone with soft paste to obtain transparent effect. Pieces much sought by collectors.

spoils system, practice developed in US rewarding loyal supporters by appointing them to polit. offices. First used on large scale by Pres. Jackson. Corruption incurred by system led to civil service reform in late 19th cent.

Spokane, city of E Washington, US, on Spokane R. Commercial centre of surrounding area. Pop. (1963) 227,000.

Spolcto, city of Umbria, C Italy. Orig. Etruscan, later Roman colony. Cap. of duchy under Lombards from 6th cent. AD, city was under papal rule for 6 cent. Roman remains include bridges, amphitheatres. Pop. 40,500.

sponges *see* PORIFERA.

spoonbill, long-legged bird with beak flattened and wide at tip. Species include white spoonbill, *Platalea leucorodia,* of Europe and roseate spoonbill, *Ajaia ajaia,* of Florida and S America.

spontaneous combustion, sudden burning of substance of low ignition point, without evident cause. Oxidation occurring within substance increases heat, causing combustion.

Sporades, Northern, Gk. archipelago in Aegean Sea. Largest island Skiros. **Southern Sporades,** also known as the Dodecanese, group of islands incl. Rhodes, Cos, *etc.,* lying off coast of Turkey.

spore, non-sexual reproductive cell found in flowerless plants. Capable of giving rise to new plant which may or may not resemble parent.

sporozoa, parasitic protozoa which reproduce by formation of spores.

sprat, *Clupea sprattus,* foodfish of herring family. Bluish green with silver underside. Lives in coastal shoals, feeding on plankton and fish eggs.

spring, natural outflow of water from earth. Mineral springs contain minerals dissolved from porous rock. Hot springs occur mainly in volcanic areas.

spring azure butterfly, *Lycaenopsis argiolus,* small blue Amer. butterfly with spotted underparts.

spring lizard, thorny devil, *Moloch horridus,* spiny desert lizard of Australia. Squat and short-tailed; covered with spines, largest on snout and above eyes.

springbok, *Gazella euchore,* horned antelope of S Africa. Stands *c.* 30 in. high, has lyre-shaped horns. Emblem of Republic of South Africa.

Springfield, state cap. and city of C Illinois, US, on Sangamen R. Centre of rich agric. region. Settled 1818; known as home and burial place of Pres. Lincoln. Pop. (1965) 111,000.

Springfield, city of SW Massachusetts, US, on Connecticut R.

White Spoonbill

Chemicals and machinery manufactured. Settled (1636) by Puritans. Pop. (1960) 174,000.

springtail, minute wingless insect of order Collembola. Found esp. in damp soil. Feeds on decaying vegetable matter.

spruce, coniferous evergreen tree of genus *Picea* of N temp. zones. Some species used for ornaments; wood,

Spoleto cathedral

Indian Giant Squirrel

straight-grained and light, commercially important. Varieties include Norway spruce, *P. abies,* white spruce, *P. glauca,* Colorado spruce, *P. pungens.* Most species provide pulp for paper-making.

spurge, woodland or marsh plant of family Euphorbiaceae, esp. of genus *Euphorbia.* Milky juice and flowers without petals or sepals.

Spurgeon, Charles Haddon (1834–92), Eng. Baptist minister, known for popularity of sermons. Metropolitan Tabernacle, London, built (1861) for his large audiences. Sermons later printed and widely read.

squall, strong wind starting suddenly and lasting only several minutes. Often accompanies thunderstorms.

square root, numerical quantity of which a given larger number is the square, *e.g.* 4 is the square root of 16.

squash bug, brownish black insect,

pest of squash plants. Species include N Amer. *Anasa tristis* and European *Coreus marginatus.*

squash racquets, game similar to RACKETS, played in 4-walled court.

squid, marine cephalopod mollusc with torpedo-shaped body. Long retractile arms have suckers at ends. Ejects inky fluid (SEPIA) to baffle enemies.

squill, spring-flowering bulbous plant of Eurasia, Africa and N America. Garden varieties include Siberian squill, *Squilla siberica.* Brit. woodland wild bluebell is *S. nonscripta.*

squint *see* STRABISMUS.

squirrel, small, usually arboreal, vegetarian rodent. Species include European red squirrel, *Sciurus vulgaris*; Amer. red squirrel or chickaree; Austral. phalanger; Indian giant squirrel, *Ratufa indica,* the largest tree squirrel. N Amer. grey squirrel introd. to Europe (1890) has become a pest.

Srinagar, cap. of Kashmir province, India, in Himalayan valley (at 5,250 ft.). Known for network of canals and streams in and around city. Silk industry formerly supplied parachute silk for Brit. army. Pop. (1966) 302,000.

Stabat Mater, medieval Latin hymn sung in R.C. services to one of many musical settings. Tells of sorrows of Virgin Mary by the Cross.

stable fly, *Stomoxys calcitrans,* insect which sucks blood of mammals. Also

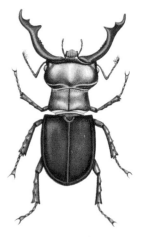

Stag Beetle

known as biting horse fly; a livestock pest in low-lying areas.

stachys, genus of cosmopolitan plants of the mint family. Includes *S. sylvatica,* hedge woundwort, with heart-shaped serrated leaves and small purple flowers, and *S. palustris,* hedge nettle.

Staël, Anne Louise Germaine de (1766–1817), Fr. writer; daughter of Jacques Necker. Exiled (1803) by Napoleon for liberal views, she lived in Switzerland. Works include novels *Delphine* (1802), *Corinne* (1807), and a romantic eulogy of Ger. literature *De l'Allemagne.*

Stael, Nicolas de (1914–55), Fr. painter. Early work abstract, later more figurative, using clear colours.

Staffordshire, inland county of C England. Area: 1,154 sq. mi.; county town, Stafford. Mainly industrial, county is centre of pottery industry. Two coalfields give name 'Black Country' to S area towards Birmingham. Pop. (1966) 1,802,000.

stag beetle, large plant-feeding beetle with antler-like mandibles. Larvae live in rotting wood. Species include *Lucanus cervus,* largest Brit. beetle, and *L. capreolis* of NE US.

stage-coach, carriage formerly used esp. in Europe and America, in early 18th cent., to convey passengers, mail, luggage. Drawn by 4–6 horses, changed at staging points.

stained glass, coloured glass used in making windows. Panes in many colours held together by lead strips. Art matured by 5th cent., but best work executed in medieval Gothic cathedrals, *e.g.* Chartres, France.

Stair, 1st Viscount *see* DALRYMPLE, JAMES.

Stair, 1st Earl of *see* DALRYMPLE, JOHN.

Still Life with Pears by Nicolas de Stael

Stained glass window in Bourges Cathedral, showing the prophet Joel

Scenes from the Old Testament portrayed in stained glass, Rouen Cathedral

Detail of a 14th century stained glass window at Freiburg, Germany

Stair, 2nd Earl of *see* DALRYMPLE, JOHN.

stalactites, icicle shaped deposits, often calcite, found hanging from roofs of limestone caves. Formed as deposits from dripping water, they may merge with STALAGMITES below them. Outstanding examples found in Carlsbad Caverns, New Mexico, US.

stalagmites, icicle shaped deposits found rising from floor of limestone caves. *See* STALACTITES.

Stalin, Joseph, orig. Joseph Vissarionovich Dzhugashvili (1879–1953), Soviet polit. leader. Exiled to Siberia for Bolshevist activity, returned (1917) during Russ. Revolution. Joined Lenin's govt., elected (1922) general sec. of Communist Party. Shared leadership after Lenin's death (1924) until 1927, when he engineered removal of Trotsky and Zinoviev. Thereafter exercised dictatorial powers as head of Politburo and premier (1941–53). Consolidated power through series of purges (1930s). Initiated massive indust. and agric. collectivization with FIVE YEAR PLAN schemes. Assumed (1941) military leadership after Germany invaded USSR. Expanded Soviet power in E Europe during meetings with other Allied leaders at end of World War 2 and by aggressive post-war foreign policy.

Stalin Peak, highest mountain (24,590 ft.) of USSR, in Tadzhik SSR. Orig. called Garmo Peak; renamed Stalin Peak (1935), Mt. Communism (1962).

Stalingrad *see* VOLGOGRAD.

stamen, male organ of flower. Consists of pollen-bearing anther on a filament.

Stamp Act, measure passed by Brit. Parl. (1765), requiring all legal documents in Amer. colonies to bear a revenue stamp. Violently opposed in America on grounds that Parl. did not have right to impose taxation without corresponding representation. Act repealed 1766.

Stanhope, Lady Hester Lucy (1776–1839), daughter of 3rd Earl Stanhope, niece of William Pitt. Settled (1810) in the Lebanon; adopted Eastern dress and customs; instigated Druses' rebellion against Egyptian rule. Died destitute.

Stanislaus [II] Augustus Poniatowski (1732–98), king of Poland (1764–95). Elected to position by intervention of Russia. Forced (1795) to sign third partition treaty, ending the existence of his kingdom.

Stanislavsky, Constantin, orig. Constantin Sergeyevich Alekseyev (1863–

Stachys sylvatica

1938), Russ. actor, director and teacher. Co-founder of Moscow Art Theatre (1898). His 'method' of total identification with role influenced many subsequent theories. Author of *My Life in Art* (1924).

Stanley, Edward George Geoffrey Smith, 14th Earl of Derby (1799–1869), Brit. politician. As Sec. for Colonies introduced Bill (1833) for abolition of slavery. P.M. (1852, 1858–9, 1866–8). After quarrel (1834) with Russell, left Whig party for Tories.

Stanley, Frederick Arthur, 16th Earl of Derby (1841–1908), Brit. politician. Fostered imperial co-operation during term of office as Gov.-General of Canada (1888–93).

Stanley, Sir Henry Morton, orig. John Rowlands (1841–1904), Brit. explorer and journalist. As correspondent of *New York Herald,* sent (1869) to Africa to find DAVID LIVINGSTONE.

Euphorbia splendens one of the Spurge family

With Livingstone, explored N end of L. Tanganyika. On later expedition, traced source of Congo R.; founded (1879) Congo Free State.

Stanley, Wendell Meredith (1904–71), Amer. biochemist. With J. H. Northrop and J. B. Sumner, awarded Nobel Prize for Chemistry (1946) for isolation of crystalline forms of virus.

Stanneries, the, [Lat: *stannum,* tin] term orig. applied collectively to tin mines of Cornwall and Devon, England. Also to surviving customs connected with them.

Stanton, Edwin McMasters (1814–69), Amer. politician. Sec. of War under Lincoln (1862–5), and then under Johnson. Resigned (1868) after resisting threatened dismissal by Johnson.

Stanton, Elizabeth Cady (1815–1902), Amer. reformer and suffragette. Organized 1st Woman's Rights Convention (1848); 1st Pres. of National Woman Suffrage Association. Author of autobiog. *80 Years and More* (1898).

star, heavenly body other than a planet appearing stationary in space due to vast distance from Earth. Nearest star Alpha Centauri is 4 light years away. Stars vary in colour, brilliance, size, density and speed of motion. Science of RADIOASTRONOMY is concerned with 'dark' stars which emit radio waves but not light.

Star Chamber, Eng. tribunal of king's councillors from Edward III's reign. Situated in Westminster Palace, name derived probably from starred ceiling. Orig. imposing restraint on nobles, Court tried criminals under Tudors, but excessive harshness towards Puritans in early 16th cent. led to abolition of Court (1641).

starch, carbohydrate occurring in most seeds, stored by plants in chains of glucose molecules. By chemical processing can be used as stiffener in laundering, textile and paper industries. Plants supply animals with necessary starch.

starfish, flattened carnivorous star-shaped marine animal. Normally has 5, or multiples of 5, arms. Smallest *c.* $\frac{1}{2}$ in., largest 36 in. across. Species include common starfish, *Asterias rubens.*

stargazer, fish of warm seas of family Uranoscopidae, related to perch.

Stark, Johannes (1874–1957), Ger. physicist. Discovered Doppler effect in canal rays (positive ions produced in gases when electricity discharged) and broadening of spectrum lines in electric field (Stark effect). This

Starling

confirmed quantum theory. Awarded Nobel Prize for Physics (1919).

starling, *Sturnus vulgaris,* gregarious bird with dark metallic plumage. Often a pest in cities, roosting in buildings. Has spread from Europe to Asia and N America. Varieties include ROSY PASTOR or rose-coloured starling, and mynah.

star-of-Bethlehem, bulbous plant of genus *Ornithogalum.* Narrow leaves and star-shaped flowers. *O. umbellatum* is common in Med. region; *O. nutans* of Asia Minor has green and white flowers.

Star-spangled Banner, Amer. national anthem since 1916. Words written by Francis Scott Key, after witnessing Brit. assault of Fort McHenry (1814). Music by John Stafford Smith, adapted from an English song.

Staten Island, island at mouth of Hudson R., in N.Y. state, US. Forms part of Richmond borough of New York City. First settled 1661.

State's Evidence *see* QUEEN'S EVIDENCE.

states of matter, term for gas, solid, and liquid forms, in which matter exists. Temperature, pressure changes can cause physical conversion from one state to another *e.g.* ice into water into steam.

States-General *see* ESTATES-GENERAL.

States' Rights, constitutional doctrine advocated by exponents of decentralized govt. in US. Arose over interpretation of 10th Amendment of Constitution. Manifested in KENTUCKY AND VIRGINIA RESOLUTIONS, NULLIFICATION crisis and ultimately in secession of Southern states leading to Civil War (1861–5).

statics, in physics and engineering, branch of mechanics dealing with bodies and forces at rest or in equilibrium.

statistics, science of collecting, classifying and interpreting numerical facts

or data. Used as method of analysis in sciences, social sciences, business, *etc.* Concerned both with description of actual events and predictions of likelihood of an event occurring.

statute, law passed by legislature and formally placed on record; unlike system of unwritten law based on custom and previous judicial decisions, known as common law.

steam engine, machine powered by energy derived from steam. Water is boiled in airtight vessel, producing steam which expands and is capable of mechanical work. Steam turbine consists of series of cylinders through which superheated steam passes at high pressure so that full driving force of steam is utilized before condensation occurs. Experiments 1st recorded (130 BC) by Hero of Alexandria. James Watt produced 1st practical version (1769); 1st steam locomotive devised (1814) by George Stephenson; steam engine for ships (1814) by William Symington.

steam organ *see* CALLIOPE.

stearic acid, colourless, odourless, wax-like fatty acid, occurring in animal fats. Used in manufacture of soap, candles, cosmetics and medicine.

steel, alloy of carbon and iron. Characterized by strength, hardness, elasticity and resistance to corrosion, fatigue, shock. Used in building construction, machinery, springs, tools. Special purpose steels are obtained by addition of specific ingredients.

Steele, Sir Richard (1672–1729), Eng. essayist and playwright. Began journal *Tatler* (1709); with JOSEPH ADDISON, produced the *Spectator* (1711–12), *Guardian* (1713). Plays include *The Conscious Lovers* (1722).

Steen, Jan (1626–79), Dutch genre painter. Works, mostly humorous (often depicting scenes of revelry) or moralistic, include *The Prince's Birthday*, *The Painter's Family*.

Stefansson, Vilhjalmur (1879–1962), Canadian Arctic explorer. Made ethnological and archaeological investigations on expeditions, adopting Eskimo survival techniques. Led longest Polar expedition (1913–18). Works include *Great Adventures and Explorations* (1947).

Steffens, [Joseph] Lincoln (1866–1936), Amer. journalist. Exposés of corruption in Amer. polit. and business life collected in *The Shame of the Cities* (1904), *Upbuilders* (1909), *Out of the Muck* (1913).

Stein, Gertrude (1874–1946), Amer. author and critic. Through her salon in Paris exerted considerable influence on writers and artists. Novels featuring experimental 'impressionist' style include *Three Lives* (1909), *The Making of Americans* (1925) and *The Autobiography of Alice B. Toklas* (1933).

Stein, Heinrich Friedrich Karl, Baron vom und zum (1757–1831), Prussian statesman, premier (1807–8). Abolished serfdom, caste, relics of feudalism; enabled peasants to buy land; instituted local self-govt. and civil service. Instrumental in forming alliance with Russia against Napoleon (1813).

Steinbeck, John Ernst (1902–68), Amer. author. Known for warm portrayals of unassuming, ordinary people. Works include *Tortilla Flat* (1935), *Of Mice and Men* (1937), *The Grapes of Wrath* (1939), *Cannery Row* (1944) and *Winter of Our Discontent* (1961). Awarded Nobel Prize for Literature (1962).

Steiner, Rudolph (1861–1925), Austrian social philosopher. Founder of anthroposophy, a theosophical cult interested in 'spiritual science'.

Steinmetz, Charles Proteus (1865–1923), Amer. electrical engineer, b. Poland. Discovered the law of hysteresis and developed methods of calculating alternating-current phenomena. Built generator for producing lightning artificially.

Stendhal, orig. Henri Marie Beyle (1783–1842), Fr. novelist, served in Fr. army under Napoleon. Novels, marked by psychological insight and sharp wit, include *The Red and the Black* (1830) *The Charterhouse of Parma* (1839); also essays, *Of Love*.

sten gun, light sub-machine gun, working on recoil principle. Limited range and accuracy; employed extensively in World War 2.

stenosis, in medicine, narrowing of passages or ducts of the body; result of disease or congenital abnormality.

stentor, pond-dwelling ciliate unicellular animal of genus *Stentor*.

Stephen, Saint (d. *c*. AD 33), first Christian martyr. Stoned to death at Jerusalem soon after Ascension. One of the 7 deacons of early Christian Church.

Romping Couple by Jan Steen

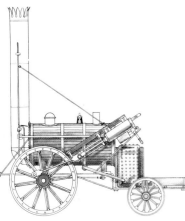

Stephenson's 'Rocket' (1829)

Stephen [I], Saint (c. 977–1038), first king of Hungary (1001–38). Crowned by Pope Sylvester II, effected widespread conversion of Magyars to Christianity, suppressed revolts of pagan nobles. Considered founder of Hungarian state.

Stephen (1097–1154), king of England (1135–54). Usurped throne from Matilda, daughter of Henry I. Reign marked by long civil wars. Eventually forced to name Matilda's son (later Henry II) as successor.

Stephens, John Lloyd (1805–52), Amer. traveller and archaeologist. Travelled in Europe and Far East, also visited ruined Indian cities of C America. Books include *Incidents of Travel in Central America, Chiapas, and Yucatan* (1841).

Stephenson, George (1781–1848), Eng. engineer, pioneer of steam locomotives and early railways. Built 1st locomotive to haul coal (1814); 1st to use steam blast (1815). His 'Rocket' won locomotive contest

The steppes of Russia

(1829), subsequently used on Liverpool-Manchester Rly. Founded Institute of Mechanical Engineers. Devised miner's safety lamp (c. 1815).

steppe, term applied to level treeless grasslands of SE European RSFSR, and SW Asiatic USSR. Mostly agric. area.

stereochemistry, branch of chemistry concerned with arrangement of atoms and groups of molecules in 3 dimensions, and the effect of these relationships on the physical and chemical properties of the molecule.

stereophonic sound, sound recorded simultaneously by microphones at various distances from sound source. In playback sound emanates from more than one speaker in order to produce realistic impression.

stereoscope, optical instrument producing 3-dimensional effect in a photograph. Consists of 2 photographs of the same subject taken from a slightly differing angle; viewed through 2 sloping lenses, thus merging the image and giving appearance of solidity or depth.

stereotype, plate providing solid printing surface. Cast from mould made from body of moveable type.

sterility, inability to reproduce species, found in man, animals and plants. Causes in humans may include impotence, glandular imbalance, disease and psychological problems.

sterilization, methods of rendering substances free of contamination by bacteria. Immersion in boiling water or in alcohol solution, or irradiation are methods used. Term also used for rendering of sexual organs incapable of reproduction.

Stoat or Ermine showing winter colouring (right)

Stern, Otto (1888–1969), Amer. physicist, b. Germany. Awarded Nobel Prize for Physics (1943) for work on measurement of magnetic properties of atoms and their components.

Sterne, Laurence (1713–68), Brit. novelist, b. Ireland. Best known for unfinished novels, *The Life and Opinions of Tristram Shandy* (1759–67) and *A Sentimental Journey through France and Italy* (1768).

sternum, in human anatomy, broad vertical bone to which front ribs are attached.

steroids, organic compounds found in animal cells esp. in human brain and spinal cord. They include bile acids, sex hormones, adrenal cortex hormones.

stethoscope, instrument used in medicine for detecting sounds in heart and lungs. Consists of chest piece connected by rubber tubes to 2 ear pieces. First devised with 1 earpiece by Laennec (1819).

Stettin see SZCZECIN.

Stevens, John (1749–1838), Amer. inventor. Instrumental in estab. of 1st US patent laws. Built (1806–8) *Phoenix,* sea-going steamboat. Received 1st rly. charter in US (1817).

Stevens, Thaddeus (1792–1868), Amer. politician, leader of radical

Republicans during RECONSTRUCTION era. Strong advocate of Negro emancipation. Proposed 14th Amendment and was responsible for impeachment of Pres. Andrew Johnson.

Stevens, Wallace (1879–1955), Amer. writer. Elegant poetry, tightly controlled; included in collections *Harmonium* (1923), *The Man with the Blue Guitar* (1937), *The Auroras of Autumn* (1951). Also wrote essays, plays, epigrams.

Stevenson, Adlai Ewing (1900–65), US polit. leader. Governor of Illinois (1949–53), unsuccessful Democratic pres. candidate (1952, 1956). US Ambassador to UN (1961–5).

Stevenson, Robert Louis (1850–94), Scot. novelist, poet, essayist. Author of popular classic novels *Treasure Island* (1883), *Kidnapped* (1886), *Strange Case of Dr Jekyll and Mr Hyde* (1886); major poetic work, *Child's Garden of Verses* (1885).

Stewart, House of *see* STUART OR STEWART, HOUSE OF.

stibnite, antimony trisulfide, lead-grey mineral associated with lead and zinc ores. Leading source of antimony. Used in ancient times as cosmetic.

stick insect, walking stick, trop., usually wingless, insect with long, slender, twig-like body. Species include N Amer. walking stick, *Diapheromera femorata,* and oriental *Casansius morosus.*

stickleback, small spiny-backed fish of family Gasterosteidae of N hemisphere. Species include three-spined stickleback, *Gasterostreus aculeatus.*

stigmata, in R.C. theology, miraculous reproduction of Christ's wounds on hands, feet, and side. Received only by persons of great piety, *e.g.* St Francis of Assisi, Padre Pio.

still, apparatus for distilling liquids by vaporization and condensation. Used in making alcohol. During US Prohibition era, numerous illegal, private stills produced alcohol.

stilt, wading bird found chiefly in marshes. Long legs, long neck and slender bill. Species include common or black-winged stilt, *Himantopus*

Stock Dove

himantopus, of S Europe, Africa and Asia, and black-necked Amer. stilt, *H. mexicanus.*

sting, piercing organ of some insects, animals and plants and the wound it makes. Pierces the skin of victim and often injects poison.

sting ray *see* RAY.

stinkbug, shield bug, broad, flat insect of family Pentatomidae. Emits disagreeable odour.

stinkhorn, foul-smelling fungus of genus *Phallus,* esp. *P. impudicus.*

stink wood, tree with foetid smelling wood esp. *Ocotea bullata.* Hard durable wood used for cabinet making.

Stirling, county town of Stirlingshire, C Scotland, on R. Forth. Centre of light industry and rail transportation. Site of royal residence for 5 centuries, coronation of Mary, Queen of Scots and James VI. University (1967). Pop. (1965 est.) 27,500.

Stirling, 1st Earl of *see* ALEXANDER, WILLIAM, EARL OF STIRLING.

Stirlingshire, county of C Scotland. Area: 451 sq. mi.; county town, Stirling; other towns, Falkirk, Grangemouth (on Firth of Forth). Hills include Ben Lomond (3,193 ft.). Industries include coal mining, textiles, distilling. Pop. (1966) 199,000.

stitchwort, annual or perennial cosmopolitan herbs of genus *Stellaria.* Species include greater stitchwort, *S. holostea,* with white flowers, and lesser stitchwort, *S. graminea.*

stoa, in Gk. architecture, long portico usually built to convey sense of perspective. Used as public meeting place.

stoat, *Mustela erminea,* small carnivorous mammal related to weasel. Found in N Europe, C Asia and N and S America. Reddish-brown coat with black-tipped tail. In winter, coat (except tail-tip) turns white; then valued as ermine.

stock, annual or perennial plant of genus *Matthiola,* native to Med. region, Asia and S Africa. Popular garden flower, esp. *M. tristis,* night-scented stock.

stock dove, *Columba oenas,* small, European wild pigeon.

stock exchange, market organized to facilitate business transactions, *i.e.* buying and selling securities. Exchange run according to fixed rules.

Stockholm, cap. of Sweden, near junction of Baltic Sea and Gulf of Bothnia. Industries include textiles, printing, ship-building, metalworking. Cultural centre, scene of presentation of annual Nobel Prize awards. Founded *c.* 1252. Pop. (1965) 1,162,000.

The Stadhuset (municipal building) in Stockholm

stocks *see* SHARES.

Stocks, Mary Danvers, Baroness (1891–   ), Eng. economist, broadcaster and writer. Held several university teaching posts; served on govt. committees.

Stoicism, school of philosophy founded by Zeno of Citium (*c.* 315 BC). World regarded as organic whole, diffused with divine active force of God. Man's true end is active life in harmony with nature, *i.e.* life of virtue, virtue being God's will. Universal benevolence and justice conceived of as duty, necessitating control of emotion and passions. Notable followers of stoic doctrine in Rome were Seneca, Epictetus and Marcus Aurelius.

Stoke-on-Trent, city of Staffordshire, England, formed from merger (1910) of 6 towns. Centre of THE POTTERIES. Pop. (1966) 276,000.

Stokowski, Leopold Anton Stanislaw (1882–   ), Amer. conductor, b. England. Conducted Cincinnati Symphony Orchestra (1909–12); founded All-American Youth Orchestra (1939).

Stolypin, Piotr Arkadevich (1862–1911), Russ. polit. leader. Premier (1906–11), pacification programme opposed in DUMA: after securing conservative majority, ruthlessly exterminated opposition. Assassinated.

stomach, bag-like organ at lower end of oesophagus, acting as temporary receptacle for food. Action of gastric juices and muscular movements of stomach wall break down food and pass it into duodenum.

Stone, Lucy (1818–93), Amer. suffra-

Stonehenge, Wiltshire, England

gette, opponent of slavery. Co-founder of Amer. Woman Suffrage Assoc. (1869). On principle, kept maiden name after marriage to H. B. Blackwell.

Stone Age, stage of prehistory when man 1st used stone implements. Divided into Eolithic, Palaeolithic, Mesolithic and Neolithic periods. In last phase (*c.* 2500 BC) tools were fashioned by grinding or polishing.

stonechat, *Saxicola torquata,* small European songbird of thrush family. Brownish plumage with black head, white collar and orange breast.

stonecrop, mossy, evergreen creeping plant of genus *Sedum* with yellow flowers. Found in temp. regions. English stonecrop, *S. anglicum,* and yellow stonecrop, *S. reflexum,* cultivated as rock garden plants.

stonefish, small, dull-coloured spiny scorpion fish of genus *Synanceja.* Lies camouflaged in stone or coral in trop. waters, esp. Indian and Pacific Oceans. Dorsal fins inject poison.

stonefly, insect of order Plecoptera, with 2 pairs of membranous wings and long antennae and cerci. Aquatic carnivorous nymphs have gills.

Stonehenge, prehistoric and pre-Druid (*c.* 1800–1400 BC) monument on Salisbury Plain, England. Remains of original arrangement include 'central altar' in horseshoe formation, surrounded by 2 upright stone circles. Probably used for religious purposes and astronomical calculations.

stoneroller, *Campostoma anomalum,* fish of carp family with black and orange fins. Found chiefly in clear streams of C US.

Stopes, Marie Carmichael (1880–1958), Brit. botanist, writer, and advocate of birth control. Founded (1921) first birth control clinic in Britain. Wrote best seller *Married Love* (1918).

stork, large migratory wading bird of family Ciconiidae related to herons. Stout body, long slender legs, short neck and long red bill. Species include white stork, *Ciconia ciconia,* and black stork, *C. nigra.*

storks bill, geranium plant of genus *Pelargonium* mostly native to S Africa, incl. ivy geranium *P. peltatum* and fish geranium *P. hostorum.*

Stormont, parl. of Northern Ireland, responsible for internal affairs. Estab. (1920) at Stormont, near Belfast.

stout, dark, sweet beer made of roasted malt, with higher percentage of hops than porter. Alcohol content *c.* 6–7%.

Stowe, Harriet Beecher (1811–96), Amer. novelist. Remembered for *Uncle Tom's Cabin; or, Life Among the Lowly* (1851–2), which influenced abolitionist movement by portrayal of slave life. Also wrote novels about New England, *e.g. Pearl of Orr's Island* (1862), *Oldtown Folks* (1869).

strabismus, squint, condition in which one or both eyes turn inwards, *i.e.* convergent, or outward *i.e.* divergent, and do not follow objects together; due to muscular imbalance or paralysis. Often correctible by exercise, glasses or surgery.

Strabo (*c.* 63 BC–*c.* AD 21), Gk. geographer and historian. Observations recorded in *Geographica* (17 vols.), constituting source of knowledge of ancient world.

Strachan, John (1778–1867), Canadian clergyman, 1st Anglican bishop of Toronto. Advocated Anglican supremacy and control of education in Upper Canada.

Strachey, [Giles] Lytton (1880–1932), Eng. essayist and biographer. Associated with Bloomsbury group. Works include *Eminent Victorians* (1918), *Queen Victoria* (1921).

Stradivari, Antonio (1644–1737), Ital. violin maker. Studied under Niccolò Amati, built renowned Cremona workshop, continued by sons.

Strafford, 1st Earl of *see* WENTWORTH, THOMAS.

Straits Settlements, former Brit. crown colony, comprising MALACCA, PENANG, SINGAPORE. Estab. 1867, dissolved 1946. Singapore became separate colony, Penang and Malacca became part of Malaya, now FEDERATION OF MALAYSIA.

Stralsund, seaport of East Germany. Founded 1209; became leading Hanseatic city. Unsuccessfully besieged (1628) during Thirty Years War. Pop. (1965 est.) 64,000.

Strasbourg [Ger: Strassburg], city of E France, cap. of Bas-Rhin department. Commercial centre of ALSACE. Industries include leather, brewing. Contains university (founded 1538). Seat of Council of Europe. Free imperial city from 13th cent. until seizure (1681) by Louis XIV. Pop. (1962) 302,000.

Stratford, city of Ontario, Canada, on Avon R. Known for annual Shakespeare Festival. Pop. (1961) 20,467.

Stratford-on-Avon, town of Warwickshire, England, on Avon R. Tourist centre, Shakespeare's birthplace (his home is preserved). Site of Shakespeare Memorial Theatre. Pop. (1963) 17,000.

Strathclyde, kingdom of medieval Britain, independent after Anglo-Saxon invasions. Stretched from W Highlands of Scotland to N Wales until confined (*c.* 7th cent.) to Clyde Valley and Cumberland. Cap. Dumbarton. Incorporated into Scot. kingdom in 10th cent.

stratification, in geology, arrangement of sedimentary rocks in layers (strata). Character of layering varies with conditions of sedimentation. Angle of strata to horizontal determined by earth movements.

stratosphere, lower portion of outer layer (ionosphere) of Earth's atmosphere. Distance from earth varies from 6 mi. at Poles to 13 mi. at equator; temperature (between −45°C and −75°C) varies little with height. First reached (1931) by Auguste Piccard in balloon ascent.

stratus clouds *see* CLOUD.

Strauss, Johann (1825–99), Viennese composer and conductor. Wrote more than 400 waltzes incl. *Blue Danube* and *Tales from the Vienna Woods*; operettas, *e.g. Die Fledermaus*.

Strauss, Richard Georg (1864–1949), Ger. composer. Influenced by Wagner. Works include symphonic poems *Don Juan* (1888), *Till Eulenspiegel* (1895); operas *Salomé* (1905), *Elektra* (1909) and *Der Rosenkavalier* (1911); and many songs.

Stravinsky, Igor Fedorovich (1882–1971), Russ. composer. Noted for use of dissonance and unorthodox rhythms. Best known works include ballets *The Fire Bird* (1910), *The Rite of Spring* (1913); and operas *The Rake's Progress* (1951), *The Flood* (1962). Naturalized French (1934); took Amer. nationality (1945).

strawberry, low perennial herb of genus *Fragaria*, native to N temp. and sub-trop. regions. Valued for fruit. *F. vesca* is the wild strawberry; cultivated strawberry is hybrid between *F. virginiana* of N America and *F. chiloensis* of Chile.

strawberry tree, *Arbutus unedo,* small European evergreen tree. Has shiny leaves, white or pink flowers, strawberry-like fruit; often cultivated for ornament.

strawflower, everlasting flower of genus *Helichrysum*. Cultivated in Med. regions, S Africa and Australia. Yellow, orange, red or white flowers.

stream-of-consciousness, in literature and cinema, technique of presenting thoughts and images as they occur to a character rather than in logical or narrative sequence. Best known example James Joyce's novel *Ulysses* (1922).

streptomycin, antibiotic substance used for treatment of tuberculosis, meningitis and other diseases. Discovered (1943) by S. A. Waksman and associates.

Stresemann, Gustav (1878–1929), Ger. liberal statesman. As Chancellor (1923) and Foreign Secretary (1923–9), strove for Germany's acceptance as respected European power and for friendly relations with France. Signed (1926) LOCARNO PACT, engineering Ger. entry into League of Nations. Shared Nobel Peace Prize with Aristide Briand (1926).

strike, work stoppage by employees, with aim of settling grievances, usually over pay, working conditions or demarcation dispute (*see* TRADE UNION). Official if sanctioned by trade union concerned; if not, termed unofficial. General Strike in UK (1926) immobilized country's industry and transport for several months. Lock-out is stoppage of work initiated by employer.

Strindberg, [Johann] August (1849–1912), Swedish author. Best known for new techniques and expressive language. Bitter, naturalistic dramas of sexual antagonism include *The Father* (1887), *Miss Julie* (1888), *Dance of Death* (1901).

string(ed) instruments, strings, group of musical instruments which derive

Stained glass window from Strasbourg Cathedral

their tone from vibrating strings. Strings may be plucked (*e.g.* harp, guitar, lute), stroked with horsehair bow (*e.g.* violin, viola) or struck with hammer (*e.g.* dulcimer, piano, clavichord).

stroboscope, lamp producing brief flashes of light at controllable, usually rapid frequency. Used in studies and photographs of cyclical motions.

stroke *see* APOPLEXY.

Stromboli, Ital. island in Lipari group, off coast of Sicily. Has active volcano (3,038 ft.).

strontium, metallic element with compounds resembling those of calcium. Found only in combined state, *e.g.* strontianite.

Struensee, Count Johann Friedrich von (1737–72), Danish statesman. b. Germany. Physician to insane King Christian VII, exercised (1771–2) absolute power. Initiated peasant reform before execution as lover of Queen Caroline Matilda.

strychnine, alkaloid drug obtained from seed of nux-vomica tree of genus *Strychnos*. Small doses used as stimulant. Poisonous in large doses; often used as rat-killer.

Stuart or **Stewart, Charles Edward** *see* STUART OR STEWART, JAMES FRANCIS EDWARD.

Stuart, Gilbert (1755–1828), Amer. portrait painter. Known esp. for 3 portraits of George Washington, incl. that on US dollar bill.

Stuart or **Stewart, House of,** ruling family of Scotland (after 1371) and of England (after 1603) until death of Anne (1714). James VI of Scotland succeeded to Eng. throne as James I. Two crowns united by Act of Union (1707). Subsequent Hanoverian rule challenged by JACOBITES.

Stuart or **Stewart, James, 1st Earl of Moray** (1531–70), natural son of

Sturgeon

James V of Scotland. Became (1567) regent after abdication of half-sister Mary Queen of Scots. Sponsored Knox's Scot. Reformation.

Stuart, James Ewell Brown ('Jeb') (1833–64), Confederate cavalry officer in US Civil War. Instrumental in victory at Chancellorsville (1863).

Stuart or **Stewart, James Francis Edward** (1688–1766), son of James II, known as 'Old Pretender'. Claim to Eng. throne frustrated by Act of Settlement (1701) excluding Stuart line. Accession of George I led to abortive uprising (1715) by JACO-BITES. His son, **Charles Edward Stuart** or **Stewart** (1720–88), called 'Young Pretender' and 'Bonnie Prince Charlie', led revolt (1745), which ended in defeat at Culloden Moor. His brother, **Henry Benedict Maria Stuart** or **Stewart** (1725–1807), was last direct male Stuart claimant. Created cardinal of R.C. Church.

Stuart, John, 3rd Earl of Bute (1713–92), Brit. polit. leader. Tory P.M. (1761–3), endorsed George III's policies. Resigned after unpopular Treaty of Paris.

Suez Canal

Stuart, John McDouall (1815–66), Scot. explorer. Led several expeditions (1858–62) into interior of Australia. Reached shore of Van Diemen's Gulf on Indian Ocean (1862).

stucco, fine plaster used on interior walls and ceilings as covering or moulded decoration.

sturgeon, cartilaginous fish of *Acipenser* genus with toothless protruding mouth below which are 4 barbels. Found in rivers, lakes and inland seas of N temp. zone. Length 12–14 ft. Valued as source of caviare, also of isinglass.

Sturluson, Snorri (1178–1241), Icelandic historian. Collection of sagas and poems and record of kings of Norway until 1177 in *Heimskringla*.

Sturm und Drang [Ger: storm and stress], literary movement originating in late 18th cent. Germany. Name from lyric drama *Die Wirrwarr: oder, Sturm und Drang* (1776) by Maximilian Klinger. Emphasized genius of individual as opposed to rationalistic ideals of the ENLIGHTENMENT. Exponents included Goethe, Schiller,

Lenz. Influence spread to Fr. and Eng. literature.

Sturt, Charles (1795–1869), Eng. explorer in Australia. Explored S Austral. river system (1828–9), discovered Darling R. Brit. Colonial Sec. (1849–51).

Stuttgart, indust. and commercial city of West Germany, cap. of Baden-Württemberg, on Neckar R. Industries include electrical machinery, textiles. Other occupations include publishing. Pop. (1967) 613,000.

stye, inflammatory swelling of eyelid resembling small boil, caused by infection of an eyelash follicle.

Styria, Steiermark, prov. of SE Austria. Area: 6,326 sq. mi.; cap. Graz. Predominantly mountainous with several tourist resorts. Timber and mining (esp. iron ore, lignite) important. Pop. (1961) 1,137,865.

Styron, William (1925–), Amer. novelist. Author of *Lie Down in Darkness* (1951) and *The Confessions of Nat Turner* (1967).

Styx, in Gk. myth., principal river of Underworld, over which souls of the dead were ferried by boatman Charon. Waters made Achilles invulnerable, but also said to contain some deadly property. Most solemn oaths sworn by Styx.

subconscious, ideas and mental processes beyond area of awareness. May be brought into consciousness by hypnotism, psychotherapy, or in dreams.

sublimation, in chemistry, process of changing a substance directly from solid to gas, by-passing liquid state.

sublimation, in Freudian psychology, direction of primitive instincts (*e.g.* sexual or maternal) into activities, such as art, social work, religion.

submarine, ship that submerges and travels under water. Usually equipped with torpedoes or missiles. In use since 19th cent.

subpoena, legal process or writ requiring presence in court of person, usually to serve as witness.

subsidy, financial aid awarded to promote worthwhile projects. Govt. agric. subsidies stabilize food prices without detriment to livelihood of farmers.

subway *see* UNDERGROUND.

succulent, plant of dry regions whose leaves and stems store large quantities of fluid. Examples include species of *Aloe, Agave* and *Euphorbia* genera, and of cactus family.

sucker, *Catostomus commersoni*, Amer. and E Asian freshwater fish, 3 in.–3 ft. long, related to carp. Feeds by sucking up small invertebrates. Often used for food.

suckerfish, fish of family Echeneididae. Attaches itself to sharks, turtles, *etc.* by means of sucking disc on head.

Suckling, Sir John (1609–42), Eng. poet, courtier and soldier. His lyrics appeared in *Fragmenta Aurea* (1646).

Sucre, official cap. of Bolivia. Founded (1538) as La Plata. Agric. and commercial centre. Contains 16th cent. cathedral and university (founded 1624). Pop. (1965) 60,000.

sucrose, sugar obtained from sugar cane, sugar beet, *etc.* Constitutes large part of maple sugar.

Sudan, Republic of the, state of NE Africa, with coastline on Red Sea. Area: *c.* 976,750 sq. mi.; cap. Khartoum. Desert in N, savannas and

swamp areas in S. Economy dependent on production of cotton; other exports include dates, peanuts. Ruled jointly by UK and Egypt (1899–1955); independence 1956. Pop. (1967 est.) 14,355,000.

Sudanese Republic *see* MALI.

Sudbury, city of S Ontario, Canada. Centre of nickel-mining region; also has reserves of gold, silver, lead, zinc, copper and platinum. Pop. (1966) 85,000.

Suetonius [Gaius Suetonius Tranquillus] (*c.* AD 70–*c.* 160), Roman historian. Friend of younger Pliny, and one of imperial secretaries under Trajan. Extant works are *De Vita Caesarum*, from Julius Caesar to Domitian, and parts of *De Viris Illustribus*.

Suez Canal, waterway (107 mi. long) through United Arab Repub., linking Med. Sea and Red Sea. Built (1859–69) by Fr. engineer Ferdinand de Lesseps. Owned by Brit.-controlled company until nationalization (1956) by Egypt. Closed (1967) by Israeli-Arab war.

Suez Crisis, international incident (1956), begun when Israel invaded Suez Canal area after nationalization by Egypt. Occupied by Fr. and Brit. troops until UN intervention. Disagreement over Brit. role led to resignation of Brit. P.M. Anthony Eden.

Suffolk, maritime county of SE England. Area: 1,482 sq. mi.; county town Ipswich. Divided admin. into E Suffolk (cap. Ipswich) and W Suffolk (cap. Bury St Edmunds). Main occupations crop and dairy farming, fishing. Formerly noted for horse-

breeding (Suffolk Punches). Pop. (1966) 519,000.

Suffolk, 1st Duke of *see* BRANDON, CHARLES, 1ST DUKE OF SUFFOLK.

suffrage, right to vote in local and national elections. Franchise extended by stages; UK reform acts accorded suffrage to all adult males by 1918; to women by 1928.

suffragettes, name given to those who campaigned for women's right to vote (*see* WOMEN'S SUFFRAGE). Often adopted measures putting themselves at physical risk.

Sufism, mystical movement of Islam, developed 10th cent.; rejected ritual and sought simpler, personal union with God, often by contemplation. Influenced Persian writers, incl. Sadi, Omar.

sugar, sweet crystalline substance mostly obtained from juice of sugar cane and sugar beet. Used as ingredient and flavouring in food, also as fermenting agent in alcoholic beverages. In chemistry, carbohydrate of same group as sucrose, glucose, fructose.

sugar beet, *Beta vulgaris,* variety of beet with white root, cultivated as source of sugar in temp. zones. Produces *c.* 33% of world's sugar.

sugar cane, *Saccharum officinarum,* tall perennial grass of trop. and warm regions, providing chief source of sugar. By-products include molasses and rum. Produces 65% of world's sugar.

sugar glider, *Petaurus breviceps,* arboreal marsupial of phalanger family. Glides between trees by means of winglike membranes.

Sugar Cane in full flower

Sugarloaf Mountain, Pão de Açúcar, granite peak (1,296 ft.), Rio de Janeiro, SE Brazil.

Sui, Chinese ruling dynasty (581–618). Reunited country after 400 yr.

The River Nile irrigates the deserts of Sudan

Superb Starling

of division and laid foundation for 2nd great imperial era. Succeeded by T'ang dynasty.

suicide, intentional and voluntary self-destruction. In UK suicide was legally regarded as a crime until 1961.

suite, in music, collection of linked pieces in contrasting rhythms. Name also applied to collection of pieces from larger work, opera or ballet, arranged to be played as concert piece.

Sukarno, Achmed (1901–70), Indonesian polit. leader, 1st pres. (1945–67). Helped estab. Indonesian repub. (1945). Assumed dictatorial powers (1959). Stripped of power (1966) after army revolt; deposed 1967.

Suleiman [I] the Magnificent (1494–1566), Ottoman sultan (1520–66), also called 'The Lawgiver'. Penetrated Europe, defeating Hungary (1526), but failing in siege of Vienna (1529); conquered parts of Persia and Arabia. Controlled Med. Sea until defeat at Malta (1565).

Sulla, Lucius Cornelius (138–78 BC), Roman general and leader of senatorial party. As quaestor under Marius in Africa secured surrender of Jugurtha (107 BC). Consul 88 BC, gained command against Mithridates by marching on Rome with army. Captured Athens, made terms with Mithridates, returned to Rome (83 BC). Victorious in subsequent civil war, exterminated many opponents and declared himself dictator. Reformed constitution, aiming to increase power of senate; carried out important reforms in criminal procedure.

Sullivan, Sir Arthur Seymour (1842–1900), Eng. composer. Wrote songs incl. 'Onward, Christian Soldiers',

'The Lost Chord' and with W. S. Gilbert numerous popular light operas incl. *Iolanthe* (1882), *The Mikado* (1885) and *The Gondoliers* (1889).

Sully, Maximilien de Béthune, Duc de (1560–1641), adviser to Henry IV of France. Supervised finances (1598–1611). Restored Fr. prosperity by encouraging agriculture and industry, estab. transportation network.

sulpha drugs, group of synthetic bacteria-inhibiting drugs used in treatment of pneumonia, venereal diseases, meningitis, *etc.* Discovered (1932) by Domagk.

sulphates, general name for salts of sulphuric acid; hence any compound containing SO_4. Calcium sulphate in gypsum form used in building or casting. Magnesium sulphate sold as Epsom salts.

sulphur (S), non-metallic element occurring as yellow crystalline solid, often deposited around volcanic craters and hot springs. Used in manufacture of gunpowder and matches, in medicine, *etc.*

sulphuric acid (H_2SO_4), thick, colourless, highly corrosive acid. Because of versatility and stability widely used in steel, fertilizers, chemical industries.

sultan, ruler of Islamic country. Term also applied formerly to reigning sovereigns of Turkey.

sumac, sumach, shrub or small tree of genus *Rhus* of temp. and sub-trop. regions. Preparation of dried and powdered leaves, bark, *etc.* used esp. in tanning. Species include staghorn sumac, *R. typhina,* of N America.

Sumatra, volcanic island of Indonesia, in Indian Ocean. Area: c. 162,000 sq. mi.; main city, Palembang. Mountains in SW, swampy lowland in E, fertile plateau. Produces rubber, petroleum, coal, coffee. Pop. (1961) 15,439,000.

Sumerian civilization, society of S Mesopotamia (5th–3rd millennium BC). Featured powerful city states (*e.g.* Kish, Lagash, Ur) with developed cultures, esp. pottery and metalwork. Eventually conquered by rival Semitic cities.

summons, in Eng. and Scots law, citation or order to appear in court of law to answer a charge. Also writ by which order is made.

Sumner, William Graham (1840–1910), Amer. sociologist and economist. Advocate of free trade. Argued in *Folkways* (1907) that imposed reforms would be ineffective against weight of social conventions.

Sun, central body of Solar System around which planets revolve in orbit, and from which light and heat are derived. Average distance from Earth c. 93 million mi.; diameter (est.)

864,000 mi. Nuclear action within Sun converts hydrogen into helium, releasing energy and diminishing mass.

sun bear, Malayan sun bear, *Helarctos* (*Ursus*) *malayanus,* small bear of SE Asia. Short broad head, short glossy, mainly black, fur.

Sun Yat-sen (1866–1925), Chinese revolutionary. Developed 3 People's Principles of nationalism, democracy and social reform as basis for polit. doctrine. Overthrow of Ch'ing dynasty in 1911 revolution led to election as 1st pres. of Chinese repub.; resigned 1912. Withdrew and estab. power in S, organizing KUOMINTANG. Became pres. (1921) of unofficial Canton govt., later agreed to work with Communists.

sunbird, brilliantly coloured songbird of family Nectariniidae, native to Africa and Australasia.

sunbittern, *Eurypyga helias,* solitary bird of C and S Amer. jungle, with long orange legs and snake-like neck. Flies little. Feeds on insects and fish.

Sundanese, Malayo-Polynesian language with c. 15 million speakers in East Indies and parts of Oceania.

Sunday school, organization for giving religious instruction to children, usually attached to church. Started in England by Robert Raikes (1780); in US introd. by Francis Asbury (1786). Movement at height by end of 19th cent. Co-ordinated by World Council of Christian Education, founded 1889.

Sunderland, county borough of Durham, NE England. Centre of glass-making in 16th cent. Industries include shipbuilding, brewing, textiles; exports coal. Pop. (1967) 219,000.

sundew, dew plant, small insectivorous bog plant of genus *Drosera,* native to temp. and trop. regions.

sundial, instrument indicating time of day by position of shadow of upright centre pin (gnomon) cast by sun on graduated flat surface.

sunfish, various fish of Molidae family, esp. *Mola mola,* ocean sunfish. Also small spiny-rayed freshwater fish of genus *Lepomis,* native to N America.

sunflower, tall, annual or perennial plant of *Helianthus* genus, with yellow-rayed showy flowers, mostly native to N America. Species include *H. annuus,* common sunflower (state flower of Kansas).

Sung, Chinese imperial dynasty (960–1279). Period notable for improvement in commercial facilities, intensive scholarship and development esp. of fine arts. Overthrown by Mongols.

sungazer, *Cordylus giganteus,* S African reptile of the girdle-tailed lizard group with whorls of large scales round the tail.

Sunnites, orthodox Moslem sect of Islamic religion. Predominant in Arabia, Turkey, N Africa.

sunrose, Eurasian shrub or herb of genus *Helianthemum.* Cultivated for showy variously coloured flowers.

sunspot, one of dark spots appearing periodically on Sun, but rarely visible to naked eye. First observed *c.* 1610. Affects terrestrial magnetism and other phenomena.

sunstroke, condition, sometimes fatal, caused by exposure to sun or excessive heat. Characterized by prostration, coma and often extreme rise in body temperature.

superb starling, *Spreo superbus,* vari-coloured starling of S Africa, related to mynah birds.

superego, in psychoanalysis, concept corresponding approx. to primitive conscience. Part of human personality heavily influenced by parental and other early models; functions to compel ego to control anti-social impulses of ID.

Superior, Lake *see* GREAT LAKES.

supernova, name given to rare, particularly bright star of NOVA type.

supersonic speed, speed greater than that of sound. At sea level, about 760 m.p.h., decreases with altitude to 660 m.p.h. at 40,000 ft. Commercial aircraft now being designed to achieve this speed. *See* SOUND BARRIER.

Suppé, Franz von (1819–95), Austrian composer of operettas, ballet music, symphonies, overtures. Works include *Poet and Peasant* (1846) and *Light Cavalry Overture.*

supply and demand, in classical economics, factors determining price. Ideal economic system equates supply and demand (supply by producers=demand of consumers).

suprarenal gland *see* ADRENAL GLAND.

Supreme Court, highest judicial court of US, final court of appeals; composed of 9 judges headed by Chief Justice. Estab. 1789 by Constitution as autonomous govt. branch with powers balancing executive and legislative branches. Role as interpreter of constitutionality of legislation or executive actions 1st developed under JOHN MARSHALL. Judges appointed by pres., subject to Senate approval; size of court determined by Congress. Recent decisions elaborating rights of individual, esp. 1954 decision ordering desegregation of schools, have

Sunflower

estab. court's interest in initiating social change.

Surabaya, Soerabaja, city of NE Java, Indonesia. Light industries include glass manufacturing. Pop. (1961) 1,008,000.

surface tension, force affecting surface of liquid, which tends to behave like membrane, supporting light objects, giving water drops pear shape, *etc.* Underlies capillary attraction in plant nutrition, *etc.*

surgery, branch of medicine concerned with treatment of injury, deformity and disease by means of manual operation with or without the use of instruments. Although practised from ancient times, major advances were not made in this field until the introduction of aseptic techniques and modern anaesthetics.

Surinam, formerly **Dutch** or **Netherlands Guiana,** autonomous Dutch territory in S America. Area: *c.*

Village, Surinam

54,000 sq. mi.; cap. Paramaribo. Produces rum, timber, coffee, bauxite. Population of Creole, Negro, Asian and European descent. Main language, Dutch. Predominant religion, Christianity. Pop. (1963) 350,000.

surplice, loose-fitting linen garment with broad sleeves, usually white, worn over the cassock by clergymen and choristers.

surrealism, in literature and art, movement (esp. 1920s and 1930s) attempting to capture imaginative expression of dreams. Founded (1924) by Fr. writer André Breton; expounded in his *Manifeste du Surréalisme.* In literature, confined almost entirely to France. In painting, international figures included Salvador Dali, Max Ernst, Marc Chagall, Joan Miró. In films, used by Jean Cocteau.

Surrey, inland county of SE England. Area: 744 sq. mi.; county town Guildford, admin. centre Kingston on Thames. Predominantly agric. with dairying and sheep-raising. Former N areas absorbed by Greater London (1965). Pop. (1967 est.) 985,930.

surveying, study and recording of land formations used to estab. relative positions on earth's surface. Branches are topographical, geological, hydrographic, mine-surveying. Basis of cartography.

Susannah and the Elders, apocryphal book of OT, appended to *Book of Daniel.*

suslik *see* SOUSLIK.

Susquehanna, river (450 mi.) flowing through indust. New York and Pennsylvania, US., into Chesapeake Bay. Extensive flood control in operation.

Sussex, maritime county of SE England. Area: 1,457 sq. mi. Divided into E Sussex (admin. centre, Lewes),

Paramaribo, Surinam

W Sussex (admin. centre, Chichester). Agriculture, dairying, main occupations. Tourism important. Pop. (1966) 1,160,000.

Sutherland, maritime county of N Scotland. Area: 2,028 sq. mi.; county town, Dornoch. Mountainous with extensive forests and moorlands. Main occupations, crofting, fishing. Pop. (1966) 13,000.

Sutherland, Graham Vivian (1903–), Eng. painter. Early works influenced by surrealism, in late 1930s began symbolic use of natural forms. Also known for portraits, esp. *Winston Churchill* and *Somerset Maugham.*

Sutherland, Joan (1926–), Austral. operatic soprano. Joined Covent Garden (1952); has toured widely. Roles include Lucia in *Lucia di Lammermoor.*

Trio Indians, Surinam

suttee, Hindu custom involving voluntary cremation of widow on husband's funeral pyre. Abolished by British colonial govt. (1829).

Suttner, Bertha Kinsky, Baroness von (1843–1914), Austrian novelist and pacifist. Works, esp. *Lay Down Your Arms* (1889) contributed to pacifist movement. Awarded Nobel Peace Prize (1905).

Sutton Hoo, village in Suffolk, England, where Anglo-Saxon ship-burial of *c.* AD 650 was found. Important decorated silver and gold jewellery and weapons were unearthed.

Suvorov, Aleksandr Vasilyevich (1729–1800), Russ. army officer. Subdued peasant revolt (1775) and Polish uprising (1794). Defeated French (1798) in N Italy during Fr. Revolutionary Wars.

Suzuki, Daisetz Teitaro (1870–1966), Jap. scholar. Authority on Zen Buddhism, contributed much to exchange of religious ideas between East and West. Works include *An Introduction to Zen Buddhism* (1949), *Mysticism: Christian and Buddhist* (1957).

Svalbard *see* SPITSBERGEN.

Svedberg, Theodor, FRS (1884–), Swedish chemist. Awarded Nobel Prize for Chemistry (1926) for research on colloids. Also studied protein molecules.

Sverdlovsk, city of Russ. SFSR, in Ural Mts.; indust. and mining centre. Founded (1721) by Peter the Great. Pop. (1967) 940,000.

Swabia, Schwaben, region of SW Germany. Formerly encompassed SW Bavaria, SE Baden-Württem-

Swallowtail with caterpillar

berg, Alsace and E Switzerland. Broke up after 1268, divided into Württemburg, Bavaria and Baden. Present area covers SW Bavaria, SE Baden-Württemberg. Noted for scenic beauty; contains Black Forest.

Swahili, Bantic language of Niger-Congo group with 8 million speakers on E central African coast. Also name for a member of Bantu races of Zanzibar and surrounding coastal area.

swallow, small, long-winged migratory bird of Hirundinidae family of cosmopolitan distribution. Noted for graceful flight and forked tail. Species include bank swallow, cliff swallow and martin.

Swallow

swallowtail butterfly, butterfly of genus *Papilio,* with elongated rear wings resembling swallow's tail. Trop. varieties frequently mimic other species.

swamp, areas of wet spongy land often with heavy vegetation and particular forms of wild life, but unfit for cultivation. Drained swamp areas include Everglades, Florida, US.

swan, widely distributed, large, aquatic bird of sub-family Anserinae of Anatidae family. Long slender neck and in adult generally white plumage. Species include trumpeter swan, *Cygnus buccinator,* of N America (largest species), mute swan, *C. olor,* and Australian black swan, *C. atratus.* Young known as cygnets.

Swansea, Abertawe, city of Glamorganshire, Wales. Centre of metal industries. Pop. (1966) 171,000.

swastika, decorative prosperity and good luck symbol dating from 4th cent. BC, orig. Asian. Adopted as symbol of Ger. Nazi party and Third Reich.

Swaziland, inland kingdom of S Africa, member of Brit. Commonwealth. Area: 6,705 sq. mi.; cap. Mbabane. Surrounded by South Africa, except for border on NE with Mozambique. Mountainous with fertile central land. Agriculture expanded by extensive irrigation. Exports iron ore. Kingdom created 1967. Pop. (1966) 389,000.

sweat, perspiration, secretion of certain mammalian glands. Most important function is to regulate body temperature.

sweating sickness, febrile epidemic disease appearing in 15th and 16th cent. Characterized by excessive perspiration; usually fatal.

Sweden [Sverige], kingdom of E Scandinavia, N Europe. Area: 173,436 sq. mi.; cap. Stockholm; main cities Gothenburg, Malmö.

Mountainous with extensive forests and many lakes. Agriculture and forestry important. Mineral resources include iron ore, lead, zinc, sulphur. Industry based principally on natural resources; also shipbuilding, motor

car manufacturing. Became kingdom 10th cent.; united with Norway (1319) and Denmark (1397). Major European power (16th cent.). Engaged in numerous wars until adoption of neutral stand (1815). Predominant religion, Lutheran Protest-

antism. Unit of currency, krona. Pop. (1968) 7,893,704.

Swedenborg, Emanuel, orig. Emanuel Swedberg (1688–1772), Swedish scientist, theologian, and mystic. Stated that Last Judgement had occurred in 1757; accepted as its prophet by New Jerusalem sect formed after his death.

Swedish, Scandinavian Indo-European language, with *c.* 7 million speakers in Sweden, S Finland and Aaland Is.

sweepstake, form of gambling in which winning tickets are selected at random. These win the money contributed by other competitors. Most famous is Irish Sweepstake.

sweet fern, *Comptonia asplenifolia,* small aromatic N Amer. shrub with fern-like leaves.

sweet gum, *Liquidambar styraciflua,* tall pyramidal tree native to N America. Hard, red-brown wood used in furniture. Exudes balsam used in medicine and perfumery.

sweet pea, *Lathyrus odoratus,* leguminous climbing annual plant native to S Europe with sweet-scented flowers.

sweet pepperbush, spiked alder, summer-sweet, *Clethra alnifolia,* ornamental deciduous shrub native to N America. Fragrant pink or white flowers.

Stockholm, Sweden

Common European Swift

Alpine Swift

bird. Long narrow wings, short tail, small feet with hooked claws; noted for rapid flight. Species include common European swift, *Apus apus,* with black plumage and light throat patch, and chimney swift, *Chaetura pelagica,* of N America.

Swift, Jonathan (1667–1745), Eng. writer, b. Dublin. Masterful satires include *A Tale of a Tub* (1704) on religion, *Gulliver's Travels* (1726) on politics. Anglican clergyman, created (1713) Dean of St Patrick's, Dublin. Wrote pamphlets on Irish problems (*e.g. A Modest Proposal,* 1729).

swift moth, ghost moth, grey or brown moth of family Hepialidae. Noted for rapid flight.

Swinburne, Algernon Charles (1837–1909), Eng. pre-Raphaelite poet. Main works include verse plays *e.g. Atalanta in Calydon* (1865); also *Poems and Ballads* (1866) and *Songs before Sunrise* (1871).

swine, any mammal, esp. domestic pig, of family Suidae of Europe and Asia, and family Tayassuidae of N and S America.

swine fever, hog cholera, acute, highly contagious and usually fatal viral disease of swine. Characterized by high fever, vomiting, diarrhoea and lethargy.

Swiss cheese plant, *Monstera deliciosa,* greenhouse climbing plant from trop. America. Hanging cord-like roots and perforated leaves.

Swithin, Saint (d. 862), Eng. monk. Chaplain to Egbert, king of West Saxons; Bishop of Winchester. According to tradition, if St Swithin's day (15 July) is wet, it will rain for next 40 days.

Switzerland, federal repub. of C Europe, composed of 22 cantons. Area: 15,950 sq. mi.; cap. Berne; principal cities Zürich, Basle, Geneva. Contains major portion of Alps, incl. some of highest European peaks; extensive lakes and forests. Agri-

culture in valleys includes wheat, oats, fruits, dairying and stock-raising. Manufacturing of electrical goods, precision instruments, clocks, watches, *etc.* Independent of Holy Roman Empire (1648); Helvetic repub. formed 1798. Policy of neutrality (adopted 1815) encourages estab. of headquarters by international organizations, esp. banking,

sweet potato, batata, long potato, *Ipomoea batatas,* perennial plant native to N America, cultivated for edible, reddish, sweet-tasting tubers. Widely grown in US, used as vegetable, dessert or preserved.

sweet william, *Dianthus barbatus,* biennial or perennial herb native to S Europe. Grown in gardens for brightly coloured single or double flowers.

sweetbriar, eglantine, *Rosa eglanteria,* European species of bush rose. Hooked white or pink single flowers, scarlet fruit.

swelltoad, name for GLOBE FISH.

swift, migratory, swallow-like bird of family Apodidae, related to humming

The Greek theatre at Syracuse, dating from the 5th century BC

This picture of a clown anemone fish living in a sea anemone illustrates symbiosis; the sea anemone's tentacles are usually dangerous, but do not harm the fish, which provides the anemone with oxygen and food, while the fish receives protection

feet. The 2 other types are hypothetical (conditional proposition and 2 statements of fact) and disjunctive (alternative proposition and 2 statements of fact).

sylphs, nature spirits. According to Paracelsus they inhabit the air, as gnomes inhabit the earth, nymphs water and salamanders fire.

symbiosis, in biology, living together of dissimilar organisms from which each benefits; *e.g.* algae and fungus (which together form lichens) are mutually interdependent.

Symbolism, movement in European literature and graphic art in late 19th and early 20th cent. Aim of exact representation of emotion achieved by suggestion instead of statement. Initiated by Fr. poets, *e.g.* Rimbaud, Mallarmé.

symphony, orchestral composition in sonata form. Climax of classical symphony reached in work of Mozart and Haydn. 19th cent. composers who influenced the form include Beethoven, Bruckner, Berlioz and Mahler.

synagogue, building designed for public prayer, religious education and other communal activities in Jewish communities. Prob. originated *c.* 6th cent. BC among Jews in exile in Babylon, unable to visit Temple in Jerusalem.

synchrotron, type of nuclear AC-

insurance. Official languages French, German, Italian. Religions, Roman Catholicism, Protestantism. Unit of currency, Swiss franc. Pop. (1967 est.) 6,071,000.

sword dance, dance originating in Highlands of Scotland, performed over 2 crossed swords to accompaniment of bagpipes.

swordfish, *Xiphias gladius,* large food fish (up to 15 ft. long) of Med. Sea and Atlantic. Elongated upper jaw forms sword-like structure. Popular as sport fish in N America.

swordtail, *Xiphophorus helleri,* small, brightly coloured freshwater fish of C America, with elongated caudal fin.

sycamore, *Acer pseudoplatanus,* genus of Eurasian maple trees. Large and deciduous, with yellow-green

flowers, planted as shade tree. Species include *Platanus occidentalis* of E and N North America.

Sydney, cap. of New South Wales, Australia. Country's largest city and port. Commercial, shipping centre. Founded (1788) as penal colony. Contains university (founded 1852). Sydney Harbour Bridge (opened 1932), Opera House (1968). Pop. (1966) 2,444,735.

syenite, coarse-grained igneous rock, composed mainly of orthoclase with hornblende and other minerals.

syllogism, in logic, method of argument drawing conclusion from 2 premises. Most common form is categorical, made up of 3 statements of fact, *e.g.* all dogs have 4 feet; a pug is a dog; therefore a pug has 4

Typical Alpine valley in Switzerland

Swordtail

Syringa vulgaris, or Lilac

CELERATOR. Used to accelerate particles to very high speeds esp. for research purposes.

syncopation, in music and poetry, shifting of stress from normal beat. Rhythmic suspension, unaccented beat, rest, or silence on beat are types of syncopation. Characteristic of modern music and of verse using speech rhythms.

syndicalism, revolutionary doctrine advocating abolition of state. Trade union is basic unit of govt. Theories developed from works of Proudhon and Georges Sorel (1847–1922).

Synge, John Millington (1871–1909), Irish playwright associated with Irish Renaissance. His plays in poetic prose include *Riders to the Sea* (1904), *The Playboy of the Western World* (1907).

Synge, Richard Laurence Millington (1914–   ), Brit. biochemist. With Archer Martin, awarded Nobel Prize for Chemistry (1952) for discovery of new method of separating compounds.

Synoptic Gospels, first 3 books of NT; *Matthew, Mark, Luke.* So-called because they give almost the same account (synopsis) of Jesus' life. Name contrasts them from more philosophical Gospel, *John.*

synthesis, in chemistry and biology, formation of compounds from their elements or simpler materials. Used in industry to provide substitutes for natural compounds, *e.g.* rubber.

synthetic fibres, artificial, chemically produced fibres. Woven as fabrics are generally quick-drying. Do not shrink and are resistant to creasing and chemical damage, but attract dirt and absorb grease. Include Acrilan, Dacron and Orlon.

syphilis, contagious disease caused by spirochete *Treponema pallidum.* Usually venereal in origin but may be congenital. Affects almost any organ or tissue of the body, esp. genitals, skin, mucous membranes, brain.

Syracuse, Siracusa, city of SE Sicily, Italy, cap. of Syracuse prov., port on Ionian Sea. Leading Gk. city (*c.* 730 BC); sacked by Romans (212 BC). Exports salt, wine, olive oil, fruit. Pop. (1965) 60,500.

Syracuse, city of New York State, US, on Erie Canal. Main industries steel, metal, pharmaceuticals. Pop. (1963) 333,000.

Syria, Arab repub. of SW Asia. Area: 70,800 sq. mi.; cap. Damascus; main cities, Aleppo, Homs. Desert in centre and SE; Anti-Lebanon Mts. in W; fertile plain in SW. Agriculture main

occupation; revenue from oil pipelines. Seat of Phoenician civilization from 13th cent. BC, became part of Persian Empire. Successively under Egyptian, Roman, Arab, Fr. rule. Repub. proclaimed 1941; independent 1944. Prov. of United Arab Repub. (1958–61). Member of Arab alliance against Israel in 1950s and 1960s. Pop. (1967 est.) 5,634,000.

syringa, genus of shrubs or trees of family Oleaceae native to Europe and Asia. *Syringa vulgaris* is the common lilac. Also the N Amer. mock orange, a shrub of genus *Philadelphus.*

Szczecin, Stettin, city and port of NW Poland, on Oder R., former cap. of Pomerania prov. Successively under Swedish, Prussian, Ger. rule, until 1945. Main industries include shipbuilding and engineering. Pop. (1965) 310,000.

Szechwan, prov. of SW China. Area: *c.* 210,000 sq. mi.; cap. Chengtu. Mountainous with central plateau. Extensive agriculture; oil and coal reserves. Absorbed Sikiang prov. (1955). Pop. *c.* 85,000,000.

Szilard, Leo (1898–1964), Amer. nuclear physicist, b. Hungary. With Enrico Fermi created 1st nuclear chain reaction (1942); important stage in the development of atomic bomb.

Krak des Chevaliers, a Crusader fortress in Syria

T

Tabasco, state of SE Mexico. Area: 9,783 sq. mi.; cap., Villahermosa. Main occupation, trop. agriculture. Pop. (1967 est.) 546,300.

tabasco, *Capsicum conoides,* variety of hot red pepper native to Mexico. Used as condiment.

tabernacle [Lat: hut], in OT, portable sanctuary 1st used by Israelites in Wilderness (*Exodus* xxv). Contained Ark of the Covenant and Mercy Seat in inner part called Holy of Holies.

Tabitha or **Dorcas,** in NT, woman of Joppa noted for good works. Raised from dead by St Peter.

Table Mountain, flat-topped mountain (3,549 ft.) overlooking Cape Town, South Africa. Summit often veiled by cloud known as 'The Tablecloth'.

table tennis or **ping-pong,** indoor game akin to tennis. Played on table 9 ft. by 5 ft. National and international championships held annually, under International Table Tennis Federation rules.

taboo, tabu, prohibition, common among primitive peoples, of certain words and actions, on religious grounds. Also setting aside of certain objects for religious use.

Tabriz, city of NW Iran, cap. of Azerbaijan prov., within earthquake zone. Varied light industries, esp. carpets. On trade route, was Persian cap. for short periods. Pop. (1966) 403,414.

Tacitus, Cornelius (*c.* AD 55–*c.* 117), Roman historian. Consul (AD 97),

Typical scenery on Tahiti

proconsul in Asia (AD 112–16). Major extant works are *Germania,* account of the German tribes, 4 books of *Historiae,* history of Rome AD 68–96, and 8 books and fragments of *Annales,* history of Rome, AD 14–68. Also *Dialogus de Oratoribus,* and *Agricola,* biog. of father-in-law Gnaeus Julius Agricola.

Tadoussac, early Fr. Canadian trading post on St Lawrence R., Quebec. Visited (1535) by Jacques Cartier. Oldest settlement in Canada. Site of 1st stone house (1600). Later settled as fur-trading post. Pop. 1,064.

Tadzhik, Tajik Soviet Socialist Republic or **Tadzhikistan,** constituent repub. of USSR in C Asia. Area: *c.* 55,000 sq. mi.; cap. Dushanbe. Includes Pamir Mts., Syr-Darya R. Became repub. 1929. Main industries agriculture and mining. Pop. (1968) 2,736,000.

taffeta, fine plain-weave fabric, smooth on both sides. Made orig. of silk.

Tafilet, Tafilelt, Tafilált, oasis on caravan route in Moroccan Sahara. Noted for dates and leather.

Taft, Robert Alphonso (1889–1953), Amer. politician. Senator from Ohio (1939–53), promoted TAFT-HARTLEY LABOR ACT.

Taft, William Howard (1857–1930), 27th Pres. of US (1909–13), Republican. US Sec. of War (1904–8), elected (1908) as Pres., succeeding Theodore Roosevelt, whose 'trust-busting' policies he continued more conservatively. Opposition within Party led to revolt of Progressives and Taft's defeat in 1912 election. Served as Chief Justice of Supreme Court (1921–30).

Taft-Hartley Labor Act, US congressional legislation empowering National Labor Relations Board to control unions more rigorously and to intervene in major strikes. Passed (1947) over Pres. Truman's veto.

Tagalog, Malayo-Polynesian language, 1 of 3 official languages of Philippines. Has nearly 16 million speakers.

Tagore, Sir Rabindranath (1861–1941), Indian writer and philosopher. Estab. (1901) Santiniketan, a school of international culture which became Visva-Bharati University. Influential in nationalist movement. Main works, collection of lyrics *Gitanjali* (1912), the verse play *Chitra* (1913), and *Sadhana,* a philosophical work. Awarded Nobel Prize for Literature (1913).

Tagus, river (*c.* 550 mi.), longest of Iberian Peninsula. Flows W into Portugal from E Spain. Meets Atlan-

tic at Lisbon, where estuary forms landlocked harbour.

Tahiti, formerly Otaheite, main island of Society group, part of FRENCH POLYNESIA, S Pacific Ocean. Area: 402 sq. mi.; cap. Papeete. Discovered 1767. Became Fr. colony 1880. Pop. (1967 est.) 52,068.

tailor-bird, small Asian bird of genus *Orthotomus.* Makes its nest by sewing several leaves together.

Taine, Hippolyte Adolphe (1828–93), Fr. critic, historian and philosopher. Applied methods and discipline of biological sciences to study of art, literature, history and psychology. Main works, *Origines de la France Contemporaine* (6 vols., 1876–93) and *Histoire de la Littérature Anglaise* (1864).

taipan, brown cane snake, *Oxyuranus scutellatus,* large brown very poisonous Austral. snake. Up to 10 ft. in length, found in trop. regions of NE Australia and New Guinea.

Taipei, city of NW Taiwan, on Tanshui R. Cap. of Repub. of China and seat of Nationalist govt. since 1949. Founded 18th cent. Produces tea, sugar, fruit. Contains Taiwan University. Pop. (1964) 1,085,000.

Taiping Rebellion (*c.* 1850–65), revolt in China against Manchu dynasty. Led by Hung Hsiu-ch'uan who declared himself leader of Taiping (Great Peace) Dynasty. After initial success, crushed with help of Western troops under General Charles Gordon.

Taiwan see CHINA, REPUBLIC OF.

Taiyuan, Yangku, cap. of Shansi prov., N China. Known since AD 450. Industrial and rly. centre near coal mining region. Pop. (1957 est.) 1,020,000.

Taj Mahal, white marble mausoleum beside Jumna R., near Agra, India. Built (17th cent.) by Mogul emperor, Shah Jahan, as tomb for his favourite wife.

Takla Makan, Taklamakan, sandy desert ringed by oases, Sinkiang prov., China. Area: *c.* 125,000 sq. mi.

Takoradi, Sekondi-Takoradi, city and port of Ghana, W Africa, on Gulf of Guinea. Major commercial and industrial centre. Exports cacao, hardwood, manganese and bauxite. Pop. (1966) 181,000.

Talbot, Charles, Duke of Shrewsbury (1660–1718), Eng. statesman. Played important part in accession of William of Orange (1688) and in securing Hanoverian succession in 1714.

talc, soapstone, very soft whitish mineral, magnesium silicate. Occurs in massive or flaky form. Used as

Table Mountain and Cape Town

lubricant and absorbant, for toilet preparations and filters.

Talleyrand-Périgord, Charles Maurice de (1754–1838), Fr. statesman. Supported Revolution. Foreign Min. under Directory and under Napoleon I, whom he helped to power. After fall of Napoleon (1814) instrumental in securing succession of Louis XVIII. As Foreign Min. at Congress of Vienna (1815), successful in obtaining relatively favourable terms for defeated France. Helped Louis-Philippe overthrow Bourbon monarchy (1830); ambassador to Great Britain (1830–5).

Tallien, Jean Lambert (1767–1820), Fr. revolutionary. Organized REIGN OF TERROR in Bordeaux (1794). Instrumental in securing Robespierre's downfall (27 July, 1794).

Tallinn [Ger: Reval], seaport and cap. of Estonian SSR, in USSR, on Baltic. Founded by Danes (1219). Member of Hanseatic League. Captured (1710) by Peter the Great. Industries include iron and steel, cotton, shipbuilding. Pop. (1966) 335,000.

Tallis or **Tallys, Thomas** (c. 1510–85), Eng. organist and composer. Wrote church music, hymns, anthems, etc.

tallow, solid animal fat. Used commercially in soap, margarine and candle-making; formerly as lubricant.

Talmud, collection of Jewish law, traditions and customs, codified c. AD 500. Regarded as 2nd in importance to OT. Survives in different versions

incl. Palestinian and Babylonian Talmuds.

Talon, Jean (c. 1625–94), Fr. colonial administrator. Intendant of New France (1665–8, 1669–72), supervised expansion of trade and settlement in N Amer. colonies.

tamandua, *Tamandua tetradactyla,* arboreal anteater of trop. America. Elongated snout and sticky tongue for catching insects; prehensile tail.

tamarind, *Tamarindus indica,* large trop. tree. Pod contains seeds enclosed in juicy acid pulp; used in beverages and food.

tamarisk, Old World trop. plant of genus *Tamarix. T. gallica,* is an ornamental Med. shrub with feathery branches and pink or white flowers.

Tamberlane, Tamerlane, Timur the Lame (c. 1336–1405), Mongol conqueror. Occupied Samarkand and made it cap. of empire extending to Persia, Armenia and Georgia. Subdued GOLDEN HORDE. Invaded India and sacked Delhi. Defeated Turks at Angora (1402).

tambourine, hand-held percussion instrument consisting of circular frame and single drumhead, with circular metal plates or jingles in frame.

Tamil see DRAVIDIAN.

Tamizhagam, Madras, state of SE India. Area: 50,132 sq. mi.; cap. Madras. Centre of ancient Dravidian culture. Colonies estab. by Portuguese (16th cent.) and by Dutch,

French and British (17th cent.). Agriculture important, esp. cereals, spices, tobacco and tea. Pop. (1965) 35,651,000.

Tamm, Igor Yevgonyevich (1895–1971), Russ. physicist. With P. A. Cherenkov and I. M. Frank, awarded Nobel Prize for Physics (1958) for studies of Cherenkov effect in radiation.

Tammany, Amer. polit. organization, dominant in New York city politics (19th–20th cent.). Founded 1786, orig. patriotic society, developed into source of corruption with such leaders as 'Boss' Tweed. Ceased to be influential after 1934.

Tammuz, in Babylonian religion god of nature, loved by Ishtar, and killed and restored to life by her. Symbolized annual death and rebirth of plants; associated with Gk. Adonis.

Tampa, city of W Florida, US, resort on Tampa Bay, at mouth of Hillsboro R. Main industry food processing.

Tamandua

Scarlet Tanager

Contains University of Tampa. Pop. (1960) 274,970.

Tampere, Tammerfors, city of SW Finland. Founded 1779. Industries include cotton, paper, leather, machinery, locomotives. Pop. (1967) 188,000.

Tampico, city and seaport of NE Mexico, on Panuco R., near Gulf of Mexico. Founded *c.* 1554, expanded with discovery of oil (*c.* 1900). Exports oil, cattle, agric. produce. Pop. (1965 est.) 139,867.

Tamworth Manifesto, election address by Brit. P.M. Sir Robert Peel at Tamworth (1835), prototype for modern electioneering. Term CONSERVATIVE PARTY first used there for Tory party.

Tana or **Tsana,** lake in NW Ethiopia, *c.* 6,000 ft. above sea level. Area: 1,400 sq. mi. Source of Blue Nile.

tana, insectivorous tree shrew of family Tupaiadae of Borneo and Sumatra. Long muzzle with an extended nose pad.

tanager, migratory, mainly tropical, songbird. N Amer. species includes scarlet tanager, *Piranga erythromelas*; scarlet with black wings, tail, beak; female green and yellow.

Tanaka, Giichi, Baron (1863–1929), Jap. general and statesman. Alleged author of *Tanaka Memorial* (1927) which set out plan for world conquest. P.M. (1926–9).

Tananarive *see* ANTANANARIVO.

Tandy, [James] Napper (1740–1803), Irish rebel, comrade of WOLFE TONE. Involved in unsuccessful invasion (1798) of Ireland. Fr. influence saved him from execution (1800).

Taney, Roger Brooke (1777–1864), Chief Justice of US Supreme Court (1836–64). As Sec. of Treasury (1833–4) supported Pres. ANDREW JACKSON's policy to charter Banks of United States. As Chief Justice, his decisions favoured states over federal govt. Ruled in favour of slavery laws in DRED SCOTT CASE (1857).

T'ang, dynasty of China (618–906), founded by Li Yuan. Period of great

territorial expansion (Korea, Manchuria, Mongolia, Tibet, Turkestan), of cultural interchange with India and C Asia. Confucianism became state religion and arts, esp. sculpture, painting and poetry, flourished.

Tanganyika, Lake, world's 2nd deepest freshwater lake. In C Africa between Congo Republic, Tanzania and Zambia.

tangerine, small, thin-skinned variety of orange belonging to mandarin orange species, *Citrus reticulata*. Deep reddish orange skin. Native to SE Asia, now widely grown in trop. and sub-trop. regions.

Tangier, seaport and major commercial city of Morocco on Straits of Gibraltar. Founded by Phoenicians. Made international zone and free port (1923) ruled jointly by UK, France, Spain and Italy. Integrated with independent Morocco (1956). Pop. (1965) 110,000.

tangle, fan kelp, large seaweed, *Laminaria saccharina* or *L. digitata. See* OARWEED.

tango, dance of Sp.-Amer. origin, internationally popular since *c.* 1915. Tempo is 4-4, similar to Cuban habanera.

Tanguy, Yves (1900–55), Fr. surrealist painter. Large canvases endlessly repeat fantasies which resemble undersea or lunar landscapes.

tank, very mobile, heavily armoured vehicle, moving on tracks, possessing large guns. First used (1916) by British in World War 1; technique perfected in Ger. Panzer Divisions in World War 2.

tanker, ship designed to carry liquid in bulk, esp. fuel oils. Often very large *e.g.* Japanese *Idemitsu Maru,* gross tonnage 108,800 t., length 1,122 ft.

Tannenberg, village in Poland where in 1410 the Teutonic Knights were defeated by the Poles. Also scene of Russian defeat by Germans (1914).

Tannhäuser (*fl.* 13th cent.), Ger. lyric poet, minnesinger. Legend of his purity used by Wagner in opera *Tannhäuser.*

tannin, tannic acid, astringent compound present in many plants, *e.g.* tea, walnut, gall nuts and acacia bark. Used in tanning, making of inks, for clarifying solutions in medicine and dyeing.

tanning, process by which animal skins are turned into leather. Designed to give durability and attractive finish. Tannin has been used for this purpose since *c.* 3000 BC; alum and chrome salts or fats and oils (for chamois leather) are also employed.

tansy, *Tanacetum vulgare,* common European flowering plant. Formerly

used as stimulant in medicine, now cultivated purely as garden plant.

tantalum, dark grey hard metallic element discovered (1802) by A. G. Ekeberg. Occurs naturally with niobium. It has great ductility and is widely used in alloys. Highly resistant to acids and corrosion, used for surgical and laboratory equipment.

Tantalus, in Gk. myth., son of Zeus and father of Pelops and Niobe. For angering the gods, punished in Hades by being set in pool of water, hungry and thirsty, but unable either to drink from the pool, or to reach fruit on tree above his head.

Tantra, group of post-Vedic Sanskrit treatises. Describe practices intended to purify the body and develop perfect self-control. Form scriptures of Shakta sects.

Tanzania, United Republic of, country of E Africa, formed (1964) by union of Tanganyika and ZANZIBAR. Total area: 342,820 sq. mi.; cap., Dar-es-Salaam. Tanganyika became Ger. protectorate (1885) mandated to UK after World War 1. Achieved dominion status 1961, became republic within Brit. Commonwealth

(1962). Mainly agric., producing sisal, cotton, coffee and timber. Minerals include diamonds and gold. Tanganyika has Mt. Kilimanjaro in N (19,300 ft.), Livingstone Mts. in S, also parts of L. Victoria and L. Tanganyika. Main languages, Swahili, English; religions, Animism, Christianity. Unit of currency, E African shilling. Pop. (1966 est.) 12,231,000.

Taoism, Chinese system of philosophy and religion attributed to Lao-Tse. Fully developed as pantheistic mystic religion by AD 5th cent., based on escape by contemplation from illusions of ordinary life.

tape recorder, electromagnetic instrument which records speech and music by effect of sound waves on magnetized plastic tape. On playback magnetic patterns reconverted into original electrical impulses and audible sound waves.

tapestry, ornamental fabric for covering walls, furniture and for curtains, of very ancient origin. Made by interweaving of plain warp threads with

Tana

Malayan Tapir

weft of varying colours and textures incl. silk, wool. European wool tapestries are extant from 10th cent. Notable centres were Arras (from 14th cent.), Brussels, Aubusson, Beauvais and Gobelins.

tapeworm, long ribbon-shaped parasitic worm of subclass Cestoda. Adults infest intestines of man and other vertebrates; larvae infest large number of vertebrates and invertebrates.

tapir, nocturnal herbivorous ungulate mammal native to C and S America and SE Asia. Largest is Malayan tapir, *Tapirus indicus.*

tar, dark brown or black viscid liquid with peculiar aromatic odour. Obtained from distillation of wood, coal or similar substances. Pitch is more solid form. Used for road-making, in medicine, as protective coating for wood, iron, *etc.* Distillation of coal tar yields bases for aniline dyes.

Tara, village of Co. Meath, S Ireland. On nearby Hill of Tara ancient pagan Irish kings were crowned and held assemblies.

Taranaki, prov. of New Zealand on W North Island. Settled (1841) but scene of hostilities between settlers and Maoris (1860–1). Pop. (1962) 101,300.

tarantella *see* TARANTULA.

Taranto, seaport of Apulia, SE Italy. Gk. settlement from 8th cent. BC. Sacked by Saracens and Normans in 10th and 11th cent. Naval base. Fishing important. Pop. (1965) 208,000.

tarantula, wolf spider, *Lycosa tarantula,* large hairy spider of Eurasia. Bite is painful but not dangerous. In Middle Ages in Italy, dancing was thought to cure bites, hence dance called tarantella.

tarboosh, fez, flat-topped, close fitting, brimless cap of Moslem countries. Once a badge of Turkish citizenship, proscribed in Turkey (1925) by Kemal Pasha.

tardigrade, microscopic, chiefly herbivorous invertebrate of phylum Tardigrada. Lives in water, on mosses, lichens, *etc.*

tare, various species of VETCH. In Bible name is used for harmful weed prob. DARNEL.

Targum, Aramaic exegetical translations of Old Testament. Originally intended for instruction of Jews who spoke Aramaic instead of Hebrew. The Onkelos Targum is best known.

tariffs, customs, duties on imported goods intended to protect native producers and provide revenue by increasing prices of imports in relation to home-produced goods.

Tarkington, [Newton] Booth (1869–1946), Amer. realistic novelist. Author of *Penrod* (1914), *The*

Magnificent Ambersons (1918) and other stories of the Midwest.

tarot, tarok, orig. European pack of playing cards used for Ital. game *tarocchi* in Middle Ages. Now used for fortune-telling.

tarpan, Przewalski's horse, *Equus przewalskii,* small half-wild C Asian horse.

Tarpeia, in Roman legend, daughter of officer commanding Romans against Sabines. Offered to betray citadel for ornaments on Sabines' left arms (bracelets). Crushed under shields (worn on left arm) of Sabines and hurled from Tarpeian Rock.

Tarquinia [Lat: Tarquinii], formerly Corneto Tarquinia, town of C Italy, 44 mi. NW of Rome. Main trades, agriculture and stone quarrying.

La Théorie des Resaux by the surrealist painter Yves Tanguy

Tattoos have been made in indelible ink on this man's back

Etruscan and Roman remains include necropolis. One of 12 chief Etruscan towns, declined after 3rd cent. BC.

Tarquinius, Lucius Superbus, 7th and last king of Rome, prob. Etruscan. Murdered Servius Tullius to obtain throne, was cruel and despotic ruler. Driven from Rome (510 BC) after son Sextus ravished Lucretia.

tarragon, *Artemisia dracunculus,* European perennial wormwood. Long slender aromatic leaves used as flavouring.

tarsier, *Tarsius tarsius,* small nocturnal arboreal insectivorous primate related to lemur and monkey. Native to E Indies. About size of rat, has large eyes, long feet and hands equipped with sucker-like discs.

Tarsus, ancient Turkish city in plain of Cilicia. Once a seaport, now silted up *c.* 10 mi. from Med. Sea. St Paul was a native. Pop. *c.* 35,000.

tartan, worsted cloth woven in chequered pattern. Tartan kilts and plaids worn by Scot. clans since 15th cent., each clan having distinctive pattern. Illegal (1746–82) after 1745 Jacobite uprising.

tartaric acid, organic compound potassium salt (potassium tartrate). Occurs in grape juice. Separates in fermentation of grape juice into wine. Used in baking as cream of tartar, and in making of fizzy drinks.

Tartars, Tatars, name given to invading peoples of Russia (13th cent.) under the Mongols. Overran and dominated parts of Eurasia until 15th cent. when GOLDEN HORDE empire dissolved. Much of Russia influenced by Tartar civilization.

Most adhere to Islamic religion, number *c.* 5,000,000 in USSR.

Tartini, Giuseppe (1692–1770), Ital. violinist and composer, 1st to discover existence of 3rd sound (sound produced when 2 notes played together). Compositions include sonatas *The Devil's Trill* and *La Didone Abbandonata.*

Tashkent, cap. of Uzbek SSR, central Asia. Centre of cotton textile producing region. Founded 7th cent.,

Tarsier

historic trade centre. Conquered (13th cent.) by Mongols. Incorporated (1865) by Russia, became cap. of Turkistan. Pop. (1967) 1,127,000.

Tasman, Abel Janszoon (*c.* 1603–59), Dutch navigator. Discovered Tasmania, New Zealand, Tonga and Fiji (1642–3); also Gulf of Carpentaria on 2nd South Seas expedition (1644). Sailed round Australia, unaware of its existence.

Tasman, Mount, second highest peak (11,475 ft.) of New Zealand, in S Alps of South Island. Named after Abel Tasman, discoverer of New Zealand; 1st climbed 1895. Popular skiing centre.

Tasmania, island state of Australia, lying SE off mainland. Consists of Tasmania and several small islands. Area: 26,215 sq. mi.; cap. Hobart. Mountainous and forested, island exports wool, fruit, metals, esp. copper, zinc. Discovered (1642) by Tasman; penal colony estab. (1803) by British. Attached to New South Wales until 1825; joined Australia at independence (1901). Pop. (1966) 371,217.

Tasmanian devil, *Sarcophilus harrisii,* burrowing carnivorous marsupial of Tasmania. Black coat with white patches,

Tasso, Torquato (1544–95), Ital. Renaissance poet. Works include pastoral play *Aminta* (1573) and epic poem *La Gerusalemme Liberata* (1581). Inspired later romantic poets.

taste, sensation caused by stimulation of taste buds, most of which are on tongue. Four basic tastes: bitter, salt, sweet and acid.

taste buds, cluster of cells at base of

papillae of the tongue, constituting organ of taste.

Tate, Allen (1899–　　　), Amer. poet and critic. Works include *Poems 1922–1947, On the Limits of Poetry, The Forlorn Demon.*

Tate, Nahum (1652–1715), Eng. dramatist and poet, b. Ireland. Wrote version of Shakespeare's *King Lear* with happy ending, and with Dryden's help, 2nd part of *Absalom and Achitophel.* Created Poet Laureate 1692.

Tate Gallery, building containing notable art collection at Millbank, London. Opened 1897, original collection given by Eng. merchant Sir Henry Tate. Contains Eng. painting and sculpture from 18th cent., foreign works of 19th–20th cent.

Tati, Jacques, orig. Jacques Tatischeff (1908–　　), Fr. film director and actor. Films include *Jour de Fête, Les Vacances de Monsieur Hulot* and *Mon Oncle* for which he received (1958) Oscar for best foreign film.

Tattersall, Richard (1724–95), Eng. horse breeder. Opened (1766) Tattersall's thoroughbred racehorse auction at Hyde Park Corner, London.

tattoo, military display or pageant, held outdoors and often at night. Also signal on drum or bugle to recall soldiers to quarters.

tattoo, practice of decorating skin by pricking it and inserting colouring matter to form pictures or designs.

Tatum, Edward Lawrie (1909–　　), Amer. geneticist. With G. W. Beadle and Joshua Lederberg, awarded Nobel Prize for Physiology and Medicine (1958) for work on genetics.

Taurus see ZODIAC.

Tawney, R[ichard] H[enry] (1880–1962), Eng. historian and economist. Chief work, *Religion and the Rise of Capitalism* (1926) explores development of modern capitalism.

tawny owl, *Tyto aluca,* carnivorous woodland bird of Europe and Near East. Feeds largely on rats, mice, shrews, *etc.*

Tawny Owl

Teal

taxation, govt. levy to provide revenue. Oldest form is land tax; other means of taxation developed as scope of govt. responsibilities widened, esp. 19th–20th cent. Direct taxes, graduated according to individual's ability to pay, include INCOME TAX (major source of internal revenue), surtax, death duties or inheritance tax, rates and corporation tax. Forms of indirect taxation, such as sales or purchase taxes, based on stipulated percentage of cost. All levels of govt. have designated taxation powers; income tax is levied by national govt., in UK by Inland Revenue and in US by Internal Revenue.

taxi, cab, passenger-carrying vehicle, esp. motor car, hired at set fee (mostly calculated by taximeter according to time or distance).

taxidermy, art of skinning and preserving animals in life-like state, mostly for exhibition. Fur or feathers are cleaned with special preparations and hide is stretched over artificial framework.

Taylor, Elizabeth (1932–   ), Brit. film actress. Received (1960) Academy Award for Best Actress (*Butterfield 8*) and an Oscar (1967) for *Who's Afraid of Virginia Woolf.* Other films, *Cat on a Hot Tin Roof, Cleopatra.*

Taylor, Jeremy (1613–67), Eng. bishop and theological writer. Works include the devotional classics *The Rule and Exercises of Holy Living* (1650) and *The Rule and Exercises of Holy Dying* (1651). *The Liberty of Prophesying* (1646) is a defence of religious toleration.

Taylor, Zachary (1784–1850), 12th US Pres. (1849–50), Whig. Served in Indian military campaigns, commanded US forces in MEXICAN WAR, victorious at Palo Alto, Buena Vista. Elected Pres. (1848), died in office.

Tbilisi, formerly **Tiflis,** historic city, cap. of Georgian SSR, on Kura R. Founded 5th cent. Centre of indust. region. Pop. (1967) 823,000.

Tchaikovsky or **Tschaikowsky, Piotr Ilyich** (1840–93), Russ. composer and conductor. Compositions melodious and romantic; popular, esp. orchestral music. Works include 5th and 6th (*Pathétique*) symphonies, ballets *Swan Lake, The Sleeping Beauty*; also fantasies *Romeo and Juliet,* and '*1812*' overture. Operas include *Eugene Onegin* and *Pique Dame,* and songs 'None But the Lonely Heart'.

tea, *Thea sinensis,* shrub with fragrant white flowers, extensively cultivated in China, Japan, India, Ceylon, *etc.* From the dried leaves a bitter aromatic beverage is prepared by infusion in hot water.

teak, *Tectona grandis,* tall E Indian timber tree of family Verbenaceae. Now cultivated in W Africa and trop. America. Hard durable reddish brown wood used in shipbuilding and furniture manufacture.

teal, small, freshwater duck of genus *Anas.* Species include N Amer. blue-winged teal, *A. discers,* and green-winged teal, European *A. crecca* and Amer. *A. carolinensis.*

Teapot Dome Scandal, incident arising out of lease (1922) of US naval oil reserve, Teapot Dome, in Wyoming. Secretary of Interior Albert Fall convicted (1929) for leasing land without competitive bidding. Senate investigations led to allegations of govt. corruption.

tear gas, gas, usually bromide compound, inducing temporary loss of sight through excessive flow of tears. Used in warfare and civil disturbances.

teasel, biennial or perennial herb of genus *Dipsacus* from Europe, Asia and N Africa. Fuller's teasel, *D. fullonum* is cultivated for its prickly

Flowering   Tea   Bush   of   the   popular,   large-leafed   Assam   variety

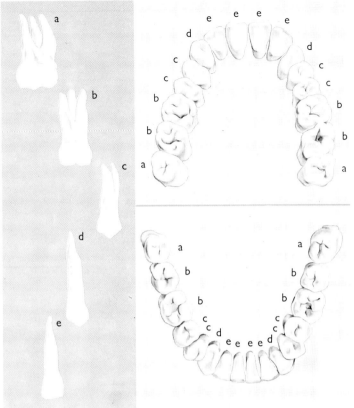

Teeth : diagram of human dentition showing types of tooth and arrangement in upper and lower jaws (a) and (b) molars, (c) bicuspid, (d) canine, (e) incisor

flower heads, used for raising the nap on woollen cloth.

Tebaldi, Renata (1922–), Ital. operatic soprano. Specializes in Puccini roles.

tecoma, genus of trop. Amer. shrubs and trees. Large showy blossoms. *T. capensis* is W Indian honeysuckle.

Tecumseh (*c.* 1768– 1813), Shawnee Indian chief. Attempt to form W confederacy failed after defeat (1811) at Tippecanoe by US forces. Assisted British in War of 1812, killed at battle of Moraviantown in Upper Canada.

Tedder, Arthur William, 1st Baron (1890– 1967), marshal of Royal Air Force. During World War 2 commanded RAF in Middle East. Deputy Supreme Commander to Gen. Eisenhower, contributed to success of Normandy invasion.

teeth, in most vertebrates, structures embedded in upper and lower jaws, serving chiefly to masticate food. In man, early set of 20 deciduous (or milk) teeth are replaced by 32 permanent teeth in 6th year. Tooth, coated with enamel, consists of dentine, surrounding nerves and blood vessels; roots attached to jaw by membrane.

Tegucigalpa, cap. of Honduras. Founded 16th cent. Includes city of Comayagüela. Pop. (1966) 191,000.

Teheran, Tehran, cap. of Iran, *c.* 70 mi. S of Caspian Sea. Created (1788) cap. by Aga Mohamad Khan, since grown steadily. Transport, commercial and manufacturing centre. Pop. (1966) 2,803,000.

Teheran Conference, meeting (Nov.- Dec. 1943) held at Teheran, Iran, between Allied leaders Churchill, F. D. Roosevelt and Stalin during World War 2. Outlined plans for invasion of Europe and role of UN in peace settlement.

Tehran *see* TEHERAN.

Teilhard de Chardin, Pierre (1881– 1955), Fr. Jesuit palaeontologist and philosopher. His philosophy is an attempt to reconcile Christian theology with the scientific theory of evolution, to establish a relationship between facts of religious experience and those of natural science. Works include *The Phenomenon of Man* (pub. 1959) and *The Divine Milieu* (pub. 1960).

Teiresias, in Gk. myth., Theban blinded by Hera and given long life and gift of prophecy by Zeus. Consulted by Odysseus; revealed truth about OEDIPUS and warned Creon of consequences of defiance of divine laws.

Tel Aviv, largest city and financial centre of Israel, on Med. Sea. Textile and clothing manufacturing, educ. centre. Founded 1909 as suburb of Jaffa (built 15th cent. BC), which it incorporated (1949). Pop. (1965) 392,000.

telegraph, method of sending messages in form of electrical impulses, by

Teheran with the Elburz Mountains in the distance

radio or wire. First developed by Samuel Morse (1844) in US.

Telemachus, in Gk. myth., son of Odysseus and Penelope. With Odysseus destroyed Penelope's suitors who had gathered at palace during Odysseus' absence.

Telemann, Georg Philipp (1681–1767), Ger. baroque composer. Extremely versatile and prolific. Wrote over 600 overtures, 40 operas, sonatas and church music.

telepathy, communication between minds by means other than physical (sensory) perception. Subject of much research but its genuineness remains controversial.

telephone, electrical instrument by which sound is transmitted and reproduced at a distance. Invented by Alexander Bell (1876) as result of Faraday's discovery of electromagnetism.

telescope, optical instrument for viewing distant objects. May utilize 2 lenses (refracting type) or a lens and a mirror (reflecting type). First used (1609) for astronomy by Galileo.

television, transmission and reception of visual images using electromagnetic radiation; pattern of electric impulses from camera reconstructed in receiver to form picture. First developed, in UK, by John Logie Baird (1926). International communication aided by use of satellites.

Telford, Thomas (1757–1834), Scot. civil engineer. Responsible for building Caledonian Canal; also c. 1,000 mi. of new roads in Scotland. Designed Menai Suspension Bridge from Wales to Anglesey and St

Buddhist temple in Kuala Lumpur, Malaysia

Katherine's Docks, London, England.

Tell, William (*fl.* 14th cent.), legendary Swiss hero. Traditionally sentenced to shoot apple off son's head with bow and arrow for refusing to recognize Austrian authority. In revenge, shot Austrian bailiff.

tellin, marine bivalve mollusc of genus *Tellina.* Thin round white, yellow, pink or purple shell.

tellurium (Te), semi-metallic element with properties similar to sulphur, discovered 1782. Appears as white crystalline form. Used to reinforce rubber and in dye manufacture.

Telugu *see* DRAVIDIAN.

temperance movement, group organized to prevent consumption of alcoholic beverages. In US, most powerful were Women's Christian Temperance Union (founded 1874) and Anti-Saloon League (founded 1893), instrumental in securing PROHIBITION.

Templars, military religious order (formed 12th cent.), called Knights of the Temple of Solomon. Achieved fame through exploits during Crusades, moved (1291) to Cyprus. Persecuted by Philip IV of France, order dissolved 1314.

Temple, Henry John, 3rd Viscount Palmerston (1784–1865), Eng. statesman. Began as Tory, but joined Whigs (1830). Foreign Sec. (1830–41, 1846–51), upheld independence of

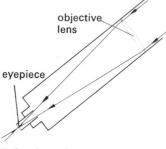

objective lens

eyepiece

Refracting telescope

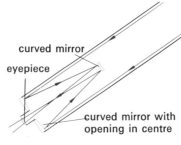

curved mirror

eyepiece

curved mirror with opening in centre

Reflecting telescope

Belgium, Turkey to counter continental powers. P.M. (1855–8, 1859–65), aided Ital. independence, dealt with Sepoy revolt in India. Antagonized colleagues with overbearing policies.

Temple, William (1881–1944), Eng. educationalist and churchman. Archbishop of York (1929–42), and of Canterbury (1942–4). Sought to relate Christian ideals to modern life. Wrote *Nature, Man and God* (1934).

temple, building, esp. large and imposing, erected as place of public worship. Term also applied to any large, pretentious public building.

tempo, in music, indication of speed at which piece should be played. Term is Italian, as are *allegro, andante, moderate, presto, etc.,* which describe different tempi.

Ten Commandments, in OT, summary of law of God as given to Moses in form of 10 statements on Mt. Sinai. Basis of moral code of Judaism, Christianity and Islam. Divided into 3 groups dealing with duty to God, personal integrity and proper treatment of others.

tench, *Tinca tinca,* European freshwater fish related to the carp. About 16–18 in. long. Olive green in colour and grey beneath.

tendon, band of dense, white fibrous tissue which connects muscle with bone. Achilles' tendon attaches muscles of the calf to the heel bone.

Tenerife, largest of CANARY ISLANDS. Area: 795 sq. mi.; chief city and port Santa Cruz de Tenerife.

Tennessee, state of S central US. Area: 42,244 sq. mi.; cap. Nashville; main cities: Memphis, Knoxville, Chattanooga. Mountainous in E, fertile plain in W. Cotton and tobacco farming; chemicals and food manufacture. Recent growth aided by TENNESSEE VALLEY AUTHORITY power project. Fr. claims in area ceased after 1763. Admitted as slave state 1796. Joined (1861) South in Civil War and was important battleground.

Tennessee, main tributary (652 mi. long) of Ohio R., S central US. Rises in E Tenn., drains area of 41,000 sq. mi.

Tennessee Valley Authority (TVA), independent, govt.-supported agency, created (1933) by US Congress, empowered to develop Muscle Shoals, Alabama, and integrate power and irrigation projects of Tennessee R. basin. Widespread programme provided stimulus for growth of region.

Tenniel, Sir John (1820–1914), Eng. caricaturist famous for cartoons in *Punch.* Also provided original illustrations for *Alice's Adventures in Wonderland* and *Through the Looking-glass and What Alice Found There.*

tennis, lawn tennis, game played by 2 or 4 players on prepared surface, either indoors or outdoors. Descended from 16th cent. European court game. Introduced as new game (1873). International championships include Wimbledon, Davis Cup.

Tennyson, Alfred, 1st Baron Tennyson (1809–92), Eng. Romantic poet. Early works, chiefly short lyrics published in *Poems* (1832), include 'The Lady of Shalott'. *Poems* (1842) immediately successful, followed by longer works incl. *The Princess* (1847), *In Memoriam* (1850). Popular narrative poems *Idylls of the King* (1859–88) based on Arthurian legend. Made Poet Laureate (1850).

Tenochtitlán, ancient cap. of Aztecs, C Mexico, on site of modern Mexico City. Founded *c.* 1325, taken by Spaniards (1521). Est. pop. at time of Sp. conquest 250,000.

tenor, in singing, highest mature male voice.

tenpin bowling, indoor bowling game, played with 10 wooden 'pins' and a composition ball. Each player aims to knock down the set of pins twice during 10 'frames' of a game.

tenrec, nocturnal insectivorous mammal of family Tenrecidae of Madagascar. Related to hedgehog and shrew; long pointed snout.

Tensing Norkay see NORKAY, TENSING.

Teotihuacán, San Juan Teotihuacán, town of C Mexico. Site of famous Toltec ruins, Pyramids of the Sun, Pyramids of the Moon, temples of Tlaloc (rain-god) and Quetzalcoatl (lord of the air and wind).

tequila, Mexican liqueur resembling brandy; distilled from agave.

Terence [Publius Terentius Afer] (*c.* 185–159 BC), Roman comedian, b. Carthage. Received patronage of Scipio Aemilianus. Plays, mostly adapted from Menander, represent scenes of Gk. life but without Roman elements; include *Andria, Hecyra, Phormio* and *Adelphi.*

Teresa of Avila, Saint (1515–82), Sp. Carmelite nun and Roman Catholic mystic. Seeking to restore discipline and a more rigorous austerity to the order, she founded (1567) the Discalced (unshod) Carmelites. Estab. 17 new convents, and with the help of St John of the Cross, 14 communities for monks on similarly reformed lines. Writings include the *Life, Way of Perfection* and *The Interior Castle.*

termite, soft-bodied insect of order Isoptera. Lives in colonies; builds or tunnels large nests and feeds on wood. Some, as Amer. *Reticulitermes flanipes* and European *R. lucifungus,* destructive to trees and wooden structures.

tern, migratory seabird of family Laridae, related to the gull. Common tern, *Sterna hirundo,* of Europe and America has white, black and grey plumage.

terpenes, in chemistry, a number of unsaturated cyclic hydrocarbons. Constituents of resins or essential oils, widely used in perfumes.

Terpsichore, in Gk. myth., Muse of Dancing.

terra cotta, reddish brick-like earthenware, porous and unglazed. Made by being slowly air-dried, then baked hard in kiln. Used since antiquity for statues, figures, vases, *etc.*

Terra Nova National Park, Canadian national park in Newfoundland. Area: 153 sq. mi.

Terramycin, trade name for oxytetracycline, a yellow crystalline antibiotic. Effective against numerous disease-causing micro-organisms.

terrapin, N Amer. edible turtle of family Testudinidae, esp. diamondback terrapin of genus *Malaclemys.* Red-bellied terrapin, *Pseudemys rubriventris,* is found in inlets of Chesapeake Bay, and yellow-bellied terrapin, *P. scripta,* in SE US.

terrier, breed of dog orig. used to dig out burrowing animals. Medium sized with short muzzle and relatively large head. Breeds include fox terriers (rough and smooth), Boston, Scotch, Skye, Cairn, and larger bull terriers.

Territorial Army, part of Brit. Army. Estab. under Territorial and Reserve Forces Act of 1907. Replaced in 1967 by a smaller Territorial and Army Volunteer Reserve.

Terry, Dame Ellen Alicia (1848–1928), Eng. actress. Played Shakespearean roles with SIR HENRY IRVING. Toured US.

Tertiary see GEOLOGICAL TABLE.

Tertullian [Quintus Septimus Florens Tertullianus] (*c.* AD 160–225), Roman theologian, b. Carthage, trained as lawyer. Became Christian priest. *Apologeticus* (AD 197) urges protection of Christians, other works advocate rigorous and ascetic Christian life. Later conversion to Montanism, reflected in writings, resulted in break with Catholic Church.

Terylene, UK trade name for polyester fibre. US trade name is Dacron.

Test Act, legislation passed (1673)

Termites' nest

by Eng. Parl. to exclude from office those who refused to swear allegiance and to receive communion according to Church of England. Repealed (1828).

testis, testicle, male reproductive gland, either of 2 oval glands located in the scrotal sac or scrotum. Produces spermatozoa and hormones controlling secondary sexual characteristics developed at puberty.

tetanus, lockjaw, infectious disease caused by bacterium that enters the body through wounds. Characterized by tonic spasms and rigidity of voluntary muscles, esp. those of neck and lower jaw. May be prevented by inoculation.

Tetzel, Johann (1465–1519), Ger. Dominican monk. His selling of indulgences (1517) at Wittenberg for reconstruction of St Peter's, Rome, provoked LUTHER's posting of his 95 theses on church door.

Teutonic Knights, medieval Ger. military religious order. Founded *c.* 1190 in Holy Land. Undertook conquest of pagan E Prussia (13th cent). Became Protestant after 1525.

Teutonic mythology, lore based on adventures of principal gods of Germanic religion, Woden, Tiw, Frey and Freyja, together with a few heroes. Developed in semi-literary form in medieval *Nibelungenlied.* Related stories, with some Christian influence, found in Icelandic Norse myths.

Common Tern

Texas, SW state of US. Area: 267,339 sq. mi.; cap. Austin; main cities, Houston, Dallas, San Antonio. Comprises part of Great Plains, with Red, Colorado and Rio Grande rivers. Explored by Spaniards (1519– 1684), became prov. of Mexico; won independence by revolution, 1836; republic 1836– 45. Admission to US as state (1845) precipitated MEXICAN WAR, after which Mexico relinquished all claims to Texas. Resources include timber, oil, natural gas and sulphur. Livestock rearing practised on large scale. Pop. (1960) 9,579,677.

Texel, West Frisian island, part of North Holland prov., NW Netherlands. Area: 64 sq. mi.; chief town, Burg. Scene of Eng.-Dutch naval battles in 1653, 1673, and 1797. Pop. (1962) 10,890.

textiles, materials made by weaving, knitting, felting, quilting, braiding, or netting from threads or fibres. Most are knitted or woven.

Thackeray, William Makepeace (1811– 63), Eng. writer, b. India. Novel *Vanity Fair* (1847– 8) satirized romantic sentimentality and pretensions of upper class society. Also wrote *Pendennis* (1848– 50), *The History of Henry Esmond* (1852) and *The Newcomes* (1853– 5).

Thai, Sino-Tibetan language. Has 18 million speakers in Thailand and SW provs. of China.

Thailand [Prathet Thai], formerly **Siam,** kingdom, governed by king and

constituent assembly, of mainland SE Asia. Area: 198,271 sq. mi.; cap. Bangkok. Main rivers Menam, Mekong, Salween. First Siamese kingdom estab. 13th cent.; visited by Portuguese 1511, but contact with outsiders limited until 19th cent. Agriculture, esp. rice and rubber, important. Main language, Thai; principal religion, Buddhism. Unit of currency, baht. Pop. (1965) 31,508,000.

Thais (*fl.* 4th cent. BC), Gk. courtesan, mistress of Alexander the Great and later of Ptolemy I. Said to have instigated burning of Persepolis.

Thales (*c.* 640 BC– *c.* 546 BC). Gk. philosopher, mathematician and astronomer. Regarded as founder of Gk. philosophy; believed water to be basic element of life. Credited with founding deductive geometry and predicting solar eclipse of 585 BC.

Thalia, in Gk. myth., Muse of Comedy.

thalidomide, drug administered as sedative. Found to cause physical defects in unborn children when taken during first 12 weeks of pregnancy. Discovery led to adoption of stricter regulations in testing of new drugs.

Thames, 2nd longest river (*c.* 218 mi.) of British Isles, flowing E into North Sea. Site of large docks in London (Pool of London) and on estuary, esp. at Tilbury.

Thanksgiving Day, US national holiday. Commemorates first harvest of Plymouth Colony and celebration feast held by Pilgrims and neighbouring Indians. Celebrated 4th Thursday in Nov.

Thant, U (1909–   ), Burmese diplomat, UN Sec.-General (1961– 71). Represented Burma at UN (1947– 61). Succeeded Hammarskjold as head, granted wider powers in re-election (1966).

Thar Desert, Indian Desert, largely uninhabited area of S West Pakistan and NW India. Area: *c.* 60,000 sq. mi.

theatre, orig. outdoor auditoriums for Gk. drama, 1st recorded *c.* 5th cent. BC. In Middle Ages European religious drama performed in churches. Palladio's Teatro Olimpico 1st indoor secular theatre. Eng. Elizabethan theatres used courtyard plan and were open to the air. By 17th– 18th cent. audience was separated from performers by raised stage, lights, curtains *etc.* 'Theatre in the round', with actors entirely surrounded by audience is 20th cent. innovation.

Thebes, ancient Egyptian city on site of modern Karnak and Luxor. Centre of worship of Amen (*c.* 2134 BC). Sacked by Assyrians (661 BC), by Romans (29 BC).

Theiler, Max (1899–   ), Amer. research physician, b. South Africa. Awarded Nobel Prize for Physiology and Medicine (1951) for development of yellow fever vaccines.

theism, belief in god or gods and the philosophy incorporating that belief. Unlike deism, does not reject belief in divine revelation or intervention.

Themistocles (*c.* 525– *c.* 460 BC), Athenian statesman and commander. Persuaded Athenians to concentrate on strengthening fleet. Prominent in 2nd Persian War, gained decisive naval victory over Persians at Salamis (480 BC). Ostracized (*c.* 472 BC) after conflict with Cimon, plotted with Pausanias of Sparta and fled to Asia Minor.

Theocritus (*fl. c.* 270 BC), Gk. poet, prob. b. at Syracuse; regarded as founder of pastoral poetry. Extant

Tower Bridge on the River Thames in London

works collectively known as *Idylls*; pastoral pieces presented in short, dramatic form. Other poems mythological in subject. Written mostly in hexameters in Doric dialect.

theodolite, portable surveying instrument with telescopic sight. Used to estab. horizontal and vertical angles.

Theodora (*c.* 508– 548), Byzantine empress. Exerted great influence on policies of her husband Justinian, esp. in religious matters. Inspired him to crush Nika rebellion.

Theodoric the Great (*c.* 454– 526), king of the Ostrogoths. Sent to Italy by Emperor Zeno, defeated (488) Gothic king Odoacer; declared himself king, ruled Italy for 33 yr., giving it peace and prosperity, and continuing tradition of imperial Rome.

Theodosian Code, Roman legal code issued (AD 438) by Theodosius II, emperor of East. Based on Gregorian and Hermogenian codes; used in *Corpus Juris Civilis*.

Theodosius [I] the Great (*c.* 346– 395), Roman emperor (379– 95). As ruler of E part of Empire, secured peace with Goths. Administered W part of Empire in name of Valentinian II, after whose death ruled as sole emperor. Responsible for estab. (380) Catholicism as official religion. Summoned (381) Council of Constantinople at which his victory over ARIANISM was confirmed.

theology, study, thought and analysis dealing with God, his attributes and relation with universe. Systematic theology concerns specific doctrine, *e.g.* Christianity.

Theophrastus (*c.* 371– *c.* 287 BC), Gk. philosopher, pupil and friend of Aristotle, his successor as head of Peripatetic school. Surviving works include 2 books on plants and parts of philosophical and scientific works. Best known for *Characters,* 30 chapters, each describing, often humorously, some human failing. Influenced 17th cent. Eng. literature, also La Bruyère.

Detail from a Greek vase (*c.* 570 BC) showing Ariadne being left behind on the island of Naxos by Theseus

Theorell, Axel Hugo Theodor (1903–), Swedish biochemist, first to extract and purify myoglobin. Awarded Nobel Prize for Physiology and Medicine (1955) for work on oxidation enzymes.

theosophy, belief that every life on earth is part of universal soul of a supreme deity. Like Hinduism, states that man undergoes many lives before achieving final unity with the supreme being. Also aims at estab. of world brotherhood of all faiths and races.

Theotocopoulis, Domenicos *see* EL GRECO.

Theramenes (d. 403 BC), Athenian statesman and constitutionalist. Attempted reimposition of moderate oligarchy of Gk. Golden Age. Opposed by Critias, forced to take poison.

therapeutics, in medicine, remedial treatment of disease. Includes OCCUPATIONAL THERAPY and PHYSIOTHERAPY.

Thérèse of Lisieux (1873–97), Fr. Carmelite nun and Roman Catholic saint, called Little Flower of Jesus. Wrote spiritual autobiography *L'Histoire d'une Âme.* Named (1945) 2nd patroness of France, after St Joan.

Thermidor, 11th month of Fr. Revolutionary calendar from 19 July to 17 Aug. Coup d'état of 9 Thermidor (1794) marked end of Reign of Terror and downfall of Robespierre.

thermionics, branch of physics dealing with emission of ions from substances under action of heat.

thermit, aluminium powder mixed with metal oxide, emitting tremendous heat when ignited. Used esp. in welding and for incendiary bombs.

thermodynamics, science concerned with relation between heat and mechanical energy, and conversion of one into the other. Applied in physics, engineering and chemistry.

thermometer, instrument for measuring temperature. Usually consists of graduated sealed glass tube with bulb, which contains mercury or coloured alcohol.

Thermopylae, Battle of (480 BC), encounter in Second Persian War. Pass of Thermopylae at first successfully defended by Greeks; Persians shown way round pass, thus surrounding Greeks. Leonidas and small force of Spartans continued defence of pass but completely overwhelmed.

Theseus, in Gk. myth., son of Aegeus, king of Athens, or of Poseidon. Heroic deeds included killing of Minotaur of Crete (with help of ARIADNE). Defeated Amazons, whose Queen Hippolyte bore him a son, Hippolytus. Married Phaedra, sister of Ariadne. Attempted to abduct Persephone; sent to Hades, but rescued by Heracles.

Thespis (*fl. c.* 534 BC), Gk. poet. Said to have introduced actor, impersonating legendary or hist. character, to reply to leader of chorus. Sometimes regarded as inventor of tragedy.

Thessalonians, 2 epistles of NT, written (*c.* AD 52) by St Paul to church at Thessalonica. Praises faith of Thessalonians, corrects false ideas about Second Coming of Christ.

Thessalonika, Thessalenike, Thessaloniki *see* SALONIKA.

Thessaly, division of ancient Greece, on E coast. Rugged, mountainous, with broad, fertile plains. Unified (4th cent. BC) by Macedonians; Roman prov. from 2nd cent. BC; ceded to Greece by Turkey, 1881.

Thetis, in Gk. myth., one of Nereids and mother of Achilles. Given by Zeus and Poseidon to Peleus because of prophecy that her son would be greater than his father.

Thibault, Jacques Anatole *see* FRANCE, ANATOLE.

Thiers, [Louis] Adolphe (1797–

Greek theatre at Epidaurus

1877), Fr. statesman and writer. Author of *Histoire de la Révolution Française* (10 vols., 1823–7). Moderate liberal, instrumental in precipitating JULY REVOLUTION (1830). Twice premier (1836,1840) under Louis-Philippe. In opposition until selected as leader of provisional govt. during Franco-Prussian War (1870–1); suppressed COMMUNE OF PARIS. Pres. of repub. (1871–3), forced to resign by monarchists.

Thirteen Colonies, name applied to Brit. colonies of N America that fought Amer. Revolution and founded United States. They were Massachusetts, New Hampshire, Rhode Island, Connecticut, New York, New Jersey, Pennsylvania, Delaware, Maryland, Virginia, North Carolina, South Carolina and Georgia.

Thirty Years War, European conflict (1618–48), fought mainly in Germany, involving religious and territorial struggle between Ger. princes, variously supported by external powers, and Holy Roman Empire of Habsburgs. War precipitated by imperial opposition to Bohemian uprising against Ferdinand (later Ferdinand II). Victory for imperial forces under TILLY followed by Danish intervention, which ended (1629) with triumph of WALLENSTEIN. Swedish participation, under Gustavus II, during 1630s ended in compromise; war spread beyond Germany after France joined Sweden (1635). Eventual settlement came with PEACE OF WESTPHALIA. Struggle between France and Sp. Habsburgs continued until 1659.

Thirty-Nine Articles, basic statement of doctrinal belief of Church of England. Drawn up orig. 1551–3; revised and adopted by Convocation (1562). Made law by Act of Parl. (1571).

Thisbe, in Asiatic legend, maiden of Babylon, loved by Pyramus. While waiting for Pyramus, Thisbe fled from a lion, and Pyramus, finding her blood-stained cloak, killed himself: Thisbe returned and stabbed herself.

thistle, prickly plant of family Compositae and esp. of genera *Cirsium* and *Onopordum*. Heads consist of many small flowers with spiny purple, rose, yellow or white bracts. Species include Scotch thistle, *O. acanthium,* the emblem of Scotland, bull thistle, *C. lanceolatum,* and Canada thistle, *C. arvense,* a pernicious weed.

Thomas, Dylan Marlais (1914–53), Brit. writer, b. Wales. Works include *Twenty-five Poems* (1936), *Portrait of the Artist as a Young Dog* (1946); verse play *Under Milk Wood* (1954).

Musk Thistle

Thomas, George Henry (1816–70), Amer. Union general in Civil War. Nicknamed 'Rock of Chickamauga' after his stand there (1863) in Chattanooga Campaign. Fought under Sherman in Atlanta campaign.

Thomas, Saint, one of the Twelve Apostles, also known as Didymus [Gk: twin]. Doubted Resurrection of Christ until saw Jesus and touched His side. Traditionally apostle to S India or Parthia.

Thomas à Becket *see* BECKET, SAINT THOMAS À.

Thomas à Kempis (*c.* 1380–1471), Ger. monk. Author of many devotional works incl. the ascetical treatise *On the Following (or Imitation) of Christ* (attributed by some, however, to Gerhard Groote).

Thomas Aquinas *see* AQUINAS, SAINT THOMAS.

Thompson, David (1770–1857), Canadian explorer and geographer, b. England. 1st European to travel length of Columbia R. Made important map of W Canada (1813–14).

Thompson, Edward Herbert (1860–1935), Amer. archaeologist. Excavated Chichen Itza, Mayan cap. of Yucatan.

Thompson, Ernest Seton *see* SETON, ERNEST THOMPSON.

Thompson, Francis (1859–1907), Eng. mystical poet. *Poems* (1893) include 'Hound of Heaven'.

Thompson, Sir John Sparrow David (1844–94), Canadian statesman. Conservative P.M. (1892–4).

Thomson, Charles Edward Poulett, 1st Baron Sydenham (1799–1841), Brit. colonial administrator. Appointed Gov.-General of Prov. of Canada (1839), achieved union of Upper and Lower Canada legislatures.

Thomson, Sir Charles Wyville (1830–82), Scot. zoologist, noted for deep-sea research. Wrote *The Depth of the Oceans* (1872). Headed *Challenger* expedition (1872–6) which laid basis for study of oceanography.

Thomson, James (1700–48), Scot. poet. His blank verse poem *Seasons* (1730) influenced later Romantic poets. The song 'Rule Britannia' appears in masque *Alfred* which he wrote with David Mallet.

Thomson, James (1834–82), Scot. writer and poet; wrote under pseudonym B. V. Works include *The City of Dreadful Night* (1874), a poem of dark despair.

Thomson, Sir Joseph John (1856–1940), Eng. physicist. Awarded Nobel Prize for Physics (1906) for study of electrical conduction through gases. Discovered electron. His son, **Sir George Paget Thomson** (1892–), also a physicist, shared with C. J. Davisson Nobel Prize for Physics (1937) for discovery of diffraction in the electron.

Thomson, Roy Herbert, Lord Thomson of Fleet (1894–), Brit. newspaper owner, b. Canada. Controls newspapers in Canada, US, UK, also TV and radio stations. Took over Kemsley Newspapers (1959), Times Newspapers Ltd. (1966).

Thomson, Virgil (1896–), Amer. composer and music critic. Works include operas *Four Saints in Three Acts* and *The Mother of Us All.*

Thomson, William, 1st Baron Kelvin of Largs (1824–1907), Brit. physicist. Noted for research work in thermodynamics and theory of elasticity. Invented reflecting galvanometer and quadrant electrometer; perfected transatlantic submarine cables and estab. Kelvin scale of temperature.

Thor, in Teutonic myth., son of Odin, and god of thunder. Represented as having great strength and wielding

Blessed Thistle

magic hammer. Thursday named after him.

thorax, in higher vertebrates, part of body between neck and abdomen. Contains heart and lungs, great arteries and veins, gullet and nerves. Supported by ribs and sternum.

Thoreau, Henry David (1817–62), Amer. writer and naturalist. *Walden* (1854) is an account of his experiment in living alone in the country to escape materialism and frustrations of society. His *On the Duty of Civil Disobedience* (1849) condemns profit-seeking, indust., urban civilization.

Thorfinn Karlsefni (*fl. c.* 1000), Scandinavian explorer, b. Iceland. Voyaged to Greenland and probably, Quebec.

thorium, silvery metallic radioactive element. Source of atomic energy. Certain of its isotopes may be used in nuclear reactors as fuel.

thorn, woody plant with briars, prickles or spines *e.g.* the hawthorn, European *Crataegus oxyacantha* and Amer. *C. coccinea.*

thorn apple, plant or shrub of genus *Datura* of warm temp. and trop. regions. Prickly fruit and large trumpet-shaped flowers. Species include jimsonweed, *D. stramonium,* a poisonous plant.

Thorndike, Dame Sybil (1882–   ), Eng. actress. Created title role in Shaw's *Saint Joan* (1924). Also noted for her roles in *Ghosts, The Linden Tree, Arsenic and Old Lace.*

thorny devil *see* SPINY LIZARD.

Thorpe, James (1888–1953), Amer. athlete. All-American football player at Carlisle Indian School. Forced to surrender awards for victories in 1912 Olympics track and field events, after discovery of earlier professional sports activity.

Thorwaldsen, Albert Bertel (1770–1844), Danish neoclassical sculptor. Works include *Jason* and *Byron.* Designed *Lion of Lucerne,* executed by his students.

Thoth, ancient Egyptian god of wisdom and magic. Inventor of hieroglyphics. Portrayed as human with ibis head. Identified by Greeks with Hermes.

Thousand and One Nights, Arabian Nights, collection of stories written in Arabic. Framework, with character Scheherazade who entertains her husband with the tales, incl. Ali Baba and Aladdin, is Persian. Translated into French (18th cent.) and English (19th cent.).

Thrace, region of SE Europe on SE tip of Balkan Peninsula, occupying NE Greece, S Bulgaria and European Turkey. Main cities, Istanbul, Adrian-ople, Gallipoli. Largely agric. area. Early inhabitants driven E by Illyrians and later by Macedonians; conquered by Romans (1st cent. BC). Subsequent ownership much disputed, esp. by Turkey and Bulgaria, latterly (World War 1) by Greece.

thrasher, N Amer. insectivorous song-bird esp. of genus *Toxostoma* of Mimidae family; related to mocking bird. Sage thrasher and brown thrasher common in US.

Three Emperors' League, informal agreement (1872) between Germany, Russia and Austria-Hungary to ensure mutual peace. Threatened by Russo-Turkish War (1877–8), superseded by TRIPLE ALLIANCE.

Three Rivers *see* TROIS RIVIÈRES.

thresher shark, large shark of genus *Alopias,* esp. *A. vulpinus.* Found near Amer. and European coasts. Threshes water with long pointed tail to round up small fish on which it feeds.

thrift *see* SEA PINK.

thrips, minute agile black, yellowish or brown insect of order Thysanoptera. Sucks sap from plants.

Throgmorton or **Throckmorton, Francis** (1554–84), Eng. conspirator. Implicated in Catholic plot to put Mary Stuart on Eng. throne (1583). Hanged at Tyburn.

thrombosis, clotting of blood in blood vessels in circulatory system as in heart, arteries, veins or capillaries.

thrush, widely distributed songbird of family Turdidae with dark spotted breast. Species include mistle thrush, Old World song thrush, *Turdus philomelos;* also N Amer. hermit thrush, *Hylocichla guttata,* with reddish tail, and wood thrush, *H. mustelina,* with reddish head.

Thucydides (*c.* 460–*c.* 400 BC), Gk. historian and general. Exiled for failure to relieve Amphipolis from Brasidas (424 BC). History of PELO-PONNESIAN WAR, covering events to 411 BC, noted for condensed, lucid, graphic style, fairness and political reasoning. Well-known speeches include Pericles' Funeral Oration.

Thugs, Phansigars, secret Indian religious sect. Flourished from 13th cent. Worshipped goddess Kali, strangled victims as sacrifices to her. Suppressed by British 1829–36.

Thule, name given by ancients to most northerly land of Europe. Variously identified as Norway, Iceland or Orkney and Shetland Is. Modern Thule is district of NW Greenland, founded 1910. US air base nearby.

thulium (Tm), metallic rare earth element, found esp. in minerals euxenite and gadolinite.

thunderstorm, electric storm, turbu-lence caused by instability of the atmosphere. Accompanied by thunder, lightning, and often violent gusts of wind, heavy rain or hail. Strong upward currents of moist, rapidly cooling air form Cumulo-nimbus clouds (*see* CLOUD) which produce violent showers of rain or hail; static electricity develops, causing lightning flashes; rapid expansion of air, produced by heat of lightning, constitutes sound of thunder.

Thurber, James Grover (1894–1961), Amer. humorist, many of whose cartoons appeared in *The New Yorker.* Wrote satire *Is Sex Necessary?* (1929) and short stories incl. *The Secret Life of Walter Mitty.*

Thuringia, historic region of C Germany. Former cap. Weimar. State dissolved 1952, divided into E Ger. districts of Erfurt, Gera and Suhl. Main cities, Jena, Gotha, Gera, Erfurt, Mülhausen. Industries include electrical machinery, optical equipment.

Thurmond, [James] Strom (1902–   ), Amer. lawyer and Republican politician. Gov. of S Carolina (1947–51). States' Rights Democratic candidate for US pres. (1948). US Senator from S Carolina (1955–   ).

Thurso, Archibald Sinclair, 1st Viscount (1890–1970), Brit. politician. Sec. of State for Air (1940–5).

Thutmose or **Thutmosis I,** king of Egypt (*c.* 1500 BC). Accomplished warrior whose principal expeditions were to Nubia and the Euphrates.

Thutmose or **Thutmosis II** (*fl. c.* 1490 BC), king of Egypt. Ruled with his half-sister HATSHEPSUT.

Thutmose or **Thutmosis III** (*fl. c.* 1475 BC), king of Egypt (1468 BC). Expanded territory, conquering all of Asia Minor.

Thyestes, in Gk. myth., son of Pelops

Sea of Tiberias, in Galilee

and brother of Atreus. Seduced Aethra, Atreus' wife, banished, recalled by Atreus and served limbs of his children at banquet. Cursed house of Atreus. By daughter Pelopia became father of AEGISTHUS, with whom he contrived death of Atreus.

thyme, perennial plant of genus *Thymus,* esp. common garden herb, *T. vulgaris.* Pungent aromatic leaves used in seasoning.

thymus gland, ductless gland found in vertebrate animals. Lies near base of neck in man, becoming vestigial in adults. Stimulates antibodies.

thyroid gland, ductless gland on each side of trachea connected below larynx by thin tissue. Secretion regulates rates of metabolism and body growth in humans.

Thyssen, August (1842–1926), Ger. industrialist. Pioneered blast furnaces and other technological innovations.

Tiber [Ital: Tevere], river (251 mi. long) of C Italy. Drains area of 6,700 sq. mi. Source of hydro-electricity.

Tiberias, town of NE Israel, on Sea of Galilee. Named after Emperor TIBERIUS; centre for Jews after destruction of Jerusalem. Modern town is centre of agric. region.

Tiberias, Sea of, alternative name for Sea of Galilee, NE Israel.

Bust of Tiberius

Tiberius (42 BC–AD 37), Roman emperor (AD 14–37), stepson of Augustus whom he succeeded. Empire prospered under his rule; regularized state finances.

Tibet, country of C Asia, autonomous region of China. Area: *c.* 470,000 sq. mi.; cap. Lhasa. Predominantly mountainous (average altitude 13,000 ft.) with agriculture in Tsangpo valley. Rich in salt, gold, radioactive ores. Under successive lamas, *fl.* 7th cent. First conquered by China (1720); independence declared 1913; retaken by China 1933. Invaded (1950) by Chinese Communists. Revolt (1959) unsuccessful; Dalai Lama fled to India; estab. as autonomous region of China (1951). Mongol population. Traditional religion, Lamaism. Pop. (1957) 1,270,000.

Tibetan, Tibeto-Burman language, with *c.* 6 million speakers in Tibet and China.

Tibeto-Burman, one of the 2 main branches of Sino-Tibetan language group. Includes Tibetan and Burmese.

Tibullus, Albius (*c.* 48–19 BC) Roman elegiac poet. Poetry, mostly on love, and idyllic country life, marked by charm and tenderness.

tick, parasitic arachnid of order Acarina with piercing mouthparts. Lives on mammal or bird blood. Some spread diseases, esp. fevers.

tickbird, several birds which feed on ticks, *e.g.* the oxpecker.

Ticonderoga, village of NE New York, US. Scene of battles in French and Indian Wars and American Revolution.

tide, alternate rise and fall of surface of sea (usually twice in 24 hr.) caused by gravitational pull of the moon and sun. Spring tide occurs when earth, moon and sun are practically in same line; high tides are higher, low tides lower. Neap tide, of smaller amplitude, occurs when gravitational pull of sun is at right-angle to that of moon.

Tieck, Ludwig (1773–1853), Ger. poet, novelist, dramatist and critic. Initially a romantic; early works include *Der Gestiefelte Kater* (*Puss in Boots,* 1797) he later turned to realism as in, *Des Lebens Überfluss* (*Life's Overflow,* 1837).

Tien-Shan, mountain range of C Asia, on border between USSR and China. Highest peak, Pobeda (24,406 ft.).

Tientsin, Tienching, city and port of N China, cap. of Hopeh prov. Economic centre of N China. Industries include chemicals, metallurgy. Two universities. Pop. (1957 est.) 3,220,000.

Tiepolo, Giovanni Battista (1696–1770), Ital. painter. Leading exponent

Tin processing plant in Malaya

of Venetian rococo style. Painted frescoes in Doge's Palace, Venice; also in Würzburg and Madrid.

Tierra del Fuego, archipelago in Atlantic Ocean, off S South America. Area: *c.* 18,500 sq. mi. E part belongs to Argentina (cap. Ushuaia); W part to Chile (cap. Punta Arenas). Main occupations, sheep-raising, timber, fishing. Pop. (1960 est.) 47,900.

Tiflis *see* TBILISI.

tiger, *Panthera tigris* or *Felis tigris,* large Asiatic carnivorous mammal, family Felidae. Coat usually orange-yellow striped with black; no mane.

tiger beetle, rapid-flying carnivorous beetle of family Cicindelidae. Worldwide distribution in sandy localities. Larvae live in tunnels in soil.

tiger moth, moth of family Arctiidae. Long brightly coloured wings; larvae are hairy caterpillars.

tiger-flower, plant or flower of genus *Tigridia,* native to Mexico and S America. *T. pavonia* has red flowers spotted with yellow and purple.

tiger's eye, yellow-orange striped gemstone formed of silicified, fibrous asbestos.

Tigris, river of SW Asia (*c.* 1,150 mi. long) rising in E Turkey and joining Euphrates in S Iraq to form Shatt al Arab. Ancient cities of Nineveh and Ctesiphon were on banks.

Tilden, Samuel J[ones] (1814–86), Amer. lawyer and politician. Defeated as democratic candidate in 1876 pres. election by apparent discrepancy in count.

till, boulder clay, material deposited by melting sheets of ice. Composed of clay matrix embedded with pebbles and boulders.

Till Eulenspiegel *see* EULENSPIEGEL, TILL.

Tillich, Paul Johannes (1886–1965), Amer. philosopher and Protestant theologian, b. Germany. Works include *Systematic Theology* (3 vols., 1951–63), *The Courage to Be* (1952).

Tilly, Johann Tserclaes, Count of (1559–1632), Flemish imperial commander in Thirty Years War. Victorious at White Mountain (1620), Wimpfen (1622), Lutter (1626). Stormed Magdeburg (1631). Mortally wounded at Lech.

Tilsit, former name of **Sovetsk,** Russ. city on Nieman R. Produces leather, cheese, timber. Pop. (1965 est.) 31,200.

Tilsit, Treaty of (1807), agreement between Napoleon I and Alexander I, restoring peace between France and Russia. Russia agreed to secret alliance against England, recognized Duchy of Warsaw. In 2nd treaty, 2 days later, Napoleon gained major concessions from William III of Prussia, incl. ceding to France of all Prussian territory W of Elbe R.

timber beetle, beetle of family Scolytidae. Larvae bore in the wood of trees. Species include bark beetle and ambrosia beetle.

timber wolf, *Canis lupus,* large wolf of E N America. Usually grey in colour.

Timbuktu, city of C Mali, near Niger R. Ancient city was centre of caravan trade routes and of Moslem culture. Modern city produces salt. Pop. (1967 est.) 8,000.

time, in music, rhythmical arrangement and relative length of notes and rests within bars.

time, measurement of duration as experienced on Earth, normally calculated in terms of recurring natural phenomena, *e.g.* night and day caused by rotation of Earth in relation to Sun.

Times, The, Brit. national daily newspaper, founded (1785) by John Walter; called *The Daily Universal Register* until 1788. Traditionally many eminent people have expressed their opinions on major issues in letters to *The Times*.

Timor, island of Lesser Sundas group, Indonesia. Area: 13,071 sq. mi. W part, orig. Dutch Timor, became (1949) Indonesian prov. of East Nusatenggera (cap. Kupang). E part forms overseas territory of Portugal and Indonesian enclave of Oe-Cusse (cap. Dili). Total pop. *c.* 2,500,000.

Timothy, 2 epistles of NT, traditionally ascribed to St Paul. Addressed (*c.* AD 66) to Timothy, bishop of Ephesus, giving counsel on the safeguarding of the Christian faith.

timothy, timothy grass, *Phleum pratense,* tall European perennial grass with long cylindrical spikes. Grown in N US and Europe for hay.

timpani *see* PERCUSSION INSTRUMENTS.

Timur *see* TAMBERLANE.

tin (Sn), soft, silvery-white metallic element. Ductile and malleable; barely affected by moisture. Used to protect other metals in alloys; compounds used in dyeing, enamels, fireproofing and medicine. Tin plate is iron or steel with thin coating of tin. Ores found in Bolivia, Indonesia, Congo, Nigeria.

tinamou, bird of family Tinamidae of S and C America, related to rhea.

tinstone, cassiterite, common mineral, tin dioxide, the principal ore of tin.

Tintern Abbey, ruined Cistercian cruciform church in Monmouthshire, England.

Tintoretto, orig. Jacopo Robusti (1518–94), Ital. painter. Subjects are mainly biblical, *e.g.* enormous masterpiece *The Paradise* (1589–90) in Doge's Palace, Venice.

Tippecanoe, Battle of, victory (1811) in NE Indiana, for troops of General W. H. Harrison against Amer. Indians.

Tipperary, Tiobraid Arann, inland county of S Repub. of Ireland, in Munster. Area: 1,662 sq. mi.; county town, Clonmel. Admin. divided into North Riding and South Riding. Hilly with rich agric. land. Main occupation, dairying. Pop. (1966) 122,778.

Tippett, Sir Michael Kemp (1905–), Eng. composer. Works include *Concerto for Double String Orchestra* (1939), the opera *The Midsummer Marriage* (1952), the oratorio *A Child of our Time* (1941) and *Magnificat* and *Nunc Dimittis* (1961).

Tippoo Sahib (1749–99), sultan of Mysore, India (1782–99). Continued his father's wars against British. Attacked (1789) Travancore, defeated and forced (1792) to give up half his dominions. Finally killed at siege of Seringapatam by British under General Wellesley.

Tirana, Tiranë, cap. of Albania, founded *c.* 1600 by Turks. Modern

Ceiling painting by Tiepolo from the bishop's palace at Würzburg

city dates from 1920. Situated in fertile region producing olives, almonds. Industries include printing, production of consumer goods. Pop. (1964) 157,000.

Tirol *see* TYROL.

Tirpitz, Alfred Friedrich von (1849–1930), Ger. naval officer. During World War 1, initiated construction of submarines, advocated unrestricted warfare.

Tirso de Molina, orig. Gabriel Tellez (*c.* 1584–1648), Sp. ecclesiastic and dramatist. Comedies include *El Burlador de Sevilla* (1630) which contained original Don Juan.

Tiselius, Arne Wilhelm Kaurin (1902–71), Swedish biochemist. Awarded Nobel Prize for Chemistry (1948) for developing method of separating colloids.

tissue, in biology, an aggregate of cells similar in form and function, such as in nerve, connective, muscle and epithelial tissue in animals, and equivalents in plants.

Tisza, Istvan (1861–1918), Hungarian P.M. (1903–5, 1913–17). Sought to crush nationalist aspirations of minorities (esp. Serbs) in Austria-Hungary.

tit, titmouse, widely distributed arboreal songbird of family Paridae and esp. of genus *Parus*. Short bill and strong claws; largely insectivorous. Species include blue tit, *P. caeruleus,* tufted titmouse, *P. bicolor,* coal tit, *P. ater,* crested titmouse, *P. cristatus.*

Titanic, Eng. passenger liner (46,000 t.). On maiden voyage, 14 Apr. 1912, struck iceberg in N Atlantic and sank with heavy loss of life. Disaster prompted stricter safety regulations and permanent iceberg patrol.

titanium, greyish, metallic element. Widely distributed but difficult to extract. Added to various steel alloys and used in jet engines, missiles *etc.,* because of heat-resistant qualities.

Titans, in Gk. myth., 12 children (6 sons, 6 daughters) of Uranus and Gaia (Heaven and Earth). Defeated in battle by Olympian gods.

tithes, form of taxation. Origins were religious, connected with offering of first fruits to deity. Later a form of tribute requiring a tenth of a man's produce or property. Used for maintenance of bishops and clergy.

Titian, orig. Tiziano Vecellio (*c.* 1490–1576), Renaissance Venetian painter, supreme master of colour.

Great Tit

Works include altarpieces *Assumption of the Virgin, La Gloria;* portraits, *Pope Paul III;* religious and mythological paintings, *Presentation of the Virgin, Bacchus and Ariadne.*

Titicaca, Lake, freshwater lake in Andes of Bolivia and Peru, at 12,600 ft. Area: *c.* 3,200 sq. mi. World's highest lake.

titlark *see* PIPIT.

titmouse *see* TIT.

Tito, Josip Broz, orig. Josip Broz (1892–), Yugoslav soldier and statesman. Led Partisan resistance against Ger. occupation in World War 2. Premier (1945–53) of new Communist Yugoslav repub., pres. (1953–). After break (1948) with COMINFORM, succeeded in maintaining independence of Yugoslav Communism in face of Soviet pressure. Assumed neutral position in international politics.

Titus [Titus Flavius Sabinus Vespasianus] (AD 40–81), Roman emperor (AD 79–81). Son of Vespasian. Captured Jerusalem (AD 70); completed construction of Colosseum.

Titus, epistle of NT, traditionally ascribed to St Paul; prob. written *c.* AD 66. Advises on govt. of church.

Tivoli, town and manufacturing centre, Latium, C Italy. Remains from ancient Romans who called site Tibur, include Hadrian's villa. Pop. (1967 est.) 23,000.

Tlinglit, group of N Amer. Indian tribes, orig. inhabiting coastal area of SE Alaska.

TNT, trinitrotoluene, explosive compound of carbon, hydrogen and oxygen formed by action of nitric acid on toluene.

toad, small, tailless amphibian of family Bufonidae. Usually brown or black, warty skin with poison glands. Terrestrial except when breeding.

toadfish, predatory, voracious fish of family Batrachoididae. Oyster toadfish, *Opsanus tau,* found along Atlantic coasts of US. Poison toadfish of S Amer. coast has poison gland at base of dorsal fin spines.

toadflax, herb of genus *Linaria*. Species include European *L. vulgaris* with yellow and orange flowers; naturalized weed in N America.

tobacco, plant of genus *Nicotiana* native to trop. America. Now cultivated in many parts of world, esp. US, India, Africa, China, USSR. Large ovate leaves, pink flowers. Dried and cured leaves of *N. tabacum* may be rolled into cigars, shredded for cigarettes and pipes; processed for chewing; powdered for snuff.

Tobago, island of lesser Antilles, West Indies, part of state of TRINIDAD and Tobago. Area: 116 sq. mi.; cap. Scarborough. Discovered (1498) by Columbus; settled by English (1616); changed hands regularly until united as Brit. colony with Trinidad (1899). Pop. (1960) 33,200.

Tobit, apocryphal book of OT. Included in canon of Douay version of Bible as *Tobias.*

tobogganing, winter sport, using light sledlike vehicle, carrying 1 or more persons. Perfected in Switzerland, using specially prepared runs, *e.g.* Cresta at St Moritz. Included in Winter Olympics.

Tobruk, Med. port of NE Libya, scene of heavy fighting in North African campaign in World War 2. Pop. (1964 est.) 15,867.

Toc H, international Christian social service organization founded (1915) by Rev. Neville Talbot and Rev. P. T. B. Clayton.

Tocqueville, Charles Alexis Henri Clerel de (1805–59), Fr. political historian. Predicted that in modern democracy his ideal of liberty would be sacrificed in interests of equality. Works include *De la Démocratie en Amérique* (1835–40) and *L'Ancien Régime et la Révolution* (1856).

Todd, Alexander Robertus, Baron Todd of Trumpington (1907–), Brit. biochemist; noted for research on chemical structure of nucleotides and nucleic acids. Awarded Nobel Prize for Chemistry (1957).

toga, in ancient Rome, white woollen garment worn over tunic, leaving right arm bare; roughly semicircular in shape, up to 6 yd. long by 2 yd. wide. Decoration varied according to rank.

Togo, republic of W Africa. Area: *c.* 21,850 sq. mi.; cap. Lomé. Part of Ger. colony of Togoland (1884), divided into Brit. and Fr. mandates (1919), became UN trusteeship (1946) part of Fr. community (1958), independent (1960). Economy based

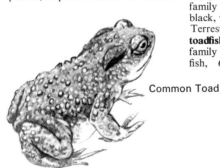

Common Toad

on agriculture, esp. palm products, cocoa, rubber. Main language

French; religions Animism, Christianity. Pop. (1965) 1,702,000.

Tojo, Hideki (1884–1948), Jap. army officer and politician. As P.M. (1941–4) instigated bombing (1941) of PEARL HARBOR; executed as war criminal.

Tokay, Tokaj, town of NE Hungary famous for sweet, golden wine.

Tokyo, city and port, cap. of Japan, on Honshu Is. Area: 265 sq. mi. Village of Edo founded 16th cent. Became imperial cap. and renamed (1868). Devastated by earthquake (1923). University city, centre of publishing and printing, varied manufacturing industries. Pop. (1965) 8,893,000.

Toledo, historic Sp. city, cap. of Toledo prov., C Spain, on Tagus R. Conquered by Romans 193 BC. Centre of Moorish, Spanish and Jewish culture in Middle Ages. Renowned for sword-making. Gothic cathedral (begun 1227) has paintings by El Greco. Pop. (1960) 40,651.

Toledo, city in NW Ohio, US, at mouth of Maumee R. on L. Erie. Shipping port of Great Lakes, rail and trade centre. Glass, metal, paint industries. Pop. (1965) 647,000.

Tolkien, John Ronald Reuel (1892–), Eng. writer. Author of popular fantasies *The Hobbit* (1937), *The Lord of the Rings* (3 vols., 1954–5).

Toller, Ernst (1893–1939), Ger. socialist and expressionist writer. Works, concerned chiefly with evils of war and exploitation of the masses, characterized by feeling of tragic hopelessness. They include *Masse Mensch, Der Deutsche Hinkemann* and *Die Maschinenstürmer.*

Tolpuddle Martyrs, six farm labourers transported (1834) to Australia as result of demands for higher wages. Pardoned (1836) after national protest.

Tolstoy, Count Leo Nikolayevich (1828–1910), Russ. writer and religious theorist. Interested in social reform. Works increasingly reflected Christian ideals of love and passive resistance to evil. Classic novels include *War and Peace* (1865–9), *Anna Karenina* (1875–7), *The Death of Ivan Ilyich* (1884) and *Resurrection* (1889–1900); also wrote dramas (*e.g. The Power of Darkness,* 1886).

Toltec, ancient (*c.* 6th–13th cent.) civilization of Mexico. Associated with archaeological sites found at Teotihuacán, Cholula, Tollán. Toltecs were skilled metal and stoneworkers, devised a calendar; religion centred on Quetzalcoatl. Supplanted by Aztecs (*c.* 13th cent.).

toluene, colourless inflammable liquid, by-product of coal-tar. Used as high explosive, as solvent, and in dyes and perfumes.

tomato, *Lycopersicon esculentum,* plant with red or yellow pulpy edible fruit. Native of S America; now cosmopolitan.

Tomonaga, Sin-itiro (1906–), Jap. physicist. Shared Nobel Prize for Physics (1965) for research on quantum field theory.

tom-tom, oriental flat metal gong of indefinite pitch. Also Amer. Indian drum played with hands, used in rituals and for signalling.

Tone, [Theobald] Wolfe (1763–98), Irish nationalist. Gained Fr. support for rebellion against English; involved in abortive efforts at invading Ireland (1796, 1798).

tone poem, musical composition of 19th cent. Characteristic of Romantic period, introduced interpretation of literary, dramatic and pictorial elements.

Tonga, Friendly Islands, group of small volcanic Polynesian islands of SE Pacific Ocean. Total area: 250 sq. mi.; cap. Nukualofa on Tongatapu. Independent kingdom under UK protection since 1900. Main exports copra, bananas. Pop. (1963) 74,000.

tongue, muscular organ in the floor of the mouth in man and most vertebrates. Covered by mucous membrane with small projections forming taste buds. Functions in mastication, taste, and, in man, speech.

tonic sol-fa, in music, notation system adapted from Fr. *solfège* and Ital. *solfeggio* systems, designed to simplify sight-reading. Notes are *doh, ray, me, fah, soh, lah, te, doh* indicating position on scale.

Tonkin, former Fr. protectorate in SE Asia, since 1949 part of Vietnam. Area now included in N Vietnam. Population largely Annamese.

tonsil, prominent mass of lymphoid tissue situated at each side of cavity at rear of mouth. Condition of **tonsilitis** characterized by inflammation of one or both tonsils.

Tonty or **Tonti, Henri de** (*c.* 1650–1704), Fr. explorer and fur trader in N America; with LA SALLE, explored to mouth of Mississippi R.

tony flower, *Oenothera fruticosa,* popular name for yellow-flowering garden variety of EVENING PRIMROSE.

topaz, mineral of acid igneous rocks. Variety used as gemstone is typically yellow and comes from Ural Mts., S Brazil and Ceylon. False topaz is citrine, a yellow quartz mineral.

topaz humming bird, *Topaza pella,* large brilliant green humming bird of S America.

topminnow, small fish of family Poeciliidae. Some used in mosquito control; others kept in trop. aquaria.

Torah, Hebrew name for first 5 books of OT. Contain Mosaic law. Gk. name Pentateuch.

Ruins of Hadrian's villa at Tivoli

The famous Kannon Temple in Tokyo

The Place du Capitole, Toulouse, with the 18th century town hall on the right

Tordesillas, town of Leon, C Spain. Treaty of Tordesillas (1494) between Spain and Portugal extended Papal Bull (1493) by giving Brazil to Portugal.

tormentil, *Potentilla tormentilla,* Eurasian herb with yellow flowers. Root contains astringent used in dyeing.

tornado, violent wind, travelling as funnel-shaped whirlwind with calm centre. Moves at 20–40 m.p.h. May devastate area 5–30 mi. wide. Esp. common E of Rocky Mts., US.

Toronto, city and cap. of Ontario, Canada, on N shore of L. Ontario. Commercial and transport centre, industries include food processing, iron and steel works. Fr. post destroyed (1759) by British. Called York, became (1796) cap. of Upper Canada; renamed Toronto 1834. Pop. (1966) 665,000.

Toronto, University of, non-sectarian university in Toronto, Ontario, Canada. Estab. (1843) as Kings College. Largest university in Canada, extensive graduate research facilities.

torpedo, self-propelled, underwater, explosive missile used in naval

Tortoise: left, skeleton; right, undershield

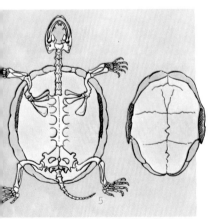

warfare. First developed (1866) by Robert Whitehead. Modern varieties propelled by jet engines, guided by remote control or automated systems.

Torquemada, Tomás de (1420–98), Sp. inquisitor-general. Took ruthless measures against heretics. Responsible for expulsion of Sp. Jews.

Torre Nilsson, Leopoldo (1924–), Argentinian film director. Best known films include *La Casa del Angel* (1956), *The Eavesdropper* (1966).

Torres Strait, channel, *c.* 80 mi. wide, between New Guinea and N tip of mainland of Australia. Contains Torres Strait Islands; area: *c.* 11 sq. mi. Pop. (1963) *c.* 4,000.

Torres Vedras, town of W Portugal. Fortifications, extending 28 mi. to R. Tagus, used by Wellington to hinder Fr. march against Lisbon in Peninsular War. Pop. 8,500.

Torricelli, Evangelista (1608–47), Ital. physicist; developed (1643) mercury barometer; improved the telescope and microscope.

torsion, type of force applied to solid body, esp. piece of machinery, having effect of twisting it spirally.

tortoise, reptile of order Chelonia, marine and freshwater varieties of TURTLE. Best known is small N African turtle, *Testudo graica.*

tortoise beetle, small tortoise-shaped beetle of family Chrysomelidae with metallic lustre.

tortoiseshell butterfly, brilliantly coloured butterfly of genus *Nymphalis,* esp. *N. milberti.* Larval state feeds on nettles.

torture, infliction of bodily pain as means of extorting confession or information from prisoners. Legally practised in England until 1640. Feature of religious persecution and totalitarian regimes.

Tory, Eng. polit. organization, began (17th cent.) as group supporting James II, later discredited for pro-Jacobite leanings. Most of 18th cent. spent in opposition to Whigs, revived under younger William Pitt. Declined after Reform Bill of 1832, evolved into CONSERVATIVE PARTY.

Toscanini, Arturo (1867–1957), Amer. conductor, b. Italy. Conducted (1898–1908) at La Scala, Milan. Principal conductor (1908–14) of Metropolitan Opera, New York; of NBC Symphony Orchestra (1937–54).

totalitarianism, system of absolute govt., in which social and economic activity of state organized hierarchically to eliminate opposition. Highly centralized govt. controlled by single official party. Doctrine usually appeals to nationalist and socialist

sentiment through aggressive foreign policy. Modern examples have been Fascist Italy and Nazi Germany.

totemism, belief of tribe or clan that its members are intimately related to, or descended from a plant or animal. Tribe symbol may be represented through tattoos, carvings. Practised in Australia and among Indians of N America.

Toubkal, highest peak (13,661 ft.) of Moroccan Atlas Mts.

toucan, fruit-eating bird of family Ramphastidae of trop. America. Black with yellow, red and white throat and breast; large bill.

touch-me-not, Eurasian annual plant of genus *Impatiens,* esp. *I. noli-me-tangere.* When ripe, pods burst on being touched, scattering seeds.

Toulon, city and seaport of SE France, cap. of Var department. Major Fr. naval base; industries include shipbuilding, tourism. Pop. (1962) 221,000.

Toulouse, historic city, cap. of Haute-Garonne department, S France. Formerly cap. of Visigoths and of Aquitaine. Has Romanesque basilica, Gothic cathedral, university (founded 1230). Now indust. centre. Pop. (1962) 329,000.

Toulouse-Lautrec, Henri de (1864–1901), Fr. painter and lithographer. His work, which includes brilliant posters for cabaret, mainly depicts scenes from life of Parisian cafe life.

Touraine, former prov. of C France, cap. Tours. Ruled by counts of Blois and Anjou (10th–11th cent.) and by kings of England (12th cent.). Fertile region, drained by Loire.

Touré, Sékou (1922–), Guinean trade unionist and polit leader. Pres. of Guinea (1958–).

tourmaline, silicate of boron and aluminium. Occurs in acid igneous rocks. Gem forms are blue, green and honey-yellow.

tournament, contest between groups of mounted knights using blunted weapons according to agreed rules. Began in 11th cent. in France and were great ceremonial occasions in Europe until 17th cent. Joust was contest between individuals.

Tourneur or **Turner, Cyril** (*c.* 1575–1626), Eng. dramatist. Wrote *The Revenger's Tragedy* (1607) and *The Atheist's Tragedy* (1611).

Tours, city of C France, cap. of Indre-et-Loire department, on Loire R. Cap. of former prov. of Touraine. Centre of rich agric. region. Manufactures silk, lace, stained glass. Contains 12th cent. cathedral. Pop. (1962) 151,000.

Tourmaline: crystals in calcite (left) and cut stone (right)

Tours, Battle of, decisive defeat of Saracen invaders between Tours and Poitiers, France, by Charles Martel (732). Effectively prevented further Saracen advance. Also called Battle of Poitiers.

Toussaint L'Ouverture, François Pierre Dominique (c. 1744–1803), Haitian patriot. Led rebellion (1791) of Negro slaves. Forced Brit. withdrawal (1793) from island. Conquered (1801) Santo Domingo, governed island until Napoleon intervened (1802). Captured and imprisoned by French.

Tower Bridge, bascule bridge over R. Thames, London, England (opened 1894). Roadway raised by hydraulic power to allow passage of ships.

Tower of London, fortress, garrison and museum in London. On N bank of R. Thames surrounded by moat and walls. Oldest part, the Keep or White Tower, built (1078) by William the Conqueror. Used as royal residence and as state prison. Tower Hill used as place of execution up to 18th cent. Brit. Crown Jewels on display in newly built Jewel House.

towhee, Amer. finch of genera *Pipilo* and *Chlorura.* Species include *P. erythnephthalmus,* of E N America, green-tailed towhee, *C. chlorura,* of Rocky Mts. and California towhee, *P. fuscus crissalis.*

Town and Country Planning, term for method of land use arranging residential, shopping and industrial areas to give pleasing appearance, maximum amenity and healthy conditions. Examples include 19th cent. Paris, Canberra (1913), Brasilia (1960).

Townes, Charles Hard (1915–   ), Amer. physicist. Shared Nobel Prize for Physics (1964) with Nikolai Basov and A. Prochorov for work on light and radio wave frequencies and for contributions to quantum electronics.

Townshend Acts (1767), legislation sponsored by Charles Townshend and passed by Eng. Parl. imposing duties on glass, lead, paints, paper and tea imported by Amer. colonies.

Ensuing colonial unrest led to Boston Massacre (1770), Boston Tea Party (1773).

toxaemia, condition of illness due to presence in the bloodstream of toxins or poisons produced by disease germ; or the abnormal function of certain organs, *e.g.* kidneys.

toxin, poisonous, usually unstable, compound generated by microorganisms or plants, or of animal origin. Some cause diseases such as tetanus, diphtheria.

Toynbee, Arnold (1852–83), Eng. pioneer economic historian and social reformer. Published *Lectures on the Industrial Revolution of the 18th Century in England* (1884). His nephew **Arnold Joseph Toynbee** (1889–   ), historian and philosopher. *Study of History* (10 vols., 1934–54) attempts to analyse rise and fall of civilizations.

Trabzon, Trebizond, colony of Byzantine empire founded (1204) by Alexius Comnenus. Included S shore of Black Sea, Georgia and Crimea. Fell to Ottoman Turks (1461).

trachea, windpipe, in man and other air-breathing vertebrates, tube extending from larynx to bronchi. Composed of rings of cartilage and muscle, lined with mucous membrane. Serves as passage for conveying air to and from lungs.

Tractarianism, doctrine of early leaders of 19th cent. OXFORD MOVEMENT towards Catholicism.

Trade Descriptions Act, legislation passed by UK parl. (1968), prohibiting misdescription of goods, services,

Scene from the life of St Martialis (13th cent.), from the cathedral of St Gatien at Tours

accommodation and facilities provided in course of trade; prohibits false or misleading indications as to prices.

trade union, association of employees in a particular trade, formed principally for purpose of collective bar-

Canadian National Exhibition Hall, Toronto

gaining over terms of employment and conditions of work. Developed (19th cent.) from voluntary associations in face of opposition on part of employers. Threat of STRIKE is union's ultimate bargaining weapon. Also *see* UNION, LABOUR.

trade wind, persistent wind of Atlantic and Pacific oceans. Blows from sub-trop. high pressure areas towards low pressure belt of Equator; towards NE in N hemisphere, and SE in S hemisphere. Name originated in days of sailing ships.

Trades Union Congress (TUC), voluntary association of Brit. trade unions (estab. 1868). Elects General Council from delegates of affiliated unions to negotiate with govt. and international labour bodies.

Trafalgar, Battle of (1805), decisive naval battle off SW Spain, W end of Straits of Gibraltar. Brit. fleet under HORATIO NELSON defeated combined fleets of France and Spain. Nelson fatally wounded.

tragedy, dramatic form dealing with subject of heroic stature whose character is flawed by some weakness which in the end causes his downfall, awakening in the spectator pity for the hero, fear at the fate which overtakes him and acceptance of ultimate rightness of the result. Evolved (6th cent.) from religious rites in ancient Greece culminating in plays of Aeschylus, Sophocles and Euripides. Fr. dramatists Corneille and Racine, influenced by plays of Seneca, adhered to unity of time, place and action, contrasting with English tragedy of Shakespeare. Modern tragedy often depicts figure of non-heroic stature in conflict with society.

Traherne, Thomas (*c.* 1637–74), Eng. writer. Metaphysical poetry (*e.g. Centuries of Meditations*) undiscovered until late 19th cent.

Trajan [Marcus Ulpius Trajanus] (AD 53–117), Roman emperor (AD 98–117), b. Spain. Conquered Dacia and much of Parthia. Constructed Forum Trajanum at Rome and founded library, Bibliotheca Ulpia.

tram, tram-car, carriage for conveying passengers. Runs on tracks of rails sunk into road surface; esp. powered by electricity. Horse-drawn introduced to UK in 19th cent.

tranquillizer, drug with sedative or calming effect without inducing sleep.

Transcaucasia, district of Asian USSR, S of Caucasus Mts. Now divided into Georgian, Azerbaijan and Armenian Soviet Socialist Republics. Combined as Transcaucasian SFSR 1923, divided 1936.

transcendentalism, in philosophy, mode of thought emphasizing intuitive and spiritual perception beyond (transcending) everyday, empirical experiences. First associated with Kant and other Ger. philosophers, developed in US in 19th cent. writings of Emerson, Thoreau.

transfusion *see* BLOOD TRANSFUSION.

transistor, electronic semiconductor device, invented (1948). Used for controlling flow of current, it is smaller, more efficient, more reliable, has longer life than equivalent thermionic valve [UK], vacuum tube [US]. Used in radio, television, spacecraft, computer engineering, *etc.*

Transkei, area of Cape prov., South Africa, set aside as native reserve of Bantustan. Area: 16,329 sq. mi. Main occupation is agriculture. Pop. *c.* 1,420,000.

transpiration, loss of water by evaporation in green plants. Generally takes place through leaves and is part of process of PHOTOSYNTHESIS.

transplant, organ, medical operation of transferring organ (heart, kidney, lung, *etc.*) from one person or animal to another. First successful human heart transplant carried out in South Africa in 1967.

transportation, punishment consisting of despatch of convicted persons overseas for varying lengths of time, often for life. Abolished in UK 1860s after extensive use of Australia as penal settlement.

Trans-Siberian Railway, line in USSR from Leningrad to Vladivostok (*c.* 5,400 mi.) on Pacific coast. Serves Moscow, Omsk, Novosibirsk, Irkutsk. Begun 1891, completed 1905.

Transvaal, prov. of NE South Africa. Area: 110,450 sq. mi.; main cities, Johannesburg, Pretoria. Settled by Voortrekkers from Cape Colony (1835) proclaimed independence (1856), annexed by Britain 1877. Boer rebellion (1880–1) resulted in self-govt.; re-annexed 1906; joined Union of South Africa 1910. Resources include gold at Witwatersrand, diamonds near Pretoria. Main industry stock raising. Pop. (1960) 6,273,477.

Transylvania, historic region of C plateau, Romania. Fertile area with vineyards and orchards, also abundant mineral resources, incl. gold, iron. Part of Austro-Hungarian empire. Seized by Romania (1918)

Part of Trajan's Column, Rome

and formally ceded by Hungary (1920). Towns include Cluj, Brasov.

trapdoor spider, arthropod of family Ctenizidae. Ambushes prey from silk-lined burrow with hinged lid.

Trappists, monks of R.C. Order of Cistercians of the Stricter Observance. Founded 17th cent. at La Trappe, France. Monks observe strict silence, live on bread and vegetables.

traveller's joy, old-man's-beard, *Clematis vitalba,* perennial woody vine of Europe and N Africa with fragrant white flowers.

traveller's tree, *Ravenala madagascariensis,* banana-like tree of Madagascar. Edible seeds; cup-like leaf sheath holds watery sap.

trawler, large fishing boat equipped for trawling, *i.e.* to catch bottom-feeding fish, *e.g.* haddock, cod. Nets are designed to be dragged through water at desired depth.

treason, crime of seriously endangering safety of country to which person owes allegiance or of attempting to overthrow sovereign or govt. In US, may be punishable by death; in UK, by life imprisonment.

Tree, Sir Herbert Beerbohm (1853–1917), Eng. actor-manager. Estab. Royal Academy of Dramatic Art; built Her Majesty's Theatre, London.

tree, perennial plant with permanent, woody, self-supporting main stem or trunk. Usually grows to considerable height, developing branches and foliage.

tree creeper, small insectivorous bird, esp. of family Certhiidae of temp.

Tree Frog

regions. Feet adapted to climbing. Species include common tree creeper, *Certhia familiaris.*

tree fern, fern of family Cyatheaceae found in trop. and sub-trop. regions, esp. in Australia and New Zealand. Trunk-like stem with foliage at top.

tree frog, arboreal frog of family Polypedatidae of trop. and temp. regions with adhesive suckers on toes.

tree mallow, herb, shrub or tree of genus *Lavatera.* Several grown in gardens, esp. *L. arborea.*

tree of heaven *see* AILANTHUS.

tree sparrow, *Passer montanus,* small European sparrow with black spot on ear coverts. *Spizella arborea* breeds in N North America.

treehopper, small leaping insect of family Membracidae. Feeds on juices of plants.

treerunner, brightly coloured Austral. NUTHATCH of genus *Neositta.*

tree-shrew, insectivorous, arboreal mammal of family Tupaiadae of SE Asia. Bushy tail and long pointed snout.

trefoil, plant of genus *Trifolium* native to temp. and sub-trop. regions. Red, purple, yellow or white flower heads.

trek, term used for migration on foot, applied to Great Trek made by Boers from Cape Colony, South Africa. In protest against Brit. rule, they moved N (1838) and founded Transvaal.

Trelawney, Sir Jonathan (1650– 1721), one of 7 Eng. bishops imprisoned (1688) by James II for signing petition against declaration of indulgence.

trematode, fluke, parasitic flatworm of class Trematoda with one or more external suckers for adhesion.

tremolite, grey-white mineral; variety of AMPHIBOLE.

Trenchard, Hugh Montague, 1st Viscount (1873–1956), Brit. air marshal. Chiefly responsible for organization of Royal Air Force on present lines and for estab. of RAF college at Cranwell.

Trent, Council of (1545–63), ecumenical council convened by Paul III, continued under Julius III and Pius IV. Discussed concessions to restore religious peace after Reformation. Protestant demands considered impracticable. Council defined Catholic doctrine and discipline and effected reform of many eccles. abuses.

Trent Affair, diplomatic incident (1861) of Amer. Civil War involving removal of 2 Southerners from Brit. ship *Trent* by Union ship *Jacento.* After Brit. protest, prisoners were released (1862).

Trentino-Alto Adige, autonomous region of N Italy. Area: 5,255 sq. mi.; cap. Trento. Bordering Switzerland and Austria, formed Austrian prov. of S Tyrol (1801–1919). Ger. population of Alto Adige has agitated for reunion with Austria. Chiefly mountainous, forested, many lakes and resorts. Pop. (1965) 790,000.

Trenton, cap. of state of New Jersey, US, on Delaware R., 1st settled by Quakers (1679). Became state cap. 1790. Industries include pottery and ceramics. Pop. (1965) 242,000.

Trenton, Battle of, incident (1776) of Amer. Revolution in which George Washington crossed Delaware R. and captured Hessians by surprise.

Trevelyan, George Macauley (1876– 1962), Eng. historian. Works include *History of England* (1926), *England under the Stuarts* (1944).

Trevithick, Richard (1771–1833), Brit. inventor and engineer. Designed water pressure pumping engine, high pressure steam-engine for land transport, steam threshing machine. Constructed (1804) 1st steam locomotive to run on rails.

triangle, in geometry, plane figure bounded by 3 straight lines. Equilateral triangle has 3 equal sides. Right triangle has one angle of 90°. Area of a triangle is the product of half of one base and the corresponding altitude.

triangle, small percussion musical instrument. Consists of bar of steel bent in shape of triangle, struck with small steel rod.

Triassic *see* GEOLOGICAL TABLE.

Tribes of Israel, in OT, name sometimes used for descendants of 12 sons of Jacob.

tribune, name assigned to various officers of ancient Rome. Military tribunes were commanders of the army. Tribunes of the Plebs were the 2 elected defenders of ordinary citizens' rights, constituting type of court of appeal.

trichinosis, disease in man and animals caused by infection with parasite *Trichina spiralis.* Principally transmitted by eating inadequately cooked pork. Characterized by fever, diarrhoea, muscular pains.

Trier, city in W Germany, on Mosel R., 5 mi. below Luxembourg frontier. Important Roman garrison; extensive Roman remains. Birthplace of Karl Marx. Pop. 90,000.

Trieste, city of NE Italy, port at head of Adriatic. Made free port (1719) by Austria, became trade outlet for C Europe. Annexed by Italy (1919). Under Allied military govt. from 1945. UN Protectorate (1947); in 1954 city assigned to Italy, coastal strip of 200 sq. mi. to Yugoslavia,

which retained use of port. Industries include shipbuilding, oil refining. Pop. (1965) 281,000.

triggerfish, fish of family Balistidae inhabiting warm seas. Erectile spines on anterior dorsal fin. Both edible and poisonous varieties.

trigonometry, branch of mathematics which deals with relations between sides and angles of triangle. Trigonometric functions express ratios of different parts. Used in mathematical and scientific calculations.

Trilling, Lionel (1905–), Amer. writer and critic. Essays published in *The Liberal Imagination* (1950), *Beyond Culture* (1965).

trillium, N Amer. plant of genus *Trillium* of family Liliaceae. Stems have whorl of 3 leaves and large solitary pink or white flower. Species include wake robin, *T. grandiflorum.*

trilobite, class of extinct marine arthropods, found in Palaeozoic rocks. Had 3-lobed body, up to 18 in. long.

Trinidad and Tobago, republic of West Indies, member of Brit. Commonwealth of Nations, comprising islands of Trinidad and TOBAGO. Trinidad area: 1,864 sq. mi.; joint cap. Port-of-Spain. Discovered by Columbus (1498). Settled by Spaniards, ceded to UK (1802). Joined as colony by Tobago (1899). In 1958 became seat of govt. of West Indies Federation, dissolved 1962.

Trinity, in Christianity, 3 aspects of Divine Being, *e.g.* God the Father, Son, and Holy Ghost. Doctrine asserted early in the religion, estab. in Nicene Creed.

Trinity House, name given to UK authority superintending lighthouses

Port of Spain, capital of Trinidad and Tobago

and pilotage. Orig. given charter by Henry VIII.

Triple Alliance, formed 1882 when Italy joined Germany and Austria-Hungary (united by Dual Alliance of 1879). Growing conflict of interest with other European states (*see* TRIPLE ENTENTE) increased diplomatic tension prior to World War 1.

Triple Entente, diplomatic accord between France, Russia and UK, developed during 1890s and 1900s. Grew out of concern over German commercial and colonial expansion. Though not formal, alliance held together at outbreak of World War 1.

Tripoli, city, Med. port and joint cap. (with Benghazi) of Libya. Cap. of Tripolitania prov. Orig. Tyrian outpost *c.* 750 BC. Acquired from Turkey by Italy (1911); fell to British (1943) in World War 2. Pop. (1964) 214,000.

Tripolitan War, war fought between US and Barbary States of N Africa (1801–5) in attempt to safeguard Amer. ships in Med. Sea from Barbary pirates.

trireme, sailing vessel equipped with 2 masts and 3 banks of oars. Prob. originated in Sidon or Tyre; copied by Greeks and Romans. When used in fighting, relied solely on slave-oarsmen; sails and oarsmen used in carrying cargo.

Tristan and Isolde or **Tristram and Yseult,** medieval tale of Celtic origin. Tells of Tristan's journey to Ireland to bring Princess Isolde to Cornwall as bride of his uncle, King Mark. On return journey, pair drink love potion which binds them eternally in love. Tale incorporated in Arthurian legend in Malory's *Morte d'Arthur.* Also used by Tennyson in *Idylls of the King* (1859–85), and by Wagner in music drama *Tristan and Isolde.*

Tristan da Cunha, volcanic island in S Atlantic. Area: 40 sq. mi.; only settlement, Edinburgh. Frozen crayfish only export. Weather and radio stations. Discovered (1506) by Portuguese; annexed (1816) by British. Evacuated (1961) after volcanic eruption; resettled 1963. Pop. (1963) 280.

Triton, in Gk. myth., son of Poseidon and Amphitrite. Represented as fish-shaped from the waist, and shown blowing on conch shell.

Triumvirate, term applied in ancient

Rome to govt. carried on by 3 men. First Triumvirate (60 BC) formed by Caesar, Pompey and Crassus, 2nd Triumvirate (43 BC) by Octavian, Antony and Lepidus.

Trois Rivières or **Three Rivers,** city of Quebec, Canada, on St Lawrence R. Pulp and paper production centre. Founded 1634 by Champlain. Pop. (1966) 58,000.

Trojan War, in Gk. myth., war waged by Greeks on Trojans to recover Helen, wife of Menelaus abducted by Paris of Troy. Gods fought on both sides. First 9 years indecisive; in 10th year occurred quarrel between Achilles and Agamemnon, Achilles' refusal to fight, death of Patroclus, Achilles' return to war and death of Hector; Trojans reinforced by Amazons and Ethiopians; Achilles slain by Paris or Apollo; summoning of Neoptolemus and Philoctetes by Greeks. Finally, Greeks simulated departure, leaving WOODEN HORSE outside Troy; despite warnings of Cassandra and Laocoon, Trojans brought it into city, enabling Gk. soldiers hidden inside to open gates to army and sack the city.

Trollope, Anthony (1815–82), Eng. novelist. Portrays Victorian characters and social structure, esp. in Barsetshire series set in ordinary but imaginary county, and the Parliamentary series. Best-known works *Barchester Towers* (1857) and *Last Chronicle of Barset* (1867).

trombone, brass musical instrument, formerly called sackbut. Known from 15th cent. Fitted with sliding tube which controls pitch. Orchestras today usually have 1 bass and 2 tenor trombones.

Tromp, Maarten Harpertzoon van (1597–1653), Dutch admiral. Victory over Sp. fleet marked end of Spain's role as great naval power. In Dutch War fought series of engagements against British under Blake and later Monk, ending in his own defeat and death off Dutch coast.

Trondheim, formerly Nidaros, cap. and ice-free port of Sor-Trondelag prov., C Norway. Founded (997) by King Olaf I; has Gothic cathedral. Industries include shipbuilding, sawmilling. Pop. (1965) 114,000.

tropic bird, sea bird of family Phaethontidae found chiefly in trop.

regions. White plumage with black markings; elongated tail feathers.

Tropic of Cancer, line of latitude $23\frac{1}{2}°$ N of Equator, passing through Mexico, S China, India, Arabia, Sahara Desert. Northernmost limit of TROPICS.

Tropic of Capricorn, line of latitude $23\frac{1}{2}°$ S of Equator, passing through South Africa, Australia, central S America. Southernmost limit of TROPICS.

tropical fish, aquarium fish requiring controlled water temperatures. Varieties include angel fish, mollys, danio, gourami, swordtail and zebra fish.

Tropics, Torrid Zone, region of Earth lying between Tropics of Cancer and Capricorn. Characterized by uniformly high temperatures, by heavy predictable rainfall, esp. near Equator. Typical vegetation is trop. rain forest, evergreen, dense luxuriant vegetation, growing all year round.

tropism, natural movement of plants in reaction to external influences. A sunflower turning to face the light exemplifies phototropism; roots turning downward exemplify geotropism.

troposphere, general name for lowest part of Earth's atmosphere, extending to *c.* 5–10 mi. above surface of Earth. Contains most atmospheric water vapour. Separated from STRATOSPHERE by **tropopause.**

Troppau, Congress of, agreement (1820), signed by Austria, Russia and Prussia, that any state in which a revolution occurred would be brought back into Holy Alliance, if necessary, by force.

Trotsky, Leon, orig. Lev Davidovitch Bronstein (1879–1940), Russ. revolutionary. Before major role in 1917 Oct. Revolution, spent years exiled from Russia for Marxist activities. After Bolshevik triumph, organized victorious Red Army during civil war (1918–20). After Lenin's death (1924), led opposition to Stalin, became foremost spokesman for international Communism. Expelled from party (1927), banished from USSR (1929). Assassinated in Mexico City, prob. at Stalin's instigation.

troubadours, lyric poets of 11th to 13th cent. in S France, Spain and N Italy. Wrote in *langue d'oc* (Provençal). Developed elaborate form of lyric poetry intended to be spoken with musical accompaniment. Subjects were love and chivalry, esp. ideal of courtly love.

trout, freshwater game and food fish of family Salmonidae, esp. of genera

Tropical fish: diamond gourami

Veiled Tuareg man

Salmo and *Salvelinus*. Species include European river or brown trout, *S. trutta*, and rainbow trout, *S. gairdnerii* of N America.

trouvères, Fr. poets of 11th–14th cent. Wrote in language of N and C France (*langue d'oïl*). Considerably influenced by TROUBADOURS. Subjects of narrative poems were mainly epic and chivalrous romance.

Troy, Ilium, Ilion, ancient stronghold of NW Asia Minor, near mouth of Dardanelles on Aegean Sea. In Gk. myth., founded by Ilus, son of Tros. Excavation of Heinrich Schliemann revealed remains of 9 superimposed cities, earliest built before 3000 BC; 6th settlement, contemporary with Middle Bronze Age in Greece (*c.* 1900–1600 BC), forms subject of TROJAN WAR; 9th settlement declined when rejected as cap. by Constantine the Great.

Troyes, city of Aube dept., France, on R. Seine. Ancient cap. of Champagne region. By Treaty of Troyes (1420) Henry V of England formally made heir to Fr. throne and received Catherine de Valois in marriage.

Trucial States, Trucial Oman, seven independent sheikdoms on Persian Gulf, in treaty relationship with UK since 1820. Total area: *c.* 32,000 sq. mi.; largest town, Dubai. Region mainly desert and mountainous. Oil reserves being developed. Pop. (est.) 180,000.

Trudeau, Pierre Elliott (1919–), Canadian polit. leader, P.M. (1968–). Liberal Min. of Justice before succeeding Lester Pearson as P.M. Imposed War Measures Act after political kidnappings in Quebec (1970).

truffle, subterranean edible European fungi of genus *Tuber*.

Trujillo Molina, Rafael Leonidas (1891–1961), Dominican army officer and politician. By military coup, became Pres. of Dominican Repub. (1930–38, 1942–52). Retained effective power until 1960. Assassinated following year.

Truman, Harry S. (1884–), 33rd US Pres. (1945–53), Democrat. Senator from Missouri (1935–45), elected (1944) Vice Pres., became Pres. on F. D. Roosevelt's death. Authorized use of 1st atomic bomb to end war with Japan. Attended POTSDAM CONFERENCE (1945) to settle post-war polit. problems. Promulgated 'Truman Doctrine' (1947) to aid European countries against spread of Communism and put into operation Marshall Plan. Re-elected (1948) in surprise victory over Thomas Dewey, 'Fair Deal' programme thwarted by Congress, 2nd term dominated by Korean War.

trumpet, brass wind instrument. A long tube bent twice on itself, opening out at extremity. Modern trumpet has 3 valves, giving pitch of B b or A.

trumpet flower, general name for various plants with trumpet-shaped flowers. *See* TECOMA; NARCISSUS.

trumpet-creeper, *Campis radicans,* N Amer. woody vine with pinnate leaves and large red trumpet-shaped flowers.

trunkfish, boxfish, brightly coloured trop. fish of family Ostraciontidae. Box-like body encased in bony plates.

trustee, one who legally holds property in trust for another. He must not make profit out of his trust and may appoint a solicitor to act as agent. Liable for loss caused by his own or his agent's negligence.

trusteeship, territorial, system of agreed control of non self-governing territories; administered by UN to promote welfare and preparation for self-govt. Supervised by Trusteeship Council of UN members. Replaces mandates operated by League of Nations.

trypsin, enzyme produced by vertebrate pancreas. Converts proteins into amino-acids and poly-peptides. Necessary for digestion processes of most animals.

Tsar, Czar, title orig. of Grand Dukes of Muscovy from 1547. Assumed by Peter the Great as emperor of Russia (1721). Nicholas II (d. 1918) was last Russ. Tsar.

tsetse fly, bloodsucking fly of genus *Glossina* of C and S Africa. Transmits sleeping sickness and other diseases to man; causes nagana in domestic animals, esp. cattle.

Tshombe, Moise Kapenda (1919–69), Congolese polit. leader. Pres. (1960) of secessionist Katanga. Charged with complicity in murder of PATRICE LUMUMBA. Exiled after breaking pledge to join Katanga with Congo. P.M. of Congo (1964–5). Went to Europe after army coup (1965). Sentenced to death, kidnapped and detained in Algiers (1967), where he died.

Tsimshian, group of N Amer. Indian tribes speaking Tsimshian or Chimmesyan dialects. Now live on reservations in Brit. Columbia and Alaska.

Tsin or **Ch'in,** dynasty of China (265–420). Unsettled period marked by expansion of Buddhism. Dynasty founded by Emperor Hwangti. He extended empire considerably, estab. centralized govt. and began building of Great Wall.

Tsinan, Chinan, historic city of E China, cap. of Shantung prov. Founded *c.* 2200 BC. Main industry textiles. Pop. (1957 est.) 862,000.

Tsinghai, Chinghai, prov. of W China, mainly grassland with salt lake Koko Nor. Area: 262,236 sq. mi.; cap. Sining. Rich mineral resources, with cattle breeding major industry. Pop. (1953) 1,676,534.

Tsingtao, seaport of Shantung prov., China, on Yellow Sea. Developed by Germany during occupation (1898–1914). Industries include textiles, engineering. Pop. (1957 est.) 1,121,000.

Tsushima, 2 Jap. islands SE of Korea. Area: 271 sq. mi. Scene of decisive naval victory by Japan in Russo-Japanese War (1905).

Tuareg, nomadic Moslem Berber matriarchal peoples of Sahara desert and Sudan. Only Saharan people among whom men wear veil and women do not.

tuba, bass wind instrument of SAXHORN family. Used in orchestras and in most brass bands.

tuber *see* BULB.

tuberculosis (TB), infectious disease of man and some other vertebrates caused by organism *Mycobacterium*

The ruins of Troy

1. Darwin Tulip; 2. Rembrandt Tulip; 3. Double Tulip; 4. Parrot Tulip

tuberculosis. Formerly called consumption. Characterized by tubercles (nodular lesions). May be acute or chronic; affects almost any tissue of the body, esp. lungs. BCG vaccine used to produce immunity.

Tubman, William Vacanarat Shadrach (1895–1971), Liberian statesman and lawyer. Became pres. 1944.

Tucker, Sophie, orig. Sophie Abruza (1884–1966), Amer. singer and vaudeville actress, b. Russia. Known as 'the last of the red hot mommas'.

Tudor, House of, Eng. ruling family (1485–1603), estab. by Henry Tudor, who took throne as Henry VII ending WARS OF THE ROSES. Succeeded by Henry VIII, Edward VI, Mary I and Elizabeth I.

Tuileries, former royal palace, Paris, France. Planned by Catherine de Medici, begun 1564, in present Tuileries Gardens. Used as residence by Louis XVI and Napoleon I. Destroyed by fire (1871).

Tula, historic city, cap. of Tula prov., Russ. SFSR, USSR. Founded 12th cent. Govt. armament factory estab. by Peter the Great. Indust. and transport centre. Pop. (1967) 371,000.

tularaemia, infectious disease of small mammals and man caused by bacterium *Pasturella tularensis.* Transmitted to man by insects or by handling infected animals. In man, characterized by headache and fever.

tulip, bulbous plant of genus *Tulipa* with large cup-shaped solitary flowers of various colours. Most garden tulips are variants of *T. gesneriana* introduced into Europe from Turkey (16th cent.).

tulip tree, tulip poplar, *Liriodendron tulipifera,* large magnoliaceous tree from E N America with tulip-like flowers. Wood used in furniture making. In Australia, an evergreen tree, *Lagunaria pattersonii,* of mallow family with pink flowers.

Tull, Jethro (1674–1741), Eng. agriculturalist, developed mechanical seed drill (1701).

tumbleweed, plant which breaks away from its roots in autumn and is blown by the wind, scattering seeds. Abundant in prairie regions as Russian thistle, *Sabola kali* and amaranth, *Amaranthus graecizans.*

tumour, tumor, abnormal or diseased swelling in any part of the body, esp. an overgrowth of new tissue that is autonomous and serves no useful purpose. Benign when localized and harmless; malignant if diseased and spreads to other parts of the body.

tuna *see* TUNNY.

tundra, area of cold deserts of N Eurasia and N America within Arctic circle. Characterized by permafrost, covered by snow and ice in winter, thawing of top soil in summer. Vegetation includes lichens, mosses and fast-growing low shrubs.

tung-oil tree, tree of genus *Aleurites,* esp. *A. fordii* of China. Seeds yield tung oil used in manufacture of paint, varnish, linoleum.

tungsten, hard, malleable, acid-resistant metallic element. High melting point and low electrical consumption make it suitable for use in lamp filaments, X-ray tubes, *etc.* Tungsten carbide used in drills and cutting tools.

Tunis, cap. of Tunisia, connected with Med. Sea by canal. Founded by Phoenicians, became cap. 13th cent. Now comprises native city, Jewish quarter, Kasbah and modern suburbs, laid out by French. Nearby are ruins of Carthage. Pop. (1966) 764,000.

tunisflower, *Oenothera fruticosa,* yellow flowering plant related to evening primrose.

Tunisia [Al Jumhuriyatu Tunis], republic of N Africa. Area: 48,332 sq. mi.; cap. Tunis. Settled *c.* 1200 BC by Phoenicians; centre of Roman power in N Africa. Ruled by Byzantines until

7th cent. Arab conquest. Held by Turkey from 1579. Became Fr. protectorate (1881); gained independence (1956). Has narrow coastal

lowlands, with Atlas Mts., fertile valleys, salt pans and Sahara desert to S. Economy largely based on agriculture and mining. Main language, Arabic; religion, Islam. Unit of currency, dinar. Pop. (1963) 4,598,000.

tunnel, passage-way cut underground to facilitate communications. Longest rly. tunnel is Simplon, Switzerland ($12\frac{1}{4}$ mi., opened 1922); longest road, Mont Blanc, France-Italy (7·2 mi., 1965); longest in world Chesapeake Bay Bridge Tunnel, US ($17\frac{1}{2}$ mi., 1963). Earth tunnels normally circular lined with rings of cast iron or pre-cast concrete. Shield tunnel driving when circular ring is pressed forward by hydraulic jacks, 1st used by Brunel under R. Thames (1824).

tunny, tuna, largest game fish of mackerel family. Widely distributed. Horse mackerel or bluefin of genus *Thunnus* is a warm water tuna, 60–200 lb. in weight. Tuna fisheries in Med., Atlantic and Pacific waters; large quantities canned.

Tupper, Sir Charles (1821–1915), Canadian polit. leader; Cons. P.M. (1896). Premier (1863–7) of Nova Scotia, instrumental in province's entry into Canadian Confederation (1867).

turbine, rotary steam engine. Developed by Sir Charles Parsons (1884). Basic forms are impulse and reaction depending on whether fluid strikes or passes over blades of motor causing it to rotate and provide mechanical energy. Widely used in ship and aircraft propulsion.

turbot, *Rhombus maximus,* flatfish of North Sea and Med. Sea. Popular food fish.

Turenne, Henri de la Tour d'Auvergne, Vicomte de (1611–75), Fr. army officer. Victorious marshal of Fr. troops at end of Thirty Years War. Sided with princes in FRONDE, but joined court party and defeated Condé in battle of the Dunes (1658). Killed after victory at Sinzheim (1674) during 3rd Dutch War.

Turgenev, Ivan Sergeyevich (1818–83), Russ. author. Concerned to alleviate social ills, esp. of serfs, he opposed destructive attitudes of contemporary revolutionaries. Works include *A Sportsman's Sketches* (1852), *A Nest of Gentlefolk* (1858), *Fathers and Sons* (1862).

Turgot, Anne Robert Jacques (1727–81), Fr. economist and comptroller-general of finances (1774–6). Attempted drastic reform of economy incl. removal of tax immunities and estab. of free trade. Dismissal forced by aristocracy.

Turin, Ital. city in Piedmont region at foot of Alps, NW Italy, on Po. R. A Roman city, became cap. of Savoy (1562), of Italy (1861–4). Motor car and silk manufacturing centre. Pop. (1965) 1,112,000.

Turkestan or **Turkistan,** region of C Asia, hist. trade and immigration route. Now divided between China, USSR and Afghanistan.

Turkey, Turkish Republic [Türkiye cumhureyti], republic partly in Eur-

ope and partly in Asia. Area: 296,190 sq. mi.; cap Ankara; major cities, Istanbul, Izmir. Rugged mountains encircle high inland plateau with narrow peripheral coastal plains.

The Turkish town of Selcuk is in the ancient area of Ionia which was the cradle of Greek civilization in the 7th-6th cent. BC

Tunisian market square

The city of Turin: in the foreground is the Ponte Vittorio Emanuele I over the River Po

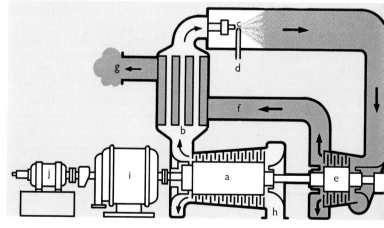

Diagram of a Gas Turbine: (a) air compressor (b) heat exchange (c) combustion chamber (d) fuel supply (e) turbine (f) channel for burning gases to b. (g) exhaust (h) air inlet (i) dynamo (j) starting motor

Turkey proper formed 11th cent. after arrival of Turkic tribes. Formed OTTOMAN EMPIRE which expanded 13th-18th cent., mainly in Med. Europe; Ottoman sultanate abolished 1922. Turkey became repub. through efforts of Nationalists under Kemal Ataturk. Islam ceased to be state religion and programme of westernization vigorously implemented. Economy depends largely on agriculture. Mining and manufacturing of secondary importance. Main language Turkish. Unit of currency, Turkish lira. Pop. (1964) 32,901,000.

turkey, *Meleagris gallopavo,* large Amer. game bird, domesticated in many parts of the world. Bronze coloured plumage; male has fan-like expansible tail; up to 4 ft. long and 35 lb. in wt. Intensively reared for flesh.

Turkic, branch of Altaic languages. Spoken in Turkey, E Europe, N and C Asia.

Turkmen Soviet Socialist Republic, C Asian constituent repub. of USSR, formed 1924. Area: 187,000 sq. mi.; cap. Ashkhabad. Lies E of Caspian, contains Kara-Kum desert. Industries mainly agric., by means of irrigation. Some mineral resources, incl. petroleum. Pop. (1967) 2,029,000.

Turks and Caicos Islands, group of small W Indian islands, N of Haiti.

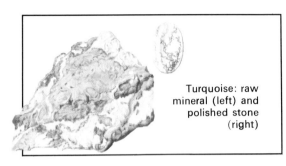

Turquoise: raw mineral (left) and polished stone (right)

Total area: 166 sq. mi. Discovered 1512. Dependency of Jamaica (1873-1962), Brit. colony. Pop. (1962) 6,000.

turmeric, tumeric, *Curcuma longa,* East Indian perennial herb with large aromatic yellow rhizome. Ground rhizome yields spice used as condiment and colouring agent.

Turner, Frederick Jackson (1861-1932) Amer. historian. Principal works *The Significance of the Frontier in American History* (1893) and *The Rise of the New West* (1906).

Turner, Joseph Mallord William (1775-1851), Eng. landscape painter. After visiting Italy, developed free, abstract technique attempting to capture effect of light on colour. Greatly influenced work of the Impressionists. Paintings include *Calais Pier, Fighting Téméraire, Rain, Steam and Speed.*

Turner, Nat (1800-31) Amer. Negro slave insurrectionist. Hanged with 19 others for killing over 50 whites in home of his master.

turnip, biennial plant with edible tubers, related to the cabbage. Cultivated in temp. zones as cattle food and vegetable. Chief varieties are *Brassica rapa* with white tubers and rutabaga or Swedish turnip, *B. napobrassica.*

turnpike, stretch of road paid for and maintained by fees collected from users at toll-gates. Authorized in England in 1346 and in N America in 1785. Now usually state-owned.

turnstone, widely distributed migratory shorebird of genus *Arenaria* related to the plover. Black and white

Interior at Petworth by William Turner

plumage. Species include black turn-stone, *A. melanocephala* of N Amer. Pacific coast.

turpentine, fluid obtained by distillation of gum or resin from pine and other trees. Used in making of wax polishes and for thinning paints and varnishes.

Turpin, Richard ('Dick') (1706–39), Eng. highwayman. Reputed to have made overnight ride from London to York, subject of several legends. Arrested for horse theft and hanged at York.

turquoise, mineral, hydrous aluminium phosphate with some copper. Valued as gemstone. Best specimens found in Iran. Colour varies from sky blue to apple green.

turtle, reptile of order Chelonia comprising aquatic and terrestrial species. Body encased in shell of bone covered by horny shields; horny-edged toothless jaws; retractile head, limbs and tail. Species include SNAPPING TURTLE; hawksbill turtle, *Eretmochelys imbricata,* which yields tortoiseshell; edible green turtle, *Chelonia mydas,* of trop. and sub-trop. seas.

turtle dove, bird of genus *Streptopelia* of Europe and Africa. European *S. turtur* has grey-blue plumage with long tail.

Tuscan, standard literary dialect of Italian. Dominant since Dante, Petrarch and Boccaccio (14th cent.).

Tuscany, Toscàna, mountainous region of N Italy. Approx. area of ancient Etruria. Area: 8,876 sq. mi.; cap. Florence; major cities, Leghorn, Lucca, Carrara, Pisa, Siena. Contains Apennine Mts., Arno R., also island of Elba. Agriculture important esp. olive growing and viticulture. Pop. (1961) 3,286,160.

Tuscarora, N Amer. Iroquoian Indian tribe. Orig. occupied N Carolina. After war with colonists (1711–13), moved N to join Iroquois Confederacy.

Tussaud, Marie (1760–1850), Fr. wax-modeller. During Fr. Reign of Terror forced to make models of important guillotine victims using heads from decapitated bodies. Moved to London where she opened (1802) wax museum.

tussock moth, dull-coloured moth of family Lymantriidae. Larvae have tufts of hair on body.

Tutankhamen (d. *c.* 1340 BC), Egyptian pharaoh of 18th dynasty. His tomb in Valley of the Kings, excavated (1922) yielded magnificent examples of jewellery, pottery, furnishings, *etc.* of ancient Egypt.

Twain, Mark, orig. Samuel Lang-

Part of a mural in the tomb of Tutankhamen

horne Clemens (1835–1910), Amer. writer, humourist. Author of classics *The Adventures of Tom Sawyer* (1876) and *The Adventures of Huckleberry Finn* (1884), which recall his Mississippi boyhood. Other novels include satirical *The Gilded Age* (1873), *The Prince and the Pauper* (1881) and *A Connecticut Yankee at King Arthur's Court* (1889).

Tweed, William Marcy (1823–78), Amer. politician. Through Tammany leadership, controlled Democratic party nominations and patronage in New York city. Achieved wealth from fraudulent activities. Died in prison after exposure of wholesale graft.

tweed, rough-surfaced woollen fabric woven in various patterns. It is durable and almost weather-proof. Best-known made in Harris, Scotland.

Tweedsmuir, John Buchan, 1st Baron (1875–1940), Brit. author and statesman. Best known for adventure novels, esp. *The Thirty-nine Steps* (1915), *Greenmantle* (1916), and for biographies of Cromwell, Julius Caesar, Montrose, *etc.* Earlier practised law (from 1901), entered parl. as Cons. M.P. (1927). Gov.-General of Canada (1935–40).

Twelfth Day, the 12th day after Christmas, *i.e.* 6 Jan. Important Christian feast, commemorating baptism of Christ and visit of Wise Men to Bethlehem.

Twelve Disciples, men chosen by Jesus to be his original followers;

Andrew, Simon Peter, James (son of Zebedee), John, Philip, Nathanael (Bartholomew), Matthew, James (son of Alphaeus), Simon, Thomas, Jude (brother of James), Judas Iscariot. Number symbolic of 12 tribes of Israel.

Twelve Tables, earliest code of Roman law. Drawn up 451–449 BC with object of stating customary law and abolishing patrician privileges. Only fragments survive.

twelve-tone system, system of musical composition utilizing 12 chromatic tones of octave. Developed by SCHOENBERG and his followers.

twelve-wired bird of paradise, *Seleucides ignotus,* paradise bird of Australasia. *See* illus. p. 564.

twins, 2 offspring born of one pregnancy. Identical twins born from division of a single fertilized egg are of the same sex and closely resemble each other. Fraternal twins born of separately fertilized eggs may differ in sex and appearance.

twite, *Carduelis flavirostris,* small N European brown moorland finch with yellow bill.

Two Sicilies, Kingdom of, union of 2 kingdoms of Sicily and Naples, achieved (1816) under Bourbon-Sicily house. Merged (1861) with Italy.

two-stroke engine, internal combustion engine having one power stroke for every 2 instead of every 4 strokes. Develops more power for less weight than FOUR-STROKE ENGINE.

Twelve-wired Bird of Paradise

Tyburn, small underground stream in London, England. Gave name to gallows at W end of Oxford Street, last used 1783.

Tyler, John (1790–1862), 10th US Pres. (1841–5), Whig. Resigned Senate seat held as states rights Democrat (1827–36) and joined Whig Party in protesting Pres. Jackson's policies on finance and federal powers. As pres. lost Whig and cabinet support by siding with the Democrats. By Webster-Ashburton Treaty, Texas annexed (1845) under his plan.

Tyler, Wat (d. 1381), Eng. rebel leader. Financial restrictions on peasant class forced PEASANTS' REVOLT, led by Tyler. Early successes ended with his murder.

tympanic membrane, ear-drum, tough membrane, separating outer ear from inner ear and bones transmitting vibration to brain.

Tyndale, Tindal or **Tindale, William** (c. 1484–1536), Eng. religious reformer; influenced by Luther. Translation of NT into vernacular suppressed by Cardinal Wolsey. Wrote tracts advocating principles of Reformation; burned at stake as heretic. His translation forms basis of 1611 Authorized Version of Bible.

Tyne, river of N England (c. 80 mi. long) flowing E to North Sea. Shipbuilding esp. at Gateshead, Newcastle, Tynemouth.

typhoid fever, acute infectious disease caused by *Salmonella typhosa* bacterium usually in contaminated food and water. Characterized by prolonged fever and diarrhoea.

typhoon, violent revolving trop. storm, similar to hurricane. Wind may exceed 100 m.p.h.; dense rain and cloud near central, calm 'eye'. Occurs in W Pacific, mostly in late winter and spring.

typhus, acute infectious disease caused by rickettsiae organisms, transmitted by lice and fleas. Characterized by severe nervous symptoms and eruption of reddish spots.

tyrannosaur, tyrannosaurus rex, large 2-legged carnivorous dinosaur weighing c. 20 t., of Upper Cretaceous era of N America. Remains found in Montana, US.

tyrant, in ancient Greece and Syracuse, ruler exercising absolute power without legal authority; often popular champion who had seized power in class dispute. Rule of tyrant frequently beneficial, but became unpopular with growth of democratic sentiment in Greece.

tyrant *see* KINGBIRD.

Tyre, former major commercial city and port on Med. coast. Founded c. 2800 BC, became famous for purple dye. Tyrians estab. Carthage in 9th cent. and prospered despite conquest by Alexander the Great c. 333 BC and Romans 64 BC, until destroyed by Moslems AD 1291. Site now occupied by Lebanese town of Sûr.

Tyrol, Tirol, Alpine prov. of W Austria. Area: 4,884 sq. mi.; cap. Innsbruck. Main industries are dairying and tourism, mining (lead, iron, salt). Pop. (1961) 462,899. *See also* TRENTINO-ALTO ADIGE.

Tyrone, largest county of Northern Ireland. Area: 1,218 sq. mi.; county town, Omagh. Main occupation, agriculture, esp. flax, potatoes. Pop. (1966) 136,000.

Tyrrhenian Sea, part of Med. Sea bounded by Corsica, Sardinia, Sicily and Italy.

Tzu-Hsi (c. 1834–1908), empress of China. Fostered anti-foreign feeling which led to BOXER REBELLION.

The famous winter resort of Kitzbühel in the Austrian Tyrol

U

U–2, type of US reconnaissance aircraft. *See* POWERS, FRANCIS GARY.

Ubangi-Shari *see* CENTRAL AFRICAN REPUBLIC.

U-boat, abbreviation of Ger: *Unterseeboot,* submarine. Also *see* Q-BOAT.

Uccello, Paolo, orig. Paolo di Dono (*c.* 1396–1475), Florentine painter, noted for imaginative use of linear perspective. Works include frescoes in Santa Maria Novella, Florence, and 3 paintings of the Rout of San Romano.

Udaipur or **Mewar,** district of NW India. Orig. princely state, now part of RAJASTHAN.

Udall, Nicholas (1505–56), Eng. dramatist whose play, *Ralph Roister Doister,* is 1st known Eng. comedy.

udder, mammary gland of cow, goat and other mammals. Mammary tissues manufacture liquids and solids forming milk for feeding of young.

Udmurt Autonomous Soviet Socialist Republic, repub. of Russ. SFSR. Area: 16,250 sq. mi.; cap. Izhevsk. Products include timber, flax, quartz. Industries, steelworks, glass-making, food processing. Pop. (1965) 1,376,000.

Uffizi Gallery, art museum in Florence, Italy. Building is 16th cent. palace built by Georgio Vasari for Cosimo I de' Medici. Contains one of world's foremost collections of Renaissance painting and sculpture.

Uganda, E African, repub., member of Brit. Commonwealth of Nations.

Area: 91,000 sq. mi.; cap. Kampala. Exports coffee, cotton, sugar and tea. Achieved independence (1962); became repub. (1967). Pop. 7,934,000.

Ugaritic, Semitic language related to Classical Hebrew. Discovered in cuneiform script on clay tablets dating from 14th cent. BC at Ugarit, W Syria. Earliest known alphabet.

Ugric, branch of the Finno-Ugrian family of languages.

Uhde, Fritz von (1848–1911), Ger. religious and genre painter. Works include *The Sermon on the Mount* and *Going Home.*

U.H.F. *see* V.H.F.

Uhland, Johann Ludwig (1787–1862), Ger. romantic poet and literary historian. Member of Swabian School. Ballads include 'Ich hatt' einen Kameraden' and 'Der Wirtin Töchterlein'.

Uigur, Turkic-Altaic language. Has over 4 million speakers in Chinese prov. of Sinkiang.

Uigurs, Uighurs, Turkic people of C Asia. Rulers of Mongolia (745–840). Founded empire in present-day Sinkiang (*fl.* 9th–13th cent.), still inhabited by their descendants.

Uist, name of 2 islands of Outer Hebrides, off NW Scotland, part of Inverness-shire. Main occupation crofting. Comprises South Uist, chief town Lochboisdale and North Uist, chief town Lochmaddy.

ukelele, small 4-stringed, orig. Hawaian, guitar. Provides accompanying chords to sung melody.

Ukrainian, Slavic Indo-European language. Has 38 million speakers in the Ukraine, and parts of Russia and Romania.

Ukrainian Soviet Socialist Republic, Ukraine, constituent republic of USSR. Area: 232,046 sq. mi.; cap. Kiev; chief port, Odessa; main cities Kharkov, Dniepropetrovsk. Chief rivers Dnieper and Donets. Agriculture is main industry, esp. cereals. Hydro-electricity is produced. Pop. (1968 est.) 46,381,000.

Ulan Bator, cap. of Mongolian People's Repub. Centre of newly developed agric. region. Industries include food-processing, timber, cement and textile manufacturing. Pop. (1962) 195,300.

Ulanova, Galina Sergeyevna (1910–), Russ. dancer. Became (1944) prima ballerina of Bolshoi ballet. Noted esp. for interpretation of roles in *Swan Lake* and *Giselle.*

Ulbricht, Walter (1893–), Ger. polit. leader. A founder of Ger. Communist Party (1919). Chief minister of East Germany (1960–71).

ulcer, destruction of skin or mucous membrane resulting in break that does not heal. Caused by infection (*e.g.* syphilitic ulcer), inadequate blood supply (*e.g.* varicose ulcer), or irritation (*e.g.* gastric ulcer).

Ulfilas or **Wulfila** (*c.* 311–383), Gothic Arian churchman. Bishop of the Goths. Translated Bible into Gothic.

Ulloa, Antonio de, FRS (1716–97), Sp. statesman and mathematician. Visited Peru (1735) and noted existence of platinum.

Ullswater, lake (7 mi. long) in counties of Cumberland and Westmorland, NW England. Popular tourist attraction of Lake District.

Ulm, city of West Germany. Important medieval religious and commercial centre. Has 14th cent. Gothic cathedral. Textile, metal, leather and chemical industries. Pop. 92,700.

Ulster, prov. of N Ireland comprising all NORTHERN IRELAND (counties of Antrim, Armagh, Down, Fermanagh, Londonderry and Tyrone) and 3 counties of Republic of Ireland (Cavan, Donegal and Monaghan). Population has Protestant majority, instrumental in refusal of Northern Ireland to join Irish Free State (1922).

Ulster King of Arms, formerly chief heraldic official of Ireland and registrar of Order of St Patrick. Office transferred to London College of Arms (1943).

ultrasonics, science of sound vibrations of frequencies higher than those normally audible to human ear. Used to detect flaws in metal, for cleansing of small and complex articles, *etc.*

ultra-violet rays, electromagnetic radiation beyond limit of visibility at violet end of SPECTRUM. Wavelength is shorter than visible light but longer than X-rays.

Ulysses *see* ODYSSEUS.

umbelliferae, large family of plants having compound flowerheads. Includes many vegetables and herbs, *e.g.* carrot, celery, dill, parsley.

umber, mixture of clay with iron and manganese oxides, used as a pigment. Raw umber is dark yellowish brown, acquires reddish tinge when burnt.

Umberto II *see* HUMBERT II.

Portrait of Federico da Monfeltro by Piero della Francesca, in the Uffizi Gallery

umbilical cord, fleshy structure uniting abdomen of foetus with placenta of mother's womb, through which the mutual blood circulates. Severed at birth, resulting scar is navel.

umbrella, portable canopy of cloth used as protection against rain. In ancient Egypt and Far East often an emblem of rank.

umbrella bird, name given to genus *Cephalopterus* of C and S Amer. birds. Males are black with umbrella-like feather crest.

umbrella bush, *Acacia oswaldi,* small bush-like Austral. acacia. Used for hedges.

umbrella tree, *Magnolia tripetala,* small deciduous tree native to N America. White flowers and large oval leaves grouped in umbrella forms at ends of flowering branches. Name also given to Austral. tree, *Porassaia actinophylla.*

Umbria, region of C Italy. Area: 3,377 sq. mi.; chief town Perugia. Mostly hilly with Apennine Mts. in E. Agriculture main industry, esp. olive and vine-growing. Pop. (1961) 788,546.

umlaut, vowel change caused by partial assimilation to a succeeding sound, usually that of i or j orig. standing in following syllable, but now lost or altered. Also sign used, esp. in German, to indicate alteration in vowel sound.

Unamuno y Jugo, Miguel de (1864–1936), Sp. philosopher and novelist. His thought anticipated Existentialism; expressed in philosophical work *Del Sentimiento trágico de la Vida* (1913). Novels include *Paz en la Guerra* (1897).

Unanimisme, Fr. literary movement of early 20th cent. Emphasized importance of group over individual, claiming that artist can achieve significance only by becoming part of a social aggregation. Leading exponents Jules Romains, Georges Duhamel.

uncertainty principle, law of quantum mechanics which states impossibility of accurately verifying position and velocity of a particle. One, but not both quantities, may be definitely fixed. Formulated (1927) by Werner Heisenberg.

uncial, term for letters having large rounded forms (not joined to each other). Used esp. in early Greek and Latin manuscripts (AD 300–900).

'Uncle Sam', personification of US govt. Orig. used derisively by opponents of War of 1812. Possibly named from 'Uncle Sam' Wilson, a govt. inspector of Troy, N.Y., or simply from initials US.

unconformity, geological structure resulting from deposition of strata on eroded and distorted older strata.

unconscious, subconscious, in psychology, area of the mind containing motivating drives and impulses of which man is normally unaware. Also contains previously conscious ideas, subsequently lost from area of awareness. Held by SIGMUND FREUD to play vital role in personality development and motivation of behaviour.

underground [UK], **subway** [US], subterranean rly. forming part of city transport system. First opened (1863) in London, England.

Underground Railroad, in US history (mid-19th cent.), system enabling Southern slaves to reach Northern states and Canada. Fugitive slaves were guided and sheltered by abolitionists on journey northward.

underwing, moth of genus *Catocala*. Red, yellow or orange bands on hind wings. Species include red underwing, *C. nupta*.

Undset, Sigrid (1882–1949), Norwegian novelist. Works, reflecting scholarly knowledge of Middle Ages and her conversion (1924) to R.C. Church. include trilogy *Kristin Lavransdatter* (1920–22) and tetralogy *Olav Audunnson* (1925–27). Awarded Nobel Prize for Literature (1928).

undulant fever, Malta fever, brucellosis, infectious disease of man and animals caused by bacteria of brucella group transmitted in goat's or cow's milk, or meat, or by contact. Frequently causes recurrent fever in man and abortion in animals.

unemployment, state in which work is unavailable to large number of people requiring it. Called structural if caused by decline or change in processes of given industry. Widespread during period 1918–39. Industrialized nations attempt to control economy in order to balance supply with demand of labour.

UNESCO *see* UNITED NATIONS EDUCATIONAL, SCIENTIFIC AND CULTURAL ORGANIZATION.

Ungaretti, Giuseppe (1888–1970), Ital. poet, b. Alexandria. Prominent in beginning of modern Ital. poetry. Verse, mostly autobiographical, collected in *L'Allegria* (1919), *Sentimento del Tempo* (1933), *Il Taccuino del Vecchio* (1960).

Ungava, region of N Quebec, Canada. Area: 239,780 sq. mi. High plateau rich in minerals and iron. Ungava Bay is inlet (200 mi. long, 160 mi. wide) extending S from Hudson Strait.

Lomonosov University, Moscow, capital of the USSR

ungulate, hoofed mammal of order Ungulata, *e.g.* cattle, camel, horse, rhinoceros, elephant.

unicorn [Lat: one horn], legendary animal with horse-like body and rhinoceros-like horn. First mentioned in classical mythology, more common in medieval literature and heraldry.

Unidentified Flying Objects (UFO), commonly called flying saucers. Objects or lights seen in the sky, believed to be non-terrestrial by some and attributed to unusual natural phenomena by others.

uniformitarianism, in geology, theory that all past geological processes are result of physical forces still at work. First advanced (1795) by James Hutton; not generally accepted until publication of Sir Charles Lyell's *Principles of Geology* (1830–3).

Uniformity, Acts of, 4 acts of Eng. parl. (1549, 1552, 1559, 1662), aimed at enforcing standard reformed practices. Last Act re-estab. Church of England rites, prescribed use of Book of Common Prayer.

Unilateral Declaration of Independence (UDI) *see* RHODESIA.

Union, Acts of, in Brit. history, 2 acts, first (1707) uniting parliaments of England and Scotland, second (1800) uniting those of Britain and Ireland.

union, labour, organization of employees set up to improve wages and working conditions. Widespread use of labour unions began with Brit. trade union movement of 19th cent. Pursuit of goals achieved primarily through collective bargaining between union and company management, ultimate weapon being threat of strike.

Union Jack, popular name for UK national flag (properly Union Flag); accurate name only when flown from jackstaff of warship.

Union Movement, Brit. polit. group, orig. New Party founded (1931) by SIR OSWALD MOSLEY. Became (1932) British Union of Fascists; declared illegal 1940. Revived after World War 2 as Union Movement.

Union of Soviet Socialist Republics (USSR), federated state of E Europe and N Asia, stretching from Baltic Sea (W) to Pacific (E) and N to Arctic Ocean. Area: 8,599,300 sq. mi.; cap.

Moscow; principal cities, Leningrad, Kiev, Kharkov, Odessa. Consists of 15 constituent repubs., largest of which is Russ. SFSR. Climatically diverse European regions include Ukrainian grain fields, indust. and population centres and sub-trop. areas of Black and Caspian seas. Separated from Asian regions (*see* SIBERIA) by Ural Mts. Rich agric. and forest areas; important coal, iron, copper and petroleum deposits. Polit. consolidation of USSR dates from founding of Russ. empire under IVAN IV (1547); subsequent disorders ended with estab. (1613) of ROMANOV dynasty. Russ. imperial gains and transformation from medieval state to European power largely achieved under PETER I and CATHERINE II. Tsarist autocracy led to increasing discontent (19th–20th cent.) among peasants and workers, culminating in RUSSIAN REVOLUTION (1917), estab. of Communist state under LENIN and creation (1922) of USSR. Economic and polit. rise resulted in Soviet challenge to West during World War

2 (under STALIN) and extension of influence in post-war world. Main language, Russian; chief religion, Russ. Orthodox. Unit of currency, rouble. Pop. (1966) 235,543,000.

Union Pacific Railroad, railway system in US. Main line built (1865–9) W from Council Bluffs, Iowa, joined Central Pacific Railroad at Ogden, Utah, forming 1st US transcontinental rly. Early history marked by financial scandals. Now operates 10,000 mi. of track in 13 states.

Unionist *see* CONSERVATIVE PARTY.

Unitarianism, form of Protestantism, founded late 17th cent. Rejects doctrine of Trinity, asserting that Jesus was human prophet and teacher.

United Arab Republic, independent Arab-Muslim repub. formed (1958) by union of Syria and Egypt. Syria seceded (1961). Area: 386,198 sq.

mi.; cap. Cairo. Comprises desert, and fertile, densely populated Nile valley. Ancient Egypt seat of highly developed early civilization. After death (30 BC) of Cleopatra, became Roman prov. Conquered (642) by Arabs; later ruled by Turks, French, British. Independent kingdom from 1922 until proclamation of repub. of

Egypt (1953). Suez Crisis (1956) followed nationalization of Suez Canal. Arab-Israeli hostilities reached level of open warfare (June 1967). Name changed to Arab Republic of Egypt (1971). Language, Arabic; main religion, Islam. Unit of currency, Egyptian pound. Pop. (1963) 30,147,000.

United Church of Canada, formed 1925, by union of Canadian Protestant churches (Methodist, Congregationalist and most Presbyterian).

United Empire Loyalists, name given to colonists who remained loyal to Britain during Amer. Revolution and migrated to Canada, esp. in 1783–4. Extensive settlement in Nova Scotia and Quebec, led to estab. of new colonies, New Brunswick (1781) and Upper Canada under CONSTITUTIONAL ACT (1791).

United Free Church of Scotland, Scot. Presbyterian Church formed (1900) by union of Free Church of Scotland with United Presbyterian Church. In 1929 main body joined Church of Scotland leaving *c.* 13,000 members in United Free Church.

United Irishmen, revolutionary Irish polit. organization, founded (1791) by Wolfe Tone. Suppressed 1794; became secret revolutionary body and sought aid from France. Leaders executed or imprisoned after failure of 1798 rebellion.

United Kingdom [of Great Britain and Northern Ireland] (UK), island

UNITED KINGDOM PRIME MINISTERS

Sir Robert Walpole	Whig	1721–1742	Viscount Palmerston	Lib.	1858–1865
Earl of Wilmington	Whig	1742–1743	Earl Russell	Lib.	1865–1866
Henry Pelham	Whig	1743–1754	Earl of Derby	Cons.	1866–1868
Duke of Newcastle	Whig	1754–1756	Benjamin Disraeli	Cons.	1868
Duke of Devonshire	Whig	1756–1757	William Gladstone	Lib.	1868–1871
Duke of Newcastle	Whig	1757–1762	Benjamin Disraeli	Cons.	1871–1880
Earl of Bute	Tory	1762–1763	William Gladstone	Lib.	1880–1885
George Grenville	Whig	1763–1765	Marquess of Salisbury	Cons.	1885–1886
Marquess of Rockingham	Whig	1765–1766	William Gladstone	Lib.	1886
Earl of Chatham	Whig	1766–1767	Marquess of Salisbury	Cons.	1886–1892
Duke of Grafton	Whig	1767–1770	William Gladstone	Lib.	1892–1894
Lord North	Tory	1770–1782	Earl of Rosebery	Lib.	1894–1895
Marquess of Rockingham	Whig	1782	Marquess of Salisbury	Cons.	1895–1902
Earl of Shelburne	Whig	1782–1783	Arthur Balfour	Cons.	1902–1905
Duke of Portland	Coalition	1783	Sir Henry Campbell-Bannerman	Lib.	1905–1908
William Pitt	Tory	1783–1801	Herbert Henry Asquith	Lib.	1908–1915
Henry Addington	Tory	1801–1804	Herbert Henry Asquith	Coalition	1915–1916
William Pitt	Tory	1804–1806	David Lloyd George	Coalition	1916–1922
Lord Grenville	Whig	1806–1807	Andrew Bonar Law	Cons.	1922–1923
Duke of Portland	Tory	1807–1809	Stanley Baldwin	Cons.	1923–1924
Spencer Perceval	Tory	1809–1812	J. Ramsay MacDonald	Lab.	1924
Earl of Liverpool	Tory	1812–1827	Stanley Baldwin	Cons.	1924–1929
George Canning	Tory	1827	J. Ramsay MacDonald	Lab.	1929–1931
Viscount Goderich	Tory	1827–1828	J. Ramsay MacDonald	Coalition	1931–1935
Duke of Wellington	Tory	1828–1830	Stanley Baldwin	Coalition	1935–1937
Earl Grey	Whig	1830–1834	Neville Chamberlain	Coalition	1937–1940
Viscount Melbourne	Whig	1834	Winston S. Churchill	Coalition	1940–1945
Sir Robert Peel	Tory	1834–1835	Clement R. Attlee	Lab.	1945–1951
Viscount Melbourne	Whig	1835–1841	Sir Winston S. Churchill	Cons.	1951–1955
Sir Robert Peel	Tory	1841–1846	Sir Anthony Eden	Cons.	1955–1957
Lord John Russell	Whig	1846–1852	Harold Macmillan	Cons.	1957–1963
Earl of Derby	Tory	1852	Sir Alec Douglas-Home	Cons.	1963–1964
Earl of Aberdeen	Peelite	1852–1855	Harold Wilson	Lab.	1964–1970
Viscount Palmerston	Lib.	1855–1858	Edward Heath	Cons.	1970–
Earl of Derby	Cons.	1858			

New York, largest city and cultural centre of the USA, with the Empire State Building in the centre background

The Capitol, Washington

Street in New Orleans, United States

nation of NW Europe consisting of England, Scotland, Wales and North-

ern Ireland. Formed (1800) by Union of Great Britain and Ireland (reduced to Northern Ireland, 1922, with creation of Irish Free State). Pop. (1967) 55,068,000.

United Nations Atomic Energy Commission, agency estab. by General Assembly (1946) to facilitate development of atomic energy for peaceful uses and recommend means of controlling nuclear weapons. Negotiations for nuclear disarmament have been deadlocked since outset of Commission's work.

United Nations Conference on Trade and Development (UNCTAD), specialized agency of UN, authorized by General Assembly. Estab. to promote world trade, esp. through aid to developing countries to accelerate economic production.

United Nations Educational, Scientific and Cultural Organization (UNESCO), special agency of UN, estab. 1946, to further exchange of ideas and achievements and aid in development of world education. Membership includes some nations not belonging to UN.

United Nations General Assembly see UNITED NATIONS ORGANIZATION.

United Nations High Commissioner for Refugees, office estab. (1951) with H.Q. in Geneva, to replace Inter-

national Refugee Organization. Chartered to alleviate refugee problem and co-ordinate activities of volunteer agencies. Awarded Nobel Peace Prize (1954).

United Nations International Children's Emergency Fund (UNICEF), agency estab. (1946) by UN to assist children throughout the world, esp. in devastated areas and underdeveloped countries. Financed by voluntary contributions. Awarded Nobel Peace Prize (1965).

United Nations [Organization] (UN), international body (H.Q. New York), estab. 1945 to maintain peace and

security and promote co-operation between countries in solving social, economic and cultural problems. Charter, drawn up at San Francisco conference, designated admin. functions to Secretariat (headed by sec. general), deliberative functions to General Assembly (comprising delegates from all member nations) and policy decision functions to Security Council (5 permanent and 10 non-permanent members). Original membership of 51 states has expanded to include most independent countries, major exceptions being Nationalist China, East and West Germany; permanent members of Security Council are US, USSR, UK, France and mainland China. As it is arbiter of international disputes, UN has had limited success, as in Arab-Israeli conflicts (1948, 1956, 1967), Indonesia (1949), Korea (1951–3). East-West division, manifested in Security Council, increased importance of sec.-general's office, esp. in Congo crisis (1960–4).

United Provinces of Agra and Oudh *see* UTTAR PRADESH.

United States Air Force Academy, founded 1954 for officer training at Denver, Colo., US; permanent site at Colorado Springs estab. 1958.

United States Military Academy, founded 1802 at West Point, N.Y., to train army officers. Subsequent reorganization estab. broader curriculum.

United States Naval Academy, founded 1845 at Annapolis, Maryland, to train officers. Opened as Naval School, name changed (1851).

United States [of America] (US), federal repub. of N America, covering S half of continent, Hawaii and Alaska. Area: 3,615,211 sq. mi.; cap. Washington, DC; main cities, New York, Chicago, Los Angeles, Philadelphia, Detroit. Bounded by Pacific (W) and Atlantic (E) oceans. Rocky Mts. dominate W interior, grain-producing C Plains drained by Mississippi system, S of which are oil-rich Texas and SW regions. SE US primarily agric., Great Lakes and Atlantic coast (also S California) are main indust. and population centres. Colonial struggle (began 16th cent.) for dominance of area ended with triumph of English in FRENCH AND INDIAN WAR. Nation estab. (1783)

with success of Thirteen Colonies in AMERICAN REVOLUTION. Westward expansion (19th cent.) facilitated by LOUISIANA PURCHASE and MEXICAN WAR. Threat of secession by South ended with Union victory in CIVIL WAR (1861–5). By 20th cent. US had become a leading indust. nation with exploitation of vast agric. and mineral resources. Emergence as world power after World War 1 challenged by rise of USSR during World War 2. Official language, English; main religion, Protestantism. Unit of currency, dollar. Pop. (1968 est.) 199,319,000.

United States Supreme Court *see* SUPREME COURT.

Universal Postal Union, international agency of UN, H.Q. at Bern, Switzerland. Founded 1875, passed to UN (1947). Facilitates international exchange of mail.

Universalist Church of America, branch of Protestant Church, founded (1780) by John Murray in Gloucester, Mass. Adherents believe in ultimate salvation for all men. Merged (1961) with American Unitarian Assoc. to form Unitarian Universalist Assoc.

universe, in astronomy, all space and all objects contained in it, also phenomena associated with them. Includes specifically Solar System as part of Milky Way galaxy, as well as other identified galaxies containing stars, gaseous clouds and radiation sources. Einstein postulated that space was curved and unlimited, making universe finite but boundless.

unleavened bread, bread eaten at Jewish Passover Feast. Made without leaven because this causes dough to ferment and is regarded as symbol of corruption.

English village, United Kingdom

Castle Stalker, Argyll, United Kingdom

UNITED STATES PRESIDENTS		
George Washington	Fed.	1789–1797
John Adams	Fed.	1797–1801
Thomas Jefferson	Rep.	1801–1809
James Madison	Rep.	1809–1817
James Monroe	Rep.	1817–1825
John Q. Adams	Rep.	1825–1829
Andrew Jackson	Dem.	1829–1837
Martin Van Buren	Dem.	1837–1841
William H. Harrison	Whig	1841
John Tyler	Whig	1841–1845
James K. Polk	Dem.	1845–1849
Zachary Taylor	Whig	1849–1850
Millard Fillmore	Whig	1850–1853
Franklin Pierce	Dem.	1853–1857
James Buchanan	Dem.	1857–1861
Abraham Lincoln	Rep.	1861–1865
Andrew Johnson	Rep.	1865–1869
Ulysses S. Grant	Rep.	1869–1877
Rutherford B. Hayes	Rep.	1877–1881
James A. Garfield	Rep.	1881
Chester A. Arthur	Rep.	1881–1885
Grover Cleveland	Dem.	1885–1889
Benjamin Harrison	Rep.	1889–1893
Grover Cleveland	Dem.	1893–1897
William McKinley	Rep.	1897–1901
Theodore Roosevelt	Rep.	1901–1909
William H. Taft	Rep.	1909–1913
Woodrow Wilson	Dem.	1913–1921
Warren G. Harding	Rep.	1921–1923
Calvin Coolidge	Rep.	1923–1929
Herbert C. Hoover	Rep.	1929–1933
Franklin Roosevelt	Dem.	1933–1945
Harry S. Truman	Dem.	1945–1953
Dwight D. Eisenhower	Rep.	1953–1961
John F. Kennedy	Dem.	1961–1963
Lyndon B. Johnson	Dem.	1963–1969
Richard Nixon	Rep.	1969–

Untermeyer, Louis (1885–   ), Amer. writer and critic. Works include volumes of poetry, *Collected Parodies* (1926), and anthologies *Modern American Poetry* (1st ed., 1919) *Modern British Poetry* (1st ed., 1920).

Unterwalden, canton of C Switzerland. Area: 296 sq. mi. Predominantly mountainous and forested. Divided into Obwalden (cap. Sarnen) and Niwalden (cap. Stans). Population German-speaking; religion Roman Catholicism. Pop. 45,323.

untouchables, among Indian Hindus, members of a caste denied social and religious privileges.

Unwin, Sir Stanley (1884–1968), Brit. publisher. His *The Truth about Publishing* (1926) regarded as standard text on various aspects of the trade.

Upanishads, Hindu philosophical treatises. Discuss nature of the universe and the deity, and relationship between spirit and matter.

upas, *Antiara toxicaria,* large tree of mulberry family, native to Java. Sap is poisonous.

Updike, John Hoyer (1932–   ), Amer. novelist and poet. Works include *The Poorhouse Fair* (1959), *The Centaur* (1963), *Couples* (1968). Collected poetry in *Telephone Poles and Other Poems* (1963).

Upper Canada, hist. region (1791–1840) of Canada, covering much of present Ontario, cap. York (now Toronto). Created by Constitutional Act (1791) after influx of UNITED EMPIRE LOYALISTS. United with Lower Canada (1840) by Act of Union.

Upper Palatinate, Oberpfalz, prov. of Bavaria, often referred to as the Palatinate. Area: 3,724 sq. mi.; cap. Regensburg. Predominantly agric. region. Historically associated with Lower or Rhenish Palatinate (*see* RHINELAND-PALATINATE).

Upper Volta [République de Haute Volta], inland repub. of W Africa. Area: 105,869 sq. mi.; cap. Ouagadougou. Predominantly semi-arid savannah. Economy based on agriculture and livestock rearing. African

kingdom until annexation by France (1896); part of Ivory Coast colony (1932–47); autonomous repub. within Fr. Community (1958); full independence (1960). Army assumed power 1966. Official language, French. Predominant religions, Islam, Animism. Pop. (1967 est.) 5,054,000.

Uppsala, city of E Sweden. Important medieval cultural and eccles. centre. 13th cent. Gothic cathedral contains tombs of Gustavus I, Linnaeus and Swedenborg. Library of 14th cent. university contains medieval manuscripts incl. *Codex Argenteus.* Pop. (1965) 183,700.

Ur, ancient Sumerian city, called 'Ur of the Chaldees' in OT, on R. Euphrates, S of Babylon. Great temple of the Moon god with ziggurat or tower and graves dating back to 3500 BC have been excavated.

Ural-Altaic languages, family of languages incl. Finnish, Estonian, Lapp, Hungarian, Turkish and Mongolian.

Urals, mountain range of USSR running from Arctic to Caspian Sea (*c.* 1,500 mi.). Traditional boundary between Europe and Asia. Highest peak is Narednaya (6,182 ft.).

uraninite, mineral found mainly in Colorado, US. Consists largely of uranium, thorium, lead, pitchblende and certain rare earth metals. When heated, yields helium.

uranium (U), heavy, radioactive, silvery metallic element; natural source of nuclear energy. Occurs in pitchblende, carnotite and other ores.

Uranus, in Gk. myth., personification of the heavens, and according to Hesiod, son and husband of Gaia, the Earth. Father of the Titans, incl. Cronus (father of Zeus); emasculated and overthrown by Cronus.

Uranus, in astronomy, planet 7th in distance from Sun. Revolves about Sun at a mean distance of 1,782,700,000 mi. in *c.* 84 yr. Has 5 satellites.

Urban II, orig. Ugo of Lagery (*c.* 1040–99), pope (1088–99). Sermon at Clermont promoted first Crusade. Furthered reforms of Gregory VII.

Urban IV, orig. Jacques Pantaléon (d. 1264), pope (1261–4). Invested Charles of Anjou with Sicilian kingdom, thus alienating House of Hohenstaufen.

urban renewal, Amer. term for TOWN AND COUNTRY PLANNING.

Urbino, town of the Marches, C Italy. Cultural centre (esp. 15th–17th cent.). Contains Renaissance palace. Pop. *c.* 22,000.

Urdu, Indic language of India. Now one of official languages of India. It contains borrowings from Persian and Arabic and as a spoken language is closely connected with Hindi.

urea, crystalline compound product of protein metabolism found in urine, blood, bile, *etc.* of all mammals. Of great importance as a fertilizer and in medicine.

Urey, Harold Clayton (1893–   ), Amer. chemist. With G. N. Lewis, discovered heavy water (1932). Awarded Nobel Prize for Chemistry (1934) for isolation of heavy hydrogen.

Uri, one of 3 orig. Swiss cantons. Area: 415 sq. mi., cap. Altdorf. Mainly agric. region. Predominantly German-speaking. Pop. (1960) 32,021.

Uriah, called 'the Hittite', in OT, one

Mosaic from Ur

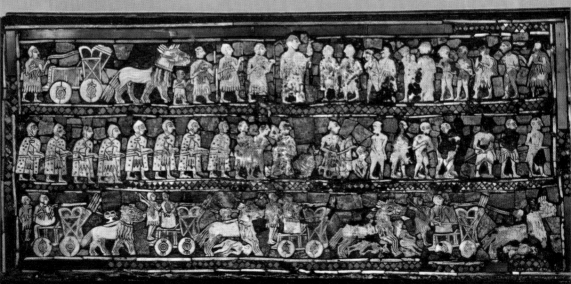

Montevideo, Uruguay

of David's warriors. David wanted Uriah's wife and arranged for his death in battle.

uric acid, chemical compound found in small quantities in urine of mammals. Main constituent of excrement of birds and reptiles.

urinary bladder, muscular, membranous sac acting as reservoir for urine.

urine, fluid composed of water and waste products extracted from animal blood by kidneys and eliminated via bladder and urethra.

Urquhart, Sir Thomas (1611–60), Scot. translator and mathematician. Translated 1st 3 books of Rabelais (1653). Also devised a universal language and wrote on mathematics.

Ursa Major, Great Bear, circumpolar constellation of N hemisphere, popularly called The Plough or Big Dipper. Pole Star (contained in constellation Ursa Minor) may be found by extending line through 2 end stars called Pointers.

Ursa Minor, Little Bear, constellation of N hemisphere. Also called Little Dipper. Contains Pole Star.

Ursula, Saint (*fl.* 4th cent.), virgin martyr of Cologne. According to legend, put to death with 11,000 companions.

Ursulines, Order of Saint Ursula, Roman Catholic order of nuns, founded (1535) in Italy by St Angela Merici. Approved as religious order (1612). First founded specifically for teaching girls.

urticaria, nettle rash, hives, skin condition, caused by allergy. Characterized by pale rash and severe itching.

Uruguay [**República Oriental del Uruguay**], repub. of S America, on N

bank of Plata estuary; bounded N by Brazil, W by Argentina. Area: 72,150 sq. mi.; cap. Montevideo. Main occupations cattle- and sheep-rearing, meat packing. Meat and wool account for *c.* 80% of exports. Claimed by Spaniards and Portuguese 17th–18th cent. Claimed independence from Spain, but occupied by Brazil (1820). Achieved independence (1827). Religion, Roman Catholicism; language, Spanish. Pop. (1967 est.) 2,783,000.

Urumchi, Urumtsi, cap. of Sinkiang prov., NW China. Industries, coalmining, chemicals, iron and steel goods. Pop. (1967) *c.* 240,000.

Ushant, Fr. island off coast of Brittany, NW France. Scene of Howe's victory over French fleet (1794).

Uskudar, suburb of Istanbul, Turkey; formerly separate town of Scutari, site of FLORENCE NIGHTINGALE's hospital in Crimean War.

USSR *see* UNION OF SOVIET SOCIALIST REPUBLICS.

Ustinov, Peter Alexander (1921–), Brit. actor, dramatist, film director. Plays include *House of Regrets* (1942), *The Love of Four Colonels* (1951). Appeared in films incl. *The Sundowners* (1961), *Topkapi* (1964), *The Comedians* (1968).

Usumbura, former name of BUJUMBURA.

usury, orig. any charge for use of borrowed money. In England fixing of maximum interest rates began in 16th cent. Now usually means the charging of an exorbitant amount of interest.

Utah, Rocky Mountain state of NW US. Area: 84,916 sq. mi.; cap. Salt Lake City. Predominantly mountainous; in E, high plateaus cut by deep canyons and valleys; in W, dry level Great Basin area with Great Salt Lake to NW. Has deposits of uranium, petroleum, copper, gold, silver and natural gas. Industries include textiles, machinery, metal refining, food processing. Settled (1847) by Mormons. Pop. (1963 est.) 983,000.

Utamaro, Kitagawa (1753–1806), Japanese artist, noted esp. for woodblock colour prints.

uterus, womb, muscular organ in female mammals in which the foetus develops. Usually about 3 in. long in humans but is greatly enlarged during pregnancy; situated in pelvis, opens via the cervix into the vagina.

U Thant *see* THANT, U.

Utilitarianism, philosophical school founded by Jeremy Bentham and later developed by J. S. Mill, who incorporated it into 19th cent. liberalism. Doctrine based on concepts that man's needs dictated by pleasure and state's concern should be the greatest happiness for the greatest number.

Uto-Aztecan, linguistic family of N America. With Tanoan and Kiowan, forms Azteco-Tanoan language group.

utopianism, polit. philosophy envisioning ideal state. Name derived from Sir Thomas More's *Utopia* (1516) where state is constructed for benefit of all citizens. Early utopian works include Plato's *Republic* and St Augustine's *City of God*; among later theorists were Saint-Simon, Proudhon and Robert Owen. Novels based on utopian themes have often been satirical; best known authors include Swift, Huxley and Orwell.

Utrecht, city of C Netherlands. Transport and communications centre. Site of Royal Dutch Industries Fair. Chemical and textile manufacturing, food processing, iron and steel foundries. Pop. (1966) 271,000.

Utrecht, Treaty of, settlement (1713) ending War of the SPANISH SUCCESSION and supplemented by Fr.-Austrian agreements of 1714. Emperor Philip V recognized as king of Spain. Sp. possessions in Low Countries and Italy transferred to Austria. France recognized Hanover claim to Eng. throne. Britain and Netherlands gained commercial advantages.

Utrillo, Maurice (1883–1955), Fr. artist; noted esp. for his paintings of street scenes of Montmartre, Paris.

Uttar Pradesh, state of N India formed (1950) by merging United Provinces with states of Rampur, Benares and Tehri-Carhual. Area: 113,654 sq. mi.; cap. Lucknow; cities, Cawnpore, Agra (site of Taj Mahal), Benares or Varanasi, Holy City of the Hindus. Chiefly agric., wheat, rice, sugar, cotton. Industries, metal work, textiles. Pop. (1961) 73,746,401.

uvarovite, mineral of GARNET group, coloured emerald-green by presence of chromium.

uvula, small, fleshy lobe of soft palate projecting downwards at back of mouth.

Uxmal, ancient city of SE Mexico, cap. of later Maya empire. Contains fine examples of Mayan Renaissance architecture.

Uzbek, Turkic-Altaic language. Has 6 million speakers in parts of Asiatic Russia and Mongolia.

Uzbek Soviet Socialist Republic, Uzbekistan, constituent republic of USSR since 1924, in Turkestan region of C Asia. Area: 158,069 sq. mi.; cap. Tashkent; other cities Bukhara, Samarkand. Agriculture is main industry, esp. cotton, rice, fruit. Pop. (1968) 11,266,000.

Uzziah or **Azariah** (d. *c.* 740 BC), in OT, king of Judah (*c.* 785–*c.* 740 BC). Rebuilt and refortified Elath on Gulf of Aqaba.

Vaal, river (*c.* 700 mi.) of Repub. of South Africa. Rises in SE Transvaal flowing SW to join Orange R. in Cape Prov. Provides irrigation and electric power.

vaccination, inoculation of weakened or killed infectious micro-organisms into blood. Produces antibodies to resist infection. Introduced by Edward Jenner (1796) to immunize against smallpox; now also used for diphtheria, typhoid, poliomyelitis, *etc.*

vacuum, in physical theory, an enclosed space having no matter. In practice, perfect vacuum unobtainable because of vapour emitted by container itself.

Vaduz, cap. of Liechtenstein. Market town for surrounding area. Pop. (1967 est.) 3,500.

vagina, in female mammals, passage leading from the womb to the exterior at the vulva.

Valais, Wallis, canton of SE Switzerland. Area: 2,021 sq. mi.; cap. Sion. Steep forested mountain slopes. Tourism, also chemicals, and food-processing. Two-thirds of inhabitants speak French. Pop. (1960) 177,783.

Valdivia, Pedro de (*c.* 1500–53), Sp. soldier, conqueror of Chile. Founded Santiago (1541). Gov. of Chile (1549–53); killed in Indian uprising.

Valencia, city and port of E Spain. Exports fruit, wine; manufactures textiles. Many architecturally important medieval and Renaissance buildings. Pop. (1965) 502,000.

Valencia, city of N Venezuela. Centre of rich agric. region producing coffee, sugar, cacao and tobacco. Industries: textiles, sawmills, tanneries. Pop. (1966) 196,000.

Valencia, prov. of E Spain. Area:

4,165 sq. mi.; cap. Valencia. Densely populated fertile coastal plain with intensive olive and vine cultivation; also produces rice, fruit and vegetables. Pop. (1960) 1,429,708.

valency, in chemistry, capacity of an element to combine with another. Comparative unit is hydrogen; measured by number of hydrogen atoms combined with or displaced by element.

Valentine, Saint (*fl.* 3rd cent.), Roman bishop, martyred *c.* 270. Traditionally patron saint of lovers; sending of valentines on his feast day, 14 Feb., originated in medieval times.

Valentinian III (419–455), Roman emperor (425–455) in West. In spite of victory (451) over Attila, reign marked by loss of African prov. and dismemberment of much of W Empire by Vandals, Visigoths and Huns.

Valentino, Rudolph, orig. Rodolpho d'Antonguolla (1895–1926), Amer. film actor, b. Italy. Silent screen's most celebrated romantic lover. Films include *The Four Horsemen of the Apocalypse, The Sheik.*

Valerian [Publius Licinius Valerianus] (d. *c.* AD 269), Roman emperor (253–60). Captured in campaign against Persian Emperor Shaipur I.

valerian, herb of genus *Valeriana* of temp. and colder regions of N hemisphere. Fragrant pink or white flowers; root used in medicine. Species include *V. officinalis.*

Valéry, Paul (1871–1945), Fr. symbolist poet and essayist. Works include poems *La Jeune Parque* (1917), *Le Cimetière Marin* (1920) and collection of essays *Variété* (1924).

Valhalla, in Norse myth., hall in which the god Odin receives souls of slain warriors.

Valkyries, in Norse myth., hand-maidens of the god Odin who fly over field of battle choosing those to be slain, and escorting them to Valhalla.

Valladolid, city and cap. of Valladolid prov., N central Spain. Industrial and agric. centre. Cathedral (1595) and university (1346). Conquered from Moors (10th cent.); replaced Toledo as chief residence of kings of Castile in 15th cent. Pop. (1965) 165,000.

Town hall in the Plaza del Caudillo, Valencia

Valle-Inclán, Ramón del (1869–1936), Sp. writer. Most famous work is 4 vol. novel *Sonatas* (1902–5). Also wrote plays and social satires.

Vallejo, César (1895–1938), Peruvian poet, lived mainly in Paris. Author of *Los Heraldos Negros, Poemas Humanos.*

Valletta, cap. and port of Malta. Founded (1566) by Knights Hospitallers. Pop. (1964) 18,000.

valley, long depression in earth's surface between uplands, hills or mountains. Formed by river erosion, sometimes further modified by passage of glacier, or by earth movement between 2 faults.

Valley Forge, winter camp (1777–8) in Pennsylvania, US, where Washington's Continental army endured great hardship. Now State Park.

Valley of the Kings, valley near Thebes, ancient cap. of Egypt. Burial place of Pharaohs of New Kingdom, incl. Tutankhamen.

Valois, Fr. dynasty founded by Charles de Valois, 3rd son of Philip III. Younger branch of Capetian line which it succeeded (1328); followed (1589) by Bourbon dynasty.

Valparaiso, city of C Chile, chief port of W South America. Founded 1536. Industrial centre and tourist resort. Pop. (1965) 276,000.

vampire, in folklore, evil spirit which leaves its grave at night to suck blood of sleeping victims.

vampire bat, blood-sucking bat of genera *Desmodus* and *Diphylla* of trop. C and S America. Incisor and canine teeth modified for slitting skin.

Van, largest lake in Turkey, in Van prov. Area: 1,454 sq. mi. Saline lake with no apparent outlet. Town of Van at E shore dates from 8th cent. BC.

Van Allen belts, 2 layers of radiation, varying in depth, surrounding Earth in outer atmosphere and extending from *c.* 600 mi. to *c.* 30,000 mi. above its surface. Possible hazard in space flights.

Van Buren, Martin (1782–1862), 8th

Vampire Bat

US Pres. (1837–41), Democrat. Sec. of State (1829–31), Vice-Pres. (1833–7), chosen by Pres. Jackson to succeed him. As Pres., supported INDEPENDENT TREASURY SYSTEM.

Van de Graff, Robert Jemison, (1901–67), Amer. physicist. Inventor of electrostatic particle accelerator, used in radiation research, cancer treatment.

van de Velde, family of 17th cent. Dutch artists. **Esais van de Velde** (*c.* 1590–1630), painter of genre and battle scenes, one of founders of Dutch realistic landscape painting. **Willem van de Velde** (1633–1707), most renowned of Dutch marine painters; worked mainly in London. **Adriaen van de Velde** (1636–72), specialized in painting pastoral landscapes in Ital. manner.

Van Diemen's Land, until 1853 name for TASMANIA.

van Dyck or **Vandyke, Sir Anthony** (1599–1641), Flemish portrait painter. Influenced by Rubens. After 1632 lived in England; noted esp. for portraits of nobility at court of Charles I.

van Gogh, Vincent (1853–90), Dutch post-impressionist painter. After dark, sombre paintings of peasant life in Holland, produced best work while living in Paris and Provence. Portraits, still life and landscapes characterized by broken brushwork, use of pure bright colour and dynamic, subjective style. Works include *Portrait of Père Tanquy, The Sunflowers* and *The Starry Night*.

van Meegeren, Henricus Anthonius [Han] (1889–1947), Dutch painter, notorious for imitations of 17th cent. painters, esp. supposed work by Vermeer, *Christ at Emmaus*.

vanadinite, lead chlorovanadate, soft mineral occurring in yellow, brown or greenish crystals.

vanadium, rare element occurring in certain minerals. Obtained as light grey powder or metal. Used to toughen steel, increase shock resistance.

Vanbrugh, Sir John (1664–1726), Eng. dramatist and architect. Comedies include *The Relapse, The Provoked Wife*. Designed Castle Howard and Blenheim Palace.

Vancouver, George (1757–98), Eng. navigator and explorer. Commanded expeditions (1791–4) to explore N Pacific coast; circumnavigated island later named Vancouver.

Vancouver, city of SW Brit. Columbia, Canada, Pacific port. Large ice-free harbour; terminus of Canadian Pacific Railway. Industries include shipbuilding, fish canning, lumbering, manufacturing of steel products and furniture. Pop. (1966) 410,000.

Vancouver Island, island of Brit. Columbia, Canada. Area: 13,049 sq. mi.; main city, Victoria. Discovered (1778) by James Cook. Industries include mining, lumbering, fishing.

Vandals, ancient Germanic tribe (5th cent.). Controlled E Med. region until overthrown (534) by Belisarius. Belief in Arianism led to persecution of Orthodox Christians.

Vanderbilt, Cornelius (1794–1877), Amer. capitalist, known as 'Commodore'. Made fortune through post-Civil War rly. enterprises.

Vane, Sir Henry (1613–62), Eng. statesman. Gov. of Massachusetts (1636). Parl. leader during Civil War; member of Long Parliament, but hostile to Cromwell's Protectorate. After Restoration, beheaded for treason.

vanilla, trop. climbing orchid of genus *Vanilla*. Pod-like fruit yields extract used in flavouring food. *V. planifolia,* native to Mexico and C America, widely cultivated.

van't Hoff, Jacobus Hendricus

Vancouver

(1852–1911), Dutch chemist. Awarded Nobel Prize for Chemistry (1901) for work in chemical dynamics and osmotic pressure.

vaporization, change of matter into gaseous state. Term vapour is commonly used to describe gaseous state of normally solid or liquid substance.

Varangians, Viking warriors and merchants of 9th cent. Founded colonies in Russia. Carried out raids as far S as Constantinople. Name also given to mercenary bodyguard of Byzantine emperors.

Vargas, Getulio Dornelles (1883–1954), Brazilian statesman. Pres. (1930–45, 1951–4) as result of successful insurrection. Carried out social reforms but ruled autocratically. After deposition (1954) committed suicide.

variable star, star of changing brightness and, sometimes, colour. Cepheid type varies according to regular pattern.

varicose vein, condition usually appearing on legs or lower abdomen, resulting in dilated, twisted or baggy veins. Caused by pregnancy, overweight, prolonged standing.

variolite, basaltic rock with prominent spherulitic texture. Spherulites or varioles, esp. on weathered surfaces, appear as pale-coloured spots.

Varley, Frederick Horsman (1881–), Canadian painter, b. England. With A. Y. Jackson, founded 'Group of Seven'.

Varna, Black Sea port of Bulgaria, known (1949–56) as **Stalin.** Manufacturing city, cotton-textile producing centre. Also popular resort. Pop. (1965) 180,000.

varnish, solution of gum or resin in oil (oil varnish) or in volatile solvent

13th cent. castle above Vaduz

Landscape in Venezuela's llano (grassy plain)

The beautiful Ponte di Rialto in Venice

(spirit varnish). On drying forms hard, usually glossy, protective coating.

Varro, Marcus Terentius (116–27 BC), Roman poet, satirist, grammarian. Of over 600 volumes, covering all aspects of learning only *De Re Rustica*, parts of *De Lingua Latina* (treatise on Latin grammar) and of *Satirae Menippeae* survive.

Varus, Publius Quintilius (d. AD 9), Roman general defeated by Germans under Arminius in Teutoburgian forest. Committed suicide.

Vasa, Swedish royal house (1523–1654). Founded by GUSTAVUS I.

Vasarely, Victor (1908–), Hungarian abstract painter. Influenced by Bauhaus theories. Uses geometric forms esp. in black and white.

Vasari, Giorgio (1511–74), Ital. artist. Best known for biographies of Renaissance artists. Translated as *Lives of the Artists, Painters, Sculptors and Architects* (10 vols. 1912–14).

vascular system, in man, heart, blood vessels and lymphatic system, which carry oxygen, nutrients and waste products to and from various parts of the body. Also applied to structures carrying out similar functions in animals and plants.

Vassar College, independent liberal arts college for women at Poughkeepsie, N.Y., US. Chartered (1861), orig. Vassar Female College, renamed (1867).

Vatican City [**Stato della Città del Vaticano**], independent papal state created by LATERAN TREATY (1929).

Situated within city of Rome, Italy, residence of pope. Area: 0.17 sq. mi. Includes Church of St Peter, Vatican Palace, admin. and eccles. offices. Pop. (1963) *c.* 1,000.

Vatican Councils, series of ecumenical councils of R.C. Church. First (1869–70), enunciated doctrine of papal infallibility. Second (1962–5), convened by Pope John XXIII, revised Church's role in modern society.

Vatnajökull, large icefield (*c.* 3,150 sq. mi.) of SE Iceland. Flooding caused by eruptions of underlying volcanoes.

Vaud [Ger: **Waadt**], canton of SW Switzerland. Area: 1,239 sq. mi.; cap. Lausanne. Mountainous region; people primarily French-speaking and Protestant. Pop. (1963) 430,000.

vaudeville, stage show of light entertainment nature. Name derived from *Vau de Vire* songs of 15th cent. France. Amer. vaudeville flourished late 19th, early 20th cent.

Vaughan, Henry (1622–95), Brit. poet, b. Wales. Metaphysical verse includes *Silex Scintillans* (1650).

Vaughan Williams, Ralph (1872–1958), Eng. composer. Works influenced by folk music. Composed operas, ballets, songs and symphonies, incl. *London Symphony*. Interest

in Tudor music reflected in *Fantasia on a Theme by Thomas Tallis* (1910).

vault, in architecture, arched ceiling or roof built with stone or brick. Roman semi-circular form replaced by Gothic ribbed vaulting.

Veblen, Thorstein Bunde (1857–1929), Amer. social scientist. Author of *The Theory of the Leisure Class* (1899), analysis of values and motivations in business; coined phrase 'conspicuous consumption'. Also wrote *The Theory of Business Enterprise* (1904).

vector, in mathematics, a quantity of direction (*e.g.* velocity) and magnitude.

Veda, general term for scriptures of Hinduism. Includes oldest *Rig-Veda* hymns and supplementary *Sama-Veda*. Classics of Sanskrit literature, concentrate on Indra, bellicose national god.

Vedanta, orthodox writings of Brahminic (Hindu) philosophy, supplementing Upanishads. Written 5th cent. BC–AD 2nd cent., express pantheistic view of universe.

Vega [**Carpio**]. **Felix Lope de** (1562–1635), Sp. poet. Influential dramas (*c.* 1,500) featured sympathetic characters and disregard for classic unities.

vegetarianism, practice of restricting diet to foods of vegetable origin, for humanitarian or health reasons. Strict vegetarians abstain from all food which comes from animals *i.e.* incl. eggs, milk, butter, *etc.*

vein, blood vessel which takes deoxygenated blood from tissues to heart and, in the pulmonary system, oxygenated blood from lungs to heart. Vein walls are thinner than those of arteries and are provided with valves.

Velásquez, Diego Rodríguez de Silva y (1599–1660), Sp. painter. Appointed (1623) court painter to Philip IV. Noted works include *Surrender of Breda*; court portraits, *Maids of Honour*.

Velázquez, Diego de (*c.* 1460–*c.* 1524), Sp. conquistador. First gov. of Cuba which he conquered (1511–14) and colonized.

veld, veldt, grassy plateaus of E and S Africa. Cattle-herding and agriculture main occupations.

vellum, fine parchment made from specially treated calf or kid skins. Used as writing surface and in bookbinding.

velvet, fabric woven with short thick pile on one side, often made of silk. Modern grades include Lyon velvet, velveteen, corduroy.

Vendée, department of W France, on the Atlantic. Area: 2,700 sq. mi.; cap.

La Roche-sur-Yon. Centre of uprising (1793) against revolutionary govt., put down (1794–6). Pop. (1962) 408,900.

venereal disease (VD), group of infectious diseases usually transmitted by sexual contact with infected person. Include GONORRHOEA, SYPHILIS. Immediate medical treatment usually effective but may be fatal if untreated.

Venezuela [República de Venezuela], South Amer. federal republic on Caribbean Sea. Area: 352,141 sq. mi.;

cap. Caracas; main cities, Maracaibo, Valencia. Coastal lowlands, rich in oil (chief export) rise to cattle-raising regions of C plain; population centres in W highlands, where coffee, cacao produced; in E are unexploited Guiana highlands. European penetration begun by Columbus (1498). Independence wars (began 1810) successful under Bolívar; became repub. (1830). Subsequent history reflects class conflict. Official language, Spanish; religion, Roman Catholic. Unit of currency, bolivar. Pop. (1966) 9,352,000.

Venice, Venezia, Adriatic seaport and cap. of Venetia, NE Italy. Built on *c.* 115 islets, connected with mainland by bridges. Renowned for palaces, churches (*e.g.* St Mark's), canals and bridges (*e.g.* Bridge of Sighs). Became (7th cent.) city-state headed by doge. Maritime power (10th–15th cent.). Lost Gk. possessions to Turkey. Taken (1797) by Napoleon, placed under Austria. United with Italy (1866). Pop. (1965) 362,000.

Ventris, Michael George Francis (1922–56), Eng. archaeologist and linguist. Identified Linear B, language of tablets found at Cnossus, as ancient form of Greek.

Venus, in Roman religion, perhaps orig. goddess of gardens, through Sicilian, Gk. and Eastern influence became goddess of love, identified with Gk. Aphrodite. Earliest temple to her in Rome dedicated 295 BC. Venus Genetrix regarded as mother of Roman people.

Venus, in astronomy, planet 2nd in distance (*c.* 67,200,000 mi.) from Sun; diameter 7,700 mi. Appears as bright star in evening sky. Continuous layer of cloud impedes observation. Surface temperature (*c.* 800°F) recorded by US Mariner 2 (1962).

Venus's fly-trap, *Dionaea muscipula,* perennial-insectivorous herb native to N Carolina and Florida. Hinged leaves close when touched; insects trapped between the halves of leaves are digested.

Venus's looking-glass, annual herb of genus *Specularia.* Species include *S. speculum-veneris,* native to Eurasia and N Africa, and Amer. *S. perfoliata.*

venus's slipper, orchid of genus *Cypripedium,* native to Americas. Also known as venus's shoe.

Veracruz, city and chief seaport of Mexico on Gulf of Mexico. Cortéz landed (1519) near site later chosen for present city (1599). Serves rich agric. region. Pop. (1967) 186,000.

verbena, plant of genus *Verbena* chiefly native to trop. America. Many species grown as garden annuals for showy flowers. Species include European vervain, esp. *V. officinalis.*

Vercingetorix (d. 46 BC), Gallic leader. Headed uprising against Rome, suppressed (52 BC) by Julius Caesar.

Verdi, Giuseppe (1813–1901), Ital. composer. Major figure in 19th cent. opera, works include *Rigoletto* (1851), *La Traviata* (1853), *Aida* (1871), *Otello* (1887) and *Falstaff* (1893). Religious works include *Requiem* and *Stabat Mater.*

verdigris, greenish deposit formed on copper, brass or bronze surfaces exposed to the atmosphere. Consists principally of basic copper sulphate.

Verdun, town in Meuse department, NE France, on Meuse R. In World War 1, Marshal Pétain and General Nivelle withstood heavy Ger. offensive (1916).

Vereeniging, city, S Transvaal, Republic of South Africa, on Vaal R. Treaty ending South African War signed (1902). Coal-mining main industry. Pop. *c.* 70,000.

Verendrye, Pierre Gaultier de Varennes, Sieur de la (1685–1749), Canadian explorer of W Canada and US. Estab. fur-trading posts; journeyed (1738) from Assiniboine river to Missouri.

Vergil or **Virgil** [Publius Vergilius Maro] (70–19 BC), Roman poet, b. near Mantua, N Italy. During stay in Rome after 41 BC joined literary circle of Maecenas, met Augustus. Works are *Eclogues* (begun 43 BC, pub. 37 BC), 10 short pastoral poems; *Georgics* (completed 30 BC), didactic poem on agriculture in 4 books; AENEID (30–19 BC), epic poem in 12 books, celebrating origin and growth of Roman empire. Much influence on later pastoral and epic poetry, *e.g.* Spenser, Milton.

Verlaine, Paul (1844–96), Fr. Symbolist poet. Early works include *Fêtes Galantes* (1869). Return to Catholic faith inspired *Sagesse* (1881). Served prison sentence for shooting his intimate friend RIMBAUD.

Vermeer, Jan or **Johannes** (1632–75), Dutch painter, b. Delft. Major works,

The Milkmaid (*c.* 1658) by Vermeer

Viaduct in Switzerland

esp. subtly-lit interiors, include *Young Woman with a Water Jug* and *The Milkmaid.*

vermilion, red water-soluble pigment consisting of mercuric sulphide. Produced by reaction of mercury and sulphur. Used in paints.

Vermont, state of NE US. Area: 9,609 sq. mi.; cap. Montpelier; main city, Burlington. Predominantly mountainous and forested; agriculture mainly dairy farming. Brit. settlement began early 18th cent. Declared independence (1777), joined union (1791). Pop. (1960) 389,880.

vermouth, liquor prepared from white wines and flavoured with bitter and aromatic herbs. Made chiefly in France and Italy.

Verne, Jules (1828–1905), Fr. novelist. One of 1st to write modern science fiction. Works include *Journey to the Centre of the Earth* (1864), *Twenty Thousand Leagues under the Sea* (1870) and *Around the World in Eighty Days* (1873).

Verner, Karl Adolf (1846–96), Danish philologist. Formulated **Verner's law,** tabulating sound changes in the Germanic languages of Indo-European family.

Verona, city, NE Italy, on Adige R. Agric. market town; printing and paper works. Roman remains and 12th cent. cathedral. School of painting *fl.* 15th–16th cent. Pop. (1965) 242,000.

Verona, Congress of (1822), last meeting held under provisions of QUADRUPLE ALLIANCE of 1814; empowered France to suppress revolution against Ferdinand VII of Spain.

Veronese, Paolo, orig. Paolo Caliari (1528–88), Ital. painter of Venetian school, b. Verona. Works, rich in colour and design and often depicting religious feast scenes, include *Marriage at Cana, Supper at Emmaeus* and *The Rape of Europa.*

Veronica, Saint, woman of Jerusalem said to have wiped Jesus' face with towel on way to Calvary. Imprint of His face was left on towel.

veronica, speedwell, perennial flowering plant of genus *Veronica,* native to temp. regions. Many species cultivated as garden flowers.

Verrocchio, Andrea del, orig. Andrea Cioni di Michele (1435–88), Florentine artist and sculptor, pupil of Donatello. Taught Leonardo da Vinci.

Versailles, city and cap. of Yvelines department, SW of Paris, France. Grew around Palace of Versailles, built for Louis XIV (1661) by Louis Le Vau and J. H. Mansart, decorated by Charles Le Brun. Home of Fr. Court (1682–1790). Made museum and national monument by Louis Philippe.

Versailles, Treaty of, settlement (1919) incorporating agreements of Paris Peace Conference (1918–19) between World War 1 Allies (UK, France, US and Italy). Germany, not represented, forced to accept terms, incl. payment of reparations and return of occupied territory. Treaty also contained covenant of LEAGUE OF NATIONS.

vertebrae, bones comprising spinal column or backbone of vertebrates. Man has 33: 7 cervical, 12 dorsal, 5 lumbar; last 9 are fused to form sacrum and coccyx.

vertebrate, animal of subphylum Vertebrata with segmented spinal column or backbone. Includes mammals, birds, amphibians, reptiles, fish.

vertigo, temporary dizzy sensation caused by disturbance in balance mechanism of the inner ear, or by eye or brain malfunction.

vervain *see* VERBENA.

Verwoerd, Henrik Frensch (1901–66), South African polit. leader. During his term as P.M. (1958–66), South Africa became repub. Advocated supremacy of whites, largely responsible for development of APARTHEID. Assassinated in House of Assembly.

Vesalius, Andreas (1514–64), Flemish physician noted for anatomical studies disproving many of Galen's doctrines. Chief work, *De humani corporis fabrica* (c. 1546, tr. 1949).

Vespasian [Titus Flavius Sabinus Vespasianus] (AD 9–79), Roman emperor (AD 70–79), founder of Flavian dynasty. Restored finances and re-organized army. Built the Colosseum.

vespers, religious office for 6th of the canonical hours: said or sung generally in early evening.

Vespucci, Amerigo (1454–1512). Ital. navigator. Explored mouths of Amazon R. (1499). Evolved system for computing almost exact longitude. Proved S America was not part of Asia; continent named (1507) for him.

Vesta, in Roman religion, goddess of the hearth, worshipped in every house. Sacred fire of state kept ever burning in Temple of Vesta, tended by 6 **Vestal Virgins,** orig. daughters of noble families. Penalty for breaking vow of chastity was burial alive. Returned to private life after serving 30 yr.

Vestris, Madame, orig. Lucia Elizabeth Bartolozzi (1797–1856), Eng. actress, opera singer and theatre manager. Introduced realistic sets.

Vesuvius, active volcano, S Italy, near E shore of Bay of Naples. Main cone, 3,890 ft.; seismological observatory at 1,995 ft. Eruption (AD 79) destroyed Pompeii and Herculaneum.

vetch, annual or perennial leguminous herb of genus *Vicia* native of N temp. regions and S America. Mostly climbing varieties; purple or yellow flowers. Cultivated for forage and soil improvement, *e.g. V. sativa.*

veterinary medicine, diagnosis and treatment of diseases and injuries of animals. Treatment by vaccines, antibiotics, *etc.* has revolutionized animal disease control.

Equestrian statue of the *condottiere* Bartolommeo Colleoni by Verrocchio

Vicuña

veto, executive govt. action witholding consent of legislation. In UK, royal prerogative last invoked 1707; House of Lords has limited delaying power. In US, pres. veto can be overruled by two-thirds vote in Congress. In UN negative vote by Security Council permanent member constitutes veto.

V.H.F. [Very High Frequency], wireless emissions using high frequencies and short wavelengths. Necessary where medium wave transmissions overlap. **Ultra High Frequency** uses shorter wavelengths and higher frequencies.

viaduct, construction of bridges or arches designed for movement of train or car over depression, esp. valley. Made of wood, stone, or reinforced concrete.

vibraphone, type of GLOCKENSPIEL having mechanically induced vibrato.

vibration, in physics, movement in one direction and back again, as of pendulum. Rate of oscillation is called frequency. Also *see* SOUND.

viburnum, tree or shrub of genus *Viburnum* native to Europe, Asia and N Africa. Used as decoration.

Vichy, town of C France. Site of famous hot mineral springs, exported as Vichy water. Pop. (1962) 30,400.

Vichy government, admin. of unoccupied France (1940–4) during World War 2, cap. at Vichy. Estab. under Marshal PÉTAIN, became Ger.-controlled under PIERRE LAVAL. Regime ended (1944) with Allied invasion of France.

Vicksburg campaign, manoeuvres (1862–3) in US Civil War, undertaken by Union army under Grant. Capture of city of Vicksburg after 6-week siege and fall of Port Hudson placed entire Mississippi region under Northern control and split the Confederacy.

Vico, Giovanni Battista (1668–1744), Ital. philosopher and historian. In *Scienza Nuova* (1744) investigated theory of recurring hist. cycles.

Victor Emmanuel I (1759–1825), king of Sardinia (1802–21). Led Sardinians against Fr. occupying forces (1792–6). Abdicated.

Victor Emmanuel II (1820–78), king of Sardinia (1849–61) and Italy (1861–78). Ruled as constitutional monarch; supported Cavour and helped create unified Italy.

Victor Emmanuel III (1869–1947), king of Italy (1900–46). Supported Mussolini's rule of Italy until 1943. Abdicated.

Victoria (1819–1901), queen of Great Britain and Ireland (1837–1901). Befriended Lord Melbourne, P.M. at her accession to throne, m. Prince Albert of Saxe-Coburg (1840).

Clashed with Lord Palmerston on foreign policy. Became (1876) Empress of India with aid of Disraeli. Reign, marked by Brit. economic and colonial expansion, known as 'Victorian era'.

Victoria, Guadeloupe, orig. Manuel Félix Fernández (1789–1843), Mexican revolutionary. Took part (1811–24) in struggle for independence; 1st pres. (1824–9).

Victoria, Tomás Lius de [Ital: Tommaso Lodovico da Vittoria] (*c.* 1548–1611), Sp. composer, lived in Rome. Wrote church music, esp. masses, motets and psalms.

Victoria, cap. of Hong Kong, Brit. Crown Colony, SE China, on Hong Kong Is. Large natural harbour; trade centre. Pop. (1961) 675,000.

Victoria, port on Vancouver Is., cap. of Brit. Columbia, Canada. Founded (1843) as trading post. Good harbour facilities; industries include sawmills, cold-storage plants. Pop. (1964) 172,000.

Victoria, state of SE Australia. Area: 87,884 sq. mi.; cap. Melbourne. Comprises Murray-Darling basin, S plains, C and S highlands (incl. Australian Alps). Settled (1834–5) as part of New South Wales Colony; separated (1851); became state (1901). Industry, esp. machinery, textiles, important; agriculture, wool and cereals. Pop. (1966) 3,217,832.

Victoria Falls, falls of upper Zambesi R. S central Africa; comprises Main Falls, Rainbow Falls, Eastern Cataract. Discovered by David Livingstone 1855. Renamed Mosi-Oa-Toenja.

Victoria Nyanza, lake of E central Africa, bordered by Uganda, Tanganyika, and Kenya. Area: *c.* 26,830 sq. mi. World's 2nd largest freshwater lake. Discovered (1856), explored (1875) by Stanley.

Victoria regia, *Victoria amazonia,* waterlily with large circular leaves. Native to S America.

vicuña, *Lama vicugna,* wild S Amer. ruminant related to the guanaco. Found in the Andes. Soft brown wool.

Vidal, Gore (1925–), Amer. novelist. Works include *Messiah* (1954),

Washington, D.C. (1967). Also dramas, incl. *The Best Man* (1960).

Vienna, Wien, cap. of Austria on Danube R. Cultural, commercial, financial centre. Roman military centre; imperial residence and centre under Habsburgs (1278–1918). Besieged by Turks 1529, 1683. Under Maria Theresa (1740–80) attracted musicians incl. Haydn, Mozart, Beethoven. During early 20th cent. noted for contributions in medicine and psychiatry. Pop. (1964) 1,639,000.

Vienna, Congress of, meeting (1814–15) of European powers to settle problems arising out of defeat of Napoleon I. Resolved boundary disputes, estab. 'balance of power' principle in international politics. Negotiated chiefly by Metternich (Austria), Castlereagh (Britain) and Talleyrand (France).

Vientiane, admin. cap. of Laos, on Mekong R. Ancient cap. of Laotian kingdom and of Fr. dependency of Laos. Trading centre, esp. wood, textiles. Pop. (1962) 162,000.

Viet Cong, Communist military force engaged in guerilla warfare in South Vietnam during 1960s. Supported by North Vietnamese govt., successfully penetrated much of area despite increasing US aid to South Vietnam.

Vietnam, former state (1945–54) of SE Asia, comprising Annamese regions of Indo-China. Divided (1954) by Geneva Conference into North and South Vietnam at end of INDO-CHINESE WAR.

Vietnam, North, repub. of SE Asia. Area: 61,293 sq. mi.; cap. Hanoi. Predominantly agric. (rice chief crop), rapid indust. gains aided by

Victoria regia

Common Vole

mineral resources, esp. coal. State estab. (1954) by Geneva Conference;

Communist govt. headed by Ho CHI MINH supported prolonged offensive by VIET CONG in South Vietnam (1960s). Pop. (1968 est.) 20,100,000.
Vietnam, South, repub. of SE Asia. Area: 66,350 sq. mi.; cap. Saigon.

Economy based on agriculture (rice, rubber) of Mekong Delta and coastal lowlands. Repub. proclaimed (1955) shortly after withdrawal from French Union. US economic and military aid failed to avert increasing VIET CONG penetration of country during 1960s. Pop. (1965) 16,973,000.
Vietnamese, Asian language, with *c.* 20 million speakers in Vietnam.
Vigeland, Adolf Gustav (1869–1943), Norwegian sculptor. Best known work *The Fountains* (1915), large group of figures representing man's development.
Vigny, Alfred Victor, Comte de (1797–1863), Fr. Romantic poet, dramatist and novelist. Works, often bleak and pessimistic, include *Poèmes Antiques et Modernes* (1826), *Les Destinées* (1864) and drama *Chatterton* (1835).
Vikings, Scandinavian sea-raiders, also called Norsemen. Colonized parts of England, Ireland, France, Iceland (8th–10th cent.). Believed to have reached N America. Traded as far S and E as Persia, Spain, Russia.
Villa-Lobos, Heitor (1887–1959), Brazilian composer. Wrote operas, symphonies, piano and chamber music. His *Chôros* draws on folk music and culture of Brazil.
villanelle, poem, usually pastoral or lyrical in style, consisting of five 3-lined stanzas and final quatrain. Has only 2 rhymes throughout.
Villars, Claude, Duc de (1653–1734), marshal of France. In War of Spanish Succession won victories at Friedlingen (1702), Hochstadt (1703), Denain (1712); defeated at Malplaquet (1709). Negotiated treaty of Rastatt (1714).
villein, peasant of W Europe under medieval manorial system. Did not own land; owed services to lord.

Unlike serf was personally free. System declined in England by 14th cent. but survived elsewhere until 19th cent.
Villeneuve, Pierre Charles Jean Baptiste Silvestre de (1763–1806). Fr. admiral. Defeated by Nelson in Battle of Trafalgar (1805).
Villiers, George, 1st Duke of Buckingham (1592–1628), Eng. politician, favourite of James I. Urged marriage of James' son Charles to Henrietta Maria of France. Assassinated by an army officer.
Villon, François, orig. François de Montcorbier or François de Loges (b. 1431), Fr. poet. Involvement in brawls led to repeated arrests and banishment (1463). *Petit Testament* (1456) facetious parody of legal testament. Best known for *Grand Testament* (1461) melancholy and bitterly humorous in parts, containing ballades and rondeaux. Became popular as Romantic rogue-hero in 19th cent.
Vilna, city and cap. of Lithuanian SSR. Founded 10th cent. Commercial and indust. centre; manufactures leather, foodstuffs, chemicals, matches. Cap. of Lithuania (1323–1795), when passed to Russia. Incorporated by Poland (1920–39). Pop. (1966) 305,000.
Vincent de Paul, Saint (1576–1660), Fr. R.C. priest. Estab. societies for relief of poor in Fr. towns. Founded (1625) Lazarists or Congregation of the Mission, secular priests working in rural areas. Later founded Sisters of Charity for work in cities.
Vinci, Leonardo da *see* LEONARDO DA VINCI.
vine, climbing or trailing plant, either woody or herbaceous, of genus *Vitis.* Grown for ornament or edible fruit. Species include grape vine, Boston ivy, English ivy, Virginia creeper.
vinegar, sour liquid consisting of dilute and impure acetic acid, obtained by acetous fermentation from wine, beer, *etc.* Used as preservative in pickling and as a condiment.
vingt-et-un, game played with 52 cards in which players aim to hold cards totalling 21 points. Also known as pontoon or blackjack.
Vinland, portion of N Amer. coast discovered by Lief Ericsson (*c.* AD 1000). Location of landing disputed, most likely S coast of New England. Also known as Wineland.
vinyl group, chem. compound with a valence of one derived from ethylene.

Forms basis of plastics and fibres industries.
viol, family of 6 stringed instruments played with bow; popular esp. 16th-17th cent. Held between player's knees. Modern DOUBLE BASS is descended from this family.
viola, term for alto member of VIOLIN FAMILY.
viola da gamba, form of viol; 6 stringed instrument with similar range to 'cello.
violet, plant native to temp. regions of genus *Viola,* esp. *V. odorata* with small bluish-purple flowers. *V. tricolor* is the pansy.
violin family, string instruments whose 4 strings are bowed or plucked. Strings are stretched across a wooden bridge which transfers their vibrations to a sound chamber forming body of instrument. Members are violin, viola and violoncello ('cello), double bass.
Viollet-le-Duc, Eugène Emmanuel (1814–79), Fr. architect. Major figure in Gothic revival. Wrote classic works on medieval architecture, restored Fr. cathedrals incl. Notre Dame.
violoncello *see* CELLO.
viper, poisonous snake, incl. true viper of genus *Vipera,* of Europe, Asia, Africa, and pit viper of America and Asia. Flattened triangular head and relatively short thick body. Adder, *V. berus,* is a true viper. Pit vipers include bushmaster, copperhead, rattlesnake, water moccasin.
viper's bugloss, blueweed, *Echium vulgare,* coarse prickly weed of Europe, naturalized in US.
Virgil *see* VERGIL.
Virgin Island of the US, territory formerly part of Danish West Indies. Area: 133 sq. mi.; cap. Charlotte Amalie. Islands include St Thomas, St Croix, St John. Sugar-cane, rum distilling; tourism. Pop. (1965) 50,000. **British Virgin Islands,** presidency of Leeward Islands colony. Area: 59 sq. mi.; cap. Road Town. Islands include Tortola, Anegada,

Baby orchid, one of the violet-scented orchids

Men working in the vineyards
of Jerez de la Frontera, Spain

Virgin Gorda. Some grazing; sea-island cotton and tobacco grown.

Virgin Mary *see* MARY.

virginals *see* SPINET.

Virginia, E coast state of US. Area: 40,815 sq. mi.; cap. Richmond; main city, Norfolk. Bordered by Blue Ridge and Allegheny Mts.; farming and mining are chief occupations. Site of 1st permanent Eng. settlement (Jamestown, 1607) in Americas; became royal colony (1624). Opposed colonial rule before Amer. Revolution, achieved statehood 1788. Centre of conflict during Civil War (1861–5). Pop. (1960) 3,966,950.

Virginia creeper, *Parthenocissus quinquefolia,* N Amer. climbing vine, naturalized in Europe. Palmate leaves usually composed of 5 leaflets.

Virginia deer, *Odocoileus virginianus,* white-tailed deer of E N America. Also found in Guyana, Bolivia, Peru.

Virgo *see* ZODIAC.

virus, disease-causing micro-organisms smaller than bacteria. Parasitic, in that they multiply only in living cells. Identified as cause of poliomyelitis, measles, smallpox and some types of common cold.

Visayan, Malayo-Polynesian language, with 5 million speakers in scattered areas of Oceania.

Visconti, Ital. family, ruled Milan (13th cent.– 1447), acquiring all Lombardy and surrounding districts. **Giovanni Visconti** (1290–1354) added Bologna and Genoa to family territories. **Gian Galeazzo Visconti** (*c.* 1351–1402) commenced systematic conquest of independent cities, incl. Verona, Padua, Siena. Purchased (1395) title of hereditary duke. On death of son **Filippo Maria Visconti** (1392–1447), duchy passed to Sforza family.

viscose, solution prepared by treating cellulose with caustic soda and carbon bisulphide. Used in manufacturing regenerated cellulose fibres, sheets or tubes, as rayon or cellophane.

viscosity, property of fluids and some gases measured according to resistance to flow. Water has a low viscosity. High viscosity of, *e.g.* oil lessens with application of heat.

Vishnu, in late Hindu religion 2nd person of Trinity, 'the Preserver'. Certain traditions attribute to him various incarnations, incl. KRISHNA. Earlier legend associates him with solar deities of Rig-Veda.

Visigoths, major group of Ger. Gothic tribes in W. Driven SW by Hun invaders into Roman Danubian provs. Under Alaric I sacked Rome (410), later conquered Spain and much of S

France. Forced to retreat into Spain by Clovis (507). Finally defeated by Moors in Spain (711).

vision, function of the eye. *See* SIGHT.

Vistula, chief river (*c.* 663 mi.) of Poland. Rises in Carpathians, flows N through Poland to Baltic at Gdansk. Navigable for most of its length.

vitamin, one of group of organic compounds, essential in small quantities to normal body metabolism. Found in minute amounts in natural foodstuffs; also produced synthetically. Vitamin deficiencies cause various diseases. Classified as vitamin A, B, C, D, E and K complexes.

Vitebsk, city of Byelorussian SSR. Textile and machinery industries. Large Jewish population depleted by Ger. occupation during World War 2. Pop. (1966) 194,000.

Viterbo, city, Latium, C Italy. Medieval section remains with noted 12th cent. cathedral and Palace used by Popes (1255–67) still visible. Pop. (1965) 49,000.

vitriol, metallic sulphate of glassy appearance, such as copper sulphate (blue vitriol).

Vitruvius [Marcus Vitruvius Pollio] (*fl.* 1st cent. AD), Roman writer on architecture. His work *De Architectura* (Eng. tr. 1915) widely used by Renaissance architects.

Vittorini, Elio (1908–), Ital. writer. Works, reflecting experiences in antifascist underground, include *The Red Carnation* (1934, pub. 1948). Also wrote *Conversation in Sicily* (1941).

Vivaldi, Antonio (*c.* 1675–1741), Ital. composer of over 50 operas. Best known for *Concerti Grossi* and violin concertos.

Vivekananda, Swami (1863–1902), Hindu mystic and teacher. Instrumental in introducing theories of Ramakrishna to Europe and US.

Vladivostok, city and cap. of Maritime Territory, Russ. SFSR, port of eastern USSR, on Sea of Japan. Ice-free port 8 months of year. Founded 1860; military base in World Wars 1 and 2. Pacific terminus of Trans-Siberian Railway. Shipbuilding, fishing and whaling industries. Pop. (1967) 379,000.

Vlaminck, Maurice de (1876–1958), Fr. Expressionist artist and writer. Member of Fauve group. Works include landscapes, esp. snow scenes.

vodka, unaged colourless spirit distilled from potatoes, rye, maize or barley. Orig. made in Russia.

volcano, opening in earth's crust formed by subterranean molten material (magma) forcing its way to surface. Accumulation of steam may result in eruption when LAVA, rock

Vineyards at Beilstein
on the river Moselle

fragments, gases, *etc.* are released. Solidified lava and rock, deposited around outlet, form conical hill with craters. Volcanic regions include Italy, Indonesia, Japan, Pacific Islands (*e.g.* Hawaii).

vole, small rat-like rodent of genus *Microtus* and related genera. Blunt nose and short legs; herbivorous diet. Species include field vole, *M. agrestis,* water vole or water rat, *Arvicola amphibius,* and meadow vole, *M. pennsylvanicus,* of N America.

Volendam, town in NW Netherlands, on Lake Ijssell. Tourist centre. Pop. (1960 est.) 6,900.

Fishing boats in the harbour at
Volendam

Volga, river (*c.* 2,300 mi.) of European RSFSR, largest river in Europe. Rises in Valdai hills; wide delta on Caspian Sea. Linked by Volga-Baltic Waterway, Baltic-White Sea Canal, Moscow Canal and Volga-Don canal. Dams and hydro-electric stations in upper Volga; irrigation in lower region.

Volgograd, formerly **Stalingrad,** city of SE European RSFSR, port on lower Volga. Indust., commercial and communications centre. Founded 1589 as Tsaritsyn; called Stalingrad (1925–61). Resisted 6-month Ger. attack in World War 2. City rebuilt since war. Pop. (1967 est.) 720,000.

volleyball, game played by 2 teams on a court. Players hit a ball with their hands, attempt to return it over net without its touching ground. Originated (1895) in US by W. G. Morgan, became Olympic event (1964).

Volstead Act, legislation passed (1919) by US Congress over Pres. Wilson's veto. Provided for enforcement of PROHIBITION of alcoholic beverages. Repealed (1933) by 21st amendment.

volt, unit of electromotive force (emf), and unit of potential difference. Named after Ital. physicist Alessandro Volta (1745–1827). Defined as difference in potential which, applied to conductor of 1 ohm resistance, produces current of 1 ampère.

Volta, Allessandro, Conte (1745–1827), Ital. physicist. Invented electrophorus, an electrostatic device (1775); also voltaic pile (1800), 1st device for producing continuous electric current. Electric unit, the volt, named after him.

Voltaire, orig. François Marie Arouet (1694–1778), Fr. philosopher and writer. Attacked organized religion and civil repression, advocated Eng. liberalism. Ideas influenced movement which culminated in Fr. Revolution. Author of tragedy *Zaïre* (1732) and *Letters Concerning the English Nation* (1733). Best known philosophical work, satirical and witty, *Candide* (1759).

Volterra, Vito (1860–1940), Ital. mathematician and physicist. Adapted discovery of basis of functional analysis to form of integral (Volterran) equations.

volume, term for measure of bulk or space occupied by a body.

volvox, genus of small chlorophyll-bearing organisms forming hollow spherical colonies common in ponds. Regarded by zoologists as flagellate protozoans, by botanists as green algae.

Von Braun, Wernher (1912–   ), Ger. scientist. Developed V-2 rocket used against Britain in World War 2. Went to US to work on guided missiles; became director (1960) of Space Flight Center, Alabama, for National Aeronautics and Space Administration; worked on Apollo Project.

Voodoo, religion originating in W Africa, now practised in West Indies, esp. Haiti, S US and Brazil. Rites linked with serpent worship and sometimes cannibalism and human sacrifice.

Voronezh, city of S central European RSFSR, on Voronezh R. Manufactures include synthetic rubber, machinery, locomotives, aircraft. Pop. (1967) 592,000.

Voronoff, Serge (1866–1951), Fr. surgeon, b. Russia. Transplanted animal (chiefly monkey) glands for human rejuvenation and treatment of thyroid deficiency. Works include *From Cretin to Genius* (1941).

Voroshilov, Kliment Yefremovich (1881–1969), Russ. army officer and statesman. Prominent during Revolution. As Commissar for defence (1925–40) reorganized army and developed air force. Directed defence of Leningrad in World War 2. Pres. of USSR (1953–60).

Vorster, Balthazar Johannes (1915–   ), South African politician; P.M. (1966–   ). Advocate of strict policy of apartheid.

vortex, term used to describe rapid rotary motion around an axis. Used mostly of fluids (whirlpools) and of air (tornadoes, whirlwinds).

Vosges, mountain range of E France. Highest peak, Ballon de Guebwiller (4,672 ft.). Pastures, pine forests, vineyards (on E slopes); tourist centre.

Vulcan, in early Roman religion, fire god, perhaps god of the smithy; later identified with Gk. Hephaestus (son of Zeus and Hera and husband of Aphrodite).

Vulgate, Latin version of Bible based largely on translation of Hebrew text by St Jerome. Chosen (1592) by Council of Trent as official version in Roman Catholic Church.

vulture, large broad-winged bird of temp. and trop. regions. Strong elongated beak and featherless neck and head; feeds on carrion. Species include the lammergeier, Egyptian vulture, *Neophron perconopterus*, turkey buzzard, *Cathartes aura*, king vulture, *Sarcorhamphus papa*.

Vyshinsky or **Vishinsky, Andrei Yanuarievich** (1883–1954), Russ. statesman and jurist. Main prosecutor during Moscow treason trials (1936–8), foreign min. (1949–53), UN representative (1953–4). Author of *The Law of the Soviet State* (Eng. tr. 1948).

The Andean Condor is the largest of the Vulture family

Waals, Johannes Diderik van der (1837–1923), Dutch physicist. Awarded Nobel Prize for Physics (1910) for equation of state of gases and liquids.

Wace, Robert (c. 1100–c. 1175), Anglo-Norman chronicler. Author of metrical chronicles incl. *Roman de Brut* (1155), derived from Geoffrey of Monmouth's *Historiae*; important source of ARTHURIAN LEGEND.

wadi, waddy, in arid regions of Asia and N Africa, a defined depression in the terrain. Esp. stream bed, dry except during rainy season.

wage, return, in goods, services or money, on labour. Real wages determined by amount of goods monetary wages will buy. Wage theorists include Ricardo and Marx.

Wagga Wagga, town of New South Wales, Australia on the Murrumbidgee R. Rich agric. district. Pop. (1963) 22,000.

Wagner, Richard (1813–83), Ger. composer, writer and conductor. Developed theory of opera as musical drama. Founded festival theatre at Bayreuth for own productions; presented 4-opera cycle *Ring of the Nibelungs* (1876), also *Parsifal* (1882). Earlier operas included *Flying Dutchman* (1843), *Tannhäuser* (1843–5) and *Lohengrin* (1850).

Wagner-Juaregg, Julius (1857–1940), Austrian neurologist. Awarded Nobel Prize for Physiology and Medicine (1927) for work on fever therapy, esp. treatment of paresis.

wagon train, means of transportation in which several wagons drawn by animals travelled together for mutual protection. Used esp. 18th–19th cent. migration to Amer. west.

Wagram, village, N of Vienna, Austria. Scene of defeat of Austrians by Napoleon I (1809).

wagtail, small, chiefly Old World bird of family Motacillidae related to pipit. Slender body with long narrow tail.

Wahabi, followers of Mohammed ibn Abd al-Wahabi (1703–87) who founded strict Moslem religious sect.

Wahabi worship in unadorned mosques, may not wear silk.

Wakefield, Edward Gibbon (1796–1862), Eng. colonial statesman. Organized association for founding South Australia (1834). Became managing director of New Zealand Association (1837); was instrumental in colonization of New Zealand.

wake-robin, various wild flowers of *Trillium* genus of N America and Eurasia. Also the CUCKOO PINT.

Waksman, Selman Abraham (1888–), Russ.-Amer. microbiologist. Awarded Nobel Prize for Physiology and Medicine (1952) for discovering streptomycin.

Walcheren, North Sea island of Zeeland prov., Netherlands. Area: 82 sq. mi.; chief cities Vlissingen, Middelburg. Agric. centre.

Wald, George (1906–). Amer. biologist. Awarded Nobel Prize for Physiology and Medicine (1967) for ophthalmological researches.

Waldenses, Christian sect formed (1170) by Pierre de Waldo of Lyon. Lived in poverty, emphasized Bible and rejected several R.C. doctrines; condemned as heretics (1215). Persecuted 15th-17th cent., recognized (1848) by Charles Albert of Savoy. Sect survives in Piedmont.

Wales and Monmouthshire, principality of British Isles. Area: 8,006 sq. mi.; cap. Cardiff; cities, Swansea, Newport, Port Talbot. Cambrian Mts. cover most of interior rising to 3,560 ft. (Mt. Snowdon). Rivers include Severn, Wye and Dee. Industries mainly in S, coalmining, heavy engineering, tinplate, iron and steel works; manufacture of textiles, nylon and plastics. Orig. inhabited by Iberians, country later overrun by Celts. Resisted Romans, Anglo-Saxons and Normans. Country finally annexed (1277) by Edward I of England, polit. integration achieved (1536). Welsh retain own language and culture. Pop. (1967) 2,709,930.

Walker, William (1824–60), Amer. adventurer. Invaded (1855) Nicaragua, captured Granada, estab. himself as pres. Ousted (1857) by Central Amer. powers, captured and shot.

Wall Street, street in Manhattan, New York City, site of Stock Exchange and financial centre of US.

wallaby, small kangaroo of genera *Macropus, Thylogale, Petrogale.* Found in Australia and Tasmania.

Wallace, Alfred Russel (1823–1913), Eng. naturalist. Originated a theory of evolution independently of Darwin, to whom he sent his findings. Joint paper published 1858.

Wallace, Edgar (1875–1932), Eng.

Wall Street, New York

author, best known for crime thrillers, incl. *The Four Just Men* (1905), *The Green Archer* and *The Hand of Power.*

Wallace, George Corley (1919–), Amer. politician. Gov. of Alabama (1963–7). 3rd party pres. candidate (1968), polled 13% of vote for Amer. Independent Party.

Wallace, Henry Agard (1888–1965), Amer. politician. F. D. Roosevelt's Sec. of Agriculture (1933–41) and Vice-Pres. (1941–5). PROGRESSIVE PARTY candidate for pres. (1948).

Wallace, Lew[is] (1827–1905), Amer. lawyer, diplomat, writer. Author of popular novel *Ben Hur* (1880).

Wallace, Sir William (c. 1270–1305), Scot. hero in struggle for independence. Led army which drove English from Stirling (1297), and took title of Gov. of Scotland. Defeated (1298) by Edward I at Falkirk. Captured and executed in London.

Wallace Collection, collection of paintings, esp. Fr., and *objets d'art,*

A mining valley in South Wales

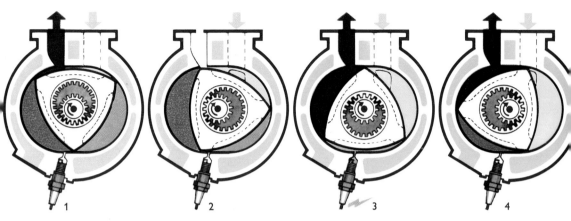

Wankel rotary engine: the diagrams illustrate its continuous cycle which lacks the 'stroke' of a conventional internal combustion engine. *Yellow* represents the induction mixture, *orange* the compression mixture, *red* the ignited mixture which escapes as exhaust (*brown*)

inherited by Sir Richard Wallace (1818–90) from his father, Marquis of Hertford. Now on view Hertford House, London.

Wallach, Otto (1847–1931), Ger. chemist. Awarded Nobel Prize for Chemistry (1910) for work on alicyclic compounds.

Wallachia, region of Romania, consisting of former provs. of Greater and Lesser Wallachia. Roman prov. of Dacia, conquered in turn by Turks and Hungarians. Union with MOLD-AVIA led to estab. of Romania.

wallcreeper, *Tichodroma muraria*, small grey-black bird of nuthatch family with crimson wing-patches. Inhabits cliffs and mountainous areas of S Asia, Europe and N Africa.

Wallenstein, Albrecht von (1583–1634), Austrian general under Ferdinand II in Thirty Years War. After several victories, dismissed (1630) for loss at Stralsund (1628). Recalled (1631) to fight Swedes, defeated at Lutzen (1632). Murdered, prob. for secret peace negotiations.

Waller, Edmund (1606–87), Eng. poet. Best known poems include 'Of Divine Love' and 'Go, Lovely Rose'.

walleye, *Stizostedion vitreum*, large N Amer. freshwater game and food fish. About 3 ft. long; large staring eyes.

wallflower, *Cheiranthus cheiri*, European plant with sweet-scented yellow or orange flowers. Many garden species cultivated.

Wallis and Futuna, Fr. protectorate of S Pacific Ocean. Comprises Wallis and Hoorn islands. Area: *c.* 75 sq. mi. Pop. (1963 est.) 10,000.

Walloons, people of Liège region of Belgium speaking Walloon, a Fr. dialect. Number *c.* 4 million. Friction between Walloons and Flemish remains element of Belgian politics.

walnut, deciduous tree of genus *Juglans* of N temp. zones. Edible fruit; timber used in cabinet making. Species include Persian or English walnut, *J. regia*, and black walnut, *J. nigra*, of E US.

Walpole, Horace, 4th Earl of Orford (1717–97), Eng. writer. Remembered for his *Correspondence* and Gothic novel *The Castle of Otranto* (1764).

Popularized Gothic revival, among 1st to write art history.

Walpole, Sir Robert, 1st Earl of Orford (1676–1745), Eng. statesman. Chancellor of Exchequer, leader of Whig administration and in effect 1st Brit. P.M. (1721–42). Restored economic stability after SOUTH SEA BUBBLE; encouraged policy of free trade, friendship with France and increase in power of House of Commons. Estab. principle of collective responsibility of cabinet and P.M. to parl.

Walpurgis, Saint (d. 779), Eng. nun. Missionary to Germany, abbess of Benedictine nunnery at Heidenheim. Walpurgisnacht, the eve of her Feast Day (1 May) coincides with pagan festival associated with witches.

walrus, either of 2 species of Arctic seal-like carnivorous mammals of family Odobenidae. *Odobenus rosmarus* inhabits NW Atlantic, Arctic and *O. divergens* the Bering Sea. Males up to 10–12 ft. long may weigh over 1 ton. Hunted for oil-yielding blubber, hide, ivory tusks.

Walsingham, Sir Francis (*c.* 1530–90), Eng. statesman and diplomat. Under Elizabeth I, joint Sec. of State. Operated govt. spy system, instrumental in condemnation of Mary Queen of Scots.

Walther von der Vogelweide (*c.* 1170–1230), Austrian lyric poet and musician. Most famous of Minnesingers.

Walton, Ernest Thomas Sinton (1903–), Irish physicist. With Sir John Cockcroft awarded Nobel Prize for Physics (1951) for work on atomic nuclei.

Walton, Izaak (1593–1683), Eng.

Wapiti

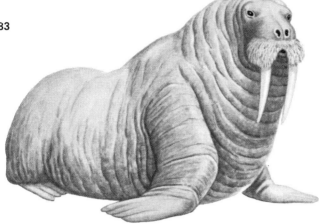

Walrus

author. Wrote biographies of Donne, Herbert and Bishop Sanderson; better known for *Compleat Angler, or, The Contemplative Man's Recreation* (1653).

Walton, Sir William Turner (1902–), Eng. composer. Works include setting of poems by Edith Sitwell, *Façade* (1923, later a ballet); oratorio *Belshazzar's Feast* (1931); film scores (*Henry V*, 1945, and *Hamlet*, 1948); opera *Troilus and Cressida* (1954).

waltz, dance in triple time developed from Ger. *Ländler*. Popularity spread from Vienna owing to compositions of Strauss family.

wandering Jew, trailing or creeping ornamental plant, esp. *Zebrina pendula* and *Tradescantia fluminensis*.

Wanganui, city of North Island, New Zealand on Wanganui R. Major wool and meat market. Pop. (1962) 34,100.

Wankel rotary engine, advanced type of internal combustion engine invented by Felix Wankel. Uses rotary rather than reciprocal motion of pistons.

wapatoo, wapata, underground tubers of arrowhead plant, *Sagittaria latifolia*, used as food by N Amer. Indians.

wapiti, *Cervus canadensis,* Amer. elk, similar to European red deer, found in Canada and W US.

war, armed conflict prosecuted by force. International war is that between sovereign states; civil war between factions within a state. Total war is waged not only against a nation's forces but against its complete population.

war crimes, actions during war for which defeated side is held criminally responsible. Legal principle estab. (1943) by UN War Crimes Commission. As result, Nazi polit. and military leaders brought to trial at Nuremberg (1945–6). *See* NUREMBERG TRIALS.

war debts, Inter-Allied debts, names given to financial obligations incurred between Allied govts. during and after World Wars 1 and 2.

War of 1812, conflict (1812–15) between US and UK; declared by US Congress. US claimed rights of neutral shipping to trade with France, disputed by Britain. In course of campaign Brit. forces took Washington before being halted at Fort McHenry (1814). War ended officially by Treaty of Ghent (1814) before final defeat of Brit. forces at New Orleans by Andrew Jackson (1815).

Warbeck, Perkin, (1474–99), pretender to English crown. Persuaded he was son of Edward IV, acknowledged by French and Scots, unsuccessfully invaded England (1496). Captured by Henry VII and hanged.

warble fly, 2-winged fly related to bluebottle. Larvae feed in skin of cattle causing rounded swellings. Cattle species is *Hypoderma bovis.*

Old market square in Warsaw

Great Reed Warbler

South and C Amer. warble fly, *Dermatobia hominis,* preys on man.

warbler, small insectivorous songbird. Old World warblers of family Sylviidae have brown plumage. Species include garden warbler, *Sylvia borin,* blackcap, *S. atricapilla.* Amer. warblers of family Parulidae are brightly-coloured; species include black-throated blue warbler, *Dendroica caerulescens,* yellow warbler, *D. petechia.*

Warburg, Otto Heinrich (1883–1970), Ger. physiologist. Awarded Nobel prize for Physiology and Medicine (1931) for discovery of respiratory enzyme.

Ward, Artemus, orig. Charles Farrar Browne (1834–67), Amer. journalist. Remembered for humorous column, 'Artemus Ward's Sayings' in Cleveland *Plain Dealer.*

Warhol, Andy (1930–), Amer. 'pop' artist and film-maker. Works include enlarged replicas of everyday objects, *e.g.* soup cans, cigarette packets, and controversial film *Chelsea Girls.*

Warlock, Peter orig. Philip Heseltine (1894–1930), Eng. composer of songs and chamber music incl. 'The Curlew'. Under own name wrote on music, edited Elizabethan songs.

Warner, Charles Dudley (1829–1900), Amer. editor and writer. Wrote travel essays, collaborated with Mark Twain on *The Gilded Age* (1873).

Warren, Earl (1891–), Amer. jurist and politician. Gov. of California (1943–52), unsuccessful Repub. vice pres. candidate (1948). Chief Justice of US Supreme Court (1953–69). Chairman, WARREN COMMISSION (1964–5).

Warren, Robert Penn (1905–), Amer. novelist, poet, critic. Southern background and ties led him to help found and edit (1935–42) *Southern Review* and are basis for novels incl. *All the King's Men* (1946) and *World Enough and Time* (1950).

Warren Commission, US commission appointed (1964) by Pres. Johnson to investigate assassination of John F. Kennedy. Unanimous but controversial report found no conspiracy, claimed Lee Oswald acted alone.

Warsaw, cap. of Poland, on Vistula R. Trading centre since Middle Ages; seat of Polish govt. from

Water Buffalo

1596. Old City destroyed in World War 2; majority of population deported or killed by Nazis. Many old buildings since reconstructed from drawings and paintings. Pop. (1965) 1,253,000.

Warsaw Treaty Organization, estab. (1955) under mutual defence treaty signed in Warsaw, Poland. Charter members: Albania, Bulgaria, Czechoslovakia, East Germany, Hungary, Poland, Romania, USSR; Albania unrepresented since 1962. Treaty binding for 20 yr., formed to counter remilitarization of West Germany.

wart, small, usually hard growth on skin. Most common on hands and neck. Treated by application of

Buddhist monks outside the Wat Phra Kao temple in Bangkok

acid or by cauterization. In some cases, disappears spontaneously.

wart hog, *Phacochoerus aethiopicus,* African wild swine with large tusks and warty skin on face.

Warton, Thomas (1728–90), Eng. poet and scholar. Works include *Poems* (1777); *The History of English Poetry* (1774–87). Made Poet Laureate (1785).

Warwick, Richard Neville, 1st Earl of (1428–71), Eng. nobleman, known as 'the Kingmaker'. During Wars of the Roses, joined Yorkists; captured Henry VI (1460), placed Edward IV on throne (1461). Later changed sides; attempt to reinstate Henry (1470) led to defeat and death in battle at Barnet.

Warwick, municipal borough and county town of Warwickshire, C England. Has castle (begun 1394) and university (founded 1965). Pop. (1967 est.) 17,700.

Warwickshire, county of C England, in Midlands. Area: 983 sq. mi.; county town, Warwick; main centres, Birmingham, Coventry, Leamington, Rugby. Extensive agric. region. Industries include iron and steel, motor car manufacturing. Pop. (1966) 2,095,000.

Wasatch range, mountain chain of US, from SE Idaho to C Utah. Av. ht. 10,000 ft.; highest peak, Mt. Timpanogos, 11,750 ft.

Wash, the, inlet of North Sea on E coast of C England, 20 mi. long, 15 mi. wide. Shallow, with shifting sandbanks and marshy shores.

Washington, Booker T[aliaferro] (1856–1915), Amer. reformer. First pres. of Tuskegee Institute (1881–1915). Believed education would best serve Negro cause. Wrote autobiog. *Up From Slavery* (1901).

Washington, George (1732–99), 1st US Pres. (1789–97), Federalist. Distinguished in Fr. Indian Wars (1753–7), served in Virginia House of Burgesses (1759–74), represented Va. in Continental Congress (1774–5). Appointed (1775) commander of

Continental Army in AMERICAN REVOLUTION, led campaigns leading to Brit. surrender (1781). Presided over Constitutional Convention (1787), unanimously elected US pres. Administration marked by split between ALEXANDER HAMILTON and THOMAS JEFFERSON, and resignation of latter. Set precedent by refusing 3rd term. In Farewell Address (1796) warned against foreign entanglements. Retired to home, Mt. Vernon.

Washington, coastal state of NW US, named after George Washington. Area: 68,192 sq. mi.; cap. Olympia; main cities, Seattle, Spokane, Tacoma. Mountainous in W, main river is Columbia. Fur-trading posts estab. early 19th cent.; became state 1889. Agriculture and lumbering important; also mining and fishing. Pop. (1960) 2,853,214.

Washington, cap. of US, located in federal territory, District of Columbia, E US. Built on land ceded by Maryland and Virginia, site selected by George Washington. Contains White House, Capitol, govt. buildings, 4 universities. Pop. (1960) 763,956.

Washington, Mount, highest peak (6,288 ft.) of White Mts., New Hampshire, US.

Washo, Amer. Indian tribe, from L. Washo area of W Nevada. Conquered by the Paiute (1862), only few remain on reservations in California, Nevada.

wasp, carnivorous winged insect of widespread distribution, incl. social and solitary species. Former have queens, sexless workers and male drones. Queens lay eggs and alone survive winter in temp. regions.

Wassermann, August von (1866–1925), Ger. bacteriologist. Discovered (1906) chemical reaction now known as Wassermann test, widely used for diagnosis of syphilis.

Wat Phra Kao, Buddhist temple in Bangkok, Thailand. A famous shrine with coloured roofs and gilded spires.

water (H_2O), transparent colourless liquid; chemical compound of hydrogen and oxygen. Tasteless and chemically neutral in pure state. Freezing and boiling points under normal atmospheric pressure: 0°C (32°F) and 100°C (212°F). Poor conductor of heat and electricity.

water beetle, black or dark-coloured aquatic beetle, esp. of family Dytiscidae. Hind legs function like oars.

water boatman, aquatic insect of family Corixidae with paddle-like hind legs, *e.g. Notonecta glanca.*

water buffalo, *Bubalus bubalis,* buffalo of S Asia and Borneo with

Water Pipit

backward curving black horns. Used as draught animal.

watercress, *Nasturtium officinale,* hardy perennial European herb naturalized in N America. Found in or around water, pungent leaves used as garnish and in salads.

water cricket, *Velia caprai,* predaceous insect with stout body and short legs. Found on water surface; feeds on insects and spiders.

water crowfoot, aquatic or marsh plant of genus *Ranunculus,* widespread in Europe and N America. Species include *R. aquatilis* with white flowers, and yellow water crowfoot, *R. flabellaris,* of N America.

water deer, *Hydropotes inermis,* small Chinese deer. Neither sex has antlers; males have tusks.

water flea, small dark or brightly-coloured aquatic crustacean, *e.g.* of genera *Cyclops* and *Daphnia.*

water gas, colourless poisonous gas, compound of carbon monoxide and hydrogen. Burns with intensely hot flame, widely used as fuel.

water gnat, marsh treader, elongated pond-surface or marsh bug of family Hydrometridae.

water hyacinth, *Eichhornia crassipes,* trop. floating aquatic plant with violet funnel-shaped flowers. Troublesome river weed.

water lily, aquatic plant of genus *Nymphaea* with large dish-like floating leaves and brightly coloured flowers. Species include *N. alaba* of Europe and *N. odorata* of America.

water louse, freshwater crustacean related to wood louse found in weedy streams and ponds. Species include *Asellus aquaticus.*

water mark, design impressed in paper. Used esp. in banknote manufacture to discourage forgery.

water mite, water spider, water tick, small arachnid of group Hydrachnellae, esp. freshwater mite.

water moccasin, cottonmouth, *Agkistroden piscivorus,* venomous pit viper of marshes of S US reaching 6 ft. in length. Olive or brown in colour; feeds on fish and amphibians.

water ouzel *see* DIPPER.

water pipit, *Anthus spinoletta,* small singing bird of Eurasia and N America. *A. s. rubescens,* a common Amer. variant, resembles the lark.

water polo, water sport devised in 1870s. Played by 2 teams of 7 swimmers; goals scored by pushing inflated ball across opponents' line. Olympic event since 1900.

Water Lily

water rat, general name for various rodents which live near water, esp. European *Arvicola amphibius.* Also N Amer. muskrat, *Ondatra zibethica,* and Austral. water rats of genus *Hydromys.*

water scorpion, aquatic predaceous insect of family Nepidae. Powerful forelegs, flat oval body and long tube at end of abdomen for breathing. Species include *Nepa cinerea.*

water shrew, semi-aquatic shrew with hind feet fringed with stiff hairs. Species include widely distributed Old World shrew, *Neomys fodiens*; shrews of genus *Chimarrogale* of Japan, Borneo and Sumatra; common N Amer. shrew, *Serex palustris.*

water skiing, aquaplaning, orig. French sport of skiing on water on short, broad skis while being pulled by motor boat. World Water Ski Union, (founded 1949) organizes world championships.

water spider, aquatic European

View of Washington, showing the Jefferson Memorial (foreground) and the Washington Monument (obelisk, in background)

Waterbuck

spider, *Argyoneta aquatica*. Constructs underwater bell-shaped silk structure filled with air bubbles brought from surface. Large Amer. species, *Dolomedes sexpunctatus*, runs over surface of water.

water thyme *see* WATERWEED.

water violet, water gilliflower, aquatic plant with spongy inflated flower stalks. Species include European *Hottonia palustris* and N Amer. *H. inflata*.

waterbuck, *Kobus ellipsiprymnus,* large game antelope with long horns. Found in swamps of S and E Africa.

watercolour, type of painting and the paint used; *i.e.* solid or semi-solid, blended with water rather than oil.

waterfall, abrupt descent of water over ledge in river-bed. Caused normally by greater degree of erosion in weaker rock strata below fall. Examples include Niagara, US-Canada (*c.* 165 ft.), Victoria Falls (*c.* 355 ft.) on Zambesi R., Africa.

Waterford, county town and port of Co. Waterford, Repub. of Ireland, on R. Suir. Centre of 18th cent. glass industry. Pop. 28,700.

Waterfall at Jostedalsbre, Norway

water-glass, soluble glass made by fusing sodium carbonate with silica. Transparent, adhesive and soluble in water. Used esp. as cement in fireproofing and for preserving eggs.

waterhen *see* MOORHEN.

Waterloo, Battle of, defeat in S Belgium (June 1815) of Napoleon (after return from Elba), by British, Dutch and Germans under Duke of Wellington, and Prussians under Blücher. Napoleon, threatened in E by Austrians and Russians, supported Marshal Ney in attack on Allies near Brussels. Fr. rout led to Napoleon's abdication (22 June).

watermelon, *Citrullus vulgaris,* annual trailing vine native to trop. Africa. Widely cultivated for large globular or elongated fruits which have a hard green rind and pink or red sweet, watery pulp.

water-milfoil, aquatic temp. herb of genus *Myriophyllum*. Submersed leaves are finely divided.

waterpower, power of water used to drive machinery, as in water mills, wheels, *etc*. See HYDRO-ELECTRIC POWER.

watershed, elevated land separating head-waters of 2 river systems or groups of systems. May be distinct mountain range, *e.g.* Andes of S America.

waterskater *see* PONDSKATER.

watersnake, harmless snake of genus *Natrix* common in E US. Found in or near fresh water; feeds on aquatic mammals. Also E Asian or Austral. snake of family Homalopsidae.

waterspout, tornado occurring at sea. Column effect is caused by revolving funnel of mist and raindrops extending from low cloud to surface of water.

Waterton-Glacier International Peace Park, S Alberta, Canada and NW Montana, US. Area: 725 sq. mi., set aside (1932) by Canadian Parl. and US Congress. Made up of Waterton Lakes National Park in Canada and Glacier National Park, US.

waterweed, ditch moss, water thyme, perennial aquatic herb of genus *Elodea* of freshwater streams and ponds. Widespread in trop. and temp. regions. Commonly used in aquaria.

Watling Street, Roman road running *c.* 100 mi. from London via St Albans to Wroxeter in Shropshire, England.

Watson, James Dewey (1928–), Amer. biologist. Shared Nobel Prize for Physiology and Medicine (1962) with M. Wilkins and F. Crick for estab. of structure and function of nucleic acid (DNA).

Watson, John Broadus (1878–1958), Amer. psychologist. Pioneer of behaviourism, shifting emphasis from conscious analysis to study of response to stimuli. Wrote *Animal Education* (1903), *Behaviourism* (1925).

Watson-Watt, Sir Robert Alexander (1892–), Brit. physicist. Developed method of locating aircraft by radio waves (radar), used in World War 2.

Watson-Wentworth, Charles, 2nd Marquis of Rockingham (1730–82), Eng. Whig statesman, P.M. (1765–6, 1782). Attempted to reconcile N Amer. colonists with repeal of Stamp Act.

Watt, James (1736–1819), Scot. mechanical engineer. His fundamental improvements to efficiency of existing steam engine (Newcomen) led to widespread use of steam power as means of propulsion in machinery, railway engines, *etc.*

watt, unit of electrical power. Represents power used to maintain a current of 1 ampère under pressure of 1 volt, measured by wattmeter. Named after James Watt.

Watteau, Antoine (1648–1721), Fr. painter of Flemish descent. Noted esp. for fanciful pastoral scenes featuring either courtiers or peasants.

wattle, name for various Austral. shrubs of genus *Acacia*.

Watts, Isaac (1674–1748), Eng. non-conformist minister and hymnwriter. Among surviving hymns are 'O God our help in ages past'. Poetry includes 'How doth the little busy bee'.

Waugh, Evelyn Arthur St John (1903–66), Eng. novelist. Satirical novels incl. *Decline and Fall* (1929), *Vile Bodies* (1930), *Brideshead Revisited* (1944); also trilogy, *Men at Arms* (1952), *Officers and Gentlemen* (1955), *Unconditional Surrender* (1961).

wave, in physics, general term for energy-bearing, self-propagating disturbance in any medium or in space,

Weaver bird

Feast in a Park by Watteau

e.g. waves of sea, sound waves, light rays. Distance between peaks of disturbance is called **wavelength** and number of crests per second is frequency.

Wavell, Archibald Percival, 1st Earl Wavell (1883–1950), Brit. army officer. Commander-in-chief in Middle East (1939–41), defeated Italians at Cyrenaica (1940). Viceroy of India (1943–7), involved in negotiations for Indian independence.

wax, substance composed mainly of esters of fatty acids and alcohols. Secreted by bees, certain plants and sperm whales. Paraffin is a mineral wax. Insoluble in water, waxes are used for candles, polishes, waterproofing, *etc.*

wax myrtle, candleberry, shrub or tree of genus *Myrica*. Species include *M. cerifera* of E N America. Small hard berries have coating of wax used for candlemaking.

wax tree, any tree yielding wax. Species include Japanese wax tree, *Rhus succedanea;* evergreen privet, *Ligustrum lucidum,* of E Asia with dark green leaves and white flowers; Chinese ash, *Fraxinus chinensis,* encrusted with white wax by insects.

waxbill, Old World weaverbird, esp. of genus *Estrilda*. White, pink or red bill of waxy appearance.

waxwing, Amer. or Eurasian songbird of genus *Bombycilla*. Brown velvety plumage and wings with scarlet, waxlike tips. Species include Bohemian *waxwing, B. garrula pallidiceps* and cedar waxwing, *B. cedrarum.*

wayfaring tree, type of VIBURNUM.

Wayne, Anthony (1745–96), patriot leader during Amer. Revolution. Held command at Brandywine (1777) and led successful surprise attack on Brit. forces at Stony Point (1779).

Waziristan, region of West Pakistan. Area: *c.* 5,000 sq. mi. Home of Pathan tribes. Until 1955 part of North-West Frontier prov. Pop. *c.* 420,000.

Weald, district of low sandstone hills in SE England in Kent, Sussex and Surrey, between North and South Downs. Site of Roman and Anglo-Saxon iron-works.

weasel, small carnivorous mammal of genus *Mustela* native to temp. and cold regions of N hemisphere. Long slender body, long neck and short legs; reddish-brown coat above, white below.

weather, state of atmosphere at given place and time. Factors include heat, atmospheric pressure, humidity, cloud cover, *etc.* Weather forecasts are based on low and high pressure areas, topography and previous re cords. *See* METEOROLOGY.

weathering, disintegration of rock at earth's surface under atmospheric influences. Rain, frost and temperature changes break up rock, gradually forming soil.

weaverbird, weaver finch, bird of family Ploceidae related to the finches. Chiefly African and Asian. Builds elaborately woven nests.

weaving, interlacing of yarns to form a fabric, usually done on a loom. Warp yarn runs lengthwise and weft, woof, or filling, runs crosswise. Basic weaves are plain, twill and satin.

Webb, Sidney James, Baron Passfield

Waxwing

(1859–1947), Brit. socialist theorist and economist. With his wife, **Beatrice [Potter] Webb** (1858–1943) and others, founded Fabian Soc., influential in Brit. labour movement. Their works include *History of Trade Unionism* (1894), *Soviet Communism* (1935).

Weber, Carl Maria Friedrich Ernst von (1786–1826), Austrian composer. Works included popular romantic operas *Der Freischütz* (1820) and *Oberon* (1826).

Weber, Max (1864–1920), Ger. sociologist. Pioneer of modern social science, esp. in analysis of leadership. In *The Protestant Ethic and the Spirit of Capitalism* (1904–5), related rise of capitalism to Protestant teachings.

Weber, Max (1881–1961), Amer. artist, b. Russia. Pioneer of abstract Cubism in US. Later works developed representational expressionist style.

Webern, Anton von (1883–1945), Austrian composer. Pupil of Schoenberg. Later works, esp. for small groups of instruments, characterized by brevity and complete abandonment of tonal structure.

Webster, Daniel (1782–1852), Amer. lawyer and politician. Participated in McCulloch *v.* Maryland case. US Senator from Massachusetts (1827–41, 1845–50). Sec. of State (1841–3, 1850–52); signed **Webster-Ashburton Treaty** (1842) settling boundary disputes with Britain, in NE US. Supported Compromise of 1850.

Webster, John (*c.* 1580–1625), Eng. Jacobean dramatist. Works include powerful tragedies, with theme of revenge, *The White Devil* (1612) and *The Duchess of Malfi* (1623).

Webster, Noah (1758–1843), Amer. lexicographer. Sought to standardize US spelling and grammar and establish a specifically Amer. usage. Compiled *American Dictionary of the*

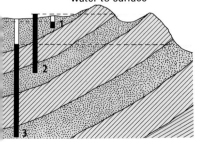

Artesian well 1) in first stratum 2) in lower stratum, producing more pressure 3) deeper still but pressure not sufficient to raise water to surface

Carl Maria von Weber

English Language (1828) which in revised forms remains in wide use.

Weddell, James (1787–1834), Eng. Antarctic explorer, b. Ostend. Discovered arm of S Atlantic Ocean named Weddell Sea after him (1823).

Wedekind, Frank (1864–1918), Ger. actor and dramatist. Plays, often with sexual themes, include *Der Erdgeist* (1899), *Die Büchse der Pandora* (1903).

Wedgwood, Josiah (1730–95), Eng. potter. Developed at Etruria, Staffordshire, new type of cream-coloured porcelain; also very hard coloured unglazed porcelain (pale blue, green and black) decorated with reliefs in white, based on classical designs.

weever, weaver, *Trachinus draco* and *T. vipera,* small European marine fish. Dorsal spines have poisoned tips.

weevil, small beetle of widespread Curculionidae family with beak-like snout. Larvae are legless whitish grubs. Grain weevil, *Sitophilus granarius,* and rice weevil, *S. oryzae,* are pests of stored cereal products.

weigela, genus of E Asian deciduous shrubs. Widely cultivated for clustered funnel-shaped white, pink or crimson flowers.

weightlessness, state of body in absence of gravitational force. Normally experienced when body is outside gravitational field of planet.

weights and measures, term for standard measurements of length and volume. Main systems currently used are metric and avoirdupois; troy system used for precious metals. International Bureau in Paris fixes metric standards.

Weil, Simone (1903–43), Fr. philosophical writer. A Jew, she became interested in Catholicism and mysticism of ancient Greece. Works include *Gravity and Grace* (1947), *Waiting for God* (1950).

Weill, Kurt (1900–50), Ger. composer. Worked with Bertolt Brecht on satirical operas *e.g. Aufsteig und Fall von Stadt Mahagonny* (1927) and *Dreigroschenoper* (based on John Gay's *Begger's Opera,* 1928). Went to US (1935) and wrote musical version of *Street Scene* by Elmer Rice (1947).

Weimar, city of East Germany on Ulm R. Cap. of duchy of Saxe-Weimar (16th cent.); cap. of former state of Thuringia (1920–47). Cultural centre since 18th cent., having associations with Goethe, Schiller, Herder, Liszt. Modern city has light industry and printing. Pop. *c.* 65,000.

Weimar Republic (1919–33), admin. of Germany after signing of Treaty of Versailles. Under Ebert and Hindenburg, made progressive recovery from World War 1 until economic crisis (1929). Repub. ended with appointment of Adolf Hitler as Chancellor.

Weinberger, Jaromir (1896–   ), Czech composer. Work includes orchestral and chamber music; also opera *Schwanda, the Bagpiper* (1927).

Weismann, August, FRS (1834–1914), Ger. biologist. Produced theory of continuity of germ-plasm; stated that acquired characteristics were not inheritable.

Weiss, Pierre (1865–1940), Fr. physicist. Discovered molecular unit of magnetic moment, called the Weiss magneton.

Weizmann, Chaim (1874–1952), Brit. scientist and Zionist leader, b. Russia. Aided production of explosives for British in World War 1. Pres. (1920–31) of World Zionist Organization. Instrumental in securing Balfour Declaration. First pres. of Israel (1948–52).

welding, process of joining metal surfaces by heating sufficiently for them to melt and unite. Required temperature obtained by oxy-acetylene flame, or electric arc.

well, excavation, usually cylindrical, in which water or oil is collected for bringing to surface. In artesian wells water is forced to surface by underground pressure.

Welland Canal, Canadian waterway connecting L. Erie with L. Ontario, 27·6 mi. long with 8 locks. Minimum depth 25 ft. Completed 1932.

Weller, Thomas Huckle (1915-   ), Amer. physician and parasitologist. Shared Nobel Prize for Physiology and Medicine (1954) with J. F. Enders and F. C. Robbins for cultivation of poliomyelitis vaccine.

Welles, [George] Orson (1915–), Amer. actor and producer. Directed notoriously realistic radio play of H. G. Wells' *War of the Worlds* (1938). Films include *Citizen Kane* (1940), *Compulsion* (1959), *The Trial* (1963).

Wellesley, Arthur, 1st Duke of Wellington (1769–1852), Brit. army officer and statesman. Aided brother Richard in Indian campaigns. Commander (1809–13) after battle of Corunna in Peninsular War, ended Fr. ambitions in Spain. Defeated Napoleon I in Battle of Waterloo (1815). As Tory P.M. (1828–30), promoted, after earlier opposing, Catholic Emancipation.

Wellesley, Richard Colley, Marquis of Wellesley (1760–1842), Brit. colonial administrator. Gov.-general of India (1797–1805), extended Brit. influence by checking power of French and native princes. Foreign Sec. (1810–12), Lord Lieutenant of Ireland (1821–8, 1833–4).

Wellington, 1st Duke of *see* Wellesley, Arthur.

Wellington, cap. of New Zealand, on North Island. First settled (1839–40); became cap., succeeding Auckland (1865). Now chief port of New Zealand with wool, meat packing and refrigeration industries. Pop. (1966) 168,000.

Wells, H[erbert] G[eorge] (1866–1946), prolific Eng. novelist. Works range from science fiction, *e.g. The Time Machine* (1895); amusing novels of social comment, *Kipps* (1905); to discussions of human predicament in a scientific world *The Shape of Things to Come* (1933).

Welsh *see* Celtic.

Welsh Nationalist Party [Plaid Cymru], political organization dedicated to obtaining Welsh independence by constitutional methods.

Welty, Eudora (1909–), Amer. novelist and short-story writer. Works mostly depict Mississippi life. Novels include *Delta Wedding* (1946) and *The Ponder Heart* (1954). Collections of stories include *A Curtain of Green* (1941), *The Golden Apples* (1949).

welwitschia, genus of desert plants of family Gnetaceae of SW Africa. Short thick trunk with 2 leaves growing at base.

Wenceslaus, Saint (d. 724), duke of Bohemia. Made peace with Henry I of Germany. Killed by brother Bolislav for attempt to enforce measures against paganism. Patron saint of Bohemia.

Wentworth, Thomas, 1st Earl of Strafford (1593–1641), Eng. statesman. After 1628 main adviser of

Charles I. Lord Deputy of Ireland (1632–9), where he estab. order and prosperity. Beheaded for treason by order of the Long Parliament, allegedly for planning to use Irish troops in Britain.

werewolf, werwolf, in medieval superstition, a man turned into a wolf. Roamed countryside eating human flesh. *See* LYCANTHROPY.

Werfel, Franz (1890–1945), Austrian poet, dramatist and novelist. Works include novels *The Forty Days of Musa Dagh* (1933), *The Song of Bernadette* (1941).

Werner, Alfred (1866–1919), Swiss chemist. Awarded Nobel Prize for Chemistry (1913) for work on molecular structure.

Weser, navigable river of Germany, 273 mi. long. Flows N from Münden past Bremen, entering North Sea at Bremerhaven.

Wesker, Arnold (1932–), Brit. playwright. Author of trilogy *Chicken Soup with Barley* (1958), *Roots* (1959), *I'm Talking about Jerusalem* (1960). Also *Chips with Everything* (1962) and other 'kitchen sink' dramas.

Wesley, John (1703–91), Eng. nonconformist preacher, founder of Wesleyan Methodist Church. Ordained in C. of E., preached doctrine of salvation in church and in open air, esp. to the poor; attracted numerous followers. Brother, **Charles Wesley** (1707–88), wrote over 6,000 hymns, incl. 'Jesus, lover of my soul', 'Love divine all loves excelling'.

Wesleyan Methodist Church, evangelical church founded by John Wesley (1739), formally organized (1784).

Wessex, kingdom of West Saxons estab. in England (6th cent.). Covered region S of Thames R. between modern counties of Sussex and Devon; cap. Winchester. Became leading power in England under Alfred the Great. Name also used for counties of Dorset, Hampshire and Somerset, esp. in Wessex novels of Thomas Hardy.

West, Benjamin (1738–1820), Amer. painter, resident in London after 1763. Historical pictures include *The Death of Wolfe*.

West, Nathanael, orig. Nathan Weinstein (1903–40), Amer. novelist. Novels, bitter in tone, popular after his death, include *Miss Lonelyhearts* (1933), *A Cool Million* (1934), *The Day of the Locusts* (1939).

West, Dame Rebecca (1892–), Eng. novelist and critic. Novels include *The Judge* (1922) and *The Fountain Overflows* (1957).

Map showing West and East Pakistan (Bangladesh)

West Bengal, state of NE India. Area: 30,775 sq. mi.; cap. Calcutta. Industries based on coal and petroleum. Part of Brit. Bengal (1764–1947). Pop. (1965 est.) 34,970,000.

West Indies, islands between North and South America, separating Caribbean Sea and N Atlantic Ocean. Total area: 91,788 sq. mi. Comprise Bahama Islands, Greater Antilles (Cuba, Haiti, Dominican Repub., Cayman Is., Jamaica, Puerto Rico) and Lesser Antilles (Leeward Is., Windward Is., Trinidad and Tobago, Barbados).

West Irian, formerly **Netherlands New Guinea,** W part of island of New Guinea. Incorporated by Indonesia (1963). Area: 159,000 sq. mi.; admin. cap. Sukarnapura. Pop. (1967) 820,000.

West Lothian, Linlithgowshire, county of E Scotland. Area: 120 sq. mi.; county town Linlithgow. Main occupations, dairy farming and mining. Pop. (1966) 103,000.

West Pakistan, region of Pakistan. Area: 310,236 sq. mi.; main cities, Karachi, Lahore. Separated from East Pakistan (Bangladesh) by India.

West Point, US military reservation, SE New York state. Since 1802 site of United States Military Academy.

West Riding, admin. district of Yorkshire county, England. Area: 2,798 sq. mi.; county town, Wakefield; main cities, Sheffield, Leeds. Industries include steel, coal and wool. Pop. (1967) 3,783,000.

West Virginia, E state of US. Area: 24,181 sq. mi.; cap. Charleston. Allegheny Mts. in E, Ohio R. on W border. Part of state of Virginia until Civil War; separated 1863. Agriculture, esp. cereals and tobacco; also

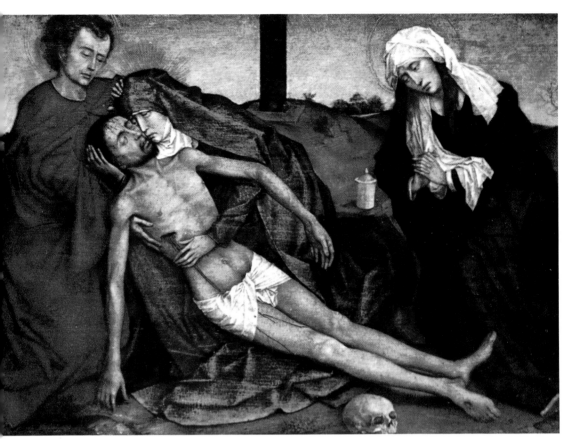

Pieta by Roger van der Weyden

coal-mining and oil refining. Pop. (1960) 1,860,000.

Western Australia, largest state of Australia. Area: 975,920 sq. mi.; cap. Perth; main port, Fremantle. Fertile in SW with vast central desert. Extensive deposits of gold and iron. Metals and machinery manufacturing. Agriculture (esp. sheep-rearing and wheat) important. Governed by New South Wales until 1831. Pop. (1966) 835,570.

Western European Union (WEU), defence association of Belgium, France, West Germany, Italy, Luxembourg, Netherlands and UK. Estab. 1955 as extension of Brussels Treaty Organization (1948).

Western Samoa *see* SAMOA.

Western Union Telegraph Company, world's largest cable and telegraph company. Completed 1st transcontinental telegraph line (1861) across N America.

Westinghouse, George (1846–1914), Amer. inventor and manufacturer. Invented air brake and automatic signalling used on railways.

Westmeath, inland county of Republic of Ireland. Area: 681 sq. mi.; county town, Mullingar; main town, Athlone. Mostly level and fertile with lakes, bogs. Main occupations dairy farming and cattle raising; textiles. Pop. (1966) 52,849.

Westminster, City of, borough of London since 1965, incl. metropolitan boroughs of Paddington, Westminster, St Marylebone. Contains Westminster Abbey, Houses of Parliament, Buckingham Palace. Pop. (1967 est.) 258,930.

Westminster, Statute of (1931), Brit. parl. enactment recognizing independence of dominions of Brit. Commonwealth. Implemented decision

Wheatear

of previous Imperial Conferences.

Westminster Abbey, national shrine and scene of coronation of Eng. monarchs since William I. Gothic in design, mainly built 13th-15th cent. with additions in 16th and 18th cent.

Westminster Assembly (1643–9), convocation summoned by Long Parliament to establish liturgy and govt. of Eng. church. Members mainly Presbyterians. Issued Westminster Confession of Faith, also Shorter and Longer Catechisms (finally rejected in England, accepted in Scotland).

Westmorland, county of NW England. Area: 788 sq. mi.; county town, Appleby; main town, Kendal. Largely mountainous; partly in LAKE DISTRICT. Dairy farming and cattle raising chief occupations. Tourism important. Pop. (1966) 67,000.

Westphalia, region of NW Germany. Made kingdom by Napoleon I (1807); incorporated as prov. of Prussia by Congress of Vienna (1815). After 1945 became part of NORTH RHINE-WESTPHALIA.

Westphalia, Peace of (1648), settlement terminating THIRTY YEARS WAR. Power of Habsburgs diminished, Holy Roman Empire dissolved into sovereign states. France, emerging as dominant power, continued war with Spain until 1659.

Wexford, maritime county of Leinster prov., Repub. of Ireland. Area: 908 sq. mi.; county town, Wexford. Low fertile land, mountainous in W. Agriculture, fishing and mining main occupations. Pop. (1966) 83,355.

Weyden, Roger van der (*c.* 1400–64), Flemish artist, also known as Roger de la Pasture. After Van Eycks, head of Flemish school. Subjects are mostly religious *e.g. Descent from the Cross* and *Nativity.*

Weygand, Maxime (1867–1965), Fr. army officer, organized defence of Warsaw against Red Army (1920). Supreme Allied commander (1940). War Min. in Vichy govt.; gov. of Algeria. Arrested by Germans 1942, released 1945.

whale, large marine mammal of order Cetacea reaching 100 ft. in length. Fish-like body, forelimbs modified into flippers, horizontally flattened head. Hunted for flesh, oil, whalebone. Divided into toothed whale and whalebone whale, Species include sperm whale, *Physeter catodon,* toothed whale valued for its oil, blue whale, *Sibbaldus musculus,* whalebone whale, the largest mammal.

whaling, industry of catching whales. Organized 1st by Dutch (17th cent.). Developed on large scale with invention of explosive harpoon (1856) and building of factory ships for extraction of oil, *etc.* Decline in whale population through over-hunting has led to international control.

Wharton, Edith (1862–1937), Amer. novelist, best known for studies of Amer. high society. Novels include *The House of Mirth* (1905) and *The Age of Innocence* (1920). Also short stories and literary criticism.

wheat, grass of genus *Triticum,* esp. *T. aestivum,* widely cultivated in temp. regions. Yields grain which is processed into flour or meal and used chiefly in breadmaking. Comprises two-fifths world's cereal acreage. Leading producers, USSR, US, China, Canada.

wheatear, small insectivorous, migratory, chiefly Old World thrush of genus *Oenanthe* with white rump. Species include *O. oenanthe* of Eurasia and N America.

wheel, name given to any disc-shaped device used as part of machine or vehicle. Effect when fitted to axle is to permit maximum mechanical effort to be applied to work requiring to be

done. Earliest vehicular wheel was Bronze Age chariot wheel 3500 BC. Potter's wheel known in Egypt from 3rd millenium BC.

Wheeler, Sir [Robert Eric] Mortimer (1890–   ), Brit. archaeologist. Best known for work at Maiden Castle, Dorset, and in Indus Valley. Books include *Prehistoric and Roman Wales* (1925) and *Early India and Pakistan* (1959).

whelk, edible marine gastropod mollusc with spiral shell of family Buccinidae. Native to N Atlantic and N Amer. coasts. Species include common whelk [UK], waved whelk [US], *Buccinium undatum.*

whidah *see* WHYDAH.

Whig, Eng. polit. party, predecessor of present Lib. Party. Name, orig. denoting 17th cent. Scot. Covenanters, applied to upholders of parl. power against Crown (1679). Supported Glorious Revolution (1688), retaining power 1714–60. Dominant figure until 1742 was Robert Walpole, responsible for party's polit. power. In early 19th cent. advocated parl. reform, culminating in Reform Bill (1832), after which Whigs known as Liberals.

Whig party, US polit. party, composed of groups formed in opposition to Andrew Jackson, joined by National Republican Party (1836). Successful in election of W. H. HARRISON as pres. (1840). Several members joined FREE SOIL PARTY (1848); despite Zachary Taylor's victory in pres. election, party split over slavery question.

whimbrel, *Numenius phaeopus,* small migrant curlew of Europe and Asia.

whin, gorse, furze, common names for spiny shrubs of genus *Ulex,* esp. *U. europaeus,* native of Europe with bright yellow flowers.

whinchat, *Saxicola rubetra,* small Old World migrant songbird of thrush family. Short tail, stocky build and white streaks on head and neck.

Whipple, George Hoyt (1878–   ), Amer. pathologist. Shared Nobel Prize for Physiology and Medicine (1934) with G. R. Minot and W. P. Murphy for research in treatment of pernicious anaemia.

whip-poor-will, *Caprimulgus vociferus,* N Amer. nightjar with brown plumage mottled with black and cream. Name derived from its call.

whipsnake, *Dryophis prasinus,* very long and slender tree-climbing snake of Malaya. Amer. whipsnake is harmless snake of genus *Masticophis.*

whirligig beetle, aquatic beetle of family Gyrinidae. Gyrates on surface of slow-moving or still water. Species

Wheat: (1) Ear of Common Wheat and (2) Hard Wheat

include the common whirligig beetle, *Dinentes americanus,* and European whirligig, *Gyrinus natator.*

whirlpool, revolving current in water caused by opposing currents, irregular formation of shore bottom, wind action or waterfalls.

whirlwind, vertically revolving current of air caused by atmospheric instability. Small dust-whirls occur in dry weather; sandstorms, hurricanes and tornadoes are more violent.

whisky, whiskey, spirituous liquor distilled from malted and fermented grain, *e.g.* barley, rye. Characteristic flavour of Scotch whisky achieved by malting of grain over peat fires. Irish variety sweeter in taste. US and Canadian whiskies mostly made with rye, some with corn *e.g.* Bourbon. Liqueur whiskies include Drambuie, made only in Isle of Skye, NW Scotland.

Whisky Rebellion (1794), uprising in Pennsylvania, US. Caused by Alexander Hamilton's excise tax (1791), thought discriminatory by whisky producers. Rioting quelled by troops.

whispering bells, California yellow bells, *Emmenanthe penduliflora,* N Amer. annual plant of Hydrophyllaceae family with pendulous yellow flowers.

whist, card game for 4 players. Originated from 16th cent. games in England giving rise to bridge (19th cent.). Variations include duplicate whist, bid whist, solo whist.

Whydah (Widow Bird)

White-tailed Deer

Whistler, James [Abbott] McNeill (1834–1903), Amer. Impressionist painter and etcher. Worked in Paris and London. Works include famous portrait of his mother.

Whit Sunday, Christian festival commemorating descent of Holy Spirit to Apostles. Occurs 7th Sunday after Easter.

Whitby, coastal town of N Yorkshire, England. Abbey founded 656. Synod of Whitby (664) chose Roman instead of Celtic forms for Eng. church.

White, Gilbert (1720–93), Eng. naturalist. Works include *Natural History and Antiquities of Selborne* (1789).

White, Patrick Victor Martindale (1912–   ), Austral. novelist, dramatist and poet. Novels include *Happy Valley* (1939), *The Tree of Man* (1955) and *Voss* (1957).

White, T[erence] H[anbury] (1906–64), Eng. novelist. Author of *Mistress Masham's Repose* (1946) and tetralogy *The Once and Future King* (1939–58), on Arthurian legend.

white butterfly, any of several white butterflies, usually of genus *Pieris*. Includes cabbage butterfly.

white corpuscle, white blood cell; *see* LEUCOCYTE.

White Fathers, Society of Missionaries of Africa, R.C. African mission society. Founded (1868) by Cardinal Lavigerie of Algiers.

White Horse, Vale of the, Berkshire, England. Named after white horse chalk hill figure at Uffington, supposedly commemorating victory of Alfred the Great over Danes (871).

White House, official residence of US pres., Washington, D.C. Site chosen by George Washington who laid corner-stone (1792). Designed by James Hogan. Burned by British (1814) in War of 1812, restored and painted white. Under admin. of Theodore Roosevelt 'White House' became official name.

white lead, heavy white poisonous lead carbonate, insoluble in water. One of earliest pigments, used in paints, putty and some pottery.

White Nile, Bahr-el-Abiad, river of Uganda and Sudan *c.* 1,500 mi. long. Flows from Lake Victoria through Sudan as Bahr-el-Jebel. At Khartoum joins Blue Nile to form main Nile R.

white poplar, *Populus alba,* Eurasian poplar naturalized in US. Whitish bark and leaves.

White Russia *see* BYELORUSSIAN SSR.

White Sea, inlet of Barents Sea, NW USSR, 365 mi. long. Chief port, Archangel. Despite being ice-bound for much of year, important for fisheries and lumber exports.

whitebait, young of several European herrings, esp. common herring, *Clupea harengus,* or of sprat, *C. sprattus.*

whitebeam, *Sorbus aria,* deciduous tree or shrub native to Europe. Oval leathery leaves, scented white flowers and scarlet fruits.

Whitefield, George (1714–70), Eng. evangelist, Methodist leader. Early influenced by John Wesley, founder of Methodists, but Calvinistic views led to breach with them, esp. on theories of predestination.

whitefish, food fish of family Coregonidae found in N Amer. lakes. Species include Great Lakes whitefish.

whitefly, small plant-sucking insect of family Aleyrodidae. Wings and body coated with white powder. Several species are crop pests.

white-fronted goose, *Anser albifrons,* wild goose of Eurasia and N America. Greyish-brown with white patch above the bill.

Whitehall, street in C London. Name refers to area containing DOWNING STREET and several UK govt. offices.

Whitehead, Alfred North (1861–1947), Brit. philosopher and mathematician. Formulated idealist philosophy of organisms, unifying principle being God. Collaborated with Bertrand Russell in *Principia Mathematica* (3 vols., 1910–13).

white-tailed deer *see* VIRGINIA DEER.

whitethroat, small songbird with white throat, esp. Old World warbler, *Sylvia communis.*

Whitgift, John (*c.* 1530–1604), Eng. divine. Archbishop of Canterbury (1583). Influential in estab. C. of E. under Elizabeth I.

whiting, *Merlangus merlangus,* common European marine food fish of family Gadidae. Found in shallow waters, esp. of North Sea. Also N Amer. fish of genus *Menticirrhus* and Austral. fish of genus *Sillago.*

Whitman, Walt[er] (1819–92), Amer. poet and essayist. Began as newspaper editor. Poetry, beginning with *Leaves of Grass* (1855), used free verse technique and pantheist themes.

Whitethroat and nest

Small White Butterfly with cater-pillar

Best of subsequent poetry contained in *Drum-Taps* (1865) and *Sequel to Drum-Taps* (1866). Prose includes *Specimen Days and Collect* (1882–3).

Whitney, Eli (1765–1825), Amer. manufacturer, inventor of cotton gin (1793). Produced 1st muskets with standard interchangeable parts.

Whittier, John Greenleaf (1807–92), Amer. poet and reformer, prominent Quaker. Advocate of abolition of slavery. Best known for poems depicting New England life, esp. in *Snowbound* (1866) and *Maud Muller* (1867). Also wrote hymns.

Whittington, Richard (1358–1423), Eng. merchant, 3 times mayor of London. Subject of legend of Dick Whittington and cat.

Whittle, Sir Frank (1907–), Brit. aeronautical engineer. Patented (1930) basic designs for turbo-jet engine, forerunner of modern jet aircraft engine.

Whitworth, Sir Joseph (1803–87), Eng. gun manufacturer. Developed screw-thread standard for rifles.

whooping cough, pertussis, infectious disease usually attacking young children. Characteristic cough terminates in 'whoop' during intake of breath.

whortleberry *see* BILBERRY.

whydah, whidah, small bird of sparrow family with long tail. Male has red breast in breeding season. Species include paradise whydah or widow bird, *Vidua paradisea*.

Whymper, Edward (1840–1911), Eng. mountaineer. First (1865) to scale Matterhorn.

Wichita, tribe of N Amer. Indians of Caddoan linguistic stock. Subsistence based on agriculture and buffalo-hunting in Kansas. Settled (19th cent.) on Oklahoma reservation.

Wichita, largest city of Kansas, US, on Arkansas R. Important meat-packing and flour-milling centre. Pop. (1965) 292,000.

Wicklow, county of SE Ireland, in Leinster. Area: 782 sq. mi.; county town, Wicklow. Hilly terrain used for cattle-grazing. Pop. (1966) 60,281.

widgeon *see* WIGEON.

Arrangement in Black and Grey by J. A. McNeill Whistler

widow bird *see* WHYDAH.

Wiechert, Ernst (1887–1950), Ger. novelist. Symbolic works include *The Baroness* (1934) and *The Forest of the Dead* (1945).

Wieland, Christoph Martin (1733–1813), Ger. Romantic poet. Works include *The Republic of Fools* (1774) and *Oberon* (1780).

Wien, Wilhelm (1864–1928), Ger. physicist. Awarded Nobel Prize for Physics (1911) for studies in heat radiation.

Wiesbaden, city and cap. of Hesse, West Germany, on Rhine R. Famous for mineral springs; centre of wine trade. Pop. (1965) 261,000.

wigeon, widgeon, freshwater migratory duck of genus *Mareca*. Male of European and N Asian wigeon, *M. penelope,* has chestnut head and neck, and green and black wings. S Amer. wigeon, *M. sibiliatrix,* has pinkish-brown plumage with white head.

Wight, Isle of, island off Hampshire coast, S England. Area: 146 sq. mi.;

White-fronted Goose

admin. centre, Newport. Scenic tourist centre. Pop. (1966) 97,000.

Wigner, Eugene Paul (1902–), Amer. physicist, b. Hungary. Shared Nobel Prize in Physics (1963) for contributions to practical application of atomic energy.

Wigtownshire, county of SW Scotland. Area: 487 sq. mi.; county town, Wigtown. Main occupation, animal farming. Pop. (1966) 29,000.

wigwam, Algonkian name loosely

Wild Ox

William the Silent

applied to houses of N Amer. Indians. Dome-shaped or conical huts made of poles lashed together at top and covered with bark.

Wilberforce, William (1759–1833), Brit. reform politician. Promoted bill (1807) abolishing slave trade. His son, **Samuel Wilberforce** (1805–73), Anglican cleric, defended C. of E. orthodoxy against Tractarians.

Wilbye, John (1574–1638), Eng. composer. Leading exponent of madrigals, *e.g.* 'Adieu, Sweet Amaryllis'.

wild boar, *Sus scrofa*, wild hog of continental Europe, SW Asia and N Africa. Coarse hair and enlarged canine tusks. Most domestic swine derived from wild boar.

wild ginger, Canada ginger, black snakeroot, *Asarum canadense*, small N Amer. perennial plant with purplish-brown flowers and creeping aromatic rootstock.

wild goat, *Capra ibex*, goat of mountainous regions of Eurasia.

wild guelder rose, shrub or tree related to cultivated cranberry bushes. Found in N America and Europe.

wild ox, gaur, large ox of SE Asia and Malay Archipelago. Height at shoulder may be 6 ft.

wildcat *see* BOBCAT.

Wilde, Oscar Fingal O'Flahertie Wills (1854–1900), Brit. writer, b. Dublin. Author of novels, *e.g. The Picture of Dorian Gray* (1891), witty drawing-room comedies, incl. *Lady Windermere's Fan* (1892) and *The Importance of Being Earnest* (1895). Convicted on morals charge, wrote *De Profundis* (1895–7) in prison.

wildebeest, *Connochaetes gnu*, large horned antelope of S Africa. White tail, long mane and curved horns.

Wilder, Thornton Niven (1897–), Amer. writer. Works include novel *The Bridge of San Luis Rey* (1927); plays, *Our Town* (1938) and *The Matchmaker* (1954).

Wilderness campaign, in US Civil War, series of battles (May-June 1864) between Union, commanded by Ulysses Grant, and Confederacy, under Robert Lee, in N Virginia. Both sides suffered heavy losses, results inconclusive.

Wilhelmina (1880–1962), queen of the Netherlands (1890–1948), daughter of William III. In exile (1940–5) during Ger. occupation. Abdicated in favour of daughter Juliana.

Wilkes, John (1727–97), Eng. polit. leader. Critic of George III, twice imprisoned and denied seat in Parl. Championed reform, became symbol of anti-autocratic rule.

Wilkins, Sir George Hubert (1888–1958), Austral. polar explorer. Participated in various reconnaissance projects; flew over N Pole (1928).

Wilkins, Maurice Hugh Frederick (1916–), Brit. biologist, b. New Zealand. Shared Nobel Prize for Physiology and Medicine (1962) with F. H. C. Crick and James Watson for work on nucleic acid (DNA).

will, in law, written declaration by person expressing desired distribution of property after his death. Must be signed in presence of 2 witnesses. Oral will is only legally recognized under special circumstances.

will, in philosophy, inner force motivating person's conscious actions. Existence denied by some philosophers, defined by others on intuitive grounds as motive force of personality, or as result of interacting elements.

willemite, zinc orthosilicate mineral of various colours. Usually green.

William Rufus *see* WILLIAM [II] RUFUS.

William [I] the Conqueror (*c.* 1027–87), king of England (1066–87). As Duke of Normandy, pursued claim to throne by invading England and defeating HAROLD at battle of Hastings (1066). Consolidated power through estab. of hierarchical chain of loyalty. Promoted completion of DOMESDAY BOOK.

William [II] Rufus (*c.* 1058–1100), king of England (1087–1100). Extravagant, opposed by subjects. Gained military successes in Normandy and Scotland. Found slain by an arrow in New Forest.

William III (1650–1702), king of England, Scotland and Ireland (1689–1702). Son of William II of Orange, made peace (1674) with English in Dutch Wars. Marriage to Mary (later MARY II) enabled him to claim Eng. throne through Glorious Revolution; forced to accept BILL OF RIGHTS (1689). Reign chiefly occupied by continental wars until Louis XIV recognized him as king (1697).

William IV (1765–1837), king of Great Britain and Ireland (1830–7), son of George III. Created (1789) Duke of Clarence, succeeded brother George IV.

William [I] the Silent (1533–84), Prince of Orange, b. Germany. Appointed Sp. stadholder of Holland (1555), led Dutch struggle for independence from Spain. Converted (1573) to Calvinism, ruled United Provs. after 1581. Assassinated by Catholic fanatic.

William I (1797–1888), king of Prussia (1861–88), emperor of Germany (1871–88). Reign dominated by BISMARCK, whom he appointed chancellor (1862). Proclaimed emperor at Versailles. Symbolized Ger. unity.

William II (1859–1941), emperor of Germany and king of Prussia (1888–1918). Conflict with BISMARCK resulted in chancellor's dismissal (1890). Aggressive colonial and military programme prompted Anglo-French entente; foreign policy

Willow: (a) female catkins (b) male catkins (c) leaves are smooth and dark green on the upper side: on the underside they are greyish white and hairy

instrumental in outbreak of World War 1. Abdicated, fled to Holland, remained in exile until his death.

William of Ockham or **Occam** (d. *c.* 1349), Eng. Franciscan scholar. Opposed temporal power of papacy, lived under protection of Emperor Louis IV. Rejected doctrines of Thomas Aquinas, advocated belief in God through faith.

Williams, Tennessee, orig. Thomas Lanier Williams (1914–), Amer. writer. Plays include *The Glass Menagerie* (1945), *A Streetcar Named Desire* (1947) and *Cat on a Hot Tin Roof* (1955). Other works include novel *The Roman Spring of Mrs. Stone* (1950).

Williams, William Carlos (1883–1963), Amer. poet and physician. Developed idiomatic free verse form through which he attacked social injustice, as in *Paterson* (5 vols., 1946–58). Also wrote essays, novels.

Williamsburg, early settlement (1632) in SE Virginia, US, between York and James estuaries of Chesapeake Bay. Cap. of Va. (1699–1779). Many ancient monuments. Pop. 7,000.

Willingdon, Freeman Freeman-Thomas, 1st Marquis of (1866–1941), Brit. colonial administrator. Gov.-general of Canada (1926–30), viceroy of India (1931–6).

Willkie, Wendell Lewis (1892–1944), Amer. politician. Unsuccessful Repub. pres. candidate (1940). Opposed Franklin Roosevelt's New Deal domestic policies, sought to liberalize Repub. party.

will-o'-the-wisp, jack-o'-lantern, pale, flickering light seen over marshland at night. Prob. caused by phosphorescence or ignition of gases.

willow, tree or shrub of genus *Salix* found mostly in N temp. and Arctic regions. Tough pliable twigs or branches used for wickerwork, *etc.*

willow pattern, design in blue and white, used to decorate chinaware.

Based on Chinese legend introduced into England *c.* 1870.

willowherb, plant of genus *Epilobium,* esp. *E. angustifolium* with narrow leaves and reddish-purple flowers.

Willstätter, Richard (1872–1942), Ger. chemist. Awarded Nobel Prize for Chemistry (1915) for work on chlorophyll and plant pigmentation.

Wilmington, city and port of Delaware, US, on Delaware R. Fort Christina built on site by Swedes (1638). Shipyards important since 18th cent. Produces chemicals, textiles. Pop. (1965) 284,000.

Wilmot, John, 2nd Earl of Rochester (1648–80), Eng. poet, courtier and wit. Author of love lyrics and satires.

Wilmot Proviso, amendment (1846) to bill in US House of Representatives stipulating absence of slavery in territory acquired through Mexican War. Failed to be passed by Senate, increased North-South rivalry.

Wilson, Angus (1913–), Brit. writer. Satirical novels include *Anglo-Saxon Attitudes* (1956) and *Late Call* (1965). Critical works include *The Wild Garden* (1963).

Wilson, Charles Thomson Rees (1869–1959), Brit. physicist. Shared Nobel Prize for Physics (1927) with Arthur Compton. Developed Wilson cloud chamber, facilitating study of ionized particles.

Wilson, Edmund (1895–), Amer. writer. Critical works include *Axel's Castle* (1931) and *To the Finland Station* (1940); best known short story collection, *Memoirs of Hecate County* (1946).

Wilson, Ethel Davis, née Boyant (1890–), Canadian novelist, b. South Africa. Sympathetic satires include *Hetty Dorval* (1947) and *Love and Salt Water* (1956).

Wilson, [James] Harold (1916–), Brit. polit. leader, P.M. (1964–70). Held office in Lab. govt. (1947–51), elected party leader (1963). As P.M., failed to curb inflation.

Wilson, [Thomas] Woodrow (1856–1924), 28th US Pres. (1913–21), Democrat. Pres. of Princeton University (1902–10), Gov. of New Jersey (1911–13). As Pres., 1st term marked by 'New Freedom' domestic reform programme, incl. FEDERAL RESERVE SYSTEM (1913). Re-elected (1916) on successful neutral stand in World War 1, led US into war (1917). Armistice of 1918 negotiated basis of his FOURTEEN POINTS. Secured covenant of LEAGUE OF NATIONS at Treaty of Versailles. Awarded Nobel Peace Prize (1919).

Wiltshire, county of SW England. Area: 1,350 sq. mi.; county town, Salisbury. Pastoral and agric., contains Salisbury Plain, ancient remains at Stonehenge, Avebury. Pop. (1966) 471,000.

Wimbledon, part of Merton, borough of Greater London, England. Home of All England Lawn Tennis Club, scene of international matches since 1877.

Winchester, municipal borough and

Wild Guelder Rose

Wild Goat

county town of Hampshire, England. Cap. of Wessex, historic centre of art and scholarship. Has cathedral and Winchester College, boys' public school. Pop. (1967 est.) 28,600.

Winckelmann, Johann Joachim (1717–68), Ger. archaeologist. Pioneered study of ancient art in *History of Ancient Art* (1764).

Winckler, Hugo (1863–1914), Ger. Assyriologist. Translated Amarna tablets and Code of Hammurabi. Also excavated Hittite cap. of Hattushash near Bogaz-Koy, Turkey.

wind, natural, discontinuous movement of air caused by differences of air pressure within atmosphere. Air flows from region of high pressure (anti-cyclone) to one of low pressure. Movement may be on local scale, *e.g.* sea breezes; regional *e.g.* mistral; or large scale *e.g.* cyclone, hurricane, typhoon. Force measured according to Beaufort Scale.

wind instruments, name given to woodwind and brass families of instruments. Sound is produced by player setting in motion column of air inside his instrument. Woodwind instruments include clarinet, saxophone, oboe, bassoon, flute. Brass instruments include horn, trumpet, trombone, bugle, tuba, *etc.*

Windaus, Adolf (1876–1959), Ger. chemist. Discovered vitamin D3. Awarded Nobel Prize for Chemistry (1928) for research on relation of sterols to vitamins.

Windermere, largest lake in England, $10\frac{1}{2}$ mi. long, *c.* 1 mi. wide, in Lake District, NW England.

windflower, common name esp. for wild varieties of ANEMONE.

Windhoek, cap. of South West Africa, trade and communications centre of the territory. Pop. *c.* 36,000.

windmill, apparatus using wind power for pumping water, grinding corn, *etc.* Usually consists of tower with revolving arms at top bearing sails to catch wind. Introduced to Europe prob. during 11th cent., widely used esp. in Holland.

Windsor Castle

Windmill Hill, site in Wiltshire, England, of one of oldest neolithic cultures of Britain, excavated 1925.

windpipe *see* TRACHEA.

Windsor, Duke of *see* EDWARD VIII.

Windsor, House of, name of royal family of Great Britain. Adopted by George V (1917).

Windsor, royal borough and market town of Berkshire, England, on Thames R. In large park is Windsor Castle, an official residence of Brit. sovereign; 1st stronghold built by William the Çonqueror, present building dates mainly from 14th cent. Contains St George's chapel.

Windsor, city and port of Ontario, Canada, on Detroit R., directly opposite Detroit City, US. Important indust. centre. Pop (1962) 120,000.

Windward Islands, chain of small volcanic islands of Lesser Antilles in Caribbean Sea. Area: *c.* 1,412 sq. mi. Controlled since 16th cent. by Brit. and Fr. govts. Since 1966 all states in association with Britain, except Martinique and the Grenadines. Pop. (1960 est.) 823,000.

wine, alcoholic beverage made from fermented juice of GRAPE. Classified as still or sparkling (*e.g.* champagne), natural or fortified (*e.g.* sherry, port), dry or sweet, depending on climate, and on variety of grape, soil where grown and treatment of grape. In red wines (*e.g.* Ital. chianti, Fr. burgundy or claret) entire grape is used, in white (*e.g.* Fr. sauternes, Ger. hock) only juice is used.

Wingate, Orde Charles (1903–44), Brit. army officer. Engaged in guerilla warfare behind Jap. lines in Burma in World War 2, with Indian troops known as 'Chindits'.

winkle, whelk of genus *Busycon*. Destroys oysters by drilling shell and rasping away the flesh.

Winnipeg, city of Manitoba, Canada, at confluence of Assiniboine and Red rivers. Incorporated 1873. Largest grain market of Brit. Commonwealth, important rly. and communication centre. Pop. (1966) 257,000.

Winnipeg, Lake, lake in Manitoba, Canada, *c.* 250 mi. long and 55 mi. wide. Connected to Hudson Bay by the Nelson R.

winter cherry, cape gooseberry, Chinese lantern, *Physalis alkengi,* perennial Eurasian plant. Whitish flowers and red fruit enclosed in orange-red calyx.

winter cress, Eurasian cress of genus *Barbarea* with yellow flowers. Sometimes cultivated for salads.

winterberry, black alder, *Ilex verticillata,* deciduous shrub of N America with oval serrated leaves and bright red berries.

wintergreen, small creeping evergreen plant of genus *Gaultheria,* esp. *G. procumbens* of N America. Yields medicinal oil. Red berries are called checkerberries. Also N Amer. *Pyrola minor.*

Winters, Yvor (1900–   ), Amer. critic and poet. Works include *In Defense of Reason* (1947) and *Collected Poems* (1960).

wintersweet, *Acocanthera spectabilis,* evergreen shrub native to S Africa. Dark green leaves and white flowers with purple-black berries.

Winthrop, John (1588–1649), Puritan leader and 1st gov. of Massachusetts. Instrumental in estab. of Colony's Puritan rule. Expelled (1636) Anne Hutchinson and followers for heresy.

wire, metal filament, usually round in cross-section, made by drawing metal through holes until desired diameter is achieved.

wireless, in UK, term for RADIO.

wireworm *see* CLICK BEETLE.

Wisconsin, state of N central US. Area: 56,154 sq. mi.; cap. Madison; main city, Milwaukee. Settled 18th cent., became state, 1848. Agriculture (esp. dairying) is major industry. Pop. (1960) 3,951,777.

Wisdom of Solomon, The, apocryphal book of OT, written in Greek, wrongly attributed to Solomon.

wisent, *Bison bonasus,* European bison, now extinct in the wild. Has longer legs and smaller head than Amer. bison, and short horns.

wisteria, climbing leguminous shrub of genus *Wisteria* native to N America and Asia. Racemes of white, blue, pink or violet drooping flowers.

witch doctor, member of primitive tribe who performs rites to cure sickness, combat evil spirits, *etc.* Sometimes called medicine man.

witch hazel, deciduous tree or shrub of genus *Hamamelis* native to N America and Asia. *H. virginiana,* of E N America has yellow flowers. Medicinal lotion is derived from bark.

witchcraft, exercise of a power,

allegedly obtained by compact with some supernatural agency, esp. the devil, to influence course of events. Prob. dates back to fertility cults prevalent in Europe in Paleolithic times. Condemned (14th cent.) by Christian Church as heresy; 300,000 people executed as witches (16th–17th cent.). In America, most noted persecution occurred (1692) at SALEM.

Witenagemot, assembly of nobles and high churchmen in Anglo-Saxon England. Appointed by king in advisory capacity.

Witt, Jan de (1625–72), Dutch statesman. Leader of opposition to House of Orange, grand pensionary (1653–71). Ended (1654) 1st Dutch War with England. Organized (1668) Triple Alliance against Louis XIV. Attack (1672) by France and England caused his resignation and call to leadership of William of Orange.

Witte, Count Sergei Yulievich (1849–1915), Russ. statesman. Promoted Russia's indust. development through extensive rly. construction, esp. Trans-Siberian Rly., encouragement of foreign investment, introduction of protectionist tariffs. First constitutional Russ. premier.

Wittelsbach, Bavarian dynasty, ruled (12th cent.–1918) Bavaria and Rhine Palatinate. Most powerful under Duke Maximilian I (1573–1651). All family lands united (1799) under single ruler who became king (1806) of Bavaria. Dynasty deposed.

Wittenberg, city of East Germany. Nailing by Martin Luther of 95 theses on door of Schlosskirche (1517) marked beginning of Reformation.

Wittgenstein, Ludwig (1889–1951), Austrian philosopher, lived mainly in England. The *Tractatus Logico-Philosophicus* (1919) played role in founding of LOGICAL POSITIVISM. Later philosophical works include *Philosophical Investigations* (1953).

Witwatersrand, The Rand, region of South Africa containing ridge 62 mi. long and 23 mi. wide with richest gold fields in world. Surface gold discovered 1884.

Witz, Konrad (*c.* 1400–45), Ger. painter, influenced both by Flemish and Ital. art. Best known for altarpieces and religious works.

woad, *Isatis tinctoria,* European plant formerly cultivated for blue dye.

Wodehouse, P[elham] G[renville] (1881–), Eng. novelist. Created caricature characters from Brit. upper-class life incl. Jeeves, Bertie Wooster.

Woden, in Germanic myth., supreme god [Norse: Odin]. Ruler of the sky,

The Miraculous Draught of Fish (1444) by Konrad Witz

god of war, learning, poetry and magic. Held court for slain warriors in Valhalla.

Wohler, Friedrich (1800–82), Ger. chemist. Synthesized organic compound, urea (1828). Devised processes for isolation of uranium, beryllium and yttrium.

Wohlgemuth, Michael (1434–1519), Ger. painter. Teacher of ALBRECHT DÜRER.

Wolf, Hugo (1860–1903), Austrian composer, b. Styria. Wrote numerous songs in Romantic *lieder* style.

wolf, large carnivorous mammal of genus *Canis,* now restricted to relatively uninhabited areas of N hemisphere. Hunts in packs, preys on small mammals. *C. lupus,* European wolf, has coarse brown or grey fur, bushy tail and pointed ears.

wolf spider, wandering ground spider of family Lycosidae. Species include European wolf spider (tarantula), *Lycosa tarantula.*

Wolfe, James (1727–59), Brit. army officer. Second-in-command to Amherst during FRENCH AND INDIAN WAR, took part in successful siege of Louisbourg (1758). Commanded expedition against Quebec, outmanoeuvred and defeated (1759) Fr. forces on PLAINS OF ABRAHAM; mortally wounded.

Wolfe, Thomas Clayton (1900–38),

Amer. writer. Lengthy lyrical novels, partly autobiog. include *Look Homeward Angel* (1929) and posthumous *You Can't Go Home Again* (1940).

Wolf-Ferrari, Ermanno (1867–1948), Ital. operatic composer. Wrote comic operas, incl. *Il Segreto di Susanna* (1909) and 1 grand opera, *The Jewels of the Madonna* (1911).

wolfhound, large dog *e.g.* Irish wolfhound, used orig. for hunting wolves; also borzoi or Russ. wolfhound.

Wolfit, Sir Donald (1902–68), Eng. theatre and film actor and manager.

Wolf

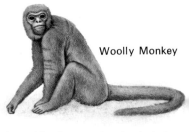
Woolly Monkey

Famous roles included Hamlet, Othello, Shylock and Volpone.

Wolfram von Eschenbach (*fl. c.* 1200), Ger. epic poet. Only extant complete work is *Parzifal.*

wolfram, extremely hard metallic element. It is ductile; also called TUNGSTEN.

wolframite, ore of tungsten, a tungstate of iron and manganese. Often found with tin ores.

Wolfson, Sir Isaac (1897–   ), Brit. industrialist. Estab. Wolfson Foundation; sponsors medical research in UK and Brit. Commonwealth.

Wollstonecraft, Mary *see* GODWIN, MARY.

Wolseley, Garnet Joseph, 1st Viscount (1833–1913), Brit. army officer. Served during Indian Mutiny. Suppressed Red River Rebellion in Canada (1869–70).

Wolsey, Thomas (*c.* 1475–1530), Eng. cleric and statesman. Created Lord Chancellor and Cardinal (1515 by Henry VIII). Acquired great wealth, founded Cardinal (Christ Church) College, Oxford, and built Hampton Court Palace. Failure to arrange king's divorce from Catherine of Aragon led to dismissal and arrest for high treason.

Wolverhampton, indust. town of Staffordshire, England. Manufacturing industries include rolling stock, motor vehicles and chemicals. Pop. (1967) 267,000.

wolverine, wolverene, carcajou, *Gulo luscus,* carnivorous N Amer. mammal of weasel family. Thick blackish fur with pale forehead; bushy tail. Hunted for its fur.

Woman's Christian Temperance Union, Amer. organization founded (1874) to press for legislation prohibiting sale of alcohol and harmful drugs and abolition of prostitution.

womb *see* UTERUS.

wombat, burrowing, nocturnal marsupial mammal of family Vombatidae, of Australia. Stocky with coarse greyish fur.

Women's Land Army, Brit. organization in World Wars 1 and 2.

Wood Pigeon

Provided agric. labour force to replace farm workers serving in forces.

Women's Royal Voluntary Service (WRVS), formerly **Women's Voluntary Service,** UK association formed from voluntary bodies set up during World Wars. In peace time work includes distributing meals to disabled, *etc.* Wartime duties included nursing, care of evacuees and air raid victims, *etc.*

women's suffrage, right of women to vote. First UK women's suffrage committee formed 1865. Among supporters was J. S. Mill in *On the Subjection of Women* (1869). National Union of Women's Suffrage Societies (formed 1897) led by Mrs. Henry Fawcett. More militant Women's Social and Political Union (formed 1903) under Emmeline Pankhurst helped achieve right to vote for married women over 30 (1918). *See* SUFFRAGETTES. Vote extended (1928) to all women at 21. Early advocates in US included Susan Anthony and Elizabeth Stanton; union of movements achieved (1890) as National American Woman Suffrage Association. 19th Amendment (1920) granted voting rights to women.

Wood, Sir Henry Joseph (1869–1944), Eng. organist and conductor (1894) of newly founded Queen's Hall Promenade Concerts. Attracted many new composers to London.

Wood, John (1704–54), Eng. architect. Helped plan Bath city and building of *e.g.* Royal Crescent.

wood, hard, fibrous substance which makes up greater part of stems and branches of trees and shrubs beneath the bark. Composed of xylem, phloem intersected with vascular rays.

wood anemone, wild anemone of genus *Anemone* with solitary white flowers. Species include *A. nemorosa* of Europe and *A. quinquefolia* of N America.

Wood Buffalo National Park, forest region of NW Territories and Alberta, Canada. Area: 17,300 sq. mi. Became wildlife area (1922).

wood mouse, *Apodemus sylvaticus,* small nocturnal Eurasian fieldmouse. Brown with greyish-white underside.

wood pigeon, ring dove, *Columba palumbus,* European bird of family Columbidae. Has ring of white patches round neck.

woodbine, name for HONEYSUCKLE.

woodchuck, ground hog, *Marmota monax,* burrowing N Amer. marmot found in woodlands and farmland. Hibernates underground.

woodcock, medium-sized insectivorous wading bird with long bill and

brownish plumage. Species include European and Asian woodcock, *Scolapax rusticola,* and Amer. woodcock, *Philohela minor.*

woodcut and **wood engraving,** terms applied to pictures printed from wood blocks cut by hand. Perfected in China by 2nd cent. AD, in Europe by 14th cent.

Wooden Horse, device used by Greeks in TROJAN WAR to capture Troy. Huge wooden effigy of horse built, warriors concealed in belly, left outside city. Trojans, persuaded it was offering to Athena, despite warnings of Cassandra and Laocoon, dragged it inside walls, causing destruction and defeat of Troy.

wood-frog, *Rana sylvatica,* common European and Amer. frog found in moist woodlands. Reddish- or yellowish-brown with dark marking on head.

woodlouse, slater, small terrestrial crustacean of suborder Oniscoida found under stones or bark. Flattened elliptical body with 7 pairs of legs; dull brown or grey in colour.

woodpecker, almost universally distributed tree-climbing bird of family Picidae. Short legs, chisel bill, long sticky tongue. Nests in holes in trees. Species include European green woodpecker, *Picus viridis,* great spotted woodpecker, *Dondrocopus major,* and Amer. red-headed woodpecker, *Melanerpes erythrocephalus.*

woodruff, plant of genus *Asperula* with small white flowers. Species include European sweet woodruff, *A. odorata,* sometimes used in perfumery, and dyer's woodruff, *A. tinctoria,* with creeping rootstock.

woodrush, plant of genus *Luzula,* esp. *L. campestris,* growing chiefly in woodlands. Short, grass-like leaves and clusters of brown flowers.

wood-sorrel, perennial herb of genus *Oxalis* native to Europe, Asia and N America. *O. acetosella* has white purple-veined solitary flowers.

Woodward, Robert Burns (1917–   ), Amer. chemist. Awarded Nobel Prize for Chemistry (1965) for synthesis of organic compounds, incl. cortisone, quinine.

woodwasp, wood-boring insect of family Siricidae. Widely distributed in N hemisphere. Black and yellow woodwasp, *Urocerus gigas,* common in UK; *Sirex noctilio* is serious pest in New Zealand.

woodwind, group of orchestral instruments. Includes flute, clarinet, oboe and bassoon.

woodworm, larva of beetles of family Anobiidae. Beetle lays eggs in cracks in wood; larvae burrow into wood; adult beetles emerge leaving holes. Most common is furniture beetle, *Anobium punctatum*. May be serious pest; preservatives have been developed to combat woodworm.

woody nightshade *see* BITTERSWEET.

wool, fibrous growth, usually curly, covering skin of certain animals, esp. sheep. Absorbent, strong, warm, crease resistant and able to hold dye; spun into yarn and used extensively in clothing manufacture.

Woolf, Virginia (1882–1941), Eng. novelist and critic. Influenced by Proust and Joyce, works characterized by avoidance of factual description and use of interior monologue. Most important novels, *Mrs Dalloway* (1925), *To the Lighthouse* (1927) and *The Waves* (1931).

Woollcott, Alexander Humphreys (1887–1943), Amer. literary and dramatic critic. Writings include *Shouts and Murmurs* (1923), *While Rome Burns* (1934), *Long, Long Ago* (1943).

Woolley, Sir [Charles] Leonard (1880–1960), Brit. archaeologist. Conducted excavations at ancient city of Ur and Bronze Age city of Alakah, near Antioch. Author of *The Sumerians* (1929), *Abraham (1936)*.

woolly monkey, large monkey of genus *Lagothrix* of Amazon basin, S America. Grey woolly coat, prehensile tail.

Woolworth, F[rank] W[infield] (1852–1919). Amer. capitalist. Opened 5-and-10 cent store in Lancaster, Pa. (1879). Opened branches in US and other countries.

Worcestershire, county of C England. Area: 699 sq. mi.; county town, Worcester. Undulating agric. land with fruit growing, mixed farming, salt mines; main industries, porcelain, carpets, glass, fireclay, metal work. Pop. (1966) 663,000.

Wordsworth, William (1770–1850), Eng. poet, leader in Romantic movement. Attempted to write about simple people and nature, in non-literary, everyday language. Later works often characterized by prosaic sentimentality. Became Poet Laureate 1843. Works include *Lyrical Ballads* (1798) written with S.T. Coleridge and containing 'Tintern Abbey', *Poems in Two Volumes* (1807) containing the 'Ode to Duty' and 'Intimations of Immortality' which expresses his belief in neo-Platonic

philosophy. Among famous shorter poems are 'The Daffodils' and 'The Solitary Reaper'.

workhouse, 18th cent. Eng. institution organized under POOR LAW to provide work and shelter for able-bodied paupers and their dependents.

World Bank *see* INTERNATIONAL BANK FOR RECONSTRUCTION AND DEVELOPMENT.

World Council of Churches, organization constituted (1948) at Amsterdam (H.Q. Geneva, Switzerland) by representatives from 150 Protestant and Orthodox churches. No legislative power, provides opportunity for practical co-operation and discussion.

World Health Organization (WHO), agency of United Nations (estab. 1948) set up with aim of attaining highest possible level of health for all peoples. Activities include medical research and training in care of sick and prevention of disease.

World Meteorological Organization (WMO), agency of United Nations (estab. 1951); replaced International Meteorological Organization (estab. 1878). Aims to standardize, coordinate and improve meteorological services throughout the world.

World War 1, conflict (1914–18) precipitated by assassination (June 1914) of Francis Ferdinand of Austria-Hungary in Serbia. By Aug. Europe was involved in total warfare, opposing alliances being Central Powers (Germany, Austria-Hungary and Turkey) and Allies (Britain, France, Russia, Belgium, Serbia, Montenegro and Japan). Rapid Ger. advance in W thwarted near Paris; followed by prolonged stalemate in concentrated trench warfare. In E, Ger. victories culminated in Russ. Revolution (1917) and Russ. withdrawal from war. In 1915, Bulgaria joined Central Powers, Italy joined Allies. Unrestricted Ger. submarine attacks (1916–17) led to US entry on Allied side and eventual end to stalemate. Successful counter-attack by Allies in 2nd battle of the Marne followed by surrender of all Central Powers except Germany. After internal revolt, Germany signed armistice (11 Nov. 1918) at Compiègne. Subsequent peace treaties, esp. TREATY OF VERSAILLES, radically altered polit. boundaries of Europe at expense of Central Powers. Overwhelming loss of life (est. 10 million dead) led to international search for peace, initially through LEAGUE OF NATIONS.

World War 2, conflict (1939–45) climaxing aggressive policies of AXIS

Wood-Frog

powers (Germany, Italy and Japan) and attempts to counter them by W European nations (UK and France). Hitler's success in Bohemia (*see* MUNICH PACT) and non-aggression treaty signed with USSR opened way for attack (Sept. 1939) on Poland. Britain (with Commonwealth) and France declared war on Germany. Hitler's quick victory in Poland followed by occupation of Denmark, Norway and Low Countries; crushed France (surrendered June, 1940) after Allies were forced to evacuate DUNKIRK. Britain, led by Churchill, resisted Ger. bombings in 'Battle of Britain'. Ger. and Ital. successes in N Africa and Balkans (1940–1) preceded invasion of USSR (June, 1941). Jap. attack on Pearl Harbor (Dec. 1941) brought US into war; Japan then occupied much of SE Asia. Axis triumphs halted in N Africa (*see* NORTH AFRICAN CAMPAIGN), by Allied landings in Algeria and S Italy, US naval victories in Pacific and USSR's defeat of Ger. forces at Stalingrad (1943). Italy surrendered (Sept. 1943), but Germany continued to resist Allies. Russ. drive through E Europe and Allied invasion of Normandy under Eisenhower (June, 1944) brought eventual Ger. collapse and surrender (May, 1945). Amer. 'island-hopping' strategy in Pacific and dropping of atomic bombs on Hiroshima and Nagasaki led to Japan's surrender (Sept. 1945). Need to ensure international peace led to formation of UNITED NATIONS; however, problems of post-war Europe remained unresolved, difficulty increasing with development of 'cold war' between East and West.

worm, elongated creeping animal with soft, often segmented body. Commonly the EARTHWORM.

worm lizard, worm-like limbless lizard of genus *Amphisbaena*. Found mainly in Africa and S America.

Worms, historic city of West Germany on Rhine R. Centre of wine-growing region. Became 1st free imperial city (1156). Scene of Diet of Worms which outlawed Luther. Has Romanesque cathedral. Pop. 55,000.

Worms, Concordat of (1122), agreement between Pope Calixtus II and

Woodworm Beetle (*Anobium punctatum*)

Wren

Emperor Henry V after dispute over investitures. Emperor conceded right of free elections of bishops, abbots. Pope granted Henry right to be present at elections and to invest those elected with lay rights before consecration.

Worms, Diet of (1521), meeting of theologians and officials of R.C. Church called by Emperor Charles V at Worms. Martin Luther appeared under safe conduct to defend his theories. On refusal to retract was outlawed, together with his followers.

wormwood, herb or low shrub of genus *Artemisia. A. absinthium,* perennial Eurasian shrubby herb, yields oil used in absinthe.

Worsaae, Jens Jacob Asmussen (1821–85), Danish historian and archaeologist. Regarded as founder of pre-historic archaeology as a science.

wrasse, marine fish of family Labridae of world-wide distribution. Compressed, brilliantly coloured body.

Wren, Sir Christopher (1632–1723), Eng. architect. Designed over 50 London churches, incl. St Paul's Cathedral.

wren, small singing bird of family Troglodytidae of temp. and trop. regions. Species include European and Asian wren, *Troglodytes troglodytes,* and house-wren *T. aedon,* of N America.

wrestling, Olympic sport in which 2

Wryneck

unarmed contestants in hand-to-hand combat struggle to trip or throw one another to the ground. Popular among ancient Egyptians and Greeks; 1st included in Olympiad *c.* 704 BC.

Wright, Frank Lloyd (1869–1959), Amer. architect. Concerned esp. to relate building to surroundings. Introduced open-plan houses. Influenced much 20th cent. architecture. Among his works are Imperial Hotel (Tokyo, Japan), Guggenheim Museum (New York City, US).

Wright, Orville *see* WRIGHT, WILBUR.

Wright, Richard Nathaniel (1908–60), Amer. novelist and short-story writer. Regarded as leading spokesman for American Negroes. Works include *Native Son* (1940) and autobiog. *Black Boy* (1945).

Wright, Wilbur (1867–1912), Amer. aviator. With brother **Orville Wright** (1871–1948), pioneered power-driven flight (1903). Founded Wright Aeroplane Co.

writing, art of forming symbols on surface of some medium to record and communicate ideas. Ancestor of alphabetic writing was Semitic script, developed 18th–17th cent. BC prob. in Sinai and using single consonant signs. Earlier method of communication was combination of ideograms (symbols representing ideas rather than images) and phonetic symbols, *e.g.* Babylonian and Assyrian cuneiform and Egyptian hieroglyphics.

Wroclaw, prov. of SW Poland. Until 1945 part of Ger. Lower Silesia. Area: 7,269 sq. mi.; cap. Wroclaw. Mixed farming, cattle-raising, cereals, potatoes, flax. Industries, coal mining, heavy engineering, glass, paper, textiles. Pop. (1960) 1,768,000.

Wroclaw, Breslau, city of Poland, annexed (1945) from Germany. Centre of Silesian coalfield. Industries, machine tools, textiles, electrical goods, iron foundries. Pop. (1964) 466,000.

wryneck, Old World insectivorous bird of genus *Jynx* of woodpecker family. Grey plumage above and yellow below. Named for habit of twisting neck while feeding. Species include European *J. torquilla* and *J. pectoralis* of central and S Africa.

wulfenite, molybdate of lead. Occurs commonly as yellow orthorhombic crystals in veins with lead ores.

Wurtz, Charles Adolphe, FRS (1817–84), Fr. organic chemist. Investigated constitution of glycerine and glycols, and of amino-acids. Wrote *La Théorie Atomique* (1879).

Würzburg, city of Bavaria, W Germany. Fine buildings include episcopal palace (1719–44), 12th cent.

Wulfenite

Marienberg Castle and Bridge of the Saints (1474). University (1403). Pop. 120,000.

Wyandot, name given to N Amer. Iroquoian Indians S of L. Superior.

Wyatt, Sir Thomas (*c.* 1503–42), Eng. lyric poet. Introduced sonnet form into English from Italy. Many poems 1st pub. in Tottel's *Miscellany* (1557).

Wycherley, William (1640–1716), Eng. dramatist. Introduced element of coarse satirical realism to essentially artificial Restoration comedy. Plays include *Love in a Wood* (1671), *The Country Wife* and *The Plain Dealer* (both 1674).

Wycliffe or **Wiclif, John** (*c.* 1324–84), Eng. cleric and scholar. Denied R.C. Church doctrine of Transubstantiation, proclaimed supremacy of scripture over eccles. authority, attacked wealth of church and feudal authority. Theories propagated by itinerant preachers (LOLLARDS). Condemned as heretic, but protected by John of Gaunt. Completed translation of Bible into English.

Wykeham, William of (1324–1404), Eng. bishop and chancellor of Edward III. Founded New College, Oxford (1380), Winchester College (1388–94).

Wylie, Elinor Hoyt (1885–1928), Amer. poet and novelist. Works include verse *Nets to Catch the Wind* (1921) and novel *The Venetian Glass Nephew* (1925).

Wyoming, state of W US. Area: 97,914 sq. mi.; cap. Cheyenne. Mountainous with high plains, extensive forests and pasture land. Petroleum, natural gas and uranium resources. Farming and tourism important. Main industries, oil refining, food processing. Flourished with discovery of gold (1876) and completion of Union Pacific Rly. (1868). Pop. (1960) 330,066.

Xanthe *see* XANTHUS.

Xanthi *see* XANTHUS.

Xanthippe, Xantippe (*fl. c.* 5th cent. BC), wife of Socrates, reputedly of shrewish disposition.

xanthophyll [Gk: *xanthos,* yellow], generic name for yellow, carotenoid pigments found esp. in flowers, fruits and leaves. Lutein, crystalline carotenoid alcohol, found in plants, animal fat, egg yolk. Zeaxanthin is chief pigment of yellow Indian corn.

Xanthus, ancient city of Asia Minor, on Xanthus R. Antiquities, discovered (1838) by Sir Charles Fellows, include friezes, now in British Museum. Modern city of **Xanthi** or **Xanthe,** in W Thrace, Greece, produces tobacco. Pop. (1961) 26,000.

Xantippe *see* XANTHIPPE.

Xavier, Saint Francis *see* FRANCIS XAVIER, SAINT.

Xenocrates (396–314 BC), Gk. Platonic philosopher. Succeeded Speusippus as head of Academy in Athens.

xenon (Xe), rare, colourless, odourless, gaseous element found in Earth's atmosphere. Used in filling radio, television and luminescent tubes.

Xenophanes (*fl.* 6th cent. BC), Gk. poet. Attacked polytheism and anthropomorphism of contemporary Gk. religion, asserting that God is single and eternal. From presence of fossils of fishes on mountains, inferred that the land had risen from the sea.

Xenophon (*c.* 430 BC-*c.* 355 BC), Gk. historian, pupil of Socrates. Joined (401 BC) Gk. expedition under Cyrus of Persia. In *Anabasis* relates adventure and subsequent retreat after battle of Cunaxa (401 BC). Later fought with Spartans against Athens and Thebes at battle of Coronea (394 BC). Banished by Athenians who confiscated his property. Lived in Elis until 370 BC. His *Memorabilia* and *Symposium* expound character and teachings of Socrates. Hist. works include *Hellenica,* a history of Greece.

Xeres or **Jeres, Francisco de** (*c.* 1504–47), Sp. historian. Participated in conquest of Peru (1530–4), bringing gold from ATAHUALPA. Author of a history of the conquest.

Xerography, commercial process similar to PHOTOGRAPHY. Does not require light-sensitive paper. Selenium coating on metal plate given charge of static electricity. Electrostatic image of original formed by attraction or rejection of thermo-plastic and carbon powder, then transferred to copying-paper and fixed by heat. Widely used for rapid copying of, *e.g.,* documents.

Xerxes [I] the Great (*c.* 519 BC–465 BC), king of Persia (486 BC–465 BC), son of Darius Hystaspas. Led expedition into Egypt. Invaded Greece in PERSIAN WARS; fleet destroyed at Salamis (480 BC). Killed by one of his soldiers. Appears in OT as Ahasuerus.

Xhosa, Bantu language with over 2 million speakers on SE coast of Africa.

Xingú, Chingú, river (*c.* 1,200 mi. long) rising in NE Mato Grosso, Brazil. Flows N through Pará state to Amazon delta. First explored 1885. Lower reaches navigable.

Xipe, in Aztec religion, god of seeding and planting. Represented as clothed in skin of a flayed man symbolizing new vegetation clothing the earth.

xiphosura, order of large marine arthropods of America and S Asia; related to spiders. Includes horseshoe, king and swordtail crabs. Amer. species is *Limulus polyphemus.* Because of ancient origin, referred to as living fossils.

Xochimilco, city of C Mexico, suburb of Mexico City. Noted for floating gardens, intersected by numerous canals lined by poplars. Produces flowers, vegetables, fruit.

Xoxe, Koci (1911–49), Albanian Communist leader. Active in partisan movement during World War 2. Min. of the Interior (1946–9). Executed for treason.

X-ray, Roentgen ray, Röntgen ray, invisible electro-magnetic radiation produced by electric current passing through vacuum tube with 2 electrodes. Penetrates substances opaque to light. Widely used in medicine to photograph internal organs, bones, *etc.* and destroy diseased tissue. X-rays discovered (1895) by Ger. physicist W.C. Roentgen.

xylene, xylol, colourless, oily liquid, mixture of hydrocarbon compounds; prepared from coal tar and used as solvent.

xylophone, percussion instrument consisting of a set of resonant wooden bars, tuned to different pitches, which are struck with hammers.

XYZ Affair, diplomatic incident (1797–8) between US and France. Reports that 3 Fr. agents, called X, Y and Z, had attempted to bribe members of Amer. delegation to offer large sum of money to Fr. Directory led to Amer. demands for war against France. Arguments settled (Sept. 1800) by Convention of Mortefontaine.

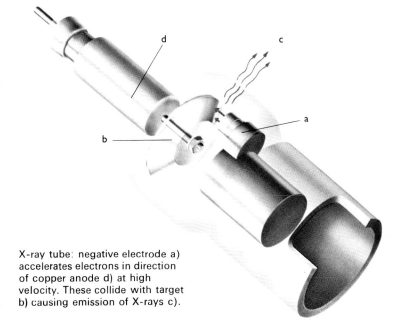

X-ray tube: negative electrode a) accelerates electrons in direction of copper anode d) at high velocity. These collide with target b) causing emission of X-rays c).

Y

yacht, sailing or power driven boat used either for racing or pleasure cruising.

yachting, sailing, sport of racing or cruising in sailing craft. Introduced (17th cent.) into England by Charles II; 1st Eng. yachting club estab. 1775. In US, racing began with foundation (1844) of New York Yacht Club. Included in Olympic Games. International ocean-racing contests include America's Cup, Fastnet Cup.

yak, *Poephagus grunniens,* stocky wild ox of Tibetan highlands. Shaggy brown hair, short legs, smooth black horns. Domesticated yak is source of meat and milk; used as draught animal.

Yakima, N Amer. Shahaptian Indian tribe of C Washington in Columbia and Yakima rivers region.

Yakut Autonomous Soviet Socialist Republic, in NE Siberia, Russ. SFSR. Area: 1,198,145 sq. mi.; cap. Yakutsk. Poor transportation has left rich mineral and forest resources unexploited. Extreme climate. Pop. (1965) 614,000.

Yale, Elihu (1649–1721), Eng. merchant, b. Boston. Amassed fortune in trade. Yale University named after him as major benefactor.

Yale University, privately endowed US university in New Haven, Conn.

Yacht (Bermudan rigged ketch)

Developed from Collegiate School founded (1701), estab. at present site (1716), given present name (1718), after benefactor Elihu Yale. Became University (1887). Undergraduate women 1st admitted 1969.

Yalta, city and health resort of S Crimea, Ukraine, USSR, on Black Sea. Pop. (1965 est.) 54,000.

Yalta Conference, conference held at Yalta, before end of World War 2 (1945). Attended by Winston Churchill (UK), Franklin D. Roosevelt (US) and Joseph Stalin (USSR). Agreements reached included insistence on unconditional surrender of Germany, holding of conference on setting up of supra-national organization (became United Nations Organization).

yam, trop. climbing plant of genus *Dioscorea* of warmer regions of E and W hemisphere. Edible starchy tuberous roots. Cultivated for human and animal consumption.

Yamashita, Tomoyuki (1885–1946), Jap. general. Led invasion of Malaya (1942); supreme commander in Philippines (1944–5). Convicted of war crimes; executed.

Yangtze Kiang, longest river (*c.* 3,400 mi.) of Asia and of China. Rises in Tibet and flows E to enter sea N of Shanghai. Navigable for *c.* 1,500 mi.; Chungking, Hankow and Nanking are chief ports.

yankee, yank, term of uncertain origin, used to refer to Americans. Within US, esp. during Civil War, term applied to people from North East US. Connotation varies.

Yaoundé, cap. and transport centre of Fed. Repub. of Cameroon. Founded by Germans (*c.* 1890), became cap. of French Cameroons. Exports cocoa products. Pop. (1965) 101,000.

Yaqui, nomadic Indian race inhabiting NW Mexico and SW US. Have begun to settle in Mexican state of Sonora.

Yarmouth, Great, county borough, resort and seaport of Norfolk, England, at mouth of R. Yare. One of world's largest herring ports. Pop. (1961) 52,860.

Yaroslavl, region of Russ. SFSR, USSR. Area: 14,250 sq. mi.; cap. Yaroslavl. Agriculture and lumbering main industries.

Yaroslavl, cap. of Yaroslavl region, Russ. SFSR. Founded 1026. Pop. (1964) 467,000.

yarrow, milfoil, *Achillea millefolium,* strong-scented Eurasian perennial plant naturalized in N America. Fine, carrot-like leaves; cluster of white, pink or red flowers. Sometimes used as tonic and astringent.

yaws, frambesia, pian, infectious contagious trop. disease caused by organism *Treponema pertenne.* Characterized by severe skin lesions and, in late stage, bone destruction.

year, term used for period taken by Earth to revolve once round Sun; usually computed at 365 days 5 hr. 48 min. 49·7 sec. A calendar year is fixed at 365 days with an extra day every 4 years (leap year), leaving an error of about 1 day every 4,000 years.

yeast, microscopic fungi. Produces alcohol and carbon dioxide in presence of sugar. Used in alcoholic fermentation of beer, wine and industrial alcohol. Also in baking, yeast acting upon carbohydrates in dough causing mixture to 'rise'.

Yeats, William Butler (1865–1939), Irish poet and dramatist. Adherent of Irish nationalism, helped found ABBEY THEATRE, wrote plays incl. *Countess Cathleen* (1899). Poetry influenced by mysticism, noted for lyrical, dramatic qualities and symbolism. Prepared *Collected Poems* (1933), incl. earlier poems *e.g.* 'The Lake Isle of Innisfree', 'Byzantium', 'Easter 1916', 'Among School Children'. Awarded Nobel Prize for Literature (1923).

yellow fever, yellow jack, acute infectious febrile disease of tropics, esp. Caribbean area, Brazil and W coast of Africa. Caused by virus transmitted by mosquito, *Aedes aegypti.* Characterized by jaundice, vomiting, haemorrhages, *etc.* First effective vaccines produced by Max Theiler.

yellow hammer, *Emberiza citrinella,* European bird of finch family. Male has yellow head and belly. Name also given to yellow flicker, *Colaptes auratus,* woodpecker of E N America with yellow stripes on wings and body.

Yellow River *see* HWANG-HO.

Yellow Sea, Hwang Hai, inlet of W Pacific, between China and Korea. Named because of yellowish silt deposited by Hwang-Ho (Yellow R.).

yellow wagtail, wagtail of genus *Motacilla,* esp. common Eurasian wagtail, *M. flag* with greenish upper plumage and yellow throat and underparts. *See* illus. p. 605.

yellow-crested penguin, *Endytes cristatus,* penguin of Falkland Is., New Zealand and Antarctic waters. Short thick bill, yellow crest and moderately long tail.

Yellowknife, town and admin. cap., S Northwest Territories, Canada, on shore of Great Slave L. Founded (1935) after discovery of gold and silver. Transport and communications centre. Pop. (1966) 3,741.

yellowlegs, Amer. shore bird of genus *Tringa,* related to greenshank. Brown-black plumage mottled with white and yellow legs. The 2 species are greater yellowlegs, *T. melanoleuca,* and lesser yellowlegs, *T. flavipes.*

yellowroot *see* ZANTHORHIZA.

Yellowstone, river (671 mi.) rising in NW Wyoming, US and flowing to Missouri R. At base of Yellowstone Lake, forms scenic falls.

Yellowstone National Park, in Wyoming, Idaho and Montana, US. Estab. 1872. Noted for geysers incl. Old Faithful, petrified forests and hot springs.

yellowwood, *Cladrastis lutea,* ornamental leguminous tree of SE US. Clusters of fragrant white flowers; hard yellow wood yields dye. Any other tree yielding yellow wood, *e.g. Schaefferia frutescens* of S Florida.

Yemen, repub. of SW Asia, on Red Sea. Area: 75,300 sq. mi.; cap. Sana'a. Mountainous except for

coastal strip. Fruits, grain, qat grown. Hist. associated with Arabia after introduction of Islam (628). After Ottoman dissolution (1918), ruled by monarchy until coup (1962) and estab. of repub. Main religion, Islam. Unit of currency, riyal. Pop. (1962) *c.* 5,000,000.

Yemen, Southern, repub. of SW Asia on Arabian peninsula, formed (1967) from South Arabian Federation and E Aden Protectorate. Area: *c.* 60,000 sq. mi.; cap. Aden. Region primarily mountains and desert, agriculture is main occupation. Aden serves as distribution port. Estab. of repub. ended more than cent. of Brit. rule. Pop. (1965 est.) 900,000.

Yenisei, Enisei, river (*c.* 2,560 mi.), Russ. SFSR, in C Siberia. Rises in E Sayan Mts, and flows W and N to Kara Sea. Middle and lower reaches navigable in summer; linked by canal system with Ob R. Hydro-electric station at Krasnoyarsk; other towns, Minusinsk, Yeniseisk, Igarka.

yeoman, term in Eng. social history for class of small landowners who worked own farms. Esp. characteristic of period between disintegration of feudal system and industrial revolution.

Yeomen of the Guard, royal bodyguard of England, now restricted to

ceremonial functions at the Tower of London. Instituted (1485) by Henry VII. Also called 'Beefeaters'.

Yersin, Alexandre (1863–1943), Fr. bacteriologist. Isolated plague bacillus and developed serum to combat it.

Yesenin, Sergei Aleksandrovich *see* ESENIN, SERGEI ALEKSANDROVICH.

yeti or **abominable snowman,** animal resembling man said to live in Himalayas of Asia. Tracks (12 in. long) found have been ascribed to it. Existence disputed but believed by some to be a remnant of Neanderthal man.

Yevtushenko or **Evtushenko, Yevgeny Aleksandrovich** (1933–   ), Russ. poet. Criticisms of Communist regime reflect desire for return to initial revolutionary stages of USSR. Works include *Stalin's Heirs* (1961) and *Babiyar* (1968).

yew, evergreen coniferous tree or shrub of genus *Taxus* of Eurasia and N America. Dark green leaves and red berry-like fruits; yields fine-grained elastic wood. Species include ground hemlock or Canada yew, *T. canadensis,* of Canada and NE US.

Yezidis, religious sect of Iraq. Combines elements of Islam and Christianity, worships good and evil, sometimes called devil worshippers.

Yggdrasill, in Norse myth., tree of life representing universe. Eagle (heaven) at top, serpent (hell) at bottom; squirrel between was symbolic of strife.

Yiddish, Germanic language spoken by many Jews. Borrows from Slavic, Hebrew languages; written in Hebrew characters. Literature little developed until late 19th cent. owing to educated Jews' preference for Hebrew.

Yingkow, city of Liaoning prov., NE China, former treaty port of Manchuria. Opened 1864, has declined in 20th cent. Pop. (1957) 131,000.

Yoga [Sanskrit: union], system of Hindu philosophy characterized by belief in possibility of union with supreme being or ultimate principle through liberation of the self; this state achieved by observance of moral rules, self-control, meditation, and breathing and posture exercises.

yogurt, yoghourt, prepared food of custard consistency. Made from curdled milk, sometimes sweetened or flavoured.

Yokohama, industrial city, C Honshu, Japan, major port on Tokyo Bay. Industries include steel works, shipbuilding, oil and chemical works, automobile manufacture; chief export, silk. Largely rebuilt after earthquake (1923). Pop. (1964) 1,789,000.

Yokuts, group of N Amer. Indians of S California. Settled mainly on Tule R. reservation.

Yom Kippur *see* ATONEMENT, DAY OF.

Yonge, Charlotte Mary (1823–1901), Brit. novelist. Numerous works, reflecting propriety and religious devotion, include *The Heir of Redclyffe* (1853).

Yonkers, residential area and manufacturing centre of Westchester Co., New York, on Hudson R. Adjoins greater New York City. Orig. Dutch settlement (*c.* 1650), chartered 1872. Pop. (1965) 201,500.

Yorck von Wartenburg, Johann David Ludwig, Graf (1759–1830), Prussian army officer. Led Prussian forces in Napoleon's attack on Russia (1812). Concluded Convention of Tauroggen (1812) withdrawing Prussian troops from fighting.

York, Richard, Duke of (1411–60), Eng. nobleman, heir to throne (1447), displaced by son of Margaret of Anjou. Protector of England during Henry VI's insanity, claims to throne began Wars of the Roses. Slain in battle of Wakefield. Son seized throne (1461) as Edward IV.

York, House of, Eng. royal family. Claimed throne through Edmund of Langley (1341–1402), 5th son of Edward III, created (1385) Duke of York. WARS OF THE ROSES resulted from rivalry between RICHARD, DUKE OF YORK and Lancastrians. Edward IV, Edward V and Richard III ruled

Wadi on the Heights of Bab el Mandeb in the Yemen

before 2 houses united under Henry VII, 1st Tudor king.

York, county borough and county town of Yorkshire, N England. As Eboracum, was military cap. of Roman Britain; in 7th cent. became cap. of kingdom of Northumbria; archbishopric founded 625. Important medieval, eccles. and commercial centre. City walls (14th cent.) and cathedral (12th–15th cent.). Industries include rolling stock, confectionery, chemicals, optical instruments. Pop. (1967) 104,468.

Yorkshire, largest county of England, divided into admin. counties of East Riding, North Riding and West Riding. Area: 6,081 sq. mi.; county town, York; main cities, Sheffield, Leeds, Hull, Huddersfield. Borders on North Sea, contains Pennine hills and Plain of York. Indust. region in W with extensive coal deposits; textiles, cutlery and machinery manufactured. Pop. (1966) 4,863,000.

Yorkshire terrier, Eng. breed of toy terrier. Long silky straight coat; dark steel blue on back, tan on head, chest and legs.

Yorktown, historic settlement (1631), SE Virginia, US, on York estuary of Chesapeake Bay. Scene (at Moore House) of British surrender (1781) during Amer. Revolution. Town besieged (1862) during Civil War.

Yorktown campaign, concluding military encounter (1781) of Amer.

Revolution. Brit. forces, led by Cornwallis, retreated from Carolinas into Virginia and awaited reinforcements. Aided by French blockade of Chesapeake Bay, Washington penetrated Brit. defences and forced surrender (Oct. 1781) at Yorktown.

Yoruba, Sudanic speaking people of Africa, orig. inhabiting SW Nigeria and Dahomey. Have spread widely in W Africa.

Yosemite National Park, Sierra Nevada, California, US. Area: 1,200 sq. mi. Estab. 1890. Includes Yosemite Valley; Yosemite waterfall, 2,425 ft.; giant sequoia trees.

Yoshida, Shigeru (1878–   ), Jap. statesman. Served 5 terms as P.M. (1946–54). Signed Jap. peace treaty with Allies (1951).

Young, Brigham (1801–77), Amer. religious leader. Succeeded Joseph Smith as leader of Mormon sect (1847). Led (1846–7) following to Salt Lake City and founded prosperous settlement where he instituted polygamy (1852).

Young, Denton True ('Cy') (1867–1955), Amer. baseball player. Winner of most games (511) in major leagues.

Young, Francis Brett (1884–1954), Eng. writer. Novels of Brit. middle-class life include *Portrait of Clare* (1927) and *A Man About the House* (1942).

Young, Sir John, Baron Lisgar (1807–76), Eng. politician and ad-

ministrator. Cons. M.P. (1831–55). Gov.-General of New South Wales, Australia (1861–7); Gov.-General of Canada and Gov. of Prince Edward's Is. (1869–72).

Young, Owen D. (1874–1962), Amer. govt. adviser. Promoted Young Plan reducing German reparation payments. Adopted (1930) by Allied nations to replace Dawes Plan, programme unfruitful with advent of Depression and rise of Hitler.

Young, Thomas (1773–1829), Brit. physicist and Egyptologist. With Helmholtz, developed a theory of colour vision; described astigmatism. Contributed to deciphering of Rosetta Stone and Egyptian hieroglyphics.

Young Men's Christian Association (YMCA), organization founded in London (1844) by Sir George Williams and in US and Canada (1851–4). Original purpose of teaching Christian principles broadened to provide residential, educ., sporting and cultural facilities. International organization with H.Q. in Geneva, Switzerland. **Young Women's Christian Association (YWCA)** founded (1855) in England.

Young Turk Movement, reform and nationalist movement of OTTOMAN EMPIRE in early 20th cent. Organized revolt which deposed Abdul Hamid II (1909).

Younghusband, Sir Frances Edward (1863–1942), Brit. explorer and writer. Explored mountains between Kashmir and China. Appointed commissioner to Tibet (1902–4) and led Brit. expedition to Lhasa.

Youngstown, trade and manufacturing centre of Ohio, US. Important steel manufactures based on local coal and iron resources. Founded 1797. Pop. (1965) 373,000.

Youth Hostel Association (YHA), organization designed to provide cheap overnight accommodation for young travellers of limited means. Formed in Germany where 1st hostel opened (1910). International Youth Hostel Federation founded at Amsterdam (1932).

Ypres [Flemish: **Jeper**], Belgian town of W Flanders. Scene of 3 battles of World War 1. Pop. *c.* 8,000.

Ypsilante, Alexander (1792–1828), Greek patriot. Led secret society in War of Independence; raised abortive revolt in Moldavia (1821) which made possible successful uprising in Peloponnese. Brother, **Demetrios Ypsilante** (1793–1832) played important part in Peloponnese in fighting against Ibrahim Pasha.

Yseult *see* TRISTAN AND ISOLDE.

Yüan, Chinese dynasty (1260–1368),

16th cent. stone bridge, Mostar, Yugoslavia

founded by KUBLAI KHAN. Saw increased foreign trade, development of postal services, improvements in roads and canals. Succeeded by MING dynasty.

Yüan Shih-k'ai (1859–1916), Chinese polit. leader. Leading imperial supporter (1901–12), advised Hsüan emperor to abdicate. Succeeded Sun Yat-sen as pres. of provisional govt., monarchical ambitions thwarted (1915).

Yucatán, peninsula of SE Mexico, Brit. Honduras and Guatemala. Area: *c.* 70,000 sq. mi. Predominantly tableland, produce includes sisal, tobacco, cotton; also trop. timber. Before arrival of Spanish (16th cent.) region was centre of Mayan civilization.

yucca, plant of genus *Yucca* of lily family. Found in warmer regions of US. Pointed, usually rigid leaves and white waxy flowers. Species include Joshua tree, *Y. arborescens,* of desert regions.

Yugoslavia [Socijalistička Federativna Republika Yugoslavija], repub. of SE Europe. Area: 98,725 sq. mi.; cap. Belgrade; principal cities Zagreb,

Sarajevo, Skoplje. Predominantly mountainous with extensive agriculture and forestry. Mineral deposits include copper, iron, lead on which

Yellow Wagtail

industry is based. Federation of Socialist Repubs. of Serbia, Croatia, Slovenia, Montenegro, Bosnia and Herzegovina, Macedonia formed after World War 2; became Communist State under TITO. Main languages, Serbo-Croatian, Slovenian. Predominant religions, Orthodox Eastern, Roman Catholicism. Unit of currency, dinar. Pop. (1967) 19,958,000.

Yukawa, Hideki (1907–), Jap. physicist. Awarded Nobel Prize for Physics (1949) for his work on the meson theory of nuclear forces.

Yukon, territory of NW Canada, bordering on Alaska. Area: 205,346 sq. mi.; cap. Whitehorse. Sparsely populated tundra and mountainous region, extensive mineral deposits. Scene of 1890s Klondike gold rush, during which town of Dawson flourished. Pop. (1966) 14,382.

Yukon, river (*c.* 2,000 mi.) in Yukon and Alaska, one of longest Amer. rivers. Formed by Lewes R. and Pelly R. Flows generally NW to Bering Sea. Navigable in summer. Lower reaches explored by Russians (1836–7, 1843); upper reaches by Canadian Robert Campbell (1843).

Yuma, tribe of N Amer. Indians in Colorado R. area, US.

Yungas, Yuncas, people of pre-Inca kingdom of N Peru. Descendants inhabit parts of Bolivia and Peru.

Yunnan, province of SW China. Area: 160,000 sq. mi.; cap. Kunming. Plateau and canyon land drained by Mekong and Yangtze rivers. Principal crops, rice, tea, corn. Important tin, copper, coal and gypsum deposits. Pop. (1957 est.) 19,100,000.

Yurok, group of N Amer. Indians of lower Klamath R. in N California. Organized by kin rather than by tribe.

The Yukon River in Alaska

Z

Zabrze, city of SW Poland, formerly in Upper Silesia. Centre of Katowice mining region, incorporated by Poland (1945). Pop. (1966) 198,000.

Zadkine, Ossip (1890–1967), Fr. cubist sculptor, b. Russia. Works, include 'Torso', 'Diana' and monument 'The Destruction of Rotterdam'.

Zagazig, town of N Egypt, in rich agric. district. Has textile industries; market for grain and cotton. Pop. (1963) 82,900.

Zagreb, city of NW Yugoslavia, cap. of Croatia. Industries include manufacturing of machinery, textiles, chemicals, paper. Seat of R.C. and Orthodox Eastern archbishoprics. Contains 11th cent. cathedral. Pop. (1964) 491,000.

Zagros, mountain system of SW Iran. Extends along and across border with Iraq. Highest peak 15,000 ft.

Zaïmis, Alexander (1855–1936), Gk. statesman. Premier 6 times (1897–1928). Pres. of Greece (1929–35); struggles between republicans and royalists ended in his exile.

Zaire *see* CONGO, REPUBLIC OF THE.

Zama, Battle of, confrontation (202 BC) in N Africa, W of Carthage. Defeat of Hannibal by Scipio Africanus Major marked end of 2nd Punic War.

Zambesi, river (1,633 mi.) of S central Africa. Rises in Zambia, flows approx. SE, forming Zambia-Rhodesia border, through Mozambique to Indian Ocean. Explored (1860s) by David Livingstone. Includes VICTORIA FALLS. Kariba Dam is important source of hydro-electric power.

Zambia, repub. of C Africa, formerly Northern Rhodesia, member of Brit. Commonwealth. Area: 290,586 sq. mi.; cap. Lusaka. Largely plateau broken by hills and drained by Zambesi R. Rich copper producing area with deposits also of cobalt and zinc. Explored by David Livingstone (19th cent.); annexed (1891) by Brit. South Africa Co.; became Brit. protectorate 1924; joined FEDERATION OF RHODESIA AND NYASALAND 1953; independent (1963). Became repub. and renamed 1964. Pop. (1966 est.) 3,894,000.

Zamboanga, city and port of SW Mindanao, Philippine Is. Exports copra, hemp, timber and rubber. Principal market of S Philippines. Pop. (1967) 158,000.

zanthorhiza, yellowroot, genus of shrubs of family Berberidaceae of N America; purplish brown flowers and bitter yellow roots.

Zanzibar, former island repub. off E African coast, now part of TANZANIA. Area: 640 sq. mi.; chief town, Zanzibar. Produces cloves, trop. fruits. Contested by Arabs, Persians and Portuguese, became (1890) Brit. protectorate. Independent (1963), repub. estab. (1964) before union with Tanganyika. Population mainly Moslem. Pop. (1965) 354,000.

Zapata, Emiliano (*c.* 1879–1919), Mexican revolutionary. After overthrow of Diaz (1911), led independent Indian movement fighting for agrarian reform. Occupied Mexico City 3 times. Killed by agent of Carranza.

Zaporozhe, formerly Aleksandrovsk, city of S Ukraine, USSR, on Dnieper R. Centre of steel, aluminium industries. Pop. (1966) 571,000.

Zapotec, Indian people of Oaxaca state, Mexico, culturally akin to Maya and Toltec. Prominent as independent nation *c.* 1st cent. BC; conquered by Spaniards (1522–6).

Zaragoza *see* SARAGOSSA.

Zarathustra *see* ZOROASTER.

Zatopek, Emil (1922–), Czech athlete. Estab. records in 5 and 10 thousand metres and marathon races with victories in 1952 Olympics.

Zealand, Sjaelland, Danish island between Kattegat and Baltic Sea. Area: 2,709 sq. mi.; principal cities, Copenhagen, Roskilde, Elsinore. Dairying and fishing important.

Zealots, Jewish party (*c.* 37 BC–AD 70) formed in opposition to idolatrous practices. Revolt against Romans (AD 6) followed by intermittent violence until Jerusalem destroyed by Romans (AD 70). Zealots disappeared as Jews left Palestine.

Zebedee, in NT, father of James and John, disciples of Jesus.

zebra, horse-like African animal of genus *Equus*. White or buff coloured with black or brown stripes. Rarely domesticated.

zebra fish, any of various barred trop. fish. Species include small Austral. sea fish, *Melambaphes zebra,* with 9 dark cross-bars; small blue and silver striped Indian danio *Branchydanio rerio,* a popular aquarium fish.

zebra plant, *Calathea zebrina,* ornamental foliage plant of Brazil. Large leaves with yellow-green and olive green stripes on upper surface.

zebu, *Bos indicus,* domesticated Asiatic bovine animal, many breeds found in India, China, East Indies and parts of Africa. Short horns, long pendulous ears, large fatty hump over the shoulders.

Zebulun, in OT, 6th son of Jacob (*Gen.* xxx, 20). Ancestor of one of tribes of Israel, settled in N Palestine.

Zechariah, prophetic book of OT. First part by Zechariah, records events in Judah (520–518 BC). Later part (2nd cent. BC) contains allegories foretelling destruction of Jerusalem and Temple. Messianic hope clearly expressed; Christ's entry into Jerusalem on Palm Sunday foretold.

Zedekiah (*fl.* 6th cent. BC), in OT, last king of Judah (*c.* 597–586 BC). Allied with Egypt despite warnings of Jeremiah, resulting in Nebuchadnezzar's invasion of Palestine and destruction of Judah. Zedekiah and his people captured and removed to Babylon.

Zeebrugge, outer port of Bruges, West Flanders prov., Belgium, on North Sea. Linked with Bruges by 6-mile canal. Ger. submarine base during most of World War 1.

Zeeman, Pieter (1865–1943), Dutch

Zebra

physicist. With H. A. Lorentz awarded Nobel Prize for Physics (1902). Discovered Zeeman effect, the splitting up of lines in a line spectrum by strong magnetic field.

Zelaya, José Santos (1853–1919), Nicaraguan politician, pres. (1894–1909). Attempted to create Central American union. Overthrown by rebels with US support. Died in exile.

zemstvo, assembly in Russia (1864–1917) which functioned as unit of local govt. After 1870 officers were elected. Made advances in educ. and health fields.

Zen Buddhism, Japanese form of Buddhism. Originated (6th cent.) in India, reached Japan by 12th cent., where it was supported by Samurai. Advocates meditation as means of achieving self-realization.

Zenger, John Peter (1697–1746), Amer. journalist, b. Germany. Acquitted in trial for libel, result helped further freedom of the press in America.

zenith, in astronomy, point in the heavens vertically above any place on Earth. Directly opposite NADIR. Zenith and nadir form the 2 poles (superior and inferior respectively) of the horizon.

Zeno of Citium (*fl. c.* 300 BC), philosopher, b. Cyprus. Founder of Stoic school of philosophy, named from fact that Zeno taught in Stoa Poikile (Painted Colonnade), marketplace, Athens. *See* STOICISM.

Zenobia (d. after AD 272), queen of Palmyra. Ruled for son after murder of husband; increased territory and power of Palmyra. Taken as captive to Rome (AD 272) after capture of Palmyra by Aurelian.

zeolite, hydrated silicate of aluminium with alkali metals. Occurs as secondary mineral in cavities in basic igneous volcanic rocks.

Zephaniah, Sophonias, prophetic book of OT (6th cent. BC). Denounces sins of Jerusalem but ends with prediction of salvation and Jews' return to God's grace.

Zeppelin, Ferdinand, Graf von (1838–1917), Ger. army officer. Invented 1st airship (1900); during World War 1, Germany used Zeppelins in bombing raids.

Zermatt, resort and winter sports centre of Valois canton, Switzerland. Situated at base of the MATTERHORN.

zero, digit signifying nothing, symbolized as O. Zero indicates mid-point on integer scale, between +1 and −1. Prob. introduced to West from Hindu India in Middle Ages, vital in development of practical number system.

The Zambesi River in Mozambique

Zerubbabel (*fl.* 6th cent. BC), gov. of Jerusalem, a prince of Judah. Sponsored rebuilding of Temple of Jerusalem.

Zetland, county of Scotland comprising SHETLAND ISLANDS.

Zeus, in Gk. myth., supreme god, son of Cronus and Rhea. Overthrew Cronus, became ruler of heaven. Husband of Hera who bore him Hebe, Ares, Eileithyia; also many children born to him by goddesses, nymphs and mortals, *e.g.* Persephone, Artemis, Apollo, Hermes, Dionysus, Perseus, Heracles; father of Athena, and, in some legends, Aphrodite. Dispensed good and evil to men, protected law, order and justice. Manifested authority with thunder-bolt; made earth fertile with rain. Regarded as father and saviour of men (Zeus Soter). Identified with Roman Jupiter.

Zhukov, Georgi Konstantinovich (1896–   ), Soviet military and polit. leader. Field marshal during World War 2, instrumental in victory at Stalingrad (1943), capture of Berlin. Appointed (1957) defence min., ousted by Khrushchev.

Ziegler, Karl (1898–   ), Ger. chemist. With Giulio Natta, awarded Nobel Prize for Chemistry (1963) for developing system of uniting hydrocarbons, used in manufacture of plastics, *etc.*

Zimbabwe [Bantu: stone house], stone ruins in SE Rhodesia. Name esp. refers to large site near Fort Victoria, where white explorers discovered stone temple and acropolis (*c.* 1870). Believed built by Bantus, *c.* 15th cent.

Zimmerman, Dominikus (1685–1766), Dutch architect. Noted for decorations in rococo style.

zinc (Zn), hard bluish white metallic element. Occurs as sulphide, oxide, carbonate, silicate, *etc.* Used in making of galvanized iron, alloys (*e.g.* brass), die-casting metal and, when rolled into sheets, as protective covering for roofs.

zincblende *see* SPHALERITE.

Zinjanthropus, fossil of man-like ape found in Tanzania, E Africa. Has low brow, large molars. Thought to have evolved in Lower Pleistocene Era, *c.* 1 million yr. ago.

zinnia, plant of genus *Zinnia* chiefly native to Mexico but widely cultivated. Many garden varieties grown for variously coloured daisy-like flowers. *Z. elegans* is state flower of Indiana.

Zinoviev, Grigori Evseyevich (1883–1936), Russ. polit. leader. Pres. of Comintern (1919–27), joined Trotsky in opposition to STALIN, but lost influence. Executed after public trial (1936).

Zinoviev letter, issue in Brit. politics. Letter (later proved a forgery) bore instructions for Communist uprising in England. Its publication contributed to Labour Party's electoral defeat of 1924.

Zinsser, Hans (1878–1940), Amer. bacteriologist and epidemiologist. Made special study of typhus. Author of *Rats, Lice and History* (1935) and medical texts.

Zionism, polit. and cultural movement seeking to re-estab. Jewish nation in Palestine. First World Zionist Congress convened 1897. Played important part in setting up Jewish State of Israel (1948).

zircon, common hard mineral, zirconium silicate. Occurs in small tetragonal crystals or grains of various colours. Used as refractory when opaque, as a gem when transparent.

zirconium (Zr), metallic element combined in zircon, *etc.* Used as structural material in nuclear re-

Zurich is built on the banks of the River Limaat at the northern end of Lake Zurich

actors; compounds used in manufacture of ceramics and refractory materials.

zither, musical instrument with 30–45 strings stretched over sounding box. Has 4 or 5 melody strings which are fretted, other strings provide accompaniment. Played with plectrum and the fingertips.

Zodiac [Gk: *zodiakos,* pertaining to animals], imaginary belt in the heavens extending *c.* 8° on each side of the ecliptic. Divided (*c.* 2000 BC) by Babylonians into 12 equal parts, each distinguished by a sign. First 6, N of the equator, are *Aries* (Ram), *Taurus* (Bull), *Gemini* (Twins), *Cancer* (Crab), *Leo* (Lion), *Virgo* (Virgin). S of the equator are *Libra* (Balance), *Scorpio* (Scorpion), *Sagittarius* (Archer), *Capricornus* (Goat), *Aquarius* (Water Bearer), *Pisces* (Fishes). Names orig. corresponded to constellations bearing same name, but due to precession of the equinoxes, now coincide with constellations bearing names next in order.

Zoë (d. 1050), Byzantine empress, daughter of Constantine VIII. Reigned jointly with 3 successive husbands, rule marked by corruption. Initiated (1042) final split between E and W churches.

Zog, orig. Ahmed Zogu (1895–1961), king of Albania (1928–43). Premier (1922–4), assumed dictatorial power 1925; proclaimed himself king 1928. Fled Albania 1939; abdicated 1943.

Zola, Émile (1840–1902), Fr. writer. Naturalist philosophy embodied in 'scientific' novel cycle, incl. *L'Assommoir* (1877) and *Nana* (1880). Advocated social reform, supported anticlerics in DREYFUS AFFAIR with pamphlet *J'Accuse* (1898); prosecuted for libel, fled to England.

Zollverein, customs union among German states in 19th cent. Began (1818) in Prussia, gradually absorbed other Ger. tariff unions. Contributed to polit. unity, achieved by creation (1871) of Ger. Empire.

Zomba, cap. of Malawi, in Shiré Highlands; founded (*c.* 1880). Region produces cotton, tobacco. Scheduled to be replaced as cap. by Lilongwe. Pop. (1967 est.) 22,000.

zombie, in voodooism, person raised from the dead by sorcerer, usually for some evil purpose. Otherwise held to be a person drugged or hypnotised by a sorcerer.

zoology, branch of biology concerned with study of animals. Early classifications made by Aristotle; Linnaeus (18th cent.) developed binomial nomenclature indicating genus and species. Field of zoology expanded by study of embryology, physiology and use of microscope.

Zoroaster [Gk: **Zarathustra**] (628–551 BC), Persian religious leader, founder of ZOROASTRIANISM.

Zoroastrianism, dualistic religion derived from Persian pantheism of 8th cent. BC, instituted by Zoroaster. Doctrines stated in *Zend Avesta* scriptures; universe dominated by warring forces of good and evil, in which good would triumph. Ceremony centres on purification rites, religion survives in Iran and India (through Parseeism).

Zsigmondy, Richard (1865–1929), Austrian chemist. Awarded Nobel Prize for Chemistry (1925) for research on colloidal solutions and development of the ultra-microscope.

zucchini *see* COURGETTE.

Zuckmayer, Carl (1896–   ), Ger. playwright. Opposed militarism and bureaucracy in satirical comedy *The Captain of Köpenick* (1931). With rise of Nazism, left Germany for US. Attacked Hitler's regime in *The Devil's General* (1946). Also wrote *The Cold Light* (1956).

Zugspitze, peak (9,721 ft.) in Bavarian Alps, on Bavaria-Austria border; highest peak in Germany. Rack and pinion rly. connects resort of Garmisch-Partenkirchen with summit.

Zuider Zee *see* IJSSELMEER.

Zulu, Bantu-speaking people of Natal,

Repub. of South Africa. Mainly live on tribal reservations in **Zululand,** annexed (1887) by Britain and now part of Natal. Tribe rose to power in early 19th cent., warred with Boers in 1830s. Finally subjugated by British forces (1879).

Zulu, Bantu language of Niger-Congo group. Has over 2 million speakers in E coast regions of C Africa.

Zuni, Pueblo people inhabiting W New Mexico; of Zunian linguistic stock. Farming on irrigated land; basketry, pottery, weaving, jewellery. Original 7 Zuni villages attacked by Coronado 1540; abandoned in Pueblo revolt of 1680.

Zurbarán, Francisco de (1598–1664), Sp. painter. Noted esp. for portraits and studies of religious subjects.

Zurich [Ger: Zürich], city of N Switzerland, cap. of Zurich canton, on L. of Zurich. Indust. and commercial centre, produces textiles, machinery. Became free city (1218), joined Swiss Confederation (1351). Zwingli began (16th cent.) Swiss Reformation in Zurich. Has university (built 1832) and Romanesque Gross-Münster. Pop. (1966) 435,000.

Zweibrücken [Fr: **Deux-Ponts**], city of Rhineland-Palatinate, West Germany. Centre of metal, leather and textiles manufacturing. Annexed by France (1797–1814); extensively damaged in World War 2. Pop. (1965) 30,836.

Zweig, Arnold (1887–1968), Ger. novelist, advocate of socialism and Zionism. Author of trilogy comprising *The Case of Sergeant Grischa* (1927), *Young Woman of 1914* (1931), *De Vrient Comes Home* (1932).

Zweig, Stefan (1881–1942), Austrian novelist, essayist and biographer. His portraits of literary figures include *Three Masters* (1920) on Balzac, Dickens and Dostoevsky; of hist. figures *Maria Stuart* (1935) on Mary Queen of Scots. Novels include *Impatience of the Heart* (1938).

Zwickau, city of East Germany, on Mulde R. Industrial centre of coalmining area; machinery, chemicals, textiles, porcelain. Founded 11th cent. Gothic and Renaissance buildings. Pop. (1965) 128,000.

Zwingli, Ulrich or **Huldreich** (1484–1531), Swiss priest, a leader of the Reformation. Opposed the papacy, monasticism and the worship of images. Advocated derivation of religious faith from the Bible. Became leader of Protestants in S Germany and much of Switzerland. Killed in battle between Protestant Zurich and Catholic cantons of Switzerland.